The Whole Language Catalog

Kenneth S. Goodman

◆

Lois Bridges Bird

◆

Yetta M. Goodman

AMERICAN SCHOOL PUBLISHERS

Macmillan/McGraw-Hill

Acknowledgments

Like the grass-roots movement it strives to represent, *The Whole Language Catalog* is the result of a collaborative effort by many. Thanks go first to our publisher, George Rosato, whose inspired idea to create a whole language resource book, in the spirit of Stewart Brand and the *Whole Earth Catalog* (Portola Institute, 1968), gave us the perfect format in which to showcase whole language. George guided us throughout the project.

Next we thank our contributors—more than five hundred classroom teachers, teacher educators, parents, students, educational researchers, administrators, writers, and others—an international community whose writing informs, inspires, delights, and compels us to work even harder to achieve the goal we share in common: quality, humane education for all.

We are indebted to our three feature authors: Herbert Kohl, Ron Miller, and Sandra Wilde, whose respective features, "Education in Turin: A Romance," "Pioneers" and "Spelling Celebrations" add much to the overall information and appeal of the book.

We are also most grateful to the international group of outstanding scholars who so kindly took time from their demanding careers to share their perspectives on language, learning, and liberating education.

We were very fortunate to have the expert advice and help of these contributing consultants in the following areas:

Literature: Katy Obringer, Supervising Librarian, Children's Library, Palo Alto, CA.

Math and Environmental Education: Doug Haner, Elementary Resource Teacher, San Francisco, CA.

Parent Education: Debbie Montgomery, Parent Education, Pre-School Family, Palo Alto, CA.

Science: Michael McGuffee, Fourth-Grade Teacher and Christa McAuliffe Fellow, Stillwater, OK.

Social Studies: Cynthia McDermott, Professor, California State University, Dominguez Hills, Los Angeles, CA.

Our heartfelt thanks to our many colleagues and students who went the extra mile—and beyond—for us. These include: Bruce Appleby, Nancy Areglado, Carol Christine, Judy Cummings, Toby Kahn Curry, Karen Dalrymple, Jayne DeLawter, Elizabeth Doerr, Carole Edelsky, Bobbi Fisher, David and Yvonne Freeman, Debra Goodman, Ron Hutchison, Debra Jacobson, Dorothy King, Mary Kitagawa, Judith Larner Lowry, Lois Mather, Heidi Mills, Robert Peterson, Gary Pharness, Lynn Rhodes, Nancy Shapiro, Carole Urzúa, Chris Weber, and Marilyn Wilson.

A very special thank you to Dorothy Watson, truly one of the best-loved and most influential leaders of the whole language movement, who helped so generously in so many ways.

Producing a book of this nature requires the work of many. We very much appreciate the professional efforts of our production crew, based in Tucson, Arizona and in four San Francisco Bay Area offices.

In Tucson, University of Arizona graduate students Joel Brown and Geane Hanson sent out several hundred letters to potential resource contributors. When Joel wasn't at the computer printing letters, he was out in whole language classrooms taking many of the photographs that appear in *The Catalog*. Graduate student Kathryn Whitmore also helped with numerous details, and inspired our historical feature, "Pioneers," through her own historical research on another project.

In the San Francisco office, Linda Gutlohn, editorial coordinator, created and managed our voluminous data base; her hardworking staff of word processors, copy editors and copy fitters included Eileen Burke, Marcella Friel, Kate Littleboy, Nancy Riddiough, David Sweet, Michelle Taverniti, and Verna Wefald. Our permissions editor, Betty Nanz, handled hundreds of permissions for us, and index coordinator Marc Savage, with help from Susan Coerr and our Arizona friends Joel Brown, Jacquie Casati, Linda Dorn, Alan and Jane Flurkey, Brian Husby, Gary Husby, Debra Jacobson, Richard Meyer, Barbara Thompson, and Janice Wizinowich, produced professional indexes.

Across the bay in Berkeley, our resource coordinator Frances Christie and her assistant, Arietta Chakos, checked and rechecked publishing references, prices, addresses, etc. on more than five hundred and forty book notes and curricular resources.

North of San Francisco, in Novato, Lynda Banks, our art director and production manager, assembled wall to wall, floor to ceiling shelving to accommodate the oversized pages. A team of computer experts working double shifts in Lynda's light-filled office, combined our page thumbnails with Lynda's superb design and gave us beautiful pages. Thanks to Rick Gordon, Stephanie Eichleay, Scott Morrow, Myrna Vladic, Johan Carlisle, and Deborah Bates. Christina Reski created and cataloged our art data base and kept track of dozens of other details as well; Sari Marks and Batya Fischer provided valuable back-up assistance; Jeri Johnston contributed to the icon and cover design. We appreciate the excellent work of our proofreaders, ably directed by Deborah Schatten: Marianne Rogoff, Elizabeth Share, Constance M. Johnstone, and Anne B. Cushman. We were most fortunate to have such a competent and dedicated crew. Overseeing it all was Lynda Banks, a creative designer, artist, master organizer, and tireless worker. We thank her and her darling daughter, Alessandra (who provided delightful respite from the project!) and patient husband, Michele Accinelli. We also thank our marketing strategist, Murrell Peddicord, for his ever-positive guidance.

On a personal note, speaking from the Palo Alto office, my deep appreciation to Carolyn Clebsch, who provided us with additional striking photographs, to Ravid Haselkorn, who cheerfully managed mountains of xeroxing and filing, to Mandy MacCalla, for her sensitive, skillful editorial assistance, to Debbie Montgomery, for her unfailing kind generosity and invaluable help with a myriad of tasks, and to Gloria Norton, for emotional support and lots of good laughter. A special thank you to my beloved parents, Hal and Alice Bridges. My father is the best writer I know; he listened, critiqued and improved upon countless details time and time again. I could not have managed without his expert guidance and loving encouragement. Thanks to my husband, Dennis, for his understanding and support, and finally, to our children, Aislinn, Erin, and Brennan. You are the loves of my life. Thank you for helping me through.

—LBB with KSG and YMG

We want to hear from you! And you may want to become a contributor to the second edition of *The Whole Language Catalog*. Please see the "Reader Response" form and "Become a Contributor" on page 445.

CREDITS

Design, art direction, production:
Lynda Banks Design
Editorial coordinator: Linda Gutlohn
Permissions: Betty Nanz
Resource coordinator: Frances Christie
Index: Marc Savage
Photography, illustration: see page 444
Manufacturing supervisor: Jean Haldorsen

For each of the selections listed below, grateful acknowledgment is made for permission to adapt and/or reprint original or copyrighted material as follows:

James V. Allen: "A Kinder, Gentler Curriculum," by James V. Allen from *The Literacy Connection,* September, 1989, vol. VII, no. 1. Reprinted by permission of the author.

American Bookseller: Excerpted from "Introducing the National Reading Initiative," by Louise Howton, from *American Bookseller,* May 1988. Copyright © 1988. Reprinted by permission of *American Bookseller* Magazine.

ArtsReach, Educational Arts Program for Indian Children: "Venado," by Fernando Duenas and "When I Was Born," by Diane Ochoa from *Dancing with the Wind: The ArtsReach Literacy Magazine,* vol. 1, 1989. Copyright © 1989 ArtsReach. All rights reserved. Reprinted by permission of the publisher.

Bamboo Ridge Press: "What Can I Say?" by Eric Chock; poem by Leslie N.; poem by Wade Kyono; poem by Calvin; poem by Sherman; "Slow Pin," by Tricia Kaneko; "The Glass Teacher," by Julie A.; and "From the Front of the Class," by Eric Chock, from *small kid time hawaii,* edited by Eric Chock. Copyright 1981, 1989 by Eric Chock. Reprinted by permission of Eric Chock.

Basic Books, Inc.: Excerpted from *In Search of Mind,* by Jerome Bruner, Harper & Row. Copyright © 1983 by Jerome Bruner. Reprinted by permission of Basic Books, Inc., Publishers, New York.

Edith Baxter: "Journeys," in a revised and expanded form titled "Journeys in the Classroom," appeared in the newsletter of The Whole Language Teachers Association, Sudbury, MA, vol. 5, no. 1, Spring 1990. Used by permission of the author.

Byrd Baylor: "Dear Bird," by Byrd Baylor, from *City Magazine,* Tucson, AZ, vol. 2, no. 7, July 1987. Reprinted by permission of the author.

Bobbi Bernstein: "Letter from a Librarian," by Bobbi Bernstein. Copyright 1989 by Bobbi Bernstein. Used by permission.

The Helen Brann Agency, Inc.: Foreword by Maya Angelou to *I Have Something to Say About This Big Trouble: Children of the Tenderloin Speak Out,* collected by Reverend Cecil Williams and Janice Mirikitani, Glide Word Press, 1989. Copyright © by Maya Angelou (foreword). Reprinted by permission of The Helen Brann Agency, Inc.

The Brookline Foundation: "A Perspective on a Child Study Group," by Laura Harwood, from *Reflections: The Brookline Educational Journal,* vol. 4, no. 2, Spring 1987. Reprinted by permission.

Marilyn Burns: Adapted from "Writing in the Math Class (K–8)," by Marilyn Burns, from *The Math Solution Publications,* Marilyn Burns Education Associates, © 1988. Adapted and reprinted by permission of the author. "Assessing Students' Understanding: Open-ended Questions for 12th Graders—A Report from the California Assessment Program," by Marilyn Burns, from *The Math Solution Newsletter,* no. 8, Fall/Winter 1989–90, Marilyn Burns Education Associates, © 1989. Reprinted by permission of the author.

California State Department of Education: "Recommended Readings in Literature: Kindergarten Through Grade Eight" from "What Is the California Reading Initiative?" excerpted and reprinted by permission, from California Reading Initiative poster *Open Books=Open Doors,* California State Department of Education, P.O. Box 944272, Sacramento, CA.

California Writing Project: Excerpted from the National Writing Project brochure, published by the California Writing Project, University of California at Berkeley. Reprinted by permission.

(Continued on page 443)

Table of Contents

11 Learning

65 Language

163 Literature

205 Teaching

279 Curriculum

335 Community

377 Understanding Whole Language

Indexes

What Is Whole Language?

Whole language is nothing short of a grass-roots revolution in education. It brings together the scientific study of learning, of language, of teaching, and of curriculum with the positive, people-centered, historical traditions that sensitive, caring teachers have always upheld. A whole language classroom is a democratic community of learners, and its curriculum is embedded in the culture and social experiences of the larger community.

For teachers, whole language means coming of age as a profession: a complete, integrated philosophical and factual base for making countless professional decisions that teachers must make to help their pupils learn as much as they can. It means putting tests and textbooks in their proper place, since they are no more than tools for professional teachers to use as they serve their pupils. It means taking charge in their classrooms, taking responsibility, and expecting authority and respect.

Neighbors for A New Fratney, a multiracial organization of parents, teachers, and community activists, have worked for more than two years to create in their inner-city Milwaukee school, La Escuela Fratney, a program that embraces whole language, bilingualism, democratic discipline, cooperative learning, and a multicultural curriculum that draws on the cultural diversity of the city. (See pp. 336; 348–349)

For learners, whole language means rich, authentic, developmentally appropriate school experiences. It means learning that is as real, relevant, and easy in school as it is outside school. It means reading real literature, not workbooks and skill sheets. It means writing when you need to write because you have a real purpose and something to say. It means problem-solving, answering your own real questions in an environment that encourages you to take the risks necessary to learn. It means supportive teachers who take the time to know each pupil, who work collaboratively with their pupils in learning, and who can make every day at school one to be cherished and remembered. In whole language classrooms there is time for thinking and time for growing. For learners, whole language isn't just an alternative to what they do in traditional classrooms. It's much more: more reading and writing, more participation, more science and social studies, more of the humanities, more opportunities to pursue personal as well as common interests and needs, more concern for building strong friendships and support systems.

A student in Sarah Costello's seventh grade reads his recently published composition aloud to an appreciative audience of his classmates, William J. Pistor Junior High, Tucson, AZ. Students in whole language classrooms write daily about topics of their own choosing. (See Graves, p.130)

For school administrators, whole language means new roles supporting teaching and learning. It means curricular leaders who provide resources, who facilitate holistic planning, and who help teachers evaluate teaching and learning to produce continuous growth in both. Whole language administrators aren't afraid to put their trust in teachers and learners, and they're not afraid to take risks themselves to change traditional piecemeal schools to holistic integrated ones. Whole language administrators lead a collaboration of professional educators, parents, community mem-

The reading loft in Debra Goodman's fifth-grade classroom is available to students for quiet reading almost any time of the day. Whole language teachers respect their students as capable, creative learners who can be trusted to make decisions, with teacher guidance, about how they spend time in their classroom. (See Goodman, p. 207)

shape and enrich the curriculum. It means their children will be reading and writing earlier, more often, and more enthusiastically; it means that their child's language, values, and cultural heritage will be treated as strengths upon which to expand. And it means the school accepts all students and helps them build knowledge and confidence in themselves as learners. Whole language is a collaboration between the home and the school, in which parents and teachers work together to expand on the home culture and to extend the learning horizons of all members of the school community.

As whole language has spread from teacher to teacher, from classroom to classroom, from school to school, from community to community, it has drawn on the best of modern research and theory, and it has built a literature of teachers writing for teachers, a network of teacher support groups, and a wealth of student experience and classroom achievement, which in turn is stimulating new research and more practical and complete theoretical understanding. Parents of all socioeconomic classes and ethnic groups have become aware of

Curiosity about the origin of their school's name led Arlene Malkin and her second- and third-grade students at Ohlone School into a three-month study of the Ohlone Indians. Students participated in a variety of learning experiences that replicated the village life of the Ohlone, including building an Ohlone hut, using reeds and saplings they collected themselves. (See p. 302)

whole language and are seeking its educational advantages for their own children.

bers, and students to create schools that are dynamic learning communities.

For parents, whole language means a commitment to providing their children, at every age, regardless of differences in ability, interest, culture, language, or physical well-being, with optimal, challenging, and appropriate learning experiences. It means hard-working, highly professional teachers who know their children and who are prepared to draw on the background and experience of parents to

WHOLE LANGUAGE umbrella

The Whole Language Umbrella, founded in 1989, is an international confederation of whole language teacher support groups. Designed to give teachers a stronger voice and greater credibility, The Umbrella offers support and networking services. For teachers, whole language means coming of age as professionals. (See p. 408)

Lucy Sprague Mitchell (1878–1967) was an educator who, during the early part of this century, worked to develop curricula for children that would capture their experiences and expand their worlds. Her concerns with humanism and science are shared by whole language educators today. (See Mitchell, p. 376)

The Whole Language Catalog is our attempt to bring all aspects of this dynamic educational movement together in a book. When we set out to put together *The Whole Language Catalog*, we visualized something as rich and diverse as whole language itself. We wanted to capture the voices of teachers, the joy and productivity of learners, the wisdom and inspiration of the pioneers on whose shoulders we stand, the strength of the philosophical base, the excitement of the classrooms, and the grass-roots momentum that is whole language today. We wanted to represent whole language well enough that parents and professionals just coming to whole language could get a sense of it. And we wanted to be inclusive enough to provide confident whole language professionals with new resources, new ideas, and new insights. We wanted not only to provide a full picture of where whole language is, but also to offer a major resource for extending it further. We hoped we'd be able

Children at Yaquina View School, Newport, OR, embrace their principal, Ron Hutchison. As curricular leaders, whole language principals are friends with their students both inside and outside the classroom. (See p. 275)

Alarmed that their children were losing their Inuit culture and language, the community rallied to create a new curriculum based on Inuit values and experiences. Local authors and artists wrote and illustrated new literature that reflects the Inuit way of life. (See pp. 284–285)

Whole language is a collaboration between the home and the school, in which parents and teachers work together to expand on the home culture and to extend the horizons of all members of the school community. (See Goodman, p. 363)

Author/Editors

Kenneth S. Goodman

Ken Goodman is a teacher, reader, writer, researcher, theoretician, professor, father, grandfather, and citizen. Throughout his career in education, which now spans six decades from the forties to the nineties, he has sought to integrate these roles. He started his career as a teacher of a self-contained eighth grade and has taught all ages from preschool to senior adult. The research he did on reading, which led to miscue analysis and a psycholinguistic transactive theory of reading, always involved real people reading whole texts. He has been active in professional organizations, starting with his teachers union and continuing as he eventually served as president of the International Reading Association, National Conference on Research in English, and the Center for Expansion of Language and Thinking. His Ed.D. from UCLA is in curriculum development; he has, throughout his career, attempted to integrate what he has learned about reading and language into a curriculum and methodology that would serve all pupils, particularly minorities and the poor.

When the whole language movement began as a grass-roots movement among North American teachers, it was not surprising that it found a philosophical and practical base in Ken's work. In fact, up until this movement began to spread, Ken's work was better known among teachers in Australia, New Zealand, Canada, and the United Kingdom than it was in the United States. He is currently professor of Language, Reading, and Culture at the University of Arizona.

Further Reading by Kenneth S. Goodman
What's Whole in Whole Language? Heinemann, 1986.
Report Card on Basal Readers, with P. Shannon, Y. S. Freeman, and S. Murphy. Richard C. Owen, 1988.
The Whole Language Evaluation Book, ed. with Y. M. Goodman and W. J. Hood. Heinemann, 1989.

Lois Bridges Bird

While teaching first and second grades in California and Arizona, Lois Bridges Bird came to realize that the learning capabilities of children far transcend the limitations of traditional classroom methods. While earning her Ph.D. in education and linguistics at the University of Arizona under the guidance of professors Ken and Yetta Goodman, she discovered the answer to those limitations—whole language.

Lois became a whole language advocate. She edited a book, and wrote articles for books and journals. She communicated the liberating philosophy as a whole language consultant and in courses that she taught at San Francisco State University, San Jose State University, and the University of California, Berkeley. And she has worked two years, so far, on *The Whole Language Catalog.*

Lois's knowledge of young children is often refreshed in her Palo Alto home. She and her husband, Professor Dennis K. Bird of Stanford University, have two daughters and a son, whose adventures provide daily lessons in the ways of inquiring young minds.

Further Reading by Lois Bridges Bird
Becoming a Whole Language School: The Fair Oaks Story. Richard C. Owen, 1989.
"Professional Development at Fair Oaks." In *Organizing for Whole Language,* ed. K. S. Goodman, Y. M. Goodman, and W. Hood. Heinemann, in press.
"The Art of Teaching: Self-Reflection and Evaluation." In *Whole Language Evaluation Book,* ed. K.S. Goodman, Y. M. Goodman, and W. Hood. Heinemann, 1988.
"Joyful Literacy at Fair Oaks." *Holistic Education Review,* Winter 1989.
"Reading Comprehension Redefined through Literature Study: Creating Worlds from the Printed Page." *California Reader,* vol. 21, no. 3, March/April 1988.

Yetta M. Goodman

When Yetta Goodman, as a student teacher, got a class of inner-city teenagers enthusiastically involved in a choral reading, her supervising teacher invited other teachers in to see it. She can still draw on that natural teaching ability when she gets an audience of a thousand teachers weepy over *Love You Forever* or *Faithful Elephants.* IRA gave her its Outstanding Teacher Educator in Reading award.

But it would certainly have surprised her primary teachers to know that Yetta, who came to school not speaking English, would grow up to be president of the National Council of Teachers of English. Her research on miscue analysis, literacy development, and the writing process has provided whole language teachers with the knowledge they need to be kidwatchers, a term Yetta made popular.

Yetta has taught at all levels and still found time to be a supermom and grandma. Ken and Yetta have three daughters, all of whom are or have been whole language teachers, and six whole language grandchildren. Like Ken, she is a professor of Language, Reading, and Culture at the University of Arizona.

Further Reading by Yetta M. Goodman
Language and Thinking in School, with K. S. Goodman, E. B. Smith, and R. Meredith. Richard C. Owen, 1987.
Reading Miscue Inventory: Alternative Procedures, with D. Watson and C. Burke. Richard C. Owen, 1988.
How Children Construct Literacy: Piagetian Perspectives. International Reading Association, 1990.

Our initials are used throughout *The Catalog*: *KSG* refers to Kenneth S. Goodman, *LBB* to Lois Bridges Bird, and *YMG* to Yetta M. Goodman.

What Is Whole Language? (cont'd.)

to fill 400-plus oversize pages, richly illustrated with graphics, pictures, and students' work. But our main job turned out to be how to fit it all in. We were overwhelmed by the response of teachers, administrators, parents, and students, as well as theoreticians and researchers. Every age from preschool to senior adult is well represented in this catalog.

There was no simple way for us to organize this book. By its nature, whole language is integrated, and every aspect is highly related to many others. So *The Whole Language Catalog* is a start-anywhere-and-read-in-any-direction book. We've tried to suggest some of the interconnec-

tions. But readers can follow their own agenda: checking out the philosophy, looking for the history, mining for ideas for bilingual pupils, preschoolers, or student teachers. They can check out favorite publishers of children's literature or find out who's producing good social studies resources for middle grades. Or they can just dip in as time permits.

As earnestly as we have worked to be inclusive and fully representative, we know we've left some things out. Whole language is too dynamic and growing too rapidly for us to be sure that we found all of it. We console ourselves by hoping that our readers will tell us of our omissions and

oversights. We expect you to tell us of any miscues or errors of judgment we might have made. As we prepared *The Whole Language Catalog,* we kept telling ourselves that the next edition will be much easier. We invite you, our readers, to share your own experiences, to offer your own contributions, to react to what you do and don't like.

Whole language is a collaborative venture. We expect our readers to transact with the book, and through it with us and with the contributors. If we've succeeded, *The Whole Language Catalog* will carry the collaboration to new frontiers.

—Kenneth S. Goodman, Lois Bridges Bird, Yetta M. Goodman

Contributors

Feature Authors

Herbert Kohl is the author of our feature "Education in Turin: A Romance". He was born in the Bronx in 1937 and attended P.S. 104, Macombs Junior High School, and the Bronx High School of Science, graduating in 1954. From the time he was in junior high school he dreamed of doing two things with his life: teaching school and writing. After four years at Harvard and two in graduate school studying philosophy and mathematics, he became a public school teacher. He also began work on what was to become his first book, *The Age of Complexity*, which was about contemporary philosophy.

Herbert started out teaching fifth grade at P.S. 145 in January 1962 and is still involved in public education. Over the past 28 years he has taught all grades from kindergarten through high school, has done teacher training, founded and directed the Teachers & Writers Collaborative, and in general has worked to make school and society more decent and just places.

Over the years Herbert has written about learning and growing, advocating the elimination, through education, of racism, sexism, and all other forms of oppression.

An expanded version of "Education in Turin: A Romance" will be published by Continuity Press. Entitled *The Romance of Education,* it will include an essay by Joseph Featherstone on the practical importance, for teachers engaged in educational reform, of understanding the history of progressive education. For information about the book, write to: Continuity Press, 40561 Eureka Hills Rd., Point Arena, CA 95468.

Further Reading by Herbert Kohl

36 Children. New American Library, 1967.
On Teaching. Schocken, 1976.
View from the Oak, with J. Kohl. Scribner, 1977.
A Book of Puzzlements. Schocken, 1981.
Growing Minds: On Becoming a Teacher. Harper & Row, 1985.
Mathematical Puzzlements. Schocken, 1987.
The Long Haul: The Autobiography of Myles Horton, with M. Horton and J. Kohl. Doubleday, 1990.

Ron Miller is the main author of our feature "Pioneers." He is the founder and executive editor of *Holistic Education Review,* a quarterly journal exploring alternative, person-centered approaches in elementary and secondary education. His doctoral research on the cultural history of American education, focusing on holistic alternatives, will be published later this year. Ron has written on alternative education for several publications, including *Mothering, New Age Journal,* and the *Journal of Humanistic Education.* He was formerly a Montessori teacher.

Further Reading by Ron Miller

What Are Schools For? Holistic Education in American Culture. Holistic Education Press, 1990.

Sandra Wilde is the author of our feature "Spelling Celebrations." She teaches and conducts research at the University of Oregon. She has been a teacher and teacher-educator for nearly 20 years, and has lived in most regions of the United States and Canada. Her major professional interests are invented spelling, whole language spelling curriculum, and the role of reading, writing, and literature in learning mathematics. Her book on invented spelling and developmental punctuation will be published by Heinemann Educational Books in 1991.

Further Reading by Sandra Wilde

"Learning to Spell and Punctuate: A Study of Eight- and Nine-year-old Children." *Language and Education: An International Journal 2,* 1988.
"Looking at Invented Spelling: A Kidwatcher's Guide to Spelling" and "Understanding Spelling Strategies: A Kidwatcher's Guide to Spelling." In *The Whole Language Evaluation Book,* ed. K. S. Goodman, Y. M. Goodman, and W. Hood. Heinemann, 1988.
"The Power of Literature: Notes from a Survivor." *The New Advocate 2,* 1989.
"A Proposal for a New Spelling Curriculum." *Elementary School Journal 90,* 1990.

Teachers, Teacher Educators, Researchers, Students, Parents, Administrators, Publishers, Librarians, Booksellers, and Authors from around the world who have contributed to this book

UNITED STATES

Alabama
Roberta Long
Maryann Manning
Bernice Wolfsan

Alaska
Shirley Ann Kaltenbach

Arizona
Byrd Baylor
Nelson G. Begay
Sigmund A. Boloz
Chris Boyd
Hal Bridges
Joel Brown
Meredith Cherland
Carol Maytag Christine
Ward Cockrum
Anna Coor
Sarah Costello
Annabel Crites
Cathy Crockett
Caryl Crowell
Alyce E. Dalzell
Susana de la Peña
Lois E. Easton
Carole Edelsky
Maryann Eeds
Alan Flurkey
Jane Flurkey

Vicci Fox
Dan Gapp
Beate Gillian
Mary Glover
Geane R. Hanson
Saundra Bryn Harmon
Lillian Hentel
Debbie A. Hickman
Aaron Hood
Wendy Hood
Pam Howard
Debra Jacobson
Terrianne Jacobson
Kitty Kaczmarek
Dorothy F. King
Jeff LaBenz
Carol Novillis Larson
Torri Vic Larzelere
Louise Lockard
Annette Maggitti
Myna L. Matlin
Yvonne Merseau
Luis Moll
John Moran
Nancy Moyer
Kathryn E. Mullarky
Sheila Nicholas
Diane Ochoa
Sandra Patton
Ralph Peterson

Gayle Powers
Pat Rigg
Elizabeth R. Saavedra
Ann Schlumberger
Lee Wayne Shainen
Shea Shochat
Kathy Gnagey Short
Henrietta Simons
Karen Smith
Mary Lee Smith
Roach Van Allen
Jeannette Veatch
Kathy M. Whalen
Kathryn F. Whitmore
Janice Wizinowich
Bob Wortman

California
Susan S. Abel
Pam Adair
Pilar Alvarez
Rachel Arnow
Rebecca Arnow
Katie Bausch-Ude
Patricia Beatty
Aislinn Bird
Brennan Bird
Erin Bird
Sally Bonner
Sharon Broadhead
Marilyn Burns

Katharine Busch
Michael Caff
Candy Heinsen Carter
Elena Castro
Penny G. Caudle
Armando Cerrillo
Arrietta Chakos
Greg Chapnick
Frances Christie
Peter Craske
Laurel Cress
Paul Crowley
Lisa D'hollande
Susan E. Davis
Jayne DeLawter
Elizabeth Doerr
Dennis Doyle
Matt Dudley
Anne Haas Dyson
DiAnn Waskul Ellis
Cecelia Estrada
Gloria Wilber Fearn
Jean W. Fennacy
Barbara Flores
David Freeman
Yvonne S. Freeman
Peter Gabel
Rick Gartner
John Gegan
Karen Goodman

Shoshana Goodman
Patrick Gonzalez
Lynne Griffiths
Michael Hagan
Doug Haner
Ravid Haselkorn
Tmirah Haselkorn
Shirley Brice Heath
Eddie Hernandez
Catherine Howard
Erin Howard
Louise Howton
Charlotte S. Huck
Beth Huntzinger
Barbara Ingram
Eleanora Jadwin
Louise Jensen
Ron Jones
Anna Joyce
Masako Kagawa
Judith Kalman
Herbert Kohl
Jill Korengold
Stephen D. Krashen
Kathryn M. Krauskopf
Debra Krencicki
Jane G. Lambert
Perry Lang
Bonnie Laster
Roberta Lee

Evelyn Logan
Jan B. Loveless
Judith Larner Lowry
Beverly Lozoff
Carlen Luke
Mandy MacCalla
Awele Makeba
Arlene Malkin
Leslie Mangiola
Deborah A. Manning
Leslie Marks
Bobbi Jentes Mason
Mary D. Maxwell
Robin Mayo
Richard McCallum
Cynthia McDermott
Israel Mendoza
James Moffett
David Montgomery
Debbie Montgomery
Lauren Montgomery
Marty Morgenbesser
Cynthia Motsinger
Jessica Nelson-Lundy
Samuel D. Nofziger, Jr.
Gloria Norton
Patricia M. Nourot
Kathy O'Brien
Katy Obringer
Patricia Paige

George K. Parrish
Lucinda Pease-Alvarez
Pamela Perkins
Susan Poplack
Katie Post
Rebecca Rapoport
Alicia Rivera
Pat Robinson
Dennis Ronberg
Linda Ronberg
Juana Arcelia Sainez
Katharine Samway
Jane Sheftel-Hara
Margaret Smullin
Jean Kerr Stenmark
Aaron Stonestrom
Janice Stradford
Marsha Umland
Carole Urzúa
Juan Manual Villa
Bob Wells
Robert Whitlow
Pat Yencho
Pat Yowell
Patricia Broderick
 Zaballos
Sharon Zinke

Colorado
Joanne Cermak
Karen Sabers Dalrymple
Aileen Fisher
Margaret A. Heath
Mary F. Hellen
Anne Henderson
Leslie A. Leyden
Kathy Mestnik
Lynn K. Rhodes
Nancy L. Shanklin
Lorrie A. Shepard
Yvonne Sui-Runyan
Mary Ellen Sweeny
Ruth L. Taravella
Judy VanDeWeghe
Dale W. Vigil
Elizabeth Walen

Connecticut
Francelia Butler
Judy Dobbrow
Linda Giordano

District of Columbia
Dorothy Rich

Florida
Robert A. Blume
Marcy Guddemi
Wendy Kasten
Linda Lamme

Georgia
Eliot Wigginton

Hawaii
Eric Chock
Donald Y. Enoki
David Hartle-Schutte
Tricia Kaneko
Gail Sakagawa
Anita Shaw
Helen B. Slaughter
Linda C. Tsubata

Illinois
Bruce Appleby
Eileen Ogintz
Diane Stephens

Indiana
Barbara Backler
Carolyn Burke

Jim Hall
Jerome C. Harste
Denise Ogren

Iowa
Barbara Hyslop Heidger
Lois Mather
Sharon Wetherell

Kansas
Gordon Gulseth
Elizabeth Schmar

Kentucky
Randy Burnett
Jean Anne Clyde
Melissa Rae Gallagher
Jason Garland
Linda Oxendine
April Kay Smith
Carrie Leigh Wilson

Louisiana
Cindy Elliott

Maine
Nancy C. Andrews
Nancie Atwell
A. Frederic Cheney
Marvin N. Higgins

Maryland
Bess Altwerger

Massachusetts
Odete Amarelo
Paula Anderson
Nancy Hyland Areglado
Edith Baxter
David Bloome
Joshua Bloomekatz
Beth Cohen
Judy J. Cummings
Jacqueline L. Finn
Bobbi Fisher
Bill Harley
Laura Harwood
Mary M. Kitagawa
Sara Lawrence
 Lightfoot
Ron Miller
Janet Palladino
Margaret Y. Phinney
Philo T. Pritzkau
Barbara Siaki
Mary Snow
Judith Solsken
Laurel Stevick
Jay Sugarman
Maureen C. White

Michigan
Mianne Adufutse
Janine Archey
Liping Chen
Toby Kahn Curry
Debby Davies
Debra Goodman
Charlotte Haun
Susan E. Kinzel
Keith Kroll
Arlene Lecours
Jude McClain
Vera Milz
Larry Pike
Julia Pointer
Tara Ransom
Connie Weaver
Marilyn Wilson
Zhenyu Zhu

Minnesota
Patrick Shannon

Missouri
Nancy Anderson
Trifona Andres
Barbara Halliwill Bell
Mary K. Bixby
Janice Henson
Kittye Copeland
Diane Gammon
Ronald B. Gillam
Carol Gilles
Jo Glaser
Janet Goo
Steven W. Graham
Candace Hamilton
Peter Hasselriis
Margaret Henrichs
Mary Anne Jennings
Nancy Knipping
Sheryl McGruder
Howard M. Miller
Robin Myers
Deborah Nieding-Allai
Elizabeth D. Nelms
Tara Nickel
Judith Oliver
Virginia Pfannenstiel
Pat Pollock
Barbara Reid
Marilyn Richardson
Karen Shroyer
LeeAnn Sinclair
Mira Soekias
Mary Jo Stockbauer
Leslie Swanda
Grace Tychsen
Kathy Waner
Dorothy J. Watson
Nancy Wildermuth

Montana
Rich Thompson

Nevada
Melisa Choroszy
Nancy L. Kelly
Ann M. Marek

New Hampshire
Donald Graves
Thomas Newkirk

New Jersey
Claudia A. Gentile
Suzanne Gespass
Arlene R.H. Pincus
Harriet Paget Ritzer
Dorothy S. Strickland

New Mexico
Martha Ahlmann
Jack Carter-North
Eddie Corona

New York
Ruth Ann Blynt
Rachel L. Bullard
Nancy Buscaglia
Lucy McCormick
 Calkins
Jason Cetron
Ardith Cole
Catherine Compton
 Lilly
Judy Cox
Amanda Crafts
Kathleen Cunningham
Clair Doyle
Dominique F. Guerin
Shelley Harwayne

Carol Hittleman
Melissa Lauren Holtzer
William Bryant Logan
Sharon Markell
Bill Martin Jr
Eileen McCormick
Barbara Means
Deborah Meier
Dot Muller
Jenny O'Connor
Susan Ohanian
Ricardo Otheguy
Richard C. Owen
Oliver Patterson
Julie Patton
Adam Christopher
 Pepitone
Laurie Pessah
Maureen Powell
Charlene Rogers
Dick Salzer
Susan Chmiel
 Schroeder
JoAnn C. Shaheen
Nancy Shapiro
Norman Sherman
Ira Shor
Sheila M. Siegfried
Heather Wahba
Lillian Weber

North Carolina
LaDonna Hauser

North Dakota
Steve Harlow

Ohio
James Allen
Rudine Sims Bishop
Alicia Brashear
Bennett Cain
Melissa Cain
Diane DeFord
Henry A. Giroux
Martha L. King
Alexa Lindquist-
 Sandmann
Susannah Loehr
Moira G. McKenzie
Hughes Moir
Don Penthal
Gay Su Pinnell

Oklahoma
Mike McGuffee

Oregon
Mary Bertun
Leonila Bonifacio
Amanda Cornwall
Julia Craig
Kati Lynn Field
Ron Hutchison
Harmony Jones
Dao Le
Judy McDermott
Madeline Moore
Hang Nguyen
Natasha L. Osborn
Rom Papish
Meredith Proost
Erik Sanchez
Chau Vu
Chris Weber
Sandra Wilde

Pennsylvania
Carol S. Avery
Carole L. Slotter

Puerto Rico
Colette Green

Rhode Island
Robert F. Carey
Helen D'Ordine

South Carolina
Bobbi Bernstein
Amy Donnelly
Janet Sloatman Files
Jacqueline L. Gmuca
Heidi Mills
Timothy O'Keefe
Laura S. Truesdale
Leslie L. Vine
David J. Whitin
Phyllis E. Whitin

Tennesee
Lois S. Vandagriff

Texas
Laurie M. Brown
Anita Castañeda
Ruth L. Galaz
Judith Wells Lindfors
Yolanda Rippetoe
Aurelia Dávila de Silva

Utah
Marjorie Coombs
Becky Reimer

Vermont
Glenda Bissex

Virginia
Nancy Larrick
Laura S. Robb
Suzanne F. Sprenger

West Virginia
Lois Blackburn

Wisconsin
Michael Apple
Barbara Dier
Barbara Miner
Robert Peterson
Angela Wegner

Wyoming
Patty Vincent

ARGENTINA
Roxana Morduchowicz

AUSTRALIA
New South Wales
Nicole Black
Mark Brennan
Trevor H. Cairney
Brian Cambourne
Kevin Comber
Phil Cormack
Fred Gollasch
Inta Gollasch
Don Holdaway
Barbara Kamler
Margie Leys
Brenda Parkes
Judy Peters
Ann Pulvertaft
Jan Turbill
Chris Weckert

South Australia
Garth Boomer

Victoria
Lesley Wing Jan
Keith Pigdon
Paul Richardson
Marilyn Woolley

CANADA
Alberta
Margaret T. Stevenson

British Columbia
B. M. Lynn Archer
Linda Calahan
Mark McCue
Norma I. Mickelson
Gary Pharness
Heinz Senger
Toby Taylor
Lee Weinstein

Manitoba
Ethel Buchanan
Catherine Ousey

Northwest Territory
Fiona O'Donoghue

Nova Scotia
Jane Baskwill
Susan Church
Ruth Gamberg
Ann Manicom
Judith M. Newman
Jim Rice

Ontario
June Gravel
Wendy McDonnell
Sharon Murphy
Adrian Peetoom
Sharon J. Rich
Gordon Wells

Quebec
Beverly DeCarlo
 Beauvais
Lorraine Gilmeister
 Krause
Myrna Guy
Peter J. H. Krause
Mary Maguire
Robert Morrison

Saskatchewan
Ted Custer
Jerline Quintal-Finell

ECUADOR
Sonia Alexandra
 Guerrero

ENGLAND
James Britton
Robin Campbell
Margaret Chan
Nigel Hall
Bronwyn Mellor
Michael Simons
Mike Torbe
Catherine Wallace
Ann Ketch

JAPAN
Mark Caprio

MALAYSIA
Nan Bonfils

NEW ZEALAND
Barbara Alaatatoa
Margaret Mooney

PHILIPPINES
David Blair
Jesse Mae de Vera
Lauren Hoyt
Yvonne T. Boiser

User's Guide

What's In It For You

Open this omnibus resource book and find:

1. Nuts and bolts ideas and strategies from experienced whole language educators for organizing and supporting whole language learning at home and in the classroom.

2. The addresses of publishers, bookstores, and mail order companies that offer a fascinating array of books and materials from the holistic, hands-on side of education.

3. Explanations of language, learning, and liberating education by internationally famous authorities that will help you develop your own philosophy of education, and help you understand *why* you are doing what you are doing.

4. Lively, informative history of progressive education—from Comenius to Piaget—presented in Herbert Kohl's "Education in Turin: A Romance," and Ron Miller's "Pioneers."

5. Candid photographs, funny anecdotes, and inspiring first person stories from the grass roots—of and by teachers, parents, students, administrators, researchers, and others—that will make you laugh and think. Our contributors come from 42 states, 7 Canadian provinces and 1 territory, and 8 other countries, yet all are united by a fervent desire to help learners, preschool through adult, discover the excitement and joy of learning.

How to Read *The Catalog*

Read it any way you choose. This is a set-your-own-agenda-or-no-agenda book. *The Catalog* is organized around four central features:

1. The framework

There are seven divisions:
  Learning
  Language
  Literature
  Teaching
  Curriculum
  Community
  Understanding Whole Language

Within each division, there are subdivisions. All entries within a subdivision—essays, book notes, language stories, resources—are related. Cross references follow many of the essays.

2. The running features

These run across all divisions. Here is a brief explanation of what you'll find in each:

As I/We See It
Commentary by Ken, Yetta, or both on the theoretical underpinnings of whole language.

Kidwatching
Yetta explains the significance of selected language samples, and shows how such information informs instruction.

Viewpoint
We invited prominent educators to address a topic of their own choosing related to language, literacy, and liberating education.

Cornerstone
Leading educators and talented whole language teachers explain the fundamental concepts of whole language and establish the foundations of student-centered education.

Whole Language Internacional
Highlights whole language teachers, schools and happenings in Argentina, Australia, Great Britain, Japan, Malaysia, Nicaragua, and the Philippines.

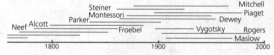

Pioneers
Ron Miller, publisher and executive editor of *Holistic Education Review*, has written biographical sketches of outstanding progressive educators, past and present. Yetta Goodman, Luis Moll, and Kathryn Whitmore provide additional portraits.

Education in Turin: A Romance

Herbert Kohl, author of many books and articles including the best seller, *36 Children*, provides an historical overview of progressive education through his fictional account of eight generations of a teaching family.

As Teachers See It
Whole language involves the professionalism of teachers. Read this feature—discussions of issues from the teacher's perspective—and see if you agree.

Principals Speak Out
Strong administrative leadership is essential as schools move from traditional ways to whole language. Here are the voices of some who are providing that leadership.

Parents' Perspective
Read what parents are saying and doing to improve education in their states and communities.

As Kids See It
Parents and teachers often wonder what kids really think. We went straight to the kids and asked them.

Classroom Demonstrations
Successful whole language teachers explain how they organize and support whole language learning.

Great Teachers
Profiles of exceptional teachers, written by colleagues who have seen them in action.

Great Schools
Great schools are created by dedicated faculties and parents. Here are inspiring accounts of their accomplishments.

Breakthroughs

First person educational success stories by teachers and parents.

Neef Alcott Parker Steiner Montessori Froebel Dewey Vygotsky Mitchell Piaget Rogers Maslow

1800   1900   2000

Network

Many teacher support groups are now assuming a leading role in the professional development of teachers, sponsoring major conferences and workshops, writing monthly newsletters, running clearinghouses for professional books. In this feature we include excerpts from teacher support group newsletters from the United States, Canada, and Australia. We also include subscription information.

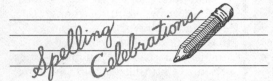

Sandra Wilde, 1987 recipient of the NCTE Promising Researcher Award for her groundbreaking dissertation on spelling, explains the significance of specific misspellings, and what they reveal about the "linguistic genius" of the speller. She also offers theory-wise tips for teachers who want to help their students become more proficient spellers.

Becoming Literate

First-person accounts of learning to read and write by adults who have recently become fully literate or by teachers who are helping adults discover literacy.

In the Mail

We share with you the inspiring and informative letters we have received from students, parents, teachers, administrators, and other concerned citizens about a variety of issues related to whole language.

To fully understand writing you must write. Whole language educators write, and they are inviting their students to do so. Here are samplings of their writing across genre.

Language Stories

Vignettes that teach, that help teachers understand what it means to learn from children.

MarvELous INVENTIONs

Young children, unfettered by social conventions, do marvelous things with both oral and written language as they attempt to discover what language is and what it can do. We present samples of their creative oral constructions, invented spellings and punctuations.

The Funny Side

Spend time with kids in the classroom or elsewhere and you are bound to smile sooner or later. Here are light-hearted, humorous anecdotes from the funny side of teaching and parenting.

It Shouldn't Happen to Kids

…or teachers and parents. These vignettes reveal the unsound thinking that has dominated our profession. The stories are all true. The names have been changed or eliminated.

I Used to Be... But Now I...

Inspired by Kenneth Koch and Dorothy Watson, this feature highlights in a sentence or two the changes teachers are making as they move from traditional schooling practices to whole language strategies.

Well-Said

Provocative quotes drawn from the writings of seminal thinkers.

WHOLE LANGUAGE CAMERA

Here are glimpses of whole language in action as viewed through the lens of a camera.

YOUNG ARTISTS

Artwork by students, preschool through high school.

3. Resources

Book Notes

We give a brief overview of professional books and, space permitting, excerpt quotes.

Resources

On nearly every page you'll find professional and curricular resources—publishers, organizations, periodicals, books, materials—that can enhance the whole language experience at home and at school. To buy, write or call the company directly. The prices, addresses, and phone numbers we have listed were accurate as of June, 1990.

Resource Essays

These relate to a specific resource, and describe in greater detail than a review just what function the resource serves or service it provides.

4. Indexes and Correlations

We provide four comprehensive indexes and cross references to help you access information:

• Literature Reference List

An index of all the literature to which our contributors refer in their essays. Please note: this is not intended as a core literature list or a recommended reading list.

• Running Features Index

This is a listing of all the titles by running feature. Suppose you are a parent interested in what other parents have to say. Using this index, you can look up "Parents' Perspective", and find all the individual titles included in this feature and the page numbers on which they can be found.

• Resources and Books Index

Want to look up a specific resource? This index, divided into seventeen subject categories, is your best bet. Keep in mind that whole language is not easily categorized. If you don't find the resource in the first category you choose, try another.

• Subject/Author Index

Here you will find the names of all authors of essays, stories, and book notes, together with salient whole language topics.

• Correlations

You can find cross references to related essays at the ends of articles.

—LBB

A Letter to Teachers New to Whole Language

Dear Teacher,

I'm aware that many teachers who read this catalog will be new to whole language. Welcome! I believe that you will find in whole language, as many other teachers have, a new sense of yourself as a professional. Many teachers see in whole language what made them want to be a teacher in the first place: the wonderful joy of helping young people learn. I know of no other movement in the history of education that has so caught the imagination of teachers and developed so strong a grass-roots base among classroom teachers as whole language.

I believe that's because the teaching profession, particularly in the English-speaking world, has come of age. Teachers are taking seriously their responsibilities as decision-makers and as advocates for the young people they teach. They are not satisfied to be treated like incompetents who must be told what to do and precisely how and when to do it. They are taking power, as professionals, in their classrooms.

Whole language brings together modern, scientific knowledge of teaching, learning, language, and curriculum and puts it into a positive, humanistic philosophy, which teachers can identify with and which offers them strong criteria for their professional decisions and teaching practice. And the premise of whole language, that each teacher must make her or his own commitment and devise a personal teaching style, is a refreshing contrast to insulting text manuals and administrative mandates.

Currently there are a number of ways that teachers come to whole language. For some of you whole language has provided a name for what you already believe in and already do in your classrooms. You are the teachers who quietly set aside the basals long ago. You involve kids in reading and writing, use thematic units, and minimize the damage to your kids from standardized tests and report-card marks. Whole language makes it possible for you to claim the respect you've been entitled to all along. But more than that, whole language enables you to examine what you are doing and to build and expand on the base as you share with others and incorporate ideas from other whole language teachers into what you are doing.

To these teachers I say thank you for what you've done. Thank you for leading the way all these years for kids and for professional, self-respecting teaching. We need you to remind us of the debt whole language owes to the past. Before anyone said "I'm a whole language teacher," there were whole language teachers. And there have always been whole language learners.

Others have become interested in whole language through colleagues, the teachers next door and down the hall, who seem to enjoy their teaching and whose pupils seem to be happy, creative, and productive kids. You may be picking up ideas, literature sets, process writing, big books, and thematic units and discovering that to use them effectively you have to rethink everything else you're doing. It helps to be able to talk over your "disequilibrium" with your colleagues, borrow some books, join a teacher support group, or go to a conference or workshop. But the transition to whole language is ultimately one you have to make yourself.

To these teachers I say we're glad you're becoming a whole language teacher. All of us consider that we also are still becoming. Few of us experienced anything like whole language teaching when we were pupils ourselves. And

even in our fondest imagination we could not predict how much our kids were capable of doing if only we freed them from the textbooks, tests, and artificial limitations of traditional teaching. So we learn from our kids and from each other. We're glad you're going to help.

Still other teachers hear about whole language at conferences, read about it in professional journals, or become fascinated with the exciting whole language professional books appearing in greater and greater abundance. But you, yourself, may not know any whole language teachers. Many of the voices of teachers and other professional educators creating this literature are represented in this catalog. New teachers are attracted by the authenticity of this

Great Teachers Featured in *The Catalog*

Atwell, p.136 Avery, p.14 Boyd, p.19 Castro, p.412 Copeland, p.48

Corona, p.331 Crowley, p.53 Curry, p.229 Easton, p.273 Gollasch, p.345

Goodman, p.314 Holdaway, p.45 Hood, p.239 Huntzinger, p.350 Jacobson, p.420

Makeba, p.186 Martin, p.167 Milz, p.404 Obringer, p.178 Paley, p.30

Siu-Runyan, p.374 Smith, p.77 Whitlow, p.372 Wigginton, p.286 Wortman, p.47

Not pictured: Bloome p. 227, Wing Jan p.152

literature. They read the language stories, see the samples of kids' miscues or writing, and are inspired by the creative energy of so many of the teachers. But the next step in turning this into a new way of teaching in their own classrooms is not easy. Any change is frightening and real change is really scary. And the risks are real if you find yourself out ahead of your colleagues and your administrators.

To you we say we're here for you. In this catalog, and in the increasing amount of whole language professional literature, we share our concepts, experiences, insights, and the growing evidence that whole language works. We share the belief system that underlies whole language. Many teachers by themselves, with no administrative support, have succeeded in making the move to whole language teaching. If you can find other teachers who also want to change, that helps a lot. My advice is take your time and find your own path to whole language. Take a personal inventory and decide what you are already doing that fits. Then decide which parts of your teaching you are least happy with, such as using workbooks, grouping, organizing time, or giving weekly spelling tests. In this catalog are many ideas of holistic alternatives. And there are many references to more information and ideas. Move at your own pace as you make the change. Don't be discouraged by temporary setbacks and don't let disparaging remarks from others deter you. Keep moving until you feel

what you are doing is consistent with what you have come to believe, and then keep moving some more as you see what you and your kids can accomplish.

And now there are teachers who find that whole language is the policy of their school or their district or that there is a strong move toward whole language, which has the support of administrators. *I fervently hope that no teacher is being forced to adopt whole language.* But even without overt pressure it is possible to feel uneasy that things are moving too fast around you and that your colleagues have lost respect for you because you haven't changed your way of teaching. You care about your kids, you work hard at teaching, and you are not about to make risky changes just because other people have decided you should. You have a right to be cautious and skeptical. Whole language is not about change simply for the sake of change.

Teachers, like their pupils, need time for growth and for change. All learning deserves patience. Try to keep an open mind as you consider whole language alternatives. You may be surprised to find that you already share some of the philosophy of whole language. The problem for many teachers comes as they realize that they can not simply add the things they like about whole language to what they are already doing: They can't add literature sets to their diligent use of basal readers, for example. There isn't time to do both, and the underlying philosophies are contradictory.

Moving from relying on the teacher's manuals to relying on your own professional judgment may be the scariest part of all. You need to be in charge of this transition, but you deserve support, respect, and assistance from your colleagues and your administrators. Share with them your misgivings; show them that you're willing to be a risk-taker, that you're open to change but that you need to be sure of yourself as you modify your teaching.

A key to making the transition to whole language teaching is having more faith in yourself as a teacher and in your kids as learners. On the one hand, it's strange that you would doubt your ability to take charge in your own classrooms, considering how well educated you are. But when you're used to being told by administrators and manuals what to do, it makes you doubt your own competence. As for the kids, don't expect miracles overnight. They need to get used to new experiences too. In time they'll amaze you. But when you start entertaining doubts about whether to go back to the old ways because the kids aren't doing as well as you hoped, ask yourself where they would be under the old program. How much actual reading and writing have they done that wouldn't have happened otherwise? What are the kids doing who would have been in your low group? What's happening with your top achievers now that the ceiling is out of their way?

It is only teachers who can make whole language happen. You're the ones who are there with the kids in the classroom. So to all of you joining or considering joining the ranks of whole language teachers, my coeditors Yetta Goodman and Lois Bridges Bird join me in saying whole language needs you. Kids need you.

Sincerely,

Ken Goodman

→ See: DeLawter, p. 389; Gillam, p. 56; Goodman, pp. 207, 215, 274, 344, 363.

"Learning is an act of creation which makes and shapes the world of the learner."

—Mike Torbe
Language, the Learner and the School

CAROLYN CLEBSCH

Learning

Contents

The Eyes of the Artist

by Catherine Compton-Lilly

The midafternoon sun filtered through the bank of windows, casting a yellow glow on Mrs. Driver's kindergarten. Most of the children worked contentedly, gluing colorful pieces of yarn onto squares of brown burlap.

I remember being surrounded by activity and staring at the guest artist seated by the windows. He sat motionless, slightly hunched with age. His voice was deep and gruff but conveyed genuine interest. The telltale white cane reminded me that he could merely feel the heat of the sunshine. A long line of children spanning the entire length of windows waited patiently for their chance to speak with him.

I was thankful that he could not sense my stare; I watched for a long time. When I was the last remaining child, Mrs. Driver gently led me to the end of the line. As I walked, my feet felt the size of an elephant's, though the rest of me felt small and vulnerable.

Tears threatened my eyes, but I refused to sacrifice my five-year-old honor. I could hear but did not listen to the conversations he was having with the other children. My mind was elsewhere.

Then suddenly it was my turn. Mrs. Driver introduced us. He asked softly what I had made, but I could not muster a reply. Instead I passed my piece of burlap into his tough gray hands. He felt each piece of yarn and looked me straight in the eye and said, "It's a lovely flower. What color is it?"

And as I answered, the sun came beaming through the windows.

Catherine Compton-Lilly is an elementary teacher at the DeWitt Road School, Webster, NY.

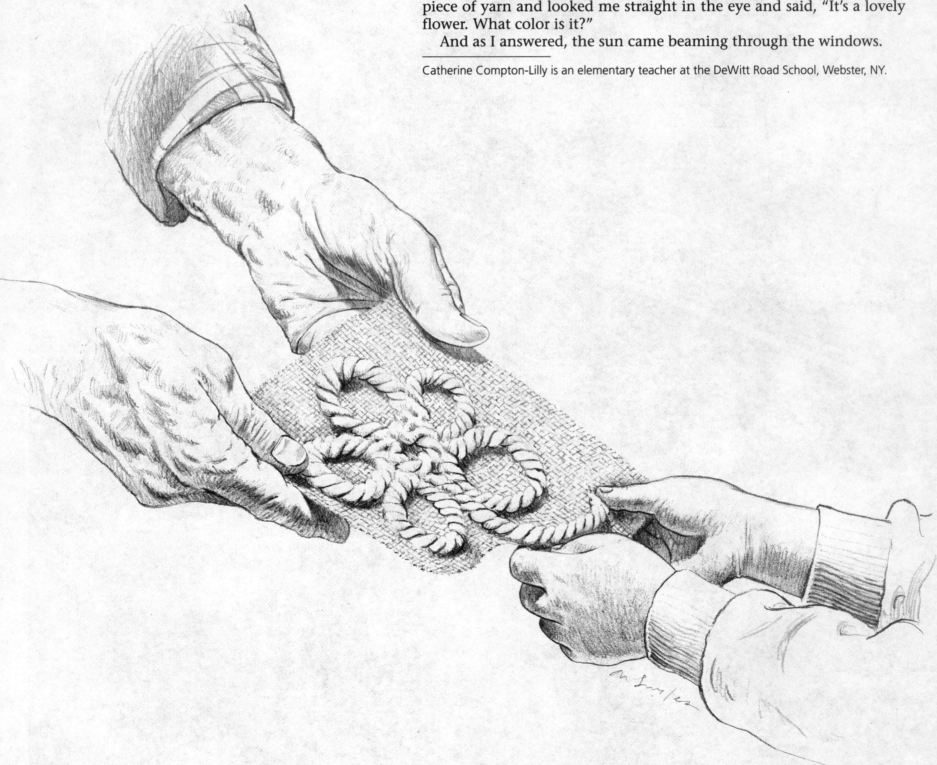

Coming to Know

As I See It:
Kenneth S. Goodman

Coming to Know

Adapted from *Language and Thinking in School*, 3d ed., by Kenneth S. Goodman, E. Brooks Smith, Robert Meredith, and Yetta M. Goodman (New York: Richard C. Owen, 1987): pp. 94–96.

And this our life, exempt from public haunt,
Finds tongues in trees, books in the running
    brooks,
Sermons in stones, and good in everything.

    —Shakespeare, *As You Like It*

Knowledge and Knowing

Children could not achieve by themselves the state of knowing that Shakespeare describes, nor could they reach it with their fellow children only. They would see the trees, the brooks, and the stones, but not being able to engage in discourse about them, they would not come to "know" them in relation to each other and to other events in the "Forest of Order." Trees can speak only when humans with the power of language observe them and make them a part of their own knowing.

Knowing is more than thinking, although thinking is one of the processes by which people come to know. Knowing is a very personal process, involving imagination above all else. Some of our thinking procedures can be isolated and scientifically explained, but perhaps only the poet has the kind of vision that can capture a full concept of knowing. Walt Whitman says it well:

There was a child went forth every day
And the first object he look'd upon
That object he became,
And that object became part of him for the
    day or a certain part of the day,
Or for many years or stretching cycles of years.

    —"A Child Went Forth"

Knowing is becoming. As events in the world become part of children's worlds and as they gain their own view of people and things about them, they begin to become persons.

Once Paumanok,
When the lilac-scent was in the air and fifth-
    month grass was growing,
Up this seashore in some briers,
Two feather'd guests from Alabama, two together,
And their nest, and four light-green eggs spotted
    with brown,
And every day the he-bird to and fro near at hand,
And every day the she-bird crouch'd on her nest,
    silent, with bright eyes,

And every day I, a curious boy, never too close,
    never disturbing them,
Cautiously peering, absorbing, translating.

    —"Out of the Cradle Endlessly Rocking"

Whitman was not the only poet to discover and extol the freshness and intimacy of childhood learning—coming to know—but certainly he showed a profound sensitivity to it in the line "Cautiously peering, absorbing, translating." Poets never seem to outgrow this quality of childlike experiencing, of meeting the world head on and coming to terms with it. Somewhere along the educational road to adulthood the wondrous quality of experiencing and coming to know in language can be lost, and personality can stagnate. Teachers can work to keep the intellectual growth going.

Language and Coming to Know

A key educational problem is the place of language in intellectual learning, what we call *coming to know*. Language may be seen as a necessary part of the personal process of experiencing and knowing. In this view, the thing is not known until it is discussed and named, and its interrelation with other things is not understood until language embodies the idea. If this function of language is accepted, intellectual education is neither the memorization of words and facts, nor the possession of significant experiences, but is the constant interplay of interrelated experiences and language. Since language is pivotal in a person's learning through experience, it is the very core of the teaching-learning process.

To Dewey and Bentley (1949), knowing is a transactional process between the individual and the environment, with language at the center. Coming to know—experience interpreted and intellectualized in language—would then be viewed as the basic goal of education.

Dewey believed that experience would not stand alone as learning but that it must be interpreted through a process of reflective thinking to be made consequential. Knowing is a transaction between the individual and the environment in which both are transformed. There is no such thing as absolute knowledge, only a process of knowing involving actions and word-meanings together. The search of young children for answers to their questions about every new item they see and handle is a natural example of the transaction between the individual

and the environment that Dewey describes. This process is always happening, and it never becomes final or fixed. The teacher's role is to keep the way open and the means available for the richest and fullest possible transactions.

One of the most powerful statements of the difference between knowledge and knowing is the one-act play *The Lesson* by Eugène Ionesco (1958). Herr Professor, his student, and his maid are the characters. The play opens innocently enough with the arrival of a new, young female student, but soon the maid interjects a note of foreboding by admonishing the professor not to let "it" happen again. However, the teacher, by impressing his knowledge (verbiage) upon the pupil through the means of monotonous recitation, finally overwhelms the pupil and symbolically (although on stage literally) kills her. The Herr Professor could have achieved the same end had he used the more subtle, but equally deadening, modern methods of tightly programmed mastery learning materials or carefully conditioned group processes. The aim would still have been the subjection of the pupil to the disembodied verbalization of the culture. The only possible rejoinder to *The Lesson* is to give the learner ownership over both language and experience and to view language as the matrix in personal knowing. Then the process of education becomes a process of personal discovery under the guidance of teachers who are aware of the validity of this process in their own learning.

➜ See: Goodman, pp. 23, 67.

References

Dewey, J., and A. Bentley. 1949. *Knowing and the known.* Boston: Beacon.
Ionesco, E. 1958. *The lesson.* In *Four plays.* New York: Grove.

Book Note

"The Having of Wonderful Ideas" and Other Essays on Teaching and Learning

Eleanor Duckworth
1987; 168 pp.; $13.95
New York: Teachers
College Press

This may be the best book about teaching and learning ever written. In a variety of fascinating essays about such topics as children making bulbs light up and teachers observing the moon and thinking about what they see, Duckworth offers a distinctly Piagetian perspective on how we come to know, and on the role schools play in that knowing. Duckworth combines a strong background in Piaget (she worked with him and was one of his translators) with a probing intelligence that is never content to take things for granted. Every page contains interesting revelations and insights. The main message to a reader of this book is that it is absolutely imperative for learners to reinvent the wheel, for it is through invention rather than transmission that true learning occurs.

Sandra Wilde

As I See It:
Yetta M. Goodman

We See What We Know

Paraphrasing Piaget—we only see what we know. I was reminded of this when we visited Heron Island, part of the majestic Barrier Reef off the Queensland coast in Australia. As we flew over the sea to reach the island, I was intrigued by the water; it was vast, blue, and beautiful. When we explored the island, we walked out on the reef at low tide and I was impressed with the shadows, the movement, and the color. However, after a nature walk with one of the reef guides who picked up and let us hold all kinds of sea creatures, talked to us about them, and answered our questions, I saw the reef anew whenever I went for a walk. The shadows became sea cucumbers and other sea animals. The flashes of color were now the

edges of clams lying disguised among rocks and coral. Small fish and tiny fast-moving crabs, which I hadn't noticed earlier, were visible all the time now. I could predict them from their movements, colors, shadows, and the holes in the sand. And as we flew back to the mainland, I realized that the circles and sand areas that I noticed on our way out were islands being born. I could see now that the reefs were coming together to support life. I noticed a tree on one formation which I knew would eventually become an island. It is, indeed, true that one *sees* based on what one knows, and both the known and the knower are never the same again.

➜ See: Piaget, p. 311.

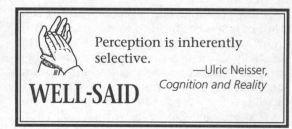

Perception is inherently selective.

    —Ulric Neisser,
    Cognition and Reality

WELL-SAID

Breakthroughs

by Carol S. Avery

Carrie

Our principal was on the phone when I walked into the office that Friday morning several years ago. He caught my eye as I heard him say, "So today will be her last day?" He hung up the phone and said, "That was Carrie's foster mother. Her temporary placement ends tomorrow."

Carrie! She had come to our school in September, a tiny first-grader whose reputation everyone knew by the end of the first week. Recess the first morning found her tussling with a group of older boys over possession of a playground ball. During art she somehow walked through the wet tempera on another child's painting that had slipped to the floor only a moment before. In the classroom, her crayons lasted a week, ending up as broken nubs scattered throughout her desk. She could rarely find her pencil, scissors, or math book in that overflowing desk.

Day after day she engaged in one fray after another with her classmates. When in frustration they tattled, "Mrs. Avery, Carrie's . . ." or turned to her and said, "Carrie, stop it!" she defiantly glared at them and shouted, "I didn't do nothin'." To every teacher and student she became known for her pouts and shouts. When these tactics failed to bail her out of difficulties, her face wrinkled into a twisted agony and she cried—an eerie, silent cry. Tears squeezed from her eyes and ran down her cheeks.

In the first weeks of school I often stewed over Carrie's progress. Was she learning anything in our daily reading and writing workshops or in math? Literature time—listening to stories—seemed to be her favorite time of the day, though she frequently pestered other children as they sat together on the carpet.

Yet, despite her obvious distrust of the world—or maybe in spite of it—Carrie made progress in her schoolwork. She was the first child to "go around the world" in the game we played with math facts. As she moved from desk to desk, at each one the first to call out the correct answer to the math fact on the flash card I held up, her sullen face softened, and by the time she reached the last half of the room she was all smiles. Not that she was perfect. She encountered several stops along the way and had to wait her turn in order to resume her journey, but she became involved and eager, a part of the group. Her astonished classmates urged her on and, at the end, cheered her success.

During free play Carrie often came up to me and said, "I can read this book to you," and then she'd snuggle under my arm and read and look up at me and giggle and read some more. Her delight came not only in the satisfaction of learning to read, but also from her involvement with characters and story lines. She loved *Cookie's Week* by Cindy Ward, the story of a mischievous cat. When she came to the page when Cookie, the cat, knocked a flowerpot off the windowsill, she commented, "In my old house our plants all died." She paused a brief moment, then shrugged and added brightly, "But I still watered them anyhow."

At the beginning of the year her writing consisted of scribbles. She filled page after page with erratic, almost wild, crayon and pencil marks. Gradually Carrie began writing letters and then stringing those letters together into fragments of thoughts. But it was the story of the Thanksgiving dinner she was to share with her foster family that engaged Carrie in writing. She wrote over and over about the turkey dinner, the visiting relatives—especially the grandmother—and

the planned trip to a movie. "Anyways, I never been to a movie before," she told me when I conferred with her about her writing.

Now, today was Carrie's last day in our school. During free play this Friday morning, she led a group of children in a puppet show based on the folktale *Rumplestiltskin*. In her version, after the queen guesses Rumplestiltskin's name, they go off to Disneyland for a honeymoon.

Later that morning, we began our writing workshop and the giggling Carrie grew somber. Fifteen minutes into the workshop, I looked up from my writing to see her tears. She glanced over at me. I held out my arms, and she got up from her desk, came to me, and with fists clenched against her chest, buried her head in my shoulder. For several minutes Carrie's silent sobs beat against me. She never made a sound. Then she left and went back to her writing.

At the end of the workshop Carrie asked, "Can I share today?" The class gathered on the rug and Carrie read her writing. "I am moving. I don't want to, but I got to. I will miss you. Miss you. You guys are all I got. I will miss you."

There was a silence before Elizabeth raised her hand.

"Elizabeth?" said Carrie.

"I think your writing's good. It made me feel sad." Then Elizabeth added, "I'll miss you too."

"Yeah," said Monica. "I agree. I'll miss you too."

"I'll miss you three," piped up Ryan.

"I'll miss you four," said Jeff.

"I'll miss you five."

"I'll miss you six." One by one, each child chimed in with the spontaneous count all the way to twenty-five. Carrie turned to me.

"I'll miss you twenty-six," I said.

Carrie giggled and said, "Thank you." The children clapped.

Carrie walked out the door that afternoon for the last time. She phoned many of the children throughout the year and wrote notes to several of us. Sometimes the children spoke of her. "Carrie liked this book," they'd say. Or, "Remember when Carrie won 'Around the World'? I miss her."

At the beginning of Carrie's five months in our classroom community, she evoked anger and frustration from both peers and adults. Slowly, although certain vestiges of these first behaviors remained, we all came to experience a different Carrie, one who appeared to relax some of her own intense anger and display behaviors that roused our compassion and laughter.

Gradually Carrie engaged in classroom learning. She set her own pace and made her own choices about writing topics and reading materials. This is not to say that I, or any of her other teachers, permitted her to avoid responsibility to her studies—though the going was rough at first. Like the other children, Carrie was required to adhere to the classroom procedures and structures as we shaped them during the first few weeks of school. Within that structure, the choices she made and the responses she received from teachers and peers enabled her to assume the responsibility of a student. Time and choice were her allies. Her classmates became her advocates. But they were not all she had. As Carrie moved on to another school and another class, I knew she took with her an involvement with learning, an especially powerful engagement with written language, and—the catalyst for it all—her wonderful imagination.

→ See: Harlow, p. 51; Literature Reference List, p. 429; Meier, p. 50; Ohanian, p. 60.

Carol S. Avery is a primary teacher with the Manheim Township School District, Lancaster, PA.

Great Teachers:
Carol S. Avery

by Carole L. Slotter

Noisy Learning

Greg and I ignored the racket around us and talked seriously for 10 minutes about reading and writing. I was a middle-aged visitor and he was a very verbal, almost seven-year-old.

"What do you do when you come to a word you don't know?" I asked.

"Sometimes I go on and come back later when I know what the story is about and I can figure out the word from its first letter. Sometimes I cover up a compound word and after I have part of the word, I can figure out the rest. Sometimes I get one syllable and then I can read the word."

Our conversation shifted to writing. "I learned to write by writing really short stories, then writing longer ones. I write about things I know," he said with a tone of authority. "Like, I know a lot about the *Titanic* and I wrote one book about it and now I am writing a sequel. I like to write to get ideas out of my head so they don't bother me when I am doing something else."

"You get ideas outside of school?" I prompted.

"Yeah, like I am waiting for the bus, I think of all of these ideas I can write about."

I changed the topic temporarily. "Tell me about Mrs. Avery."

"I like her. She lets us read together when we are quiet enough, and she lets us have a nice reading time. But I like writing a lot, because she comes around to us and if we're stuck, she can help. Like, I was writing and she said to read it over, and I found out that the end of the sixth chapter was good enough. It was an end."

Greg was one of 23 children in the classroom that day in late May. I've reported our conversation because it was typical. Greg talks with strangers about literary activities as he might discuss a game at recess, but he also can be boisterous, mischievous, and inattentive. His behavior is the norm for a group that Carol Avery insists was one of the most difficult of her career and was on its worst behavior the day I visited.

I didn't see "worst" behavior. Yes, it got noisy. Some of the youngsters strayed from the assigned activity, and some were rambunctious. Carol called them "a handful." Keeping active, wiggly, mouthy kids working diligently all day might be accomplished with 12 burly drill sergeants placed between desks, but that's not the kind of class Carol runs. She allows a level of personal freedom that encourages individual commitment to learning. I saw that commitment and I saw kids excited about learning. Several youngsters carried books to me, pleading, "Let me read you a great story."

Though the class was most enthusiastic over reading and writing, students still had fun with math. Carol started math with a class game called "Around the World." I witnessed a breakthrough. Monica, who had never won the game, suddenly had a streak of right answers and moved halfway around the class. There were moans when she got knocked off by one of the class math brains, but a few minutes later, she got another turn and she won. Everyone cheered.

Then Carol distributed a paper with just one addition problem at the top: 21 plus 38. She explained to children that they hadn't been taught how to add two-digit numbers, so it was all right if they couldn't do the problem. She asked them to try to do it and to write on the paper how they did it or why they couldn't. Carrying writing into the math lesson produced some thoughtful expository paragraphs, along with several correct answers to the problem.

Three daily components of Carol's class are writing workshop, reading workshop, and literature time, which have similarities among them that reflect her philosophy of teaching. Writing workshop is a time for each child to work on a piece of writing. The choice of topic is the child's. After a first draft is completed, the child shares the writing either in a small group or in the whole group. I saw drafts on a wide range of topics, from "Dinosers," a story I was told was "part fiction and part nonfiction," to a contemporary excursion to the Three Bears. Monica wrote memories of her late grandfather, recalling a water fight with him in her backyard.

In the sharing, the child is in charge. The class sits on a rug in the corner of the room, and the child who is sharing sits in the "author's chair." The author reads the piece and then calls on classmates with raised hands. Comments of praise precede the questions for clarity. After sharing a piece, the child uses feedback from his classmates to revise. When the child is satisfied, the piece is published. Carol types the text (in standard English), and the child adds the illustrations. The pages are stapled into an attractive cover, and the book joins the class library.

Sharing is part of literature time too. Both the teacher and the children read books aloud and then analyze what they read. The child reader calls on peers who ask about the reader's opinion of the story. When Carol reads, she asks open-ended questions that bring out speculation about the author's intentions. In these discussions, there are no right or wrong opinions. And everyone has an opinion!

Bright-eyed Megan told me, "Write that Mrs. Avery likes books. She has books everywhere."

"Okay, I will. Is there anything else she likes?"

"Unicorns and *us*," she replied.

There must be at least 400 trade books, maybe more, stacked on every possible surface. Most of the books are Carol's, and she makes them available to the children. In literature time that day, though, Elizabeth shared a book from home: *Too Many Hopkins,* autographed by the author, Tomie dePaola. These first-graders know authors, and dePaola is a favorite. Photographs of children's authors are pinned on the wall, and the children write to and receive letters from many of them.

When it was time for reading workshop, Carol made an announcement the kids applauded: "Today you may pair up and read to one another." Minutes later, tucked into every cranny of the room were 11 pairs and one trio, their efforts on the book of choice producing a hubbub of expressive voices. I moved around the room, listening to the reading. The children enjoyed the adult audience and shared the illustrations with me. I found Jody, Matt, and Jeff under the teacher's desk where the three had claimed a cozy private place to share their selections. By the time I got to them, they had finished reading and were talking about ghosts and the ship the *Queen Mary.*

"So, what's the best part of your class?" I asked.

"Authors parties, publishing books, and reading together," they responded.

"Now tell me what's the not-so-good part of this class."

The Magdeberg Hemispheres: Grade Eleven

by Robert Morrison

Mr. Trassler places the Magdeberg Hemispheres on the demonstration table. Two black handles protrude like overdeveloped ears from each half. For some reason, a childhood flashback occurs. I am explaining to my mother that the kids from the apartment block have been teasing me about the way my ears stick out, something I had not realized before but of which I am now very much aware. My mother tapes my ears back and assures me that if I leave the tape in place for a long time my ears will grow in just the way I want them. The tape falls off by the next morning, but so has my concern for the shape of my ears. A sharp elbow in the side from the Tick draws my attention back to the teacher. The Tick is concerned not for my welfare but his own. He doesn't want to draw Mr. Trassler's attention our way. This teacher has been known to throw challenging questions at the class, and it is obvious that he is up to something this morning from the way he grins as he attaches a vacuum pump to the now-joined hemispheres and explains how he is about to draw out all the air. And the challenge comes, offered to the class as a whole but probing straight at the heart of our egos.

"I wonder if anyone in this room is strong enough to pull the two halves apart."

The hemispheres dangle by one ear as he holds them aloft for each of us to see. We look at him astonished. This is 11F, the all-boys class that has been kept together throughout its high school career, the collectivity of individual personalities from which the real students in 11A through E are to be kept shielded. Twenty-eight James Deans stiffen, flick glances about the room. To survive in this room you must be the class clown or the class bully. I am the class

---

"Everyone knows what that is," Jeff answered. "What's that?"

The three voices answered loudly in unison: *"Noise!"*

A major characteristic of this classroom was the large amount of choice and responsibility given the children. The children had control of their reading and writing. That appeared to nurture independence and self-reliance, qualities that encourage kids to be active—in fact, to talk. Forced passivity might result in quiet classrooms, in classes that are easier to handle, but, I think, would squelch excitement for learning.

In Carol's class, the teacher doesn't give all the answers. In fact, I saw her, in subtle ways, throw the learning task back to the child, who went off enthusiastically to find the answer to the question she had just asked. In the groups, the young authors know that their peers would ask questions; they anticipated them and asked themselves those questions as they worked on a draft. That process produced independent and analytical thinkers.

Most children who leave Carol Avery's class, I predict, will be lifelong learners who can solve problems. But last year's group won't be quiet learners—and who says that's a problem?

➜ See: Literature Reference List, p. 429.

Carole L. Slotter is the director of public relations at Millersville University, Millersville, PA.

---

clown and search quickly through my repertoire, looking for a way to turn the moment to advantage. George Spano beats me to it. He raises a languid hand.

"I think I can handle that little chore."

The class snickers; the jabs of Spaz Spano are not usually so verbal in nature. Trassler grins, the hemispheres swing slowly in his hand as he holds the drama of the moment. We grin too, knowing our teacher's downfall to be inevitable, secure in the knowledge that we like The Traz.

"In fact, I'm sure that none of you young gentlemen are strong enough to pull the two halves apart. I'll give a quarter to any of you who can do it."

The Traz has gone too far. The grins disappear. The Spaz reaches out to take the hemispheres by the handles and stands frozen, holding his own moment of attention. A quarter clatters onto the demonstration table, riveting our attention as it spins and settles. We hear the intake of breath; we hear the grunt as Spano's arms flex to separate the halves; we watch wide-eyed as nothing happens. Red-faced, The Spaz tries again and red-faced, fails. Hughsey holds up his hands to take the hemispheres. Hughsey tries and fails. Pat, Richard, Don, and Archie try and fail, as the black globe is passed down the length of the table, until it is set before me, the class clown. The class expects a quip, expects a rescue in humour, and again, nothing leaps to mind. The Traz smiles, and walking slowly toward the hemispheres, lets the class off the hook.

"I've tricked you today. I would try this demonstration in this class where you all know how strong you really are. But you see, we are sitting at the bottom of an ocean of air, an ocean so deep and heavy that it presses down on the outside of those hemispheres with a pressure of 14.7 pounds per square inch. Think about how many square inches are on the outside of that globe Robert is holding. Look at the picture on page 176 of the textbook."

There, we are astonished to find two horses straining against chains, two horses trying to pull the two halves of the Magdeberg Hemispheres in opposite directions.

"George, you might as well have tried to lift my car."

The class bursts into laughter. Trassler's Volkswagen Beetle is an institution in my lexicon of class antics. He looks at me, expecting the quip that will bond the class together and allow him to draw further on the point of the lesson. For a moment I am panicked until my brain kicks in—and—it happens. I twist my hands in opposite directions, the hemispheres separate with a loud pop, and as the class bursts into an uproar, I place the two halves in his outstretched hands.

I don't really remember what happened after that, except that I didn't get the quarter. It became important 20 years later when I bumped into Mr. Trassler at the checkout counter of Pascal's Hardware and told him what every teacher thirsts to hear—that he had been a great teacher. I also told him I was speaking as a professional, for I too was a teacher and had been in the classroom for 15 years. I even confessed that it was I who had attached the stink bomb to the bottom of his gas pedal one cold January day when all the windows in the Beetle were sure to be frozen shut. And for some reason, I told him of the Magdeberg Hemispheres, the long-forgotten memory of that day tricked out of me by the unexpected contact. I could see the astonishment, the confusion, the pleasure, flickering across his face. He reached into his pocket and handed me a quarter. We stared at each other, smiling awkwardly, until I asked him for the 20 years' accumulated interest. With a laugh, we shook hands and went our separate ways.

Robert Morrison is the vice-principal of Lindsay Place High School, Pointe Claire, Quebec.

Behind and Beyond Whole Language

Successful teachers I have known operate from a global perspective based on concepts and values, which brings order to a complex situation. There is a logical interrelatedness of the numerous facets of the design that becomes apparent as the learning events, personal relationships, shared responsibilities, and available resources are synchronized into a working environment. Language, spoken and written, arises within an activity. It supports, influences, and enriches learning. The main focus of attention, however, is not on language itself but generally on what is going on—the task, the story, the learning underway. Teachers, aware of the role language has in forming and conveying meaning, make sure that learning events are organized so that children will need to use a wide range of oral and written language for various purposes in different contexts.

Symbolization and Representation

For most of us, language is the major medium for learning, but behind it lies symbol-making, one of the most primary of human activities (Langer 1942). Thinking and learning do not result from raw experience with objects, events, or encounters with a natural phenomenon; rather, these experiences are mediated through signs and symbols which represent that reality. Our minds abstract from what is experienced and symbolically represent phenomena to ourselves and others. Cultures are formed, preserved, changed, and passed on through systems of meaning encoded in signs and symbols. Learning involves knowing the sign systems operating in the culture, using them for our own purposes, changing or abandoning outworn symbols, and creating new ones. Young children display skill as symbol-makers in a range of media and situations. In play, for example, they project themselves into new roles, reenact previously experienced events, and use objects to represent other objects, people, or animals (a pillow can be a mother, father, animal). Later they use skills in drawing and writing to signify, explore, and reflect on firsthand experiences as is illustrated in the following example produced by Chris, a kindergartner, after viewing a football game one Saturday.

Notice how he distinguishes the Michigan players (M) from the Ohio State players (B, for Buckeyes). In the original drawing he colors the team uniforms appropriately and draws in their face masks. He pictures himself in front of the TV with arms raised as if cheering. On each side of Chris are two symbols, the helmets, clearly labeled MESH A GEN and OHIO. At the top of the page he writes what the text is all about: ME WATCHING FOOTBALL. Overall, the text reveals much about Chris's knowledge of the culture as well as his skill in using two modes of representation.

In recognizing the role of language in making and sharing meaning, teachers must make sure that the primacy of language doesn't crowd out the use of other symbol systems and forms of representation. Music, mathematics, drawing, painting, sculpture, drama, poetry, and story are important areas for study in themselves. They can allow children to learn subject matter and express their understanding in multiple ways. Such opportunities not only stretch children's perceptive powers, but also offer them forms of expression that go beyond the logical and linear.

Context of Situation

The most useful concept for whole language teachers, in my view, concerns the social context of learning and its influence on the nature of talk, writing, or other forms of communication. It is not simply the physical setting (as important as it is in education) that makes the difference, but *what is going on at the time.* What is the activity, the subject matter? What is being achieved through language? Who is involved and what do they bring in terms of purpose, knowledge, culture? Is the classroom formal and institutionalized, where hierarchical relationships predominate? Or more flexible, where responsibility is shared and role relationships can vary?

Michael Halliday (1975) proposed a model of "language in use" that explores the multiple factors that affect the way meanings are expressed in speech. He includes cultural codes, dialects, grammar, and phonology as well as the functional components of language. Of particular interest here, however, is his analysis of *context of situation,* because those components are ones that teachers can most directly influence, making them extremely valuable conceptual tools. Halliday describes those components as *environmental determinants* of verbal interaction and identifies them as *field, tenor,* and *mode.*

Field is the focus of attention, the concerns of the participants and their reasons for interacting; it's a composite of the subject matter being considered and any activities or materials of the physical context that are part of the interaction.

Tenor represents the nature of the relationships as perceived by the participants. In working through a project, the relationship between partners may be close and collaborative as they experiment and observe. Talk is likely to be concerned with action, observations, and outcomes. Their language and relationship with each other changes when they report their work to the whole class or an interested adult visitor.

Mode refers to the forms of communication used in message transmission. In working with light, children will not only talk but make some notes or sketches, perhaps a chart or table, as they go along. In reflecting on their work or reporting it, they may produce a poem, play, or mock interview with an important scientist.

These are variables that teachers work with all the time, often unconsciously and sometimes without recognizing how change in one affects the other. Just how this functions in the classroom can be seen more clearly, perhaps, if we consider the concept of *frame.*

Framing Knowledge

Whatever the special curriculum requirements, the teacher usually has considerable scope in how it is framed, that is, how it is taught and studied. The frame focuses the attention of the learners, specifies what in a larger field of inquiry is to be considered, and determines the degree of control teachers and pupils have in selecting, organizing, and pacing the work to be done. There is generally an overarching topic or concept that bridges relevant fields of knowledge. There is likely to be less emphasis on just acquiring facts and more on creating knowledge. (Bernstein 1975; Goffman 1974). Framing allows students to experience knowledge in many forms and explore it from different perspectives.

An example from Peggy Harrison's class of 10-year-olds illustrates framing. The children were investigating the customs, rituals, homes, tools, crafts, and so on used by the different tribes of Ohio Indians. Their work at first required considerable reading and discussion, of both fiction and nonfiction, to get a sense of the time and people. They also visited a museum and Indian mounds in the area and viewed films. Children made models, replicated Indian tools and crafts, and wrote stories and reports.

An outcome of their visit to the museum was a decision to establish one of their own. This had a profound effect on the class. The shift in frame specified a new perspective, a different stance toward the study; children saw their investigations differently. No longer were they working on projects to please themselves and the teacher. Now they were a team making decisions about possible artifacts and ways of presenting them in the museum. They reread and discussed again what they had learned, and remembered specifics about their visit to the museum. The class appointed a committee to set standards and select those artifacts to be included.

Roles and role relationships changed, as did the focus of responsibility and power in the classroom. The committee learned to exercise power responsibly. The range of talk—planning, discussing, arguing, pleading, explaining—was intentional, sometimes emotional, and often very specific as accuracy and detail became more important. The writing varied from careful labeling and brief descriptions to making proposals for exhibits and producing stories and explanations of "how things were done" by the early Ohio residents. One group decided to share its work by preparing a volume on Indian Life, e.g., Hunting, Preparing Food, The Squaw's Life. The drama frame continued when the museum opened and children assumed roles as guides and docents.

In the Ohio Indian Study concern for language was always present. It became the focus of attention when children were struggling to find appropriate ways to write down what they wanted to say, or were closely attending to the language of a particular story or poem. It was the center of attention at other times when language itself was the content of learning.

➔ See: Britton, p. 69; Dyson, p. 46; Moffett, p. 70; Short, p. 18.

The author wishes to thank Jean Sperling, kindergarten teacher, Westerville, OH, and Peggy Harrison, teacher, Upper Arlington, OH.

References

Bernstein, B. 1975. "On the classification and framing of educational knowledge." In *Class, codes and control: Towards a theory of educational transmission.* London: Routledge & Kegan Paul.

Goffman, E. 1974. *Frame analysis.* New York: Harper & Row.

Halliday, M. A. K. 1975. "Talking one's way in: A sociolinguistic perspective on language and learning." In *Problems of language and learning,* ed. A. Davis. London: Heinemann.

Langer, S. 1962. *Philosophy in a new key* (1942). New York: Mentor Books.

Martha L. King, professor emerita, Ohio State University, has been an elementary school teacher, curriculum consultant, and professor of language arts in elementary education. She has researched and written about critical reading, language arts, informal education, and children's development. In the early 1970s she was cofounder of EPIC.

Patterns That Connect

Whole Language Internacional
by Brian Cambourne

Helping Students Seek the Patterns Which Connect: A View of Literacy Education from Down Under

There is an important issue that politicians, employers, educators, and the community in general urgently need to address. It is this: What kind of literacy do we want for our nations as we enter the 21st century? Should we aim to increase the levels of what some term *functional literacy* (i.e., "enough to get by on"), or should our schools aim to produce graduates who demonstrate a kind of literacy that goes well beyond mere functional literacy?

I believe that we have no choice. If we are to survive as nations, we need more than mere functional literacy. We need to produce more and more school graduates who have access to and control over the range of those forms of oral and written forms of language that make higher level thinking and knowing possible. We need school graduates who can use both oral and written forms of language to seek out and understand what one of the seminal thinkers of the 20th century, Gregory Bateson, called "the patterns which connect" (1979). One of the most powerful ways to get access to and control over these forms of language is through sustained engagement with text. If this is true, then it means that we need to ensure that our schools produce graduates who regularly read, write, talk, and listen, and who continue to do so long after they have left school. My thesis is that persons who do this inevitably internalise the forms of language that support thinking and knowing. They seem better equipped to discover those patterns to which Bateson refers.

Some teachers in Australian classrooms are achieving this kind of language learning with their pupils. This is especially true with respect to children who have been classified as *educationally disadvantaged*. When data from such classrooms are analysed, they show that pupils in these classes have similar kinds of experiences:

- They are immersed in appropriate texts;
- They receive appropriate demonstrations of how reading, writing, talking, and listening are done and what they can be used for;
- They are given responsibility for making some decisions about when, what, and how they read, write, talk, and listen;
- They have high expectations about themselves as potential readers, writers, talkers, and listeners;
- They are given high expectations about their abilities to complete the reading, writing, talking, and listening tasks that they attempt;
- They are given opportunities to approximate mature and/or "ideal" forms of reading, writing, and talking without fear of punishment or ridicule;
- They are given time to engage in the acts of reading, writing, talking, and listening;
- They are provided opportunities to employ developing reading, writing, talking, and listening skills in meaningful and purposeful contexts;

A classroom teacher himself, Brian Cambourne was awarded a Fulbright Fellowship and a postdoctoral fellowship at Harvard University in the midseventies. He has been a visiting fellow at the Program for Language and Literacy, University of Arizona, and at the Center for the Study of Reading, University of Illinois. Presently, he is head of Centre for Studies in Literacy at the University of Wollongong, New South Wales, Australia, where he has been working since 1982.

- They are given responses and feedback from knowledgeable others, which both support and inform their attempts at constructing meaning using language;
- They are provided plenty of opportunities to reflect upon and make explicit both how and what they learn.

In Australia, classrooms that conform to these principles are regarded as examples of the movement that has become known as *whole language*. At the core of this view of whole language is the "wholeness" of the demonstrations that learner-reader/writers receive. Essentially they are demonstrations of language that are "whole" enough to enable learners to engage with the way language is organized. This is because the teachers who run these classrooms appreciate that one can really only "know" a language when one knows how all the systems and subsystems that make it up "fit" together. We are finding in Australia that this principle of "knowing" through understanding "the patterns which connect" is not restricted to language learning. Teachers are beginning to apply it to the learning of mathematics, music, and other curriculum areas.

These teachers also understand that learning language can be seriously complicated if learners are expected to engage with demonstrations that make it difficult to seek out and discover these patterns. This is what typically happens when language and/or language processes are fragmented and the fragments become the demonstrations that learners receive. An example would be the traditional grammar, phonics, or spelling lesson. In the traditional grammar lesson the grammatical subsystem of language is stripped clear of the complex web of other linguistic subsystems (e.g., the meaning system, the phonological system, the pragmatic system, etc.) and taught as a system in its own right and with its own integrity. The learner is presented with demonstrations of how grammar "works" in isolation from its role in shaping and moulding meaning. The subtle patterns that connect each of the linguistic systems that work cooperatively to produce intended meanings are thus broken. Similarly, in the traditional phonics and/or spelling program, the graphophonic system is peeled away from the syntactic and semantic systems of language and the patterns that connect each to effective reading and writing are lost. The learner is left to discover what the patterns that connect are, in contrived and artificial ways. Sadly, many find this process of orchestration so difficult that they give up and opt out.

Bateson (1979) recognised how such a situation would seriously complicate the process of learning when he wrote:

Break the pattern which connects the items of learning and you destroy all quality.

I believe that this statement should become

Reference
Bateson, G. 1979. *Mind and nature: A necessary unity.* London: Wildwood House.

Further Reading by Brian Cambourne
◆ *Coping with Chaos,* with Jan Turbill. Australia: Primary English Teaching Association, 1987 (available through Heinemann).
◆ *The Whole Story: Natural Learning and the Acquisition of Literacy in the Classroom.* New Zealand: Ashton Scholastic, 1988.

Book Note

The Meaning Makers: Children Learning Language and Using Language to Learn

Gordon Wells
1986; 256 pp.; $16
Portsmouth, NH: Heinemann

My copy of this book plainly shows the exhilaration I felt when I first read it; the text is heavily underlined and notes fill the margins. Based on the Bristol Study, in which language samples were collected in home and at school from over 100 children during a ten-year period, the book provides striking evidence that children are active learners who use and control language as they work to make sense of their world. Wells also presents evidence that soundly refutes the notion that some children are linguistically disadvantaged. As Wells shows again and again, limited language use at school is more often an indictment of restrictive schooling practices than proof that some children are handicapped linguistically. The book, inspiring from start to finish, ends with Wells's recommendations for theoretically sound teaching.

LBB

Book Note

The Whole Story: Natural Learning and the Acquisition of Literacy in the Classroom

Brian Cambourne
1988; 210 pp.; $12.80
Auckland, New Zealand: Ashton Scholastic

For the past decade, Brian Cambourne has been researching how learning, and especially literacy learning, occurs. He has conducted this research in the naturalistic mode he prefers: sitting in classrooms for many hundreds of hours. This book arises from what he has observed in those classrooms.

Cambourne argues that teachers who are dissatisfied and/or frustrated with their literacy teaching methods are prisoners of a view of learning that is based on invalid assumptions. This view seriously complicates the process of learning to read and write. The book presents an alternative view of learning and an approach to teaching literacy that liberates teachers. Furthermore, it leads to the development of highly literate, critically aware, confident readers and writers. These are liberated learners who will continue to read and write long after they have left school.

part of the creed of all who profess to be implementing a whole language philosophy.

→ See: Cairney, p. 345; Edelsky, p. 72; Goodman, p. 344; Torbe, p. 232.

Cornerstone: Kathy Gnagey Short

The Role of Intertextuality in Reading and Learning

Peter Rabbit

Peter's mother said to Pinky and Blacky and Peter, "Go outside and pick carrots." Before they went outside, Mother said, "And don't go in Mister Vegetable's garden. He will make you into pancakes." Then they went outside. Pinky and Blacky went to pick carrots but Peter didn't. He went into Mister Vegetable's garden. He didn't pick carrots. When Mister Vegetable saw him, he wanted to kill him but he didn't. But he did cut some of his tail off. Pinky and Blacky were about done picking carrots when Mister Vegetable caught Peter and put him in a cage. Pinky and Blacky went home. They never got Peter Rabbit back but they had a baby and named him Peter Rabbit and lived happily ever after.

—Amy, age 6 (Short 1986)

Harold Rosen (1984) gets at the heart of intertextuality when he points out that a story exists *only* because of the existence of other stories. Amy's story about Peter Rabbit came into existence because of the other stories she had read, written, and experienced in the past. There are obvious connections in her story to *Peter Rabbit* (Potter 1902), the nursery rhyme "Three Blind Mice," and fairy tales that end with "and they lived happily ever after." While Amy's connections are more obvious than many, all stories come into existence because of their connections to the past stories of the writer and the reader.

De Beaugrande (1980) defines intertextuality as the process of interpreting one text by means of connections to previously constructed texts. In reading a text, the reader draws connections from other texts that he or she has written or read. Those connections change both the current evolving text and understandings about the past texts.

A text includes any chunk of meaning that has unity and that can be shared with others. A piece of art or music, a dance, an oral story, or a poem can all be texts. Rosen argues that narrative, creating a story about our experiences, is a basic thinking process that we use to make sense of our experiences. It provides us with one way to organize those experiences in a meaningful way. Otherwise they remain fragmentary and unconnected and therefore virtually meaningless. From the endless stream of experiences in which we are constantly involved, we select, organize, and bring meaning to those experiences through storying. We must construct our own stories by connecting our current experiences with our past experiences.

As we read, draw, or dance, we search for unity within the evolving text and between the evolving text and our past texts. Tensions are created as we search for unity, and this propels learning forward. As we search, we discover both suspected and unsuspected connections between current evolving texts and past texts. These connections result in new understandings of these texts and of our general constructions of reality.

Inventing a story is not enough. According to Rosen, a story must be told. It must be made public. In telling a story to others

by expressing it in some public form, we not only bring the story to life, but we also make new connections and create new meanings.

Once we share a story, that text becomes a source of further dialogue and storying by both the reader and the writer—a process of endless intertextuality. In this process, we gain a richer understanding of texts. We create bigger stories that are more encompassing and better stories because of more complex intertextual ties.

Intertextuality involves connections and disjunctions. The connections allow us to link things, help us see new relationships, and allow us to bring unity to a text. The disjunctions, the things that do not fit, force us to go back and reconsider our stories. This reconsideration can lead to fundamental changes in our thinking about the text and the world.

The following classroom example illustrates the complexity of the intertextual ties made by children.

[Figure: connections around "NO ROOM"]

- The Three Bears (run away—looking for something)
- "Stay away from things that are already full."
- Bremen Town Musicians (run away)
- "Always run away from bees."
- It Could Always Be Worse (animals all go in a house too full)
- "Don't hog. If everyone wants the same thing, nobody gets it."
- Bus Ride (all get in—bee chases them out)
- "Finders Keepers"
- NO ROOM
- "Share"
- Rosie's Walk (bee chases fox)
- "Don't fight."
- Personal Experiences with Animals (natural enemies)
- "Don't run away from home."
- Giants (large mitten)
- "Pick a home. Stay there and be happy with what you've got."
- "The animals will find another mitten and start over."

![photo] Kathy Gnagey Short teaches children's literature at the University of Arizona where she is an assistant professor in Language, Reading, and Culture. She has worked extensively with elementary teachers in their efforts to develop curricula that actively involve students in using reading and writing to learn. Much of her work has centered around integrating children's literature into the curriculum.

A small group of children were engaged in a literature circle (an open-ended discussion) of the folktale *No Room* (Clymer and Venezky 1982). In this story a series of progressively larger animals crawl into a large mitten to get warm. Finally a fly crawls into the mitten and the mitten bursts apart. The figure below shows the variety of connections that the children made with other stories as they attempted to construct a meaning for this story during their discussion.

A number of children made an easy connection with several past stories that created a unity for the story that depended on a bee stinging the animals, thereby causing the mitten to fall apart. However, when someone in the group pointed out that this story involved a fly, this unity was disrupted. An anomaly was created that required the children to search for new connections, so they again began searching both their own past texts and the printed text.

The new texts that each constructed required children to reorganize their knowledge and to generate new rules that they could later use as anticipatory frames to make predictions in future literacy

events. The figure lists what the children felt that this story had taught them.

The figure also traces how one child, Amy, carried her theme from this story, "Don't run away from home," into her writing and art over the next month. She used the theme of running away and getting lost in a variety of stories and connected it with a larger theme of getting along with other people.

Amy's connections in "The Smiling Cat" demonstrate the complexity of the intertextual ties that children make with past texts. Amy took the idea of a baby and a cat from several of her earlier stories and wrote a story about a girl who has an unhappy cat and who finally asks her mother if she had ever had a cat and what she did to make it happy.

This process of creating a new unity through intertextual ties is what learning is all about. Learning involves bringing meaning to our experiences by searching for and creating a new unity from those experiences through intertextual ties. In schools, when we break learning into separate parts, we make that search for connections more difficult. It is only when learning occurs within the natural complexity of life experiences that learners are able to make connections that are more varied and personal.

Learning is a process of authorship, of constructing our own stories. It is not a process of authority, of submitting to someone else's story. As educators, we need to work with our students to create environments that support learning through authorship.

→ See: Dancing on the Edge, p. 190; Creating Classrooms for Authors, p. 24; Rich, p. 27; Short, p. 194; Strickland, p. 20.

References

Clymer, T., and R. L. Venezky, eds. 1982. *No room.* Boston: Ginn.
De Beaugrande, R. 1980. *Text, discourse, and process.* Norwood, NJ: Ablex.
Potter, B. 1902. *The tale of Peter Rabbit.* London: Warne.
Rosen, H. 1984. *Stories and meanings.* London: National Association for the Teaching of English.
Gnagey Short, K. 1986. "Literacy as a collaborative experience." Ph.D. diss., Indiana University.

Further Reading by Kathy Gnagey Short
- *Creating Classrooms for Authors,* with J. Harste and C. Burke. Heinemann, 1988.
- "New Potentials for Teacher Education: Teaching and Learning as Inquiry," with C. Burke. *Elementary School Journal* 90(2), January 1990.
- *Talking About Books: Creating Literate Classrooms,* with K. M. Pierce. Heinemann, 1990.
- "Teachers and Students as Decision-Makers," with G. Kauffman. In *Portraits of Whole Language Classrooms,* ed. H. Mills and J. A. Clyde. 1990.

Marvelous Inventions
You Need, You Invent

Seven-year-old Julio sent a note to his friend Ana and invented two new punctuation marks to get his point across: ʔ means "Guess Who?!" and ⌇ means "from."

TO ANA! ⌇ JULIO

—Julio is the neighbor of Ann Schlumberger, a doctoral student at the University of Arizona, Tucson, AZ

Great Teachers:
Chris Boyd
by Carole Edelsky

The Flow of Learning
by Chris Boyd

"Oh sure, she can do this with these kids, but my kids can't do all that," says the visiting teacher.

"I don't see how I could even keep up with all the planning," worries another.

"Jeez, it's like walking through a jungle—so much stuff hanging like vines," grumbles a third.

Visitors to Chris Boyd's kindergarten in midyear or later are indeed often overwhelmed by the complexity of what they see in the physical environment, the curricular content, and the children's capabilities. The large windowless room with the loft built by parents years ago is divided into areas for blocks, art, books, manipulatives, live animals, and group discussion. Each of these locations serves many functions. The block

area, for instance, may house a big-block rendition of the *Mayflower* with a fan blowing the sails. On the walls are lists and graphs for current use, products of group study for informing others, and statements about what the teacher believes. Hanging from the ceiling may be children's artwork, poems someone brought in from home, or strips of paper representing rain (during the time when the room is divided into climactic zones). And taped to the ceiling may be a line showing just how long a blue whale is in comparison with a gray shark.

In any one curricular unit or topic of study, Chris Boyd and the children will be attending to all of the following: the topic (e.g., Italy or fish or hearts); Chris's chosen lens for viewing that topic (e.g., studying the heart in connection to symbols or studying Italy through the lens of change); how these concepts connect to the children's daily world; and how new concepts in this unit relate to those from prior units.

And the children's interactions with this content, with Chris, and with each other are equally stunning. Here are kindergartners who in school look just as competent as they look outside of school. Just as they do outside, they expect events, talk, and each other to make sense. They display those expectations in their personal and scientific writing. And they expect sense when they discuss each other's writing and when they listen to and respond to each other during group discussions.

But looking at the evolution of this classroom from the start of school to when things are in "high gear" is even more impressive. Then it is possible to see how the increasing density of the physical classroom ("how the room piles up," in Boyd's words) is deliberately related to the teacher's overriding whole language goals and beliefs.

In late summer, when school begins, the room is relatively bare. The only things on the walls are statements and pictures about the teacher's philosophy and one curriculum goal chart. These announce to parents that Boyd believes that teaching is always about learning and that the learner is the main character of this drama. The one chart of district curriculum goals in math and reading is for administrators' and parents' benefit, reassuring the worried ones by charting how these goals will be met in this non-traditional classroom. On the shelves at first are only the toys, manipulatives, and books that are likely to be familiar to the children on the first day and that are likely to have been used at home in interaction with others. This lets the children know that what they know from home is welcome here, and it encourages them to continue to see learning and doing as social events.

During the first week (and continuing throughout the year), Chris and the children begin "piling up" the room. They bring in animals, games, new equipment, books—things they will do and use together, things that begin to mark a shared history. As Chris Boyd says, "The walls and shelves become a scrapbook."

Next to go up is children's artwork. They paint, they title the work, they choose the best place to display it, and they tell others what they were thinking of when they added certain marks or colors. Some years, children will have one-person shows or group galleries.

Another addition is objects that are "intellectual stimuli": graphs (e.g., of the number of seeds in each child's slice of watermelon), lists of things to do and to remember, repositories of information (which eventually begin to to be saved in individual books). These charts, lists, and graphs are created together, publicly; and they are used (as informational resources for children's individual writing, as reminders of work to be done, etc.).

As the class becomes a learning community, more group productions go up. Out of a several-week study of Italy came a group-built corner featuring prints and children's renditions of Rembrandt and DaVinci paintings, artifacts from Italy, group-created maps, and a cassette tape of *Aida*. Groups of children might transform certain areas of the room so that the housekeeping corner becomes a hospital or the block area becomes a heart and lungs (when one walks through the lung area one inhales and exhales loudly).

Through this increasingly dense trail of curriculum-in-the-making, Chris Boyd's beliefs shine through. To her, the whole language classroom is not synonymous with "freedom of expression" or "child-centeredness" or thematic units or literature study or writing or even all these ideas and activities taken together. She believes strongly that curriculum has to center on connections—connections between one curricular area and another and between in-school concepts and out-of-school daily lives. One of her major goals is for children to become aware of their own struggles and problems as they are learning, whether they are struggles with how

In kindergarten this week we began looking generally at cause and effect and more specifically at temperature. Reading a thermometer requires learning to count by twos, fives and tens. The Fahrenheit and centigrade scales demonstrate two ways of recording the same information. Estimating temperatures using some general knowledge and the senses, and testing those estimates with a thermometer, help children apply what they learn to everyday experiences. Graphing experiences seem limitless as we plot low city temperatures; the temperatures of classroom areas, objects, and food; the cooling down of hot chocolate and pancakes; and the rising temperature of ice water.

After watching weather reports on TV, children explore the globe and discuss lifestyles in other countries. They are now very aware of the proximity of any particular country to the poles or the equator and how that affects the temperature range for that country.

Literature is an integral part of these discussions as children look at the world in different ways. Our study of Russia was enhanced by our discussions of cold and snow in literature. Clothing was of particular interest to the children as we studied the illustrations in Russian folktales and discussed effects of climates on wardrobe and lifestyle.

This Russian theme included other arts as well. A study of Marc Chagall inspired an interest in stained glass and vivid colors in paintings. Peter Tchaikovsky's Symphony no. 6 became our favorite "working music." We discussed the effect the art and music had on us (Symphony no. 6 made the children's stomachs "feel funny and go up"). Our investigation of cause and effect led us to consider the possible reasons for artistic style and how environment affects it.

This flow of learning comes from an honest desire to learn. It becomes manageable for me through my own involvement as a learner and because I have a clear picture of what we're doing conceptually. Since I know that we are looking at cause and effect as we study temperature, a skill such as thermometer reading has its place as a tool for learning that is related to what is going on in the room. Skills are acquired in a useful and appropriate context. This is the difference between a learning community such as ours and a classroom that does thermometer reading exercises, current events, weather, news, and reworded encyclopedia reports on selected countries.

➜ See: Edelsky, p. 72; Goodman, p. 306, 308.

Chris Boyd is a kindergarten teacher at Roadrunner School, Phoenix, AZ.

written language works or with how some piece of new information about snakes fits what they knew yesterday. Child-centeredness and freedom of expression in this classroom are side effects, then, of the teacher's beliefs in the following: the importance of real reading and writing; the importance of making content (including literary content) the center of the curriculum; the importance of increased awareness of one's own and others' thinking and learning processes; and the importance of individuality within community.

➜ See: Edelsky, pp. 72; Goodman, p. 207.

Carole Edelsky is a professor at Arizona State University, Tempe, AZ.

Multiple Paths to Meaning

 Viewpoint: Dorothy S. Strickland

The Child as Composer

David, a first-grader, is drawing an airplane. As he draws, he talks to himself about a recent trip he has taken. At times he lifts the crayon from the paper and waves it through the air making sounds like a jet engine. Following each excursion his crayon magically finds the paper. His picture acts as a convenient landing strip as he continues to draw/talk his story.

Jennifer's eighth-grade class has just finished Paula Fox's The Slave Dancer. The class has been divided into groups. Each group has been asked to discuss the story and collaborate on a report or interpretation of their impressions to be shared with the entire class. Jennifer's group has decided to have one member serve as a narrator, reading from the text as the others reenact the "prisoners" dance. They select the passage to be read, decide on music to hum, and the type of movement appropriate for the dance. They are ready to perform.

Angel and Patrick are sitting at the computer. They are writing a mystery story about a stolen Lamborghini. At one point the two boys have a disagreement about how the thief might behave. Patrick gets up and begins to act out his ideas. Angel watches and then suggests a slight modification. They reach an accommodation and the two fourth-graders return to their writing.

Dr. Dorothy S. Strickland is the State of New Jersey Professor of Reading, Rutgers University. She was formerly the Arthur I. Gates Professor of Education at Teachers College, Columbia University. A former classroom teacher and learning disabilities specialist, Dr. Strickland has held elected office in both the National Council of Teachers of English and the International Reading Association. She was recipient of an NCTE award for research and IRA's Outstanding Teacher Educator of Reading Award.

Seemingly, the vignettes above describe children engaged in very different activities. A close look, however, reveals some important similarities. In each case the children are in the process of creating something. They think about it, generate ideas they might wish to convey, and set about expressing those ideas in a rather deliberate manner. The expression of ideas takes many forms: talking, drawing, writing, music, and movement. Sometimes the forms are interwoven and interdependent. There are many stops and starts. They revise and polish until they are satisfied that everything is "just right." Finally, they may share what they have created with others. Each child and each group of children is engaged in the composing process.

What constitutes the composing process? When whole language teachers think of composition, they most often think of the writing process—a model that includes prewriting, drafting, revision, conferring, and editing. If we were to extend that model beyond writing to include other forms of expression, we might find the thinking processes to be very much the same. For example, whether children are composing through art, drama, music, movement, writing, or speaking, they are apt to engage in: (1) idea stimulation and planning, (2) drafting or trying out their ideas, (3) conferring with others, (4) revising and polishing their ideas, and (5) sharing or going public with what has been created.

I am not suggesting that these modes of expression are identical; however, I submit that there are underlying processes that bond these models of communication within a communicative data pool not unlike the "linguistic data pool" offered by Harste, Burke, and Woodward (1984). These researchers suggest that children operate from a "linguistic data pool" into which they feed what they learn from each language encounter and draw what they need in subsequent language encounters. Thus, oral language encounters provide data for written language encounters and vice versa.

The principle of a "linguistic data pool" is basic to whole language theory. The interdependence of meaning, form, and function is well understood by teachers as it relates to reading, writing, listening, and speaking. For example, in whole language classrooms, written and oral language are not divided into time slots. Instead, they are integrated with each other and with various subject matter areas, such as science and social studies, so that students may learn to communicate through topics of interest and importance to them.

Interestingly enough, even in whole language classrooms, efforts to extend the communicative framework beyond listening, speaking, reading, and writing to include other modes of communication rarely go beyond the incidental level of instruction. While art, music, and drama are not unimportant in these classrooms, they may not be valued as important modes of communication. Consequently they may not seem worthy of inclusion in that interdependent communicative network, providing support for each other and for the traditional language arts—listening, speaking, reading, and writing.

Jan Olsen (1987), an art teacher in Brookline, Massachusetts, tells how she helped a sixth-grader use his visual skills to enhance his writing:

Paul's language arts assignment was to write a descriptive paragraph about a character he would later use in a story. He called his character "The Big Guy."

Paul's Original Paragraph

James weighed 240 pounds and use to be champ. He beat Mohamad Ali for the crown. He's 38 know and he has drugs and pot. He's been put in jail for 5 years and that ended his carrear. He's had a tough time finding a job. His face is scared. He wares a ripped T shirt with knee pants. He's trying to make a comeback in the boxing world. He's black. (spelling not corrected)

Paul had worked hard on it and it was similar in quality to his previous writing. I knew that Paul had very high visual skills, so I decided to see what would happen if Paul drew a picture of his character and translated the information into a new paragraph.

Paul's New Paragraph

The lonely man stood in a ring holding tight to the ropes. His head was bald. His chest was hairy and sweaty. His legs looked like they were planted to the ground like stumps. His muscels were relaxed in the dark ring. His mouth looked mean and tough they way it was formed. He was solid looking. His boxing gloves had blood stains on them. His still body structure glowed in the darkness. He braced himself against the ropes. His white pants had red stripes. The hair on his chin prickled out like thorns.

Research suggests that children use many different communication systems to construct meaning for themselves and to convey what they know to others. What is known about one system is used to support understanding of other systems. The notion of a "communicative data pool" has the following implications for classroom practice: (1) children need frequent opportunities to compose; to express what they know and what they feel; (2) children need opportunities to compose in many different ways; (3) all modes of expression/composition deserve respect and time in the classroom; and (4) teachers need to observe children's natural tendencies toward self-expression and build on what they do well. Help students use their strengths as bridges to other means of expression.

→ See: Family Storybook Reading, p. 359; Goodman, p. 67; Short, p. 18; Sprenger, p. 202; VanDeWeghe, p. 22.

References

Harste, J., V. Woodward, and C. Burke. 1984. Language stories and literacy lessons. Portsmouth, NH: Heinemann.

Olsen, J. 1987. Drawing to write. Research report. New York: Teachers College, Columbia University.

Excerpted from The California Reader 21(3), March/April 1988.

Further Reading by Dorothy S. Strickland

◆ Family Storybook Reading, with D. Taylor. Heinemann, 1986.

◆ The Administration & Supervision of Reading Programs, with J. Feeley and S. Wepner. Teachers College Press, 1989.

◆ Emerging Literacy, with L. Morrow. IRA, 1989.

📷 **WHOLE LANGUAGE CAMERA**

Studiously studying statues at Stanford, Stanford University Museum, Palo Alto, CA.

Classroom Demonstrations

by Phyllis E. Whitin

Responding to Novels through Visual Representations

Intrigued by the potential of expressing ideas through alternative communication systems, I invited my seventh-graders to create visual representations based on the Civil War novel *Across Five Aprils* by Irene Hunt. They could use color, geometric shapes, and symbols to represent important ideas in the book: theme, conflict, characterization, or character relationships. They could use any medium, and the background could be in any shape. The students would also attach a summary statement to explain their work.

The students created collages, charts, graphs, diagrams, mazes, and paintings, all of which brought new insight to the novel. We taped them to the bulletin boards and walls, and circulated around the room, studying them to discover the ideas they communicated.

Emily portrayed major events of the novel in a cloth collage. The lace across the top signifies a wedding. The burning barn shows the height of the town's intolerance of the Creighton family. The cannon, made of cloth swirled with black and gray, conveys the evil of war. Emily also denoted character change by dividing human figures into two sides. Jethro, for example, wears a lighter cloth on the left because he was dazzled by the glory of war at the novel's beginning. Emily showed his change of character by using a darker material to represent his later disillusionment.

Kevin drew four circles in his representation. A single black circle was at the top, a solitary red one on the bottom. In the middle were two circles side by side, green on the left, blue on the right. A sketched rifle was glued so that it divided the green and blue circles, and stretched from the lower red circle to the top black one. Kevin explained:

> The two circles, green and blue, symbolize the blue skies and the green grass of southern Illinois. They also stand for all the women. The soft colors represent signs of happiness and peace of the home.
>
> On the other hand, the two circles, black and red, show the feelings of war. The rifle that links these two colors together is a representation of lust, greed, and anger of war. The gun, in effect, is an object that divides the two sides and wells up hatred for each other. One side wants to conquer the other every minute. Bill, a rebel soldier, and John, a Union soldier, join up as brothers and make a special bond between all the colors!

Kevin used his visual representation to show the great paradox of the novel. The rifle, a symbol of war, shattered the peace and happiness of home. However, the two sides of war could never totally divide because of the bonds of two brothers. I found it interesting that even though we had not discussed the term paradox in class, Kevin was able to demonstrate this concept through colors and symbols.

As I reflected upon our experience, I realized many benefits:

- Exploring with alternative communication systems created new possibilities of understanding. As Jenny G. commented, "When I created my visual, many ideas flowed into my mind."

- By using color, texture, and shape, students developed new appreciation for figurative language, symbolism, and literacy style.

- Creating a personal artistic response enabled many students to respond to the novel in an aesthetic way. They participated in the novel at the feeling level. Amy N. noted, "When I created my visual, I thought of Jenny and

how she felt." Chris added, "It made me realize I don't want war."

- Students and I learned from one another's representations. Amy M. said, "When I thought about someone else's visual, I learned even more about the story and saw their ideas put down on paper."

Amy M.'s comment captures the potential of visual representations. They serve to record feelings and ideas that may otherwise be elusive. I'm beginning to see other ways to use visual representations in the classroom. Next I am planning to have groups of students create collaborative representations. This variation might open up a whole new range of possibilities as students share and extend their thinking during the creative process.

➡ See: Literature Reference List, p. 429; Rapoport, p. 176; Sprenger, p. 202; Whitin, pp. 41, 354.

Phyllis E. Whitin is a middle grade teacher at the Irmo Middle School/Campus R, Columbia, SC.

Considering Creativity

by Bob Wells

Captain Alfred Haynes was flying his DC–10 from Denver to Chicago in late July, 1989, when one of the engines blew up, sending jagged metal through the protective barriers, cutting all three hydraulic lines. Without hydraulic pressure, the pilots had no control over the aircraft. It began a downward spiral. Luckily, an off-duty DC–10 captain, Dennis Fitch, was sitting in the passenger section. He rushed to the cockpit, got down on his knees, and manipulated the throttles of the two remaining engines, regaining limited control of the aircraft. No written procedure existed. As he later explained, "We were making it up as we went along." One hundred eleven people died when the plane crashed. One hundred eighty-five people survived because these men were creative.

What about the engineers who designed that plane? They were highly trained professionals, but they just hadn't imagined an emergency in which a plane could lose all three independent hydraulic systems.

I had to take statistics again in graduate school. We were assigned a problem that I just could not do, even with the help of my computer and a statistical software program. Rather than just not do it, I did another statistics problem. I wanted to hand something in. During the next class, the professor criticized an "anonymous" student who didn't do what had been assigned. He said creativity was fine in its place, but . . . He went on to explain how, when he travels in an airplane, he likes to think that the pilots are not going to do anything creative, that they will go strictly "by the book."

Although an airplane in an emergency and a classroom are not analogous places, I believe that in these two little stories there is philosophical food for thought for all classroom teachers.

Bob Wells is an entrepreneur and a junior in the school of life, Sunnyvale, CA.

WELL-SAID Imagination is more important than knowledge. Knowledge is limited, whereas imagination embraces the entire world—stimulating progress, giving birth to evolution.

—Albert Einstein

Book Note

Authors of Pictures, Draughtsmen of Words

Ruth Hubbard
1989; 192 pp.; $16
Portsmouth, NH: Heinemann

Ruth Hubbard sees children as they are. Her "ethnographic informants," the first-graders, describe their perceptions of time, space, movement, and color in pictorial, written, and oral form. I picked this book up and couldn't put it down! Its emphasis on discovering the child's point of view is a refreshing change from adult-centered interpretations of children's drawings. The children's words and pictures together create a window through which we as adults can better view and understand their meaning.

Debbie Montgomery

Language Stories

Free Choice

As a kindergartner, Shoshana had endured a very long year of a teacher-controlled skill-and-drill regimen that had her sitting in her seat, working on stacks of dittos. She was delighted when she entered first grade and encountered a teacher who believed in giving kids a say in planning their day. Shoshana bounded home after that first day of school and announced to her mother, "Guess what! We had this much work"—she held her hands two inches apart. Then she stretched her arms out wide—"and all the rest was choosing!"

—As told to LBB by YMG

➡ See: Goodman, pp. 32, 360.

Resource: Periodical

Creative Kids

$17.97/year (8 issues)
from:
P.O. Box 637
100 Pine Ave.
Holmes, PA 19043
1-800-345-8112
1-800-662-2444
(PA only)

Creative kids—are there any other kinds? How nice that all kids have a professional-looking magazine in which to publish their creations: poetry, fiction, games, photographs, interviews, comics, artwork, book reviews, editorials, and the like.

LBB

Classroom Demonstrations
by Judy VanDeWeghe

Shaping Meaning with Emergent Readers

Over the years I've discovered that beeswax is a wonderful, clean, and relaxing modeling medium for young children to create with while listening to stories being read aloud. As the children engage in both listening and shaping wax into small story characters or props, they integrate characters, key ideas, and story grammars, and they internalize good literature. The action provides young children with the concrete experience needed to shape and represent their thinking.

This action-sparked synthesis was clearly evident most recently with my prekindergartners when I used modeling as a way to create story props for "miniature world literacy play." I reread "The Ugly Duckling." After a quick review of the characters and problem, many chose to model the ugly duckling while listening intently, others modeled the mother duck, eggs, and ducklings; or the fierce hunting dog; or the white swans.

Next, I invited the children to build a miniature world for their story props in an emptied water table; this was a large contained space around which four or five children could comfortably work during daily free choice periods. The children began by combining small wooden town buildings, a farm, and little people with natural grass, twigs, bits of paper, small pebbles, and even a pretend pond—along with the various wax characters they had created—to play out (as they would time and again) the story of the ugly duckling.

Over the days, I stepped in to facilitate their play with questions and suggested other creative construction materials they could use in their evolving miniature setting; for example, one child's NO HTNGN sign eliminated a fierce hunting dog from the set. I observed that children were able to reconstruct story language with confident approximations; and their symbolic play reflected the actual story events. In contrast, it was also interesting to note how some were able to construct delightful new extensions, which reflected personal meanings and related fantasy elements, transforming the ugly duckling into a well-liked playmate. In another version, a fairy godmother appeared on the scene and solved the duck's problem! As they became immersed in literacy play, I noticed the children returning to the text to check the correct sequence of events through illustrations—as rehearsal for their retellings with the props; or they asked to hear special phrases and pages again; others snuggled in pairs, to do "pretend readings" with the text.

For the modeling I recommend natural beeswax or try a modeling wax that Stockmar produces in a variety of beautiful colors. It can be ordered through Hearth Song (for catalogs and orders, call 1-800-325-2505). Each 1½" x 4" piece is an ample amount to create a small one- to two-inch inch character or object. The props tolerate frequent handling; once formed, the wax becomes firm until warmed in hands and modeled again.

This medium invites young emergent readers to become more meaningfully engaged with a text. They share and extend their comprehension with their peers, combine integrated and discovery learning, and experience what more fluent readers do when they give whole texts their passionate attention.

➜ See: Paley, p. 30; Parkes, p. 36; Rich, p. 27; Short, p. 18.

Judy VanDeWeghe is an early childhood educator, Denver, CO.

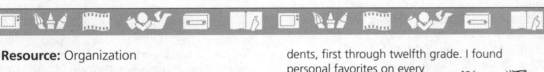

As Teachers See It

Daydreaming
by Geane R. Hanson

All through school I can remember hearing that I had such potential, if only I would stop daydreaming. I don't believe that experience is unique. Through my conversations with others I am beginning to think it synonymous with schooling. Why is there such prejudice against daydreaming in the classroom?

A mounting body of research indicates that daydreaming is not time spent disconnecting from reality. Rather, it is often time spent connecting our outer experiences to our interior domains. Outside experience only has meaning because we can see it as meaningful, and such vision comes from within. Daydreaming is not a time when kids disintegrate, but a time when they integrate.

Jerome Singer (1976) suggests that children who daydream appear to be happier, more curious, more creative in their thinking, and more readily able to deal with frustration and boredom. Fiona Mackie (1985) says that in school, children's unity of life purpose is compartmentalized and segmented. According to Mackie, this segmentation, and ultimately, limitation, is imposed in school when daydreaming is forbidden. Children's daydreaming activity is a natural process through which they blend internal and external realities. It is not a way to avoid meaning but a way of making meaning.

At a time when we hear so much about how kids can't think for themselves, how they expect easy answers, and how they cannot sustain self-initiated learning and interest, we must consider how we regard time spent in more interior states. By not valuing our students' internal time, we foster their dependence on outer processes that may not be personally meaningful.

To understand reality we must not attend solely to what is objectively measurable. Such expanded awareness facilitates the emergence of our own meaningful schemas. By acknowledging the value of daydreaming in our own lives and in the lives of our students, we move another step closer to the gifts given to us when we are born whole, human, and conscious. Our acknowledgment allows us to create and respond from the inside out as we evolve.

I have always daydreamed. I believe we all do. It is one of those threads that naturally and continually recur throughout the tapestry of our lives in a form that makes it uniquely our own.

➜ See: Short, p. 18.

References
Mackie, F. 1985. *The status of everyday life.* Boston: Routledge & Kegan Paul.
Singer, J. 1976. *The inner world of daydreams.* New York: Harper & Row.

Geane R. Hanson is a graduate student at the University of Arizona, Tucson, AZ.

> Learning is, most often, figuring out how to use what you already know in order to go beyond what you currently think.
>
> **WELL-SAID**
> —Jerome Bruner,
> *In Search of Mind*

As I See It:
Kenneth S. Goodman

Whole Language Learners

Everyone is a whole language learner. We learn in the real world as we encounter new situations and live through experiences. Learning is continuous in authentic problem-solving situations. Learning isn't different in school and out of school. But in traditional schools there has been a tendency to narrow and confine learning. Often, schools have disconnected school experience from life experience and broken sensible wholes into nonsensical fragments. Success in school is not the same as learning.

Some of us, after years of schooling, have learned to survive in classrooms and in curricula where what we are learning is broken down into bits and pieces. We have learned to separate success in school from learning, by regurgitating undigested "facts"—dates, names, procedures. We have become good at what David Bloome calls *procedural display*, acting the way we think teachers want us to act.

But ultimately, for learning to take place we must integrate, we must "get it all together." If some insight or understanding is really functional or important to us, we will work it over for ourselves until it all fits and makes sense. Most of the rest is forgotten as quickly as it was "learned" because it never really was worth knowing in the first place—or we never recognized a reason for knowing it.

What E. D. Hirsch doesn't understand when he raises cries about "cultural literacy" is that we learn easily what is relevant and meaningful and we forget easily bits and pieces of knowledge that never come together. Learning is natural to human beings, and we'll work very hard at it if it is part of authentic experiences with the real world. In whole language classrooms we recognize the nature of human learning, and we try to make learning as authentic and easy in school as it is outside of school.

Learners Construct or *Invent* Their World

Simply speaking, we learn what we need to learn to survive and make sense of the world. And we do so as we confront situations that need to be understood and as we are confronted with problems we need to solve. Piaget, the great Swiss psychologist, has helped us to understand that learning is a very active process, that children expect the world to make sense, and that they actively attempt to construct a sensible world around themselves. They keep modifying their constructions until there is some equilibrium between their own view and the real world. Things are easy to learn if they are important to the learners and if the learning takes place in authentic contexts. It may help scientists studying things to take them apart and see what their smallest parts are, but for functional learning things must be kept whole and in functional, meaningful contexts.

Language Is Essential for Human Learning

Language makes human learning very different than the learning of other species. Language is the most remarkable and universal human achievement. But because every human society and virtually every human individual learns at least one language easily and well, we have underestimated this achievement.

To understand the importance of language in human learning, we must understand the two factors that make it possible and essential. Humans have the ability to think symbolically,

that is, to create symbols that represent things, ideas, relationships, or experiences. Languages use symbols in complex ways to represent the world and our experiences and relationships with it. So the first factor in language development is this ability to think symbolically. That makes language possible. But what makes it necessary is that we are social animals born incapable of surviving alone. As we mature, our need for others becomes increasingly complex. We need to communicate not just simple needs but complex feelings, emotions, and understandings. We need to share our experiences and try out our understandings. So we desperately need language. We don't just develop language because we *can*, we develop it because we *must*.

Human interaction is dependent on language, so human language is the means of communication and of thought. It is also the medium of human learning; our ability to think symbolically is transformed by language into an ability to represent anything we experience or think. Thus we can reflect on experience, and we can present our understandings through language to others—we can think together. We can pool our experience and our intelligence through a common social language. Alone among living things we have language to think, learn, and communicate.

Each human being has the ability to invent language. But if we each had to do so ourselves, the task would be overwhelming. Furthermore, our social need to communicate would not be met if each of us invented our own private language. Fortunately, we don't have to do the whole job. Each of us is born into a family and a community, which already have language. Language surrounds us in every social situation. As we begin to invent language, and we do, people respond to us in the social language. Our personal inventions come in contact with the social conventions of the language. Two forces are at work: the constructive personal force of invention, which expands our language outward, and the conventionalizing force of the social language, which moves the personal language toward the social.

In the context of real life situations, this dynamic process of language development goes on. Eventually the personal language becomes social; that is, the learner seems to internalize the social language. With the social language, the learner also takes in the way of viewing the world that the culture has developed; we learn how to use language to mean things the way others in our society do. Halliday, the British linguist, calls this "learning how to mean." Halliday points out that we learn language while we are learning about the world through language. That's because language is never learned for its own sake but always as a means to communication, thinking, or learning.

Throughout our lives this interdependence between learning language and learning through language goes on. It is what makes it possible to build our vocabularies and our concepts, to widen the range of our language genres as we widen our interests and needs, to develop new ways of expressing new ways of thinking. It makes it possible for us to learn second languages as we need to and to learn alternate dialects of our first language when that is useful.

Reading and writing are also learned most easily in the context of using them to learn. That's why throughout our lives we remain whole language learners.

The term *whole language* is a response to these key understandings. In school, as well as outside of school, we must keep language whole and in the context of its use. Language must be kept whole because only when it is whole is it meaningful and functional. Language learning in school will be like language learning outside of school if learning experiences in school are authentic, that is, like the real world. Children must have the opportunity to use their own language in school to express their thoughts, to talk about their experiences, and to present their insights. So whole language teachers are continuously aware of providing children the opportunity to use language in all of their school activities. They realize that that will build both their language and their conceptual schemas.

The same opposing forces of invention and convention that produce language learning also produce conceptual learning. Human beings do not learn simply by being told what they must know. They learn by inventing their own hypotheses of how the world works and then trying them out against reality. Whole language teachers understand that they help learning happen by creating conditions in their classrooms that will focus on real questions, real issues, and real problem-solving.

There have always been whole language learners. But they haven't always had whole language teachers. Because we kept learners dependent on teachers and materials, we're only now getting an inkling of what they are capable of achieving given holistic learning environments and supportive whole language teachers. We've had too little faith in learners and assumed that they were only capable of doing what we let them do. Children in whole language classes are reading and writing earlier and more independently, because they have ownership over their own learning and choice in what they read and write. They are producing projects in thematic units that show depth of understanding and insights that surprise both their teachers and their parents. They're simply learning a whole lot more.

➜ See: Bausch-Ude, p. 26; Goodman, pp. 13, 67, 363; Holdaway, p. 44.

Resource: Organization

National Association for the Education of Young Children (NAEYC)

1834 Connecticut Ave., NW
Washington, DC 20009-5786
1-800-424-2460

The nation's largest professional organization of early childhood educators offers a wealth of professional development resources, information on federal legislation affecting early childhood services, audiovisual materials, and up-to-date information on innovative early childhood projects. Perhaps its most important contributions are the little pamphlet *Appropriate Education in the Primary Grades*, which maps out the do's and don'ts of theoretically sound educational practice, and the superb journal, published six times a year, *Young Children*.

LBB

by Debra Goodman

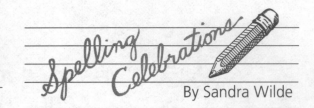

Thank You, Clara Jane Thompson

This year is the first year of our new whole language school, The Dewey Center for Urban Education in Couzens Elementary School. I enrolled my son Reuben in the third-grade class. His teacher is Clara Jane Thompson, who has taught in this Detroit inner-city school for a good number of years.

Reuben started school this year very reluctant to read and write. When he was six, he wrote a story to warm his mother's heart. "Once a little bear lived with his mom. One day the bear said, 'Mother, will you play with me.' 'No son,' said the bear's mother, 'I'm too busy now.'"

When Reuben went to first grade, his entire writing experience was limited to copying things down from the board and writing words in workbooks. Evaluation was based on proximity to the adult model, which my bright son knew he could never match. "I can see it in my head," he said, "but I can't do it."

For homework one day, he was to write out the alphabet. I had him do it on the computer. "Computers are okay," his teacher told me, "but on the test this spring, he'll have to use the three lines to write on." It seems her whole class was planned around the test in spring.

When Reuben was two years old, he knew at least 30 stories by heart. In first grade, he was never invited to read a story unless it was in a basal reader. In first grade, Reuben learned that reading was knowing a lot of words. He didn't want to read anything with words he might not know. He learned that reading is sounding words out. Though sounding out was a little funny to him (If "G" says /g/ and "O-O" says /u/ and "D" says /d/, then my name should be "gud-man"), he never doubted that sounding words out was the right way to learn to read.

He did doubt that reading and writing was something he was good at. His first-grade teacher loaded the kids down with assignments to keep them busy so that she could meet with her reading groups. Reuben knew he could never finish all the assignments, so he decided not to do any. He refused to work, acted up, and gave his teacher a headache.

Reuben's teacher said his reading and math progress was fine. The problem was, he wouldn't do his work. It seemed to me that if he was good in reading and math without doing his work, he was probably correct in assuming his work was a waste of time. This didn't occur to his teacher.

Second grade was more of the same. "You don't learn anything in second grade," Reuben told me. "It's just review." Reuben's second-grade teacher was concerned about Reuben's work habits and his handwriting. "If he acts like this in second grade, how will he do in third grade?"

Almost all of Reuben's second-grade work involved writing, usually copying. Reuben tried to do the minimum. Reuben wrote T (true) or F (false) for science and social studies tests, though his teacher wanted him to write the sentences out. When Reuben did write, his teacher responded, "I can't read this."

Reuben became a real problem. Instead of sitting in his seat in its neat row and doing his work quietly, he talked with his friends. His teacher moved his friends away and he had to crawl on the floor to talk to them. "She hardly ever caught me," he reported later.

Reuben's second-grade teacher wasn't concerned about his knowledge or ability. She was concerned about his behavior. He wouldn't do his work. He wouldn't stay in his seat. He wouldn't be quiet. In fact, she was having the same problem with a number of children, but it didn't occur to her that she might change. She insisted that Reuben change. Reuben did change. He became unhappy and anxious. He

reported that he was the worst writer in the class. He refused to read or write at home.

Now Reuben is in third grade. Clara Jane Thompson adjusts her teaching to each child. When Reuben told his teacher that he couldn't write because his finger was sore, she put a Band-Aid on it and told him not to write too much at home so that he could do some writing in school.

Mrs. Thompson invited him to sit at a table where he can talk quietly with his friends. She invited him to choose a book to read for 20 minutes each day. On the fourth week of school he decided to read *Ramona and Her Mother*, a book that I read to him last year.

His teacher invited him to use a picture to write a story. Reuben began the first story he's written since he was six. He wrote three pages and he's not finished yet. "The problem is," he told me, "once I get a good idea I just can't stop writing."

Reuben has just finished his fourth week of school. He came home with a star for being the best independent reader of the day. He likes school. Mrs. Thompson has insightful things to say about my son. She writes back to him each day in his journal, and so has conversed with him a great deal in his first weeks of school. She observes with a practiced eye his interests, his work, and his movements around the room. She has reading conferences with him twice a week.

C. J. is a kidwatcher. She has been watching children for close to 30 years. In the classroom she is patient and calm, and the children feel accepted and cherished. She has that experienced calm that I, as a 10-year veteran, envy. As one third-grader said, "When you're in your fifties, you have these little ways of getting children to behave."

C. J. loves to read. She immerses her kids in stories and poetry, author studies and literature response. C. J. has read every book in her room and haunts bookstores for good titles. During her talky-reading time (the second- and third-graders enjoy sharing during reading time), she holds conferences with children and keeps records of their independent reading. Some of the students are hard to keep up with, so they write out their own records for her looseleaf notebook.

C. J. also keeps and collects copies of old basal readers and reading collections that other teachers have discarded with new adoptions. She knows all of the stories in these books and keeps them for students to share. She has basal reading groups twice a week, but they are rather untraditional. She announces what story will be read and invites anyone in the class to join the group. The children really enjoy rereading old favorites.

C. J. and I are on our school personnel committee. I was surprised when she asked a candidate, "What have you been reading lately?" She explained later that whole language teachers must be readers themselves.

As a teacher, I have had conferences with ecstatic parents who are thrilled with the change in their children. I have gotten excited about my own students. But this is *my* Reuben. I have watched him growing for the last eight years. I have shared his unhappiness and his defeat. My Reuben—excited about reading and writing. My Reuben—happy to be going to school.

I never really knew how much a good whole language teacher offers each child until Reuben met Clara Jane Thompson.

→ See: Bell, p. 48; Blynt, p. 360; Goodman, pp. 274, 360; Literature Reference List, p. 429; Quintal-Finell, p. 361.

Debra Goodman is a teacher at Dewey Center for Urban Education, Detroit, MI.

Invented Spellings: Letter-Name Spelling

One day *.E.T.* went to the *.R.K.* (arcade). He had some quarters he played pac-man.

Dina, 4th grade

When young children begin their first explorations with invented spelling, they use the names of letters to construct written representations of words. An example of such a spelling might be *BKZ* for *because*, where a spelling is made up from the letter names associated with consonant sounds in the word. (William Steig has written an entire children's book, *CDB*, or *See the Bee*, in letter-name spelling.) For the most part, our spelling system reflects more complex relationships between sounds and letters, but in the case of abbreviations, such as *E.T.*, the word is spelled by writing the names of the letters heard in it. Dina merely extended this principle to the spelling of the video *.R.K.* where one can play Pac-Man. Notice also that she understood that periods may be used in such words; her overextension in this case involved also using a period *before* the word, bracketing it the way one does with quotation marks.

Book Note

Creating Classrooms for Authors: The Reading-Writing Connection

Jerome C. Harste and Kathy G. Short, with Carolyn Burke
1988; 416 pp.; $22.50
Portsmouth, NH: Heinemann

Harste, Short, and Burke present lesson ideas and demonstrations for teachers who want to create process-centered reading and writing classrooms. The authors organize their theory around the authoring cycle, a metaphor for learning. They elaborate on the practical components of the cycle itself, as well as on other specific curricular strategies.

Kathryn F. Whitmore

❝ Authoring is a form of learning. As we use language, art, or drama to communicate ideas, the process of working with the words, paints, or gestures allows us to construct and generate meaning for ourselves and others. As Elliot Eisner (1982, p. 52) has commented, 'the demands of the occasion motivate the creation.' Literacy is a process of outgrowing our current selves to solve our communicative problems. Reading and writing are transactions whereby language users begin with concepts and beliefs, but in the process free themselves from what they presently think, feel, and perceive. The same is true for other forms of literacy. ❞ (p. 9)

Viewpoint:
Peter Gabel

New College of California

As we approach our 20th anniversary, New College remains one of the most creative and progressive educational institutions in the country. While most of the nontraditional schools that sprang up in the late sixties and early seventies have either retreated to a more traditional stance or simply have been unable to survive the conservative climate of the last 10 years, New College has remained true to its original vision and, in addition, can claim an impressive list of accomplishments.

Starting with only $2,500 and a handful of students who met in Father Jack Leary's living room, we have steadily expanded and strengthened our undergraduate humanities program, while adding a widely praised public interest law school and innovative graduate programs in psychology and poetics. Accreditation by the Western Association of Schools and Colleges was granted to the college only five years after its founding.

I believe the most important reason for our success has been our ability to create a learning environment in which people feel genuinely respected and appreciated for who they are—for their own unique qualities and interests, their own diverse cultural experiences, their own distinctive intelligence and way of knowing the world. At New College, we have no desire to reproduce the kind of standardized, other-directed education that tends to fill students with an underlying insecurity and self-doubt while fostering a compliant and uncritical deference to external authority. Our aim is to empower students by "confirming" them—by providing them with the kind of empathy and validation that is a prerequisite to true self-development.

We confirm our students in many ways. We do it through our emphasis on the advising or mentor relationship between each student and a member of the core faculty. We do it through our small, discussion-oriented classes. We do it through encouraging students to become actively involved in self-designed community projects. And we do it through requiring each student to take substantial responsibility for his or her own course of study. Through these approaches, which are centered more on the student's active learning than on his or her ability to adapt to whatever is taught, we seek to elicit each person's distinctive curiosity while providing the personal guidance needed to channel that curiosity in a constructive direction.

Finally, I want to emphasize our effort to link the goal of personal development with social responsibility and committed social action. The confirmation and respect that we value so highly here are qualities of human interaction that should, in significant measure, shape every aspect of our society, and our hope is that the educational experience students have here will give them the confidence and knowledge they need to help bring this kind of society into existence.

➜ See: Horton, p. 74; Stephens, p. 361.

Peter Gabel is the president of New College of California, San Francisco, CA.

Parents' Perspective

The Boy Who Could

by Amy Donnelly

Not so long ago there was a five-year-old boy who longed for his mother's undivided attention. His mother enjoyed playing games, reading, and talking with him, but she also enjoyed learning herself. This meant that he had to learn how to live with his mother's divided attention.

One day he complained, "Mom, I have nothing to do!"

"Well, I could use your help with my homework," his mother said as she continued reading. He was very quiet. "Please will you help me?"

"Okay," he replied glumly, "but I don't know how."

"All you have to do is write a story."

"You know I don't know how to write words!" the boy snarled as he stomped his foot.

"Write anything you feel comfortable writing."

The boy walked slowly over to the kitchen table and sat staring at the blank piece of paper. His mother continued studying. In a few minutes, he returned to her side and whined, "I don't know what to write about."

"I know exactly how you feel," she sympathized. "Well, when I can't think of anything to write, I write about something I know a lot about."

Once again the boy returned to his chair at the kitchen table. For a while, he sat motionless. He frowned. Finally, he picked up his pencil. Almost as quickly, he put the pencil down. He wiggled and squirmed in his chair. His mother could feel his struggle as he pondered what to write. "What do I know? What do I know?" she heard him whisper as he looked around the room. Again he picked up his pencil and this time called to his mother, "How do you spell 'things'?"

"Spell the best you can and I will be able to read it." As if by magic, the room suddenly felt electrified with energy as the boy picked up his pencil and wrote. The frown on his face disappeared, replaced by an expression that conveyed the excitement and concentration of an artist pursuing his craft. Now he wrote fast and furiously as if his thoughts would evaporate if not quickly captured in print.

After some time, he hopped over to his mother. "I'm finished!" he announced with a big grin. "Read it to me."

Silently his mother prayed that she could read his inventive spelling. Cautiously, she took his paper and read, "Things in the house!"

"You're right!" (Luckily for the mother, he had drawn pictures to go with his text.) "I never knew writing could be so much fun!" he exclaimed.

And to this day the mother basks in the rewards of that day's divided attention. As for the boy, he boasts about the story he wrote for his mother and remembers that her homework (and support) helped him feel more confident that he could truly read and write.

Amy Donnelly is a doctoral student at the University of South Carolina, Columbia, SC.

The Funny Side
Sweet Stimulus

My daughter took my two-year-old grandson shopping for his first Halloween costume and was telling him about trick-or-treating.

"See, Kyle, you put on your costume, and you go up to our neighbor's house, ring the doorbell, and say 'trick or treat!' Do you think you can say that?"

Kyle promptly responded, "Can't."

"C'mon, sweetie. You'll have a trick-or-treat bag and you'll say 'trick or treat!' I bet you can say that."

"Can't."

My daughter thought a moment, then tried one more time.

"When they open the door, you hold up your bag, you say 'trick or treat!' and *then* . . . they give you some *candy*."

"Trick or treat!"

—As told to LBB by Evelyn Logan, special education teacher, Abbot School, San Mateo, CA

Liquid Nitrogen
by Debra Goodman

Two young men
in a haze of drink
wander into the Science Center
on Children's Day
because it's free.
The young black woman,
full of fun,
announces a liquid nitrogen demonstration.
And they stumble into the brand-new
    auditorium.
Sit—and trade jokes,
cushioned in grant-funded blue carpeting.
Kids file in from summer schools and camps—
tots with eyes wide and mouths open,
skeptical adolescents full of questions.
The woman begins her script.
The two men, front and center,
try catcalls.
"Hey baby, what you doing after the show?"
She calls out right to the top row seats,
"Do you know what this is?"
Frosted steam rolls out of a thermos
like Morticia's glass.
"That's dry ice," one man answers—
suddenly caught up in school days
left behind the city streets.
"No, dry ice is actually frozen carbon dioxide.
This is liquid nitrogen."
Her lab coat gleams,
her voice is crisp with confidence,
her life shines—
filling the room like fluorescent light.
The young men sputter and grow silent.
Out of place.
The demonstration continues
and they watch as the woman
tosses deadly frost at their feet.
The children scream,
but it evaporates before it hits the floor.
The two men stare
as the boiling ice
disappears like a dream.
They have stumbled face to face with younger
    selves.
They rise and hurry out
after the children have gone.

➜ See: Goodman, p. 266.

Debra Goodman is a teacher at Dewey Center for Urban Education, Detroit, MI.

A Man Who Learned with Love

I met Carl at Eastern Michigan University where we happened to live in the same dormitory. I noticed him as I first moved in on September 5, 1988. His special elegance as well as his politeness caught my attention. My heart started pounding seriously whenever he said hi to me. We kept greeting and watching each other for more than three months before he finally came to me and said, "Liping, I have something to tell you, but you don't need to respond if you don't want to." I noticed that his hands were trembling as he hesitantly said, "Please allow me to tell you the truth that I like you very much." He showed his concern on his face and his love in his eyes. I knew that he really meant it, and I also knew that the happiest moment of my life had come.

Being a native speaker of English, Carl really had a hard time when I first introduced him to my Chinese friends. He wished to integrate with my friends, but he couldn't because he did not speak any Chinese at all. Pretty soon Carl recognized the necessity to learn my language. He had strong desire to communicate with Chinese people, especially my parents, who did not speak any English. Therefore, we started our Chinese lessons.

Carl was an active learner. He knew what he wanted to learn and how to collect all the information he needed. I never forced him to learn anything, because he was the person who made the lesson plans. "How to address Chinese people," and "How to behave in a Chinese family," were two of his favorite topics. He kept asking questions about the usage of words, phrases, and sentences. I always gave him a lot of examples to make him familiar with the situations in which our language was used. I set up chances for Carl to practice what he had learned of each day. I gave him positive responses whenever he made progress. I encouraged him to speak to Chinese people, and he did at the bus stop, on

the street, and in the supermarket, regardless that he did not know them at all.

Carl was an eager learner. Not only did he learn Chinese from me, he also asked for help from his Chinese classmates. One day at midnight, he called me and said, "Wo ai ni, Liping!" which meant "I love you, Liping!" I was so surprised to hear that, because I didn't teach him this sentence. Maybe Carl sensed that I'll never teach him this, so that he learned it from someone else. Carl used to be a very good singer before he got hurt in his throat by an accident. He likes music very much and he borrowed most of my cassettes. He listened to Chinese music every day. He mimicked the sounds as well as the melodies and sang them to me. Most of the time we would sing together, and then I would explain the meaning of the songs to him. "Sleep, My Love" was one of Carl's favorites: "Ching-ching yung ni dzai hwai jung. Jin-jin ba ni kan ge gou. Dzai jiang ni shwang shou jin wo. Rang wo de ai gen swei ni ru mung" ("I want to hold you. I want to look at you. Let my love follow you into your dream"). We sang the song together every night before he went back to his room.

Carl was a smart learner. He knew how to please his teacher—me. After I gave him a Chinese name, he started to sign his notes in Chinese. Once we were eating in a Chinese restaurant where the waitresses were impressed by Carl's perfect use of chopsticks. As a proud teacher, I told the waitresses that Carl could speak Chinese. Besides, he also could write his name in Chinese. The waitresses were too surprised to believe. One of them passed Carl a pen and asked him to prove it. Carl quickly wrote down his name on the napkin without hesitation. Then we both proudly looked at each other without saying a word for about five minutes. At that moment, we preferred to be silent, because we already knew what we wanted to say to each other.

I haven't seen Carl for more than five weeks since I came to San Francisco for TESOL Summer Institute. As I know, he is still making progress with his Chinese. We talk to each other every other day on the phone. Instead of saying "hello," Carl answers the phone by saying "wei," and "good night" is replaced by "dzai jian." Based on the strong motivation of learning and his courage of practicing, Carl is able to carry on a general conversation in Chinese now. His proficiency of Chinese is growing every day. However, he still has much more to learn. By the end of August he'll fly to Taiwan to see my parents. He may need to study even harder for the time being. He has a very difficult mission on his trip to Taiwan. He needs to present himself to my parents and seek for the permission of marrying me. I have no idea how my father is going to treat him. We all look forward to seeing the positive result. So far, what I can say is "Good luck, Carl!"

→ See: Kagawa, p. 353; Krashen, p. 86.

—Liping Chen, TESOL student teacher, Eastern Michigan University, Ypsilanti, MI

The Funny Side
Two Lunches

In this story, we join three-year-old Gibson at the sign-in sheet, where one's signature serves the dual purpose of providing both an attendance count and a lunch count. Watch as he uses print to signal a special request.

The prebreakfast sing-along at our day-care center had just ended, and the last of us stragglers were on our way out to the breakfast table. As I happened by the sign-in desk, I noticed that Gibson was perusing the day's sign-in sheet.

"Jean Anne, I signed my name two times," he informed me, pointing to the sheet. Sure enough, his name appeared twice on the form. "Why did you do that?" I asked him, curious about his intent.

"I want two lunches."

→ See: Clyde, p. 49.

—Jean Anne Clyde, professor, University of Louisville, Louisville, KY

The varied manifestations of thought, such as writing, mathematical formulae, and musical compositions are the end products of the multiple transformations of thought.

WELL-SAID

—Vera John-Steiner, *Notebooks of the Mind*

 **As Teachers See It**

Immigrant Children Share Real Lives

by Katie Bausch-Ude

I am called the "teacher" in the classroom of 22 pre–first-grade students of diverse cultural and linguistic backgrounds. In reality, we spend our days learning from and with each other as we share language to communicate about our lives. We try to make *real* reading, writing, listening, and speaking a priority. After all, people like Sambath, a six-year-old Cambodian student, have *real* lives to share.

Let's face it, as educators in North America, we are no longer teaching the same children we did even 10 years ago. Demographic studies prove this on paper. Stories such as Sambath's prove it in the heart . . .

> We have to move because it was the other person that play with the gun and the managers went to my dad and they get madder and say, "Tell your people about stop playing with the gun." The manager say it was my brother but it was not Sokchear. The manager say we have to move but my dad get so angry that he move, but he can't find a house.

> When I was at my house all the Cambodian peoples came and they talk about my brother, about the gun . . . he's shooting a window at the back of their yard. But it's not Sokchear, it's the brother of my big brother friend. The people say it's Sokchear because they don't know his name, they only know Sokchear's name. Then the people climb the manager's stairs and tell him to call the cops and I feel bad.

> My dad tried to tell my mom about the cops, then my dad go outside and tell them it's not my brother. Then my mom came out and blame them back because they were blaming us, but my sister tell them because my mother was so angry and she can't speak English. Then my dad said, "Stop blaming us." But my brother can't go outside anymore.

To make matters worse, Sambath's family is already on a special waiver to attend our school. They may lose this privilege if they move. It's hard for me to imagine being six and having concerns like eviction, mistaken identity, cultural shock, and even betrayal, not to mention the acquisition of a second language. Yet Sambath is not alone . . . we are the teachers of thousands of children with similar concerns, and all too often, *what* we're teaching and *how* we're teaching hasn't caught up with *who* we're teaching today.

→ See: Edelsky, p. 72; Goodman, p. 23; Urzúa, p. 42.

Katie Bausch-Ude is a curriculum specialist with the Fresno Unified School District, Fresno, CA.

📷 **WHOLE LANGUAGE CAMERA**

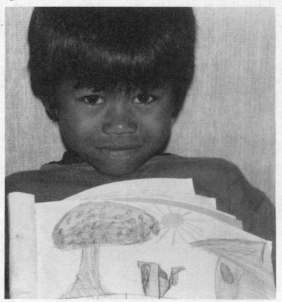

A young immigrant from Cambodia beams with pride over his newly published book in Janice Stradford's primary classroom, Santa Rosa, CA.

Cornerstone: Sharon J. Rich

Playing with Literacy: Developing a Sense of Story in the Early Years through Whole Language

Children's play is a complex process through which they recreate the world and, in the re-creation, come to a better understanding of the world and of words. Children need concrete experiences with new concepts and ideas. By manipulating materials in sand and water play, children learn many things ranging from conservation through cooperation. Opportunities to play with books and the language of books need to become a part of every preschool program, because books and literacy are a natural part of the child's world. Books, reading, and writing demand a place in any good early childhood program, because they provide access to a world beyond the here and now. Children need time to experiment with text, story, and language in a safe, risk-free environment.

Some teachers have added sign-in sheets and environmental print to the classroom housekeeping or block centres. Other teachers have focused on writing; in a writing centre four- and five-year-olds are systematically invited to write. Still other teachers have used big books with a simple predictable pattern in kindergarten. Each of these procedures goes a long way towards increasing the literacy environment. Early childhood classrooms now more closely resemble real life. However, understanding the concept of playing with literacy is limited. What is neglected is the notion of helping children understand who they are through story. By providing children with a sense of story, we help them to come to understand their culture and their lives. To do this the centre of the early childhood curriculum must be story. Story provides a much needed source to "language about."

As children hear and read stories, they develop a sense of character and of the way book language works. As teachers read to young children, they talk about title, author, illustrations, words, characters, and story. A question as simple as "What did you like about the story?" causes children to begin to adopt a reflective stance towards the story and themselves. The story helps to develop imagination and extend the awareness of other possible worlds.

Stories are about someone else trying on a different version of the world. By reading or hearing a story, children extend their notion of play. They will often experiment with an author's "play," perhaps by participating in a story drama or simply adopting an author's word or phrase.

Young children surrounded by print and story demonstrate echoes of story in their play, in their art, and in their writing. Three-year-old Courtney, taken by the wonderful illustrations in *Jillian Jiggs*, spontaneously begins to hang her own paintings in her room. The story informs her art and her play, and she becomes Jillian.

Galan prefers dramatic play. He organizes others into dockworkers or he creates flying dragons. He does not read well yet. But Galan's teacher recognizes that his well-developed sense of narrative in his dramatic play is the basis on which his literacy development will be struc-

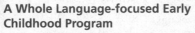

Sharon J. Rich is coordinator of Core Curriculum Studies of the Faculty of Education at the University of Western Ontario. Widely known for her work in helping teachers come to understand the whole language approach to teaching, she has conducted inservice sessions across Canada and the United States. Research activities extend from language and reading curriculum implementation across all grade levels. In her research, Sharon examines the role of self-understanding in the professional development of teachers.

tured. She knows Galan's narrative thought enables him to plan, predict, anticipate, and confirm, all of which are strategies for literacy. Continued exposure to story develops his personal literacy storehouse. He demonstrates comprehension not by writing answers to questions but by organizing a dramatic representation. Drama is a way of interpreting stories. His play brings him into the world of literacy.

Meek (1982) suggests that good stories teach reading because the stories draw readers back for repetition and practice. Literature helps children come to understand the universality of experience and the nature of their world. When children read stories they create a context or a framework for their understanding of the world. Thus they will become critical readers and critical citizens. Through literature, children learn how to make sense of the world. Courtney uses art and Galan dramatizes.

A Whole Language-focused Early Childhood Program

In establishing a sound program for young children, the principles of a good whole language classroom are most appropriate. The first principle suggests that children, in order to learn language, need to be surrounded by it. In the early childhood classroom there are many opportunities for children to use their own language. Centres such as sand, water, visual arts, library, cooking, drama, housekeeping, and writing are vital aspects of the program. Print that occurs naturally in children's home environments appears in the preschool classroom. The housekeeping centre has telephone books, note pads, pencils, and pictures posted on the fridge. The block centre has signs, some ready-made but others blank for the children to fill in as they create their own signposts to their own "storied" worlds. In their drama centre the props are open-ended . . . a piece of material from old drapes, a bit of carpet, a lantern, scarves—all fodder for the imagination. The library and writing centres are close to each other, together the focal point of the classroom. Comfortable chairs and many books fill the room. Books are displayed so that covers can be seen, inviting children to read. Lists of class favourites are posted. There is a place for an adult and child to sit side by side to read.

Children need many opportunities to participate in story drama. One day the children, together with Max in *Where the Wild Things Are*, may seize power and control their world; another day they, like Franklin in *Franklin in the Dark*, may discover that we all have something that frightens us; still another day they may echo a character's thought that "I need a rest." The teacher may ask for a wild rumpus to begin or a scary cave to be constructed with blocks. Barry, a lonely boy who sometimes arrives at school with dark circles under eyes, may produce a picture of a child huddled in a corner, afraid to go home. The picture echoes Franklin, but it may also echo Barry's story. The teacher watches, records, and plans. The teacher will be better able to help Barry acquire literacy if she begins to better understand the social and emotional

being that is Barry. Offers of alternative worlds and alternative routes to literacy are made through the teacher and through the story.

Demonstrations are also provided through other children's stories. The teacher asks, "Do you have something to share?" At times a simple retelling of an event at home is offered; at others an author's story and a child's story are interwoven. At still other times the child picks up a book and reads. The story is owned, held, and remembered as teacher, child, and story negotiate meaning.

In this whole language early childhood classroom, the child who tells a story from pictures or who reads from memory is celebrated. The child who builds on an author's story is acknowledged as attending to a story, rather than reprimanded for copying. The child who mixes up Goldilocks and Red Riding Hood in a story drama is noted as having some control over two stories, not as lacking control over one. The teacher's attitude towards approximation can have the most positive or negative effect on the child's move towards literacy. The teacher collects data on the child's emergent literacy and shares it with all of those who interact with the child.

Children are rewarded psychologically by the stories offered to them in their whole language program. As previously suggested, we "story" our lives and we each have a story to tell. The reward of our life story is the way in which we make meaning of it. As adults we need to recognize that response is individual. Stories are shaped by experience. We, and children, are "meaning makers." Stories, by their very nature, satisfy our need for routine and for closure. They actively engage our minds and in their unfolding provide us with confirmation of our predictions and of our humanity. Our early childhood classrooms need to become places in which our children's stories are heard, respected, and shared. Our treatment of story provides the foundation for our children's move towards literacy learning.

→ See: Baskwill, p. 168; Dyson, p. 46; King, p. 16; Literature Reference List, p. 429; Parkes, p. 36; Short, p. 18; Van DeWeghe, p. 22; Watson, p. 40.

Reference
Meek, M. 1982. *Learning to read*. London: Bodley Head.

Further Reading by Sharon J. Rich
◆ "Restoring Power to Teachers: The Impact of Whole Language." *Language Arts* 6(2), 1985.
◆ "Learning in Whole Language" *Classroom*, March 1987.
◆ "Whole Language: Changing Beliefs About Language Learning." *FWTAO Newsletter*, 1988.
◆ "Informal Teacher Support Groups," with J. Weiss. *Orbit* 20, 1989.
◆ "Teachers' Willingness to Apply Reading Comprehension Strategies," with M. Pressley. In *Teacher Education and Special Education*, 1990.

Children like to figure out how things work. From their earliest days, they are endlessly poking and pushing and pulling apart to find out what makes things **WELL-SAID** go. This is how they learned to talk. They listened to the talk on all sides of them and they began experimenting and figuring out how talk works. Once they began to figure out what they needed to know, they made talk work for them.

—Bill Martin Jr, *Sounds of Language*

Cornerstone: Dorothy F. King

Matthew: Aspects of the Growth and Development of a Child's Written Language

At four and a half years old, Matthew is an accomplished language learner and user who is very adept at finding out more about language. Matthew is bright, wise in the ways that most children are. He is creative and verbal. He does amazing things, but they are probably typical of most children who are allowed to experiment. Basically, Matthew is allowed to learn on his own—and he is an excellent strategist.

Matthew, age 4

David Doake (1979) says that there is no such thing as reading and writing readiness as it is presently popularly conceptualized in our educational system. Dr. Doake says that children begin to learn to read and write from the time they first hear and see language.

Matthew has been read to daily since he was four days old. He has always seen people around him read and write. When he was two, Matthew was reading to his stuffed animals, pretend friends, and any real people who would listen. He used, and still does use, both memory reading (called "memorization" by some) and semantically and syntactically correct reproduction of meaning in which he tells the meaning of the story in words different from the author's.

One of Matthew's favorite ways to share a book is when the reader stops at a specific point in the text and lets him fill in words.

Rose Red continued <u>walking</u> (on her way), but later in the day <u>she saw him</u> (she saw the dwarf) again. He was busy counting <u>the jewels</u> (the jewels) from the sack, and had them <u>laid on the ground</u> (piled up on the ground). How they glittered in the <u>sparkly sun</u> (light from the setting sun)!

Matthew expects print to make sense in its setting. He was quite excited the day he got his Mickey Mouse glass. That evening, as he sat at the dinner table with the glass in front of him, a guest asked Matthew if the glass were his. He said it was. She then pointed to the name Mickey Mouse on the glass and asked him what it said. "Matthew's glass" was the matter-of-fact reply. It certainly made sense to Matthew that those words should be there.

When print doesn't seem to make sense, Matthew asks questions. I became aware of how much he already knew about print and context when he was three years and eight months old. We were at Wal-Mart. Matthew was in the shopping cart seat, keeping up a steady monologue as we went through the store. He asked, "Why is the K mart sign in the Wal-Mart store?" I said, "Show me what you mean." Matthew pointed to a sign on the wall that hung over the sewing supplies: **Knit-Sew**.

Given the similarities, I had to reply in all honesty, "That's a very good question."

Recently Matthew had to resolve another problem. He has long known the logo for the TV program "Sesame Street," and invented a song using its spelling: S-E-S-A-M-E, S-E-S-A-M-E, Sesame, Sesame, Sesame.

Later he found a can in the spice rack and said, "These must be sesame seeds, S-E-S-A-M-E. It says sesame seeds."

Apparently Matthew is very confident about his response to the print display: sesame. But look what happened when he encountered this word in a setting that didn't seem to make sense to him.

Matthew was looking through the *Reader's Digest* and came across an advertisement for nuts. "Mommy, look what I found!" he said, pointing to the word "sesame." I asked him what it said and he paused. He looked up at me and said, "Peanuts." The next day he pointed to the print under the jar of nuts and asked me to read it to him. I asked him what he thought it said. Matthew said, "It's gonna tell me why it says *sesame* on those peanuts."

As far as we can tell, Matthew began to think of himself as a writer as early as three years of age. He left notes for us telling us where he had gone or what he had done or inviting us to shows. Writing was functional to him, though some people would classify his notes as scribbling.

This is an example of a conversation Matthew wrote when he was three years and four months old. He enjoys written conversation and reads it to himself and to others.

Here is written conversation that Matthew initiated. "My name is Matt." "My name is Mommy." "Your name is Dottie." "Yes, you are right. What is Daddy's name?" "Max. Not Matthew." "Matthew" is written in spiral counterclockwise form.

Notice also the ways Matthew makes the letter *a*, capitalized in his name and lowercased in his father's. Matthew attends a nursery school three mornings a week. When he started writing his name on his papers, one of his teachers intervened. Matthew originally made a fairly conventional-looking capital *a* with a pointed top. He switched to a lowercase *a*, then to drawing a square, and now he is presently content with the boxlike *a* you see here. His switch to the lowercase *a* occurred at the time we received a communique that said: "Dear Parents, Attached is a sheet showing the proper way to make letters."

One day last September he worked very hard to produce these:

Matthew calmly announced, "Oh, by the way, I can write now." This seems to me to imply that Matthew was judging his work by the print around him. Though he had used his writing functionally before, he now assumed new status.

The examples above are not to imply that Matthew's writing has been simply a linear progression of refinement. He continues to use scribbles as well as more conventional forms. And, even when a conventional form is achieved, he continues to experiment with it.

The next illustration is a letter he wrote to Dorothy Watson saying he wasn't able to go and see her:

Notice the control he shows, his conformity to adult standards.

Now look:

Here is evidence of a language user and learner who experiments —and enjoys it—a language user who obviously feels in control. (H...E "look, I'm putting four of them on it!" ...L "backwards"...L—before the H...O "down here" below the first L..."Now Matthew all mixed up"..."I'm making an O for the H"...lots of laughing.)

Matthew has a wordless book made for him by his grandmother from illustrations from her books (Howard 1985). He wanted to write his story down, so we made photocopies of all the pages and he wrote a story about Kitty and Frog. Here are two pages from his story:

Matthew read this story frequently for about three weeks. During this time one of his favorite

books was *Too Many Lollipops*, by Robert Quackenbush. It has a refrain: "And eat a lot of lollipops." One day Matthew rewrote his Kitty and Frog story so that it too had a refrain. Matthew's refrain was "And they played." The rest of the text remained the same even though he chose to write the same "words" again at the top of each page.

Here is an example of the functional ways that Matthew uses written language. This exam-

ple is part of a joke, a trick. Matthew wrote this, then hid it behind his back and said, "I bet I can make you say what's on this." The reply was, of course, "No, you can't." Matthew said, "Ha, ha! It says no."

Matthew also understands that writing can be duplicated and disseminated to others who are strangers. After watching a news program about the MX missile Matthew made a poster saying "Stop MX" and asked me to photocopy it so he could pass it out to everyone "so they'll think."

So far Matthew's writing is limited to spellings that he knows or knows where to find and copy. Only recently has there been evidence that he may use invented spellings. The first example shows a word he "spelled" orally last summer: S-O-M, or swim.

Dorothy F. King is president of the Center for Expansion of Language and Thinking. In addition to teaching in special education, Dorothy has taught students of all ages, from preschoolers to graduate students. Currently, she and her family live in the Navajo Nation, where she is an educational consultant.

Matthew watches a show on TV called "Dusty's Treehouse," and here is his spelling of Dusty. Note that both of these examples are done with movable letters, not with letters he writes.

Matthew uses written language naturally and seems quite able to learn more from the environment in which he lives.

Should Matthew attend the school program in our district, he will spend much of kindergarten doing exercises to help him identify letters, doing matching exercises, and coloring within the lines. Matthew has been able to identify letters since he was two years old. He can match according to his own criteria and to a criterion that is given to him. He does not consistently color within the lines, but he has already demonstrated the ability to draw letters.

Matthew demonstrates that language use does not progress linearly but is a recursive phenomenon in which users experiment and develop rules and strategies. We need to keep in mind Jerry Harste's admonition (1980) that we not judge children's language works by adult standards or preconceived stages of development.

➜ See: Files, p. 355; Goodman, p. 32; Kalman, p. 34; Ketch, p. 39; Literature Reference List, p. 429; Watson, p. 40.

References

Doake, D. 1979. "Preschool book handling knowledge or book experience and emergent reading behavior." Paper presented at IRA National Convention.

Harste, J. 1980. "Alison: On language learning." Paper presented at IRA National Convention.

Howard, G. 1985. *The Mark Twain book* and *Don't be a silly.* New London, MO: Ralls County Book Company.

Quackenbush, R. 1975. *Too many lollipops.* New York: Scholastic.

Further Reading by Dorothy F. King

◆ "Real Kids or Unreal Tasks: The Obvious Choice." *Kentucky English Bulletin,* Winter 1990.

◆ "Toward Excellence in the Education of Navajo Children: One School's Journey." *Journal of Navajo Education,* Winter 1990.

◆ "Whole Language: Cherishing Learners and Their Language," with K. Goodman. In *Language, Speech, and Hearing Services in Schools,* in press.

◆ "Assessment and Evaluation in Bilingual, Multi-Cultural Classrooms." In *Assessment and Evaluation in Whole Language Programs,* ed. W. Harp. Christopher-Gordon, to be published 1991.

◆ Proceedings of the First Annual Whole Language Umbrella Conference, ed. with S. Ohanian. Richard C. Owen, to be published 1991.

Marvelous Inventions

A Cool Kid

Judith carried her daughter, Molly, age three, into the bedroom and gently laid her down on her bed for a nap, not noticing that the window directly above the bed was open. Soon after she had tiptoed from the room, she heard Molly cry out, "Bring me a blanket, Mom! I'm refrigerating!"

—As told to LBB by Judith Larner Lowry, Bolinas, CA

					Steiner			Mitchell
					Montessori			Piaget
				Parker				Dewey
		Pestalozzi	Neef	Alcott				
Comenius	Rousseau					Froebel	Vygotsky	Rogers
								Maslow
1600	1700			1800		1900		2000

Pioneers: Jean-Jacques Rousseau (1712–1778) by Ron Miller

Holistic education was introduced to modern Western culture by the romantic writer Rousseau in his book *Emile* (1762). Rousseau did not invent a system of holistic education; he simply observed that the scientific, technological, urban, nationalistic culture that was beginning to emerge in the 18th century would seriously interfere with children's natural ways of growing and learning. For Rousseau and the romantic tradition that followed him, the realm of nature is our physical, emotional, and spiritual home; the romantic poets and philosophers—Blake, Goethe, Coleridge, Wordsworth, Emerson, Thoreau, and others—asserted that humankind must reclaim a sense of reverence for natural processes and the natural environment, rather than accept only a scientific-technological view that seeks to control and conquer nature for shortsighted utilitarian ends.

Rousseau argued that there are organic patterns in human development that must be respected and followed if the child is to grow into a healthy adult. For example, he observed that young children do not think or reason in the same ways as adults and should not be forced to do so. "The first impulses of nature are always right," he declared in *Emile.* "There is no original sin in the human heart." By emphasizing that natural tendencies are healthy rather than evil, he sought to make education an art of nurturing rather than a science of discipline. Education should allow and encourage natural energies to express themselves, rather than seek to instill the fixed ideas, beliefs, and habits of the adult generation.

Rousseau recognized that children must, of course, live in society; but he raised the point that adult society is neither perfect nor finished, that we do not know enough about natural human development to presume we are giving children what they truly need. If we instill social knowledge and skills, we should at least do so with an attitude of humility and respect toward the young life in our care.

Unfortunately, Rousseau's writing, like his personal life, was uneven and inconsistent. His name has been used to discredit holistic approaches as being irrational and disordered; a typical example was the attack on progressive education during the 1950s, in which one critic dismissed Rousseau as an "unbalanced romantic." His name has become the symbol for anarchism and sentimentalism in education. But this is to ignore the core message of his educational theory—that human development unfolds according to an inherent order, direction, and wisdom which transcend our cultural and ideological prejudices. Rousseau, and holistic educators who followed him, argued that education must start by understanding and respecting organic human development.

Hold childhood in reverence and do not be in any hurry to judge it for good or ill. Give nature time to work before you take over her tasks, lest you interfere with her method . . . Nature wants children to be children before they are men. If we deliberately depart from this order we shall get premature fruits which are neither ripe nor well flavored and which soon decay. We shall have youthful sages and grown-up children. Childhood has ways of seeing, thinking and feeling peculiar to itself; nothing can be more foolish than to substitute our ways for them.

WELL-SAID

—Jean-Jacques Rousseau, *The Educational Theory of Jean-Jacques Rousseau*

📷 **WHOLE LANGUAGE CAMERA**

"TDE" spells "Teddy." First grader, Fernando, a student of Annette Maggitti's Desert Winds School, Tucson, Arizona, beams at his accomplishment.

Book Note

Language Stories & Literacy Lessons

Jerome C. Harste, Virginia A. Woodward, and Carolyn L. Burke
1984; 288 pp.; $17.50
Portsmouth, NH: Heinemann

Harste, Woodward, and Burke explore early literacy by observing young children's interactions with their world. The authors view children as informants who reveal how they become language learners and users. Kidwatching is used as a research tool to make generalizations about the literacy lessons children can teach us. The authors differ with Piaget in that they regard language learning as first and foremost a social event.

Lois Mather

❝Research is not simply the business of testing hypotheses, but rather the business of getting hypotheses to work in exploring and expanding the nature of literacy, literacy learning, and literacy instruction. These we see as the real and potential lessons of studying young children. ❞ (p. xx)

❝The most salient home factor relating to literacy learning is one we have termed 'availability and opportunity to engage in written language events.' Homes where books were out and readily available, where paper, pens, pencils, crayons, magic markers, and other instruments were handy, where children seemed quite naturally to be included and involved, seemed to provide the key conditions for children to go exploring and for parents to involve themselves in using and encouraging reading and writing, whether they 'technically' reported that they knew what they were doing or not. In fact, some of the worst disasters in terms of literacy development for both parents and children seemed to occur and revolve around those times when the parents set out to formally 'teach letter names,' 'teach the alphabet,' or engage in other school-like reading and writing tasks. ❞ (p. 42)

Great Teachers:
Vivian Paley
by Eileen Ogintz

Kids' Fantasies Set the Stage for Play

His finger pointed straight . . . Then he found the treasure map and he went to the treasure. And then he goed back home and he was rich again and he turned into a cat.

—A four-year-old's story about his magic ring

Every school day, a class of 24 exuberant Hyde Park preschoolers gets a chance to do what adults only dream about. They act out their fantasies, even choosing who will help bring them to life.

"Absolutely, they are using their fantasies to cope with the world," explained Vivian Paley, their teacher at the University of Chicago Laboratory Nursery School. "They are creating worlds they can understand."

Paley, a 30-year teaching veteran and author of five books about children in her classroom, is as excited about the youngsters' forays into fantasy as they are. Her latest book, *Bad Guys Don't Have Birthdays: Fantasy Play at Four*, follows a group's fantasy play throughout a school year.

She calls the preschoolers' play "universal theater" and says that if we "really listen" to fantasy play, we will see that it uses imagery, ideas, and logic, just as adult theater does.

Paley, considered a pioneer in the classroom use of fantasy dramatization, stresses that through fantasies—be they about parents and babies, animals, or superheroes fighting bad guys—children are able to express their pleasure and curiosity as well as their ominous feelings and fears. Paley says she believes that children aged three to five spend three-fourths of their time engaged in some sort of fantasy play.

One recent morning, Paley was seated on a small chair, bent over a child-sized table. She seemed oblivious to the chaos swirling around her as the children jumped and yelled, played with blocks and Legos, painted large, vibrant pictures, and built sand castles.

One by one, the 13 children who had asked to be "on the story list" that day got their turn to tell Paley a tale, which she copied verbatim, grammatical errors and all. She also taped the storytelling sessions for use in her writing. The children, intent on getting their stories across, paid no attention to the small tape recorder.

One five-year-old told how Superman, Robin, and Batman fought with Plutar and Joker "till 21 [meaning someone counts to 21], and then they all ate tuna fish and pasta."

Paley, who recently won an award from the Erikson Institute for service to children, believes there is increasing interest in this concept.

"There is a growing feeling that more and more teachers find this a welcome common meeting place between themselves and children—a curriculum truly based on the thinking of the children themselves, coming out of their

> I have studied nursery school and kindergarten children for 32 years, as their teacher and classroom biographer. The teaching and writing go together, and I cannot do one without the other. I record each day's play and storytelling and conversations, then create my own stories about what is happening. The next morning, in the classroom, my reality is measured alongside the children's. As with play itself, the process is never-ending. The children invent new images and symbols every year and I continually expand my definitions of what we are doing in the classroom. My books evolve out of the persistent theme of a particular child, the urgent preoccupations of the developing classroom culture, and my own curiosity about the mystery of making connections in a classroom.
>
> —Vivian Paley

play," Paley explained, noting that she is now being asked to demonstrate the technique around the country.

She stressed that no child is forced or required to participate in the story sessions, but added that they invariably become one of the children's favorite parts of school.

Later in the morning, after the toys had been straightened up, the children and their teachers gathered at the theater, a small room where a six-foot-square "stage" on the floor has been marked off by green tape. Each child's story from that day's list is acted out here, the author picking the actors from those who volunteer.

Some parts, predictably, are more popular than others. There were a lot more actors who wanted to be giraffes and cats, for example, than to be bad guys. If no one volunteers, Paley said, the part must be imagined. The author usually grabs the choicest role.

"The desire to play and to have friends, to transpose private fantasies into public, ongoing play is the strongest motivation a child has to expand communication skills," Paley explained. "The payoff of friendship and fantasy is so important to any child."

"The very act of dramatizing an idea enables it to be seen more clearly," Paley said. "This offers the young imagination the opportunity to see the images in the mind more clearly."

"Yet typically the same themes are recounted year after year," Paley said. The younger children first reenact their lives at home, being Mommy and Daddy, siblings, perhaps a baby-sitter and a baby, all eating, sleeping and playing.

Paley's book centers on a boy named Frederick, who is distressed by the arrival of a new baby brother and the attention the baby is getting. At one point, Frederick announces to a classmate, "I'm the new borned person, okay? No father and no brother. Mommy and the baby. Don't let anyone come in, okay?"

No matter whether their mothers hold paying jobs or not, the girls tend to continue to act out more domestic scenes, often being mothers or big sisters, while boys gravitate toward action involving cars, boats, ships, and of course, bad guys, Paley said.

For both boys and girls, Paley added, the fantasies enable these young children to feel in control of their environment, to feel powerful. "Power is any ability to feel stronger, happier, and bigger," she said. That might be as Superman or as a college girl or simply by changing the circumstances of their lives.

Paley recalled the child who complained that his older brother hated him. He told stories about two brothers who love each other. And there are lonely only children who like stories about lots of siblings.

Who wouldn't, she asked, like to create a world where bad feelings can instantly be changed to good feelings, where one can have a say in who all of the characters are—and what they do?

Occasionally, Paley said, a child uses his story to convey a problem at home. "If the child is upset, I'll always ask if they are sure they want to act that story out," she said.

And the child may well say no. "Fantasy is useful," Paley observed. "But one must protect children from exposing what they don't want to expose."

→ See: Dyson, p. 46; Nourot, p. 31; Rich, p. 27; Short, p. 18; VanDeWeghe, p. 22.

Excerpted from *Chicago Tribune*, 9 February 1988.

Further Reading by Vivian Paley
- ◆ *White Teacher*. Harvard University Press, 1979.
- ◆ *Boys and Girls: Superheroes in the Doll Corner*. University of Chicago Press, 1984.
- ◆ *Mollie Is Three: Growing Up in School*. University of Chicago Press, 1986.
- ◆ *Bad Guys Don't Have Birthdays: Fantasy Play at Four*. University of Chicago Press, 1988.
- ◆ *The Boy Who Would Be a Helicopter*. Harvard University Press, 1990.

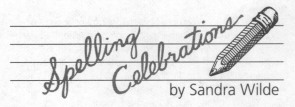

Spelling Celebrations
by Sandra Wilde

Patterns and Strategies: The Importance of Spelling

It's important to be a good speller because "they're going to ask you to spell something when you go to high school . . . and you're not going to know what it is and they're going to get mad."

Elaine, 4th grade

It's important to be a good speller because if you are "police ladies or men you have to write nice so they can understand."

Gordon, 4th grade

If you were to ask a cross section of adults why spelling is important, their answers would probably fall into the two categories exemplified by Elaine and Gordon. Some would see spelling as primarily a matter of etiquette in the low-level sense of minding your p's and q's; correct spelling is something you do to make a good impression, to stay out of trouble, so that people won't think you're ignorant. (Elaine also said that even adults need to be good spellers because otherwise "everybody's going to think that you don't go to school . . . and your mother doesn't care.") By contrast, other people, like Gordon, think of correct spelling as primarily a communication tool, a courtesy to others, etiquette in the higher-level "golden rule" sense. Which attitude would we rather have our students hold? Through interviewing children, we can discover what beliefs they hold about the importance of spelling. Through communicating our own attitudes, we can influence those beliefs.

Cornerstone: Patricia Monighan Nourot

Storyplaying in the Kindergarten

It's Wednesday morning. As I arrive at the school to work in the kindergartens, I hear two children whispering: "I'll put you in my story—a wolf one—if I can be in yours," Josh says to Amir.

In Mrs. Cole's classroom, 6 of the 29 children have signed up for my station—storyplay, a technique developed by Vivian Paley for dictating and enacting stories. As we sit around the table, Rebecca and Mika tell me they want to complete pictures before they dictate their stories while Ricardo, John, and James offer to start pictures and then dictate. Only Michelle declines the option of drawing a picture, saying, "I'll do the words first and then *maybe* I'll do a picture."

I write what Michelle dictates: "Once upon a time there was a little girl and a fox. And Dorothy played with the fox. They were dressed up like trees. A pond comed and a fish and a butterfly. A purse comed and an Easter bunny gave the kids eggs." She pauses. "How many people, so far, Mrs. Nourot?" I read what she has dictated, underlining the characters. "Seven," she counts. "Make that six kids gots eggs." I insert "six." She continues, "An arrow comed and u-umm . . ." Michelle pauses and scans the room. "And a piece of paper and . . . an earring! The end."

Patricia Monighan Nourot is an assistant professor of education at Sonoma State University in Rohnert Park, California. Before completing her doctorate, she taught elementary school for eight years and preschool for five years. She is the coauthor of *Looking at Children's Play: A Bridge Between Theory and Practice* (Teachers College Press, 1987), and this year is serving as visiting educator to the Child Development Division of the State Department of Education.

We count the characters again and discuss how she will manage them when we enact the play. She plans to direct her actors to wait offstage until I read aloud their roles. I ask her what part she would like to play when the story is performed. She thinks for a moment and says, "The fox—and Kim can be the fish 'cause she likes to swim." She skips across the room to tell Kim her intentions.

Later that morning classmates Michelle has selected enact the story as I read it aloud. As the last character arrives on stage, Michelle interjects, "Wait, that's not all! I forgot a part. The fox covered everybody up."

"Shall I write that into the story?" I ask. Michelle nods enthusiastically as she carefully covers each character with a make-believe blanket. And I add "The fox covered everybody up" to her written text.

Michelle is not the only one to struggle with how to include all her friends in the cast. John solves his dilemma in another way. He dictates the following "Ninja Turtle" story:

One time there was trouble and a bad guy was killing people. And then the Ninja Turtles killed the bad guy. Six bad guys. The Ninja Turtle killed the bad guys.

When John finishes, Ricardo and James immediately try to cajole him into selecting them for the coveted turtle roles. "But I promised Josh, Jeff, and Andrew," he states hesitantly, caught in the emotional dilemma of casting his storyplay without violating his friendships. He listens to the boys sitting near him for a few minutes, then carries his picture of the four Ninja Turtles over to the cubbies, where he painstakingly copies "Josh," "Jeff," and "Andrew" from the cubbies onto three of the four turtles, finishing with "John" on the fourth. "There," he announces as he returns to the table. "This is the sign about my play and it has all the names on it."

Other children use drawings to accompany their dictated stories in different ways. For example, Rebecca's story begins with a poem: "Roses are red, violets are blue, and most of all I like you."

"It's about friends," Rebecca comments.

Once upon a time there was me and my friend. I climbed a tree and I hurt myself and had to go to the hospital. My friend came with me in the ambulance. And I had a broken leg. They took me home and my friend brought me flowers. I went on crutches. The end.

After the story is enacted, Rebecca shows her picture to her classmates and asks them to guess which part of the drawing was the poem and which scene in the story the drawing depicted. A lively discussion centers on how each part of the drawing represented a piece of the story. Rebecca tells why she made the drawing and listens to her classmates' interpretations of them.

As the year progresses, this process of figuring out which parts of the drawing carries particular meanings is often extended during the story dictation process. Children ask me to reread their stories and we discuss the features of words and letters. They also copy words from their stories onto their drawings.

In another kindergarten the teacher schedules free choices for the hour, and children individually come to me to dictate and draw their stories. Story characters in all four kindergartens are remarkably similar, although each "classroom culture" develops unique conventions for expressing stories in dramatic play.

Media characters such as John's "Ninja Turtles" and the ever-popular *Ghostbusters* flourish. We adults chuckle together when we realize that the names Michelangelo and Raphael, used so freely in story dictations, represent the children's brand of "cultural literacy" rather than our own. These are two of the names for cartoon characters in "Teenage Mutant Ninja Turtles."

Conventions are also derived from children's television. One example is a rainbow marking the end of a television program. This convention is often seen in the girls' stories, which gives rise to the theatrical convention of the rainbow character waiting, bending over, hands to toes, in the corner of the stage until the end of the story. Then the rainbow triumphantly stands with radiating arms as the audience applauds.

Characters, themes, and story structures are also gleaned from fairy tales and other children's literature. The character Dorothy is included in Michelle's story following discussions of *The Wizard of Oz*, which was read at school. Daniel is more explicit about the source of his story:

There was a person and then he had a hat. The hat came alive. The hat chased after the man. The fox chased after the hat. The cow chased after the fox. The horse ran after the cow. The bull chased after the horse. The duck ran after the bull. The bear chased after the duck. Then everybody stopped chasing and kicked each other. The end.

"You know that book *The Gingerbread Man*?" Daniel asks as I finish writing the last word. "Well, I was kinda thinking about it for this story. Get it?"

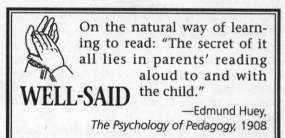

Book Note

Wally's Stories

Vivian Gussin Paley
1981; 232 pp.; $8.95
Cambridge: Harvard University Press

This is one of my favorite books to read aloud to my university students and workshop participants. I use *Wally's Stories* to help emphasize points that I hope to make about important developmental moments in the lives of young children. The impact of stories on children's oral language development is obvious as Paley shows what happens when children are actively involved in acting out not only the stories written by classic children's authors, but also the powerful stories dictated by the children themselves. Paley, a consummate kidwatcher, helps readers peer into the magical world in which children live.

YMG

I do "get it" and so much more, as each Wednesday morning I share with children and their teachers the power and authority of storyplay, which gives form and content to beginning experiences with written language.

→ See: Dyson, p. 46; Paley, p. 30; Rich, p. 27; Short, p. 18.

Cornerstone:
Sandra Wilde

Trusting the Learner: Elaine Learns to Punctuate

Anyone looking at Elaine's writing would have said that she didn't understand punctuation at all. Periods seemed to be scattered all over the page, as in this example:

I. [went] to the fun house i got scared
then i started to cry I. was a ghost . . .
we were really ghosts we had
a pumpkin pie. we ate it it
was good me and m.s wilde went to
go out to eat then we went to go
watch a movie we bought a pop and
some popcorn. we watched. Annie.
then we went home then we
went to the carnival the next
morning we went to the.
carnival in m.s wildes car my
mom does not let me use our car to go.

(Elaine's spelling has been regularized, but her capitalization and line divisions have been preserved.)

When I interviewed her, however, I discovered that she did have some idea about where periods went; her ideas just weren't very coherent. In some cases, she said, they go at the end of a sentence—but she couldn't define how she knew where the end of a sentence was. In some cases, like in the middle of "m.s," she said she used a period because "that's how they write it"; i.e., "just because." My favorite explanation, though, was when she explained the periods that she put after "I" by saying that "periods and capitals go together," a rule she'd been taught but of course didn't really understand. Because of this conglomeration of half-baked ideas, Elaine's punctuation looked pretty chaotic.

One day, however, to my surprise, Elaine wrote a story in which virtually all the periods were placed correctly. When I asked her how she knew where to put them, she said, "It's at the end of a sentence." She explained that she knew where sentences ended by just listening. After talking to her teacher, I discovered the reason for her new level of understanding. One day, Sr. Maria (Elaine's teacher) had sat down with Elaine and read aloud a story she had written, asking her to tell where the sentences ended. Although Elaine couldn't define what a sentence was, she could hear in her own writing where one ended and the next one began. From then on, her sentences were, for the most part, punctuated correctly. She left out a few periods and put a few at the ends of clauses, but she never used them weirdly anymore.

Elaine, who was not a very strong writer, had been taught two rules about punctuation. Rule #1 ("periods and capitals go together") was simple but not very accurate. Rule #2 ("a period goes at the end of a sentence") was vague but accurate; unfortunately, without advice about applying it, it was useless to her. It is impossible to give children hard and fast rules about punctuation because there aren't any. You can, it's true, say that a period goes at the end of a sentence, but you can't operationally define a sentence to someone who doesn't already know what one is. The standard definitions such as "a complete thought" and "something containing both a subject and a predicate" are not precise enough for reliable identification. However, when Elaine was helped to draw on her own instinctive knowledge about sentences, it became apparent that she knew enough about them to tell where they end, without needing a definition at all. And, of course, once you know where the sentences end, you know where the periods go. A vague rule (#2) worked when she realized she could sense how to apply it; a rule

that sounded definitive (#1) only led her astray. This vignette shows that trusting the learner involves two components: providing learners with appropriate experiences, trusting that they will learn from them; and realizing that we can guide learners to trust themselves as they expand upon and use their own knowledge base.

→ See: Spelling Celebrations; Wilde, p. 406.

—Sandra Wilde is an associate professor at the University of Oregon, Eugene, OR.

Kidwatching
Yetta M. Goodman

Shoshana

Shoshana is six years old and has just finished first grade. She was visiting with her grandparents for two weeks during summer vacation. She wanted a special notebook where she could write her activities each day so that when she went back home, she could tell her mother everything she had done while she was away.

Her first entry was as follows:

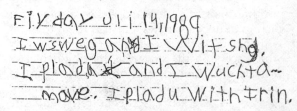

Fiyday Jli 14, 1989. [Grandma suggested the year]
I wsweg and I wit shg [She read aloud as she wrote: "I went swimming and I went shopping."]
I pladu and I wuchta . . . [She read, "I played and I watched a . . ." I put the dots because it is not the end of the sentence.]
move. [movie—I put the dot because it's the end of the sentence. She then looked back at her writing, read it aloud, and placed a period after shopping (shg). "That's the end of a sentence, too," she said. She then finished her entry reading as she wrote and placing a period at the end.]
I pladu with IRIN. ["I played with Aaron."]

We could evaluate many things in Shoshana's journal entry. We could examine her use of WENT first attached to the beginning of the word SWIMMING as a single letter and then written as an separate word (WIT) prior to SHOPPING. She represented the IN with an E in SWIMMING and did not represent it in SHOPPING. She ended the word PLAYED with a U representing the way she read the word with a plosive sound at the end.

But what interested me in this kidwatching opportunity was her awareness of sentenceness. She easily and without encouragement of any sort placed final sentence punctuation in the appropriate places. Shoshana provides a good example to refute the notion of sequence. Within this particular piece of writing Shoshana shows greater awareness of the concept of sentenceness than of the concepts of wordness or letter-sound correspondence. Shoshana is just becoming aware of the alphabetic nature of the English language. This is evident when she reads, too. She is willing to take the time to use her developing knowledge when it comes easily to her, but because she has so much to say as she writes and is eager to get the meaning of what she is reading, she makes greater use of her developing knowledge at some times more than other times.

She knows word boundaries in reading almost all the time, but as shown in her journal entry there are times when the concept of word boundaries is not fully conventional in her writing. Although Shoshana seems very confident of sentenceness, she shows growing awareness of all three concepts at some level. Since we trust her to continue to construct knowledge about words, letter-sound correspondence and sentences, we will continue to find many ways to involve her in reading and writing experiences and enjoy Shoshana-watching as we do.

Later, when I read Shoshana this piece to verify what I had written, I asked her how she knew where to put the periods at the end of her sentences. Her answer reveals the ability of learners to know more about concepts than they are able to verbalize.

"My teacher told me where to put them. When you think that's enough writing for one sentence, then you'll put a period so they'll know."

→ See: Goodman, p. 360.

Book Note

The Craft of Children's Writing

Judith Newman 1985; 72 pp.; $6 Portsmouth, NH: Heinemann

Intention, organization, experimentation, and orchestration are concepts developed by Harste, Woodward, and Burke in their award-winning *Language Stories and Literacy Lessons* (Heinemann, 1984) to explain the process of written language development. Newman illustrates each with striking samples of children's writing, including an in-depth case of six-year-old Shawn. A slim text simply organized around these four concepts, it's a good one to hand parents or teachers unfamiliar with literacy as a developmental language process.

MarVELOUS INVENTIONS

Repairments

THE BOAT WENT TO
A BOAT SHOP
TO GET REE
PAIR MENTS
Did it get fixed? YES

—Contributed by Pat Robinson, primary teacher, Ohlone School, Palo Alto, CA

Education in Turin: A Romance by Herbert Kohl

The Common Schools:
The Rise of Jonathan Stokes

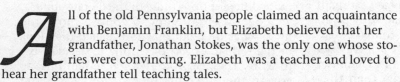

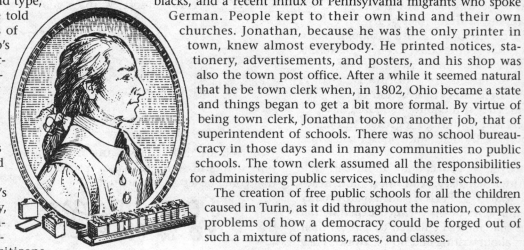

All of the old Pennsylvania people claimed an acquaintance with Benjamin Franklin, but Elizabeth believed that her grandfather, Jonathan Stokes, was the only one whose stories were convincing. Elizabeth was a teacher and loved to hear her grandfather tell teaching tales.

Jonathan Stokes was born in Philadelphia in 1760. At the age of 16 he joined the Pennsylvania militia on their mad march to Amboy, New Jersey, to support Washington's effort to hold New York. He was wounded in the right leg and, as his friends used to joke, limped his way through the Revolutionary War.

After the war, Jonathan worked for a printer in Philadelphia, trying to scrape enough money together to buy a press and type, and set up his own shop. It was during that time, he told anyone who would listen, that he attended meetings of the Junto, a club set up by Benjamin Franklin. The club's members were working people—joiners, printers, surveyors, shoemakers—interested in science, politics, education, community service, books, and, in its early years, revolution.

The Junto met once a week in a local tavern. Questions were set for study and research for the next meeting, and then the previous week's questions were discussed, with occasional pauses for toasts and rounds of ale.

Jonathan was particularly interested in the group's deliberations on the role of education in a democracy, and one of his prized possessions was a copy of Benjamin Franklin's 1749 book *Proposals Relating to the Education of Youth in Pennsylvania*. The education of citizens prepared to play an active role in the new democracy was one of Jonathan's obsessions, though he had no formal schooling himself.

There was a lot of movement west in the 1790s. People like Jonathan Stokes felt constrained on the East Coast. There were too many printers in Philadelphia, too little opportunity. Ohio was opening up and growing, and might even become a state. In 1794, the fifth year of our republic's existence, the Stokes family moved to southeastern Ohio and settled in the small town of Turin.

The town had been settled by people from Connecticut, though there were also Virginians who had fought in Ohio during the war, some remnants of the Indian communities, a small number of free blacks, and a recent influx of Pennsylvania migrants who spoke German. People kept to their own kind and their own churches. Jonathan, because he was the only printer in town, knew almost everybody. He printed notices, stationery, advertisements, and posters, and his shop was also the town post office. After a while it seemed natural that he be town clerk when, in 1802, Ohio became a state and things began to get a bit more formal. By virtue of being town clerk, Jonathan took on another job, that of superintendent of schools. There was no school bureaucracy in those days and in many communities no public schools. The town clerk assumed all the responsibilities for administering public services, including the schools.

The creation of free public schools for all the children caused in Turin, as it did throughout the nation, complex problems of how a democracy could be forged out of such a mixture of nations, races, and classes.

Continued on page 55

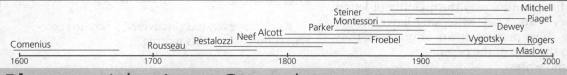

		Steiner			Mitchell
		Montessori			Piaget
	Parker			Dewey	
	Alcott				
Neef				Vygotsky	Rogers
Comenius	Pestalozzi			Froebel	Maslow
Rousseau					
1600	1700	1800		1900	2000

Pioneers: John Amos Comenius (1592-1670) by Kathryn F. Whitmore

Considered the greatest educational theorist and practical reformer of the 17th century, Comenius viewed education as a positive learning experience that should include freedom, joy, and pleasure. Among his contributions were such significant advances as using illustrations in textbooks and training the senses as the basic methodology for education.

Three prominent revolutionary themes accented the work and writing of John Comenius.

1. That a universal compulsory education is necessary for all children:
The following reason will establish that not the children of the rich or the powerful only, but of all alike, boys and girls, both noble and ignoble, rich and poor, in all cities and town, villages and hamlets, should be sent to school (Parker 1912, p. 141).

2. That teaching methodology should be through the senses:
Those things, therefore, that are placed before the intelligence of the young, must be real things and not the shadow of things. I repeat, they must be things; and by the term I mean determinate, real, useful things that can make an impression on the senses and on the imagination. . . . From this a golden rule for teachers may be derived. Everything should, as far as is possible, be placed before the senses. Everything visible should be brought before the organs of sight, everything audible before that of hearing. Odours should be placed before the sense of taste and touch respectively. If an object can make an impression on several senses at once, it should be brought into contact with several . . . (Morrison 1976, p. 25).

3. That education should be pragmatically rooted in the students' real lives:
Nothing should be learned solely for its value at school, but for its use in life (Comenius 1986, p. 84).

The work of John Comenius not only radically changed the educational practices of his time, but broke the ground for the theorists who followed, especially John Locke and Jean-Jacques Rousseau. Many of his beliefs endure in educational theory, particularly in early childhood education.

References
Comenius, J. A. 1986. *The great didactics*, trans. M. W. Keating. London: Adam and Charles Black.

Morrison, G. S. 1976. *Early childhood education today*. Columbus, OH: Charles E. Merrill.

Parker, S. C. 1912. *A textbook in the history of modern elementary education*. Chicago: Ginn.

Kathryn F. Whitmore is a doctoral student at the University of Arizona, Tucson, AZ.

The Funny Side
Injured in Past Tense

An elaborate hospital is set up in the center of a kindergarten classroom as two classes of five- and six-year-olds study the human body. Four children have chosen to work and play in the hospital, and they have assumed a variety of roles for their play. One child records information from another at the desk in the area. Another child covers one eye to read an alphabetic eye chart. Karl, a Korean-American child, is stretched out dramatically on the bed, most of his head and body wrapped in gauze bandages and adhesive tape. Me Me, a black child, hovers over him, stethoscope in one hand, syringe in the other. Her face is covered with a green mask, and her hair and shoes are covered with surgical garb.

The teacher observes momentarily, silently considering the children's activity. Deciding to play the role of a visitor to the hospital, she puts on a dramatic face and moves quickly over to the bed and poor Karl. "Oh my, Karl, you look terrible! Whatever happened to you?" Karl looks up at his teacher happily because she has accepted the reality of the entire scene. Me Me answers, "Can't you tell, Kathy? Karl drinked and drived!"

—Kathryn F. Whitmore, doctoral student, University of Arizona, Tucson, AZ

Cornerstone: Judith Kalman

Who Invented Invented Spelling?

We all know what invented spelling is, don't we? It's that funny way kids write when they are just learning and are in the process of putting all the puzzle pieces together. Some of it is easier for the adult to decipher than others. Rebeca's "I lic tet the A's wr winig" is clearly about Oakland's major league baseball team, while we aren't sure if John's "Ttloiof2tl$" ("The rocketship is going to find some money") is about finances or not.

By the time children write the way that Rebeca does, they have traveled a long learning road of trying to make sense out of print. Although many researchers have contributed to our understanding of literacy acquisition, two Latin American women, Emilia Ferreiro and Ana Teberosky, unearthed the child's construction of the writing system. They contend that children discover that letters and sounds go together, through a long process of thought and conceptualization. (See note 1.)

To discover the conceptions implicit in children's written language acquisition (both reading and writing), Ferreiro and Terberosky developed a series of open-ended experimental situations that allowed children to express their own ideas about writing and how it works. They built their research on two simple but very important premises: first, that children learn language from authentic language environments, and second, that all children (with the obvious exceptions) will learn. Using Piaget's theory of knowledge in which the learner is actively engaged in learning—categorizing, establishing relations, constructing hypotheses, and looking for regularities, they set out to understand how children read and write before they can do so conventionally. (See note 2.)

Young Writers' Writing Inventions

Ferreiro and Teberosky assumed from the very beginning that children do not depend on formal schooling when they learn about written language. (See note 3.) Their first ideas about reading and writing develop before formal schooling begins, and many of these ideas do not necessarily coincide with an adult's understanding of writing.

Very young children may believe that there is a direct relationship between the objective characteristics of the object being represented in writing and the size of the writing used to represent it. As part of a study done in Mexico City during the 1980–81 school year, Ferreiro asked incoming first-graders to predict the number of letters needed to write a series of words. In individual interviews, she asked them: "Do you know what a butterfly and a horse are? . . . Which of the two is bigger? . . . How many letters do you think you need to write 'butterfly'? . . . Okay, write 'butterfly'. . . . How many do you think you need to write 'horse'? . . . Okay, write 'horse'." Many children either would not anticipate how many letters might be used to write these words or just made up an answer off the top of their heads (54 percent). However, 37 percent of the children who were asked these questions systematically stated that they needed more letters to write "horse" than they did to write "butterfly," because a horse is bigger than a butterfly. It is also important to note that *only 8 percent* of these children made their prediction based on some aspect of the sound composition of these words! (See note 4.)

While California is Judy's native state, she called Mexico home for 17 years. She has taught at the primary, junior high, and high school levels. In 1985 Judy was appointed to the faculty of the Universidad Pedagógica Nacional as coordinator of the Language Arts Program. She is currently working toward a Ph.D. at the University of California at Berkeley.

For the youngest children, writing means to recreate the characteristics typical of what they identify as writing. If they're most familiar with printing, then they tend to make well-separated letters or letterlike shapes. If they are most familiar with cursive writing, then they will do their own writing with curved and connected type lines.

Children's initial writing graphically varies a great deal from the beginning. Some very early writing, like David's, looks like long, curvy lines across the page.

Mi hermano va a la escuela.
(My brother goes to school.)

Other children, like Rosie, invent geometric-type shapes or squiggly marks—pseudoletters—that could be letters but are not.

I like you. I like the way you sing. I like school.

It is also common for children to use a single letter when they write the name of an object or a person as Claudia does.

Other children do exactly the opposite. They do not have control over the quantity of letters that they write. They write long letter strings, putting their pencils down only when they come to the edge of the paper.

Ricardo writes:

i t a m m c t a í l
lápiz (pencil)

s t h ñ c a a i c o
pizarrón (blackboard)

s h a i t c i a o
gis (chalk)

At first glance, these writings may look very different from each other, and yet they share several underlying ideas. To begin with, these written productions are truly writing, in the sense that when the children wrote them they did it with the specific purpose of graphically representing language and in doing so, communicating something. To the children who produced them, they are not just little marks, or isolated letters, or strings of letters made at random; they are real writing. When Claudia writes

U   for *gato* (cat),

A   for *mariposa* (butterfly),

      or

E   for *caballo* (horse),

she is not writing a U, an A, and an E as isolated letters, but *gato*, *mariposa*, and *caballo*.

None of these children understand that letters represent sounds and that this is the principle underlying the placement and variation of letters in a given written representation. Not having come yet to the realization that letters in some way represent the sounds of oral language, children use rules when they write that are quite different from those of the literate adults.

As children attempt to control more and more what they put down on paper, they look to the formal aspects of writing to decide what to write. They begin to develop certain rules to govern the different combinations and letter sequences that they produce. Their inner questions begin to deal with issues of length and letter variation. Can the same letter be used more than once in the same word or string? Can the same letter be used twice in a row? Does writing have a fixed sequence—always starting with the same letters or series of letters? Do I always have to write the same number of letters? What is the minimum number of letters that I need for writing to be real? Is there a relationship between the referent and its written representation? (i.e., Do I write "bear" with a lot of letters because it is very big and "butterfly" with only a few letters because it is very small?)

Alejandro, for example, writes with a fixed sequence. No matter what he wants his writing to mean, it is the same over and over again. Though he has plainly come to control both quantity of letters and their order, he is not yet concerned with using different combinations to say different things. The author's intention is enough to determine the meaning of a written text.

A o 8   A o 8
mar (ocean)   *gato* (cat)

A o 8   A o 8
mariposa (butterfly)   *caballo* (horse)

Raul, however, has discovered a way to represent differences in his writing.

A o e i   A o e l
gato (cat)   *mariposa* (butterfly)

A d o i   A o l b
caballo (horse)   *pez* (fish)

Although he always starts with the same letter (A) and requires that his writing always has four letters, he manages to invent a different written sequence for *gato, mariposa, caballo,* and *pez* in spite of his very limited repertoire of letters.

Inventing Letter-Sound Relationships

When children are hard at work creating ways to differentiate their written sequences, they begin to turn their attention toward a new aspect of language. Their focus shifts from the formal aspects of the written word to the possibility of using letters to represent the sounds of oral language.

When children begin to invent a way of representing the sounds of oral language, their first analysis is not phonemic but syllabic. As they begin to break spoken words down into their component parts, they tend to divide the words into syllables. This in turn serves as a basis for determining the number of letters in each word. As a result, their writing becomes predictable and much easier for the adult to interpret. The child represents each syllable with a letter; for example, "elephant" is written with three letters, "cafeteria" with five, not unlike written Hebrew or Japanese.

John writes:

rainbow

elephant

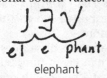

cafeteria

Each letter represents a syllable, but the letters do not have a stable sound value. For example, the T in "cafeteria" represents the syllable "ca" at the beginning of the word, and "a" at the end of it. The exact same letter represents "rain" in "rainbow" and "e" in "elephant." John is able to control the length of each word as a means of assuring variety in writing: Longer words get more letters, shorter words get less. Notice how John's attention has shifted from the meaning of the word (as when "elephant" would have to have more letters because it is a big animal) to analyzing how it sounds.

Another aspect of syllabic writing is the way in which children use the letters and assign them sound values. If they write as John does, then their writing is syllabic without conventional sound values; however, if they write as Katy does, their writing is syllabic with conventional sound values:

elephant

butterfly

Each of the letters that Katy chose conventionally represents some of the component sounds of the words she writes. However, when she writes B for the "but" in "butterfly," she is not representing the letter *b* but the whole syllable. Also note how stable her repertoire is; in both cases she uses V to represent the letter *f*.

When children begin to write syllabically, they do not automatically abandon their former beliefs, and this may create conflict. As early writers, many of them think that a word must have more than one letter to be considered "real writing," which contradicts their syllabic hypothesis when they are trying to write words like *pan* or *gis* in Spanish or "shark" or "cake" in English. One solution that children use is to divide the word in two: "Shark" becomes "sha-ark"; "cake" becomes "ca-ake." They can then jus-tify writing these words with two letters as Rosy did:

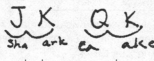

shark   cake

John had another solution: When trying to write "shark," he wrote only one letter and tried to read it, but was unsure because it was a single letter. He looked up at me and then wrote "JAWS." When I asked him what he had written, he proudly read, "Shark!"

Once children begin using a syllabic writing system, they are on their way! Their analysis of the component sounds of language becomes more acute, and they begin to represent inter-mediate sounds. This type of writing, which Ferreiro and Teberosky call "syllabic-alphabetic writing," combines two writing systems: At times, a letter is used to represent a syllable, and at other times, a phoneme. Using this system of analysis, Pedro wrote:

ca·s·a   m·a·ri·po·s·a   ga·to

In each of these sequences, some letters repre-sent a syllable and others represent a phoneme.

By the time children write like this, we can readily read it with them or follow along in their text as they proudly read it back to us. As they become more sophisticated and experi-enced writers, the syllabic representation gives way to the alphabetic principle.

Children work diligently analyzing writing from the whole to the parts, and back to the whole again, searching for meaningful regulari-ties and trying to explain the exceptions. Who invented invented spelling? Why, children did, of course. And they continue to do so time and again, as they emerge as confident and capable language learners.

➔ See: Files, p. 355; Flores, p. 218; Kalman, pp.148, 245; King, p. 28.

Notes

1. "A child who makes an approximate correspondence between sounds and letters may have spelling difficul-ties, but he is already functioning within the alphabetic system of writing," writes Ferreiro. "In order to under-stand how he has reached this point," she goes on to say, "it is necessary to understand also those children who, for example, have started to use the alphabet, but who do not see any need for two words starting with the same sound to start with the same letter. We also need to understand the conceptions that are at work even earlier, such as with those children who use uncon-ventional signs but organize them in a linear order that is very different from the order of elements of a drawing." From Ferreiro, E. 1983. "The development of literacy: A complex psychological problem." In *Writing in Focus,* ed. Coulmas and Ehlich. Berlin: Mouton Publishers.

2. Reducing Ferreiro and Teberosky's work on the genesis of writing to a set series of stages can be deceiving and can lead to some very unsound educational practices. For the sake of written exposition, I have presented a some-what clean-cut version of the process involved in the child's reconstruction of the writing system, but most children do not neatly pass from one stage to another in an orderly way. Many times their old beliefs coexist with new ones—as in the case of the conflict between the syl-labic hypothesis and the minimum number of letters required to make a word.

3. In 1978 Ferreiro wrote: "Children living in an urban envi-ronment constantly encounter written texts on all kinds of objects: books and newspapers, toys, tins and boxes, calendars and street signs, television sets, posters, etc. We know that in many other fields, children don't wait until their first year of school to start thinking about complex problems." From Ferreiro, E. 1978. "What's written in a written word," *Harvard Educational Review.*

4. Throughout this text I will present examples of children's writing in Spanish and English. In individual interviews, children were asked to write without a model to copy or being dictated letters by an adult. They were encouraged to write the way they thought a word might be written. The Spanish samples are taken from: Ferreiro and Teberosky. 1979. *Los sistemas de escritura en el desarollo del niño.* Mexico City: Siglo Veintiuno Editores; and Fer-reiro, E., and M. Gomez Palacio. 1983. *Análisis de las perturbaciones en el proceso de aprendizaje de la lecto escritura.* Mexico City: Secretaría de Educación Pública.

Book Note

Literacy Before Schooling

Emilia Ferreiro and Ana Teberosky
1982; 304 pp.; $17.50
Portsmouth, NH: Heinemann

Book Note

Awakening to Literacy

Hillel Goelman, Antoinette A. Oberg, and Frank Smith, eds. 1984; 256 pp.; $18.50 Portsmouth, NH: Heinemann

Without formal instruction, but simply through the demonstrations of the peo-ple around them, children learn constantly about things that make sense to them, including a great deal of information about what written language is and how it works. This was the major finding of a group of 14 interna-tionally known researchers (including Yetta Good-man) who gathered in Victoria, British Columbia, for a symposium organized by Frank Smith. These researchers had observed the literacy achieve-ments of children in a variety of countries and cultures: Alaska and Mexico City, Puerto Rico and Papua-New Guinea, Africa and Europe; black, white, Chinese, Mexican-American; some rich, some poor, but all powerful learners with a pen-chant for learning what they needed to get on in their worlds. The book includes an introduction by Smith and chapters from each of the partici-pating researchers.

LBB

66 My two main points will be that children in the first few years of their lives know how to learn to read and write because written language presents them with problems similar to those they solve with spoken language, and that social interaction is required to make literacy learning possible but can also confound learning. Society cannot impose literacy on children, either through pre-scription or instruction. Rather, society must make literacy learning possible. Children require a par-ticular kind of interaction to become literate. I shall characterize this interaction as an appren-ticeship, or engagement with relevant demonstra-tions. 99 (p. 143)

Book Note

Opening Moves: Work in Progress in the Study of Children's Language Development

Margaret Meek, editor
1985; 84 pp.; $7
Portsmouth, NH: Heinemann

This set of five papers exploring children's lan-guage development is edited by Margaret Meek, who hopes the collection will remind teachers that collaborative research is one way to examine the depth of narrative interactions. The relation of language and learning is explored, as well as the nature of narrative and the roles of parents and teachers. The volume is a rich source of informa-tion about children's language learning.

Carol Christine

66 We still know less than we believe about pre-literate activity . . . . The kinds of assessments that are made as the result of examinations need to be supplemented by the understandings that teachers increasingly bring to their view of their task and the pupils' comprehension of what they are about. 99 (p. 10)

Immersion: Listening to Stories

 Cornerstone: Brenda Parkes

Sarah's Story

For the past two and a half years I have been engaged in a collaborative naturalistic study with two families and their preschool children, and their interactions with favorite storybooks. The study began when the children were two years old. I have been particularly interested in the strategies that the young learners use to negotiate meanings, both with the books and with the experienced language users, and the links that they make between story experiences and story language and other literacy and life experiences.

The following is a brief extract of one child's self-initiated responses to just one of her stories during this time.

Two-year-old Sarah and her mother were sharing "The Enormous Turnip" for the first time. With Sarah snuggled beside her, the mother read the title, running her hand under the print as she did so. Then together they looked at the illustration on the front cover and wondered what the story might be about. From the outset, Sarah's mother "invited her in" to the text by continually sharing her thinking and gently engaging Sarah in this.

At first, Sarah mostly listened, occasionally asking a question, repeating and lingering over some part of the language that had particularly caught her attention, pausing to inspect carefully some detail in an illustration and instigating discussion about it. Her mother responded to her overtures, occasionally making links between "The Enormous Turnip" and other known stories or real-life experiences to make the story more meaningful. As Sarah recognized the repetitive refrain "the old man pulled the turnip, the old women pulled the old man . . . ," she began to join in, the mother subtly cuing her in by a slight stressing of the patterning and intonation.

As with other language and literacy learning in Sarah's life, story reading was a meaningful experience, with the experienced language user demonstrating how picture books work and naturally engaging the learner in the experience, with every expectation that she would succeed. The language and social interaction that accompanied the text were as much a part of the story sharing as the text itself. Sarah was continuing to learn language, and about language, through language.

Over many months Sarah returned to this story over and over again for further shared and independent readings and retellings. Sometimes she would ask for the story to be read to her, and her only response would be a soft "yes" as each page was read, a confirmation that this was how she expected it to be; sometimes she would join in with self-selected parts of the story, or take over the repetitive refrain; sometimes she would tell the story in her own words from the illustrations; sometimes she would attempt to read it exactly as it was, asking for help when she was not sure of something; sometimes she would just use the book as a reference to discuss a particular aspect of the language or an illustration; sometimes she would substitute other characters as a game with the story. She read the book to her toys, her cat, any audience she could find, and herself. In every instance, the readings and retellings were

Brenda Parkes taught for many years in New Zealand and Australian schools before taking up her current position as lecturer in language and literature at Griffith University, Queensland, Australia. Deeply interested in young children's literacy development, Brenda frequently acts as a consultant to parents and teachers, and has played a leading role in the implementation of whole language in her state.

in some way different as Sarah's linguistic facility, life experience, and her strategies continued to expand.

Links were continually made between "Turnip" and life experiences. One morning both Sarah and her father were dressed in jeans and braces. She remarked, "We both like man in turnip book." As her mother pulled some large weeds from the garden, Sarah spontaneously put her arms around her mother and said, "We pull and pull but could not pull it up." This became a popular garden game for a few weeks. In a new book, *Ten in the Bed*, she immediately connected an illustration of toys in a line all pulling another toy from under the bed with "Turnip" and, pointing to each toy in turn, said, "Rabbit pulled Hedgehog, hedgehog pulled . . . ," transferring the text from "Turnip" to this as-yet-unknown text. Other references appeared in her writing, drawing, and painting. "Turnip" became intricately interwoven in Sarah's knowing about books, literacy, life, and language.

The data that we have collected over the two and a half years hold many similar kinds of responses and references to stories. For the children they have become living experiences that can be expressed not only through language, but art, drama, and music. Indeed, any appropriate response that a particular text evokes frames of reference for other books and other language and literacy events; a storehouse of language to be lingered over, savored, chanted, and loved; and a limitless source of interpretations each time learners return to them with further world and linguistic knowledge. They are both reassuring and challenging.

As the use of whole language principles and practices becomes more evident in our classrooms, parents and teachers are making increased use of children's literature and big books. I believe that our research provides compelling evidence both for their use and the ways in which they can be used, so that all children have the opportunity to take ownership through response and find their own voice in favorite stories and big books.

→ See: Huck, p. 188; Martin, p. 96; Rigby, p. 37; Short, p. 18; Shroyer, p. 41; Watson, p. 40.

Further Reading by Brenda Parkes
◆ *Beginnings: Contexts for Early Language Learning*, with J. Smith. Distributed in the United States by Rigby; in Canada by Ginn.
◆ *Who's in the Shed?; The Enormous Watermelon; McBungle's African Safari; McBungle Down Under; Goodnight, Goodnight; A Farm's Not a Farm; You Can't See Me;* and *When the Circus Comes to Town.* Predictable books by Rigby.

 One essential aspect of literary training . . . is the art of listening to stories. This sounds like a passive ability, but it is not passive **WELL-SAID** at all: it is what the army would call a basic training for the imagination.

—Northrop Frye, cited in *Child as Critic* by Glenna Davis Sloan

---

Language Stories

Christopher

When I visited friends last spring I brought picture storybooks for their three children: Elizabeth (6 1/2 years old), Christopher (2 1/2), and Jonathan (1 1/2). After I read the three books to them, Jonathan left to play with his trucks and Elizabeth went to find some of her special books to show me. Christopher asked me to read *The Farmyard Cat*, by Christine Anello, to him again. This time he echoed and then joined in as the dog, the bull, the nanny goat, and the horse each said, "I'll get you, cat! I'll get you."

Several days later, I visited my friends again. As we ate lunch, Christopher leaned over from his high chair, caught my forearm gently in his hand, and said, "I'll get you! I'll get you!"

Christopher repeated this pair of "I'll get yous" several times during the meal, inviting me to respond with my own "I'll get you." So, I said in turn, "I'll get you, Christopher. I'll get you," and caught his arm. After he finished his lunch, he looked at me and said, "Miss Nancy got me a new book." He clambered down from his high chair and brought *The Farmyard Cat* from his bedroom. Then he pulled me to the sofa to read it to him twice more.

I had not connected Christopher's playfulness at the table with the book I had given him, but he had obviously connected the book with me. He had incorporated the refrain into his speech and play. He used the refrain to initiate and carry on his conversation with me at lunchtime. In doing so, he continued and transformed the social interaction we had begun when we shared the book five days earlier. Christopher took a social experience with a text, modified it into his own version of an oral story/game to reestablish our interaction, and then recreated the experience of the shared book.

For Christopher and for me the social aspects of sharing the book and the game he invented based on the book have made "I'll get you" a part of our language and our lives in a way that goes far deeper than the words themselves.

→ See: Baskwill, p. 168; Literature Reference List, p. 429; Rich, p. 27; Shroyer, p. 41.

—Nancy Andrews, Language Arts consultant, Maine Department of Education and Cultural Services, Augusta, ME

Resource: Book

Classics to Read Aloud to Your Children

William F. Russell
1984; 320 pp.; $15.95
New York: Crown

For the teacher or parent who wants to explore the classics with children, this book presents text to be read aloud. The selections are divided into three listening levels: ages five and up, ages eight and up, and ages eleven and up. Each story has notes about the story, the approximate reading time, and a pronunciation and vocabulary guide. This author has a new book about mythology: *Classic Myths to Read Aloud: The Classic Stories of Greek and Roman Mythology (Specially Arranged by an Education Consultant)*, published by Crown in 1989.

Katy Obringer

Resource: Publisher

Rigby

P.O. Box 797
Crystal Lake, IL 60014
1-800-822-8661

Do you know what a "Hobyah" is? I do because my five-year-old has demanded I read *The Hobyahs* by Brenda Parkes and Judith Smith a dozen times. You know you've got a winner when it's requested over and over again, and the Rigby books we own—many written by our essayist Brenda Parkes—are favorites with our three children.

One of several New Zealand/Australian publishing companies selling books in this country, Rigby, a whole language publisher, has grown by kangaroo leaps—a testimonial to the growing power and appeal of the whole language movement. Just looking through the catalog is a lesson in whole language: There are sets of small books, big books, and audiocassettes for shared reading, guided reading, and listening centers. Many titles are now available in Spanish (two of our essayists, Barbara Flores and Aurelia Dávila de Silva, served on the translation panel). Rigby also offers exciting materials across content areas—math, social studies, science, and music. Any whole language publisher worth its salt offers professional development resources; Rigby sells a video series that features Andrea Butler, as well as a variety of excellent professional books.

LBB

Resource: Audio/Video Distributor

Spoken Arts

Catalog from:
Dept. F
P.O. Box 289
New Rochelle, NY 10802
1-800-537-3617
FAX 1-914-636-1539

Here, in one catalog, is a literary and historical treasure trove. Spoken Arts offers on audiocassette "hundreds of master recordings ranging from Shakespeare to Yeats, Poe to Langston Hughes, and from Whitman to Robert MacNeil reading his unabridged memoir *Wordstruck*." Spoken Arts' cassette libraries for young, intermediate, and advanced listeners provide the best in children and adult literature and poetry. And to help make history a living experience for your students, try Spoken Arts' recorded historical speeches. John F. Kennedy's inaugural address and Winston Churchill's "Sinews of Peace" address are two that are available. The selections are made all the more exciting in that many are read by the authors themselves.

LBB

Resource: Book, Film, Audiocassettes

The New Read-Aloud Handbook

Jim Trelease
1989; 290 pp.; $9.95
New York: Penguin

Jim Trelease on Reading Aloud

$7.95 audiocassette;
$135 film (rental only)
from:
Reading Tree Productions
51 Arvesta St.
Springfield, MA 01118
1-413-782-5839

Jim Trelease reminds us of the importance and the joy of reading aloud. His book, his lectures, and his film are inspirational. If money is available, I strongly recommend that you bring him to your area to share his contagious enthusiasm with principals, librarians, teachers, and parents.

Katy Obringer

❝ If we wish children to believe poetry is important, the *worst* way to teach it is to develop a two-week poetry block, teach it, and then forget it—because that's what children will do with it. The *best* way is to incorporate meaningful poetry throughout the day. ❞ (p. 74)

Resource: Books

Books Kids Will Sit Still For: A Guide to Using Children's Literature for Librarians, Teachers, and Parents

Judy Freeman
1984; 210 pp.; $12.95
Hagerstown, MD: Alleyside Press, an imprint of Freline

Another useful library reference that addresses reading aloud, book talks, creative dramatics, read-aloud fiction selections for grades K to 6, storytelling, poetry, books for celebrating, and more.

Katy Obringer

For Reading Out Loud! A Guide to Sharing Books with Children

Margaret Mary Kimmel and Elizabeth Segel
1988; 240 pp.; $16.95
New York: Delacorte Press

The authors explain the importance of reading aloud, how to make time for reading aloud, how to read aloud effectively, and what to read. Selections include books for children in grades K to 8.

Katy Obringer

 WHOLE LANGUAGE CAMERA

"Brown bear, brown bear, what do you see?" Debbie Montgomery reads aloud from a Bill Martin Jr classic to her 18- to 24-month-old students in the Toddler class, Preschool Family, Palo Alto, CA.

Language Stories

"Rewind It"

While bookstores and libraries are virtually nonexistent throughout the vast Navajo reservation, video rental shops have begun to spring up in most communities. Though I would much prefer bookstores and libraries, cable TV and videos have brought mixed blessings, including more exposure to outside culture, language, experiences, and concepts.

Each day, I read quality children's literature to my second-grade students for many of these same purposes. These children, who had few or no books of their own, looked forward to story time each day. Garrison, arriving to class late one day, was extremely disappointed to see that the story had already begun. Wanting to hear the story from the very beginning, he searched his mind for the appropriate request and pleaded, "Rewind it! Rewind it!"

➜ See: Hartle-Schutte, pp. 38, 87, 172, 396.

—David Hartle-Schutte, assistant professor, University of Hawaii, Hilo, HI

The Funny Side

Batteries Not Included

Our son David was two and a half years old when his grandmother came to Puerto Rico for an extended visit. David loved books and especially loved being read to, and could sit for hours, listening with great appreciation. The only deterrent to his literary pleasure was the vocal apparatus of the reader. One evening my mother, a loving and accommodating grandparent, had read aloud about 20 books when her voice gave out. Now raspy and hoarse, she sounded similar to the voice in a Speak 'n' Spell after many hours of use. Making the analogy, with the innocence of a toddler, David exclaimed, "Grandma needs a new battery!"

—Colette Green, ESL teacher, University of Puerto Rico, Mayagüez, PR

WELL-SAID [Another] point that we are trying to advance as a practical conclusion is the requirement that writing be *taught* naturally . . . the best method is one in which children do not learn to read and write but in which both these skills are found in play situations . . . In the same way as children learn to speak, they should be able to learn to read and write.

—L.S. Vygotsky

From *Mind in Society* by L.S. Vygotsky (Cambridge: Harvard University Press, 1978).

Language Stories

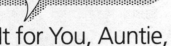

"I'll Read It for You, Auntie, if You Can't"

In the past, Navajo children who attended school often served as translators and readers for their older relatives in transactions with federal and state bureaucracies. This literacy function for children has declined over time, as a much larger percentage of Navajo adults are now literate in English.

However, one three-year-old Navajo girl still wants to assume that role. On a trip to a large city off the reservation with her aunt (who is a teacher assistant), she wanted to stop for ice cream. The aunt, who was in a hurry, claimed that there was no place to buy ice cream along the way, and that they would have to wait until they got to the city.

The niece, however, was undeterred and, pointing out several Dairy Queen billboards, said, "That's okay auntie; if you can't read the signs, I'll read them for you."

➜ See: Hartle-Schutte, pp. 37, 87, 172, 396.

—David Hartle-Schutte, assistant professor, University of Hawaii, Hilo, HI

Whole Language Internacional
by Melisa N. Choroszy

Preschool Print Awareness in American Samoa

In the middle of the South Pacific, American Samoan preschool children learning English as a second language demonstrate the same print awareness as their counterparts the world over.

The children's relationship with print is a pragmatic one. English is a second language in Samoa, but since Samoa is an American territory, its language of business and education is English. Three-year-olds recognize the stylized print of "Pago Banana Chips" or New Zealand "Morning Coffee" Biscuits. Four-year-olds are able to identify that the print does the telling. Five-year-olds recognize such words as *milk* and *stop* out of context.

Samoan preschoolers have less experience in the book-handling arena than their counterparts around the world. The Samoan culture reflects a strong oral tradition. Story reading is limited mostly to the Bible, while storytelling is encouraged and enjoyed by all. Samoan families are very close, and those who live in the lush green mountains keep in close touch through written correspondence. The language of letter-writing is eloquent and elaborate, similar to the oral storytelling tradition.

Marie Clay found that the Samoan children were far less at risk in New Zealand than the native Maori children. Their foundation in literacy was strong as a result of traditional story-telling, Bible reading, and letter-writing. Writing to relatives was a valued activity necessary for the preservation of the family structure. The closer "in touch" relatives remained, the greater the opportunity to maintain family cohesion and traditional family social structures.

The strongest of all the Polynesian cultures, the Samoans have adopted many aspects of westernization while retaining strong traditional values. Literacy is a Western value consonant with and complementary to *fa'a Samoa* (the Samoan way).

Melisa N. Choroszy is director of admissions and registrar at the University of Nevada, Reno, NV.

The Funny Side
Reading Environmental Print

The kindergarten teacher asked the children to draw pictures of their neighborhoods. She said they should put any signs in if there were any. Later a girl brought her picture to show the teacher. "This is my house," she said. "And this is the stop sign on the corner by the house." The teacher was startled to discover that on the red sign, the child had printed SHIT.

That afternoon the teacher walked the child home. Sure enough, someone had spray-painted over the stop sign. The teacher knocked on the door. "Have you seen the sign on your corner?" she said to the child's mother. "Yes we have," said the mother. "But we haven't done anything about it. Our kids can't read yet."

—KSG

The San Ramon Grocery Store is open for business in Leslie Marks's kindergarten class, San Ramon Elementary School, Novato, CA.

Book Note

Write from the Start: Tapping Your Child's Natural Writing Ability

Donald Graves and Virginia Stuart
1985; 238 pp.; $16.95
New York: E. P. Dutton

In this clear and concise book with convincing examples throughout, the second chapter, in particular, is a standout. It provides one of the best descriptions available on the difference between a skills approach, in which everything is broken down into its component parts, and a holistic philosophy that respects the children's natural learning strategies.

Graves and Stuart provide undeniable evidence that children focus on the meaningful whole before attending to the fine points of form. Following my recommendation, my daughter's preschool bought the book for their parent-teacher professional library. The result has been a group of parents who will now push for whole language as their children enter elementary school.

LBB

Book Note

The Emergence of Literacy

Nigel Hall
1987; 112 pp.; $10
Portsmouth, NH: Heinemann

After succinctly reviewing the recent literature on emerging literacy, Hall ties the research to recommendations for effective school practice that support literacy development.

Kathryn F. Whitmore

❝ The emergence of literacy is a fact not a fiction and provided children are given appropriate opportunities to display their knowledge they are only too ready to give demonstrations. What schools must do is allow them the chance to do so and not refute their hard-won, and generally reasonable, assumptions about written language. Children have an extraordinary capacity for making sense of their experience. We must not present them with a narrow and distorted world of literacy in which making sense is almost impossible. ❞ (p. 91)

In this store, you can buy all that you can carry, San Ramon Elementary School, Novato, CA.

The Funny Side
Enough Already!

As we drove by The North Face mountaineering store in downtown Palo Alto, California, my five-year-old daughter, Sarah, looking out the car window, noticed that "North Face" was written several times over around the storefront in huge red block letters. "Hmpf," she scoffed. "You'd think they could have written it just once."

—As told to LBB by Suzanne Gespass

Whole Language Internacional
by Ann Ketch

The Delicious Alphabet in Great Britain

The Delicious Alphabet is a collection of photographs of candies and drinks arranged to correspond to each letter of the alphabet. The book's purpose is to identify one way in which "community print" can be used to support literacy development. By community print, I mean the range of texts that are used in day-to-day life, such as labels, greeting cards, invitations, tickets, and signs.

The volume of community print has increased considerably over the past 20 years, but we have not monitored its impact on literacy development. Children entering school are unlikely to have their experience with this print acknowledged and extended. Support material for reading instruction centers on storybooks, phonics, and a school-defined sight vocabulary. Support for writing may involve dismantling what children already know and starting with a clean slate. There are frequent comments about children writing in uppercase letters before they start school, and the difficulty this causes teachers. Parents are admonished for teaching writing the wrong way. Yet children's preference for uppercase letters may stem from their experience with community print.

I wanted to find a way to integrate community and school experiences so that they could become mutually supportive. When I first constructed the book, I hoped it could be used to support writing by helping children to locate appropriate letter symbols. Would they be able to visualise *K* for Kit-Kat (a chocolate bar) more easily than *K* for King? The packaging of products offers word pictures that might be more accessible to the inexperienced than conventional alphabet books, which require an understanding of a sound-symbol relationship.

I used it with five-year-old children in groups of four. I wanted to see if they could name any of the labels and how they would respond to it as a book. My observations of them led me to consider the potential of a book like this for supporting reading as well as writing. As I watched the children share the reading of the book, I recognised aspects of reading behaviour:

- Response to an area of interest
- Reflection
- Defining the text
- Drawing on knowledge and experience from other contexts
- Collective knowledge

Drawing on an Area of Interest

The book relates to eating and drinking that are of universal interest. It also draws on children's love of naming things, particularly those things that reflect their personal experience:

- What they recognise because they have seen it a lot of times;
- What older members of the family eat;
- What they are not allowed to eat—"I'm not allowed to eat those Smarties [a candy-covered chocolate button], they make me bad-tempered."

Reflection

It is common to reflect on experiences or memories triggered by what is being read, and that applies especially here, because the memories tend to be very personal and pleasurable:

"Auntie Eileen always has a packet of Polos [a mint with a hole in it] in her pocket."

"We put them [Hoola Hoops—a snack in the form of a ring] on our fingers and then eat them."

Defining the Text

Defining what a text is about and adjusting this definition whilst reading is part of the reading process. One child was defining *The Delicious Alphabet* as a book about sweets, and was clearly surprised to find a picture of a canned drink, and even more surprised to find Hoola Hoops in the book. She then seemed to adjust her definition, because later, Quavers (another snack) and Vimto (a drink) did not surprise her.

Linking with Knowledge and Experience of Literacy from Other Contexts

The last page in the book shows Smarties laid out in the shape of a *Z*. Some children recognised it as the picture of a letter, some as a word, saying "Sm-ar-ties" as they traced the *Z* with their finger. The colours of the Smarties were named; the candies were counted.

Other pages of the book prompted children to say, "I've got one of these in my name," referring to one of the letters in the name of the product.

Collective Knowledge

When a group of children were sharing the book, they each brought to the reading their individual knowledge and experience. The child who ate a particular biscuit at home was able to name the package, and this was accepted by the rest of the group. They all knew more at the end of the reading than at the beginning.

For me, this book has changed how I look at children reading. Though I am not yet certain how to explain it, it's the difference between reading behaviour and reading performance, which has to do with saying words out loud. Some of the things the children talked about did not relate to the print per se but do relate to "readerly behaviour": the reflection on experience, the search for connections, and so forth. That's the next thing I will examine as I develop this work.

→ See: Hamilton, p. 59; King, p. 28.

Ann Ketch is a primary advisory teacher at the ELM Bank Teachers' Centre, Coventry, England.

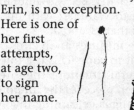

Signature

Young children love to explore their written names. My daughter, Erin, is no exception. Here is one of her first attempts, at age two, to sign her name.

—LBB

Resource: Organization

Association for Childhood Education International (ACEI)

Membership: $20 (student); $38 (professional); plus $20/year for biannual journal from:
11141 Georgia Ave., Ste. 200
Wheaton, MD 20902
1-301-942-2443

The Spring 1989 issue of ACEI's journal, *Childhood Education*, contains an excellent essay on whole language by Irene Fountas and Irene Hannigan —just one indication of the organization's commitment to education from infancy through early adolescence that is based on the cutting edge of research. Besides this fine journal, published five times annually, membership in ACEI buys you its newsletter and discounts (some as high as 40 percent) on professional conferences and materials, including its new publication, *Journal of Research in Childhood Education*.

LBB

Book Note

Print Awareness in Pre-School Children

Yetta M. Goodman, Bess Altwerger & Ann Marek
$3 from:
Program in Language and Literacy
Arizona Center for Research and Development
402 Education, Bldg. 69
College of Education
University of Arizona
Tucson, AZ 85721

Goodman, Altwerger, and Marek explore preschool children's awareness of environmental print and their knowledge and familiarity with the print in books. They found that the more context supported the print, the more readily able were children to respond appropriately. When the print was presented without supporting context, the children not only gave inappropriate responses but also became restless and bored. The study demonstrates the importance of context in making sense of language and print, and should cause teachers to rethink their use of noncontextualized reading and writing materials.

Lois Mather

It Shouldn't Happen to Kids

Grotesque Grouping

In one New England second-grade classroom, children are ability grouped for handwriting: The top group is known as "The Polishers," the middle group is "The Try Hards," and the lowest group is "The Have Nots."

—LBB

Network

Connections

When Is Language Too Much Too Soon?

by Dorothy Watson

Introduction

In the real world, reading, writing, listening and speaking make sense and make sense to do. Because of this, given half a chance, which includes receiving never-ending invitations, children learn to read and write—naturally. This naturalness and authenticity make whole language learning compelling. It also makes the role of parents and teachers as the primary invitation givers extremely important. Step into a whole language classroom and you will find the teacher constantly inviting children to recognize and use language in all its forms, and to see language doing the job it is meant to do—make meaning. Sometimes teachers must point out to learners how natural and authentic language is. Usually the children who need this reminder are those who for some reason have been deprived of the wholeness of language.

The Issue

All of the above is prelude in response to a comment made by a well-intentioned educator recently. It seems that the question of "too much, too soon" for written language arose. The worrier felt that exposure to print too early would in some way stop learners in their linguistic development. The concern resulted in the suggestion to remove print from the young child's world—from bulletin boards and school walls, even to substitute wordless books for traditional literature.

A Response

My response is not to the person who voiced this concern, but to those of us who live whole language theory and practice. What did we say or do that would cause anyone to come to such a conclusion?

Did we fail to point out to this concerned educator that children live in a world of print that is a major part of the tapestry of meaning that young inquirers enjoy getting sorted out? Where do we begin removing print? Take the names off students' coat hooks and lunch boxes? Do we obliterate the name of the school, cover the stop sign, and wrap the candy bars in plain brown paper? Do we remove the markers and paper from the classroom and refrain from encouraging students to inquire through writing (including scribbling)?

Did we fail to point out that one of the reasons visual language (reading and writing) comes naturally for children is the same reason that oral language (listening and speaking) comes naturally—the learner is surrounded by it from birth? You might protest that kids aren't exposed to street signs from the moment of birth—right, but infants are, from the first time they hear those loving voices of their parents, beginning to fill up what Carolyn Burke calls their linguistic pool. That pool is not divided into an eddy for listening, one for speaking, one for reading, and one for writing; rather the source of life for both oral and visual language is the entire pool.

Did we fail to point out that children in whole language homes and classrooms are not forced to participate in reading and writing, but they are invited to look and listen? Look at print in the environment and make guesses about what it means. Listen to those who have things sorted out—the big people who use print naturally and authentically. Children in whole language settings make choices about what is important to pay attention to and what to believe about it. Doing so is tied closely to risk-taking. When learners begin to inquire about the print that surrounds them they use that risk-taking attitude to make meaning.

Did we fail to say that no matter how much print is available *in natural situations* the child will not overload? Just as children will not bore themselves to death by reading the tenth horse story, they will not burn out or turn off by being surrounded by print. For proof follow a four-year-old around the supermarket. The visual information, including print, makes for a lively trip, but it doesn't constitute overexposure.

Did we not point out that children enjoy the delightfully difficult? I'm not talking about asking learners to deal with the fragmented text of worksheets and workbooks or of contrived stories—those have no place in a whole language setting. But print that children can make sense of—either by writing it or reading it in supportive context—that's a learning matter!

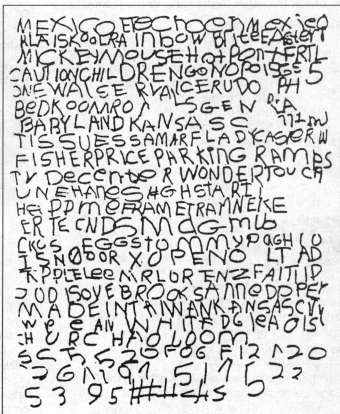

A Kindergartner Answers the Question

An educator who continues to worry about this issue should go to the ones most directly involved—the children. Interview them about print. Ask them the tough questions. My hunch is that any child informant will set the matter straight.

Would we want to remove the print from Christy's world? She brought the following to her kindergarten teacher, Becky Wundram. "Ms. Wundram, I went to Wal-Mart with my daddy. This is what I read that I wanted."

Spend just five minutes analyzing the text that Christy saw fit to copy. This is a fine example of how in natural situations the interpretation of context often precedes the interpretation of words. Whole language learning involves the child and everything in the child's world —including oral and visual language—early in life. Reading and writing aren't held back

 ## As Teachers See It

How Do We Learn to Read?

by Greg Chapnick

My son is just on the verge of making intelligible statements to replace the isolated words and babbled sentences he uses now, but it is obvious how much more he means by each single word. His favorite word these days is "bubble," but he is not just pointing out the bottle of soap to me. He is saying, "Blow some bubbles for me now!" Even when he doesn't use words, he is saying a sentence. When he grabs my arm and pushes me up and points to the tape recorder, he is saying, "I want to hear some music now!" With one word or no words, he has grasped the "whole" process of communication. Later on, he will begin to discover the separate parts of sentences, and eventually he will use the complex language of an adult. No one sat him down and explicitly told him how to do any of this. He learns by watching his parents talk to one another and trying to imitate as best he can. We are naming things and prompting him with questions, providing him with an opportunity to speak, but we are not teaching him how to make the individual sounds. He is doing that himself. We could read and recite poetry and talk to him forever, but if he didn't try it himself, he would never learn. My son is learning to speak by speaking.

Why is reading different? Why is it separated from speaking? Why is it taught from part to whole, without letting kids read real books from the beginning? This piecemeal instructional approach contradicts all natural learning. When I was learning how to make films, the first thing we did was to watch them from beginning to end. Only after we had seen an entire film would we break it down into its component parts. When it was time to go out and make a film, the only way to do it was to do it. Talking and theorizing about it didn't provide any experience at all. It helped with the overall learning process, of course, but it didn't get the film made.

I still remember the time I watched a group of physics students discuss the aerodynamic properties of a frisbee in flight. After a lengthy analysis they decided to test the theories they had so painstakingly developed. They all stood back as one of their number ceremoniously grasped the mystical saucer. With breath drawn, the pilot guided his craft out into the gleaming sunlight—it flew three inches and careened straight down into the ground. I rest my case.

→ See: Chapnick, p. 406; Goodman, p. 98.

Greg Chapnick is an elementary teacher at Fairview School, Hayward, CA.

till listening and speaking are "mastered." Children have it all. Invite them to take all of language in all its forms and modes. As long as it's natural and authentic it won't be too much too soon.

→ See Huck, p. 188; Parkes, p. 36; Rich, p. 27; Shroyer, p. 41.

From *Connections* 4(3), Spring 1989.

Dorothy Watson is a professor at the University of Missouri, Columbia, MO.

Subscription Information: *Connections* magazine is published three times a year. Subscription rates are $10 for one year, $18 for two years. Send check or money order to CEL Inc., c/o Hazel Stoyko, 246 Barker Blvd., Winnipeg, Manitoba, Canada R3R 2E4.

Parents' Perspective

by Karen Shroyer

Learning to Read Naturally

Whitney was eight months old when he had his first experience with a book. My sister handed him a board book. I warned her he'd just tear it up, but she assured me he wouldn't. He was intrigued with the pictures and seemed to enjoy hearing the simple rhymes. He immediately took to books.

Whitney had been played with, talked to, and sung to from birth. That he might also enjoy books at such an early age had not occurred to me. Books became a part of our daily routine. Books were read when he was fussy, before naptime, and at bedtime. Books accompanied us on car trips.

"Read" was one of the first words Whitney said. Books took the place of the bottle and the warm, comfortable feeling that accompanied it. "Read it again" was a frequent request. Whitney was internalizing the language, making the story his own. He wasn't yet three years old when he told his Aunt Koni, "Well, I must be going on," a line out of a favorite *Winnie-the-Pooh* book.

We began visiting the public library when Whitney turned three. Whitney's father contributed to the reading fun. He intentionally renamed or added characters and changed the plot or events just to hear his young son exclaim, "Dad, you're not reading it right!"

Whitney also corrected me. After one or two readings of a book, there was no way I could get away with skipping pages or paragraphs. When I miscued on the most insignificant word, he corrected me.

Inside, Outside, Upside Down by Stan and Jan Berenstain was an all-time favorite. He could hardly wait for the last page of this simple, predictable book, so that he could chime in with "Mama! Mama! I went to town. Inside, outside, upside down!"

One day when Whitney was approaching four, I found him in his rocking chair reading. He had a book with an extensive story line, and he was "reading" it word for word. He had learned the story we had read and talked about many, many times. I didn't realize at the time what an important leap Whitney had made in becoming a reader. Adults don't value this memory reading enough.

I didn't read to Whitney to give him a head start in learning to read. I read to him because it was such a delightful way for us to interact. Whitney watched "Sesame Street" and we sang the alphabet song, but we never practiced letter identification. He began asking questions about letters when we read or when he saw print on the television, on cereal boxes and other labels, or on signs as we were driving.

Many years later I discovered that the way Whitney learned to read is called the "lap method," and the many children who learn to read in this manner discover that reading is a relaxed, satisfying way to have a significant adult's attention. As the child enjoys the pictures and text, he begins to notice that pages are turned from right to left. In time he realizes the story is coming from the black marks (the print) on the page as well as from the pictures, and that the story is consistent from reading to reading. Still later, the child realizes the marks are words. He begins to recognize some words and to note letters within words.

The child also learns that the language of stories sounds different from the way people talk. The child discovers common beginnings and endings and similar plot structures. He also learns vocabulary and conventional knowledge. When children share and talk about stories, they expect print to make sense and to have meaning.

Whitney was reading by the time he began kindergarten. He didn't often choose to read to us, but he frequently pointed out words or chimed in on the repetitive parts of stories.

In the primary grades Whitney was a competent, confident student, but when he was in the fourth grade he could not figure out which syllable received the stress mark on either the practice sheets or the end-of-level test. He came home from school confused and dismayed, saying he couldn't make sense of the task. He could pronounce the words, but he couldn't solve this problem. I assured him that he was still a successful reader, even though he hadn't mastered stress marks.

This was really the first time Whitney questioned his own ability as a reader. I think about the young children in kindergarten or first or second grade who should be perceiving themselves as readers. When the criteria for being a reader come from skill pages rather than the successful reading of real books, we put children's self-esteem at risk.

Whitney brought the book *Tom Sawyer* home from the public library the summer before fourth grade. The dialect made the story difficult for him to read, so I read it to him. He also began writing his first book that summer. Writing was not part of his past school experiences. It was something that seemed to be a natural extension of his reading. His manuscript was heavily influenced by the Superhero comic adventures that made up a major part of his reading that summer, and by *Tom Sawyer*. His book too ended with the line, "Thus endeth the story."

I began college when he was four years old. I learned in my reading methods classes that children learn to read by learning the skills of reading first. I taught learning disability classes, then remedial reading classes, from this theoretical frame for four years. I reasoned that I didn't have time to both read to children and teach skills when I had the children for only thirty minutes a day. I blamed students' failures on their low abilities.

Then I attended a conference where I heard a classroom teacher, Kittye Copeland, talk about how her first-graders learned to read by reading real books, and learned how to write by using invented spelling. The obvious hit me. Whitney had learned to read this way; why couldn't my students? I began reading to my students daily and allowing them time to read real books in my class.

The next year I moved to a first-grade classroom. I used the basal reader and traditional reading groups, but also spent at least an hour a day, in three sessions, reading to the class. Over the years I made gradual changes in my curricula until the classroom took on the appearance of a workshop. Children spent their mornings reading or writing alone, with a partner, or in groups. Collaboration was the key. Two children together could solve problems that one alone couldn't solve. My students became independent. They relied on me less

It Shouldn't Happen to Kids

A First-Grader's Perspective of School

Rebecca entered first grade as an eager reader and writer. Within a few days she became discouraged. The teacher was leading the entire class through methodical preprimer lessons.

During a family journal time Rebecca poured out her indignation: "It is boring at school. Circle *A* because it's the first letter of the alphabet. Fifteen minutes to wait!"

When Rebecca shared her writing aloud with the family, she added a dramatic tone of sarcasm as she read, "Fifteen minutes to wait!" She loved to write; she wanted to write; the drill and the waiting made no sense to her. The saddest irony of it all is that she used a whole piece of writing as a vehicle to express her feelings about a drill designed to teach her how to write.

➔ See: Goodman, p. 360; Whitin, pp. 21, 325, 354.

—David J. Whitin, professor, College of Education, University of South Carolina, Columbia, SC, and Phyllis E. Whitin, middle grade teacher, Irmo Middle School/Campus R, Columbia, SC

Language Stories

Hold the Fort

Mr. and Mrs. Skolnick had some play equipment shaped like a fort built in their backyard for their six-year-old who attended a "developmental" first grade. The day it was finished the boy was ecstatic. The next day the handyman who built it added a sign: FORT SKOLNICK.

When the boy came home from school his mother found him standing looking at the sign and crying bitterly. "You said it was for me!" he sobbed. "It is for you, dear," said his mother. "Then why does it have a FOR SALE sign on it?"

—As told to KSG by Shirley Rapoport, Muskegon, MI

and less. Basal reading groups gave way to individual reading conferences. Literature study groups gave children the opportunity to pick the books they wanted to study and allowed children of all abilities to come together to read and respond to real pieces of literature.

It has been an exciting seven-year journey for me as I've watched first-graders become enthusiastic, confident readers. My wish is for all young children to find the satisfaction and joy that comes from knowing real books.

Whitney is just completing his freshman year at the University of Missouri. He is a National Merit Scholar, majoring in English and journalism.

➔ See: Huck, p. 188; Literature Reference List, p. 429; Parkes, p. 36; Rich, p. 27; Swanda, p. 48.

Karen Shroyer is a primary teacher at Chillicothe R-II schools, Chillicothe, MO.

Learning What Language Can Do

 Cornerstone: Carole Urzúa

Thank You, Miss Gladys

The air-conditioned van twists and turns down narrow roads that are the only things keeping the thick jungle forest from closing in. We pass rice fields, fat water buffalo, and thin men turning over the mud. We make a turn in the road, and a flat meadow stretches before us. We see a sign that proudly announces the Philippine Refugee Processing Center, the world's largest English as a Second Language program, where thousands of refugee families prepare to fly to the United States. Here is a great educational experiment for elementary school children: a whole language, meaning-centered program in the middle of the jungle!

Southeast Asian refugee children between the ages six and eleven attend the Preparing Refugees for Elementary Programs (PREP), which was begun in April 1987 and is operated by World Relief Corporation. The goal is to prepare children for successful entry into elementary schools in the United States by teaching linguistic, academic, and interpersonal skills. During the 18 weeks of instruction, children participate in warm-up activities, such as calendar, singing, reading, writing, oral language units, math, and enrichment.

In 1986 the Bureau for Refugee Programs at the U.S. Department of State asked a panel of teachers and scholars in second-language learning to recommend an ideal program for children. Calling on their knowledge of first- and second-language acquisition and pedagogy, as well as their growing knowledge of meaning-centered literacy learning, these educators described a program that would revolve around thematic units with topics familiar to elementary schools: weather, seasons, clothing, family, feelings, animals, and so on.

The panel suggested English language units that would contain activities from science and social studies and hands-on experiences for children to integrate the language arts with authentic content. In the area of literacy, the panel suggested that the meaning-centered approaches in reading and writing that are being celebrated in children using English as a first language are even more appropriate for children learning a second language. Students need to be introduced to meaningful print; they need to make the link between oral and written language as naturally as possible; and they need to be given the opportunity to enjoy reading and writing.

The State Department accepted the panel's recommendations, and in two brief years, working around the clock, created PREP, which has become a showcase for meaningful second-language learning.

Many children who arrive on the classroom doorsteps have had little contact with English, but a lot of contact with terror and sorrow. Some children go without talking for six months. More common, however, are children who at first quietly watch the activities suggested by the teacher, but then become confident and eager to learn within a short time, making enormous progress in oral and written language.

Each day children participate in shared reading with big books that are frequently associated with the thematic English language units. Children participate as listeners, choral readers, actors,

Carole Urzúa is professor in residence in the Lodi Unified School District, Stockton, California, where she works in elementary classrooms with teachers and children. She has taught a wide variety of students, from preschoolers in the Philippines to graduate students at Lewis and Clark College in Portland, Oregon, and at the University of the Pacific in Stockton, California. For many years, Carole has tried bringing together insights from first- and second-language development to help teachers make informed decisions for teaching all their children. She has published articles in Language Arts and TESOL Quarterly, as well as in several anthologies. She has also authored a book on oral language development entitled Speak with a Purpose.

and responders. Several classes of Hmong children wrote, performed, and videotaped sequences from various big books to create a travelogue. The Southeast Asian children are excited literacy learners, eager to read again and again the predictable, engaging books. During Sustained Silent Reading time, which is rarely silent, children love picking up the smaller versions of the big books and demonstrating their extraordinary facility with literacy.

The children aren't the only excited ones. As a group, the teachers are positive, loving, and hardworking. Every inch of classroom space is filled with gorgeous examples of children's work: children sit at large low tables that are covered with labeled pictures; charts are in abundance, sometimes placed on the ceiling for lack of any other space. Music, chants, dance, and movement are all regular parts of each day; lyrics are printed on tagboard and hung on easels. Early each morning, as they board the bus at the dormitories, 80 teachers carry out new books, charts, guitars, radios, and an extraordinary commitment to children's learning.

It is this faith in the natural development of oral and written language that is making the critical difference in PREP. Nowhere is this confidence in half-filled rather than half-empty glasses more evident than in the area of writing.

From the very beginning, children are urged to write in dialogue journals. At first they fill their journals with pictures or one-word entries. Teachers sometimes label the journals and always respond in an encouraging way, using language that is slightly ahead of the child's. As with children who learn English as a first language, the teachers often find it necessary to interact face to face with the Southeast Asian children in order to get enough context to interpret their entries. The integration of the written and spoken word is also evident in dictated stories based on experiences the children have had in the current English language unit. For instance, when the children are studying foods, they might visit one of two markets at the camp, buy things, and note available items, practicing English with the Filipino sellers. Back at class they might discuss the experience, noting the sequence of events, the items bought, or individual behavior. While the children are talking, the teacher might write their words and sentences on the board or on a large newsprint. When finished, the children have a fairly cohesive dictated story that they can copy and take back to read to their parents.

A new aspect of the program at PREP is Writers' Workshop. As teachers become more informed, they often choose to engage their children in writing about their own topics for real audiences. Teachers note with joy that when children sense others caring about their ideas, they use every available means to convey their message. Lai, an eight-year-old Vietnamese

girl, for instance, wanted to share with her teacher some of the things she likes. Because the complexities of what she wished to convey far outstripped her emerging sense of the English graphophonic system, she called on what she knew best: her understanding of how her native Vietnamese functioned.

> ai lai do hen bi kho da hen da ti phun.
> (I like the hen because the hen beautiful.)
> ai lai do bo bi kho do bo ve ri gut.
> (I like the bird because the bird very good.)
> ai lai do khat be kho do khat veri hangxam
> (I like the cat because the cat very handsome.)
> ai lai do Dac bi kho do Dac no toc.
> (I like the duck because the duck no talking.)

The teachers share their writing in the two-hour daily training they receive. Few are credentialed teachers; most are college graduates in areas such as communication, engineering, pharmacy, and food service. These dedicated people are chosen for their openness to new learning in addition to the traditional teacher qualities. They know when they arrive that the experience may be the most exhilarating they'll ever have. They are also realistic about the amount of time they'll have to spend gathering resources from the Materials Center, figuring out how to use the English language units, looking through writers' folders. And they know the PREP staff is committed to their development as teachers.

YOUNG ARTISTS

—Dao Le, 11, Portland, OR, from *Treasures 2*. See p. 162.

But perhaps the one thing they cannot adequately prepare for is the extraordinary progress the PREP children make in a few weeks. Beginning with short, formulaic sentences, many children are able to write lengthy autobiographies at the end of the cycle. They write letters about life in the camp to their pen pals. They recognize the variety of purposes literacy serves. They create lists and notes. And for many, writing becomes a means by which they can come to understand themselves.

One little Hmong girl, whose cycle was finished but who had not yet left the camp for the United States, taught us this lesson. After hanging around her former teacher's class and glaring at the new students from Vietnam, she finally burst out, "Miss Gladys, you no longer like Hmong. Now you teach Vietnamese." She returned the next day and handed Gladys a note.

> Dear Miss Gladys,
> You no more teach Hmong. You teach Vietnamese.
> It OK.

A few words written on a page speak volumes to us about the positive attitudes PREP children have toward literacy, about the confidence they have in themselves as users of literacy, and about the trust they have in the power of literacy to convey their message.

Thank you, Miss Gladys.

➔ See: Bausch-Ude, p. 26; Boiser, p. 344; Goodman, p. 23; Krashen, p. 86.

Classroom Demonstrations
by Sheila M. Siegfried

Note This

As a writer and a teacher, I consider myself a list maker. Lists of goals, objectives, telephone calls to be made, groceries, and even accessories needed to complement an outfit, are written in my appointment book. My appointment book goes wherever I go. We are inseparable. I begin each day writing:

Dear Sheila,
I'd like to accomplish . . .

Although I allow for flexibility in my life, I organize my day on paper. If I can write what I want to do—then I feel I can do it.

My need to organize my daily life on paper has followed me into the classroom. The children I teach in a Montessori classroom watch as I jot down a note to myself or cross out a completed activity in my appointment book. They watch as I jot down notes about them: notes stating what work they are choosing and what work they have completed; notes listing information they know and information they are learning.

It was only natural that the children began to write their own notes. They now write notes to themselves—listing books they have read or want to read. They list writing topics, favorite sports, TV shows, food, and of course one another's telephone numbers. They write personal editorials. They write notes critiquing substitute teachers:

we have sub Teachers
won Is named Juoce
I hate her she is meen
and bossy
The end

They write collectively in order to problem solve a bothersome situation:

Dear Jacob
we want to be your Friend
But we Don't want you To
FowlliING US AROUD
PlayGrond ALL THE TIME.
SOMETIMES WE JUST WANT
TO PLAY GIRL GAMES ALSO IT
SCARES US WHEN YOU
ALWAYS WANT TO TALK
ABOUT THE BURGALAR ALL
THE TIME.
FROM:
CAITLIN   KATHY   HOPE   MARIA
DREME GIRLS

They write about their own behavior:

my Esay on fighting
I was fighting too
But I was dueing
it becuse Everybody
was. I was Kictded
on the hede Punched
on the bake 5
times and pushed
7 times. I do
not like fites!

And, they write notes to their teacher;

by Aaron
Dear sheila, you are the
best teacher in the hole
world! but i dont'
no about any others
but in our room

Best of all, they write! Writing is a part of our everyday life. It is meaningful and definitely something worth *noting*.

Sheila M. Siegfried is a primary teacher at the Bennett Park Montessori Center, Buffalo, NY.

"There is a kid in someones clas I won't say the name
That dos not like math at all the end"—by Misha Hoffman

The Whole Language Catalog: **Learning** 43

MARVELOUS INVENTIONS
The Boss

At the age of five, my daughter, Aislinn, exercised elder-sister tyranny over her two-year-old sister, Erin. As Halloween approached, Aislinn pondered what character she would be and what Erin would be as well. Here is her note to me announcing her decision.   —LBB

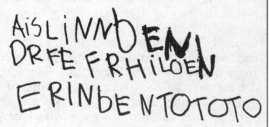

[Aislinn being Dorothy for Halloween, Erin being Toto]

WELL-SAID   The teaching [of reading and writing] should be organized in such a way that reading and writing are necessary for something . . . Reading and writing must be something the child needs. Here we have the most vivid example of the basic contradiction that appears in the teaching of writing . . . namely, that writing is taught as a motor skill and not as a complex cultural activity. Therefore, the issue of teaching writing . . . necessarily entails a second requirement: writing must be "relevant to life"—in the same way that we require a "relevant" arithmetic.   —L. S. Vygotsky

From *Mind in Society,* by L. S. Vygotsky (Cambridge: Harvard University Press, 1978).

MARVELOUS INVENTIONS
Aaron's Passover List

Aaron, age six, and his mother, Wendy, were preparing for a trip to Los Angeles to celebrate Passover with relatives. Wendy suggested to Aaron that he write as she dictated the list of clothes that he should bring with him. He agreed but said that to save time he would just use initials. Here's the result:

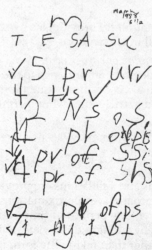

[5 pair underwear; 4 T-shirts; 2 nice outfits; 1 pair of pj's; 6 pair of socks; 4 pair of shoes; 2 pair of pants; 1 tie]

Aaron Hood is now in third grade at Hollinger School, Tuscon, AZ. This was contributed by his mother, Wendy Hood.

MARVELOUS INVENTIONS
The Organized Life

Not one to trust the important details of daily living to happenstance, Lauren Montgomery, age six, devoted every evening for two weeks to composing a list to guide her through the next day. Here is one of her lists:

[Wake up Friday!; Get up!; Get dressed; Eat breakfast; Brush teeth; Brush hair; Go to school; Come home; Get a rat; Hold the rat; Ask Aislinn and Erin if they want Mousey; Eat dinner; Get jammies on; Brush teeth; Go to bed]

Lauren Montgomery is now in second grade at Ohlone School, Palo Alto, CA.

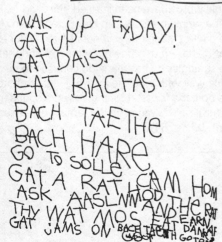

Towards Joyful Language Teaching through Homely Models

Whole language teaching has taken much of its energy and its structure from the principles of natural developmental learning which is so manifestly powerful in acquiring spoken language. Modern linguists, following the lead of Chomsky, saw it as so astonishing that children had almost mastered the grammar of their language before schooling began, that they found it necessary to construct a new concept to bypass "learning" as understood in instructional settings. They called this early language development "acquisition."

It should be said with some clarity that the models for whole language teaching are fundamentally models of *acquisition*, rather than models of instruction. But we still fail to take the acquisition models as seriously as common sense and our responsibility to children demand. This is partly because there is no deep tradition in schooling for the use of these homely models, and our presuppositions and metaphors about learning inhibit our practice.

Models of successful learning uncontaminated by formal instruction:

Some startling comparisons with formal teaching follow each.

1. *Spoken language "acquisition"*
   Learning governed by progressive approximation rather than atomised into right/wrong responses.
2. *Emergent literacy*
   Use of rich and memorable text, predictable as in the "bedtime" story, rather than vocabulary-controlled.
3. *Developmental learning*
   Massive, self-motivated and self-regulated practice or "drilling" without supervision.

Some principles these models have in common:

a. *Immersion.*
   Natural community provides a rich display of use beyond current needs or levels of the learner.

b. *Demonstration.*
   The community provides authentic models of the skill in efficient use.

c. *Participation or engagement.*
   These demonstrations engage the learner in fascinated observation, emulation, and hand-in-hand participation when permitted.

d. *Expectations.*
   The community provides positive prophesy fulfillment.

e. *Approximations.*
   Rewards and validations are provided for very small, progressive approximations towards skill over long periods of time—they are guided by a longitudinal view of developing skill rather than taking the form of corrective invasions on a right/wrong basis.

f. *Self-regulated practice—responsibility. Role-playing. The reflexive principle.*
   The learner takes independent responsibility for his or her own processing of the skill. Per-

haps the most complex and surprising part of the process, and the most difficult to describe—the learner chooses to practice the skill without direction or audience, monitoring every detail of his or her own performance, and confirming, disconfirming, and correcting as appropriate.

g. *Performance, response, use.*
   The learner takes a natural part of the communal use of the skill for all its real purposes, and is accepted as a genuinely contributing member of the community of skill.

And if all of these conditions are met, there will be:

h. *Joy and laughter—both in "teaching" and in the children's learning.*
   (And because these are universally apparent conditions of natural developmental learning as it actually operates in all human communities, they have as much scientific sanction for their necessity as any feature of sound instruction.)

From 1983 to 1986, Don Holdaway was chief consultant to a developmental literacy project in the Cambridge, Massachusetts Schools initiated by a joint effort of the city school department and Lesley College. His dynamic teaching, speaking and consulting reached an ever-widening circle of teachers in the region, who are vigorously carrying on the legacy today.

These three models provide the visible structure of Acquisition Learning and rightfully provide directions for research, touchstones for problem-solving, and patterns for school and classroom environments. To the extent that a language classroom or curriculum reflects these models, it is likely to be highly fruitful. To the extent that it departs from these models, it is likely to be ineffective, or even harmful, to many children—and certainly in need of justification.

Since school instruction has never approached the success of these hardy and homely models, we would be arrogant in the extreme to regard them as irrelevant to our professional undertakings—especially in the case of literacy. We have a clear mandate from this knowledge to teach with confidence and joy.

→ See: Cambourne, p. 17.

Further Reading
For a detailed discussion of the characteristics of natural developmental learning, see the following:

Smith, Frank. 1983. "Demonstrations, Engagement, and Sensitivity." In *Essays into Literacy.* Portsmouth, NH: Heinemann.

Holdaway, Don. 1986. "The Structure of Natural Learning as a Basis for Literacy Instruction." In *The Pursuit of Literacy,* ed. Michael Sampson. Dubuque, IA: Kendall/Hunt.

Cambourne, Brian. 1987. In *Read and Retell,* ed. Hazel Brown and Brian Cambourne. Sydney: Methuen.

———. 1987. *Natural Learning and Literacy Education.* Sydney: Ashton Scholastic.

From the *Whole Language Teachers Association Newsletter,* Fall 1988.

Further Reading by Don Holdaway
◆ *The Foundations of Literacy.* Heinemann, 1979.
◆ *Independence in Reading.* Heinemann, 1980.
◆ *Stability and Change in Literacy Learning.* Heinemann, *1985*

 **Book Note**

The Foundations of Literacy

Don Holdaway
1979; 232 pp.; $13.50
Portsmouth, NH: Heinemann

"Learning to read and to write ought to be one of the most joyful and successful of human undertakings. Notoriously, it is not so." Thus begins Holdaway's 1979 classic. Through a historical overview of the traditional approaches to literacy instruction, he exposes the misinformed thinking about language and learning that underlies the language-splintering skill-and-drill activities that have sadly turned the joy of learning to read and write into a nightmarish struggle for many children. In nuts-and-bolts detail, he outlines a developmental literacy program that will guarantee children and teachers both joy and success.

LBB

66 Parents should be encouraged to look closely at the *successful* learning in which their children engage with them, and to remember their approach and attitude when their children were learning to walk and talk. They then need to be encouraged to delight in the early stages of literacy learning and support them in the same manner as they supported the early stumblings of walking and the early bumblings of talking. The acquisition of literacy needs to be demystified for them by taking them back to a clear recognition of the principles of developmental learning which form a natural part of their recent experience with their children. 99 (p. 189)

 Book Note

What Did I Write?

Marie M. Clay
1979; 80 pp.; $10
Portsmouth, NH: Heinemann

Clay examines the child's first attempts at writing. She helps teachers and parents of early writers understand the concepts and principles children naturally follow as they become conventional writers. An easily read, quickly grasped overview of early writing development, this book is a must for preschool and primary teachers.

Lois Mather/Kathryn F. Whitmore

66 At some point beyond the attainment of the sign concept and probably after some letters and single words have been learned, the child realizes that a whole message can be written down. At the earliest stage of awareness the child hopes that he has written down a message, and that the squiggles he has made do correspond in some way with what he is saying, although he has no basis for establishing this correspondence. At this level his message is a fantasy expressed in print. 99 (p. 51)

Great Teachers:
Don Holdaway
by Bobbi Fisher

Laying the Foundations of Literacy

The first time I saw Don Holdaway he was on stage at the New England Kindergarten Conference, reading big books with a group of children. The children were enjoying the process of learning from him, as was a young teacher sitting next to me. She told me that Don had worked in her school, that she had heard him speak many times, and that she goes to see and hear him whenever she can.

I have known Don Holdaway more than five years, and like that teacher in the audience, I also return again and again to hear him, whenever I can, along with many others, whose familiar faces appear at each of his presentations.

The first time I *met* Don Holdaway was when he arrived in class at Lesley College in Cambridge, Massachusetts, a briefcase precariously balanced under one arm, and a cardboard box full of books under the other. I had never even

seen a big book, and here I was, signed up for a course that listed Marie Clay's *The Early Detection of Reading Difficulties* as its text.

Don never let on that my background knowledge was limited for the course. Instead, he lent me *Hairy Bear* and *Mrs. Wishy-washy* and told me to "have a go" with them in my kindergarten. Although I didn't know it at the time, I was about to experience natural learning. Throughout the semester, Don demonstrated to the class, and we participated, each at our own developmental level. We returned to our classrooms to practice and came back to celebrate our successes with Don, who was always eager to hear them.

Don was delighted when his students and colleagues at the Cambridge/Lesley Literacy Project started the Whole Language Teachers Association (WLTA). We knew he would be returning to Australia soon, and we wanted to be certain that the momentum for developmental learning, which he had promoted in the Boston area, would continue building after he left.

The growing number of teachers and children enjoying whole language learning, as demonstrated by the success of the WLTA, is a tribute to Don Holdaway. His hard work and ability to communicate his educational philosophy have helped lay the "foundations of literacy."

Bobbi Fisher is a primary teacher at Josiah Haynes School, Sudbury, MA.

Breakthroughs

by Margaret Smullin

Troubleshooting

While observing in other classrooms before I got my own, I was disappointed in the way some teachers brushed off their students' problems. I knew I wasn't going to do that. I would deal with each student's fight or complaint. I'd get to the root of the problem and teach lifelong problem-solving skills. I would never resort to such a superficial response as, "Say you're sorry and that you won't do it again." Boy, was I idealistic! It was all I could do to simulate some semblance of what a class should look like, much less help students with their social problems. Problem-solving lessons got reduced to "Go sit by yourself and put your head down."

When I realized that problem-solving could take up every hour of every school day I decided to make problem sheets just to keep the kids out of my hair with their constant pleas for help. The simple ditto says, "I have a problem with... about ..." on one side and "Tengo un problema con... sobre..." on the other. Under each heading is space where the children can describe the problem, suggest a solution, and make a drawing of it.

Kal and Tory pulled me at the shirt and I cried. They will help me put my jacket away.

The problem sheets caught on immediately with little explanation. I am relieved of handling every insistent complaint by reminding them to "Fill out a problem sheet." The children work with such absorption drawing their mishaps and writing about them that by the time they finish, much of their anger and hurt is diffused.

→ See: Bird, p. 90; Hagan, p. 242; Laster, p. 246.

Margaret Smullin is a primary teacher at Fair Oaks School, Redwood City, CA.

The Power of Cooperative Collaboration

by Mary Snow

During the early 1960s, in Auckland, New Zealand, Don Holdaway led a group of gifted educators in pioneering a developmental approach to literacy learning. They applied new insights about first-language learning, reading, and writing based on research from all over the world and in many disciplines to the restructuring of literacy education. The results were so powerful that the government decided to adopt their "natural learning" model and to initiate a national retraining project for teachers. In devising the inservice course, Don worked cooperatively with professionals from both the university and the schools. *Together* they developed an entirely voluntary system that within a few years had effectively revolutionized literacy education in New Zealand.

Collaboration among equals is the key to Don's concept of the relationship between teachers and the university. He sees the classroom teacher as the natural authority on children's learning. The university's contribution is to provide an arena for reflecting on what's happening in that classroom and to help document it.

Don proposed just such a collaborative relationship between Lesley College and the Cambridge, Massachusetts, schools. The inspired example of his own demonstrations, in which theory, practice, and monitoring are inextricably woven, communicated instantly. Teachers in the project and many others who took his

courses became experienced in implementing the natural learning model. Interest in their work grew, and they began to share their understanding and expertise. They became presenters at workshops, institutes, and conferences.

Teachers have taken their rightful place at the heart of the whole language enterprise. Respected as thinkers as well as doers, linked in active partnership with college people who learn along with them, they have released a creative energy that is powering a genuine grassroots movement. Grounded in research and theory and focused on close observation of and appreciation for children's active learning, Don's dynamic concept of collaborative partnership is offering renewal of our schools from the elementary through graduate levels.

Mary Snow is a professor at Lesley College, Cambridge, MA.

A Magical Dance

by Janet Palladino

I pulled out my copy of *The Foundations of Literacy* by Don Holdaway. It's falling apart now, unglued at the binding. I keep it in a plastic bag. I've read it cover to cover, I think, three or four times. I read it first during the summer of 1983, just before Don came to Cambridge.

He had come to Longfellow School to help us establish a Literacy Center Project. One purpose of the program was to train teachers to teach reading and writing through a natural learning model. The primary grade staff had committed themselves to the pilot program for one year. I was a member of the Longfellow staff and shared a feeling of being somewhat scared and unsure of many of the other teachers.

Don has a uniquely beautiful face. It can tell stories, sing songs, and dance ballet. When Don did a shared reading with a class, his eyes sparkled, his eyebrows arched expectantly. He'd glow with anticipation. Sharing would often begin with a quick poem or song.

Today, it was a favorite song from Bill Martin's *Sound of Language* series:

Hey la la, ho la
My donkey and I,
Trotting to market
For cheeses and pie!

The children were enchanted, craning their necks to look a bit closer at the words that had been printed in enlarged text on a square of cardboard. They all joined in, as it had a catchy, rhythmic tune. After a few rounds, it was time for a story. Don usually shared between four and eight texts in a shared reading lesson.

"What shall we read today?" he asked. *Yes Ma'am* was the overwhelming choice of this first-grade class.

Twenty-two pairs of eyes were glued to the pages, scrutinizing the print and the illustrations. Their bodies swayed in anticipation of the rhythm and patterns. Carlos and Joe were practically climbing into the text, their noses two inches from the book.

We miss Don's guidance and gentle encouragement, as he's living in Australia now and visits Cambridge infrequently. We are proud to have been his students. He has launched us well.

→ See: Martin, p. 96.

Janet Palladino works with the Cambridge-Lesley Literacy Project and teaches at Longfellow School, Cambridge, MA.

A Community of Learners

 Viewpoint: Anne Haas Dyson

On Friends and Writers in a Community of Learners

There are volumes about childhood in five-year-old Ethan's simple drawing of two friends playing together. If we could read that drawing well enough, the wisdom therein could help us revolutionize our ways of thinking about literacy development and, more broadly, about the role of schools in the lives of young children.

Most often, when we think about literacy and classrooms, we see them in reference to the adult world. In schools, children are "apprentices" and "approximators" of the ways of adults. And children's ways are shaped by and reflect the adult-structured activities they participate in both inside and outside of school.

Two friends playing together

But the dynamics of children's lives together in classrooms has a distinct rhythm of its own. Developmentalists like Piaget have long argued that children are not miniature adults. In contrast to the more contained movements of teachers, young children's actions reveal their sensitivity as symbol-makers. Five-, six-, and seven-year-olds play, sing, draw, dance—sometimes all at once! Never again will they be as alive to the possibilities for sounds, lines, and bodies to capture the emotional and physical qualities of life (Gardner 1982).

Children also have their own social concerns (Corsaro 1985; Dyson 1989; Paley 1986). Their skills as symbol-makers are intertwined with their increasing skill as people who can exchange stories with their friends, collaboratively play out adventures, or reason about the sensibleness of drawings. These qualities of young school-age children—their symbolic inventiveness and social attuneness—are major resources for literacy growth.

Lamar: Symbol-making and Socializing with Friends

Consider Lamar, one of the children I observed during the four and a half years I spent visiting and studying Ethan's school (Dyson 1989). Lamar, an African-American, is a calm, serious child and capable of great concentration. He draws intricately detailed pictures of boys, motorcycles, rockets, and ships, and he builds carefully balanced houses of Legos and blocks. He can, however, be quite silly with his good friends, his "bloods" Greg and, especially, Tynan, as happened the day an alphabet-card matching game became a romantic comedy. The L cards, with their pictured lips, and the H cards, with their hearts, kissed madly.

Lamar's urban classroom allows him space for making some decisions about how to spend his time and, also, about how to do many of his required activities—like the daily drawing, dictating, and writing in his journal. As he makes his choices, Lamar does not seek out Margaret, his teacher, although she seeks out Lamar, as she does all her children, for general conversation and for talk about his activities. Lamar, however, attends to his friends. Indeed, sometimes he does nothing but wait for Tynan to finish an assigned task.

While he does not like Tynan's tendency to tease him with language play ("You chili dog"),

he is loyal to his friends. He pats them on the head when they are sad. And during their playing and constructing, he sometimes negotiates on their behalf with others, often stretching intellectually in the process, as children do with their peers (Mueller and Cooper 1986).

For example, Lamar is just developing concepts of number grouping. One day, Lamar and Tynan were allowed by Aaron, a classmate, to sit with him and look at his muscle men dolls, an honor given only to them. Aaron gave Lamar two dolls, Tynan one, and kept three for himself. Tynan asked for another.

"No," said Aaron, adding that Tynan was bad.

"No, he's not bad," said Lamar reassuringly. And then he added, in his most enthusiastic voice, "I got a good idea. You have enough for two, cause there's only three people in here." (This was an impressive observation for a child who counts separate cards, rather than pairs, in matching games—and thus sometimes concludes, incorrectly, that he has won.)

But Aaron was not complying. "I changed my mind," he said. "For him, nothing."

Lamar tried again, "We could all could get two." Finally Aaron gave in. "OK. OK. I'm giving him two. We're *all* getting two."

Tynan then gave his reason, which Lamar did not require before acting on his behalf. "Yes," said Tynan, "because this is going to be a wrestling match."

"No," said Aaron.

"Yes," said Lamar. And the matches began.

A Place for Literacy

Lamar's daily activities illustrate how intertwined Lamar's social life is with his symbol making. He and his friends play, draw, and construct airplanes from paper and buildings from blocks. Within the supportive context of this symbol making among friends, literacy is taking root. At the block center, he and Aaron made a "cowboy town" with the Lincoln Logs and then made signs to label their buildings. Sometimes, at the work tables, Lamar explores letters and writes well-known names and labels and then challenges his friends to read and spell the words too.

Most central to this classroom is the daily journal activity. Lamar, like many of his peers, studies his *own* lines as he draws and sometimes talks to himself about his work. He is also curious about the drawing and talking of others (Garvey 1986). He even knows his friends' typical themes: Tynan "always" does skateboards, Greg does designs with hidden letters that his peers have to find.

Friends must negotiate with and on behalf of each other during journal time, too. Lamar defended Tynan from a peer who mistakenly thought Tynan had drawn a vampire in the midst of water. Tynan was insulted: the wavy lines were "grass." Lamar reasoned calmly on his behalf: water could be holy and "no vampire can't be in holy water."

Another day, Tynan objected to Lamar's dictated text about a monster that "was gonna jump out [from under the ground] and scare the boy to eat him." Scaring the boy might

cause the boy to run away, Tynan reasoned, and "that would not get him to get to eat him." Lamar silently considered Tynan's logic and then, with help from a parent, eliminated the words "to eat him."

Tynan's and Lamar's comments about each other's work are an extension of the social give-and-take that fills the children's world. In Lamar's school, during the primary (K–3) years, this interaction—this social life—gradually infuses the children's artistic efforts and outlines the dimensions of the composing act. The children call each other's attention to the relationship between the real world and their imagined ones ("That wouldn't happen."), as well as to the delicate negotiating between authors' and readers' evaluations of constructed worlds ("So? This is *my* story."). The children call attention also to the internal tensions of their multimedia efforts—to the compatibility of their pictures, talk, and words ("I don't see the boy [in your story] in your picture.")

In this way, the children play out in childlike ways the negotiations we all face as composers: How does a writer transform the colors, forms, and rhythms of experienced worlds into little black and white marks on a paper? How does one use those marks to help others enter and accept those worlds? (And what kind of imaginary—playful—manipulations of the real world can an author make in order to better reveal its affective truth, its essence—like fear or comfort . . . or friendship?)

The Teacher's Role

The children's urge to symbolize and to socialize allows *whole* children to invent *whole* worlds for themselves. Yet, as adults responsible for those worlds, we often feel as teacher-author Sylvia Ashton-Warner (1963, pp. 103–104) did, that all this social talk can be

> the worst enem[y] to what we call teaching . . . If only they'd stop talking to each other, playing with each other, fighting with each other and loving each other . . . In self-defence . . . I harness the communication, since I can't control it, and base my method on it.

Teachers cannot stop children like Lamar from seeking the relationships that matter to them. But they can drive children's social concerns outside the academic world (Gillmore 1983; Labov 1982). Lamar's teacher, Margaret, does not so much harness the children's talk as negotiate with it (Genishi 1989). She values the community of children she helped to found. So, while making clear her expectations for, interest in, and her appreciation of their efforts, she also gives them interactive space and ample materials for symbol making. Her own interest in the children as people and as artists and composers influences their responses to each other. The children's symbolizing and socializing thus helps define their developmental challenges and goals—that writing serve them as a means of social connection and individual expression.

A Closing Note: On Boundaries and Connections

Teachers reach out to connect with children, and children reach out, not only to teachers, but to each other as well. This is the wisdom of Ethan's simple drawing. As in many young children's drawings of people, each friend has a clear boundary (Goodnow 1977)—one child's hand reaches for but does not touch that of the other. They are distinct but together, each defining his own boundary by the way he fits the other's, like pieces of a puzzle. This is, in the

Anne Haas Dyson began her career in Texas as a preschool and elementary school teacher. Her strongest interest has been in children's lives in classroom settings, and most of her research has been conducted in kindergarten and primary grade rooms, studying children's symbol-making and socialization. In 1984 she joined the faculty of the Language and Literacy Division of the School of Education, University of California, Berkeley.

end, what we want the children to know. In Margaret's words, "Schooling is all about learning to be yourself and part of a community at the same time." Literacy is a tool for this defining and connecting, as Lamar and Ethan are both learning.

→ See: Copeland, p. 48; King, p. 16; Nourot, p. 31; Paley, p. 30; Rich, p. 27; Rigg, p. 237.

References

Ashton-Warner, S. 1963. *Teacher.* New York: Simon & Schuster.

Corsaro, W. 1985. *Friendship and peer culture in the early years.* Norwood, NJ: Ablex.

Dyson, A. 1989. *Multiple worlds of child writers: Friends learning to write.* New York: Teachers College Press.

Gardner, H. 1982. *Developmental psychology.* 2d ed. Boston: Little, Brown.

Garvey, C. 1986. "Peer relations and the growth of communication." In *Process and outcome in peer relationships,* eds. E. Mueller and C. R. Cooper. Orlando, FL: Academic Press.

Genishi, C. 1989. "Research currents: The worlds of children, what Maisie knew." *Language Arts* 66.

Gillmore, P. 1983. "Spelling 'Mississippi': Recontextualizing a literacy-related speech event." *Anthropology & Education Quarterly* 14.

Goodnow, J. 1977. *Children's drawing.* Cambridge: Harvard University Press

Labov, W. 1982. "Competing value systems in inner-city schools." In *Children in and out of school,* ed. P. Gilmore and A. A. Glatthorn. Washington, DC: Center for Applied Linguistics.

Mueller, E., and C. R. Cooper, eds. 1986. *Process and outcome in peer relationships.* Orlando, FL: Academic Press.

Paley, V. G. 1986. *Mollie is three: Growing up in school.* Chicago: University of Chicago Press.

Further Reading by Anne Haas Dyson

◆ *Language Assessment in the Early Years,* with C. Genishi. Ablex, 1984.

◆ "Staying Free to Dance with the Children: The Dangers of Sanctifying Activities in the Language Arts Curriculum." *English Education* 18, 1986.

◆ *Multiple Worlds of Child Writers: Friends Learning to Write.* Teachers College Press, Columbia University, 1989.

Book Note

Joining the Literacy Club: Further Essays into Education

Frank Smith
1988; 154 pp.; $13.50
Portsmouth, NH:
    Heinemann

Frank Smith uses the metaphor of a club to describe the social context created by students and teachers in classrooms. In this second collection of essays, Smith describes contexts that invite students to join and contexts that discourage membership. "One of the most important communities any individual can join is the 'literacy club,' because membership ensures that individuals learn how to read and write, and because reading is the entrance to many other clubs." The issue is who gets invited and who doesn't.

Carol Christine

It can be astonishing to adults how much children are learning.

WELL-SAID

—Frank Smith, *Insult to Intelligence*

Great Teachers:
Bob Wortman
by Myna L. Matlin

When I walked into Bob Wortman's classroom at Borton Primary Magnet School I immediately realized that what I saw was a community of learners. Children and adults were working together to learn. Two children, five and six years old, were sitting in an old-style bathtub filled with cushions and reading alligator books to each other. Several more were up in a brightly painted reading loft, reading fiction to themselves. When one of them needed help, it was offered gently by another. Four children wearing headsets were following the text as they listened to a tape recording of *What Do You Do with a Kangaroo?*

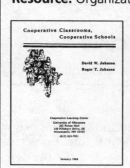

Other children were writing. Some were sitting at small tables, surrounded by pencils, markers, and writing papers of different types. Others were lying on the floor writing in journals. A low hum was heard as children discussed the content of their writing and edited work together.

Robbie's grandfather was teaching a five-year-old to play chess while two other children watched and discussed moves with the chess players. Graciela, the teaching assistant, had a group of children with her binding books they had written and edited the previous week. The principal, who had just walked into the classroom "for a minute," was looking up volcanoes in a reference book with another child. A third-grade peer tutor was using math manipulatives with two students who were learning about place value.

Four students were talking to Bob about a Picasso art print and how they were going to incorporate elements of Picasso's style into their own illustrations. Bob's voice was heard slightly above the hum of the busy five-and six-year-olds. He made a pun that was greeted by a laugh from those near him and then he laughed heartily as Bridgett returned his pun with one of her own. As Bob and the children talked on, a child working on bookbinding looked up at the art prints and incorporated a Picasso-like abstract on his front cover.

Everyone was a learner in this setting. The students developed strategies for learning about the world around them through science, social science, the fine arts, and humanities. Literacy and numeracy became part of their daily lives. They learned to live with humor and to work as members of a learning community.

The grandparent was able to see his grandson in action and the child was able to see his grandfather as a teacher and someone with whom "everyone" wanted to learn. The principal learned about whole language so that she was able to explain it to her supervisors, parents, and other principals. The teaching assistant enhanced her knowledge of child development and was encouraged to take classes at a local college. As an observer, I learned about planning and structuring a classroom where everyone is a learner.

Yet the greatest learning was Bob's. With increasing knowledge of literacy development, his classroom became more child-centered and more focused on the learning needs of individual students. He improved his observation of children, restructured his record keeping for parents, and developed alternative methods of assessments. He became an expert in children's literature and in children's written language development. He used that knowledge daily to improve the learning of his students.

Now Bob is the principal at Borton. When I walk into his school, I still see him with a book in his hand reading with his own community of learners of students, parents, teachers, and support staff, and I see everyone learning.

→ See: Literature Reference List, p. 429; Matlin, pp. 240, 398; Teachers and Research, p. 402; Wortman, p. 245.

Myna L. Matlin is the principal of Warren Elementary School, Tucson, AZ.

Resource: Organization

Cooperative Classrooms,
Cooperative Schools

David W. Johnson
Roger T. Johnson

Cooperative Learning Center
University of Minnesota
202 Pattee Hall
150 Pillsbury Dr., SE
Minneapolis, MN 55455
(612) 624-7031

January 1988

Cooperative Learning Center

University of Minnesota
202 Pattee Hall
150 Pillsbury Dr., SE
Minneapolis, MN 55455
1-612-624-7031

International Association for the Study of Cooperation in Education (IASCE)

136 Liberty St.
Santa Cruz, CA 95060

To me, cooperative learning is like a stick house—the structure may look nice, but the foundation is missing—and the big bad wolf of traditional education can blow the whole thing down. In classrooms that focus just on the structure of learning, kids can work in cooperative groups as they fill in worksheets together. What are the cooperative learning people saying about curricular content? In a student-centered, content-rich whole language classroom, cooperative learning occurs naturally without the need for a teacher-imposed, artificial cooperative grouping. There is no doubt, however, that the cooperative learning movement is helping to shake the foundation of sit-in-your-seat-and-do-your-own-work traditional education. In that regard, it only makes sense for whole language educators to join hands with the cooperative education folks. We've listed two of the leading organizations.

LBB

Great Teachers:
Kittye Copeland
by Leslie Swanda

What Her Kids Say

Each whole language classroom is different, but all share an enthusiasm for learning. This enthusiasm inspires trust, laughter, collaboration, experimentation, and risk-taking. Whole language teachers view themselves as facilitators, rather than dispensers of knowledge, and they know that they learn as much from children as children learn from them. It is this philosophy that guides whole language teacher Kittye Copeland.

Kittye teaches at Stephens Elementary Children's School in Columbia, Missouri, in a multi-aged, ungraded, self-contained classroom. There are approximately 35 children ranging in age from five to twelve. Kittye and her coteacher, Lynda Baker, plan and facilitate the learning needs of their students.

To help me tell others about Kittye, I turned to the members of Stephens Elementary Children's School, and invited them to write descriptions of their teacher and classroom. These were some of the things they shared.

> Ms. Copeland,
> The things I like about Ms. Copeland is that she gets to know the kids she teaches to. She also listens to the kids' comments and suggestions, which is something not all teachers do.
> —Aaron Bell

Kittye knows her students on a personal as well as an academic level. She takes time to visit with them individually and conducts surveys throughout the school year in order to keep abreast of their current interests and concerns.

Stephens Elementary begins and ends each school day with a class meeting. This is a time when the children share personal interests and events. They discuss current events in the community, nation, and world. Class members bring in newspaper clippings and magazine articles. The class meeting is also a time when students can discuss events taking place in the classroom and on the playground. They talk openly about conflicts with their peers as they work together to find solutions. They feel free to make real suggestions about the class routine as well as the curriculum. For example:

> Mrs. Copeland is a nice teacher because she buys books to read for us so we can learn.
> —Steve

Books are abundant in the Stephens Elementary classroom. The children view books as good friends. They choose a variety of books to read for pleasure, to find information about topics they are studying, and to share with their peers in literature study groups.

Kittye reads to her students daily, modeling appropriate reading strategies, while helping to cultivate in her students a love of literature and an appreciation for different literary forms.

> I like this school because the teachers are nice and they tell the children to write stories. I love to do math and reading in school. I think Ms. Copeland is a good teacher because she lets us write the things that we want to write.
> —Sierra

The children are engaged in authentic writing experiences every day. Writing is a way of learning in Kittye's class. She confers with students throughout all stages of the writing process; she encourages peer conferencing. She invites students to draft, revise, and edit, always allowing time for them to share and celebrate their writing.

Kittye provides ample opportunities for publication, which give students real reasons for writing. Each week students are invited to submit articles to a class newsletter. They also submit stories and poems to children's magazines and local contests and displays. Twice a year they organize, edit, and publish a class magazine. Students also complete research projects at various times throughout the school year. Their written reports are placed on the reference shelf in the classroom for use in future research projects.

Bookmaking supplies, including a book binder, are available to the students at all times. When a book is completed, a time of celebration is shared by all. Students may choose to donate their books to the class library, enabling it to grow and expand with works authored by students as well as by professional authors.

> Miss Copeland
> Makes learning fun!
> She makes games out of learning,
> and learning out of games.
> Miss Copeland's an O.K. teacher.
> —Kate

Laughter abounds in this classroom. Learning is viewed as a natural, exciting event, not a laborious process. There is a true sense of community; members are always eager to share their new discoveries, thoughts, feelings, and experiences. They enjoy working, laughing, and learning together. I have often heard Kittye say that peer collaboration is what holds the classroom together. When kids help other kids, learning can only be enhanced.

As I read through the student descriptions of the classroom and Kittye, a common thread emerged. Kittye Copeland is much more than just a teacher. She's a good friend. Nicholas speaks for me and for all other children and adults who know this great teacher.

> Through all my years at Stephens what I have enjoyed most about Ms. Copeland is that she can really communicate with us in games, reading, and working, whatever age we are. And that makes me happy to have her as my teacher.

Leslie Swanda is at the University of Missouri, Columbia, MO.

Parents' Perspective
by Barbara Halliwill Bell

Aaron

One of the first big snows of the season had fallen the night before. I was talking to Kittye Copeland on the telephone, and she asked if Aaron, my five-year-old son, was excited about the snow. Of course he was. Kittye asked Aaron to draw a snowman and bring it to her the next time he came over.

Kittye and Aaron had been friends for over two years, so he was used to such requests. However, as much as he cared for and trusted Kittye, he was reluctant to draw or write anything for her—or me for that matter. But he did sit down and attempt to draw a snowman.

Aaron was dissatisfied with his first "imperfect" effort; he scribbled through it. I cajoled him into trying again, but he was even more upset with his second less-than-perfect attempt (in his eyes) and tore it into several pieces. He refused to try again. He would not take a risk. I tried to convince him that trying was the important thing, but he was not about to believe it. If he couldn't do it perfectly, he wouldn't do it at all.

In the fall, Aaron began attending kindergarten. The teacher was humanistic but had a traditional, skills/phonics orientation. She was concerned about Aaron's inability to differentiate between uppercase and lowercase letters, especially the two *a*'s that begin his name. I saved a whole box of Aaron's circle-the-same-sound and draw-a-line-to-the-picture worksheets from this year.

Early in October he also began attending the new afternoon Step Ahead Program at the Stephens Elementary School, where Kittye had recently become head teacher. In this multiage, whole language classroom, in which kindergartners worked with kids from across grade levels, Aaron began to blossom.

It was easy for Aaron to begin reading. I had read to him a lot, asking him to finish a line or guess what would fit. He would say, "Just read to me, would ya, Mom." The supportive atmosphere of the whole language classroom, the assisted reading, big books, tapes and books, and sustained silent reading helped Aaron take off as a reader. But the writing and drawing took a little longer. He was still unwilling to take a risk, unwilling to settle for less than perfection. Again, the support from teachers and other kids helped. They wrote in journals, did language experience stories together, and wrote letters to one another as often as they wanted. By April Aaron was a risk-taking writer.

In public school, Aaron's reversal of his *b*'s and *d*'s, poor small motor skills (as evidenced in his printing), almost total lack of conventional spelling and punctuation, and low to mediocre standardized test scores would have made him a candidate for the low or, at best, middle reading group. Little weight would have been given to his use of such vocabulary as "investigate," "unconscious," and "illusion." His knowledge of phonics rules (as evident in his functional spelling) and of story schema would not have been considered.

I decided that I would not put him in an atmosphere that did not accentuate the positive. So I enrolled Aaron in the first grade at Stephen's Elementary for two reasons—Kittye's attitude toward children and the whole language program. He is finishing his fifth year in the program as an avid reader, writer, and learner. He has read only good literature (he would be so bored with basal stories); written for real purposes ("fill in the blank" is not in his schema); learned to spell by writing for real audiences (he's never taken a traditional spelling test or even seen a spelling book); integrated information that made sense in the context of his overall learning through reports that were researched, written for, and shared with others (he can't imagine multiple choice tests since he writes about what he knows); and learned for the sake of learning (not to pass a test on what someone thinks he should know). Aaron reads in the car, while waiting in line, on his way to lunch, and at any time he can. He is eager to talk and think about the books he reads. He writes stories, reports, news articles, letters, advertisements, notes, journal entries—anything that has a real purpose. He knows he can learn anything he wants to because he *is* a reader, writer, learner.

Aaron's attitude about reading and writing, and learning in general, comes from his own sense of self-worth, something that has been nurtured in Kittye's whole language program. My son has never had to endure a "low group" or "high group" stigma, nor has he faced immediate correction for a nonstandard use of written or oral language. He has always been celebrated as a learner and as a real user of language. He is one of the lucky ones.

➜ See: Goodman, p. 24.

Barbara Halliwill Bell is a graduate teaching/research assistant at the University of Missouri, Columbia, MO.

As Teachers See It

by Kittye Copeland

Learning Is Social

A classroom should be a community with one common goal: the education of every individual. The children in our class have become so responsible for their own learning that they now can guide others to become self-motivated and self-sufficient learners.

This became apparent when a new third-grader arrived in our classroom in late March. He had come from a different system where his learning was controlled and directed by the teacher. Tom was not allowed to make any curriculum decisions on his own. At the end of his first day I asked him what he thought of his new school. His reply, "It seems easier because you have no desk and you can lay on the floor," indicated that he had not been motivated academically. He had stared at the wall most of the day because he couldn't think of anything to write, and he had tried to get other students to play when it was silent reading time.

Tom was a child who hated school as much as one could at the old age of nine. His teacher had stated that he was nothing but a problem, always off task, refusing to try. I saw the tough shell of a child who had been hurt because he didn't like or could not do what he had been told to do. I knew that he would not accept many suggestions or invitations from me, so I decided to let the other students help him become a member of the literacy classroom that we had been developing all year. Tom would require some expert help in order to move into our community of readers and writers.

The next day I asked Chris to show Tom the ways of our community. I observed closely to see whether another student could motivate a new class member, jotting notes in my journal. Tom found children using reading and writing in personally satisfying ways and seeing themselves as successful language users, not competing for a grade or for the teacher's praise. These were foreign ideas to Tom.

During silent reading time Chris explained to Tom that he could choose any selection he wanted to read. He should find a comfortable place to be on his own to enjoy his reading. Tom replied, "I don't like to read." Chris, with a stunned look, replied, "Then look at pictures. You have to respect others."

The next proof of Chris's ability to help Tom become a member was during the selection of literature study books. Tom had been asked to select a book he would like to read and then discuss it with others who chose the same book. As the other students began looking at the back covers and discussing the authors or the book, Tom just sat.

Chris shared his selection process with Tom, recommending that they choose the same book so that he could help him. After the selections were made the students began to read the first chapter. Tom had a hard time with the book and wanted to stop. He began to whine about his poor choice. Chris quickly assured him that I would let them trade books. When the boys came to me and received a new book without hassle, Tom was astonished. Chris then explained how to write reactions to the book. Tom was unable to think of a thing to respond to, so Chris read his reactions and then asked Jack to share his. When that didn't work, he generated a written conversation with Tom. Chris realized that modeling is a key factor in teaching. I could see that Tom was becoming actively involved in the learning process through this interaction with Chris. When I asked about his day, this time Tom replied he had enjoyed reading his new book.

The next day Tom was asked to write a story for the class newspaper, but he said he couldn't think of anything to write about. At this point others began to assist Tom. Jack asked for back issues of the paper so that Tom could see the stories that had been published. Tom then wrote his first story.

Someone was always ready to give Tom advice. Nicholas showed him how to take notes for report writing. Before Tom gave his oral report, Chris reminded the class that it was Tom's first time; however, because of the help he had received when practicing with Sarina, you couldn't tell.

The children had all become actively involved in helping Tom. Because they are responsible for their own learning, they have learned not only how to help themselves, but how to guide and counsel others.

When I asked Chris how Tom was doing, he replied, "He sure does read and write more."

→ See: Copeland, pp. 411, 419; Dyson, p. 46.

Kittye Copeland is a teacher at Stephens Elementary Children's School, Columbia, MO.

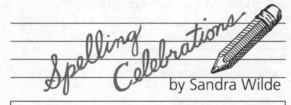
Spelling Celebrations

by Sandra Wilde

Patterns and Strategies: Living off the Land

We would have to cell (call) OFF Christmas.
Darren, 4th grade

Once their was a PARROT named DRAW TOW (two).
Gordon, 3d grade

Donald Graves talks about children "living off the land" as writers. When children write in a print-rich environment, they'll use the resources of that environment to help them spell. Aside from the usual sources like dictionaries and word charts, children also find spellings wherever there is written language. Darren, while writing one day, jumped up and ran over to look at the light switch by the classroom door, came back, and wrote *off*. (We often wondered if he had done it merely to impress the researchers who were watching him write!) Gordon asked the researcher sitting next to him how to spell *parrot*. She didn't tell him, but she had written his question in her field notes and he copied *parrot* from there. His parrot's unusual name came from the "Draw Two" card for the *Sorry* board game, which he had miscopied. The more we fill our classrooms with written text, the more children will be exposed to spellings and the more resourceful they will be able to be.

I Used to Be... But Now I...

I used to worry when my students talked among themselves,
But now I celebrate their learning together.
—Nancy Anderson

Breakthroughs

by A. Frederic Cheney

Writer to Writer

T he other day I called an elementary school principal to ask if he would introduce me to one of his students. I was working on a book of student writing samples, and I needed to talk to one of his fourth-graders. He was happy to arrange our meeting and not at all surprised that his student's work had attracted attention.

We met in a quiet corner of the office lobby. She was a delightful young lady, bubbling over with insights and strategies on writing. She told me of the stories she had written: the science lesson on lions she had written as a radio talk show, in which the whole pride was interviewed (there's one Geraldo hasn't thought of yet); the fantasy about the "Land of the Garbage People," where the entire economy was fueled by garbage. She told me that she makes her most important decisions about revising just before she falls asleep at night. She told me what a special thing it is to have a father who can make good suggestions on your writing but does so only when asked.

She asked me about the book I was doing. How many other fourth-graders would be in it? How much was I writing, and how much was I collecting? Who would be reading it? Had I ever written a book before? Had I ever written anything before? What?

We had a delightful chat, writer to writer, and then went on with our day. When the principal came back through the office, I thanked him and told him what a special little person she was. He asked, "Were you able to get two words out of her? She's one of the shyest kids I've ever seen."

When I told him that we'd had a very animated discussion, the office secretary was moved to substantiate my claim. "That's right. She talked a blue streak over there."

We hear talk these days of a community of writers. I don't have to be convinced that it exists. Why else would a shy child open up to a total stranger? We shared a community of interest, and she was secure in her role there. Because I too am a writer, I have a new neighbor. And that's reason enough for me to keep writing.

→ See: Alvarez, p. 141; Graves, p. 130; Kamler, p. 140.

A. Frederic Cheney is a consultant in the Division of Assessment, Maine Department of Education, Augusta, ME.

Marvelous Inventions

"C" for Clark

While scanning the sign-in sheet one morning, Susie, our assistant teacher, noticed something peculiar: Either we had a guest or we had a new classmate, for someone named Clark had signed in on the sheet.

To a casual observer of our program, the appearance of this boldly printed signature would have meant nothing. But those of us who knew about Ravi's interest in superheroes and had seen him repeatedly hauling his Superman book to and from school were quick to account for the mystery signature. Having donned a new identity, Ravi had signed in as Clark Kent.

→ See: Clyde, p. 26.

—Jean Ann Clyde, professor, University of Louisville, Louisville, KY

Revaluing (Special Education)

As We See It:
Kenneth S. & Yetta M. Goodman

Teachers Supporting Learners: A Transactional View

In *Crow Boy* by Taro Yashima, we are introduced to Mr. Isobe, a new teacher to the village school who is "a friendly man with a kind smile." Things are very different with Mr. Isobe as teacher. He often "took his class to the hilltop behind the school." He responds to Chibi, the tiny boy in the class who has been an isolate for six years, a "forlorn little tag-along."

> He [Mr. Isobe] was pleased to learn that Chibi knew all the places where the wild grapes and wild potatoes grew . . . He liked Chibi's own handwriting, which no one but Chibi could read, and he tacked that up on the wall . . . And he often spent time talking with Chibi when no one was around . . . But when Chibi appeared on the stage at the talent show of that year, no one could believe his eyes. "Who is that?" "What can that stupid do up there?" . . . Until Mr. Isobe announced that Chibi was going to imitate the voices of crows. (pp. 19–25)

Chibi learned from staring at ceilings, gazing out of windows, wandering the hills, and listening with great attention and interest to birds. But it wasn't until Mr. Isobe appeared that he found out that he could also learn in school and that what he had learned outside of school was important, valuable, and of interest to others. Mr. Isobe saw no clear distinction between teachers and learners. He saw himself as a learner and suspected that even the least of his pupils knew a lot and had a lot to teach him. He was a kidwatcher who evaluated his pupils by talking with them, observing them, and transacting with them. Like Chibi, all children are whole language learners. Unfortunately, also like Chibi, they don't always encounter whole language teachers.

Teaching and learning are transactional processes. We adapt the term *transaction* from John Dewey's use of it. In transactions all the elements involved in the processes are changed. So in classroom transactions teachers and learners are changed. The idea that teaching can control learning or that each act of teaching results in an act of learning in each learner is too simplistic. Teachers learn and learners teach and as they transact each is changed. Whole language teachers recognize the power of classroom transactions and plan for them. One key to their success is building an atmosphere of mutual respect in their classrooms where they value each learner, help the learners to value themselves and each other, and win the respect of their pupils.

→ See: Goodman, pp. 23, 207, 215, 247, 249, 252; Literature Reference List, p. 429; Ohanian, p. 60.

Reference
Yashima, T. 1955. *Crow boy.* New York: Viking.

Cornerstone: Deborah Meier

Labeling Students "Easy-to-Teach"

There are lots of labels that kids, school people, and the world use to sort young people. It starts very early—often in nursery school or kindergarten. And the words we start using begin to shape us, and after a while we begin to believe that the words are US!

I've invented a new label for the one school people usually use for "top students": "easy-to-teach students." The students, in short, teachers generally feel most successful with!

What are the *differences*? It's possible physical limitations prevent some people from using their full human intelligence. But more of the difference has to do with "person-made" cultural differences, things schools can *affect*.

How? Changes in the way we go about organizing schooling, teaching subjects, grading, timing, pacing can affect learning.

After all, why *are* some kids "easier-to-teach"?

1. Kids who like to please adults, who enjoy adult company, who attend to what adults say and respond to their ideas are usually easier to teach. It's flattering. And besides, such kids learn more from teacher (and adult) talk. The other kids, who care more about peers, don't do as well in school, especially if peers are not *allowed* to be coteachers.

2. Kids who can sit quietly for long periods without appearing to go to sleep handle life in school more easily. Girls seem to know how to do this better than boys, especially in the early grades. Of course, in schools where you can learn *and* move, this doesn't matter as much.

3. Kids who ask a lot of "why" questions aloud (we call that curiosity) are more likely to do well. Kids whose curiosity is more silent, or who enjoy savoring and appreciating rather than questioning everything seem duller to teachers. Schools that make room for artists, for appreciators, nurture their *kind* of intelligence.

4. Being a practical organizer, a good fixer, socially adept, or a good reader of other people's feelings may be very critical traits in the *real* world, but it's often annoying in schools, or irrelevant.

5. Some people are quick on the draw. Others are slow and deep. The latter usually get run over fast in classrooms. By the time they raise their hands, ten other kids have answered. Gradually they give up trying. They may even stop listening. If schools didn't put such a premium on quickness . . . maybe? (Consider: the word "quick" is often a synonym for "smart.")

6. If most people learn one way, then *that way* is the norm. People who do things differently have a handicap, just because it's different, *not* because it's worse! But in school, where efficiency means we usually teach things only one way, being different *is* worse! Try convincing a kid that being different is nothing to feel bad about! Ha! But it's true, it isn't bad. We all are "learning disabled" in some areas. If we're lucky, it's in an area that's unimportant to school. (My inability to memorize anything word for word could have doomed me to the dummy class in any traditional, decent Chinese school.)

What Can We Do About This?

We can try to organize [schools] so that more kids are "easy-to-teach." We can try not to give up on any kid. We can try to remember that the bad habits kids have developed are often defensive—they're trying not to seem dumb. We can offer lots of different ways to learn things, and different deadlines for those who truly need more time, and ways to learn from peers not just adults. Once kids get to be 14 or 15—almost adults— they have to work out ways of accepting who they are and then planning the best strategies for learning. We promise we'll try to work with them in making their strategies work in [schools]. We won't *lower* our standards, but we will alter our routes.

→ See: Avery, p. 14; Ohanian, p. 60.

From *Changing Schools*, CPEES Newsletter 17.

Viewpoint: Steve Harlow

The Medicalization of the Classroom:
The Constriction of Difference in Our Schools

A subtle but thorough transformation has occurred in the schools. When we deal with difference that provokes any type of tension in school settings, we turn to the medical model rather than educational models for a solution. With this transformation have come diagnostic categories that essentially keep labeled children from participating in the same educational experience as their nonlabeled peers. But even more than that, the process of sorting freezes the child at the level of objective description with preset limits drawn from the category of disability, while not freely permitting the process of discovery and growth. It is not long before the label replaces the child. With this an insidious reduction occurs; *difference* becomes equated with *inferiority*.

Special Education

If, by sorting out differences according to *educational* needs, a qualitatively better education —something that could be truly deemed "special"—resulted, then the practice would be defensible. In the final analysis it is the type of education the child participates in that becomes the touchstone of our efforts. Let us briefly examine the quality of education the child with a school-related handicap receives.

What should we mean by education? Richard Mitchell (1987) has pointed out the importance of framing basic questions with the sense of "shouldness." He says that in such matters as intelligence, love, or education we are dealing not with questions of fact, but rather with questions of moral consequence. In education we are reminded that our work is with human potential and human struggle. It begins with the meeting of a child with his or her teacher and classmates. Such a meeting should neither be clouded by labels nor deny the presence of the difficulties a child may bring into a setting. Education does not have as its prerequisites an optimum bioanatomy, a difficulty-free learning style, a compliant disposition, or a harmonious home life.

Education should be an elevating process that enables the child to gain increasing knowledge of self and a deepening sense of the world. In reality, the children designated with handicaps are treated quite differently from their non-handicapped peers. First they have a specialist (e.g., special education teacher, learning disabilities teacher) who makes the major educational decisions for them. They may also have a special classroom provided. Both of these factors underscore and reinforce their difference. Knowledge of self is thus distorted.

Second, the educational regimen calls for a selection of tasks that the child can readily achieve—a *reduced* rather than deepening sense of the world. IEP's for most children are legal agreements that guarantee the child's attainment of concrete and uninteresting objectives. Exclusive emphasis is placed on what John Passmore (1980) has described as closed capacities. Closed capacities are those areas of learning that allow for total mastery. They are by their nature objective and prescriptive. When dealing with closed capacities, we see that the personal quali-

Steve Harlow is currently the chair of the Special Education Department, Center for Teaching and Learning, at the University of North Dakota, where he has also held positions with the university's Medical School. He is host and coproducer of the regional public radio program "Considering Children," which is concluding its fifth season. He also works with teachers and parents in developing ways of engaging children who reveal some area of difficulty.

ties of the learner are secondary to *what* is to be learned. In contrast, open capacities are those areas that one can gain a deepening knowledge about, while permitting a sense of self-expression; they cannot be totally mastered (e.g., interpretation, chess, writing, storytelling, and sculpting have no final state of completion).

Open capacities involve personal ways of knowing and expression. The emphasis is on the extension of meaning as students immerse themselves in the educational setting. The rhythms of the open capacities are process and form, concept and feeling. Closed capacities, as Passmore notes, are readily converted into routines.

In teaching, staying with closed capacities has the advantage of being able to gauge and manage the progress of an activity. The purported value for the student of staying with the easily achievable is a steady current of success. Yet such success is an impostor. To the student these tasks are unrelated to discovery of self or the world. They are dehydrated of meaning. How can we enable a child who might have attentional difficulties to look and grasp when we pay so little attention to what is alive in him and around him? No, the answer to such a child's difficulties lies elsewhere. In the end the true value of emphasizing closed capacities for the special student is the predictability that the routine brings. However, curiosity, imagination, and self-expression are not well nourished by routine.

A paradox may be discerned. The special education program focuses upon the problem area of a child's being, while at the same time attempting to create a setting where few problems confront him or her. Children with a school-related handicap are thought by those who plan and care for them to be unable to handle much of the real world. Their special teacher mediates the demands of school and life by drastically reducing such demands to fragmented and closed capacities. Few accommodations are made by regular teachers to permit adjustment to the regular classroom. Rather than aiding children in their understanding and involvement of the world, the school removes them from it. In the process the children are subtly convinced that they cannot handle much of what is ordinarily to be explored and learned. The authority of the school, after all, has mirrored to them that as children possessing a handicap they can handle so much and no more.

What is denied the children in all of this is their sense of uniqueness and personal experience. As Malcolm Ross (1978, p. 62) contends, "People need to feel whole and must be responsible for their own wholeness. That means they must be helped to make their own sense of the whole of their experience, body and soul, mind and feelings." Such is the type of education that should be available to all youngsters, but particularly to those who are experiencing difficulties in school. A piecemeal education that uproots children from their peers is not conducive to the wholeness Ross describes. Inclusion in the community of the classroom is a requisite for children to come to terms with their unique-

ness. Short of this we are imprinting within the children's conception of themselves that they are members of a special subspecies of students: the handicapped.

Difficulties in functioning can be met with patience, flexibility, and accommodation. It is not the absence of struggle and tension that makes us human, but rather the quality of our engagement. With support and understanding, struggle may prove to be a catalyst to gaining self-knowledge and self-agency. Education in this sense is truly special.

➔ See: Avery, p. 14; Meier, p. 50; Murphy, p. 57; Ohanian, p. 60.

References

Mitchell, R. 1987. *The gift of fire*. New York: Simon & Schuster.

Passmore, J. 1980. *The philosophy of teaching*. Cambridge: Harvard University Press.

Ross, M. 1978. *The creative arts*. London: Heinemann Educational Books.

From *Holistic Education Review* 2(2), Summer 1989.

Further Reading by Steve Harlow

◆ *Obstacles to Mainstreaming: How We Face Difference.* Association of Childhood Education International, 1979.

◆ "Change Triangle: A Way of Dealing with Functional Difference." *Prospector,* June 1983.

◆ *Computers: The Humanistic Perspective,* ed. Haworth Press, 1985.

◆ "The Constriction of the Classroom: The Submergence of Difference." In *Readings on Equal Education, 10 Critical Issues for a New Administration* and Congress. AMS Press, 1989.

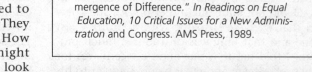

Resource: Organization

Talking Books

National Library Service for the Blind and Physically Handicapped
Library of Congress
Washington, DC 20542

In cooperation with a network of regional libraries, the Library of Congress provides a free library service to persons who are unable to use standard printed material because of visual or physical disabilities. Books and magazines in recorded form and in braille are delivered to eligible readers by postage-free mail and returned in the same manner. Phonographs and cassette players are also loaned free to borrowers. *Talking Book Topics* is a free (to blind and physically handicapped individuals) bimonthly publication that lists recently added titles to the national collection. For more information, contact your local library or the address above.

 It Shouldn't Happen to Kids

Color Her Crazy

According to standardized tests, five-year-old Jeffrey has a third-grade vocabulary and is squarely on grade level in all academic areas. His teacher, however, has recommended that he be retained because she has had to remind him all year to put his crayons away.

—As told to LBB by Gloria Norton, resource teacher, Fair Oaks School, Redwood City, CA

Parents' Perspective

by Aurelia Dávila de Silva, Ruth L. Galaz, and Yolanda Rippetoe

Perspectives on Billy

In a highly literate society, children come to school and expect to learn to read. As teachers, we can maintain this normal expectation and curiosity about the world. Learning to read requires a risk-taking environment, a tolerance for miscues, and a propensity toward self-correction while seeking to have the print make sense.

Billy's case illustrates the damage that can be perpetrated by programs that deny children this route to learning. His story is told by his mother and two classroom observers.

Yolanda (Billy's Mother)

Billy was on the free lunch program. During the first week of school, Billy came home saying that he didn't want to work for his lunch. He said that Ms. C. had told him to work for his lunch by taking the lunch money to the office. While Billy may not have understood the full meaning of the comment, I as a parent certainly did.

By September 23, Billy had made F's on three spelling tests. I called the teacher to express our concern. I asked her what she thought was happening with Billy and what we could do to help him at home. She told me to write the words on popsicle sticks and play games with the sticks. Ms. C. did not know me in person. All she knew was that we were Hispanic with a "funny" last name and that Billy was on the free lunch program. I told her that our main concern was for Billy's self-esteem and what would happen to his self-confidence if he continued to fail.

Some weeks he did very well and some weeks he failed. I remember only a couple of times when he brought home all passing grades in one day. I quickly came to resent the harsh grading system. Every paper had a number grade and a letter grade, 30/F or 90/A. One time Billy made 100 on one of his papers, but Ms. C. took off 5 points because he forgot to write his name on his paper.

I asked Ms. C. for a basal reader. I felt that if Billy could practice reading the stories at home he would have a more successful experience at school. The teacher wrote back that she could not comply with my request because it was not fair to the rest of the children in the class for Billy to have this privilege.

The week of January 23, Ms. C. called my husband at his office to tell him that she was retaining Billy in the first grade because he was not mature enough for the second grade. My husband said, "Absolutely not." He scheduled a conference for February 7.

During the conference with Ms. C., I again expressed my concern over Billy's deteriorating self-esteem. I told her I felt that Billy responded more positively when he was praised and spoken to in a warm manner. She commented that she had discovered that herself, but she had 19 other children in the class and did not have time to give Billy individual attention. Toward the end of the conference, I asked her if immaturity was the only reason for her wanting to retain Billy. She said yes.

Billy was tested on April 6, the third and last day of the Texas Educational Assessment of Minimal Skills (TEAMS) test, and testing was administered through his lunch period. Though Billy qualified for special education, we refused.

Aurelia (Observer)

Yolanda came to ask about what she needed to do to help Billy. She felt she had to communicate with the teacher so that she could get Billy extra help. Billy attended a school district that had a low minority attendance. It had a reputation as a refuge for teachers who do not want to work with minorities. I told her that poor, darkskinned minority children were usually placed in lower-level reading groups. This school district usually has lower expectations of these children. Ordinarily, children love to run errands for the teacher. In Billy's case, when the teacher said he had to work for his lunch, he was not receiving the message that this was a special thing to do.

When I visited Billy's classroom, I was not surprised. The class consisted of 15 Anglo children and 3 Mexican-Americans. Ms. C. believed in imparting information. She drilled the entire class in short and long vowels. She divided the classroom into three reading groups. Children did not have the opportunity to read books; the concentration was on skills. There was no classroom library, and except for the worksheets and copying, no other writing occurred.

This teacher did not support Billy's learning or growth. Instead, she resorted to standardized testing and decontextualized language to describe Billy's lack of achievement in the skill areas.

Ruth (Observer)

Yolanda had brought me a foot-high collection of Billy's papers. The main feature that caught my attention was a numerical score followed by a slash and a letter grade on each paper. The scores varied from high 30s to high 50s and invariably the grade was F. I found the visual impact so forceful (and I did not even know Billy) that I wondered about its impact on him.

Late that semester, a colleague asked if I could sit in for her at an ARD conference on Billy. I agreed. The moderator informed the parents of their options, emphasizing that they could place the student in the special education program and monitor him, that they could place him on a "pullout basis" or that they could choose not to place him in the program.

Yolanda voiced her preference clearly, noting that her son would be involved in summer tutoring. The moderator then verified that it was her understanding that the parents' decision was *not* to put Billy in special education. In resolute tones, a staff member said, "I would disagree; I think he needs some help."

The father rose to the occasion. In general, he said, he also disagreed with Yolanda's decision. "But she has studied the problem carefully, and *you* have given me just enough doubt to decide to give her a chance to work with Billy the way she thinks best. You tested him at *lunchtime*. Anyone, educator or not, knows that the opportune time to test a child is not on his lunchtime. And not only that—you tested him on the same day as the TEAMS tests. You have definitely placed some doubts in my mind as to your having my son's best interests in mind *and* as to your judgment in handling his education."

There were more protests from the staff. Even as the papers were being signed, one said, "I am puzzled over your attitude toward special education programs," she said. "I've worked in four districts and I've never seen a problem with one."

And another said, "It's going to be hard to teach him nine months' work in six weeks."

I sat there and watched and heard the system reach out for Billy's mother—*not* in a supportive, reassuring way, but waiting to close in around her. Afterward, the parents and I held our own three-way conference under a shade tree in the parking lot. The father's parting words contrasted vividly with the assorted lines of the nine: "For all we know, he may be an Einstein!"

Lucky kid! With parents like these, he certainly will not fail.

Our "horror" story ends on a bright note. Billy attended summer school and had a teacher who encouraged him to read. He has been enjoying reading all summer. He will start attending school in a new school where the former teacher's biases, as expressed in his permanent record forms, may not be perpetuated. Billy enjoys going to the library so that he can read real books.

→ See: Bell, p. 48; Goodman, p. 360; Smith, p. 58.

Aurelia Dávila de Silva and Ruth L. Galaz are assistant professors at the College of Social and Behavioral Sciences, University of Texas, San Antonio, TX. Yolanda Rippetoe is a music teacher with the San Antonio Independent School District, San Antonio, TX.

Further Reading
Jackson, Philip. 1968. *Life in Classrooms.* Holt, Rinehart & Winston.
McDermott, Ray. 1987. "Achieving School Failure: An Anthropological Approach to Illiteracy and Social Stratification." In *Education and Cultural Process,* ed. George D. Spindler. Prospect Heights, IL: Waveland Press.

Network

Chuska School: Empowered Children Discovered, Defined

by Martha Ahlmann

In our inservice on whole language, we always hear about how children are "empowered." One day in October, I discovered what that empowering means.

Our class went to visit a kindergarten classroom. We had been invited to share popcorn and we were going to read to them. I had several volunteers who wanted to read, one of whom was my least-able-to-sit-still boy. I wasn't sure how he'd do, but I decided I'd let him try.

When I next looked, he was asking one of the kindergarten boys if he needed help tying his shoes, and then proceeded to do it for him. A few minutes later I found that he had his group of four children completely enthralled as he went through his wild-animal book.

He had noticed some plastic animals on the shelf, and as he got to each new animal in the book, he picked up the model and compared it with the picture in the book. He pointed out the parts of the body, the head and neck, just as if he'd been teaching for years.

This child, in a skill-oriented classroom, would have been referred to special education. But in our program, he succeeds and has self-worth and self-esteem . . .

From *Diné Ba Hane'* 9(2), Winter 1989.

Martha Ahlmann is a primary teacher at Chuska School, Tohatchi, NM.

Newsletter Information: *Diné Ba Hane'* is the newsletter of the Chapter 1 programs in the Navajo Agencies' schools. *Diné Ba Hane'* translates into English as something close to "stories of the *Diné,* or people." The newsletter is published three times a year by the U.S. Government Printing Office, and features sections on successful learning activities, community involvement, professional development, recognition of excellence, and the catch-all "etc." To receive copies of the newsletter, write to Catherine Begay, newsletter coordinator, OIEP-Chapter 1, Box 110, Ft. Defiance, AZ 86504.

Great Teachers:
Paul Crowley

by Mary Bixby

"Everyone Is An Expert"

Paul Crowley taught seventh-, eighth-, and ninth-graders labeled learning disabled at Jefferson Junior High School in Columbia, Missouri, for five years. At the same time, he worked toward his doctoral degree in reading education, linking theory to classroom practice. Paul also served as our TAWL president for two years and shared his teaching experiences at professional meetings and in articles for professional journals. Yet his knowledge base and professional involvements were only part of what made Paul so successful with his kids.

Two of the most noticeable and endearing things about Paul are his fine sense of humor and his ability to see the potential for fun in nearly any situation. Paul's programs have

Paul Crowley reads to Lauren & Beth Perez.

always been natural extensions of his personality. His attitude in the classroom was that language and learning were like a party—they are social functions, and in that setting his students were always invited to "come as you are." Vygotsky's portrayal of a "zone of proximal development" (1978), in which students learn and think about experience through interactions with peers and teachers, became the impetus for Paul's focus on "kids helping kids."

Everyone in Paul's classes was an "expert" on some subject. In fact, Paul told his students that they were actually the "unlabeled gifted." One particular seventh-grade class consisted of four boys who had never viewed themselves as successful students. They were quite a crew. Robbie needed to talk to make sense of his world. Josh always dressed in olive drab or camouflage-print garb, and was a quiet but enthusiastic reader and writer with a passion for the military, especially for World War II. Kevin had the long, slender hands of an artist. He was a very reluctant reader and writer, but he loved to draw. His pictures, the envy of everyone, were prominently displayed in the classroom. John wrote wonderful stories, but he always stopped, frustrated by his inability to control technical correctness.

Paul's classroom was tiny, cluttered with books and decorated with posters, reprints of famous works of art, students' drawings, poems, and clippings from newspapers and magazines. As the second bell rang, these four students entered the room and retrieved their journals from a file cabinet drawer. They searched for Paul's latest comments in their journals as they settled into their seats. There was giggling and an exchange of knowing glances about their shared secrets with Mr. Crowley.

Their journals were for *them*; they knew they could write about anything and their writing would be valued. New entries were eagerly created, even by Kevin, who sketched what was on his mind, but who had also begun to risk adding written comments.

After journals, each student had the choice of working on a pressing assignment from another class such as English, geography, American studies, or to work on a project in process. Individual work and collaboration occurred simultaneously. While Josh was looking at the illustrations on the wall and trying to copy Kevin's style of drawing so he could finish a picture of a tank for a history report, John was asking Josh how to spell certain words for his story

about motorcycles. Kevin was trying to fill in a worksheet on "important places in Europe" for geography class. Robbie was reading a paperback novel and helping Kevin with his map, since he had the same assignment and had already completed it. Everyone was talking, exchanging materials, checking on everyone else's progress.

Meanwhile Paul was writing in his journal, in which he kept his kidwatching notes— observations of the students' activities and progress. When John leaned over to show Paul his draft of his motorcycle paper in order to ask about the correct spelling of a word, Paul read the draft and responded, "This is amazing. Tell me more about this." As John began to explain the further intricacies of motorcycle engines, he realized that he had much more to write, so he took back his draft, saying, "Gosh, maybe I should write about that, too."

Paul was a kidwatching member of the group. He was as likely to need to borrow a pencil as one of the boys, and was as quick to crack a joke. Casually and unobtrusively, he discovered what each boy was working on, and built on each learner's strengths.

Robbie, Josh, Kevin, and John all grew as learners that year. They began to think of themselves as capable readers, writers, speakers, and listeners. As their confidence grew, so did their interest and engagement in all their classes. Paul helped his kids come to believe in themselves, and in doing so, he taught them the most important lesson of all.

➔ See: Bixby, p. 402; Meier, p. 50.

Mary Bixby is an assistant professor and learning resource specialist at the University of Missouri, Columbia, MO.

Book Note

Readers and Writers with a Difference: A Holistic Approach to Teaching Learning Disabled and Remedial Students

Lynn K. Rhodes and Curt Dudley-Marling 1988; 344 pp.; $18 Portsmouth, NH: Heinemann

Since I really am a novice both in special education and in whole language, I concentrate on understanding the theories of each area. This book integrated a holistic approach to teaching in special education, so that it all came together for me.

Anita Howard

❝ We've learned that if you wish to understand parents of handicapped children you must examine the "whole" family, a system that is affected by a variety of factors, including the personalities of individual family members, religious beliefs, socioeconomic status, culture, and so on. ❞ (p. 8)

Breakthroughs

by Lois Bridges Bird

Loving Lawrence

When I taught first grade on the Tohono O'odham Indian Reservation, there was one student in my class who stood out. Lawrence (not his real name) was easily twice the size of any of his classmates both in height and weight. When I first saw him, I thought that perhaps he had been retained several times, but his records revealed the astonishing fact that he was only six years old.

Lawrence stood out for another reason. He was unable to control his bowels. I learned from the school nurse that it was a problem that had developed the previous year in kindergarten. After lunch, Lawrence would defecate in his pants. It happened every day. His mother had given up alternately pleading, cajoling, bribing, punishing, and shaming him. She simply sent a change of clothes for him in a grocery sack, and every day, after lunch, school personnel took turns washing Lawrence and helping him put on his clean clothes.

My students were as loving as any I've ever had the privilege of working with—remarkably kind and considerate toward one another. But they could not resist the vulnerability of this man–child who routinely emptied his bowels in his pants. When Lawrence was near they would feign fainting from an imagined odor. They would smell the chair he had been sitting on and pretend to gag. Lawrence bore their taunts in shamefaced silence.

One day, after lunch, we gathered in a circle on the threadbare rug for a story. Lawrence was not with us. We all knew he was in the bathroom for his ritual cleaning. We talked openly about his problem. We discussed possible reasons why it might be happening. And then I laid down the law: There would be no teasing, no taunting, no mention of his difficulty.

I could do that at least. I could prevent the open cruelty toward Lawrence in my classroom. But what else could I do? I could love Lawrence. It was so simple, and yet . . . Lawrence was not a six-year-old who could be lifted onto a lap and cuddled. He was so big. His T-shirts never covered his huge belly, which rolled out over his jeans, looking disturbingly like the gut of a beer guzzler. His jeans, unable to hold that belly in, inevitably slipped, revealing the crack of his bottom.

But I did hold Lawrence. I embraced him often. I held his hand. I talked with him quietly about everything, anything. And I began to know him. He was a talented artist. He drew with dramatic accuracy the black vultures that circled the desert sky. He was a whiz in math, quickly grasping patterns that escaped the understanding of the other children. And Lawrence was a writer. I remember especially his stories about hunting rabbits at dusk. With the skill of a poet, he took his readers to the scene of the kill: We heard the screams of the rabbit and saw the dark blood that pooled beneath the dying animal.

I grew to love Lawrence, and as the weeks passed, the children and I forgot about his problem. Then one day, after lunch, it struck me that Lawrence was part of our circle. Relaxed and comfortable in an old bean–bag chair, he sat with his legs outstretched, his arms folded across his stomach, listening intently to the story I was reading. I'm not sure when it happened, but Lawrence had started using the restroom.

Becoming Literate

by Linda Calahan

Finding My Real Voice

Expressing myself has never been easy. Sometime between childhood and adulthood, I lost the spontaneity of meaningful and honest expression of feelings. Growing up in a household where one's emotions were not to be let loose, explored, or talked about, I soon learned to shove down all the bad feelings far down into my body's inner depths, then stuff tons of food on top to keep them down under control.

Years went by when I did not shed a tear, since I had been told as a child to "shut up or I'll give you something to cry about." I recall many times during my teens when I felt that I would go crazy from all the disturbing feelings that were tumbling around in my body, begging to be heard. There was no one willing to listen, obviously I thought these feelings were unimportant and stupid. I would stuff more food into myself, temporarily relieving the pain. I came to believe that I was an insignificant person.

At an early age I learned to smile and say what I thought people wanted to hear, but as time passed and more feelings went unexpressed, more pain swallowed, I began to experience a lump blocking my throat, choking off my voice, whenever I was put in a conversational setting. I couldn't share myself. I felt what I had to say was boring and trivial.

Abused as a child and teenager, I could never chance exposing what was happening in my life. This caused more denial of feelings. I built a shell around myself to keep feelings inside and the hurt and pain out.

Years went by and I was unable to free myself from this shell. This fear that would overtake me when I was placed in a room with people—parents, family, friends, or strangers—and expected to talk. I always projected the attitude that no one could hurt me, although I was in extreme pain from holding my emotions tightly in control.

Marrying and raising children served as a distraction from my pain for many years, but my inability to show and express my true emotions caused problems in my relationship with my husband and children. Many times when I was alone with my children I would want to have a conversation with them to see how they were feeling about things. Since I had few skills in this area because of my own childhood, I often found myself at a loss for words. I don't think the kids noticed, but I felt uncomfortable and I felt something was wrong with me because of my lack of words. I couldn't understand why the words wouldn't come out. It felt as if there were a tight wire around my throat cutting off everything except my breath.

Parents should be careful when expressing the well-worn phrase that "children should be seen and not heard," because it may truly be the last time that that small voice, with its honest need to express itself, may be heard out loud.

Growing up in my house meant there was never an exchange of conversation. My parents weren't interested in how my day had gone. We never discussed whether the day was good or bad, or if I had learned anything of interest or had met any interesting people. When my family sat at the dinner table, only my father spoke. He would express his anger at his job, would give us our orders for the next day, or criticize what we had done on that particular day. There was no chance for me to experience a normal give-and-take conversation. There was also a great fear of speaking up and saying how I felt. My father had a quick hand that I would feel on my face if I spoke out. It was very restricting and out of those experiences grew my reluctance to express myself, and the feeling that what I thought and felt were wrong and of no importance.

I've found it very difficult to discover and understand many things about myself because I have never had a means to examine my life and feelings. Everything went in and nothing came out.

Presently, I have nothing left to distract me from the emotional turmoil that has left me voiceless for so long. I refuse to let my feelings go unheard; they are screaming to be released from the bondage of my constricted body. How can I free myself from this emotional shackle that was placed on me so early in life? How does one let that inner self out to "test the waters," to check out the safety of exposing one's feelings?

I feel strongly that for my own physical and mental well-being these feelings need to be set free. I went to a therapy group for one and a half years, and the therapist kept telling us to write our feelings down. I could hardly bring myself to write a letter, but my desire to get healthy was so strong that I tried writing. Writing only sporadically, mostly when feeling disturbed, I felt inadequate and this added to my hesitation. As I went further into therapy and as my life seemed to fall apart, I realized my need to seriously write about my feelings. There were many emotions inside of me, fighting to get out.

Finally, I decided to take an evening writing class to increase my writing skills and to see if I had any ability, or if I'd be wasting my time. I soon discovered that a person does not learn how to write, necessarily. It only takes a little courage to be honest and a willingness to put your pen on the paper and let your feelings rush through your arm, down the pen, and onto the paper. It also demands a teacher willing to let you write about what you know best—yourself!

Sometimes I get so excited when I write that my mind is way ahead of my pen. I write furiously not wanting to lose my important thoughts.

This is an exciting time in my life. I have gained self-esteem and self-confidence at a very crucial time. I'm still not a great conversationalist, but through writing I am examining feelings that have been tucked away and kept secret all these years, and I feel a new sense of freedom in mind and body as I put it all down on paper, read it out loud, and share these important pieces of myself with the class as they share their writing and feelings with me.

At last, my inner self has a voice by which to be heard.

"In my life I've had several occupations: wife, mother, hairdresser, and community development worker, and I've owned three businesses. I've always become bored with what I've been doing and have looked for bigger challenges.

In writing, I find the challenges unlimited. There are no boundaries. I doubt I will ever be bored with writing."

From *Voices: New Writers for New Readers* 2(1), Fall 1989.

Linda Calahan attends Invergarry Learning Centre.

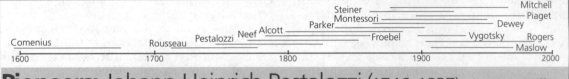

Pioneers: Johann Heinrich Pestalozzi (1746–1827) by Ron Miller

The Swiss humanitarian Pestalozzi accepted Rousseau's idea that "the first impulses of nature are always right," and sought to provide an educational setting where natural development could flourish. In his boarding schools for orphan and pauper children (the most famous of which was at Yverdon from 1805 to 1825), Pestalozzi attempted to provide a loving, nurturing environment for young people. He believed that emotional security is the necessary foundation for any true learning, and said that the task of education is to enable young people to develop their own unique personalities.

Consequently, Pestalozzi discouraged the use of coercion and corporal punishment in his schools and rejected the traditional methods of rote memorization and recitation. He insisted that the teacher begin the educational process with the student's own experience. For the younger child, this meant using real objects from the child's daily life as the starting point of instruction. "Life itself educates," said Pestalozzi. Abstraction and complexity should be achieved only gradually, through the evidence of the child's own senses. This was the heart of Pestalozzi's famous "object method."

Pestalozzi sought to cultivate the balanced development of his students' intellectual abilities, moral sensitivity, emotional life, and physical and manual skills, as well as to prepare them for leading productive lives in society. Education should aim to develop the whole person, not only limited, abstract mental skills.

The work of Pestalozzi has had a far-reaching influence on educational theory and practice. The national school system of Prussia adopted Pestalozzian techniques and thus captured the imagination of many educational reformers in the early 19th century, including Horace Mann and Henry Barnard in the United States. In the 1860s, an education professor named Edward A. Sheldon popularized the "object method" for a new generation of American teachers. As a result, Pestalozzi has been called "the father of modern pedagogy." The modern science of education has largely discarded rote memorization and recitation, and (in most modern nations except South Africa and the United States) has outlawed corporal punishment.

Still, it is mainly the letter, not the spirit, of Pestalozzi's approach that has been applied in modern education. Pestalozzi's own profound respect and love for each individual child—his insistence that emotional security and personal development must be cultivated alongside academic learning—have been practiced more faithfully by the *holistic* educators who have followed him: Friedrich Froebel and Joseph Neef, Bronson Alcott and Francis Parker, and Maria Montessori. In the work of these educators, Pestalozzi's ideas were not reduced to an "object method," but remained intact as a holistic philosophy of education.

Further Reading
Barlow, Thomas A. 1977. *Pestalozzi and American Education*. Boulder, CO: Este Es Press.
Silber, Kate. 1965. *Pestalozzi: The Man and His Work*. 2d ed. London: Routledge & Kegan Paul

Education in Turin: A Romance by Herbert Kohl

Continued from page 33

The Common Schools:
Jonathan's Granddaughter

Jonathan Stokes was surprised and delighted to see his granddaughter Elizabeth spend hours reading and teaching her cousins and younger brothers and sisters. He liked to read her quotes from Benjamin Franklin's book on education, *Proposals Relating to the Education of Youth in Pennsylvania*. One particular quote stuck with her and formed the basis of her teaching when she took charge of the one-room school at Turin in 1828:

> I say that even children are capable of studying nature, for they have eyes and don't want curiosity; they ask questions and love to be informed; and here we need only awaken and keep up in them the desire of learning and knowing, which is natural to all mankind. Besides this study, if it is to be called a study, instead of being painful and tedious, is pleasant and agreeable. . . . it is inconceivable how many things children are capable of, if all the opportunities of instructing them were laid hold of, with which they themselves supply us.

Elizabeth began her work in a small shed behind the print shop/post office. Her one regret was that the four black children in Turin were excluded from the school, but she hoped that when she was older she could do something about that. She was committed to the development of common schools, of free schools for all children. She considered herself liberal and enlightened, and loved to help children learn to read and think for themselves. She felt her main role as a teacher was to develop the spirit of inquiry in her pupils.

As soon as 20 families supported Elizabeth's work, she requested that they build her a schoolhouse. The one-room school was built with donated labor and furniture, and was supported by income from the sale of land set aside by the federal government in Ohio's statehood charter to support public education. The school was, for many people in the community, a symbol that their dream of a democratic society would be realized, through education, by their children and grandchildren.

There was another school in Turin that grew out of one of the fundamentalist churches. As John Clayton, the teacher, put it, "The role of education is to instill respect for the Bible, discipline, and the spirit of hard work." John's school started in the home of his brother, a minister, and then moved to the social hall of the newly constructed church. In 1827, when a school tax of one dollar a year on each household was established, John also asked the parents of the children he served to build a schoolhouse. As was quite common at the time, separate one-room schools were built to serve different parts of the community.

The atmosphere of Elizabeth's school was informal, more like a home than a formal place of learning. She had students who ranged in age from 7 to 16. They learned to help each other and to take responsibility for keeping the school in good repair. Elizabeth read novels to her students and kept them up on local and national political events. Her family was abolitionist, and every year she taught lessons on the evils of slavery. She told her students that she vowed to take in a free black student one day even though the state law prohibited mixed schools.

Elizabeth had been teaching for almost 10 years when something happened that changed her life. In 1836 Calvin Stowe, then a professor at the Western Literary Institute and College of Professional Teachers in Cincinnati, had been sent to study schools in Europe by the Ohio state legislature. Stowe was born in 1802, the year of Ohio's admission into the Union. As Stowe said in his report to the legislature:

> In some of the old communities of central Europe, where it happened to be known that I was born in the same year in which Ohio became a sovereign state, it seemed to be a matter of amusement as well as gratification, that a man who was just as old as the state in which he lived, had come with official authority to inquire respecting the best mode of education for the growing population of his native land; and they remarked that our Governor and Legislators must be very enlightened and highly cultivated men.

The Report on Elementary Public Instruction in Europe was submitted to the Thirty-sixth General Assembly of the State of Ohio on December 19, 1837. Ten thousand copies of the report were printed and distributed to every school district in the state.

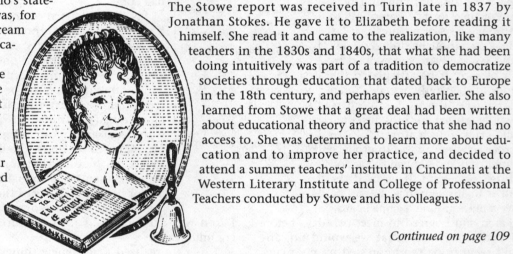

The Stowe report was received in Turin late in 1837 by Jonathan Stokes. He gave it to Elizabeth before reading it himself. She read it and came to the realization, like many teachers in the 1830s and 1840s, that what she had been doing intuitively was part of a tradition to democratize societies through education that dated back to Europe in the 18th century, and perhaps even earlier. She also learned from Stowe that a great deal had been written about educational theory and practice that she had no access to. She was determined to learn more about education and to improve her practice, and decided to attend a summer teachers' institute in Cincinnati at the Western Literary Institute and College of Professional Teachers conducted by Stowe and his colleagues.

Continued on page 109

Resource: Periodical

Understanding Our Gifted

$30/year (6 issues) from:
Snowpeak Publishing
P.O. Box 3489
Littleton, CO 80161
1-303-798-0986

The note under the title of this newsletter reads: "Dedicated to helping gifted children reach their full potential." Most whole language educators take the position that *all* children are gifted. Indeed, many of the educational practices traditionally reserved for the school-sanctioned gifted are good whole language practices to which all children have a right. This is not to deny that some children do have extraordinary abilities that the educational system needs to recognize and support; the newsletter, however, appears to contain very little that doesn't apply to all children. I'm inclined to think that, given the opportunities of the gifted, all children would shine.

LBB

Resource: Book

The Bookfinder: A Guide to Children's Literature About the Needs and Problems of Youth Aged 2–15

Sharon Spredemann Dreyer
Vol. 1: 649 pp.; $54.95 cloth
Vol. 2: 519 pp.; $54.95 cloth
Vol. 3: 703 pp.; $29.95 paper, $64.95 cloth
From:
American Guidance Service, Inc.
Circle Pines, MN 55014

The Bookfinder categorizes 1,031 current children's books according to more than 450 psychological, behavioral, and developmental topics of concern to children and young adolescents, aged 2 through 15. Use it to locate books that might help children cope with the problems of life. Accessible by subject, author, or title, the entries are fully annotated.

Katy Obringer

Resource: Book

Health, Illness, and Disability: A Guide to Books for Children and Young Adults

Pat Azarnoff
1983; 259 pp.; $39.95
New York: R. R. Bowker

This guide describes books on young people's experiences with their bodies and with disabilities, hospitalization, and medical treatments. It categorizes and annotates some 1,000 fiction and nonfiction books for children and youth about health and illness, ability and disability, function and dysfunction of the human body, including abortion, acne, cancer, death, nutrition, retardation, self-esteem, and sexuality. Access is by author's last name, title, or subject. All listings suggest appropriate grade levels.

Katy Obringer

Beyond Behaviorism

Cornerstone: Ronald B. Gillam

A Personal Paradigm Shift

Soon after completing the requirements for a master's degree, I began working as a speech-language specialist in a small school district. At that time, I thought I knew everything I needed to know about normal language development, language learning difficulties, and language teaching.

During my first year of teaching, at an elementary school, the teachers decided to swap classrooms for part of a school day. I reluctantly decided to participate. Karen Dalrymple, a second-grade teacher who didn't seem to have much time for us "special-ed types," was assigned to swap with me.

Unfortunately, the swap was scheduled during the part of the day when I saw Jay, a kindergartner who was the most severe language and articulation-disordered child on my caseload. Jay typically spoke in two- to three-word utterances, and he articulated more than 50 percent of his words incorrectly. He was also a behavior problem.

I knew the hour would be a disaster if I didn't devise detailed plans for Karen to follow. Therefore, I wrote out my lesson plans step by step so the session wouldn't be a waste of time for Jay: Karen was to go through a set of pictures that Jay had been continually drilled on. Jay would say the word represented by each picture. If he articulated the sounds in the word correctly, Karen was to give him a plastic chip. When Jay earned 20 chips, he could put a sticker in a notebook. In another activity, Jay was to produce a sentence that described the action pictured on a card. If he used the word *is* in his sentence, he got to move a piece around a game board.

Karen and I agreed to meet two days before our swap to discuss what we would do. She didn't seem to be too impressed by my plans. Her instructions for me were much less elaborate. Her students were to do a book response. She suggested that after I finish reading, I should encourage the students to talk about the book as a group, have them draw and write a response, and then have them share what they had written. The next morning, I made my first trip ever to the school library to check out a book. Another teacher happened to be there and kindly suggested a book for me to use.

When Karen came to my classroom on the day of the swap, I had the therapy stimulus items ready for her and showed her how to present them so that Jay would stay on-task and respond correctly. Karen, with a children's book in her hand, nodded and assured me that all would go well.

My hour in Karen's classroom flew by. I hardly got a word in during the book discussion. The enthusiasm with which her students went about writing and sharing was surprising. I had planned for the children to draw and write for 10 minutes, but they begged for 20 more. Few students interpreted the story in the same way I had, and all seemed to focus on different elements of the text. At first I tried to explain to them where they had gone wrong. However, they persuaded me to listen carefully to their ideas. As they explained their responses to me, I began to realize that their interpretations of the

Ronald B. Gillam is assistant professor in the Communicative Disorders program at the University of Missouri at Columbia. He teaches courses in language development, language disorders, and literacy instruction for special needs children. Dr. Gillam's research interests include transactions between spoken and written language, literacy development in special needs children, the supervisory process, and applications of whole language teaching with mentally retarded, autistic, cerebral palsied, and deaf children.

story were no less valid than my own. I kept thinking to myself, "How creative normal children are. It's too bad the kids I work with aren't capable of functioning on this level."

During the next couple of days, I couldn't help thinking about the experience I had had in Karen's room. The children in her classroom, unlike the children I worked with, were eager to communicate, enjoyed their classroom activities, and were genuinely interested in learning. I recognized that my approach to teaching was not as successful as it should be. I wanted my students to be eager learners like the students in Karen's classroom, yet I was unsure of talking to her about my questions.

A few days later, I dropped by Karen's room to find out how things had gone with Jay. She confessed that she had not followed my plans. Instead, she and Jay had done a literature lesson very similar to the one I had done in her second-grade class. She showed me the picture Jay had drawn about the story they had read together, she told me what Jay had said about his picture, and she showed me the writing she and Jay had done.

Jay had not acted out once with Karen. He had attended to the story, predicted events, and even asked Karen a couple of questions about content. Jay had been excited about talking about the book and recreating the story with toy people. He had illustrated his picture with detail and, most surprising to me, had used language to tell Karen about his picture that was more complex than I had thought possible for him. Unlike any of the other teachers Jay had worked with, Karen was excited about Jay's potential as a communicator.

I quickly realized Karen knew things about language, communication, and teaching that I didn't. We began to discuss language learning and language education on a regular basis. Karen saw children differently than I did. I was looking for disorders, and saw disabilities. Karen was looking for abilities, and saw learners. I thought language was composed of various subskills, Karen knew language was an inseparable communicative process. I thought communicatively handicapped children needed to be taught language through structure and drill, Karen knew that all children learned language through its functional use.

Karen encouraged me to try whole language. At first I thought, "This stuff may work for normal kids, but language-disordered children are different." As I experimented, I began to see children differently. As I read and discussed the literature with Karen, I moved from a "neobehaviorist" thought collective to a "sociopsycholinguistic" thought collective. With Karen as my guide, I was initiated into a different thought style.

Karen believed her philosophy of learning applied to adults as well as children, and she dealt with me in a manner that was consistent with her whole language teaching philosophy. Even though she knew we had significant philosophical differences, she trusted me as a learner. By simply telling me to read a book to her class,

discuss the book with them, allow the students to respond to the book, and share their responses, she was giving me a general structure to work within that enabled me to see the communicative potentials operating within a whole language setting. Karen trusted that her students would teach me more than I taught them, and she was right!

Karen didn't push me into discovering that whole language strategies enabled language learning to a greater extent than behaviorally based subskill drill. She waited until I had made it clear that I was ready to talk to her about our differences. She described the whole language lesson she had done with Jay, and how he had responded, and then let me draw my own conclusions. Later, she encouraged my development by giving me articles and books to read, and discussing ways that I could apply whole language strategies in my work as a speech and language specialist. Karen continually challenged me to find my own way and supported my explorations.

When we trust each other as learners, empower each other to take educational risks, and create learning experiences that correspond to each other's worlds, we open the door to better communication. And, who knows, maybe a few personal paradigm shifts will result.

→ See: DeLawter, p. 389; Heath, p. 422; Phinney, p. 425.

Further Reading
Fleck, L. 1979. *Genesis and Development of a Scientific Fact.* Chicago: University of Chicago Press.

Further Reading by Ronald B. Gillam
◆ "Development of Print Awareness in Language-disordered Preschoolers," with J. Johnston. *Journal of Speech and Hearing Research* 28, 1985.
◆ "Problem-solving in Supervision Research with Single Subject Design," with C. Strike. In *Clinical Supervision: A Coming of Age, Proceedings of the National Conference on Supervision,* ed. S. Farmer. New Mexico State University, 1987.
◆ "Toward Practical Research Supervision," with C. Strike. In *The Supervisory Process in Speech–Language Pathology and Audiology,* ed. J. Anderson. Little Brown/College Hill, 1988.
◆ "Facilitating Changes in Supervisees' Clinical Behaviors: An Experimental Investigation of Supervisory Effectiveness," with C. S. Roussos and F. Anderson. *Journal of Speech and Hearing Disorders,* in press.

Breakthroughs
by Linda Tsubata

A Late Bloomer

Pi-Ae had attended school for two years and still refused to write anything. During journal time he sat staring at his book, seemingly hoping for some kind of magic to overtake him. His standard excuse was, "I don't know how to write." Quickly I'd reply, "Oh, yes, you can, but you've got to try!" After several months, with much encouragement, Pi-Ae was finally convinced. As if by magic, he began to "scribble" and then quickly progressed to true alphabetic writing and invented spelling. As spring blossomed, so did Pi-Ae. His writing began to make sense. He wrote in simple sentences, and he began to recognize words that he had written. His last journal entry was, "Thank you. I smart now."

Linda Tsubata is an ESL teacher at Kaewai Elementary, Honolulu, HI.

Cornerstone: Sharon Murphy

A Holistic Teacher-Education Program in Special Education: Canadians Lead the Way

Changes Afoot in Special Education

From the lockstep behavioristic approach of task analysis to the perceptually and neurologically based views of learning disabilities, special education has been enamoured with the technologizing of education. This romance between special education, medicine, science, and technology has been pursued in the name of seeking out effective and efficient means to identify and educate both those who cause/experience no difficulty in whole-class instructional settings and those who are special.

However, in recent years, there has been increasing discomfort with both special education diagnosis, which has been described as "a duke's mixture of politics, science fiction, medicine, social work, administrative convenience, and what-not" (Glass 1983, p. 65), and educational practices within the field of special education, which are at best an ad hoc mix. Although the voices of critique are increasing in number (Barton and Tomlinson 1984; Coles 1987; Franklin 1987; Kavale and Forness 1985; Poplin 1984; Sigmon 1987; Tomlinson 1982; Ysseldyke 1987), the move beyond critique toward a provision of alternatives is much slower.

The Emergence of an Alternative

One Canadian university program that offers an alternative is the graduate program in Language and Learning Problems at York University. This program looked fairly traditional when it began in 1981; however, over the course of the past eight years it has moved steadily toward holistic views of special education.

The graduate program drew from the strengths and the holistic philosophical base inherent in the undergraduate program at York:

- A program that has focused on the integration of subject matter, and on the greater community as a social context for learning;
- A curriculum that places emphasis on direct experience, pupil activity, individual interests, and independent learning; and
- A program in which teachers become "less dispensers of curriculum information and more managers of information resources . . . [and] human resources" (Overing 1973, pp. 21–22).

The graduate faculty, building on the strong philosophical and pedagogical base of the undergraduate program, evolved a graduate program "with the areas of academic, interpersonal, and intrapersonal functioning treated in a holistic, integrated, and meaning-based manner" (York University 1989–1990, p. 2). The interest in communication in the undergraduate program sowed the seed of a strong language and literacy-based graduate special education program. The focus on integration of subject matter and on the importance of the pupil in education led to a holistic view of the learner and of the curriculum. The interest in the contexts of learning led not only to a "revaluing" (Goodman 1986) of special learners but an appreciation of the role of situation and context both for instructional interactions in particular and for the field of special education in general.

Sharon Murphy is an assistant professor in the Faculty of Education at York University, Toronto. She has also taught primary and elementary special education and worked as a consultant with the Department of Education in Newfoundland. Sharon's research interests include the analysis of text materials used in classrooms, assessment, and the use of computers in writing.

What Does the Program Look Like?

The program is a M.Ed. in Language and Learning Problems with specializations available in Learning Disabilities and Hearing Impairment.

It continues to provide access to and evaluation of the traditional paradigms within special education while it builds the new. While candidates must take prerequisite courses in Special Education assessment and programming, they must also take courses on the acquisition and function of language and on reading and writing before being admitted to the graduate program. This focus on knowledge of divergent positions in the field of special education is itself a theme that runs throughout the graduate program.

There are only two required courses. The first grounds candidates in the major paradigms in science. It examines how these paradigms impact on the social sciences in general and on their chosen field of specialization. The second provides a choice between quantitative or qualitative research methods depending on the research in the required thesis or project of the student. The rest of the program clusters around and echoes the themes that have been pivotal in the undergraduate program. One strand focuses on the broader historical and social context for learning problems. Another strand focuses on a critical examination of literacy curriculum and assessment. Still another strand focuses on oral and/or alternate communication systems. Special topics courses are available for those who are interested in a specific area within their area of specialization.

One word that is repeated throughout course descriptions is the word *critical*. Part of understanding where special education needs to go comes from investigating and understanding where it has been. This is what the program at York attempts to provide. For instance, testing is critically "re-viewed" as educational decision-making replete with the social, political, economic, and pragmatic considerations that enter into it. An attempt is made to go beyond critique and provide alternatives to the problematic approaches of the past.

The view of educational assessment in reading, writing, and language courses is one in which assessment occurs as part of ongoing classroom activity rather than as isolated and contrived experiences. Neither reading nor writing is reduced to a set of subskills that must be discretely tested. Instead, theoretically driven observation that focuses on whole reading and writing acts becomes the basis for knowledge about students and about strategies to promote learning.

The faculty at York continually reworks both courses and programs to reflect the emerging consensus towards a holistic view. One matter that poses a problem is whether the word *disability* should be in program descriptions. This is a paradoxical issue because, on the one hand, the term attracts the audience that the faculty wants to reach, but at the same time it echoes the reductionistic deficit-orientation that the faculty is trying so hard to avoid. Instead of *Language and Learning Problems*, the phrase *Language and Literacy* has been suggested to describe a doctoral program currently being developed. In any case, we will build on our holistic perspective to create a positive new future in special education.

→ See: Gillam, p. 56; Harlow, p. 51; Meier, p. 50.

References

Barton, L., and S. Tomlinson, eds. 1984. *Special education and social interests.* New York: Nichols.

Coles, G. 1987. *The learning mystique.* New York: Fawcett Columbine.

Franklin, B. M., ed. 1987. *Learning disability: Dissenting essays.* Philadelphia: Falmer.

Glass, G. V. 1983. "Effectiveness of special education." *Policy Studies Review* 2(Spec. 1).

Goodman, K. S. 1986. "Revaluing readers and reading." In *Revaluing troubled readers. Program in language and literacy. Occasional paper 15,* ed. K. S. Goodman, G. Williams, and D. Jack. Tucson: University of Arizona.

Kavale, K., and S. Forness. 1985. "Learning disability and the history of science: Paradigm or paradox?" *Remedial and Special Education* 6(4).

Overing, R. L. R. 1973. "Toward a redefinition of teacher education." *Interchange:* 4 (2–3).

Poplin, M. 1984. "Toward an holistic view of persons with learning disabilities." *Learning Disabilities Quarterly* 7.

Sigmon, S. B. 1987. *Radical analysis of special education: Focus on historical development and learning disabilities.* London: Falmer.

Tomlinson, S. 1982. *A sociology of special education.* London: Routledge & Kegan Paul.

York University. 1989–1990. *Master of education in language and learning problems.* North York, Ontario: Faculty of Graduate Studies and Faculty of Education.

Ysseldyke, J. E. 1987. "Classification of handicapped students." In *Handbook of special education: Research and practice. Vol. 1: Learner characteristics and adaptive education,* ed. M. C. Wang, M. C. Reynolds, and H. J. Walberg.

Further Reading by Sharon Murphy

◆ *Report Card on Basal Readers,* with K. S. Goodman, P. Shannon, and B. Freeman. Richard C. Owen, 1988.

Resource: Publisher

Turman Publishing

200 W. Mercer St.
Seattle, WA 98119
1-206-282-6900

Instructional programs for reluctant teen and young adult readers have typically relied on the worst excesses of language-splintering tactics. To add insult to injury, the materials they use are often first-grade primers or the like. Thank goodness for Turman Publishing, which publishes a variety of high-interest, easy-reading paperbacks and magazines. The content tends to be the stuff of *People* magazine, which only makes good sense. There is no denying that adolescents and young adults love reading breezy feature articles on entertainment and sports stars. They are inherently interesting—I confess that I read the Turman paperback *Cher* cover to cover. To Turman's credit, however, not all of their reading material is based on media fluff. For instance, one of the issues of *Stars* magazine celebrates Black History Week and features solid biographical sketches on such leaders as Nelson Mandela, Maya Angelou, and Jesse Jackson. The Turman novels are written by able professional authors. The only thing I object to in *Stars* is the inclusion of worksheets at the end of each story. The paperbacks are free of these basal-like quizzes.

LBB

Questioning Ability Grouping, Tracking, and Retention

 ## Cornerstone:
Mary Lee Smith and Lorrie A. Shepard

What Doesn't Work: Explaining Policies of Retention in the Early Grades

According to current policy reformers and popular wisdom, children who fail to demonstrate grade-level competence ought to be retained, for their own good and to assure high overall school achievement levels. Children who are unready for first grade ought to be placed in transitions or two-year kindergartens. Available research contradicts these assumptions. Controlled studies show conclusively that children who repeat a grade or are placed in transition programs are worse off, on both achievement and adjustment, than comparable children who were promoted (Shepard and Smith 1989).

The question of effectiveness aside, retention and extra-year programs increase the costs of educating a pupil by 8 percent (assuming the pupil remains in school to graduate)—a cost that runs into the billions nationwide. Such alternatives to retention as tutoring and summer school are both more effective and less costly. Given the large amount of downtime in school, there are more efficient ways of recycling children through the curriculum than making them sit through a second dose of field trips, music programs, and fire drills that are as much a part of a given school year as the curriculum for that grade.

Pupils who are retained pay with a year of their lives. No matter how sensitively teachers and parents handle the retention, the children understand that they are being taken from their age-mates because of some failure. This upsets them and causes them to feel shame, according to Deborah Byrnes and Kaoru Yamamoto (1984), who found that, next to blindness and the death of a parent, children rate the idea of retention as most stressful.

Retention and extra-year programs raise questions of fairness. Males and pupils who are relatively young or small for their grades are more likely than others to be retained (Shepard and Smith 1985). The validity of using such characteristics as criteria for retention is dubious, and doing so assigns pupils to a treatment that offers them no benefit and is potentially harmful.

Clearly, a major contradiction exists between the policies of school reformers and the available evidence. In what follows we explore the nature of this contradiction, drawing on the experience we gained in our own policy study of retention practices and effects in the Boulder, Colorado, school district (Shepard and Smith 1985).

When we studied Boulder, the district had no uniform policy on retention, so each elementary school had fashioned a policy of its own. In some schools, no kindergartners were retained; in others, as many as one-third completed two years in kindergarten before entering first grade. The high-retaining and low-retaining schools were not distinguishable by socioeconomic level, by level of academic ability or achievement, or by ethnic or linguistic composition. Yet something in the traditions of the low-retaining schools permitted them to get along without a practice strongly defended as essential in the high-retaining schools.

Our efforts were directed toward discovering what might account for the differences among the schools and whether any particular advantage was associated with the individual policies that had evolved. The following five issues represent our best explanation for the persistence of the practice of retention and for the wish to expand it, even in the face of research evidence that is overwhelmingly negative.

Teachers' Beliefs About Retention

Teachers in our study tended to exaggerate the perceived benefits of retention. Many believed that retention took children from the bottom of their class to the top of the class into which they were retained. They believed that a retention in the early grades prevented a retention later on, when the stigma attached to retention would be more serious. Neither belief is substantiated by research. Some teachers believed that academic failure, teenage use of drugs, pregnancy, and delinquency were the legacy of children who needed to be retained but were not. Most notable was the claim that retention is free of cost and risk. Under close questioning, none of the teachers could remember a single instance in which a child had been hurt in any way by being retained, a belief clearly at odds with what affected pupils and their parents report.

Teachers generally lack feedback on what happens to their pupils after they move on to other grades. Pupils who did not seem out of place on entering first grade at age seven can later drive themselves to junior high and are sometimes legally eligible to buy alcohol and to be drafted for military service well before it is time to graduate from high school. It is more difficult to keep adults in a public school program, and those who study the dropout problem note that the tendency to drop out prior to graduation is increased for the students who are overage for their grade. "Holding students back a year or more in elementary school increases the probability of dropping out," according to a recent study by Floyd Hammack (1986).

Beliefs About Child Development

From our clinical interviews with kindergarten teachers, we constructed a typology of beliefs about how children develop readiness for school. A sizable proportion of teachers expressed beliefs we labeled "nativist." These teachers viewed development as a physiological unfolding in a series of stages, governed by an internal timetable.

The nativist view holds that the teacher can do little for a child who is unready for school; altering the method of instruction, supplying remedial help, tutoring, and personal guidance are believed to be fruitless. In fact, remediation is thought to be irrelevant and possibly dangerous. As one teacher put it, "If they're not ready, I'm not going to push them, because that would be pushing them out the door." Therefore, the best thing a teacher can do is to "take the pressure off," cut back on instruction, and provide another year to develop by retaining the child or placing him or her in a transition program prior to first grade.

These beliefs contrasted sharply with those of teachers we labeled "remediationists." These teachers viewed all children legally eligible for school as teachable, if they are given enough appropriate opportunities at home and in the classroom. Unlike the nativists, remediationists claimed that they work individually with the "unready" child, arrange for a tutor and remedial work, maintain high expectations, and vary the mode of instruction to meet individual learning styles. "We try everything we can, and

we don't give up on a child," said one such teacher. In the view of the remediationist, labeling a child as unready and marking him or her for retention is "giving up."

Among the teachers we studied, there was an obvious relationship between beliefs about development and the rate of retention in their schools. High-retaining schools were those with nativist teachers. Low-retaining schools had a preponderance of remediationist teachers who looked for alternative means for solving the problem of "unready" pupils.

Schoolwork in Kindergarten

What was once an idyllic time for coloring, singing, reciting numbers and letters, and learning to cope with one's mittens and the class bully has too often become a fast-paced academic experience. Now incorporated into the public schools, kindergartens have fully adapted to public school purposes.

The kindergarten curriculum has become the curriculum of literacy, a purposeful preparation for what comes next. What was once considered the curriculum of first grade—that is, learning readiness—is now the province of kindergarten. Kindergarten as adults remember it is now what makes up preschool programs. According to Evelyn Weber (1986), the downward movement in the school curriculum reflects a new conception of schooling: the purpose of schooling is literacy and numeracy, narrowly defined; the curricular content that will achieve this purpose is known and can be broken down into small units, carefully sequenced, and taught directly; the teaching methods, like the content, are the same for everyone; the cure for educational disadvantage is more and earlier infusion of drill in letters, sounds, and numbers, along with practice in writing.

Although the kind of schooling that derives from this new view may be successful for some pupils, it also results in increased numbers of retentions in the early grades. The logic of these retentions is straightforward: there exists a standard body of knowledge (X); if a child does not master X, he or she must be recycled through X. Or, in nativist language, if a child is not developmentally ready for X, he or she should be held back from X until ready. An alternative view would be to examine X for its philosophical and psychological justification. When a teacher concludes that a child is "not ready for what I have to teach him," that teacher is thinking about the child's psychological characteristics rather than examining the appropriateness of "what I have to teach him." *When the curriculum is taken for granted as correct, the child who does not keep pace is labeled as a failure.*

Parental Pressures

Parents are ever more eager to provide their children with every possible educational advantage, from *in utero* Mozart to better-baby flash cards. Many parents whose children were previously enrolled in preschools with academic curricula or instructed at home have pressured kindergarten teachers to step up the academic pace of their classrooms.

In some schools, parents keep children home who are of legal age for kindergarten but who would be among the youngest in the class. After spending a year in a preschool or at home, these children then enter kindergarten at age six, and they are among the oldest in the class. In the district we studied, parents frankly admitted that they did this to give their children a competitive advantage in school. Teachers applauded this decision and claimed that the district's entrance cutoff date (September 30) was too late. Boys with summer birthdays were not ready for school, they said. One parent recalled that, at the prekindergarten orientation meeting, the school principal had warned them that boys with summer birthdays would almost certainly be retained.

As we have reported elsewhere (Shepard and Smith 1986), the relatively youngest child in a classroom achieves slightly lower than the oldest child. About nine percentile ranks separate the oldest from the youngest on first-grade reading tests. By third grade, the oldest and youngest are indistinguishable. However, if teachers seize upon this small and temporary difference as a sign of failure or immaturity, they may wrongly label a child, withhold instruction that the child might find meaningful, and retain the youngest children.

Moreover, there will always be someone in any class who is youngest and whose parents wish to intervene and provide an advantage. As the kindergarten is increasingly made up of older children, their needs will become the norm for the class as a whole. Older and more educated kindergartners will demonstrate readiness for more advanced instruction in reading. Unfortunately, children whose parents must work or who cannot afford private preschools are not as likely to perform at the same level as their older and more schoolwise classmates. Thus children of working-class or poor families are more likely to be the ones retained, while the children of upwardly mobile families will receive at least a temporary boost. In the district we studied, low-retaining schools resisted parental pressure to increase the academic rigor of the kindergarten as a whole, and they neither encouraged nor discouraged the practice of keeping relatively young children out of kindergarten for a year.

Bureaucratization

Schools are caught in a dilemma of conflicting aims. The desire for education based strictly on merit runs deep in this country. But to be fully merit-based, schools would have to have continuous performance testing, so that a child who successfully demonstrates a predetermined level of competence could proceed through the ranks and graduate at any age. Failure to pass the tests would result in as many recyclings as necessary. As a result, any given classroom would contain pupils of widely varying ages.

The competing value for U.S. schools is the desire for a democratic system of education in which every child would be provided with the best education possible. The promise of American education is to disrupt the stratifications and class distinctions of other nations and of previous generations. Since early research (Borg 1965) on tracking, some 20 years ago, showed that homogeneous ability grouping enhances the achievement of the fast group and retards the achievement of the slower groups, it has been clear that such institutional arrangements that serve meritocratic ends subvert democratic goals. That is, the quality of education for all suffers. Like retention, homogeneous ability grouping helps advantaged groups, creates further barriers for the disadvantaged, and promotes segregation and stratification.

Explaining Versus Justifying

Let us not mince words; we see little justification for retentions or for programs that add a year to a pupil's career in school. The evidence is quite clear and nearly unequivocal that the achievement and adjustment of retained children are no better—and in most instances are worse—than those of comparable children who are promoted. *Retention is one part of the current reform packages that does not work.* Moreover, retention and the practices associated with it are costly both to taxpayers and to the pupils affected. These practices are also inherently discriminatory to boys, poor children, the relatively young, and the relatively small.

Taking our low-retaining schools as models, we can suggest some alternatives to retention: a rejection of nativist beliefs about child development; flexible standards of competence in the primary grades; the delay of testing for purposes of accountability; flexible arrangements that decrease grade isolation; a variety of curricula and the use of instructional practices that take into consideration natural variations in achievement, ability, linguistic competence, and background; and the provision of services that enhance opportunities to learn and prevent failure, such as tutoring, summer school, learning laboratories, guidance services, parent education, and individualized instructions. In particular, teachers in the low-retaining schools taught us about the possibilities of managing heterogeneity without the need to sort, label, track, and retain—all practices that may meet the needs of the system, but fail to address the needs of the students.

➔ See: Dávila de Silva, p. 52.

References

Borg, W. R. 1965. "Ability grouping in the public schools." *Journal of Experimental Education* 34.

Byrnes, D., and K. Yamamoto. 1984. *Grade repetition: Views of parents, teachers, and principals.* Logan, UT: Utah State University, School of Education.

Hammack, F. M. 1986. "Large school systems' dropout reports: An analysis of definitions, procedures, and findings." In *School dropouts: Patterns and policies,* ed. G. Natriello. New York: Teachers College Press.

Shepard, L. A., and M. L. Smith. 1985. *Boulder Valley kindergarten study: Retention practices and retention effects.* Boulder, CO: Boulder Valley Public Schools.

———. 1986. "Synthesis of research on school readiness and kindergarten retention." *Educational Leadership* 44.

———. 1989. *Flunking grades: Research and policies on retention.* Philadelphia: Falmer Press.

Weber, E. 1986. *Ideas influencing early childhood education.* New York: Teachers College Press.

Excerpted from *Phi Delta Kappan,* October 1987.

Book Note

Keeping Track: How Schools Structure Inequality

Jeannie Oakes
1985; 232 pp.;
$10.95 paper/$30 cloth
New Haven, CT:
Yale University Press

This book offers a useful study of the tracking and streaming systems in American high schools. The conclusions must be taken seriously by those involved in the ability group practices in elementary schools as well.

YMG

❝ This book began with the proposition that a serious gap exists between what school people—and parents as well—hope and intend will be accomplished by tracking secondary school students and what actually happens as a result of tracking. The school board member cited in Chapter 1 who defended tracking so vehemently did so because he sincerely believed that tracking was in the best interests of the students in his school district. But as we know from the research it does not appear to be related to either increasing academic achievement or promoting positive attitudes and behaviors. Poor and minority students seem to have suffered most from tracking—and these are the very students on whom so many educational hopes are pinned. If schooling is intended to provide access to economic, political, and social opportunity for those who are so often denied such access, school tracking appears to interfere seriously with this goal. ❞ (p. 191)

Breakthroughs
by Candace Hamilton

Mom, I Can Read

Through an experience with my son Bryan, I have learned how important learning to read is to a young child and how we can crush that desire by what we do in the classroom.

Bryan is in kindergarten this year. The children are divided into two reading groups based on ability.

Bryan and I spend the 30 minutes before bedtime reading and sharing books. This past month his favorite book has been *When Will I Read?* by Miriam Cohen. This book describes a boy in the first grade who is wondering when he will be able to read. The first few times I read the book to him, he asked to hear it again. At the end of the fourth reading, Bryan began to cry and asked me when *he* would be able to read.

I couldn't understand why he was being so emotional, so I asked him what was wrong. He said that at school he was in the "dumb" reading group, and his reading group didn't read like the other group.

I had no idea he was experiencing these feelings, and I really wasn't sure how to respond. I gave him a hug, dried his tears, and helped him get his coat on. When he asked where we were going, I told him we were going for a ride.

I began driving through the business district of town, and I pointed at signs and he would tell me what they said. We played this game for about 15 minutes, when out of the blue Bryan shouted, "Mom, I *can* read!"

I smiled and said, "Yes, you can read." I proceeded to tell him that one day his reading group *would* read stories, but until then he and I could share the joy of reading together!

➔ See: Bell, p. 48; Henrichs, p. 59; Ketch, p. 39; Literature Reference List, p. 429.

Candace Hamilton is a primary teacher at Shepard School, Columbia, MO.

It Shouldn't Happen to Kids
Hitting Bottom

Lee began first grade with the usual enthusiasm of a six-year-old child. School was wonderful. He ran all the way home from school, filled with pride, to tell his parents that he had been placed in the top reading group. As the days passed, Lee was progressively moved downward, and within three weeks hit the bottom reading group. The excitement of school waned; Lee no longer talked about school but there were no outward signals to cause concern for Lee's parents. By second grade Lee had been told that he should not participate in a reading group at all because he could not read. He was made to sit in the back of the class during the reading period. One day, when he was in third grade, Lee's grandmother came to class to pick him up for an appointment. She was astonished to find that Lee was the only child in the room not allowed to read. He was removed from the public schools for good. In a sense, Lee was more fortunate than others who have experienced difficult school situations. He was curious, bright, well loved, and he was discovered. In time, in another school, he regained his self-confidence.

➔ See: Hamilton, p. 59; Meier, p. 50.

—Margaret Henrichs, associate professor, Westminster College, Fulton, MO

Teaching the Hearing Impaired

Breakthroughs

by Susan Ohanian

Love, Leslie

Leslie and I started third grade together. I arrived from 10 years of teaching seventh-graders. She arrived carrying a hastily scrawled note from the secretary, "Leslie is deaf. We are trying to get her folder." My colleagues and I held a minicaucus in the hallway: "Can she hear at all? Can she speak? Do you know what to do?"

Of course we had a right to be angry and the Special Ed supervisor would soon know it, but I smiled and said, "Welcome to our class." Leslie stared at me, her face solemn. A tear ran down her cheek. She put her head down on her desk and didn't look up for an hour.

Leslie didn't say a word to me or the other children for two days. I soon discovered, however, that she and I could communicate. I gave everybody a small spiral notebook with a welcoming note inside. My note to Leslie, like the others, explained that I would write her every day and I hoped she would write me back every day. Leslie read my note and suddenly her solemn little face broke into a wide grin. She grabbed a pencil and wrote:

Dear Mrs. O,
Thank you thank you thank you for writing to me. I will write you every day. I will write you 2 times a day. I will write you 10 times a day.
Good bye.

That note cheered me up. Not only could she read, she could write with a real voice, and she liked repetition and exaggeration. I put a copy of *Pinkerton, Behave!* on her desk along with my next note, saying, "You write like Steven Kellogg, so I think you will like his book."

Leslie was thrilled, showing my note to Dougie, whose desk was next to hers—her first attempt to communicate with another child. "Wow! Can I have that book when you finish, Leslie?" he asked. Leslie grinned and nodded. So now we knew some more important things: Leslie could lip-read, and she was willing to reach out to other children.

Suddenly I realized that no expert was going to step forward and tell me what I needed to know about Leslie. I remembered what Ned O'Gorman wrote in his lovely little book *The Wilderness and the Laurel Tree*, "A teacher will learn about children by watching them first of all; not by reading about them or talking to experts about them." I resolved to watch Leslie and base my plans on what I saw.

In her next note Leslie wrote, "Thank you for that funny dog book. It is a nice story and I love the pictures but I like cats better. Do you have any cat stories?"

Now the kid was talking my language. Asking me for cat stories is definitely carrying coals to Newcastle.

Long before Leslie's special equipment arrived, a microphone for me and a receiver for her, we knew she could talk. During that first week, I wrote her a note about my cats and she responded with a note about her cats. I looked up from her note and asked, "What are your cats' names?" Leslie told me.

"Leslie can talk!" exclaimed Dougie.

"Of course I can talk!" Leslie was indignant. "What did you think?" There was a moment of silence as we all stared at her. I hugged her. "We weren't sure. You've been here two days, and you haven't said a word."

Susan Ohanian first refused to use the basal reader in 1969 and since then has written letters and read books with students in grades one through fourteen. She has authored several hundred articles on teaching and learning for leading journals, and she contributes to the Vital Signs *annual volume (Heinemann, Boynton/Cook), bringing together reading and writing. Currently teaching part time, Susan is an active lecturer and freelance writer.*

"I was scared," she whispered. "I'm handicapped and I've never done this before. And besides, I didn't know if you could understand the way deaf people talk." This was a litany Leslie repeated all year long whenever she faced something new. She cried, stamped her foot, and wailed, "I'm handicapped."

Leslie was spoiled, overprotected; she cried a lot. She was also brave, determined, exuberant, strong-willed, loving; she laughed a lot. I spent a lot of time hugging her, wiping her tears, finding special books to delight her, writing her notes. And she wrote back. Neither of us missed a day.

Dear Mrs. O,
Thank you for showing me that new book. I love pretty books. Even if I don't read them I still love them.

Dear Mrs. O.
Rumpelstiltskin makes me so happy I get goose bumps.

Dear Mrs. O.
I love you so so so so much. Millions and billions and trillions and super de dooper.

Like her classmates, Leslie sprinkled her notes with snippets from books she loved. This one is quite an accomplishment: Leslie has squeezed in allusions to e. e. cummings, Wanda Gag, and Dr. Seuss.

Leslie taught me important lessons about handicaps and bravery and kids' ability to stick together and help one another. And Leslie showed me that unlike most writing assignments that are completed and then forgotten, personal notes live forever.

When Leslie and her classmates couldn't think of anything to say, they'd go back through the spiral bound notebooks, rereading old notes, trying to find something they could use as a springboard for new communication. They loved to look back and count all the notes they'd written, and then report their findings in very large letters, "THIS IS THE 85th NOTE I'VE WRITTEN YOU!!!!!!!!!!!"

I like to reread notes too. There's no way that Leslie would part with her notebook in June. "It's my souvenir of third grade!" she announced. But she lent it to me to photocopy, and it's my souvenir too.

Dear Leslie,
My cat begged and begged for turkey for dinner. So I gave him some. I hate to see a cat cry.

Dear Mrs. O,
I love it when your cat cries. I laugh a lot. Goodbye.

Dear Leslie,
I love it when you laugh. When you laugh, you are beautiful.

Dear Mrs. O,
I know you think I'm beautiful. My pop does too. My pop says I'm beautiful and my mom says I'm beautiful and I am happy. My mom and me love you. Jesus loves you too.

Even more lovely to behold was the way the benefits of letter-writing moved outward from the teacher's desk. One day Leslie, who was very proud of her artistic talents, drew a beautiful picture on the board. Carol, participating in a math contest nearby, accidentally erased Leslie's picture. Leslie had hysterics, and nobody could have hysterics the way Leslie could.

Carol felt unhappy she had caused the crisis but soon became aggrieved at all the fuss. After Leslie ran out of sobs and sighs, she buried her head in her arms on her desk. After half an hour of this, Carol wrote a note to Leslie:

Dear Leslie,
I am sorry I erased your picture. It was a nice one. I like you and I like the way you draw and I want to still be your friend.

Carol folded this note up into a tiny square and made an envelope for it, which she then sealed shut with half the tape in my dispenser. Then she pushed the note under Leslie's elbow.

Of course Leslie couldn't resist it and soon became engrossed in getting all that tape off the envelope. She was thrilled with the note—showed it to me and immediately started a reply:

Dear Carol,
It's OK. I want to be your friend still. You can come to my birthday party. Don't worry. Your friend, Leslie, LOVE.

These children were no more than two feet away from each other during the crisis. They never exchanged a spoken word but settled their differences and soothed their wounds through the note exchange.

One dismal day during my annual February panic, when bureaucratic nonsense combined with the conviction that winter would never end and that I hadn't taught the kids a thing, Leslie hugged me as she left the room. Very earnestly she said, "Now don't you worry. It's OK. We're going to get it. You are doing a good job." And her note that day recounted a new adventure with her cat. She added, "P.S. A lot of people love you."

When, in November, Leslie's parents began to panic, fearing that "regular" school was too difficult for her, when they wanted to put her back in a sheltered environment for the handicapped, I fought against it. I used her notes as proof of her ability to cope and even triumph in public school. In June, Leslie's mother wrote me a lovely thank-you letter. In it, she said, "I was going to phone you, but Leslie insisted that I write. She said if I write it down you will know that I really mean it, that when you really care about a person you write them a letter."

Leslie still writes. In the spring before she graduated from eighth grade, she wrote to tell me she was in a regular program and on the honor roll. She said she owed her academic success to me and to Jesus. I gladly accept my half of the credit because I'm the one who taught her knock-knock jokes. But that's another story. . . .

→ See: Literature Reference List, p. 429; Ohanian, p. 176.

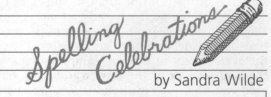

Spelling Celebrations

by Sandra Wilde

Patterns and Strategies: Placeholder Spellings

One day I was in the CHIEKCSEROS (circus).
Elaine, 4th grade

Elaine wrote many unusual spellings like this that didn't seem to be even very good invented spellings. Is this a sign of a learning disability or a visual/perceptual problem? Educators are often too quick to conclude that there are medical reasons for problems that can be explained far more simply. In Elaine's case, she explained to us that she wrote unusual spellings when she was in a hurry and wanted to focus on what she was saying rather than how she was spelling the words. When she took the time to attempt a *real* invented spelling (i.e., an attempt at representing the word accurately), she did much better. The moral is: When in doubt, ask the writer where the spelling came from.

Classroom Demonstrations
by Nancy L. Kelly

A Total Communication Class for the Profoundly Deaf

Standard reading tests show that deaf children rarely exceed fifth-grade reading levels by the time they leave school (Quigley, Russell, and Powers 1977). Wood et al. (1986) ask, "Why, after years of dedicated teaching, do so many deaf children leave school essentially illiterate, with lower educational achievements than hearing children and unable to understand or communicate with hearing people?"

I am the teacher in a total communication classroom for profoundly deaf kindergarten students. Even though my students use manual communication and are delayed three to four years in their receptive and expressive speech and language, I will not accept for them a future as illiterate adults. I know a whole language classroom will allow my students to read and write with success.

In *Back to Basics: How to Help Your Child Become a Success in School*, Hollingsworth, Templeton, and Johns (1986) say ". . . young children surrounded with written language will learn to write." In an effort to surround my students with print I did the following:

1. I printed and posted signs labeling objects such as desk, sink, refrigerator, toys, table, chairs, pencils, crayons, blocks.
2. Above the table with the auditory training equipment, I wrote a simple list of rules for testing and replacing hearing aid batteries.
3. On the bulletin board are calendars, poems, notes to and from other teachers, the class schedule, and the lunch menu.
4. On a corner of my desk I placed a small box, which contains the forms for absentees and the lunch count. On the outside of the box is a list of instructions for filling out these forms.
5. There is a table with a telephone and an old telephone book. Also a small telephone book made using the phone design from the Ellison Letter machine, which has the names and phone numbers of the students, teachers, and classmates. Above the phone is also a list of names and phone numbers.
6. A special board made from laminated poster board and labeled WE ARE WRITERS is on the wall in front of the students' desks. There is a picture of each of the three students with pictures and writing they have given me underneath.

Daily Discussions and Chart Writing

I usually begin the day with class discussions. The children tell me about what they had for breakfast, about the weather, about something that happened on the way to school, or about whatever is of immediate interest to them, such as a fight on the playground. After the discussion I ask them what they shared, and I write it down. For example, Neville said, "Me bike new blue black fun." Vanessa's first dictation was "Me Mama truck school." Julie's was "Howard me went ice cream Baskin-Robbins Howard chocolate me white Mama Daddy no like ice cream."

Although the children could reread their dictations because it was their language, I decided to expand on their utterances to make them more like English. If Neville said, "Me clothes new Mama buy," I would write "Mama bought me new clothes." I would go over the sentences with the kids and show them the words they didn't know. They have difficulty with inflectional endings such as past tense, plural, possessive, and *-ing*. I always show them how to sign using these inflectional endings. They are still able to read my expanded versions of their sentences as fluently as their own language.

Writing

"Much of the language play that is so beneficial to hearing children can be done by deaf children through writing" (Ewoldt 1985).

I began encouraging my students to write by buying each of them colorful spiral notebooks to use as journals. The first day, I let them choose their favorite color and gave them new pencils on which is marked the sign for "I Love You." We talked about writing in our journals. I told them they can pretend to write anything or they can just draw a picture.

In two weeks, the children began to do their own writing about their own ideas. One of the early writing attempts by Neville was to rearrange the letters of his name over and over in a variety of ways. He is making use of the generative principle as described by Clay (cited in Ewoldt 1985). Neville has begun to understand that the same components of his name can be rearranged to form new "words." Throughout his journal he continues to copy words from around the room, the alphabet, the days of the week, and the lunch menu.

Julie wouldn't attempt to write because she "didn't know how to spell the words." She copied words from around the room, wrote the words that she knew from her environment, such as Mom, Dad, McDonald's, Kmart, car, and truck. One day she wanted to write Kmart and asked me how to spell it. I told her to try it herself. She wrote "Kay Mart." She kept saying that it wasn't right. That night she pleaded with her parents to take her to Kmart. The next day she came to school and corrected her spelling!

Our next adventure in writing was letter-writing. Every morning I wrote short notes and letters to the students. Soon they were all scribbling notes and drawing pictures to mail to me and each other. One day each of us received a letter from Neville. On mine he wrote at the top "Mrs. Kelly" and at the bottom "Love Neville." In the middle of the page he pasted a picture of a necklace cut out from his mother's Avon catalog. He told me that was my present for next Christmas. The other students received similar letters.

My class frequently receives gifts from charitable organizations. The students usually copy a thank-you letter. When they each received a ceramic bunny candy dish filled with Easter candy, they decided to write their own letter. They each cut out an Easter figure—a bunny, an egg, and a basket—and wrote their own letters. Julie wrote, "I love you thank you candy Love Julie." Vanessa wrote, "Candy thank you Vanessa." Neville wrote, "Neville candy love." They are not content to copy my letters anymore!

One of the morning rituals in our class is to fill out the absentee and lunch slips. Vanessa would peer over my shoulder as I marked the roll book, count hot lunches, and fill out the forms. Two weeks later she said, "Me do myself." I showed her how to mark if anyone was absent and fill in their names on the line. She then went to each student and asked, "Hot lunch?" She counted on her fingers and wrote down the number on the form.

After I return from an absence due to illness, I always have a special treat waiting for me. There is usually a stack of "Get Well" and "I love you" notes. Once Julie decided to raid her mom's "Get Well" cards and wrote one for me. On the blank side of the card she wrote,

> For
> You
> From Julie
> Nancy
> Kelly
> Daddy
> Love
> Me

She was so proud of herself and asked me to put it on the WE ARE WRITERS bulletin board.

One day during free play, the students wanted to play restaurant. They took a piece of red construction paper and cut out a big M to represent McDonald's. They set up a table and chairs, made a little notepad by stapling scraps of paper together, and a menu from a piece of folded construction paper with pictures of food cut from magazines on the inside. They took turns being the waiter/waitress and took orders on their notepad. All of the words were scribble or letter strings. I believe my students know that print can serve a purpose in their lives. They see their writing getting things done for them.

My shiniest moment came one day recently when I told them they could have 10 minutes of free time before lunch to play. All the students grabbed a stuffed animal and their favorite book. They sat in a corner and read uninterrupted the whole 10 minutes. They asked me to wait a minute so they could finish their books when I said it was time to go.

Clearly they are learning to love the world of books and print!

➔ See: Cambourne, p. 17; Holdaway, p. 44.

References
Ewoldt, C. 1985. "A descriptive study of the developing literacy of young hearing impaired children." In *Learning to write and writing to learn*, ed. R. Kretchmer. Washington, DC: Alexander Graham Bell Association for the Deaf.
Hollingsworth, P., S. Templeton, and K. Johns. 1986. *Back to basics: How to help your child become a success in school*. New York: Monard.
Quigley, S. P., W. K. Russell, and D. D. Powers. 1977. *Linguistics and deaf children*. Washington, DC: Alexander Graham Bell Association for the Deaf.
Wood, D., H. Wood, A. Griffiths, and I. Howarth. 1986. *Teaching and talking with deaf children*. Chichester, England: John Wiley.

Nancy L. Kelly is an elementary teacher at Veterans Memorial School, Reno, NV.

Resource: Organization

National Association of the Deaf (NAD)

Membership: $25 (individual)
814 Thayer Ave.
Silver Spring, MD 20910
1-301-587-1788

In its promotional brochure, NAD states that it is "the oldest and largest consumer organization of disabled persons in the United States, with more than 22,000 members and fifty affiliated State Associations. It serves as an advocate for the more than 16 million deaf and hard-of-hearing people in America." Members, deaf and hard-of-hearing adults, parents of deaf and hard-of-hearing children, professionals and students in the field of deafness, get discounts on selected publications and a subscription to both the *NAD Broadcaster* and the *Deaf American*. NAD sponsors a variety of youth and rehabilitation programs, as well as symposiums.

LBB

Teaching the Developmentally Disabled

As Teachers See It

by Virginia Pfannenstiel
& Elizabeth D. Nelms

A Class-Within-a-Class Experience

What influenced my decision to place three high school students labeled moderately mentally handicapped in a basic writing and literature class? What made this experiment possible, and why did it work? How can we instigate programs so that mainstreaming traditionally segregated students is an option? To preface our study, we need to describe the self-contained program in which the three students have been enrolled during their two years at Hickman High School.

It's housed in a public high school and uses the community at large to teach students to work and live independently after graduation. Nineteen students, labeled moderately to severely handicapped with IQs from 19 to 60, work at jobs with trainers providing support, plan and cook meals at an apartment, and coordinate and participate in supervised leisure activities. They bring their experiences back to the classroom for academic instruction involving reading, writing, speaking, and listening. These students are doing exciting things and making great strides, yet they lack recognition from their regular peers; within the building, students with more severe handicaps often feel isolated and removed from the social structure of the high school. It is this exclusion from teenage life that creates feelings of inadequacy that intensify their handicapping condition. The absence of interaction with more capable peers creates a void in language development.

Meet our students: Max, a conversationalist aware of diverse issues and holder of informed opinions; Terry, a quiet student who beams when she talks about her life outside of school; and Pam, who loves reading and writes copious journal entries and letters and notes to friends, neighbors, and teachers. They are being penalized by their labels.

In the self-contained classroom, these three students were participating in reading literature and making progress on their journal responses with teacher guidance. They were writing about and discussing their feelings of segregation. They resented being called retarded in the hallways and felt that they were singled out because they weren't enrolled in any classes outside of Room 206. I had a gnawing concern for their emotional well-being and knew the effect of self-esteem on learning. This led me to mainstream them into a class in which they could read, write, speak, and listen as respected learners of their community.

The first step was the beginning of a great relationship with an English teacher who was willing to take a risk and allow three more learners into her already crowded basic writing and literature class. We discovered that we shared a whole language concept of teaching and that we had a firm theoretical base with which to support our program. Next was her introduction to Max, Pam, and Terry.

—Gennie Pfannenstiel
special education teacher

◆

I first met Gennie's three students when I slipped into their classroom; I wanted to see their school environment. The three students chosen for integration into the regular classroom had attention spans and responses observably higher than their classmates. Max became a super host, very much at home talking with a new friend.

I joined Gennie and the two girls for a book discussion. Pam and Terry were both shy but proudly showed me their reading journals. They both spoke with ducked heads and seemed reticent when I gently asked them to tell me more about their books.

—Beth Nelms
English teacher

Virginia (Gennie) Pfannenstiel is a special education teacher at Hickman High School, Columbia, MO.

Elizabeth D. Nelms is an English teacher at Hickman High School, Columbia, MO.

From Our Dialectical Journal:

September 6

Pam and Terry sat near me in class. Max sat across the room. They all participated independently in the two writing assignments: write to Mrs. Nelms and Ms. Pfannenstiel (1) "what you need to know" and (2) "three places you would rather be than at school." The girls wrote and Max drew a picture. Max and Pam both made spontaneous comments. Afterwards, Mrs. Nelms commented that they seemed to feel comfortable in class. A big part of that was her interest in them as individuals.

—Gennie Pfannenstiel

◆

September 6

I liked the way the students settled into their chosen seats. Terry and Pam snuggled in close, side by side, whereas Max sat commandingly and self-assuredly in the front. Each one seemed at ease as I eagerly sought to read the 30 new faces waiting for me to begin.

—Beth Nelms

◆

September 7

The students were assigned to do snapshot writings—choosing one of the three places they preferred to be (from the previous day) and capturing a picture of themselves in words. They also were to complete a survey. Later they told me they were excited about their new class and said it felt so good to be in a regular class. No one has labeled them in any way. They have the dignity of being members of a regular class.

—Gennie Pfannenstiel

September 8

Pam got irritated today because the students' voices were loud while working in pairs writing snapshots. She started to get uptight, and, based on previous experiences with Pam, I thought she was going to cry. When I asked her if she needed to go somewhere to calm down, she got up and dragged her chair out in the hall. Beth told her to come back in and not worry about the paper—she could take it with her to work on outside of class. Mrs. Nelms uses peers as partners as well. I'm starting to see the beauty of the more capable peer work. I hope my students pull into that collaborative energy.

—Gennie Pfannenstiel

◆

September 8

When I saw Pam's agitated state, I knew immediately she was trying to get herself under control. Later I learned from Gennie about Pam's way of coping with stress. We both saw that in this new situation with peers, Pam would have more impetus to control herself since she didn't want to set herself off from others.

—Beth Nelms

◆

September 19

Gennie and I have kept a watchful eye on the way the students paired into partners. We identified two students who made unkind observations under their breath about the three integrated students. We watched to be sure these two were seated away from the three who might have their feelings hurt by careless comments. A few students became real supporters of the three students. They encouraged them and included them in group activities if the three acted hesitant to join.

Max may not have been able to keep up with the others in reading, but he quickly became recognized as a good listener and an astute thinker. His answers in class were keen and to the point, so that I never hesitated to call on him when he raised his hand. Sometimes he figured things out faster than any other student.

—Beth Nelms

◆

September 20

The students were given an assignment that involved working in pairs. Max didn't have a partner and asked me to be his. Amy said, "Come on, Max, I'll be your partner!" He is so good at answering thought-provoking questions but needs help getting it down on paper. They made a fantastic duo. My prediction is coming true—there are supportive peers in this class.

—Gennie Pfannenstiel

◆

October 17

I have noticed that Max feels free to participate in class discussion. He introduced a rock group to the class and explained that it was an underground group.

—Gennie Pfannenstiel

◆

January 4

Pam cried today in class. Carol quickly took her in the hall to comfort her. She was crying because she said Mark had called her retarded. Mrs. Nelms talked to Mark, and he denied it. In response to Mrs. Nelms's request, Pam wrote what had happened; when she had entered the room Mark had walked in behind her and called her retarded. Later, on the way out of class, Mark said, "Hey, Pam, I don't know what you are talking about." Pam gave him a direct challenging stare until he walked away.

—Gennie Pfannenstiel

◆

January 5

In Art, Charles asked me why she was crying during class. I told him that yesterday she was upset because someone called her retarded. He said, "Yeah, I figured that and that's too bad." I told him the word retarded cuts like a knife to someone who has that label. Interestingly, Charles was one of the few students at the beginning of the school year who sensed a difference in Pam. At first he didn't know quite how to feel. Connections: That's what life is all about, accepting one another.

—Gennie Pfannenstiel

This experience for these three students, and their twenty-some peers and English teacher, has made an incredible impact on their lives; but greater still is the impact it made on me as a special education teacher watching them grow "in the real world." It was their bravery and willingness to try the unknown that gave us all the opportunity to learn more about learning. In one of those glorious spontaneous moments-

Max testified:

I used to be afraid to write. I always asked for help and wouldn't try to write on my own because I couldn't read. Now I just go ahead and try to do the best I can because I'll never learn to read if I don't write by myself. I was nervous when I first took the English class because I didn't want anyone to know I can't read. I was embarrassed to draw pictures when everyone else was writing so I decided I needed to start writing along with drawing my pictures. If you guys want to read, take my advice and don't give up. You have to try to write on your own, even if you don't know how to spell a word, you just write it anyway. That is a hard class but I like it because I get to be with other kids. If other kids see me in their class, they won't make as much fun of me because they won't think I'm just a special ed. kid.

I feel the same way Max does. Being in a regular class makes me feel like I'm a member of a community of teachers. I know that being valued for oneself is a basic human need. I know that acceptance of oneself is what life is all about.

—Gennie Pfannenstiel

◆

The key to our success in this class-within-a-class was the mutual respect we felt as professionals, and the respect we both had for each learner in our community. We thrilled at the learning that took place every day, both in ourselves and in our students.

—Beth Nelms

➜ See: Harlow, p. 51; Meier, p. 50.

WHOLE LANGUAGE CAMERA

A highlight for the children is to make a class scrapbook. Children are allowed to check it out for two nights to share our classroom activities with family and friends. Contributed by Susan Chmiel Schroeder, special education teacher, Sweet Home Schools, Amherst, NY.

Resource: Book

More Notes from a Different Drummer: A Guide to Juvenile Fiction Portraying the Disabled

Barbara H. Baskin and Karen H. Harris
1984; 485 pp.; $39.95
New York: R. R. Bowker

An annotated guide to fiction books for infants to adolescents. Included are chapters that discuss disabled people in contemporary society and the disabled in literature. In addition to being indexed by author, listings are also accessible by title and subjects. A sampling of subject headings include alcohol, anorexia nervosa, asthma, burn victims, cosmetic impairment, dyslexia, neurological impairments, orthopedic impairments, seizures, stuttering, and visual impairments.

Katy Obringer

I Used to Be...But Now I...

I used to worry about perceptual deficits, amblyopia, strabismus, etc.,
But now I realize all students can grow when given choices in what and how they'll come to know.

—Mary Jo Stockbauer

As Teachers See It

There Is No Child Who Can't Learn
by Karen Sabers Dalrymple

Aerin was so confused by print teachers thought she couldn't learn. Yet Aerin would see the word *dad* and say "father," the word *ranch* and say "farm," and she retold a beautiful story by Jane Yolen (1982) entitled "The Dawn Strider". Aerin talked about John Schneider and how he walked through the early morning. Aerin could learn.

Randy couldn't learn, his teachers thought, so they sent him out of the classroom to sit in the hall. Randy knew the exact second each bell would ring, he could remove a stuck key from a lock, he could repair the broken pencil sharpeners, and he could mend people's broken hearts. Randy could learn.

It was rumored about the school that Jay Bee couldn't learn. Yet Jay Bee was morally outraged by the misuse of nuclear energy. He would deliver orations in beautiful language as he tried to alert others to the dangers ahead. Jay Bee could learn.

Mark couldn't learn, and look how oversized he was for his group! Yet, when given time and quiet, Mark constructed a tremendous perpetual motion machine by studying the cover of an *Omni* magazine. Mark could learn.

Margie couldn't learn—she could only move about in her wheelchair, smile, and drool. Why was she in school? Yet Margie managed to forge a note from her parents. Margie could learn.

Every child can learn. We teachers just can't give up on the children. Our expectations and supportive environments make all the difference.

➜ See: Dalrymple, pp. 204, 210, 257, 426; Hamilton, p. 59; Henrichs, p. 59;

Reference
Yolen, J. "The dawn strider," In *Neptune rising*. New York: Atheneum, 1982.

Karen Sabers Dalrymple is a junior high teacher at the Eagle Valley Middle School, Eagle, CO.

Resource: Organization

Recording for the Blind

RECORDING for the BLIND News

20 Roszel Rd.
Princeton, NJ 08540
1-609-452-0606

Recording for the Blind (RFB) is a national, non-profit service organization that provides recorded educational books free on loan to blind and other print-handicapped people. The books range in level from elementary through postgraduate and beyond, and they cover all subjects, from social sciences through philosophy and law to the pure and applied sciences. RFB also provides reference and bibliographic services. If a book is not in the RFB tape library, a borrower can request that it be recorded. The tape of that book then becomes accessible to other borrowers, too. Borrowers pay a one-time only $25 registration fee.

writers

The Hunter
by Torri Vic Larzelere

Ms. Donna Crafts, the special education language arts teacher at Whiteriver Middle School in Whiteriver, AZ, invites her Native American (Apache) students, categorized as mentally handicapped, emotionally disturbed or learning disabled, to write for a class magazine, published monthly.

My Dad, Larry and I and Hutch decided to go hunting at Butterfly Lake on Friday afternoon. We went in my Dad's pick-up truck. All of us had guns. I had a .22 rifle. We loaded our weapons at Butterfly Lake.

The plan was to split up with two people each and circle around, looking for elk or elk tracks. My Dad and me and Hutch and Larry were paired up. Hutch and Larry went one way; my Dad and me went another. It was raining and snowing. After a while we spotted two elks. We sneaked up on them by going behind trees. The elks were eating grass. When we got to them, we shot them. Both were one-shot kills.

They were both big like horses. We called out to Hutch and Larry and told them to back up the truck. We started to put the elks in the truck. First we put the rope around the chest of the elk. Then we wrapped the rope around a tree. We backed up the truck. Larry and me pulled on the rope to help get the elk into the truck. We got both of them in there that way.

We drove home and saw two turkeys crossing the road. Me and Hutch were standing in the back of the truck. We shot both turkeys. Both were Tom Turkeys. It took two shots to kill them. We both jumped off the truck and picked them up. Then we went back home.

We took the turkeys off first. We gave them to my grandma and one to my Dad. We went back to my Dad's house and took off the elk. We started to skin them at the same time. My Dad showed me and Hutch how to skin them. He showed us to skin from the legs up and around. My Dad cut both of them open from the throat to the stomach. Then we had to turn them over to drain the blood. My Dad took out all the guts by himself. We helped a little. We threw the guts away to the dog. Then we started to cut the legs off. We put the legs and the ribs in the house (and the neck, too) so we could eat them later. We cut the rest of them up into little chunks. We saved some of them and gave part of them to my cousin Ernie Crocker.

My grandma, back at her house, was taking all the feathers from the turkey. She takes them out by hand. She washed the turkey next and took the guts out of his body. She heats up the guts (the gizzard, the liver, the heart and the neck). Then she throws it to the dogs so the dog will like it. Then she puts it in the icebox until Thanksgiving.

Happy Thanksgiving!!! I had a good time hunting.

From *Thanksgiving Tales*, stories submitted by Resource Room II, Whiteriver Middle School, November 1988.

Torri Vic Larzelere is a student at the Whiteriver Middle School, Whiteriver, AZ. This was contributed by Barbara Nelson, special education director.

Breakthroughs

by Ron Jones

Never Lost a Game

In the world of *x*'s and *o*'s San Francisco has a basketball team that has never lost a game. Against competition that includes local schools and colleges, the San Francisco police and fire departments, prisons, churches, corporations, and even the Chinese Consulate—San Francisco Special Olympics Basketball Team boasts a record of 135 wins, no defeats, one tie, two arrests, and one conviction. Of course they cheat! I mean what else would you call it when the San Francisco center opens each game by bear-hugging his opposition, and their wheelchair guard has a "talking basketball," and their scorekeeper loves to twist the dials but can't interpret the numbers.

So why do teams keep playing them? Well, part of the answer is the character of the San Francisco team. They have perhaps the world's largest team. On game day they suit up 70 players of all ages, sizes, and disabilities.

San Francisco Special Olympics Basketball Team.

The skill level of these hoopsters is equally varied. Some can shoot from 30 feet and never miss. Others are still waiting for that first swish. Some run with the ball, others cradle it like a baby. And one athlete indicates success by wiggling an eyebrow. Since their "tuxedo-clad" coach also serves as referee, it's not uncommon for one of his players to be given a free throw into a "substitute basket"—the circled arms of a fellow player. Or "time out" will be called so an autistic player can carefully wend his way to a spot on the floor for his "once-in-a-game shot."

This unusual team also has some unusual "secret plays"! In a recent game against a group of jugglers riding six-foot unicycles, the Special Olympics Team countered by bringing out a ladder and dropping the ball through the hoop. And in the annual Police Department game, their secret was a Vanna White look-alike who periodically spun a huge dial to determine the number of free throws against the gawking officers. It also helped to bring out their surprise guest—a 6'10" Masked Player who double-dipped for the home team before vanishing into the night. Of course their most famous trick is the "telephone play." During a tip-off the opposing team is called to a ringing phone while the Special Olympics Team cranks up shots at a defenseless basket. And if that doesn't work, there is the "pizza defense." If things get out of control, Coach Jones and his team invite the opposition out for a pizza!

Perhaps the most captivating and refreshing experience when you play this team is that they cheer for you! In fact they yell every time anyone does anything exciting. It's infectious! When their mascots Hot Dog and Milk Shake start dancing and their conga pep band starts hooping it up, the game is alive with affection—for the game and all who take part.

If you have the impression that these games take on a madcap quality, you are right. Surrounded by surprises and changing rules, the challenging team must create situations that are playful, exciting, and fair. The game becomes a form of improvisational theater in which every performer will hopefully star. In playing "the team that never lost a game," it's important that "everyone wins." A team of high-schoolers accustomed to competition and only one winner might try playing with their weaker hand, skipping on defense, or trying shots they've only dreamed of. For the police it might mean a secret "wedge play" in which they march down the floor protecting their ball carriers; or hefting their children onto their shoulders for a finger roll shoot.

In a game in which the score changes without reason and the home team cheers the visitors, victory can only be measured by feelings. There is the feeling of revelry as you invent a new shot or tickle your opponent or wear a funny hat; and wonderment as "the team that never lost a game" rejoices at your very presence. It's a great feeling being wanted and valued, appreciated and successful. And it's fun to try the unusual; to play with your friends and discover fireworks of diverse talents and personalities; to find sympathy replaced by jubilation and fear of the stranger replaced by friendship and a strange kinship. For just a moment in this game without rules and expectations, there is celebration of life—a feeling that we are all a part of some mystic game; that our differences are acceptable, even valued; that the scorekeeper is turning the dials at random and it doesn't matter.

For this game everyone is invited to play and find success. In this game we all win!

➜ See: Goodman, p. 50.

Ron Jones is the director of the San Francisco Center for the Handicapped, San Francisco, CA.

B-Ball, a book by Ron Jones about the San Francisco Special Olympics Basketball Team, will be published by Bantam in May 1990.

Children who are treated as if they are uneducable almost invariably become uneducable.

WELL-SAID

—Kenneth Clark,
Education Almanac

Resource: Periodicals

Highlights for Children: Fun with a Purpose

$2.95 each; $19.96/year
  (11 issues) from:
2300 W. Fifth Ave.
P.O. Box 269
Columbus, OH 43272-0002
1-614-486-0695

Adults don't get to "do" their magazines—other than using *Newsweek*, *Time*, or the *New Yorker* as a flyswatter, there's not much you can do besides read them. *Highlights for Children* is another story. I can remember "doing" *Highlights* at the doctor's office as a child. It must be one of the oldest children's magazines in existence, and the reason may be all the great games and puzzles it invites kids to do.

LBB

Hidden Pictures Magazine

$2.95 each; $12.97/year
  (6 issues) from:
2300 W. Fifth Ave.
P.O. Box 269
Columbus, OH
43272-0002
1-614-486-0695

Kids never seem to tire of searching a picture for some hidden object. Now there's a whole magazine devoted to hidden pictures. It also offers a variety of puzzles and riddles, some of which are pretty sophisticated and provide an excellent opportunity to talk with children about the diversity and eccentricities of language.

LBB

"To a child,
language
and the world
must be
indivisible."
—Frank Smith
Insult to Intelligence

LYNDA BANKS

Language

Contents

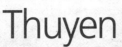

Thuyen

by David Blair

The van pulls up beside Thuyen's billet. As I step out, she comes down the sidewalk, arms stretched out. "Hello, Papa! Please come in!"

Thuyen is 14 years old, a Vietnamese refugee on her way to the United States. She calls me "Papa" perhaps because this is a form of address for older people, perhaps because my daughter, Anna, tutors her at the high school in this refugee camp. I have visited her in her home, and she comes to ours. We took her family to the beach. We'll see them off to the United States tomorrow.

Thuyen reaches out to those around her. She holds your hand. She also talks to you. Thuyen is blind. Language allows her to find out about the world around her, to connect with people. She appreciates the importance of words.

One day, Thuyen visited our office. As Anna took her from desk to desk, she took people's hands and spoke to them—in Tagalog as well as in English! She knows the power of language to open doors.

On our way back from the beach, I paused in Morong and spoke a little Tagalog with someone. "Oh, Papa speak Tagalog!" She took notice of my effort and appreciated it. And tonight, when I visited her, she greeted me and we carried on a short conversation in Tagalog. Thuyen has found that a language foreign to both of us can bring us closer!

While Catherine and Anna roll out the cookie dough, Thuyen sits at our kitchen table. Sometimes she is busy doing things with Anna, but now she is just listening. The banter between her two friends does not escape her. She joins in. She has learned to joke, to initiate and continue a conversation—in this case, a fantasy about stealing Anna's handbag —that engages those around her. We are intrigued. We want to continue the conversation. Through words, Thuyen pulls us all into a group experience where she takes the center.

We have been teaching Thuyen English, and she has been teaching us about language.

➜ See: Boiser, p. 345; Chen, p. 26; Hoyt, p. 214; Kagawa, p. 353; Krashen, p. 86; Urzúa, p. 42.

David Blair is a curriculum specialist at the Philippine Refugee Processing Center, Morong, Bataan, the Philippines.

Whole and Authentic

As I See It:
Kenneth S. Goodman

Language in Personal Knowing

Adapted from *Language and Thinking in School*, 3d ed., by Kenneth S. Goodman, E. Brooks Smith, Robert Meredith, and Yetta M. Goodman (New York: Richard C. Owen, 1987): pp. 97–98, 100–101, 102, 103, 112, 116.

Philosophers Ernst Cassirer and Susanne Langer have been particularly interested in the place of language in personal knowing. Their insights into language and other presentational forms in the symbolic transformation of experience are useful for whole language educators.

Langer (1956, pp. 105, 109) built upon Cassirer's ideas and extended them:

> The transformation of experience into concepts . . . is the motive of language.
>
> For language is much more than a set of symbols. . . . Its forms do not stand alone, like so many monoliths each marking its one isolated grave; but instead, they tend to integrate, to make complex patterns, and thus to point out equally complex relationships in the world, the realm of their meanings. . . .

The transformation of experience into concepts symbolically represented is a personal, humanizing process. In our daily living we respond to most happenings habitually because we come to know them early in life and develop routine reactions to them. Being served eggs for breakfast requires no cognitive or affective reorientation. However, every so often a slightly novel experience comes our way. We must come to terms with it by comparing and contrasting it with the familiar and, finally, by formulating it into a revised and extended version of what we already knew. We may inquire of others, even do some reading, but all the time we are transforming the experience into our own symbols. The process may be slight and only momentary when, for example, we are served an omelet for the first time instead of scrambled eggs. But were we to experience a traditional Japanese breakfast built around fish, a great deal of symbolic processing of fact and feeling would occur before we fully understood and appreciated this experience and could make it our own.

Teachers have a responsibility for fostering personal knowing in their students by developing strategies for evoking personal response to experiences and making symbolic representations of them. Many teachers sense this when they plan discussions before and after field trips or other experiences. In the same sense sharing a book, discussing a play, or reenacting an event extends learning.

Learning, conceived as coming to know through the symbolic transformation and representation of experience, involves three phases of mental activity:

1. *Perceiving* new data in the environment
2. *Ideating* upon the perceptions
3. *Presenting* ideations to oneself and others

Perceiving is that first contact through the eyes, ears, nose, or skin with an object or event that people are drawn to or select from the vast complex that surrounds them. Children stimulate the part of the environment that attracts them at a certain moment. Something from their past experience reaches out and pulls in the object or event for closer view and consideration.

Students looking out a school window at rain coming down may perceive many different happenings, depending on their previous experience with storms, their attitudes toward thunder, or what they were planning to do during recess.

Others may not have noticed the rain at all because they were absorbed in some activity.

All sensory input is organized according to schemas we have formed for our transactions with the physical world. When we have encounters that cannot be assimilated to our existing schemas we often reject them, not seeing them at all, or transform them into something we can assimilate. Otherwise an accommodation occurs in which the schemas themselves must be reconstituted; that is, we literally change the way we view the world. A good curriculum is constantly confronting learners with experiences that they must assimilate or accommodate. The teacher's role is to monitor the ways in which pupils perceive and cope with what they encounter, to push the pupils to examine and consider their perceptions, and to assist in what may be difficult accommodations.

By knowing the pupils' cultures, values, and life experiences, teachers can anticipate students' perceptions and help them build perceptual bridges.

The moment individuals talk and think about what they have perceived, the phase of **ideating** has begun. We must come to terms with what has been perceived. Language, feelings, and cognitive energy come into play as the new "percept" is brought into relation with previous ideas, beliefs, and values built through past experience.

As Langer (1956, p. 32) suggests, this need to transform perceptions of experience into one's own symbols is a

> primary activity of man, like eating, looking or moving about . . . It is the fundamental process of his mind and goes on all the time. Sometimes we are aware of it, sometimes we merely find its results, and realize that certain experiences have passed through our brains and have been digested there.

Language is crucial to the conceptualizing of both words and images perceived. Language frames the thought and imbues it with meaning so that it may be held in memory and used again in interplay with other thoughts. Minor (1964) describes this as an act of "owning" words in which children take possession of the word through a "multiplicity" of their own experiences; the language becomes their personal property.

After conceptualizing an event that they have perceived, people **present** their conceptions back to the world to be tested by others. They announce to themselves and the world that these are their ideas of the situation. In a real sense, the presentational symbols that they construct are their world. They can know no other, and the only way they can make sense of what they know is to present their conceptions for self-reflection or response from others. This is as vital an aspect of knowing as is the need to transform experience into symbols. The media of symbolic representation are language, art, music, dance, film, dramatics, or any combination of them.

Presenting occurs in all the available modes. Indeed, modern social life would be more interesting if people were encouraged to express themselves in the art, music, and dance modes as folk cultures do. Youth, usually outside of school, often use the musical mode to present their ideas. Young musicians improvise raps of social commentary. Puerto Rican children in Spanish Harlem create festive street music on oil drums and tin cans during summer evenings. Children

of the city have always been sidewalk artists while their country cousins have been whittlers and sampler makers. The school curriculum should make good use of the many natural modes of presentation used by children and youth.

The concept of symbolic transformation of experience through perceiving, ideating, and presenting gives new focus and significance to some conventional classroom activities and suggests new instructional strategies to explore. Perceiving, ideating, and presenting overlap and interplay simultaneously, although a delineation of the symbolic transformation of experience into phases can be useful in helping teachers to see the potential for symbolic learning and to construct appropriate teaching strategies for fostering such learning.

Each individual in each generation rediscovers, in part, the world's phenomena and their interrelationships. The excitement of discovery must be maintained as students traverse the conceptual paths. In the words of Whitman, the students "peer," "absorb," and then "translate."

➜ See: Altwerger, p. 295; Cambourne, p. 17; Goodman, p. 13; Short, p. 18; Whitin, p. 21.

References

Langer, S. K. 1956. *Philosophy in a new key*. New York: Mentor Books.

Minor, F. 1964. "A child goes forth: Ideas invite involvement." In *Individualizing instruction*. Washington, DC: ASCD.

Book Note

Language and Thinking in School: A Whole-Language Curriculum, 3d ed.

Kenneth S. Goodman, E. Brooks Smith, Robert Meredith, and Yetta M. Goodman
1987; 418 pp.; $27.95
Katonah, NY: Richard C. Owen

WELL-SAID

The French have a lovely proverb: "The fish will be the last to discover water." When the Institute at Nijmegen was "founded," I presented it with a gift of a seventeenth-century print, a map of the heavens, in the four corners of which are engravings of the observatories at Greenwich, Leiden, Copenhagen, and Padua. It was to wish them good luck in mapping the world of language. That mapping task will be harder than mapping the heavens. The heavens stay put while you are looking at them. Language changes when you think about it. . . . In the end, probably, full linguistic mapping will be impossible. For you cannot exhaust the subject by studying language "just" as a symbol system with its inherent structure—or "just" in any single way. Language is for using, and the uses of language are so varied, so rich, and each use so preemptive a way of life, that to study it is to study the world and, indeed, *all possible worlds*. (p. 176)

—Jerome Bruner

From *In Search of Mind*, by Jerome Bruner (New York: Harper & Row, 1983).

Viewpoint: James Britton

One Stupendous Whole

> All are but parts of one stupendous whole
> Whose body Nature is, and God the soul.
> —Alexander Pope, *Essay on Man*

Whole—a catalogue of the senses of the word as it moved through history would be fascinating. In the day of King James I, as the Authorised Version indicates, it very often described a state of recovery from some disease or accident—"whole again." And long before that, the word was certainly second cousin to that other word *holy*—in fact the *w* of *whole* only appeared, we learn, in the 15th century.

While we do, of course, speak of the wholly destitute and the wholly despicable, there are far more cases of the positive sense of *whole*—whole-hearted, (not half-hearted), wholesome, whole in body and mind, wholly desirable and—much in focus today—*a whole earth policy*. So what of *whole language?*

As a policy for the learning and teaching of language it is, I suggest, a corrective that traditional practices of schooling have necessitated. Infants at home require no such correction: using language is for them first and foremost a means of satisfying their own desires, achieving their own ends, by whatever means—and whatever forms of language—are to hand. And while at first they have only the spoken language at their service, as they begin to make the acquaintance of the written language they are likely to show the same pleasure and the same purposefulness in using it as they have exhibited with respect to speech. There have even been claims from time to time suggesting that infants take over control of language almost as though they had invented it—and indeed that some of the features that characterise adult language have come about as means of enabling infants to make good use of it on early acquaintance.

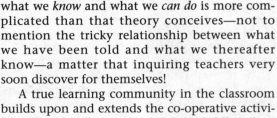

James Britton, M.A., Hon. Lld., emeritus professor of education and previous head of the English Department, Institute of Education, University of London, is a former English teacher in British secondary schools and educational editor to John Murray, Publishers. Director of the Schools Council Writing Research Unit from 1966 to 1972, he was awarded an honorary doctorate in 1977 by the University of Calgary and the David H. Russell Award for Distinguished Research in the teaching of English by the National Council of Teachers of English.

However, when the time comes to go to school, children have, of course, a great deal still to learn in order to become proficient language users—to master the range of modes and registers and styles that are required to meet all the needs of adult private and professional life. There is every reason why they should continue the kind of learning that has stood them in good stead so far: learning by co-operating in enterprises that call upon linguistic abilities—social activities within the classroom community and beyond it—in the family and in the larger community of the neighbourhood.

But the chances are that won't happen. Bruner and Olson (1977, p. 125) pointed out years ago that school practises tend to be governed by what they called "a naive psychology"—a psychology that promoted learning through media—principally language—out of the context of the experiences represented—"book learning" one might say—rather than learning from experience, the kind of active learning that we have come to call hands-on learning. Such a psychology, they state, argues that "the effects of experience can be considered as knowledge, that knowledge is conscious, and that knowledge can be translated into words. Symmetrically,"—and this is where the rub comes!—"words can be translated into knowledge; hence, one can learn, that is *one can acquire knowledge, from being told.*"

To put it at its simplest, the relation between what we *know* and what we *can do* is more complicated than that theory conceives—not to mention the tricky relationship between what we have been told and what we thereafter know—a matter that inquiring teachers very soon discover for themselves!

A true learning community in the classroom builds upon and extends the co-operative activities that characterised an active childhood—a community in which students learn with each other and from each other, with the teacher and from the teacher—by taking part in co-operative activities—many of which will be instigated by the students.

This message goes back over the years to Vygotsky—writing and studying in the USSR in the twenties and early thirties. Human consciousness, he believed, is achieved by the internalisation of shared social behaviour. That is to say, what we learn by talking with and working with other people becomes, in turn, our own modes of thinking and feeling, and what we achieve first in co-operation with someone else provides "experience traces" that empower our own behaviours (Vygotsky 1978, chapter 6). Language, as the medium of social interaction in the many forms of activity involved, clearly plays a crucial role: it will demand active listening and talking, reading and writing and will play its part in those internal monologues and dialogues that constitute our thinking: *whole language* indeed.

A whole language policy in the classroom will not neglect the language that might be described as "poetic." I have visited elementary school classrooms that were models of organised activity—*where space was carefully planned and time rather left to look after itself:* where a child's own initiative was encouraged and where co-operation rather than competition was the climate of the learning. But something was missing: the language of inquiry was much in evidence—enlivening scientific and mathematical speculations and discoveries: but for lack of suitable models and suitable encouragement the voice of poetry was not part of the classroom conversation. In other classrooms I have visited, that voice has spoken in unexpected accents—simply because (one must assume) the speaker knew such contributions to classroom discourse were acceptable:

"I saw a dead lamb and my heart fell upon it" (From Philippa, age eight, Bristol)

"I saw a tree and then I walked away from it for ever" (From a kindergartner, Vancouver)

"Why didn't you try to stay alive? You are gone for good. But you have bought my life, that is fine for me, But I am sad that you died for me, I would have liked to see you around." (From a fourth/fifth grader, Toronto, trying to respond to an Armistice Day poem)

And finally there was from Malcolm, an 11-year old from London:

My Tiger

"Sir, can I have two pieces of paper?"

"Yes, you can, Malcolm. What do you want it for?"

"To do a picture of a tiger, sir."

"All right then, Malcolm."

"It took me two weeks to do that picture, but when he was finished, he was Lord of the Jungle, he was magnificent, Lord of Lords, Master of Masters."

"The way I felt I just could not describe, but it was just the way Mrs. H. [his teacher] felt."

"Well, no one in this world could describe him. He was magnificent."

Whole Language—one stupendous whole!

→ See: Cambourne, p. 17; Dyson, p. 46; Language, the Learner and the School, p. 230; Moll, p. 413; Torbe, p. 232.

References

Bruner, J., and D. Olson. 1977. "Learning through experience and learning through media." In *Media and symbols: The forms of expression, communication and education,* ed. David Olson. *73d Yearbook of the National Society for the Study of Education,* Part I. Chicago: University of Chicago Press.

Vygotsky, L. S. 1978. *Mind in society.* Cambridge: Harvard University Press.

Further Reading by James Britton

◆ *Language and Learning.* Pelican, 1970.
◆ *The Development of Writing Abilities, 11–18,* editor and joint author. Macmillan Educational, 1975.
◆ *Prospect and Retrospect,* ed. G. Pradl. Boynton/Cook, Heinemann, 1982.
◆ *English Teaching: An International Exchange,* ed. with M. Gill, W. Washburn, S. Middleton, M. Torbe, and A. Applebee. Heinemann, 1984.
◆ *Language, the Learner and the School,* with D. Barnes and Mike Torbe. Boynton/Cook, 1989.

 WELL-SAID

In his autobiography, Frederick Douglass tells how his master caught his mistress teaching him the alphabet. The master was enraged. Not only was it against the law to teach a slave to read, but it would make him unmanageable and unfit to be a slave. "From that moment," Douglass says, "I understood the pathway from slavery to freedom. Whilst I was saddened by the thought of losing the aid of my kind mistress, I was gladdened by the invaluable instruction which, by the merest accident, I gained from my master. Though conscious of the difficulty of learning without a teacher, I set out with high hope, and a fixed purpose, at whatever cost of trouble, to learn how to read."

—Cited in Katherine Paterson's "The Secret Life of Katherine Clements Womeldorf"

From Once Upon a Time . . .

📷 **WHOLE LANGUAGE CAMERA**

A mother reads to her four-year-old daughter, Palo Alto, CA

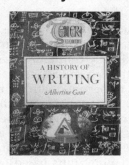

MarvELous INVENTIONS

Short-Changed

Aaron Hood, age seven, thought his tooth was worth $1 rather than the 25¢ left by the tooth fairy. He left this note under the pillow with the quarter because the tooth fairy failed to recognize the true monetary value of his tooth.

—YMG

I wath my tuth Backo

Aaron Hood

[I want my tooth back.]

Book Note

English Teaching: An International Exchange

James Britton, editor
1984; 208 pp.; $16.50
Portsmouth, NH: Heinemann

This thought-provoking look at our profession from around the English-speaking world won't tell you what to do Monday, but it will help you understand why you must do what you do Monday.

If you want to see Freire in action, for example, read the chapter, "'Strangers No More': A Liberatory Literacy Curriculum," which first appeared in *College English.* It describes how community college women in the Bahamas learned to write powerfully about one of their most basic concerns: the role of women in Bahamian society.

The title of one section sums up the effect of the book: "And Gladly Teach." My favorite chapter, an article by Peter Medway, states:

❝ We are responding as if our pupils had been saying, "Talk to us in language we can understand, and give us the chance to use the resources and skills we already possess to make sense of the things you are showing and telling us." The 'linguistic deprivation' to be taken seriously is the one for which we ourselves have been responsible, since denial of the opportunity to talk and write in personal modes is a reduction in the chance to learn. It is in effect a human rights issue. ❞(p 157)

Medway compares this position to earlier demands that the Bible be printed in the vernacular as opposed to Latin, so that the layperson could understand and discuss it.

Mary Kitagawa

Book Note

A History of Writing

Albertine Gaur
1984; out of print
London: The British Library

This is a very readable history, richly illustrated with color and black-and-white reproductions of writing over the full span of the use of writing. Much of the material comes from the British Library and the British Museum. The book takes an anthropological view. It rejects a simplistic view which still is quite common that all writing may be viewed as the evolution of the modern Roman alphabet. Instead it looks at writing in the context of each culture as a means of information storage. Though the book is written for adults, children of all ages would enjoy seeing the wonderful variety of writing systems and materials that have existed all over the world.

KSG

❝ The story of writing is a tale of adventure which spans some twenty thousand years and touches all aspects of human life. It is important in universal, not just in scholarly, terms. ❞ (p. 7)

❝ Many materials were primarily designed for a different purpose and for different use. These are silk, cotton, linen, metal, ostraca (pieces of broken pottery) and various utensils and objects such as swords, glass lamps, bronze vessels, furniture, fans, etc. In terms of information storage, the status of metal, in particular that of bronze, is very similar to that of stone: both guaranteed permanence. The Roman laws are supposed to have been kept on the Capitol, inscribed in bronze. In India and Southeast Asia, where until very recently the main writing material was the highly perishable palm-leaf, important legal documents, especially entitlements to land, were usually engraved on specially fashioned copper plates. Occasionally Jain, Buddhist and Hindu scriptures were accorded similar treatment. ❞ (p. 69)

by Sandra Wilde

Invented Spellings: Meaning Relationships

I was in *EXCELLERATED* classes all the way through school.

Sheila, adult

As adults, we often write words that are part of our oral vocabulary that we assume we know how to spell. If the word is one that we've seen in print and remembered, we may spell it correctly. If we haven't seen the word in print or haven't remembered its spelling, we may still spell it correctly as we use our knowledge about word meanings and analogies to other words. Sometimes we use the same knowledge base and come up with an incorrect but eminently logical spelling. This is what Sheila did here. *EXCELLERATED* classes are for those who excel, right? An important point to remember is that when spellings are constructed out of our knowledge about language rather than just remembered, the spelling is an invented one even if it happens to be correct. Invention refers to the process, not the product.

Resource: Organization

Modern Language Association of America (MLA)

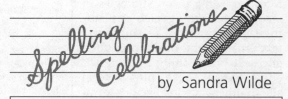

10 Astor Pl.
New York, NY 10003-6891
1-212-614-6317

The MLA is a professional organization primarily for language professors. As evidenced by its cosponsorship of "Responsibilities for Literacy: Communities, Schools, and Workplaces," the second MLA conference on literacy (to be held in Pittsburgh, Pennsylvania, in September 1990), the association has recently extended its interests to literacy. It publishes *PMLA* six times a year and the quarterly *MLA Newsletter,* as well as scholarly books. Subsidiary organizations include the Association of Departments of English, the Association of Departments of Foreign Languages, and the Association of Teachers of Technical Writing.

LBB

by Sandra Wilde

Patterns and Strategies: How Many Ways Could You Spell *Circumference?*

PSOLOKHOEGMPPHOURIADNZ
(circumference)

Ernest Horn, adult

No, Ernest Horn (1929, pp. 47–55) didn't really use this spelling of *circumference,* but he did invent it. In an exploration of the predictability of English spelling, Horn came up with every possible spelling of each phoneme in *circumference* and then figured out how many possible combinations there would be. He came up with nearly a trillion! (Even using only relatively common spellings of each phoneme resulted in 396,900,000 possible spellings.) Of course, in practice not all combinations of spellings can go together, but there is enough unpredictability in the spelling system that every word has at least several reasonable spellings (e.g., *SERCUMPHARANCE* for *circumference*), if you're going mainly by phonetic information. This should make it very clear that "sound-it-out" cannot possibly be an effective spelling strategy! Oh, by the way, *ps* as in *psychology, olo* as in *colonel, kh* as in *khaki, oe* as in *does, gm* as in *diaphragm, pph* as in *sapphire, our* as in *journey, ia* as in *parliament, dn* as in *Wednesday,* and *z* as in *quartz* equals *PSOLOKHOEGMPPHOURIADNZ.*

Reference

Horn, Ernest. 1929. "A source of confusion in spelling." *Journal of Educational Research* 19.

Viewpoint: James Moffett

Whole Language, Whole Learner

Laypeople and many educators may not understand the significance of the term *whole language*. What other kind is there? What is *partial* language? It may be difficult to contrast language wholes and parts unless you're a classroom teacher familiar with the way in which schools atomize a subject into artificial units incarnated in textbooks and tests.

What is now called *whole language* I have always called *whole discourse*. Though not, unfortunately, a common school term, *discourse* has the advantage that one can speak of *a* whole discourse such as a conversation or an improvisation, a poem or an ad, and thus easily contrast some complete speaking or writing act with a mere fragment such as a sentence, word, or syllable.

The traditional curriculum decomposes discourse into parts and enshrines them in teaching and testing units. These units may be based on language elements such as phonics, spelling, vocabulary, and grammar; on rhetorical concepts such as metaphor, coherence, and foreshadowing; or on strategies in reading and writing such as planting topic sentences, teasing out a text's main point, or drawing inferences. It is one thing to acknowledge that all these (plus several zillion others) are involved in learning to discourse. It is quite another to organize the consciousness of learners and teachers around them by making curriculum and testing units out of them.

The whole language approach, as I understand it, never forgets the parts but insists that these are better learned through complete and authentic discourse acts, which are nothing less than the language arts themselves—speaking, listening, reading, and writing. So teaching holistically is teaching directly to the main goals. This is important, because in current ed lingo *direct instruction* refers to drills and the particle approach on the assumption that basic skills are fragments and get learned only by being singled out. But the truly basic skills are thinking and verbalizing, making and taking meaning—the big things.

This means that we should organize curriculum around actual kinds of discourse, so that learning units are, for example, various sorts of made-up stories like fables and tales, or of true stories like memoirs and case histories, or of essays like editorials and reviews. I have spent a great deal of my career trying to illustrate a repertory of actual kinds of discourse, oral and written, practiced in our culture. (See note.) If students constantly practice these various modes of discourse, they will not only master the language arts (becoming culturally literate as a secondary effect), they will also learn the parts of discourse—like spelling, vocabulary, and grammar.

The holistic approach has never come anywhere near being realized even by its most ardent advocates, who have had our hands so full clearing a way for it that we have not fully envisioned how it might best work. Talking, reading, and writing for real, as the vocal and literate community does outside of school, entails radically altering the very processes of schooling. Textbooks and tests will have to go. Students will have to gain far more power in deciding what to read and write and talk about. The holistic approach will not work unless learners become

James Moffett taught English and French for ten years at Phillips Exeter Academy, then spent three years at the Harvard Graduate School of Education as a research associate developing a student-centered curriculum in language arts and English. Moffett was a participant in the Dartmouth Seminar of 1966, a forerunner of the whole language approach. He has served on the faculties of the University of California at Berkeley and San Diego State University, and occasionally teaches at Middlebury College's Bread Loaf School of English.

decision-makers. Such choosing must itself be a major focus of learning, but it cannot be programmed or standardized, only constantly exercised in collaboration with peers and adults.

Schooling will have to become both more personal and more social. Fitting students to the right kind of language activity means that they will be working in different kinds of discourse at the same time, sometimes alone and often with partners. The new curriculum units based on discourse types will not be marched through in unison but experienced in different individual sequences and circumstances. At the same time the very social nature of discourse and of the process approach to learning it, including much feedback and partner decision-making, calls for peer interaction on a scale few teachers are prepared to accommodate.

Successful implementation of a holistic approach will eventually need to override both the curricular division into subject courses, as the movement toward reading and writing across the curriculum has merely hinted at so far, and the segregation of learners by ages, as current efforts at cross-age teaching have barely begun to intimate. Whole language implies a new integration of the total school curriculum, since discourse may be about anything, and content courses are heavily discursive. Content courses also badly need reform in the areas of thinking and inquiry, and would benefit enormously from integration with each other. Math needs to be much more closely coordinated with regular language with which it shares the job of symbolizing the content of the subject courses. Regular language does this qualitatively, mathematical language quantitatively.

Segregating students by age excludes from classrooms the extremely powerful learning force that I call *rippling*, whereby older learners work constantly with younger learners so that every student is both teaching and taught. I'm certain that basic literacy and most else that we try to teach in school could be learned far more effectively if we permitted knowledge to be passed down this way, as it is so effectively, for good or ill, outside of school.

As the whole language movement gains momentum, resistance mobilizes against it. The particle approach enjoys all the advantages of incumbency, despite the obvious failure of isolated skill drills. The holistic approach is expected to "prove itself." Most administrators, industry executives, school board members, and even teachers prefer the particle approach because it is easier to organize (it seems), more profitable commercially (since whole language does not need all the special materials that skills drills need), and more familiar to politicians and the public. But I think that to save schools and hence their own jobs, public educators will have to reform the curriculum drastically. This will necessarily take the direction of integrating both knowledge and the knowers—the language arts with each other, the "subjects" with each other, and the human resources across ages and "ability" groupings.

What makes integration inevitable is that learners must have experiences that make or keep them whole. Students now stumble forlornly among the bits and pieces, baffled by the

arbitrariness of the materials and activities that have been set up for them, until they drop out physically or mentally. What I have always called *student-centered* learning corresponds to what is now called *whole language*. The connection is that once you shift learning focus from the parts of discourse to whole, authentic discourse, you are featuring people, not things—language *users*—and the circumstances within which they exchange speech and texts. Teachers have to know about and work with what goes on within individuals and between individuals and not remain usherettes in a bought curriculum, pretending that language is an external object. Students have to exercise themselves throughout the discourse repertory with a will awakened by the mandate to make decisions and think for themselves in a community set up for maximum practice in speaking, reading, and writing. The functioning of an individual is naturally integrative if it is not confused by the environment. The mind is striving to make sense of experience and put everything together in a way that best allows an individual to survive and thrive. Whole language is for whole people.

➔ See: Edelsky, p. 72; Van Allen, p. 307.

Note: For professional samples see *Points of Departure: An Anthology of Nonfiction* and *Points of View: An Anthology of Short Stories* (New American Library). For student samples from upper elementary through college see the series *Active Voices, I, II, II, IV* (Boynton/Cook and Heinemann). Though now out of print, *Interaction: A Language Arts and Reading Program, K–13* (Houghton Mifflin) is still available in some school systems and contains the fullest illustration at all grades of the whole-discourse repertory.

Further Reading by James Moffett
◆ *Student-Centered Language Arts and Reading, K–13*, 3d ed., with B. J. Wagner. Houghton Mifflin, 1983.
◆ *Teaching the Universe of Discourse.* Boynton/Cook, 1983.
◆ *Coming on Center: Essays in English Education.* Boynton/Cook, 1988.

Resource: Book

Children's Literature in the Reading Program

Children's Literature in the Reading Program

Bernice E. Cullinan, editor
1987; 171 pp.; $18
Newark, DE: International Reading Association

This excellent publication gives helpful teaching ideas for primary, intermediate, and upper grades. It also contains guidelines for enriching children through literature.

Katy Obringer

📷 **WHOLE LANGUAGE CAMERA**

Seventh graders in Sarah Costello's class play "literary jeopardy", quizzing each other on literature references, writers conferencing responses, and library skills, William J. Pistor Middle School, Tucson, Arizona

Book Note

Storm in the Mountains: A Case Study of Censorship, Conflict, and Consciousness

James Moffett
1988; 280 pp.; $12.95
Carbondale and
   Edwardsville, IL: Southern
   Illinois University Press

This fascinating book, written by a major foundational thinker of the whole language movement, examines a textbook censorship incident as the jumping-off point for a meditation on literature and human values. James Moffett is best known as the developer of *Interaction*, a Houghton Mifflin language arts series, which was published in 1973. Based on the principle that readers should be exposed to the entire "universe of discourse," *Interaction* was a series of anthologies of pieces from varied genres of text: literary forms such as memoir, fiction, and drama, as well as books of maps, riddles, comics, and so on. The teacher's manuals were sourcebooks of ideas rather than scripts. Unfortunately, *Interaction* was too different and went out of print.

But while it was still on the market *Interaction*, along with other materials, became the object of the famous Kanawha County, West Virginia, book bannings beginning in 1974, which are the subject of *Storm in the Mountains*. The great value of this book is that Moffett takes his adversaries seriously, in two ways. First, he doesn't condescend to their motivations but appreciates their religious commitment: "I feel closest to the book protesters in their insistence on a spiritual framework." In addition,

however, he takes their objections to books seriously enough to analyze and criticize them in detail, and eventually concludes that he can in no way support or appreciate the values that the book banners uphold.

Storm in the Mountains kept me thinking throughout about what reading and literature are, about parents' rights versus children's right to read, and about education in a multicultural society.

Sandra Wilde

66 'God believes in the beauty of phonics' means that those who see themselves as God's spokespeople prefer phonics, precisely, I think, because it shuts out content by focusing the child on particles of language too small to have any meaning. In other words, what phonics really amounts to for those who are sure they have a corner on God's mind but are very unsure of being able to hold their children's minds is *another way to censor books* (unconsciously, of course) *by nipping literacy itself in the bud.*

"Literacy has from the beginning enabled individuals to liberate themselves by permitting them to bypass the oral culture, the local group, on which they would otherwise have to depend for knowledge. Serfs can bypass masters, merchants the government, Christians the priests, and children their parents. Literacy is dangerous because books bring minds together across the limits of time and space. Books build broader identities. They give access to that planetary perspective so feared by the part of us clinging to lesser group identity. Once literacy supplants or competes with oralcy, we may 'lose our children' to other ways of thinking. 99 (p. 225)

Children's Minds

Margaret Donaldson
1978; 166 pp.; $6.95
New York: Norton

When I first read about Piaget's work, there was one thing that always puzzled me. In experiments in which children were asked to compare parts of a set of objects to the whole set, the phrasing seemed unnecessarily confusing. When children were shown a set of four red and two white flowers and asked whether there were more red flowers or more flowers, they tended to answer that there were more red flowers. Piaget took this as evidence that children could not think about both part and whole simultaneously. But, I thought, what an odd way to phrase the question. In everyday speech, if you asked the question at all, wouldn't you be more likely to say something like, "If somebody asked you how many flowers you had, and then asked you how many red flowers you had, which number would be greater?" Margaret Donaldson had the same idea, and this classic book describes a variety of research that

shows that children's thinking is necessarily embedded in both language and social context. Donaldson makes a persuasive case that both teaching and evaluation of children must be contextualized and related to children's own purposes. *Children's Minds* is an important corrective to some of the oversimplification of Piaget's ideas, which is still all too common.

Sandra Wilde

66 To conclude, then, here is the heart of the matter. By the time they come to school all normal children can show skill as thinkers and language users to a degree which must compel our respect, so long as they are dealing with 'real-life' meaningful situations in which they have purposes and intentions and in which they can recognize and respond to similar purposes and intentions in others. (Sometimes, as in the story context, it is enough that they recognize them in others.) These human intentions are the matrix in which the child's thinking is embedded. They sustain and direct his thoughts and his speech, just as they sustain and direct the thought and the speech of adults—even intellectually sophisticated adults—most of the time. 99 (p. 127)

YOUNG ARTISTS

"Waiting for cookies at the bakery," Rachel Arnow, 6, Palo Alto, CA.

Book Note

Coming on Center: Essays in English Education, 2d ed.

James Moffett
1988; 224 pp.; $13.50
Portsmouth, NH:
   Boynton/Cook

This new edition adds seven new articles to the 1981 edition. The 16 articles center on Moffett's convictions about inner speech and meditation. He describes and demonstrates these with his poetic "Bajan Bestiary" and his analysis of the shortcomings of English teaching. But the essence of his message is to be found in the longest chapter, "Writing, Inner Speech, and Meditation."

Mary Kitagawa

66 Writing and meditating are naturally allied activities. . . . Relating the two by means of a bridging concept, that of inner speech, brings out aspects of all three that can illuminate old educational goals and identify new ones. 99 (p. 90)

66 Why does poetry always precede prose in the history of literature? . . . Because in addition to, or beyond, any symbolization or conveying of meaning, it *summons power.* . . . Perhaps for the very reason that language is learned in an early state of susceptibility and internalizes the world, it evokes, invokes, conduces, induces, vibrates, and resonates. 99 (p. 128)

Teaching the Universe of Discourse

James Moffett
1983; 230 pp.; $14.00
Portsmouth, NH:
   Boynton/Cook

We often say that teachers cannot claim to teach writing unless they write themselves. But teachers cannot claim to plan curricula either unless they consider what the composing process entails. Moffett beautifully describes the range of discourse situations in a couple of hundred pages of deep but pleasant reading.

The spectrum of discourse Moffett outlines ranges from what is happening, such as drama and rhetoric, to what has happened, such as different kinds of narrative, including biography and autobiography. He discusses generalizing and exposition, and also theorizing and logical argumentation. Each kind of discourse is related to the content of language study and the choices the teacher makes in creating and selecting curriculum.

Mary Kitagawa

66 My concern is greater for a curriculum that helps semiliterate, nonverbal types of children than one that fosters the gifted. The very profound relationship that exists between literary and everyday discourse—some of which I hope I have demonstrated in this essay—is such that to work in one is to work in the other. Nearly all the assignments I am recommending have multiple goals. A student who writes a play is learning how to converse, to appreciate an art form, to understand himself, to describe, and, very generally, simply to write. 99 (p. 108)

Authentic Reading/Writing Versus Reading/Writing Exercises

Whole language posits a difference between language in its entirety (language *in use* or whole language) and language fragments (language exercises). Whole language people also believe that learning language (not learning language exercises) offers the best implications for educational practice. Therefore, whole language stresses authentic reading/writing as distinguished from simulations. It urges us all to understand that distinction, to aim for the authentic, to realize that even though conditions (e.g., test giving, mandated districtwide essay contests, teacher fatigue, etc.) may sometimes require exercises, it is absolutely necessary to recognize them as exercises and not to try to fool ourselves into thinking a simulation is the same as the real thing.

Without constant, honest examination of assignments and projects planned by ourselves or with our students, it is easy to see the creative exercise as much better than the usual mind-dulling exercise. It is more interesting, more fun, more engaging—it *is* better. And then because it is better, it is easy to think of it as real. But there is a world of difference between the cutest, cleverest, most creative simulation and real language use.

What we know about language—oral and written—is that it is learned through real use. Real use constitutes language-as-a-whole; and it is real use we must at least *aim* for in classrooms. What must we know to understand the difference, then, between real language *use*—that is, real reading and writing—and reading/writing exercises? Most importantly, we have to know that the subsystems of language—the phonological (or graphic and orthographic), syntactic, semantic, and pragmatic systems for offering cues to meaning—are implicated in distinguishing authentic reading and writing from imitations.

Just because vocal sound can be heard does not mean talk is occurring. Parrots and wind-up "talking" dolls are not talking. Intentionality (part of the pragmatic cuing system) as well as other pragmatic cues are missing, so the noises are not considered talk even if they are well-formed utterances. And just because someone is reciting based on a graphic display or making marks on paper does not mean she or he is reading or writing. Pronouncing words off a flash card is not reading. Cuing systems are missing. While there are graphic, orthographic, and pragmatic cues offered by the flash card, the genre of flash card (a pragmatic cue) does not help one predict syntax or semantics. Neither does putting spelling words in a story constitute writing. Relationships that should obtain among cuing systems are severed or distorted (e.g., the "writer's" purpose—complying with the assignment, displaying competence in spelling—does not fit possible purposes associated with the genre or story such as entertaining, moralizing, soothing, warning.)

What makes something reading or writing is the use of cues from all language subsystems, with those systems working together. Filling in blanks does not make worksheet "writing" a simulation of writing. Job application forms

Carole Edelsky received her Ph.D. from the University of New Mexico in 1974, where her dissertation won the Popejoy Outstanding Dissertation Award. She has been named Distinguished Visiting Professor at New Mexico State University and at Appalachian State University, a Fellow of the Center for Inquiry into Literacy at the University of Pennsylvania, and is currently professor of Curriculum and Instruction at Arizona State University.

require blank-filling too. But if one is filling in an application "for real," then the semantics required by the form (pertaining to past job history, worker qualities) fit the writer's purpose (to get a job); and the spellings (abbreviations) and syntax (deletions) would fit the genre of application form. The purpose of doing a worksheet, however, is to comply with an assignment or to display competence. The semantic cues in that case (possibly pertaining to ducks or farms or airplanes or a myriad of other topics) are no longer related to the pragmatic system. Technically, that is what renders the activity unauthentic. Assigning children tasks that necessarily eliminate cuing systems or distort relationships among cuing systems deprives children of whole language.

Another way of saying this is that it prevents children from *using* language and forces them to merely practice, to simulate use by means of fragments. A fragment can be as small as a letter or as big as a story. Language that is whole can also have that range (putting an initial on a key chain is whole language; so is reading any novel for entertainment). Missing cuing systems fragment language (for example, the spelling demons list offers no syntactic cues to narrow down possible parts of speech, but my grocery list does—it won't contain conjunctions, for instance). Another way of creating a fragment is to sever normally interrelated systems, usually by distorting the influence of the prag-

matic system. Thus, a lengthy school report is still most often a fragment. The content and form (e.g., information on sharks) has nothing to do with the *student's* purpose for writing (to prove one knows how to write reports; to fulfill the assignment); the genre expectations (that the author will inform a readership) are belied by the fact that the chief reader (the teacher) knows more than the author. In other words, dealing with fragments (missing cuing systems, distorted connection among systems) is not real language use, is not real reading or writing, is not whole language. And exercises deal with fragments.

In teaching written language exercises (rather than real written language use), one does not *use* language *with* the learner; one administers it *to* the learner. A telltale sign that one is teaching language exercises rather than language use is the focus of the lesson. With language exercises, the focus is most often on the convention(s) relating to some language point (e.g., spelling or punctuation) or on the language act itself (e.g., reading, pronouncing). With real language use, the focus is most often on what one is *doing* with the language—the ideas being wrestled with, the goal being sought. Reading and writing are like that outside the classroom. They could be like that inside the classroom too, but only if we can clearly distinguish language-use wheat from exercise chaff.

➜ See: Edelsky, p. 19; p. 77; Literature Study: One Classroom, One Session, p. 196; Moffett, p. 70. Writing in a Bilingual Program/Habla Una Vez, p. 87

Further Reading by Carole Edelsky
◆ "Hookin' 'Em in at the Start of School in a Whole Language Classroom," with K. Draper and K. Smith. *Anthropology and Education Quarterly* 14, 1983.
◆ *Writing in a Bilingual Program/Había Una Vez.* Ablex, 1986.
◆ "Whole Language: What's the Difference?" with B. Altwerger and B. Flores. Heinemann, in press)
◆ "One More Critique of Testing—with Two Differences," with S. Harmon. *English Education* 20, 1988.

Classroom Demonstrations
by Jane G. Lambert

Communication Hub: The Message Board

I set up a message board, an idea originated by Carolyn Burke at Indiana University, in my classroom after reading Reta Boyd's article, "The Message Board: Language Comes Alive" (1985). As Boyd points out, the message board serves as a "vehicle for communication," in addition to helping the students develop language fluency for different purposes. I hung a small bulletin board in an area of the classroom most accessible to traffic. I put the title "Message Board" at the top and provided paper, pencils, and thumbtacks at the site. I explained to the students that the message board is an ongoing activity that will give them the opportunity to send and receive personal messages to and from fellow classmates and me. I told them that they could post messages after recess and lunch and when they had extra time during the day.

All of my students got involved with the message board. At first I think they were simply thrilled about the opportunity to write notes, legally, in class. Over time, they began to use this medium as a communication device to convey their concerns, opinions, ideas, compliments, and inquiries. I used the medium to communicate with my students as well, but also to witness the development of writing fluency, particularly among my less proficient writers.

From these messages I developed strategy lessons for highlighting particular problems that recurred in my students' writing.

➜ See: Lambert, p. 151.

Reference
Boyd, R. 1985. "The message board: Language comes alive." In *Whole Language: Theory in use*, ed. J. M. Newman. Portsmouth, NH: Heinemann.

Jane G. Lambert is an elementary teacher at Bell Gardens Intermediate School, Bell Gardens, CA.

📷 **WHOLE LANGUAGE CAMERA**

A student in Sarah Costello's seventh grade class reads his classmates' compositions, posted on the bulletin board, William J. Pistor Middle School, Tucson, AZ.

Resource: Periodical

Written Communication

$28.80/year (4 issues) individual; $76.50/year institutional from:
Sage Publications, Inc.
P.O. Box 5084
Newbury Park, CA 91359
1-805-499-0721

We received a brochure about this new journal, but we haven't seen the journal yet. Have you? Let us know what you think. It's described as a "scholarly journal that publishes application, research, and theory about the written word." The illustrious editorial board, which includes our essayists Anne Haas Dyson and Shirley Brice Heath, tempts us to subscribe.

LBB

As kids see it

Tragedy in China

by Zhenyu Zhu

Zhenyu Zhu is a 13-year-old boy from China. He came to Detroit on January 5, 1989. He wrote this account based on a phone call he made to his grandmother the day after the June 1989 massacre in Tiananmen Square. It was written for our seventh-grade program, the culminating activity of our thematic unit on the struggle for equal rights. Meagan Atkinson, a fellow classmate, helped him edit his original draft.

—Toby Kahn Curry, teacher,
Dewey Center for Urban Education, Detroit, MI

On Sunday morning, June 4, 1989, I called China. My grandmother told me that all Saturday night soldiers killed students, maybe more than one thousand. The soldiers moved from the north of the square to the south of the square, killing students like they were sweeping a floor. When they saw people who disobeyed them they killed them. In just maybe 2 hours the very large square was quiet, not any noise. There were tons of students' bodies in the square. The square became red. The hospital didn't have enough time to clean the square. On Sunday morning my grandmother went to the square. She had permission because she is an officer of Chinese hospitals. She saw a student who wasn't dead. He tried to move his body, but he couldn't move, he just cried. Another student was caught in an explosion. His mother found all of his body except for his left leg.

I am very angry about things. When one student dies he will fall down, but ten or more hungry people will stand. The government can kill thousands of students, but they can't kill all of the Chinese people. The students may die, but people will always remember them. They will be remembered in our minds and in our hearts.

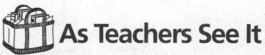

As Teachers See It

My Own Experience

by Alexandra Guerrero

I've wished to learn English since I was a little girl. I started to learn it in elementary school. I did everything the teacher said in order to learn it. I remember sitting in my classroom, repeating whatever the teacher said; at the beginning the alphabet, and then the new words. I remember how boring the homework I had was, to write down every word I learned 30 times. While learning vocabulary, we used to write down the words and then copy the meanings the teacher wrote on the board. To memorize all those words was the lesson for the next day. I remember that back home, sitting at my desk and closing my eyes, I memorized all those new words. I got tired of sitting in that same place, so I used to go outside and memorize all the rest. When I knew all the words, I used to recite them in front of my mom. I tried my best to get the meaning of all of them. When reading something in front of the classroom, I tried not to make mistakes and to pronounce every word the best I could. What a happy day when I got back my homework without any corrections on it, but what a sad day it was when I saw big red circles on my final written exam.

It was something special, my love for learning English, and my goal was to speak it the best that I could. I went into an English language career as soon as I finished high school. After four years of study, I got my degree as an English teacher. I was happy to reach my final goal. Certainly, I learned a lot from the teachers, dictionaries, and books. My parents were happy, but I didn't feel the same way. When I had to talk, I couldn't express myself spontaneously and naturally, whatever came to my mind. I had to think for a moment until I remembered the words that I'd memorized before. I had an empty space inside of me; my goal was not complete. I thought what I really needed was to put in practice everything that I'd learned. In order to have personal and real experiences using the language, I came to the United States. With more experience, I could more naturally express myself. I finally had reached my goal after such a long time.

Now I feel really happy and eager to teach with my knowledge of English and my experience of life in an English-speaking country. I know my students cannot learn the way I learned. They will learn from what they like and from their own personal experiences. I won't force them to learn long lists of new words. I don't want them to memorize what has no meaning for them. They will learn from their own mistakes, and the more they make, the more they will learn. Just give them the freedom to learn and they will.

➜ See: Chen, p. 26; Hoyt, p. 214; Kagawa, p. 353; Krashen, p. 86; Wallace, p. 88.

Alexandra Guerrero is the owner of English Seeds Center, Cuenca, Ecuador.

Marvelous Inventions

PLES DOt toth the WOSPS nast

Or the Wasps!

[Please don't touch the wasps' nest]

—Katie Post, 7, student of Catherine Howard, Ohlone School, Palo Alto, CA

Book Note

Transforming Literacy Instruction

Nancy Leavitt Shanklin and Lynn K. Rhodes
Educational Leadership (March 1989): pp. 59–63

As proponents of whole language, Shanklin and Rhodes developed a school-university collaboration that affected the way reading and writing were taught in the Denver Schools' Chapter 1 program. They established a supportive learning environment for teaching and learning by offering choices in staff development, providing instructional materials, and encouraging risk-taking in instruction. They encouraged teachers to reflect on their teaching and learning. Teachers simulated a whole language classroom to help elementary principals experience whole language instruction and to provide a basis for discussion. Principals were encouraged to learn about whole language so that they could support their staffs.

This article has more meat in it than most textbooks on staff renewal and curricular change. It is a good overview of the process used to bring about change within a school system. A must-read for staff developers.

Lois Mather

Resource: Organization

Language Experience Special Interest Group (LESIG) of the International Reading Association

c/o Rich Healy
Waubonsee Community College
Rte. 47 at Harter Rd.
Sugar Grove, IL 60554
1-708-466-4811

Language experience, the process of capturing children's experiences in print for later use as reading material, is a component of whole language, and here's a group dedicated to promoting its application. In addition to sponsoring an annual meeting held before the International Reading Association conference, LESIG publishes a periodic newsletter and the *Journal of Language Experience*, which serves as a forum for holistic theory and practice.

LBB

As kids see it

The Writer's Journal

by Adam Christopher Pepitone

What's a journal? A journal is a tool that you use when you write. It is a blank book. In it you write memories, stories about people, lists of things you wonder about, and many other things. Authors use journals all the time. They carry them with them. Whenever they see or think of something interesting, they write it down. They look in their journals for ideas.

Adam Christopher Pepitone is a third-grader at Curtis Estabrook School, Brooklyn, NY. This was contributed by his second-grade teacher, Maureen Powell.

Becoming Literate

by Myles Horton with Judith Kohl & Herbert Kohl

Reading to Vote: The Citizenship Schools

Myles Horton founded the Highlander Center in 1932 and worked and lived there until his death in 1990. The Center, located originally in Monteagle, Tennessee, and now in New Market, has been active in labor, civil rights, and environmental struggles for over 55 years. It is one of the central forces in the world for social change through democratic education. This selection is an excerpt from Horton's autobiography, The Long Haul, *written with Judith Kohl and Herbert Kohl and published by Doubleday in 1990. The Citizenship Schools described in the selection succeeded in registering over 50,000 African-Americans for voting in the South in the years immediately preceding the Civil Rights Movement. Many people who participated in the schools, including Septima Clark, Fanny Lou Hamer, and Bernice Robinson, became leaders during the Movement, and Highlander's work in the 1950s laid the infrastructure and helped create the leadership for the struggles of the 1960s.*

In the early 1950s the staff at Highlander made the decision to do something about racism—we were having workshops with black and white people to figure out some answers—but we didn't know how to tackle the problem. . . . At this time Eleanor Roosevelt was looking for people to do unofficial support work for the United Nations, and we thought that might be a way to work with people in other countries. In 1955 we decided to have an exploratory workshop to see how interested people would be in using the United Nations volunteer organizations as a possible basis for relating to other countries. It was a shot in the dark.

As it turned out, we did a lot of analysis in that workshop, but it was analysis of the South, not the United Nations. We had economists there, political scientists, people connected with the United Nations, just trying to find out if there was an interest in the subject. The Highlander board had decided we had to deal with the problem of racism. It was on the basis of attempting to do something about racism that we were exploring these other possibilities and trying to find out from people themselves how we could go about it. We had set ourselves a goal, but we didn't have the slightest idea how to achieve it.

Some of the people who came to the U.N. workshops were from the Sea Islands of South Carolina, a chain running north and south of Charleston down into Georgia—little islands that were populated by the last group of slaves brought over to the United States before slave trading stopped. Many of the people there speak Gullah, a mixture of an African language and English. It's a little difficult to understand at first, but once you listen closely, you can figure it out.

The people who began coming to Highlander from the Sea Islands started talking about their problems. One man, Esau Jenkins, was an enterprising businessman from Johns Island who had a restaurant and a motel, and also ran a bus for people from the island who worked as domestics for the rich folks in Charleston. On the trips back and forth across the bridge, he would try to teach them to read well enough to pass the examination that was required for people to vote in South Carolina. But the trip was only 30 minutes long, too short to do much, and he also discovered that, although a few people had passed the test, some were only memorizing the Constitution and not learning to read at all. Esau said that he wasn't interested in the United Nations, but he was concerned about getting

teachers to help people to read and write, so that they could vote. Another U.N. workshop participant, Septima Clark, got interested in Esau's program. She was a teacher from Charleston, South Carolina, who had taught on Johns Island and knew the situation there.

Now Highlander doesn't initiate programs; we help former students carry out the programs that they themselves ask us to help them with. I went down to Johns Island and was in and out for almost a year trying to figure out how to help Esau. I'd get acquainted by going fishing with the people. I'd spend the night with them, work with them on their farms, and play with their children.

We weren't thinking of it primarily as a literacy program, because teaching people to read and write was only one step toward their becoming citizens and social activists. The immediate goal was getting the right to vote. Becoming literate was only a part of a larger process. We tried to fit literacy into a program that would be clear enough to be effective, and one the people could run themselves.

STATE HISTORICAL SOCIETY OF WISCONSIN

John's Island Citizenship School, 1957. At right, Alice Wine, one of the first people to register for a Citizenship School.

It didn't take long to learn that there was money available for literacy education in South Carolina. In fact, they couldn't spend the money they had. There was federal money and state money, there were literacy teachers on the payroll who hadn't had a student for years, so it wasn't a matter of money or teachers. Obviously we needed to look for something else. Once we put our minds to it, it was easy to find out that all the past efforts at trying to teach the Johns Islanders to read and write were demeaning programs carried on by rather dominating, opinionated teachers who made the students feel so inferior that they didn't want to have anything to do with them. We were looking for the opposite approach, one that would be based on respect and make people feel as comfortable as possible in a new and difficult learning situation.

I knew from the early days of Highlander that you couldn't carry on an educational program with the kinds of people we were interested in working with until you could forget many of the things learned in college and start listening to the people themselves. I was trying to apply this "learning from the people" idea to the residents of the Sea Islands. As I got acquainted with them and acquired more

understanding, it became quite simple. The only reason problems seem complicated is that you don't understand them well enough to make them simple. We needed to determine what the motivation would be, who could best facilitate learning, and what would be the best learning environment.

Then we decided that it would be threatening to people to bring them into a formal classroom. Some unsuccessful literacy programs brought these people into the schools, where their grandchildren went, and made them sit at desks so small that they couldn't get their legs under the tables. The children called the adults "daddy longlegs." We decided to find an old building of some kind where they'd be comfortable and feel at home, and since there was already a cooperative store on the island, we decided to use its back room for the school. We put in a potbellied stove, tables to write on (there were no desks) and some chairs.

Before the first Citizenship School started and the Highlander staff members were working on the idea, I did something that I've found very useful. I pretended that we had already started one of the schools in an informal place, with a nonjudgmental person in charge. The adults were there to learn to read so they could register and vote and perhaps learn other things they might want to know. I could just see these people in my mind's eye in an informal non-school setting. Then I could see somebody who hadn't been a teacher before struggling along learning with them and working with them and drawing them out. I went through the next night and the next, and then I decided the students couldn't take it every night, so they would go twice a week. In almost the same way, I decided the program had to be condensed into a period short enough that they could see an end to it, say, the three-month period between crops, when they would have some leisure time on their hands. I figured out the length of the program primarily on the basis of the crops, not by intellectualizing about learning. . . .

When I thought I had it all worked out in my mind, Esau Jenkins and Septima Clark and I decided it was time to find a "teacher." Septima recommended her niece, Bernice Robinson. She had been to workshops at Highlander and had told us that if she could ever do anything for Highlander to let her know, but when we told her what we had in mind, she said, "Oh no, not that, I'm not a teacher." I told her, "That's exactly why you're going to do this. You know how to listen, and you respect the adults who want to vote."

Bernice was a black beautician. Compared to white beauticians, black beauticians had status in their own community. They had a higher-than-average education and, because they owned their own businesses, didn't depend upon whites for their incomes. We needed to build around black people who could stand up against white opposition, so black beauticians were terribly important.

That's how we started the initial class. Bernice and her 14 students decided to call it a Citizenship School. The first thing Bernice put up on the wall for them eventually to learn to read was the United Nations Declaration of Human Rights. Since we were operating from the basis that these were adults with dignity, it was important to challenge them with something worthy of the attention and concern of an adult. Our objective was to help them understand that they could both play a role at home and help change the world.

Bernice began the first class in the back room of the cooperative store by saying, "I am not a teacher, we are here to learn together. You're going to teach me as much as I'm going to teach you." She had no textbooks or teacher's manuals. Her only materials were the U.N. Declaration of Human Rights, the state constitution and some materials for teaching schoolchildren, which she quickly realized were too juvenile for mature adults.

Bernice and the students developed the curriculum day by day. They learned to write letters, order catalogs, and fill out money orders. They made up stories about the vegetables they grew and the tools they used.

"They tell me a story," Mrs. Robinson told us, "a story which I write down, then they learn to read the story. It's their story in their words, and they are interested because it's theirs." She gave priority to their immediate interests so they could experience the usefulness and joy of learning.

At the beginning there was a problem over pencils. Many of the people in the class were in their sixties, and most of them were used to holding a plow or a hoe, or throwing out a fishing net. When they'd first hold a pencil, nine times out of ten they'd break it. The physical adjustment isn't easy. You could hear those pencils snapping all over the room. We decided right there that no teacher should ever show any concern about pencils, because that would be intimidating, but simply hand students another one and say there're plenty more. Because they had so many other obstacles to overcome, we tried to make unimportant things like that as insignificant as possible.

This first Citizenship School, which met twice a week for three months, grew from 14 to 37 students, and 80 percent of them graduated and got their certificates, that is, they registered to vote. People on the neighboring Edisto Island heard about the Citizenship School students' success in registering to vote and asked if they could also have a school. Although we hadn't thought beyond that first experimental class, we said, "All you have to do is find three people and a teacher. That's all. We'll furnish the pencils." They asked for some help, so Bernice went over and helped them set up their school. What we believed in was starting people on a path of group action. Along with becoming literate, they learned to organize, they learned to protest, they learned to demand their rights, because they also learned that you couldn't just read and write yourself into freedom. You had to fight for that and you had to do it as part of a group, not as an individual.

All the time Highlander was involved in the Citizenship School program, we insisted that, while voter registration was a great goal, voting wouldn't do the job alone. We don't hold with those who say that you mustn't challenge people, that you have to be very cautious and tell them that if they take this first step, they'll win. That's an insulting thing to say to a person. We say, "That's the first step, but it's only the first step. If you're black, white folks aren't going to pay any attention to you even if you can vote. Sure, get in there and vote, but then you've got to demonstrate."

The idea was to stretch people's minds. One way we did that was to bring in visiting black activists from other places in the South to share their experiences with the students. We believed this all had to be done by black people for themselves in order for it to be educationally sound. By the time the Citizenship School students finished their classes, they knew that voting by itself was not enough. Even before the school was over, they'd go to Charleston and demonstrate and make demands that public facilities be opened up for them. These were people who only a short time ago had believed they couldn't do

anything. They felt confident now; they were being challenged; and most of all, they were forcing whites to treat them with respect. . . .

Soon the Citizenship School program started island-hopping. We never brought anybody into that system from the outside. After it started island-hopping, it began to move into other states, and within two years it was growing by the hundreds. It was very spontaneous because it was so simple. Then Highlander was asked to help work out a program to orient more teachers. We found that by bringing 20 potential teachers at a time to Highlander for a residential training program and using Citizenship School teachers to train them, we could use these new recruits to come back the next time as teachers for the next group. They were not only successful in helping people in their own communities learn to read and write and become citizens and learn to protest and demonstrate, but they got the dignity and satisfaction of training other people. Part of their job was to keep the process going.

We finally said, "Look, you don't need to come to Highlander if you're down in Louisiana. Get a place for the class to meet. You can do exactly what we did. You know who the teachers should be. You can do the whole thing yourselves." And so it became a self-perpetuating system. We just mixed in the yeast at the beginning and set the process in motion. With Septima Clark to provide the leadership, the program expanded into Georgia and other parts of the South.

Highlander's chief interest is in starting up programs. Sometimes we start off programs that get people going, and our job is to get out of the way before we are run over. The Citizenship School project eventually became too big for us; in fact, it became bigger than all the rest of Highlander put together. When it gets to that stage, other people can take it over and operate it. Martin Luther King, Jr., whom I met when he was a junior at Morehouse College, asked if we would set up an educational program for the Southern Christian Leadership Conference (SCLC), and I asked him exactly what he wanted. After we talked about it several times, I said, "We've got a ready-made program that you can have. Take the Citizenship School program, it's too big for us." He backed off at first, but then he very meticulously went over the records and the costs and finally decided this was a program he wanted to recommend to his board. SCLC took that program over and we helped set it up. Septima Clark and Andrew Young (who had come to Highlander earlier in the year to work with the program) joined the SCLC staff.

In February of 1961, when we turned the Citizenship Schools program over to SCLC, I gave the following farewell talk to the prospective teachers who were in training at Highlander, the people who would be working on spreading the program throughout the South:

> People learn faster and with more enjoyment when they are involved in a successful struggle for justice that has reached social movement proportions, one that is getting attention and support outside the movement, and it's socially big enough to go far beyond the individuals involved. It's a much bigger experience than anything you've had before as an individual. It's bigger than your organization, and it's qualitatively different, not just more of the same. I want the struggle for social and economic justice to get big and become so dynamic that the atmosphere in which you're working is so charged that sparks are darting around very fast, and they explode and create other sparks, and it's almost perpetual motion. Learning jumps from person to person with no visible explanation of how it happened.

Excerpted from *The Long Haul*, by Myles Horton, with Judith Kohl and Herbert Kohl (New York: Doubleday, 1990): pp. 97–108.

Book Note

The Long Haul: An Autobiography
Myles Horton, with Judith Kohl and Herbert Kohl
1990; 231 pp.; $21.95
New York: Doubleday

Resource: Publisher

Teachers College Press
P.O. Box 2032
Colchester, VT 05449
1-800-445-6638;
(802) 878-0315
(call collect in VT)
FAX (802) 878-1102

Teachers College Press offers some of the best titles available in education today. Of particular interest to whole language educators are Anne Haas Dyson's new book, *Multiple Worlds of Child Writers*, and Catherine Loughlin and Mavis Martin's book, *Supporting Literacy*. In addition, whole language educators won't want to miss a new language and literacy series, which Dorothy Strickland and Celia Genishi are currently editing.
LBB

WHOLE LANGUAGE CAMERA

A junior high student's home away from home, Palo Alto, CA.

Whole Language Internacional
by Roxana Morduchowicz

Argentina: Teaching Freedom of Expression in a New Democracy

For eight years (1976–1983) the people in Argentina lived under a military dictatorship. Nobody in the country could ask any questions. Nobody in the country could give any answers. To talk and to listen were verbs of dangerous conjugation. Few young people studied at the university. Censorship and fear filled the air. People who spoke freely disappeared. Thousands of Argentine people were tortured. Some of them, the minority, were able to return home after being kidnapped by the military regime. Others, the majority, were killed after being tortured. Their bodies never appeared. They are known as *desaparecidos,* the "disappeared people."

For eight years, schoolchildren and old people lived under the same conditions: fear, silence, censorship. The school's front door was locked to ideas, and the problems of the real world could not be discussed.

April 2, 1982, was the beginning of the end for the military regime. The Malvinas war against Britain was their last attempt to stay in power. But the thousand young Argentinians who died were enough to make us understand the meaning of seven years of dictatorship. In 1983 the country awoke from its nightmare. In free elections, the people chose a democratic government, the first in eight years. The time of silence was over.

But people were still afraid. It was hard for everybody to realize that democracy meant more than voting for a president. Almost everybody forgot how democracy worked. Children under eight had never before breathed the air of freedom. Children under 14 had never gone to school in freedom. That year, 1984, those children went to democratic school for the first time.

How could we teach children who had known only authoritarianism that suddenly they lived under democracy and were allowed to speak freely? How could we teach children what democracy meant and what freedom of expression was?

A New Magazine: *Entre todos*

Two months after democracy returned to Argentina, the answer came. Sponsored by the Department of Education, 10-, 11-, and 12-year-old children in 460 public elementary schools in Buenos Aires would be the "journalists" of a monthly publication in which they could write whatever they wished. The new magazine, written by and for the students, would communicate to schools and teach children what freedom of expression means.

In March 1984, I became the journalism teacher working with these children directly in the schools. In a city as large as Buenos Aires, with more than six million people, we decided to begin with one neighborhood, a poor one, where a thousand sixth- and seventh-grade students studied. Once a week, I would work with the students in 10 schools in this school district.

In the beginning, the main goal was to promote free discussion at school. Children had to understand that the new democracy brought freedom of expression to the country and to their own classroom. Journalism classes were planned just to talk about democracy, freedom, everyday life at school, and the new era for Argentina.

The students practiced their new right to speak freely for two months. Then they started to write what they thought. They wrote letters, poems, stories, jokes, games. They wrote about politics and their hopes for democracy. They interviewed the secretary of education and asked him about the past and the future. And they named the magazine *Entre todos* (Among Us All).

In May 1984, the first issue—20 newsweekly-sized pages in color—rolled off the city government's press and went out free to all the children, teachers, and principals in this district.

Entre todos taught them to speak and write without fear and to trust the media again. The magazine also allowed children who did not know each other to communicate: They learned that the world did not consist of just their classroom, school, or street. More than 60 percent of the stories students published during the first year were related to democracy and freedom.

In 1985, with four assistants, the program grew. More schools became involved in this magazine and had journalism classes. By the beginning of 1987, we reached 25,000 students, and journalism is now a subject for the 21 school districts in the city. There are journalism teachers for every district involved in the program. These special teachers work with the students once a week, helping them to write stories, to interview people, to organize surveys, and to discuss everything. We do not work by mail. We want the children to know who the coordinators are, so each of them goes to the school once a week and works directly with the children and their teachers.

The magazine enables the children to see that many children in their big city feel the same things they feel. In that way, they discover Argentine society as a whole, not only their own immediate world. The magazine had a basic goal: to promote free expression and to teach children what democracy means. After eight years of the military regime, the whole society had to wake up. The magazine was an initial step along this path.

The Daily Newspaper

Each of the six newspapers in Buenos Aires has a different bias. The Department of Education signed an agreement with the six of them, and since 1986 every sixth- and seventh-grade student gets a daily newspaper for free every Wednesday. Every week the newspaper is a different one, so that during the year the students get to know all of them.

The teacher uses the newspaper to teach math, language, social studies, and natural sciences based always on reality. Ten years ago a math teacher could say, "If you have 100 candies and you give your friend 75, how many will you have then?" This is not real at all. No child will have 100 candies, and even if he has them, he will never give away 75.

Now the same teacher says: "Look at the classified ads section in the newspaper. Choose a job you would like to have. Find out the salary offered for this job. Then look at the next page in your newspaper and find out how much money you have to pay if you want to rent a two-room apartment. Which percentage of your salary do you have to use to pay the rent?"

In both cases, the teacher teaches math. The difference is that the second situation is related to everyday life.

In the same way, in social studies the chil-dren learn about government issues, the congress, politics, international conflicts, new laws, and the economy. And in natural science students must learn to understand the nuclear era, hunger, lack of housing, pollution, the country's natural resources, drugs, and sex education.

The Department of Education hired more than 15 coordinators for this program. Each works with one school district. The coordinator advises every sixth- and seventh-grade teacher in the district. The coordinator goes to every school in the district once a week, just to talk with the teachers and ask them about the program: the ways in which they use the newspaper, areas of difficulties, new ideas, students' reactions and questions. In this way, teachers are not alone. If there is any problem, coordinators will be with them to solve it. Twice a year there is a meeting between all the district teachers to evaluate the program and think about changes for the next year.

Not every teacher accepted the newspaper at school. "Politics should stay outside the classroom," many of them said.

Many of them preferred the textbook as the only tool from which to teach. They already knew the textbook, because it never changed. On the other hand, the newspaper was different every day. And teachers would have to read it if they wanted to use it at school.

Others felt like they had in years before: controlled and fearful of speaking freely about reality in the classroom. Sometimes the principal did not allow them to use the daily newspaper, and he discussed all the news with the teachers before starting the class.

The students enjoyed the journalism instruction as well as the use of the daily newspaper at school. This was the best sign for the Department of Education to go on with the program.

The Radio Goes to School

Children already showed they had a voice and were able to produce their own messages. A weekly radio program produced by and for children was another way to express themselves freely.

Since 1987, every Tuesday at 9:00 A.M., every sixth- and seventh-grader in 460 public elementary schools in Buenos Aires listens to a radio program produced by students. Every Tuesday the program is broadcast from a different school. In this way, every week a different class is responsible for the program, and all the neighborhoods, poor and rich, have the same opportunity to broadcast from their own schools.

At the beginning of each program, the school announces its phone number, and the other 459 schools are able to call and communicate. Two students usually sit in the principal's office to answer the phone calls from other students in different schools.

The school usually has four weeks to prepare a program. As with the magazine, students produce the stories with their journalism teacher. They choose the major topics they want to speak about: the music, humor, news, and whatever else they'd like to share.

As soon as they choose the main subject, they start to work: interviews, surveys, editorials, research on books, newspapers, radio, and TV. They feel like journalists, but more than this, they feel that 11- and 12-year-old children are able to do research on any subject, publish, and give their own opinions about it.

Last year, one of the government's basic projects was moving the capital south. One school decided to prepare a program about this subject because the students in Buenos Aires thought they would also have to move south with the capital. The children selected news from daily newspapers, read books, went to the Brazilian embassy to find out what happened in that country when they changed their capital and built Brasilia; they interviewed sixth-grade students from the south to see how they felt about this idea; they organized a survey of their neighborhood and found out what the society felt about it.

Finally, after the research, they wrote and broadcast their own opinions.

Since the beginning of this program, the topics children chose were:

* Are children able to vote in national elections?
* Will democracy live with us forever?
* What is love for us (children)?
* Which television programs do we like?
* What games do we usually play?
* What does fear mean to us?
* What kind of music do we listen to?
* What is humor?
* What do we know about drugs?
* Do we want sex education in school?
* Is pollution a problem in Buenos Aires?

The radio went to school, and the children learned to use it. They learned that to be responsible for a program means to inform with responsibility, to say the truth, not to censor the answers, and to give everyone the right to express themselves freely.

They learned what freedom of expression is, and what a free press means. They came to understand what happened to the media and to the people's right to speak between 1976 and 1983. They learned that democracy was the only system in which they could express themselves freely and that democracy is more than voting for a president or having national election. Through reading and writing, newspapers and broadcasting, children are learning what democracy means. If democracy is to survive, Argentinians, especially children, will have to learn to use their freedom.

➔ See: Apple, p. 418; Bird, p. 93; Edelsky, p. 72; Giroux, p. 419; Horton, p. 74; Shannon, p. 223.

Roxana Morduchowicz is the author and director of these programs at the Department of Education in Buenos Aires, Argentina.

Book Note

And None of It Was Nonsense: The Power of Storytelling in School

Betty Rosen
1988; 176 pp.; $13.50
Portsmouth, NH: Heinemann

This book about "the power of storytelling in school" is effectively described by a quote from the postscript by the author's husband, Harold Rosen.

Kathryn F. Whitmore

❝ Teaching and learning never change without a special kind of imaginative act, which all the curriculum guides in the world cannot render unnecessary. You may be persuaded that it is important to become more conversant with narrative theory. You may be inspired to turn your classroom into one where stories flow and become a major means of learning and developing linguistic powers. But then you need to translate your enthusiasm into day-to-day practices. How will you make your first move? How do you learn to tell stories? Where will you find them? How, in a phrase, do your principles undergo that amazing metamorphosis into everyday encounters? Only by your own imaginative weighing of your students and their history, and yourself and your history. You must trust your own inventiveness. That is what this book is about. ❞ (p. 172)

Great Teachers: Karen Smith

by Carole Edelsky

There's no doubt about it: Karen Smith's fifth/sixth grade combination self-contained classroom in a barrio of South Phoenix turns every generalization about poor, minority-language kids on its head. It's not the room that's an attention-grabber—no snappy hi-tech equipment, few amenities (though there are many books)—it's the kids. Instead of seeing children who are educational slouches, visitors see considerate self-starters who all look like they are academically gifted. The more sensitive visitors notice not only a room full of seemingly gifted *individuals* but a marvelously competent *community*. Through Karen Smith's brilliant teaching, even the least mature, least interested children become interested and competent.

One organizational feature of this classroom is especially helpful in augmenting what Karen (hereafter known as KS) does. The children stay in her room for two years. Every fall, half the class consists of old-timers, last year's fifth-graders who enact norms and directly teach the newcomers. Their memories of how special events went last year (e.g., the potluck dinner, the bill of rights convention) and the stories they tell about both special and mundane doings provide everyone with a vision of what can be achieved. And of course, the old-timers' stories are usually exaggerated. These exaggerations improve the visions (goals) for this year's classroom life. For instance, when KS first started to require that children campaigning for election to class office make platform statements, the first candidates promised their constituents parties and dances if they were elected. Gradually, following stories about the great ideas in last year's campaign, the platforms shifted to promises about daily schedules (more free time). Now, campaign promises are curricular—one candidate promised more writing time; another offered more romance novels for literature study and the right of students to plan their own day.

While having the same children for two years is an interesting feature of KS's classroom, other dimensions have been present for years. The "two-year plan" just makes it all better. For instance, there is a solid sense of community here. The room is homey in that it offers homelike freedoms and demands. At home, children can go to another part of the room or some other space within the house without having to be supervised every minute. At home when children break something, they clean it up. At home when someone gets hurt someone else helps. At home, people engage in a lot of incidental talk with others. The same is true for this classroom.

Another dimension to KS's classroom concerns control—children's control of the curriculum and of the room. KS and the children share this control in very complex ways. Overall, KS is clearly in charge (she can take back control at any time); but on a day-to-day basis, control over some areas is shared (i.e., negotiated); in other areas control has been turned over to the children to the extent that KS *refuses* to take it back. The children, for example, are in charge of choices of books for literature study, what will be studied in science, how their day will be spent, what they will do with topics they've chosen for social studies, who will work together to study books, and so on. One result is that they take *their* work seriously, respect it (and themselves as academic workers), become *eager* students (wanting to study much more than they have time for), and weave their work into their nonschool lives (e.g., they can be overheard talking at home about their literature study book while working

on a bike chain or about the rocket they're building for science when they are eating lunch).

Class government is the vehicle through which the children control the room. KS ensures that they succeed. She meets with class officers, makes sure the president has an agenda, teaches them how to delegate tasks to committees and how to establish time lines and follow through, but the power to act is theirs. The children control the budget, deciding how much money will be spent for books, field trips, and equipment, knowing that lost books have to be paid for first out of the treasury. The children initiate subcommittees to take care of disputes and lost items (KS says she is simply not involved in that kind of thing anymore). They are the ones who amend the class bill of rights each year.

This dimension of classroom community, children's caring, and children's collective and individual control of curriculum and classroom, grow out of KS's beliefs and one crucial stance. That stance is trust. She truly trusts them—and follows through on that trust even if a twinge of suspicion arises.

She believes all children are capable of learning and of making sense, that all children have a rich history to draw on, that every person is both a teacher and a learner. She watches particular children who are especially good at teaching in particular ways (e.g., Sarah's uncanny ability to intuit when a writer needs a direct lesson and when he needs an interested listener) in order to get tips for her own teaching. KS sees curriculum and children's abilities as reflexive; in her words, "As we act on the world, it acts on us." Thus, she believes that as children discuss literature, the literature changes for them, becoming something powerful in their own lives.

She highlights the idea that language is one of the most basic classroom resources, that it has to be allowed to happen however it happens, that it can be trusted to be productive ("off-task" is an irrelevant idea to her). The model she uses for how the classroom should work and what children should be doing there is her ideas about what we adults do with oral and written language and ideas in our own world. That is, *our* talk goes on and off topic, on and off task; *we* get up and walk around when we're writing something; *we* seek out advice and opinions from friends; *we* bring content we've learned into our mealtime conversations and leisure activities. So, she believes, should children in school. And so KS enacts her model—and that enactment is a model for all of us.

➔ See: Bird, p. 196; Dyson, p. 46; Edelsky, pp. 19, 72; Literature Study: One Classroom, One Session, p. 196.

Carole Edelsky is a professor at Arizona State University, Tempe, AZ.

Logo from the Bloomington, Indiana TAWL group created by Jim Hall; contributed by Barbara Backler.

Expanding Oral Language

 Viewpoint: Lillian Weber

Comments on Language by a Silent Child

My own language experience leaves me—as I reflect on some of what I read about language—more than a bit doubtful about some of the stereotypes and generalizations that people pose. The fact is that I had been called a "dumb doll" when I was a child. And people didn't mean that I was dumb as in mute; but that it seemed I was determined to be silent. Of course, many children were described in this way in the past and not much was made of it, one way or another; it was not a terrible handicap to be this way, provided you *did* speak and *could* answer, because, after all, the school structure didn't really expect an enormous amount of performance. The teacher did most of the talking. The teacher asked the questions and you answered to the point of the information. You certainly weren't expected to have every range of function or to be imaginative in your language.

It had not been a handicap to me in school to be a rather silent child, which was natural for my placement as a middle child in a large family, because I was the kind of child who was constantly searching to catch on to what was going on, to comprehend—and there was a lot going on, because it *was* a home with a lot of "language surround." My mother was a poet and my father was a kind of political arguer. There were always people there, at home, where big issues and things were being argued: There was immigrant talk and angry talk and this kind of talk and that kind of talk. It isn't that it came from us necessarily. You listened to it and you appreciated it.

I met up with many very silent children, even more silent than I, who were my classmates in the South. That silence was typical of my peers. There's a whole history of the two- or three-word speech of the Vermont farmer or small storekeeper. When I was in Norway, I again heard that the rural children hardly speak, and this was a widespread cultural phenomenon for children from working-class families on school entrance. The academic descriptions of disadvantaged children have never rung a bell in my head. These descriptions go on as if the limited answer on a test or in an interview is a strange new phenomenon.

Vera John-Steiner wrote about how Pueblo children grow up in a culture that treats the development of language as wisdom (John-Steiner and Osterreich 1975). In the Pueblo culture, language is wise words, and one doesn't use it profusely and fluently or easily; it develops very slowly. Professor John-Steiner's description evoked memories of language in my own home, evoked all the cultural experiences with language I have had—of being the "dumb doll" and the silent "stone face," always listening and holding myself impassive while I sought comprehension, but not yet ready to take a chance on speaking.

Language Develops Over Time

Language development is part of the whole cultural setting in which a person grows up; it is influenced by what is expected in the family, and a child's or adolescent's "silence" or shyness does not mean an incapacity for further development later. This is part of what I knew had to be communicated in the understanding of language

> Lillian Weber, professor of education at City College, CUNY, until 1987, founded the City College Workshop Center in 1972, after five years of work in public schools in New York City, making changes intended to better support the child's active learning process. She was a founding member of the North Dakota Study Group on Evaluation, has been on the board of directors of the National Consortium on Testing, and has served as a member of the board of the Prospect Center. Her current major interests, whether in science, in language, or in politics, all have a coherence around advocacy of inclusion.

acquisition—not only how children as infants develop language, but how they do it as part of a whole time-sweep, and a cultural sweep.

We must always remember that the functions of language are just that—functions. There has to be a need for that function, there has to *be* that function for its development. Basil Bernstein observed that the struggle for civil rights was a greater asset to the development of functional power in many blacks than anything a school could do. *What is going on* is extremely important in language development.

Language acquisition isn't a vocabulary list. It occurs around an object. When I said something about a baby to a two-year-old whose mother had just had a baby, his immediate response was, "Oh, the baby! The baby crying! Change the baby!" And as a very enterprising, working child, he pulled up his shirt to demonstrate himself and said, "I feed him. Baby crying, I feed him." It is not only the words that he has learned but the intonation, the expression. Talking about the baby, his voice is mellifluous; talking about playing ball, it's big boy talk.

In school, the tape recorder is a tool that can help bring back some of this language. In addition, the teacher, having joined the discussion, can help by saying, "You know, when I was watching you people I heard somebody say something like this." You will then find a tremendous energizing of the children. We have done this a lot. In one instance, the same thing was played back four times to the children, at their request, these were just four-year-olds, because they got so interested in their own words.

The "rich life" is fostered in the school by these methods; the "rich life" is what I'm saying teachers have to be aware of. You need to be aware of the fact not that the child has a limited vocabulary, which you will fill up, but that the child has a richer vocabulary than you know. Even if it is limited compared to someone else's, it is still richer than when you elicited it, and it can be built on. Nor is it simply a case of a child's syntax development, but the special nature of the way in which this child has constructed a language that is common to all of us, and how he or she uses it. If we don't respect this in children, we may actually be *cutting across* the path of their development, instead of *using* it.

There are many, many ways of putting together language. One child with great deliberation savors the sound, the syllables; another will chatter part of the time to hear himself. Another child is succinct, another child speculates, another child story tells. And none of this contradicts what has been observed about how children acquire syntax and grammar. Each is working within his or her style. Style is relevant to understanding children's language and how you support children; it must be. After all, we identify each other in part by the style of our speech—not only its pace and rhythms but in the characteristic ways we put speech together.

If you are concerned about a child having a range of language function, what kind of language do you suppose results if language is drawn only from the one-to-one contact—the adult talking back to the baby—as essential as this may be? How much range is there in the language of the teacher, even when it is more than question and answer and the giving of

orders? Function, diversified function, does not develop that way. It develops where the child hears higher level language, lower level language, street language, love language: contrastive language. At a very early age, children do hear contrastive language and they understand it. "Grandma is coming to dinner. Be sure you talk nicely for Grandma." The contrasts of language have to do with what is proper. Just as teachers need, constantly, to ask themselves whether they have offered enough life in the classroom to bring out any discussion, they must question whether they have provided a "language surround" with sufficient contrastive elements.

I'm not saying that the child is expected to use it. I'm saying that that is what he lives with, and is around. We provide it, in part, when we read poetry to children, when we read them stories. These activities introduce new language, new pauses, new phrases, new rhythms, extended phrases, all kinds of things that are not in the spoken language. For teachers, it is a question of looking at the range of possibilities, and what the situation elicits, in order to stretch the situation.

The Shared Human Context

I would like to suggest that shared experience really emerges from the human context, and comes from very ordinary things. My experience is that the familiar encourages a tremendous use of language. You don't get a great language extension out of a new experience with, say, magnetism. You get a few additional vocabulary words; you don't get a proliferation of the use of language or a diversification of function. It's too strange to do anything with except name it: "Oh, yes. Magnetism!" But you don't have a whole story about it. What you have a whole story about is your own soap opera, and your own soap opera—the basic human drama—is something that we all share. We all know about mothers, fathers, babies, harshness, illness, vomiting, sore throats. It is not difficult to share tons of things that are just simply part of the human condition.

It is on the basis of this that children should have a continuation of the house corner, the hospital corner. We keep thinking that new experiences are what's going to extend children's language, and what is really meant is extending their vocabulary slightly.

I am in no way derogating the value of new experiences. I'm simply saying that the teacher's ability, using the classroom setting—its focus on the ordinary natural materials and shared experiences—to evoke in children memories of their earlier experiences is basic.

There has been a certain arrogance about teaching "open classrooms," and a certain arrogance about the child's learning. We've talked in terms of children working up to capacity, of stimulating children, without a real awareness

📷 **WHOLE LANGUAGE CAMERA**

The joy of sharing, Palo Alto, CA

Cornerstone: Judith Wells Lindfors

Children's Talk

When Joe's first-grade teacher asked him what writing is, he told her, "It's a different way to be talking." Why does Joe see writing as a way of talking? Talk has been this six-year-old's major way of communicating throughout his short life, an early, close, and constant friend, enabling him to communicate his meaning to others. For Joe, talk is really a synonym for communication.

Joe has been expressing meaning since birth. Like all humans, he has been attempting to

• Connect with others;
• Understand the world;
• Reveal himself.

At first Joe expressed himself nonverbally through facial expressions and gestures. In his waving, his pointing at objects of interest, his taking turns at peekaboo, he reached out to connect with others. In the puzzled looks he directed to others, he elicited help as he tried to understand the world. And in his smiles and cries and chortles, he revealed himself, a unique being in the world.

After a year came *words*—that major milestone. Joe reached out to others with his "hi's" and "bye-bye's." He tried to figure out the world through his early questions: "Dat?" (What's that?) or "Daddy?" (Is it Daddy that I hear?) He revealed his feelings, opinions, likes, and dislikes by saying "no!" and "mine" and "gain" (I want to do that again).

And all through Joe's early years, talk worked for him, carrying out the social and cognitive and emotional purposes that he as a human being was born to carry out.

Some teachers fail to see a child's talk as anything special during the school years. Many see

Judith Wells Lindfors's work in language education has focused on both first- and second-language development. She has taught at primary, secondary, and college levels in Africa and the United States. Her book, *Children's Language and Learning* (now in its second edition), won the Modern Language Association's Mina Shaughnessy Medal, which is awarded in recognition of a significant contribution to language education. Her current research is on dialogue journal writing with African (Zulu) and Indian students for whom English is a second language.

it as a way station on the road to literacy. So while they nurture literacy development, they assume that the child's talk needs no special attention. It's just *there*. It doesn't need tending to.

Not so. It does need tending to because talk carries out some expressive work better than any other form of communication. Immediacy: That's the specialness of talk; it's also the great paradox of talk. Talk enables the individual to go *beyond the immediate* while keeping the individual entrenched *within the immediate*. This is because talk involves informational and interactional aspects—We talk *about something* (informational) *with someone* (interactional). Joe's talk enabled him to go beyond the immediate situation that his earlier nonverbal expression depended on. His smiles, points, gestures, and touches could relate only to what could be seen, pointed to, gestured toward, and touched. Thus, what the communication was about (informational aspect) was limited to that which was immediately perceptible. But talk allowed Joe's communication to be about things that were not present—things past, things future, even things feared, wished for. In its informational aspect then, talk allowed Joe to go beyond the immediate situation. But in its interactional aspect, talk held him within the immediate, face-to-face, here-and-now, me-and-you encounter. This togetherness of participants is often important in communication, which is why some stories are told in books and others are told around the campfire, in the kitchen, or in first-grade sharing time.

Which brings us back to Joe. In his talk, he brings the "beyond" into the classroom—Star Wars, his baby sister's antics, his parents' arguments, his nightmares, his wonderings. And in his talk, he is entrenched in the shifting, moment-to-moment partnerships that foster his membership within that classroom community. Joe knows nothing of "paradoxes involving interactional and informational aspects of oral language." Not in the abstract, anyway. But he *knows* these from the communication events of his classroom—when he tells his friend a joke,

when he invites a friend to come home to play with him after school, when he asks his teacher a question, when he responds to a classmate's anecdote, when he argues or comforts or challenges or asserts or... In these events Joe's talk is with someone about something. He *knows* the interactional and informational aspects of talk.

Joe is luckier than many other first-graders. His teacher appreciates, encourages, and fosters his talk in the classroom with her and with his peers. She recognizes the crucial communication Joe does through his talk.

• She hears him connecting with others when he compromises, invites, offers, comforts.
• She hears him trying to understand his world when he seeks confirmation, wonders aloud, attempts to clarify an idea, makes a connection, generalizes.
• She hears him revealing himself when he asserts an opinion, makes a joke, refuses to comply, evaluates another's action, expresses fear.

Joe's teacher pays Joe and his classmates what Thoreau calls "the greatest compliment": "The greatest compliment paid me was when one asked me what I thought and attended to my answer." His teacher attends to what Joe says by asking him more about it, by picking up and building on it. Many teachers respond to children's classroom talk by evaluating it. They lavishly sprinkle through their own talk what they call "positive reinforcement": "I like the way you told us that." Joe's teacher makes such comments, but she is careful to limit them, for these evaluations often serve to close off and dismiss the interaction event. Too much positive reinforcement tells the child, "I am the approval-dispenser and your job is to please me." So Joe's teacher responds more by listening carefully, by questioning him further, and by building on what he has said. In these ways she tells him she cares about what he thinks and is attending to his ideas. At*tending:* That's the ultimate *tending* to the child's talk.

Vivian Paley (1981, p.113) pays her kindergartners the greatest compliment when they discuss matters of importance to them.

Deana:	Did even Martin Luther King have to sit in the back of the bus?
Teacher:	All black people did.
Deana:	That was really no fair.
Jill:	That reminds me. Why do we have to always sit at the same lunch table?
Teacher:	What would you rather do?
Jill:	Sit anywhere we want. That's more fair.
Teacher:	That might become confusing. Most people would rather know exactly where they sit, Jill.
Deana:	I don't would rather know.
Eddie:	Me neither.
Teacher:	How does everyone else feel about this? (There is unanimous approval.) Well, then, it's okay with me.
Jill:	Free at last!

Talk entrenched *within the immediate*: the joint construction of talk made possible by the world these children and their teacher share, and enhancing their sense of themselves as a community. Talk going *beyond the immediate*: the consideration of Martin Luther King, Jr., of fairness, of freedom— a heady "curriculum" for five-year-olds. Yet not surprising, for the power of children's talk is great in classrooms where it is *attended* to.

For these kindergartners as for first-grader Joe, talk was an early, close, and constant friend in communication. It's going to be a lifelong friendship.

→ See: Bloome, p. 82; King, p. 16; Paley, p. 30; Shor, p. 223; Weber, p. 78.

Reference
Paley, V. G. 1981. *Wally's stories.* Cambridge: Harvard University Press.

---

of the private spaces, of the river that must exist with much deeper meanings to feed the child's further progress, and that are not yet accessible to them. When we talked about comprehension, we actually thought we had something. Well, we do have something, but we are only beginning to understand what it is, and it is *our understanding* of this interesting phenomenon that needs to be examined, not the child's comprehension—as if that were an entity.

→ See: Bloome, p. 82; Goodman, p. 83; King, p. 16; Lindfors, p. 79; Peterson, p. 79; Shor, p. 223.

Reference
John-Steiner, V., and H. Osterreich. 1975. "Learning styles among Pueblo children." *Report to the National Institute of Education,* August.

Adapted from *The Urban Review,* 1976, pp. 172–184.

Further Reading by Lillian Weber
◆ *The English Infant School and Informal Education.* Prentice-Hall, 1971.
◆ "The Open Corridor: Experiment in Redefining Public Education." Proceedings of Conference, SUNY, Cortland, NY. *Open Education,* April 1972.
◆ "Comments on Language by a Silent Child." Urban Review, Fall 1976.
◆ Review of Bennett's "Teaching Styles and Pupil Progress." *Review of Education* 4(5), September/October 1977.
◆ "Adapting Classrooms for All the Children." In Special Education and Development, ed. S. Meisels. University Park Press, 1979.

The Funny Side

Jaws-on Learning

A young mother in Colorado was helping her 18-month-old daughter, Alicia, learn to talk. Alicia had nearly learned the word "dirty," which she heard almost every time she tested with her mouth some interesting thing she picked up from the floor. One sunny summer morning when she was playing on the front porch, Mom glanced through the screen door and saw urgent need for more learning. "Dirty!" she cried.

"Durry," said Alicia as she quit chewing on the giant earthworm.

—Hal Bridges, professor emeritus of history, University of California, Riverside, CA

Cornerstone: Lucinda Pease-Alvarez

Cross-Age Tutoring: An Opportunity for Student Talk and Reflection

Cross-age tutoring is a truly authentic learning encounter that connects communities of learners. Tutor and tutee participate in social interactions that support and extend their learning during the tutoring sessions. After the tutoring, tutors meet to discuss any problems they may have encountered.

Initially, tutors talk like traditional classroom teachers; they do almost all of the talking and they ask too many questions. This pattern was certainly apparent in the early interactions involving Rigoberto and his kindergarten tutee, Raul. For the most part, Rigoberto spent the tutoring time reading to his tutee. He seldom made the book available to Raul or pointed out any illustrations. Occasionally he would ask Raul a question about what had occurred in the story he was reading.

Like many tutors, it was not easy for Rigoberto to relinquish the role of all-knowing teacher. He struggled with two other tutees, insisting that they behave like model students. He complained when they would not listen to the stories he read or when they refused to answer questions. Finally, after listening to the suggestions of his classmates he tried something new. He let his new tutee read to him. Soon he was encouraging her to write about what she had read. Instead of Rigoberto dominating the sessions, his tutee was the one who did most of the talking as well as the reading and writing.

Tony's tutee, Hugo, also did more and more talking as the year progressed. He even began to initiate and pursue his own topics during tutoring sessions. On one occasion he interrupted Tony to talk about a subject of great importance to him.

Hugo: You know what, my mom said, "Umm, que quieres hacer when you be, umm, big?" And I said, "I wanna be a teacher."

Tony: I wanna be a snake driver [makes motor noises], and then I'll fall off and I'll hafta have an operation and then I'll retire.

Hugo: I didn't wanna say that. I wish I be a racer but a motorcycle you know that little motorcycles.

Tony: Yeah.

Hugo: They're bad, man.

Because tutors were so intimately involved with their tutees' learning, they began to talk about it. They returned from tutoring sessions full of information about how their kindergartners were progressing. They would proudly point to a piece of writing and comment on a special characteristic (e.g., "He writes from bottom to top," "She writes the first letter where the last letter should go," "Now he knows how to write accent marks"). As problems arose, students began to share and reflect upon their experiences. Often they would work together to resolve these problems.

Ana: Pedro was a brat. He didn't want me to read to him....All he did was hear himself talk in a tape recorder....Pedro said, "Why are you doing this?" and I said, "I'm teaching you guys to read and write."

Linda: Maybe you could ask him why he doesn't want you to read to him? Is he bored?

Ana: Yeah.

Teacher: What would you do if you had a tutee—

Linda: Ask him what kind of things they like. Tell him what it's like when they grow up and they don't know what it's like to read or write.

Teacher: What do you do with a kid that's bored?

Iris: Umm, get both your arms [makes hugging gesture].

Sara: Let him read to her 'cause sometimes some of the big kids they don't let their tutee read and that's what they want...

Teacher: You say he likes to color?

Mary: Let him color and tell you what the picture is about.

Sara: Or write down something.

Mario: [Have him] tell a story about the pictures.

Iris: Or he could write words under it.

Discussions like this provide students with frameworks for self-reflection. Oftentimes students who share their experiences with others come up with their own solutions and insights. At one point Ana, the tutor who was experiencing difficulties in the preceding exchange, was seriously considering abandoning her tutee, Pedro. After much deliberation, she finally reached her own solution, which she referred to in the following fieldnote entry:

> after all I am going to stey with pedro because I lourd a lesen dont let go to a person you like...I read 5 books and he like them

> [After all, I am going to stay with Pedro because I learned a lesson. Don't let go (of) a person you like....I read 5 books and he likes them.]

➔ See: Alvarez, p. 141; Bird, p. 93; Dyson, p. 46.

Lucinda Pease-Alvarez is an assistant professor at the University of California at Santa Cruz, CA.

Breakthroughs

A Time to Celebrate

Courtney, age 10, had been working with her five year old tutee, Lilly, for eight months when one day Lilly suddenly wrote in invented spelling:

Cuano esi a la casa (When I'm at home).

Courtney shrieked with delight, hugged Lilly and then asked, "Why didn't you tell me you could do this?"

Lilly looked down shyly. "It was a secret."

"Oh no, Lilly, this is much too big to be a secret! Come on. We have an announcement to make!"

Courtney walked over to Lilly's kindergarten teacher, Mrs. Short, whispered in her ear, then returned to Lilly. "OK, Lilly. Tell the class!"

Lilly stood up in front of the class. "I can read and I can write."

Her classmates cheered and applauded. Lilly, holding onto Courtney's hand, beamed.

—As told to LBB by Leslie Mangiola, elementary teacher, Fair Oaks Elementary, Redwood City, CA

📷 WHOLE LANGUAGE CAMERA

As part of a schoolwide cross-age tutoring program, a fifth grader reads aloud to a kindergarten student, Fair Oaks School, Redwood City, CA.

MARVELOUS INVENTIONS

BBP! LmP RUMP YmP This is me falling down.

[Bump! Lump! Rump! Yump! This is me falling down.]
—Pilar Alvarez, 6, student of Catherine Howard, Ohlone School, Palo Alto, CA

Resource: Book

Three Generations Speak

Jerline Quintal-Finell, editor
1985; 25 pp.; $4 from:
Jerline Quintal-Finell
Box 770
La Ronge, Saskatchewan,
S0J 1L0
Canada

Historically and culturally rich in detail, this student-authored and illustrated booklet provides the reader with a glimpse into the past and present lives of the Cree of Pelican Narrows. The sixth- and seventh-grade author/historians relate their own stories as well as the stories of their parents and grandparents, whom they interviewed. *Three Generations Speak,* an inspiring model for teachers and students in other communities, demonstrates what is possible when students are allowed to step beyond the narrow confines of the classroom.

LBB

 **writers**

Grandfather's Gun
by Ted Custer

A long time ago my grandfather had a pirate's gun. It was black and made out of copper and wood. He loaded the gun with silver bullets, which all pirates used in those days.

"We were the pirates," my grandfather said. "We got in the ship that took us to North America. I got shot in the back. My brother was not so lucky. He got one eye taken out in that fight. A few days later, they came back for him and finished him off. He left a wife and two children behind. We buried him in the ocean." My grandfather paused and handed me the gun he had been clutching, while he told his story. "I cannot hold on anymore."

My grandfather died a week later and we buried him along the great shores of North America. There are no more pirates, just the evidence of the gun, which I store as part of my valuable memories of a great storyteller, my grandfather.

From Three Generations Speak, 1985.

Ted Custer was a seventh-grader when he wrote this.

Viewpoint: Ralph Peterson

The Voices of Critique and Dialogue

Dialogue requires risk-taking for both teachers and children. A basic rule of dialogue is that participants—teachers and students—do not enter the encounter with a plot in mind to be acted out. Spontaneity is essential. It is the immediacy of the responding, the calling forth of the other, and the listening that moves participants to insights that cannot be realized through solitary thinking.

A clear alternative to dialogue is that of making children consumers of textbook views, or projects of someone else's thinking rather than self-projects.

Ralph Peterson teaches in the College of Education at Arizona State University. His chief interests are studying the building of holistic learning communities, teaching about literature, and working for teacher empowerment.

Dialogue is at the same time difficult and enjoyable. It requires initiative, inquiry, critical thinking, and invention from all involved. Dialogue ceases when participants exempt themselves from exerting intelligence and imagination. Students must be active in dialogue, sharing what it is they understand to be true, based on their "lived" meaning and intent. And it is enjoyable not only because we have a chance to see ideas dramatically come to life on the spot, but because the possibility exists that a fresh perspective for interpreting experience will evolve.

Partners in dialogue, whether they are examining possible interpretations of a text in a literature study, working together to understand unexpected phenomena in a science experiment, or contributing to the clarity of a classmate's piece of writing, seek to accurately interpret their experience. In dialogue students are asked to see for themselves, to share their interpretations, and not to rely on secondhand meanings developed for their consumption.

Teachers work alongside students to help them examine facts for themselves and draw their own conclusions. Teachers are listeners who avoid dominating students with knowledge and intent. They act collaboratively to build shared meanings so that children can construct knowledge about the subject that reflects their experience and intentions. In emphasizing the process of coming to know, teachers work to help students take charge of their learning.

Imagine a class studying the transfer of energy. Since ice makes the presence and absence of heat observable, the teacher has outfitted the students with ice and warm water to initiate inquiry. The teacher supports students in their inquiry and critical thinking by extending the dialogue whenever possible, by outfitting them with needed equipment and information, by helping students to make sense of their observations, and by aiding them in the design of experiments. One group of students begins to devise a way to insulate ice from heat. Another group examines how surface area affects melting rate. The directions the students' inquiries take are far less important than their sustaining the inquiry, attending to facts, and working together in dialogue to critique what happens and formulate testable hypotheses.

This is not to say that teachers are indifferent to whether students acquire knowledge. They are concerned that students will not only learn, but also engage in meaning making that allows them to critique, receive feedback, and benefit from contributions made by others seeking to know.

Students use what they learn about meaning making in dialogue with classmates when they work independently. Students capable of taking a critical perspective on their experience within the classroom dialogue bring this skill to their independent work when they interpret a text, revise their writing, and study the meaning of a historical event. Equally important to independent meaning making is the opportunity for students to see how others bring their mind to bear on experience. Classroom dialogue is an occasion to practice thinking with others. What students learn about how others take action, reflect, make inquiries, and critique contributes to their own meaning making.

The demands of living in a democracy and the responsibility teachers have for caring for the young require that teaching and learning be free from a standardized curriculum. The unrehearsed voices arising from critique and dialogue must be heard. When they are silent, classrooms become boring places; science learning is hobbled, literature fails to be a way of knowing, history is unseeing, and thought and speculation are without imagination.

➜ See: King, p. 16; Lindfors, p. 79; Shor, p. 223; Weber, p. 78.

Further Reading by Ralph Peterson
◆ *Grand Conversations: Literature Groups in Action,* with M. Eeds. Scholastic, 1990.

Resource: Book

If Only I Could Fly: Poems for Kids to Read Out Loud

Brod Bagert
1984; 53 pp.; $12.95
Juliahouse Publishing
13223 Briar Hollow
Baton Rouge, LA 70810
1-504-769-5655

Cindy Elliott, a whole language teacher in Baton Rouge, Louisiana, who represents poet Brod Bagert, wrote and asked if we could include information about Brod. The answer was yes. Here it is.

Brod Bagert is a New Orleans trial lawyer and former City Council member turned poet/author. A guest speaker to parent and educator organizations nationwide, Bagert appeared at the 1989 IRA convention in New Orleans. Designed to be read out loud by children, his poetry is meant to create a dramatic interpretation—it is work "about the fun, fear, silliness, challenge, and sorrow of childhood." Bagert visits schools where he, as well as students, perform his work to great acclaim. In addition to *If Only I Could Fly,* Bagert has also published poetry books about New Orleans and Alaska.

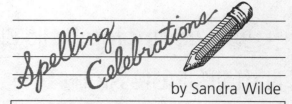

by Sandra Wilde

Invented Spellings: Using One Letter Many Ways

The *BADE* (body) has legs. Some *PEEPLE* are *MESEN* (missing) one leg.

Tammy, 1st grade

In three words here, Tammy had a number of different uses of the letter *e.* Yet look at what she has revealed about her knowledge of phonetics and language! In *BADE,* the E represents the long *e* sound. Tammy is just not yet aware that this sound is often spelled with a *y* at the end of a word. In *PEEPLE,* the double *E* also represents the long sound of *e,* and she shows an awareness here that it is often spelled with two letters, particularly in the middle of a word. (If the word had been *steeple,* her *ee* spelling would have been correct.) Two *e*'s occur in *MESEN.* The first one is a common children's spelling for the short *i* sound, which really sounds a lot like the letter name *e.* The second one may appear to be the same, but my hunch is otherwise. Don't many of us really pronounce the second syllable of *missing* not as "sing" but as "seen"? I think she's spelling long *e* again here! One final note: In addition to these four misuses of the letter *e,* Tammy used it correctly seven times in the sentence.

 ## The Funny Side

It's Grandma!

Two-year-old Jason shows promise of becoming an accomplished lexicographer. Every time he gets to talk on the phone it's with his Grandma Gloria. Therefore, with impeccable logic, he calls the phone "Grandma Gloria."

—As told to LBB by Gloria Norton, resource teacher, Fair Oaks School, Redwood City, CA

📷 WHOLE LANGUAGE CAMERA

Will it spin off the desk? Two boys watch a top with excited anticipation, Palo Alto, CA.

Linguistic Diversity

 Viewpoint: David Bloome & Judith W. Solsken

Naftali's Profession

In Herman Melville's "Bartleby the Scrivener," Bartleby's job is to copy documents. Day after day, he copies legal documents. In the absence of photocopy machines or similar mechanical devices, Bartleby's job is an essential one. Only with multiple written copies can agreements be kept, and the sophisticated economic, legal, and political system of Western society function. But Bartleby prefers not to: not to copy, not to work, not to participate in the system. Eventually, he dies. Another of Melville's protagonists also dies because of language, or perhaps more accurately, the lack of it. Billy Budd, a seaman on a British warship, unable to speak on his own behalf, strikes out and kills an officer. For that act, Billy is killed.

Compare the portrayal of language and literacy in "Bartleby the Scrivener" and *Billy Budd, Foretopman,* with language and literacy in Isaac Bashevis Singer's "Naftali the Storyteller and His Horse, Sus" in his *Stories for Children.* As a small boy, Naftali loved stories and storybooks so much that he decided to be a traveling bookseller and storyteller when he grew up.

> Naftali said, "When I grow up, I'll travel to all the cities, towns, and villages, and I'll sell storybooks everywhere, whether it pays me or not."
>
> Naftali had decided on something else, too—to become a writer of storybooks. He knew full well that for this you had to study, and with all his heart he determined to learn. He also began to listen more closely to what people said, to what stories they told, and to how they told them. Each person had his or her own manner of speaking. Reb Zebulun told Naftali, "When a day passes, it is no longer there. What remains of it? Nothing more than a story. If stories weren't told, man would live like the beasts, only for the day."
>
> Reb Zebulun said, "Today we live, but by tomorrow, today will be a story. The whole world, all human life, is one long story."

Naftali becomes a bookseller and storyteller, traveling in his wagon from village to village, collecting and telling people's stories.

In "Naftali the Storyteller and His Horse, Sus," language and literacy make people—ordinary, everyday people—visible and historical. In *Billy Budd, Foretopman,* lack of language condemns an ordinary person, a conscripted sailor, to death and invisibility. Billy doesn't even get to tell his own story, either in court or in the newspaper accounts. In "Bartleby the Scrivener," literacy makes people invisible and ahistorical. Only by "preferring not to," can anyone become visible, and when that happens, one is pushed to the margins, out of sight.

When we look at schools, we see much of literacy tied to being invisible and ahistorical. Students—especially students from ordinary, everyday families—are not asked to tell their stories, each in their own manner of speaking. They are asked instead, like Bartleby, to reproduce the privileged language and texts of our society—by literally copying them or by memorizing snippets of them to parrot back. Because this language and these texts are privileged, we are surprised when students resist—when, like Bartleby, they prefer not to, or, like Billy, they strike out. We don't see that what students are resisting is their own invisibility, their own quiet deaths in classrooms and in society. But it doesn't have to be that way.

As whole language teachers, we have the opportunity to define our profession, like Naftali's, as collecting and sharing stories of ordinary, everyday people. To do this we must

> David Bloome is an associate professor in the School of Education, University of Massachusetts. He is the founding editor of *Linguistics and Education: An International Research Journal.*
>
> Judith W. Solsken is associate professor of education and director of the Reading and Writing Program at the University of Massachusetts at Amherst. She holds a Ph.D. in linguistics from Cornell University and was formerly a high school English teacher. She has conducted ethnographic research and published articles on children's reading and writing at home and in school.

recognize, like Naftali, that this is a demanding intellectual profession. We have to study, for there is much to learn about language and literacy, about the many ways ordinary people use language and literacy every day, to define themselves and their relationships with each other. We must listen more closely to what people say, to what stories they tell, and to how they tell them. We must listen to help capture, not to correct, the richness of people's language and stories, for it is through their own authentic language that people become visible.

Naftali's profession will be demanding for us in other ways as well. For when we really listen to people's stories, their pain becomes visible to us, too. Their stories give us a window on a world that is not itself whole, an economic, legal, and political system that silences and makes invisible large numbers of people. Alice Walker shows us the pain and brutality of invisibility in *The Color Purple.* But she also shows an underlying beauty and power, which are not at all romantic, but the basis of a continued struggle for voice. In an essay describing her attempt to capture Celie's voice in *The Color Purple,* Walker (*Living by the Word,* Harcourt Brace Jovanovich, 1988, p. 64) says:

> Celie's words reveal not only an intelligence that transforms illiterate speech into something that is, at times, very beautiful, as well as effective in conveying her sense of her world, but also what has been done to her by a racist and sexist system, and her intelligent blossoming as a human being despite her oppression demonstrates why her oppressors persist even today in trying to keep her down. For if and when Celie rises to her rightful, earned place in society across the planet, the world will be a different place, I can tell you.

In defining our work as Naftali's profession, whole language teachers take on political as well as intellectual challenges as we choose to work within schools. Whole language, for us, is not just a vision of education, but a vision of the world and the way people connect with each other. For it is in the sharing—in the telling, the listening, the recording, the reading, and the retelling—of our stories that we become visible to each other, that we become part of human history, and that we begin to change that history together.

→ See: Bissex, p. 209; Bloome, pp. 228, 359; Curry, p. 228; Lindfors, p. 79; Literature Reference List, p. 429; Shor, p. 222; Weber, p. 78.

Reference
Melville, H. "Bartleby the scrivener." In *Billy Budd.* New York: Penguin, 1983.

Further Reading by David Bloome
◆ *Literacy and Schooling,* Ablex, 1987.
◆ "Analyzing Teacher-Student and Student-Student Discourses." In *Multiple Disciplinary Perspectives on Classroom Discourse,* ed. J. Green and J. Harker. Ablex, 1988.
◆ *Classrooms and Literacy,* Ablex, 1989.
◆ "Children and Basal Readers." In *Theory into Practice,* with S. Nieto. In press.
◆ "Procedural Display and Classroom Lessons." In *Curriculum Inquiry,* with P. Puro and E. Theodorou. In press

Further Reading by Judith W. Solsken
◆ "Discourse Structure: Expectations of Beginning Readers and Readability of Text." Published under the name of Judith Gourley. *Journal of Reading Behavior* 16, 1984.
◆ "Authors of Their Own Language." *Language Arts* 62, 1985.

Resource: Periodical

Linguistics and Education: An International Research Journal

David Bloome, editor
$27.50/year (4 issues) individual; $65/year institutional from:
Ablex Publishing
355 Chestnut St.
Norwood, NJ 07648
1-201-767-8450

As we've grown in our understanding of language and learning, we've come to realize the critical role of linguistics in both exploring and explaining educational processes. Catalog essayist David Bloome, the founding editor of *Linguistics and Education,* explains the format of this important journal.

LBB

❝ *Linguistics and Education* provides a forum for researchers from diverse linguistic perspectives to share and discuss their inquiries into educational perspectives both in and outside of school. As researchers explore educational processes, they are raising questions about the linguistic perspectives extant in the field and providing new directions. The Journal publishes high quality research and related scholarly work on all topics related to linguistics and education, broadly defined. Such topics include, but are not limited to, classroom interaction, language diversity in educational settings, language policy and curriculum, written language learning, language disorders in educational settings, and the application of linguistics, sociolinguistics, psycholinguistics, discourse analysis, social semiotics, conversational analysis, and ethnomethodology to educational issues. ❞

The Funny Side

A Rose by Any Other Name...

Child: Teacher, can I go to the terlit (toilet)?"
Teacher: Did you say "can"?
Child: No, I said "terlit"!

—As told to YMG by Marion Edmond

📷 **WHOLE LANGUAGE CAMERA**

Art and laughter at Fratney School, Milwaukee, WI

As I See It:
Kenneth S. Goodman

The Dialects of English

Adapted from *Language and Thinking in School*, 3d ed., by Kenneth S. Goodman, E. Brooks Smith, Robert Meredith, and Yetta M. Goodman. (New York: Richard C. Owen, 1987): pp. 67–69.

Does a peach or a cherry have a *pit, seed, stone,* or *bone* in it? Your answer will be different depending on where you live and where you grew up. Do you carry the groceries home in a *bag,* a *sack,* a *poke,* a *tote,* or a *package?* One or more sounds natural to you, and the others are either strange-sounding or they have quite another meaning. A speaker from southern Illinois amuses his Chicago listeners when he says he will "warsh" his clothes and then "arn 'em." A listener in Milwaukee notes inwardly the lack of culture of an educated Kentuckian who says "dived" instead of "dove."

All these are aspects of the differences between the well-established regional dialects of the United States. Such differences have been studied and documented by linguistic atlas field workers to determine the boundaries and overlaps of dialect regions. Three major dialects emerged: northern, midland, and southern. But each of these can be subdivided. Furthermore, some eastern dialects developed that didn't move west. Eastern New England, New York City, and eastern Virginia are examples. Another such dialect developed in the hollows of the Appalachian Mountains. The influence of the generally westward population movement across the northern, middle, and southern states since colonial days explains the division of the country into the basic dialect groups. Insularity explains the more contained dialects of New England, New York City, eastern Virginia, and Appalachia. The areas of earliest settlement on the East Coast developed the smallest and most easily defined dialect areas.

When the mapping of American dialects is finally completed, it will partly represent an extension of the westward movement, and partly reflect major changes in the speed and methods of transportation in recent decades. The population movement into California, Florida, Texas, and the rest of the Sun Belt, for example, often represents leap-frogging from distant parts of the country.

The dialect patterns of the major northern cities are influenced by a south-to-north movement as industrialization became a magnet to those leaving more rural areas. This has led to complex socioeconomic dialect patterns within the major cities. The different social classes have been recruited from different parts of the country. After the immigration of Europeans in large numbers ended in the 1920s, industrial workers were recruited from among the black and white poor in the South and Midlands. World War II accelerated that migration.

Studies of socioeconomic dialect patterns within urban complexes of the United States are relatively recent. In the geographic atlas work there was a strong tendency to concentrate only on the most stable and well-established language forms. Studies of urban dialect patterns require a look at the speech of all groups in an area, across ethnic, racial, and class lines. The patterns of dialect distribution within a metropolitan complex relate to the population shifts in that complex. Immigrants have tended to arrive in the inner city, to spend a generation there, and then to shift outward toward the outer part of the city and the suburbs. Successive waves of European immigrants replace each other, followed by black and white immigrants from the South. In more recent decades a major Hispanic migration from Puerto Rico, Mexico, Cuba, and Central America has been underway. Even more recently there has been an immigration of Asians, particularly from the countries of Indochina.

Transplanted regional dialects are superimposed on preexisting ones in the cities; and all are in continuous evolution, as is language everywhere. The net result is a picture of great variation with social-status factors becoming intermixed with linguistic, ethnic, and racial ones. Some language forms—phonological, grammatical, and semantic—become prestigious, while others are accorded the low social status of their users. Some folks' language seems archaic to others. And those who stay "down home" snicker at the changes in the language of their city cousins.

All dialects influence each other to some degree, but upwardly mobile individuals will tend to shift toward prestige forms to gain greater acceptance from high-status groups in the community and to conceal their more humble beginnings (Shuy 1967).

While many Canadians speak a dialect close enough to the northern U.S. dialect that they are mistaken for American tourists when they travel overseas, there is a range of Canadian dialects too. Isolated areas such as the "outports" of the maritime provinces have quite distinct dialects. And, of course, French Canadians speak a dialect notably different from the modern dialects of France. New Zealanders and Australians can differentiate their dialects and are particularly surprised when North Americans think they sound British.

Needless to say, English that stayed home did not remain static. The world changes even without travel. Sometimes English changed faster than its emigré cousins. Sometimes the language left behind was more conservative. The Anglo-Saxon settlers in Britain set up seven kingdoms and left the stamp of their differing dialects, which survive to the present day. An age of slow communication and identification with the land maintained distinctness. There were centers of political power and literary brilliance, which pulled at the extremes of Lancashire, Yorkshire, Lallans, and Cockney, but through it all the dialects of England and the English-speaking areas of Scotland, Wales, and Ireland maintained their strong identity. The United States has only a handful of dialects compared to some 29 in the United Kingdom.

For whole language teachers what is important is that each dialect is a bona fide language system. Speakers of low-status dialects do not speak standard English poorly; they speak their home dialects well. Teachers need to be well aware of this fact in daily instruction. In recent years both politicians and writers have recognized the myth of a pure form of English and the value of dialect differences. Class dialects, as Shaw demonstrated in *Pygmalion*, while more clearly recognized in Britain, exist in all other English-speaking countries. That requires a careful educational response, lest difference be confused with deficiency.

Whole language implies celebrating language in all its variety. We start in whole language, as Dewey advised, where the child is. The goal is never to reject one language form and replace it with another. Rather, the goal is to expand on the base of the home dialect and to support learners as they add other dialects and registers to their repertoire.

→ See: Literature Reference List, p. 429; Weber, p. 78.

Reference

Shuy, R. 1967. *Discovering American dialects.* Champaign, IL: National Council of Teachers of English.

Book Note

Black English: Its History and Usage in the United States

J. L. Dillard
1973; 364 pp.; $8.95
New York: Random House

The language of African-Americans has a complex and fascinating history, stemming from the days when a dialect of English, intermingled with African vocabulary and usage, developed among slaves. The general public tends to think of black English as merely "incorrect" English, but Dillard's history and description of it prove that this is not so. He shows that black English, like other dialects, has its own rules and grammatical structure, and describes how its use is affected by social and cultural factors. His final chapter, on black English and education, is still timely. All teachers of black students should read this book; since whole language teachers are those who work at understanding the language and culture of their students. *Black English* is also valuable for any teacher who would like to learn something about language history, sociolinguistics, and relationships between language and learning.

Sandra Wilde

❝ Misunderstanding of the grammatical patterns of the disadvantaged Negro's speech frequently leads to the conclusion that he has no grammar, a completely untenable position from the point of view of any linguist. The child who says *Mary hat* and *he book* has a possessive grammatical category (possession by juxtaposition) just as surely as the one who says *Mary's hat* and *his book*. Yet a widely used teaching device is to draw a picture of the hat on Mary's head in order to "show" the child that it is Mary's hat.❞ (p. 273)

I Used to Be...But Now I...

I used to think that the students ought to talk like Peter Jennings,
But now I know they have a right to their own dialect.

—Anonymous

The Funny Side
Get It Rat!

Child: How do you spell "rat"?
Teacher: R-A-T
Child: No, I don't mean "rat" mouse, I mean "rat now."

As kids see it

Will Lingoism Overtake the Schools?

by Ravid Haselkorn

"Jen, listen, there was a totally rad rager at Phil's last night. Yeah, and Charlotte met a totally fine guy named Rod but found out he was dealing with Susan. So she decided to shine him. But later Charlotte felt totally bummed because he's so awesome. That's why she got wasted and they ended up scamming after all. Yeah, can you believe it? But she says she's gonna dog him sooner or later because everyone's ragging on her for scamming with him."

Translation: Charlotte went to a party last night, met a handsome boy named Rod, and liked him until she found out he had relations with a girl named Susan. Charlotte became very depressed, ended up getting drunk, and eventually kissed Rod anyway. Her friends were unhappy with the way she behaved so she plans to break up with him.

Any questions? This exemplifies the life of the typical teenager. Where do all these special words come from? Do they develop in the schools themselves, or are they imported? What explains this phenomenon?

In any profession, a neophyte will encounter and be forced to learn a new language. Doctors, lawyers, journalists, and teachers have developed their own jargon. In the case of professions, a need for specialized languages arose because there was no other way to describe certain situations. A doctor couldn't discuss medical ailments with other doctors by saying, "You know the patient in Room 406 who feels off-balance, extreme dizziness, nausea, and has flickering eyes?" That would take all day and cause extreme confusion. Instead, scientists gave those particular ailments a name, and a doctor says instead,"You know the patient in Room 406 who has labyrinthitis? He needs to have a....

But why do people who are not involved in specific professions develop their own language? A particular group will develop its own form of communication when one or more of the following conditions exist:

1. A tightly-knit group.
2. A similar background and/or common experience.
3. A pervasive feeling of alienation from the society.
4. A need for secrecy, often in connection with illicit activities.

Gangs are a perfect example. As a result of their illegal drug activities, territorial wars, and jingoistic beliefs, they have developed their own language. In fact, since gangs fulfill all of the above conditions, it may be said that Lingoism has taken over. Lingoism is a deviationist language used as a symbolism of "sovereignty," resulting at times in the development of an entire sublanguage.

But can we compare the schools to the gangs? Is Lingoism spreading in the educational system, or are students borrowing certain words from the gangs and other groups? Has the Tower of Babel come crashing down on the schools?

It is no secret that drugs are present on most school campuses. Consequently, the need for secrecy definitely exists among the participants in this "trade." However, for the most part, drug trafficking has not reached the point in the school system where an entire sublanguage has emerged. Rather, the students use their own jargon as a means of distinction. Students seek to separate themselves from the teachers and the judgmental adults. Accordingly, when an adult, especially a teacher, attempts to relate to the students by using Lingoism, the "offenders" are barred through ridicule. Often the teacher is labeled as "lame," in this case, a "student" word in itself. This occurs because the students resent the imposing adult's trespassing into the teenagers' world. The language of the schools is picked up from the outside, and for the most part, from groups not considered proper by the adults, such as the gangs, rock groups, and so on. Using the special language in school creates status akin to a class system within the student body. Those who have mastered the unique language are considered the "cool" people, the "in" people. Cliques have seized the opportunity to use the "cool" language to strengthen the ties within their particular group and to keep secrets from others. The rest of the students just follow their lead, trying to keep up with the trend.

But the question often raised is, "Doesn't this student Lingoism harm the student-teacher relationship?" Although most people would respond in the affirmative, claiming the phenomenon mars communication between the two, I strongly disagree. Students converse with the special language only among themselves, not with the teachers. It is not the only language used by students at the schools; rather it is the only language used among themselves. The use of a different language is part of teenagers' search for identity and a benign form of releasing their rebelliousness. Thus, it could be said that Lingoism *aids* the student-teacher relationship. If one can express himself in the way he wishes, isn't he more willing to cooperate, more willing to learn?

Lingoism will not overtake the schools. It is a natural outlet for students, and is necessary for maintaining a healthy elementary and high school atmosphere.

Ravid Haselkorn was graduated from Palo Alto High School in the class of 1990 and is currently a freshman at the University of California at Berkeley.

WELL-SAID

I do not believe I had a problem with English after kindergarten. I could switch from Spanglish to Street to Standard at will. I read. I didn't fear writing. I could mimic the prestige dialect—both the spoken and the written. I could even add "however" to essays on the basis of sound, although not often on the basis of sense. I was, however, apparently unable to mimic the school's way of viewing the world, the ways reflected in rhetorical patterns. The literacy we [Puerto Ricans] acquire tends to be of the wrong sort, even when the dialect is right. Basic literacy wields little power.

—V. Villanueva, Jr., "A Rhetorically Critical Literacy," *Information Update* 4(3)

Language Stories

A Concrete Experience

Janey came home from her first day in the first grade looking puzzled. She talked happily about her new teacher, which of her kindergarten friends were in her room this year, and other important first-day facts. After a while she asked, "Mom, do we have any cement things?"

"We have some cinder blocks in the bookcases, but I think that's as close as we come to cement things." I responded. "Why do you want to know?"

"Well, the teacher wants us to bring cement things tomorrow to tell about ourselves."

"Ohhh . . . did she ask you to bring a concrete object?" Janey nodded, her mouth full of a chocolate cookie. "That means you should bring in something real—like a favorite toy or one of your collections—something that will help the other children get to know you better. Sometimes those real things are called 'concrete objects'," I explained.

"That's weird," Janey said, going off to find something to take to school the next day. Concrete and cement were synonyms Janey had learned for the hard stuff curbs and sidewalks were made of. She also knew about rubber cement as a kind of glue to use on paper but probably had never heard concrete used to refer to anything other than pavement. Her teacher may have been unaware of Janey's confusion, and even unaware that concrete and cement were synonyms in our mid-Atlantic dialect, though they may not have been in an Indiana dialect.

At any rate, Janey recognized her dilemma when she began to plan how to get a "cement thing" to school and asked the question in the best way she could manage: "Do we have any cement things?" She was only partially aware that her confusion was in her substitution of the word "cement" for "concrete."

Janey's confusion and our conversation provided both of us with new insights into our language. Janey learned a new meaning for an old word and continued her developing sophistication about nuances of word meanings. She wouldn't use the word "concrete" to mean "real" until many years later, but her understanding of it began on the first day of first grade.

I had that conversation with Janey 17 years ago. It has been near the surface of my mind ever since. I recall it when I see puzzled looks on children's faces as they listen to adult conversations and when I hear a person use a word in an unexpected way. Dialect differences are often subtle, and nuances of words are learned through using language in social situations where it is safe to take risks and try out new meanings. In safe social situations a person's language grows richer, more precise, more sophisticated.

➔ See: Andrews, pp. 36, 171; Goodman, p. 83; Weber, p. 78.

—Nancy Andrews, language arts consultant, Maine Department of Educational and Cultural Services, Augusta, ME

WHOLE LANGUAGE CAMERA

A seventh-grader participates in Nancy Moyer's classroom discussion, Amphitheater Junior High, Tucson, AZ.

As I See It:
Kenneth S. Goodman

Dialect Differences and School Programs

Adapted from *Language and Thinking in School*, 3d ed., by K. S. Goodman, E. Brooks Smith, Robert Meredith, and Yetta M. Goodman. (New York: Richard C. Owen, 1987): pp. 74–76, 78, 84, 91.

The Myth of Nonlanguage

A myth has grown up among the general public, and among many teachers and educators as well, that may be called the myth of nonlanguage. Somehow, the belief has developed that children, labeled variously as "culturally deprived," "culturally disadvantaged," "low income," "language deprived," or just slum kids, are virtually without language. This belief is reinforced for many teachers by their observation of youngsters who are inarticulate and unresponsive in the classroom. But the overwhelming evidence of linguistic research should begin to clear up this myth. All people ever studied have language. All normal children learn the language of their subcultures, and they use it on the playground, at home, and in the street. The observed "lack of language" of some children in the classroom, then, is not a real lack of language but a reluctance to use language in school, perhaps because when it is used it is rejected or ridiculed.

When children enter school, they bring to it five to six years of language and experience. Because their world, prior to entering school, has been largely confined to their family, their home, and their immediate neighborhood, both their language and experience are heavily rooted in the home culture. The language they speak is their mother's tongue. No matter what language learning they achieve in their lifetime, this first one is most deeply rooted.

This language has been so well learned that no conscious effort is involved in its use. It is deeply internalized. Children's language is as much a part of them as their own skin. Rejection of children's language may be more deeply disturbing than rejection of their skin color. The latter is only an insult, the former strikes at their ability to communicate and express their needs, feelings—their selves.

When they hear language, children can judge whether it sounds right or wrong on the basis of the language norms of their dialect. They can detect very fine differences in sounds when these differences are significant in their dialects. They have learned to ignore differences in speech sounds that are not important to their dialects. They have learned to use their dialect's patterns of rhythm and pitch with great subtlety. They enjoy, at an early age, puns in the language that depend for their humor on slight differences in stress, pitch, or phrasing. The puns may be funny only within one dialect of English.

Children of school age have virtually mastered the grammar of their dialect to the point where they can create sentences they have never heard but that are grammatical within their dialect. Their vocabulary falls largely within the vocabulary of their speech community. They have begun to develop concepts based on experiences common to their culture and have learned to express these concepts in their mother tongue.

In all respects, the process of language learning and development is the same whether the child is learning a socially prestigious dialect or learning one with low social status. When they enter school, their language is well learned and is just as systematic and just as important to them, regardless of the social value attached to their dialect in the general culture.

Perhaps the greatest handicap to more effective language programs in the schools has been the mistaken assumption that language that deviates from the standard (however defined) is bad, sloppy, or ineffective. Linguists are often surprised that anyone believes that any dialect of any language could exist without a system of its own. Linguists have learned through studies of countless dialects of countless languages that speakers of each dialect use its system with great consistency.

As long as the schools treat learners as poor users of standard English rather than as speakers of their own systematic dialects, schools will be unable to deal adequately with the language learning of all children.

Children who do not speak high-status English have language that has been adequate for their needs up to the time they begin school. That same language continues to be an effective means of communication in the child's daily life, outside of school. This effectiveness is increased, and the dialect is reinforced through contact with adults and peers at home and in the community. The teacher may say that "I done it" is wrong, but the culture says over and over again to the child that "I done it" is right.

It is only when children come into increasing contact with other groups in the general society that their language may become inadequate for their changing needs. Normally, new communicative needs will stimulate the expansion of children's language. But teachers may frustrate the language development rather than facilitate it if they continually attack that speech as incorrect or substandard. Children may be driven to defend themselves, their families, their friends, and their culture by resisting all attempts to change their language. They may be forced to regard rejection of their language as rejection of themselves.

Sometimes high-status speech becomes low status when people move from one region to another. What should happen to transplanted pupils when they arrive in the Boston or London, Toronto or Sydney classroom? What complicates the problem is the ethnocentrism that most people feel for their language. If language is different, it must be bad. Too often, children are shunted into "speech-correction" classes because they have phonemes that differ from those of their new speech communities. Sometimes the children are admonished when they have said a word or gleaned the meaning of a phrase, but in their own dialect.

Teachers cannot plead ignorance in the case of language phenomena. Educators need to know what regional speech is, what immature speech is, what a lisp is, what an idiosyncrasy of one child's idiolect is. Surely, schools must not attempt to stamp out individuality in speech. A federal judge ruled in the widely publicized Ann Arbor Black English case that school insensitivity to language difference was a handicap to school achievement even when no prejudice exists (Smitherman 1981).

The significance of dialect differences in general has been neglected in teaching language and literacy skills. Children who are divergent speakers are often doubly handicapped. Not only is their language rejected and their form of expression misunderstood and thwarted, but they also tend to be children who are not highly motivated to meet school demands and achieve. They will give up easily and reject education if the school rejects their language.

If teachers and schools are to achieve success with divergent speakers, they must first accept and understand the mother tongue of the learners.

Divergent speakers can build on the base of their own language. They can be encouraged to experiment with language and to meet the increasing need for societal communication by expanding their language. The goal is to move outward from the mother tongue, not to replace it or stamp it out. Dialect differences are inherent in language, and teachers must come to accept difference and to work with it.

→ See: Goodman, p. 83; The Meaning Makers, p. 17; Weber, p. 78.

Reference
Smitherman, G. 1981. *Black English and the education of black children/youth*. Detroit: Center for Black Studies, Wayne State University.

Poem

by Leslie N.

Uno da odda night ha
me and my friend
wen go see one bad movi you know
and was real bad you know
but everybody like dat kine movi
cuz they bad das why
I wanted to leave da teata
but my friend said we go stay
I said why and she said cuz
she need experience

→ See: Chock, p. 156.

From *small kid time hawaii*, ed. Eric Chock (Honolulu: Bamboo Ridge Press, 1981).

Leslie N. was a student at Nanakuli High when she wrote this.

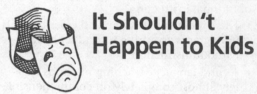

It Shouldn't Happen to Kids

No Speak Pidgin

Miss Kim on that first morning of her first year of teaching kindergarten in Hawaii, told her bright-eyed island pupils how exciting school would be. When she finished she said,"And now that you're in school all of you will speak good English and no one will speak pidgin."

Six weeks later she was at her wit's end. No matter how she tried to stimulate interest in her class she couldn't get them to say anything. They wouldn't even answer questions. "Why do you just sit there," she said. "Why won't you talk in class?" Finally, one boy burst out: "You wen' say no talk pidgin, so we no can talk."

—KSG

WHOLE LANGUAGE CAMERA

William and Eric, students in Lisa D'hollande's kindergarten, consult each other as they examine seeds with magnifying glasses, Ohlone School, Palo Alto, CA.

Second-Language Learning

 Viewpoint: Stephen D. Krashen

The Input Hypothesis and Language Education

A simple concept unites first-language acquisition, second-language acquisition, and the development of literacy: the Input Hypothesis, the idea that comprehension of messages is necessary for language acquisition and that focusing on form (conscious learning) is not. In other words, we acquire when we attend to what is said to us or what we read, not how it is said or written.

Evidence

There is massive evidence showing that comprehensible input is the major source of our linguistic and literacy competence. Here is a brief look at some of the evidence (for details, see Krashen 1989, 1990):

1. More comprehensible input results in more language and literacy development.
   - Better second-language acquisition and literacy development are associated with longer residence in the country where the language is spoken.
   - Better reading comprehension, writing style, grammar, vocabulary, and spelling are associated with more access to print outside school and/or more leisure reading.
   - More comprehensible input in the form of listening to stories is associated with better vocabulary development.

2. The development of language and literacy can occur without conscious learning and without formal instruction.
   - There are many documented cases of adult immigrants acquiring second languages without instruction.
   - Second-language teaching methods that rely almost completely on comprehensible input produce clear progress in second-language acquisition.
   - First- and second-language speakers can acquire rules of grammar without instruction.
   - Children can learn to read and spell before starting school.
   - Very few people with large vocabularies claim to have developed them through vocabulary programs.
   - Estimates of yearly growth in children's vocabulary are far larger than the number of words school programs even attempt to teach.
   - Children can spell many words they have not been taught.
   - Children improve in spelling even when they are excused from spelling or when no spelling instruction is given.

Pedagogical Research

Methods based on comprehensible input have been shown to produce excellent results when compared with "traditional" methods. Comprehensible input-based methods, such as Terrell's Natural Approach and Asher's Total Physical Response, have been declared the winner in beginning second-language teaching method comparison studies. "Sheltered" subject matter teaching has also been shown to be very effective (in sheltered subject matter teaching, second-language acquirers learn subject matter through a second language). Children who participate in Sustained Silent Reading and Self-Selected Reading programs that last for at least

> Stephen D. Krashen received his Ph.D. in linguistics at UCLA in 1972, and is currently professor of linguistics and codirector of the USC Writing Project at the University of Southern California. His awards include the Modern Language Association of America: Karl Mil Outstanding Book in Second Language Acquisition; the Robert J. Ludwig Distinguished National Leadership; and the Paul Pimsleur Award. An active speaker, Krashen has presented for the Teachers of English to Speakers of Other Languages, and the International Congress of Applied Linguistics.

seven months do at least as well as, and often better than, children in traditional programs on tests of reading comprehension and vocabulary.

Bilingual Education

The success of certain bilingual programs confirms the validity of the Input Hypothesis. Two points need to be made before we can see how this is so:

1. *The importance of background knowledge.* Simply put, background knowledge provided in the first language can make English input more comprehensible. A limited English proficient child who has had a good education in science in the first language, and who understands photosynthesis, the basic structure of the atom, and why the seasons change, will be much better prepared in a science class taught in English, even if his or her command of English is incomplete. A child with this kind of background knowledge will not only do better in science, but will also acquire more English, because the input will be more comprehensible.

2. *Literacy transfers.* Once literacy is developed in the first language, the development of literacy in the second language comes much more easily. We can distinguish two kinds of literacy that transfer:
   - "Lower-level" literacy is the ability to read and understand ordinary texts. If children learn to read by making sense of what is on the page (Goodman 1982; Smith 1982), it will be easier to learn to read in a language they understand. Once children can read in their first language, this ability transfers rapidly to the second language.
   - "Higher-level" literacy is the ability to use language to solve problems and make yourself smarter. It entails reading texts selectively, making notes, underlining, following an outline, discovering ideas as you rewrite, and so on. Once you can do these things in one language, you need not learn to do them in another.

Successful bilingual programs provide comprehensible input both directly and indirectly. They provide it directly by effective ESL and sheltered subject matter teaching, and indirectly but powerfully by teaching subject matter in the first language, without translation. Subject matter teaching in the first language gives students background knowledge, which makes English input more comprehensible. In successful bilingual programs, literacy is also developed in the first language, which then transfers to the second language.

The Role of Output

I have attempted to show that comprehensible input plays a key role in language education. Input, however, is not the entire story: We also need to consider the role of output. According to the Input Hypothesis, output, or speaking and writing, is a result of language acquisition, not the cause. Although language output does not directly cause language acquisition, it has several important functions.

1. Output can encourage input, through conversation and discussion. If you speak, someone else may speak to you. In addition, a less competent conversational partner can influence comprehensibility of input by indicating when problems occur ("What?" "Would you repeat that, please?") and by influencing what is talked about.

2. Output can have affective results as well. As Smith (1988) has argued, production in the form of writing can make the writer feel more like a member of the "literacy club," like someone who reads and writes. The writer will "read like a writer." Similarly, actually speaking French can make a second-language student feel like a member of the French-speaking world, which can lead to more interaction/comprehensible input and a greater receptivity to input.

3. There is also a growing amount of research showing that output, especially writing, can have very positive cognitive consequences. Writing helps us clarify our thinking and solve problems (Langer and Applebee 1987).

Practitioners in language arts, second-language teaching, and bilingual education are members of the same profession: language education. Teachers (and researchers) in these subfields have a great deal in common and have a great deal to learn from one another.

→ See: Bird, p. 93; Chen, p. 26; Freeman, p. 90; Heidger, p. 89; Hoyt, p. 214; Kagawa, p. 353; Otheguy, p. 91; Wallace, p. 88.

References

Goodman, K. S. 1982. *Language and literacy: The selected writings of Kenneth S. Goodman,* ed. F. Gollasch. London: Routledge & Kegan Paul.

Krashen, S. 1989. "We acquire vocabulary and spelling by reading: Additional evidence for the Input Hypothesis." *Modern Language Journal* 73.

———. 1990. "The Input Hypotheses and some competing hypotheses." In *Comprehension-based language teaching: Current trends.* Ottawa: University of Ottawa Press.

Langer, J., and A. Applebee. 1987. *How writing shapes thinking.* Urbana, IL: National Council of Teachers of English.

Smith, F. 1982. *Understanding reading.* Hillsdale, NJ: Erlbaum.

———.1988. *Joining the literacy club.* Portsmouth, NH: Heinemann.

> **Further Reading by Stephen D. Krashen**
> ◆ *The Input Hypothesis.* Longman, 1985.
> ◆ *Inquiries and Insights.* Alemany Press, 1985.

 📷 **WHOLE LANGUAGE CAMERA**

Treetop companionship, Palo Alto, CA.

Language Stories

"What Language Are You Speaking?"

The metalinguistic knowledge and generalizations that language users develop are limited by their experiences. Growing up on the Navajo reservation, our son came to believe that if he couldn't understand a speaker, then they must be speaking Navajo. For the most part, he was right. An exception came when visitors from Norway were speaking Swedish, Norwegian, and Finnish. He wondered aloud how they learned to speak Navajo so quickly.

When we moved to Tucson, an area with a large Spanish-speaking population, he came to believe that whenever he couldn't understand the speaker, they were speaking Spanish. Yelling to his sister, who was in the bathroom at the other end of the house brushing her teeth, he was unable to understand her replies. Finally, after numerous attempts, he gave up and yelled, "I can't understand you! Are you speaking Spanish?"

→ See: Hartle-Schutte, pp. 37, 38, 172, 396.

—David Hartle-Schutte, assistant professor, University of Hawaii, Hilo, HI

Book Note

Experiences with Literature: A Thematic Whole Language Model for the K–3 Bilingual Classroom

Sandra Nevarez, Raquel C. Mireles, and Norma Ramirez
1990; 352 pp.; $24
Reading, MA: Addison-Wesley

Three bilingual whole language teachers in Cerritos, California, have drawn on their own rich use of Spanish-language children's literature to provide a collection of 21 thematic literature units for the use of other teachers. This book would be valuable just for its exhaustive treasury of Spanish-language books, organized around themes. The units are built around a flexible model that teachers can use or adapt to build their own units.

The model encourages lots of reading aloud to children and integration with other areas of the curriculum. Related English-language books are also listed.

The teacher-authors have as their purpose to provide: "a meaningful program of learning experiences for children and a viable alternative to lock-step skill-building language arts programs. Instead, children are encouraged to explore themes via literature as a means to develop their language, literacy, and cognitive abilities; to expand their experiences; and to nurture their love for reading" (p. xiv).

KSG

📷 WHOLE LANGUAGE CAMERA

"The apple is happy when she's sweet."
—Ardith Cole, first grade, Lockport, NY.

Book Note

Writing in a Bilingual Program: Había Una Vez

Carole Edelsky
1986; 242 pp.; $27.50
Norwood, NJ: Ablex Publishing Corporation

As Edelsky states in the preface, "Though this is one book, one overall tale, there are actually three stories here." The first story is an in-depth analysis of the writing development of 26 first-, second-, and third-grade bilingual children. Edelsky examines their language proficiency, invented spelling, writing content, audience awareness, and their pragmatic awareness of text and context. The second story is a description and critique of the bilingual program in which the study took place, and the third, a remarkable account of Edelsky's own evolving understanding of "authentic" reading and writing. All three tales have far-reaching implications for research and instruction, for both bilingual and monolingual populations.

LBB

❝ It had been slow in coming, but at last the light flashed on! The problem with most school literacy activity was not just purposelessness. (In fact, it was produced with purposes of compliance and evaluation.) It was not assignment vs. spontaneity or in-school vs. out-of-school. It was that most of what is called reading and writing in school is inauthentic, only a facsimile, not the real thing. Some of the activities masquerading as reading and writing are inauthentic because meaning-creation is not a central goal. Some are inauthentic because they don't require that children wrestle with all the cuing systems. Some are inauthentic because one set of pragmatic constraints prevents the operation of another set. ❞ (p. 168)

Resource Essay

Poetry Books *en español* for Whole Language Classrooms

Recommended by Yvonne S. Freeman and Carolina Cervantes

Tortillitas para mamá (Little tortillas for mom), trans. by Margot C. Griego, et al., (New York: Henry Holt and Company, 1981). This collection of nursery rhymes from Spanish-speaking communities in the United States includes English translations. Text includes directions for finger plays and dramatization.

Adivinanzas indígenas (Indigenous riddles), by Elisa Ramírez (Mexico City: Editorial Patria, 1984). This collection of Mexican Indian riddles varies in complexity but provides ample opportunity for success for all ages.

La oración de la noche (The night prayer), by Manuel Ponce (Morelia, Mexico: Instituto Michoacano de cultura, 1988). This book includes two short yet sophisticated poems about the natural beauty and peace of the night. The content, rich imagery, rhythm, and illustrations are superbly complementary.

→ See: Freeman and Cervantes, pp. 184, 312, 320.

Book Note

Reading in the Bilingual Classroom: Literacy and Biliteracy

Kenneth Goodman, Yetta Goodman, and Barbara Flores
1979; 50 pp.; $5.25
Silver Spring, MD: National Clearinghouse for Bilingual Education

A slim volume that contains a wealth of information, this book dispels the most common myths surrounding bilingualism–biliteracy, answers the questions teachers of bilingual children inevitably have, and carries the inspiring message of respecting and valuing all children in all their diversity.

LBB

❝ Nothing will facilitate language development more than the true love for language in all its many forms that teachers can help children to share. In the context of that love of language, both pupils and teachers can come to appreciate that to have two languages is to be twice blessed. ❞ (p. 43)

Spelling Celebrations
by Sandra Wilde

Invented Spellings: Suffixes

One day a queen and her prince got *MARDIT* (married) in a castle.

Anna, 3d grade

Then we *WACHT* (watched) a little t.v.

Anna, 3d grade

We *TRYED* (tried) to shot (shoot) it.

Vincent, 3d grade

The man *DIED*.

Gordon, 4th grade

As children become more familiar with words, one of the ways that they begin to move beyond phonetic spelling is to abstract out features like suffixes; for instance, to understand that past-tense words almost always end with *-ed*, even though the ending is pronounced three different ways in words like *jumped*, *played*, and *wanted*. The three invented spellings shown here suggest three different levels of evolution in the spelling of the *-ed* suffix. In *MARDIT*, Anna isn't even using a phonetic spelling but instead has created a fairly rough approximation of the word. *WACHT*, however, is a very phonetic spelling, including a *t* to represent the /t/ pronunciation of *-ed*. Vincent's spelling shows an understanding of the constant spelling of the suffix, but no awareness of rules for changing the root word. The one correct spelling, *died*, doesn't tell us anything for sure. Gordon *might* understand the e-dropping rule, but could have just seen the spelling somewhere and remembered it without understanding its underlying structure. Which child could benefit from instruction about rules for changing root words before suffixes (if, and only if, these spellings are typical ones for them)? Only Vincent! Anna is not yet ready, and Gordon probably already knows the rules, whether consciously or not.

Cornerstone: A Conversation Between Catherine Wallace & Margaret Chan

Reading and Writing from the Beginning

Margaret and Catherine met on an inservice course offered at Ealing College of Higher Education for teachers who teach in multicultural/multilingual schools. Margaret is an experienced infant school teacher who is now a language support teacher at an infant school (for ages five to seven) in Hounslow on the outskirts of London. She is part of a team that supports language development both in English and in the children's home languages. Over 90 percent of the children in Margaret's school speak a home language other than English. Many languages are represented in the school but the first language of the majority is Punjabi. Most of the children come into the nursery school that feeds into the infant school speaking no English at all.

CW: Margaret, would you like to say a little bit about the overall ethos of the school?

MC: We take a whole child approach so that all our teaching is solidly based on the children's experience.

CW: And this involves also respecting the languages and cultures of the children, doesn't it?

MC: Yes. Our aim is to give institutional support to bilingualism so that the children can choose whether to use English or their first language, whichever is appropriate. In fact, they will use their first language in school in many contexts.

CW: And presumably the whole school environment reflects the number of languages spoken in the school?

MC: Yes. We have multilingual texts throughout the school—both as material on display and as books. And in our staff we have multilingual competence. For instance, I have a multilingual colleague who can support five Indian languages, as well as English.

CW: Would you like to say a little bit about the collaborative environment you encourage in the school?

MC: We aim to foster collaborative skills—we want the children to support each other's learning. In fact, we discourage a competitive approach. We work collaboratively ourselves as a staff and with the children and their parents. At the same time, the children work collaboratively with the teachers and with their peers and their parents.

CW: There's also collaboration, isn't there, between you as a language support teacher and your colleagues who are dealing with the traditional subject areas?

MC: Yes. My job is to point out the demands of the curriculum upon our children, the majority of whom are second-language learners of English. An awareness of the children's language needs informs our approach to all parts of the curriculum.

CW: So you are talking about drawing people's attention to the language demands of math or early science, not just of reading and writing activities?

MC: Yes. We take a theme-based and cross-curricular approach to learning, so we don't in fact isolate the areas of the curriculum in the traditional way. We start from a particular theme. Then the teachers will brainstorm on the possible ramifications of the theme. My particular role is to look out for the language demands that could arise from the area of work proposed.

CW: Would you like to say a little bit about the approaches to learning in the classroom itself?

Catherine Wallace is a senior lecturer in EFL/ESL in the Department of English Language Teaching at Ealing College of Higher Education in London. She teaches a range of courses for teachers who either teach in multicultural contexts in the local community or who are overseas teachers of English from many parts of the world. Wallace's major responsibility is as course director of an M.A. program, Language in the Multicultural Community.

MC: We use the integrated day system by which the children are offered a variety of activities round which they progress fairly freely during the day. In order to complete the activities they must interact with other children. Our approach to reading, for instance, is based on the paired reading approach which is essentially interactive and collaborative.

CW: One hears a lot about paired reading in British schools at the moment. Could you say how it's done in your school?

MC: Well, first it involves the parents' undertaking to read with their children two or three times during the week. They also correspond with the teachers about the sorts of choices of book the child is making and that brings in cooperation between parent and teacher.

CW: What if the parents can't read English?

MC: The reading doesn't have to be in English—the children can take home books that are in the mother tongue. The important thing is for the children to share a story with a parent—or, of course, it could be an older brother or sister.

CW: I believe you also have paired reading between children themselves in school, don't you?

MC: Yes, the paired reading approach is also used between teacher and child and child and child—they may be either peers in the same class or older children may come and read with the younger children, which enhances the experience for both.

CW: I think you also sometimes use the big books, don't you, for class storytelling?

MC: Yes. This is a very good way of sharing a story among a group. In fact the children get to know the books so well that they can "read" the stories to each other, though they aren't able to read the particular individual words on the page. We don't, in fact, make any demarcation point as to where reading as such starts—we refer to it as reading right from the beginning. We encourage the children to use any clues they can—in the early stages, of course, that's usually the pictures and their memory of the story from previous tellings.

CW: I think, too, you're interested in children not just reading stories but in reading a whole range of material.

MC: Yes, we realize that reading is a multifaceted experience. Our children will read a variety of different texts for a variety of different purposes during the school day. And we no longer give precedence to one sort of reading experience over another. We don't even have a reading scheme [basal reader] any more.

CW: So this means you've got a lot of "real books."

MC: Yes, we've got real books with real stories.

CW: But it's not just reading for pleasure that's important is it, but rather for information, to take action or make decisions—a whole range of purposes?

MC: Yes. There are a hundred reasons for reading throughout the school day—there'll be the menu for school lunch, the calendar, and the weather chart. However, reading for pleasure is especially important. That's something the chil-

dren didn't get when we stuck rigidly to a reading scheme. The books were not real stories; they were not written with any appreciation for how language should sound. The children were not reading for enjoyment—they were just acquiring a skill in isolation. An important part of our approach now is that enjoyment should be there from the beginning.

CW: The aim generally is to demystify the process of reading, isn't it?

MC: Yes. Right from the earliest attempt at reading we say that they are *reading* and this also spills into the approach to writing. So right from the beginning when the child takes a pencil and makes a mark on the page and is trying to communicate, we call that *writing*. We don't only call it writing when it's conventionally written in conventional scripts using orthodox spelling.

CW: So you get rid of this idea of children saying that they "can't read" or they "can't write."

MC: Yes. Quite recently some of the older children did a survey about reading and writing, and all the children from the nursery up said they could read. They feel they can read right from the beginning when they first get an idea as to what a book is. And, equally, they feel they can write from the beginning. They gradually start to incorporate conventional letters not only in English but also in their mother tongue, so our children may, for instance, use a recognizable Arabic word form or a Punjabi or English word form in the middle of a page of writing.

CW: Do they talk about this? Are they aware of this themselves?

MC: Oh yes—part of the process of demystifying is to make the children very aware of what they're doing.

CW: So you encourage the children to talk about their own reading and writing strategies—to make them more generally aware of their own language use. And I think you also said they use their own writing—even when it's "invented" or developmental—to tell their own stories?

MC: Yes. Our children are authors. From the beginning they're producing books—and we call them books. They may be produced in many different ways. They may be developmentally written, typewritten, or produced on a word processor. And lots of the books are produced collaboratively with a friend, either from the outset or at the draft stage. Also, older children will write for younger children, which means that the older children need to adapt their language.

CW: And they will be writing in languages other than English, won't they? They may be producing bilingual books. I've seen collaborative work for instance, where bilingual learners who speak only a little English write a story in their mother tongue and attempt to tell it in English to an English-speaking peer who then writes an English version in a way that is accessible for a second-language learner. So this is another good language awareness activity, making the children aware of the need to adjust one's language according to one's audience.

MC: And of course they use writing in many different real contexts—writing a thank you letter after a visit, writing a class newspaper, or writing off for particular information in connection with project work.

CW: Could we turn to project or topic work, which is the framework for many of the literacy activities we have been describing? Would you like to talk about a particular theme that you recently used in your school, which highlighted the multicultural and cross-curricular perspectives we've been talking about?

MC: Yes, with our very youngest children, who are five, we took the theme of time and we

Margaret Chan is a community language service teacher in the London borough of Hounslow, England.

As Teachers See It:

by Barbara Hyslop Heidger

No Need to Panic

Lucky the newcomer to English who lands in a whole language classroom. The supportive, affirming, kid-based, language-filled environment is the ideal situation for learning to speak, read, and write in English. As a pull-out teacher in a K through 6 whole language school, I am awed by the rapid progress made by students in these classrooms. There is no need to panic when you receive a new ESL child, because the whole language practices you already use will provide for the language, literacy, and emotional development that the child needs. You should feel good about doing the following in your teaching:

1. You have high expectations and confidence in ESL children. You know that they have rich experiences, knowledge, and language skills, and that they can be successful in English. Children don't sit and vegetate in your class "until they know English," deciding that school is a spectator sport. Something productive is expected from each child all the time. You adapt tasks, use cooperative learning and peer teaching, and use everything that everyone has for communication (nonverbal gestures, pictures, first language, etc.)

In spite of all the adaptive procedures you are using, there will be times when the class activity is too difficult. At such times, new,

looked at it in a cross-curricular way, so that art, craft, music, and math—every curricular area was linked to the theme. And one of the ways to develop a concept of time was through the medium of a story. We chose "The Hare and the Tortoise." The story was chosen because it illustrates certain concepts of time.

I started by making a big book with pictures of the story, but no writing at all, so the story could be told and retold not just in English but in other languages, and the bilingual support teachers could use it to support mother tongue activities. I made a tape of the story in English and a tape was also made in Punjabi so that the children could listen to the story using headphones. Now the children were beginning to make up their own stories as they played the game. So, from a given story, they were now creating their own story. They had puppets based on the story. They used these in any way they wished, so the link with the original story became quite tenuous.

CW: And did any writing emerge from this?

MC: We made a photo story book about it.

CW: So what emerged was a collaborative account of an experience that the class had shared.

MC: Yes, and my bilingual colleagues who support the mother tongue also made sure that they focused their activities on the same topic.

CW: So Margaret, if I can sum up, what you're describing is a holistic approach to language development in the sense that all the children's language abilities are engaged in tasks that arise naturally from a theme-based approach and from a real need to communicate.

MC: Yes. You really can't draw the threads apart. The whole thing has to be integrated.

→ See: Heidger, p. 89; Hoyt, p. 214; Krashen, p. 86; Urzúa, p. 42.

Further Reading by Catherine Wallace

◆ *Advanced Reading Skills.* Longman, 1981.
◆ *Learning to Read in a Multicultural Society: The Social Context of Second Language Literacy,* reprint. Prentice-Hall, 1988.

---

non-English-speaking fifth-graders get a basket that contains special tasks: a book on their home and family (or later, one on their former school and their new school), which they are making by drawing pictures or adding photos and then writing captions in English and home language; their own homemade bilingual dictionary; a children's book in first languages; a number-word matching game, and English children's books, some with accompanying commercial or teacher-produced tapes for a personal listening center. They can keep track of the work they are doing by checking off what they have worked on and want to continue.

2. You surround ESL children with written and oral language in meaningful contexts. Upper grade teachers often borrow materials and ideas from primary colleagues. Good children's literature and predictable books, such as *The Very Hungry Caterpillar*, *The Three Little Pigs*, good songs, and chants are ageless and provide wonderful language and literary models.

3. You also realize that your new ESL children can be a boost to the confidence of all your readers by providing purposeful and socially acceptable shared reading experiences. Tutors profit from a "tutor support" session, in which they discover ways of establishing meaning.

You and your students may work together to label the classroom in functionally appropriate ways. You might even have corresponding labels written underneath in the first language(s), getting help from the ESL children, parents, and bilingual picture dictionaries. Some classes even learn new words and phrases daily in the first language of the ESL students.

4. You, as teachers applying whole language, include ESL children from the beginning in writing activities such as dialogue journals. You celebrate whatever form the writing may take—pictures, home language, or invented English spelling and syntax. If the writing is in the child's first language in the beginning, it is helpful to have the parent or someone else in the school or community help translate if you don't know the language. Then you can make an appropriate response in English, and have a wonderful reason to transcribe into English to "help me remember." This same translator may also give you some ideas about the children's writing in their first language. Encourage beginning English writing attempts as soon as children seem to be comfortable.

5. Finally, you validate the children's home language and culture in all possible ways, incorporating pictures, objects, folktales, children's literature, food, and music from their country.

Your class celebrates the national holidays of your second language children (Chinese New Year, Cinco de Mayo, etc.). Your emerging English speakers and their parents and ethnic community become experts and invaluable resources. They have reason to share pictures and stories of holiday events "back home." The whole class has rich opportunities to read about the customs, stories, and histories and plan the decorations, music, food, and activities.

As whole language teachers, you *do* have the ability to teach and reach the ESL children in ways that are adding to the education of all your children, creating a whole child and whole world classroom.

→ See: Freeman, p. 90; Hoyt, p. 214; Krashen, p. 86; Literature Reference List, p. 429; Urzúa, p. 42; Wallace, p. 88.

Barbara Hyslop Heidger is an elementary ESL teacher at Kirkwood Elementary School, Coralville, IA.

Resource: Organization

Teachers of English to Speakers of Other Languages (TESOL)

1600 Cameron St., Ste. 300
Alexandria, VA 22314
1-703-836-0774

The work of *Catalog* essayist Stephen Krashen has done much to promote interest in authentic literacy experiences within the TESOL organization, and *Catalog* essayists Lucinda Pease-Alvarez, Pat Rigg, Katharine Samway, and Carole Urzúa have been instrumental in developing the whole language component of TESOL. The organization's mission is to strengthen the effective teaching and learning of English around the world while respecting individuals' language rights. TESOL supports and seeks to inspire those involved in English language teaching, provides leadership and direction through the dissemination and exchange of information and resources, and encourages access to and standards for English language instruction. Publications include a scholarly quarterly and the *TESOL Newsletter,* a classroom-oriented publication with referenced articles, job listings, calls for conferences, and book reviews.

LBB

Breakthroughs

Tawana

Bonnie Laster tells this story about Tawana, a five-year-old black child enrolled in Bonnie's bilingual, whole language kindergarten:

It was September. School had just started. I had a pretty even mix of black and Hispanic students. One morning just before lunch, we were singing songs: "Old MacDonald," "The Itsy Bitsy Spider," "If You're Happy and You Know It." Then I suggested we sing "Venga a Ver Mi Charca," a favorite of my Hispanic students.

Tawana listened to the song sung in Spanish by her Hispanic classmates, then scowled, covered her ears, and shouted, "Stop that! I can't stand the sound of that!"

I knew it was Tawana's first real exposure to Spanish. But I knew in time she would grow accustomed to it because throughout the school day, Carmen, my Hispanic instructional aide, and I use both Spanish and English interchangeably with the children. I don't believe in the old ESL exercises. We just give our kids lots of opportunities to explore and use both languages just as kids do in multilingual homes and communities.

The message to the kids is clear: Both languages are valued, both languages are respected, and they are invited to explore, enjoy, and learn both.

Tawana got the message. In May she handed a story to Carmen. As in her other stories, she had used invented writing—with one important difference. As Tawana explained, this one was "written in Spanish."

—As told to LBB by Bonnie Laster, primary teacher, Brentwood Oaks School, East Palo Alto, CA

Classroom Demonstrations

by Yvonne S. Freeman and David E. Freeman

Ten Tips for Monolingual Teachers of Bilingual Students

Whole language teachers build on the strengths and background knowledge that their students bring with them to the classroom. These teachers strive to develop their students' language resources, and they know that all students, including non-English speakers, come with a linguistic system that functions well enough to meet all their communication needs. As teachers plan activities to expand the range of language uses for their students, they provide consistent opportunities for their bilingual students to develop listening, speaking, reading, and writing in their first as well as their second languages.

When teachers have a group of bilingual students who all speak the same first language, which the teacher also speaks, and for which there are written materials available, those bilingual teachers can provide experiences with literature and content materials using their students' primary language as the language of instruction. This will involve some effort on the teacher's part, particularly in gathering appropriate instructional materials.

However, even teachers who are not bilingual, or who are not teaching a class of students who all speak the same language, can find ways to support the development of both English and the primary language(s) of their students. We have worked with whole language teachers who have successfully supported the first languages of their bilingual students despite the fact that the teachers themselves were not bilingual. The teachers did make extra efforts to prepare themselves to meet the needs of all their students. They read the current research on bilingual education by Cummins (*Empowering Minority Students*, CABE, 1989), Krashen and Biber (*On Course*, CABE, 1988), and others. This research calls for first language support for the academic success and building of self-esteem of language-minority students. As a result of reading, taking classes, and talking with other professionals, teachers we have worked with have developed a number of ways to support the language development of their bilingual students. We have listed below some of the ideas that they feel have worked well in their classrooms.

1. Arrange for bilingual aides or parent volunteers to read literature written in the primary language to the students and then to discuss what they have read.

2. Plan for older students who speak the first language of the children to come to the class regularly to read to or with the younger students and to act as peer tutors. For example, sixth-grade students might come to a first-grade class two or three mornings a week to share reading. This often proves beneficial to the older students as well as the younger students. Younger students can choose books to read to older students on certain days.

3. Set up a system of pen-pal letters written in the primary language between students of different classes or different schools.

4. Have students who are bilingual pair up with classmates who share the same primary language but are less proficient in English. This buddy system is particularly helpful for introducing new students to class routines.

5. Invite bilingual storytellers to come to the class and tell stories that would be familiar to all the students. Using context clues, these storytellers can convey familiar stories in languages other than English. Other well-known stories such as "Cinderella" have their counterparts (and origins) in non-English languages.

6. Build a classroom library of books in languages other than English. This is essential for primary language literacy development. At times, teachers within a school may want to pool these resources.

7. Encourage journal writing in the first language. A bilingual aide or parent volunteer can read and respond to journal entries. Give students a choice of languages to read and write in.

8. To increase the primary language resources in classrooms, publish books in languages other than English. Allow bilingual students to share their stories with classmates.

9. Look around the room at the environmental print. Include signs in the first language as well as articles and stories in English about the countries the students come from. One teacher made bookmarks which were laminated and left in a basket for visitors. On one side was a proverb in English and on the other the equivalent proverb written in a language other than English.

10. Have students engage in oral activities such as show and tell using their first language as they explain objects or events from their homelands.

These whole language teachers who teach whole children by supporting their strengths, including their first languages, have witnessed academic success in two languages for their students and increased self-esteem. These teachers and their students have revalued the importance of bilingualism in a classroom where the whole language of all students is celebrated.

➔ See: Freeman, pp. 110, 189, 212, 294, 368; Heidger, p. 89; Krashen, p. 86; Urzúa, p. 42; Wallace, p. 88.

Yvonne S. Freeman is the director of Bilingual Education and the codirector of the Language Development Program at Fresno Pacific College, Fresno, CA.

David E. Freeman is codirector of the Language Development Program and the director of the Secondary Teaching Program at Fresno Pacific College, Fresno, CA.

As Teachers See It

by Laurel Cress

Fulfilling a Need

In his book *What's Whole in Whole Language* Ken Goodman writes, "Bilingual children learn more than one language for the same reason that monolingual children learn only one: they learn what they need." I've been teaching a whole language, bilingual kindergarten for four years, and the truth of this statement is revealed to me daily. I know it's true; in fact, this year I refused to do a formal English as a Second Language (ESL) program that entailed flashing picture cards at students and recording the cards they can name in English.

My students were tested at the beginning of the year on the LAS test and again at the end. I got the results back the last week of school. All the children had made significant progress; some gained over 30 points on the test. Several of my NES kids jumped two levels.

Where did they get this English? From everyday whole language classroom activities: from shared reading with the whole class, dramatizing and discussing books in English, singing many, many songs in English, and doing cooperative learning activities in which they were seated with monolingual English speakers. And of course they make friends with English-speaking children and played together in the playhouse, built block towers, and interacted with their English-speaking friends in any one of a hundred ways in the classroom and on the playground.

How much English they learn has a lot to do with the initiative of the individual child. For example, this year I had a pair of twins, José and Sandra, who started the year as NES kids. José is very outgoing, likes to be a leader, and soon made many friends among both English- and Spanish-speakers. Toward the end of the year he tried to communicate with me exclusively in English, only using Spanish when he was unable to get his point across in English.

Sandra is a timid child who seldom speaks unless adults address her first. She chose her playmates from among the other Spanish-speaking children in class, and I never heard her trying to speak English alone though she participated in the shared reading in English and sang along with all the English songs.

Although I believe my observations are more valuable and valid than standardized tests, nevertheless, I was happy when the LAS test results corroborated what I was seeing in my classroom. Sandra scored 10 points higher, José, 30 points. Sandra learned the English she needed to participate in classroom activities. José learned more because his goal was to be a classroom leader.

➔ See: What's Whole in Whole Language, p. 381.

Laurel Cress is a bilingual primary teacher at Longwood School, Hayward, CA.

The Funny Side

Speaking of Specifics

When Gloria Norton was working for her bilingual teaching credential she had to take the language proficiency test. At the same time she took the Spanish version, she also mistakenly took the English proficiency exam. The results came back several weeks later, and to Gloria's extreme surprise, she discovered she had failed the English composition. The testing agency's reason? She hadn't developed her theme with enough "specifies."

—As told to LBB by Gloria Norton, resource teacher, Fair Oaks School, Redwood City, CA

Cornerstone: Ricardo Otheguy

Frequently Asked Questions About the Role of Minority Languages

The role that languages other than English should play in the education of children from linguistic minorities is a subject of great interest in the United States. The widespread perception is that teachers who work with language-minority children, especially those teaching in public school bilingual programs, use a great deal of Spanish, Chinese, and other foreign languages. Research points in the opposite direction. In general, throughout public schools in the United States, there is very little use of languages other than English in bilingual programs, and very little interest in preserving those languages.

The overwhelming majority of bilingual programs (about 85 percent) are subtractive; that is, their purpose is to make children English monolingual (Crawford 1987). Those bilingual teachers who do speak Spanish in classrooms in the United States use it on an average only 23 percent of total classroom time. For Cantonese the figures are even lower. Teachers who speak it the most use it 8 percent of the time.

But what about the popular notion that classes in a bilingual program are supposed to be conducted in other languages, whereas English as a Second Language (ESL) programs are supposed to be in English? Although bilingual programs differ widely, they all place a great deal of emphasis on ESL. They all have a lot of subject-matter instruction in English. Though it is generally agreed that all bilingual programs should

Ricardo Otheguy is professor of linguistics and education at the Graduate School and the City College, both of the City University of New York. He was a visiting Fulbright scholar in the Humanities Faculty of the University of the Republic in Montevideo, Uruguay. His publications deal with Spanish grammar and semantics, bilingual education, and languages in contact. He has helped develop innovative bilingual programs in New York City public schools.

make consistent use of the child's home language, in fact only a few do.

Many people like the idea of children growing up bilingual. But they feel that languages other than English do not have to be developed by the school. They reason that the minority child already knows the home language by the time schooling starts. Remember that this assumption is never made for American-born children from English-speaking families. Teachers whose students speak the majority language don't think for a minute that children have completed the development of their native language. Bilingual children are no different. Their home language needs nurturing no less than that of monolingual children. The evidence suggests that without the help of the school those children who start their education being potentially bilingual will almost certainly finish it as English monolinguals.

But what do we get from developing skills in languages other than English anyway? For example, does developing a minority child's home language contribute to academic achievement? Research shows that development of the home language contributes to higher academic achievement. For Hispanic children in secondary schools nationwide, proficiency in Spanish is one of the two most important correlates of high scores in tests of math and reading (Nielsen and Fernandez 1981). The home language plays another important role in the acquisition of a second language. By using the native language, teachers can provide a context that will then facilitate understanding of, and growth in, the second language (Crawford 1989).

What about the public? Do people want bilingual programs? Opinion polls show that parents, and the public at large, favor bilingual education. Many people pay good money to send their children to private and church-sponsored bilingual programs. In the city of Miami, there are more than 10 fee-charging schools whose main attraction is that they conduct classes in Spanish. These aren't expensive, elite institutions, but schools for working-class people (García and Otheguy 1985, pp. 3–20; 1987, pp. 83–95).

So these programs are popular and the public at large wants them. The evidence is that they work. Educational activities are not easy to evaluate. This is true for bilingual programs and for every other type of educational enterprise. Yet positive evidence of success is easily available (Castellanos 1983; Crawford 1989).

➜ See: Krashen, p. 86; Wallace, p. 88.

References

Castellanos, D. 1983. *The best of two worlds: Bilingual-bicultural education in the United States.* Trenton: New Jersey State Department of Education.

Crawford, J. 1987. "Bilingual education: Language, learning and politics. A special report." *Education Week,* 1 April.

———. 1989. *Bilingual education: History, policy, theory and practice.* Trenton, NJ: Crane Publishing.

García, O., and R. Otheguy. 1985. "The masters of survival send their children to school: Bilingual education in the ethnic schools of Miami." *Bilingual Review* 12.

———. 1987. "The bilingual education of Cuban-American children in Dade County's ethnic schools." *Language & Education* 1.

Nielsen, F., and R. Fernandez. 1981. *Hispanic students in American high schools: Background characteristics and achievement.* Washington, DC: National Center for Educational Statistics.

Further Reading by Ricardo Otheguy

◆ "Thinking About Bilingual Education: A Critical Appraisal." *Harvard Educational Review* 52, 1982.

◆ "The Masters of Survival Send Their Children to School: Bilingual Education in the Ethnic Schools in Miami," with Ofelia García. *Bilingual Review* 12, 1985.

◆ *English Across Cultures: Cultures Across English (A Reader in Cross-cultural Communication),* ed. with Ofelia García. Mouton de Gruyter, 1989.

◆ "Transferring, Switching, and Modeling in West New York Spanish: An Intergenerational Study." *International Journal of the Sociology of Language,* 1989.

 WHOLE LANGUAGE CAMERA

A stationary ride, Palo Alto, CA.

Book Note

Empowering Minority Students

Jim Cummins
1989; 143 pp.; $17 from:
California Association for Bilingual Education (CABE)
1926 J St., Ste. 810
Sacramento, CA 95814
1-916-447-3986

There are, in this country, groups of minority students who are disempowered by our educational system. Whole language teachers, however, are committed to providing an empowering curriculum for all their students. The information contained in *Empowering Minority Students* can help whole language teachers make informed decisions concerning their language-minority students.

In his book Cummins places education for bilingual students in its historical and political contexts, presents the research that supports bilingual education as the best means of achieving academic success for bilingual students, discusses the disinformation about bilingual education that the public has been subjected to, and explains the importance of a new kind of curriculum that empowers language-minority students. Cummins argues that politics and racism are two reasons that an empowering curriculum, including bilingual education, has not been implemented with bilingual students.

David E. Freeman and Yvonne S. Freeman

The Funny Side

The Right Sentiment

Refugees in the Philippines Refugee Processing Center love to give flowers as gifts to their teacher, especially on their graduation day at the end of the cycle. Children in the PREP programs are no exception. They present a festive sight as they wait by the roadside for the arrival of their beloved teacher. Everyone is eager to present their token of appreciation. A box of candy, a garland, an album, a small purse, paper roses, a Vietnamese hat, a Lao pen-holder, and even self-made greeting cards are small things that will forever remind you of them.

There was a seven-year-old boy I will always remember, not for his gift but for the note that he sent with it. He obviously wanted to impress me for the last time with his newly acquired vocabulary.

Dear teacher Miss Mae,

I thank you for teaching me many things. I give you this gift as a symbol of my deepest sympathy.

Your student,
Minh

—Jesse Mae de Vera, teacher, World Relief Corporation, the Philippines

Joyful Literacy at Fair Oaks School

by Lois Bridges Bird

At the south end of a barrio, between dilapidated apartment buildings, their balconies draped with laundry hung out to dry, and Raychem, a huge industrial complex, sprawls a salmon-colored stucco school building, enclosed in an asphalt yard. This is Fair Oaks, a whole language, bilingual school in Redwood City, California, a working-class community 15 miles south of San Francisco. The student population is 85 percent Hispanic, and 10 percent other minorities such as Tongan, Asian, and black. The majority of the children arrive speaking only their native tongue; by fourth grade, most have made the transition to English instruction. It is the poorest school in the district. Many of our students are recent arrivals in the United States, fleeing the war in Central America or economic problems in Mexico. Our principal has estimated that 10 percent of our children live in garages without facilities most of us take for granted. They do not have a head start in anything related to school, but they do have, like children everywhere, a natural propensity to learn.

This propensity was not evident when Fair Oaks followed the traditional skills regimen of basals and workbooks. According to test scores, our students were three and four years below grade level, well below the test band set for schools like ours. In 1975, alarmed by the low scores, the California State Department of Education sent a team to Fair Oaks to investigate, thus initiating several years of soul-searching on the part of the Fair Oaks faculty. Spurred on by this visit, the faculty, with the help of resource teacher Gloria Norton began taking a long hard look at their educational program. A grant from the neighborhood corporation, Raychem, helped pay for intense inservice and summer courses for the teachers with leading authorities in the field, and helped to fill classroom libraries with fine children's literature. In 1984 Redwood City School District made it official: Fair Oaks was designated a bilingual, whole language school.

Through whole language our students are gaining access to the full power, beauty, and joy of language and literacy. The benefits are many, but perhaps best understood as four broad themes: (1) experimentation, (2) authenticity, (3) self-reflection, and (4) empowerment.

Experimentation

At Fair Oaks, we reject the behaviorists' theories that reduce language and learning to a system of isolated skills; instead, we follow children's natural and powerful learning strategies. We embrace Shirley Brice Heath's advice and provide children with models of "joyful literacy." We immerse them in rich, functional print (the walls in whole language classrooms are said to "drip with print"!). We read to them —three, four, five times a day—beautiful literature, poetry, and song. We give them control and ownership of their reading and writing, and, with our guidance, allow them to experiment and approximate, to play with literacy in the same way they play with all they are attempting to learn. We understand that literacy, like oral language learning, is a developmental process.

Authenticity

Fair Oaks teachers try to avoid lessons involving "unauthentic language"—language stripped of pragmatic purpose, occurring only in compliance with teacher-directed assignments. The focus is always on meaning. Children write across the curriculum for a wide range of authentic purposes: to protest government policies in Central America, to explain to friends how to construct a backyard tent, to note information gathered from spending the afternoon in the library researching the life of manatees.

Here is an example of language use for a very pragmatic purpose:

Mr. smiTh,
we have a brocen
TebR. iT nios scRs.
can same baff FiseT
Piis?

ThanK ⅄ou
Chris #14

[Dear Mr. Smith, We have a broken table. It needs screws. Can somebody fix it, please? Thank you.]

Book Note

Becoming a Whole Language School: The Fair Oaks Story

Lois Bridges Bird, editor
1989; 151 pp.; $14.95
Katonah, NY: Richard C. Owen

This book tells the story of one school's evolution into whole language. The voices of primary and intermediate classroom teachers, resource teachers, university specialists, the principal, the superintendent, and one school board member are heard as their individual enthusiasm and frustrations in this project are retold. This description includes: (1) practical how-to tips from teachers involved in supporting emerging readers, facilitating writers workshop and literature studies, and organizing a cross-age tutorial program, (2) a historical overview of Fair Oak's entry into whole language, and (3) a theoretical and philosophical discussion of the universal truths concerning children and teachers as learners.

Mary Ellen Sweeny

This was written by a Spanish-speaking five-year-old self-transitioning into English. It is typical of the notes we receive daily in the school office.

Self-Reflection

Although there is some debate as to the actual value of metacognition and metalinguistic awareness—the ability to reflect upon one's own cognitive and linguistic processing—there are those, such as Courtney Cazden, who consider it the very essence of education. Debate over its significance notwithstanding, students in whole language classrooms frequently and spontaneously examine their own thinking, reading, and writing. While participating in a literature study, nine-year-old Karla explains how she thinks Robert Smith composed his delightful *Chocolate Fever:*

He saw first in his mind . . . what the author did is first, he saw the . . . what he was going to write down. Because what I do is as soon as I'm writing, ideas come to my head like this when I'm writing, writing, writing, writing. Sooo, I think he did the same thing! He sees the picture in his mind before he writes it down.

Karla is a writer. She understands her own writing process, and she senses what Robert Smith must do as he puts pen to paper, or sits in front of his keyboard.

Empowerment

Through the freedom and support and respect for the language learner that whole language provides, our students have come to believe in themselves as capable, creative learners, knowing what they need and how to get it.

Three years ago, a young woman, only weeks out of her credential program, was hired to teach sixth grade at Fair Oaks. It soon became apparent that she was overwhelmed and needed help. Thinking it might ease her burden, Gloria suggested that she use a basal for a few weeks while

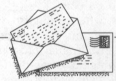

she got herself established. She accepted that advice; her students, however, did not. Many of them had been at Fair Oaks since kindergarten and had never seen a basal, much less used one, and their first reaction was, "Hey! What happened to our *real books?*" Their second reaction was to go on strike and refuse to read until the literature books were returned. Now that's empowerment, and that was the end of the basal!

Perhaps nine-year-old Karla explains empowerment best. When I asked her what she liked the most about Fair Oaks, she thought long and hard before answering, but when she finally found the words she wanted, I felt my pulse quicken and goosebumps creep up the back of my neck—it was the kind of response whole language teachers live to hear. She said, "At other schools, they teach you about other people's ideas; at Fair Oaks, they help you discover your own ideas."

At Fair Oaks we will continue to help our students "discover their own ideas," and, in the process, they will expand and refine our understanding of what it means to be joyfully literate.

→ See: Edelsky, p. 72; Literature Reference List, p. 429.

Adapted from *Becoming a Whole Language School: The Fair Oaks Story,* by Lois Bridges Bird, ed. (Katonah, NY: Richard C. Owen, 1989) and "Joyful Literacy at Fair Oaks School," by Lois Bridges Bird, *Holistic Education Review* 2(4), Winter 1989.

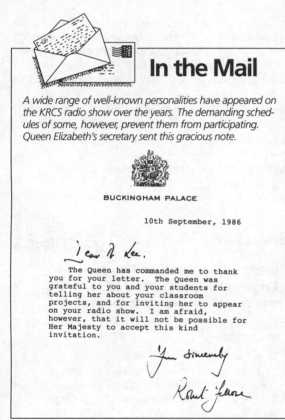

In the Mail

A wide range of well-known personalities have appeared on the KRCS radio show over the years. The demanding schedules of some, however, prevent them from participating. Queen Elizabeth's secretary sent this gracious note.

BUCKINGHAM PALACE

10th September, 1986

Dear Mr Lee.

The Queen has commanded me to thank you for your letter. The Queen was grateful to you and your students for telling her about your classroom projects, and for inviting her to appear on your radio show. I am afraid, however, that it will not be possible for Her Majesty to accept this kind invitation.

Yours sincerely,

Robert Fellowes

Classroom Demonstrations

by Lois Bridges Bird

An Interview with Roberta Lee

Roberta Lee is a sixth-grade bilingual teacher at Fair Oaks School who has been teaching for 24 years. Eight years ago she created a radio show in a bilingual barrio school. The show has won numerous educational awards including the prestigious California School Board's Golden Bell Award. The Whitney Foundation, which provided grant funding for the radio show equipment, has recommended this project for exemplary status at the federal level and inclusion in the National Diffusion Network.

LBB: What equipment did you need and how did you obtain it?

RL: The Whitney Foundation is a San Francisco-based organization that promotes teacher initiative in language arts and reading. I wrote a proposal that they funded. With a $2,000 grant we were able to purchase basic radio equipment—two record players, a tape recorder, a mixer, two microphones, two headphones, and jacks.

LBB: How is the show organized?

RL: It is broadcast every Friday morning for one-half hour. We open with some music, read student-submitted stories, poems, and so forth. From there we give a brief news report including newsworthy events on local, state, and national levels. Often we have a separate sports report. Then we might have a guest speaker—the kids interview someone special from the community. The chosen guest often coincides with a unit of study. Next on the show, we give public service announcements, note items of interest to the school and community, and often the school nurse will provide some pertinent health tips. Then we announce sensational citizen awards —certificates given to students, staff, and community members for service to the school or for academic achievement. Finally, we end with some sort of contest—questions about geography, for instance, and sign-off with more music.

LBB: How do you organize the kids who do the actual broadcasting?

RL: Student broadcasters serve a four-week shift so that all students have the opportunity to participate. They select an area of production reflecting their own special interests, skills, or job aspirations—they can choose to be directors, scriptwriters, actors, engineers, announcers, disc jockeys, or secretaries. Students can pool their skills to produce musical shows, radio dramas, interviews, and challenging contests.

LBB: How do the children learn their chosen job?

RL: They learn by doing! We do have lessons on scriptwriting. We have lessons on writing invitations and thank-you letters to people who appear on our show. I also help the kids learn and practice proper telephone etiquette, since they often use the telephone to contact people and conduct the general radio show business. The kids also learn how to conduct an interview. They learn to avoid questions that lead to dead-end, yes-no answers. And we have lots of opportunities to learn about and practice effective deliveries over the air. The kids begin to notice—and critique —the professional disc jockeys and news broadcasters they hear on their favorite radio stations.

LBB: What goes into producing each radio show?

RL: We work on it all week long. The kids are constantly researching and writing up material for the show. They have authentic, compelling reasons to do that research, and a real audience out there who will hear what they've learned. We allow two days for rehearsal prior to each program so broadcasters have enough practice to sound polished and professional. They quickly learn that radio personalities cannot be seen so their voices must communicate to the listeners. The benefits are tremendous for all children, but especially for children who are learning English as a second language. ESL drills can't begin to compare!

LBB: What help do you have with the show?

RL: Teachers, parents, and community people are willing to help with such an exciting project, and many senior citizens from various organizations are willing to donate their time. The relationship established between the children and senior citizens is genuine and lasting, and it allows both groups to have a feeling of importance. Every year we dedicate one radio show to a theme of "giving" and honor our volunteers.

LBB: The benefits of this experience for kids seem obvious, but what stands out in your mind as the major benefits?

RL: It has enhanced bilingual strategies by accelerating English acquisition and providing varied and authentic opportunities to read, write, and speak; it has increased multicultural awareness in the schools and in the community and brought in parent and senior citizen volunteers. Students are submitting more written work of a higher quality than ever before, and their oral broadcasting skills show marked improvement as well. All in all, it has proved to be a rewarding, stimulating, and fun way to promote functional language and literacy development. I can't imagine now teaching any other way!

→ See: Morduchowicz, p. 76.

Further Information: The radio show, known as KRCS (Redwood City Schools), is now broadcast from two other schools in the district besides Fair Oaks. For more information regarding the establishment of a school radio show, you can purchase Ms. Lee's handbook, "On the Air with KRCS," for $2.50 by writing to her or calling: Fair Oaks School, 2950 Fair Oaks Ave., Redwood City, CA, 94063, (415) 368-3953.

Great Schools — Fair Oaks School

Meet Fair Oaks School Literacy All-Stars

by Janet Nielsen

Viewers of the PBS Literacy special, "First Things First," got a close-up look at the cross-generational tutoring program at Fair Oaks School in Redwood City. The Project Literacy U.S. (PLUS) special, broadcast on PBS last October, examined families-at-risk and programs across the country that are working creatively and effectively to break the cycle of intergenerational illiteracy.

"The show was significant in exploring schools and programs which are actively engaged in changing expectations for low income, minority children," according to Gloria Norton, resource teacher at Fair Oaks School. The stu-

dents at Fair Oaks are predominantly recent Hispanic immigrants from one area of Mexico. Working with Stanford University anthropologist and linguist, Shirley Brice Heath, the school has made cross-age tutoring and the study of literature the key to instruction.

"We have received calls and letters from all over the United States from viewers who want to know more and who are anxious to reach these students who traditionally are at the bottom of the educational structure," reported Norton. "The program helped our parents and children feel a great sense of pride in their school."

From *Vision,* the KQED instructional television newsletter,

YOUNG ARTISTS

Armando Cerrillo, 9, student of Elizabeth Doerr, Fair Oaks School, Redwood City, CA.

Whole Language Internacional
by Mark Caprio

Japanese Students' Reaction to Whole Language

Akiko: Now, understanding English and saying what I want to say in English, I think, kills me. [translation]

Maki: When I heard this remark "You must speak in English" for the first time, I think, "It is impossible. To be sure, I studied English until now in order to pass the entrance exam, but I hardly speak in English." I had a fear of my English ability about conversation.

Takako: When I began to talk, inside my head became white. [translation]

The fears expressed by these three female students are real. Even though they have studied the English language for a total of at least six years, the majority of students entering a university have never been asked to use the language for any purpose of communication. As Maki tells us, most of her study was concentrated on preparing for university entrance exams. Maki's teacher had told her that it was not important to learn how to speak, just to read, write (through a grammar-translation method), and hear (not listen). Thus, when they entered my class for the first time and heard me, a native speaker of English (also a first for most) ask them to converse in English with a classmate, it figuratively made them "turn white inside."

The class consisted of 31 female students and 1 lucky male student. They were members of the newly formed Japanese studies department designed to prepare them to teach Japanese as a foreign language. The class met for 90 minutes three times a week. Our class time was divided into two sections with half of the students spending the first 45 minutes in the language laboratory (LL) and the other half in the classroom with me. After the 45 minutes were up, they switched.

Although the primary objective of the class was listening and speaking, I felt it necessary to include writing and reading. The students would progress faster, I reasoned, if they were engaging in all four basic language skills.

Classroom	LL
first day: group work	listening
second day: free conversation	listening
third day: free reading/writing	free listening

Speaking

The greater part of the class time was spent on speaking activities. The first day was usually reserved for group activities designed to engage the students in conversation. These activities included values clarification activities, group presentations to the class, and activities requiring cooperation among and between groups.

The second day was used for group discussion. In groups of four, the students talked on a topic of their choice. Afterward, a reflection time took place in which they evaluated their performance. Students felt it took too much time in the beginning to decide on a topic, and in their midterm evaluations of the class, they asked me to assign a topic. I suggested we use a "rotating group leader" who would take turns deciding on a topic and leading the discussion. This appeared to help the students.

Listening

Listening, for the most part, was handled by a teaching assistant (TA) in the LL. There the students worked through two popular movies, one while reading the movie script and the other while reading the book, as well as other shorter American television shows such as "Family Ties" and "60 Minutes." They also listened to stories and other recorded material. Also, rather than using the LL just for listening, the TA was encouraged to allow the students time to discuss the stories or movies.

The third day of the class was a free listening period for the students. On this day, the students were able to use any listening material they were interested in. They could also use the individual audiovisual room on the floor above. The TA was present to help the students choose materials and to assist them if they had questions or problems.

Reading and Writing

In my class, the third day was set aside for a silent period to be used for reading and writing. It was also a time when I could meet with the students on an individual basis. The writing requirement for the class was an exchange journal that the students kept with fellow classmates. The students were also asked to read at least four books over the course of the year.

Students' Reactions

The students reacted to this class both positively and negatively. Some students felt a need for more structure in their learning. They wanted to know *the* correct way to speak English. Kaori remarked, "I do want to speak correct English, not Japanese English... If you find some Japanese English in our talking, please correct it." They have been taught for six years to believe that there is one and only one correct way to speak English. (Some Japanese high school teachers drill the students to get them to pronounce "what" as "hwat".) In response to this need, I asked the students to write down any problems they had in free conversation during the reflection time that follows. These we then discuss during the free writing and reading period.

Another problem is not so easily remedied. Up until the time they entered the university, most of the students' study has been in preparation for the entrance exam. This has involved a lot of rote learning of grammar rules and vocabulary words. Most of what they "learned" goes by the wayside soon after the tests are over. Yet many students felt that their English ability had faltered because they could no longer remember all the vocabulary they studied. I am still at a loss for a way to convince the students that their English ability is not deteriorating because they do not remember what they memorized in high school.

On the positive side, 27 out of the 30 students who answered the final class evaluation felt that they had made significant progress in English. Takako wrote, "I believe my English ability came to a high. First, when I speak in English, I feel easier and more joyful than before. Second, it takes shorter time to write Kokan [exchange] diary and to read English books."

Many students felt that the relaxed atmosphere of the class allowed them to feel free. Indicative of the students' feelings toward the class was the fact that as a whole, they attended the class more than 97 percent of the time—a very high rate for Japanese university classes.

Many students felt that they had come to feel more comfortable while conversing in English. Kyoko, who stated that speaking English confused her at the beginning of the year, wrote that she noticed the pleasure of speaking English. While throughout most of the year the topics they chose for discussion were those that concerned things directly involved with their daily lives and thus were less threatening to talk about, in the end, they were able to discuss a news story taken from CBS News's "60 Minutes."

Students also learned to read and write faster in class. The exchange journals were very popular with the majority of students. Each student averaged about 25 pages over the course of the year. For many, it was the first time they had ever written something for someone to read rather than

correct. Chika stated that it became easier to write as she did not mind if there were some mistakes in her writing.

Although many students complained that they could not completely understand the books they read, they had come to understand more of the content of the stories and to read at a faster pace. To them, this was success. Other students came to enjoy reading in English.

Much of what was said about reading and writing can also apply to listening. Whereas some students still felt frustrated at not being able to understand everything in the movies they were watching, others noticed improvement in their understanding. Akiko said, "At least when I am hearing English, I came not to throw it out, even if I can't understand it. Now I enjoy our English class because I came to be able to understand a little part of our teacher's jokes."

She also mentioned that she now watches TV at home in English (when the program is broadcasted bilingually).

Although the students may not have gained as much linguistic knowledge as they would have in a traditional (teacher-centered, textbook-based, test-evaluated) class, they did begin to use their linguistic knowledge. Perhaps more important, many of them came to realize that language is not a static array of words and rules but a living and growing tool for communicating with their fellow human beings.

Akiko: Lately, I want to communicate with others what I think in English. And, if my English can be understood, I am very happy. I remember these feelings of these pleasure. This is the biggest success.

Maki: In this class, I can express what I want to say in English.

Takako: I feel easier to speak in English than before. I can make myself understood in English easier.

→ See: Caprio, p. 226; Freeman, p. 90; Krashen, p. 86.

Mark Caprio is a professor at Nanzan University, Nagoya, Japan.

Book Note

Integrating English: Developing English Language and Literacy in the Multilingual Classroom

D. Scott Enright and Mary Lou McCloskey
1988; 368 pp.; $30.25
Reading, MA: Addison-Wesley

"What should I do with my students who don't speak English?" Enright and McCloskey ask in the introduction to their book. They provide cogent answers. Designed as a handbook for teachers, administrators, and teacher educators, it combines a thorough explanation of our current research-based understanding of language and literacy development with a practical guide to creating an integrated curriculum for second language learners. The guide lists as its educational goals: joy, community, access, literacy, and power.

LBB

❝ The experience of war belongs to no single culture, nor does the experience of hunger, fear or losing a loved one. On the other hand, the experiences of safety, of accomplishing something, of joy, of loving and being loved also do not belong to a single culture. These experiences are an intense and living part of our classrooms. If they are recognized, they can be tapped to facilitate instruction and to strengthen the classroom community.

"English and the larger North American culture can also be incorporated into the classroom community as they are found in the world of people outside the classroom—either by taking the students directly out to the real world (e.g., school tours, field trips) or by bringing the real world directly into the classroom (e.g., invited guests and speakers, use of radio or television, use of realia, or corresponding with persons outside the classroom). ❞

Parents' Perspective

by Lois Bridges Bird

A long way down, Palo Alto, CA.

Interview with Lucinda Pease-Alvarez

In recent years, as immigration to the United States from Mexico and Central American countries has dramatically risen, American parents have become increasingly interested in bilingual education. However, many of the old fears about bilingualism remain. Parents wonder, If my child is learning two languages will his or her language development be stunted? Will the two languages interfere with each other? Dr. Lucinda Pease-Alvarez, visiting professor at the University of California, Santa Cruz, is a language researcher, fluent in both English and Spanish, and the mother of two bilingual daughters, Laura, 12, and Pilar, 6. I asked about her experiences as a bilingual parent, and what advice she would offer parents who want their children to become bilingual.

Lois: How did you learn Spanish?

Cindy: I had the usual four years of Spanish in high school, picked up some more in college. But I really learned to speak the language when I joined the Peace Corps in 1974 and was assigned to Colombia. Five weeks after arriving there, I met Antonio [her husband] who spoke no English. Working to maintain a romantic relationship made me bilingual!

Lois: And your children? How did they learn their Spanish?

Cindy: To understand Laura and Pilar's bilingualism, you really have to know the larger context. Tonio and I were married in Colombia and spent the first year of our marriage there. We really spoke nothing but Spanish. Tonio still knew little English, and no one in his family spoke any English at all.

Everything that counted happened in Spanish. It was our family language, the language of our home. Then Tonio was accepted to graduate school at Stanford University and suddenly had a major incentive to learn English. So we decided that on certain days we'd just use English, but that would last about three seconds and we'd be back in Spanish again.

When Laura was born, I made a deliberate decision that I would speak just Spanish to her. By that time we were back in the States, living in married student housing at Stanford, and I figured that unless *I* spoke Spanish to her, just being around Tonio, who was so extremely busy with his graduate studies, wouldn't work. She wouldn't really learn Spanish. So right from the very beginning, in all our interactions, I spoke Spanish to her. My mother, who lived nearby, took care of her during the day and spoke only English to her.

This was not a contrived use of Spanish, because it had been our family language from the very start of my relationship with Tonio. Tonio was learning English, but he was most comfortable with the English jargon of his field [engineering]. When he came home, he was tired and slipped naturally back into Spanish. So it felt very natural to use Spanish exclusively with Laura. I'm not sure how it would work to use a language with a child that wasn't really authentically functional for you.

Lois: What about the old worries that many people associate with bilingualism, namely stunted language development and first-second language interference?

Cindy: A colleague of mine and I charted the first eighteen months of Laura's language development, and, by all measures, she was highly verbal. There was no lag whatsoever. By eighteen months, she was aware that there were two dif-

ferent language systems and she could use both appropriately. She spoke English exclusively with her grandparents, Spanish with me and Tonio.

Her lexical development was balanced across both languages. She showed more incidence of Spanish phonological features, particularly the Spanish aspiration. But basically, she went back and forth between the two languages with ease.

Lois: And this developmental pattern held?

Cindy: Absolutely! When Laura was two, we took her to Colombia. Within minutes of boarding the plane, she spoke Spanish exclusively and continued to do so for the duration of our month-long stay. Once in a while, if she didn't know a word in Spanish, she'd use the English counterpart.

Spanish really became salient for Laura when I started taking her to a Peruvian baby-sitter who was a dominant Spanish speaker. This clenched Spanish for Laura. When she was four, I enrolled her in a preschool program on the Stanford campus. It was at this point that her English took a giant leap. Peers, of course [who were exclusively English-speaking], became all important to her.

Lois: And Laura's bilingualism today?

Cindy: She can hold her own with a monolingual Spanish speaker. It's not easy, but when Fernando, Antonio's brother, who speaks no English, was here Laura served as his interpreter. She can read Spanish and write as well—using invented spelling.

Lois: What about Pilar?

Cindy: Pilar is a different child who has had very different language experiences, primarily because she had a sister who was five years older than her and who spoke mostly English to her. Her receptive control of Spanish is excellent, but productively, she never had a strong enough Spanish background. When Pilar is addressed in Spanish, she replies in both Spanish and English. In fact, I think that she thinks that monolingual Spanish people are actually bilingual and can understand both Spanish and English.

Lois: How do Pilar and Laura feel about being bilingual?

Cindy: Well, Pilar is definitely proud. She says, "I am a Colombian person and an American person." And she lets people know she's bilingual. "I can speak in *español*." Laura, I'm not as sure of. She's moving into adolescence when kids want to be anything but different. It's hard, too, because we don't live in a bilingual community or in a society that really supports bilingualism.

Lois: Is there anything now, with the gift of hindsight, that you would do differently in regards to your daughters' bilingualism?

Cindy: Yes, read more Spanish literature! That's the one thing I regret not doing more of.

➜ See: Chen, p. 26; Hoyt, p. 214; Kagawa, p. 353; Krashen, p. 86; Wallace, p. 88.

On the fence, Palo Alto, CA.

Book Note

Bilingualism and Learning Disabilities: Policy and Practice for Teachers and Administrators

Ann C. Willig and Hinda F. Greenberg, editors
1986; 214 pp.; $18.95
New York: American Library Publishing Co.

This collection of short articles is in touch with recent holistic trends in special education (*Exceptional Children*, October 1989). The book sets out to explore several important questions: Why are bilingual minority students overrepresented in special education classes? Do these students truly have learning problems, or are they reflecting cultural and linguistic differences that are misunderstood? Who in the education community should make decisions about these children? Who will train the decision-makers? What policy issues must be resolved for accurate assessment? What are effective ways to correct true language disorders?

The contributors to this book come from a wide range of experiences and backgrounds. Yet they seem to agree on several issues, such as the following: Traditional assessment puts language minority students at a disadvantage. Part-to-whole instruction does not meet the needs of students labeled learning disabled. Policymakers need to be better informed. For readers looking for an introductory overview of the issues, this book would be a good beginning.

Yvonne Freeman

Robbie Parry, 5. Contributed by Lisa D'hollande, kindergarten teacher, Ohlone School, Palo Alto, CA.

Becoming a Reader

Classroom Demonstrations

by Bill Martin Jr and John Archambault
Pictures by Peter Lippman

Saturday Night at the Fair

Story and illustrations
courtesy DLM, Allen, Texas
© 1990, *Sounds of a Pow-Wow*

We're dancing,
We're prancing,
We're simply
    romancing,
Saturday night at the fair,

We're whirling,
We're twirling,
our dreams
    are unfurling,
Saturday night at the fair,

OH! Where's Nellie?

Mama,
Nellie's
lost!

Angel, you were
supposed to hold
her by the hand.

I did, Mama, I did

Where are you, Nellie?

Here I am,
Mama.
Look what I
found.

We already have a dog,
a cat, a parrot, a lizard,
and ten hamsters.
We don't need
a monkey.

Oh, Mama ...

Mama and Papa and all of us kids
strolling along hand in hand,
Hot dogs and popcorn
    and sweet cotton candy
spun to the beat of the band . . .

We're dancing,
We're prancing,
We're simply romancing,
Saturday night...
Yes, Saturday night...
Saturday night at the fair.

Often a song or a jingle or a chime-along story can spontaneously engender the mind-set of a drama, freeing both children and teacher to new heights of awareness, joy, and acting out. That's what John Archambault and I hope happens with this rhythmic routine, "Saturday Night at the Fair." We want it to turn kids on, like Mother Goose. The spurt of personal drama that interrupts the flow of a family outing, hopefully, is familiar enough to evoke in the reader an appropriate range of voices and images, and the necessary skills for an artful reading.

By observing and appreciating the children's successes in dealing with this little bit of theatrics, the teacher is impressing them with genuine respect of their efforts. A dozen well-chosen scripts is enough to provide children with a multifaceted minicourse in dramatic reading, writing, storytelling, and acting. Here are some of my favorites:

1. "Overheard on the Saltmarsh," a poem by Harold Monroe
2. "The Night before Christmas," a poem by Clement Moore
3. "The Sea Wolf," a poem by Violet McDougal
4. "The Gunny Wolf," a folktale
5. "Daddy Fell Into the Pond," a poem by Alfred Noyes
6. *Whose Mouse are You?,* a story by Robert Kraus
7. *Sheep in a Jeep,* a story by Nancy Shaw
8. "A—You're Adorable," a song by Buddy Kaye, Fred Wise, and Sidney Lippman
9. "The Mice Who Loved Words," a story by Daniel Weiss
10. "The Maestro Plays," a jingle by Bill Martin Jr
11. *White Dynamite and Curly Kidd,* a story by Bill Martin Jr and John Archambault
12. "The Grandmother," a story by Jan Simpson
13. "This Is the House That Jack Built," Mother Goose
14. *The Carrot Seed,* a story by Ruth Kraus
15. "Does Your Chewing Gum Lose Its Flavor on the Bedpost Overnight?" a song by Billy Rose and Marty Bloom

➜ See: Hara, p.104; Literature Reference List, p. 429; Martin, p. 167.

From *Sounds of Laughter* (Allen, TX: DLM, 1990).

writers

The Making of a Literary Heretic

by Janet Sloatman Files

My brother Bill had the secret. He had the letters. The letters from school. We sat working in deep concentration on the red formica kitchen table. "That's it, Shorty. That spells JANET." I grabbed the paper and ran with it in an overflow of energy through the dining room into the living room and back. Somehow, seeing the letters in my name gave me a new sense of maturity, a step toward more secrets, more doors to be unlocked. The letters in the books, on the cereal boxes, and especially on the papers my big brother Bill brought home from school, were becoming mine.

I learned to love books and the words caught within from the nursery rhymes and fairy tales my mother read to me at bedtime. I recall knowing where my favorite rhymes were in the book. Little Bo Peep was sandwiched between Jack and Jill and Humpty Dumpty, my first fictional heroes. They took on a life of their own, far beyond the reaches of the Golden Book pages. This richness added to my pleasures at naptime. I could keep myself company by imagining a personal relationship between myself and the three-dimensional Bo Peep that hung above my crib. This was the first of many relationships that extended beyond the pages of books I enjoyed.

When I graduated from crib to narrow studio bed, my mother, warm and soft and comforting, squeezed next to me at bedtime to visit with old friends in stories we read over and over again—friends like the saggy baggy elephant, the pokey little puppy, and Cowboy Small. Later, as I grew beyond read-alouds, the place my mother had hollowed next to me in bed was filled with books of my choosing.

I chose (and still choose) to go to bed with books first. I would hide them like secret friends beneath the blankets on my bed, placing them there reluctantly, half-consciously, when sleep would not wait for one more chapter or page. The characters between their covers would not remain bedridden. They peopled my waking fantasies. During the "great horse period," when Marguerite Henry's and Walter Farley's ponies and black stallions galloped through my dreams, I had imaginary hoofed friends that accompanied me to school. They were so numerous that my memory was stretched to its limit recalling their individual names, until one sad day I could no longer remember them all, and had to face the fact that they were indeed imaginary.

The places where books were kept were almost like sanctuaries. There was the secret room behind the parlor on Grandma's farm. The bowfront oak library desk held Edgar Allan Poe and Grandfather's turn-of-the-century veterinary books. I would sit on rainy or hot, fly-buzzing afternoons and read with horrible fascination of telltale hearts, and pits and pendulums, and emergency tracheotomies on horses' esophagi.

Mrs. Webster shared books with me for six years as the librarian at Willard Elementary School. She introduced me to the real books that later lived in piles next to my bed. I can still remember where on the bookshelf she led me to *The Secret Garden* and *Hans Brinker, or the Silver Skates*, and that wonderful book about the masthead that came to life. Her quiet, gray-haired, spectacled demeanor was only a cover, for I discovered through leaked stories that Mrs. Webster had actually broken wild mustangs out West without the specs.

I recall the ritualized tribute we paid to new books. Mrs. Webster taught us how to hold the book upright and crease the binding carefully on each side to prevent breaking the back. The ceremony held the right amount of sanctity for the reverence I felt for books then.

Books are still piled beside my bed, but I enter their pages boldly now. I look for the author as much as for the author's characters. I insist upon the author's voice no matter how academic the text. I don't limit myself by thinking I must understand everything the author says, for I realize that I too am authoring. In learning to hear my voice I can join the author's voices more fully. The doors are opened now. The secrets have become clues. I enjoy stepping into my literary maturity.

➜ See: Files, p. 355; Literature Reference List, p. 429; Parkes, p. 36.

Janet Sloatman Files is a consultant and graduate instructor at USC Coastal College, Myrtle Beach, SC.

Reading for pleasure is an extraordinary activity. The black squiggles on the white page are still as the grave, colorless as the moonlit desert; but they give the

WELL-SAID

skilled reader a pleasure as acute as the touch of a loved body, as rousing, colorful and transfiguring as anything out there in the real world. . . . [These are] the paired wonders of reading: the world-creating power of books, and the reader's effortless absorption that allows the book's fragile world, all air and thought, to maintain itself for a while, a bamboo and paper house among earthquakes; within it, readers acquire peace, become more powerful, feel braver and wiser in the ways of the world.

—Victor Nell, *Lost in a Book: The Psychology of Reading for Pleasure*

—Contributed by Bruce Appleby, University of Southern Illinois

In the Mail

May 17, 1984
Dear Parents,

Some weeks ago, each of the second-graders in Room 7 began a new language arts project—creating a picture book. During hours of writing, editing, copying, drawing, reading aloud, talking, listening, and reading again, the children (with spontaneous enthusiasm) engaged in the process of writing and illustrating and finding an audience. Their joy is evident in their work (is it not?).

But of course, the children have had years of preparation for such an assignment. And their good start began (where it continues) at home—with you. The conversations, stories, books, jokes, all the experiences you share with your children encourage them to love fact, imagination, stories, ideas, and words. At school, we continue your work by making reading and literature, speaking and listening, writing and sharing central to our curriculum. Literacy is not a simple matter (each child approaches aspects of language in a unique way), but its acquisition is rewarding and fun for a child, and it does happen—with patient effort (and faith, even) and with consistent adult support.

Fortunately, in all of this, none of us is alone. There are books—hundreds of books, thousands of books, millions and billions and trillions of books: folktales and fables; poetry and song collections, picture books, chapter books, classics, biographies, and more. They are all there to extend the wonder, the understanding, the vocabularies of all children. As your children already know, books are too good to miss.

So congratulations to the children, to you, to teachers, librarians, authors, illustrators—to all of us. We are doing our job well, together.

Sincerely,
Alicia Rivera

➜ See: Rivera, pp. 166, 202, 358.

Alicia Rivera is a primary teacher at Hillcrest Elementary School, Oakland, CA.

Resource: Publisher

Ballantine/DelRey/Fawcett/Ivy Books

Education Dept. 89/HS
201 E. 50th St.
New York, NY 10022
1-800-638-6460
1-800-492-0782 (MD)
1-301-848-1900 (AK and HI—call collect)

A wide spectrum of titles is available from Ballantine/Del Rey/Fawcett/Ivy. As a result of publishing merger mania, these are all divisions of Random House, as are Vintage, Pantheon, and Knopf, which are also included in the catalog. You'll find many classics in paperback, as well as contemporary young adult fiction. The Language Arts division has an interesting selection of international writers including Chinua Achebe, Yashar Kemal, and Murasaki Shikibu. Teachers' guides authors include Dr. Arlene Pillar, a distinguished literary advocate.

Resource: Organization

Reading Is Fundamental (RIF)

Smithsonian Institution
Ste. 500
600 Maryland Ave., SW
Washington, DC 20560
1-202-287-3220

Through RIF, children can participate in free activities designed to motivate reading and book selection for their personal ownership. To further encourage reading in the home, RIF offers a range of low-cost publications for parents, teenagers, reluctant readers, and brand-new readers. These publications, including brochures, posters, booklets, and books, are helpful and filled with positive, upbeat suggestions.

Arrietta Chakos

As I See It:
Kenneth S. Goodman

Reading: The Psycholinguistic Guessing Game

In 1967, I presented a paper at the American Educational Research Association in Chicago in which I called reading a psycholinguistic guessing game. That was early in my career, so when a relatively small journal, then called *The Journal of the Reading Specialist,* wrote and offered to publish it right away, I readily agreed. Since then it has been included in at least eight major anthologies and translated into several different languages.

Though the concept grew out of my miscue research, I have some quite diverse people to thank for my ideas coming together in that paper.

The first is Jeanne Chall. In 1965 she recommended me to Harry Levin, a psychologist at Cornell University who had one of the first major grants for research on reading from the U.S. Office of Education.

So Harry Levin is the second person I must thank. He brought me to Cornell University in Ithaca for a month that summer. Among the people I met and interacted with were Eleanor Gibson and Joanna Williams, psychologists; Rosemarie Weber, a linguist; and Andrew Biemiller, a developmental psychologist. A high point of the month for me was the three days that Noam Chomsky, the linguist, spent with us.

Noam Chomsky used a term that struck a responsive chord with me: *tentative information processing.* He suggested that readers make tentative decisions as they strive to make sense of text, and they remain ready to modify their tentative decisions as they continue reading.

That idea fit very well with what I was learning from my miscue research. It helped explain why people made miscues (which I had defined as *deviations from expected responses to the print in oral reading*) and why they did or didn't correct them as they continued reading. The most common view of reading up to that time was that it consisted of successive accurate identifications of the words in the text. Few had considered that getting to sense in reading might not involve accurate identification of every word

Language Stories

Acquainted through a Book

When Melisa Chorozsy, whom we fondly call Aunt Melisa, accepted a position at the University of Hawaii, she made a limited edition picture book entitled *Aunt Melisa Lives in Hawaii* for the children of some of her closest friends, including my daughter, Sarah. In it were photographs of Melisa in her new office, at Waikiki Beach, in front of Diamond Head, and so on, with captions beneath each photo. It quickly became a favorite of Sarah's. We read it often, and even shared it with Sarah's new sister, Jane. Sarah had just turned five when Melisa called to say she was coming for a visit. "You've met Aunt Melisa," I reminded Sarah, "but Jane never has."

Sarah looked thoughtful for a moment, then said, "Jane has never *met* Aunt Melisa, but she knows her through her book."

—As told to LBB by Suzanne Gespass, Princeton, NJ

and might involve information not in the words on the page at all.

Tentative information processing. And as I put that idea into my own developing view it meant that reading was a *psycholinguistic guessing game.* In my research I found readers anticipating what was coming. They predicted grammatical patterns; they reworded the text; they inserted, omitted, substituted, and changed the word sequence. Sometimes they lost themselves in the process, but often they produced sensible text readings that differed in remarkable ways from an expected reading.

The story that follows is one I've used for a long time to demonstrate the guessing game. Read it through once to yourself and then write down, without looking back, what you remember reading. Don't cheat now! Don't look back!

The Boat in the Basement
A woman was building a boat in her basement. When she had finished the the boot, she discovered that it was too big to go though the door. So he had to take the boat a part to get it out. She should of planned ahead.

Now, let me tell you what happened as you were reading. You read along trying to make sense of the little story. It's a retelling of a familiar folk story, so you anticipated where it was going. Your focus was not on letters and words except as they helped you to get to meaning. Most of you reached a point in the third line where you felt an almost irresistible urge to regress, to go back and check what you just read. You got information that didn't fit with your predictions. This is a story about a *boat.* Why does it say *boot* there? For some the urge was so strong that you disobeyed my order not to reread! What did you do in your retelling? Did you write *boat* assuming a typo or a trick, or did you keep *boot?*

Research with this little story has shown that virtually every reader understands it and can retell it, though seldom in the original words. By the way, look at your own writing of the story. Did you use your usual cursive handwriting? Did you print? One thing you didn't do was to accurately reproduce the print font of the original. My instruction was to write what you remember reading. But you, as reader, represented what you *understood* in your own writing; you didn't reproduce the text.

Some of you are aware that you read more tentatively after you found the first problem in the text. And most of you found another "typo" or two. Actually there are six problems in this short text. And it is very unlikely that you noticed all of them. Even when readers have been told in advance that there are errors in the text, they almost never find all of them.

I Used to Be...But Now I...

We used to phonicate, syllabicate, and flash, But now we use whole texts and listen to the meanings students construct.

—Professors Bernice Wolfsan, Maryann Manning, and Roberta Long

If reading were accurately identifying words in succession, then you would have been much more likely to notice each problem. Actually, it is much more a matter of psycholinguistic guessing. In reading you use three kinds of information:

Graphophonic. You use the spellings, you use the sounds of oral language, and, yes, you use phonics—the relationships between spelling and sound patterns. But it's not a matter of simply sounding out. Yes, you noticed *boot* when it didn't fit your prediction. But look at the word after *go* in line 5 of the story. Aha! Virtually none of you noticed that it isn't *through,* which you expected. It must be that when we read we only use enough information to confirm what we expect. And we know that there's not much use in dwelling on those "ough" endings.

Syntactic. Language isn't just a string of words. It uses complex grammatical structures to express meaning. Most of you were jarred to find *he* at the end of line 5. You expected a female pronoun because the story is about a woman. You expected a preposition where you actually saw *though* but that looked enough like *through.* It fit the grammatical pattern you had assigned. On the other hand, somewhat less than half of those who read the story notice that the last line should've said *should've* and not *should of.* That's a very common misspelling in print and not a grammatical error at all. It sounded right to you so you didn't notice the misspelling. High school English teachers are most likely to catch that one. If you noticed that *a part* was two words and should've been one, that's because the two-word phrase doesn't fit the syntax here.

Semantic. You must bring sense to a text to get sense out of it. In our culture, even if you don't have a basement you know what one is. You have experience with doors, stairways, and boats, so you have a sense of the reason why the poor woman had to take the boat apart to get it through the door. But it did not surprise us that several Australians told us that in their rewriting they had written *shed.* There are few basements there and the shed is a much more likely place to build a boat.

Guess what? You read with your mind and not your eyes! The brain is the organ of human information processing. The eye is one of its important tools. But the brain tells it where to look and what to look for. The brain uses only a little of what the eye reports, and it predicts the rest. Perception, what we make of what we see, is very different from vision. To prove that I will tell you that there is an extra word in the story and that few of you will have noticed it. Got it yet? I'll wait.

Not yet? Oh, well—there are two *the*'s in a row. It isn't that your eye didn't see that; it's that the brain—which is very smart—knows that you can't have that in English. So it says to itself, "I've got that information already."

In the reading guessing game we use strategies to make sense of print. We sample or select from the print—it would be too slow and distracting to use it all. We predict what will be coming ahead from what we already know. We make inferences and merge them with what we explicitly know so that we can't tell when we're done what we took from the text and what we put into it. And we have strategies for correcting when we lose the meaning.

You couldn't help yourself when you read "The Boat in the Basement"; you had to make sense of it. That's what effective reading is, making sense of print. Efficient reading is doing that with the least amount of time, effort, and input. So congratulate yourself if you didn't let the errors distract you from proficient reading—you had a well-played psycholinguistic guessing game.

➜ See: Freeman, p. 110; Goodman, pp. 100, 102.

How the Story Ends
by Bill Harley

When you read a book you read it line by line
The story comes to life as the tale unwinds
You make a guess at how the ending goes
But you turn the page because you don't know

Chorus:
You don't know if it will come out right
You are afraid it won't but still you think it might
And so you turn the page and hope the good guys win
Because you don't know how the story ends

Water swirled over a young girl's head
They watched in horror as if she were dead
She went under and left no doubt
Till two hands reached in and pulled her out

(Chorus)

When I was young and people asked of me
I had no answer to what I'd be
Now I have watched all this time go by
And still I stumble when I reply

(Chorus)

The world turns round day by day
Darkness leads our dreams astray
So some say they know and they place their bets
But the ending isn't written yet

(Chorus)

We don't know if it will come out right
We are afraid it won't but still we think it might
So we turn the page and do the best we can
'Cause we don't know how the story ends

Bill Harley is a performer who reaches both adults and children with a unique blend of song and story. In the past nine years, he has given over a thousand performances, including appearances at the National Storytelling Festival, the International Children's Festival in Ottawa, Canada, and on American Public Radio's "Good Evening" show. He has six recordings of songs and stories for both children and adults and has won a variety of awards, including the Parent's Choice Gold Award for his record *Fifty Ways to Fool Your Mother* and for a series of filmstrips he wrote and narrated for Learning Tree Films. Bill now lives in Seekonk, Massachusetts with his wife, Debbie Block, and two sons, Noah and Dylan.

'Tis the good reader that makes the good book.
—Ralph Waldo Emerson

WELL-SAID

📷 **WHOLE LANGUAGE CAMERA**

Puppetry play, Annette Maggitti, first grade,
Desert Winds School, Tucson, AZ.

Book Note

How Texts Teach What Readers Learn

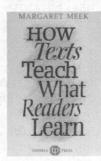

Margaret Meek
1988; 48 pp.; available from:
The Thimble Press
Lockwood, Station Rd.
S. Woodchester
Stroud, Glos.
England

This is a little book, only 48 pages, but it packs a powerful wallop to help teachers and researchers consider how it is that readers learn to read by reading. Margaret Meek calls her book a workshop, because she asks the reader to participate in a number of activities during the course of the book to help support her exploration—the role of the text as reading teacher. For example, she asks the reader to examine how the text teaches by taking the reader carefully through a number of well-known texts written for a wide range of readers. Margaret Meek, who works in teacher education at the Institute of Education, University of London, has been having significant influence on the teaching and understanding of reading in England. Her other books on the teaching of reading and literature also make important statements about the field of reading, reading instruction, and reading research. Some of them include *Achieving Literacy, Cool Web,* and *Learning to Read* (distributed in the United States by Heinemann).

YMG

66 The most important single lesson that children learn from texts is *the nature and variety of written discourse,* the different ways that language lets a writer tell, and the many and different ways a reader reads. Go back again to your own learning. How did you know when you were reading a joke? Didn't you practise asking them before you fully understood the puns of the 'Knock, knock" game? Wasn't it the conspiratorial feeling of the exchanges that pleased you? Irony—not saying quite what you mean—is likewise socially learned. 99 (p. 21)

Resource: Organization

Institute for Readers Theatre

P.O. Box 17193
San Diego, CA 92117
1-619-276-1948

Lights, camera, action! With the aid of the Institute for Readers Theatre script packets, complete with a director's prompt book and instructions, you can make reading come alive for your students through dramatic enactments of literature. Featuring both old and new literary classics for primary ages through adults, the scripts invite participation from even reluctant readers. The institute also offers a six-unit, three-week international workshop (last summer's workshop was held in Madrid) as well as shorter, inservice workshops.

LBB

Resource: Book

Readers Theatre: Story Dramatization in the Classroom

Shirlee Sloyer
1982; 134 pp.; $12.95
Urbana, IL: National Council of Teachers of English

You don't need professional scripts to use readers theatre in your classroom; in fact, students gain much from writing their own scripts. This practical guidebook shows how to choose literature for dramatic translation—everything from poetry to prose to folklore—how to script the literature and how to block and present the production. If you haven't tried readers theatre in your classroom, you and your students are in for an exciting experience.

LBB

Resource: Video Series

Reading Planet

Landmark Films
$795 whole series; $225 each
from:
3540 Slade Run Dr.
Falls Church, VA 22042
1-800-342-4336

We aren't familiar with this program, but at the urging of *Catalog* essayist, Barbara Flores, Reading Planet producer Henrietta Simons sent us the description below.

LBB

Reading Planet, a unique four-part video series designed by reading teachers to promote literacy and language development, has received high ratings from the California Instructional Video Clearinghouse and the Department of Education, Melbourne, Australia. A youthful alien teacher/hero transports five students into outer space, where, after many dramatic and exciting adventures, they discover that reading can actually become fun. Clues to the goal strategies of Reading Planet are revealed by the titles of the segments: Visualization (*Turn on the TV in Your Head*); Context Clues (*Escape from Lethargia*); Time Sequence (*Time Scrambler*); and Inference (*Hope of the Future*). Thorough classroom testing reveals that children 6 to 10 are most receptive.

Henrietta Simons

Resource: Publisher

IEM Publishing Company

8 Irving Pl.
Nutley, NJ 07110

IEM (Inexpensive Education Materials) Publishing brings back children's titles that are out of print. Working with the Office of Migrant Education, IEM provides colorful children's picture books in cloth editions for $1.46 to $1.94 per book (75 copy minimum order).

Knowing Students as Readers: Miscue Analysis

As We See It: An Interview with Kenneth S. & Yetta M. Goodman
by Bronwyn Mellor and Michael Simons

The Miscue Head

Kenneth and Yetta Goodman have studied the reading process by analysing the miscues, or unexpected responses, of children reading written texts aloud. They argue that reading is as much a language process as speaking and listening, and suggest that reading miscues can provide "windows on the reading process at work." Their work with children learning to read has become well known to teachers because of its theoretical insights into the reading process and its particular relevance for teaching children with reading difficulties.

The headline that's associated with your work is the description of reading as a "psycholinguistic guessing game." Do you feel happy about that identification?

Kenneth: I feel better about that than about several others that people have used. The key thing is first of all information processing, in the sense of having access to a lot of information, using it selectively, and on the basis of that making inferences and predictions. It was important to find a phrase to describe it that would make clear that this was not an exact kind of thing; that it involved a human intellect and an attempt to leap towards meaning on the basis of a fairly efficient kind of process.

What helps teachers take on your view of what is involved in words and language and then building them back up again?

Yetta: Two things: One is to get teachers to look at themselves as readers. We have a number of

> It is important to add that *reading* my world, always basic to me, did not make me grow up prematurely.... **WELL-SAID** Exercising my boy's curiosity did not distort it, nor did understanding my world cause me to scorn the enchanting mystery of that world. In this I was aided rather than discouraged by my parents.
>
> My parents introduced me to reading the word at a certain moment in this rich experience of understanding my immediate world. Deciphering the word flowed naturally from *reading* my particular world; it was not something superimposed on it. I learned to read and write on the ground of the backyard of my house, in the shade of the mango trees, with words from my world rather than the wider world of my parents. The earth was my blackboard, the sticks my chalk.
>
> —Paulo Freire and Donaldo Macedo
> ➜ See: Freire, pp. 222, 346.
>
> From *Literacy: Reading the Word and the World* (South Hadley, MA: Bergin & Garvey, 1987): p. 32.

texts which we use in our seminars that have errors built into them. Teachers are shocked when they realise that they've read something and haven't detected the errors.

Kenneth: We get them to set aside for a moment what they think reading is like and to confront the reality of it. As long as teachers believe that in order to become readers and writers you have to go through successive stages of perfection, then they're constantly frustrating themselves and the kids. That way they're so concerned with the mistakes that the kids are making that they do not see the strengths and the progress made. Miscue analysis helps people to realise that many of the miscues kids are making are sensible, even remarkable sometimes, in what they reveal about the language processes that the reader would have to go through to have produced them.

Could you comment on your recent work with children whose first language isn't English?

Yetta: We did major miscue analysis with eight different linguistic populations: Four of them are low-status dialect speakers of American English, and four are second-language readers. All were reading English, although some of them were reading in English and retelling in their native language. Ken wanted to see whether the reading process looked the same across all of these kids, and there is tremendous similarity.

Are we right in presuming that the thorough use of miscue analysis was a way of providing you with the tools for subsequent strategies? How does that fit with the fact that many teachers feel daunted at the thought of using the full inventory?

Yetta: First of all, the more you know about miscue analysis itself, the more you know about the reading process, the more you can help a child who has problems. Once you are aware of what is involved in miscue analysis, you are always listening with what I call a "miscue head"; you have the scheme of miscue analysis in your head. Sometimes, working with youngsters whose strategies are not very efficient, you may need to do a very full, complete miscue analysis, but if kids are developing appropriately, it's not necessary to use a miscue inventory because you know that they're using the strategies in an appropriate way, and you just keep monitoring it yourself.

Kenneth: We would argue that, although to use miscue analysis as formally as it is set out in the Reading Miscue Inventory you need to do nine or ten before you get fast enough, this isn't any more time-consuming or difficult a procedure than using a number of popular tests that don't actually provide much information.

Yetta: Certainly when you collect the battery of tests that are used in remedial classes, I think that one miscue inventory can provide more information than all of them for kids who seem to be having problems. I say "seem to be having problems" because one of the amazing things is that often, doing a complete reading miscue inventory, you find a kid really doesn't have a problem at all; that often he or she didn't have enough to read or was constantly interrupted or

thought that what he or she was supposed to do was sound out everything. Context is so important: Give the child a different story, a more predictable story for example, and you change the miscue patterns. Also, miscue analysis helps the teachers ask themselves, How do I respond when the child's reading for me? Often teachers say when they hear themselves, "I asked such bad questions" or "I interrupted the child" or "I redirected the child." As such, it becomes a teacher-training tool.

Kenneth: A key thing is that miscue analysis isn't any use at all unless you have some sense of the theoretical context and the view of language and reading that's involved. If you try to use it from a clinical, medical, diagnostic point of view, then a miscue is just another name for an error, and all you're preoccupied by is what the kids are doing wrong so that you can get them to stop doing it.

Yetta: Insertions and omissions can give you tremendous insight into whether a reader is proficient or not. Proficient readers tend to make insertions more than less proficient readers; certain kinds of omissions tend to be things that are acceptable to the syntax and semantic structure of the text, and good readers make them all the time. Other kinds of omissions indicate kids who want to leave out words that they are afraid to try and identify.

Could you generalise on the kinds of support teachers can offer to pupils?

Yetta: Get out of the reader's way more and more, certainly when they're reading the text. Offer no help whatsoever, not even a positive response. I have begun to believe that too much positive response is as behaviouristic as negative reinforcement. Constantly put the process back in the reader's hands. "You don't have to look in my face to see if you're right. Does it make sense to you? If it does, then keep going." At the end, let the kid take the lead in retelling what they remember. You learn so much about how good  the child's comprehension has been by being careful not to provide the information yourself, even to the point of not asking a question like "Tell me about the woman in the story." It's unlikely but possible that the child didn't even know that there was a woman in the story. Instead, say "Tell me more about the people in the story." We've also begun to get kids to talk about what the reading process is about by looking at their own miscues; and in a small group they can discuss each other's miscues.

Kenneth: Often kids are surprised to find that they are not alone in making errors and then, when asking themselves "Why did I do that?" realise they did have a pretty good reason for doing it.

Yetta: This notion of talking about the reading process with other people is very important. "Readers at risk" actually believe that good readers remember every single thing that they've ever read.

Kenneth: The concept I put in the place of "remedial" is "revaluing"; that is where the intent of the teacher is to help the child to revalue himself or herself as a reader and to revalue the process; to help the child move away from the process of sounding out and attacking words, and toward making sense out of print and legitimising the kinds of productive strategies that the kids have been using and had thought were cheating. These kids are often their own worst enemies in that their beliefs about themselves and their ability to learn get in their way constantly; they're very easily discouraged. So a lot of patient time taken to help them revalue themselves is the most essential thing.

For a teacher who is daily supporting children who have reading difficulties, there is often a certain tension about whether the kid is going to make it through the text. The teacher wonders, Will I ever get this kid to read if the struggle is so deep?, and also, If the struggle is so deep and so long, is anything coming out of this text at all given the very laboured way in which the text is being read?

Yetta: I think the struggle is not due to the complexity of the text itself but  what the kids don't know about the content within the text. It's when the meaning or the ideas are totally foreign to the reader that you feel you're struggling with the text. If kids are very excited about something—say motorcars or bikes—they'll find a way to dig at that information in a text. The role of the teacher is to help kids get excited by the content, and then working out the text becomes "I need that text. I want that text."

Kenneth: If you understand reading as a transactive process, and that the sense that the reader brings to the text is at least half of what is going on, then we understand that strategies develop that are necessary to deal with the print in the context of that. You can't make reading easier by pulling the process apart and teaching reading skills as such. The older the kids get, the more ludicrous and less profitable that kind of thing is, because all you are doing is digging the hole deeper underground. The one thing that kids who have problems have in common is that as they get older they can do the phonics, they can identify the words on flash cards; what they can't do is make sense of what they're reading because everything is focussed on trying to get words right.

What's your attitude to devices like cloze procedure?

Yetta: It depends on how they are used. Cloze can become a very limiting, narrow experience. Directed thinking activities like asking children to predict what is going to come next in the text can be good, but I've seen prediction used so often in one story that it's become tedious.

Kenneth: Any strategies that you use like that have to be subordinate to the basic fact that you learn to read by reading. If any teacher finds that more time is being spent on even good activities like this rather than reading, then there's an imbalance in the programme.

What should teachers bear in mind about the relationship between silent reading and reading aloud?

Yetta: Kids should probably be spending most of their time reading silently in school. If you believe that language should have function and purpose whenever it's used, then there are very few occasions when we would use oral reading functionally and purposefully. One may be listening to kids read in a one-to-one situation: This has to be a sustained piece, as it may take a kid two pages to get into a story. The only other two ways are, one, to back up statements about a book in a class, and two, as a dramatic art.

Kenneth: The big difference between oral and silent reading is that in oral reading, besides comprehending, you're also producing an oral representation. It's interesting that people seem to have the ability to produce with their mouth representations of what they have read, at the same time as processing the text further ahead to decide what it means and where they're going. The second thing is that oral reading for proficient readers is much slower than silent reading, and the miscues don't reflect any lack of control over the process. It's just that they are not used to reading at so slow a pace.

Could you comment on the implications of what is sometimes called "the voice on the page"?

Kenneth: I believe that when people read there are always two texts: There's the published text, and the text which the reader is constructing in transaction with that—that's as much the reader as the text. If I'm reading a story by Hemingway, what I understand from it is certainly going to be dependent on what Hemingway is trying to say and the experiences he represents; but it's also going to be my own experiences, my value system, my dialect and language as compared to his, and the text that I construct is the only one I could really know.

Most children learn to read and continue to learn to read using fiction; do you think that there is an overemphasis on narrative?

Yetta: Kids should be encouraged to read all kinds of materials. Both in reading and writing, there has been a tendency to concentrate on stories and to forget other aspects of reading, such as the role of environmental print or print embedded in context. The work that I have done with little children suggests that environmental print is probably the universal route into literacy. If we believe that we should build on what kids already know, we've got to begin to think of functional literacy as important and make kids aware that these are legitimate reading experiences.

→ See: DeFord, p. 113; Goodman, p. 98; Marek, p. 105; Pinnell, p. 112.

Excerpted from *The English Magazine* 16, Spring 1986, London.

 WHOLE LANGUAGE CAMERA

Students in Nancy Moyer's seventh-grade class debate miscue markings on the board, Amphitheater Junior High School, Tucson, AZ.

Book Note

Reading Miscue Inventory: Alternative Procedures

Yetta M. Goodman, Dorothy J. Watson, and Carolyn L. Burke
1987; 240 pp.; $18.95
Katonah, NY: Richard C. Owen

Reading Miscue Inventory is the basis for my current understanding of whole language, reading, and, to a large extent, writing. It introduced me to psycholinguistic reading theory, and there's no turning back. I have changed the way I look at kids, education, and the classroom.

Alan Flurkey

❝ Miscue analysis is to reading what radiology is to the examination of the human body. It includes a number of procedures to view what readers do when they read in order to understand the reading process, just as radiology uses X-rays and sonograms to achieve an understanding of the inner workings of the skeleton and organs. Miscue analysis evaluates reading problems at the same time as it provides a view of the knowledge readers bring to their reading and the strategies they use to solve their problems. Miscue analysis shows how readers use various systems of language and a variety of strategies to construct meaning. ❞ (p. 3)

Book Note

Reading Strategies: Focus on Comprehension

Yetta M. Goodman and Carolyn Burke
1980; 253 pp.; $18.95
Katonah, NY: Richard C. Owen

Here's how the authors describe this book:

❝ *Reading Strategies: Focus on Comprehension* is a practical book, applying psycholinguistic concepts to reading with specific lesson plans. The book is appropriate for use in courses in reading diagnosis, reading comprehension, and methods in reading at both the graduate and undergraduate level. It is also written for classroom teachers who want to keep reading in a whole language context, rather than focusing on isolated skills, and is particularly well suited to the development of individualized reading programs....

"*Reading Strategies: Focus on Comprehension* has two parts. Part One sets the theoretical perspective, which places reading—where we believe it must be—within a language framework. We explore the process of reading as it relates to the other processes of listening, speaking, and writing, and use knowledge about language and learning to develop a rationale for reading instruction....

"Part Two presents specific strategy lessons growing out of this theoretical framework that can help readers become secure in their quest for meaning. ❞ (p. *v*)

Kidwatching
Yetta M. Goodman and Wendy Hood

Miscues and Aaron's Reading

Aaron, a seven-year-old just starting second grade, is reading *The New Baby Calf* by Edith Newlin Chase and illustrated by Barbara Reid (1984) to his three-year-old brother cuddled with him on the sofa. The book is one Aaron has never seen or heard. He reads the title on both the book jacket and the title page, taking in the picture as he reads.

The first page (p. 4) of the written text is:	Aaron reads somewhat slowly with a steady voice:
Buttercup the cow had a new baby calf, a fine baby calf, a strong baby calf.	Buttercup the cow had a new born calf, a fine born calf, a st . . . stug . . . starn . . . soft baby calf.

page 6

Not strong like his mother, But strong for a calf, for this baby calf was so new.	Not sarn . . . sarg . . . like his mother, But . . . for a calf, for this born calf was so new.

We are observing Aaron in a comfortable home setting that provides a good opportunity for miscue analysis. This procedure involves listening to the unaided oral reading of a complete story or article, asking readers to reflect and retell following their reading, and analyzing the responses they make to the text (Goodman, Watson, and Burke, 1988). The unexpected responses readers make are known as miscues.

In miscue analysis procedures, instead of comparing the text and the reader as we did above, a typescript of the text is used so that the observer can record all the reader's miscues and rereadings while the reader reads the original text. The reading is tape-recorded to provide opportunities to check the typescript markings and to maintain a permanent record for thorough analysis later. In miscue analysis, we don't examine a few miscues at random; we analyze a minimum of 25 consecutive miscues in order to discover the quality of the miscue, the knowledge the reader has about the language cueing systems, the reader's concern for maintaining the grammatical structure and the meaningfulness of the text, and how the reader changes strategies throughout the reading.

The next few pages of Aaron's marked typescript follow.

page 8 Buttercup licked him with her strong warm tongue. Buttercup washed him with her strong warm tongue.

page 10 And the new baby calf liked that!

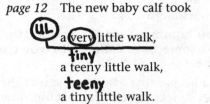

I Used to Be...But Now I...

I used to point out every mistake,
But now I investigate the miscues and we learn from them.

—Grace Tychsen

page 12 The new baby calf took

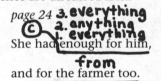

a very little walk,
a teeny little walk,
a tiny little walk.

page 14 His skinny legs wobbled

when he took that little walk,
and the new baby calf fell down.

The New Baby Calf has 31 pages with the printed text on the left hand page and fine illustrations of farm life on the right. Whenever he turned a page, Aaron's eyes always went to the illustration first. He examined the picture quickly and then read from the printed text starting at the top left of the page and returning to the beginning of the next line. He returned to the illustrations when he was reading, always using them selectively. He seemed to know when the pictures would be helpful. He never used them when he was reading function words such as *the, with, that, had*. In fact, Aaron handles high frequency words well. With words such as *very* (p. 12), he seemed to know that illustrations were of no help, so he reread the sentence twice, omitting the intensifier each time. He used the pictures for help with nouns such as *farmer* (p. 24). The miscues in this sentence are discussed later.

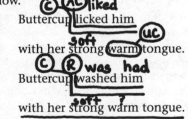

page 24 She had enough for him,
and for the farmer too.

Aaron's miscue analysis provides a wealth of information about his reading. It is obvious by the tone of Aaron's voice, his continuous reading, and his use of the illustrations, that he knows he's reading a story. His predicting strategies are evident when he substitutes *new born*, a common idiom, that fits well with *calf* (p. 4). *Baby* is usually a noun and may not be as predictable in this structure. He does read *baby* as expected in the last sentence (p. 4), substitutes *born* again (p. 6), and then reads *baby* as expected the next eight times it occurs.

Rarely does Aaron self-correct his predictable miscues that result in acceptable sentences. But Aaron responds differently when his predictions are unacceptable. These different responses show his ability to use his confirming strategies to self-correct appropriately.

He predicts *fall down* (p. 14) but self-corrects immediately. The example (p. 24), *she had everything* shows an appropriate predication, but when it doesn't fit with the following sentence portion, he makes four more attempts, finally self-correcting to the expected response. He reads all the way to the end of the sentence, rereads to the point of the miscue, and in so doing corrects *farmer* as well.

Aaron often reads to the end of the sentence with an unacceptable miscue before he decides to reread and self-correct. It seems that he is not yet confident enough to self-correct more quickly and needs the additional context to confirm or disconfirm his miscues. His confirming and self-correcting strategies can also be seen on page 8. He initially reads *licked* as expected, then abandons his correct response

(AC) and substitutes *liked* for *licked*. He again reads to the end of the sentence before he returns to self-correct *licked* although he omits *warm* and substitutes *soft* for *strong*. In the next sentence he reads *warm* but with a questioning intonation, indicating that he is not quite sure of the phrase *soft warm tongue*.

Examining the same word across the text adds to Aaron's reading profile. Aaron reveals his knowledge of the graphophonic system in his sounding-out strategies for *strong* on pages 4 and 6 (st . . . stug, starn, sarn, sarg). He initially uses the *st* blend with the appropriate lax vowel, but when this doesn't work he moves to using other graphophonic information. *Strong* has an unusual English spelling with one vowel in the middle of five consonants. In addition, Aaron's problem is compounded by the syntactic and semantic complexities of the context. Aaron uses his graphophonic system selectively.

When he is unsuccessful using his sounding-out strategies (p. 4), he looks at the illustration quickly, and reads *soft baby calf* making use of graphophonic cues and producing a meaningful structure. The second time the word *strong* occurs (p. 6), Aaron produces two nonwords that retain sound and graphic similarity to the text (both are possible pronunciations in English). The next time *strong* occurs (p. 6), Aaron hesitates momentarily, omits it, and continues reading, leaving an unacceptable sentence. Then on page 8, without hesitation, Aaron substitutes *soft* for *strong* both times. Whenever he can, Aaron produces a real word substitution that results in an acceptable and meaningful sentence like the substitutions of *soft baby calf* (p. 4) and *soft tongue* (p. 8). Both these substitutions fit the story and allow him to continue building his meaning.

It may be that Aaron's concepts of babies and tongues interfere with his ability to infer that babies and tongues can be strong, and, therefore, he is unable to predict as expected in these contexts. On page 20, when the baby calf takes a little walk, the text says: *A little longer walk, a little stronger walk*. Aaron has no problem predicting *A little stronger walk*, even though this is much more complex syntactically (tongues and babies can indeed be strong but walks cannot). He has had time to build more context about the growing independence of the calf and is now more familiar with the poetic form and rhythm of the language that helps him make more competent predictions. *Strong* occurs only once more in the story (p. 28): *his legs grew strong so he could run and kick*. Aaron simply omits it here, and it results in an acceptable sentence. Aaron is comfortable omitting words to maintain the flow of the story, especially adjectives such as *strong* (p. 6 and p. 28) and *skinny* (p. 14), which are not necessary to retain the structure of the sentence. But he does not omit often, only six times in a 240-word story.

By analyzing how readers respond to the same word in different linguistic contexts throughout a text, it becomes obvious that readers do not treat words that look and sound alike the same in different story contexts. Often readers produce the word as expected in one context and seem to not know it in another. This shows the impact of all the language cueing systems on individual words. Words are not the same simply because they look alike and sound alike. *Stronger* walks have little relation to *strong* warm tongues, which are in turn different than a *strong* baby calf, or than growing *strong*. Adults may be able to show some semantic relationships between the meanings of the words, but actually these words represent different meanings and concepts in each context: size and consistency of animal tongues, moving distances, and growing legs.

In summary, Aaron shows his ability to use all the language cueing systems at the same time—the graphophonic, the semantic, and the syntactic—in order to construct the meaning of the text. He selects cues when he needs them, makes inferences about text meanings, and predicts and confirms continually. He changes his strategies when he needs to. He has learned, during the reading of this story, to broaden his strategies and become a more confident and flexible reader. If he can't produce something meaningful that fits the grammatical structure, he omits. If the same word occurs in a more predictable context, he is able, by the end, to use the new cues to read words that he could not at the beginning.

Prior to reading this book, Aaron had been reluctant to read past any word he was unsure of. His previous strategies were either to sound the word out until he was satisfied or to close the book.

We know much more about Aaron's reading of this story, although we don't have room to discuss it all. We not only analyzed all the miscues he made, but we also know that in his retelling, he understood the story line, reconstructed most of the events, and related the warm and caring mood.

Aaron's miscue profile allows us to plan appropriate reading experiences for him. (Goodman and Burke, 1984.) Following the reading and retelling, with his little brother safely tucked in bed, we discussed Aaron's reading with him. We focused on his strongest strategies. We talked about why omitting is sometimes a good strategy. He said it helps him "keep the story going." Looking at some of his substitutions, we also talked about reading through to the end of a sentence and substituting a "best guess" that makes sense. Aaron needs to continue reading stories that he enjoys. As his teachers, we might read *The New Baby Calf* to him at this point, have him read it silently, and then read it to the whole class. He might want to direct a puppet show about the story. Since Aaron's mother is going to have another baby soon, Aaron might write a story about the things he and his younger brother will do with the new baby. When Aaron knows the story very well and if he continues to be interested in it, the teacher might place small squares over some of the adjectives like *strong, born,* and *skinny* and ask Aaron (perhaps with some other students) to write on the squares other words that would be acceptable in those places. The teacher would select only some of these activities, taking into consideration Aaron's interests.

Initially, as teachers use miscue analysis, they follow the procedures as presented in the RMI. Eventually, as teachers become comfortable using miscue analysis, they internalize the miscue process and begin to understand reading in a new way. Miscue analysis not only provides a profile of the reader, but it also helps teachers develop new insights into the reading process.

As teachers work with miscue analysis, there are two common responses. Teachers become excited about what they are learning about reading and their students. Reading specialists say that they have never known as much about their students as they know when they do miscue analysis. The second common response is "I will never be able to listen to a student read in the same way again."

→ See: Goodman, p. 98; Literature Reference List, p. 429; Marek, p. 105; Rigg, p. 239.

References

Chase, E. N. 1984. *The new baby calf.* New York: Scholastic.

Goodman, Y., and C. Burke. 1984. *Reading strategies focus on comprehension.* New York: Richard C. Owen.

Goodman, Y., D. Watson, and C. Burke. 1988. *Reading miscue inventory: Alternative procedures.* New York: Richard C. Owen

Wendy Hood is a primary teacher at Hollinger School, Tucson, AZ.

Book Note

Understanding Reading: A Psycholinguistic Analysis of Reading and Learning to Read, 3d ed.

Frank Smith
1986; 264 pp.; $19.95
Hillsdale, NJ: Lawrence Erlbaum Associates

After reading this book you may understand more about the reading process than you bargained for, but rest assured, you will never again be able to assign a language-splintering skill sheet without guilt. Smith deftly dismantles the logic behind the popular traditional approaches to teaching reading, and in uncompromising detail explains what reading is and what teachers can do to support it. Interwoven throughout is his sociopsycholinguistic theory of learning.

LBB

❝ The primary role of reading teachers can be summed up in very few words—to ensure that the children have adequate demonstrations of reading being used for evident meaningful purposes, and to help children to fulfill such purposes themselves. Where children see little relevance in reading, then teachers must provide a model. Where children find little interest in reading, then researchers must create more interesting situations. No one ever taught a child to read who was not interested in reading, and children cannot be told to be interested. ❞ (p. 182)

❝ Failure to learn is explained in terms of fad rather than fact. The specialized insights of students of the brain are important in many respects, but they do not yet explain reading or reading problems. The relating of subtle differences in learning, behavior, attitude, and personality to gross differences in the architecture of the brain should not become a new phrenology, as unscientific as making judgments about people's character from the bumps on their skull. ❞ (p. 68)

Book Note

Reading Process and Practice: From Socio-Psycholinguistics to Whole Language

Constance Weaver
1988; 512 pp.; $27.50
Portsmouth, NH: Heinemann

During the last year the faculty of Orion School in Redwood City, California, has been conducting a study group around one of the best compendiums of whole language theory and practice currently available—Constance Weaver's *Reading Process and Practice.* The book lends itself beautifully to a group study; it's big and meaty and has thought-provoking exercises throughout; each chapter ends with study guide questions as well as a very helpful bibliography for further reading. Much more than a text on reading, it includes material that embraces the entire elementary school spectrum, including developmental literacy, content area reading, and special education. An added bonus is a very complete chapter by Dorothy Watson and Paul Crowley, "How Can We Implement a Whole Language Approach?" which served as the basis of an all-day study session at Fair Oaks School.

LBB

📷 **WHOLE LANGUAGE CAMERA**

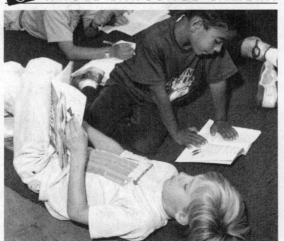

Second-graders in Alicia Rivera's classroom relax with a good book, Oakland, CA.

The Funny Side

The Sinless *Señor*

We bring our own experience to bear on every reading transaction. Gregg Jennings, son of a minister, proves this point.

Our family visited some friends several years ago and they took us out to a Mexican restaurant to eat. Our son, Gregg, who was seven years old, was given directions to the restroom.

He came back quickly and confessed that he could not tell which was the boys' and which was the girls'. I thought this was strange, but being engrossed in conversation, I did not consider the reason for Gregg's inability to read what was on the door of the restroom.

Our friends gave him specific instructions this time, relating that the boys' room was down the hall on the left. We were ready to leave, so while Gregg was gone, we walked toward the cashier to pay.

Gregg came back and stood beside me. He said nothing and seemed to have no particular concern. In my typical motherly chitchat, I whispered, "Do you feel better?"

Gregg shook his head. "I couldn't go, Mom."

"You couldn't go?" I was shocked, remembering how anxious he had been previously. "Why couldn't you go?"

"Mom, the door said 'Sinners,' and I was afraid to go in," Gregg replied.

We all got a good laugh and Gregg received his first Spanish lesson as we discussed the meaning of *Señores.*

Mary Anne Jennings is a graduate student at the University of Missouri, Columbia, MO.

📷 **WHOLE LANGUAGE CAMERA**

Consultation, Palo Alto, CA

Classroom Demonstrations

by Jane Sheftel-Hara

This Kid Loves to Sing

Remember those old cartoons that had song lyrics shining out at you and one of the animated creatures would invite you to sing along to some familiar song, and all you had to do was follow the bouncing ball? "Come on," he'd say with his big wide mouth, "It's easy; all you have to do is *follow the bouncing ball*." Well I remember those cartoons, because when I was a little girl I loved to sing, and I read and sang those song lyrics as the ball bounced over them, even though I hadn't been taught to read them phonetically. I did the same kind of reading in our family songbooks. I knew the songs by heart because my parents and older sister sang them a lot, and when my sister showed me the words in a book, I began to follow along with her and read them as I sang.

Today I still love to sing, and I especially love to sing with kids. As a teacher and continuous student of how to help kids like reading, I have noticed that children of all ages are drawn to the magic of songs and their lyrics. In realizing that as a child I had fun learning to recognize many words within the context of songs, the idea for a reading project came to me when my five-year-old son expressed a wish to read like his older brother. If the magic I felt in music was the force that motivated me to learn to read those lyrical words, maybe my son Andrew would feel the same way.

So I chose three songs that Andrew enjoyed: the 1950s popular song "Cupid," sung by Sam Cooke; "Twist and Shout," sung by the Beatles; and a long and sophisticated folk song called "The Dutchman," by Mike Smith. When at home or driving in the car with Andrew I played cassette tapes of the songs and sang along; sometimes I sang them without the recordings to accompany me. Andrew loves to sing, and he caught on quickly to the tunes and some of the words. Once the melodies and rhythms were very familiar to him, I presented Andrew with a self-made big book containing all of the song lyrics in very large, bold print, with space available for his own illustrations. Now he saw that the lyrics were represented in printed words.

At a natural pace I sang each song with him while running my hand under the words. (Later Andrew decided that he wanted to run his hand under the words as we sang.) My main objective for Andrew was that he would gain a sense of what fluent reading feels like and have enough success to ensure greater confidence in his ability to read.

Sometimes we would stop singing to talk about the meaning of concepts or words. These conversations were usually initiated by Andrew's curiosity about some of the "big" words. Often I'd ask him what he guessed they meant in relation to the rest of the song lyric. Valentine's Day has since taken on a whole new meaning for him since we talked about the myth of Cupid. After two months of singing "The Dutchman," Andrew and I investigated Dutch motifs, such as tugboats, canals, wooden shoes, Amsterdam, Rotterdam, the Zuider Zee, and the story of the boy who kept his thumb jammed in the dike. As for "Twist and Shout"... well, you know the Beatles. Sometimes I think that Andrew's deep learning of those words happened so quickly because he was usually dancing in place and clapping his hands while singing the lyrics.

Though kinesthetic is a "big" word, we didn't need to discuss that approach to learning. But I noticed that as Andrew's dancing or clapping blended with the rhythm of the lyrics in song, his reading was pushed ahead naturally to the beat, so that getting stuck on one word just didn't feel right to him. The system had a built-in mechanism that helped Andrew to read ahead with fluency. When he did reach an unknown word, he skipped over it and read on so as not to break the rhythm at hand. Andrew's success was exciting, but the nagging teacher part of me kept asking, "Uh-huh . . . but can he read these words if they're presented out of context?" So I printed about a hundred song words onto flashcards. Sometimes I'd put four in front of him and ask, "Which one of these words is 'distress'?" or "Choose the word 'jammed' from this group of words." At times I would shuffle a small pile of cards and have Andrew pick one at a time to read; he got to keep those he could read, and I kept a checklist of them. Even in the flashcard game Andrew was a playful participant.

After two months of simultaneous singing and sight-reading the three songs, Andrew was able to recognize over two-thirds of the words presented to him out of context. I believe that this success in word recognition is remarkable.

As for Andrew's gaining a sense of what it feels like to read with fluency and confidence, the evidence was clearly seen in the pride on his face and the enthusiasm in his responses as he read and sang the songs. Andrew was proud of his accomplishment, and that is very moving to me, both as a teacher and a parent. He was given the freedom to sing and have fun while developing his reading, and he was rewarded with success.

Today Andrew is seven years old and a second-grader who loves to read all kinds of text. He is not afraid to read books that have a lot of "big" words; he just skips over them and talks on and on about his latest discovery made through reading. And I'm thinking, Isn't it great that this kid loves to sing?

➔ See: Blackburn, p. 331; D'Ordine, p. 298; Martin, p. 96.

Jane Sheftel-Hara is an elementary language arts teacher with the Richmond Unified School District, Richmond, CA, and an ESL reading instructor at the College of San Mateo, San Mateo, CA.

Breakthroughs

Make Way for Books

Florida University sponsored a whole language conference that featured Yetta Goodman as the keynote speaker. On returning from the conference the following Monday, one of the participants conferred with her principal and reached a decision. She walked into her second-grade classroom and, while her students watched in surprise, took the basal readers off the selves, packed them in boxes, and sealed the boxes with tape.

"Why are you doing that?" her students wanted to know.

"What do you read when you are at home?" she asked.

"Books."

"And that's what we are going to read in here from now on!"

—As told to LBB by Linda L. Lamme, professor, University of Florida, Gainesville, FL

Cornerstone: Ann M. Marek

Retrospective Miscue Analysis: An Instructional Strategy for Revaluing the Reading Process

Retrospective miscue analysis (RMA) is a procedure that engages readers in reflecting upon and evaluating the reading process through analyzing their oral reading miscues. Many readers who do not read as well as they would like have misconceptions about good reading. They believe good readers know all the words they encounter, never make mistakes, and remember everything they read. Measured against this mythical good reader, many find themselves lacking. This awareness of their inadequacies immobilizes their attempts to grow as readers, and they become "their own worst enemies" (Goodman 1982, pp. 87–95).

> Ann M. Marek is an education consultant working for the State of Nevada. Her work on Retrospective Miscue Analysis as an instructional strategy for adult readers is described in Occasional Paper No. 19 (University of Arizona, Program in Language and Literacy) and in *Whole Language Evaluation* (Heinemann, 1988).

Through analyzing their own reading, readers discover for themselves that reading is a process of predicting, sampling, confirming, and correcting. They become aware that graphophonic, syntactic, and semantic cuing systems in language provide information to readers as they construct meaning from print. Most important, they dismantle their notion that good reading is represented by error-free reproductions of text. Research has shown (Marek 1987) that as their models of the reading process shift from "text reproduction" to "meaning construction," their reading strategies (analyzed through miscue analysis or through less formal observations) reflect an increase in miscues, are syntactically and semantically acceptable, and do not disrupt meaning.

Retrospective miscue analysis is most effectively used by teachers and researchers who understand miscue analysis and psycholinguistic theory. With these theoretical underpinnings, educators will be able to explore adaptations of the following procedures, based on their knowledge about language and about their students as language learners. Possibilities for adaptations are discussed throughout.

RMA Procedures

Prior to RMA Session

1. Meet with a reader to tape-record a reading of a text. At the conclusion of the reading, ask the reader to retell what he or she remembers about the text. (See *Reading Miscue Inventory* by Goodman, Watson, and Burke for a complete discussion of aided and unaided retellings.)

   The text may be fiction or nonfiction, and the reader should read the entire chapter, short story, or article. Texts may be selected by either the teacher/researcher or the student. Although some readers may be reluctant to select materials at first, they will show greater willingness to do so as they begin to feel more confident about their reading.

2. During the next week, analyze the reader's miscues, using Procedures I, II, or III in *Reading Miscue Inventory*.

   Although it is not necessary that each reading be fully analyzed through miscue analysis, this data can provide ongoing evidence of the reader's development of efficient and effective strategies.

3. Review the miscues made by the reader, noting any *patterns* that exist. Select between 5 and 15 miscues for discussion during the upcoming RMA session.

The miscues teachers select will be directed by their assessments of readers' attitudes and abilities. The "Reading Interview" described in *Reading Miscue Inventory* provides insights into readers' models of the reading process. Readers for whom this technique is appropriate are likely to believe that all their reading strategies are ineffective. Selecting miscues that demonstrate effective strategies is critical for initial sessions in order to help these readers begin to revalue the reading process. Over time, teachers may have readers listen to the tape recordings and select for themselves the miscues they wish to analyze.

4. Prepare a list of the miscues to be discussed during the RMA session. Include the tape recorder counter numbers to find points in the text where the selected miscues occurred.

Conduct RMA Session

1. Approximately one week later, meet with the reader to conduct the RMA session. Play the tape recording of the previous reading and proceed through the selected miscues, discussing them one at a time. The following questions can be used as guidelines for discussion:

   - Does the miscue make sense?
   - Was the miscue corrected? Should it have been?
   - Does the miscue look like what was on the page?
   - Does the miscue sound like what was on the page?
   - Why do you think you made this miscue?
   - Did the miscue affect your understanding of the text?

   These questions are merely suggestions. Some teachers do not ask whether the miscues look and sound like language, concerned that these questions may inadvertently encourage an overreliance on the graphophonic cuing system. But other teachers do ask readers to consider whether the miscues sound and look like language in order to help them explore the importance of syntax as a language-cuing system.

   In the beginning the questions guide the sessions. In subsequent sessions, readers begin to "take control" of the discussions. They begin asking the questions themselves without much prompting from the teacher. After considering whether the miscue makes sense, readers and teachers engage in discussions that ultimately focus on issues like self-correction, the reasons why readers make miscues, and the effects of miscues on comprehension, though not in any particular order. Teachers can use these discussions to share with readers what they know about reading and about good readers. For example, a reader may begin to assert that all miscues do not need to be corrected. At that moment the teacher can comment, "In fact, we know that good readers tend not to self-correct miscues that fit the passage and make sense." Such "teachable moments" abound during RMA discussions.

2. The entire RMA session may be tape-recorded to document shifts in attitudes and perceptions about the reading process. Particularly interesting discussions may be transcribed or anecdotal notes may be prepared.

3. Ask the reader to read and retell another selection for use in the next RMA session, if one is to be held.

These procedures describe an RMA session conducted by a teacher with one reader. Several teachers have experimented with RMA in small and large group settings, and with readers working in pairs. The configuration used will be guided by the purposes set by teachers for engaging readers in this kind of self-reflection and self-evaluation.

Ken Goodman (1973, p. 3) has stated that "everything we know we have learned from kids." Retrospective miscue analysis is one way of sharing what we know with readers in an attempt to help them become better readers. In the hands of knowledgeable teachers, the potential for this technique is limitless.

➜ See: DeFord, p. 113; Goodman, pp. 98, 100; Peters, p. 114; Pinnell, p. 112.

References

Goodman, K. S., ed. 1973. *Miscue analysis: Applications to reading instruction.* Urbana, IL: National Council of Teachers of English.

———. 1982. "Revaluing readers and reading." *Topics in Learning and Learning Disabilities* (January).

Goodman, Y. M., D. J. Watson, and C. L. Burke. 1987. *Reading miscue inventory.* New York: Richard C. Owen.

Marek, A. M. 1987. "Retrospective miscue analysis as an instructional strategy with adult readers." Ph.D. diss., University of Arizona, Tucson.

The Funny Side
Real Conflict

This year the fifth-grade students in Leslie Mangiola's classroom are exploring issues across content area through the overarching theme of "conflict." An analysis of conflict routinely arises in their literature studies since literary plots often entail the resolution of some sort of conflict. During a general discussion one morning, Leslie asked her students if they could think of an example of conflict from literature. Not wasting a second, Omar piped up, "Oh you mean like when one kid has a book and another kid wants it?!"

—As told to LBB by Leslie Mangiola, elementary teacher, Fair Oaks School, Redwood City, CA

Resource: Publications

Occasional Papers

$3.50 from:
Program in Language and Literacy
504 College of Education
University of Arizona
Tucson, AZ 85721
1-602-621-2211

Occasionally published but always of interest to whole language educators, papers from the University of Arizona Program in Language and Literacy, directed by Ken and Yetta Goodman, include the Goodmans' now classic "A Whole Language Comprehension-Centered Reading Program," which helped launch the whole language movement.

LBB

Knowing Students as Readers: Interviews and Surveys

Classroom Demonstrations

by David Hartle-Schutte

Reading Interviews

The following two interview forms were used in my ethnographic investigation of the home environments of Navajo children who have become successful readers. These forms may be useful to anyone wanting to find out more information from children or their parents about what they remember about learning to read. This approach provides a retrospective view, rather than a detailed longitudinal study, and is much less invasive and disruptive than observations over long periods of time.

Student Interviews

The students were questioned about their memories of their literacy development. The open-ended interview begins with general questions; gradually, the questions become more specific. Many of the questions are similar to those found in the *Reading Interview* (Goodman, Watson, and Burke 1987, p. 219). Other questions focus on the literate environment at home. Durkin's interview (1966) and those based upon it (Doake 1981; Haussler 1982; Romero 1983) used very structured and detailed questions that forced the interviews in a direction predetermined by the interviewer. Durkin noted that the interviews were often boring for both parties involved, and that she got much more valuable information through casual conversations with the participants. For these reasons this study intentionally used open-ended questions.

The student interviews in this study were also designed to have some overlap with the parent interviews, providing for "triangulation" of data (Kamil, Langer, and Shanahan 1986) as a means of verifying or questioning data from different sources.

By beginning the parent interviews prior to completing many of the student interviews, it was possible to have different perspectives on the same child's literacy development, to cross-verify information provided by the students and their parents, and to modify some of the questioning techniques. Initially, I had not expected that the students would provide much information about their early literacy development. However, by comparing information from both student and parent sources, I discovered that the students were often an excellent source of information. This led me to put more emphasis on the later student interviews.

The interviews were conducted in a conversational tone; follow-up questions were asked about information provided by students. All interviews were tape-recorded, with student permission, and notes of the responses were written on the inter-

view form. The length of these interviews varied from 15 to 35 minutes, depending upon how willingly the students spoke and how much they remembered. The tape recordings were reviewed, and additional written notes were made to complete the transcripts of the interview.

STUDENT INTERVIEW QUESTIONS

(Interview to be conducted in a casual, informal manner to put the student at ease as much as possible. Specific questions and wording vary depending upon student responses.)

- **Tell me what you remember about learning to read.**
  Was it easy/hard? Who helped? When did you learn? Before or after starting school? In school? At home?

- **Do you think you're a good reader now? Do you like to read?**
  What? Do you read anything at home besides school assignments? Does this reading help you to do better in school? Is reading important to you?

- **Is there anything at home that you think helped you learn to read?**
  What is important? People? Things? Activities?

- **Do you know anyone who has trouble reading?**
  What do you think would help them?

- **Do you speak or understand Navajo?**
  Which language did you learn first? Do you think that made any difference in learning to read?

- **Do other people in your home read?**
  Who? What? How much?

- **Do you have things in your home to read?**
  What? How much? For kids or adults? Own books? Library books? Magazines? Newspapers? Who reads them?

- **Do you remember anyone reading to you at home?**
  Who? When? How much/often? Now, or as a young child?

- **Was there ever a time when reading was hard for you?**
  What do you remember about that? What changed things?

- **Did you/Do you ever do writing at home that isn't homework?**
  What? When? How much?

- **You have a younger brother/sister, right?**
  Do you think he/she will become a good reader? Why?

- **Does your family do anything now that you think will help [brother/sister] become a good reader?**
  What? How do you think that will help?

Parent Interviews

Interviews were scheduled at the families' homes rather than at the school for three reasons: (1) home interviews were more convenient for the families; (2) the families were more relaxed and comfortable in their own homes; and (3) visiting in the home would give me the opportunity to observe the literate environment of the home, and ask to see certain materials mentioned by the parents.

As with the student interviews, the parent interviews were open-ended, beginning with general questions and progressing to more specific ones. I audiotaped the interviews, and added written notes and field observations of the

home environments. The full-length interviews lasted between 50 and 130 minutes, with most taking about 90 minutes. The interviews were conducted in a conversational manner. At the conclusion of each interview, I orally summarized each parent response to each question, and asked for verifications, corrections, and clarifications from the parents. These summaries and responses were also audiotaped, and the additions and changes were made to my written notes. Immediately following each home interview, I wrote notes of my observations of the home environment, the types of literacy materials observed, and the interactions between the parents and the children.

During the interviews, if specific materials were mentioned by the parents as being important to their child's literacy development, I asked to see those materials, if they were still available. One couple mentioned a tape recording they had made of their fifth-grade son when he was three years old, reading a favorite story aloud. I was able to listen to this recording. Other parents showed children's and adults' reading materials, favorite storybooks, dictionaries, encyclopedias, storybooks with cassette tapes, and stories that their children had written. Parents who had read to their children were asked to describe or demonstrate their procedures.

PARENT INTERVIEW QUESTIONS

- **How do you think [child] does in reading now?**
  Has he/she always been that way? How do you know if someone is a good reader?

- **What do you remember about [child] learning how to read?**
  When did it happen? Before school age or after starting school? Did [child] rea anything at home before attending school?

- **What do you think has been (most) important in [child] becoming a good reader?**
  How do you think that helped?

- **Did [child] ever have trouble in reading?**
  In what way? What changed it?

- **Were there things that someone at home did or does that has helped [child] become a good reader?**
  How do you think that helped?

- **Are there things that you had or now have in your home that you feel helped [child] become a good reader?**
  How did they help? How were they used?

- **Do you/Did you (or someone else in the house) read to your children?**
  How often? How long? Can you describe what you did? How did you decide to do this?

- **Is there anything about [child]'s personality that has helped him/her become a good reader?**
  How do you think that helped? Did he/she talk early or show a lot of curiosity about things? Quick learner?

- **Is [child] generally a good student, or just good in reading?**
  Did the good reading help in these other areas, or not?

- **Do you consider your family traditional?**
  In what way? Who in the family speaks Navajo? How much? Are there any other things that makes your family traditional?

- **Did [child] grow up hearing mostly Navajo, mostly English, or both?**
  Do you think that had any effect upon his/her learning to read?

- **What are your memories as a child of learning to read?**
  When did you learn? Was it easy or hard? Why?

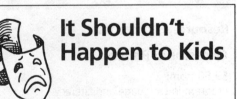

It Shouldn't Happen to Kids

The Trouble with Lists

A kindergarten teacher, who has always loved *Charlotte's Web* ever since she first heard it as a child, was reading it aloud to her five-year-old students when she was asked by her principal and colleagues to stop. She was incredulous, but they were adamant. As they reminded her, *Charlotte's Web* is on the core literature list for *third* grade.

—LBB

➡ See: Literature Reference List, p. 429.

- **What type of schools did you attend?**
  How many years? Was it easy or hard for you? Would you consider yourself a successful student? Do you think [child]'s experience in school is different from yours?

- **Do you have children that aren't old enough to go to school?**
  How old are they? Do you think they will become good readers? Why?

- **Do you do anything differently with your younger child[ren] than you did with [child]?**
  What? Why do you think you do things differently? Is [younger child] reading anything yet? What? Is this different from [child] ?

- **If you had to give advice to someone about how to help their child become successful in reading, what would you suggest?**

- **Do you have any comments or suggestions about what the schools are doing or should be doing to help children become good readers?**

I'd like to quickly summarize from my notes what you've told me to see if I have everything correct, and to see if you have anything to add or change.

If I have any other questions later, can I get in touch with you?

Are you interested in me sharing with you some of the information I get from other families when I finish?

➜ See: Hartle-Schutte, pp. 240, 264, 265; Marek, p. 105.

References

Doake, D. 1981. "Book experience and emergent reading behavior in preschool children." Ph.D. diss., University of Alberta.

Durkin, D. 1966. *Children who read early.* New York: Teachers College Press.

Goodman, Y. M., D. Watson, and C. Burke. 1987. *Reading miscue inventory alternative procedures.* New York: Richard C. Owen.

Haussler, M. 1982. "Transitions into literacy: A psycholinguistic analysis of beginning reading in kindergarten and first grade children." Ph.D. diss., University of Arizona.

Kamil, M., J. Langer, and T. Shanahan. *Understanding reading and writing research.* Boston: Allyn & Bacon.

Romero, G. 1983. "Print awareness of the pre-school bilingual Spanish-English speaking child." Ph.D. diss., University of Arizona.

David Hartle-Schutte is an assistant professor at University of Hawaii, Hilo, HI.

Classroom Demonstrations

Reading Survey

At the beginning of the school year Debra Goodman uses this form to become acquainted with her students as readers.

—LBB

READING SURVEY

Do you like to read?
Do you think you're a good reader?
What is (are) your favorite book(s) right now?
Who is your favorite author?
What do you like to read besides books?
List some of the books you read in fourth grade.
List the books you've read this summer.

Debra Goodman is a teacher at Dewey Center for Urban Education, Detroit, MI.

Grade Seven Reading Class

by Catherine Ousey

Out on the playground
Covered with silent
Trampled snow
Blue shadowed footprints

In the classroom
Eyes moving,
Pages rustling, whispering
Secrets

As we read,
Soft strains of
Christmas carols
Meander

From the Music room
Charlie looks at me

Her black eyes
Laughing at the
Tentative
Notes

We smile at each other
And read on

Catherine Ousey is a junior high teacher at Nordale School, Winnipeg, Canada.

Book Note

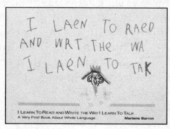

I Learn to Read and Write the Way I Learn to Talk: A Very First Book about Whole Language

Marlene Barron 1990; 32 pp.; $5.95
Katonah, NY: Richard C. Owen

So what is this thing called whole language? When a puzzled parent asks the question, we recommend *I Learn to Read and Write the Way I Learn to Talk*. The author, an ardent advocate of whole language ideas, is head of the West Side Montessori School in New York. She wrote the book to help concerned parents appreciate the similarities between achieving literacy and the natural process of learning a first language. The brief text is supplemented with abundant examples of children's writing. It helps the reader formulate additional questions, and it directs the interested reader to more challenging material.

❝Whole language is a way of looking at children and how they learn. It is grounded in research from many fields: linguistics, language development, sociolinguistics, anthropology, and education. It is an attitude, a set of beliefs about how children learn.

"What's more, it's a full-time program. It can't be done just a few hours a day. It's being with children in a way that flows through the curriculum, the classroom, the home. Every school day and weekends, too. Whole language is a part of everyday life. It can't be stuffed in a textbook or done between taking attendance and lunch.❞ (p. 5)

Resource: Publisher

Nellie Edge Big Books

Resources for Creative Teaching
P.O. Box 12399
Salem, OR 97309-0399
1-503-399-0040

Jacque Wuertenberg says that if we invited kids to sing their way into reading, there would be no such thing as a fifth-grade nonreader. Nellie Edge invites primary age children to do just that with a line of big books, which feature such traditional songs as "Oh, A-Hunting We Will Go" and "Goodnight, Irene." The books, printed on tagboard with black-and-white illustrations and plastic spiral binders, look like giant coloring books. Homespun looks aside, kids love them (and, in fact, *can* color them). The publisher, Resources for Creative Teaching, also offers blackline masters for making little accompanying books that kids can take home.

LBB

Resource: Publisher

LINK: The Language Company

1430 Larimer Sq., Ste. 304
Denver, CO 80202
1-800-637-7993

LINK, Language Instruction Natural to Kids, edited by *Catalog* essayist Lynn K. Rhodes, promises to link kindergarten through sixth-grade students with literature, language, and experiences across the curriculum. Founded on the principle that literature is the heart of an effective curriculum, LINK provides activities written by classroom teachers to extend literature. There are a number of packaging options, but the basic LINK PAK consists of one trade book plus extension suggestions. Recognizing that many whole language teachers prefer to create their own materials, LINK also offers Rhodes's practical guide for designing literature units and invites teachers to submit their own curricula for possible publication.

LBB

The Funny Side

A Future Politician

A second-grader was asked by his teacher, "Which is easiest—reading, writing, or talking?"
He responded, "Talking, because you don't have to know anything to talk."

—Carol Hittleman, director of Language Arts, Huntington Public Schools, Huntington, NY

Classroom Demonstrations

Perspectives on Reading Group Strategies

by Karen Sabers Dalrymple

I'm often asked about reading grouping strategies and how they relate to our Integrated Curriculum Program.

Expectations for Readers: All children will read at some point in time if they are engaged in an environment of meaningful print. Unlike the commercialized reading programs, we do not hold "grade-level" expectations for our students. As a result, several children may begin third grade with a love of literature and knowledge of their world, yet they may not be independent readers. Within units of study, children are given purposes for reading, and eventually the students begin to use the print meaningfully. Literacy develops as children use print to learn about their world.

Materials and Use of Materials: The five classrooms within our Integrated Curriculum Program have large classroom libraries to support our teaching of reading. The materials vary in textual difficulty and in genre.

As we are designing our units of study, we look for the many genres of literature, both factual and nonfactual, that will support comprehension of ideas about a particular theme. We use the literature in large, small, and individual settings so that students will become aware of and learn to comprehend a wide range of literature. We offer opportunities for students to respond critically to read-alouds, self-selected readings, and small-group shared readings through art, discussion, writing, and drama.

Reading Groups: Reading groups develop only after teachers become knowledgeable about their students. Groups are flexible and are formed on academic, social, or intellectual needs or interests. Time, materials, and activities for the groups' work depends upon the purpose of the group.

For example, during a unit on space study, third-graders were webbing information with their teacher, when the question of shuttles and rockets and their differences arose. Children interested in the question were asked to meet in the discussion area. Perusing texts that were available in the classroom for the study, they read about shuttles and rockets and developed two definitions. This was a one-time group that met for about 40 minutes for a specific task.

➔ See: Dalrymple, pp. 63, 204, 210, 426.

Karen Sabers Dalrymple is a teacher at Eagle Valley Middle School, Eagle, CO.

More Grouping Strategies

by Sharon Broadhead

The children in my class each have an "I CAN READ" folder in a file box, which they use to store the books they have made or are working on. They also keep an "I CAN READ" recording book. Each time they finish a selection in their reading group they write the title of the selection on one page of the "I CAN READ" book. There are six lines on each page underneath the space for the title. When a child reads that selection to someone in the class, that person signs his or her name on one of the lines. That way both the children and I have a record of what selections they have worked on and with whom they have read.

Class members are encouraged to read to each other and to teach each other to read. Children who are more advanced readers are encouraged to work individually on more challenging reading material during work time and silent reading. My reading groups are a mixture of less proficient and more proficient readers; who works best together and what language they are working in are my only criteria for placing a child in one group over another. As a group reads I can observe which children have a better understanding of the reading process. The members of a group are expected to help each other.

➔ See: Bird, p. 92; Dalzell, p. 241.

Excerpted from "Questions and Answers Concerning Emerging Readers," *Becoming a Whole Language School*, ed. Lois Bridges Bird (Katonah, NY: Richard C. Owen, 1989).

Sharon Broadhead is a primary teacher at Fair Oaks School, Redwood City, CA.

How I Group for Literature Study

by Pat Yencho

Initially, students choose from the books available to them and are, therefore, in a group based on the book they have selected. With succeeding book choices probably 90 percent of the group members opt to stay together as a group. As Edelsky explains, a "sense of community" develops around every book read as members of the literature study groups come together and share their personal reading experiences. Because of this group bonding (a bonding that transcends class friendships or playground cliques) my students are forced to select a book every member in their group wants to read. It is fascinating to observe their process in negotiation and compromise as they work to find a book that meets with everyone's approval. There is certainly merit in groups staying together, especially since some shy children may feel more comfortable with the same group and may, therefore, be more likely to risk sharing their thoughts and ideas.

Ideally, at any given time there are four groups: two work independently, reading new books and recording their reactions in their literature logs, while the other two participate in discussions with the teacher. This ideal arrangement often changes depending on the length of the books chosen. Some children are able to finish reading the book before the due date for discussion. These children may read other good literature while they wait for the rest of the group to finish. Children usually have at least two books going: a book for literature study and a library book.

➔ See: Bird, pp. 92, 196.

Excerpted from "My Escape from Basals," *Becoming a Whole Language School*, ed. Lois Bridges Bird (Katonah, NY: Richard C. Owen, 1989).

Pat Yencho is an elementary teacher at Fair Oaks School, Redwood City, CA.

Books Are Full of Adventures

by Elizabeth Archibald

I love to read because books are full of adventures. You can put your nose in a book and won't want to stop until your dinner is cold. When you open a book, what are you going to find? Maybe you'll find a lion who likes to leap around with children on its back. Or maybe you'll find a little boy who gets turned into a mouse or some kids who think a junk pile is a treasure.

All you have to do is turn the pages and you aren't in your living room any more. If you want to leave your adventure, all you have to do is put in a bookmark. You can read anywhere—in bed, on the bus, in the reading corner, in the bathtub, even on top of the washing machine. Anyone who doesn't love to read is missing giggles, magic islands, monsters, clocks ticking in the walls, and lots of things you never thought of. I love reading.

Elizabeth Archibald is a second-grader. This essay, which won a 1989 National Mott's Apple Award, appears exactly as she wrote it.

The Mott's Apple Awards are a national public service program designed to encourage children to value reading as a lifelong skill and pleasure, and to focus national attention on the importance of reading in children's lives.

Primary teacher Cathy Howard and her daughter, Erin, sent us this "whole language" passage from their favorite book, Understood Betsy *by Dorothy Canfield Fisher.*
—LBB

WELL-SAID

"Betsy sighed, took out her third-grade reader, and went with the other two up to the battered old bench near the teacher's desk. She knew all about reading lessons and she hated them, although she loved to read. But reading lessons! . . . You sat with your book open at some reading that you could do with your eyes shut, it was so easy, and you waited and waited and waited while your classmates slowly stumbled along, reading aloud a sentence or two apiece, until your turn came to stand up and read your sentence or two, which by that time sounded just like nonsense because you'd read it over and over so many times to yourself before your chance came. And often you didn't even have a chance to do that, because the teacher didn't have time to get around to you at all, and you closed your book and put it back in your desk without having opened your mouth. Reading was one thing Elizabeth Ann had learned to do very well indeed, but she had learned it all by herself at home from much reading to herself. Aunt Frances had kept her well supplied with children's books from the nearest public library. She often read three a week—very different, that, from a sentence or two once or twice a week."

➔ See: Literature Reference List, p. 429.

Excerpted from *Understood Betsy*, rev. ed., by Dorothy Canfield Fisher (New York: Henry Holt, 1946, 1974): pp. 68–69.

Education in Turin: A Romance by Herbert Kohl

Continued from page 55

The Common Schools:
Elizabeth and the Reformers

Cincinnati changed Elizabeth Stokes's life, or at least that's what she's always said. At the Institute, she met Calvin Stowe himself and his father-in-law, Lyman Beecher. The whole Beecher family overwhelmed her with their fervor and their eccentricity. In Catherine Beecher, Lyman's oldest child, she met the most remarkable woman she'd ever encountered. They took walks together, and Catherine convinced her of the importance of education for women.

Henry Ward, one of the sons, impressed her with the vehemence with which he opposed slavery. Harriet, Calvin Stowe's wife, was more reflective, and Elizabeth remembered years later that it seemed natural to her that Harriet would write a book that would become world famous and help free the slaves. Her copy of *Uncle Tom's Cabin* was one of her most prized possessions. She gave it to her daughter Alice when, years later, Alice decided to become a teacher. She liked to point out her favorite quote from the book: "Your little child is your only true democrat."

The ideas discussed in Cincinnati and the books Elizabeth discovered there had a profound effect on her thinking and teaching. There was Rousseau's *Emile;* there were the works of Pestalozzi, the great Swiss educator, who taught children of the poor; and there were the works of Froebel, the German who created gardens for children called *kindergartens.* Elizabeth was particularly struck by Froebel's ideas about the role of play in learning, which confirmed her own observations. When she returned to Turin she transcribed in a flowing and graceful hand a quote from Froebel and hung it up behind her desk. The quote read:

Play is the first means of development of the human mind, its first effort to make acquaintance with the outward world, to collect original experi-

ences from things and facts, and so exercise the power of body and mind.

Elizabeth returned to Turin in the fall of 1838 with a renewed sense of the importance of her work. However, Elizabeth wasn't the only educator in Turin who had encountered new ideas. John Clayton, the teacher at the church school, learned of the American Sunday school movement and traveled to Philadelphia to meet John P. Crozer and spend time at his Baptist Sunday school. Crozer and other ministers were strong proponents of public support for education. However, they believed that public education should also be Christian education and that the United States should become a Christian democracy based as much on the Bible as on the Constitution. They suspected deists like Horace Mann, the Stowes, and the Beechers who, though professed Christians, didn't believe in received authority and put too much emphasis on thinking things out for themselves.

When John returned to Turin he convinced his congregation that their school should be a Christian public school, and they applied for funds, forcing Elizabeth for the first time to break her uneasy truce with John. The fight over God in the schools was fought in Turin and throughout the country in the years leading up to the Civil War, and resulted in an uneasy compromise in Turin as in most other places. John's school received some tuition reimbursement in exchange for conceding to Elizabeth's school the title Turin Common School.

➔ See: Literature Reference List, p. 429.

Reference
Marenholz-Bulow, Baroness B. von. 1877. *Reminiscences of Friedrich Froebel,* trans. Mary Mann. Boston: Lee and Shepard.

Continued on page 139

						Steiner					Mitchell	
Comenius			Rousseau	Pestalozzi	Neef Alcott	Parker	Montessori	Froebel		Vygotsky	Dewey	Piaget Rogers Maslow
1600			1700			1800			1900			2000

Pioneers: Joseph Neef (1770–1854)
by **Ron Miller**

In 1805 William McClure, an American philanthropist, visited Pestalozzi's school at Yverdon and was highly impressed. McClure believed that the Pestalozzian method would succeed grandly in the young American republic, and he invited Pestalozzi to come teach in the United States. The great educator declined, but Joseph Neef, one of the teachers at his school, agreed to follow McClure and accept his patronage. Neef emigrated in 1806, taught himself English, and in 1808 published one of the first systematic explanations of holistic education, *Sketch of a Plan and Method of Education.*

In this work, Neef defined education as the "gradual unfolding" of the child's innate "faculties and powers." He condemned traditional educational approaches that set up the teacher as authority figure and argued that with proper guidance young people can discover truth for themselves, through their own "senses and understanding." He criticized traditional teaching methods harshly for suppressing children's natural curiosity. Neef's views on reading instruction were especially radical for his time, when children were drilled to memorize and recite long passages from adult books. "My pupils shall pry into no book," Neef wrote, "till they are able not only to comprehend what they are to read, but also to

distinguish perfectly well, good from bad; truth from falsehood; reality from chimera; and probabilities from absurdities." Perhaps this statement is overly dramatic (who among us can make any of these distinctions "perfectly well"?), but the point he was making is a foundation of the whole language approach: Reading should be a *meaningful* activity that engages the person authentically with the real world he or she lives in.

Neef put these ideas into practice in schools he opened in Philadelphia (1809) and Kentucky (1813). A century before the progressive education movement, Neef encouraged his students to ask questions and to think critically (he would deliberately make mistakes in his talks, encouraging his students to correct him). He led his students out of the schoolroom into the woods and fields for firsthand lessons in natural science. But McClure had been wrong about American culture's openness to these new methods; Neef's schools were criticized and quickly failed. A gifted teacher whose talents were unrecognized, Neef farmed in Kentucky for 13 years. In 1826 he joined McClure and the British reformer Robert Owen at the utopian New Harmony community in Indiana, and was the head teacher at its school. But New Harmony failed the next year, and Neef returned to his farm.

Further Reading About Joseph Neef

Gutek, Gerald Lee. 1978. *Joseph Neef: The Americanization of Pestalozzianism.* Tuscaloosa, AL: University of Alabama Press.
Neef, Joesph. 1969. *Sketch of a Plan and Method of Education* (1808). New York: Arno/New York Times.

Resource: Book

Magazines for Children

Donald R. Stoll, editor
1990; 48 pp.; $5.25
Newark, DE: International Reading Association/ Educational Press Association

B. Cullinan introduces this topic and publication with an article that justifies magazines as an important part of children's literacy at home and at school. She argues that magazines are easily accessible and affordable sources of current information that are fun for children who enjoy a variety of content areas. The length and variety of magazine articles, as well as the typical photographic illustrations, capture children's interest and fit their life-styles.

Included in Cullinan's article and the remainder of the publication are ideas for magazine uses at home and at school, and an annotated bibliography of available magazines, including publication and distribution information as well as descriptions, a subject index, and an age/grade index. This informative and handy resource will be helpful for teachers, parents, librarians, and anyone who is involved in encouraging children to read a variety of materials. *Kathryn F. Whitmore*

WHOLE LANGUAGE CAMERA

First graders in Ardith Cole's class take turns reading aloud from their journals, Lockport, NY.

Questioning Vocabulary

 Cornerstone: David E. Freeman

Teaching Vocabulary: What's in a Word?

One practice that is absent in most whole language classes, but predominates in traditional classrooms from kindergarten through twelfth grade, is the direct teaching of vocabulary. Kindergartners listen to their teacher read *Brown Bear, Brown Bear,* and then pick out all the words that start with the letter *b.* The teacher lists those words on the board. A fifth-grade teacher using a story from a basal teaches 10 words from the teacher's guide. A twelfth-grade English teacher prepares students for the SAT by having them use 20 difficult words from a blackline master to write a story. Subjects such as social studies and science are often considered "hard," owing to their heavy vocabulary load. Because at least some students are able to pass the tests or write the sentences containing the vocabulary words, teachers conclude that students have learned them. Vocabulary learning is seen as a necessary prerequisite for engaging in reading and writing.

Given this emphasis on direct instruction of vocabulary in traditional classes, it is not surprising that there has been considerable research on the best ways to teach and learn new words. The assumptions are that vocabulary items can be learned from the direct teaching of individual words and that knowing a word is essential for reading the word.

In contrast, though whole language teachers pay attention to words, they keep vocabulary building in the context of student reading and writing. These teachers begin with whole texts and focus instruction on constructing meaning. Students may choose to try out new words they have heard or read in stories, but the choice is made by the students. Vocabulary acquisition results from engaging in meaningful reading and writing activities and from real life experiences. As Freire and Macedo (1987) state, one must read the world before reading the word.

Considerable evidence shows that teaching vocabulary directly is not time well spent. Studies show that our vocabulary is so big that it cannot be learned from direct teaching. Instead, as Krashen (1985) argues, vocabulary develops by our receiving comprehensible input as we listen and read.

Seashore and Eckerson (1940) estimated that the average vocabulary of a college undergraduate is 156,000 words. Lorge and Chall (1963) challenged this figure, claiming that educated adults have a minimum of 50,000 words in their vocabulary. Both of these figures are too big to be learned in school. If a student learned 20 words per week for a school year of 36 weeks, she would learn a total of 720 words per year. If she learned at this rate for 12 years, the total would come to only 8,640 words. In other words, the sheer size of our vocabularies indicates that vocabularies cannot be learned from direct teaching. Instead, we must acquire words in natural contexts by listening and reading. George Miller (1987) estimated that children between the ages of four and six pick up an average of 14 new words per day. At that rate, a child would learn over 5,000 words per year.

It could be argued that direct teaching augments vocabulary that is picked up naturally.

David E. Freeman is codirector of the Language Development Program and director of the Secondary Teaching Program at Fresno Pacific College in Fresno, California. Freeman has worked with both elementary and secondary teachers interested in applying whole language with bilingual students. He has written in two areas: what miscue analysis shows us about text cohesion, and using whole language approaches with students who speak English as a second language.

However, even for supplemental vocabulary development, direct teaching is not as effective as reading. The Center for Reading in Urbana, Illinois, conducted studies showing that students learned an average of .02 words per minute by direct instruction and .25 words per minute by reading. This means that they learned 1.2 words for each hour of skills and practice, and 15 words for each hour of reading.

A study carried out with adult speakers of English and college students who were learning English (Saragi, Nation, and Meister 1978) showed that both groups were able to recognize many new vocabulary items just from reading a novel. Subjects read Anthony Burgess's novel *A Clockwork Orange,* which contains words in a made-up language, words the subjects could never have seen before. The novel comes with a glossary in the back, but subjects were given copies of the novel without it. After they read the novel, they were given a multiple choice test on 90 of the 241 new words from the novel. Scores ranged from 50 percent to 96 percent correct, with an average score of 76 percent. This meant that subjects on the average learned over 183 new words.

Reading and listening add to our vocabulary because we actively construct, rather than passively receive, a meaning for each word in a variety of contexts. We connect the printed symbol, the word, with an object or idea we already know in the world. In this process, we learn a good deal more than just a definition of a word.

Words and Word Parts

Some teachers argue that it is possible to help students increase their vocabulary through direct instruction focused on word roots and affixes. This argument is appealing. If students know the meanings of certain roots and affixes that occur commonly, they can deduce the meaning of a great number of words. Knowledge of the Greek and Latin building blocks is also helpful.

The critical questions are these: Does knowledge of word roots and affixes allow students to predict the meaning of words? Is the whole equal to the sum of the parts? A tenet of whole language, however, is that the whole is actually greater than the sum of the parts.

Let's look more closely at teaching vocabulary through its parts. Herr (1959, p. 75) says:

> A root word is a small word from which a larger word is made. About sixty-five percent of the words in our dictionary come from Latin and Greek roots. A few of the most-used Latin and Greek roots are given below. It will help you increase your word power if you know these. When you come to a word you do not know, try to pronounce it with your knowledge of phonics, then if you still do not recognize the word or its meaning, look at a base word and then look for the prefix and suffix.

Prefix	Root	Suffix
re- (back, again)	*cogn* (know)	*-ize* (to make)
con- (with)	*bene* (good)	*-tion* (state or condition)
un- (not)	*dic(t)* (say)	*-al* (relation to)
de- (from, down)	*greg* (flock)	*-ate* (to make)
	capit (head)	

con + greg + ate + ion + al = relation to the state or condition of being with the flock

un + re + cogn + ized = not made known again

bene + dic + tion = the condition of saying something good

de + capit + ate = to make the head (go) from

In order to use word parts to determine meaning, you have to decide which parts are prefixes, roots, and suffixes, and which meaning of a root or an affix applies. For example, is *cognate* made up of *co + gnatus* or *cogn + aten*? Which meaning of *re* should you use to determine the meaning of *retire*, "back" or "again"? These problems are not apparent to someone who *knows* both the meaning of the word and the meanings of the parts. To teachers this method makes sense.

Try using your knowledge of roots and affixes to define the following words: *capitation, capitular, cognomen, benefice,* and *beneficiate.* Now try defining these words: *regregation, unconcapitize,* and *decognal.*

Here are the answers for the first five words:

capitation direct uniform tax imposed on each person (head)

capitular of or relating to an ecclesiastical chapter (chapter = head)

cognomen surname or nickname

benefice an ecclesiastical office to which revenue for an endowment is attached

beneficiate to treat so as to improve properties

It would be difficult to arrive at the dictionary definition of these words if you depended only on roots and suffixes. As you may have suspected, the last three words I made up. Knowledge of the meaning of word parts does not necessarily lead to the meaning of the words.

On Knowing Words

Studies in linguistics suggest we have phonological, morphological, syntactic, semantic, and pragmatic information about each word we "know."

Phonological Information. There may be words that we recognize when reading but can't pronounce. Nevertheless, we would probably recognize those words if someone else pronounced them. Examples would be names of characters in Russian novels and scientific names such as *tachistoscope.*

Morphological Information. We know the various forms a word can take: noun plurals, verb tenses, comparative and superlative adjectives, and so on. For example, if we know the word *Xerox,* then we know that the past tense is *Xeroxed* and that we can talk about the *Xeroxability* of a document.

Syntactic Information. We know a word's part or parts of speech. We might question whether the word *mother* can function as a noun and a verb. To take another example, *blessed* can be a verb (he blessed me when I sneezed), and an adjective (blessed are the meek). In order to know how to pronounce this word, we have to determine the part of speech. Finally, especially with verbs, we know what other elements of the sentence must be present. For example, *put* requires both a direct object and a prepositional phrase. This can be understood by considering these odd sentences: *I put the cat. I put in the garage.*

Semantic Information. We know what the word means, what it refers to. We know both direct and extended meanings. For example, *chicken* can be an animal or a cowardly person. We also know what words go with a word. For example, we can make or send our condolences, but can we say them or mail them to someone? What helps us in our reading is that we can predict words that go together. In a story about baseball, we could predict *bat* or *player* or even *tiger*, but not *whale* or *shoulder pads*. And the kind of bat is the stick, not the animal.

Pragmatic Information. Finally, we know something about the level of formality of the word. We know the contexts in which it would be appropriate or inappropriate to use the word.

If knowing a word entails all these kinds of information, then it becomes apparent that students need to see, hear, and use words in a variety of contexts in order to come to know them.

→ See: Freeman, pp. 90, 212; Goodman, pp. 98, 100; Krashen, p. 86; Literature Reference List, p. 429; Saavedra, p. 111.

References

Freire, P., and D. Macedo. 1987. *Literacy: Reading the word and the world.* Granby, MA: Bergin & Garvey.

Herr, S. 1959. *Improve your reading through phonics.* Los Angeles: Instructional Materials and Equipment Distributors.

Krashen, S. 1985. *Ideas and insights.* Hayward, CA: Alemany Press.

Lorge, I., and J. Chall. 1963. "Estimating the size of vocabularies of children and adults: An analysis of methodological issues." *Journal of Experimental Education* 32.

Miller, G. 1987. "How children learn words." *Scientific American* 257(3).

Saragi, T., P. Nation, and G. Meister. 1978. "Vocabulary learning and reading." *System* 6.

Seashore R., and L. Eckerson. 1940. "The management of individual differences in general English vocabularies." *Journal of Educational Psychology* 31.

Further Reading by David E. Freeman

◆ "Assignment of Pronoun Reference: Evidence that Young Readers Control Cohesion." *Linguistics and Education* 1(2), 1988.

◆ "Language and Literacy for Bilingual Learners: Two Papers," with Y. Freeman. *Occasional Papers.* University of Arizona, May 1988.

◆ "Bilingual Learners: How Our Assumptions Limit Their World," with Y. Freeman. *Holistic Education Review,* Winter 1990.

◆ "New Attitudes for New Students," with Y. Freeman. *Holistic Education Review,* in press.

◆ "Practicing What We Preach: Whole Language with Teachers of Bilingual Learners," with Y. Freeman. In *Organizing for Whole Language,* in press.

Language Stories

The Lens of Experience

I last taught first grade on the Tohono Oodam Indian Reservation, located some 60 miles west of Tucson in the spectacular Sonoran desert. I would periodically hold individual reading conferences and ask each student to read aloud so that I could do an informal miscue analysis. During one session, Vernon asked to read "Lost in the Woods" from an old basal reading series. He opened to the title page and read, "Lost in the Desert." And for the next seven pages, every time he came to "woods," he substituted "desert." I knew that later there would be time to dig out past issues of *National Geographic* and look at glossy photographs of the New England woods and talk about the concept of forests. Now I just listened, with growing excitement. I knew Vernon was a reader—able to enter the world of print and share the fear of the lost child. Together they found their way out of the wilderness—the book child escaped the grasp of the dark woods, Vernon, the vast expanse of the desert.

—LBB

As kids see it

My Coon Dog Bob
by Randy Wayne Burnett

I have a dog named Bob. He is a coon dog. He is white and black. One night my Dad and I took him hunting down the river. We had hunted for a long time when Bob treed a coon. My Dad shot the coon out of the tree and we took it to the truck. Then we left to go to another place to hunt. He treed another coon and then he ran off. He got far away from us and started crying. My dad didn't know what was wrong. He was caught in a steel trap. We got him out and took him home. We put him up and never hunted him too much again.

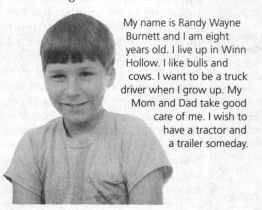

My name is Randy Wayne Burnett and I am eight years old. I live up in Winn Hollow. I like bulls and cows. I want to be a truck driver when I grow up. My Mom and Dad take good care of me. I wish to have a tractor and a trailer someday.

From *Great Mountain Tales,* written by Linda Oxendine's second-grade class, G. R. Hampton School, Barbourville, KY, 1989.

YOUNG ARTISTS

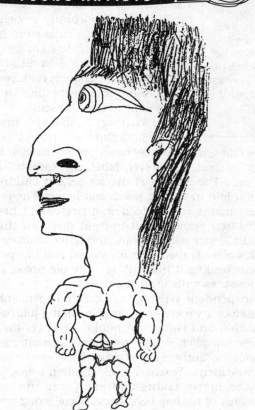

—Patrick Gonzales, 9, Elizabeth Doerr, fourth grade teacher, Fair Oaks School, Redwood City, CA.

WELL-SAID

I go with Robert Louis Stevenson, who said that an intelligent reader with imagination can make an "Iliad" out of a newspaper.

—Carl Sandburg, *Writer's Notebook*

Language Stories

Reading Word Lists: Are They Harder for Teachers or for Children?

When I was a classroom teacher for the Albuquerque Public Schools, we were required to give Individual Reading Inventories to all our students during the first month of school. These inventories consisted of word lists, which began at the preprimer level and worked up to the eighth-grade level. We were required to ask the students to begin reading the first word list and continue until they missed a total of five words on the list, which was labeled frustration level. Then we were required to give the student a story at that particular level.

One day I was administering the IRIs to some of my students. It was late in the morning, and I thought I could squeeze one more student in before we had to begin preparing for lunch. I asked Kenneth if he would come join me at the back table. I gave him the instructions and he began reading the words on the first list. He completed the word list without error, so I asked him to continue on to the next list. He did well again, so I just signaled to keep going. He recited word after word, and my eyes grew heavier and heavier. I shifted and shifted as he continued his delivery of words. I sat and he read. I am not sure how much time had elapsed, when I opened my eyes and found Kenneth just sitting patiently in silence. I asked Kenneth to continue with the list, but he meekly informed me that he had completed reading all the lists quite a while ago, and was waiting for me to wake up and let him know what to do next.

The following year, I found myself in the same situation asking students to complete the word list. I asked Vincent to read the list of words aloud to me. Vincent looked over the list, studied the words, mouthed them in silence, and deep in thought, crinkled his face. I sat watching, wondering why he was studying the words with such intense concentration. I asked him if he could read the words and he replied very confidently, "Oh yes, I can read these words. I know how to read." Then I asked him if there was a problem with the lists. He responded, "Yeh, there is. You see, I know how to read, but I can't say what these words are because I haven't learned typing yet." What a confident reader Vincent was!

→ See: Freeman, p. 110; Jensen, p. 104.

—Elizabeth R. Saavedra, doctoral student, University of Arizona, Tucson, AZ

Language Stories

The Impact of Gender

In an attempt to distinguish real versus fantasy in his ever-widening worldview, my five-year-old son David wanted to know if "dynamite" is a real thing.

"Yes, it's a man-made explosive," I explained.

"You mean a *man* made it?

"Well, a man or a *woman* could make it in a factory."

"Why isn't it *woman*-made?"

"That's a good question."

"It should be 'man/woman-made'!"

—Debbie Montgomery, Palo Alto, CA

Strategies for Helping Readers

 Cornerstone: Gay Su Pinnell

The Early Literacy Study Group

Literacy Learning for At-Risk First-Graders

The Early Literacy Study Group is a group of teachers who are concerned about working effectively with young children who are having difficulty learning to read and write. The group's ultimate goal is to improve literacy instruction for children in kindergarten through second grade.

The group is a collaborative project of Ohio State University and the Columbus public schools. Two years ago, the group began to meet with Ohio State teachers Charlotte Huck and myself. The project was facilitated by John Hilliard, director of Chapter 1, and Edwina Bradley, supervisor of Reading. Teachers in the group were experienced in Reading Recovery. They had learned how to observe and analyze children's reading and writing, and how to "follow the child's intentions" in order to develop effective strategies. Now they were focusing their attention on classroom and group teaching. They knew that Reading Recovery is designed for one-to-one teaching and that the procedures are neither directly transferable to group or classroom nor appropriate for all children.

The Early Literacy teachers based their planning on the assumption that literacy skills are best learned within the context of reading and writing whole texts. When children are hearing, reading, and writing whole stories, messages, or other texts, they can more easily see the purpose and construct meaning from the activity. There are opportunities to work at any level of language—letter, word, sentence, or story—necessary to get the whole job accomplished. This complex, constructive process is supported by constant talk between teacher and children and among children.

Children's literature offers a readily available and rich resource from which literacy instruction can emerge. The group selected books that represented good children's literature and could promote knowledge of reading and writing. These "power texts" not only introduced children to the joy of reading, but also provided a base for teaching specific skills within a meaningful context.

The group created a flexible framework within which they could work and explore these powerful texts. They met weekly to share their observations of children, to analyze their own responses to children, and to evaluate the potential of different teaching techniques.

Used flexibly, the framework serves as an overarching conceptual guide. Teaching for strategies and helping children make connections come as teachers interact with children and children with each other. Throughout the process, the teacher is aware of and tries to emphasize the interrelatedness of reading and writing in literacy learning. Using the basic framework as a guide, they began to use a variety of reading and writing experiences that are linked by a particular theme or focus. Many experiences emerge from the interactions with one book.

Gay Su Pinnell is associate professor in the Department of Theory and Practice at the Ohio State University, where she teaches graduate and undergraduate courses on reading, language arts, and children's literature. She is an experienced elementary teacher and has coordinated the teacher education approval process for the state education department in Ohio. In 1988 she received the Governor's Award for Outstanding Service for her work in initiating Reading Recovery in Ohio. She is codirector of the Reading Recovery Project at Ohio State University and principal investigator for the Early Literacy Research Project, sponsored by the John D. and Catherine T. MacArthur Foundation. Her current interests include creating kindergarten programs that help children develop language and literacy in meaningful ways.

Components of the framework, not listed in any order of importance, represent a range of activities. It is not necessary that each component be practiced daily.

Reading Aloud to Children. Reading to children every day demonstrates good reading and helps children learn the language of books and how stories are constructed. Teachers try to be aware of children's responses; they reread favorites and children join in. Hearing a story many times helps children create their own "in-the-head" texts that later serve as the basis for writing.

Familiar Rereading. Children independently read many books, including literature that has been read aloud and books written by individual children. It does not take long to build up a collection of books that children can read either alone or with assistance from each other. This gives teachers a chance for a brief reading session with a child or for taking a running record of one child's reading.

Shared Reading. In shared reading, teacher and children read and enjoy text together. Big books, recipes, lists, letters, story maps, dramatizations, and other material help children become involved in reading in a highly supported way. Shared reading is a transitional experience that helps children to match up the knowledge gained through hearing stories with the visual aspects of print. The teacher can take the opportunity to teach for early strategies such as word-by-word matching, left-to-right directionality, and locating words. The teacher can also encourage fluency and phrasing, and instill the notion that reading must make sense.

Shared Writing. In shared writing, teacher and children create a text together. The text may be a story retelling, alternative text, list, letter, label, or "speech balloon." The teacher is the scribe, but children soon join in writing words and letters. The process makes it easy to demonstrate, and have children practice, left-to-right directionality, sound-letter relationships, and letter formation. This piece is used later for shared and independent reading. Children's favorite big books are those they write for themselves.

Independent Writing. Children independently produce a variety of writing, including journals, stories, and their own books. Teachers make time for quick writing conferences, sharing sessions, or "authors chair" activities.

Assessment. Teachers track children's progress by regularly taking and analyzing running records of reading behavior and collecting writing samples and other information. They use Clay's Diagnostic Survey (1972) at the beginning and the end of the year.

It is evident that teachers in the Early Literacy Group draw heavily from the literature on whole language curricula, informal education, and literature-based classrooms. The description provided here may imply that teachers in the group were using whole language. However, the similarities between whole language and the group's framework are yet to be determined. We suspect that the structure of Early Literacy lessons is more visible and that the teachers are deliberately teaching and demonstrating processes more than is usual in whole language classrooms. The Early Literacy Group is still testing and revising the framework, keeping in mind the particular needs of at-risk readers. Though profiles of individual learners indicate good results, we do not have enough information to judge the effectiveness of the framework. We can say, though, that we have expanded our knowledge of how children acquire literacy and how the social context can be a rich source of that learning.

➜ See: Cairney, p. 116; Goodman, p. 98; Hauser, p. 115; Marek, p. 105; Peters, p. 114; Teachers and Research: Language Learning in the Classrooms, p. 402.

Reference
Clay, M. 1972. *The early detection of reading difficulties: A diagnostic survey.* Portsmouth, NH: Heinemann.

Further Reading by Gay Su Pinnell
◆ *Up from Excellence,* with W. W. Wayson and B. Mitchell. Phi Delta Kappa, 1988.
◆ "Reading Recovery: Helping At-Risk Children Learn to Read." *Elementary School Journal* 90, 1989.
◆ "Success of Children at Risk in a Program that Combines Reading and Writing." In *Reading/Writing Connections: An Instructional Priority in the Elementary School,* ed. J. Mason. Allyn & Bacon, 1989.
◆ *Teachers and Research: Language Learning in the Classroom,* ed. with M. Haussler. IRA, 1989.
◆ *Bridges to Literacy,* ed. with D. DeFord and C. Lyons. Heinemann, in press.

Resource: Periodical

Literacy Matters

Martha L. King Language and Literacy Center
$12/year (3 issues) from:
Literacy Matters
  Subscriptions
Instructional Materials
  Laboratory
College of Education
842 W. Goodale Ave.
Columbus, OH 43212

Also available:

Eminent Scholar Videotapes $25 each

**Educational Reports
(occasional papers series)** $3 each

Staying abreast of innovative classroom practice matters, and one way to do just that is to subscribe to this slim but meaty journal, published three times a year by the Martha L. King Language and Literacy Center of Ohio State University. The journal publishes research-based classroom practice across content areas. The issue we received included three excellent articles by classroom teachers on the ways in which they have involved their at-risk first-graders in literature. The Martha L. King Language and Literacy Center also offers an occasional paper series and an Eminent Scholar Videotape Series, which includes presentations by such scholars as Courtney Cazden, Charlotte Huck, and Margaret Meek-Spencer.

LBB

Cornerstone: Diane DeFord

Reading Recovery

The program that is now called Reading Recovery began as a collaborative effort between Dr. Marie Clay and teachers of the Auckland, New Zealand, schools in the early 1960s. Classrooms are based upon the informal/infant schools concepts utilized in Britain. Children enter school on their fifth birthday and soon merge into the junior class (generally six- to eight-year-olds). Although this instructional program is very holistic, teachers were concerned about children who did not take on the reading process in a way that allowed them to be successful in school. The Reading Recovery program that evolved out of this collaboration is outlined in *The Early Detection of Reading Difficulties* (Clay 1985).

Children are tutored in a one-on-one instructional program for a half hour each day of the week until they are able to read classroom materials within an average range for their class. When the strategies are well orchestrated, the Reading Recovery teacher works with the classroom teacher to devise a plan for discontinuing the individual tutoring. The Reading Recovery teacher is simultaneously involved in a unique teacher education program that incorporates teaching/peer observation/critique on a regular basis throughout the instructional program for the child. The combination of individual, intensive tutoring and teacher collaboration is a dynamic process that has produced impressive results in New Zealand, Australia, Canada, and the United States.

In 1983 Diane DeFord joined the faculty of Language Arts, Children's Literature and Reading at Ohio State University. She is an associate professor and coordinator of the program area. She teaches courses in reading and writing methodology and evaluation in addition to her work as codirector of Reading Recovery.

Reading Recovery is based upon many of the same concepts found within the whole language philosophy. Teachers must observe closely what children are saying and doing. They use good children's literature or instructional materials that have good story lines and predictable language. Teaching must be related to the strengths the reader has shown rather than to the reader's weaknesses. Instruction must emphasize strategies, not isolated bits of language. The program is also based upon the belief that teachers cannot learn about teaching without careful study and reflection on their work with children. If something is not going well with the child's learning, the teacher must first question what has occurred in lessons.

Because Reading Recovery was devised to solve some problems found in holistic teaching/learning settings, it also incorporates concepts not typically articulated in whole language theory. It is based upon the notion of early intervention: Children may not mature into reading, and waiting two or three years will not help. Because accelerated learning is one of the goals of the program, the teacher must discover what strategies should be taught from an analysis of the child's work with text (both reading and writing). Direct teaching occurs, which might take the form of letter work, learning to hear sounds in words while writing, generating new words from known items, and cutting apart language in the cut-up sentence so that the child may put it back together. Any single instance of direct teaching must be related to specific needs and approached in a variety of ways throughout the lesson in order to be effective. Overemphasizing any aspect of reading or language over another in teaching will have a negative impact on learning.

Reading Recovery fulfills an important purpose for those first-grade children who have difficulty learning to read. The teacher seeks to use children's personal meanings in devising a program of ongoing learning, to instill a sense of risk-taking, to facilitate growth in orchestrating reading strategies, to continually extend children from where they are to where they can go next (a Vygotskian notion), and to develop a system of checks within readers themselves so that they may monitor their own reading, gain meaning, and devise a self-improving reading process.

→ See: Cairney, p. 116; Goodman, p. 98; Hauser, p. 115; Marek, p. 105; Peters, p. 114.

Reference
Clay, M. 1985. *The early detection of reading difficulties*. Portsmouth, NH: Heinemann.

Further Information: For more information about the program, contact Reading Recovery, 200 Ramseyer Hall, 29 W. Woodruff, Ohio State University, Columbus, OH 43210.

Further Reading by Diane DeFord
◆ "Validating the Construct of Theoretical Orientation in Reading Instruction." *Reading Research Quarterly* 20(3), Spring 1985.
◆ "Children Write to Read and Read to Write." In *Children Learn to Read and Write: A Cooperative Effort*, ed. J. Kerber and D. Tovey. IRA, 1986.
◆ "Classroom Contexts for Literacy Learning." In *The Contexts of School-based Literacy*, ed. R. Raphael. Random House, 1986.
◆ "Why Don't You Write About a Tan Ant? A Question of Knowledge and Control in Teaching and Learning." In *Literacy, Learning and Instruction*, ed. M. Sampson. Kendall-Hunt, 1986.

Classroom Demonstrations

by Keith Kroll

Using Reader Response in an American Literature Course

To put it as directly, and perhaps as brutally as possible, we must stop "teaching literature" and start "studying texts."

—Robert Scholes, *Textual Power*

As described in the Kalamazoo Valley Community College (KVCC) catalog, English 203: American Literature 1 "is an introduction to, and survey of, American literature from the colonial period to the beginning of the Civil War." As is typical with elective literature courses at a community college, the course mainly attracts students who are interested in literature or are planning to transfer to four-year schools.

For fall semester 1988, I decided to incorporate into the course several new approaches: short response papers to the week's reading, two longer response papers, student collaboration, individualized reading assignments, and writing conferences and workshops.

In my directions to students concerning their short responses, I told them:

The short responses are a way for you to explore and express your original ideas; to raise questions you have about the text(s); to provide possible answers to questions you have about the text; to discuss how texts are similar or different. Your short responses should not merely be a recounting or paraphrasing of what the text is about, although

they should be a response to what the author has to say and how he or she says it.

The short response papers *and* the student responses to the short response papers served as the basis for class discussion. In these, students repeatedly raised interesting and provocative questions and made interesting comments about the readings.

In the longer response papers, students were allowed to select the authors who appealed to them. I also held writing conferences and workshops on each of the longer response papers. Rather than simply submitting a final draft, students brought a rough draft to a writing conference, where I discussed the draft with them. After our conference, they then rewrote the draft and brought it to a writing workshop, where two other students in the course read and commented on the draft.

A large percentage of students considered the class a success. While I was generally pleased with the course, there are several changes I plan to make in the course:

1. Arrange the course by themes or topics rather than chronologically;

2. Give students questions to guide their responses;

3. Bring more aspects of American culture into the course, for example, architecture and clothing.

→ See: Senger, p. 192.

Further Reading About Reading Response
Bergstrom, Robert R. 1983. "Discovery of Meaning: Development of Formal Thought in the Teaching of Literature." *College English* 45 (December).
Bleich, David. 1969. "The Subjective Character of Critical Interpretation." *College English* 31 (October).
Corcoran, Bill, and Emrys Evans, eds. 1987. *Readers, Texts, Teachers*. Upper Montclair, NJ: Boynton/Cook.
Eagleton, Terry. 1983. *Literary Theory: An Introduction*. Minneapolis: University of Minnesota Press.
Erlich, Victor. 1975. "Reading Conscious and Unconscious." *College English* 36 (March).
Flynn, Elizabeth A. 1983. "Composing Response to Literary Texts: A Process Approach." *College Composition and Communications* 34 (October).
Hillocks, George, Jr. 1980. "Toward a Hierarchy of Skills in the Comprehension of Literature." *English Journal* 69(3), (March).
Hunt, Russell A. 1982. "Toward a Process-Intervention Model in Literature Teaching." *College English* 44 (April).
Petersen, Bruce T., ed. 1986. *Convergences: Transactions in Reading and Writing*. Urbana, IL: NCTE.
Petrosky, Anthony R. 1982. "From Story to Essay: Reading and Writing." *College Composition and Communication* 33 (February).
Rosenblatt, Louise. 1983. *Literature as Exploration*, 3d ed. New York: MLA.
Sampson, G. P., and N. Carlman. 1982. "A Hierarchy of Student Responses to Literature." *English Journal* 71 (January).
Scholes, Robert. 1985. *Textual Power*. New Haven: Yale University Press.
Tompkins, Jane, ed. 1985. *Reader-Response Criticism*. Baltimore: Johns Hopkins University Press.

Keith Kroll is an instructor at Kalamazoo Valley Community College, Kalamazoo, MI.

Network

Reading Difficulty: A Blueprint for Action

by Judy Peters

It is hard to say when students begin to see themselves as failures. It may be that they are frequently struggling with material that is too difficult for them, or that they feel guilty about not showing the same degree of interest in reading as others, or that they find themselves not understanding what they read. The number of successful experiences they have had when reading may be few and decrease each year.

This sense of failure can cause anger, frustration, anxiety, and the feeling that they can't succeed in reading no matter what they do. A focus on decoding and pronunciation may lead to the idea that correct oral performance is the goal of reading, rather than understanding the text, and minimise the amount of risk-taking attempted.

Parents' natural concern may result in placing undue pressure on the child to achieve, and attempts to help at home can end in frustration. Teachers' low expectations of the child may be communicated in a variety of subtle ways. Well-meaning attempts to make classroom work easier for these children may confirm their poor opinions of their own reading ability.

The cumulative effect of these negative feelings produces a vicious circle for readers experiencing difficulty. They may become less confident in their own attempts to solve problems and more and more dependent on the teacher to direct their every effort. This can drastically limit their chances of developing strategies for independence.

Here are some possible strategies for responding to lack of confidence:

- Structure reading situations that are fun and guarantee success, for example, oral readings of predictable but high interest material such as Dr. Seuss, the children's own written material, and a great deal of poetry.
- Provide a wide range of materials, including comics, magazines, picture books, nonfiction, and the children's own writing.
- Demonstrate self-selection techniques such as reading cover summaries or reading the first page or two for level of interest and difficulty.
- Ensure that most reading is self-chosen material for enjoyment.
- Provide opportunities for group and class discussion and sharing of books.
- Read to the children daily and model enjoyment of reading and reading strategies at every opportunity.
- Treat all children as successful readers and monitor interactions for subtle communications of lower expectations for some children.
- Use every opportunity in all curriculum areas or social situations to build up children's self-esteem. Celebrate successes that occur in the playground, socially, or at home, as well as those in learning.
- Create a classroom environment that encourages risk-taking and praise children when they "have a go."
- Communicate with parents about the importance of encouragement.

Limited Reading Strategies

Good readers do have good decoding skills, but they also rely heavily on their abilities to predict what is coming, use contextual clues, monitor their version of what is on the page for sense, and generally read passages for the meanings they contain. Part of this reading for meaning depends on their being able to tie what they read into their personal conceptual framework.

Reading difficulties occur for some children when they have not developed all or some of these strategies to the point where they can progress independently, by making informed guesses at unknown words, which they then monitor using context and visual characteristics. From this monitoring comes the child's ability to self-correct to something that is more acceptable.

A child who has good phonic attack skills but does not read for overall sense will flounder on every phonetically irregular word. Alternatively, a child who makes good guesses based on meaning, but makes no use of graphophonic cues, will have trouble ascertaining if the attempt was correct. Children who only attend to saying the words correctly and don't realise that the most important outcome is understanding the message will have little understanding of what they have read.

Here are some possible teaching strategies for helping children develop as "strategic" readers:

Begin by making an assessment of the strategies the child does use.

For children who are not using prediction and context clues:

- Build up fluency on easy materials.
- Use the "repeated reading procedure" in which they read a story over and over, or reading in unison with a fluent reader or taped version of the story.
- Ask them to predict what is going to happen next.
- Encourage them to skip an unknown word, read to the end of the sentence, and think about what word would make sense.
- Give practice on cloze passages.
- Get them to stop at the end of each sentence and ask, "Did that make sense?"
- Model fluency, prediction skills, appropriate phraseology, and reading the punctuation, using big books, or group reading of the same story.
- Encourage children to listen to themselves read and develop an "ear for error" whereby they notice if a word doesn't make sense.

For children who are not using graphophonic cues:

- Direct their attention to the beginning letter of the word to confirm their attempts. Gradually add in looking at the end and middle part of the word also.
- Ask them if the word looks like the one they have suggested.
- Show them other words with the same sound pattern and if they recognise any, get them to transfer the sound to the word they are attempting.
- Use shared book or group reading to point out words with similar sound patterns, endings, etc.

For children who do not understand what they read:

- Give them many opportunities to write and then read their own writing.
- Provide them with many chances to relate what they read to their own experiences, in discussion with peers or in individual conferences. Encourage retelling of the story orally or through dramatisation or drawing; provide opportunities for group interpretation of stories.
- Help them to pose questions they would like answered.
- Practise sequencing the parts of a story, try macro cloze, where they have to predict the missing element of a story, and rewrite endings of stories or pick changes that have been made to them.
- Help children to read nonfiction for information by choosing considerate texts and providing background information.

Lack of Purpose/Personal Motivation

Where readers have had little success or personal enjoyment from their reading experiences,... they will view reading as something that is only important as a school activity, undertaken mainly to satisfy the teacher. Students may be unable to relate what they read to their own experiences or make connections between the ideas presented in their reading. This naturally affects their ability to comprehend what they read.

It seems that good readers approach texts with personal intentions to be met, possibly even framing questions they would like answered as they go. Thus their involvement with a text is an active one and they are continually processing what they read in terms of what they know. The children who read only because they have to don't interact with print in the same way, and meaning suffers. It is important to help these children find ways that reading can be purposeful and personally important for them; otherwise, as soon as they are allowed to, they will abandon it.

Here are some possible strategies for building personal motivation:

- Match reading materials with children's interests and provide opportunities for group discussion of interest-related reading.
- Make use of real-life reading materials such as advertisements, manuals, and newspapers.
- Encourage children to think about purpose and audience when they write. Publish their writing and make sure they receive feedback on it.
- Introduce children to a wide range of forms of writing such as plays, written directions, letters, and class newspapers.

Book Note

Using Big Books and Predictable Books

Priscilla Lynch
1986; 30 pp.; $6.28
New York: Scholastic

Shared Reading: Safe Risks with Whole Books

Adrian Peetoom
1986; 32 pp.; $6.28
New York: Scholastic

A Teacher's Guide to Shared Reading

F. L. Barrett
1982; 32 pp.; $6.28
New York: Scholastic

If you don't know how and why to use real books with kids, you will after you've read these three handy booklets from Scholastic. Not to be missed, especially for teachers new to whole language.

LBB

• Help children to set their own purposes for reading, in the form of questions they want answered or specific points to look for.

Lack of Practice

Children who are having difficulty with the reading process are likely to slip further and further behind their more successful peers, simply because they do not read as much and so have less practice.

Because they are perceived as needing special attention, such readers may have been required to spend some of their reading time on activities such as word attack skills. A high emphasis on oral reading, which is much slower than silent reading, will also decrease the amount of text read in any session.

There may also be the problem that children have continually been given, or have chosen, material with which they have missed out on the opportunity to read with the fluency and accuracy which develops appropriate phrasing and the ability to predict what is coming and necessary background to self-correct when errors are made.

A dilemma, then, is to find ways of increasing the time spent on reading by those children who show the need for it, without causing them to miss other important aspects of their education. In fact if they are to regain lost ground, they will need to spend more time on reading than their more successful peers.

Lack of Recognition of Importance of Parents

Kemp found that parents who wished to seek help for or assist their own children had mostly received no support from the teacher, and had finally given up their attempts in frustration and fear of doing more harm than good. It would seem that in assisting children with reading difficulties, we need to communicate fully our plans to parents and involve them at as many levels as possible.

Here are some possible strategies for involving parents:

• Communicate with parents at the earliest opportunity, as a valuable source of learning about the child, to build up a reading profile. Show them the completed profile and plan of action and modify both in accordance with their feedback.

• Negotiate with them as to what involvement they would like in the planned action.

• Keep regular contact in regard to the child's progress.

➡ See: DeFord, p. 113; Goodman, p. 100; Marek, p. 105; Meier, p. 50; Pinnell, p. 112.

Excerpted from *English Language Arts Newsletter*, no. 4, November 1987.

Subscription Information: The *English Language Arts Newsletter* is published four times a year. Overseas educators can subscribe to *ELAN* by sending $40 (Australian currency) to *ELAN*, Ingle Farm Curriculum Unit, 15 Darrang Ave., Ingle Farm, SA 5098, Australia.

📷 WHOLE LANGUAGE CAMERA

Students browse in school library, Sunnyside High School, Tucson, AZ.

Breakthroughs   by Ray Dawley

Actions Speak Louder…

After lunch my fourth-graders and I participate in a sustained silent reading period that we call DEAR time—"Drop Everything And Read." At the start of this school year, I was having a hard time getting the kids to settle down and get into their books. After repeated reminders and reprimands, I decided to quit talking and show them what I meant. I grabbed my book, sat down, put my feet up, and said just once, "Hey you guys, please quit your yapping! I want to read!" Then I opened my book and started reading. The kids watched me for a while, then took up their own books and followed suit. DEAR time is no longer just a name in our room.

Ray Dawley is an elementary teacher at Fair Oaks School, Redwood City, CA.

 **Classroom Demonstrations**

by La Donna Hauser

Supporting Emerging Readers

I begin each year with a 10-day unit on primary literature I call "Books You May Have Missed!" I surround students with primary books and begin a typical lesson by reading a personal favorite. I consciously try to model good read-aloud techniques and also question students to get them to predict, infer, analyze, and compare the stories. We talk about types of fiction, story grammar, vocabulary, authors, and fix-up strategies to use when something doesn't make sense. Students are then allowed to read silently for 20 minutes. They choose the book they want and get into small groups to discuss and answer questions I give them. After 5 or 10 minutes of discussion, they share their answers. Reading class ends with a read-aloud simply for enjoyment.

Sample Questions for Groups to Answer:

• *When you come to a word that you don't know, what do you do to figure it out? Can you think of other ways you could help yourself?*
I want students to realize what they do as they read. I'd like them to discover these word-level strategies: (1) skipping an unknown word, (2) using context clues, (3) looking for structural clues within words, (4) sounding out the word, (5) using a dictionary, and (6) asking for help. I accept all productive strategies that students use.

• *What do you do when you get to a part of the story you don't understand? How do you go about understanding it?*
I look for these answers: (1) ignoring the difficulty and reading on—the information may not be important to the story, (2) not judging—the problem may be cleared up later so keep reading, (3) rereading the sentences, (4) rereading the previous passage, and (5) getting help (Wilson and Gambrell 1988).

• *What do all the stories you've read have in common?*
I want them to have a sense of story: characters, setting, plot, conflict, and theme. Students don't use these terms, but they can often explain what they are.

• *Give an example of an unusual word you found in the books. What did it mean?*
We often make a chart of words we find in the books. I'm trying not only to get them to notice words, but also to appreciate the variety of vocabulary in these books, and the fact that the vocabulary is not always easy.

• *Research the life of an author whose book your group is reading. Make a chart telling about the author and his or her books.*

• *How are pictures used in books?*

• *All the books you've read today are fables. What are the characteristics of fables?*

During this time I introduce "Buddy Reading" and record each child reading a literature book aloud, which is less threatening to read aloud than a basal story. I use that tape to give children feedback on their reading and to diagnose any problems they may be having.

➡ See: Goodman, p. 100; Marek, p. 105; Peters, p. 114.

Reference
Wilson, R. M., and L. B. Gambrell. 1988. *Reading comprehension in the elementary school.* Boston: Allyn & Bacon.

La Donna Hauser is an elementary teacher at Bradley Creek School, Wilmington, NC.

Book Note

Chapter 1 Reading Instructional Strategies Guide for Elementary Chapter 1 Reading Teachers

$15 plus $3 postage and handling from:
Julian G. Baca
Chapter 1 Office
Albuquerque Public Schools
Albuquerque, NM 87125

Three years ago we had the good fortune to learn about and acquire a copy of the *Chapter 1 Reading Instructional Strategies Guide for Elementary Chapter 1 Reading Teachers,* published through the Elementary Field Office of Albuquerque Public Schools. The booklet lists strategy lessons, "helping hands" (a helpful directory providing examples and further explanations), a glossary of strategies, information about evaluation procedures, references, and an appendix of books for whole language. Even though this booklet is intended primarily for use with younger children, the information is useful to upper elementary teachers also. It addresses strategies that are global and can be applied to the Reading Miscue Inventory, the writing process, literature studies, and thematic units. Given the dogmatic nature of most school district materials and manuals, this book is very progressive. We recommend it to any teacher who is new to or involved in whole language.

Alan and Jane Flurkey

Classroom Demonstrations

by Trevor H. Cairney

Six Whole Language Strategies That Integrate Reading and Writing

If one accepts a constructive view of reading comprehension then the next consideration is "What do I do on Monday?" Let me outline six strategies that I have found useful.

COLLABORATIVE STORIES

Introduction

I devised the term *collaborative story* to describe a strategy that requires children to create their own versions of a story using a no-text version of a picture book as a stimulus. I use the term *collaboration* because it is a collaboration between original and new (child) author. I have used it successfully with children of varying abilities. For example, I have seen nonreaders make great strides towards independence using this technique, and talented children "stretched." Its great strength is that it gives children the opportunity to create meaning at the text level.

Procedure

To use the strategy you need a wordless picture book. A number of books of this type are available commercially today; however, it is easy to create your own.

Once you have your wordless book, you share the original story with the child, group, or class. With less proficient readers (e.g., kindergarten or nonreaders) you read it to them; while more proficient readers might read it themselves. Once the text has been read (this doesn't have to be the same day; you may have read it many times in the past), the children are ready to produce their own versions. The decision may be made to reproduce a similar story using the children's own language (without looking back at the text), or the children may decide to try to produce a completely different version.

Your role in the composing process will vary depending upon the ability of the children and the size of the group you are working with. For example, if you are working with young readers, you will need to scribe the text for them (although they might do their own drafts) while they compose. More proficient readers might work independently or in groups with your role reduced significantly. No matter how you use the activity, the composing should be done by the children.

The strategy lesson ends when the new text is shared with other readers. Some children might then like to go back to the original text to see how the new text is different. Each text that is produced in this way is then read orally by the pupil to different audiences, and silently as often as he or she wishes.

Variations to This Strategy

A useful variation is to use the pictures from a text that your students have not seen before. This changes the nature of the lesson; however, your children still have to use similar knowledge of language to construct the text. What this variation offers that is different is complete freedom from the constraints of the original text stored in memory.

TEXT SHUFFLE

Introduction

This is an old technique, which has been used successfully by many teachers. It involves cutting a text into pieces (using logical divisions based on meaning) and presenting the pieces to individual children or small groups of four to six. It requires the reader to create meaning at the text level. In particular, it creates a need for the use of story structures, which may or may not have been intuitively learnt through the experience of literature.

Procedure

I usually use a text of 200 to 500 words for this strategy. Making the materials is relatively easy. You might use old readers, or school magazine stories.

Once you have your text segments, glue them to uniform-sized pieces of cardboard and provide each child with a segment (if working in groups). Then, ask the group to try to reconstruct the text. At first you might need to help them by asking questions like: Who thinks they have the first part? and How do you know that piece comes next? However, it doesn't take long for most children to learn how to negotiate the meaning without your assistance.

STORY FRAMES

Introduction

Story frames are a form of probed text recall (Cairney 1985). The story frame is a skeletal outline of the text; in a way, a story level cloze. The skeleton contains just enough information to probe the child's recall of the story constructed and stored in memory. This technique is not designed to test memory of text. One of the difficulties that some readers face is not being able to organise the information generated by the text. These readers remember only isolated segments of a text that they have created while reading. This technique helps them to construct a coherent representation of the text.

Procedure

The frame you construct should not be too detailed. If it is, the activity becomes far too restrictive. Children can complete this individually or in small groups.

The presentation of the original text can be done in a variety of ways. For example, you might use picture books beyond your children's current reading level and read the texts to them. On the other hand, you might use a text that the children can read, and have them read it silently.

After the story is read, a leader asks the members to suggest the content to be placed in each slot. Once the frame is complete it is read right through and the content discussed.

Michael Magee lived on the Outer Barcoo in an old shanty. Hardly a soul passed by nor any man of religion. He lived with his unchristened son and wife.

One day a priest happened to pass by.

Now his son had never been christened so the preacher agreed to christen him straight away.

But it just so happened that the boy listened through the keyhole of the door and thought christening was like branding sheep.

So straight away he ran out of the house to the bush with his father and everyone chasing,

but they started to catch him so he crawled into a log. They got a stick to poke him out, and the priest got ready to sprinkle him,

and his parents and the priest realized they had no water and had forgotten his name.

The priest decided to throw a whisky bottle at him as he ran out, and he christened him Maginnis after Maginnis' Whisky. And so that's why even today people still joke with him and ask where he got his name.

—A story frame written for *A Bush Christening* by Scott, age 11

STORY TRANSFORMATION

Introduction

This strategy is a modification of one I have previously referred to as *Lap Stories* (Cairney 1985). In using a new label I am simply widening its scope.

This revised strategy aims to encourage children to use alternative ways to make meaning. It reflects the belief that excursions into other methods of creating meaning help the reader to construct a more enriched personal representation of the text. (Cairney, in press). It also helps readers to learn more about written language as part of the process.

Procedure

Children might use silhouettes on an overhead projector, a time line, dramatisation, mime, puppetry and so on. Once the children have transformed their story in some way, I encourage them to share the meaning they have created with other children. The part that the original text plays varies depending upon the medium used to transform the text. If drama has been used, the text is modified to provide a script. However, with silhouettes, the original text is read as the silhouettes are shown.

To introduce this strategy lesson, it is essential to model it first. This is usually done with the participation of the class. For example a year-one class might help to prepare silhouettes for the text "There Was an Old Lady Who Swallowed a Fly." The text could then be read by one or two storytellers, with other members of the class manipulating the silhouettes.

NEVER-ENDING STORY

Introduction

This strategy is a truly integrated reading and writing activity. Children are provided with a story beginning and are then asked to continue to write for a limited amount of time, until told to pass the story on to another child for it to be continued. This technique requires the child to read and write in an interactive way. First reading, then writing, reading, then writing, and so on. Each time a new text is passed on to the child, it is necessary for him or her to read the text already written, predict what the author was trying to create, and plan how to extend the text. In a sense, this activity is forcing the reader to "read like a writer" in a way difficult to achieve simply through conventional writing lessons.

Procedure

I always introduce this strategy by modelling it on the overhead projector. After taking a story beginning, which has been written on the overhead prior to the lesson, I write the next section of the text. I stop after writing several sentences, read the text out loud, and ask the group to suggest what might come next. I then take someone's suggestion and write the next section of the text. I continue in this way until the text is completed to the group's satisfaction.

I usually start by providing a story beginning of no more than two or three sentences. The beginning introduces a character, sets a little of the scene, and perhaps provides some initiating event. You then ask the children to start writing. After a set period of time (e.g., three minutes) you stop them and ask them to pass the text on. No matter how long you provide for each segment of text, always warn the group just before stopping them. You might simply say, "In one minute you need to pass it on, so finish the sentence you're on." The only variation to this pattern is that you should provide extra time for the ending to the text. In fact, I normally allow each child to write until satisfied with the ending.

CHARACTER INTERVIEWS

Introduction

This strategy is a highly creative form of literary response. It requires a thorough understanding and appreciation of the text, and encourages the reader to "get inside the character," as well as elaborating upon the text. If our aim is to create readers who see reading as a constructive meaning making process, then there is no better activity to help achieve this.

Procedure

I explain that the aim is to interview a character from a story that they know well. I take a story that I've shared with them, select a character (and give my reasons for the choice), and then proceed to act out the interchange between a detached interviewer (i.e., someone not part of the story) and a real character from the story.

Once I have demonstrated how an interview might unfold, I ask them to brainstorm characters from stories they know who could be interviewed. I then explain that their job isn't to retell the story, but to take one aspect of it and use it for the interview, as if it were part of real life. The group is then split into pairs and each pair encouraged to select a character, decide who will fill the separate roles of interviewer and interviewee, and then proceed to prepare an interview, recording all questions and answers.

When sufficient time has been allowed the group re-forms and the pairs present their interviews, one acting as interviewer (I), and the other as character (PBP).

I: We welcome warmly the Paper Bag Princess [1980]. As you may recall, she heroically saved her prince from the dragon's lair. Tell me, did you plan right from the beginning to tire out the dragon so you could save the prince?

PBP: Well, it was just one of those "on-the-spur-of-the-moment" ideas.

I: Weren't you worried that the dragon might have burnt your scanty paper bag dress?

PBP: Now that I think of it, I don't believe I thought of it at all. Indeed, I was lucky to find it to wear when my palace burnt down. The burning of my clothes etc., was a most unfortunate happening.

I: Ah, I see. Weren't you downhearted when Ronald rejected you because you were a mess?

PBP: I was feeling a little downhearted at first, but then I realised that Ronald was a conceited, spoilt, immature young man, and I would not have got along with him.

I: Did you think that the dragon was rather foolish and simple-minded to fall for your tricks?

PBP: Oh yes, certainly, I think he also wanted to show off a bit. The ostentatious prig!

I: The story goes that you didn't get married with Ronald after all. Have you anybody in mind?

PBP: I met him coming back from saving Ronald (groan). He took in my situation at once, and bought me my choice of clothes. We'll be getting married in the spring.

I: Well, I'm afraid that we must conclude this interview, and I am sure that you will join me in all the best wishes for the Paper Bag Princess.

—A character interview prepared for the character Elizabeth in *The Paper Bag Princess* by Clementine, age 12.

The six strategies outlined above have been provided to show that there is an alternative to traditional comprehension instruction. While these activities are all different, they share many common features. First, they help readers to create meaning as they encounter texts. Second, they require the readers to construct a coherent understanding of whole texts. Third, they encourage excursions into other forms of meaning making (such as writing, drawing, dramatisation, etc.) to create a more complete understanding of the text read. Fourth, the teacher is vitally involved as a facilitator, modelling and demonstrating strategies that effective readers use to make sense of texts. Finally, they recognise the important social nature of reading and allow children to learn from each other.

References

Cairney, T. H. 1985. "Linking reading and writing." In *Literacy: Strategies and perspectives*, ed. D. Burnes, H. French, and F. Moore. Adelaide: Australian Reading Association.

———. In press. *Teaching reading comprehension: Meaning makers at work*. Milton Keynes, U.K.: Open University Press.

Munsch, R. 1980. *The paper bag princess*. Toronto: Annick Press.

Patterson, A. B. 1976. *A bush christening*. San Francisco: Collins.

To appear in a modified form in a forthcoming book, *Teaching Reading Comprehension: Meaning Makers at Work*, Milton Keynes, U.K.: Open University Press.

Trevor H. Cairney is an associate professor at the University of Western Sydney, Nepean, Australia.

YOUNG ARTISTS

—Ben Adams, 17, Cornelius, OR
(from *Treasures 2*, see p. 162)

Language Stories

Knowing What Works

Erin, age four, was stretched out on the couch pretending to read, in a dramatic voice, *Molly Learns a Lesson*, from Janet Shaw's popular American Girl Series.

As I walked by with a load of folded laundry, she turned to me and said, "Pretend reading helps you with real reading."

"Who told you *that?*"

"No one. I just knowed it in my head!"

I walked on thinking, "Wouldn't it be great if all adults who work with young readers knew that in *their* heads?"

—LBB

➜ See: Literature Reference List, p. 429.

WHOLE LANGUAGE CAMERA

Linda Oxendine reads from her 70-year-old father's second-grade McGuffy Reader,
G.R. Hampton School, Barbourville, KY.

Cornerstone: Robin Campbell

The Whole Language Teacher Responding to a Reader's Miscues

A teacher actively listening to a primary school child reading from a book that engages the child's attention provides an interesting study. The teacher does far more than listen; he or she also guides, supports, and facilitates the reading. The teacher first shows support by becoming involved in a genuinely shared literacy event. The teacher demonstrates by both word and deed an empathy for what the reader is trying to achieve. An extract from Brian's oral reading of *Six Little Kittens* is indicative of this support.

Brian: Next—next they find a house made of—a house made of jelly [or Jell-O].

(Ha ha!)

This will not do—this will not do, says one of the little kittens. The children will eat it all up.

(And it will wobble!)

—all up and then there will be no house left.

(And it would wobble.)

Teacher: It would wobble, wouldn't it?

Previous reading encounters with his teacher had taught Brian that a

Robin Campbell is a former primary school teacher who is now head of the Division of Education and Training at Hatfield Polytechnic in England. He taught 5- to 11-year-old children for 15 years in four schools. In one school he served as head teacher before moving on to teacher education. His doctorate included an exploration of the support that teachers provide for young beginning readers in the classroom. He now teaches literacy development courses with undergraduate and postgraduate students.

real sharing would take place. He could enjoy the story and comment on it, safe in the knowledge that the teacher would respond to what he was trying to achieve rather than telling him to get on with his reading.

However, at times a reader will miscue and the teacher will need to consider how to respond. The whole language teachers whom I have worked with do so in particular ways.

Nonresponse, waiting, restarting the sentence, a soft *no*, and the occasional telling of the word all may be part of the teacher's repertoire, depending on the teacher's knowledge of the reading process and his or her understanding of what the reader is doing. These strategies allow minimal disruption for the reader. They help the child to stay involved with the text. They provide some information about how predictions are working out.

The whole language teacher listens to the reader but does not intervene in order to correct. Instead, there is a trust in what the reader is trying to do, and the teacher acts as a mediator to guide and support.

➔ See: Goodman, pp. 98, 100; Marek, p. 105.

Further Reading by Robin Campbell

◆ "Oral Reading Errors of Two Beginning Readers." *Journal of Research in Reading* 10(2), 1987.
◆ *Hearing Children Read.* Routledge, 1988.
◆ "Is It Time for USSR, SSR, SQUIRT, DEAR, or ERIC?" *Education 3–13* 16(2), 1988.
◆ "Learning About Reading During Pupil-Teacher Reading Interactions." *Cambridge Journal of Education* 18(3), 1988.
◆ "Shared Reading in an Infant Classroom." *Primary Teaching Studies* 5(1), 1989.
◆ "The Teacher as a Role Model During Sustained Silent Reading (SSR)." *Reading* 23(3), 1989.
◆ *Reading Together.* Open University Press, 1990.

Breakthroughs
by Patricia Broderick Zaballos

The Whole Language Difference

I am an undergraduate assigned to a depressingly traditional basal, phonics, linguistics ("What's the morpheme?") reading classroom. I have noticed that when the students sit around the little table and wait for their turn to read or ask a question, many of them become bored.

One day I sat by Katie, a second-grader, and noticed that she was looking at the clock at least every two minutes. Another girl entertained herself by looking ahead in the book or working on her workbook pages before she was supposed to. I don't blame them—I nearly fall asleep myself when I am in this classroom. The teacher constantly reprimands Katie, oftentimes unfairly, for things that she doesn't even notice in the other students. I feel for Katie, because it is obvious to me that she is smart. But the teacher doesn't seem to recognize that she is misbehaving because she is being presented with an uninteresting, inappropriate reading program.

Today there was some time left after the students finished their workbooks, so I sat next to Katie and asked her what she liked to read. She brought me a short story that especially appealed to her. I asked her what she liked best about the book, and she talked about her favorite part. We looked at the picture on one page and discussed whether the story was taking place at night or on a rainy day.

While I was getting my things together to leave, Katie walked up to me and said, "I know you're going to be a good teacher." I asked her why. She thought about it for a moment and then said, "Because you're nice."

That really meant a lot to me. When I thought back I realized that I hadn't lavished any special praise on her; I had simply sat with her for a while, listened to her read a book that she liked, and talked with her about the book briefly. All this student needed was a little positive interaction. She needed to feel valued as a person.

Whole language can do this. It gives kids the chance to read what they want to read. And it lets them discuss what they find important about the book. But most important, I think it helps kids realize that their thoughts and input are important. What a difference that can make!

➔ See: Ohanian, p. 176; Reader's Workshop, p. 175; Wildermuth, p. 197.

Patricia Broderick Zaballos, an elementary teacher at Hillside School, San Lorenzo, CA, wrote this when she was a student teacher.

Book Note

Hearing Children Read

Robin Campbell
1988; London: Routledge
Available from:
Associate Book Publishers
North Way, Andover
Hampshire SP10 5PE
England

"Hearing Children Read" is a central activity in the primary classroom. In this book Robin Campbell, a principal lecturer in Education at Hatfield Polytechnic, gives a detailed description and analysis of children reading to their teachers and of the teachers responding to that reading. Campbell draws on his

observation and analysis of teachers at work in normal classrooms, and provides practical guidelines for hearing a child read.

Campbell discusses the purposes for hearing children read, and examines the preliminaries to that reading, such as where it takes place, how to reduce interruptions, and so on. He gives many examples of what actually goes on when a teacher is hearing a child read, and uses the words of teachers and children wherever possible to bring the book to life and made it recognizable to teachers.

Hearing Children Read is specially relevant to primary school teachers and student teachers, and will also be useful to parents who are interested in their children's reading development.

Classroom Demonstrations

by Debra Jacobson

Strategies for Helping Readers in Literature Study

When students need all the support they can get in order to tackle a literature study book, take it slow and stick with your readers. Instead of giving the same book to everybody, let two kids share one book. Meet with them and predict about the book together, looking at pictures, chapter headings, and so on. Then read some of the book to the group and talk about it some more. Agree as a group on a small number of pages to read and let them discuss the selection with partners. Write the names of the partners on the board, and tell the kids that when they have read the pages, talked about it with their partners, and written a potential discussion item on a Post-it, they should put a check on the board by their

names and then go about other appropriate literacy/language workshop activities. Call the group together again that day, or the next, to discuss the book and plow ahead slowly.

I have also asked kids to preview potential literature study books and tell me if they think it would be worthwhile to buy more copies of the book. We conduct little book talks and share what we know, and then I put the books out for kids to read.

➔ See: Bird, p. 196; Jacobson, pp. 160, 365; Kitagawa, p. 420; Peters, p. 114; Yencho, p. 108.

Debra Jacobson is an elementary teacher at Coronado Elementary School, Tucson, AZ.

Materials: Consumer Beware

As We See It:
Kenneth S. & Yetta M. Goodman

Consumer Beware! Selecting Materials for Whole Language Readers

As we were projecting the format for *The Whole Language Catalog,* we envisioned a section called "Consumer Beware!" We wanted to help thoughtful consumers in response to the voluminous selection of materials published for children to read and to use either in school or at home.

We weren't too concerned about the materials that most of us would reject as suitable for whole language classrooms. Certainly traditional basal readers, spelling, language arts, and handwriting textbooks, workbooks with lists of fractured language divorced of meaning or simpleminded questions would not be considered by whole language advocates.

We have, however, become concerned about the growing use of the label *whole language* on a host of materials that reflect little knowledge about the philosophy of whole language. An ad for one basal reading series, for example, shows a teacher's plan book with "whole language" penciled in as an activity on Monday from 1:00 to 2:00 P.M. Workbooks have been developed to accompany trade books (adolescent and children's literature) with mindless questions and skills. Since they have virtually nothing to do with the original literature, they can be published without permission from the author or the original publisher. Some of them have such silly ideas as "circle every letter *b* on page 32" of a children's literature classic. Some companies slap the label *whole language* on materials at teachers' conferences, but remove them when promoting those same materials for other audiences.

At the same time, there are some teachers and administrators who have come to believe that they are "doing whole language" as long as they are using big books, literature sets, or individualizing the reading program with little regard for the quality of the material or its relationship to the rest of the curriculum. Even materials that are part of a holistic program should be subject to evaluation and scrutiny and not simply accepted at face value.

So we thought that we would evaluate materials in the catalog that we believe are using the label *whole language* in an unprofessional way. However, as we began to consider the huge number of good, mediocre, and downright bad materials, we realized that our responsibility is not to place a *Good Housekeeping* seal of approval on materials.

First, we occasionally disagree among ourselves about what is "good literature" or good whole language materials. Second, selection of material is a continuous procedure in whole language classrooms for librarians and teachers. Thousands of new children's trade books alone are published yearly, and companies are producing increasing numbers of big books, text sets, and nonfiction materials for schools to take advantage of the growing interest in whole language. Although a consumer's report of whole language material might be appropriate in some form, there is no real room in this catalog for such an enterprise. Third, each teacher, school, or district should be setting up its own criteria for material selection, involving parents as well as students in the process. They shouldn't have to wait for experts to tell them what is good. Setting sound criteria empowers those involved in material selection and evaluation and at the same time educates them.

With these reasons in mind, we decided to help the readers of the catalog think through criteria that can easily be adapted to fit their needs.

Predictability, Not Readability

An important issue often raised is how to choose a book to meet the reading ability of the reader. We reject "readability formulas" that focus on simplistic notions of the text. Such formulas are concerned with the number of words, clauses, sentences, and sound patterns, suggesting that longer language units and more "complex" language structures are harder to read. On the contrary, our research indicates that longer texts often are easier to read than shorter texts, and that texts that are complex grammatically because they show clearly the relationships between ideas and people can be easier to read than simple sentences.

Readability formulas are developed to judge texts apart from the transactions readers have with them. With readers out of sight and mind, the most important criteria to consider such as predictability, background knowledge and experience, appropriateness, relevance, interest, and purpose are ignored. We do not believe that counting features provides any helpful yardstick to match readers with any written material. The age ranges book publishers and librarians place on literature for children and adolescents are a better guide for teachers and parents than readability formulas because they are based on experiences that teachers and librarians have had. But the age ranges are simply guides. Only the *reader* can really know whether a book is easy or difficult.

We believe that what is most important is that reading material be predictable for readers. Predictability factors include the following:

- Language that is natural for a particular context and for the reader. The reader has had real-life experiences and is familiar with the way in which the language of this type of text is used.
- Conceptual information is known by the reader to a considerable extent though it often contains new information which interests and captures the imagination of the reader.

When readers can predict language and conceptual possibilities as they read, they can cope with relative complexity in linguistic form and conceptual information.

Criteria for Selecting Reading Materials

When considering reading materials, the following criteria need to be addressed:

1. Literary quality—this will always be personal. Individual readers need to develop their own criteria.
2. Authentic social/cultural significance—this includes the truth value, validity, and honesty of the reading material; knowledge that is most accepted by scientists; concerns for ethnic diversity and stereotyping; and a sense that the material fits pragmatically what is known in the social and cultural world.
3. Cohesion and coherence—the way in which the text hangs together.
4. Illustrations—illustrations help to create a context and add an extra meaning dimension to the written text.
5. Teaching possibilities—the many opportunities to use the materials to support the rest of the curriculum.
6. Psychological possibilities—a wide range of materials to serve many different interests and purposes.

By considering such criteria, groups can construct lists of questions to answer as they are involved in material selection. Margaret Mooney offers just such a list in her book *Developing Life-long Readers,* published by the Department of Education in New Zealand and now available in the United States from Richard C. Owen, Publishers.

Questions such as Mooney's, adapted for particular grades and communities, provide a format to help us think through the complexity of material selection. As teachers and librarians become comfortable using them, these questions become internalized and are used whenever material selection takes place.

Students can also be involved in developing similar questions for their own personal selection of reading material and for selection for their classroom and school libraries. Involvement in such discussions is a powerful teaching tool for the development of students' critical reading.

➡ See: Dalrymple, p. 426; Edelsky, p. 72; Goodman, p. 122; Huck, p. 188; Larrick, p. 173; Mooney, p. 120,121; Ohanian, p. 176; Owen, p. 414; Peetoom, p. 415.

 It Shouldn't Happen to Kids

Don't Expect a Happy Ending to This Story

Five third-graders were doing well in reading, and their own teacher and the reading teacher got together and decided that this group might as well read library books instead of their readers. So they went to the principal, and guess what? It was decided that these kids could do that for a while, and then the teachers would report to the principal on what happened.

Well, the kids really flew. They read *Charlotte's Web* and some other books and talked about them, and the teachers were happy and gave a good report to the principal. The principal said, "Let's give them the tests from the reading series." Well, the teachers didn't think that was a good idea, because the group hadn't read those stories, but the principal really wanted them to give the test, so they did.

The teachers were still happy after the testing, because there were 26 questions and one kid got them all right and the others missed one but one kid missed two. But the principal thought about it and said, "Well, then, they had better read the stories in the reader also." So they did.

➡ See: Literature Reference List, p. 429; Salzer, pp. 231, 409.

—Dick Salzer, professor, SUNY at Buffalo, NY

📷 **WHOLE LANGUAGE CAMERA**

A ride into fantasy in the Children's Library, Palo Alto, CA.

TEACHERS NETWORKING
THE WHOLE LANGUAGE NEWSLETTER

A Good Book Is a Good Book Anywhere

by Margaret Mooney

Recently I had the opportunity to meet with teachers in various parts of the United States to discuss the principles, practices, and materials used in early literacy programs in New Zealand. It has been interesting to note that as teachers are influenced by the movement towards whole language, they become more discerning in the selection and use of books in their classrooms. Titles hitherto used solely for "teaching reading" or "practicing skills" are bypassed for books that work as books, books that first and foremost tell a story, and books that are springboards to exploration and discovery in the various language modes, including speaking, listening, writing, reading, moving, watching, shaping, and viewing.

This concern has also received considerable attention in New Zealand, especially during the development of *Ready to Read,* the series published by the New Zealand Department of Education for use in all primary schools. The following criteria, established by teachers, editors, and reading specialists, proved effective in identifying the most suitable scripts for trial and later for publication. Although the examples in this article are from titles in the *Ready to Read* series, teachers and editors are continuing to use the criteria when considering any material for use in programs at all levels of the elementary school. The criteria identify scripts that help the reader develop positive attitudes to and understandings about books and about him/herself as a reader.

First, does the piece have charm, magic, impact, and appeal? This element is hard to define but relatively easy to identify. It's what demands the repeated "read it again" response and causes chunks of language or meaning to reappear in the reader's mind. For this to happen, the impact and lasting, pleasurable quality has to be intrinsic, both in the story and in the author's style. Charm, magic, impact, and appeal make a text succeed as a story, whether it is read aloud or silently, and provide further delights on each reading, as reflected in *Old Tuatara* (1982).

> Old Tuatara sat in the sun./He sat and sat and sat.
> "Asleep," said the fantail./"Asleep," said the gull.
> "Asleep," said the frog./"Asleep," said the fly.
> "Not asleep," said Old Tuatara.

Second, does the piece say something worthwhile? Does the story merit the reader spending time getting the message? Does the author's idea always remain uppermost, avoiding any overt presentation of a moral or lesson? Does the story

say something new or present a familiar theme in such a way that the reader doesn't feel he's heard it all before?

Children are very quick to see when they are being conned or sold short. They are discerning readers who seldom give an author a second chance. Their years of learning, living, and loving enable them to draw their own conclusions and make appropriate judgements. The readers can decide whether their sympathy lies with the fly or with Old Tuatara.

Third, is the shape and structure appropriate? Consideration here includes the flow and pace

of the story, the unfolding of the story and its resolution, and the author's technique in leading one episode into the next and in signalling a change of mood and pace. Does the story set its own pace and carry the reader through the text, leaving a willingness to share the experience again? The patterned structure of *Blackbird's Nest* offers opportunities for much rhyming and repetition. The format generates its own pace as it takes the reader through the cycle of growth.

> Four speckled eggs in a blackbird's nest.
> Blackbird sat/Blackbird sat,
> Blackbird sat in a blackbird's nest.
> Four bare babies in a blackbird's nest.
> Blackbirds fed/Blackbirds fed,
> Blackbirds fed in a blackbird's nest.
> Four big babies in a blackbird's nest.
> Babies grew/Babies grew,
> Babies flew from the blackbird's nest.
> Now what is left in the blackbird's nest?
> One small feather/and one dead leaf.
> A lonely,
> empty
> blackbird's nest.

Fourth, is the language effective? Does the language suit the subject and the characters? Do the characters talk naturally? Does the language aid the reader in making sense of the author's idea?

The effective use of language, and the balance of what is said with what's not said, establishes a nod-nod-wink-wink trust between the author and the reader. This criterion is another where condescension (as opposed to simplicity) diminishes the story's chance of becoming a well-loved favourite. The children will quickly see that the story was chosen for the words it teaches. Text for beginning readers should include the language of books as well as language the reader would use in natural conversation. There is no place for collections of words

selected from readability formulae.

Lastly, is the piece authentic? Does the piece achieve what it claims? Does the author fulfill all the promises engendered by the title and text? Is the message genuine? Does it avoid the sham, the misleading, the prejudiced, the stereotyped, and the superficial?

As with the other criteria, this section applies to both fiction and nonfiction. Justice must seem to be done in stories of fantasy as well as those of fact, and safety must always be a concern. In the case of nonfiction, all the facts should be accurate, so that children do not have to relearn correct details later. This means that nonfiction, like fiction, should be specific rather than general.

The readers feel they know Old Tuatara and know exactly what to expect when they peep into a blackbird's nest. They feel this intimacy with the text and ownership of it because both stories meet the criteria outlined above. Each text acknowledges the reader's responsibility in discovering the author's message and controlling the unfolding of it in the story line.

I am convinced that these criteria are not relevant exclusively to New Zealand. I hope you find them useful. Children in any country will learn best on books that are rewarding and have meaning, and a good book is a good book anywhere!

➜ See: Goodman, p. 119; Mooney, p. 121; Owen, p. 414; Owen, p. 414.

References
Cowley, J. 1982. "Old Tuatara." *Ready to read.* Wellington, New Zealand: Department of Education; Katonah, NY: Richard C. Owen Publishers, Inc.
Harvey, O. 1982. "Blackbird's nest." *Ready to read.* Wellington, New Zealand: Department of Education; Katonah, NY: Richard C. Owen Publishers, Inc.

From *Teachers Networking* 8(2), December 1987.

Margaret Mooney is a teacher and educator and, for the last seven years, has been editor of *Ready to Read* in the New Zealand Department of Education.

Subscription Information: Subscriptions to Teachers Networking are by school year. A four-issue, one-year subscription costs $15.00 for U.S. residents, $18.00 for Canadian residents. (Subscriptions should be paid for in U.S. dollars.) Send your name and address along with a check or money order to Richard C. Owen Publishers, Inc., Rockefeller Center, Box 819, New York, NY 10185.

Book Note

Developing Life-long Readers

Margaret Mooney
1988; 30 pp.; $5.95
Katonah, NY:
    Richard C. Owen

Classroom Demonstrations

by Sharon Zinke

Turnaround

During the past four years I have begun to look closely at literature and research related to literacy development. As this study has heightened my awareness of the need for some change in the public schools, I have become engaged in some political situations. I have recently become aware that politics is a condition that affects a person who demonstrates a consistently high level of commitment to one side of a controversial issue.

I could feel it coming three years ago. We had been using Ginn 720 as our districtwide basal reading series for 12 years, and were nearing the end of our second seven-year adoption period. We had just been informed that, because of a delay in the math adoption, our new language arts adoption would be postponed for an extra year. I remember standing before our school's neatly stacked supply of *May I Come In* and *A Duck Is a Duck* basals, a slight wave of nausea washing over me as I contemplated three more years of *ip*'s and *ipe*'s and forced reading by teachers and students of those same old contrived stories. I had already gotten into trouble for suggesting that our first-grade teachers replace *A Pocketful of Sunshine* with some delightful children's literature. Could I last three years? I began to feel the tug of the upcoming Textbook Selection Committee.

As Hayward's selection process began, I felt certain that any of the new basals would be an improvement over the old Ginn 720 with its memorized words and word parts, its endless isolated "comprehension skills," its worn-out, grade-leveled stories with their accompanying questions, and, worst of all, its intricate system of Criterion Referenced and Mastery Tests. Yet I had the haunting feeling that the new basals, although proudly displaying good literature, would still have as their major thrust the sequential teaching of reading skills and would still dominate the language arts program with step-by-step procedures, taking power from teachers. Nearly all of our site administrators, backed by district administrators, were still requiring teachers to follow the Ginn system, as they were afraid that teachers using literature and left to their own devices might not cover all the skills. The new basal readers would provide a comforting structure. Although several of us on the committee felt that our state money would be better spent filling classrooms with real books and providing substantial inservice for teachers, it looked as if we would have to choose two of the eleven possible basal programs and put it to a districtwide vote.

Holt's *Impressions*, a Canadian "whole language anthology," was the only adoption, in my own opinion, that could allow us to move with any speed at all toward a literature-based, meaning-driven, integrated language arts curriculum. Teachers could choose to be heavily involved with the anthology and teacher's guide, or the anthology could be a useful supplement to a program based on a curriculum negotiated between students and teacher. I began to bring the *Impressions* materials to meetings and to voice my concerns and discuss possibilities with anyone who would listen. We were up against incredible odds. The Holt materials were in the process of being Americanized and did not get on the state matrix in their entirety; a waiver was required. For the same reason, piloting materials did not arrive until it was too late to pilot them. Many teachers and administrators perceived the teacher's guide as too sketchy, requiring too much teacher judgment and planning. We had a vocal phonics-first contingent on our committee, one of whom attempted to convince the board to override our committee's decisions. The Houghton Mifflin series, which was competing with Holt in the districtwide vote, was beautifully packaged, full of ideas for teachers, and was being piloted in nearly every elementary school in the district.

The miracle is that a whole language anthology claimed the vote in our district. Somehow a process began in our committee that empowered teachers to move in a new direction. I see this adoption as a positive step toward implementation of our new state framework. The assessment segment alone will force us as a district to look at children and learning in a new way. A turnaround. A positive step toward literacy for all children.

➜ See: Freeman, p. 189; Huck, p. 188; Larrick, p. 173; Zinke, pp. 408.

Sharon Zinke is a Language Arts specialist at Fairview School, Hayward, CA.

As Teachers See It

by Margaret Mooney

Selecting Books for Use in Reading Programs

Does the story have charm, magic, impact, and appeal?
- Will the children demand that the book be reread, or will they revisit it by themselves?
- Will chunks of language and meaning resurface at later times?
- What is the book's lasting appeal?
- Will the book stand repeated readings?

Is the idea worthwhile?
- Does the author's message have merit for its own sake? (Many stories contain a moral, but morals should be inherent in the story and not presented as a reason for the reading.)
- Is the idea worth the time and effort spent on the reading?
- Does the story say something new, or, if a familiar theme, does it offer a new view?

Is the story's shape and structure appropriate?
- Does the shape and structure help to carry the reader through the story?
- Does the story have a beginning, a middle, and an identifiable climax with an acceptable resolution?
- Does the story create its own pace?
- How has the author linked the episodes?
- What gaps is the reader required to fill?
- How does the author signal a change of pace, mood, or action?

Is the language effective?
- Does the language suit the theme and the characters?
- Does the language spark the child's imagination, and inspire thought?
- Are there memorable phrases and/or sentences?
- Do the characters act and speak naturally?

- Does the author use book language to heighten the story's shape?
- How much does the author leave to the reader's imagination?

Is the story authentic?
- Is the story credible to the reader?
- Does it avoid condescensions, stereotyping, and inaccuracy?
- Does the author fulfill the promises engendered by the title, theme, and story shape?
- Will it lead the child into further reading and learning?

Do the illustrations help the reader gain meaning from the text?
- Are they appropriate for the theme and characters?
- Do they make the meaning of the text clearer?
- Do the illustrations reflect the mood of the story and give rise to feelings and emotions?
- Do they complement the text, rather than compete with it?

Is the format of the book appropriate?
- Do the book's size and its shape suit the content and the reader, or do they merely fit a series format?
- Do the typeface and size, spacing, and line breaks match the reader's stage of reading development? (pp. 4–5)

➜ See: Dalrymple, p. 426; Goodman, pp. 119, 416; Owen, p. 414.

From *Developing Life-long Readers,* by Margaret Mooney (New York: Richard C. Owen, 1988).

Book Note

Borrow-A-Book: Your Classroom Library Goes Home

Linda Hart-Hewins and Jan Wells
1988; 26 pp.; $5.32
New York: Scholastic

Education should be a shared endeavor between home and school, a concept Linda Hart-Hewins and Jan Wells give new meaning with their inspiring guide for helping parents surround their children with the joy of literature. Through a Borrow-a-Book program, children are able to borrow a book of their choice from the classroom library each afternoon and carry it home in a special oilcloth book bag. Parents read the book aloud, discuss it with their children, and fill out a simple card: name of the book, who read it, and parents' and children's comments about the book and the reading experience. The program has spread to 30 other schools in the Toronto school system and has drawn rave reviews from all involved. *Borrow-a-Book* includes helpful suggestions for financing the program, book selection and storage, a pattern for making the book bag, ways to enlist parental support, and how to keep track of the books. You won't want to just borrow *this* book; it's one to own.

LBB

As kids see it

But It Doesn't Say Much

by Becky Reimer and Linda Hunsaker

Red-haired, blue-eyed Rachel sidled up next to Becky as she was busy recording an interaction between two other first-graders. It was partner reading time in Linda Hunsaker's classroom, and children were reading their *Scholastic News*. Rachel peeked at Becky's writing and quietly asked, "Are you writing in your journal, Mrs. Reimer?"

"No, not exactly, Rachel. I think I'd call this a writing log and not a journal. I'm writing down interesting things I hear and see happening in your class."

"Oh. Well, have you seen this?" Rachel handed Becky her copy of *Scholastic News*.

"No, what's it about?" Becky inquired.

"Well, it's about these birds." Rachel pointed to the brightly colored bird on the front cover.

"Yes, I can see that. Strange-looking bird all right. I've never seen them around here. I've only seen them in zoos. That's funny, look at his beak. It looks like feathers surround his beak," said Becky as she chatted with Rachel.

"Well, I think the bird has fish in its mouth," Rachel gently suggested, offering a differing alternative for what they were both seeing.

"What kind of bird is that?" Becky asked.

"Well, I don't know. But I think this will tell us." Rachel answered by pointing to the two-paragraph text about puffins. She began to read the text aloud.

"Here it says puffins. They're called puffins." She shared a bit of the information she had learned from her reading. She continued to read aloud to herself. She finished the last line, looked up at Becky, and stated, "Hmmmmm. That didn't say much about puffins. So where do they live?"

Her remark took Becky by surprise. She was right, that article gave very little information about puffins.

> Puffins live where it is very cold. For most of the year, they fly and swim. In June and July, they live on the land. Baby puffins are born then! (*Scholastic News* 43[14])

Rachel's insight spurred all the students to reread those two paragraphs written about the puffins. As a class, they retold the information contained in that short piece:

> Puffins swim.
> Puffins fly.
> Puffins live where it is cold.
> Puffins eat fish.
> Puffins live on the land in June and July.
> Puffin babies are born in June and July.

The class agreed they had learned very little about puffins, and they brainstormed unanswered questions about these interesting birds. Listed below is a sample of the 45 questions generated by this first-grade class:

> Do they fight other birds?
> Do they stay out in bad weather?
> Where do they live?
> What do they eat?
> Do they drink?
> Do they kill men? Do men kill them?
> How do they protect themselves from danger?
> Do they use tools to help them?
> Are they like penguins?
> What do penguins do about nests, eating, swimming in the water, and their babies?
> Do puffins do the same?

Erik discovered that the very smallest print on the page addressed to the teacher contained the information that puffins lived in the Arctic.

As I See It:
Yetta M. Goodman

Grid of Reading Materials

There is much written material available for students in libraries, bookstores, and homes. To facilitate the bridging of reading instruction into silent, independent, and self-selected reading, the teacher should be aware of the wide range of reading material to which students should be introduced and which should be readily available to them to help them develop proficient use of reading strategies.

The Grid of Reading Materials may be used by the teacher as a guide in setting up or enriching a comprehension-centered reading program.

Grid of Reading Materials

	A. Newspapers and magazines	B. Research materials	C. Symbolic materials other than books	D. Problem-solving materials	E. Trade books	F. Primary sources
I. Social Studies	Current events Controversial issues Feature articles Political news	Encyclopedias Biographies Texts Journals Research reports Histories	Globes Maps Morse code Photographs Fine art Music sheets Political records Cartoons Ballots	Building models Making clothes from patterns Reconstructing human culture from artifacts	Nonfiction books Biographies History Poetry Anthropology Geography Political science Economics Human relations	Family documents Letters Government documents
II. Science	Weather Science editor Science news	Encyclopedias Texts Journals Histories Logs	Graphs Chemical symbols Films Thermometers Scales	Experiments Cooking recipes Computer printout	Biographies Physical science Natural science Nonfiction Poetry	Conservation records Notes of original scientific records Prescriptions
III. Mathematics	Business news Want ads Stock-market reports Financial section	Technical journals Histories	Films Formulas Expanded notations Scales Number systems	Solving problems Computation	Biographies Nonfiction Poetry	Written problems Business ledgers
IV. Literature	Book, play, and movie reviews Narratives in magazines	Bibliographies Biographies Texts Histories	Text illustrations Format (book, play, script) Music Works of art	Theme and plot analysis	Fiction Poetry Nonfiction	Creative writing by students in class

From *Reading Strategies: Focus on Comprehension*,
by Yetta M. Goodman and Carolyn Burke (New York: Richard C. Owen, 1980): pp. 37–38.

Erik asked why that part was only addressed to the teacher. At this point in the discussion, students began to brainstorm possible reasons why the author may have written the article in the manner he or she did. For example:

1. There was not enough room on the page.
2. They didn't know enough about puffins to write more.
3. Maybe they didn't think about it.
4. They had other things to do.
5. Maybe they didn't want us to learn that much about them.
6. They wanted us to find the information on our own.
7. They wanted the teacher to tell us more.
8. They thought we already knew a lot about puffins.
9. They thought we wouldn't be as interested in studying about puffins if the publisher told us everything.
10. Maybe the publishers thought we couldn't read more words.
11. They didn't think it necessary to use the whole page to write about the puffins.

Linda asked students if they thought the author chose to write so little because he or she didn't think first-graders could read hard words. The students refused to accept word difficulty as a possible reason for lack of content. After all, in their own writing, hard words were not an issue. Joshua wrote the word "perchance" the day before in his story and that was a hard word, but it was a word he felt he needed to use for his topic.

Linda suggested to her students that they write letters to the publisher of the newspaper informing them of their concerns and recommended changes. In addition, the students inquired about how decisions are made about the inclusion of articles in the paper.

In previous years, Linda would have followed the teacher's edition plan, requesting the students to read the article, and then asking the children "Where do the puffins live?" "What do they do most of the year?" Such questions test for recall of facts and signal to students that comprehension is nothing more than remembering isolated details and answering teacher-posed questions.

The Comprehension-Based Literacy Project's goal is to help children and teachers become

(Continued on page 124)

Fighting Censorship, Sexism, Racism

Book Note

Trust Your Children: Voices Against Censorship in Children's Literature

Mark I. West
1988; 150 pp.; $19.95
New York: Neal-Schuman

Mark West has conducted an intriguing series of interviews with children's authors, publishers, and activists against censorship. His subjects include authors whose work has been most frequently banned, such as Judy Blume, Robert Cormier, and Maurice Sendak, and the topics discussed include censorship of sexuality, political content, and racism. These thought-provoking interviews are important background reading for whole-language teachers who want to encourage their students to read widely from the works of a variety of authors. The section on activists includes the addresses of groups such as People for the American Way (P.O. Box 96200, Washington, DC, 20077-75220) and the National Coalition Against Censorship, as well as information about their work.

Sandra Wilde

Resource Essay

International Reading Association Stands Out Against Censorship

For some time, the International Reading Association has monitored the censorship issue through an Intellectual Freedom Committee, which now operates as an advisory group. The group is currently chaired by M. Jerry Weiss of Jersey City State College in New Jersey. Recently, *Reading Today* interviewed Weiss about some of the current concerns relating to censorship.

"Censorship is a rising concern," says Weiss. "We have had more and more problems with books than ever before. I get many letters from people who are having problems with censorship. Many times, the people complaining about books have not even read them, but are objecting on the grounds that they have received lists (of so-called objectionable books)."

Both trade books and textbooks are affected by censorship pressures. "Textbook publishers have given in, and one of the concerns I have is that in many of the 'literature-based textbooks' there have been adaptations of stories that have not been clearly marked," says Weiss. "Teachers should know when even minor changes have been made. Trade books are under more attack in the high school and junior high since more books are used there as regular texts. However, school libraries are affected at all levels. Even a book that has excellent reviews may not be purchased if it is likely to be challenged. The whole 'what if' syndrome greatly affects children's access to books."

Although recent court cases in Tennessee and Alabama involving materials that were challenged were decided in favor of the schools, Weiss says that there are really no winners in such cases. "Even when the books stay, the pressures are so great that there is a tendency to give in," says Weiss. "You need lots of attorneys and lots of resources in order to win, and even if you win, you have to put up with those members of the community who are going to start the process all over again. No part of the curriculum is sacred."

Weiss calls for better communication between schools and parents as one way to alleviate the problem. "Parents have to talk to teachers about their concerns, and there should be a variety of books for kids to choose from," says Weiss. "I believe that there is a real need for greater flexibility and the adoption of more than just a single text. If we had greater flexibility, we would have fewer cases. If a parent objects to a book being in a library and says that no child in the school should read a book, that's censorship. It's a different situation when the parent says they would prefer that their child should not read the book."

"We have urged that every school have a clearly stated policy in writing on school adoption and purchasing policies for books for classroom use and library use," notes Weiss. "There should be a clear-cut procedure whereby anyone objecting to materials must fill out appropriate forms stating why they are objecting and what they recommend, and these should be referred to a school review council, which should consider the request in light of the objectives of the school curriculum for the best education of each child. These policies are very, very important."

Weiss adds that the Young Adult Services Division of the American Library Association has available a useful packet with sample forms that schools have used. For information, contact: American Library Association, 50 E. Huron St., Chicago, IL 60611.

Weiss also encourages IRA councils at all levels to run programs dealing with academic and intellectual freedom issues so that teachers can be aware of the positive things that can be done to prevent censorship. "We're here to support teachers and answer their questions and to work with publishers," says Weiss. "Only through united efforts can we protect the rights of authors and teachers and students."

➔ See: Ohanian, p. 176; Storm in the Mountains, p. 71.

Excerpted from *Reading Today* 6(4), February/March 1989.

Resource: Organization

Women's Action Alliance

370 Lexington Ave., Ste. 603
New York, NY 10017
1-212-532-8330
FAX 1-212-779-2846

The Alliance, a national organization, is committed to the goal of full equality for all women. It provides educational programs and services to assist women and women's organizations accomplish their aims. Working as an information and referral source, the Alliance operates a number of programs: the Information Services Program; the Sex Equity in Education Program; and the Women's Centers Program.

A catalog of excellent publications is available; titles include *Non-sexist Education for Young Children* and *Equal Their Chances: Children's Activities for Non-sexist Learning*. The biannual journal *Equal Play* ($12.50 annual subscription) and the newsletter *Alliance Quarterly* are outstanding. The alliance sponsors national projects on women and drug education; teenage pregnancy prevention; and children of single parents and the schools. Computer equity for girls is another vital issue the group promotes through publications and training projects.

Arrietta Chakos

Resource: Book

Girls Are People Too! A Bibliography of Nontraditional Female Roles in Children's Books

Joan E. Newman
1982; 195 pp.; $12.50
Metuchen, NJ:
  Scarecrow Press

Girls Are People Too! was written for three reasons: to stress that these books are not for girls only, but about girls; to aid parents, teachers, and librarians in selecting books to purchase and recommend to young readers; and to update other bibliographies and approach literature from the perspective of accenting role models. A comprehensive appendix contains a chronology of notable events and personalities in the history of women.

Katy Obringer

Resource: Pamphlet

Ten Quick Ways to Analyze Children's Books for Racism and Sexism

Council on Interracial Books for Children
1841 Broadway, Rm. 300
New York, NY 10023
1-212-757-5339

As a good teacher you are concerned with racism and sexism and try to screen them out. Accordingly, you may want to write for a copy of "Ten Quick Ways to Analyze Children's Books for Racism and Sexism," a simple but effective checklist that recommends looking at 10 factors: (1) the illustrations, (2) the storyline, (3) the lifestyles, (4) the relationships between people, (5) the heroes and heroines, (6) the effects on students' self-esteem, (7) the author's and illustrator's background, (8) the author's perspective, (9) loaded words, and (10) the copyright date.

LBB

WHOLE LANGUAGE CAMERA

Reflection in Annette Maggitti's first-grade classroom, Desert Winds School, Tucson, AZ.

Homing in on Honey.
—Contributed by Catherine Howard,
Ohlone School, Palo Alto, CA

Media

Resource: Organizations

Media Network

Membership: from $25 (individual) and $50 (organization) to $250
MediaActive only: $10/year (4 issues)
from:
Alternative Media Information Center
121 Fulton St., Fifth Fl.
New York, NY 10038
1-212-619-3455

The Media Network is a membership organization that fosters the development, distribution, and educational application of outstanding films and videos. The network knows how hard it is to find films that deal with the social issues of our time—homelessness, decline of the family farm, poverty, teenage hopes and fears, alcohol and drugs, and so on—thus it is the nation's premier information broker of issue-oriented, cultural, and political media. In addition to videotapes and film rentals, they provide printed guides to available media and have a computerized information center. Their newsletter, *MediaActive*, has informative articles about media use in education.

Doug Haner

Association for Educational Communications and Technology (AECT)

1025 Vermont Avenue, NW
Suite 820
Washington, DC 20005
1-202-347-7834

This organization is dedicated to improving instruction through the utilization of media and technology. Its main purpose is to enhance the professional skills of its members—education administrators, librarians, instructional designers, curriculum developers, teachers, trainers, and others—by keeping them current on advances in technology. One benefit of membership in AECT is a subscription to its periodical, *TechTrends*, which explains the latest developments in educational technology. Other member services include a discount subscription to the quarterly journal *ETR&D*, reports to members, a membership directory, and job referral service.

Doug Haner

National Information Center for Educational Media (NICEM)

P.O. Box 40130
Albuquerque, NM 87196
1-800-421-8711
Indexes available from:
Plexus Publishing
143 Old Marlton Pike
Medford, NJ 08055
1-609-654-6500
FAX 1-609-654-4309

If you are looking for the fastest way to locate the rental or purchase source for any audiovisual materials, NICEM is the organization to contact. They publish printed-and-bound indexes for all types of nonprint educational media. If you have telecommunications equipment available, their materials, in the form of their A-V Online data base, can be accessed through DIALOG File 46 (1-800-227-1927). The data base is also available for purchase on CD-ROM.

Doug Haner

Resource: Book

Children's Media Market Place

Dorothy Blythe Jones, consulting editor
1988; 397 pp.; $45
New York: Neal-Schuman

Children's Media Market Place is a directory of sources for locating children's materials, including books, software, audiovisuals of all types, television and radio programs, and periodicals, for preschool through grade 12.

Katy Obringer

Resource: Audiovisual Producer

Society for Visual Education (SVE)

1345 Diversey Pkwy.
Chicago, IL 60614-1299
1-312-525-1500
1-800-829-1900
FAX 1-312-525-9474

From the company that introduced the use of motion pictures and filmstrips to schools comes a variety of valuable multimedia resources for teachers of primary and elementary grades. SVE's catalog is filled with books, cassettes, study prints, computer software, videos, and filmstrips that make language and literature come alive for children. The resources are critical in a dynamic, multifaceted classroom.

Their catalog devotes several pages to whole language and details several thematic units for teachers: Seasons, Journeys, Heroes and Heroines, and Animals. Even if you don't intend to buy from SVE, the thematic unit ideas are valuable in themselves.

Doug Haner

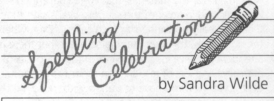

As kids see it

Daddy's Cane Patch
by Carrie Leigh Wilson

One Morning I was getting up to get ready for school. I got up and got dressed and I was five years old. I went outside and I was going as fast as I could go. I was knocking down a lot of cane stalks. I was jumping on it and pretending like I was riding a horse. Dad said, "Carrie, get out of there!" I got in big trouble. The cane was for making molasses. We made some. I will tell you how to make molasses. First you twist it and then you boil the juice. They are good!

> Hi my name is Carrie Leigh Wilson. I got the name Carrie from my grandmother. I live on Walker Park Road. My road is next to Dr. Thomas Walker State Park. I like dogs and cats and spaghetti. I want to be a teacher when I grow up because school is fun. My family is special because they love me. I have a brother and a sister. I wish I had a baby sister.

From *Great Mountain Tales*, written by Linda Oxendine's second-grade class, G. R. Hampton School, Barbourville, KY, 1989.

(Continued from page 122)

thoughtful, skillful readers and writers. In the project classrooms, teachers guide students to critically examine and self-question the texts they read. Students' questions, concerns, and observations are used to discuss text.

Project teachers help their students take action on their reflections. In this case, Linda helped Rachel and her peers use their thinking about the puffin article to write a letter to the publisher.

Within this puffin episode, the students were exposed to some fundamentals about reading and writing, such as:

1. Writers have to make decisions about what to include in a written text.
2. A writer's decision reflects knowledge of subject matter and assumptions about the intended audience.
3. A reader has to be an active thinker about the author's message.
4. A reader must pay attention to more than words on the page because pictures, size of print, and so on also communicate meanings.
5. A reader can question the quality and thoroughness of an article.

The children in Linda's classroom are learning the satisfaction of acquiring reading and writing by experiencing language activities through integrated processes, and not as separate subjects. They are discovering that reading and writing go hand in hand with the fulfillment of life purposes.

Excerpted from *Contemporary Issues in Reading,* Utah Council of International Reading Association, Fall 1987.

Becky Reimer teaches at the University of Utah, Salt Lake City, UT. Linda Hunsaker is a first-grade teacher in the Salt Lake City School District, Salt Lake City, UT.

Spelling Celebrations
by Sandra Wilde

Invented Spellings: Flap Consonants

It is *EVRY BUTEES* (everybody's) brthtey (birthday).
Ellen, 1st grade

EVREBUTEY (everybody) is a Animil (animal).
Hannah, 2d grade

BLATER (bladder) (on a labeled diagram of the body)
Kris, 2d grade

Isn't this strange? Three different children have used the letter *t* to represent a sound that clearly sounds like *d* and is spelled *d*. These examples, however, represent a special case of the letter *d*. When either /d / or /t / occurs between two vowels in English (as in the words *ladder* and *latter*), it turns into a sound called a "flap consonant," so called because the tongue flaps against the roof of the mouth. (Try it and see!) It sounds more like /d / than /t /, but is actually not quite the same as the /d / that occurs, for instance, at the beginning of a word. Many words that are familiar to children have flap consonants that are spelled with one or two *t*'s (*later, butter,* etc.). It is therefore not at all surprising that they would use *t* to represent the flap in a word whose spelling they don't know. It is important to remember that children's hypotheses about spelling grow out of their own experiences with words and their spellings, and that they will not necessarily categorize language in the same way that adults do.

Becoming a Writer

Aileen Fisher

So You Want to Be a Writer?

by Aileen Fisher

How does a writer go about becoming a writer? Where does the inspiration come from? How do you get started?

These questions are often asked by boys and girls who think they want to write poems and stories. And I suppose every writer gives a somewhat different answer.

My answer to the first question is very brief: read, read, read. See how different writers use words to make things happen or to point up a thought or a feeling. Then write down some of your own words and hide them away for a while. When you take them out, read them aloud. How do you think they sound? In the meantime, keep reading!

Where does the inspiration come from? From all around you. From the people you know, the sights you see, the things you do and remember, and particularly from the way you feel. Writers aren't all inspired by the same things. Some of them turn to nature, some of them love the city with its beehives of lighted windows, some of them live in a world of fancies. Open yourself to whatever means the most to you, and ideas will flow in. And in the meantime, keep reading.

How do you get started? By doing, by practicing . . . just as you learn to throw a Frisbee or play a musical instrument. You don't start out being a writer any more than you start out being a violinist. You build up to it. You practice patiently. It usually takes a while before a writer can get something published. But in the meantime you can make progress by reading what other writers have written.

As far as my own writing is concerned, I was no child prodigy by any means. I occasionally thought up verses when I was in grade school (we didn't learn about haiku and other verse forms in those days). And I contributed to the school column in the weekly newspaper when I was in high school. But it wasn't until my senior year in college that I began seriously hoping I might become a writer. And what do you think I turned to for inspiration? My childhood in the Upper Peninsula of Michigan. I have been turning to it ever since!

I had a lucky childhood. When I was five years old, my father was advised by the doctor to give up his business in town and move to the country where life would be less strenuous. And so in the fall I entered the first grade, we were living in a big white house on the bank above a river, two miles from town. I couldn't imagine a better place to live.

We always had cats and dogs to play with (I have written many verses about them), and we had horses that knew how to twitch their skins to scare off the flies, and cows that knew how to turn green grass into white milk and yellow cream, and chickens that were expert at making eggs. It was my job to gather the eggs each evening.

I wonder how	You'd think the yolk
an egg's begun.	and white would run
The yolk	before the shell
is yellow as the sun.	was ever done . . .
The color of the white	But hens don't lay a
is . . . none.	scrambled one!

writers

Reading! A Writer's Way

by Jessica Nelson-Lundy

This is how it happened. I was 12, and like most kids I had waited until Saturday morning to tell my parents that *National Geographic* magazines were needed to complete a class project—due (of course) on Monday. Irritated, but ever enthusiastic about her children's education, my mother agreed to take me to a bookstore. My punishment, however, was to endure an all-day shopping trip that covered all of Wisconsin Avenue in downtown Milwaukee in the middle of winter's cold and snow. I was grateful to finally step into a bookstore; warm and delightfully dusty with a hush of voices that told me this was a place of reverence. Stacks of books and rows of shelves produced small corners and pockets just big enough for one person to squeeze into and find, quite by accident, something vaguely interesting; to thumb through the pages absently, and before long to find a seat on a short stack of books, absorbed in the words painted across the page. At least that is where my mom found me and asked what I was doing. A school librarian, my mom almost fainted when I, a nonreader, asked for the book. Acting before the spell that had just taken over her daughter could break, she bought me Willard Motley's *Knock on Any Door.*

I possessed the book; the book possessed me. Apart from my "physical" ownership of the book, Motley's characters had faces in my mind. I saw Nick Romano's dark curling hair, his smooth olive complexion, and the angle at which his hat sat on his head. I heard their New York accents, smelled Momma Romano's pasta cooking, and tasted it when she set it on the table. I knew the homes they lived in, saw the crowded, filthy streets where the children played, and prayed these conditions would not corrupt these people that I had come to care about.

These images, tastes, and smells played out the novel's drama in my mind, giving me an experience that was uniquely personal. No one else saw the Nick Romano that I constructed with Motley's description (my Nick had a scar on his right cheek from chicken pox) or tasted that pasta and thought, as I did, "Egh . . . perhaps a pinch of salt." When I finally finished the book and the fantasy ended, I set the book down and thought—God, I want to do that! I want to create a world so real, so complete, that images are created in the reader's head.

That is how I became a writer. Through reading I, too, became hooked on the quest for self-expression with words. While *Knock on Any Door* was the first novel to stir this desire in me, it was not the

---

Yes, ideas for poems lie all around us, in the everyday things we see and do and think and feel and remember, as well as in unusual sights and happenings. In the city as well as in the country, poems are waiting to be discovered, yours for the taking. Who knows . . . perhaps you are living a poem right now which some day you will put down on paper.

From "So You Want to Be a Writer," *Highlights for Children,* 1980; the poem "An Egg" from *I Wonder How, I Wonder Why,* by Aileen Fisher (NY: Abelard-Schuman, 1962).

Aileen Fisher is an author and poet, in Boulder, CO.

last. With each reading experience I am inspired by the author's skill in creating a world and the characters that populate it to continue that quest. I am fascinated by the author's ability to draw me into that world, prompt my participation in it and my involvement with the characters.

With each reading experience, I am convinced of the infinite possibilities with which the human experience can be conveyed. While *Go Tell It on the Mountain* and *East of Eden* both focus on the coming of age of two young men, each depicts this common experience in vastly different ways. For Alice Walker's Miss Celie of *The Color Purple* and Toni Morrison's Sethe of *Beloved,* the challenges of becoming women are strained by sexism and racism, yet the two authors tell very different stories. In spite of the variances of these and other literary works, the commonality of humankind is displayed, allowing the reader to empathize with the conditions and obstacles a character faces.

Nonfiction too must be important to the writer. It is here that the facts to accurately construct a setting or sketch a character are found. History, psychology, philosophy, the sciences, provide writers with the background information that lends fiction credibility. James Michener is a writer of fiction, but the basis for many of his novels is the history of a people or place. Facts provide writers with significant, sound, and valid details that buy the trust of readers and efficiently establish a setting, set a mood, or create an attitude.

With the tools of nonfiction and the inspiration of fictional works, I find myself, like many writers, compelled to write. Provoked by an idea, a thought, an image, I am forced to take pen in hand, even when the clock reads 2:00 A.M. and I'd much rather be in bed. It is the result I crave; the well-turned phrase, the vivid metaphor, the description that excites all the senses; that one line that will just possibly compare with one of Morrison's, one of Faulkner's, one of Baldwin's, or, dare I, Joyce's. I cannot not write and see reading as the most valuable tool in that endeavor, thus I cannot not read. And each time I take a book in hand, there is still a place inside myself where I become 12 years old again, take a seat on a stack of books in an old dusty bookstore, and go on a splendid journey. Bye!

→ See: Literature Reference List, p. 429.

Jessica Nelson-Lundy is a graduate student at San Francisco State University, San Francisco, CA.

WELL-SAID I remember the hours I spent off in a corner with my book. I would go into another world. I couldn't have guessed that some day I would create worlds of my own.
—Virginia Hamilton, *Reading Is Fundamental*

📷 **WHOLE LANGUAGE CAMERA**

Writers at work. Desert Wind School, Tucson, AZ.

writers

Dear Bird: Heck, Anyone Can Start a Day. But How Do We Stop It?

by Byrd Baylor

My mailbox is always stuffed with letters from children who read my books. Sometimes they enclose lucky pennies, feathers, samples of good dirt, small rocks, pictures of themselves, moss, spiderwebs and even pencils they want me to use to write new books.

These letters are often signed Your Best Reader, Your Fiend, Your Fiend Forever, Good Luck in the Feature, Your Mane Animal Lover, Me and You Forever, Your Only Pal, Send Books, Good Typeriting Forever, and Here's Hoping You Can Amount to Something.

And here are some of the letters:

Dear Arthur,

Everybody has to write to a arthur. You are the arthur I have to write to. Please send a lot of interesting things to put on the bulletin board. If anything interesting ever happened to you, please tell me what it was. If nothing happpened that is okay just so it is two pages long. Send a lot of stuff right away because I only gots one more week to do my report. I forgot to write before.

Well, goodby Arthur.

Henry.

P.S. Now I only gots four days so you better hurry.

Dear Bird,

I have made up my mind to come out there to live with you. My mom says I can go in seven years. The only thing is I need a map. If you are busy you can just send it in six and a half years. I can't wait, can you?

Your happy fan,

Estelle

P.S. Keep in touch.

Dear Byrd,

I read that book about secret places. You are the only one I am telling about my place. It is out by Mr. Horn's old place on the other side of where the chickens used to be. Chickens die a lot. I drug five big boards over that way and fixed up the gully with branches and eveything. When I get married I think I'll still live here. If she wont live here I'll get a different lady. I already got a box with food in it. I am already 8 years old.

XOXOXOXO,

Billy

Dear Ms. Baylor,

My dad is writing this for me but I am saying what to say. We read your book, *The Way to Start A Day*. So now we know how to start a day, but how do we *stop* it? Please let me know because I want to do it right.

Love,

Kevin

Dear Byrd Baylor,

We studied about the desert and Native Americans and we read two of your books. I have a lot of information. I think I know what arrowheads look like, kind of like Christmas trees. Some have turquoise in them for a picture. Indians put arrowheads on sticks and they turn into spears. Right? The Basketmakers were some of the first to live 2,000 years ago. I have more information.

Good luck in the desert,

Debbie

Dear Byrd Baylor,

This is a complante which you probably wont like.

It is about your book where the coyote steals that dog puppy and you probably remember how she comes sneaking back to the sheep camp at night to see that puppy one more time. You probably remember how they touch noses. Well I know they aint never going to see each other again.

Well I don't read a lot of books but I thought they was supposed to be about sports or famous people or at least funny. So I get to reading about this coyote and I think its pretty good.

Then see its free reading time in our school which means you aint supposed to do nothing but read for 15 mins. So there I am reading that book which I thought was pretty good and I come to that real sad part and before I know it theres tears coming out of my eyes and Im wiping my nose like a pure fool.

Im a real tuff guy and I get a lot of respeck for that and here I am sniffling. It was about the most emberesing thing that ever happened to me except maybe one other thing, so in free reading time your not supposed to even go the bathroom, your just supposed to read but I jump up and get out of there and put water on my face and just hang out for awhile by myself. Boy, was I mad at you. You ought to think of things like that before you go putting sad parts in books.

I tole my frien Jarvis to read that book and tell me how it ends up and he might because he has a lot of respeck for me but you can write and tell me the ending if you want to. If you ever write a book thats funny or about sports let me know. Also please write back as soon as you can because I cant get that stupid coyote off of my mind. Maybe what you wrote was real and you couldnt help yourself just trying to tell the truth. Thats the only reason I can think of why anybody would write a book like that.

Will J.

Dear Byrd Baylor,

I have your book *One Small Blue Bead*, about that brave boy back in prehistoric times living in that cave and wondering if there were other tribes out in the wilderness somewhere. That book really seems close to me. I've read it seven times already. The reason I like it so much is that I'm a lot like that boy myself, only I live in an apartment and I'm fatter and Jewish.

Louis

Dear Byrd,

My Aunt Helen heard you talk at the university. She told us you said walking around on cement too much will make you crazy. It is better to walk on dirt. I didn't know people could say that at the university. Do you have scientific proof? Lately I've tried walking off the cement and I feel real good. Please say something private to me about this.

Your fellow walker in the dirt,

Elizabeth

Dear Ms. Baylor,

We are GEM students studying the qualities of leadership and success. How do you feel you demonstrate leadership, scholarship, courage, attention to detail and task commitment? What are your physical attributes?

(Signed by five sixth-grade girls)

I'm trying to answer that one right now. I hate to disappoint them, but I'm not much in any of those departments, and I may not even have enough task commitment to finish this letter . . .

→ See: Literature Reference List, p. 429.

From *City Magazine* 2(7), July 1987, Tucson, AZ.

Byrd Baylor is the "arthur" of several award-winning children's books and a novel about Indians in Tucson, *Yes Is Better Than No.*

Resource: Video Series/Audiocassettes

Southwest Series

The Byrd Baylor Family Video Series Videocassettes from $24.95 to $49.95 Audiocassettes from $5.95 to $7.95

P.O. Box 2911

Tucson, AZ 85702

1-602-623-2255

Southwest Series was formed in 1986 by Byrd Baylor and others to produce educational media materials based on her children's books. Three of her titles are in the Byrd Baylor Family Video Series as dramatizations narrated by Will Rogers, Jr.: *Hawk, I'm Your Brother, The Other Way to Listen,* and *The Way to Start a Day*. These stories are also available in Spanish in both video and audio.

New products include Byrd Baylor: Storyteller, which features Byrd reading her stories to the camera, and will include *I'm in Charge of Celebrations, Amigo, The Best Town in the World,* and others. Two more Byrd Baylor stories, *Everybody Needs a Rock* and *The Desert Is Theirs,* read by Will Rogers, Jr., are also available.

As kids see it

Animal Personalities
by Dominique F. Guerin

Make your story extraordinary by changing yourself into an animal that's like you. I'm very shy, so I changed myself into a turtle. If you are brave, you can change yourself into a lion.

Great Expectations
by Heather Wahba

When you write, make your audience feel like they're in the story. If you keep on writing and become a great writer when you are little, you may become a professional writer when you grow up. If you keep on writing books, people will keep on reading your books. They might think that you write so well that they will want to write like you.

Dominique F. Guerin and Heather Wahba are third-graders at Curtis Estabrook School, Brooklyn, NY. These were contributed by their second-grade teacher, Maureen Powell.

Little Lies

by Meredith Proost

It all began one Tuesday when Melinda and I lost all track of time and found we couldn't possibly finish our practicing before our mom came home from grocery shopping. Before she left, we had agreed to do all our chores and practice piano.

"Yes," we said together when mom asked if we had finished our practicing. But when she walked into the living room, there was the piano music, stacked just as she had stacked it that morning. And the lesson book was on the table where we had left it after our piano lesson the day before.

Mom knew we were lying. She had a sad look on her face. Before Melinda or I could make an excuse, Mom told us that she was going to tell us a lie sometime during the next few days. We wouldn't know when she was lying, and the lie would be something very important to both of us.

That night mom told us that the next morning when we woke up, breakfast would be waiting: hot cereal with lots of cream and even more brown sugar, just the way we like it. Melinda and I looked at each other knowingly. That must be the lie.

But the next morning when we woke up, in the kitchen we found our bowls of hot cereal with lots of cream and even more brown sugar, just the way we like it.

On Wednesday, Mom told us that she would pick us up right after school so that we could go shopping for spring clothes. Melinda and I looked at each other knowingly and said to ourselves that had to be the lie. We decided we would be going home on the bus as usual.

But after school, there sat Mom in the parking lot ready to take us shopping.

The following day our dad was on a business trip. Mom told us to pick a restaurant, Italian or Chinese, and the three of us would go out for dinner that night. Melinda and I looked at each other knowingly. That must be the lie. If we said Chinese, Mom would take us out for pizza. If we said Italian, we knew we'd be having chow mein for dinner.

We said, "Chinese," and that night we had won-ton soup, chow mein, fortune cookies, and tea.

When we arrived home from school Friday, Mom greeted us with, "Guess what! I just reserved two airplane tickets. You two get to fly—all by yourselves—to visit your grandma over spring vacation!" Now that is something we had always wanted to do. We had dreamed about traveling alone and talked about it for years. Ordinarily we would have run to our rooms to start packing, even though spring vacation was three weeks away. But we looked at each other knowingly. That had to be the lie.

Mom may have been surprised at our lack of excitement, but she didn't say a word. She waited until the following day to ask us if we had discovered her lie.

Melinda said, "Yes, we know. We won't be flying to Grandma's for spring vacation. Everything else you have said has been true, so the airplane trip must be the lie."

"I'm glad it's finally over," I said.

Melinda said, "Yes. It has been awful for days thinking we couldn't trust you. I guess we deserved that little lie about flying to Grandma's."

➜ See: Bonifacio, p. 160; Treasures, p. 162.

From Treasures: Stories & Art by Students in Oregon, *comp. by Chris Weber (Portland, OR: Oregon Students Writing and Art Foundation, 1985).*

Meredith Proost was 12 years old when she wrote this.

★ **T R I B U T E** ★

Alvina Treut Burrows: A Tribute

by Nancy Larrick

As members of the Reading Hall of Fame gathered in New Orleans for the 1989 IRA Conference, we learned of the death of Alvina Treut Burrows on April 19, just a few days before her 84th birthday. A memorial service was held for her on April 29 at Fairhaven, where she had lived very happily for several years in her own cottage with her own grand piano and other cherished furnishings.

As I wandered through the vast exhibit area of the New Orleans Convention Center, I thought again and again of Alvina Burrows. Glaring lights and fast-talking salesmen with shopping bag of printed matter were advertising "The NEW Reading Initiative," "The NEW Reading-Writing Connection," "The NEW Whole Language Approach."

"What's NEW about all of this?" I wanted to ask. This is just the approach, the philosophy, that Alvina Burrows had arrived at through her work with children and which she presented so persuasively 50 years ago in *They All Want to Write: Written English in the Elementary School*, written with Doris C. Jackson and Dorothy O. Saunders. It is a remarkable book now in its fourth edition. Alvina Burrows described herself as one of those "who have teaching in our bones from a lifetime of experience." Her philosophy comes through clearly: "that a child could indeed become the minstrel of his own free spirit and a careful scribe as well." Her tribute to children reflects her own approach to learning and teaching: "to children whose literacy flourished as they talked, read, and wrote; as they painted, studied, and sang; as they played, argued, and grew as persons; we shall be always joyously grateful." And to Alvina Burrows, thousands of children and teachers will "be always joyously grateful."

Reference

Burrows, A. T., D. C. Jackson, and D. O. Saunders. 1984. *They all want to write: Written English in the elementary school.* Hamden, CT: Library Professional Publications, The Shoe String Press.

Nancy Larrick is an author and one of the founders of the International Reading Association. She is a resident of Winchester, VA.

When I Grow Up

by Kati Lynn Field

When I grow up, I'm going to be a writer.
I'm going to write those big fat books like the ones in the library.
People will open those books, and there will be all the words that I wrote for them to read.
I like writing a lot.
It makes me feel like magic.
Sometimes it makes me excited, and
sometimes it makes me peaceful.
I didn't learn my writing,
I came with it.

Kati Lynn Field is a first-grader at Yaquina View School, Newport, OR.

How I Became a Not-Writer

by Lee Wayne Shainen

My first extracurricular writing was probably the jokes and character sketches about teachers I passed along to amuse my classmates. I was bored with my classes, and it was much more important to me to be liked than to do well in school. It seemed to work. I was popular, but along with it came the tag of talent. Parents and teachers especially would always throw in words like "creative" "talented" "writer" when talking about me. I bought it. The appellation of writer stuck.

I grew into it, not so much writing as being a writer. It was my identity: Lee, the writer. That's who I was supposed to be. So I cultivated the look, the postures, the trappings. I stayed up all night smoking and drinking with other writers, blustery in bars, conspiratorial in coffeehouses. I studied other writers, got degrees and rejection slips, and taught writing.

When I wasn't getting published it was because I was too far ahead of my time, or I wouldn't sell out, or I was committed to "quality" fiction in a comic book era. So I traveled to gain experience, became a loner to fathom my own soul, searched for that special hideaway where the great novel in me would be enticed out of me onto paper. Toward the end I became an editor, smugly tearing apart in others what had given me so much anguish, while all I wrote were letters seeking seduction or solace from women.

I had played all the parts except actually sitting down day in, day out, and writing. I had become a not-writer. I couldn't let the image of being a writer go, and I wasn't writing. I was shut down from rejection, paralyzed with fear and doubt about my ability, and angry that others expected me to write.

Recently, in therapy, I discovered a deeper source of my not-writing. I opened a door I had refused to in my writing. Behind that door I found a frightened and angry child who wanted to be loved for who he was, not for what he could do. Slowly we're becoming friends. He's beginning to trust me to take care of him. We're no longer writing or not-writing to please or punish, but because sometimes we just like to write. And when anyone asks me what I do, I tell them I'm a tile contractor.

➜ See: Shainen, p. 148.

Lee Wayne Shainen is a freelance writer, performance poet, and substitute teacher living in Tucson, AZ.

Book Note

They All Want to Write: Written English in the Elementary School, 4th ed.

Alvina Treut Burrows, Doris C. Jackson, and Dorothy O. Saunders
1984; 238 pp.; $20
Hamden, CT: Library Professional Publications, an imprint of The Shoe String Press, Inc.

Becoming Literate
by Gary Pharness and Lee Weinstein

Writing Set Me Free: An Interview with Jack Hutchison

Voices *is produced because we believe adult student writers have something important and powerful to say. They deserve the opportunity to read their work and be read in a dignified format.*

The following interview is with Jack Hutchison, who attends Invergarry's evening literacy classes. Jack is a 41-year-old welder. The interview sheds some light on how Jack views the writing process.

Voices: Jack, it's been over two years since you enrolled in the literacy program for the purpose of studying the welding manual. You were able to tell us what all of the welding words meant, but you couldn't read the words.

Jack: That's right, I know how to weld. I've been doing it for years and years, but I've never been any good in reading and writing. If I can't read something, I can't understand it. I enrolled in the literacy program to try to be in a position to read and write better. I had in mind that I could possibly take another chance at my welding test. I've taken it before, but I got about 100 percent wrong because I couldn't read it.

Voices: After a couple of months you left the literacy programme knowing you could re-enter at any time. How do you feel about coming back?

Jack: Good. I knew I had to finish this business of learning to read and write if I ever wanted to get on with my life. It's been on my mind for a long time.

Voices: Has your reading and writing changed since coming back to school?

Jack: At first it took me a long time to do any writing. A lot of times I'd get confused about what I should say and what I shouldn't say. Now I find it a lot easier. In fact, I even enjoy writing.

Voices: What do you feel after you've written a story?

Jack: I feel good in the respect that I get something out that I'm thinking about. It doesn't answer all my questions. Just because you write about something that's troubling you, or something that's on your mind, doesn't mean writing's going to solve it; a person has to realize that, too. It makes a person feel better knowing that here at school somebody else is going to read it.

Voices: Jack, do you think of the people out there who might read your story when you're writing it, or do you write just for yourself? What kinds of things get your writing started?

Jack: It all depends on what I'm writing about. I might write about something that I've had on my mind for years and years and I've never had anybody to talk to about it. I lived with a lot of things that I remember when I was a kid that I never did talk to anybody about. And since I started writing, I wrote some of them down and it's sort of a relief to get them out, and now they're gone.

Voices: So much of your writing is about bad times or you could even say bad experiences. Do you take any happiness from your writing of these experiences?

Jack: I do. Because I pulled through it. Some of the things that have happened might be hard on a person when they're young, but some of the things you can sort of laugh at if you're older.

Voices: In one of your pieces, you talked about having difficulty with your speaking. Do you find it easier writing than speaking?

Jack: Yes I do. I find I can express myself a lot better on paper than I can with my words. I feel I'm a lot freer on paper than I am speaking.

Voices: Do you find it difficult talking about yourself in this interview?

Jack: I do. I know on paper it doesn't matter to me, but to speak one on one, I do.

Voices: How do you feel about writing about yourself?

Jack: It doesn't bother me. At first it did a lot, but not anymore. I don't know why it doesn't bother me in the least. Once I start writing, it seems I keep writing.

Voices: Do you think it's contributed to being able to talk more about yourself?

Jack: Yes, it's helped quite a bit. I think I'm a little bit more open with what I really have to say and what I don't say.

Voices: After having written for a while, do you recognize one point, or a series of events, that were important to you seeing yourself as a writer? Was there a point or a time when you could sit down and say, "Well, I'm writing now?"

Jack: When you guys published that "Pipeline" story. It really amazed me to read something I wrote in a magazine. I never thought I'd see the day I'd write something that would be in a magazine. It really lifted my confidence that I could do it.

I fill out applications by myself which I've never done. Before, my wife has had to do it for me. On unemployment I had to get somebody else to do the card. If I needed to write somebody a letter I wouldn't dare. I knew they'd never read my writing because they'd never understand what I wrote. Now I'm not scared, I wouldn't be scared to sit down and write someone a letter. That makes me really happy.

Voices: How do you see the relationship between yourself as the storyteller and me as the reader?

Jack: A relationship? Sort of. I don't think I'd be able to sit down and tell you something that really bothered me. And yet I can turn around and write on a piece of paper and give it to you and, for some reason, it makes me feel good because I give it to you and you're reading it. If you want to say something about it or talk to me about it, then I can talk about it. But I can't talk about it right from the start.

Voices: How does your writing influence what you do outside of school?

Jack: I wouldn't even look at the newspaper before. I pretty well every day look at the newspaper now.

Voices: Do you talk about some of the things you read about with others?

Jack: To my wife. Or I'll be having a cup of coffee in a restaurant and I'll start talking to the different waitresses about the different things I read. Before I came to this school, I'd never do something like that.

Voices: We've talked about your reaction to seeing your "Pipeline" piece in *Voices*. What did you do right afterwards?

Jack: Well, the first person I gave it to was my son to read. And he was totally amazed. That sort of brightened up his life for him. It really brightened up his face. Then I showed it to my wife and my other two kids and to different people I knew and they were really amazed.

Voices: Jack, before beginning to write yourself, what was your notion of what a writer is?

Jack: I always thought writers must be bullshitters. Now, after writing myself I've found that writing from the heart is a different kind of writing than I see at the newsstand. I guess I find writing about life, especially my life, very interesting.

Voices: Do you have anything to say to other adults who have difficulties reading and writing?

Jack: Yes, I never thought I could do it until I started doing it. And even after I started doing it, I still wasn't convinced. If you stick in there, after a few months you soon realize that if you go over some of your work, you're amazed at what you find.

This teacher in literacy class told me I helped her student the other day. The teacher said she had been trying to get her student to be more open. She hadn't been having any success until she had her student read my story. The student said reading that story had changed her life. That just made my whole day, because I really feel good that I could actually help somebody in that respect.

→ See: Brennan, p. 228; Calahan, p. 54; Taylor, p. 185.

From *Voices: New Writers for New Readers* 2(1), Fall 1989.

Gary Pharness is a co-founder of *Voices* and administrator of Invergarry Learning Center, Surrey, British Columbia. Lee Weinstein is co-founder of *Voices* and is developing a Workplace Literacy Program for the city of Vancouver, and a Community-Based and School-Based Literacy Program for Little Mountain Neighborhood House and the Vancouver School Board, Vancouver, British Columbia.

📷 WHOLE LANGUAGE CAMERA

An absorbed young writer, Chandler, AZ.

Resource: Periodical

Voices: New Writers for New Readers

Editorial Office: Lower Mainland Society for Literacy and Employment
14525–110A Avenue
Surrey, British Columbia,
V3R 2B4
1-604-584-5424
$12/year (3 issues) from:
Delta Systems Co.
570 Rock Rd. Dr., Unit H
Dundee, IL 60118-9922

Voices provides an opportunity for new readers and new writers to meet and to talk across distance, cultures, national boundaries, and time. It is published as a professional literary magazine, with exquisite graphics and photographs, respecting the dignity and the power of the new writers' voices. And it means that literate adults have no excuse for saying that we do not know about the lives, the struggles, the aspirations, and contributions of new readers and writers—we have only to open our hearts and our minds, and to read publications such as *Voices*.

Dr. Hanna Arlene Fingeret

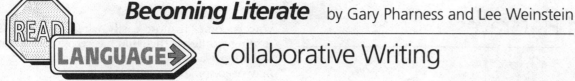

Becoming Literate by Gary Pharness and Lee Weinstein

Collaborative Writing

In the preceding interview Jack Hutchison writes he has "found that writing from the heart is a different kind of writing than I see at the newsstands."

This phrase answers the most fundamental questions faced by writing teachers: How do we get our students to write? As literacy teachers, we recognize unorganized expressions of the mind or heart as legitimate attempts at writing. This recognition enables students to gradually learn more sophisticated ways of expressing feelings and thoughts.

We are convinced that in the private act of writing about their aspirations and tragedies, students enter a collaborative undertaking with all those writers who have written before. This assumption creates an exciting paradox: Writing becomes a collaborative act, not the solitary effort generally presented to students.

To stimulate collaborative writing practices, instructors and administrators first need to identify successful instructional strategies. Research on how practicing writers pursue their craft and analysis of successful programs offer insight into how and why one methodology works while others do not.

As administrators and instructors who hope to establish quality writing programs, we must respond to the following basic questions, if we are to genuinely assist students to open the door to writing:

• What and how important is student writing in ESL/ABE/literacy programs?
• How much of the curriculum and instructional pie do we budget for student writing each year?

Writing and reading are the focus of our literacy program. We freely use students' writing, from the simplest, tentative first efforts, to accomplished prose found in anthologies, as reading instruction within the syllabus. We consider students' writing to be their most valuable resource and, therefore, we do not hesitate to use it as formal curriculum.

Students, in the process of becoming literate, come to understand that what happens outside of the classroom represents the core of their literacy development and is the raw material for their curriculum.

Students' understanding of this idea puts the classroom, and by extension the role of teacher, in the proper perspective, because it removes the idea that classroom and teacher are the repository of all knowledge, thus setting the stage for creating a student-oriented writers workshop.

This workshop format helps students understand how writing is a democratic process, and how it presents the same problems—accurately communicating ideas, experiences, and feelings— for all writers. We believe that most literacy students receive insufficient time for processing and reflecting on these problems. It is in the act of disclosure through writing that adults learn. In many instances adult new readers create their own writing and reading curriculum and come to fully appreciate the significance of life experience writing.

This process only occurs for students when there is a conscious effort by instructors to genuinely appreciate the value of students' lives. To ensure that this happens, instructors must be curious, not about what students do not know, but about what they do know.

Students achieve from this powerful combination of disclosure and instructor validation the knowledge that they possess the most powerful text: their own history.

Students' writing describes the full range of life experience, from laboring in sweatshops to success in business; from early memories to marriage and family deaths. Through their efforts to put personal histories on paper, student writers are connected to each other.

In recognition of that connection, and because students deserve the inherent opportunities of a writing workshop, we use such a format.

In Invergarry's workshops, the students and the instructor bring in photocopies of their work. During discussion the class explores the functions of language. In addition, instructors introduce writing that may speak to student experience, and that shows learners how their work fits into literature as a whole—into the social and cultural patterns explored by earlier and present-day writers.

Writers are strengthened in each other's company. Whether in a workshop setting or in the presence of other authors' books, they grow from seeing how authors in similar circumstances use writing to understand and empower themselves. In this context, learners have the opportunity to find out what print may have to say to them.

What we have been describing is a process. It only suggests how students' experiences can be used to help themselves and others as they work toward literacy. Individual instructor initiative and imagination and not blind obeisance to prescribed curriculum bring this process to fruition.

This collaborative writing process recognizes that all language learners, whatever their age, linguistically construct their own version of the world. Therefore, literacy work begins with the learner's world.

In this framework, the learner's experience is the core of learning. This perception dictates a free and open learning environment that makes skills practice secondary to the learner's experience.

Keys to implementing this collaborative approach are intuition, trust, spontaneity, and the willingness to happen upon things. As well, instructors must possess or acquire a knowledge and passion for language and literature. Though academic background is not required, instructors must have a far-ranging understanding and knowledge of what kind of literature is relevant to their students' work, and how published writing and student writing are connected.

This process invites instructors to struggle with their own practices . . . to use learners' writing and writing created from their experiences as the foundation for ESL/ABE/literacy curriculum.

From Voices: New Writers for New Readers 2(1), Fall 1989.

As kids see it

Write What You Know
by Rachel L. Bullard

When you're writing a story, don't just write anything down. Write about something you know. It's more interesting if you write about something you know. Write about your dog or your cat or your family or someone in your family. That's how you make stories more interesting.

Rachel L. Bullard is a third-grader at Curtis Estabrook School, Brooklyn, NY. This was contributed by her second-grade teacher, Maureen Powell.

The Funny Side

Too Much of a Good Thing

Christopher, age six, was given the assignment in his "Rapid Learner" class to interview someone about his or her Christmas memories. He was to write the story down and bring it to school the next day. He chose his Grandma Gloria and called her on the phone that evening.

"Hi, Grandma! Do you have a special memory about Christmas?"

"I do, Chrissy. When I was about your age, I got a little blackboard with chalk and an eraser, and I just loved it. It was just what I wanted. I put it under my bed and when I woke up the next morning, it was the first thing I thought of. I just couldn't wait to get out of bed and use it!"

"Grandma?"

"Yes?"

"Do you want me to write *all* that or should I just write 'no'?"

—As told to LBB by Gloria Norton, resource teacher, Fair Oaks School, Redwood City, CA

Book Note

Experiment with Fiction

Donald H. Graves
1989; 88 pp.; $7.50
Portsmouth, NH: Heinemann

Investigate Nonfiction

Donald H. Graves
1989; 128 pp.; $7.50
Portsmouth, NH: Heinemann

Do you find you cannot get to a Donald Graves workshop as often as you'd like? The solution is to buy some of his books and take them home. Here are two of an eventual five-volume series, *The Reading/Writing Teacher's Companion*. Many chapters include Actions, which are suggestions and examples of activities. These make the text resemble a series of workshops with the author, for the Actions are the type of hands-on experiences you'd do in "A Day with Donald Graves" or classroom experiments you'd try between weekly support group meetings. Many are invitations to develop your own writing.

Mary Kitagawa

❝ The approach to more formal reporting in the Actions in this chapter will begin with the exploration of what you and the writer know. Younger students in the primary years are more confident about what they know than older students. It doesn't mean that they do know more than older students, only that they haven't been through the usual school socialization process, which fails to help children establish what they already know at each succeeding grade level. Report writing of the type I am discussing here attempts to establish turf, a sense of what the child knows and controls, and solid content that allows the child's own voice to emerge from the material. ❞
(p. 81, *Investigate Nonfiction*)

Understanding the Writing Process

 Viewpoint: Donald H. Graves

Thoughts on Writing: An Interview by DiAnn Waskul Ellis

DiAnn: Don, let's start with a general but probably one of the most critical questions: "What is literacy?"

Don: For me literacy is more the stance a person takes toward the world. A literate person is a person intentioned with the world. And a person who wants to see beyond what may be on the surface.

For example, I had a great uncle who never went beyond the sixth grade. But my dear uncle Nelson—who was a Democrat—took no quarter when it came to pushing my Republican parents and family. "How can you people be against a man who is making it possible for a poor man to live through the Depression?" And, of course, they had a difficult time answering him saying he is just giving stuff away.

The saying is that a literate person is one who sees things in a very broad and yet a very specific way. Although my great uncle Nelson didn't do an extensive amount of writing or reading, I call him literate. Literate in the sense of using language for the power it is intended to be used for.

DiAnn: How did you come to realize how writing should be taught?

Don: I think I got a little bit of an inkling first from children. When I did my dissertation I did extensive observations of children and saw what they could do. That was one place.

Secondly, I got involved in writing because I was very upset with what was happening in reading. I was a director of reading and everything was clinical. I was going through my doctoral studies and everyone was studying what kids couldn't do—all kinds of disabilities, this, that, and the other thing. Well, there is no question that children do have reading problems, but I was getting fed up with all this "couldn't do." That was one thing that launched me.

It was also significant for me that I met Donald Murray. He is my real mentor, if you could call someone that, because he's the greatest writer and teacher of writing that I have ever known.

DiAnn: What are some of the things he taught you?

Don: He taught me to find my own voice. He taught me how important it was to write from the standpoint of authority—the authority of my own facts. When you present a dissertation, unfortunately committees tend to remind you of what you didn't know, and you leave feeling so ineffectual and so apologetic about everything it's a miracle you ever rebound on your feet. And I had a good committee. But that process unfortunately works to make you think you don't know. Murray helped me find my voice. He was my voice coach.

DiAnn: Did you say that when you were a teacher in the classroom, you came to realize how writing should be taught because you were doing something incorrectly?

Don: No, that's only in retrospect. I had no realization whatsoever when I was teaching writing. I went from that "Fascist" approach where I corrected everything to sort of a permissive approach where I cheered everything they did. But the writing process didn't come in until much after I finished teaching—that is before I had left my classroom teaching days. I'm a late bloomer, very late. After 50, shall we say.

DiAnn: How do writers change as individuals and grow into becoming better writers?

Don: I think the biggest thing is they find they have things to say. So from that, the teacher should be focusing on the child in his or her broadest perspectives. I'm focusing on the child's making of meaning, not just doing writing. From the minute the child walks into the room until the child leaves, I'm working on helping the child realize that he or she has the power to make meaning. That to me is essential. It may be making meaning in drawing, painting, or drama. Writing is just one thing in the child's total day as far as making meaning, so I'm working hardest on that. If you focus on all that, then the writing comes. I think one of the dangers I may have communicated is that you do it all through writing and it just isn't the case. Writing is just one tool for making meaning.

DiAnn: How do the best teachers of writing operate? You have had a chance to observe quite a few good teachers.

Don: Number one, they write themselves. Number two, they share their writing. Number three, their students have different voices. They don't all sound like the teacher. And that requires, on the part of the professional, a fair amount of knowledge about the teaching of writing. Usually they are people who, on the one hand, are quite outspoken and who have real tension with the world and the issues of the world. On the other hand, they respect you for your unique perspective of the world—but they're going to challenge you too.

DiAnn: They're usually literate individuals, aren't they?

Don: Yes, literate in the sense that they ask big questions of the world and do not settle for just a few facts here and there.

DiAnn: How would you suggest that teachers teach writing with emergent readers?

Don: I would reverse it and say, how do you teach reading with emergent writers, because it's more natural to begin with the writing. The child makes his own marks on paper more easily than he translates the arbitrary marks of someone else. So the biggest thing is to provide lots of pencils and paper. Write to children yourself. In fact my book, *Write from the Start,* is about all this. The thing you are trying to do is to show children what writing is and to recognize the power they have on paper. It is the way they learn to talk.

The child says "ball." And I say to my wife, "My word, Bill just said 'ball.'" I respond with the joy of communication and would that we would respond with the joy of communication to these marks, drawings, consonants—usually not vowels yet—but responding specifically, not in general.

DiAnn: Can you give me an example?

Don: I'll use it two ways. The child says "ba." I don't say, "Wait a minute, Bill, you missed the final consonant. Now repeat after me, 'ball.'" I don't do that. I rejoice, trusting that Bill is going to pick up from me what that final consonant is.

On the other hand, here is a child who has written maybe just "bl" with no vowel in the middle here at the moment. We know that the vowels come later and usually with just the consonants, the child can reread it. I find that the vowels come in more easily when the child is reading work that the child has recognized, than the other way around. On the other hand, they may need some help with the sounds.

DiAnn: You said that drawing is also very important.

Don: Very, because the child can show what he or she means. For example, the beginning of a narrative can show in the drawing. If you notice early children's drawings, they are very static and usually face the camera straight out. Next in the picture you have a house with a chimney smoking like a howitzer at right angles to the roof and a sun in the sky—but nothing is happening.

Then you see a change when, instead of facing straight out, you see the child in profile. The minute the child is in profile—or the mother or the father or the dog—the child can act inside the picture. When you can act on the picture then you can have narrative, because something will unfold and something will happen.

So we're watching the child's drawings to see how they show things happening. I had a child who drew a tree over here with a hole in it and another tree with a hole next to it. You see these footprints go down the tree, across the bottom, and up into the other hole. That's a narrative—something happened.

DiAnn: And this would be true with ESL children?

Don: Sure. This is a human thing. The dilemma from the time of the cave man is, how do you show the lapse of time. That's the challenge. In reality, if you look at the most sophisticated art in a museum, you see it is the artist's ability to choose the precise moment in time, and everything centers in the moment. The children have to first discover that there are moments and gradually get more and more sophisticated until they pinpoint a moment. If you take the painting of the Creation in the Sistine Chapel, it is that gap between the palm and the finger that is the moment.

Well, in order to choose a moment, you have to exclude all others. Which is really artistic expression. True art is more what you don't say than what you do say. Young children first have to say it all and then start to choose what they don't say.

The child who wrote about her mother losing her job noticed that her mother didn't "get on her" for kicking the table or spilling the milk. The mother didn't say anything. The sophisticated part is that the child noticed what the mother didn't do—which is highly literate artistic expression. So we see it in drawing, we see it in painting, and we see it in writing. It's that child who said the one-liner about Miss Smith, you see. Think of all the things he didn't say. That's the brilliance of that thing.

DiAnn: Will you share the anecdote?

Don: This is a child in downtown Boston who was writing a character sketch and was stuck. What he said was—and he had only written one line—"When Miss Smith yelled, everybody's ass tightened just a little bit." He said, "I don't know what to write next." I said, "Don't write anything. You've got the whole thing in one line."

That's art! It's that magnificent selection because out of all the things Miss Smith said, he chose—I don't know if she appreciated it—the essence. She was a screamer and it affected everybody in the class.

DiAnn: Should computers be used in the teaching of writing?

Don: Yes. The miracle of the computer is the word processing. You can change things. You get a clear visual image of the word. You can put space in. You can add information in the right place so you don't have to copy it all over.

> Donald Graves has been a teacher, school principal, and a language supervisor for a city school system. He is currently Professor of Education at the University of New Hampshire and the Director of the Writing Process Laboratory.

For children who have motor problems, they get a magnificent machine text. You can print multiple copies. You can go to instant publication. You can use modems for children to communicate with each other. Heavens, we don't remotely know the limits yet. It's going to rely on our professional literacy and how we use it—just like everything else.

DiAnn: Some teachers are afraid of trusting students with inventive spelling because they fear the children will misspell the word many times throughout the selection. How would you suggest they deal with this problem?

Don: First of all, our data show how children change their inventions over time. You're quite right when you say that the child will misspell the word in the middle of a piece and then misspell it two or three other times. In fact, you may see three different inventions of the same word. The word is still in flux. So that does occur—there is no question about that.

However, what we need to look at is, do those words change over a six-month period? Well, they should. That's how we have to evaluate it. It's the same way that a child acquires language. If we were afraid that a child would make a mistake with a pronunciation early on—as speech therapists know—and start calling attention to these elements early in the game, children start to have speech impediments. But make no mistake, we look for full spellings wherever they can occur. We help children with high frequency words. We help them with their "bugaboo" spelling words. I ask students to do a self-evaluation—finding words they think may be misspelled.

So there's a lot of work left to be done, and I think that is the cause of a lot of fear in the public. As you know, if you surveyed the public for the most important curriculum areas, number one is reading, number two is mathematics, and number three is spelling. Composition is number eight. Handwriting and spelling are ahead of composition. This goes way back. It's visible. If you misspell a word, you must have a low level of literacy. If you cannot write with a clear hand, that's also a mark of not being literate. It's the surface feature game.

DiAnn: How would a teacher help children who are using defective spelling—where the spellings appear different? Would you circle those words? Would you tell the children that there are a certain number of misspellings?

Don: It depends on where the child is in the piece, and it depends on the age. Do you want to specify an age?

DiAnn: Let's say a second-grader.

Don: A second-grader should have more discrimination now. If the child is reading extensively, then the child should begin to discriminate more. It may be that the child will need to listen more carefully to final consonant sounds. Maybe the child will need some visual memory work. I would be expecting some changes there. I may say, "Underline all the words which you think are full spellings. Put a double line under three words that you wish you could spell but you can't right now. Write down the four words you studied this week that you need for your writing."

This means you not only need to remember what the four words were but also be able to write them. I'm not doing that with first-graders, but toward the end of second grade I'm doing that.

DiAnn: And it's a very natural process where they can see why they are writing these words and needing to use them.

Don: You need them for your writing. That is what spelling is for. That's what handwriting is for. It is all for writing.

DiAnn: Can you talk a little about conferences and about how, why, and how often you conference with children when they are writing?

Don: Some I only see once a week. Others I need to see every day and I do it very quickly. I'll start with the writing period and I'm around to their desks like a rocket. They know I'm coming and usually need help. They're afraid to work alone.

DiAnn: How many minutes do you spend? Give us an example.

Don: A quick conference like those I just mentioned would take about 30 seconds.

DiAnn: What do you ask?

Don: "What are you going to write about?" They should know, depending on the age, what the piece is about. Then I ask them where they are in the piece, and where they need help. I usually carry my clipboard, and I write down what they're writing about and indicate with a plus if I think they know what they're doing, a zero if I can't tell, and a minus if I need to get back to them before this is over. So I have long-term notes and these show the progression of their written pieces.

DiAnn: In which areas of writing do you feel we need more research?

Don: Well, certainly we need a lot more with regard to writing and reading. We need a lot more research on how children become more self-discriminating in critiquing their own work and in discovering what they think are the weaknesses and strengths of their own pieces. We need a lot more research on how genres emerge for children. I see too much that's just personal narrative of fiction. There's no question that children can write poetry. They can write plays. They should be doing much more work in scientific observation, recording data, and generalizing on that data. Above all, we need data on teachers demonstrating these things themselves.

DiAnn: Do you think that teachers as researchers can gather that data?

Don: They can, provided there is someone working with them. And I stress "with them," not from the standpoint that they can't do it alone but because all researchers work in teams.

DiAnn: Maybe a university link as a resource aid?

Don: Yes, that could be a help. The teachers are helping me on a study of fiction. They're helping in gathering data and making some preliminary observations. I'm helping on the classifications. Now I'm going to give the data back to them and they'll go to work on it.

DiAnn: Actually, wasn't that the method Piaget used in his work in Geneva?

Don: Yes, it was.

DiAnn: Do you feel that most of what goes on in the classroom is teacher-generated as opposed to student-generated?

Don: Yes. Our textbooks are set up that way. Our objectives for systems are set up that way. I have rarely seen objectives set up so that we learn from the children. And that, once again, comes back to the level of literacy of the professional. If a professional is highly literate, then you can listen. If a professional doesn't know what to do with what children say, then he's back to the textbook and back to prescribing.

DiAnn: It's more difficult to be teacher-generated, because you constantly have to devise new ideas and techniques, and the truth of the matter is it's all right there. The children have so much to generate.

Don: That's right. It's just a matter of knowing what we see. You have to be very organized, and it takes a very structured room where it's very predictable in order for unpredictable magnificent literate occasions to occur.

DiAnn: If teachers wanted to learn more about the teaching of writing, which books would you recommend?

Don: *A Writer Teaches Writing* by Donald Murray, *In the Middle* by Nancie Atwell, *When Writers Read* by Jane Hansen; *Clearing the Way* by Tom Romano is excellent for high school, and *Writing Well* by William Zinsser is also very good.

DiAnn: Do you have a favorite piece of literature?

Don: All my life I've been interested in Russian literature and I think my favorite is *Anna Karenina*. In that story, my favorite character is Levin, and he is someone who loves to work in the fields and to watch and learn from the people. He hates the city—I'm a country boy—and he is very nervous there. Also, his beautiful love of Kitty, his wife.

DiAnn: How old were you when you read that book for the first time?

Don: About 18. I tried *War and Peace* before that, but I crashed. I started it in the seventh grade, because my mother told me it was one of the longest books ever written, so I charged into it and I got impaled in the opening scenes.

DiAnn: It goes to show how significant pieces of literature encourage us to read more and learn more from books.

Don: Very much, indeed!

DiAnn: Thank you, Don, for sharing your thoughts. I hope these ideas have stimulated our readers to think more about the writing process. They certainly have for me.

➜ See: Blynt, p. 134; Brown, p. 133; Crafts, p. 136; Kamler, p. 140; Kitagawa, p. 132; Literature Reference List, p. 429.

From *The California Reader* 21(3), March-April 1988.

DiAnn Waskul Ellis is a professor at San Francisco State University, San Francisco, CA.

Book Note

Writing: Teachers & Children at Work

Donald H. Graves
1983; 336 pp.; $15
Portsmouth, NH:
Heinemann

In this landmark publication, which has revolutionized the teaching of writing, Graves looks at the writing process and how to make it operational within the classroom. Evaluation techniques and ways to share children's writing with parents are included in the volume. Graves strongly recommends that teachers write, so they know how the writing process feels, and so children will want to join the writing club. Graves also states: "At every single point in our research in the last 15 years, we've underestimated what kids can do."

Lois Mather

MARVELOUS INVENTIONS

Moon, Sun, Mars, Earth, Mercury, Jupiter, Pluto, Uranus, Venus, Saturn, Neptune

"All this writing is making my hand bloodshot."

—Contributed by Linda Giordano, second grade, Hawley School, Newtown, CT

Viewpoint: Mary M. Kitagawa

Seikatsu Tsuzurikata

Editor Lois Bird asked me to write about *seikatsu tsuzurikata*, "life experience composition." My husband and I have described this philosophically oriented writing education model in *Making Connections with Writing* (1987).

Even for those who have no academic interest in the movement or in Japanese education, there is good reason to learn something about its theory and practice. For one thing, it illustrates ways of promoting children's linkage of inner speech with writing (even though the Japanese teachers who began this movement in the late twenties had no more knowledge of Vygotsky's term "inner speech" than we had in the West). *Seikatsu* also enacts James Britton's exhortation for teachers to build upon children's writing in the expressive mode. And on a practical note, we can learn from Japanese teachers a way of responding to journals that enhances the writer even more than the usual dialogue journal responses do.

As James Moffett (1988) says in *Coming on Center:*

> What is new in composition are *connections.* Composing connects. The bits and pieces of thought, memory, feeling, and imagery lie within already, it's true, but old habits keep turning these over in the same patterns or simply ignoring them. . . . The act of composing necessarily rearranges our store of inner material.

Moffett recommends *telling what is happening* as a step close to inner speech. In an article about his first-graders, Masao Hino described how he slowed and dramatized each step of making pancakes for his class, stopping periodically so they could transcribe their on-the-spot perceptions (inner speech focused on *what is happening*) into external language (as either *what is happening* or as *what just happened*). I have tried the same exercise with older students and found their descriptions detailed and elaborate.

For what Britton calls expressive writing, my husband and I chose to use the term "writer-biased prose," meaning, as he does, writing that remains close to the self of the writer. *Seikatsu* proponents considered such writing the basis of all writing. Apparently Donald Murray and others who promote "discovery drafts" would agree. Nurturing the writer-self as opposed to the product, and the writer above the audience, is a fundamental aim of the Japanese *seikatsu* teachers. Much of the children's writing rings clearly with the authors' voices, but that is a byproduct, since the primary aim of this writing education is the enhancement of the self, apart from what is produced.

In my experience as a writer-biased teacher in this country, I have been able to observe the growth of self in many students through journals and reading logs. Students who began the year writing tentatively, generically, or by mere manipulation of literary-sounding phrases begin to express themselves with a clear-cut sense of "I say . . ." It is particularly dramatic with pre-adolescents, who are reluctant to take an individualistic stance orally before their peers but will do so in writing, even in a revolving journal that gets passed from student to student.

The primary nurturing of the child's self, as well as of the child's writer-self, comes for Japanese teachers through extensive responses

Mary M. Kitagawa currently teaches fourth and fifth grades in Amherst, Massachusetts, and has taught in eastern Massachusetts, Michigan, and Arizona. With her husband, Mary spent eight months in Japan learning about a writing-education/life-guidance educational movement called *seikatsu tsuzurikata.* Because of their continued interest in the parallels between that movement and whole language, they are working to facilitate dialogues between the proponents of both.

that they write in the margins of students' compositions and journals. With their extremely large classes, this avenue has even more importance than it does in classes in which support can also come in face-to-face conferences. But we too can use the margins to good advantage in dialogue journals. I have students turn back about one-third of the page from the left so that there is a fold when reopened. By leaving me that space, they anticipate an almost line-by-line response from me, their personalized reader. I enjoy this homework every evening. It complements the oral exchanges we have during the day, because I can pause to consider what I want to say and can be more thorough in my attention to details. If the writer's intentions are not clear, I can reread the text in various ways to try to find the strength I really want to highlight. In a conference, sometimes my hesitation would be misinterpreted by an unconfident writer. Japanese teachers write books and articles to help each other make effective written responses. In their circle group support meetings, the most common format is to bring samples of student writing with teacher replies, so that all the teachers can develop their skill at writer-strengthening responses.

Here is an example of a reluctant writer's journal and my backing of Octavio as both a person and as a writer.

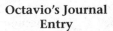

Octavio's Journal Entry	My Response
Saturday at one o'clock I had a soccer game. At the beginning of the game I played defender. I really hate playing defender because you have to stay back and help the goaly, but my coach switched me with a boy named Jose he played forward. I thought to myself now thats my pacition, I went up to the line to start the ball. I asked my teammate what the score was. He said one to zero. Adomadically I thought up a plan. So we tried it. It was going good until I got the ball.	Here is a very precise opening. You describe your place and how you felt playing that position. That helped me see the game through your eyes, Octavio. I can just picture your expression changing as you got to take over as a forward.

"Automatically" you felt a sense of leadership and put the plan into action. |
| I was dribeling it and a boy hit me with his knee. I fell to the ground in pain. I felt like if a rig was running me over. Then I heard a whisle. | What a sharp description, "like a rig running me over." |
| The refery came running to see if I was ok. I got up and I got a free kick. I was nervous. The reff whistled. That was the sign to kick the ball so I did. The ball went flying though the air. The goaly dove for it but he mist it and it went in, it was a goal.... | You may have still been in pain, but you got up.

Careful description of every detail, even for someone who might not know the game as you do. |

Many aspects of *seikatsu* writing and writing education parallel the process approach (sometimes with cultural differences, such as a heavier emphasis on reality than fiction, and with logistical differences due to factors such as class size). The strongest parallel between *seikatsu tsuzuri-*

kata and the process approach, I believe, is in trusting the child's authority, the child's language, and the child's message. That is an awesome shift from traditional language arts instruction. The exciting news is that dedicated teachers on both sides of the ocean have come to the same zealous conclusions about the importance of this.

➔ See: Brown, p. 133; Graves, p. 129; Kamler, p. 140; Kitagawa, pp. 420, 212.

References
Kitagawa, M., and C. Kitagawa. 1987. *Making connections with writing: An expressive writing model in Japanese schools.* Portsmouth, NH: Heinemann.
Moffett, J. 1988. *Coming on center: Essays in English education.* Portsmouth, NH: Boynton/Cook.

Further Reading by Mary M. Kitagawa

◆ *Making Connections with Writing: An Expressive Writing Model in Japanese Schools,* with C. Kitagawa. Heinemann, 1987.

◆ "Creating a Mosaic in the Context of Cultural Diversity." In *Stories to Grow By,* ed. J. M. Jensen. Heinemann, 1989.

◆ "Guise, Son of the Shoemaker." In *The Whole Language Evaluation Book,* ed. K. S. Goodman, Y. M. Goodman, and W. J. Hood. Heinemann, 1989.

◆ "Letting Ourselves Be Taught." In *Richness in Writing: Empowering Minority Students,* ed. D. M. Johnson and D. Roen. Longman, 1989.

◆ "Observing Carlos: One Day of Language Use in School." In *Teachers and Researchers Language Learning in the Classroom,* ed. G. S. Pinnell and M. L. Matlin. IRA, 1989.

◆ "When the 'Wrong' Students Come Through the Door." (possible title) In *The Whole Language Organization Book,* ed. K. S. Goodman, Y. M. Goodman, and W. J. Hood. Heinemann, in press.

Book Note

Making Connections with Writing

Mary M. Kitagawa and Chisato Kitagawa
1987; 200 pp.; $17.50
Portsmouth, NH: Heinemann

Through their research of the *seikatsu* philosophy of education in Japan, the Kitagawas provide an entirely different perspective on writing development. Rather than viewing writing as a way to communicate with the world, *seikatsu* views writing as a way of making inward connections to the outside world. The gentle responses of the *seikatsu* teachers are a powerful and touching model for engaging with students and their writing.

Janice Wizinowich

66 The *seikatsu* curriculum begins with children writing in expressive prose. Their topics are their direct experiences. Helping them make a strong connection to reality is more important than teaching them to persuade, influence, entertain, or impress a reader. To accomplish this, the readership is controlled by the teacher, just as a parent tends to act as a buffer for the toddler's speech audience so that expressive qualities are preserved during development. Teachers exert this control by interjecting themselves as readers who are so empathetic that redundancy, gaps in information, and lack of conventional punctuation do not distract them from the writer's desire to share an experience. 99 (p. 13)

Classroom Demonstrations

by Laurie M. Brown

Seikatsu: Giving Authors Voices, or How to Silence Freddy Krueger

Agonizing screams and machine-gun rattle reverberated off the walls of our writing lab as my students read their pieces filled with bloody nightmares and army tanks. My students listened in fascination to each Freddy Krueger and Rambo retelling.

Five months ago I had introduced process writing to the class, stressing the importance of writing from personal experience. I continually modeled this and stressed the point in several minilessons, yet the power of cable television prevailed, permeating much of the students' writing. I winced repeatedly and wondered how I could get away from the horror tales without taking back the freedom of choice that the entire writing process celebrates.

Fortunately, a friend recommended *Making Connections with Writing,* by Mary and Chisato Kitagawa, which answered this haunting question. The text examines *seikatsu* (pronounced say-kah-tsoo), a form of personal writing aimed at anchoring the author in reality. I told my students about it and asked them to "write what remains strong in your mind about a certain day, a certain time" (p. 17).

This brought in a new era to our classroom. Delving into our experiences, we giggled, wept, and learned about ourselves and our fellow writers. Freddy Krueger was pushed aside—our family, our feelings, stepped to the forefront of our writing. This piece is about *seikatsu* and how it encouraged growth for a community of writers. Still believing in choice, I view *seikatsu* as a way to help writers find their voices. Next year, I will begin the year with *seikatsu,* then branch out into fiction writing once my students have established themselves as writers.

One student, Idris, immediately adapted to this new form. Typically a tough, reluctant learner, Idris authored and allowed me to share the following piece:

> Oooo it hurts. Well if you keep still it won't hurt so bad. Oh I love my mother when she's like that. I could hear the roar of alcohol, I could feel it splash against my paper cut. It finally soaked in. My mom kissed my paper cut. Her lips felt warm like butter. She reached in a small box and pulled out a bandage. She ripped the paper off slowly and carefully so she wouldn't damage the band-aid. She removed the two slips of paper then carefully put the bandage on my paper cut. I stood up and kissed my mom. She's a real hero.

Idris smiled as I read; the class warmly received his piece. "I like the way he wrote that his mother's kiss felt warm like butter," commented Rita. Frequently in the past, the class had enjoyed Idris's stories, delightful tales of football and humorous moments. Yet this time my students glanced at each other. Nate's nervous giggle melted. He realized, as the rest of us did, that Idris had pulled back his calloused exterior and shared tender feelings.

Mattie came into our classroom just as we began writing *seikatsu.* Although she was reluctant to share her pieces with the other students, her emotions poured onto paper and formed vivid images. Mattie shared with me her piece about ShaQuetta:

> I have a sister named ShaQuetta . . . On Sunday my sisters went outside to play and a girl put ShaQuetta on her bike. And when they were going they fell down . . . . She let go of my sister and my sister fell slowly down to the ground. When I found out I was really mad at her. I cried. I can feel the water going down my face. My knees were coming together and my hands were red like a silk coat.

Later, in a note, Mattie thanked me for listening to her. I might not have heard Mattie's tales if we had not written *seikatsu.* This form encourages students to look again at their own experiences, create their place in reality, and paint their view with words.

As with Mattie, Sara's voice came through in her *seikatsu.* Writing diligently throughout the fall, Sara produced many clear and grammatically correct stories. Yet I couldn't find Sara in her pieces. Then one day she brought in "Bond":

> Tonight my dad and I were working on a list of materials we were going to need for my science project. My dad was explaining in his rough, low voice Ohm's Law and why it works. Each time he would start a new sentence I felt a chime in my chest. I felt a bond, a brand new bridge between my dad and I that was never there before. I was kind-of sad when it was over. But half of me felt glad, not because it was over but because it had ever started.

Every word shouts Sara—celebrating her individuality and a strong bond with her father.

Idris, Mattie, and Sara were three of many in my class who blossomed as writers once *seikatsu* was introduced. They found their voices and shared their perspectives on life with eloquence. The sounds of blood and ammunition receded from my room like low tide. My children had found their voices, and crashing waves of media would never again drown them out.

➜ See: Blynt, p. 134; Brown, p. 351.

Laurie M. Brown is an elementary teacher at Landis Elementary School, Alief, ISD, Houston, TX.

Book Note

Clearing the Way: Working with Teenage Writers

Tom Romano
1987; 216 pp.; $15
Portsmouth, NH: Heinemann

Learning to write well is exacting. It is hard work for both students and professional writers. Unlike professional writers, however, students possess neither the vast experience to see them through writing slumps nor the luxury of an editor to alert them to the bits of stupidity and dishonesty that inevitably creep into writing. And never is it more agonizing to appear stupid or dishonest than during the teen years. Tom Romano's concern for honesty in writing comes through in the way he opens himself and his teaching to us in this book. He is the teacher you wanted to have in high school, someone there for you as a real human being when you tended to see *establishment* in the rest of your dealings with adults.

Mary Kitagawa

❝ Common decency. The student is a human being, not a mechanical writing device to be shaken like a candy machine until the desired product pops out. If a teacher has had initial success in cutting students loose and the students therefore feel secure enough to write honestly, then their feelings are real and run deep, whether they are expressed in nonstandard usage, written with run-on sentences, or asserted with unsupported generalizations. ❞ (p. 89)

Book Note

Expecting the Unexpected: Teaching Myself—and Others— to Read and Write

Donald M. Murray
1989; 288 pp.; $15
Portsmouth, NH: Boynton/Cook

This book is slow reading for me. It's not that the reading is arduous or the text is dense; quite the contrary. I keep having to stop and attend to the inspiration it gives me to write. One of the nice things about surprise is that after you've had one or two or three surprises, then you become a veteran of surprise and will begin to recognize it. I am convinced that every one of us is a writer once we discover how to ride the roller coaster of ups and downs and twists and turns that make up for us our own style of doing it. What Murray shares are his own roller coaster rides and his own ways of helping students discover theirs.

Mary Kitagawa

❝ Our students will recognize surprise when we share our surprise at what we are writing, when we allow members of the class to share their writing and their surprises with us, and when we, as teachers are surprised at what they are writing. They must see the great range of surprise that is possible when writing becomes exploration. ❞ (p. 9)

❝ Writing should be hard. We are asking of writing nothing less than an understanding of the world in which we live. ❞ (p. 112)

Book Note

Forming/Thinking/Writing

Ann E. Berthoff
1978; 224 pp.; $16
Portsmouth, NH: Boynton/Cook

Among the books I have read and worked with on the teaching of composition, this one has had the greatest impact. Berthoff illuminates the art of composing as an act, rather than simply translating what's "up there" in ephemeral spheres in the head into words on paper. This work suggests that students experience art forms other than those to which we expose them. Berthoff recommends sending students into nature, allowing them to grasp branches, twigs, stones, feathers, and other organic elements: "Let them write about the experience of transaction. How do they view these specimens, as static objects, things that are undergoing process/growths? . . . The way we see things is a reflection of how we see ourselves in the act of transforming images into forms." Overall, *Forming/Thinking/Writing* is a wonderful sourcebook with a humanistic tone.

Beate Gillian

Writers Workshop

Classroom Demonstrations
by Ruth Ann Blynt

Writers Workshop, 1987–88

We have to trust the kids. I say this even though I know it will make some of my favorite colleagues leap from their worn seats in the faculty room to pelt me with erasers, paper clips, and cold coffee. We have to like the kids; and we have to *let* them think, not *teach* them to think. We are presumptuous if we believe we have that kind of power. Kids are born knowing how to think. Our job is to let them think and to give validity to their thoughts.

There's no better way to do this and accomplish that monumental shift in responsibility—by which "I learned" becomes more important than "I taught"—than to redevelop curriculum so that it mirrors whole language philosophy. Writing workshop proved it to me.

Let some of my kids prove it to you:

Joanne was a teacher's type of student. Intelligent, conscientious, and open-minded, she'd give any program a fair shot. She embodied the whole language philosophy from her first poem, "The Cold War," which decries the clique rivalries in our school, to her final exam essay on the important things she learned about writing:

> That it is an individual sort of thing. Everyone has their own style of writing and it shouldn't be changed. Restraints, limits or other things like that can cripple a writers originality. A writer should be able to write about what he wants, when he wants and how he wants.

Joanne wrote notebooks of poems. She published in-school periodicals. She entered her writing in out-of-school contests. She never failed to come prepared, follow procedure, and be a constant reminder to me and the other students that it could be done.

But Joanne would have thrived in any educational setting. So though I know she benefited from writers workshop, she doesn't really prove its necessity.

Maybe Scott does. Scott was not a good student in English. But he came to class nearly every day. And he was a real likable kid. He just didn't like to read or write. He probably still doesn't. But now he knows he can do it if he has the need and the desire. "The most important thing that I learned is that reading and writing isn't so bad after all. Writing stories on your life is great. You can put down your feelings and no one can say anything. I didn't know that." Scott was allowed to spend the better part of 12 years in a school system not knowing that.

Becky was the bravest of us all. She didn't follow the rules of workshop time as far as when to do what. But she was constantly writing or planning writing. Sometimes she would sit for days at a time with her head in her hands on her desk, producing nothing visible. Then a day or two later, she'd rush into the room, sheaves of papers flying, thrust them in front of my face, and breathlessly command, "Listen to this." Invariably she gave me a piece of her heart on that crinkled notebook paper with the hard-to-read backhand flourish. She volunteered to read aloud to the class and thus initiated the "group share" procedure that took us from early embarrassing moments of reading a single sentence aloud to our friends, to reciting entire works to an audience of educators at our year's end Authors Tea. Her first piece was about a recurring dream. Becky's voice is low and

scratchy, and she often sounds about to cry when she speaks. But she made us realize that what she told us in her work was true, and she made us care. She followed with a highly controversial poem about what boys do to girls that she allowed us to display on our classroom bulletin board with her name on it.

Becky's masterpiece, though, was the story of her cousin Michael. Michael and Becky had that one-of-a-kind relationship in which two people sort of breathe as one. She narrated incidents from their common past, which involved helping one another to quit drinking and taking drugs. She mesmerized us with a scene of closeness so vivid it stung our eyes with tears: a picture of her cousin after having jokingly shoved her into a leech-infested swamp and quickly retrieved her; the two of them standing on the dock. "I wasn't crying, but he was." Finally, as all good storytellers do, she built with suspense and ample foreshadowing to her sad story's climax: her cousin's suicide, and her own later attempt to follow him. He returned to her and stopped her. "Just put your finger down your throat, Becky, and throw up these pills. You'll be all right," he assured her. And she was. She was more than all right. She was terrific. "I know where Michael is," she closed. "He is a star. I talk to him every night." Symbolism isn't too hard for these kids, as long as the symbols have meaning for them.

Griffin, a senior, upper-tracked student, was "the writer" among his classmates. But he produced virtually nothing in workshop: some fascinating poetry, a worthy sketch once in a while. But he worked only when his Muse visited, never rewrote, and avoided and disputed every attempt I made to coax him to do otherwise. The most productive writing he did all year was in his journal. I asked him once, via this conduit, if it bothered him to see his classmates so successful in a field that formerly belonged to him. There was no response until the end of the year. The workshop's final exam required that students come prepared with a preliminary draft of a new piece, and focus, edit, and produce the final draft during the required three-hour time slot. Griff was elated when he handed me his finished product. And "Shuckernut and Pinkerball" was his best effort of the year. But it was another test question that finally answered my journal query.

> I learned this year that everybody has some serious talent out there at something, especially writing. Not that everyone is good at all types of writing but everybody has their own story to tell, and, if they tell it their own way, then it can be great. People in my class who I expected couldn't write on a bathroom wall, wrote some exceptional stuff.

I Used to Be...But Now I...

I used to think teachers sat back while the class wrote,
But now I write, too.

—Anonymous

"All the trust I had in everyone walked out the door one June morning, when my mother left." That line in Emily's journal took my breath away. "Is there a story here?" I wrote back. "No," she assured me later. "I couldn't." And she didn't for quite a long time. But when she finally did, it was as good a piece of writing as I've read anywhere, at any time. In a cold and straightforward manner, Emily disclosed the story of her mother's leaving. The depth of the underlying emotions was revealed only in clincher lines that shake the psyche of the reader. "My mom took my sister and me to Perkins's Park and told us that she and my dad were separating," Emily offered. "The park never seemed the same after that." When, "later that evening my dad, my sister, and I went out for ice cream," Emily provided the caustic observation that ice cream is "a very popular separation dessert." She questioned the validity of grownup perceptions when, after she and her father "had a talk," the result was "I found out 'I don't know' isn't an answer," which put an end to "our 'attitude' discussions." The cathartic release of writing is one rarely considered on lists of behavioral objectives. But it is one of the most valid reasons for engaging in the activity.

One of the great things about workshop is that everyone does something memorable. It's possible to really know kids, more kids than ever before. The ultimate celebration of our year's accomplishments came with our Authors Tea, when students performed their finished work to an engrossed and enthralled audience. But overall, I don't suppose that was really any more important than our monthly classroom group shares, or any of the small response group readings that took place every day. What mattered was the writing, and the reading of that writing.

Final exam answers proved that to me, if I'd retained any doubts. Karen summed it up for all writers everywhere with, "The most important thing I learned this year about writing is that you give a piece of yourself to someone who reads what you wrote. It is something that is all your own. You make it. It gives you a sense of accomplishment."

→ See: Crafts, p. 136; Graves, p. 129; Kitagawa, p. 132.

Ruth Ann Blynt is a writing instructor at Utica College, Utica, NY.

Resource: Book

Inspiring Young Authors Year-Round: A Handbook for Teachers and Parents

Nancy Oster Steffel, Ed.D. and Susan Griffis Swenson, M.S.Ed.
1989; 144 pp.; $8.95
Racine, WI: Treetop

Whole language educators are often wary of cookbooklike idea books, but here's one that is chock-full of theoretically sound ideas for bookmaking, as well as strategies for inspiring writers using children's literature and recordings, many of which are thematically related to seasons and holidays. It also includes helpful computer applications for producing both text and illustrations.

LBB

As kids see it

Thumbs Up for Writers Workshop

Here's what Ruth Taravella's middle school students have to say about writers workshop:

"You can't show your own ability by using a textbook, but when you write, you find out what you're capable of, and you find out about your own mistakes."

"You learn without realizing you're learning in the writers workshop. A textbook is boring."

"I like the workshop. My grades have come up from D's and F's last year to C's this year."

"It's not the same old thing; it's always something different."

"I'm still getting language skills, but in a fun way."

"I make a lot of mistakes, but the more practice I get the better I am getting."

"It enables us to be more creative and express ourselves more freely. We learn by doing instead of out of a textbook."

This was contributed by Ruth Taravella, middle school teacher, District #70, Pueblo, CO.

Resource: Organization

The Center for the Study of Writing (CSW)

the
center
for the
study
of
writing

5513 Tolman Hall
Graduate School
of Education
University of California
Berkeley, CA 94720
1-415-643-7022

The Center for the Study of Writing provides national leadership to schools, colleges, and universities as they work to improve the teaching and learning of writing. In an increasingly complex, technological, and multicultural society, the questions that surround writing—how it develops; how it connects to such processes as reading, speaking and thinking; what its relationship is to identity and power; and how we can best teach it—take on urgency and demand answers.

The Center supports an extensive program of educational research and development, in which some of the country's top language and literacy experts work to discover how the teaching and learning of writing can be improved from the early years of schooling through adulthood. Underlying Center research is the belief that research must both move into the classroom and come from it; thus the Center supports "practice-sensitive research" for "research-sensitive practice."

CSW publishes an ongoing series of technical reports and occasional papers about current issues in the field, including reports on CSW research. In conjunction with the National Writing Project, CSW publishes *The Quarterly,* a journal on writing and the teaching and learning of writing, which goes to CSW subscribers and to teachers at NWP sites throughout the country.

Classroom Demonstrations
by Nan Bonfils

What Makes Good Writing? Ask the Kids–They Know!

Holistic assessment of samples of student writing can serve a variety of purposes when used as an inservice activity for staff. It stimulates dialogue about what faculty members value in writing and how they teach it; it gives administration a handle on how well the general school population writes; and it generates criteria for evaluating subsequent writing.

But in my opinion the really potent and too often neglected value of the faculty's assessment is when it is stimulated in the classroom. Our young writers, even seven- and eight-year-olds, can cash in on the same benefits. Holistic writing assessment in the classroom can provoke conversation about writing, propel self-examination of writing, and produce guidelines for evaluating writing. Here's a report on a third-grade classroom.

Set-up

I selected four papers that spanned a wide range of quality. The papers were anonymous, labeled W, X, Y, and Z, and none of the four were written by anyone in the room. However, the samples were genuine and current, as I selected them from an adjacent classroom that same week. Each student had photocopies of all four papers. As soon as they skimmed the papers, the students recognized the topic as the one that we had used for holistic writing. I advised them that this was an experiment, the same experiment that their teachers had performed. I was curious to see if I would get the same results from students.

Procedure

1. We read each paper out loud without comment.
2. Students reread the papers silently and sorted them into two piles—highs and lows: "ones I liked a lot and ones I didn't like a lot." Rule: You have to have at least one paper in each pile.
3. Students worked independently to refine the sorting to the point of ranking the papers one to four "with a score of four going to the best and one to the one you didn't really like at all."
4. Students took time to jot notes individually about how they ranked the papers. "What makes number four the best?"—a fine exercise in supporting an opinion.

Record

1. We tallied our votes with great emphasis on my part that these were only opinions and could change.

Sample format:

	W	X	Y	Z
Mary	4	2	1	3
Claes	4	3	1	2
Geoffrey	4	2	1	3
Tad	4	3	1	2

2. In some classrooms a more anonymous grid will suffice.

Sample format:

	4	3	2	1
W	✓✓✓✓	✓		
X	✓	✓✓	✓✓	
Y				✓✓✓✓
Z		✓✓	✓✓✓	

1. We looked for consensus about the highest and lowest ranked papers. (In my experience, both students and teachers are quick to reach agreement about fours and ones. It's the middle that's fuzzy.)
2. Based on their notes and rereading the papers, we began to list the qualities of the top paper. "What makes sample W so good?"

3. We listed the traits of not-so-good writing by describing sample Y.

Results

We had a list of criteria for what makes good writing to post in our classroom. Its value as a guidepost for these young writers was that *they* wrote the list.

What Makes Good Writing

- It makes sense.
- The event is clear.
- You can understand the words.
- It's neat enough to read.
- It's long because it had to be—to tell a complete story.
- It's short—it told a lot in a little.
- Interesting.
- Details.
- Action words make it exciting.
- There may be spelling mistakes but we can figure it out.

These self-selected standards gave students a measuring stick for their own efforts and the writing of others they encountered in the world of print. The framework was open-ended, so the list expanded as writing and reading experience strengthened throughout the year.

Our students may not have the vocabulary for discussing or labeling quality, but they have the analytical ability to recognize good stuff. Just ask them!

→ See: Goodman, p. 252.

Nan Bonfils is an elementary teacher at the International School of Kuala Lumpar, Kuala Lumpur, Malaysia.

📷 **WHOLE LANGUAGE CAMERA**

Kristen Cummings, age 5, at her home writing center, North Adams, MA.

Resource: Periodical

Bread Loaf News

$9/year (3 issues) individual; $12 institutional from:
Dept. A
Bread Loaf School of English
Middlebury College
Middlebury, VT 05753
1-802-388-3711

The Bread Loaf School of English, a graduate English program, publishes this magazine to report on the work done by its teachers. The issue we received included articles on assessment, minority recruitment of teachers and educational faculty, a cross-age tutoring project in South Carolina, Newcomer High School in San Francisco, where new immigrants spend their first year of high school, and an interview with Myles Horton, book reviews, letters, and news about upcoming conferences, workshops, and anything else of interest. Several theme issues are planned for the magazine. Contributors include names well known to whole language exponents, such as James Armstrong, Shirley Brice Heath, James Moffett, Ken Macrorie, and Eliot Wigginton.

Great Teachers:
Nancie Atwell
by Amanda Crafts

On the first day of eighth grade in 1983, I sat with my friends at a small cluster of desks in a cheerful classroom, listening to my reading and English teacher, Nancie Atwell. She was briefly telling us what her plans for the year were. We were to go to her room twice a day for 50 minutes—once for English, once for reading.

I was relieved to hear that for the second year our class had writing workshop during English. The year before, English class had been different from any I had known previously. Our seventh-grade teacher introduced us to a kind of English class in which lessons about parts of speech, punctuation, and spelling were not daily headaches, and inane ditto sheets concerning these topics were almost nonexistent.

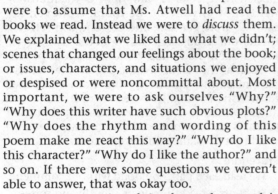

Nancie Atwell

Ms. Atwell then explained our reading class. She was planning Sustained Silent Reading for almost the entire class period five days a week! I was excited about this, but wary too. Several of my past teachers agreed that SSR was a good thing, and in seventh grade we were even allowed to read during three periods a week. Yet, there always seemed to be a catch—sometimes we had to complete book reports or questionnaires upon finishing a novel; sometimes we were assigned books, or we had only a limited choice between three or four books picked by our teachers. Other times the problem was just a matter of very little SSR time in school. However, I realized it was a far cry from the SRA kits and literature anthologies that I had suffered through in the past, and this gave me hope.

When the excitement of the first day wore off, I was able to see even more clearly just what constituted our new habitat. First was the feeling of comfort and closeness present. For one thing, the placement of our desks was left largely up to us. Rarely did people misbehave enough to have assigned seats. Lounging while reading or writing was our choice.

The second aspect immediately evident was the vast library of books—more books than I had ever seen in any classroom library. They weren't all the "right" books in the way of literature meticulously picked exactly for our age level, by educators who had long since passed this level. There were selections from every genre, about countless subjects and in varying levels of difficulty, from perhaps sixth grade to a collegiate level. For a voracious reader like myself, these books were a gift.

There were several areas in our room that housed the tools we used as writers and readers. There were a dozen types of paper, as well as an assortment of stationery. Decorated coffee cans were filled with pencils, markers, crayons, pens of every color, felt-tip markers, chalk, and a lot of red-inked instruments. There was white-out, carbon paper, stencils, rulers, hole-punches, and various other tools. Small bookcases were filled with dictionaries, thesauruses, "bad-spellers' dictionaries," rhyming dictionaries, address books, and other guides.

On the opposite side of the room were four coatrack partitions, leaving five small areas for writing conferences or for privacy while reading or writing. There was also an area cleared of desks and chairs for our "group share" response sessions. This was an area in which to share a work in process or a finished piece. These were held for the last 10 or 15 minutes of writing workshop and consisted of the entire class.

The back wall was covered in posters, messages, poems, schedules, pictures, and whatever

we wanted to put on display. One corner of the front of the room held Ms. Atwell's desk; the other held a large conference table and file cabinet. We were at liberty to look at our permanent writing folders at any time. The blackboard covered the front wall. It was easy to feel comfortable and well supplied in this room. Soon we began to settle into a regular routine.

I was not disappointed in the reading class. We were allowed to read whatever we desired. Ms. Atwell encouraged us to look into the school and town libraries and local bookstores, as well as referring students to others who owned certain books. Often she would loan us her own books.

The catch I had been fearful of turned out to be one of the most wonderful discoveries of the year. Every student had a reading log—a folder filled with paper where we were to correspond with Ms. Atwell about what we were reading. We had specific instructions not to treat this as a series of book reports. We were to assume that Ms. Atwell had read the books we read. Instead we were to *discuss* them. We explained what we liked and what we didn't; scenes that changed our feelings about the book; or issues, characters, and situations we enjoyed or despised or were noncommittal about. Most important, we were to ask ourselves "Why?" "Why does this writer have such obvious plots?" "Why does the rhythm and wording of this poem make me react this way?" "Why do I like this character?" "Why do I like the author?" and so on. If there were some questions we weren't able to answer, that was okay too.

Literature was viewed simply as other people's writing, and we were free to comment on or criticize it as if we were giving response to a classmate. Soon we were drawing parallels from our own lives and our own writing in the books we read. This is exactly what Ms. Atwell had in mind when she changed the format of our SSR time.

Nancie Atwell had been directing the Boothbay Writing Project for three years by the fall of 1983. Some students had been taught for at least one year by a teacher involved in the project. The writing process is taught as early as kindergarten. It is simple to follow at all age levels, and it consists of nine basic steps.

Rehearse
This is a way of brainstorming—first for a writing topic and then as a basic plot-line of the writing piece.

First Draft
For some students, this is often the most difficult step. Ms. Atwell kept telling us, "Just *write*—everything and anything."

Conference
With the pages of (often) mass confusion in hand, the writer and one or two other students went to a conference area to read the work. When reading, the responders ask questions, make comments, and advise from notes they made. The writer then takes his own notes from their observations to remind him of trouble spots and possible changes.

Second Draft
After the conference, the writer contemplates this response and decides on what changes will take place because of it. The second draft is formed by re-writing, including all the changes made as a result of the decisions.

Second Conference
This second conference ideally should have both responders who have heard the original

and others who have not. The procedure is the same as the first conference.

Confer with Self
This step is often the most arduous for me. The writer must read through the piece several times, taking into account the response just given and the writer's own ideas of what has been accomplished.

Self Edit
This draft is the first to be read by others, so it must be legible and orderly.

Edit
When the writer has corrected everything circled, the piece is placed in a rack of material to be edited by Ms. Atwell.

Final Copy
The next day, the piece is handed back to the author, with any mistakes that may have been missed pointed out by Ms. Atwell. She spends a few moments with the writer, explaining, making comments, and discussing the piece. Any grammar, punctuation, or spelling rules that we have used in the context of our writing are discussed, and a note is made on the sheets of paper clipped to the front page of our daily writing folders. Then the writer transcribes it once again, this time making sure it is totally error-free. When that is done, it is placed on another rack on Ms. Atwell's desk, so that she can check it over and insert it in our permanent writing folders.

Ms. Atwell is very organized, and I'm sure that fact helps differentiate between being not only creative and innovative, but an effective teacher as well.

At the beginning of every class, Ms. Atwell took a "status of the class" roll call, so our progress was always documented. This way she was able to see if we weren't working up to our potential and if we were aware of what our peers were working on.

As each ranking quarter ended, the class had individual conferences with Ms. Atwell. At this time we went through our permanent writing folders to see what we had accomplished in reference to the goals we had decided upon at the beginning of the quarter.

➜ See: Cermak, p. 137; Goodman, p. 252; Graves, p. 129; Rapoport, p. 176.

Amanda Crafts is a student at Syracuse University, Syracuse, NY.

As kids see it

Punctuation Power
by Jason Cetron

Punctuation and capitalization are very important. If you don't use them, it will be very hard to read your sentences. I'll show you what I mean. once there was a lady she had sheep goats and chickens she loved them very much one day she had a baby she loved the baby more than the animals Do you see what I mean? Punctuation and capitalization are very, very important.

Jason Cetron is a third-grader at Curtis Estabrook School, Brooklyn, NY. This was contributed by his second-grade teacher, Maureen Powell.

Book Note

In the Middle: Writing, Reading, and Learning with Adolescents

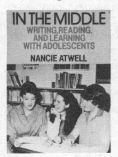

Nancie Atwell
1987; 320 pp.; $16
Portsmouth, NH: Boynton/Cook

I spent late summer and early fall with my Nancie Atwell "bible" tucked under my arm, hoping to absorb her philosophy. I followed her advice to the letter, checking and rechecking with it after each new writing/reading workshop class. I haven't spent so much time with a book since I read Dr. Spock and Karen Pryor while breastfeeding my firstborn.

Ruth Ann Blynt

❝ The word *story* can be traced to the Greek word *eidenai,* which means "to know." As a reader, I look to stories to help me understand and give meaning to my life. As a writer, I tell stories so I may understand, teaching myself and trying to teach others through the actions and reactions of those "people on the page," Donald Murray's "little scenes in which people reveal both themselves and the subject." This book tells stories because it's the best way I know to reveal myself, my students, and my subject: helping adolescents put written language at the crux of their emotional, social, and intellectual worlds. Framing these is my own story, the evolution that brought me out from behind my big desk and allowed my students to find their ways inside writing and reading. ❞ (p. 3)

Book Note

Lessons from a Child: On the Teaching and Learning of Writing

Lucy McCormick Calkins
1983; 182 pp.; $13.50
Portsmouth, NH: Heineman

This book reads like a novel because, as Susie and her teachers and some of her classmates come to life for us through Calkins's account of two years' observation, we see the writing process unfold just as the plot of a novel does. But the plus factor in this case is that, entwined within the "plot" of Susie's growth, the author provides direct information about theory and other research.

Lessons from a Child portrays the struggles and benefits of teacher and researcher in collaboration. Many of those are presented in direct quotations, such as: "'My hands are sore from sitting on them,' she (the teacher) joked with me. 'But it's the only way I can keep from wielding my red pen.'" (p. 33)

Mary Kitagawa

❝ It is significant to realize the most creative environments in our society are not the ever-changing ones. The artist's studio, the researcher's laboratory, and the scholar's library are each deliberately kept simple so as to support the complexities of the work-in-progress. They are deliberately kept predictable, so the unpredictable can happen. Similarly, Mrs. Howard and I became convinced that the juxtaposition of a complex, changing craft such as writing and a simple consistent environment freed the children to make choices as they wrote. ❞ (p. 32)

 ## As Teachers See It

by Joanne Cermak

Inspiration from Atwell

As a fourth-grade teacher, I took Nancie Atwell's book *In the Middle* hesitantly when it was suggested by sixth-grade teacher and favorite discussion partner, Karen Dalrymple. It was for middle school teachers; however, I was surprised. I found it inspirational, a model for my own teaching goals, and, with some adaptation, appropriate and meaningful for the teaching of fourth-grade students.

As an elementary teacher I had no formal training for teaching writing. Having discovered the works of Donald Graves and Lucy Calkins, I had been using the writing workshop model in my classroom for five years, and each year its advantages became more apparent. Each fall I began the year attempting to model writing by taking the first 10 minutes of our writing time to write myself. In a week or two, I no longer had the urge to write, too eager to get to conferring, hoping to touch everyone and to ask the right questions. After reading *In the Middle*, I became determined to write with my students. Nancie inspired me to try to use myself as a writing resource; discovering for myself techniques that worked, experiencing the problems encountered, and gaining insights about the process. She led me toward looking at myself not just as a teacher, but as a writer. I shared my stories with my students, as well as what I learned about writing. They tried what I tried; I tried what they tried.

Their interest in my writing encouraged me further. In October I shared a story about my childhood, detailing an argument I had with my sister. In April my sister, visiting from New York, stopped by our classroom. She was immediately surrounded by students demanding to hear her side of the story. She did not recall the incident at all.

Nancie motivated me to take the time to write, to trust myself with what I discovered, and to become a researcher in my own classroom, observing and learning from my students and myself. She had written on a topic she cared about, experimented on, and researched. She used her students, her husband, and her colleagues as conference partners. This is how she instructed her students to write; this is how she wrote. Just as she claimed students needed to see adults who write, I needed to see teachers who use their classrooms as ways to learn about teaching.

I began to experiment with learning logs. At first this was frustrating. Students responded by saying that a book was "good," characters were "nice." Remembering the beginnings of writing workshop, I realized that too had not come easily. I had struggled with conferring. Our early peer conferences were of little help. The students had needed an internal reserve of good questions to ask and ways to look at writing. They had needed experience with the process. Then we modeled good conferences, discussed the rationale for conferences, and practiced techniques that were helpful. Now they demand quality conferences, seeking out partners with good conferring reputations.

I determined that what the fourth-graders needed for their reading was an internal reservoir of ways to respond to literature. We began using our read-aloud books. We did activities as a whole class, discussing aspects of character, setting, plot; I served as recorder, putting our class answer on chart paper to display. Students then tried the same or similar activities in small groups, using multiple copies of literature books. Within their literature groups, students voiced their own views, heard differing views, and added, deleted, modified, or changed their opinions. Becoming more comfortable with these types of activities, students then tried responding in their logs to specific questions I posed about literature. If necessary, they were free to discuss their thoughts with a partner before writing in the log. Often I asked them questions about their opinions of a certain task or their thinking process. By the end of the year the students were choosing their own reading materials and responding as they saw fit. An internalized "idea bank" had been formed from which they could draw future ideas. I was able to watch their progress, observing what students chose to focus on and how they created new ways and activities for evaluating a book.

Students learned to incorporate these ideas and extend them in new ways or to other books. Tasks were kept open-ended and thought-provoking, and students' reactions to a particular task were always considered. I am grateful to *In the Middle* for motivating me to look at myself as a writing resource and for outlining a structure for reading upon which I could build a foundational program for younger students.

➔ See: Crafts, p. 136; In the Middle, p. 137.

Joanne Cermak is an elementary teacher at Eagle Elementary School, Eagle, CO.

Tribute to Nancie Atwell
by Amanda Crafts

It's coming to a finish.
Now we're almost through;
But that won't diminish
My knowledge that's come from you.

I won't forget
The things you've shown me.
I won't regret
The things you've done for me.

Our reading journal
(for it really is *ours*)
Will be kept eternal;
It certainly filled the hours!

English class was a joy
Discovering what I could do.
It was like unwrapping a new toy
And all with the help of you.

It's coming to a finish,
Now we're almost through;
But that won't diminish
Our friendship: me and you.

Love—
Amanda

Amanda Crafts is a student at Syracuse University, Syracuse, NY.

 ### WHOLE LANGUAGE CAMERA

An author at work in Vicci Fox's class, Sunnyside High School, Tucson, AZ.

Computers

Resource Essay

Micro-computers in the Whole Language Classroom

by Fred Gollasch

In London a six-year-old girl is sitting by a BBC computer using a Quinkey, a small hand-held keyboard about the size of a paperback book. Each finger of her right hand operates a button, and the thumb alternates between two others. These six simple keys enable her to generate all the letters of the alphabet, punctuation, and numbers. She shares the computer screen with three other children, each producing text on a quarter of the screen. They obviously enjoy the writing, which is punctuated with chat. They have learnt to master the Quinkey in about a third of the time it takes to master a conventional keyboard.

In the next room a nine-year-old visually impaired boy writes by himself at the side of the classroom. He fingers the Quinkey easily as his eyes focus steadfastly on the screen.

In Boston, Massachusetts, first-grade children use a talking word processor. As they type the computer reads what they have written. The teacher has the option of choosing whether the computer will respond after each letter, word, sentence, or all three. Although the voice is still somewhat artificial and there are problems with the pronunciation of difficult words, it is a sign of things to come.

In Cambridge, England, a ten-year-old composes a poem that moves on the screen. Anyone reading it is compelled to read it with the emphasis the author intended as appropriate pauses are included. The impact of this moving text brings the poem to life as his friends read it aloud.

At the next computer three children give their own emphasis to a well-known poem using the same program. They laugh as they respond to this magic movement on their screen.

In a primary school in Sydney, Australia, it is lunchtime. Children of all ages gather in bunches around the school's micro-computers armed with pens and paper. Peering from each screen is the round, friendly face of a little character called "Podd." Above him are the words "Podd can . . ." When a child types in a word such as "cry" or "wink," Podd performs the act before their very eyes. If it is something he can't do, the screen reads "No he can't."

The children are members of the Podd Club, dedicated to solving the problem of how many things Podd, the star of this delightful BBC software program, can actually do. They have formed the club themselves to help the kindergarten class add to their lists of what Podd can and can't do. They have now discovered more than 70 actions. They have only another 40 or 50 to go.

In Alaska a sixth-grade classroom buzzes with excitement as the children gather around a monitor. Text appears on the screen. They have just been successful in establishing telecommunication links with 11-year-olds in a school in Mexico. A loud cheer echoes through the room, adding to the warmth from the central heating. In this land of cold isolation, they are delighted to have made this link with another country. There will be much reading, writing, listening, and talking involved in their joint projects as they struggle to make themselves understood and to understand the halting English of their new-found friends.

The above are just a few glimpses into recent language developments in micro-computing in schools around the world. In Australia there are pockets of high energy involving teachers, consultants, lecturers, and software producers, who are helping to keep the country at the forefront of

world developments. However, the speed of development in computing and, to a lesser degree, literacy learning theory makes it difficult, particularly for the busy classroom teacher, to know in what direction to go.

This situation compels us to take a careful look at how we might use micro-computers for literacy development. Primary teachers can use micro-computers wisely for literacy development in the classroom. If we are going to use micro-computers effectively for literacy development in primary schools, we need to:

1. understand language learning principles,
2. integrate micro-computers into the classroom,
3. see the computer as a tool,
4. understand the role of the teacher as a facilitator,
5. understand how to establish classroom environments that nurture literacy development,
6. be selective in the use of software, and
7. plan carefully.

References

Chandler, D. 1984. *Young learners and the micro-computer.* Milton Keynes, England: Open University Press.

Chandler, D., and S. Marcus. 1985. *Computers and literacy.* Milton Keynes, England: Open University Press.

Gollasch, F. 1985. "Developing quality writing in the classroom," *Literacy Centre Publication.* Wagga Wagga: Riverina-Murray Institute of Higher Education.

Pulvertaft, A. 1984. "Learner choice—learner power," *Australian Journal of Reading* 7(4), November.

Wray, D. 1986. "Too much software? An update on computer-assisted learning in language and reading," *Reading (U.K.R.A.),* July.

Excerpted from *Micro-computers in the Whole Language Classroom* (Wagga Wagga, New South Wales: Centre for Teaching & Research in Literacy).

As Teachers See It

by Claire Doyle

Creative Applications of Computer Assisted Reading and Writing Instruction

I have recently conducted several inservice training sessions for teachers and teacher aides at elementary and high schools on the Navajo Indian Reservation. These workshops have been devoted to computer assisted instruction for remediation in reading and writing. It has been unusual, exciting, and rewarding work. Each visit leaves me impressed by the innovation, daring, and competence of the teachers and students in these remote schools.

Each visit also leaves me impressed by the amount of money spent on computer hardware and software at these schools. I continue to be disappointed, however, by the lack of quality of a great deal of packaged instructional software that I see there and advertised in catalogs, magazines, and newsletters everywhere.

Essentially, the slick software packages available today, carefully structured and limited in vocabulary, are like the basals and workbooks of yesterday. In sharp contrast, word processing and other applications software including data base and spreadsheet—the unstructured, limitless, creative, uncanned alternative to the multitude of education packages marketed today—are being underused and overlooked.

For students who have experienced years of phonics work, dictionary skill building, reading what someone else has chosen, and writing what they are told, computers with word processing software (and other applications packages) offer a new start. An emphasis on the

reading and writing process, not on the subskills some define within that process, may be accomplished with activities like the following:

- Writing letters to each other/electronic mail
- Writing journals
- Writing stories and publishing collections
- Responding to the writing of others by writing comments, reviews, questions to them on the computer—a sort of writers network
- Encouraging free writing and "play" with word processing
- Conversing with another computer on a shared computer
- "Musical computer"—chain writing
- Creating data bases about each student in the class
- Exploring startup costs of a small business and making calculations with a spreadsheet

Computer assisted instruction is not the panacea for our students' struggle toward literacy. It is, however, the opportunity for a new approach to an old problem. It requires creativity, careful thought, and effort by dedicated teachers. Instead of resorting to the "electronic workbooks" that publishers are desperately pushing, we need to explore the great potential that computers offer us.

Excerpted from *Journal of Reading,* December 1988.

Claire Doyle is an instructor at North Country Community College in Saranac Lake, NY.

Resource: Computer Group

Teachers' Idea and Information Exchange (TI & IE)

$8/disk; first 30 disks and next 6 disks for $249.95; next 6 disks for $39.95; sampler disk and catalog for $12.95; StoryWorks program for $49.95 from:

TI & IE
Dept. N
P.O. Box 6229
Lincoln, NE 68506
1-402-483-6987

Resource: Periodical

The AppleWorks Educator

$24.95/year (8 issues) from:

c/o AACE
P.O. Box 60730-TI
Phoenix, AZ 85052

As TI & IE asks, why wait for the software you need? Create it yourself using AppleWorks and then send your file to the "largest AppleWorks educators' group in North America," to share with other educators through its network. More than 900 files (on 30 disks) are available. The *TI & IE Bulletin* describes how the group works. *TI & IE News* is an occasional newsletter with useful hints and information.

LBB

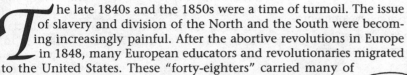

Education in Turin: A Romance by Herbert Kohl

Continued from page 109

From the Civil War to the New Century:
An Uneasy Truce

The late 1840s and the 1850s were a time of turmoil. The issue of slavery and division of the North and the South were becoming increasingly painful. After the abortive revolutions in Europe in 1848, many European educators and revolutionaries migrated to the United States. These "forty-eighters" carried many of Froebel's, Pestalozzi's, and Rousseau's ideas to the United States, and many people heard about kindergartens for the first time from them.

In 1851 kindergartens were banned in Prussia as being revolutionary. Froebel, an old man by this time, was heartbroken but dreamed of developing kindergartens in the United States, a place where the dream of democracy was still alive. Elizabeth remembered hearing Elizabeth Peabody, the sister-in-law of Horace Mann, a Froebelian, and leading American feminist educator, lecture on Froebel and was particularly struck by some of Froebel's (1877) last words:

> If people will not recognize and support my cause in my native land I will go to America, where life is freely unfolding itself and a new education of man will find a footing.

Elizabeth married in the late 1850s and her only daughter, Alice, was born just before the Civil War. Elizabeth tried to protect Alice from many of its horrors, but it was impossible not to feel the physical and psychological wounds the war left on its participants. Turin, divided during the war, needed to heal and Elizabeth decided to do something. Because there were so many problems, she decided to focus on those she knew best, those relating to the common schools.

The town experienced an influx of blacks from the South whose education had to be provided for. There were also new migrations from Pennsylvania, New England, and Europe. By 1868 the potential student population was near 150, too large to be accommodated in a one-room school or the Christian School. If the community was to build a new school, there had to be some way to reconcile all the differences that existed in the community. Elizabeth, with the assistance of the teachers at both schools, convened a series of town forums on education quite unaware of what she was opening up. On the first night parents from the fundamentalist school came in a large group. Some members of the business community attended, as well as several of the farmers from the surrounding area. A handful of parents from Elizabeth's former school also came. Only two black adults came. They were friends of Elizabeth's and came more as a favor to her than out of their own conviction. The racism that was generated by the defeat of the South and the influx of blacks led most blacks in Turin to keep to themselves for safety.

From the outset the meeting was dominated by representatives of the business community. An eloquent plea by both teachers almost convinced the business people that it would be in the children's and town's best interests to build a new school. In a hesitant way, one of the farmers suggested that it would be possible to save money and solve a problem by giving one of the old schools to the local blacks. With the exception of Elizabeth and her friends, everyone was relieved. Blacks and the town each would have a school. The only thing to be worked out was how progressives and fundamentalists could get along in the same building. As the fundamentalist teacher put it, "My students are quiet and orderly and they won't disturb anybody. The other students are the ones who talk and move around so much. If you can find a way for your students not to disturb mine we'll get along fine."

The compromise created more problems than it solved. The black community was relegated to an old school, and the new school became increasingly fundamentalist in educational style if not religion. An uneasy truce reigned among the teachers, and there was no unity of purpose or philosophy in Turin's schools.

Reference

Marenholz-Bulow, Baroness B. von. 1877. *Reminiscences of Friedrich Froebel*, trans. Mary Mann. Boston: Lee and Shepard.

Continued on page 169

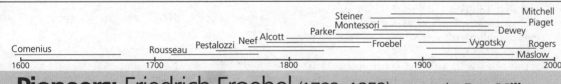

Pioneers: Friedrich Froebel (1782–1852)   by **Ron Miller**

Froebel was an idealistic, romantic young German who worked with Pestalozzi from 1808 to 1810 and then set out to conduct his own schools. Froebel's most lasting contribution to modern education was the kindergarten—literally a garden for children, where their inner nature could be carefully tended and nurtured. Less well known is the fact that Froebel's educational theory had a significant influence on later educational pioneers, including Francis W. Parker, Maria Montessori, and many other progressive educators.

In 1826 Froebel wrote *The Education of Man*, expressing his view that the purpose of education is to unfold "the divine essence of man." Froebel saw the human being as a growing, creative force, and argued that the adult must not attempt to determine the limits to the child's potential growth; he wrote that "it is unspeakably pernicious to look upon the development of humanity as stationary and completed"; education must not make the child "an external dead copy" of the adult generation, but must allow the inner, creative force to express itself. This is an important philosophical basis for whole language approaches; the student is not to be seen as a passive recipient of curriculum, a tabula rasa, but as a purposeful, creative individual who brings to all learning, especially reading and writing, unique personal characteristics and meanings.

Froebel did not intend for the kindergarten to be the child's last chance to learn in a free and nourishing environment; the kindergarten was to become the foundation of a wholly transformed system of education. Unfortunately, in many cases the very opposite has occurred: As educators and parents have grown more concerned about academic "excellence," there has been increasing pressure to hurry young children into academic achievement. Many of the trappings of conventional education, including basal readers and tests, have unfortunately found their way into the children's garden. Froebel would, no doubt, be appalled.

Further Reading

Froebel, Friedrich. 1893. *The Education of Man* (1826). New York: Appleton.

As kids see it

The Big Turtle
by Melissa Rae Gallagher

One day we went fishing. We stayed for two hours. I thought I caught a big fish when I pulled it in I saw that it was a gigantic turtle head. I jumped backwards about six feet. As I thought it was a big snake. We stayed a little bit longer after that. Then we went home. We kept the turtle for one night. The next day we took it up to my Papaw's house and we fried the turtle and we ate it. It was good turtle meat.

Hello my name is Melissa Rae Gallagher. I am eight years old. I live on Walker Park Road. I like to go bowling and swimming. I like pizza, hamburgers, and hotdogs. I got my name from my papaw, uncle, my Uncle Ray, and my cousin Jennifer. When I grow up I want to be a nurse because when my Papaw gets sick my Mom and Dad does too. I want to take care of them all. I love my Mom and Dad and papaw because my Papaw makes me things. My Mom makes me clothes and makes me meals. My Dad makes a living for us. I wish I had a convertable and more puppies and a little brother. My best friends are everyone in my class.

From *Great Mountain Tales,* written by Linda Oxendine's second-grade class, G. R. Hampton School, Barbourville, KY, 1989.

Strategies for Helping Writers

Cornerstone: Barbara Kamler

A Researcher Learns to Listen: Lessons for Conferencing

Most educators are familiar with the term *writing conference* from the work of Don Murray and Don Graves of the University of New Hampshire in the United States. I was fortunate to work with both during my six-month study leave in 1980. I think of the writing conference as a workman-like conversation about writing in progress (Sowers 1982); I think of the writer as an apprentice at the workbench with a master craftsperson, a senior colleague, stopping by once in a while for a quick chat about the work (Murray 1982).

Such chats are short and frequent and imply that the senior colleague also practises the craft of writing. Chats are not search-and-destroy missions. They are not signs to show the apprentice everything he did wrong, nor the time to teach everything he needs to know to perfect his craft.

We know that children learn language because they are amongst people who respond to meaning before form. Consider Rachael, aged three, learning to talk at home. She might be sitting in her high chair yelling "Soo-soo" as she bangs her cup loudly. Because her father has knowledge of the context in which she yells "Soo-soo" (it's lunchtime, they are in the kitchen, the cup is banging), he can figure out her meaning, respond to it, and give Rachael a cup of juice. "Soo" is an essentially meaningless noise. It is far from conventional. This *form* of child language, however, is accepted. The father does not say "Soo-soo" properly, nor does he wait until Rachael can say "juice" before he gives her a drink. He does not, in fact, focus on the *form* of her language at all. Figuring out Rachael's meaning and responding to it are central to this exchange.

Now consider Rachael four years later learning to write at school. Her grandmother has just died. This is Rachael's first encounter with death. She tries to make sense of this experience by writing about it, and her teacher responds thus:

Death

7-5-81
mourn
Heaven
hapiness

I don't think people should ~~I mama ever~~ when people die, because if you know they are going to ~~heaven~~ they will have internal hoppiness while we morn on earth. We will go and see them some day.

Heaven always has a capital letter.

While the absurdity of attending to form before meaning is apparent in the home context, this is not obviously so in the school context. As a three-year-old, Rachael was focussed on meaning. As a seven-year-old, Rachael is still focussed on meaning, on expressing something important to her. The adult/teacher, however, is now focussed on the *form* of language, on *how* the message has been expressed rather than on *what* has been said. Correct spelling, neat, legible handwriting, and punctuation are primary, the message only a vehicle, it would seem, for learning the conventions.

While it might seem ridiculous to hold one set of beliefs about oral language and a completely different set of beliefs about writing, this is more often than not the case among writing teachers. We need to examine the consistency of our beliefs about language.

Here are my beliefs about writing development:

1. Writing development must be viewed as part of a continuous process of language development.
2. Writing is a process of discovering meaning. The child learning to write is learning how to mean in written form.
3. In learning how to mean, the child is constantly constructing and inventing ways to participate with others in the social process of making and sharing meanings.

Learning to conference is not a matter of learning a new recipe, formula, method.

- Learning to conference involves an understanding of how children became language users in the first place.
- Learning to conference involves understanding writing as a process of discovering meaning.
- Learning to conference involves understanding the student writer as an individual who is learning to use language to discover meaning in experience and communicate it.

What's at stake is shifting our attitudes and beliefs about the nature of teaching and learning. The barriers are enormous: Attitudes and beliefs do not shift easily. We have been trained as teachers to be critics and judges, imparters of facts and directors of learning. We do not trust children to learn unless we directly act upon them. Any change depends on putting aside a belief the cognitive psychologist Howard Gruber calls *magical thinking* (Emig 1981).

We wish the child to grow up and in fact he does: We therefore attribute his growth to our own desires and our efforts (Piaget 1980). The questionable causal attribution provides the main justification for adult efforts to educate children.

In recent years we have become increasingly aware that adults do not teach children some of the most fundamental ideas; at best, we help to provide circumstances in which children discover what they must know.

I remember well the first conference I had with Don Murray. I had written about a Stephen Stills concert I had trudged through the New Hampshire snow to watch, and I was ready to get some advice about the piece as well as to "watch the man" in action to see how "real conferencing" was done. The best way I can describe how I felt at the end of our 10 minutes is to say I felt like humming that Peggy Lee tune, "Is That All There Is?"

I remember that I spoke a great deal and Murray said little. I talked about how I had come to write the piece and what I wanted to do. I spoke about Stephen Stills, my distress at the burned-out zombie he had become, my awkwardness sitting with a student audience who had no knowledge of the political history Stills and I shared. Murray listened but I remember him saying I had packed an enormous amount of information into two pages and had I considered making it into a short story. At the time this seemed ridiculous. Getting out two pages was hard enough for me; the idea of a short story was impossible.

I was disappointed in the conference. It seemed to me that nothing happened. I did no further work on the Stephen Stills piece. In the course of that semester, however, I learned the most important thing I have ever learned in my academic life: to have faith in myself as a writer.

I did not know that I could write. But Murray believed I could. He expected a good paper every week and I gave him one.

Two years ago I discovered that I had finally begun to learn how to do the same for my students. I had just run my first writing workshop for teachers, with my colleague Gary Killar, where the teachers spent a week writing a piece for their own satisfaction. Somehow at the end of six days, several of them credited me with having taught them to write, an impossible task in six days. What I did give them, however, was the knowledge and faith that they could write. I shared strategies that were useful to them. I asked hard questions. I expected great writing. I got it.

What then are the lessons I've learned from conferencing?

Primarily, conferencing is not *the answer*. While conferencing is a powerful kind of teaching, there are other teaching formats and strategies to help writers find their own voices and accept responsibility for the writing. It seems to me that attitude and belief are more at stake here than methodology.

- We need to look at the way we talk to writers.
- We need to examine the patterns of interaction in our classrooms.
- We need to examine when, how, and with what information we will enter each individual student's writing process.

We can then begin to conference even before we know how to do it, just as children begin to talk and write even before they know how to do it. Like the language learning process, the teaching process will be developmental and recursive. The only difference is that we *must* also introspect on the process we are going through, as without reflection there will be no growth or change.

We need to be hard on ourselves. We need to examine our beliefs about language and learning. We need to examine the relationship between our theory and our practice.

At the same time we need to be patient with ourselves and realise that such change takes time. We need to beware of easy answers, beware of orthodoxies, and most of all, beware of not listening to kids.

→ See: Bissex, p. 209; Cheney, p. 49; Graves, p. 129; Goodman, p. 208; Hellen, p. 144.

References

Emig, J. 1981. "Non-magical thinking: Presenting writing developmentally in schools." In *The nature, development and teaching of written communication*, vol. II, ed. C. Fredrikson, M. Whiteman, and J. Dominic. Hillsdale, NJ: Lawrence Erlbaum.

Murray, D. M. 1982. *Learning by teaching: Selected articles on writing and teaching*. Portsmouth, NH: Boynton/Cook.

Sowers, S. 1982. "Reflect, expand, select: Three responses in the writing conference." In *Understanding writing: Ways of observing, learning and teaching*, ed. N. Atwell and T. Newkirk. NEPEX.

Excerpted from *A Researcher Learns to Listen: Lessons for Conferencing* (Wagga Wagga, New South Wales: Centre for Teaching & Research in Literacy).

As kids see it

The Writer's Voice
by Melissa Lauren Holtzer

Voice means hearing yourself in a story. Write about something you like, so your audience will hear you in the story. Write something no one else can write.

Melissa Lauren Holtzer is a third-grader at Curtis Estabrook School, Brooklyn, NY. This was contributed by her second-grade teacher, Maureen Powell.

As Teachers See It
by Lucinda Pease-Alvarez

"Ya tuve una conferencia con mí misma":
Conferencing as a Bridge to Self-Reflection

According to Calkins (1986), writing conferences provide us with the kind of support that helps us ask questions of our emerging texts. Experiences with conferences help us develop and internalize thinking and writing skills. To achieve this aim, writing conferences should "teach the writer, not the writing."

Student conferences often mirror the kind of conferencing that involves teachers and students. Student authors begin these conferences by reading their pieces out loud. Listeners receive these pieces by summarizing or paraphrasing what they have heard and commenting on the parts that they liked. Depending on the circumstances, they may ask the author a few questions or offer suggestions. Some authors conclude conferences by making decisions regarding the future of their pieces (e.g., whether or not to revise, the nature of revisions, whether to pursue another topic).

Calkins argues that this kind of predictable format helps the writer internalize the structure of a conference. Once internalized, the writer calls upon the format as he or she reconsiders the emerging text. Despite the predominance of this approach to writing conferences, sometimes students take a critical, almost prescriptive stance toward another student's piece. For example, the peer conferences between Graciela and Irene consisted primarily of suggestions and evaluative remarks that included the following:

"You begin too many sentences with 'My Little Sister.'"

"You need to talk about only one thing, not about all the things you did at Santa Cruz."

"What did the little girl in your story look like?"

"Real people don't talk like that."

"*Le falta emoción.*" (It lacks emotion.)

Graciela and Irene's conferences do not represent the kind of facilitative event that Calkins advocates. Instead of thoughtful questions that direct their attention to a particular technique or process, their conferences are often a litany of specific suggestions. Despite the heavy-handed tone of these conferences, these two girls addressed concerns that writers must face over and over again (e.g., leads, focus, redundancy, description, and plausibility). Moreover, the girls have begun to take on more responsibility for their own writing. They now begin conferences by identifying specific areas where they need help ("*No suena bien por aquí. ¿Tienes algunas ideas?*" [It doesn't sound good here. Do you have any ideas?]). Instead of relying on feedback from others, they even come up with their own solutions (e.g., "*Aquí voy a escribir más descripción de la niña.*" [Here I'm going to write more description of the girl.]) They are no longer so dependent on one another and are now conferencing with other students. They have even gotten to the point of internalizing the conferencing process. Recently, Irene announced "*Ya tuve una conferencia con mí misma.*" (I just had a conference with myself.)

Through the process of talking with teachers and peers about her writing, Irene has reached the point where she is able to reconsider her writing on her own. In short, the conferencing that routinely goes on in her class has contributed to her ability to reflect.

➜ See: Pease-Alvarez, p. 80; Hellen, p. 144; Kamler, p. 140.

Reference

Calkins, L. 1986. *The art of teaching writing.* Portsmouth, NH: Heinemann.

Lucinda Pease-Alvarez is an assistant professor of education at the University of California at Santa Cruz, CA.

 ## Book Note

The Art of Teaching Writing

Lucy McCormick Calkins 1986; 360 pp.; $17.50 Portsmouth, NH: Heinemann

This book, perhaps more than any other available on the market now, has made the pioneering work of Donald Graves accessible to teachers. In 1978, Don and his two research assistants, Lucy Calkins and Susan Sowers, embarked on a study that was to revolutionize what we know about young children and writing. That knowledge is reflected in this book. It inspires as it teaches, challenges as it explains: what to expect from children at different points on the developmental continuum, how to organize and schedule a writers workshop, detailed guidelines for conducting writing conferences, time-tested strategies for working with developing writers, reading-writing connections, and exploring writing across genre and purpose. And throughout, Lucy masterfully interweaves theory with practice, research with classroom vignettes, examples of student writing with her own self-reflections as a teacher of writing.

The result is a book jam-packed with the sort of nuts-and-bolts information teachers need to develop a successful writing program for youngsters in kindergarten through sixth grade, as well as a fascinating personal account of Lucy's evolution as a writing teacher. It's an account that may inspire teachers to take the most important step of all—to become writers themselves.

LBB

 ## Classroom Demonstrations
by Anna Coor

Writing Process Grouping: A Management Strategy

Hands waved all over my first-grade classroom. Voices cried, "Teacher. Teacher." Insistent little fingers tapped me on the back. Eager students held their writing in front of me begging, "Read mine to the class."

This was a typical situation during writing time. My notes showed that I had met often with the children who were most productive and most insistent, and that about half the class was getting little or no attention. Children who were motivated and enthusiastic were developing: writing copiously, revising, editing, publishing. Others were getting left by the wayside.

To develop the sense of shared endeavor, which I had experienced in a writing workshop, with my students, I began to sit down and write with them. We would write together for about 10 minutes. Then I would conference with children for another 10 to 15 minutes. Finally, several of us would share what we had written.

As I insisted upon my need for uninterrupted time, the children learned to focus on their work and to rely upon themselves. In this new working atmosphere, students wrote and shared more than before. Sharing continued to be dominated by the eager, however, and I still needed more individual contact with all the children for conferencing, revision, editing, and assessment.

To achieve this I began to work with one small group at a time, while a second group shared in an activity or lesson directed by my classroom aide or a parent volunteer, and a third worked independently at learning centers around the periphery of the room.

We devoted an hour a day to writing workshop. During that time I worked with each group for 20 minutes. The children and I brought our writing materials to the reading table. As each person arrived at the table, he or she began to write. After about five minutes I would begin to conference with each child as others continued working. During the last few minutes, one or two of us would share with the group.

Conferences could deal with any aspect of the writing. Some children became very involved with revision. Some wanted to edit their final work to perfection. Only a few were satisfied with first draft work. After a brief conference, a child in the writing group might be directed back to his or her desk, where there was more room to spread out for revising, editing, or illustrating.

All but two of the children published at least one book during the three-month period we held small group writing workshops. I conferenced with each child every day. Children began to grasp and incorporate grammatical forms more readily than they had in our whole group workshop. Children participated in all levels of the process: prewriting, writing, revision, editing, and publishing.

I was able to assess each child's development consistently and to give each frequent, appropriate feedback and direction. Peer feedback came as a natural outgrowth of the sum of the children's experiences in the intimate setting of the writing workshop. Sometimes one child would respond to something in another's story, or in literature, developing his or her story in a new and interesting way.

Writing and sharing in small group settings helped to develop a more nurturing and productive atmosphere in my classroom. I became a part of the writing community and was able to attend to the needs of each individual student. Each child was actively engaged in the total writing process and had ample opportunity to share with others.

Working with small groups solved the management problems I had experienced with writing workshop and increased the sense of shared endeavor in my class.

Anna Coor is an elementary teacher at Villa de Paz School, Phoenix, AZ.

 **Classroom Demonstrations**

Writers Workshop Forms

As they initiate a writers workshop, many teachers feel the need for forms to help monitor the process.

—LBB

The three forms below and the one at right are a sampling of teacher-created forms to help kids with peer conferencing:

Conference with a Friend

1. I read my story to:

2. Here is what my friend <u>learned</u> or <u>liked</u>:

3. Here are some <u>questions</u> my friend had:

4. This is what I'm going to do now:

—Contributed by Pam Adair, primary teacher,
Fair Oaks School, Redwood City, CA

First Check

	Writer		Reader	
	Yes	Needs work	Yes	Needs work
Is the message clear?				
Do things go in order?				
The writer likes:				
The reader likes:				
Suggestions for revision:				
Writer: Reader:				

Final Check

	Writer		Reader	
	Yes	Needs work	Yes	Needs work
Spelling:				
Punctuation:				
Capitals:				
Words I need help spelling:				
Other problems:				
Writer: Reader:				

Here is a form middle school teacher Karen Sabers Dalrymple developed to help her keep track of the writing her students do:

Writing Workshop Report

Teacher _____ Grade/Year _____ Student _____

Type of Writing	Quarter 1		Quarter 2		Quarter 3		Quarter 4	
	No. of Pieces	No. Publish	No. of Pieces	No. Publish	No. of Pieces	No. Publish	No. of Pieces	No. Publish
Personal Narrative								
Poetry								
Fiction								
Nonfiction								
Comments:								

Conference Worksheet

Author _____
Response Team 1. _____
2. _____

Directions:

1. The author reads the paper aloud to the team members.
2. The team talks together and writes down what they like about the author's writing.
3. The team writes down questions they have about the author's writing or suggestions as to how the author can improve the story.
4. The author writes down how he or she will change the story to improve it.

A. What did you like about the story? Why did you like these parts?
1.
2.
3.

B. Give the author some suggestions as to how he or she can improve the story. Be specific.
1.
2.
3.
4.
5.

C. The author should write what he or she will do to improve the story.

The student writing folder is the mainstay of writers workshop; the following three forms are from a folder developed in Calgary, Canada, that provides both the teacher and students with a complete record of the writing process as well as the written outcomes:

Personal Writing Folder Record

Card No. _____
Student: _____ Grade: _____

Use the following numbers and letters to complete assignment code sections:

Some Possible Formats
1. Journals/Diaries
2. Biography/ Autobiography
3. Anecdotes
4. Invitations
5. Descriptions
6. Letters (Personal)
7. Letters (Business)
8. Essays
9. Summaries
10. Requests
11. Applications
12. Memos
13. Poems
14. Plays/Skits
15. Stories
16. Fantasies
17. Dialogues
18. Editorials
19. Fact Sheets
20. Newspaper Stories
21. Proposals
22. Songs
23. Poster Displays
24. Reviews (Books)
25. Reviews (Film, TV)
26. Observations
27. Chapter of Novel
28. Interviews
29. Directions
30. Dictionaries
31. Reports
32. Position Statements
33. Booklets
34. Scripts
35. Cartoons
36. Articles
37. Broadcasts
38. Advertisements
39. Legends
40. Tall Tales
41. Monologues
42. Other

Some Possible Roles
A. Self
B. Character in Story
C. Parent
D. Reporter
E. Storyteller
F. Specified Person
G. Scientist
H. Famous Person
I. Object
J. Other

Some Possible Audiences
I. Self
II. Specified Person
III. Specified Group
IV. Friend
V. Classmates
VI. Famous Person
VII. Teacher
VIII. Other Authors
IX. Public
X. Editor
XI. Other

Some Possible Purposes
a. Record
b. Report/Narrate
c. Describe
d. Explain
e. Speculate
f. Summarize
g. Defend
h. Convince/Argue
i. Apologize
j. Request
k. List/Categorize
l. Move
m. Compare/Contrast
n. Imagine

Possible topics for me to write about	My titles	Work in progress	Final draft	Assign-ment code • Format • Roles • Audiences • Purposes	Group or individual project	My personal response to the writing project	Elements I have under control
				G I			

Thinking About My Writing Process

	Record assignment number beside strategies used	My goals as a writer
Prewriting		
Drawing/Diagramming		
Observing		
Listening to Reader		
Listening to Speaker		
Brainstorming		
Reading for Information		
Role Playing		
Interviewing		
Questioning		
Sharing in Small Groups		
Contributing to Discussion		
Viewing Activities		
Exploring Writing		
Note-making		
Story Boarding		
Revising		
Reading Work Aloud		
Listening to Work Read		
Conferencing with Teacher		
Peer-editing		
Individual Revision		
Individual Proofreading		
Sharing		
Taping of Writing		
Displaying of Writing		
Reading Final Drafts		
Publishing Writing		
Dramatizing Writing		
Putting Writing to Use		
Other Sharing		

 **WHOLE LANGUAGE CAMERA**

A student in Sarah Costello's seventh grade reads aloud from his newly-published piece to an appreciative audience, William J. Pistor Middle School, Tucson, AZ.

Resource: Book

Where Do You Get Your Ideas? Helping Young Writers Begin

Sandy Asher
1987; 83 pp.; $12.95
New York: Walker

This book shows how to find ideas for writing stories, plays, and poems with wonderful suggestions by noted authors.

Katy Obringer

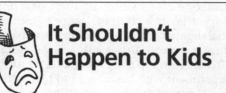 **As Teachers See It**

by Catherine Ousey

Some Thoughts While Reading Students' Work

Many of my colleagues commiserate with me because I am a teacher of language arts to grade six, seven, and eight students. They sympathize with me because of the many student papers I have to read. In his book, *Writing with Power*, Peter Elbow writes about the drudgery of reading pieces by student writers who have not yet acquired the skill of an experienced writer. I feel that way sometimes, of course, especially if the student has not organized the piece for me with punctuation and paragraph breaks. But I get a great deal of satisfaction out of reading the work of students too.

The first challenge for me is to see that piece of work from a writer's point of view, to pick out the successful elements or the skills shown by the writer. And, of course, I must also find the weaknesses. I ask myself: How will this affect the intended reader? Why are certain parts suc-cessful? How can this piece be more successful? What one aspect of this piece can be improved so that the whole piece will be more successful?

After I figure out how the piece can be made more lively or clearer for the reader, I must communicate my evaluation to the writer in a persuasive and positive way. That is the hardest part of my job. For the writer still has the power to make the decisions about his or her own writing. I feel I have done my job if I can present a new idea to a student or help him or her to see another point of view.

And then there *are* some really good pieces written by students. A student will often produce some very exciting writing. Some pieces make me chuckle. Some writing makes my heart ache with the picture it shows me of a student's life, the despair or loneliness. Some pieces intrigue me with the cleverness the writer has shown. I am often touched by my students' writing.

Helping students look more closely at their work encourages growth. It makes me feel important that I may be able to do that. Who knows what effect my evaluation of their work may have? Sometimes I cast my mind to the future wondering what is in store for a particular student. I hold close to my heart the feeling that I may be helping to create a good future for him or her. Perhaps by helping them to feel successful, I can increase their self-confidence and affect their future positively.

➜ See: Brown, p. 133; Crafts, p. 136; Goodman, p. 249; Kamler, p. 140.

Catherine Ousey is a junior high teacher at Nordale School, Winnepeg, Canada.

It Shouldn't Happen to Kids

Cornflakes and Cream

In honor of Mother's Day, a fourth-grade teacher instructed her kids to complete the sentence, "I love my mother because…" Marlene, a writing teacher who travels to schools in the district and works with teachers and writing, came in to help with the assignment. "Please work with that kid," the teacher instructed Marlene, pointing to a small, dark-haired boy in the corner. "Tommy can't do anything right."

Marlene walked over to Tommy, knelt down beside him, and discovered that he had already written, "When my mother isn't home it's like cornflakes and milk. When she *is* home, it's like cornflakes and *cream*—with bananas and strawberries on top."

Marlene was amazed and delighted. "We've got to go show your teacher, Tommy. This is great!" She took Tommy's piece and hurried over to the teacher, who sat at her desk, observing the class at work. "Look at this," said Marlene, handing the teacher Tommy's paper.

The teacher glanced at the paper and then said, "See, I told you he can't do anything right. The assignment was 'I love my mother *because.*'"

—LBB

As kids see it

Writing Is Therapy
by Jason Cetron

Keep writing, keep crying. When you write you might write something sad, and you might start crying. Ignore the crying, and keep writing. If you can't ignore the crying, just keep writing and cry at the same time.

Jason Cetron is a third-grader at Curtis Estabrook School, Brooklyn, NY. This was contributed by his second-grade teacher, Maureen Powell.

Resource: Book

The Young Writer's Handbook

Susan and Stephen Tchudi
1984; 160 pp.; $13.95
New York:
Charles Scribner's Sons

This book covers many aspects of writing, including history, plays, journals, poems, school writing, letters, editing, fiction, and publishing.

Katy Obringer

Resource: Distributor

The Writing Company

P.O. Box 802
Culver City, CA
90232-0802
1-800-421-4246

First the good news about the Writing Company: It carries many important works that secondary whole language educators shouldn't be without, such as books by Ann Berthoff, Peter Elbow, and Toby Fulwiler, as well as Mina P. Shaughnessy's classic, *Errors and Expectations*. The company also carries a variety of desktop publishing software, literary classics on video, and posters. Now the bad news: They sell skill-and-kill worksheets, workbooks, and software. Our recommendation? Get their catalog and, as with all distributors, go for the good stuff.

LBB

Classroom Demonstrations
by Marjorie Coombs

From the Inside Out: Starting with the Main Course

Why begin at the beginning? Writing a story "from the inside out" is a kind of writing my eighth-grade students like. Inside-out writing allows students to concentrate on the excitement first and to invent situations and story lines without the mechanical restraints of producing first a beginning, then a middle, and finally an ending. Sometimes stories written in that sequence contain long introductions and surprisingly short conclusions, because students are tired of writing when they near the end, and their chief goal is to finish. With an inside-out approach, students are free to create a story by dealing with the most dramatic event first, and their imaginations lead to stories that are well paced and balanced, although sometimes farfetched.

Beginning a story in the middle does not mean that the writing lacks either control or logic. It does mean that the control of the writing is given to the student. Students assume responsibility for the development of the topic, including their ideas for a beginning and an ending. Thoughtful sequencing and a logical story line develop naturally.

The assignment is inspired by Margaret Grant, who is a third-grade teacher in Missoula and a teacher/consultant with the Montana Writing Project. Her ideas are based on her own sound research.

"Draw a bull's-eye in the center of the paper," I tell my students, passing out sheets of white typing paper. "Now, imagine that you are in a lonely, deserted place; a dark forest . . . or an old, deserted building . . . or some place where the wind is howling. Think of a person or creature you'd least like to meet there. Put some names in the center of the bull's-eye." Students spend a few minutes writing names: Bigfoot, Count Dracula, a grizzly, a werewolf, a rattler.

"Choose one of the creatures you've listed," I say, "and outside the bull's-eye add the most vivid adjective you can think of to describe the horror of that creature." Robin is absorbed with *Bloom County* books and chooses Bill the Cat, drooling. Catica writes about a dangerous murderer on a lonely street late at night. I am writing too, modeling my own topic on the chalkboard at the front of the class. So far I have considered "tarantula, convict, pit bull," and settled on "ax murderer"; listed "menacing, hostile, sneering," and finally decided on "desperate." I don't erase; I cross out what I don't like and circle what I like.

We share some of our adjectives for a list on the chalkboard. It is okay for students to use someone else's words in their descriptions. I hope that my students' papers look like the chalkboard; that they feel free to change their minds, choose other subjects or descriptions after listening to their classmates' contributions, experiment with language, and play with words.

"Now add a verb," I say. "What do you picture this creature doing? Then add a word or phrase to make the verb stronger. Finally, build the words you have into a powerful sentence." The sentence will become the nucleus of the inside-out story. Once this main component of the situation has been developed, the whole story can be built from it. On the board I add "blocked the doorway" to the desperate ax murderer and then expand the sentence: "There the desperate ax murderer planted himself, blocking the doorway confidently, staring at me with his steely, ice-blue, clear-filmed eyes, his mouth in a sneer."

"Now choose a partner and read your sentence aloud. Ask your partner to read it back to you." It's important for students to hear what they've written, first read by themselves and then by their partner. I want my students to stop frequently to consider the clarity and effect of their writing on their audience.

"Write your reaction to your own sentence: You have put yourself in this situation; what do you do next?" I ask. To my own sentence on the board, I add the following reaction: "I froze. My knees were weak, like jelly. My mouth dried up. I opened it and a little gurgle sounded from far away. I couldn't swallow." After students have written their reactions, I ask them to trade with a partner and read each other's writing, first silently and then aloud. Listening to their words read by someone else gives students some distance from their writing. Frequently, student writers think they've included all the information necessary, because the situation is familiar and clear to them. Students then are given the chance to explain further, adding the details.

Finally, it is time to write the introduction. "How did you get into this situation?" I ask. "What's the setting? Describe it, using sensory images. Make your reader feel and see what it was like." After students have set up the situation, they can arrange the parts of their story in any way they choose. Robin decides to arrange his story with the powerful sentence at the beginning and weave the setting into the narrative. Catica follows the order of the story parts as they have been presented in class and adds a unique ending. Writing from the inside out by starting with the main course provides both direction and incentive for the student authors.

From *Inside Out: Creative Writing in the Classroom*, Utah Arts Council.

Marjorie Coombs is a teacher and the assistant principal at Rowland Hall, St. Mark's Middle School, Salt Lake City, UT.

Breakthroughs
by Mary Hellen

Real Writers, Real Response

Share time, the last 15 to 20 minutes of writing workshop when children shared their pieces, was fairly routine that first year Mary Lou and I worked together. As part of a Chapter 1 in-class delivery model, I collaborated daily with Mary Lou Keirns, a first-grade teacher, during her writing workshop. Through our coaching, the kids made "typical" comments: "I like your pictures," "I like the way you left spaces between your words," "I liked your story." The author enjoyed the praise, but it didn't lead to revising or rethinking of his piece. As the year progressed, we knew the children had learned much about writing, but their questions and comments during share time did not reflect it.

Year two was quite different. Because of the growth we'd seen in the previous class's writing, and because of our growing comfort with the children being in charge of their learning, we set up share time differently. We didn't start the class with definite rules for sharing, for example, "First, you tell the author what you heard. Then you can tell what you really liked about the piece," and so on. The second year we just explained that authors like to get feedback about their writing and to make sure their readers understand their piece, but beyond that, response was open. We wanted children to respond more naturally to writing than they had the first year.

We started by modeling, but we made sure our comments were honest ones. If we didn't understand a part, we asked the author just what he meant. If we loved a part, we told the author specifically what we liked. When the kids made some general remark, we encouraged the author to ask for more information—letting the author know it was up to him to get what he needed from the other children. We also let the author know it was okay to ask for more specific information or clarification.

For example, if the author shared his piece and a child commented, "I liked your story," it was up to the author to ask, "Why?" or "What did you like about it?" We put an end to round-robin responses—when the author sits in the author's chair and quickly calls on one child after another with no thought or talk in between. If a child in the audience made a comment and the author looked confused, we asked the author, "Did you understand what she meant?" or "Did you agree with her?" If the author said no, we followed up with, "Then ask her to tell you more." Other times, when comments were made to the author, we asked him (before he could move on to the next raised hand), "What do *you* think about that?" If he started to talk to Mary Lou or me, we said, "Don't tell me, talk to him."

It wasn't smooth at first—many of our kids weren't used to defending what they said or thinking about their questions. But as the year progressed, share time became our favorite part of the workshop. Mary Lou and I often sat in the back, just watching the children take over another part of their learning. We continued to make comments and ask questions, serving as models for the kids, but we were just part of the group. Authors took charge and demanded help from the listeners. Share time became very purposeful. The author often had a definite area in which he needed help, and once he knew he was in charge, directed all comments toward his goal. When a child in the audience suggested something inappropriate, or made a remark that had nothing to do with the author's request for help, it was not unusual for the author to respond, "*That's* not what I want to do! That doesn't help me!" Kids learned to use share time to get the help they needed, and these skills carried over to other areas like self-conferencing and peer conferencing. As a result, the writing flourished in Mary Lou's room.

I don't believe the second year was magical or the group especially gifted. What we learned from that group of children works with all kids. By trusting that all children, including first-graders, can learn to give honest, helpful feedback to classmates, and by not constraining them with rote "story-starter" responses, great "shares" can happen in any writing workshop. Just as we have to believe that, kids *do* have something to say in their writing, so too, we must believe that, when given the chance, they are quite capable of responding naturally to writing.

➜ See: Alvarez, p. 141; Kamler, p. 140.

Mary Hellen is a Chapter 1 teacher with the Adams Twelve Five Stars Schools, Denver, CO.

Classroom Demonstrations

Classroom Use of Autobiography
by Debby Davies

It worked for the classes I taught winter term, 1989, at Jackson Community College in Jackson, Michigan. My goal was to encourage exploring and expressive writing. I combined four approaches:

1. Use of autobiography to help students make connections between their lives and literature;
2. Use of thematic writing units, entitled Growth, Work, and Change;
3. Use of writing samples that were emotionally accessible: that is, writing in which emotion is important and easily understood; and
4. Defining my role as an enabling member of a learning community.

My students are predominantly white teenagers and returning adults. Many live in rural areas and attended small schools where narrative writing and the "I word" are discouraged. Many are parents, or single parents, and are economically vulnerable. A number have had some sort of trauma in their lives: death of a parent at an early age, sexual or physical abuse, school labeling, an alcoholic parent.

The program resembled Bartholomae and Petrosky's, in *Facts, Artifacts, and Counterfacts*, but with less emphasis on academic discourse.

In a 15-week term, students:

* Freewrote;
* Did response writing, both directed and open-ended (e.g., what do you think you will remember about this text?);
* Wrote autobiographical essays;
* Wrote persuasive papers supported with narrative; and
* Chose one paper to include in a class autobiography.

The material read included:

* Journal samples from Macrorie's *Telling Writing*;
* Oral history (*Smithsonian Collection of American Folklore*);
* Autobiographical excerpts from Alice Walker's essays;
* Contemporary poetry;
* Excerpts from Feldman and Bertzold's *End of the Line* (interviews with autoworkers);
* Excerpts from Terkel's *American Dreams: Lost and Found*; and
* "I search" papers from Macrorie's *The I Search Paper*.

Conferences were held after students handed in initial work; all graded papers could be rewritten until the last week of class; response work was ungraded.

This project worked wonderfully! Students who characterized themselves as "slow" or "poor" readers got through the reading material and wrote their hearts out with well-developed ideas. They exhibited meaningful risk-taking in their writing.

The student anthology made an immediate, dramatic difference. Most students saw their own work "in print" for the first time. They discovered they were in a class where people wrote well.

Students liked it! A survey showed that a majority of students felt the autobiographical material had increased their comfort with the class, their own writing, and other forms of writing. They also felt the "emotionally accessible material" had interested them more than other English class material. No student responded negatively. All but one student said they would recommend the approach.

Students were unusually open about individual writing problems; as a result, progress occurred. They became more authoritative discussing social issues. Some became more political and involved in their education.

I loved this project and will repeat it, using the student anthology from this term as one text. I think the program has implications for empowering writers regardless of age or ability.

→ See: Literature Reference List, p.429.

Further Reading
Bartholomae, D., and A. Petrosky. 1986. *Facts, Artifacts, and Counterfacts*. Portsmouth, NH: Boynton/Cook.
Coles, N. 1986. "Democratizing Literature: Issues in Teaching Working Class Literature." *College English* 48.
Horning, A. 1987. "The Climate of Fear in Teaching Writing." In *Teaching Writing: Pedagogy, Gender, and Equity*, ed. Caywood and Overing. Albany, NY: State University of New York Press.
Rosmer, M. 1987. "Which Reader's Response," *College English* 49.

Debby Davies is a developmental writing teacher at Jackson Community College, Jackson, MI.

Written Conversation
by Margie Leys

As mature writers we know that writing is *not* just speech written down. We know that oral and written language vary in some degree in syntactic patterns, vocabulary, organisation of text, and functions. But we also know that what we learn in one language context (speech) can be useful in another language context (writing). We have learned to apply all we know of oral language usage in our usage of written language.

This written language strategy can be useful for beginning writers and reluctant writers—particularly those who are afraid to take risks both with spelling and the creation of a message (Shelly, a third-grader who refused to write without her bottle of white-out, is a prime example). It can also be used to encourage logical thinking and, with a slight adjustment, provides an interesting "creative" activity for writers of all abilities.

In its simplest form two writers, usually a teacher and a student, converse on paper. This provides an informal and supportive context for writing where the focus is on the message, *not* the surface features of the writing. Also, the audience is available to provide feedback immediately!

The following conversation took place between Kate, a first-year college student, and Amelia, a fourth-grade student. Kate used this strategy for two reasons. One was to "break the ice" with Amelia. As this was their first meeting, it provided Kate with a novel way of introducing herself and learning something about Amelia. And two, it was a nonthreatening way to learn about Amelia's writing and spelling strategies.

As you know, my name is Kate. My last name is Morris. I come from Ganmain. Have you heard of it? It has a fairly well known football team called the Lions. It also has famous Ganmain pies. Have you ever tasted one of them?

yes I have tasted a pie. I now Ganmane. My name is Amelia Sharpe I live 43 brown st.

I don't live in a street. I live on a farm. It is a few miles out of town. We have sheep and wheat crops on our farm. Do you know anybody who lives on a farm? Is there anyone in your family who lives on a farm?

yes I have a mum and a sister. My mum's name is Mary and My Sister's name is Christine. My mum Dvorst Dad. Mum has a Boyfriend He's name is Dave. He live on a fram. Have you any Sister's or Brother's?

A variation that can extend the better writers and yet still support the weaker writers is to have students write conversations in character. For example, after reading Judy Blume's *The Pain and The Great One*, pairs of children wrote as either a parent and The Great One, a parent and The Pain, or as The Great One and The Pain to extend the story. Following is a portion of a conversation between the father and The Pain.

Daddy, do you love me more than The Great One?
We love you both the same.
Why does The Great One get to play blocks?
You do too.
Why does The Great One get to use the phone?
Because she knows how to use it.
I can count the numbers on the phone too.
But how come you always get the wrong number?
Because the operator can't count like me.

The creation of this entertaining and perceptive dialogue required the children to draw on their daily experiences at home and school, their understanding of the story, of the flow of conversations, of how to create a written message and of the conventions of written language. In short, they had to use what they knew about how language works in both the oral and the written forms. As with the previous example, they were writing in an informal and supportive context, and it was their message that mattered, not the surface features of the product.

MarvELous INVenTioNs

End of Conversation

A written conversation that Yetta initiated with her grandson, Aaron, age six, ended abruptly:

My name is Yetta
I work at the university
I have an office at the University of Arizona.
I do't not wait to paly this game
[I do not want to play this game]

What game do you want to play? hedi and go cek
[Hide and go seek]

→ See: Bird, p. 216; Literature Reference List, p. 429; Nelms, p. 248.

Note: Written conversation was developed by Dr. Carolyn Burke at Indiana University.

Further Reading
Bean, Wendy, and Chrystine Bouffler. 1987. *Spell by Writing*. PETA.
Brennan, Mark. 1986. "Talkwrite: The Gentle Art of Written Conversation." Wagga Wagga, New South Wales: Centre for Teaching & Research in Literacy.

Resource Essay

Teachers & Writers Collaborative

by William Bryant Logan

The first thing I learned when I started to work for Teachers & Writers Collaborative three years ago was that teaching writing is hard on the knees. If I am not dancing in front of the blackboard, trying to keep up with the flow of lines shouted out for a collaborative poem, I am jumping from chair to chair asking questions, encouraging, suggesting alternative approaches. And here on a spring morning, when masses of dandelion seeds were invading the classroom through an open window, was a fifth-grade girl who had written "the sun rising over the horizon."

"Well, that's true," I said. "Do you want it to rise over something more specific? Think about it."

I leaped away, my knees crackling, and on my next circuit, remembered what I'd asked. By the expectant look on her face, I figured she'd got the sun coming up over the windowsill or the red mailbox. This is what she'd written: "the sun rising over the continuous universe."

Hallelujah.

Every one of the more than 400 writers, filmmakers, artists, and dancers (plus one radio personality) who have worked through Teachers & Writers (T&W) in New York area schools over the last two and a half decades has a fund of similar stories. They might collectively be titled "Reasons to Go On." At the least, they are the source of energy that has made the Collaborative able to survive and prosper.

T&W began in 1967, on a $78,000 grant from the Office of Education, thanks in large part to the drive and outright pushiness of maverick educator Herbert Kohl, T&W's original director. It was the first organization to send poets and writers into the schools for extended residencies. It also made use of the journals that resident writers were required to keep, created "living textbooks" to accompany the writers into the classrooms, and helped teachers teach writing.

Other, ancillary goals have fallen by the wayside, but these four have kept T&W a vibrant enterprise. The reason may be that they form a recirculating set: experimentation, verification, reflection, publication. As large a part as T&W plays in daily teaching—T&W writers are working with over 8,000 students right now—the wider application of its work comes through the fine, hands-on publications that it produces, things like the two *Whole Word Catalogues*, Meredith Sue Willis's *Personal Fiction Writing*, Alan Ziegler's two-volume *The Writing Workshop*, Inky Penguin's *The Writing Book* and its Spanish version, *El libro de la escritura*, the collaboratively composed *Handbook of Poetic Forms* (which spawned a radio show and audiotapes), and the award-winning *Teachers & Writers Magazine*. T&W's *Publications Catalogue* lists more than 35 T&W-published titles and an equal number of volumes from other publishers, including important books by Teachers & Writers veterans, like Herbert Kohl's *36 Children*, Kenneth Koch's *Wishes, Lies and Dreams*, and Phillip Lopate's *Being with Children*.

"Living textbooks" is not a bad description for T&W volumes, since unlike many education titles, they are records and suggestions drawn from the daily experience of writers teaching.

Any teacher wants something that will "work." The central question for T&W's efforts is, "What does it mean for ideas to 'work'?" Or put more baldly, "What are we doing here anyway?" T&W writers have a very free hand in the schools, so it's impossible to give a pat answer. Still, if there is a consensus, it is this: We are not training little poets or novelists. We are trying to help kids make the connection between their own living experience, the language they speak, and the language they write. This is the link that makes a line or a paragraph sing, that infuses the sense of reality with wonder, that makes for true clarity and precision. Furthermore, it gives the child a feeling of power and worth that is hard to match in other activities, particularly after his or her writing is set in type in an anthology and given to the child to take home, as happens at the conclusion of every series of workshops.

With these ends in view, T&W writers and artists will try anything. When I first applied to teach, veteran Dan Mack told me to consider all the kinds of writing I do. "Look," he said, "why not propose something to do with journalism or translation? If Nancy [the director] thinks it will fly, she'll let you do it." Mack should know. He had helped organize and produce a kid-written and spoken radio show out of P.S. 75 in Manhattan, while his wife Teri oversaw the creation of films scripted, acted, and shot by children at the same school. Some of the latter ended up at a film festival at New York's Bleecker Street Cinema. Another T&W project, a dramatic work, became the Emmy-winning CBS documentary *We Don't Act Our Age*. On another front, T&W writers involved in the General Electric Science Writing Project, produced the volume *The Art of Science Writing*. Then there was the dance that involved children creating costumes to make themselves a part of the human body, so that in the course of the performance, the dispersed members might finally turn into a few complete humans, who dance together. Or the bilingual workshop where the students were found one day trying to create and repeat elaborate Spanish tongue twisters. Recently Stephan O'Connor, the current head of the long-running P.S. 75 project, organized a public reading that matched his best students with established adult writers, to the delight of both.

The most elusive and sought-after of the Collaborative's four goals, however, is contained in its own name: Teachers & Writers Collaborative. This was the link that Kohl had insisted upon back in 1966. Today it takes the form of teacher workshops organized as part of ongoing residencies or as special events, and of course it happens through the publications. But the real exchange that makes these possible must take place in the classroom.

The teacher-writer relationship can be full of jealousy, feelings of inadequacy on both sides, and passivity. Or it can be glorious. Recently I got to work with a very committed teacher at P.S. 84 in Manhattan. She wrote right along with her class, earnestly and well. I like to think I brought some lightness and surprise to the skills that she was already developing in them. But one morning, when I'd come in with a poem I loved about travel to an exotic place and was bulling along about it in front of 26 bewildered faces, she cut me off. "You see, what Mr. Logan means is," she said, "how will you get to this strange, new, wonderful place?" That day, three of the least active members of the writing class suddenly produced terrific work, based on the one idea she had articulated so clearly. She taught me a lesson in tempo and relaxation that will take me a long time to master, but once I've got it, I can teach it too.

➜ See: Horton, p. 74.

William Bryant Logan is a writer-in-residence at the Cathedral of St. John the Divine and works for Teachers & Writers Collaborative, New York, NY.

Four Days

We were studying the first act of *Othello*. The discussion centered on Iago's pathological jealousy and paranoia. As evidence for this I focused on

And it is thought abroad that 'twixt my sheets (Othello) has done my office. . . .

"Anybody understand that?" Blank. So I start taking it apart. What does 'twixt mean? If *office* is understood as duty or a job, what now?

"Oh, I get it," shouts Carol from the back of the room and starts cackling loudly. She explains to her tablemate the sexual connotations as she scribbles in her book the interpretation she has grasped.

"Hey, this stuff would be terrific," she says, "if it was in English."

Excerpted from "Four Days," a selection from *The Year of the Teacher,* a book-length manuscript.

—Marvin Hoffman, former director of Teachers & Writers Collaborative and author of *Vermont Diary* (T&W)

Book Note

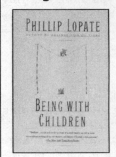

Being with Children

Phillip Lopate
1989; 400 pp.; $9.95
New York: Poseidon Press, a division of Simon & Schuster

This classic is a vivid account of a writer's experience teaching writing to children in a Manhattan elementary school (in a program sponsored by Teachers & Writers Collaborative): the visionary principal; the harassed but courageous teachers; and the children, white, black, Latino, children of university professors and the streetwise children of parents on welfare, all struggling to express their true and interesting experience of the world. Lopate's hilarious and poignant adventures are touching, powerful, always alive. This edition features a new afterword by the author.

❝ Learning by Doing is a credo so deeply absorbed into the American educational ideology that it has become axiomatic, like the law of gravity. It has had the effect of making activity appear to be a positive good: so long as the kids are busy doing something, the quality and meaning of the experience are to some degree assumed. Learning by doing has a good deal of common sense behind it. Where the thinking goes wrong is in forgetting to ask (as in our national involvement in Vietnam): What are we doing exactly? Why should I do this? How does my little job connect to the other parts of the process? Who is going to use this thing I am doing, and toward what end?

"Learning by doing, while good as far as it goes, is short on preliminary analysis and shallow on ethics, and it lacks historical perspective.❞ (p. 327)

It Shouldn't Happen to Kids

Meeting Louis Untermeyer
by Francelia Butler

When I was about 10, my mother and father took me to Cleveland, Ohio, to see Louis Untermeyer, the anthologist and poet who was autographing books in Halle Brothers Department Store. Beaming, they brought me up to the celebrity, who was sitting at a small table with a stack of books beside him.

"My daughter writes poetry, too," my father announced proudly.

"Oh, she does!" Mr. Untermeyer exclaimed. "Then tell her to sit down and write me a poem."

I felt like the Miller's daughter must have felt in "Rumpelstiltskin" when her father boasted that she could weave straw into gold. I panicked.

"Do as you're told," Father said.

"Just a short one," Mother added. "Do it right now."

I wrote down something and I knew it was dreadful. My brain, my hands, and my heart were frozen.

"Now take it to Mr. Untermeyer," Mother commanded. I even had cold feet. I could barely shuffle across to his table and push the paper before him.

He took a look at the piece of paper. His face was expressionless.

Just then, Father came up with the book he had purchased. Mother and Father waited expectantly while Mr. Untermeyer autographed it.

"Just look what Mr. Untermeyer wrote," Mother exclaimed. "Now aren't you glad we made you write that poem he wanted?" She read the inscription out loud:

To Francelia—
Sure that she will become the poet she deserves to be.
                    Louis Untermeyer

My parents thought it was a good omen of my poetic future. It was the last poem I ever wrote.

From *Teachers & Writers* 18(2), November/December 1986.

—Francelia Butler, editor-in-chief of *Children's Literature* (Yale University Press) and professor of English, University of Connecticut, Storrs, CT

Resource: Book

Return of the River of No Return

This is a stimulating collection of poetry—one of which is reprinted here—written by students and teachers in Salmon, Idaho, during 1989 while working with two writers-in-residence from Teachers & Writers Collaborative.

Students and Teachers of Salmon, Idaho
Teachers & Writers Collaborative
5 Union Sq. W.
New York, NY 10003
1-212-691-6590

Beverly Lozoff

 As Teachers See It

Memory
by Julie Patton

I believe that you can't force kids to connect with an idea in a real way unless you find a way to put it in their bodies—center it so that they want to dance with it, feel it as something profound or mysterious.

In dealing with the idea of cultural legacy, I wanted to work with and around the idea of memory as something whole, organic. Where does memory reside? Can you say that the earth has a memory and that we are a part of it, a part of everything that has ever happened on this planet? How are we a part of it? We talked about body memory—genetic memory—and what we sense through hands and fingers, what we remember hearing, smelling. You know an orange the minute you smell it. I ask, what does the river remember, how does it flow through you, become you, connect you to the earth; and what does this earth remember?

From *Time Made My Grandmother's Hair Turn Grey*, Teachers & Writers Collaborative, 1989

To me, heritage and legacy are about developing a reference point—a point from which to take in the whole world before focusing on our own threads of personal history. With my fourth-graders we began with memories; the third-graders began with "Nothingness" and worked their way forward.

Julie Patton is a writer-in-residence at Community School District 5, Arts in Harlem Project.

 **writers**

Poem
by Bessie Babits

I used to be afraid of our stove
that looked like a dragon
Under my bed little white puffs that had fangs
When my closet was open
and all alone

But now I'm afraid of
nothing except liver
and the wind and knives
strangers & the carrot peeler

From *Return of the River of No Return*, Teachers & Writers Collaborative, 1989.

Bessie Babits is in third grade at the Pioneer School in Salmon, ID.

Resource: Book

Time Made My Grandmother's Hair Turn Grey

Teachers & Writers Collaborative
5 Union Sq. W.
New York, NY 10003
1-212-691-6590

This anthology represents the eleventh year of the Arts in Harlem Project, a cooperative endeavor between Teachers & Writers Collaborative and Community School District 5 in New York City. Emphasis in this 1989 anthology was placed on fostering "the creative imagination and language as an art." An additional focus was one combining research in personal and cultural history with creative writing.

Beverly Lozoff

Book Note

The Whole Word Catalogue

Rosellen Brown, Marvin Hoffman, Martin Kushner, Phillip Lopate, and Sheila Murphy, editors
1972; 72 pp.; $8.95

The Whole Word Catalogue 2

Bill Zavatsky and Ron Padgett, editors
1977; 352 pp.; $16.95
Teachers & Writers Collaborative
5 Union Sq. W.
New York, NY 10003
1-212-691-6590

The best collection of ideas, themes, materials, and strategies for developing writing I've seen.
Herbert Kohl

YOUNG ARTISTS

From *Return of the River of No Return*

As Teachers See It

by Judith Kalman

Exploring Revision with Kindergartners

Any adult who has spent time with young children knows what active learners they are. They meticulously pour water or sand into measuring cups over and over again; they draw outer space-like creatures time after time; and they diligently count bottle tops, little bunnies, and anything else they can get their hands on. They seem to know that experience is not a one-shot deal and that learning best takes place as a result of it.

And anyone who has spent time with young children also knows how outrageously creative they are, unafraid to explore and try new things and ways of doing them. Pink bows for elephants, long spider fingers, rainbows that follow people around wherever they go are common fare. Nobody teaches them those things and yet they do them all! They have neat explanations for everyday events. When I asked one of my kindergartners where rain goes he answered matter-of-factly, "It all runs down a big hole and falls out the other side of the ground!"

For years we have celebrated their drawings, their speech, and their explanations, but we have assumed that young children can't write on their own. We think that they are waiting for an adult to teach them how. They need letter shapes, letter names, and letter sound correspondence step by step before they can write anything at all.

Actually, the young child's exploration of written language comes from the same enthusiasm he or she has for exploring anything else. Young children have been showing those researchers and teachers who have taken the time to watch just how capable of writing they are. They create stories (Graves 1983, Calkins 1986); they relate pictures and plot (Dyson 1988); they discover the rules of the writing system (Ferreiro and Teberosky 1979); they reflect on written language (Goodman 1980); and they use writing in a functional manner, creating signs, lists, instructions, and letters (Bissex 1980).

How do children learn to do these things? The same way they learn to do anything else: through multiple attempts at writing and approximations of language written by others. Through their struggle learning takes place. Any written product represents their knowledge at a given moment in time. As their understanding deepens, their writing is transformed.

Revision and Teaching Writing

Of all the concepts developed to explain the writing process, the one that intrigues me the most is revision. Somehow, the idea of going back to something that I have already done, trying to look at it from another point of view, rethinking it and doing it again, neatly summarizes the learning process itself.

Response groups, revision partners, and multiple drafts sound great for intermediate primary kids and junior and senior high-schoolers, but are they really relevant for the early primary years?

When I considered proposing revision to my students, the first thought that came to my mind was how "here and now" they are. I wanted to try to tap the involvement that the children display in their experiential play during writing activities. I wanted them to write and rewrite in the same way that they measure sand over and over again. I thought that if I could somehow keep their writing alive over a couple of days, they would go back to it and work on it some more. I hypothesized that if I could show them a way to redo some parts without copying the whole thing over, then they would be willing to take that second look and revise.

Revision in My Kindergarten Class

A frequent activity in my classroom is book-making. Children are encouraged to write about anything they want or about some topic that we are currently working on. When I decided to introduce revision we were working on a unit about animals. We had read many animal stories, fiction and nonfiction; we had drawn animals on a big piece of butcher paper; we had classified animals by the way they were born, where they lived, and what they liked to eat. On this particular day I handed out little books that I had made for them. At the top of each page was a symbol suggesting the different ways we had classified animals. I had also made a big book with the same symbols at the top of each page. We discussed what they might write in their books about animals.

As children wrote in their books, I walked around the classroom, talking to children about their pictures and stories and listening to them read their writing. (I like to write down what they read in light pencil on their page, but only after they have written it themselves.) I praised their writing and shared my way of writing with them. When they were finished I picked up their books and carefully put them away for the next day.

When the children went home I looked at the books carefully. The children had done different things with the same assignment. Some had chosen one animal and written their whole book about it. Others had chosen a different animal for each page. I tried to find something in each book that could be revised.

The following day I used the books for a minilesson with a small group. We read each book, praised each author, and talked about their favorite parts. Then I handed back the books. I suggested that perhaps there were some parts they would like to redo. Maybe there was a picture that they wanted to finish or color. Maybe they wanted to add a page or make a cover. We looked at the books again one by one and tried to think what could be done to make them better.

Then I presented the children with cards that I had cut a bit smaller than the pages in their books. I suggested that they could use these cards to revise their books and that we would staple them in the right place when they were done. Most of the children readily accepted this challenge while a few expressed a certain unwillingness to try. But once they were all seated, they began to work intently.

Two Examples

Four pages from the first version of Michele's book are shown below:

A bear is brown.

There is a monkey in the cage.

A cat is born from its mother.

The bear eats fish.

When given the opportunity to revise, Michele added many pages, some new and others replacing existing pages, to her second version.

A bear.

A bear is brown.

There is a monkey in the cage

A cat is born from its mother.

Michele made two important modifications to her text. First, she changed her pictures, replacing one that she had hastily scribbled with a cleaner drawing. But what I found more exciting was how she systematically went back to her book, practically page by page, and added information to it. Although her use of the writing system is far from conventional, Michele remembered what each page was about and added a new thought to it.

Nick also did a very good job of revising his text. On each page he had only scribbled in a picture and a word or two, as if he were answering some of the questions we talked about. His first version looked like this:

Ju (Bear)

Ho (Mountains)

That was it. I was amazed because Nick usually worked intensely at writing, and this time he seemed to be very disinterested. When he revised his text, I was in for a big surprise. He carefully rewrote two of the four pages with invented spelling and near conventional usage, and he added information and details. His second version looked like this:

BAR R FRE
(Bears are furry.)

I U (Mountains)

HO (Born alone.)

BAR ET FESTE
(Bears eat fish.)

In their revisions Michele and Nick went way beyond what I expected them to do. They were more than willing to take another look at their books, think about them, and extend their writing or rewrite parts. Their revisions revealed

Questioning Spelling

 As Teachers See It

by Marty Morgenbesser

The Right Notes

A while back I learned to play the accordion from a musician by the name of Jehan Paul. "JP," as he is known in folk circles, is a colorful character who lives in a van somewhere in Mendocino County. "Wheel Estate," he calls it. JP also happens to be one of the best button accordion players on the West Coast. He plays by ear, and teaches that way, playing a tune over and over, while you play along.

One morning, JP was teaching a rather intricate Tex-Mex tune. I was struggling to keep up. In frustration I lamented, "I can't play it right!" JP's advice was simple, "Just play the wrong notes, but don't lose the beat."

Later it hit me: That's the same advice I give the children when they get frustrated because they're not sure how to spell a word. "Spell it the best way you can, but keep writing."

JP went further, however. With just the right touch of Zen, he posed the rhetorical question, "Who's to say what the right notes are?" Considering the differences between American and British dictionaries, the same query might be raised with respect to spelling.

→ See: Morgenbesser, p. 210.

Marty Morgenbesser is a primary teacher at San Miguel School, Santa Rosa, CA.

Book Note

Spel...Is a Four-Letter Word

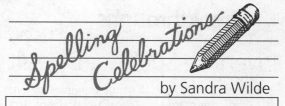

J. Richard Gentry
1987; 56 pp.; $6
Portsmouth, NH: Heinemann

In a short, readable book, Gentry examines myths about the teaching of spelling and questions traditional practices. His advice for parents helped me get up the courage to tell parents I was not going to teach spelling this year. Not a single parent has made a fuss, and the growth in children's spelling is very obvious.

Caryl Crowell

❝Children move through developmental stages of invented spelling as they move through developmental stages of speech. Parents should understand that invented spelling doesn't lead to the formation of bad spelling habits. When children encounter new information about standard spelling, they readily modify their hypotheses and have no difficulty adopting standard spelling. Ultimately, the expert speller is able to use information from visual memory, as well as knowledge of phonetic, contextual, and meaning relationships to determine the correct spelling of a word. But the process takes time. Important foundations of learning to spell are set with the use of invented spelling. ❞ (p. 39)

Book Note

Children's Categorization of Speech Sounds in English

Charles Read
Urbana, IL: National Council of Teachers of English
1975; 189 pp.; out of print; available from:
ERIC Clearinghouse Language and Linguistics

Children's Creative Spelling

Charles Read
1986; 192 pp.; $35
New York: Chapman & Hall

Any teacher who is interested in learning how we first came to understand children's invented spelling should read Charles Read's classic monograph, *Children's Categorization of Speech Sounds in English*, which was based on his doctoral dissertation. Read was primarily interested in exploring how children classified the speech sounds of English, and happened upon several children who had begun writing with their own spellings before starting school. He was able to provide a linguistic explanation for spellings such as SEK (sink), CHRAC (truck), and CIDEJCHES (cottage cheese). As a result of his work and that of Carol Chomsky, who also wrote about invented spelling in 1970, writing in the elementary school classroom has changed dramatically: Teachers now realize that when children use their own spellings they not only can write more fluently but are exploring and hypothesizing about the spelling system itself. Although Read's monograph is somewhat technical, and easier to understand if you have some background in linguistics, it is important reading for anyone who is interested in one of whole language's important research foundations.

Read's 1986 follow-up, *Children's Creative Spelling*, is a nice summary of his work and that of other researchers, including studies of dialect and spelling and of spelling in other languages. He concludes with an overview of current theory about spelling development, as well as a few suggestions for parents and teachers. He also provides an excellent bibliography.

Sandra Wilde

---

their knowledge about the subject, about the writing system, or about their sense of audience.

Teachers should understand that the most important part of doing revision with emergent writers is not the finished product but the experience the children get from trying to revise. The ways they revise are many: They color, add on, rewrite, delete, or do a combination of these. All their revisions are valid, reflecting thought, learning, and knowledge.

→ See: Kalman, pp. 34, 245.

References

Bissex, G. 1980. *GNYS AT WRK: A child learns to read and write.* Cambridge: Harvard University Press.

Calkins, L. 1986. *The art of teaching writing.* Portsmouth, NH: Heinemann.

Dyson, A. 1988. *Drawing, talking, writing: Rethinking writing development.* Berkeley, CA: Center for the Study of Writing.

Ferreiro, E., and A. Teberosky. 1979. *Los sistemas de escritura en el desarollo del niño.* Mexico City: Siglo Veintiuno Editores.

Goodman, Y. 1980. "The roots of literacy." Keynote address presented at the annual Claremont Reading Conference.

Graves, D. 1983. *Writing: Teachers and writers at work.* Portsmouth, NH: Heinemann.

Judith Kalman is currently working toward a Ph.D. at the University of California at Berkeley.

 **writers**

The Real Importance of Spelling

by Lee Wayne Shainen

Writing is magic
reaching into chaos
bringing forth thought

in imitation
of the word
made flesh.

Magic.

God and man
casting spells exactly
to make it so.

→ See: Shainen, p. 127.

Lee Wayne Shainen is a freelance writer, performance poet, and substitute teacher living in Tucson, AZ.

Spelling Celebrations

by Sandra Wilde

Invented Spellings: Low-Frequency Words

We went to the *PLANA TEREUM* (Planetarium) . . . We went on the *ESKLADER* (escalator) . . . We had *CEREL* (cereal) with *BANNAS* (bananas) and *STRAWBEERRS* (strawberries).

Anna, 4th grade

Anna used the italicized words above only once during her fourth-grade writing. They are also long and fairly difficult words. It should come as no surprise that, just as children are very successful in spelling the words they use most often, they are likely to produce invented spellings for words they have never used before. This means that, unless their vocabulary growth stagnates, children are likely to continue to have a small proportion of invented spellings in their writing. This is not a problem! As children continue to read widely, they will become familiar with the written forms of more of the words that are already in their speaking vocabulary. As they develop strategies for finding out the spellings of words, they will get better at correcting spellings for final-draft writing.

As I See It:
Kenneth S. Goodman

Dictionaries in Whole Language Classrooms

Those who have been persuaded to think well of my design, will require that it should fix our language, and put a stop to those alterations which time and chance have hitherto been suffered to make in it without opposition. With this consequence I will confess that I flattered myself for a while; but now begin to fear that I have indulged expectation which neither reason nor experience can justify. When we see men grow old and die at a certain time one after another, from century to century, we laugh at the elixir that promises to prolong life to a thousand years; and with equal justice may be lexicographer derided, who being able to produce no example of a nation that has preserved their words and phrases from mutability, shall imagine that his dictionary can embalm his language, and secure it from corruption and decay, that it is in his power to change sublunary nature, and clear the world at once from folly, vanity, and affectation.

—Samuel Johnson, *A Dictionary of the English Language*, 1755

Those who have made dictionaries have always known, as Samuel Johnson did, that dictionaries record meanings in current use; they don't establish meaning or preserve the language. Neither do they establish spellings. Noah Webster did manage to change some spellings when he published his American English dictionary. But that's because he was one of a group of literary leaders who wanted to make American literature easy to distinguish from the British. They led a movement to make American spelling different in words like centre/center, colour/color, and jewellery/jewelry. But that was an exception. Most of the time the job of the dictionary maker is to record the standard spellings.

Dictionaries and other resource books like thesauri and encyclopedias are useful in whole language classrooms. Most whole language teachers try to have several dictionaries that vary in complexity and size. Pupils need to have easy access to these. One way is to put them on a movable cart with other reference material. The dictionary can help confirm what a pupil thinks a word means. It can confirm the standard spelling(s) of a word. It can, for what it's worth, suggest the history of a word. And it can indicate at least one possible pronunciation, though that may vary from dialect to dialect.

But teachers need to help pupils understand that dictionaries are limited too. Even very complete ones can't include every insect species, every fruit variety, or every technical meaning particular to a certain science or discipline or even hobby. They can't include all the dialect variations in meaning or keep up with the constantly changing current slang. Nor can dictionaries tell the precise meaning of a word in a given context. Words contribute to the meaning of a whole sentence, paragraph, or story. But the meaning of the whole is much more than the sum of the meanings of the words. The meaning of any given word depends on the meaning of the whole.

Other resource materials, no matter how useful, are also limited. A five-year-old encyclopedia is out of date when it comes to the moons of Neptune or cancer-causing foods. When dictionaries or other resources are prepared for young people, the editors deliberately exclude many things to simplify their use. Theirs is only an educated guess about what to put in and what to leave out.

The best time to help pupils learn how to use these resources is when the information they contain is needed to write or research the answers to questions or solutions to problems. Meaningless, detached assignments that teach "reference skills" prior to their use are of little value. They're unlikely to lead to increased or effective use. But in the context of needing information, learners will respond to learning how to use reference materials. Whole language makes kids conscious of both the utility and the limitations of reference materials. And that would, no doubt, please Sam Johnson. Probably Noah Webster, too.

Breakthroughs
by Elizabeth Schmar

Inventive Spelling: Does It Really Work?

I met my first skeptical whole language parent at fall open house. I had been preparing myself for this meeting, because I know parents need convincing just as I needed convincing. My explanations of journals, big books, and book buddies were well rehearsed. But when I came to inventive spelling, I could see a look of disbelief cover Alicia's mother's face like a dark cloud.

I went on to explain how children's spelling develops gradually, just like their speaking and reading. As the children write and read more, they become aware of words and their spelling. The children are moving toward correct spelling. All the while we emphasize the writing of ideas rather than the exactness of spelling.

Alicia's mother quickly raised her hand and said, "I really do not think this new way of spelling is going to work. When I was in school, I hated spelling! I received terrible grades in spelling, and to this day I am not a good speller. I do not think just writing whatever you want to is going to teach Alicia how to spell."

I asked Alicia's mother if she had learned to spell with workbooks and spelling lists. She nodded her head yes, but with a look of disgust at the thought of memorizing endless lists of meaningless words. I explained, "Alicia will be learning to spell words as she needs to use them in writing and reading. The words will be important to her, so she will gradually learn to spell them."

I could tell that Alicia's mother was only pacified for the moment. Her look of skepticism still remained. I decided I needed some evidence to convince Alicia's mother and myself of the growth through inventive spelling.

I randomly selected 10 words from the spelling book, which we were not currently using. These words were used as a spelling test to record the progress of spelling development. The children were orally given the words and asked to try their best at written spelling. This list was given at the end of each quarter. The following examples show Alicia's growth in spelling during first grade.

October	January	March	May
can	can	can	can
did	did	did	did
run	run	run	run
kep	keep	keep	keep
go	go	go	go
kyt	kut	qut	kutt (cute)
lik	like	licke	like
cam	came	came	came
fom	from	from	from
so	snow	sonw	snow

I shared this information with Alicia's mother at parent-teacher conferences in the fall and spring and at the end of the year. She was thrilled to see Alicia's progress in reading and writing, and described herself as a "whole language convert."

I was also thrilled to have written evidence of spelling development. What I believed so strongly about spelling could actually be seen by others. Because the growth could be followed easily, I shared the four lists with children, parents, and an administrator.

The children were pleased to actually see their improvement over the year. We discussed their uncertainty about spelling at the beginning of the year, and their gain of confidence as the year progressed. I emphasized that each word may still not be spelled exactly, but they are constantly improving in spelling development.

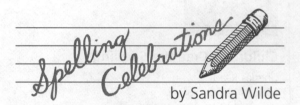
by Sandra Wilde

Patterns and Strategies: Dictionaries and Definitions

Little Nife got *SACRED* (scared) when his farther (father) said that he can cary (carry) the deer with him.

Gordon, 4th grade

At first glance, this appears to be just a permutation, a flipping of two of the letters in the word *scared*. But having watched Gordon write this, I know what *really* happened! On his first try at writing *scared*, he wrote *SCERE*, then erased it, commenting, "I used to know how to write it, but I forgot how to spell it." He then got a dictionary, began skimming all the words starting with s and stopped when he got to *sacred*, copying it onto his paper. When I asked him how he knew he'd chosen the right word, he began reading the definitions (which he hadn't looked at yet). His face lit up as he looked up and said, "See! It says right here that they 'play scary music in church.'"

The parents seemed to appreciate a display of growth that is easily understood, as opposed to standardized test scores and grades. The administrator considered this evidence as further justification for not using spelling books. And I gained confidence in my philosophy about spelling instruction and grew in my conviction of the appropriateness of whole language.

➜ See: Busch, p. 152; Goodman, p. 252; Kalman, p. 34.

Elizabeth Schmar is an elementary teacher at Elmont School, Seaman District, Topeka, KS.

Classroom Demonstrations

by Sandra Wilde

Classroom Demonstrations

by Jane G. Lambert

Spelling's Greatest Hits: A Top Twelve List

Teachers often ask me what would be useful for them to read about spelling. Although a lot has been written about the topic, it's not always easy to sort out which is truly worthwhile, since so many books and articles about spelling have focused on how often to test, what words to memorize, and other issues that aren't really consistent with a whole language approach. This list of references is meant to be provocative rather than comprehensive: a selection of articles and books that will get you to think about English spelling and how it might be learned, and to see how it has been thought about in the past. The references have been arranged chronologically.

"The Influence of Past Experiences Upon Spelling," by Ernest Horn. *Journal of Educational Research* 19 (1929). This article is a fascinating historical document. Horn talks about how complex and phonetically unpredictable our spelling system is, and includes dozens of invented spellings of the words *circus, tease,* and *miscellaneous,* thereby proving that invented spelling didn't suddenly evolve in the 1970s!

"Word Frequency as a Factor in Learning to Read and Spell," by Gertrude Hildreth. *Journal of Educational Research* 41 (1948). Hildreth, sounding surprisingly contemporary, talks about how spelling curriculum should focus on helping children spell the words they want to write rather than on memorizing long lists of words that they seldom use. The article includes a wonderful graph showing how infrequently most words are used.

The Structure of English Orthography, by Richard L. Venezky. (The Hague: Mouton, 1970). Although this is not a book to read at one sitting, and is most accessible to readers who know a little about linguistics, it's the best reasonably short description of the English spelling system available.

"Dialect and the Teaching of Spelling," by Frederick H. Brengleman. *Research in the Teaching of English* 4 (1970). This article is also somewhat difficult, but it's an important discussion on how spelling reflects *all* dialects by representing a level deeper than that of pronunciation.

"Pre-School Children's Knowledge of English Phonology," by Charles Read. *Harvard Educational Review* 41 (1971). This classic article explains why young children spell the way they do and shows that their spellings are phonetically based rather than random. The whole invented spelling movement grew out of this article.

"Write Now, Read Later," by Carol Chomsky. In *Language in Early Childhood Education,* edited by Courtney B. Cazden (Washington, DC: Association for Education of Young Children, 1971). Roughly contemporaneously with Charles Read's work, Carol Chomsky's article shows how children can begin writing through creating their own spellings. Like Read's, this is a groundbreaking article.

Developmental and Cognitive Aspects of Learning to Spell, edited by Edmund H. Henderson and James W. Beers. (Newark, DE: International Reading Association, 1980). This collection of articles picks up where Read left off by looking at how invented spellings change as children grow older. These studies, mostly carried out at the University of Virginia, show that children *don't* stay stuck in the same invented spellings forever!

"Kids *Can* Write the First Week of School," by Mary Ellen Giacobbe. *Learning* 10 (1981). A brief article about a teacher who discovered that "first-grade children were able to write far more than I ever imagined." This was one of the first articles that led to invented spelling's really catching on in classrooms.

"Social Interaction and Invented Spelling," by Constance Kamii and Marie Randazzo. *Language Arts* 62 (1985). This article demonstrates that spelling, like writing, can be a social activity and can be learned collaboratively.

"American Spelling Instruction: Retrospect and Prospect," by Richard E. Hodges. *Visible Language* 21 (1987). This is one of several articles Hodges has written about the history of spelling instruction, and his work is grounded in a sophisticated understanding of how English spelling works. Such articles are valuable because it's always nice to know where we've come from.

"Invented Versus Traditional Spelling in First Graders' Writings: Effects on Learning to Spell and Read," by Linda K. Clarke. *Research in the Teaching of English* 22 (1988). This may be the first study to carry out a statistical comparison between writers in invented spelling classrooms and traditional spelling classrooms. The findings, which are complex and should be read in their entirety, show that invented spellers not only wrote more but spelled better.

"A Proposal for a New Spelling Curriculum," by Sandra Wilde. *Elementary School Journal* 90 (1990). This article shows what a whole language spelling program might look like and why it's a good idea.

The Funny Side
Kids Know the Score

I was making the rounds, checking in with each of my five-year-old kindergartners during our writing time, when I noticed red-haired, freckle-faced Brandon bent so far over his paper that his nose almost touched it. "Whatcha working on, Brandon?" I asked as I knelt down beside him. He kept his head down and continued to work. "A story about the Three Bears," he mumbled. I peeked over his shoulder and, much to my surprise and delight, noticed that he had actually spelled the word "hot." "Brandon, how did you learn how to spell 'hot'?" This time he looked up at me and said, with some exasperation, "Mrs. Laster, I've been in school. I'm learning!"

—As told to LBB by Bonnie Laster, primary teacher, Brentwood Oaks School, East Palo Alto, CA

📷 **WHOLE LANGUAGE CAMERA**

Word search; a student in Jenny Ore-Giron's class uses the dictionary, Amphitheater High School, Tucson, AZ.

Spelling Strategies

My fifth-graders generated a class list of strategies for double-checking spelling accuracy. These strategies were tied to publication purposes only. The students brainstormed possible ideas and then debated the feasibility of each. Ultimately, they generated the following list, which I wrote on tagboard and displayed in the room:

If you are not sure of the spelling of a word:

1. Invent a spelling until you are ready to publish.
2. Ask a partner or a friend to double-check it for you.
3. Double-check it against the same word from a story that you have read.
4. See if the word is posted in your environment, and use that spelling.
5. Look it up in a dictionary if you are sure of most of the spelling.
6. Use a spell-check on a computer, if available.

Having this list of strategies displayed in the classroom reinforced a more functional, realistic way of dealing with spelling, as opposed to memorizing the spelling of individual words.

➔ See: Lambert, p. 72.

Jane G. Lambert is a graduate teaching assistant in the Department of Curriculum, Teaching, and Special Education at the University of Southern California, Los Angeles, and an elementary teacher at Bell Gardens Intermediate School, Montebello, CA.

Language Stories

How Dare U, Teddy!

"[Theodore] Roosevelt...took a licking over spelling. In 1906, he ordered the Public Printer to set his reports in a simplified system—"dropt" for "dropped," "thru" for "through." These modest proposals enraged Congress... The House of Representatives moved to forbid the printer to spend any money on such heresies. Then it spent four days debating the President's constitutional right to spell as he wished versus the legislature's right to disapprove. When Congress unanimously voted that public documents must 'adhere to standard orthography,' Roosevelt meekly gave in."

Excerpted from "When—spelling—Pow! - wurdz can get you down," by Joseph Kastner, *Smithsonian,* August 1989.

—Contributed by Joel Brown, graduate student, University of Arizona, Tucson, AZ

It is a damn poor mind indeed which can't think of at least two ways to spell any word.
—Andrew Jackson

WELL-SAID

Cornerstone: Katharine Mitchell Busch

Spelling Proficiency Develops Naturally Through Written Language Experiences

Children learn to spell through reading and writing rather than practicing spelling lists. I became aware of this phenomenon when I was a second-grade teacher beginning to develop a whole language curriculum. Not only did I focus on authentic language events, but I tried to create a classroom environment that supported risk-taking by the students. I encouraged them to concentrate on getting their thoughts on paper and not to be concerned with the mechanics of writing or conventional spelling in their first drafts.

At the beginning of the school year I told children: "Spell the best you can. You will know what it says when you read it." The children had no trouble accepting this procedure and used functional spelling when they wrote. I audiotaped the reading of their stories so that I would have a record of each child's interpretation of his or her text.

Katharine Mitchell Busch is an assistant professor at San Bernardino's California State University's graduate reading program where she teaches courses in oral and written language development, sociopsycholinguistics of reading, and models of reading. Her research interests in children's literacy began in 1977 when, as a second-grade teacher, she developed an integrated reading/writing/language arts program. Through this project she became interested in children's invented spellings and natural uses of genre.

At first, when I analyzed the children's writing, I focused on the kinds of stories the children wrote, observing their sense of "storyness," cohesiveness, mood, and audience awareness. But then I realized that I had collected a profile of spelling development for each child as well.

There are two indications of language growth in spelling. One is an increase of words spelled conventionally. The other is a change in the type of functional spelling.

I learned that children's spelling strategies are not illogical but illustrative of the child's knowledge of language and how it works. Children are active participants in the use of language and are constantly generating hypotheses that serve their purpose for each occasion.

If children are encouraged to work through spellings of unknown words, they will become sensitive to conventional spellings when they encounter them in print settings and respond, "Aha, so that's the way it's spelled."

Teachers who are concerned with correctness should keep records of their students' language growth and periodically analyze conventional and functional spellings in their writing. As part of their writing program, they can teach revision and editing processes that will help students learn convention in language.

→ See: Goodman, p. 252; Kalman, p. 34; Schmar, p. 150.

Further Reading About Spelling Proficiency
Bouffler, Chrystine. 1983. *Spelling*. Wagga Wagga, New South Wales: Centre for Teaching & Research in Literacy.
Busch, Katharine. 1977. *Children's Interactions with the Expressions of Language*. Bloomington, IN: Indiana University.
Harste, Jerome, Virginia Woodward, and Carolyn Burke. 1984. *Language Stories and Literacy Lessons*. Portsmouth, NH: Heinemann.
Read, C. 1975. *Children's Categorization of Speech Sounds in English*. Urbana, IL: National Council of Teachers of English.

Further Reading by Katharine Mitchell Busch
◆ "A New Lens for the Learning Disabled: A Cognitive Approach to Reading." In *Landscapes: A State-of-the-Art Assessment of Reading Comprehension Research 1974–1984*, ed. A. Crismore. Indiana University Language Education Department, 1985.
◆ "Teaching Strategies: 'Getting the Picture,' 'New Friends,' 'Say it Again.'" In *Celebrating Learner*, ed. with M. Atwell. California State University Thirteenth Annual Reading Conference, San Bernardino, 1989.
◆ "Letter Writing: A Collaboration Between Teacher Education Students and First Graders." In *The Blending of Theory and Practice*, ed. M. Ice. California State University Third Annual Reading Conference, Bakersfield, 1990.

Great Teachers: Lesley Wing Jan

by Keith Pigdon and Marilyn Woolley

Challenges, Charts, and Celebrations

Charts featuring peace studies, environmental issues, factual reports, explanations, limericks, and funny poems present themselves in kaleidoscopic colour as you move into Lesley's classroom. A closer look reveals storage of children's publications alongside those of authors and illustrators, a special chart featuring an Author of the Week chosen by the class, hosts of challenging questions to prompt children to consider other alternatives, outline research skills, group responsibilities, and collections of class dictionaries.

It is apparent from Lesley's planning that she believes that science and social studies content sets a context for learning and using language appropriate to children's purposes.

Her conceptual framework takes seriously the notion that curriculum that engages children's real world issues will empower them to understand their world more fully, gain a sense of control over it, enjoy it, and work to conserve their natural environment.

One of Lesley's greatest strengths is that she puts a high value on collaboration and reflection. She plans jointly with other teachers and eagerly seeks feedback on her selection of resources, her teaching strategies, her organisational devices, and her record-keeping. She welcomes visitors to her classroom so that she can continually engage in interaction. We were involved in school-based professional development and were delighted by her invitation to visit her classroom on a weekly basis. We negotiated that we would do some teaching each week and discuss the literature models and strategies used after each session. We were interested in exploring children's responses

to factual texts within an integrated curriculum framework and asked if we could model these through analysis of published material or through jointly constructed texts with the children. Lesley reflected on her own growth as a teacher in the following comments:

I'm more aware of the purpose of modelling specific texts to children either when I'm constructing a text in front of them or when I'm sharing a published text with them. I have extended the type of texts I use and I have greater knowledge to impart to the children, so they can make better choices.

She was aware that she had developed and refined her teaching repertoire and her knowledge of what to look for and analyse in children's writing:

I'm sure that I have focussed much more on looking into children's writing. Last year I did process writing and as I conferenced I would write down comments, but I really wasn't looking beyond this or observing them while they were writing or observing their actual writing behaviours.

I'm much more aware of the children as individuals and the ways they set about particular tasks. This became evident to me in the parent-teacher interviews. The parents were amazed at the amount of information I had about their children.

Children's perceptions of their learning in exciting, eventful classrooms provide good insights into the characteristics of successful teaching. The following is an excerpt collected from children in Lesley's classroom:

Before a Topic:

She gets your ideas down so you can use them later. Sometimes to see what we know before we start a topic.

After a Shared Experience:

You can learn things when other people say things that you don't know—like about the different animals. We share ideas that way.

Revising:

She makes lots of charts to help us with our writing. She comes back and gets us to help her change her draft. She talks to us about the most interesting bits to make us think about our writing.

We look at how words work and we can then use better words in our writing. As people suggest things she crosses out words or uses a caret to put better words in.

We learn how to use commas better. This helps us so we don't always use "and." We know how to do proper long sentences. I want to learn about other languages and how words work. I know lots of new words like containers, marsupial and encyclopaedia. I can spell them.

Classroom Demonstrations

by Lesley Wing Jan

Spelling in a Whole Language Classroom: One Teacher's Approach

Introduction

I teach spelling within the context of a whole language classroom. I do not want it to be perceived that spelling is isolated from the writing process; however, to explain the organisational techniques used within my program, I have separated it from all the interdependent strands of my program.

I have been strongly influenced by Brian Cambourne's (1988) Conditions of Language Learning. These seven conditions of Immersion, Demonstration, Expectation, Responsibility, Use, Approximation, and Response are the basis of my language program and particularly my written language program.

My programs are developed within an integrated curriculum that is jointly planned with my teaching colleagues with some pupil negotiation. My language activities and focuses are drawn from the content areas of the curriculum. The children have time for personal writing each day, during which they are engaged in their own topic choice and writing style. Modeling is a very important aspect of my program and a valuable strategy for showing children how writers write: how writers deal with spelling demands and how writers write for different purposes and audiences. Factual and fictional texts are an integral part of my literature-based approach. The factual texts provide opportunities to discuss the author's intent and how the information is organised. We compare the tasks of both fiction and factual text authors. I also model the writing of various forms of factual texts and often use jointly constructed texts as planned demonstrations of the many purposes and uses of our language. The children are encouraged to select their own reading material and to share their reading discoveries in conference situations—either peer conferences or individual conferences with me. Cooperative group work is utilised as often as possible.

A Dual Approach

I have developed a two-strand approach to spelling. The first strand deals with the personal spelling needs of the individual children as revealed in their writing. They use proofreading skills prior to publishing, locating their spelling errors with the help of teacher or peer conferencing. It also involves a "have-a-go" approach to discovering the correct spelling of the words. The children keep a record of the words they have mastered as a means of celebrating their

developing spelling competencies. These words are recorded in personal "Words I Know" books.

The second strand addresses the problem of extending the children's knowledge of how our written language works and developing a common or shared language with which to discuss spelling strategies. Ultimately this allows the children to discover, classify, and organise their knowledge about spelling patterns and apply this newly found knowledge to their personal writing needs.

This second strand is based on focus studies that are drawn from the written language activities of the content or subject areas of the integrated curriculum. I draw the children's attention to particular spelling strategies or knowledge using any of the written material within the content area of the curriculum. This written material can be either commercially produced texts (e.g., big books, poetry, etc.), jointly constructed texts (e.g., wall stories, class books, etc.), or any written work produced by the children.

The focus study strand allows the relationship between reading and writing to be firmly established and enables pupils to be truly immersed in the print related to the topic being studied. They are exposed to the many ways written language is used within each subject area and have many opportunities to hear, see, say, write, and use the words related to the topic. Spelling thus becomes an integral part of all the written language activities.

The Role of the Teacher

I have identified the following teacher roles as important in achieving control of spelling:

1. Providing models of the writing process and demonstrating how writers go about solving spelling problems;
2. Generating curiosity and interest in the patterns of our language system;
3. Providing an expectation that all children will become better spellers;
4. Establishing a classroom atmosphere that encourages risk-taking in order that the children are prepared to "have a go" at all spelling demands;
5. Using the content areas as a source of language activities;
6. Planning a spelling program that caters to individual, group, or class spelling needs;
7. Observing and recording the children's writing progress;
8. Keeping cumulative, dated samples of the children's written work to demonstrate the child's spelling development in different contexts.

Assessment and Evaluation

Because of the very nature of a whole language classroom, monitoring and evaluating the language development of each child is continuous and ongoing and not divided into meaningless parts taken out of context. I build a profile on the individual child's writing and spelling development:

- Dating samples of the children's writing;
- Keeping anecdotal records in writing conferences;
- Observing children during writing;
- Examining the individuals' "Words I Know" books;
- Studying and noting the nature of spelling attempts on the children's "have-a-go" cards;

- Providing proofreading activities that will reveal the ways children go about locating and correcting spelling errors; and
- Using a spelling interview such as provided in Bolton and Snowball's book *Springboards—Ideas for Spelling* (1985).

As part of the learning cycle the children need the opportunity to reflect on their learning, assess their own progress, define their achievements, and identify the areas for further development. I use the following to develop pupil self-evaluation:

- Things I Can Do Chart. Children record their achievements. It is a celebration of their developing competencies.
- My Spelling Check. Periodically the children reflect on their attitudes towards spelling and record their findings on a pupil self-evaluation checklist that I have devised based on PETA's *Am I Becoming a Good Speller?*
- Spelling Conferences. During these conferences the children are encouraged to discuss their spelling and focus on an aspect they can try to improve.

➔ See: Busch, p. 152; Cambourne, p. 17; Goodman, p. 252; Hartle-Schutte, p. 106; Schmar, p. 150; Wilde, p. 151.

References

Bolton, F., and D. Snowball. 1985. *Springboards—Ideas for spelling.* Australia: Nelson.
Cambourne, B. 1983. *The whole story.* Auckland: Ashton Scholastic.

Further Reading About Whole Language Spelling

Baskwill, J., and P. Whitman. 1988. *Evaluation: Whole Language, Whole Child.* Ontario: Scholastic.
Bean, W., and C. Bouffler. 1987. *Spell by Writing.* Rozelle: PETA.
Bouffler, C., and W. Bean. 1987. "Spelling It Out to Parents." *P.E.M.* 65. Rozelle: PETA.
Bolton, F., and D. Snowball. 1986. *Spelling in Context.* Australia: Nelson.
Cripps, C. 1988. *Catchwords—Ideas for Teaching Spelling.* Sydney: Harcourt Brace Jovanovich.
Education Department of Victoria. 1984. *The Teaching of Spelling.* Curriculum Branch.
Education Department of South Australia. 1987. *Spelling R–7 Language Arts.*
Goodman, K. 1986. *What's Whole in Whole Language?* Portsmouth, NH: Heinemann.
Hudson, C. 1983. *Spelling: A Teacher's Guide.* Victoria: Landmark Educational.
Jenkin, R., ed. 1986. *Spelling Is Forever.* Victoria: ARA.
Kelly, B. 1985. "What's in a Word?" *P.E.M.* 50. Rozelle: PETA.
Parry, J., and D. Hornsby. 1985. *Write On: A Conference Approach to Writing.* Australia: Martin Educational.
Turner, J. 1984. "Spelling in the Total Language Program." *P.E.M.* 46. Rozelle: PETA.

Lesley Wing Jan is an elementary teacher at Eltham East Primary School, Melbourne, Victoria, Australia.

The following author blurb written by Michael Millard, a child in Lesley's classroom, provides a more personal perspective:

Michael was born in Melbourne in 1978. He grew up in Australia very well and by the time he was in Grade 1 he was a very good writer. In Grade 2 he wrote quite a few stories and got them published. In Grade 3 he had a teacher called Lesley Wing Jan. Lesley was extremely interested in poems, stories, reading and writing, so of course he became an even better writer.

➔ See: Cairney, p. 345; Goodman, p. 344.

Keith Pigdon and Marilyn Woolley are professors at the Institute of Education, University of Melbourne, Carlton, Victoria, Australia.

Writing to Learn

Classroom Demonstrations
by Carol Gilles

Heartfelt Dialogue

Doug was a big-boned, blond eighth-grader. He liked trucks, truck meets, and girls, and carefully avoided writing, his homework, and his learning-disabled label.

Doug was one of six large eighth-grade boys I met every morning in a "resource class," where it was my task to build on "strengths" and remedy "weaknesses" while helping these students

pass eighth grade. It was soon obvious that I would either spend my whole time tutoring these students in someone else's curricula or let them accept low grades in order to read, write, speak, and listen in my class. Of course they would continue to stay in my class more and more if all of them failed!

A compromise had to be reached. All of these young men were in the same American studies–English block class, and I decided to use the resource class to prepare students for concepts in social studies, help connect those concepts to the lives of my students, and use those concepts in our reading, writing, talking, and listening.

One of the first units in American studies was on the South American Indian culture. Students studied the Mayans and Aztecs of Mexico and finally the Incas of Peru. Since my husband had spent some time in Peru, I brought in slides of Machu Picchu to give my students an idea of the steep Peruvian mountain slopes, the terraced farming, and the remains of the Incan civilization.

Journals were a part of our classroom, and after we watched the slides and talked a bit, I asked students to take a few minutes to react to the slides in their journals. As I read the entries that evening, I was struck by Doug's. Normally Doug's writing was minimal, yet this piece captured the vast loneliness that we had seen in the slides. I responded quickly in writing from a reader's perspective: *(see Fig. 1 above)*

The next day during journal time, I noticed Doug, John (a good speller), and Tony conversing on and off and passing Doug's journal between them. Since they were obviously involved in literacy activities, I left them alone. The next time I picked up Doug's journal to respond, I found this: *(see Fig. 2)*

Fig. 2

Doug had taken my quick response and decided to extend this piece of writing. With Tony's and John's help the reaction had become a poem. What made Doug move from his reaction to the poem? It wasn't an assignment; although journals were a part of our day, I never assigned topics.

I think that Doug liked his journal piece; he felt good about his description. My response

---

assured him that he was onto something. Perhaps the subtle suggestion "This is like a poem" was all he needed to try his hand at poetry. Although Doug had never written poetry, it was a part of our classroom; our class listened to poems daily.

Doug proved to me that response must be a part of every classroom. Responses aren't happy faces (or the junior high equivalent "good job"), percentages marked on the top of the page, or didactic marginalia. These marks are evaluations of a product.

True response begins a dialogue. The teacher responds as a reader, another language-user, not to "teach," but to converse. In dialogue each participant builds on what the other has said or written—questioning, extending, expanding, connecting, often offering another perspective to consider.

Fig. 1

The "heartfelt dialogue" that Ralph Peterson believes happens when a group of people try to create meanings in literature study groups can happen in journals and in writing conferences as well. This kind of dialogue moves both participants toward meanings. It acts as a catalyst, pushing readers and writers into unexplored areas. It nudged Doug into poetry and beyond.

➜ See: Gilles, pp. 270, 306; Peterson, p. 81.

Carol Gilles is a research/teaching assistant at the University of Missouri, Columbia, MO.

Book Note

through teachers' eyes: portraits of writing teachers at work

Sondra Perl and Nancy Wilson
1986; 296 pp.; $16
Portsmouth, NH: Heinemann

Why is it we like teacher-to-teacher talk best? Why is it we prefer to have inservices conducted by other on-the-line teachers? Why is it we ask so many questions of fellow teachers?

through teachers' eyes is an ethnographic study of six Writing Project teachers from first through eleventh grade. One of the strengths of any writing project is the cross-age-level sharing by teachers. This book offers an advantage in that these teachers let you visit their classes over the year, and they also are very open about their successes and failures. (I found myself most drawn to the eighth-grade teacher who was having a "bad" year. I loved it for being so real!) There are many opportunities to see how other teachers solve their problems through various approaches, not all instantly successful.

If you've ever asked for a day off to visit other teachers at work, here is a chance for many such days—opportunities to see fine teachers at work.

Mary Kitagawa

❝ Watching Audre experiment and flounder, I stopped worrying about the unevenness of my own teaching. Good teaching, I could see in Audre's classroom, didn't have to be smooth. Like Audre's writing, her teaching was continually evolving—continually, as she wrote herself, 'in process.'

"Like her students, I could see that it didn't bother Audre to take chances, make mistakes, stumble, and recover. She knew from previous experience that she would eventually 'get it right'—or nearly right. And that for her, as for her students, the pleasure would come in the quest, the questioning, the making of discoveries; it would come, as she put it, 'not in the treasure but in the hunt.' ❞ (p. 61)

As Teachers See It:

Journal Writing in First Grade
by Leslie Vine

The word *journal* used to conjure up memories of college classes in the sixties in which I wrote often inane comments and sometimes important insights on life but never garnered a response from any teacher. Hence, the thought of forcing journal writing on beginning writers kept me from using it as an avenue in the writing process.

I've now changed my mind because I've discovered the value is not in the child's writing entry upon entry, but in the response of the teacher. The journal can become a place of written communication that develops a unique teacher-student relationship. It is in these short writings that I "hear" the children's inner thoughts; thoughts I couldn't possibly take the time to address orally when bombarded with 20 stories first thing in the morning.

➜ See: Dalrymple, p. 210.

Leslie Vine is an elementary consultant and tutor in Florence, SC.

Resource: Newsletter

Dialogue: The Newsletter about Dialogue Journals

$10/year (3 issues) from
  Handbook Press
Dialogue, CAL
1118 22d St., NW
Washington, DC 20037

On the front cover of *Dialogue* the editors quote Albert Camus: "The world needs real dialogue. The only possible dialogue is the kind between people who remain what they are and speak their minds." *Dialogue*, a newsletter about dialogue journals, published three times a year, enables educators to do just that. It explores a wide range of interactive writing in this country and abroad across such educational fields as literacy development, reading, ESL, special education, and adult education. Back volumes in bound sets are available and reasonably priced.

LBB

WELL-SAID

I saw that "writing across the curriculum" wasn't just a method of getting students to write who were afraid of writing. It was also a method of getting students to learn who were afraid of learning. I was once such a student, morbidly afraid of the sciences and other disciplines that looked alien and forbidding. Now I began to think that I could have written and thereby reasoned my way into those disciplines—far enough, at least, so that they would have lost their terrors.

—William Zinsser, *Writing to Learn*

Classroom Demonstrations

Learning Journals Across the Curriculum

by Susan E. Kinzel

I knew from research by Toby Fulwiler and Art Young at Michigan Technological University that, in writing across the curriculum courses, journals can be used as write-to-learn tools, not write-to-show notebooks. During the first 10 weeks of a 20-week composition course, I had my students keep a personal journal. During the second 10-week period, my students kept a learning journal in a course of their choice. This journal had clear guidelines. The first part included entries students made while reading course texts and library material related to the course. The second section, written immediately after class, was student responses to class lecture or discussion. In the final section, I asked the students to speculate each week about the meaning and theory behind the day-to-day course work. My goal was to see if learning journals would benefit my students. Would writing help them become better learners?

When I handed out the journal guidelines at the beginning of the second 10-week term, I gave an introduction to the theory behind this assignment. Using Pat Juell's guidelines (Juell 1985, p. 187), I emphasized the process of becoming "independent thinkers directly involved in and aware of their learning." I wanted the students to become "creative thinkers who develop new connections rather than memorize 'facts.'" And I asked students "to use writing as a process for discovery and clarification of ideas." I checked the journals every two weeks (five times per term) to note changes in their writing and answer questions that they might have. I compared end-of-the-term responses from the fall term personal journals to the end-of-the-term responses from the winter term learning journals. I interviewed students during our conferences and kept an informal teacher log, recording notes when reading and reacting to individual journals and interviews. I hoped that students would learn more effectively by writing to learn and think, not just by memorizing facts. I expected that the students would find value in their personal journals, but I was not certain about their response to a course journal with such specific guidelines.

Even though 63 percent clearly enjoyed the personal journal in the fall term, 52 percent found the learning journal valuable. A majority of the students, both in their journal entries and conference interviews, told me that the journal helped them study for exams. As a representative student response, one student pointed out that the journal forced her to reread and recopy her notes after each class, helping her to better understand the class lecture. Another finding is the unexpected difficulty that some students had with speculative thinking entries. The students need to learn what Ralph S. Stevens (1985, pp. 211–221) said in "Writing and Learning: What the Students Say": "Explaining the matter to oneself encourages the student to make connections between the subject and her or his own life" (p. 217). I was asking my students to change their approach to learning.

I found the learning journals to be a benefit for the students, especially in organizing material and class notes. Many had found the journals helpful when studying for exams or term papers. I learned that it would be valuable to have the students share their speculative thinking entries together in small groups each week. Through peer interaction, students could help each other by sharing their writing and answering questions.

References

Juell, P. 1985. "The course journal." In *Roots in the sawdust: Writing to learn across the disciplines,* ed. Ann Gere. Urbana, IL: NCTE.

Stevens, R. S. 1985. "Writing and learning: What the students say." In *Roots in the sawdust: Writing to learn across the disciplines,* ed. Ann Gere. Urbana, IL: NCTE.

Further Reading About Writing to Learn

Britton, James. 1970. *Language and Learning.* Coral Gables, FL: University of Miami Press.

——. 1988. "EJ Focus 2: Journals, Logs, and Freewriting." *English Journal* 77, pp. 47–62.

Emig, Janet. 1977. "Writing as Mode of Learning." *College Composition and Communication* 28 (May): pp. 122–128.

Fulwiler, Toby. 1980. "Journals Across the Disciplines." *English Journal* 69, pp. 14–19.

——. 1987. *The Journal Book.* Upper Montclair, NJ: Boynton/Cook.

Fulwiler, Toby, and Art Young, eds. 1982. *Language Connections: Writing and Reading Across the Curriculum.* Urbana, IL: NCTE.

Gere, Ann Ruggles, ed. 1985 *Roots in the Sawdust: Writing to Learn Across the Disciplines.* Urbana, IL: NCTE.

Herrington, Anne. 1981. "Writing to Learn: Writing Across the Disciplines." *College English* 43, pp. 379–387.

Young, Art, and Toby Fulwiler, eds. 1986. *Writing Across the Disciplines: Research into Practice.* Upper Montclair, NJ: Boynton/Cook.

Susan E. Kinzel is an instructor at Michigan Technological University, Houghton, MI.

Expanding Kindergarten Journal Writing

by Denise Ogren

My kindergartners have been writing in their journals since the first day of school. They write and draw on blank pages in a three-pronged folder, and each page is dated with a rubber stamp. Usually the children draw a picture and then write a sentence to go with it. I encourage them to write about interesting things that happen to them, but I still have several children who are stuck with repetitive picture identification such as, "This is my house."

One day we were going to draw pictures for a birthday book, but because we had limited time, I told the children to write just a sentence and not bother with a picture. The children could not write a sentence, however, because there was nothing to label. They began telling me about interesting things that had happened to them, and I asked them to write these things down. Chris wrote, "My grandma bought me new shoes." This pushed some children to craft sentences that were less repetitious and more original. Now I tell children at least once a week, "Don't worry about the picture; just write me a message about yourself."

→ See: Ogren, p. 214.

Denise Ogren is a primary teacher at Stinesville Elementary School, Stinesville, IN.

Why I Like Journals
by Julianna Lin

My favourite lesson is journal because I like to write things. When I'm doing journal, I can write down anything on any topic. One day I can write the beginning of a story. Since I'm not obliged to finish the story, the next day I can write a poem. When I'm writing a journal I'm free to explore "The Forest of Topics." Then after picking a tree or topic, I explore my topic further. If I happen to have crossed "The Field of Imagination," I'd write an imaginative story (or poem). I'd search around my tree (topic) to find some imaginative thing to write.

If I happen to have splashed through "The River of Humour," I'd write a funny story (or poem) or a story (or poem) with many jokes in it. If I happen to have taken a swim in "The River of Knowledge," I'd write a story (or poem) with true facts in it. If I happen to have waded across "The River Twist," I'd write a story (or poem) with a twist at the end.

However, before exploring this "forest" I must decide whether to write a story or a poem. That is all one needs to know before entering the forest.

When I'm writing my journal, I can explore this forest that extends farther than the eye can see, even more. That is why I like journal.

Julianna Lin is a fifth-grader in Montreal, Quebec. This was contributed by Mary Maguire, a professor at McGill University, Montreal.

Book Note

How Writing Shapes Thinking: A Study of Teaching and Learning

Judith A. Langer and Arthur N. Applebee
1987; 154 pp.; $9.50, NCTE members $7.25
Urbana, IL: National Council of Teachers of English

This two-year study was conducted with content-area teachers in a secondary school to analyze how writing affects learning. The researchers concluded that writing assists learning, but that teachers need to be selective about the writing forms they assign with relation to the kinds of learning they seek. Summary writing and note taking lead to a comprehensive but superficial focus on the whole text, while analytic writing leads to a comprehensive but superficial focus on a particular part of the text, resulting in deeper reasoning about less information. Short-answer study questions focus attention on particular information with little attention to overall relationships.

Teachers wishing to effect literacy learning through academic area instruction are advised to consider their understanding of the goals in any instructional activity, and to work with their students so that the goals are shared.

Karen Dalrymple

Principals Speak Out

by Arlene R. H. Pincus and Harriet Paget Ritzer

The Magic of Writing and the Writing of Magic

As a school immersed in the process of whole language teaching, we actively cultivate the reading-writing connection, seeking opportunities to have students think of themselves as readers and writers. In the context of creating the most literate environment possible, we invited a published author to speak to students about her craft. As a published poet who was actively engaged in discussing the teaching of reading and writing with teachers, Lindamichellebaron became the natural choice for our school's visiting author.

We'd planned a short assembly to introduce our poet to Tuscan School at which three classes would welcome her with choral speaking of several of her poems. Ordinarily, the guest would have been introduced by the principal. But first-grade teacher Betty Murphy, who shared the following letter with the principal, changed a child's life.

Jan. 6, 1989

Dear Mrs. Murphy,
I am writing this little letter to say I will always remember you. You proudly thougt now that I am dder I forgot you egsist. But it's not true. I'm in therd grade in mrs Jacksons class I'm Learning my times tables and cursve. I hope you had a merry chistmas and a happy new that wish is deliverd late

Love,
Robyn

Robyn, who had given a teacher a gift of her writing, would be the perfect one to introduce poet Lindamichellebaron.

Robyn had never even heard of Lindamichellebaron, and she certainly didn't know anything about introducing a speaker. But the principal and reading specialist Harriet Ritzer took care of that. The day before Lindamichellebaron's arrival, Robyn was invited to read the author's poems and to write a bit about how they made her feel. She came back with a few sentences that she had discussed with her teacher, Barbara Jackson.

Lindamichellebaron is here to tell us what its like being a poet. She writes about growing up and how it feels to be child. When I read her book, *the Sun is on* I felt like I wanted to read more.

"Which poem made you so sure she knows about being a child?" Dr. Pincus asked.

"'Hair Prayer'—the one about not liking her mother to hot comb her hair," Robyn immediately replied.

"Put that kind of thing into your speech, Robyn," Mrs. Ritzer urged.

Then Robyn was invited to read the poet's letter to her readers, which appears at the end of her book. It tells the story of how Lindamichellebaron first came to think of herself as a poet at the age of six when she wrote her first two-line poem.

By the next morning, Robyn's speech had gone through several revisions. She'd been rehearsed by her parents and Mrs. Ritzer. And then she met Lindamichellebaron, to whom we had already repeated Robyn's comment: Her poetry reminded Robyn of herself.

There was an immediate connection between the two. When Robyn's mother arrived and was introduced, Lindamichellebaron told Mrs. Ross that Robyn actually reminded her of her own younger self.

At the assembly, Robyn waited impatiently for the choral speaking to end. Then she stepped forward and read expressively into the microphone. She'd added to her speech:

The reason I like that book so much is because what happens to her happens to me like not wanting my mom to hot comb my hair and wanting to grow bigger and liking to read and write and I like to talk a lot too. I might be a Poet.

We had forgotten to prompt Robyn on what to do when she finished, but she proudly stationed herself on one of the "author's chairs" on the stage. Lindamichellebaron stepped forward and acknowledged the choral speaking and Robyn. She told the young audience she'd have more time for them in separate sessions right after the assembly, and the special day continued.

At each session, we were reminded we hadn't just invited a poet, we'd invited a teacher. Children were invited to ask questions. In one session, a child wanted to know what *ain't* was doing in a poem. Lindamichellebaron explained the concept of *poetic license.* "Changing language makes it more exciting. You can write the way you need to. When an idea bounces around inside your head and the ideas and words join together and come home at last, it is a poem. A poem celebrates what is unique about the poet. When pictures are painted in a way people haven't seen before, the words become a poem."

As each session ended, Lindamichellebaron invited children to continue their thinking and writing back in their classrooms.

The next day, Robyn received the following note:

January 12, 1989
Dear Robyn Elizabeth,

I have been thinking about the wonderful day Tuscan School spent with Lindamichellebaron, and I start with your outstanding introduction. Not only were your words well chosen but you understood why we chose you to do such an important job, and your delivery was sen-sa-tion-al! I don't think you will ever forget that day. I don't think our poet will ever forget Robynelizabethross. I know I will always wear a smile when I think of both of you.

Love,
Mrs. Ritzer

The reply was prompt:

Dear Mrs. Ritzer,

I will always remember the day I met Lindamichellebaron! I just wish I could see her again. When I try to think of the person who helped me the most I think of you.

Love,
Robynelizabethross

→ See: Logan, p. 146.

Arlene R. H. Pincus is the principal of Tuscan School, Maplewood, NJ. Harriet Paget Ritzer is a Chapter 1 Reading and Math specialist at Tuscan School.

Poet-in-Residence

Larry Pike has spent several days in our school each year for the last six years. Larry is a Detroit-area poet with a real gift for helping young writers find the poetry that is buried within their hearts. Larry says poetry appeals to the senses. He asks the kids to describe a place by what they can see, hear, smell, touch, and taste. Here is a sample:

I Love Tiger Stadium

All the sights;
fans yelling, Lance Parrish playing,
Alan Trammel playing,
hot dogs, flags saying "Go Tigers!"
and beach balls.
All the sounds;
when the bat hits the ball it sends
100 deciliters through my ears,
fans cheering "LOU! LOU!"
All the smells;
hot dogs and mustard, misty chalk dust,
sweet summer sweat, and fresh grass
perfect for digging cleats into.
So, you see, I love Tiger Stadium.
Gibby, Parish, Lou, and Chet the Jet
just to name a few.
It just sends nice shivers through my body
to go and see the Tigers play.
It's great to see people going around yelling,
"Yearbook! Yearbook!"
It's just a classic place.

—Jeremy Young, 5th grade

This was contributed by Debra Goodman, teacher, Dewey Center for Urban Education, Detroit, MI.

As kids see it

Road blocked for poetry

Wed. May 31, 1989.

At Tuscan School, the famce poet Lindamushelbaron came to Tuscan School. There was a poetry celebrashone that began In the atatorealm. Richard Shocin was very onered to introdos Lindamushelbaron. At the asebly we resitede "The Lonly shoe" and "Growing like a weed." At 9:30–11:00 there were junyer workshops. Lindamushelbaron gave ideas to the yong poets of Tuscan School.

In the afternoon the school children went outside and resitid grate poems of the studints of Tuscan School. The anthalgy is named Tuscan kids say.

We should give a lot of credit to the Maplewood Polece for the butay of quwiet so we could here the butay of poetry. The Maplewood cops blocked Tuscan Rd. for poetry just as tha waud for crime. The selabrashone endid with Lindamushelbaron saing a short spech. Dr. Pinkes seaid that sints Lindamushelbaron inspierd our love of poetry she was the perfickt poet to leade our celebrashon.

This press release was written by Mrs. Bonsher's first-grade class at Tuscan School for a local newspaper, the *News Record,* which published it exactly as it was written—invented spellings and all.

Resource: Book

small kid time hawaii

Eric Chock, editor
1981; 204 pp.; $6
Bamboo Ridge Press
P.O. Box 61781
Honolulu, HI 96822-8781
1-808-599-4823

The catalog we received describes Bamboo Ridge Press as a "literary small press founded in 1978 to publish literature by and about Hawaii's people." The inspiring *small kid time hawaii* is a compilation of poetry by eight-to twelve-year-olds, collected by Eric Chock while serving as poet-in-residence in Hawaiian schools. It is of exceptional lyrical quality. Chock believes that "poetic self-understanding can help students develop to their fullest self-potential as human beings." Reading this collection will make you a believer too. Chock explains how he works.

LBB

writers

What Can I Say?
by Eric Chock

At one school I visited I knew that they expected little, because I was told from the start that "*our* kids aren't very interested in poetry." In addition, they gave me their lower achieving levels of fourth- fifth- or sixth-graders, as if testing my insistence that their reading and writing abilities didn't matter to me.

As it turned out, the kids were more interested in poetry than many of my other classes, especially when they found out I was sincerely interested in their thoughts and feelings being creatively expressed, no matter how ungrammatical or misspelled the initial drafts might have been. Once they realized it was a game played with the imagination more than with the pencil, poetry became enjoyable.

When I go into the schools I sometimes see myself as a poetry salesman displaying an array of poems, looking for the ones that most students will identify with, ones that will inspire them to write their own. And when they write, I am on the lookout, not so much for polished writing, but for writing of substance.

This does not mean I am only looking for self-expression. I am looking for images and feelings a child projects in writing which make connections. I am looking for the relationships he or she makes with the world. I am looking for his or her view of the way things are, and hopefully, the way things can be, for the individual child and for the group. This kind of substance, this kind of beauty, is essential to art.

Treating student writing with an artistic attitude is, I believe, the best way to help the student approximate his or her potential for creating and appreciating poetry.

→ See: Chock, p. 226; Logan, p. 146.

Excerpted from *small kid time hawaii,* ed. Eric Chock (Honolulu: Bamboo Ridge Press, 1981).

Slow Pin

Everything's
in slow
motion, bodies
entangled,
legs, arms,
one overpowering
the other.
Then the move,
slowly,
slowly the
pin and a
sharp whistle
and the
sound of a
slap on the mat.
—Tricia Keneko

Wouldn't it be nice if there was nothing but space between your ears with a couple of stars shining?
—Wade Kyono

A crab scurried like a gathering of ashes
—Calvin

YOUNG ARTISTS

—Debbie Smith, 16, Salem, OR
(from *Treasures 2,* see p. 162)

Classroom Demonstrations
by Leslie Leyden

Poetry Celebrates Itself

Poetry used to scare me. I did not know much about it, and I had always viewed it as something one had to pick apart and analyze for symbolic meaning. I just did not feel confident enough with my own knowledge of poetry to try to impart that to my students. However, I read them lots of poetry, purely for enjoyment, or so I thought. I read them Shel Silverstein, Jack Prelutsky, the very playful and safe kind.

One day, after I had read poetry aloud for about 30 minutes, I overheard a few of my students making up some clever rhymes as they were going to lunch. I was amused. It was so easy for them. Then I realized the same thing had happened to me: After sharing poetry with my students, I had found rhymes running through my head, too.

I started exploring. I talked to people who loved teaching poetry. I talked with friends of mine who write poetry. I gathered information on the many varieties of poetry. I brainstormed with one of my teammates a list of attributes common to poetry. But most important, I gathered books filled with poetry, armloads of them. I displayed a large bulletin board filled with poems, and posters depicting the different types of poetry and samples of each. We filled our room with poetry. I made poetry books with blank pages for children to compose their own poetry. We were ready to begin.

Poet's Workshop began each morning. I started out the first week reading poetry to them for about 40 minutes each day. They were completely engrossed. I read a large variety of poetry, everything from narratives to free verse to haiku. I would not tell them specifically what types I was sharing with them; I simply read to them and they loved it.

At the end of the first week, I gave them their blank poetry books. I was apprehensive. What would they do? They amazed me. They could not wait to put pencil to paper. They emerged as poets before my eyes. They filled the pages with their own creations. They clamored to share a new poem with me and each other. The excited, busy hum in our room was filled with statements like "Listen to mine!" and "Oh, I wrote a really funny one!"

After about two weeks we began to discover more about some of the specific varieties of poetry we had been reading. We would feature a type of poetry each day, aptly titled "Poetry of the Day." I would choose selections of our featured poetry and we would explore it. I would never tell children to return to their seats and write a haiku, or whatever type we were featuring. Amazingly, some of them obviously felt confident enough to try it. We also began to investigate and compare the differences between poetry and other genres. We looked at word choice, stanzas, punctuation, form, senses, rhyme, and length, to name a few. The children continued to amaze me. Through listening, reading, writing, and sharing poetry they were truly becoming knowledgeable poets. I was realizing more and more that reading poetry is teaching poetry.

As time went on, their poetry began to take shape, reflecting the types of poetry they were experiencing. The children began to recreate images and patterns they were discovering in poetry, but with unique "voices" all their own.

It all made such sense. By simply immersing them in poetry, they had begun to internalize the rich and unique language of poetry. It did not matter if they knew how many syllables were in the third line of a haiku. What mattered was that they had emerged as confident readers and writers of poetry.

Leslie Leyden is a second-grade teacher at Sand Creek Elementary School, Douglas County Schools, Highlands Ranch, CO.

These strategies were adapted from Mary Johnson, Douglas County Schools.

Resource: Performance

Poetry Alive!

P.O. Box 9643
Asheville, NC 28815
1-704-298-4927

Yetta Goodman has seen Poetry Alive! in action, and says they're wonderful. They offer a 45-minute theatrical presentation of 15 to 20 poems designed to help students "familiarize themselves with poetry and accept poems as friends." The group also offers workshops in which they "demonstrate the use of memorization and poem performances as a means of teaching poetry and developing creative writing."

LBB

 **Classroom Demonstrations**

Test Panic: Poetry to the Rescue
by Deborah Nieding-Allai

Just before the Missouri Mastery Achievement Test (MMAT) was to be given, I began to familiarize myself with the test. I realized that my eighth-graders would be required to determine specific parts of speech and apply the respective labels. It was not enough that my students could use these components of grammar effectively and proficiently, which I knew to be true from mountains of writing. I needed to find out how well they could label the parts of speech.

The next day, at the end of class, I gave each of my students a 3"× 5" card and asked them to write the definition of an adjective (thinking that adjectives would be easy for them, since their writing displayed abundant, effective use of adjectives) on the front of the card, and on the back of the card, they were to write any additional information they desired. I knew for a fact, from previous teaching experiences, that adjectives are taught as early as third grade and are a repeated part of the curriculum each year, and I expected to find mastery of this task among many, if not all of my students.

To my dismay, none of the cards revealed a correct definition or description of an adjective. Obviously, the previous traditional methods of grammar instruction were ineffective, and I needed a more interesting and meaningful approach. I decided to play with language and use one of my favorite books, one that my students love as well. It took me about two seconds to find a poem from Shel Silverstein's book *Where the Sidewalk Ends*, which was full of adjectives.

The first task at hand was to define the term *adjective*. If this lesson was going to have meaning to the students, they had to be involved in the definition. So, on the following morning, I handed several of the students a copy of a grammar book. My room was stocked with an ample supply of three different texts, and we referred to all three. Through a class discussion, some synthesizing, and a great deal of negotiating, we determined our working definition of an adjective to be a word that "describes, limits, qualifies, or in any other way modifies a noun or pronoun." The students had a great debate over the definitions of the terms *limits, qualifies,* and *modifies,* but once we personalized these words, all was agreed upon (i.e., you modify a skateboard when you make it fit your personal style and needs).

With this arduous task accomplished, I asked the students to put everything away and listen to a poem. I asked them to consider the definition of adjectives that we had determined and to listen for these kinds of words. I wanted them to relax and enjoy the language of the poem and to listen for adjectives in a risk-free atmosphere. I had rehearsed the poem "Sarah Cynthia Sylvia Stout Would Not Take the Garbage Out" and read it with all the expression and intonation that I could. After this reading, I asked for volunteers to name any adjectives.

Donald Murray says that ideas are not concrete until they are written down, so that was their next task. I gave the students a long, narrow strip of paper and asked them to listen to the poem again, this time to write down all the adjectives that they heard.

After the second reading of the poem, the students and I reviewed our definition of an adjective, and then the students formed small groups to discuss their lists. I encouraged them to debate any words on any list that were in opposition to our definition. As the students discussed their lists, I moved around the room and briefly joined in each group's discussion. Several students were in a debate over whether nouns could be used as adjectives (as in the Golden Gate Bridge and coffee grounds) and asked me to tell them the "right" answer. I referred to the definition on the board and asked them what they thought. In each case, the students determined the right answer without my direct instruction. I wanted the students to confirm what they had learned, so I gave each student a copy of the poem to work with. In their same small groups, they looked at their adjectives, especially those in question previously, and used the context of the sentence to confirm or negate their decision.

We returned to one large group and discussed why Shel Silverstein might have used so many adjectives and what the poem would be like without adjectives. I wanted the students to have a genuine understanding of the function of adjectives. We discussed the types of writing that required adjectives as well as types that didn't.

To evaluate this activity, I once again used the exit-slip strategy. After erasing the definition of an adjective from the board, I gave the students colored 3"× 5" cards and asked them to write their definition of an adjective on the front and to write any additional information regarding adjectives on the back. All of the students gave acceptable definitions, and many gave examples to illustrate the meaning and function of an adjective.

This activity went so well that I decided to invite the students to extend it with a writing activity. The following day, I handed back their strips of adjectives and suggested we make our own poem from these "utterly disgusting descriptors." As always, my students had a better idea. Some of the students collaborated and wrote a menu for a dormitory cafeteria, while others devised the "Sure-Shot Diet."

As the year progressed, I saw my students beginning to develop their own style of writing from their knowledge of language and its function. Not only did I feel that this lesson was successful, it was a lot of fun. Thank you, Shel Silverstein!

➜ See: Freeman, p. 110.

Deborah Nieding-Allai is a whole language consultant and works for the Campus Writing Program at the University of Missouri, Columbia, MO.

Poetry: The Greatest Risk?
by Laura S. Truesdale

Poetry. The very word conjures up memories of the dreaded high school English class where poetry was interpreted line by boring line. Never was the student's opinion valued. We simply parroted the teacher's lofty translations. And never were we qualified to write even a line of poetry. These memories seem more like nightmares! How could I bring poetry into my eighth-grade language arts class? Because of these past experiences, I was afraid of poetry.

"You hypocrite," my conscience raged. "Aren't you the one who is always telling your students to take risks with their writing?" I had to overcome this fear. My students and I had experienced a great deal of success in our writing. Yet very few had taken risks with poetry (including me). I wanted all of us to experience the joy of reading and writing poetry.

My heart and mind continued to do battle. "Could I really expose my deepest and darkest feelings to the sometimes insensitive crass eighth-grader?" My heart won out, "How could you forget the most basic of whole language principles? 'Trust the learner, of whom you are one.'"

I studied the examples of poetry in *The Art of Teaching Writing* by Lucy Calkins (1986) and *In the Middle* by Nancie Atwell (1987) and I took the plunge. We decided to begin by reading poetry from selected anthologies we chose from our school library. We spent two weeks reading, sharing, and discussing the poems we liked. I tried to emphasize the fact that poetry seems to evoke feelings for the reader with very few words. We also tried to find poems that provided us with vivid imagery.

Now for the true test of my faith in the process; we were to begin writing. We worked very hard on our poems. We brainstormed, shared our rough drafts, edited (and edited), and finally published our anthology. I believe that our poems are funny, deep, and full of imagery and true feelings.

I would like to share these observations.

- Poetry should be read aloud.
- Demonstrations need to be provided in order to bring about fruitful results.
- Publication makes the process meaningful.
- Risk-taking is also crucial and must be demonstrated.

When some of the other teachers of these students read our poems, they could not believe that these were the same unmotivated students that they had in their classrooms. Language arts teachers, take what I formerly perceived as the greatest risk. Try poetry with your middle schoolers. The results will surpass your wildest dreams!

References

Atwell, N. 1987. *In the middle: Writing, reading, and learning with adolescents.* Portsmouth, NH: Boynton/Cook.
Calkins, L. 1986. *The art of teaching writing.* Portsmouth, NH: Heinemann.

Laura S. Truesdale is a language arts teacher at North Central High School, Kershaw, SC.

 **writers**

Broken Trust
by Susannah Loehr

She colored her feelings
And hid them from me.
They were no longer private.

She leaked all my secrets
I mentioned in trust.
Our friendship was ruined
Like the way metal rusts.

From *Reflections* 8(2), June 1989.

Celebrating Authors

Classroom Demonstrations
by Catherine Howard

Celebrating Authorship

"Guess what? Now everyone in Room Five has published a book!" I announced to my first- and second-grade class one day at class meeting. "I think it would be fun to celebrate somehow."

The children agreed with me, and we went on to make plans. After much discussion over several weeks, we came up with our plan for an Authors' Party. It would be held in the evening, so parents who work during the day could come. The children would have time to read their published books to their families, and, of course, refreshments would be served.

In discussing the children's ideas with parents, we came up with two further possibilities: invite parents and older siblings to share their writing, and try to find a local children's book author who would come. The children liked both ideas. Authors are always eager to promote their books, and as it turned out, we quickly found a local writer who was about to publish her first children's book. She was delighted to come and talk about the process of planning, writing, editing, and publishing her book.

Everyone was excited as the day for our Authors' Party drew near. We voted on which refreshments we would serve, and baked the edibles at school. We practiced reading our published books to each other, and we cleaned and decorated the classroom.

We had set the time for our Authors' Party as 6:45 to 8:00, but families started arriving at 6:30. Children found their books and settled in to read them to their guests. By 6:55 every possible niche in the classroom was taken, and the

room was filled with a happy buzz of voices. Approximately 80 people came, including many older and younger siblings.

At 7:00 I welcomed our guests and introduced our featured author, Dayle Dodds. Dayle began her presentation by describing how she had thought of the idea for her book, titled *Wheel Away!* She described planning, writing, rewriting, editing, and searching for and working with a publisher and illustrator. She had prepared placards to illustrate each step of the process. The children especially enjoyed Dayle's description of receiving that exciting phone call from Harper & Row saying they would publish *Wheel Away!*—she answered the phone with popcorn in her mouth, in the middle of her daughter's birthday party!

After Dayle's presentation, an older sibling and three parents read from and/or talked about

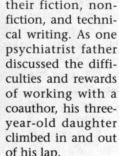

their fiction, nonfiction, and technical writing. As one psychiatrist father discussed the difficulties and rewards of working with a coauthor, his three-year-old daughter climbed in and out of his lap.

The questions the children asked Dayle Dodds and the other authors showed not only how curious and attentive they were, but also how closely they identified with the speakers as authors themselves.

"Where did you get your idea?"

"Did you and your partner (coauthor) agree on everything? What happened when you didn't agree?"

"What do you do when you run out of ideas?"

Overall, the evening was a smashing success, both as a celebration of writing and authorship, and as a family gathering. The parents expressed delight at being part of an evening that involved and interested the whole family. The children put it simply: "I'm glad we had a real author come," "It was really fun," and of course, "I liked the cookies."

→ See: Howard, p. 258.

Catherine Howard is a primary teacher at Ohlone School, Palo Alto, CA.

Resource: Periodicals

Stone Soup: The Magazine by Children

$20/year (5 issues) from:
Children's Art Foundation
P.O. Box 83
Santa Cruz, CA 95063
1-408-426-5557

Ms. Magazine called *Stone Soup* the "*New Yorker* of the 4 to 12 set." This literary magazine—a savory blend of stories, poems, book reviews, and art by children—is published five times a year. Unlike the old woman in the traditional tale, you won't need to con your students into contributing to this literary feast; any student would be proud to publish here. Every issue of *Stone Soup* contains guidelines for potential contributors.

LBB

Merlyn's Pen: The National Magazine of Student Writing

$14.95/year (4 issues) individual rate: 1–10 subscriptions;
$7.95/year (4 issues) classroom rate: 11–20 subscriptions;
$5.95/year (4 issues) classroom rate: 21 or more subscriptions;
from:
P.O. Box 1058
98 Main St.
E. Greenwich, RI
02818-9946
1-800-247-2027

After reading the magical offerings in this fine literary magazine, you might think that they had sprung from Merlyn's pen, but in reality they represent the top 2 percent of almost 5,000 submissions annually accepted for publication by students in grades 7 through 10. Besides providing a professional outlet for student writing, *Merlyn's Pen* makes for superb reading. My one concern is the Activity Guide for teachers that accompanies each issue. Some of the activities are open-ended and relatively harmless, but nonetheless, it saddens me to see lesson plans for "teaching" this beautiful student-created literature. To submit work (writing or art): Enclose a large, self-addressed, stamped envelope. Staple manuscripts and write your name on every page. Type double-spaced, using 1 1/4 inch margins. Include your name, grade, address, and phone number; your school's name, address, and phone number; and your teacher's and principal's name. You should receive a response within 11 weeks.

LBB

Resource: Periodicals

Reflections

$5/year (2 issues); $3 each; $2 back issues from:
P.O. Box 368
Duncan Falls, OH 43734

The subtitle of this periodical reads *The National Student Poetry Magazine for All Ages.* Sound impressive? It is, especially when you realize that the magazine is published by seventh- and eighth-grade journalism students at Duncan Falls Junior High in Duncan Falls, Ohio. *Reflections* is published twice a year (January and June). It contains poetry, short stories, essays, plays, teaching ideas, humorous articles, and interviews. Manuscripts may be handwritten (if they are legible), typed, or computer printed. Please include name, age, school, address, and teacher's name. Send to Dean Harper, the editor, at the above address. Be sure to include a self-addressed, stamped envelope with manuscripts. Include a statement that the work is original; then sign and date it. A teacher or parent should also sign it. Acceptance is normally made within 10 days.

LBB

Magpie: A Magazine of Literature for Children

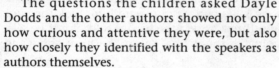

Glen Huser, editor
$12.50/year (4 issues) from:
Edmonton Public Schools
Centre for Education
One Kingsway
Edmonton, Alberta, T5H 4G9
1-403-429-8230

Each issue of *Magpie* focuses on a theme, such as celebrations, changes, creepy crawlies, irks, and quirks. All illustrations and writing are by kindergarten through twelfth-grade students. Edmonton teachers have come up with other ways of celebrating children's writing as well. Groups of schools work on a project called WOW (World of Writing) that places displays of children's writing in shopping centers and other public buildings. Other schools have "language fairs," where students have the opportunity to read their work in small groups to a wider audience of students and adults.

Arrietta Chakos

Principals Speak Out

Creating a Learning Community

by Kathleen O'Connell Cunningham

Early one November day, I met Norman Sherman, principal of P.S. 201, talking to a teacher in the main office. He introduced me as the writing process coordinator and asked the teacher what help she would like for her writing workshop. She answered, "None. I know everything about writing process." Norman smiled at her, tugged at his neatly trimmed salt-and-pepper beard, and said, "Perhaps you could help some of the newer teachers." She seemed delighted with his suggestion and walked out.

I sat down and asked Norman how he supports writing process. I expected that he would tell me a list of things, and I was ready with clipboard in hand to take notes. Instead, something wonderful happened. He began to tell me about Norman Sherman, the person who makes the principal. I put down my pen and listened for an hour. Norman told me about his days in the classroom, teaching in South Chicago and East Harlem, and about being a principal in Flushing.

"I was chosen to teach a six-week summer program to improve kids' reading. South Chicago is a poor area, we had no guide, and we had no materials. So we made use of what was around us. I set up a program that seemed sensible to me: A Study of Chicago. Since all the kids lived there and the resources were available, it was perfect to research. My students and I questioned and researched how Chicago got its water, the history of Chicago, etcetera. We toured the city with clipboards in hand. The kids read and questioned and wrote about their city. At the end of the program the reading levels doubled, and best of all, the kids loved learning.

"Junior High School Ninety-nine in East Harlem was labeled the worst school in New York City the year I was hired as a science teacher. After talking with the students in my class, I discovered that they never read. I was so upset that I started a morning reading club.

"I also found ways to build reading into my science class. Since I live near La Guardia Airport, I worked out an arrangement with the airlines to take their old flight magazines. Each Friday afternoon, I would load up my old yellow VW with boxes of *Time, Sports Illustrated,* and so on. These magazines were high-interest reading material for my students. We often would have discussions about a science article and, more important to me, I began to see my students feeling happy about reading. I had my students keep journals, just to get them writing. I guess that is why I like the writing process, it feels right for me."

Donald Murray describes a good classroom as one where "the space is shared, responsibilities are shared, reading and writing are shared, experiences are shared, above all learning is shared. The teacher works hard to help the children develop their ability to capitalize on their collective power for the common good" (Graves and Stuart 1985, p. 53). Norman Sherman creates this learning environment and allows his students and teachers to capitalize on their collective power.

➜ See: Sherman, p. 352.

Reference

Graves, D., and V. Stuart. 1985. *Write from the start: Tapping your child's natural ability.* New York: E. P. Dutton.

Kathleen O'Connell Cunningham is the Writing Process coordinator, District 25, Queens, NY.

Mrs. Laxcie

by Leonila Bonifacio

It was July 20, 1980. It was the ending of a beautiful day. I got up early that morning and went to the barn to play with my goat named Mrs. Laxcie. I called Mrs. Laxcie to come to me, but she didn't come. I went toward her. I saw her lying down on the soft hay that I fixed for her the night before. I knelt beside her and asked her, "What's wrong, Mrs. Laxcie?" She didn't reply. She was just lying there like a piece of rug.

I ran to the house like a leaf being blown by the wind. I went to my grandma's room and shook her like thunder. My grandma didn't wake up the first time I shook her. Then I shook her again. That time she woke up.

As my salty tears rolled down on my cheek, my grandma asked me, "What's wrong?" I answered with my sad voice that Mrs. Laxcie was sick. My grandma got up quicker than usual. We went to the barn very quickly.

Grandma touched Mrs. Laxcie on her head and said that she had a fever. Grandma went in the house to wake my uncle to get a doctor. I stayed with Mrs. Laxcie. I sat beside her and put my head against her stomach. With my head against her stomach, I felt her temperature rising. I knew that very moment that Mrs. Laxcie was going to be sick for a long time.

One hour later the doctor came. He checked Mrs. Laxcie. I asked him if she would be all right. The doctor looked straight at my eyes with fire in his eyes. He said that Mrs. Laxcie was going to die any day or days from that very moment. I stood frozen like the world was going to close in on me.

My uncle said, "I will get the gun and shoot her." My uncle left the barn to get the gun. As he was entering the door, I saw him carrying the long killer gun. I ran toward him, took the gun, and threw it over the barn. I told him if he was going to shoot Mrs. Laxcie, he must shoot me too. He said that Mrs. Laxcie was just an animal.

"What!" I yelled back at him. "Mrs. Laxcie is not an animal. She is my friend, my very best friend."

My uncle called my grandma out of the house and said, "You have to talk to Lennie about the goat, Ma."

My grandma saw me sitting down with Mrs. Laxcie. Grandma turned to my uncle and said, "We have to give her some time."

Day and night I spent my time in the little barn with unpleasant smells and mosquitoes hovering over me. As time passed, day and night never came, only mosquitoes. Rain and cold nights came. The barn's roof was leaking, and the window was broken by the hard blow of the wind. When it was really cold, I fixed a fire so Mrs. Laxcie would be warm.

The morning came when my grandma said it was time for Mrs. Laxcie to be put to sleep. My tears were beginning to fall on my cheeks. I begged my grandma not to shoot Mrs. Laxcie yet. But she said, "The time has come. She will be shot tomorrow morning."

I spent another night with Mrs. Laxcie. I was crying all night thinking of Mrs. Laxcie being shot. I knelt down on the hard ground and prayed to God to take my best friend Mrs. Laxcie to his kingdom. The morning came. I took my last look at Mrs. Laxcie. Her body was wrinkled and thin. Her eyes were bulging out and her hair was long.

My uncle came in the barn and carried Mrs. Laxcie out of the barn like a log and shot her. I thought I couldn't bear it, but I tried to hold my feelings inside of me. Mrs. Laxcie died on August 5, 1980 at 10:00 A.M. Wherever Mrs. Laxcie is now, I know I will always remember her.

➜ See: Proost, p. 127; Treasures, p. 162.

From *Treasures 2: Stories & Art by Students in Oregon,* comp. by Chris Weber (Portland, OR: Oregon Students Writing and Art Foundation, 1988).

Leonila Bonifacio lives in Beaverton, OR, and was 14 years old when she wrote this.

 ## Classroom Demonstrations

by Debra Jacobson

The Keeling Publishing Company

At Keeling Elementary, students are able to publish their writing either in individual books or in the *Keeling Magazine,* which is printed twice a year.

When students want to submit something to the publishing company, they fill out a form, attach their writing to it, and give the packet to their teacher, who then puts it in my mailbox. I put it in the basket labeled "incoming text" in the tiny publishing room. Linn Lane, the writing consultant, reads the submission Tuesday or Thursday. She's a local writer, and her salary is part of the publishing company's budget. If a piece is accepted, Linn puts it in the basket to be typed. If it is rejected, Linn types a response explaining why.

Bookmaking: The year we had a $1,000 grant, we bought cardboard and contact paper, and held a parent bookmaking party to make covers. Since then we've scrounged up cardboard and free books of wallpaper samples, bought 2" cloth tape, and made patterns. When a book is published, Linn makes two copies: one for the student to take home and the other for the classroom.

Magazine: Our district has a materials center that prints and binds the school magazine. At the beginning of the school year I establish two dates when the magazine will come out. We set deadlines and put reminders in the weekly announcements. A few weeks before the deadline, I ask volunteers to enter the text on my computer. I make copies of the printout and ask students to read the stories to see which ones they want to illustrate. Each student gets a magazine to take home.

➜ See: Howard, p. 159; Kasten, p. 161; LaBenz, p. 316.

Debra Jacobson is an elementary teacher at Coronado Elementary School, Tucson, AZ.

Cornerstone: Wendy C. Kasten

Books Beget Books

Like many areas of the country, South Florida has an extensive young authors program. Children who have written books visit a university campus to meet a well-known author and share their own writing. Following the Arizona model (Goodman, Cox, Milz, and Haussler 1977, pp. 5–10) for such programs, the University of South Florida has been sponsoring the Suncoast Young Authors Conference and its extended programs since 1986 on the campuses in Sarasota, Saint Petersburg, Fort Myers, and Tampa. In the Sarasota area, the books that are generated for and collected at the conference are sent to every elementary and middle school, both public and private, in Sarasota and Manatee counties during the next year.

"Kids Really Wrote These Books?"

This comment, made by an elementary student when he visited his school media center, is typical. This student was both surprised and impressed by the collection of student-authored books; not because the writing is particularly outstanding, but because a certain mystique about books was broken down for him.

From their comments I have learned that many children still view books as remote works by people who died hundreds of years ago. In their schema, children do not see authors as real-life people. The collection of student-authored books sends a strong message to children that real people write stories, and that people like themselves have something worthwhile to say. These stories have come from real children, and whether the stories are fantasy, personal narrative, or nonfiction, real children have presented them in book form. When we promote and display these books, we are celebrating the writing of children.

In organizing the conference each year, we request that children write a biography and include a photo for the back cover of their books. This is usually the first part of the book that children read. Children often remark: "Wow, this kid is only in second grade!" and "Wow, this author goes to *our* school!"

In each collection that arrives at a school, there are several titles written by children from that school. These books become especially pop-

Wendy C. Kasten taught elementary school both in Bangor and in Searsport, Maine. Wendy has been an advocate for Young Authors conferences, and founded the Suncoast Young Authors Conferences at the University of South Florida. Her research interests include emergent literacy, the writing process, and Native American education. She presently teaches at the University of South Florida at Sarasota.

ular, and the children who wrote them become school celebrities.

"Did You Read the Book About Divorce?"

Children begin discussing the writing of other children. In each collection there are several titles that are particularly popular. Some teachers have heard children talking about these books while passing in the halls or waiting in line at the cafeteria.

One such popular title was a child's description of her parents' divorce and her adjustment to it. Students were eager to read about a topic close to their experience. They connected with this book just as they do with a school library book.

The traveling book collections are made available in the media center for teachers to use in their classes. Children *choose* to read these books. No motivation is necessary. It would be more descriptive to say that children dive into the books, excited to find out what other kids have to say.

Many teachers capitalize on this interest by incorporating student-authored books into their reading instruction. Besides reading selected titles, students critique them. Some teachers choose titles to read aloud to the entire class and then discuss them.

"Can We Write Some Books, Too?"

Perhaps the most exciting aspect of the traveling collections is that books beget books. Because each school has the collection for only a few weeks, and because the books are so popular, schools take steps to develop and promote their own collections.

Interest in student-authored books is often student initiated. The Suncoast Young Authors collection gives the implicit message to children that they can do it, too. Some classes have made direct requests to their teacher to write and publish their own books. In some schools, the media center has become the school publishing center. Libraries have made purchases of binding machines or arranged for volunteers to assist teachers in school-based publishing. One school formed a "young authors club," which meets weekly after school under the direction of the media specialist and another faculty member. The purpose of the club is to encourage reading and writing with a goal of completing a bound book. This school plans a "publishers party" for children who meet their goal.

The collection, as it travels, supports teachers in the writing curriculum. Teachers who are reticent about teaching writing see their students' response and then want to learn more about teaching and improving their writing curriculum. Other teachers, who feel limited support from their administration for a dynamic writing curriculum, also report benefits. The focus on school-based writing during the collection's visit, the resulting publicity, and the obvious enthusiasm for the books from both students and visiting parents, lend additional fuel for curriculum change.

Many educators see school-based publishing as a regular aspect of writing. They often coordinate this effort with a young authors conference at the school, and invite an author of children's books who lives in their vicinity. Classrooms and media centers have become places to regularly celebrate and display the children's writing.

WHOLE LANGUAGE CAMERA

Kristen Cummings reads one of her original stories to her dad, Bill Cummings, at an Author's Day celebration in Nancy Areglado's kindergarten, West Stockbridge, MA.

A Guide to Classroom Publishing

Jane Baskwill and Paulette Whitman
1986; 24 pp.; $5.32
New York: Scholastic

There is hardly a child alive who won't respond to the joyful sense of accomplishment and wonder that publishing one's own book engenders. Now, classroom publishing is made easy with this guide by two veteran whole language teachers who have followed many student authors through the writing process—from their first tenuous drafts to full-blown beautifully published books. Don't miss the chance to share the joy of publishing with your students because you don't know how. Get this book and you will.

LBB

Resource: Books

Bare Books

Treetop Publishing
2200 Northwestern Ave.
Racine, WI 53404-2519
1-414-633-9228

What better way to celebrate your students' authorship than to give them a bound, hardcover book in which to publish their written creations? Treetop Publishing, the creator of Bare Books and Big Bare Books, makes it possible with blank books, 28 pages of high-quality white paper sewn between two hard covers. Thirteen cover designs that kids can color are available; I prefer the books with blank covers so that kids can create their own. Treetop also offers line guides that students can place under the page and use to keep their writing neat and straight for a true polished, published look.

LBB

The student-authored works serve as a catalyst for more student-authored works, which are written, produced, and shared. Books beget books.

→ See: Sprenger, p. 202.

Reference
Goodman, Y., V. Cox, V. Milz, and M. Haussler. 1977. "Encouraging young authors and young readers." *Reading Education* 2.

Further Reading by Wendy C. Kasten
◆ "Planning Your Own Young Author's Conference." *Livewire* 2(1), 1985.
◆ "Celebrating Child Authorship in Southwest Florida: The USF Regional Campuses." *Florida ASCD Journal* 4, Fall 1987.
◆ "Medicine Men, Bethlehem, and Pacman: The Intersection of Cultures in Native American Children's Writing." *Anthropology and Education Quarterly* 18(2), 1987.
◆ "Reaching All Young Authors." *Teachers' Networking* 8(1), 1987.
◆ "A Study of Third- and Fifth-Grade Students' Oral Language During the Writing Process in Elementary Classrooms," with B. K. Clarke. Florida Educational Research and Development Council. *Research Bulletin* 19(4), 1987.
◆ "A Secondary Model for a Young Author's Conference," with M. Freeman. *Journal of Reading* 33(5), 1990.

Resource Essay

Treasures

by Judy McDermott

To an eight-year-old boy, the stories were difficult to comprehend, light-years removed from his life in the bustling Willamette Valley.

But Jeremy Parker listened intently as his grandfather described what it was like to grow up black in the Deep South at the turn of the century. "It was hard for me to understand exactly what he meant," said Parker, a 15-year-old sophomore. "Now that I look back, I know that what he was saying was true."

Two years ago, Parker did more than look back. An eighth-grader at the time, he penned "My Granddad," a poignant remembrance of the master storyteller who was his grandfather.

"My Granddad" is one of 105 pieces of writing in *Treasures 2: Stories & Art by Students in Oregon.* The new anthology, a publication of the Oregon Students Writing and Art Foundation, is meant to inspire, and to showcase, the artistic talents of Oregon's schoolchildren. More than 2,000 students, grades K–12, from 56 communities competed for a place in the book.

Treasures 2, like its predecessor, the 1985 *Treasures,* is the brainchild of Chris Weber, an English-as-a-second-language teacher at Atkinson Elementary School in Southeast Portland and the foundation's editor.

To be considered for the anthology, young people across Oregon entered the Starfire Writing and Art Contest. Atkinson children named the contest, one of them saying it reminded her of "a place you imagine has words flying with intensity, with the star denoting a special glowing place."

Certainly, any number of enthusiastic teachers and parents nurture the state's creative young writers, Weber said. But the literary world isn't exactly brimming with publishing opportunities for children, he said.

"Writing excels when students see something tangible. They see that their writing is valid, that people will spend dollars to read what they have written. It can be the first step in a professional career."

Emotionally, too, publication has its rewards, Weber said. "You can see the children's pride when people express their congratulations. There is a building of self-esteem and a sense of personal worth."

Weber said the *Treasures 2* project also was marked by the young people's obvious work ethic, plus "a cooperativeness—among students, teachers, parents. There was a group spirit, and that was more important than almost anything else."

Powerful Writing

For Weber and the selection committee he assembled, the most impressive written entries possessed two special qualities: honesty and voice. "We asked ourselves, how involved was the writer and how powerful the language?"

The most successful pieces, Weber believes, share a personal moment in a young person's life.

Children write of the getting of wisdom, of overcoming fears, of the desire for acceptance, of nerve-wracking first days at work.

A Chance to Experiment

The Starfire contest represented a rare opportunity for young people to write experientially, said Tom Pattee, a former middle-school English teacher. "That was one of the things that intrigued me about the contest,"

said Pattee. "A lot of children like an opportunity to express themselves, especially if given an environment in which they can do it without criticism."

Sarah Creedon, who wrote "Song of the Harmonica" as a seventh-grader at Waluga Junior High School in Lake Oswego, has been able to share the excitement of publication with the subject of her story, her 78-year-old grandfather.

"He loved it," said Creedon. "He was really shy about it at first, but he's heard from so many friends."

Altogether, the book was more than two years in the making, from the appearance of posters announcing the competition to the book's appearance shortly before school ended last spring.

The $9.95 paperback is available at Portland bookstores or may be ordered directly from the Oregon Students Writing and Art Foundation, P.O. Box 2100, Portland, 97208.

The budget for *Treasures 2* was $21,000, including minimum-wage salaries for the assistant editors.

More to Come

Weber hopes young people whose work was not selected will not be deterred from entering the competition he is already planning for *Treasures 3.*

"It's a good experience to take the risk. If you never try, you're never going to know. These students can say, I got rejected and survived."

Jeremy Parker, who wrote the piece as a final assignment for English class, remembers his teacher was complimentary, saying, "That's perfect." Many months later, he was standing in the school office listening to the principal say, "Congratulations. Your poem got published."

"I guess it's like hitting a home run," said Parker. "It's totally exhilarating, like a surprise birthday party."

Excerpted from *The Sunday Oregonian,* 4 September 1988.

Treasures: Stories & Art by Students in Oregon

Treasures 2: Stories & Art by Students in Oregon

$9.95 each plus $1.60 shipping and handling from:
Oregon Students Writing and Art Foundation
c/o Chris Weber, editor
P.O. Box 2100
Portland, OR 97208-2100

➜ See: Bonifacio, p. 160; Osborn, p. 217; Proost, p. 127.

One of the artists who is featured in *Treasures 2,* Rom Papish, 14, stands in front of his art work, Eugene, OR.

As kids see it

Review of *Treasures 2: Stories & Art by Students in Oregon*

by Amanda Cornwall

Imagine how you would feel if you were a 14-year-old girl, as confused about life as any teenager could be. Then pretend you found a book of true stories and artwork by students that expressed exactly your hopes, dreams, thoughts, and fears. What you're imagining is how I feel about *Treasures 2.*

As I began to read, an intense feeling of excitement grew in my mind. I knew the book would be good, but this good? I was flabbergasted. Several times I did a double-take at the artwork. I found myself thinking—nine! A child of *nine* drew this! This was especially true with my favorite drawing in the book—a whimsical raccoon intertwined in a branch, drawn by Paul Haidle. The stories made me want to shout—yes! That's exactly how I feel! "Leaving," by Serena Hamm, a story about a girl who goes on her first trip out of the country, took me back to the first time I went away. The honesty, combined with dry wit and humor, in "Methods of Torture for Getting Up in the Morning," by Joe Findling, expressed my own dread at facing a new day sometimes.

Even the stories I couldn't relate to with personal experience touched me deeply, like "Through the Eyes of Love," a story by a girl my age dealing with death for the first time. Although no one close to me has died, I cried for Shari Pritchard, the author.

I think the word that best describes *Treasures 2* is inspirational. It is the kind of book that inspires readers in their own way—dreamers to dream, teachers to teach, mothers to mother, fathers to wipe the stubborn tears out of their eyes and toss the ol' pigskin around with their sons, and most importantly, student writers and artists to write and draw. It inspires teenagers like myself grappling with such daily horrors as self-worth, love, and school to come out of their ruts and greet the world with a fresh new attitude.

Treasures 2 has touched my life, and I know it will touch everyone who reads it. From crayon to watercolor to words, the art and stories in the book combine the laughter and tears of everyday life we young people experience with the honesty and purity that only student writers and artists can express.

From *Shoe Tree Magazine* 4(3), Spring/Summer 1989.

Amanda Cornwall is 14 years old and lives in Lake Oswego, OR.

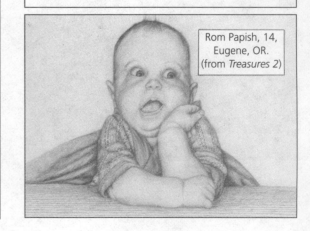

Rom Papish, 14, Eugene, OR. (from *Treasures 2*)

"Great literature,
past or present,
is the expression
of great knowledge
of the human
heart."

—Edith Hamilton
The Greek Way

—Jay Smith, Mott's Apple Award Winner, first grade, Cartersville Elementary School, Cartersville, GA, Sharon Vosburgh, teacher.

Literature

Beatrix Potter at Ohlone School

by Peter Craske

"Once upon a time there was a wood-mouse, and her name was Mrs. Tittlemouse..." It is the first Wednesday morning of the school year at Ohlone, and again I am sitting in my faded blue-and-white overalls facing 28 small strangers spread out on the rug at my feet. For them Room 2 is new and a little frightening.

Pat Robinson has taught here in Palo Alto for nearly 30 years. Tall, gray-haired, and reassuring, she has already rung the bell and taken the roll. Yet two or three mothers still linger along the wall—safe, familiar faces in these strange kindergarten surroundings.

"She lived in a bank under a hedge... " Slowly I move the opened page from right to left so that each child can see the picture of Mrs. Tittlemouse herself, standing bright-eyed at the moss-encircled front door of that funny house with its yards of sandy passages. The children crane forward to see the tiny drawing more clearly.

Already the magic is taking hold. Beatrix Potter's language, precise and without compromise, serves these California children no less well than it did English children 80 summers ago in the years before the Great War.

I have been reading the Peter Rabbit books to Pat Robinson's kindergartners every Wednesday morning for several years now. Mrs. Tittlemouse, Pigling Bland, Tom Kitten, and Timmy Willie—they were the very essence of my early childhood in rural Devonshire. It seemed important to share them with my own two sons, starting out their lives in suburban California, in a landscape so different from the rain-swept hills of Potter's Lake District.

When John, our younger child, moved into Room 2, I asked Pat if I could read a Beatrix Potter book in class. She agreed, and soon I became part of the Wednesday routine, smuggling from home a new story in the pouch of my old overalls and greeting an enthusiastic chorus of little girls and boys.

John is now long departed from Room 2, eagerly clambering up the ladder that leads to junior high and the wider world beyond. Yet I am content to stay in Pat's classroom. Familiarity with the wider world beyond only serves to make Wednesdays the more precious, a haven—at least for a few minutes—from the freeways and the supermarkets and the endless exhortations to buy.

There is shared happiness in these weekly visits. Happiness for the children, no matter whether the encounter between the fastidious Mrs. Tittlemouse and the corpulent Mr. Jackson is familiar or new. And happiness for me in watching their faces and in being the fortunate bearer of such a gift.

Peter Craske is a senior partner with Mueller, Craske and Associates, a marketing and development consulting firm with nonprofits only, Palo Alto, CA.

Viewpoint: Rudine Sims Bishop

Literature for Every Child

Story Is a Way of Knowing

Barbara Hardy, in *The Cool Web*, tells us that "narrative is a primary act of mind," a basic way of making meaning, really a cognitive strategy, a way of ordering the world. She says that "in order really to live, we make up stories about ourselves and others, about the personal as well as the social past and future." Stories, it seems, have been so important a part of life in some groups that they have invented stories to explain where stories came from.

The Ashanti in West Africa say that all stories were once the property of Nyame, the sky god. Anansi, the trickster spider, had to earn them by capturing MMboro, the hornet who stings like fire; Osebo, the leopard of the terrible teeth; and Onini, the great python. And he had to deliver all three to Nyame. Only after accomplishing these deeds, which no one else had been able to do, was Anansi able to get all the stories in the world. Fortunately, he has shared them with all the world.

The Seneca Indians tell how, long before people were on earth, Skunny Wundy was able to trick the fox into telling all his stories. Skunny Wundy placed them all in an otter-skin bag and hid them away for people to find them when they came to earth.

The Hungarians have a legend about a fairy tale tree that says that

> beyond endless mountains, beyond endless rivers, at the very remotest end of the earth and whither no bird has ever yet flown, there is a deep blue sea, and in this sea there is a small green island, and on this island is a stately tree, all of gold with shapely branches, twelve in all, and on each branch there is a nest, and in each nest, a nestful of eggs—a nestful of eggs of clearest crystal. You've only to break the crystal shell, and each has a fairy tale to tell.

Three different cultures, but each has made the origin of story a part of their folklore—a powerful statement about the traditional importance of story.

Dr. Rudine Sims Bishop, a former elementary school teacher, is a professor of education at Ohio State University where she teaches courses in children's literature. She earned her doctor's degree at Wayne State University, where she participated in the Reading Miscue Research studies. She is active in NCTE and IRA, and has published a book and several articles and chapters on reading and literature. Her most recent work is a critical examination of Walter Dean Myer's novels for adolescents, to be published late in 1990.

The importance of this point in the context of literature for every child is that this universality of narrative, the telling of stories, is a way to connect to the lives of all children in our classrooms, no matter what social group they are a part of. They all have stories to tell. Further, there are stories that are a part of their own particular cultural traditions. Sharing their stories is another way to help children learn to celebrate both the distinctiveness of each cultural group and the universality of human experience.

If story-making is a cognitive strategy, then literature can also offer children a model of one of the possible ways to make clear for themselves and others what it is they are learning in our classrooms. Literature can be an invitation to tell stories about their learning, whether the stories are in writing or drama or music or any other creative art. Story is a way of knowing.

Literature Exercises the Imagination

This is, arguably, the greatest gift that literature has to offer every child. Albert Einstein said, "When I examine myself and my methods of thought, I come to the conclusion that the gift of fantasy has meant more to me than my talent for absorbing positive knowledge." It is imagination that leads us to invention, to innovation. Neal Armstrong could not have walked on the moon had someone not been able to imagine that it could be done. Science fiction writers move us by imagining what our future will be like if certain possibilities come to fruition.

Jane Yolen, in an essay entitled "The Mask on the Lapel," traces the connections between wisdom and imagination. She starts with the magician, or the *mage*. A mage was a person of great wisdom and learning. It was a mage who told Ged in *A Wizard of Earthsea* that to light a candle is to cast a shadow. The mage had his *magic*, which was the power to produce surprising phenomena and seemingly unnatural effects. The mage in *A Wizard of Earthsea* could, for instance, seemingly transform an object into something else. What they did was to produce *images* that pass for reality, that change our understanding of what is real, that push us past our initial perceptions into the world of *imagination*. And so the connection *mage, magic, image, imagination*—all from the same root.

Good literature keeps alive the connections between wisdom and magic and imagination in ways no other medium can. It is that connection that underlies the power of literature to speak to every child.

→ See: Literature Reference List, p. 429.

Excerpted from a speech entitled "Literature for Every Child," presented at Ohio State University, Mansfield Campus, 22 September 1989.

Further Reading by Rudine Sims Bishop

◆ *Shadow and Substance: Afro-American Experience in Contemporary Children's Fiction*. NCTE, 1982.
◆ "Children's Books about Blacks: A Mid-Eighties Status Report." In *Children's Literature Review 8*, ed. G. Senick. Gale Research, 1985.
◆ "Extending Multicultural Understanding Through Children's Books." In *Children's Literature in the Reading Program*, ed. B. Cullinan. IRA, 1987.

WHOLE LANGUAGE CAMERA

Within a few hours of Kaeli's birth, big sister Monica, age 2-1/2, introduces her to literature.

Book Note

Shadow & Substance

Rudine Sims
1982; 112 pp.; $8.95
Urbana, IL: NCTE

Shadow and Substance is a rare and important survey of the African-American experience in contemporary children's fiction. As Sims reports on 150 books published from 1965 to 1979, she characterizes them as "social conscience," "melting pot," or "culturally conscious" works that set a framework for the changing context of black children's literature. Sims describes the image makers in black literature—those authors and illustrators who are witness to the African-American experience—and in closing answers the questions "Where are we?" and "Where do we go from here?" There is still not enough black literature published; nor is enough effort made to reach the potential market for African-American literature. By raising these issues and through her great knowledge of children's literature, Sims brings the potential within reach.

Kathryn F. Whitmore

❝It is interesting to note that the one controversial book in this subset focuses on the experience of picking cotton. *Oh Lord, I Wish I Was a Buzzard* is based on the experiences of a Black woman and has much to recommend it—repetitive, rhythmical, lyrical language, and illustrations that capture the beauty of the land. However, the book appeared in 1968, a time when the plantation imagery it evoked and its unfortunate references to a Black child's wishing to be such animals as a snake and a buzzard were unwelcome contrasts to the then-current emphasis on the more positive and lesser-known aspects of Afro-American history and culture.❞ (p. 53)

Resource: Book

Values in Selected Children's Books of Fiction and Fantasy

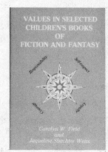

Carolyn W. Field and Jaqueline Shachter Weiss
1987; 240 pp.; $27.50
Hamden, CT: Library Professional Publications, an imprint of The Shoe String Press, Inc.

Field and Weiss have compiled 700 annotations of books for children, preschool to eighth grade, covering ten values: cooperation, courage, friendship and love of animals, friendship and love of people, humaneness, ingenuity, loyalty, maturing, responsibility, and self-respect.

Katy Obringer

WHOLE LANGUAGE CAMERA

High school student,
Sunnyside High School, Tucson, AZ

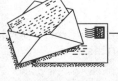

As Teachers See It
by Alicia Rivera

Children, Teachers, and Books

Displayed above my classroom doorway is a poster for Robert McCloskey's *Make Way for Ducklings*. This is a small secret, but I have put that banner there for myself; I need to see it each day. Make way for children, it reminds me; make way for children and make way for books.

Inside my second-grade room, there are 30 boys and girls and many hundreds of books. "School is like home," a student confided recently. The luckiest of children find books wherever they spend hours each day; but how important and necessary that all children find books in their classrooms: books of great variety, books of rare quality, books in large number, books worthy of celebration. From the start, and ever thereafter, children need stories that will touch their hearts, tingle their funny bones, and challenge their intellects, stories that will ignite their imaginations and fashion their dreams. Children, and teachers, need classrooms filled with beautiful, wonderful books.

And so it is in my classroom. Throughout the room there are low, labeled shelves with picture books, chapter books, nonfiction titles, biographies, poetry collections, songbooks, dictionaries, atlases, children's magazines. A partner-reading shelf holds duplicate copies of books, and group-reading shelves store sets of six or more copies of the same title. Selected books stand on the chalk tray and on top of the upright piano. Within easy reach, these are available to all of us whenever we need them during the day. "You love books," children tell me. "And so will you," I invariably reply. And, indeed, knowing what I have learned as a teacher, I know what I know, and I know that they will.

Faithfully, I read to the children each day. I begin with fairy tales by Hans Christian Andersen, that incomparable storyteller. Next, I read folktales by the Brothers Grimm, stories retold by Virginia Hamilton, and stories of Isaac Bashevis Singer. I ask the children to imagine their own illustrations, which they draw with crayon in large newsprint booklets. Then, for many weeks, I share picture books, starting with those of Randolph Caldecott and including examples from Wanda Gag to Virginia Lee Burton, from Maurice Sendak to Barbara Cooney, Chris Van Allsburg and dozens more, from this country and from around the world. We study the artwork closely and consider the relation between picture and text. And all along, we are taking time for poetry, rhyme, and song, reciting Mother Goose and other traditional verse as a matter of course and singing out often. In January, I read the children a chapter book. With their own copies, they can choose to follow. Titles are usually by Laura Ingalls Wilder, Beverly Cleary, or E. B. White. Later come the 23 small books by Beatrix Potter.

Meanwhile, children are reading often: alone or in small groups with me, with partners, by themselves, or at home with family. Children visit the school library each week to select two books from a collection that has been purposefully built to support our literature curriculum. Week by week, children keep a written homework book log arranged by theme: fairy tales and folktales, picture books, Caldecott Medal books, nonfiction books, biography, poetry. These are shared regularly at school.

Thus, ever so gradually, from one month to the next, each child's involvement with books, with reading, and with language grows. One child volunteers to bring books to school from home or from the public library; another follows her lead. Children plan and present dramatizations of favorite tales. We read more and more, discussing characters, story events, and story settings. We talk about authors and illustrators and notice patterns in their work. Children want to write and illustrate their own stories, poems, and books. And there are other projects, too: written responses, poetry recitations, letters, posters. Someone discovers classroom books in other languages. "Is this written in Chinese? I have a book from Greece. I'll bring it tomorrow." And he does.

And, inevitably, springtime arrives. "Will you read us folktales again?" "May we take our books out to recess?" We consider the conventions of book design: endpapers, frontispieces, title pages, and borders. A parent comes once a week to read, in her soft accent, picture books from her native New Zealand. And another parent writes, "Yesterday J. said something that had a great impact on me. He told me that he wished he had been born at the time of Laura Ingalls Wilder. Now this coming from a boy who was until very recently mostly interested in afternoon cartoons . . ." Many children are reading chapter books independently, and some are reading several titles in a series (from Nancy Drew mysteries to the Narnia series). "I love books," a child tells me. "I love to read," another writes in her journal. "What if there were no Beatrix Potter?" she goes on to ask herself. "Don't stop now!" the class calls out at the end of a literature period.

Stop now? Oh, I will not. Nor will you, I think to myself, not ever. We will never stop now, teachers or students, none of us, for a reason quite simple: We can't! We have learned what it means to make way in our lives for books.

Little by little, throughout 23 years in the classroom, I have learned ways to bring children and books together. My students have been my best teachers. At the same time, through courses and conferences, journals and books, and through professional organizations, both national and international, my work has been enriched by the many people whose ideas and insights about literature for children have helped shape my own.

➡ See: Dalzell, p. 239; Huck, p. 188; Literature Reference List, p. 429; Lockard, p. 236; Rivera, pp. 95, 202, 358.

Alicia Rivera is a primary teacher at Hillcrest School, Oakland, CA.

Resource: Book

Fantasy Literature for Children and Young Adults: An Annotated Bibliography, 3d ed.

Ruth Nadelman Lynn
1988; 771 pp.; $39.95
New York: R. R. Bowker

Over three thousand American and English fantasy novels and story collections for third-through twelfth-graders are listed by themes that range from allegorical fantasy to witchcraft and sorcery; a research guide is included for author studies.

Katy Obringer

In the Mail

At the beginning of a new school year, Alicia Rivera received this note from two of her former students, who are now in the third grade.

Dear Miss Rivera,
Guess who we saw outside in Discovery Center. We saw the Emperor in the parade! A little girl was saying that he had no clothes on. Then we went to the bathroom and saw a miniature little Mermaid in the sink. Then we saw her go down the drain. Then we saw the Princess at the School door. The sun was shining bright and she was driping wet. And there were peas scattered in front of the Office. And there were 20 Mattreses and Fether Beds stacked on the bed in the Nurses Room. Oh, and we forgot to tell you ..... Peter Rabits (+ him) send there love.

From us..
(and Betrix Potter + Hans Christian Anderson and all the charecters from both of them.)

How to Capture Live Authors and Bring Them to Your Schools

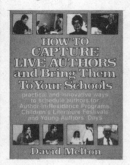

David Melton
1986; 99 pp.; $14.95
Kansas City: Landmark Editions

The subtitle of this book explains it all—practical and innovative ways to schedule authors for author-in-residence programs, children's literature festivals, and young authors' days. The publisher also sponsors the National Written & Illustrated By . . . Awards Contest for Students, publishing the three winning students' books.

Katy Obringer

Sounds of Language

Bill Martin Jr
From:
DLM (Developmental Learning Materials)
One DLM Park
Allen, TX 95002
1-800-527-4747

Whole language educators rejoice! DLM is republishing Bill Martin's *The Sounds of Language* series. Viewed by some in the seventies as too innovative for the classroom because it emphasizes the literary beauty and power of language rather than the skill regimen of basals, this magnificent anthology of fiction and nonfiction, poetry and songs invites teachers and students into the limitless world of the imagination with every turn of the page. The reissue will include a high percentage of the original material, as well as numerous new stories and illustrations. Among the new titles available in summer 1990 are *Sounds of an Owly Night* and *Sounds of Children at Play on the Hill*. The teacher guides are most helpful and enhance— rather than hinder—the literary experience.

LBB

WELL-SAID

I have sometimes dreamt, at least, that when the Day of Judgment dawns and the great conquerors and lawyers and statesmen come to receive their rewards— their crowns, their laurels, their names carved indelibly upon imperishable marble—the Almighty will turn to Peter and will say, not without a certain envy when He sees us coming with our books under our arms, "Look, these need no reward. We have nothing to give them here. They have loved reading."

—Virginia Woolf,
The Second Common Reader

Great Teachers:
Bill Martin Jr
by Peggy Brogan

Bill Martin is perhaps the most creative educational innovator of our times. He is both a visionary and a doer. His name is synonymous with faith in children and their ability to learn.

His philosophy pinpoints language as the most important tool for carving out human destiny, and therefore places the school in the responsible position of helping children develop a practical repertoire of human-centered language skills.

"Learning to read," he says, "can be a natural acquisition for children growing up in a world of print such as ours. Reading instruction is best when it helps children verbalize and refine their intuitive knowledge about language and how it works.

"Tuning the child's ear to the music of language is basic to learning to read. If children are to read sensitively, they must bring the sound of the language to the printed page. No reading lesson is complete unless it leaves children with the sound of sentences ringing in their ears and the sharp taste of words lingering on their tongues. Over the years we have made such a fetish of teaching word recognition as the only means to reading that we have all but destroyed children's appreciation of language itself."

Bill Martin came by his love of language naturally. He grew up in a Kansas environment that

As kids see it

Why I Love to Read
by Matthew Taylor

There I was standing in front of the castle. The dragon was coming towards me. I was frightened but I had my armor, sword, and shield. Fire was squirting out of his mouth. He was getting closer and closer and closer... SLAM! I closed the book. It was one of my favorite books, *The Fire-Breathing Dragon* and it seemed like I was the Knight-in-Shining Armor fighting the dragon. It was so real that it seemed like I was really there. That's why I love to read. I can be anywhere or anyone I want to be when I read a book.

Whenever I want to get away, I can just pick up my book, start to read, and ZAP—I'm in another world. My imagination takes over and I can go anywhere. I can learn many things from the olden days all the way to the future and I can pretend like I am experiencing it myself.

But the best part of all is that no matter how many times I read my book, I always get to slay the dragon.

➜ See: Literature Reference List, p. 429.

Matthew Taylor is a third-grader. This essay, which won a National 1989 Mott's Apple Award, appears exactly as he wrote it.

The Mott's Apple Awards are a national public service program designed to encourage children to value reading as a lifelong skill and pleasure, and to focus national attention on the importance of reading in children's lives.

was rich in folklore and tale-telling, with the special influence of a grandmother who threaded the family history into story form, to the continual delight of the Martin children. Here began his deep belief that at the heart of all language learning is the quest for humanness. Today he is considered to be one of America's outstanding teachers and educational lecturers. He also is a storyteller par excellence.

Millions of children and teachers and librarians in every state of the Union and throughout Canada have responded wholeheartedly to Bill Martin's unique ability to make a story come alive with meaning, humor, and drama, and to his understanding of children, language, and literature revealed in his lectures and writing. His lecturing is itself an art form, interrelating storytelling, reciting, singing, and philosophizing, often to musical accompaniment.

He served as principal of Crow Island Elementary School in Winnetka, Illinois; as editor of elementary classroom materials for Holt, Rinehart & Winston; and has been a visiting professor at more than ten universities.

His two television series, "The Storyteller," filmed in 1955, and "Bill Martin," filmed in 1968, are still widely used on educational stations across the country.

His publications include *Sounds of Language*, a literacy-based reading program for grades kindergarten through eight; the *Owl Books*, four libraries totaling 120 books for individualized reading instruction; the *Instant Readers,* 30 rhythmic read-aloud books that help children expand their intuitive knowledge about language and literacy structure; the *Freedom Books*, a set of 10 social studies books that help inculcate in children the disciplines of democracy; 18 storybooks including *Little Squeegy Bug, Smoky Poky*, and *The Brave Little Indian*, all illustrated by his brother, Bernard; and *The Human Connection*, a treatise on children, schools, and language, published by the Association for Elementary/Kindergarten/Nursery Education.

"Our job," he says, "is to give children a rich storehouse of buoyant language models, which, when securely anchored in their ears, transfer readily to the tongue and to the eye for reading, writing, and speaking."

Something About the Author: Facts and Pictures About Authors and Illustrators of Books for Young People, Vol. 57

Anne Commire, editor
1989; 300 pp.; $70
Detroit: Gale Research

Designed primarily for reference librarians, this continuing reference series, with 57 volumes now in print, provides excellent biographical information on authors and illustrators, together with photos of the authors and illustrations from their books.

Katy Obringer

Cornerstone: Jane Baskwill

From Turkey Traps to Balloon Trees

As I stood doing the dishes, I watched out my kitchen window as Nicholas and Amanda attacked the newly deposited dirt pile. "It's a good thing Steve never runs out of projects around the yard that require sand," I mused. "The children certainly have a wonderful time with it." It made me think of sand castles on the beach, sand castings, and the occasional beach burial. I wondered what these two were up to as Nicholas was handed the shovel for his turn to dig. Meanwhile, Amanda unfolded the plan as her face and hands expressed its finite details. She took one last turn with the shovel just as I wiped my hands and prepared to call them inside.

"So, what's up?" I inquired of the two sand urchins who were now before me.

"We made a trap," Nicholas said excitedly.

"A Midnight Turkey trap," Amanda corrected.

"So now what?" I wondered.

"Now we wait!" they both said confidently.

I smiled the way a mother does when she knows her children's expectations may not be fulfilled, and we all headed upstairs to begin the bedtime routine. I wondered if I should go put something in the trap. Perhaps I should check the Midnight Turkey book, which was one of their favorite stories. Maybe I'd get an idea. Bedtime stories came and went, and I never did check the Turkey book.

The next morning Nicholas and Amanda bounded down the stairs, fully dressed at 6:30 A.M., and raced out the front door without so much as a hi or good-bye. A few minutes later they returned, faces beaming, smiles from ear to ear, clutching a few bits of paper.

"The turkeys were here! Look what they left!" they said.

I was so surprised I could hardly speak.

Jane Baskwill has been a classroom teacher for the past 20 years. She is presently acting as teaching principal at Parker's Cove Consolidated School in Annapolis County, Nova Scotia. Jane has twice received an Education Quality Award from the Nova Scotia Teachers Union and recently received a Distinguished Achievement Award from the Educational Press Association of America for her series of articles in *Teaching K–8* magazine.

"What is it?" I asked.

"It's a recipe," Nicholas offered.

"For cereal sandwiches!" Amanda explained.

"And two membership cards," Nick went on, "in the Midnight Turkey Club!"

I'm still not sure if the Midnight Turkeys came or not. Steve insists he didn't leave the recipe or the membership cards. And I never did decide if the gleam in those two young pairs of eyes was delight at their find or really the gleam of a Midnight Turkey.

A few months later, exhausted after a long day at school, I drove in my yard not looking forward to the evening routine of dinner and dishes. To my surprise, the flowering crab shrub in our yard was colourfully festooned with paper balloons blossoming from every branch. Nicholas and Amanda once again greeted me with that magical look in their eyes shouting, "We're saved! We're saved! She saw the signal!" I then recognized that I was about to step out of my car into the world of *The Balloon Tree*, a book by Phoebe Gilman.

Over the years, as I have watched my children grow, I have had porridge with Goldilocks, helped Jack escape from the giant, set sail for the land of the Wild Things, and have applauded the mystery-solving expertise of any number of detectives.

For Nicholas (age seven) and Amanda (age nine), books are a natural part of their lives. There has never been a need for me to search out additional activities related to the book they were reading or a need to be sure there was a balance of written or oral responses. There has never been a need for me to check comprehension or written formats they were using or even to go out of my way to mention any other stories by that particular author.

These children made the stories come alive for themselves. They responded to the authors' playfulness with whimsey and imagination, which far surpassed anything I might have conjured up for them. They also knew what was appropriate behavior for them within the context of our family.

At school, whenever I am tempted to regulate or control my children's responses to the literature they are reading, or worry about covering specific material according to a predetermined timeline, I think about that Turkey Trap and Balloon Tree. I think about the trust I have in my own children to learn at home in natural, meaningful ways. I think about their inborn sense of play—that imagination—that is their reality. With them in mind I am able to value the other Nicholases and Amandas in my classroom and concentrate on creating an environment which allows a "Turkey Trap" to be built or a "Balloon Tree" to blossom. We are a com-munity of learners, a family, in which each member is valued, supported, invited, and trusted to share his or her involvement with literature.

If you haven't had any "Turkey Traps" built in your classroom lately, perhaps it is time to go out and dig one of your own. But be prepared. Before long, your children will come join you.

→ See: Andrews, p. 36; Literature Reference List, p.429; Rich, p. 27.

Further Reading by Jane Baskwill

◆ *Evaluation: Whole Language, Whole Child.* Scholastic TAB, 1988.
◆ *Moving On.* Scholastic TAB, 1988.
◆ *Parents and Teachers: Partners in Learning.* Scholastic TAB, 1989.
◆ *Pass the Poems Please.* Wildthings Press, 1989.

Book Note

Heidi's Alp: One Family's Search for Storybook Europe

Christina Hardyment
1988; 272 pp.; $7.95
New York: Atlantic Monthly Press

Wouldn't it be fun to climb the same alp that Heidi did? Wouldn't it be grand to see the Pied Piper leading the children of Hamelin away in an on-site reenactment of the old story?

Christina Hardyment and her four daughters think so; this book is the story of their tour of the settings of European fairy tales and children's literature. Although the writing style of this British author is somewhat dry and restrained, the contents of the book are wonderful. The bibliography of European children's literature and related scholarship is excellent, and Hardyment also includes a four-page list of useful addresses (e.g., the Hans Brinker Collection in Holland, the Hans Christian Andersen Museum in Denmark, and Pinocchio Park in Italy). Won't somebody do a similar book for the United States?

Sandra Wilde

YOUNG ARTISTS

—Corey Dickinson, 9, Portland, OR
(From *Treasures 1,* see p. 162)

Book Note

Pipers at the Gates of Dawn: The Wisdom of Children's Literature

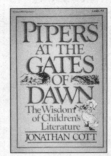

Jonathan Cott
1985; 325 pp.; $8.95
New York: McGraw-Hill

This collection of interviews/essays on authors of children's literature, including P. L. Travers, Dr. Seuss (Theodor Geisel), and Maurice Sendak, goes deeper than most. Cott talks to Travers about mysticism, compares Pippi Longstocking to Hercules, and explores the history of children's culture with Iona and Peter Opie. Cott is a poet and journalist who writes on a variety of subjects and for a variety of publications, including *Rolling Stone*. This book is a delight for teachers who would like to learn something about what their favorite writers for children are like. At an average length of 45 pages, these essays are far more extensive than is usually possible in children's literature journals. Maurice Sendak's thoughts on public reactions to the nudity in some of his picture books and Dr. Seuss's comments on subversiveness are just two examples of the unusual contents of *Pipers at the Gates of Dawn*.

Sandra Wilde

❝Adults will take their kids to museums to see a lot of peckers in a row on Roman statues and say: That's art, dearie, and then come home and burn *In the Night Kitchen*. Where's the logic in that? Art in people's minds is desexualized, and that would make the great artists sick.

"In the illustrations I did for Randal Jarrell's *Fly by Night* . . . I have an eight-year-old boy flying naked in a dream. I tried to draw the boy first with pajamas—he looked too much like Wee Willie Winkie. Then I tried him in underwear, and it looked like an ad for Fruit of the Loom. I tried him wrapped in sheets and blankets, but it looked too baroque. He had to be naked. But I know they're going to say it's typically me, arbitrarily making somebody nude. I had a picture showing a girl with her vagina in full view in *The Light Princess*, and nobody made a fuss about that, which makes me think the whole world is male chauvinist—vaginas don't count.❞ (p. 54)

❝'I'm subversive as hell!' Geisel replied. 'I've always had a mistrust of adults. And one reason I dropped out of Oxford and the Sorbonne was that I thought they were taking life too damn seriously, concentrating too much on non-essentials. Hilaire Belloc, whose writing I liked a lot, was a radical. *Gulliver's Travels* was subversive, and both Swift and Voltaire influenced me. *The Cat in the Hat* is a revolt against authority, but it's ameliorated by the fact that the Cat cleans everything up at the end. It's revolutionary in that it goes as far as Kerensky and then stops. It doesn't go quite as far as Lenin.'❞ (p. 28)

Education in Turin: A Romance by Herbert Kohl

Continued from page 139

From the Civil War to the New Century:

Alice and the Romance of Teaching

Elizabeth's child, Alice, hated school until Christmas in 1871 when one of her uncles gave her a copy of Louisa May Alcott's *Little Men*. He knew she loved *Little Women*, and supposed, correctly, that Alice would like to know what happened to Jo when she grew up.

"Jo became a teacher!" Alice told her mother. At first Alice was a little disappointed, but as the book unfolded it became clear that Jo's school was not like the one Alice attended. There was an understanding of child life she hadn't experienced in Turin. She asked Elizabeth about Louisa May Alcott.

Elizabeth knew of the Alcotts, not just Louisa May but the whole family. She took down a book to show Alice—Elizabeth Peabody's *Record of a School* published in 1835 in Boston. It was the story of the Temple School run by Bronson Alcott, Louisa May's father.

Elizabeth explained to Alice that Bronson Alcott tried to create a school where boys and girls of all classes could go to school together and grow

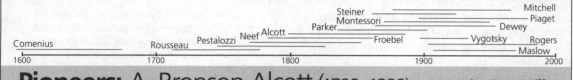

naturally and with love for each other and the world. He even took in a black student at a time when there were hardly any other integrated schools in the country. The school didn't last long, but Bronson's daughter Louisa May made it live on in *Little Men*. Jo, the wild one of *Little Women*, became what was called a "modern teacher" in the 1860s and 1870s. She believed in child-centered and experiential learning.

As Alice got older she toyed with the idea of teaching. When she was 18, her mother gave her a book called *Reminiscences of Friedrich Froebel*, written by Baroness von Marenholz-Bulow and translated into English by Mary Mann, the second wife of Horace Mann and sister of Elizabeth Peabody.

Alice was particularly moved by this quote from Froebel: "The kindergarten is the free republic of childhood." She found herself caught up in the romance of teaching and volunteered as a tutor at the Turin Common School.

➡ See: Literature Reference List, p. 429

Continued on page 204

					Steiner				Mitchell
						Montessori		Parker	Piaget
				Parker	Montessori			Dewey
Comenius			Pestalozzi	Neef Alcott			Froebel	Vygotsky	Rogers
	Rousseau								Maslow
1600		1700		1800			1900		2000

Pioneers: A. Bronson Alcott (1799–1888)   by **Ron Miller**

At the age of 24, this itinerant peddler from rural Connecticut turned to teaching in local schools near his home. Apparently the young man possessed an unusual sensitivity to children's natural ways of thinking and learning, and during the next several years, he developed a variety of innovations in his teaching that addressed natural development. He taught through conversations, journal writing, and physical activities, and encouraged imagination and self-expression. He introduced more comfortable desks, slates for writing, and real objects to manipulate and count for math lessons. When he read of Pestalozzi's work and heard of Neef at New Harmony, he identified himself with their ideas, calling his school "Pestalozzian." He attracted the attention of several liberal intellectuals who were concerned about education, and was touted in the Boston press as the "American Pestalozzi."

But Alcott encountered as much resistance as had Joseph Neef. Parents were shocked by his innovations and the fact that their children enjoyed school so much they followed their teacher home for more lessons. The angry parents opened competing schools, forcing Alcott to move several times. In 1828 he went to Boston and encountered a wider intellectual world that excited and challenged him. One of his mentors was the Unitarian leader William Ellery Channing, who passionately preached about the "infinity of resource in the human soul" and wrote that the purpose of education is to unfold these hidden powers. In 1830 Alcott moved to Philadelphia to run a school but returned to Boston in 1834. For four years, under Channing's sponsorship, he conducted the famous Temple School, with Elizabeth Palmer Peabody (later a pioneer in the American kindergarten movement) as his assistant.

During these years, Alcott became a leading member of the Transcendentalist group and lifelong friend of Ralph Waldo Emerson. Unlike most members of this group, Alcott was not a Harvard-trained scholar, but he was the most mystical and otherworldly among them. Still, he earned their respect for his idealism and integrity; Thoreau considered him to be a prophet. Unfortunately, his idealism again alienated the parents of his students; he was forced to close Temple School after the publication of his *Conversations with Children on the Gospels,* which parents (and the Boston press) considered radical, irreligious, and even obscene. He opened yet another school, but again the parents withdrew their children—this time when he refused to dismiss a black child he had accepted. Only five pupils were left, three of them his own daughters, including six-year-old Louisa May.

Thus, in 1839, Alcott's teaching career was over. He did serve as superintendent of schools in his adopted hometown of Concord, Massachusetts, but spent most of his later years as a wandering lecturer and even something of a celebrity, for Americans looked at the Transcendentalist period with a certain nostalgia. Largely forgotten, however, has been his contribution to educational theory. His innovations and writings from the 1820s and 1830s are an important chapter in the history of holistic education. Alcott advocated education for "the complete development of human nature" beyond the dry, sterile book learning that comprised it in his time. He insisted that the educator should "look to the child" rather than attempt to impose a predetermined system.

Further Reading

Alcott, A. Bronson. 1960. *Essays on Education,* ed. Walter Harding. Gainesville, FL: Scholars' Facsimiles & Reprints.

Dahlstrand, Frederick C. 1982. *Amos Bronson Alcott: An Intellectual Biography.* East Brunswick, NJ: Associated University Press.

McCuskey, Dorothy. 1969. *Bronson Alcott, Teacher* (1940). New York: Arno/New York Times.

Network

Bookwords
by Maryann Eeds

LCED inc.

My friend Ralph Peterson often talks about literature as another way of knowing. This truth was confirmed for me one more time as I read Hermann Vinke's beautiful book *The Short Life of Sophie Scholl.* Sophie Scholl (with her 23-year-old brother and other young college students) was executed at 21 for her part in resisting Hitler's policies. The story is told through interviews with Sophie's sister, Inge, who survived to tell what happened. I was struck by the influence that reading had on the lives of Sophie and the other resisters. Inge said that the reading of banned books became the first intimation of resistance. She said that "friends told one another about books . . . [but] they came to grasp that experience arises not from what you read, but from what you do. Books could stimulate, could impart an insight, could light a candle. But all of this would be relevant to your own life, your true self, only when you put into practice what you had determined was right." Through Vinke's interviews with Inge, through Sophie's diaries and letters, and through photographs and drawings, this book is a chronicle of how the group of young people who came to be called "The White Rose" put into practice what they, despite the ascendancy of incredible evil, determined was right.

Inge says that their father often quoted a line from a Goethe poem: "Braving all powers, Holding your own." Sometimes their father would simply call out, "Braving!" and the family would know what he meant. This book is a testimony to such braving. It is said to be one of the most important books ever written for young people.

➡ See: Literature Reference List, p. 429.

Excerpted From "Bookwords," *Centerspace* 2(5), May/June 1988, p. 2.

Maryann Eeds is a professor at Arizona State University, Tempe, AZ.

Subscription Information: *Centerspace* is published by The Center for Establishing Dialogue in Teaching and Learning, 325 E. Southern, Suite 14, Tempe, AZ 85282, (602) 894-1333

The Basal Failure

As I See It:
Kenneth S. Goodman

The Basal Report Card

Adapted from *Report Card on Basal Readers*, by Kenneth S. Goodman, Patrick Shannon, Yvonne S. Freeman, and Sharon Murphy (New York: Richard C. Owen, 1988): pp. iii–iv, 124–131.

The American people have a deeply ingrained belief that technology, in and of itself, can solve human problems. In education both the public and the educational profession have come to accept tests and textbooks as an infallible technology, the product of the best that science has to offer. In no other aspect of education does this total trust in technology reach the level that it does in reading instruction. And this is no accident, since the technology of reading lessons is embodied in a huge, brightly illustrated package, the basal reader, which makes an attractive promise. Basal publishers have convinced most reading experts and many school officials that basal programs are sequential, all-inclusive sets of instructional materials that can teach all children to read. If teachers follow the directions in the basal teacher's manual faithfully, the basal technology will provide universal literacy for all Americans.

Basals are now so dominant that they have become the reading curriculum in nearly all American schools. Both teachers' and students' performances are judged by the basal manuals and the basal tests. When children fail to learn to read easily and well through basal instruction, the blame goes either to the teacher for not following the basal carefully or to the children as disabled learners. In many American schools promotion from one grade to another is based on success or failure in the basals. Rarely are lesson content and instructions examined for their possible contribution to the students' problems.

The absolute dominance of basal readers led the Commission on Reading of the National Council of Teachers of English to initiate a study into basal reading programs. The concern of the Commission is with the promotion of literacy in the United States. Toward that end, *Report Card on Basal Readers* takes an advocate's position in favor of students and teachers and seeks to answer many questions: Why do teachers and students find themselves in a position of powerlessness during reading instruction? Who benefits and who suffers from the present reading programs? What are the consequences of perpetuating the status quo? How possible is change toward greater freedom for teachers in control of their teaching, and for students in control of their learning and literacy?

So What About Basal Readers?

In a nutshell, we found the basals to be seriously limited by the criteria for design that basals were founded on. They still cling to behavioral *Laws of Learning;* they still assume a teacher who is not competent to plan instruction; they still represent an industrial management view of schooling. They are more alike than different.

The basals' main strength is their tight organization and sequence. This creates a sense of scientific rigor. Everything is precise, direct, and goal-directed, from the lesson organization, to the controlled vocabulary, to the complexly labeled questions that precede, accompany, and follow the reading of the stories and other texts. They appear to offer to schools and to teachers the complete programs they have promised.

But their major strength is also their major weakness, because the essential elements of the organization and sequence do not easily permit modification in any but superficial ways. New understandings of the reading process, and new insights into teaching and learning, find their way into the language of the manuals, but they do not change the essential nature of the basal or how learners and teachers experience it. They remain locked to the notion that the learning of reading can happen skill-by-skill and word-by-word and that learning is the direct result of teaching.

Furthermore, at each point where the apparently tight system and goal-orientation of the basal is carefully examined, there appear to be misconceptions, inconsistency, misdirection, and misapplication. Lessons and test elements do not do what they claim to do. Labels are used inconsistently. And poor execution is found throughout the programs: mismatching of questions and content; incoherent, unreadable texts; awkward grammar and phrasing; unanswerable questions. The basals are not in reality what they appear to be. They are not consistent with their own design criteria.

More than anything else the basals are built around control: They control reading; they control language; they control learners; they control teachers. And this control becomes essential to the tight organization and sequence. That's why publishers admonish teachers not to wander from the manuals; that's why administrators require teachers to be faithful to the program.

If tight control were necessary to the development of reading, then we might grudgingly tolerate it. But the evidence from science —recent theory and research—is that reading, like all language, only develops easily and well in the context of its use. Learners need the freedom to experiment, to take risks, to raise questions in the process of trying to make sense of comprehensible written language. In the basal there is little choice for learners, little self-control, little sense of ownership of their learning and their reading. That's not just bad for their reading development. It's also bad for their development as thinkers, as learners, and as participants in a democratic society.

Shannon (1987, p. 311) says:

Professionals control their work and make critical judgments about what procedures and materials are most suitable for specific situations.

Duffy, Roehler, and Putnam (1987, p. 357) conclude:

As more is learned about the nature of reading and the effective teaching of reading, the need for elementary school teachers who will make substantive curricular decisions becomes more apparent.

But just as it must control reading, language, and learning, the basal's central premise requires that it control the teacher. And the control of teachers, far from assuring their effectiveness, limits both their authority and their responsibility for the development of their pupils. One of the great tragedies of the basals is the dependency they have created in teachers.

Why do publishers adhere to a discredited and narrow model of teaching? The answer, again, is control. How can they control teaching unless they make it specific and sequential? And further, how can they justify the basal if good teaching is responding to what the child is trying to do?

Clearly most of the generations of children who have experienced the basals over the past six decades have learned to read. Partly this is a tribute to the learners themselves. Partly it is a tribute to the teachers who found ways of making the basals interesting and found ways of supplementing or varying their use to fit the needs of the learners. And partly it must be due to some aspects of the materials themselves: Whatever their faults, they did focus the attention of teachers and learners on reading.

Clearly, however, the blame for the limitations and lack of success must also be shared. The basals have not fulfilled their promises: They have not taught all children to read easily and well. Basals have in fact become a rigid technology that is highly resistant to change and improvement.

If the current basals were regarded as one among several alternative approaches to materials for reading instruction, then we could assume that those teachers and administrators who prefer them could continue to use them. Others would find alternatives, and over time the merits of the competing systems would become clear. At present basals lock out alternatives and lock in teachers and learners.

→ See: Freeman, p. 110; Goodman, pp. 98, 100, 102.

References

Duffy, G., L. Roehler, and J. Putnam. 1987. "Putting the teacher in control: Basal reading textbooks and instructional decision making." *Elementary School Journal* 87.

Shannon, P. 1987. "Commercial reading materials, a technological ideology, and the deskilling of teachers." *Elementary School Journal* 87.

Book Note

Report Card on Basal Readers

Kenneth S. Goodman, Patrick Shannon, Yvonne S. Freeman, and Sharon Murphy
1988; 180 pp.; $9.95
New York: Richard C. Owen Publishers, Inc.

WHOLE LANGUAGE CAMERA

Second graders in Charlene Rogers' class display their favorite authors' books, East Aurora, N.Y.

I Used to Be...But Now I...

I used to think that basals were best,
But now that I've found 75 changes in one chapter in *Wind in the Willows*, I've changed my mind.

—Anonymous

As Teachers See It

The Problem with Basals

Basals reflect the publishers' desire to profit. The texts are overstuffed with isolated skills and seem to include everything—including the kitchen sink! Basal writers have limited knowledge of children, the reading process, and teaching.

A basal doesn't even look like a book! Basals don't teach kids how to read in the real world. For all their "skills," basals do not help children develop reading strategies. Teachers don't teach when they are using basals; they are told what to say.

Basals are flawed because:

- The material is not up to literary standards; if real literature is used it is often rewritten, and the language becomes colorless, flat, and dull. Often missing altogether are patterned vocabulary, literary context, and real language.

- Kids don't learn to sustain their reading of a book nor how to abandon a book.

- Kids don't learn to personalize their reading; for example., "My favorite book is . . ."

- Kids can't binge with basals; basals don't invite rereading.

- Kids must be read with and read to a lot. The basal technique with its teacher's manual and workbook does not lend itself to the joyful oral sharing of literature.

—As told to John Gegan by Barbara Bosworth, a dedicated whole language teacher and a member of the Bay Area Reading Project

Language Stories

The Power of a Book

We four adults had been sitting at the table in the restaurant talking for an hour or so when we suddenly realized that we hadn't seen the two little girls for some time. I finally found them crouched behind a large potted plant in the corner of the lobby, staring intently at the base of a large grandfather clock that stood against the opposite wall. When I asked what they were doing, they replied that they were watching to see if Pod and maybe Arrietty might be coming out. There was a hole in the base of the grandfather clock just like the one in *The Borrowers*. Janey's teacher had just finished reading the book aloud to the second grade, and Janey had faithfully recounted each day's adventures to Robin, who was only in the first grade.

Both girls, now college graduates, are still convinced that the Borrowers live in the Court Hill Inn and that if we had let them keep watch on that clock after everyone had gone home, they would have seen at least one of them. I think they might be right!

➜ See: Andrews, pp. 36, 84; Literature Reference List, p. 429.

Reference

Norton, M. 1952. *The borrowers*. New York: Harcourt, Brace & World.

—Nancy Andrews, Department of Education, Augusta, ME

Resource: Book Publishers

Children's book publishing has grown immensely in the last decade. The variety and quality of available titles is a pleasure to contemplate for anyone involved with book selection for children, whether teacher, librarian, parent, or child. Listed below are some publishers to look into, but they are only the tip of the iceberg.

Frances Christie

Picture Book Studio

10 Central St.
Saxonville, MA 01701
1-617-788-0911
1-800-462-1252

The catalog for Picture Book Studio is as gorgeous as the books published by this small press. Among their illustrators are Eric Carle, Lisbeth Zwerger, Yoshi, Lark Carrier, and Ivan Gantschev. Each page offers beautiful four-color examples of the illustrations inside each book. Picture Book Studio also distributes Rabbit Ears Books, picture books accompanied by audiocassettes featuring such talents as Meryl Streep and Robin Williams doing the reading, Bobby McFerrin and Ry Cooder making the music.

Albert Whitman & Company

5747 West Howard St.
Niles, IL 60648-4012
1-800-255-7675

Whitman publishes a wide range of titles for preschool through eighth-grade readers. Catalog groupings, such as concept books that deal with children's problems and concerns, picture books, and reading preparation titles, help in book selection.

Holiday House

40 E. 49th St.
New York, NY 10017
1-212-688-0085

Holiday House is a children's book publisher. Ask for a look at its catalog at your local bookstore or library. The catalog features storybooks, fables, and science books, as well as sections on holiday reading and Judaica. Titles are also grouped by grade level. If you live outside New York State, you can order books directly from the publisher.

Book Note

Broken Promises: Reading Instruction in Twentieth-Century America

Patrick Shannon
1989; 208 pp.; $14.95
Westport, CT: Greenwood Press (Bergin & Garvey, original publishers, taken over by Greenwood)

Anyone interested in why things happen in schools the way they do will be fascinated by Patrick Shannon's *Broken Promises*. Shannon sees himself as an advocate in the "political struggle over rules, definitions and meaning in everyday life" as they relate to reading instruction. Shannon places reading instruction in its social, political, and economic contexts as he explains the rise of the dependency of school personnel and the public on reading experts and commercial publishers. He explores how this dependency gives "undue power" to experts and publishers, and has negative consequences for teachers and students.

I had to go to England on a sabbatical to realize that understanding the political nature of schooling highlights the possibility of change impacting schools, teachers, and children. It was in England, where issues of class, racism, and sexism are more obvious than in the United States, that I heard discussions among professionals and in classrooms between teachers and students relating the nature of literacy and reading instruction to political issues.

Shannon provides a critique of contemporary workbooks, yearbooks on reading, basal texts, teacher's manuals, reading methods textbooks, and professional journals. He describes how both the publishing industry and reading experts have consistently imposed on teachers and the public the view that teachers are not capable of developing reading instruction within their own classrooms. They have thereby participated, whether willingly or not, in the deskilling of American teachers of reading.

School literacy, he claims, is reduced to the completion of materials; the role of teachers is reduced to the management of commercially produced reading materials, and kids are left to develop the real aspects of literacy on their own. Teachers have lost control of the skills of planning and implementing reading on a daily basis in their classrooms.

His presentation of issues supported by a strong historical base provides the opportunity for healthy debate surrounding reading instruction.

YMG

➜ See: Shannon, p. 222.

I Used to Be...But Now I...

I used to tell children when to read and what books they were to read,
But now they choose their own books and I no longer have to remind them to read.

—Janet Goo

WELL-SAID

At school my teachers were listening to me stumble through the Dick and Jane readers. They would have been amazed to know about my secret life in which I was feasting on great fat books with many-syllabled words I've never learned how to pronounce properly.

—Katherine Paterson, "The Secret Life of Katherine Clements Womeldorf," *Once Upon a Time . . .*

In the Mail

March 6, 1989

Commissioner of Education
Tallahassee, Florida

Dear Commissioner of Education:

Recently I learned that the Instructional Materials Council is about to make a decision on reading textbooks for elementary schools, and there is a question about a "whole language" alternative. I would like to urge you to give this matter very careful study and not to rely on textbook publishers as your primary source of information. The facts are these:

1. Before the current craziness with phonics began following the publication of Rudolph Flesch's *Why Johnny Can't Read* in the early 1950s, children were learning to read very well, either with *or* without a basal reader. Many teachers used "individualized reading" programs, which relied on trade books instead of basal readers. (I was one of those teachers.)

2. By convincing school boards that children can learn to read only through a tightly structured skills program, publishers of basals have reaped huge profits. They are going to be reluctant to give up those profits, and can be expected to spend millions of dollars trying to defeat the ideas of whole language.

3. Publishers are now trying to cash in on interest in whole language teaching by publishing "whole language basals." The simple fact is that a basal is not needed with whole language. Furthermore, basals are a poor substitute for beautifully written and illustrated children's literature.

4. Although whole language teaching requires an understanding of the learning process, and the more the teacher knows about literature and reading the better, it does not take a super teacher to make the transition to whole language instruction. All teachers who want to do it can do so.

5. Children who do a lot of writing and a lot of reading of trade books do as well on standardized tests as children who learned to read through basal readers. Beyond the question of their ability to read, their attitudes toward reading are far superior; they enjoy reading and take library books home for the pleasure of reading.

My field is elementary curriculum and social studies. You are well aware of the problems in social studies: Children hate it; teachers do not have time for it; children in Texas cannot name the country to the south of their state; and most 18- to 25-year-olds do not vote. By using trade books and reference books as reading material in elementary classrooms, teachers are able to teach social studies in an enjoyable way, and children grow in their knowledge of the world around them. Children write notes from reference books, and they write reports about their state's history, which they present orally to their classmates. This is a beautiful marriage between language and social studies, and no longer do children say they dislike social studies.

I urge you to recommend to the Instructional Materials Council that teachers be allowed to choose how textbook monies are to be used in their individual classrooms. If they choose basals, give them basals. If they choose no basals, let them spend the same dollar amount on trade books. Treat teachers like other professionals and let them use their best judgment about appropriate learning materials for their specific children.

Basal textbook publishers have dominated the elementary school curriculum for too many years. It is time for teachers to take charge and to decide for themselves how they will teach reading. Whole language teaching has a good research base, as well as a long history of success. It is time for Florida to free itself from a narrow skill-based approach and give children a rich smorgasbord of reading material to help them become adults who not only can, but do, read.

Sincerely,
Robert A. Blume

Robert A. Blume is a professor at the University of Florida, Gainesville, FL.

Language Stories

Tortured Language

In my Reading Methods course, we compare various types of texts that are used in reading instruction and discuss the difficulties that many of these supposedly simple texts pose for emerging readers. One text, "Pam and the Pup" (Lippincott's *Basic Reading, Book A*, 1975), relies almost totally on the graphophonic cueing system, neglecting the syntactic and especially the semantic cueing systems:

> Pam ran up the ramp,
> Up the ramp ran the pup.
> The pup and Pam nap.

My undergraduates were able to point out the drawbacks of using such texts. The best critique, however, came from a fourth-grader who asked: "What is this? Is it from a beginning book of tongue twisters?"

—David Hartle-Schutte, professor, University of Hawaii, Hilo, HI

It Shouldn't Happen to Kids

A Classic Destruction

I was out on playground duty when a group of kids who had been my students the previous year walked up to me.

"Hi, guys. How's it going?" I asked.

Their response was a unanimous groan.

"What's wrong?"

"Ms. P. is making us read *The Diary of Anne Frank*. Boy, we can't wait until Anne dies."

I just couldn't believe their response to this extraordinary, deeply moving book. "How can you say that?"

"Because Ms. P. asks so many dumb questions: 'Who coughed first when they were hiding? What was Anne wearing? What did Anne say to so and so about such and such?' It's sooo boring. We just want Anne to die so we can get the book over with."

—LBB

→ See: Literature Reference List, p. 429.

Viewpoint: Nancy Larrick

To Ride a Butterfly

The California Reading Initiative, launched statewide in 1986, has attracted the attention of the world of education in the United States. It recommends a literature-based program, which will allow children to read in an enjoyable, thoughtful manner. The recommended list of over 1,000 children's trade books, as distinguished from textbooks, is splendid.

But questions are being raised concerning implementation of the initiative. Some administrators have said they don't feel confident that teachers can teach without step-by-step, word-by-word directions. And how can a teacher read so many books? they ask—1,000 on the 1986 list of recommended books! (And I must add that close to 3,000 new children's books have been published each year since the California list came out.)

How can we measure progress, people ask, if the children in a class are all reading different books? How can we score a test if we teach children to come up with different answers?

When I was in California in March 1988, I talked with a young man who was a fourth-grade substitute teacher for the semester. His pupils were all reading *James and the Giant Peach* by Roald Dahl and enjoying it. "All are reading the same book at the same time?" I asked.

"Yes, we keep together," he said.

I persisted: "But for the cost of 30 identical books, you could have purchased a variety of books and thus encouraged more reading."

He was ready with his answer: "I can't do that because I wouldn't have time to work out a study guide, vocabulary study list, activity sheets, and comprehension questions for so many different books."

In other words, he felt he needed a teacher's guide for each book, with prearranged questions and acceptable answers spelled out. He assumed there should be a basal-reader teacher's guide for each trade book. Evidently he was more comfortable continuing in the lockstep teaching of reading, rather than branching out. That is certainly not my interpretation of the California Reading Initiative.

I have thought of this young teacher again and again as I have read the ads and now the materials being published to aid teachers in using children's literature in the teaching of reading. These teachers' guides are coming out in profusion with breathless advertising copy about this new development in the teaching of reading. As I have examined some of these guides, I note common features that leave me wondering.

Reproducible graphics stand out boldly in the new teaching aids I have seen. There are Attribute Webs, Feeling Charts, Cause-Effect Maps, Circle Charts (one involving 32 circles), Story Maps, T Comparisons, Venn Grams, Mood Plotting Charts, Relationship Diagrams, and Decision Grids.

Vocabulary building is fostered by directions for choosing one word out of eight that best describes a certain character in a book, for playing Hangman, Alliterative Add-a-Word Games, and Word Pantomime.

Writing assignments include writing a new title for a book, writing a new final chapter for

Nancy Larrick, a resident of Winchester, Virginia, was one of the founders of the International Reading Association and served as its second president. In 1977 she was awarded the IRA Citation of Merit for her contribution to reading and the Drexel University Citation for her contribution to children's literature. Larrick is perhaps best known to adults as the author of *A Parent's Guide to Children's Reading*, 5th edition (Westminster Press, 1982).

the book, and telling what the book is about in A-B-C order using 26 words.

Rewriting has its place too: Rewrite the last sentence eliminating any word that begins with the letter *A*, and you have your writing partner fill in the correct words. Copy two sentences from the book, leaving out the vowels and have a partner fill these in. Best of all: Rewrite a title in exactly 10 words. (The example given: Scott O'Dell's *The Black Pearl* grows into *An Ebony Jewel Residing in the Shell of an Oyster*. Poetry comes into all of this also: Rewrite a passage from a poem avoiding words beginning with a certain letter (avoid all *A* words, for example)—or, select a favorite passage of prose and "translate" into a poem.

Literary analysis takes over intermittently. Once, in the middle of consideration of a popular realistic modern novel, literary analysis leads to a poem by William Wordsworth. I can think of no poem that would take us further from the mood and the significance of the book being studied. Why does such diversionary thinking interrupt a breathlessly exciting book?

There are Listening Activities, Springboards to Thinking, Problem-Solving Strategies, Critical-Thinking Activities.

In one place I found this provision: "Independent Reading Time (Teacher calls a stop 3–5 min.)."

I found no reference to reading aloud.

Why are so many games and gadgets introduced? Why do proposed discussion questions and activities seem to get us off the track so often?

Why must a reader stop at the end of each section or chapter to evaluate the predictions made earlier? And then to predict for the next chapter? Surely one of the joys of reading is to become so involved that stop-and-go signs are intolerable. Why not let children read without interruption of questions and cause-and-effect charts? Why so many interruptions to thought and mood?

Think of some of the characters of children's literature whom both children and adults hold dear to cherish as lifetime friends. At the top of my list would be Charlotte the Spider, Gilly Hopkins, Sarah (Plain and Tall), Ramona Quimby, Anastasia, Cracker Jackson, and those three valiant animals who made it across Canada in *The Incredible Journey*.

I would also include the narrator in *A Taste of Blackberries* by Doris Buchanan Smith. But suppose I had had to stop reading that remarkable book in order to make out a mood chart, an attribute web, or even a "syllocrostic quiz."

I rejoice that I was never asked to come up with titles for the untitled chapters in *A Taste of Blackberries*. Or to provide a new ending for that gripping little book.

Instead, I raced on, reading almost breathlessly. After all these years, I still feel the emotional impact of that amazing story.

I am glad I have never been asked to "translate" one of Doris Buchanan Smith's paragraphs into poetry. My so-called translation would not make it poetry by any means. It would only have mutilated the beautifully cadenced language and sensitivity of the original author. To try to do that would have broken the spell that

Book Note

A Parent's Guide to Children's Reading, 5th ed.

Nancy Larrick
1982; 271 pp.; $12.95
Louisville, KY:
Westminster Press

Nancy Larrick's advocacy of active parental participation in children's reading is widely recognized. Her well-loved *Parent's Guide,* in existence since 1958, has helped parents learn that by filling our children's lives with a love of words and with the pleasures of music and art, we act as their conduits to reading.

Larrick emphasizes the importance of the oral tradition in preparing children for literacy and gives practical suggestions for incorporating storytelling, poetry, and music into everyday life.

Arrietta Chakos

good literature can cast over the readers—a spell that keeps them reading and questioning.

So where are we?

Will teachers trying to implement the California Reading Initiative resort to these high-priced packets of teachers' guides built on the basal-reader model of predict, read, interrupt, predict, read, and review, then read again?

Will they come around to actually reading the library books for children instead of the brief synopsis given in the teacher's guide?

Will they read aloud to children every day? And provide time for the children to read independently just for the pleasure of it? (And not "call a stop in 3–5 minutes.")

Will they see to it that there is a goodly supply of appealing children's books in the classroom for quick and easy borrowing? Will they make sure that children have access to the school library at any time? Will they arrange to borrow packets of books from the school library to enrich various science and social topics as they come up?

Will they arrange for children to read and discuss books in groups, using open-ended questions?

Will they be flexible enough to read, experiment, and create?

Will they take a chance?

Several years ago, Madeleine L'Engle gave the commencement address as Smith College. Although she was addressing her comments to new, young college graduates, I think she would not mind if I turn her words to inservice teachers as well.

So to those teachers who find themselves in this transitional period of the teaching of reading, who are trying to adjust their thinking and their way of teaching to meet new possibilities and new dreams, I would say, as Madeleine L'Engle said:

"Take with you your vulnerability, your tears, and your laughter. Don't be like the two caterpillars who were crawling along on the ground when a butterfly flew over them. One caterpillar said to the other, 'You'll never catch me going up on one of those.'

"But," says Madeleine L'Engle, "I'll ride a butterfly any day. I hope you will too."

→ See: Dalrymple, p. 426; Freeman, p. 189; Goodman, p. 119; Huck, p. 188; Literature Reference List, p. 429; Rapoport, p. 176.

Adapted from "To Ride a Butterfly," *Reading in Virginia* 14, Spring 1989, pp. 1–4.

Resource: The California Reading Initiative

What Is the California Reading Initiative?

In 1985, the California State Department of Education launched a language, literacy, and literature campaign for California's nearly five million students. The goal: to gift our students with lifelong positive attitudes toward reading and writing. Many of our students miss out on the rewards of reading because they do not comprehend what they read and because they do not see reading as a meaningful choice in their lives.

Superintendent of Public Instruction Bill Honig has recruited a coalition of educators, parents, and business and community leaders to help address this critical problem. The 12,000-member California Reading Association has joined with publishers, booksellers, librarians, and professional organizations in promoting and disseminating materials that will support the literacy thrust.

For the past several years, educators throughout the state and the nation have been working on publications that will help your school assess the quality of your program. These publications include:

- *Celebrating the National Reading Initiative*
- *Effective Language Arts Programs for Chapter 1 and Migrant Education Students*
- *English-Language Arts Framework for California Public Schools, Kindergarten Through Grade Twelve*
- *English-Language Arts Model Curriculum Guide, Kindergarten Through Grade Eight*

It Shouldn't Happen to Kids

What? Me Read?

In response to the California Reading Initiative, which calls for the gradual elimination of basal readers, a California elementary school decided to introduce literature into the reading program. One afternoon, the staff gathered in the teachers room to discuss the changes and how they should take place. They decided that each class should receive 30 copies of two or three trade books. That way, every child in the class could read the same book. One whole language teacher on the faculty, who had been using literature sets for years, suggested that the school purchase a number of different books in smaller sets of six to eight copies as a way to provide the students with a much wider choice. Her suggestion was immediately met with a loud protest from her colleagues.

"That's impossible!" they argued. "Then we'd have to read *all* those books!"

—LBB

WELL-SAID

Adult readers do not choose novels based on some sequence planned by B. Dalton. Neither should children.

—Carole Edelsky,
"Living in the Author's World,"
The California Reader

- *Handbook for Planning an Effective Literature Program, Kindergarten Through Grade Twelve*
- *Handbook for Planning an Effective Writing Program, Kindergarten Through Grade Twelve*
- *Model Curriculum Standards, Grades Nine Through Twelve*
- *Practical Ideas for Teaching Writing as a Process*
- *Recommendations of the Curriculum Development and Supplemental Materials Commission: 1988 Adoption, Basic Instructional Materials in English-Language Arts*
- *Recommended Readings in Literature, Kindergarten Through Grade Eight*
- *Recommended Readings in Literature, Kindergarten Through Grade Eight, Annotated Edition*
- *Secondary Textbook Review: English*

Your School and the California Reading Initiative

Your school already reflects many of the characteristics of an effective English-language arts instructional program. Because the first phase of the *Open Books=Open Doors* effort in California involves taking a close look at your present English-language arts program, this checklist should be reinforcing as well as helpful in identifying program strengths and needs.

Open the door to our schools and find:

- Visible evidence in halls and classrooms that our school values reading: an abundance of good books easily accessible to students, displays of students' writing and reading-related projects, honor rolls for readers, and plaques citing community and business contributions toward our schools' literate environment.
- Teachers reading aloud to students every day from selections that model the best of all kinds of print classics, contemporary fiction, biographies, newspaper and magazine articles, and folktales.
- Teachers using read-aloud time to engage students in *thinking* about the content and ideas by encouraging them to predict, to relate personal experiences to the content, and to make applications to their own lives.
- Students reading extensively on their own in materials self-selected from the recommended reading list with encouragement to share their enjoyment and information.
- Teachers modeling their own pleasure in reading.
- Students who can describe the value and purpose of reading and writing to their lives now and in the future.
- Students involved in many kinds of formal and informal speaking activities, including storytelling.
- Teachers providing students with direct instruction in reading for meaning and emphasizing that language must make sense to listeners, speakers, and writers.
- Teachers actively involved in expanding their own knowledge and techniques by participating in effective staff development.
- Teachers and librarians working together to provide students with a rich literature base.
- Students who write every day . . . all types of writing from letters and descriptions to stories and reports.
- Students and teachers discussing how to be strategic readers and writers and what to do when their strategies don't work.
- Visible evidence that parents and the community are actively involved in supporting our school's English-language arts goals.
- Students engaged in integrated listening, speaking, reading, and writing activities in all subject areas.
- Students who value and use the resources of their classroom, school, and community libraries.
- Students using a wide variety of technology, including computers, word processors, and audiovisual equipment.
- An assessment of English-language arts programs that goes beyond standardized measures and provides information useful in planning instruction.

- Classrooms with reading nooks that feature a variety of print, including reference materials; classrooms with writing centers that encourage students to *want* to write; classrooms with student-developed books and writing; and classrooms with displays that feature and promote reading.
- An *articulated* English-language arts program that reflects our goals and objectives that emphasize ideas from literature and other subject areas.

→ See: Freeman, pp. 184, 189; Huck, p. 188.

Excerpted from the California Reading Initiative poster *Open Books=Open Schools*, California State Department of Education. For information on ordering publications, write to: California State Department of Education, Bureau of Publications, Sales Unit, P.O. Box 271, Sacramento, CA 95802-0271.

Resource: Book

Celebrating the National Reading Initiative

California State Department of Education
1989; 86 pp.; $6.75 plus CA sales tax from:
Bureau of Publications Sales Unit
California State Department of Education
P.O. Box 271
Sacramento, CA 95802-0271

This publication for parents, teachers, and librarians offers a wealth of activities gathered from across the nation to promote reading: celebrating at home, at school, in the library, and around the town and the world.

Recommended Readings in Literature: Kindergarten Through Grade Eight

California State Department of Education
1986; 78 pp.; $2.25 plus CA sales tax from:
Bureau of Publications Sales Unit
California State Department of Education
P.O. Box 271
Sacramento, CA 95802-0271

These lists were designed to help schools and parents select good literature for students in kindergarten through grade eight. The main categories of core and extended materials, and recreational and motivational materials, are subdivided into different genres and literary forms.

Resource: Pamphlet

English-Language Arts Framework

English-Language Arts Curriculum Framework and Criteria Committee
1987; 52 pp.; $3 plus CA sales tax from:
Bureau of Publication Sales Unit
California State Department of Education
P.O. Box 271
Sacramento, CA 95802-0271

Revolutionary in many ways, this publication comes close to developing a philosophy of whole language without actually using the term.

LBB

Cornerstone: Louise Howton

Introducing the National Reading Initiative

Booksellers nationwide have reason to rejoice, for there's a new development in the teaching of reading! Those of us who have been involved in selling children's books and introducing kids to the excitement of reading have known for years that the solution to our nation's illiteracy woes lies in using the wealth of literature available to children. However, the prescribed methods of teaching reading in most of the United States have traditionally dismissed literature as a supplementary tool, rather than including it in the core material used in the classroom. Now that illiteracy has reached crisis proportions, school districts across the country are realizing that the so-called literature-based curriculum can be a powerful tool in motivating children to want to read. This major trend in primary education offers booksellers not only an important new market, but also a chance to work within what promises to become a major literacy movement.

In May 1988 the "National Reading Initiative" was launched at the annual convention of the International Reading Association. The NRI is essentially a nationwide expansion of the "California Reading Initiative," or CRI, which was launched by the Superintendent of Public Instruction for California in May 1986. The CRI is a long-term, multifaceted effort designed to promote reading and enjoyment of literature and, in turn, reduce illiteracy, Within this initiative, teachers are working with librarians and parents to bring literature-based instruction of reading, writing, listening, and speaking into California classrooms.

Specifically, a CRI committee composed of teachers, librarians, and educational consultants developed a list of 1,000 recommended titles that in turn have been identified and classified into three categories: core, extended, and recreational. Those titles, fiction and nonfiction, that have been designated as core curriculum materials because of their "compelling intellectual, social, or moral content" are used on an alternating basis with basal reader textbooks during the 60 to 90 minutes per day devoted to reading and language arts instruction. At the end of each basal reader unit, a teacher and a reading group will devote a week or two to the reading of a core title with subsequent discussion and follow-up activities. California teachers using the CRI reading list have found that their students are motivated by the trade titles to want more to read after finishing a book. Core titles are also used within the reading groups in conjunction with science and social studies curricula.

"Extended literature" titles—those that demonstrate "emotional, intellectual, and aesthetic substance"—are used largely to establish and enrich the classroom libraries, which are often much more accessible to children than the main school library. These titles are used for additional classroom reading and reading at home, with the happy result that readers from lower reading groups are more frequently progressing to higher levels. The recreational titles are provided primarily by parents for use in the home and for summer reading to complete the total reading program.

The implementation of the California Reading Initiative necessitated a major shift in focus on the part of the curriculum planners within the state's 1,000 school districts. Major assistance for this refocusing was provided by the Harper & Row Junior Books Group, which established a pilot program, choosing 17 elementary schools to serve as models of how a literature-based curriculum can and should work, and also donated books. Those schools have showcased the use of trade books in the classroom as well as the teaching practices and lesson plans that accompany the use of trade books. Pilot schools were also established in Massachusetts, Rhode Island, North Carolina, South Carolina, and New York. These and other states are in the process of developing their own approaches to the concept and are likely to become leaders in the National Reading Initiative.

➜See: Howton, p. 180; Literature Reference List, p. 429; Ronberg, p. 181.

Excerpted from *American Bookseller*, May 1988, p. 165, where this material first appeared.

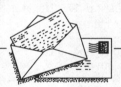

In the Mail

As Teachers See It

Readers' Workshop

by Judy Cox

Providing the Time

One major element of Readers' Workshop is that it provides students with 30 to 40 minutes of uninterrupted reading time each day.

Research has shown that youngsters learn to read by reading, just as they learned to talk by talking.

"Yet under the basal program, they spent frighteningly minimal time actually reading," says Westmere fourth-grade teacher Gail Robinson. "One study tells us that it was only six minutes a day, with the rest of reading time being spent on prereading activities, completing worksheets, and studying vocabulary words in isolation, rather than in context."

Research also has reinforced that children learn to read by being read to, and yet that happened on an all too irregular basis.

"I remember when I used to save the story till the end of the day," says Lynnwood kindergarten teacher Diane Martiniano. "My lesson plan even said 'story, if time.' But now I don't just read one story a day. I read three or four."

Sharing Ideas

Not all teachers in the district are using Readers' Workshop, and even among those who are, they vary in style.

"You will not see the same thing in every classroom. We're all trying different ideas and sharing with each other," says Lynnwood third-grade teacher Marna Foster.

The one commonality though is a sense of cautious enthusiasm.

"From the beginning, the concept of Readers' Workshop both intrigued and scared me," concludes Westmere fourth-grade teacher Gail Robinson. "Now that I've tried it, I love it, and I think it's working out well. That's not to say it's the panacea for everything, but if our goal is to build lifelong readers, writers and thinkers, then I think we are on the right track."

Excerpted from "Reading—It's Taking on a Whole New Meaning," *School's In!*, December 1988, Guilderland Central School District, Guilderland, NY.

As kids see it

Speaking as a Reader
by Jenny O'Connor

I love reading so much that whenever I can get my hands on a book, I try and read it. I read in the evening, at school, in the library, at home, on the bus, at night, and before I go to bed. When my teacher says Readers' Workshop is over, I don't want it to end.

Excerpted from *School's In!*, December 1988, Guilderland Central School District, Guilderland, NY.

Jenny O'Connor is a third-grader at Guilderland Elementary School, Guilderland, NY.

Viewpoint: Susan Ohanian

How to Create a Generation of "Aliterates"

Despite a promise that he wouldn't "be putting out Bill Bennett's list of books for the American people," William J. Bennett does indeed have a little list. In his model curriculum "James Madison Elementary School"—his last hurrah as U.S. Secretary of Education—Mr. Bennett suggests reading materials to accompany English instruction from kindergarten through eighth grade. (See *Education Week*, 14 September 1988.)

What good news! *Pilgrim's Progress* missed the cut. What bad news! So did Paddington, George and Martha, Miss Nelson, the Stupids, Anastasia Krupnik, Ginger Pye, Homer Price, Louis the trumpeter swan, and Dorothy.

What good news! The poet Jack Prelutsky made the list. What bad news! Shel Silverstein, whom children and teachers adore, did not. Myra Cohn Livingston missed the cut, too, as did Eve Merriam, Beatrice Schenk de Regniers, Charlotte Zolotow, Mary Ann Hoberman, Ted Hughes, X. J. Kennedy, Arnold Adoff, and many other poets loved by youngsters and their teachers.

A list—any list—is such a paltry thing. And in the hands of cultural elitists and their followers, a list can be terribly dangerous. Rather than including children in some sort of common cultural foundation, it excludes them from the rich possibilities of language and literature.

Force Mr. Bennett's curriculum on schoolchildren, and we will train a generation of aliterates: People who can read but choose not to.

When I look at Mr. Bennett's recommendations, I think of Sylvia. Dubbed the Zulu chief by many teachers, Sylvia was probably the toughest, most belligerent seventh-grader in our urban school. But she read—with pleasure—Langston Hughes, Lawrence Ferlinghetti, Christina Rossetti, Gwendolyn Brooks, and Basho.

Mr. Bennett's list avoids charges of ethnic bias by offering the contemporary poet Nikki Giovanni along with the traditional canon of Emily Dickinson, Robert Frost, Edgar Allan Poe, and Shakespeare. That's his entire poetry list for seventh and eighth grade.

I doubt that Sylvia ever read "The Raven," but I remember that foul-mouthed, hostile child sneaking into my room in times of great stress to listen to a tape of John Ciardi reading poems with his son Benn.

Sylvia gained 18 months in her reading scores during seventh grade, finishing above grade level, but she failed every class except reading. Occasionally, she cursed teachers, threw chairs, and fought with other kids. Finally, the authorities labeled her incorrigible, and at age 14 she was permanently excluded from the city school system.

During her final week at school, Sylvia gathered up some of the books she had enjoyed: *His Eye Is on the Sparrow, I Always Wanted to Be Somebody, Nigger, Autobiography of Malcolm X, Manchild in the Promised Land, Soul Brothers and Sister Lou.* Needless to say, none of these titles made Mr. Bennett's list. But Sylvia ran her hands over the books and said, "You know, it just proves that people who start out bad can do okay for themselves."

It has been my sustaining belief as a teacher that Sylvia was right. And such people need books to help them do okay. Powerful literature enhances children's lives, showing them a world of possibility.

I know that Ethel Waters and Claude Brown showed Sylvia possibilities that would have elud-

ed her in Mr. Bennett's list, featuring such authors as Charles Dickens, Lewis Carroll, Sir Walter Scott, Jules Verne, Alexandre Dumas.

Sylvia was a unique student, and in the nearly 20 years since I was her teacher I have never given the stack of books she devoured to any other seventh-grader. Others needed different books, and it was my job—my sacred calling—both to help each child discover books he needed and to find books the entire class could explore together.

Teaching grades seven through nine for more than 10 years, I never came up with a "must read" list. Because the makeup of a classroom changes from year to year, a teacher's resources for orchestrating the magical connection between kids and books are ever-changing.

But lists, once we let them in our doorways, have an insidious way of becoming entrenched and intransigent. They end up driving the curriculum, making us forget that the needs of individual students must be more important than the demands of any prescribed set of titles.

Mr. Bennett's little list is demeaning to children, their teachers, and the whole wonderful world of children's literature. As one might expect, it is heavily weighted toward the classics: Aesop, *Heidi*, Kipling, *Robinson Crusoe*. I wish there were some way of conducting an honest poll at the Education Department and finding out how many of its functionaries have managed to work their way through *Great Expectations, The Three Musketeers, Frankenstein,* and *20,000 Leagues Under the Sea* within the last 10 or 20 or 30 years.

As I study these recommendations, I am reminded of Mr. Bennett's observation in a recent speech: Acknowledging that he felt aggrieved when he heard that his old high school no longer required Latin, he said, "I went through it; I want them to suffer, too."

But is having suffered through *Ivanhoe* ourselves any reason to drag 11- and 12-year-olds of the 1990s through it? I would suggest that educators dust off Scott's novel and try to read it before rushing out to photocopy Mr. Bennett's recommendations.

If we are to educate for genuine literacy, then we must help children find pleasure in books, not push them through a committee's notion of the classics.

I would ask you to consider Mildred, a 15-year-old seventh-grader. She was, as she told me, "a little slow in reading." On standardized tests, she scored on a second-grade level. And her recorded IQ of 76 made her ineligible for the special help designed for "underachievers."

The choice is simple. Do you pretend that Mildred is going to read *The House of the Seven Gables* or *The Red Badge of Courage*? Do you make her feel inferior because she can't? Or do you help her find something she can read and enjoy?

Mildred was a basketball fan, able to quote all the rebounding and free-throw data about her favorite teams. I gave her a book of basketball biographies, each chapter profiling a current pro. The book was written on a fourth-grade level, and that child worked very hard to decipher its pages. After three weeks, she handed the book back with tears in her eyes. "The best book I ever read," she affirmed. "And I read it. I really did. The whole thing."

And then came the magic words, "Do you have any more?"

How many eighth-graders at Mr. Bennett's

Susan Ohanian first refused to use the basal reader in 1969 and since then has written letters and read books with students in grades one through fourteen. She has authored several hundred articles on teaching and learning for leading journals, and she contributes to the *Vital Signs* annual volume (Heinemann, Boynton/Cook), bringing together reading and writing. Currently teaching part time, Susan is an active lecturer and freelance writer.

Why My Sister Julie Hates *Across Five Aprils*
by Rebecca Rapoport

My sister and I were recently discussing some of our favorite historical fiction such as *Johnny Tremain, Spartacus, Citizen Tom Paine, The Witch of Blackbird Pond,* and *Across Five Aprils.* I was surprised to hear that Julie thinks *Across Five Aprils* is a silly book not worth the paper it's printed on. I asked Julie why she didn't like it and her response was, "I read it in school." She needed to say no more. I've read books in school and seen some of my favorite books turned into so much busywork. Teachers have a knack for that. It's pitiful.

It would be criminal just to let us enjoy a good book. Instead, teachers load us down with homework questions so that kids skim for the answers and drop the book as soon as they spot them all or have copied them from a friend. Then they give us "little quizzes" on the chapters in which we have to analyze all of the characters' actions or remember what the main character's little brother's pet iguana did at three in the morning. After the quiz, the teacher spends the whole period discoursing on the symbolism in the scene where the main character rubs the sleep out of her eyes while standing in a beam of light in front of the window.

Now I must admit that I have, on occasion, enjoyed a book I read in school, but usually I had already read it at home without the "benefit" of a teacher's help. The only other way I can enjoy a book is when I read the entire book the first night it's assigned so that my view is untainted by my teacher's assessment of the book. It's ironic that in trying to help us understand books teachers turn so many people off reading. Fortunately my sister Julie only hates *Across Five Aprils.* She still loves to read.

➔ See: Huck, p. 188; Larrick, p. 173; Literature Reference List, pp. 429; Whitin, p. 21.

Rebecca Rapoport is a high school junior. Her sister Julie is going into ninth grade.

James Madison Elementary and its spawn would, upon finishing *Ivanhoe,* have the strength or spirit left to ask, "Do you have any more?" Mildred did not read a single title from Mr. Bennett's list while she was in my care, but she and I were successful. She left our school confident that she could find pleasure in books.

We teachers must ever ask ourselves, *reading for what?* The culturalists are long on tradition but terribly short on pleasure.

Mr. Bennett exhorts educators to "jealously retain and guard" the goals of "mastery of a core curriculum of worthwhile knowledge, important skills, and sound ideals." Not once does he state that children must find joy in words if they are to become literate.

If a student leaves eighth grade knowing Dickens but detesting reading, is he a winner or a loser? If we want children to read these books so their scores will improve on another national scorecard, we are participating in a deceitful sham. We are cheating and dishonoring both the children and our calling.

➔ See: Huck, p, 188; Literature Reference List, p. 429; Ohanian, p. 60.

Excerpted from *Education Week* 7(6), 12 October 1988, p. 32.

Whole Language Internacional

An interview with Jill Korengold
by Lois Bridges Bird

Nicaragua

*S*mall children bend over their desks, trying to write on three-inch squares of paper. This struggle between abject poverty and the desire to learn occurs daily in Bluefields, Nicaragua, a community of about 38,000 people, located on the Atlantic coast, a four- to five-hour river trip through dense jungle from the capital city of Managua. It is a scene whole language teacher Jill Korengold and three colleagues from New York and California are working hard to change. Every summer, for the past five years, Jill and her group, Nicaragua Bilingual Education Support Project, an affiliate of the Educators' Committee on Central America, make the 2,000-mile journey to Bluefields with precious supplies of paper, books, and other school materials. In a recent interview, Jill's deep sympathy for these young victims of war and poverty came through strongly.

Lois: How did the bilingual project originate?

Jill: In the fifties, Somoza declared Spanish the official language of Nicaragua. The problem in Bluefields is that standard Spanish is a third language; Creole English is the first, and standard English is a second language. When Spanish was declared the official language, Creole speakers had to learn Spanish or drop out of school. This is why the new government is calling for bilingual education.

Lois: So how did you get started?

Jill: Our first trip was in 1984. We designed workshops that addressed the issue "why bilingual education?" There was a big division between people who think you can use Creole in the classroom and those who consider it completely inappropriate. Another problem is that there is very little written in Creole. Materials would have to be in standard English.

The first year we had eighty teachers from Bluefields and surrounding communities attending our workshop. We had Spanish, English, and Creole speakers; also, Rama and Miskito Indians. We decided to do the workshops in English and have someone translate to Spanish. The monolingual Spanish speakers were furious with us. "But we don't understand English! How can you do this to us?" they demanded. We said, "Do you see how your Creole kids might feel when they walk into your Spanish-only classrooms?" That made them think. People view Creole as bastardized English and not okay to use in the schools, so we explained that Creole is a complete language system and why learning in your first language is important.

I also explained how kids learn to read. We knew the schools didn't have books, but we thought the teachers could make books. As we found out, they had no paper, no crayons; how could they make books? We had come with a completely wrong idea of what was available to them.

In 1985, my friend Laura and I decided to put together a teacher's tour because we wanted to see the schools. We visited schools on both the Pacific and the Atlantic coasts. What teachers really needed was information on how to get kids to participate, how to interact with kids and actively involve them in the learning process. What we saw in the schools was so stilted. The teacher would ask a question, the kids would give a brief answer. Or the teacher would write on the blackboard and the kids were expected to copy it, often without any idea of what they were writing.

We met with government officials and told them what we had seen in the schools, and explained that we wanted to design workshops for teachers that would help them interact with kids beyond a question-answer format. "Fine," they said. "That fits with our philosophy."

One reason whole language works there so well is because they don't have any materials. They do have some old readers that are very sexist. "This is Jim. This is Father. Jim can help Father. This is Jeana. She cannot help Father. She can help Mother." So we worked at adapting the text, showing them how you can change it. And we brought posters that showed men holding pots and women, saws.

Lois: How did they respond to that?

Jill: Well, they laughed at first, but they liked it. After all, Nicaragua talks about the "New Man." I think it should be the new person. But they are trying to do away with sexism and traditional roles, so they were receptive.

We have also worked a lot with oral language development and have shown teachers how they can write down and use the kids' own language. This is really a revolutionary idea for them. The kids get to school and clam up, so we tried to get them to talk—we went on sound and color walks. Everything we do is built around the children's language. The themes we repeatedly emphasize with the teachers are that children are active learners and need to participate in class in an active, engaging way. They need lots of opportunities to express themselves.

As I said, they have so little in the way of materials. The first year we brought things that were durable and nonconsumable. We brought flannel boards, and tons of books. A friend of Laura's had found a warehouse where they were throwing out language-based readers. They were essentially books of stories—old tales, folktales, scary tales, jump rope rhymes, a story written in Creole. We brought as many as we could carry.

This year they wanted us to go to the schools in the outlying communities so we could actually see what was there. That was very helpful. When you're trying to make books and there's no paper, it's very difficult. The kids had these tiny three-by-three-inch squares of paper, but we found that they could still make books. We stressed creating a literate environment, surrounding the kids with written language, but then we realized the schools are built out of cement cinder block. How do you put things up on the cement walls? We figured out how to cement clothespins to the walls, and then you can just clip things up. One year we had a lot of paper—the end rolls of newsprint. But the next year there was a paper shortage, so you never know what you're going to find.

One thing we feel really feel good about is that we've managed to bring a library for every school. Each school got a suitcase with at least fifty books. Otherwise, there are no books; there are hardly any books in the town. This year they told us, "Reading is in an absolute crisis!" They had tested the kids and found out that they were not reading. Parents were threatening to take their kids out of the bilingual program. So the teachers sat with the kids in groups and just read to them and with them, and it made a tremendous difference.

Lois: Is the bilingual program voluntary?

Jill: Yes, and most parents want their kids in it. The bilingual program gets extra materials. But, as it turns out, most of what they have, we've brought. We've been the sole supplier of crayons. We've brought about five hundred boxes—we developed a crayon bank; teachers could check out a box. And now each school has about one hundred books.

Lois: And how long do you work there each summer?

Jill: About three weeks. Some of us stay on longer. I have a sabbatical coming up; instead of just several weeks, perhaps I could stay for six months. As I said, we did lots of bookmaking and continued to show teachers how to do variations on the text. We showed the teachers how to make their own big books—using the kids' words and adapting the text. They took "It looked like spilt milk," and changed it to "It looked like a tortilla!" *Caps for Sale* was rewritten to read *Fish for Sale*. Fishing, of course, is a major industry there. Another book was changed from a quiet night to a noisy night in Bluefields, which featured a drunken soldier and a Contra attack.

Lois: Have you encountered any fighting yourselves?

Jill: Well, we try not to think about it but it's out there. Just one week after we'd been up the river, the Contras attacked the boat and killed two people.

Lois: Jill, who sponsors you?

Jill: We sponsor ourselves. We write letters to friends and relatives. We got the mailing list for Global Education, thinking that group would be open to helping us. Most people who contribute are people who know us. One woman in Union City went around to the all the schools and said, "Can you help us? What can you donate?" The problem is shipping. Because of the embargo [the United States has imposed an embargo against Nicaragua], it's very, very hard to get supplies through. Quest for Peace has found a way; they send large containers. We are going to start working with them to get educational materials through. The fund-raising is hard work. It never ends—we work at it all year long.

Lois: What do you know about the teacher education program there?

Jill: I'd like to find out. I do know that teacher salaries are so low that many good teachers are quitting. The government said, "We can't raise your salaries because that will contribute to inflation, but we'll offer you the fourteen basic foods—oil, flour, beans, rice, et cetera—at a fraction of their cost." But it's still very hard for people who are used to having more choices.

We feel good, though. We feel like we've been able to make a difference for both the teachers and the kids. The teachers told us that our workshops were the best they've ever had. And given the choice of materials or us, they said, "We want you. We need your expertise."

And when we went into the schools this last summer, we saw evidence of our work. They had pocket charts up and were involving the kids in wonderful calendar activities. And we even encountered *Mrs. Wishy-washy!* [a predictable book from the New Zealand "Story Box"]. You know, it rains all the time there, and the roads aren't paved, so it's very muddy. So everywhere we went, we heard the refrain from *Mrs. Wishy-washy:* "Oh, lovely mud! Oh, lovely mud!"

In mid-October 1988, Hurricane Joan slammed into Bluefields and reduced it to a pile of rubble; 90 percent of the community was destroyed. Jill has not been able to get through, although she has had word that her good friends there were not harmed. What about the schools and all the materials Jill and her colleagues have brought over the past five years? Jill doesn't know. "The books were in suitcases. Maybe they were protected. Next summer we'll probably go with a hammer and nails and try to help rebuild."

LBB

➡ See: Literature Reference List, p. 429.

Great Teachers:
Katy Obringer
by Pat Yowell

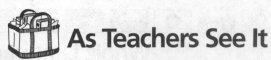

As Teachers See It

A Librarian's Influence
by Peter Hasselriis

Mix a vivacious, energetic, fun-loving person who has a dynamic personality with high ideals and goals, years of professional experience with children, in-depth knowledge of children's literature, creativity, and vision, and who do you get?—Katy Obringer, supervising librarian of Children's Services for the Palo Alto City Library system.

Unlike the schools, the public library does not have a captive audience. But when children come to the Children's Library and meet Katy, they are captivated by her warmth and genuine interest in them and their needs, and her ability to find just the right thing for them. The right thing that day might be a ride on the carousel horse, a poster for their room, the third book of a series, music for a birthday party, learning how to use the computer catalog, finding an article in a magazine, or any of a hundred other things.

Katy's professional philosophy is that a child's needs come first. To begin, she creates a physical environment that says, Welcome! This place is for you. She says this by having a fire in the fireplace on cold days, a display of artwork by children, comfortable chairs and couches just the right size for children, a picnic table in the garden, games and puzzles, a listening station for records, signs to make clear where things are located, attractive displays, plants, and decorations for special programs and holidays. The very fact that Palo Alto has a whole library devoted exclusively to children says to a child, You are important. Everything here is for you.

When you see the smiling faces, and hear the laughter and animated conversation among children and adults, you know this is a happy place to be. Children are allowed freedom to explore and test out everything the library has to offer. Katy lets them know how happy she is that they have come to the library, which gives them a boost in self-esteem. Children leave with positive feelings not only about themselves but also about the library and reading in general.

Children's Services strives to reach every child in Palo Alto. Katy is very egalitarian in her approach. No age is more or less important. Service is for all. She does not support a sign-up for programs or put any limitations on who can come to events. Every child interested in an activity is welcome. Flexibility and adaptability could be Katy's middle names. She uses every means at her disposal to entice and encourage children to develop library skills and to expand their choice of reading material. Katy believes that the process of learning to read begins as soon as a child can sit on a lap and hear a story or look at pictures. She takes every opportunity to speak to parent groups, teachers, and workers at infant and preschool centers, as well as to teachers and librarians. Moms, dads, and grandparents frequently call or come to the library for her recommendations on the best material for their little ones. The weekly toddler story hours increase her contact with this age group, and parents get practical ideas on how to develop their child's language skills with appropriate books, songs, games, and poems.

Katy's knowledge of children's literature is extensive. Her phenomenal memory enables her to identify books and characters from a tiny bit of the plot or a brief (and even inaccurate) description of a character. When asked for help, Katy always follows through and makes sure the child leaves satisfied. Children and parents catch her enthusiasm and leave prepared to like the books she has found for them. Children often gain confidence about school projects, because they know they have an ally at the library.

In order to maintain her high service standards and refine her skills, Katy keeps professionally "tuned" to the trends, research, and practices related to children's services. She continually makes the effort to go to workshops on storytelling and book reviewing. She also attends author symposia, conferences, classes, and conventions; participates on special committees and task groups; and networks with writers, teachers, and librarians.

It is pure pleasure to see this gifted and talented librarian in action. Katy radiates with the joy that comes only from a genuine love for what she is doing and for those she is serving. She has that rare gift of knowing how to listen to children and develop rapport with them.

Pat Yowell is manager of Branch Libraries and Children's Services, Palo Alto, CA.

Miss Chambers ran an honest-to-goodness library at the Greene Avenue Elementary School in Sayville, New York. It had a big oak checkout counter and matching golden oak tables and chairs. A full-time librarian, Miss Chambers took tremendous pride in having every issue of *National Geographic* that had been printed and in showing you that Sayville had been given prominent notice in one of its issues. Even greater than her pride was her belief that significant use could be made of the *Reader's Guide*, because the periodical collection in her library was so rich.

My fondest recollection, though, is of our weekly visits to her library. Miss Chambers would be waiting for me with new books that she knew I would like and, particularly, with the books of Howard Pease. Pease wrote books just for me: The Tod Moran stories were of a boy who adventured on tramp steamers. Sayville was on salt water, and it was through Tod's eyes that I could travel to a fantasy world that I knew lay just beyond the shores of "the crick" and Great South Bay. Miss Chambers would take me aside and say, "I've got a new Howard Pease book for you," or "Howard Pease has just come out with a new book, and I saved it for you." I still remember this with a glow of pleasure and think of it now as a magnificent statement about librarians, books, authors, and lifetime reading habits!

I also have memories of regular bike treks to the Sayville town library, where Mrs. Haff was the librarian. The two most vivid are of finding the Babar books, whose cursive script I could read, and of Mrs. Haff's calling my mother because I wanted to check out a book from the adults' side of the library. I think I was in eighth grade, and my mother, to her eternal credit, said, "Let him have any book he wants." To Mrs. Haff's credit, that's all she needed to hear. I don't remember what the book in question was; I know I never read anything with truly "adult" content until *From Here to Eternity* later. The seeds for the massive censorship-hating tree that I nurture at all possible opportunities were sown within me at an early age.

➜See: Hasselriis, p. 193.

Peter Hasselriis is a professor in the College of Education at the University of Missouri, Columbia, MO.

Book Note

The Child as Critic: Teaching Literature in Elementary and Middle Schools, 2d ed.

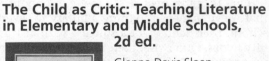

Glenna Davis Sloan
1984; 168 pp.; $15.95
New York: Teachers College Press

If one needs convincing of the efficacy of literature to inspire, to inform, and to liberate both hearts and minds, this is the book to read. Sloan makes a passionate yet practical case for making literature the center of the curriculum. Theory is interwoven with specific guidelines and bibliographies for whole class read-alouds, independent reading, small group discussions, and literary criticism. The last chapter provides strategies for helping students write their own poetry and stories. After reading this book, elementary and middle school teachers will know not only the *how* of literature as the core of their curriculum, but also the *why*.

LBB

66 Criticism, properly undertaken, is a study of how imagination works in the creation of art in words. In the process, the student's own imagination is developed and his capacity for vision enlarged. Criticism, properly undertaken, leads to a conception of literature as a coherent structure. With this conception comes awareness of its significance in one's own life, and in the lives of all. 99

Classroom Demonstrations

by Katy Obringer

Children's Services

Children's Services serves children, their parents, and other adults interested in children, children's literature, and related topics such as storytelling. As a staff we work hard in our outreach services to reach as many community members as possible. We serve Palo Alto, California, and the surrounding communities.

The following is a list of some of our activities:

- **Summer Reading Programs** encourage reading for the fun of it. We work cooperatively with all the libraries in Santa Clara County and promote the program through themes such as Mysterious Reader and Company, Space Readers, Race to Your Library (Olympics), Choose Your Adventure, Tickle Your Reading Bone, Byte into Books, and Reading Safari.
- **Library Child Care Link (LCCL) Grant.** We have increased outreach to child-care centers, preschool centers, and home-care providers. We visit schools and centers and provide a story time for children and a learning experience for teachers. We do workshops on children's literature, storytelling, making flannel boards, and so on.
- **Sleep Over at the Library** encourages fifth-, sixth-, and seventh-graders to finish the summer reading program.
- **Annual Storytelling Festival** promotes the joy of listening to a story. Fifteen local storytellers told stories on a Sunday afternoon in January.
- **Author Celebrity Series,** a highly successful joint program of the Palo Alto Unified School District and the Menlo Park School District, schedules at least nine authors per school year. School librarians work with teachers in preparing students for each author's visit.
- **Preschool Story Times** incorporates stories, songs, puppets, and so on into the weekly theme for preschool children.
- **Toddler Story Time,** developed out of a need to provide a library experience for the many babies in Palo Alto, serves children 18 months to three years. Parents, nannies, and child-care providers sit with children and help them participate in the stories and songs.
- **Bedtime Stories** is a family story time for children and parents who are invited to come to the library in their pajamas.
- **Family Films** is a Saturday event for families to view films together at the library. Nearly all the films are from books we have in the library. We display the featured books for families to check out.
- **Focus on Books** is our newest program. This year we are having our first fall reading program to continue the summer reading programs.
- **Library Card Campaign** is an ongoing effort to promote libraries and ensure that every child has and uses a library card.
- **Year of the Young Reader** is another national effort to reduce illiteracy.
- **Community Support.** The community has been wonderful in lending its support for our reading programs; for example, one of the grocery stores even printed material about books and libraries on grocery bags.
- **Read-Aloud Tapes** are made by children and circulated as one of our regular audio cassettes.
- **Emporium Back-to-School Storytelling Festival** invites storytellers in to the stores in September to celebrate going back to school.
- **Friends Across the U.S.A./ Pen Pals Across America.** Children sign a card and indicate their hobbies. Their names are sent to children throughout the United States.

- **Lectures.** I give a number of lectures about books every year to such groups as Twin Support Group, New Mother's Group, preschool groups (on literature for specific ages), colleges, private schools, and corporations.
- **Storytelling and Storytelling Workshops** are held for various groups in the community, such as local public and private schools. We also sponsor storytelling fairs.
- **National Library Week and Children's Book Week** are observed as special events every year.
- **Halloween Spooktacular** is sponsored by the Recreation Department. We always participate in this community event by telling spooky Halloween stories.
- **Libraries in Other Countries.** I have assisted organizers of children's libraries in the Philippines, Spain, and Pakistan. We had a book party at Children's Library to help get books for our sister city Palo Leyte in the Philippines.
- **May Fete Parade** is an annual event in Palo Alto. The Children's Library is represented in the parade with children dressed as favorite book characters or with book covers depicting favorite books.

- **Annual Children's Book Sale** sells all books withdrawn from the collection. Gift books are sold by Friends of the Library for 35¢ or three for $1, enabling children to have books of their own.
- **Displays.** We do numerous displays to promote reading—holiday books, new books, themes of the week, shelf sitters (wonderful books that children and parents don't find on their own), and books centered about specific programs such as a magic show. After a puppet show, puppet books are checked out like crazy.
- **Special Events.** We have lots of special events. *Clifford the Big Red Dog* was a big hit. The publishers have an adult-size Clifford costume that they loan out to schools, libraries, bookstores, and so on free of charge. We had a Clifford week with treats, stickers, bookmarks, activities, with dog (Clifford's friends) story times.
- **Support School Librarians.** We work with the librarians in the Palo Alto School District on a request basis. We are often called upon to do storytelling.

The ideas in the California *Language Arts Framework* are not new to me. I have been teaching this way for 23 years and loving every minute of it.

➜See: Rivera, p. 358; Wetherell, p. 300.

Katy Obringer is the supervising librarian at Children's Library, Palo Alto, CA.

Marvelous Inventions

It Has Mystery

Cindy Elliott of Baton Rouge, Louisiana, sent us this marvelous invention. I don't know what book her first-grade student was reviewing, but I intend to find out—and read it myself. —*LBB*

It has mysitory, exsitement Thrills and chills, and sometimes hart taching Parts.

Letters from a Librarian

by Bobbi Bernstein

Dear Teachers...
BACK TO BASICS is what the experts say —
Drill and skill them till ignorance goes away.
But using workbooks, basals, phonics, and tests
Robs you of your power, and takes away your zest.

You ask, what is the best way to make our kids literate?
I say, don't force it, or teach it bit by bit.
The answer's so simple, it's almost too good to be true:
Read books aloud, write together often, and see what they do.

Dear Administrators...
Much research has been done on how reading is learned.
It parallels language development and the process can be fun!
Try Goodman, Clay, and others to see what works and is true.
The whole language approach is really nothing new!

Dear Librarians...
What can *we* do to get kids to read?
Why, we've got what most learners need!
On the library shelves are many treasures

That can be used for read-aloud pleasures.
(Welcome the kids. Let them feel at home.
Show them a good biography, mystery, or poem.)
Spread the word, let everyone know
That the library is a good place to go.
Literacy does not result from force-feeding.
It happens when people learn to *love* reading.

Dear Professors...
Lead the way and let your students see
That whole language immersed is the best way to be!

Dear Parents...
Turn the TV off! Put away the workbook sheet!
Choose a great book to share! Read-aloud just can't be beat!
The kids'll learn to read. You just wait and see.
It'll happen quite *naturally*, and that's, for sure the key.

Dear Kids...
We love and respect you—
And want you to know
That reading and writing every day
Will help all learners grow!

Get to a library often.
Ask adults to read to you.
That magic of a good story
Will make you *happy* through and through!

Bobbi Bernstein is a songwriter and musician as well as a children's librarian at Chapin Memorial Library, Myrtle Beach, SC.

Children's Booksellers Associations

These associations produce membership lists which people can use to find the names and locations of their area booksellers.

Association of Booksellers for Children

Caron Chapman, Executive Secretary
175 Ash St.
St. Paul, MN 55126

Northern California Children's Booksellers Association

c/o Sharon Larson
The Storyteller
23 Lafayette Cr.
Lafayette, CA 94549
1-415-284-3480

New England Children's Booksellers Association

c/o Terri Schmitz
The Children's Bookshop
237 Washington St.
Brookline, MA 02146
1-617-734-7323

Texas Association of Booksellers for Children

c/o Toad Hall Children's Bookstore
3918 Far West Blvd.
Austin, TX 87831
1-512-345-8637

Southern California Children's Booksellers Association

P.O. Box 2895
La Jolla, CA 92038

Louise Howton

As kids see it

Wonderland

by Arwen Bunce

Of all the books I read
Fantasy and Adventures
are the best. I read until
my heart beats of listening
and seeing. In my mind
dragons, antelopes and
other things so great are
all tripping gaily into wonderland.

From *A Book of Fantasy and Adventures*, by 100 students from Alternative Community Schools (Summertown, TN: National Coalition of Alternative Community Schools, 1982).

The literate person…is not one who knows *how* to read, but *one who reads:* fluently, responsively, critically, and because he wants to…Children will become readers only if their emotions have been engaged, their imaginations stirred and stretched by what they find on printed pages. One way—a sure way—to make this happen is through literature.

WELL-SAID

—Glenna Davis Sloan, *The Child as Critic*

 Viewpoint: Louise Howton

The Role of Trade Publishers in the Whole Language Movement

The current whole language movement is rooted in the belief that children's learning of reading and language arts, as well as many other content areas, can be greatly enhanced by the use of literature. But where can we find the literature we need? you may well ask.

Trade publishers are today's ultimate best source of complete and original works for children of all ages on all subjects. My purpose in writing this article is to define the function of trade publishers and, I hope, to give enough guidance so that the reader will no longer feel as though the world of trade books is terra incognita.

Trade books are those that are produced "for the trade." That is, they are intended to be sold to consumers. Although they may teach a multitude of ideas, they are *not* textbooks. They are the books that comprise the majority of the stock to be found on the shelves of retail bookstores and libraries. Trade publishers are, naturally, the producers of trade books. There are several major publishing houses that have both textbook and trade divisions, but the two arms typically function separately in all aspects of their operations.

In recent years, the publishing industry has been experiencing truly explosive growth in the area of trade books produced specifically for children. This growth has been paralleled by an increase in the number of bookstores catering exclusively to children as well as an increase in the space within general bookstores devoted to children's books. Interestingly, this growth period actually began in the mid to late 1970s at a time when government funding to libraries had been severely diminished, and the bottom seemed in danger of falling out beneath the feet of children's book publishers, who until then were accustomed to garnering 80 percent or more of their revenue from the libraries.

Fortunately for the publishers, as well as for the American reading populace, this was also the time of a dramatic shift in family structure, with an ever-increasing number of women adding to family incomes by establishing their own careers, and in many cases having their children at a later age. There seems to be a correlation as well between the recent baby boom and awareness on the part of parents of the value of establishing books at an early age in their children's lifestyles. Those children who are exposed at an early age to a good quality and quantity of literature not only learn to read more easily, but also acquire a lasting love of reading. All of these factors have combined to create a much stronger demand for children's books that can be purchased, rather than simply borrowed from the library.

Naturally, the publishers responded to this increased demand by publishing more books for children—more titles and more copies of those titles. Some publishers who were previously involved only in adult publishing rushed to join the venture. Consequently, there is now an astounding and exciting array of titles available for children and adolescents on every conceivable subject and appealing to every taste.

The goal of the best children's publishers is generally to produce books that relate to children's intellectual frame of reference, but simultaneously stretch their minds and excite their imagination. Controlled vocabulary is practically unheard of in this corner of publishing. Instead, authors assume, and editors concur, that children are fully capable of learning long and intriguing new words by encountering them in the context of an absorbing story.

From the point of view of the publisher of quality trade children's books, there has probably never been a more exciting time to be working in this field. The increased sales volume has provided the financial support needed to afford publishers the opportunity to acquire the works of highly talented writers and artists. Today's sophisticated technology permits the publishers to lavish the best design and production treatment on these wonderful manuscripts and paintings, thereby producing books that have an intrinsic value beyond the words themselves.

The plentiful selection may actually prove overwhelming to a teacher. There are several categories of sources of information, however. Children's librarians are, as they have been for years, aware of the range of literature available, and are happy to make recommendations. Children's specialty booksellers constitute a newer group of dedicated professionals in this field. They usually have access to newly published books long in advance of the libraries, and are in most cases very willing and able to suggest not only titles, but also creative uses of these titles in classroom settings. There are excellent journals that review children's books. Among the most respected and reliable are *The Horn Book, School Library Journal*, the American Library Association's *Booklist*, and *The Bulletin of the Center for Children's Books*. In addition, there are several noteworthy books containing annotated lists of children's titles, and in some cases, selections from recommended books. (Please refer to the bibliography following this article for specific titles.)

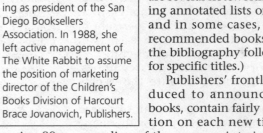

Louise Howton's career in children's books began in 1978 when she opened The White Rabbit, a children's-only bookstore in La Jolla, California. She has been active in various booksellers associations, including serving as president of the San Diego Booksellers Association. In 1988, she left active management of The White Rabbit to assume the position of marketing director of the Children's Books Division of Harcourt Brace Jovanovich, Publishers.

Publishers' frontlist catalogs, produced to announce forthcoming books, contain fairly detailed information on each new title, including a sampling of the cover or interior art. Most trade publishers also maintain a backlist catalog, containing annotated listings of all their available titles. Those backlist catalogs featuring an index cross-referenced by subject are particularly useful for teachers. And finally, visiting the publisher's exhibits at professional conferences is another way, along with frequenting bookstores and libraries, to see the books and even meet the authors.

This selection process can be a time-consuming one, for sure, but it is hard to imagine a more enjoyable task.

→ See: Howton, p. 175; Owen, p. 414; Peetoom, p. 415.

Some Books to Aid in Selecting Children's Titles

◆ *I'll Tell You a Story, I'll Sing You a Song: A Parents' Guide to the Fairy Tales, Fables, Songs, and Rhymes of Childhood,* by Christine Allison (New York: Delacorte, 1987).
◆ *Taking Books to Heart: How to Develop a Love of Reading in Your Child,* by Paul Copperman (Reading, MA: Addison-Wesley, 1986).
◆ *The RIE Guide to Encouraging Young Readers,* ed. Ruth Graves (New York: Doubleday, 1987).
◆ *Choosing Books for Children,* by Betsy Hearn (New York: Delacorte, 1981).
◆ *For Reading Out Loud: A Guide to Sharing Books with Children,* by Margaret M. Kimmel and Elizabeth Segel (New York: Delacorte, revised 1988).
◆ *Eyeopeners: How to Choose and Use Children's Books About Real People, Places, and Things,* by Beverly Kobrin (New York: Penguin, 1988).
◆ *The New York Times Parents' Guide to Best Books for Children,* by Eden R. Lipson (New York: Random House, 1988).
◆ *Classics to Read Aloud to Your Children,* by William F. Russell (New York: Crown, 1984).
◆ *More Classics to Read Aloud to Your Children,* by William F. Russell (New York: Crown, 1986).
◆ *The Read-Aloud Handbook,* by Jim Trelease (New York: Penguin, revised 1989).

 **As Teachers See It**

Bookstores

by Katy Obringer

There are many superb children's bookstores in the United States. Comb your city to find them and form library-bookstore/school-bookstore links or use the yellow pages of your phone book to find the bookstores nearest you.

Your local children's bookstore or the children's department in a bookstore is an outstanding source for a wide selection of materials. Many children's bookstores are run by people who are very knowledgeable about children's literature. Contact them about book fairs and other special events. Have them add your name to their mailing list if they offer a newsletter containing information about special events, book reviews, and services they provide.

Encourage parents and children to take advantage of the special events sponsored by bookstores such as author visits. Connect with your local bookstore to see if you can have the author visit your school when he or she is in the area.

Katy Obringer is the supervising librarian at Children's Library, Palo Alto, CA.

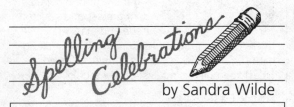

by Sandra Wilde

Patterns and Strategies: How Did Kids Spell 60 Years Ago?

SRCUS (20),
SRKS (10),
SRKUS (8),
CIRCUS (6),
CRCUS (5)

Spellings of circus *by 49 children, 1st grade*

Ernest Horn (1929. pp. 283–288) took a look at children's own spellings before the term *invented spelling* had even been invented. He asked 195 first- and second-graders to write the word *CIRCUS* and received 148 different spellings, 61 of them (by 108 children) at least somewhat reasonable phonetically. The five most common spellings are those above. Two patterns explain all of the invented features of these spellings: *c* is often replaced by *s* when it sounds like /s/ and *k* when it sounds like /k/; vowels before *r* and schwa vowels tend to be omitted. We can draw two conclusions. First, invented spelling is something children have been doing for a long time; it's just that nobody understood how to look at it 60 years ago. Second, children's spelling certainly hasn't deteriorated from some "golden age" in the past; I would guess that 195 first-graders in today's reading/writing classrooms would produce far more than five correct and 108 reasonable spellings of *CIRCUS*. Does anyone out there want to replicate Horn's study?

Reference

Horn, E. 1929. "The influence of past experiences upon spelling." *Journal of Educational Research* 19.

Resource Essay

Linden Tree

by Dennis Ronberg
and Linda Ronberg

Aside from the rather few books that deal with the philosophy and methods of whole language teaching, the majority of books housed in the teacher's resource room are very familiar to the children's bookseller and to many parents if not to all teachers. The whole language book is simply, but essentially, the book that appeals to children. Some clearly lend themselves especially well to teaching reading; books with patterned texts, predictable refrains, definitive picture-word relationships, books that sing (picture books based on and including songs), and stories that children love to hear and read again and again.

Linden Tree has also made space available for workshops in family math, whole language, and special subjects in music or education and for authors' visits and book signings. Currently a local chapter of Teachers Applying Whole Language (TAWL) is meeting monthly at Linden Tree to share ideas, discuss problems, and become familiar with new and newly reissued children's books.

Like whole language itself, Linden Tree brings together music, literature, and education to help fulfill the aspirations of teachers and parents: children who are literate and enlightened and who love to read.

Linden Tree Children's Records and Books is one of the largest children's bookstores in Northern California. It is located in Los Altos, a small suburban town midway between San Jose and San Francisco in the heart of Silicon Valley and adjacent to Stanford University. The area has experienced frenetic growth in recent years, bringing families from all over the United States and the world. The resulting rich cultural and social mix provides an unusually high interest in education and the arts.

We opened Linden Tree in 1982, primarily as a source for quality children's recordings. This was at the beginning of the surge in popularity of children's music, which emanated primarily from Canada and was led by the singer-songwriter Raffi. Since then children's recordings have increased in phenomenal proportions, aided by the accessibility of cassettes for children and by artists appearing on television.

Linden Tree has also played an active role in developing community interest in children's music through its annual series of live performances. These events range from formal concerts in large auditoriums to small, informal sing-alongs in the store. Each year these concerts bring hundreds of children into direct contact with many of their favorite recording artists, as well as many lesser-known local performers.

Soon after Linden Tree opened, we began to develop a book inventory. As with music, the children's book industry has seen tremendous growth during the past five to ten years. In 1987 the book inventory at Linden Tree had become so large that the store moved to a new location about three times larger. At present Linden Tree stocks approximately 20,000 titles, including infant board books, picture books, fiction and nonfiction for intermediate readers, science and nature, poetry and religion, and young adult literature. In addition, there is an extensive selection of parenting, special needs, foreign language, and teacher's resource books.

The growth of children's music and literature as an industry parallels the national attention now being focused on education in general and the teaching of reading in particular. The proclamation of the Year of the Young Reader, the California Reading Initiative introduced by Superintendent of Public Instruction Bill Honig, and the resurgence of the whole language method for the teaching of reading, have contributed to the increased need for and interest in children's books.

It is the application of the whole language concept, however, that has created the greatest need for increased resources for teachers. Linden Tree has responded by opening an annex above the store, which is devoted exclusively to books, materials, and information related to whole language teaching. This additional space also provides room for reading, research, and meetings.

➜ See: The California Reading Initiative, p. 174; Howton, p. 175; Whole Language Umbrella, p. 408.

Dennis Ronberg and Linda Ronberg are the owners of Linden Tree Children's Records and Books, Los Altos, CA.

Resource: Periodical/Poster

Jump! into Good Books for Children!

Quarterly. Free from:
Northern California
Children's Booksellers
Association
The Storyteller
23 Lafayette Circle
Lafayette, CA 94549
1-415-284-3480

This publication-plus-poster is published by the active and resourceful NCCBA as a community outreach to young readers. In it are reviews and recommendations on new or soon-to-be-released titles available at local bookstores or libraries. The lively layout is peppered with ideas and activities that practically leap from the page.

Arrietta Chakos

Resource: Bookstore and Mail Order

Children's Book and Music Center

Catalog free from:
2500 Santa Monica Blvd.
Santa Monica, CA
90404
1-800-443-1856 (outside CA)
1-213-829-0215

The Children's Book and Music Center is the largest store of its kind. Staffed by experienced consultants trained to assist teachers, parents, grandparents, and librarians, it has been a unique single source of books, audio, video, and enrichment material since 1950. Works by authors and performers who are dedicated to the growth and pleasure of young audiences are available through the catalog, which includes sections on multicultural and foreign language materials.

Katy Obringer

Finding Good Books

Resource: Books

Prizewinning Books for Children: Themes and Stereotypes in U.S. Prizewinning Prose Fiction for Children

Jaqueline Shachter Weiss
1983; 480 pp.; $22
Lexington, MA: Lexington Books, an imprint of D. D. Heath

Dr. Weiss provides a rare guide to themes in quality children's literature in this valuable reference work. She analyzes and summarizes the primary and secondary themes of 717 prizewinners, noting the association of certain recurrent themes with particular genres. She also gives descriptions of the sponsoring organizations and bases for judgment of children's literature awards. In addition, Weiss deals with the issues of racial and sexual stereotypes in classic books.

Lists of Award-winning Books

Information from:
American Library Association
50 East Huron St.
Chicago, IL 60611

The John Newbery Medal is an award given annually by the Children's Services Division of the American Library Association to the authors of the most distinguished American children's book published during the previous year. The award, named for the famous 18th-century publisher and seller of children's books, was established in 1922 as an incentive for better quality in children's literature.

The Randolph J. Caldecott Medal goes annually to the illustrator of the most distinguished children's picture book published in the United States during the previous year. Named for the famous English illustrator of children's books, the Caldecott Medal originated in 1938 as a testament to "the joyousness of picture books."

Lists of the Newbery and Caldecott winners and honorable mention books are an excellent source for outstanding children's literature. Some of the older titles are now out of print; check school and public libraries for these books.

Newbery and Caldecott Medal and Honor Books: An Annotated Bibliography

Linda Kauffman Peterson and Marilyn Leathers Solt
1982; 458 pp.; $50
Boston: G. K. Hall

This is a scholarly publication, designed for use as a reference. It lists all Newbery and Caldecott award-winners by year, from 1922 to 1981.

Children's Books: Awards and Prizes; Including Prizes and Awards for Young Adult Books

The Children's Book Council, editor
1986; 276 pp.; $50
New York: Children's Book Council

This reference book listing American, British Commonwealth, international, and multinational awards since each award's inception is out of print, but still available in libraries.

Children's Literature Awards and Winners: A Directory of Prizes, Authors, and Illustrators, 2d ed.

Dolores Blythe Jones, editor
1988; 671 pp.; $92
Detroit: Neal-Schuman in association with Gale Research

This is a comprehensive reference source that describes awards granted in English-speaking countries for excellence in children's literature. A total of 211 awards are covered, including major awards that are no longer given. In addition to award and subject indexes, this second edition incorporates title and author/illustrator indexes.

Children's Books of the Year

The Child Study Children's Book Committee
Bank St. College
610 W. 112th St.
New York, NY 10025

This committee has been compiling booklists since 1916 as a guide for parents, teachers, and librarians in selection of the best children's books, for the earliest listener to the fourteen-year-old.
Arrietta Chakos/Katy Obringer

Resource: Book Distributors

A good distributor can sometimes make all the difference by being a more direct route to the source of the book you want. The following list is just a beginning.

Butternut Books

WELL Associates, Inc. (Whole Education in Language and Learning)
RDI, Box 121A
Morris, NY 13805
1-607-263-5620

WELL Associates, a consulting firm dedicated to holistic education language and literacy development, started Butternut Books in conjunction with its workshops. All books in the catalog are selected and evaluated using whole language criteria. The company offers resource books as well as fine quality children's literature.

Bookpeople

2929 Fifth St.
Berkeley, CA 94710
1-800-999-4650

Bookpeople is the largest distributor of small press books in the world, offering the best of independent presses and selected trade and mass market titles. The monthly publication, *Bookpaper,* along with subject checklists (for example, Children's Titles) keep buyers abreast of new books.

Book Call

59 Elm St.
New Canaan, CT 06840
1-800-255-2665

Book Call publishes *Bibliomania,* an annotated list of new and forthcoming titles of interest. Customers can order 24 hours a day, seven days a week—a boon for serious book lovers.

Beyda Books

6443 Valjean Ave.
Van Nuys, CA 91406
1-818-988-3102 or
1-213-893-1148

Beyda Books is a wholesale specialist in books, records, audiocassettes, and videotapes for children and young adults. They stock all California Reading Initiative Books and all Caldecott and Newbery award-winners, and publish a bimonthly review newsletter, *Hot Off the Press.*
Arrietta Chakos

Resource: Organization

United States Board on Books for Young People

c/o International Reading Association
800 Barksdale Rd.
P.O. Box 3139
Newark, DE 19714-8139

The USBBY is the American section of the International Board on Books for Young People, which promotes "international understanding through children's books." It encourages literacy in a number of ways: promotes wide distribution of children's books; furthers the establishment of public and school libraries; aids in the continuing education of those involved with children and children's literature; and advocates the use of literature in education. A semiannual newsletter is published for members.
Alicia Rivera

Resource: Periodical

The Web

$10/year (4 issues) from:
Ohio State University
Rm. 200, Ramseyer Hall
29 W. Woodruff
Columbus, OH 43210

A good source of ideas that extend the book; each issue focuses on a particular topic ("Celebrating Snow") or person ("Getting to Know an Author: Madeleine L'Engle") in children's literature.

Resource: Publisher

Pantheon Fairy Tale and Folklore Library

Catalog from:
Pantheon Books
Dept. HS 27-3
201 E. 50th St.
New York, NY 10022

This series is splendid; its coverage of traditional lore from all over the world is unique. The lyrical translations and spritely prose will engage readers of all ages. African folktales, American Indian myths and legends, and stories from classical Greece are only a few of the selections.
Arrietta Chakos

Library Resources
Reviewed by Katy Obringer

The Best in Children's Books: The University of Chicago Guide to Children's Literature 1979–1984

Zena Sutherland
1986; 512 pp.; $35
Chicago: University of Chicago Press

This guide comprises very thorough annotations of the best fiction and nonfiction books from 1979 to 1984 for preschoolers through high school-age students. Titles are selected for inclusion principally on the basis of literary quality.

Children's Catalog, 15th ed.

Isaason, Hillegas & Yaakov, editors
1986; 1,298 pp.; $72
New York: H. W. Wilson

Annotations are included for over 6,000 titles for children in preschool through sixth grade. The catalog can serve as the primary reference tool in building a library collection, or can be used to supplement a library's collection. For those interested in listings for junior high, there is a separate volume, *Junior High School Library Catalog.*

The Elementary School Paperback Collection

John T. Gillespie
1985; 306 pp.; $17.50
Chicago: American Library Association

The collection lists more than 3,800 recommended titles by theme with brief annotations. The titles are listed in fiction and nonfiction groupings, and by grade categories one through three and four through six.

Reading for the Love of It: Best Books for Young Readers

Michele Landsberg
1989; 272 pp.; $10.95
Toronto: Prentice-Hall Press

Discussing books for ages 4 through 13 plus, Landsberg, a Canadian newspaper columnist, includes books of all types—adventure, time travel, fantasy, growing up, and humor. The book comprises a comprehensive discussion of different types of literature to share with children.

Choosing Books for Children: A Commonsense Guide

Betsy G. Hearne
1990; 226 pp; $9.95 paper; $16.95 clothcover,
New York: Delacorte

Chapters are organized by book types: picture books, readers, fiction and nonfiction, poetry, and young adult fiction. More than 100 titles of the best authors and illustrators are listed with suggested age groupings. The guide includes valuable information about each type of book.

Choosing Books for Children: How to Choose the Right Book for the Right Child at the Right Time

Barbara Brenner, Joanne F. Oppenheim, and Betty D. Boegehold
1986; 345 pp.; $9.95
New York: Ballantine Books

This annotated source on books for toddlers through twelve-year-olds has helpful hints on borrowing and buying books, and on locating sources for audiovisual materials to supplement literature. These may include cassette-book sets and book-related TV programs.

Best Books for Children: Preschool through the Middle Grades, 4th ed.

John T. Gillespie and Corinne J. Naden
1990; 650 pp.; $39.95
New York: R. R. Bowker

A thorough guide listing books—1,200 titles in all—by approximately 32 broad subject categories, including wordless books, mythology, crafts, music, sciences, and personal development. Particularly comprehensive in covering all areas of the school curriculum, this guide would be valuable for selecting books to incorporate into units of study.

School Library Journal: The Magazine of Children's, Young Adult and School Librarians

$56/year from:
School Library Journal
P.O. Box 1978
Marion, OH 43305-1978
1-800-431-1713

This journal features articles of interest to adults working with children. Included are reviews of books, computer software, and audiovisual materials. The *School Library Journal* also publishes an annual list of the best books published that year—a good selection tool for people wanting to purchase or read the best current books.

The New Hooked on Books

Daniel Fader
1981; 294 pp.; $2.75
New York: Berkley Books

An update of a classic book for junior and secondary teachers and parents on how to use literature to turn on the turned-off adolescent reader. Particularly appropriate for minority readers in urban schools. Out of print but still found in libraries.

KSG

Booklist

$56/year (22 issues) from:
American Library Association
50 E. Huron St.
Chicago, IL 60611
1-800-545-2433

Booklist contains adult, juvenile, reference, and audiovisual reviews and publishes an annual list, "Children's Editors Choice," featuring the best books of that year. The list can be found in the January issue, or can be ordered as a reprint for a small fee.

The Bulletin of the Center for Children's Books

$24/year (11 issues) from:
The University of Chicago Press
Journals Division
P.O. Box 37005
Chicago, IL 60637

This bulletin, for librarians and children's literature specialists, reviews the most current books for children and young people. It rates each title, gives suggested grade or age level, and includes ordering information. Particularly helpful as a selection tool, the bulletin includes a rating guide to help the selector choose the most meaningful titles for their collections.

Emergency Librarian

$15/year (6 issues) from:
Dyad Services
Box C34069
Department 284
Seattle, WA 98124-1069
(Also published in Canada)

This magazine comprises a variety of elements: feature articles of interest to librarians and other professionals, reviews of current trade books as well as professional books, lists of outstanding new books for children in grades K–12, lists of recommended audiovisual materials, information on microcomputers, and reviews of computer software.

Resource: Publisher

Children's Book Press

Catalog and ordering information from:
5925 Doyle St., Ste. U
Emeryville, CA 94608
1-415-655-3395

Children's Book Press is the only children's publisher offering contemporary legends based on tales from the minority and immigrant communities in North America. This nonprofit publisher's books and audiocassettes are an excellent way to incorporate literature from Latin America and the Caribbean, as well as African-American, Asian-American, and Native American literature, into any whole language curriculum. The multicultural, bilingual books are astonishing visual treats—the colorful, dramatic illustrations will entice any new reader. Fanciful stories, classic folktales, and epic tales combine to make a list unique in children's literature. The press has recently published a guide designed to help teachers incorporate these books into existing reading or language arts programs.

Arrietta Chakos

YOUNG ARTISTS

Laura and Pa "Little Town on the Prairie."
May 1990

The second-graders in Alicia Rivera's class celebrated a new year by creating their own literary calendar. Each month is illustrated with a scene from one of Laura Ingalls Wilder's books, Hillcrest School, Oakland, CA.

Literature Books *en español* for Whole Language Classrooms

by Yvonne S. Freeman and Carolina Cervantes

When whole language teachers plan their curriculum, they know that it is essential to take the whole child into consideration. Whole language teachers, both bilingual and monolingual English speakers working with Hispanic students, realize the importance of drawing on the background knowledge and strengths of all students in their classroom.

When whole language teachers celebrate the first language and culture of bilingual children, they are promoting self-esteem and pride that will help language-minority students become empowered learners. Whole language teachers reject the assumption held by English Only advocates that "more English equals more English," because they know that Hispanic children "submerged" in English Only classrooms with no support for their first language or culture are disempowered. One way to empower Spanish-speaking students is to provide quality children's literature for them in their primary language.

A stumbling block for whole language teachers of bilingual children is finding quality literature that children can read in their primary language. The following annotated reading list of literature in Spanish is not only for bilingual Spanish/English teachers; it can also be used by nonbilingual teachers to select books for their Spanish-speaking students to read independently.

Literature Books *en español* for Emerging Readers

◆ *Mi casa* (My house), by Francisca Altamirano (Mexico City: Editorial Trillas, 1986). Simple text and colorful illustrations show items commonly found at home. Ideal for independent reading.

◆ *La naturaleza* (Nature), by Francisca Altamirano (Mexico City: Editorial Trillas, 1986). This picture book about the sky and earth is ideal for science themes and independent reading.

◆ *El viaje de Isaac* (Isaac's trip), by Francisca Altamirano (Mexico City: Editorial Trillas, 1986). Two children teach each other about their different cultures. Colorful illustrations of Mexican village and city life.

◆ *Elisa y Palín,* by Francisca Altamirano (Mexico City: Editorial Trillas, 1986). This readable text with colorful illustrations is about a young girl who befriends a baby bird. The book is ideal for wildlife themes and discussions about freedom.

◆ *Triste historia del sol con final feliz* (Sad story of the sun with a happy ending), by Elena Climent (Mexico City: Editorial Trillas, 1986). The sun no longer shines and the people of the world cooperate to solve the problem.

◆ *Bety y su ratón* (Betty and her mouse), by Elena Climent (Mexico City: Editorial Trillas, 1986). This readable book with bold, colorful illustrations is about a girl who cannot find her favorite stuffed animal.

◆ *Pájaros en la cabeza,* (Birds on my head), by Laura Fernández (Mexico City: Editorial Trillas, 1983). This first-person narrative describes the adventures of a young girl who awakens to find birds nesting on her head.

◆ *Los derechos de los niños* (The rights of children), by José Luis García Sánchez and Miguel Angel Pacheco (Madrid: Altea, Taurus, Alfaguara, 1988). This collection of ten books expounds on inalienable rights for all children of the world. Themes include respect, empowerment, individuality, responsibility, education, individual roles, and handicaps. The titles are as follows:

> *Los niños de los cuentos* (Storybook children)
> *Los niños que no eran como niños* (The children who were not like children)
> *La niña sin nombre* (The girl without a name)
> *El niño llorón* (The crybaby)
> *El niño que tenía dos ojos* (The boy who had two eyes)
> *El niño y el robot* (The boy and the robot)
> *Los niños que no tenían escuelas* (The children who did not have schools)
> *El pueblo que se quedó sin niños* (The town that ended up without any children)
> *El niño gigante* (The giant boy)
> *La niña invisible* (The invisible girl)

◆ *Castillos de arena* (Sand castles), by Sara Gerson (Mexico City: Editorial Trillas, 1986). Little Diana shares creative ideas while building a sand castle.

◆ *Pedro aprende a nadar* (Pedro learns to swim), by Sara Gerson (Mexico City: Editorial Trillas, 1986). Colorful illustrations provide clear context for a story about an adventurous boy and his dog.

◆ *Luisa y el arco iris* (Luisa and the rainbow), by Sara Gerson (Mexico City: Editorial Trillas, 1986). This is a predictable and creative story about how a rainbow and a little girl color her town.

◆ *El escondite* (The hideout), by Sara Gerson (Mexico City: Editorial Trillas, 1986). In simple, natural language this story introduces the topics of the sentimental value of objects and bonds between generations. The illustrations help make text predictable.

◆ *Chiquito pero listo* (Small but smart), by Zoraida Vásquez and Julieta Montelongo (Mexico City: Editorial Trillas, 1984). Humorous Mozambique folktale about a rabbit who is ridiculed for his small size by larger animals.

Literature Books *en español* for Independent Readers

◆ *El viaje del joven Matsúa* (Young Matsua's trip), by Mada Carreño (Mexico City: Editorial Trillas, 1987). Retelling of a legend of Mexico's Tarahumara people, this story is about how young Matsua and his family come to be accepted by the *Rarámuri* (Tarahumara people).

◆ *Marita ratita y los duendes* (Marita the rat and the goblins), by Mireya Carrera Bolaños (Mexico City: Editorial Trillas, 1987). Marita Ratita finds herself in a book and helps the characters escape into the real world.

◆ *La historia de Benjamin* (Benjamin's story), by Carmen Esteva (Mexico City: Promociones Editoriales Mexicanas, S. A. de C. V., 1984). A curious mouse discovers the magical power of books and shares his discoveries with other small animals.

◆ *Luis y su genio* (Louis and his genie), by Laura Fernández (Mexico City: Editorial Trillas, 1986). This first-person narrative is about an unusual young genie who—instead of granting wishes—asks that they be granted to him. Book is highly imaginative with colorful illustrations.

◆ *Una rana en un arbol* (A frog in a tree), by Judy Goldman (Mexico City: Editorial Trillas, 1986). This story is about boasting and its consequences. Colorful illustrations are finely detailed and artistic.

◆ *Las dos caperucitas* (The two riding hoods), by Graciela González de Tapia (Mexico City: Editorial Trillas, 1984). In this parody of the traditional story, Little Red Riding Hood and Little Blue Riding Hood, her older cousin who loves to solve problems, devise a plan to outwit the wolf. Language is natural, but the text is extensive. Colorful illustrations are quite detailed.

◆ *El gato Cui* (Cui the cat), by Graciela González de Tapia (Mexico City: Editorial Trillas, 1984). In this narrative Cui, a stuffed animal, tells about the love of his owner and what she experienced when she lost Cui temporarily. Illustrations are large, vibrant, and detailed. Though the text is very readable and has a predictable beginning, middle, and end, it is dialectic and quite extensive.

◆ *Un día en la vida de Catalina* (One day in the life of Cathleen), by Berta Hiriart (Mexico City: CIDCLI, S.C., 1984). Fatherless Catalina, a first child, adjusts to the birth of a second. Illustrations are bold and colorful. Readable text is extensive.

◆ *Principio y fin, tiempo de vida que transcurre entre el nacer y el morir* (Beginnings and endings with lifetimes in between), by Bryan Mellonie (Mexico City: CECSA, 1984). This is a translation of the English language original. Colorful illustrations are extremely artistic. The text tells of birth and death for plants, animals, and people in a beautiful way. Language is natural.

◆ *José, un libro sobre el divorcio* (José, a book about divorce), by Gianni Padoan (Milan: Plaza Joven, S.A., 1987). With colorful, detailed illustrations, the story tells of the inner struggle of an only child whose parents become divorced. Presents issues clearly, though story may be a bit idealized. Language is readable but dialectic.

◆ *El columpio* (The swing), by Ana María Pecanins (Mexico City: Editorial Trillas, 1986). This story about a little girl and the animals she invites to ride on her swing has a surprise ending. Though the text is not extensive, some of the language may be technical.

◆ *El papalote y el nopal* (The kite and the cactus), by Aline Pettersson (Mexico City: CIDCLI, S.C., 1988). This symbolic story tells the adventure of a kite that gets caught in a cactus. Contains dramatic illustrations of Mexico's desert flora and fauna.

◆ *¿Adónde vas, Tomás?* (Where are you going, Thomas?), by Eduardo Robles Boza (Mexico City: Editorial Trillas, 1983). This story about children and a toy car that suddenly appears in their village supports themes of materialism, patience, and problem-solving.

◆ *Una historia con color* (A story with color), by María Teresa Romero (Mexico City: Editorial Trillas, 1986). This predictable book with impressively painted illustrations has technical and extensive vocabulary, which makes it a good read-aloud text. Could be used for themes and units about the sun, rain, color, and cooperation.

◆ *La pelota* (The ball), by Luís Solé Serra (Barcelona: Ediciones Hymsa, 1988). This translation of the Italian original version *La pelota* has colorful illustrations. The text which tells the story of the adventures of a soccer ball has a predictable beginning, middle, and end. Dialectic language is natural. Creatively presents topic of materialism.

Literature Books *en español* for More Proficient Readers

◆ *Historia verdadera de una princesa* (True story of a princess), by Inés Arredondo (Mexico City: CIDCLI, S.C., 1988). This historical biography of Malinche, friend of Spanish Conquistador Hernán Cortés, includes her childhood.

◆ *Que sí, que no, que todo se acabó* (Yes, no, everything's over and done with), by Miguel Angel Tenorio (Mexico City: CIDCLI, S.C. and Editorial Limusa, 1985). A poor prince searches for his beloved princess. Rhythm, rhyme, and plays on words will produce smiles and laughter.

◆ *Celestino y el tren* (Celestino and the train), by Magolo Cárdenas (Mexico City: SEP and Libros del

Rincon, 1986). This chapter novel tells the heroic adventure of a muleteer's young son and his unusual blue donkey in Mexico.

◆ *Cuentos de Pascuala* (Pascuala's stories), by Teresa Castelló Yturbide (Mexico City: SEP, 1986). This is a collection of imaginative and amusing Mexican short stories told by nannies throughout Mexico.

◆ *Las tres manzanas de naranja* (The three apples from an orange tree), by Ulalume González de León, (Mexico City: CIDCLI, S.C., 1988). The cubist illustrations fit this tale about a king who will marry his daughter to the wise man who can present the king three apples from an orange tree.

◆ *La calle es libre* (The street is free), by Kurusa (Caracas: Ediciones Ekaré—Banco del Libro, 1983). This Venezuelan story about ghetto children who want a safe place to play includes themes of urbanization, exploitation, democracy, and self-actualization.

◆ *Pintorín y el espíritu del lago* (Pintorín and the spirit of the lake), by Francisco Javier Larios (Morelia, Mexico: Instituto Michoacano de Cultura, 1988). A spirit assigns an artistic mission to a young boy who becomes an artist.

◆ *Al otro lado de la puerta* (On the other side of the door), by Marinés Medero (Mexico City: SEP and Libros del Rincon, 1986). Young Ana, daughter of a Mexican-born Spaniard, experiences the excitement of Mexico's quest for independence.

◆ *Si ves pasar un condor* (If you see a condor passing by), by Carlos Ocampo (Mexico City: Editorial Amaquemecan, 1986). This story addresses issues of old age and animal incarceration.

◆ *La abeja haragana* (The lazy bee), by Horacio Quiroga (Mexico City: SEP and Edilin, 1985). This story about a lazy bee, who is punished for not meeting his work responsibilities, can be symbolically interpreted.

◆ *Cuentos de puro susto* (Sheer fright stories), (Mexico City: SEP, 1986). By modern standards, these Mexican stories of the early 1900s are not frightening, but some are amusing and others have deeper levels of meaning.

➜ See: Freeman and Cervantes, pp. 87, 312, 320.

Yvonne S. Freeman is a professor and Carolina Cervantes is a graduate student at Fresno Pacific College, Fresno, CA.

Spanish Language Books Ordering Information

Fresno Pacific Bookshop
Attn: Richard Wiebe
1717 S. Chestnut Ave.
Fresno, CA 93702
1-209-453-2078

Lectorum Publications
137 W. 14th St.
New York, NY 10011
1-212-929-3833

Mariuccia Iaconi Book Imports
1110 Mariposa
San Francisco, CA 94107
1-415-255-8193

Puvill Division Mexico
Atención: Carmen Esteva de Garcia M.
Empresa 109
Mixcoac C.P. 03910
Mexico City, Mexico

Santillana Publishing Co.
World of Literature Catalog
Books in Spanish
924 S. Gerhart Ave.
Los Angeles, CA 90022
1-800-526-0107

Scholastic Inc.
Spanish Big Books
P.O. Box 7520
Jefferson City, MO 65102

Becoming Literate

by Toby Taylor

Life in Prison

When I first came into prison I was scared of the unknown just like everyone is when they first come in the gates. It's like dying and going to Hell, and then being reborn to start all over in a new world, which is not like any world you have ever known. Prison is a place where everything is the same and everyone is a number. A place where the strong lead and the weak follow. It is a place where you have got to live in fear, hate, and resentment. Time after time I've sat in my room and said to myself, I wish I had something to do. But it's the same old thing day after day. Long boring hours and constant idleness which never seems to end. It is a routine that you get used to after some time has passed, and you stop thinking about the outside, because when you don't see the outside for so long you just don't think or worry about it any longer. Sometimes I think to myself how nice it would be if I was out on the street with my little girl looking in at a place like this. And then I would say to myself that it was not nice at all to look in at people that could not look out at me. The only people that know about the prison are the people that have got to live in prison. The officers don't know about it because they just work eight hours a day and five days a week. So I don't know how they could say that they know all about prison. Some people say prison is like a big city with no women and no cars, and you have to eat just about the same thing every week. One meal is the same as the next. Some people say that we are in prison to be rehabilitated, but I have not seen one person in prison that has been rehabilitated. The only good thing in prison is that you can get a free education if you want one. Just about everyone I know in prison has their GED, except for me. And before I leave I will have mine. Before I came into prison I could not read a book, but I got help from some of the best friends that a man could have. And from my teacher at Deberry, who has helped me so much in so many ways.

I will never forget any of these people for as long as I can see to read a book. And I can see damn good right now.

➜ See: Brennan, p. 227; Voices: New Writers for New Readers, pp. 128-129.

Excerpted from *Voices: New Writers for New Readers* 1(2), Lower Mainland Society for Literacy and Employment (Surrey, British Columbia: Winter 1989): p. 32.

Snowflakes

by Harmony Jones

Snow, softly, slowly
settles at dusk in a dance
of white butterflies.

➜ See: Treasures, p. 162.

From *Treasures 2*, Oregon Students Writing and Art Foundation, 1988.

Harmony Jones was eight years old when she wrote this poem; she lives in Eugene, OR.

Resource: Periodical

Perspectives

$7.50 Ohio residents, $10 out-of-state/year (3 issues) from:
Cooperative Services for Children's Literature
College of Education and Allied Professions
University of Toledo
Toledo, OH 43606-3390
1-419-537-4300

Perspectives is a review journal of CSCL, a project of the University of Toledo in association with teachers and librarians, designed to aid new book selection and promote the varied use of literature in school programs. Included are specific projects teachers and parents can pursue with children to enhance and extend the reading experience—activities that go beyond the boundaries of the books while complementing their spirit. "Point—Counterpoint," another intriguing feature, presents opposing points of view about significant new books by well-known authors and illustrators.

Katy Obringer

Resource: Organization

The Children's Book Council

568 Broadway
New York, NY 10012
1-212-966-1990

The Children's Book Council (CBC) is a publishers' association that encourages the enjoyment of children's books in a myriad of ways. As sponsor of National Children's Book Week, CBC prepares colorful materials (posters, bookmarks, mobiles, friezes) to promote reading. The Council offers three annual booklists: science and social studies trade books and *Children's Choices*, a selection compiled by 10,000 U.S. schoolchildren. *Choosing a Child's Book* is a pamphlet that describes basic concepts in book selection for preschool through junior high age students. A good handout for parents, it also lists other selection guides. *CBC Features* is the official newsletter of the Council and contains articles about publishers, trends, people, places, and information on inexpensive materials available from publishers.

Katy Obringer

Resource: Periodical

The Horn Book Magazine

$32/year (6 issues) from:
14 Beacon St.
Boston, MA 02108
1-800-325-1170

Founded in 1924 "to blow the horn for fine books for boys and girls," *The Horn Book Magazine* contains reviews of the best new books for children and young adults, and its articles, often written by authors and illustrators, cover a variety of issues dealing with children's literature. The June issue carries a short listing of the previous year's books considered most outstanding. *The Horn Book Guide* is a biannual review of all hardcover trade children's and young adult's books published during the previous season.

Katy Obringer

Great Teachers:
Storyteller Awele Makeba
by Gwenne Culpepper

Making the World a Better Place

She widens her eyes a lot. Her eyebrows go up and down in constant animation. She shakes her body and uses words like "zoop" and "cha-link" and "boogety," and talks about a giant named Abiyoyo who eats people for lunch. She also dances, prances, sings, bares her teeth, and sticks out her tongue.

Talibah-Awele Ruth Makeba tells stories for a living.

She has traveled across the United States and to the Soviet Union and Australia to weave her tales of wonder and excitement, and will soon visit Taiwan. A native of St. Louis who makes her home in Oakland, California, she was recently in Jesup, Iowa, as a resident artist with Cedar Arts Forum.

Although the exaggerated movements and varying voice tones seem to be the key factors enthralling her listeners, Awele dismisses them. "What makes a good storyteller is that, first and foremost, you want to share, and you have a love for stories and books that you want to share. Second, you have to work on the stories, and memorize and perfect them, so it's the best you can give."

Her colorful dresses—tailored in Nigeria —and her varying voice tones are just style. They aren't mandatory for good storytelling. Some storytellers use props, some use costumes. Awele uses movement.

While her stories are thoroughly entertaining, Awele fervently hopes she is more than just a one-woman show, forgotten by the audience as soon as the curtain comes down. She wants her listener to be excited, and to think about the story's theme and message.

Awele believes storytelling is one of the best teaching methods around. "It's what teaching is all about," she says. "Sharing, and creativity. Not pounding someone over the head with names and dates. You can put a broken record on and get that."

She suggests that if reading and storytelling were more prevalent in the nation's schools, a lot of the problems there would disappear. "Teachers are faced with discipline problems, and overcrowding and they're burned out," she says. "They need ways to excite the students about schoolwork. If they [students] were challenged, they wouldn't have time to think of ways to be problems."

Reading aloud and telling stories is the way to excite and challenge children, she says. "Teachers should read to kids every day. And they should get into it; laugh if it's funny, cry if it's sad. The kids need to see the teachers interested," she points out.

Parents should get involved, too, to reinforce the concept of sharing ideas. Awele says children today don't have "that special time, right after dinner where the family spent time together, talking." Their free time is taken up with television, arcades, and movies. As a result, the family spends less time together, and that special time is lost. With it is lost a sense of familial and cultural pride. Both, says Awele, can be recovered through storytelling.

From *Courier*, Waterloo, IA, 15 January 1989.

Swimming in Books
by David Updegraff

Have you ever been bored to death. Well, I almost was because of my sister. My sister is a junior olympic swimmer. In order to be a junior olympic swimmer she practices 6 days a week for 2 hours and swims in swim meets each week-end. There is nothing worse than a hot, steamy, chlorine-smelling pool when you aren't a swimmer. Swim practices are long. Swim meets take forever! I used to complain a lot about her swimming by saying: "Mom, how many more hours?" My second grade teacher gave me some good books to read at the meets.

Last year my sister went to Indianapolis for a swim meet. I went to Klickat Street in *Henry and the Club House*. We went to St. Louis for a meet. I went to Narnia in *The Lion, the Witch and the Wardrobe*. Then we went to Milwaukee, but I was solving a mystery with the *Hardy Boys*. I have a new way of judging swim meets. Some meets are two book meets, some, three and real long ones are four. My sister only gets to be a swimmer, but I've been everything. I've read forty books since September and usually read a hundred by the end of the swim season. Books saved my life and I never have to worry about writing a book report.

➜ See: Literature Reference List, p. 429.

David Updegraff is a fourth-grader. This essay, which won a National 1989 Mott's Apple Award, appears exactly as he wrote it.

The Mott's Apple Awards are a national public service program designed to encourage children to value reading as a lifelong skill and pleasure, and to focus national attention on the importance of reading in children's lives.

YOUNG ARTISTS

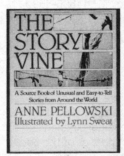

"The Storyteller"
—Nelson G. Begay, Nazlini Boarding School, Navajo Nation, AZ

Resource: Books

The Story Vine: A Source Book of Unusual and Easy-to-Tell Stories from Around the World

Anne Pellowski
1984; 116 pp.; $7.95 paper; $14.95 cloth, New York: Collier Books, an imprint of Macmillan

Pellowski, a storyteller for more than 25 years, has gathered a wonderful collection of stories from around the world. She employs a variety of unusual objects in her storytelling, such as strings and yarn, a thumb piano, sand paintings, nesting dolls, trouble dolls, and chalk drawings. Stories using finger plays, cat's cradle, and musical instruments are also included. Detailed directions for each story are given, and illustrations are provided where necessary. Scattered throughout the book you'll find useful lists of further storytelling resources.

Frances Christie/Katy Obringer

The Flannel Board Storytelling Book

Judy Sierra
1987; 216 pp.; $34
New York: H. W. Wilson

This book contains the patterns and text for 26 tales and 10 poems and songs—over 250 patterns in all. Sierra includes simple directions, ideas for parallel activities, and a useful bibliography.

Katy Obringer

Picture Book Story Hours: From Birthdays to Bears

Paula Gaj Sitarz
1987; 190 pp.; $18.50
Littleton, CO: Libraries Unlimited

Sitarz prepares the teacher, librarian, or interested adult for putting together a story-hour program, organized around one of 22 topics. For each program, she suggests different books, songs, filmstrips, and activities, incorporating finger plays (with directions), poetry, and rhymes. Ideas for publicity and decoration are some of the useful tips given, and a list of further resources and aids for storytellers is included.

Frances Christie/Katy Obringer

Cornerstone: Awele Makeba

The Educational Benefits of Storytelling

As an educator-storyteller, my first objective is to educate; to foster personal, social, cultural, and intellectual growth. My second is to create a sustained interest in literature and to excite children to read, read, read! My third, to teach about other cultures through their literature, and my fourth, to use storytelling and drama as a vehicle for addressing social and political issues.

My stories come from folktales around the world, children's literature, adult fiction, and the oral tradition. Storytelling is not just for kids, although it is aimed primarily at preschool and elementary school children. Teenagers and adults benefit from storytelling too. Storytelling is universal and infinitely compelling. "It taps issues of personal importance and real collective memories in all the listeners." And it's fun.

Storytelling is new for many people in this hi-tech/media-oriented society. Dominated by radios, movies, television, and VCRs, we are slowly losing an art form that's been around for thousands of years. In the past, storytelling brought families and communities together, as it was used to teach morals, ethical values, customs, and traditions. As I weave tales with sounds, voice colorations, rhythm, gestures, facial expressions, pantomime, dance, and song, my task is to shape a character or an event so that I can teach, motivate, and inspire. I look for stories with good, strong morals and values that teach customs and traditions, international understanding, cultural awareness, as well as literature appreciation. It is important to me as an African-American to share stories that develop self-esteem, cultural pride, and identity.

When tales are told and shared from one's heart, the stories live. The storyteller creates a vivid experience that becomes a part of the mind and person of the listener. Storytelling stimulates creativity and imagination. Some of the educational benefits of storytelling are

- Developing and deepening an enjoyment of literature; motivating children to read;
- Connecting reading, writing, and speaking;
- Providing practice in visualizing characters, events, settings, and the mood of the story; improving sense of story structure;
- Increasing awareness and interest in various genres of literature;
- Enhancing oral language and vocabulary development;
- Expanding social and cultural awareness; developing cultural pride and identity; enhancing self-esteem; and
- Inspiring children to become storytellers.

In addition to the benefits I've listed, storytelling creates a "relational bridge and closeness between teacher (teller) and students." Teachers can become great storytellers if they are willing to take time to find the right story and learn it well, and if they have the sincere desire to share their enjoyment and love of story. Schools should support professional storytellers and storytelling in the schools through in-service training, visits by librarians, and artists-in-the-schools programs. Take advantage of this stimulating means of communication, for with each telling the story lives, the oral tradition continues, and we show our children a wonderful way to look at the world.

Awele Makeba is a professional storyteller, a first-year teacher at Synergy School in San Francisco, and a master's candidate in the Elementary Education Department at San Francisco State University. She has woven her tales throughout Australia, the Soviet Union, and the United States.

 WHOLE LANGUAGE CAMERA

"I know an old lady who swallowed a fly..." Yetta shares a story with primary students at Mangere Central School, Auckland, New Zealand.

Storyteller

Awele Makeba
TELLER OF ALL TALES

415-272-0312

2501 Ivy Dr. #3
Oakland, CA 94606

As Teachers See It

Storytelling

by Katy Obringer

Use commercial storytelling tapes for extension and enrichment. Many tapes are now available by professional storytellers like Jackie Torrence, and are a delightful way to develop imagination, listening skills, and so on.

Katy Obringer is the supervising librarian at Children's Library, Palo Alto, CA.

Resource: Book

The Family Storytelling Handbook: How to Use Stories, Anecdotes, Rhymes, Handkerchiefs, Paper, and Other Objects to Enrich Your Family Traditions

Anne Pellowski
1987; 150 pp.; $15.75
New York: Macmillan

A highly useful and motivating source of stories for anyone to share, its subtitle really says it all. Pellowski, a noted authority in the storytelling field, suggests when to tell what sorts of stories and gives examples of various kinds to use. The use of visual aids and great ideas for nonsense stories are just a few of her original approaches to the oral tradition.

Arrietta Chakos

Resource: Television Series

Long Ago and Far Away

To receive free mailings and list of distributors of programs, write to:
STS—Print Projects
WGBH TV
125 Western Ave.
Boston, MA 02134

Masterpiece Theatre for children, this superb children's literature series aired on public television invites young viewers into a world of enchantment. In its first season, such classics as *The Pied Piper of Hamelin*, international folktales, and original contemporary screenplays were brought to life. They're now available on video to rent or buy. The *Long Ago and Far Away* newspaper supplement for students is filled with puzzles, games, and background information, to promote reading and discussion and enhance the literary experience.

Katy Obringer

Resource: Periodical

Short Story International

Seedling Series:
   $3.95 individual copies,
   $14/year (4 issues);
Student Series
   $4.45 individual copies,
   $16/year (4 issues);
SSI Series: $4.95 individual copies, $22/year (6 issues)
from:
Short Story International
P.O. Box 405
Great Neck, NY 11022
1-516-466-4166

The three series of *Short Story International* have won numerous awards, including the United Nations medal for their contribution to international understanding, and yet publisher Sam Tankel told me, "Classroom teachers don't know about us." We hope our listing here changes that because *Short Story International* is a treasure that belongs in every classroom, elementary through high school. The

Seedling series is published quarterly for grades 4 through 7; the Student Series is for grades 8 through 12; and there is a bimonthly series for high school and college students. Published by the International Cultural Exchange, a nonprofit, nonpartisan organization, each issue contains award-winning, unabridged, illustrated stories from around the world. These stories have a long reach—they promote a love of reading while providing sensitive insights into other peoples and other cultures.

LBB

The Basalization of Literature

 Viewpoint: Charlotte S. Huck

Literature in the Whole Language Classroom

Literature, the reading of real books not basal readers, should be at the heart of every whole language program. The development of the whole language movement grew out of the research that showed that young children were not merely imitating the language they heard around them, but were actively constructing the rules for how language worked. Their speech errors, for example, revealed their implicit understanding of how plurals were usually formed. Thus the child who says, "I'll put my socks on my feets," tells us that he knows how to say more than one. He has been listening, processing, and experimenting without explicit instruction. No one explicitly teaches a young child to talk, yet nearly all children learn.

Many children from literate homes also learn to read and write in this same natural way, for the roots of literacy develop way before schooling. In *The Meaning Makers*, Gordon Wells compares Jonathan, who he estimated had heard over 6,000 stories before he came to school, with Rosie, who had never been read to before kindergarten. Jonathan, of course, was a top achiever in reading and writing while Rosie tested out on the bottom of her class and *stayed there* throughout school. Learning to read held no threat for Jonathan, only the fulfillment of a real desire. It was all so natural and joyful. And our schools have made it so difficult and hard.

Presently, there are three kinds of literature-based reading programs operating in our schools—only the last one described would be worthy of whole language teachers.

Publishers eager to take advantage of the interest in literature-based programs have produced all kinds of little books, big books, and basal readers filled with stories and poems (but seldom a whole book). Since the texts are drawn from literature, they are better written than the old Dick and Jane readers, but they still look like basal readers and have the same kinds of workbooks, teachers manuals, ditto sheets, and end of unit tests. Teachers are using these texts much as they used basal readers, with three ability groups of children reading aloud in round robin fashion. The emphasis is still on the skills of reading with the greatest amount of time given to filling in the blank exercises. Children are given no choice of what to read and little time to discuss their responses to the story.

Another kind of literature-based reading program uses "real trade books," but uses them *as if* they were basal readers. Many teachers trained to use teacher guides for basal readers do not feel secure about their own ability to teach without them. In many instances, they do not know the field of children's literature well enough to identify the strengths of the books themselves, and so they turn to commercial guides. These guides remind one of a teacher's manual and a workbook all rolled in one. They advocate word study and phonic skills with such superb books as *Charlotte's Web* or *A Wrinkle in Time*, and they suggest every imaginable activity for each book. One study guide for the *Frog and Toad* Series is 109 pages long! Although a few guides do present

the strengths of the book and suggest appropriate learning activities (from which teachers may *choose*), most of them are merely making basal readers out of some of our best children's literature. Such basalization of fine books will never develop a love of reading; in fact, it may kill real enjoyment of literature forever.

The third kind of a reading program uses books naturally and appropriately, introducing them in kindergarten and first grade the way they would be shared in literate homes. Children are surrounded by books—books in their classrooms and books in their libraries. Teachers read aloud to their boys and girls not just once, but four and five times a day in the kindergarten and primary grades and at least twice a day in the middle grades. They read to the whole group, to small groups, and to individuals, and they reread the same book over and over again just the way a young child hears a bedtime story read again and again. One first-grade teacher told me that it was not unusual for her to read the same book as many as 20 times in one month!

Reading *with* children is as important as reading to children. When children have heard a story such as Tolstoy's *The Great Big Enormous Turnip* many times, they can join in on the repeated phrases about pulling the turnip. Reading "The Three Little Pigs," they can chant with the wolf when he says, "I'll huff and I'll puff, and I'll blow your house in." During this shared reading time children learn such concepts of print as directionality, what constitutes a word, a letter, and the purpose of punctuation. Hearing repeated readings helps boys and girls to develop a sense of story. They learn how stories begin and end; they recognize the story structures of three in such folktales as "The Three Bears," "The Three Little Pigs," and "The Three Billy Goats Gruff." They begin to understand the role of such characters as the princess, a wolf, a wicked stepmother. This knowledge then helps children predict the action of the story, for they have learned how the rules of the story are transferred to the print on the page.

Retelling stories or writing them in their own words frees children from the difficulties of composing; at the same time they are coping with the mechanics of writing. Yet writing the story of "The Three Bears" requires far more knowledge and skill than filling in a blank on a workbook page. Creating pictures develops more knowledge of a sense of story than coloring within the lines of a ditto sheet.

All children from kindergarten on should have an opportunity to read books of their own choosing every single day. They should have a wide variety of books to select from until they find one that they love and want to read over and over again. They should feel free to read quietly with one or two classmates, for reading can be a social activity. Our purpose should be to help children want to read, because our children today are not reading. We need to reorder our priorities and give children, all children, time to read books of their own choosing for

Charlotte S. Huck is best known for her college text, *Children's Literature in the Elementary School*, now in its fourth edition. She was a professor at Ohio State University for 30 years. Upon her retirement, the university established a fund in her name for the first endowed professorship in children's literature in the United States.

their own enjoyment. For wide reading produces fluent readers, children who know how to read and delight in reading.

Literature should not be confined to just the reading period. The use of real books should extend across the curriculum to include historical fiction and biography and the other superb informational books which are available on almost every subject. I'd love to study dinosaurs with a group of fourth- and fifth-graders today because we have such fascinating new books about them. Patricia Lauber's *The News About Dinosaurs*, an intriguing state-of-the-art book, discusses the latest scientific thinking about these fascinating creatures. Her other book, *Dinosaurs Walked Here*, discusses fossils as if they were entries in an ancient diary. Here children discover how scientists learn about dinosaurs. This book would be a perfect lead-in to Pam Conrad's exciting novel titled *My Daniel* that tells how a young boy and his sister discover the skeleton of a dinosaur in Nebraska during the late 1880s. A teacher would also want to read some appropriate poems from Lee Bennett Hopkins's excellent collection of poetry, *Dinosaurs*.

By reading aloud, giving children time to read, using books across the curriculum, and teaching reading with real books, we can replicate the rich literacy environments of literate homes. It lies within the power of every teacher and librarian to give children a deep experience with literature, not a watered-down one. Only then will our children become real readers who will look forward to a lifetime of pleasure in the reading of good books.

➜ See: Dalrymple, p. 426; Goodman, p. 119; Literature Reference List, p. 429; Ohanian, p. 176; Parkes, p. 36; Rivera, p. 166; Shroyer, p. 41; Watson, p. 40.

Children's Literature in the Elementary School, 4th ed.

Charlotte S. Huck, Susan Hepler, and Janet Hickman
1987; 816 pp.; $29.95
New York: Holt, Rinehart & Winston

Huck's compendium is an indispensable guide for any teacher working up a literature curriculum. Her extensive framework for study is embellished by lovingly retold stories, wittily concise plots, and carefully chosen illustrations taken from books she obviously knows and enjoys. A good deal of practical information is included: annotated lists of books by type or subject matter; recommended references and related readings; and helpful synopses of classics and little-known gems.

Arrietta Chakos

Further Reading by Charlotte S. Huck

◆ "Children's Literature as the Content of Reading." In *Theory into Practice*. Ohio State University, December 1987.

◆ *Children's Literature in the Elementary School*, 4th ed., with S. Hepler and J. Hickman. Holt, Rinehart & Winston, 1987.

◆ "Developing Readers," with Kristen Kerstetter. In *Children's Literature in the Reading Program*, ed. B. E. Cullinan. IRA, 1987.

◆ "No Wider than the Heart Is Wide." In *Children's Literature in the Classroom: Weaving Charlotte's Web*, ed. J. Hickman and B. E. Cullinan. Christopher-Gordon, 1987.

◆ *Princess Furball*. Greenwillow, 1989.

Viewpoint: Yvonne S. Freeman

Literature-based or Literature: Where Do We Stand?

Those of us involved with whole language need to be careful that the new literature-based programs are really different from the basal programs we have opposed. California's *English-Language Arts Framework* (1987) suggested that the new literature-based English-language arts curriculum should provide for (1) "in-depth study of core literary works... ," (2) "reading of literature that extends the core work, captures students' individual interests, and challenges them to explore new avenues on their own," and (3) "recreational-motivational reading that is based on students' natural curiosity and that encourages them to read for pleasure." A careful look at literature-based programs produced by commercial publishers, and those being planned and implemented by different school districts in California, reveals that literature-based programs may not be very different from old basal reading programs.

We need to compare *literature-based* programs with real *literature* programs. By looking at (1) the assumptions underlying each type of program, (2) what learners and teachers do in using one program as opposed to the other, and (3) the contents of the two kinds of programs, we, as whole language educators, can perhaps better articulate needs we have for programs that do really allow for whole language literacy instruction.

Assumptions: Literature-based or Literature?

Many school districts are adopting commercial literature-based materials for their reading programs. Other districts have organized committees of teachers and administrators to choose works of literature and plan a literature-based curriculum to be implemented in their schools.

In both cases, literature is organized so that all children at certain grade levels read the same

Yvonne (Bonnie) S. Freeman is the director of Bilingual Education and the co-director of Language Development at Fresno Pacific College in Fresno, California. She has pre–sented at local, state, and national conferences and worked with teachers in school districts in several states. She also works with Hispanic parents helping them to see the important roles they have in their children's school success.

books. In fact, in some districts, teachers are not allowed to read books or give their children books that are designated to be used at a different grade level. For example, *Bridge to Terabithia* by Katherine Paterson (1977) may be used only in the fourth grade in one local school district.

Both commercial materials and the locally produced curriculum guides provide summaries of stories, comprehension questions, units, workbook exercises, and vocabulary lists. These turn the stories into practice materials for skills and vocabulary. If all children in one grade are assigned the same books, there is also the implicit assumption that all those children have the same background knowledge and interests.

Whole language teachers approach literature from a different perspective. They understand that good literature is appreciated by people of all ages, that readers need choice in what they read, and that readers get different meanings from text because they have different interests and backgrounds. By doing different kinds of literature studies with their students, whole language teachers provide experiences appropriate for the range of learners.

Learners and Teachers in Literature-based and Literature Classrooms

Since the literature-based programs are organized and planned generically, neither learners nor teachers have any real choices when reading programs are implemented. Both are controlled by the materials since they are told what to read, when to read, and how to read. In some schools whole classes are required to read a single book at the same time. The units, workbooks, comprehension questions, and exercises provided for the literature-based programs force students and teachers alike to search for someone else's meaning and responses to the texts. Instead of following the students' leads and interests, the materials force participants to follow the directions given in the guides. Even when choice is included in reading or writing activities, the choices have been provided by someone outside the classroom, by someone who is not part of the unique context that is created in each individual classroom.

Teachers and students in the whole language classroom choose what they will read, explore literature together, ask their own questions, and create units based on their own questions. The teacher follows the children's lead as members of the community discuss what they have read and write their own responses and stories.

Materials in Literature-based and Literature Classrooms

The literature-based program does usually

include real, unadapted, but often abridged literature, sometimes in single, separate books and sometimes in anthologies. This literature is assigned a level of appropriate use. Literature-based programs often include workbooks, units, activity guides, summaries, vocabulary lists, and comprehension questions.

In literature programs, the materials list consists of a large choice of real, unabridged literature. The texts are not graded. Instead, teachers offer students a wide range of choice in what they read. Good literature is appropriate for any age level assuming there is interest. Recently, I read to a group of adults a book that most might consider a counting book for preschoolers, Molly Bang's *Ten, Nine, Eight* (1987). After I finished, one woman said, "That was beautiful. Would you read it again?" I have read Robert Kraus's *Leo the Late Bloomer* (1971) and Judith Viorst's *Alexander and the Terrible, Horrible, No Good, Very Bad Day* (1972) to children of all ages as well as adults, and all have loved them and gotten their own meanings from them. Yet both these books are assigned to be used only at the second-grade level in one district's literature-based program.

Basalization of Literature

Many literature-based programs are really not very different from the basal programs that we have been objecting to for some time. Ken Goodman (1988, pp. 29–41) described what has happened to texts when they are adapted and modified as the "basalization" of good literature. In many literature-based programs texts are not being modified. Full, unadapted, and unabridged pieces of literature are being provided to students to read. However, other features of the old basal programs that control readers unnaturally are still present in these new programs. As educators who have seen the power of literature in classrooms where children are given choices and where children explore their own responses to text, we must carefully examine alternative reading programs that are offered to us. When we provide real, unabridged literature along with opportunities for choice and exploration, we can capture students' interest, challenge them to explore new avenues, and encourage them to read for pleasure.

➜ See: California, p. 174; Freeman, p. 87, 184, 212, 312, 320, 368; Literature Reference List, p. 429.

References

Bang, M. 1987. *Ten, nine, eight.* New York: Viking Penguin.

California State Department of Education. 1987. *English-language arts framework.* Sacramento: California State Department of Education.

Goodman, K. 1988. "Look what they've done to Judy Blume!: The basalization of children's literature." *New Advocate* 1(2).

Kraus, R. 1971. *Leo the late bloomer.* New York: Prentice-Hall.

Paterson, K. 1977. *Bridge to Terabithia.* New York: Harper & Row.

Viorst, J. 1972. *Alexander and the terrible, horrible, no good, very bad day.* New York: Aladdin Books.

Excerpted from *Teachers Networking,* Summer 1989.

Further Reading by Yvonne S. Freeman

◆ *Report Card on Basal Readers,* with K. Goodman, P. Shannon, and S. Murphy. Richard C. Owen, 1988.

◆ "Evaluation of Second Language Junior and Senior High School Students in the Whole Language Content Classroom," with D. Freeman. In *Whole Language Evaluation Book,* ed. K. Goodman et al. Heinemann, 1989.

◆ "Whole-language Approaches to Writing with Secondary ESL Students," with D. Freeman. In *Richness in Writing: Empowering ESL Students,* ed. D. Johnson and D. Roen. Longman, 1989.

◆ "A Road to Success for Language Minority High School Students," with D. Freeman. In *When They Don't All Speak English: Integrating the ESL Student into the Regular Classroom,* ed. P. Rigg and V. Allen. NCTE

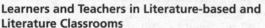

Literature-based Versus Literature: Where Do We Stand?	
LITERATURE-BASED	**LITERATURE**
Assumptions	**Assumptions**
• Literature can be organized into grade levels.	• Literature is universal across grade levels.
• Children at certain levels should read the same books.	• Children at all levels need choice in what they read.
• Children will get the same meaning from a piece of literature.	• Children get different meanings from the same text.
• Children at each grade level have the same interests and background.	• Children have varied interests and backgrounds.
Learners	**Learners**
• Have no real choices	• Have choices
• Are controlled by the materials	• Control the materials
• Find someone else's meaning	• Find meaning for themselves
• Answer someone else's questions	• Answer their own questions
• Write what is suggested	• Write their own responses and stories
• Follow directions	• Make decisions
Teachers	**Teachers**
• Follow the lead of the materials	• Follow the lead of the children
• Are told what to teach and when	• Decide with the children what to do and when to do it
• Use prepared materials	• Allow children to produce materials
Materials	**Materials**
• Real, unadapted literature	• Real, unadapted, and unabridged literature
• Literature graded or leveled	
• Anthology pieces abridged	
• Include workbooks, units, activity guides, summaries, comprehension questions	

Sharing Literature

Great Schools — Awakening Seed School

Dancing on the Edge

by Yvonne Mersereau, Mary Glover, and Meredith Cherland

It's 2:00 P.M. in the multipurpose room. The class watches. The children are taking turns interpreting scenes from *The Garden of Abdul Gasazi*. Matt and Alexei begin by standing beside each other leaning over at the waist, with arms outstretched and heads bent. Then they melt down and begin jumping around playfully like dogs. They use abrupt, shocked movements to portray the magic of Abdul Gasazi. They change quickly to flying and flapping movements, ending with both of their backs on the floor, heads together and legs up over their bodies so that their feet are touching.

Later in discussion Alison comments, "Your dance looked like yoga because you used some of the yoga shapes that we learned from Amy last year."

Mary, the teacher, asks, "What about the melting down part? Why did you happen to choose that idea?"

Matt explains, "Well, there are different ways of perspecting a dog." Discussion continues and it becomes clear that Matt has gotten this idea from the way Chris Van Allsburg has illustrated the book using varied perspectives.

Matt, Alexei, and Alison are members of a third- and fourth-grade class at Awakening Seed School, an alternative elementary school in Tempe, Arizona, where teachers worked together recently to bring dance into a whole language curriculum. Mary Glover, the school's program director and a dancer, and Yvonne Mersereau, the children's classroom teacher, collaborated on a new idea, offering dance as a complement to writing and to the study of literature. Meredith Cherland, a researcher from Arizona State University, was invited to work along with Mary and Yvonne and the children to study the process.

Awakening Seed School began in 1977 when people came together who were interested in giving children the kind of education that would help them to become better human beings. Their idea was to help children to grow toward self-actualization, and to develop an appreciation for their fellow human beings and the planet upon which we live. The school's curriculum has grown out of those ideals and has been continually adjusted and revised. A whole language curriculum has emerged and it continues to unfold daily. Teachers have realized that watching children learn informs their theory and practice. This understanding is central to the school's curriculum: As teachers learn from children what and how they need to know about their world, they can adapt the curriculum to meet their needs.

The Awakening Seed curriculum is built on the following principles:

1. Education for young children must engage the body, heart, and mind.
2. Education is a process of growth and discovery. This process takes time.
3. Learners construct and reconstruct meaning. Therefore, education must invite children to search for meaning and significance in their lives.
4. Learning and teaching involve risk-taking; children and teachers need a safe school environment where they can feel secure as learners and are supported in taking chances.
5. People learn together. Learning together involves sharing and negotiating varied perspectives. Curriculum must be structured so that people can collaborate.
6. Human beings have a need to grow. Children who help shape their own curriculum can be trusted to learn.

In Yvonne's Classroom

As a community of learners, the children in Yvonne's class are immersed daily in reading and writing, participating in the world of literature both as readers and authors.

Yvonne and the children engage in transactions with literature in a variety of ways which enable each child to develop both a personal and a social history of reading: They read stories individually, they read and study stories in small groups, and they share experiences with stories read to them. Time is set aside every day during which the children select and read books independently. The children record their choices in a reading log, documenting their personal reading history.

The Dance Begins . . .

Many of the children experienced creative movement during the 1986–87 school year, when Mary worked with them on developing an understanding of the vocabulary of movement. In working with the children, and through dialogue with others interested in holistic education, Mary and Yvonne came to see the potential for using dance to enrich and extend the study of literature. They made plans to focus on exploring literature and dance together the following year.

When the 1987–88 school year began, an hour was set aside on Monday afternoons for dance workshop. Mary planned to use picture books to help children explore the individual elements of story and the elements of dance together. At first the hour consisted of an introduction (usually reading a book with a follow-up discussion) and a segment of time for exploration of the dance elements presented. Also included in the class period was a collaborative time to work in small groups to create simple dances. Each class ended with the showing of dances to the whole group. This was frequently followed by a short discussion. When the children needed more time to talk about their work and do reflective writing in their dance dialogue journals, Mary negotiated for a second hour.

During a month-long study of the Maurice Sendak trilogy (*In the Night Kitchen, Outside Over There, Where the Wild Things Are*) the children examined commonalities in the content and construction of those stories.

The children used the patterns they saw in Sendak's work to name movements which they then used to create dances representing those stories. They followed their study of Sendak's work with William Steig's *Sylvester and the Magic Pebble*. At this point in their development they found that the specificity of Steig's language hindered them from interpreting it in dance. Sendak's more open and abstract language allowed them more freedom of interpretation.

Mary was encouraged by this work with the Sendak trilogy. She began to have a sense that they were all benefiting from having been immersed in dance and literature for a long period of time. The children were able to understand dance and literature more deeply because they had been given time to do that. Nancie Atwell (1987) has pointed out that time and ownership are crucial factors in the writing process. Mary and Yvonne found them to be crucial factors in the making of dances as well. The children had time to develop ownership of their work, and it was through that sense of ownership that they were willing to spend time on the work.

Jumanji . . . the Dance Continues

In February the children pressed Mary to return to work with Chris Van Allsburg's *Jumanji*. They felt that they had learned so much that they needed an opportunity to "revision" their previous interpretation of that work. They knew that they wanted to create a performance of *Jumanji*. They worked in pairs or groups of three. Mary suggested that each group take a scene from the story to represent through movement. After several weeks of planning and exploring possibilities for their dances, the children decided that music could help them to finalize their pieces. They responded to the music in a variety of ways. Some used it to enrich their dances, some used it to revise their dances, and others were inspired by it.

One outcome of this work was that the children came to see the effects of revision clearly through constructing dances. They found it easy to revise movement because it is such a malleable form. Their satisfaction with the final product led them to a deeper understanding of the potential of revision. That understanding extended itself to the writers' workshop. Jaymie and Nicole demonstrated a new tolerance for revision as they reworked their research paper on slavery. They kept coming back to the text repeatedly as writers with a more educated awareness of their audience. They had a new vision for the potential of their text.

Insights

We were all learners in this process. Adding dance to the curriculum had benefits for the children and teachers alike. We have come to new understandings and confirmed old beliefs. Here is what we have seen:

- We came to see that learning in one mode can serve as a metaphor for learning in another. Choreographing dances can help children understand composing as both readers and writers.

- We need to educate the body, the mind, and the heart. Children are disposed to approach learning in different ways at different times in their lives. Teachers need to provide children with a variety of avenues for making meaning. For example, some children will come to the understanding of literature most readily through the dance, while others will approach it from a less physical and more analytical perspective.

- Schools need to educate the imagination. Dance provides one more way to do this. It allows children to enter a "lived-through" experience (Frye 1964) physically, through their kinesthetic sense.

- Aesthetic development takes time. The curriculum needs to include time for children to do exploratory work and allow them the freedom to negotiate meaning together.

- Learning is social. Teachers learn through collaborating with each other and with children. Children learn through collaborating with each other. Curriculum must be negotiated so that there is time for the process of collaboration to occur.

- Children need time to reflect on their work and teachers need time to reflect on their practice. Time and reflection empower teachers and learners.

- Learning requires that children become risk-takers. If children are to do more than memorize facts, they need to feel safe enough to extend themselves physically, emotionally, and intellectually.

- Teaching requires that we risk. Risk may be

The Awakening Seed Republic

Glover
Page 1
25¢

Friday, February 17, 1989   Tempe, Arizona   1st Year, Issue 3

What's Going On?

Wants and Wishes for 1989

Taken from interviews by
Ryan Sandell, Billy Robertson
and K.C. Atwood.

 he Letts Class

Scott Thelander wants a T.V.
Michael Paul Cotter wants a toy.
Laura Robertson wants a T.V.
Stephanie Atwood wants a T.V.
Molly Mullins wants a new car.
Sara Parker wants her mommy
to have a baby.
Brian Yunt wants a horse.
Billy Robertson wants a good
education.
Bill and Mary Glover wish for
world peace.
Kathy Graham wishes for fewer
harmfull chemicals in our food.
Brithany Oliver wants a trip to
San Diego.
Baegon Oliver wants 119 Barbies.
Mary Dayley wants a scooter.

Winter Soltice

By: Patrick Plehn

Our school had a Christmas play
on December 15, 1988. It started at
7:30. It was fun. At the end we sang
Christmas carols, and had cookies and
cake. We all had a fun time. Then it
ended and we went home. Then everybody talked about it at school. Helen's
and Kathy Ostrand's classes performed
a play called Santa's Favorite Story.
Then there was a dance by Kathy Graham.
The Nutcracker was performed by Kerri's
class. Carols were sung by Kathy and
Mike's class, and the story of Frederick
was danced by Mary's and Yvonne's classes.

Jastin Crasmas   Program

Studying Martin Luther King Jr.

By: Helen and Cherry's class

Helen and Cherry's class studied
Martin Luther King Jr's life. We read
books, newspapers and magazine articles.
We watched a movie about Martin Luther
King Jr. growing up, and one about Miss
Jane Pitmann. She was the first black
woman to drink out of a whites only
fountain in Alabama. We made a heart
shaped mural of poems and illustrations.
Elsie Moore and Wade Smith came to
teach us about Martin Luther King Jr.,
and to tell us what their lives were
like when there was segregation. It
made us feel bad because it wasn't fair.
We learned that blacks were made to do
things they did not want to do. We ended
with a song by Stevie Wonder.
At least Martin Luther King Jr. still
lives in our hearts.

 Natchral BY Justin

Martin Luther King, Jr.

Martin Luther King had a dream.
The dream was that he wanted
Everyone to be free.
He marched for peace.
He fought with Love.
I hope
That the country
Is peaceful
          Forever.
                    by
                    Jesse Brown

BY: KC

Helen's Baby

By: J.T. Benton, Jesse
Brown and Ben Dubasik

Helen had a baby. She
brought it Wednesday, January 4, 1989. It was a girl.
Her name is Alyssa Cotter.
She was born on December 22,
and the time was 12:12 P.M.
Saint Joseph's hospital was
the place where she was born.
She is very cute.

By Ben

Cecelia
by Noah Underwood and J. J. King

Cecelia was born in Ecuador, South
America. May 15th is her birthday.
Cecelia came to America to be a teacher.
Cecelia took nine hours and took two
airplanes to get to America. They speak
Spanish. They eat lots of potatoes where
Cecelia lives. Where Cecelia lives, Ian
lives.

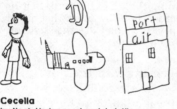 Port air

Hong Kong

Moon Lake

By: Meghan Draper

This is written by Ivan
Gantschev, the same author who
wrote Santa's Favorite Story,
the play that Helen's class
animated for the Christmas play.
The Moon Lake is about a
lake where the moon takes a bath
and leaves dazzling stones. If
you want to know what happens
there, read the book.

Joke

What's a favorite place for a
thirsty cat?
THE MILKY WAY!

Taken from the soon
to be published book:
100 Super Silly Jokes
by: Derek Cheung
     Billy Robertson
     Ryan Sandell
     K.C. Atwood

Japan

By: Nica Kolasa

Japan is very nice. The
[peop]le are very kind. There
[is] also a great many festivals.
[For in]stance: the Doll Festival,
[t]he Summer or Winter Festivals.
[Japan] is not just out of a book.
[I've] been to Japan. In Japan,
[usu]ally the clothes are the same,
[exc]ept when there is a festival.

 by Nica

---

Westchester

POEMS   FREDR
BY
ARTHUR SMI

The Nursing Home
by Jennifer Wood

On Monday, January 30th, the re[...]
were doing much better. Alta w[...]
lot better. She isn't crying anymo[...]
is nice because he gave us cand[...]
haven't been going to the nursing[...]
for awhile because Christmas ca[...]
we didn't see them on Christmas[...]

Santa's Visit

Santa's Visit

By: Baegan Oliver, Ryan
Sandell and Brithan
Oliver

When Santa came to our [...]
program he said, "Ho-Ho-Ho a[...]
He." Part of the audience [...]
He-He." The other part of t[...]
said "Ho-Ho-Ho." He was ta[...]
the Christmas Spirit.

Penpals with Nea's Class
by Denise Davey and Jessica Rod[...]

Our penpals are really special. [...]
our penpals write letters to each [...]
We help them write. Our penpal[...]
is Nea. She used to be in our sc[...]

The Japan Study
by Mia Segura

Our class is studying Japan. It was [...]
the kids' ideas to study Japan. We w[...]
lucky we had Nica and Jessica Rodd[...]
we made books about Japan. We r[...]
book that had Japanese people in it. Its
title is The Big Wave.

the street. The
school.

---

involved in making curricular changes, in trying new approaches in our classrooms, and in
relationships of personal trust with children.

An Invitation to Dance

Anne Haas Dyson has compared teaching to
a dance. "Teaching is not the doing of
activities—it is a . . . dynamic interactive dance;
teachers and children interact to create activities: to create curricula as they work to reach
their respective goals" (Dyson 1986, p. 135). We
have found that image to be an appropriate
metaphor in our work as well.

Like dance, teaching is an art, a form of self-
expression, a joy. Adding dance to the curriculum has provided us with a new version of what
teaching and learning can be. We invite you,
our fellow teachers, to add something startling
and new to your curriculum. We invite you to
use all your talents in the classroom and to collaborate with teachers who have different talents. We invite you to take chances, and to
model risk taking for children. We invite you to
follow your obsessions, and as Shelley Harwayne
(1987) encourages all of us, to stay on the frontiers of thinking.

➜ See: Cairney, p. 201; Literature Reference List,
p. 429; Short, p. 18; Whitin, p. 21.

References

Atwell, N. 1987. *In the middle.* Portsmouth, NH:
Boynton/Cook.

Dyson, A. H. 1986. "Staying free to dance with children:
The dangers of sanctifying activities in the language arts
curriculum." *English Education* 18.

Frye, N. 1964. *The educated imagination.* Bloomington, IN:
Indiana University.

Harwayne, S. 1987. Presentation for C. E. D. Writing
Workshop, October, Tempe, AZ.

Sendak, M. 1970. *In the night kitchen.* New York: Harper &
Row.

———. 1981. *Outside over there.* New York: Harper &
Row.

———. 1983. *Where the wild things are.* New York:
Scholastic.

Steig, W. 1969. *Sylvester and the magic pebble.* New York:
Prentice-Hall.

Van Allsburg, C. 1979. *The garden of Abdul Gasazi.*
Boston: Houghton Mifflin.

———. 1981. *Jumanji.* Boston: Houghton Mifflin.

Excerpted from *Language Arts* 66(2), National Council of
Teachers of English, February 1989.

Resource: Pamphlet

A Community of Learners: An Insider's View of Whole Language

Mary Kenner Glover
1986; 16 pp.; $3
Awakening Seed Press
1130 W. 23rd St.
Tempe, AZ 85282
1-602-829-1479

This account of a
whole language school
is "one classroom
teacher's daily experience with a community of
learners" at the Awakening Seed School. Glover
begins by asking the fundamental question
"What is whole language?" and goes on to
answer via examples of student writing and art.
She supplies in this simply written but expressive
pamphlet the inspiration to make the leap into a
holistic curriculum. Glover lists professional texts
as well as children's book authors as departure
points for interested readers.

Arrietta Chakos

Classroom Demonstrations

by Heinz Senger and B.M. Lynn Archer

Great Explorations: Journey through a Novel, a Screenplay, and a Film

I learned how to express my *own* opinions about the novel, screenplay, and movie of *Sounder*.

When was the last time a unit sparked such comments? How often do students become active explorers of written and visual texts? With Louise Rosenblatt's transactional theory of reading in mind, we developed a unit involving the novel, screenplay, and film of *Sounder* where the students experienced literature as something to be "lived through," rather than directed by the teacher (1976, p. 240). We wanted the ninth grade students to trust their own responses and feel comfortable in sharing their insights with each other and the two teachers who team taught this unit. This involved the teachers and students abandoning their typical classroom roles in favour of becoming co-explorers and co-creators of the texts.

The Journey Begins

We started by giving the students an overview of the unit; we explained that they would be responsible for exploring the three forms of text and that their responsibility as explorers included cooperating with the other students in their seven heterogeneous groups of four.

In order to draw on their prior knowledge and experience, the students generated ideas about the words "my childhood." Next, the students viewed *My Childhood: James Baldwin's Harlem*, the film version of James Baldwin's essay. After viewing the film, they worked with their group to list the differences and similarities between their childhood and that of the author.

Before handing out the novel, we read the first three pages aloud. During this reading, the students focussed on their own images created from what they had heard. After the reading the students generated a word cluster based on their images as a way to create a concrete and visual representation of their initial responses.

The students were then asked to write a response journal entry for every chapter. The entries could take the form of personal associations, exploratory questions, interpretive analysis, or individual feelings. Their entries would become the basis of small group and whole class discussions. If we were to be faithful to reader-response theory, the students had to be free to develop their own responses to the text without the overt direction of the teacher (Rosenblatt 1976). As expected, a few students asked how to write the response journal entries. After receiving the reply to trust their own thoughts and feelings, most students appeared satisfied. Nevertheless, one student remained after class to ask for help because he was confused by what he had read in the novel so far. Instead of asking him to talk about what was confusing, which may have led us to offer an explanation of the text, we encouraged him to ask questions and explore his confusions. With a smile of relief, he left the classroom. We remained, wondering where the journey would take us.

An Excursion with *Sounder*

Next day, the class followed the procedure that would be used for the succeeding three days. First, they assembled in heir groups to read aloud response journal entries for chapters one and two. After sharing their insights about William H. Armstrong's novel *Sounder*, one member of each group reported the highlights of the discussion to the class. During the reports, the students' ideas directed the discussion. Our role was to be active listeners in order to clarify points, ask questions, and note similarities and differences.

Later, we talked about the variety and quality of the students' responses. For us, it was interesting to hear what the students had to say instead of hearing ourselves talk about *Sounder*. Throughout the next three days, everyone continued to discuss the novel with energy and honesty. Our excursion into *Sounder* was establishing our belief that student initiated writing and talking about books is the heart of exploring literature. As Robert Weinberger (1972, p. 72) states, in "Talk in the Classroom," "for most students in school, talking about what they read may be more important than the act of reading itself."

Writing in their response journals seemed to liberate the text of *Sounder* for the students. The entries became another form of talk. For example:

I like the way Armstrong described the road as "a thread dropped on a patchwork quilt." And how he continued to describe the countryside as sewn together.

I've noticed that this author skips from season to season or year to year. I never know what is going on concerning the time.... I think that he didn't want the readers to really know what or how much time had passed. I don't like that style of writing but it is definitely interesting.

In these journals, we could clearly see the students' engagement with the novel. Once the reading of *Sounder* was completed, we were ready to continue the journey on to the screenplay.

To connect the novel to the screenplay, the student groups collaboratively wrote a letter to an imaginary film director. The letter was to persuade the director to turn the novel into an entertaining film. As the students were brainstorming scenes to include in the letter, it became apparent to them that the whole novel was not filmable. "How can you make an entertaining film out of a boring book?" "Can't we disagree?" "What if some scenes can't be adapted to film?" As a result, the students decided to include in their letters both possible and impossible scenes for film adaptation. The process brought the novel alive for the students. It turned literature from something dusty and dead to something pleasurable and personal (Corcoran 1988).

Studying the Map

Students explored Lonne Elder III's screenplay (1986) of *Sounder* by reading it aloud within their groups. It served as the map for the film. In addition to reading the screenplay, students chose three scenes which they believed would be the most effective on screen. The three scenes were to be part of a "Selling Your Screenplay" group presentation to another director. As they were rehearsing, students began to understand more fully the experiences of their characters. Previously restricted to images derived from reading and writing, the students' images now became three dimensional. By acting three scenes from the screenplay, students not only prepared themselves for the film, but helped to connect their whole selves to it. As stated by Probst (1988),

Literature is experience, not information, and . . . the students must be invited to participate in it, not simply observe it from outside (preface).

After viewing the presentations, student groups were asked to become prospective directors. The directors, or groups, each wrote a letter to their presenter. These letters indicated whether or not the director was willing to produce the screenplay. The director groups varied in their decisions about the screenplay. One group wrote,

Thank you for your presentation of your three scenes from *Sounder*. We think we will consider your scenes for the movie. It was a touching moment when the father came home paralyzed, ready for that good old home cooking.

The *Sounder* Express

The opening scenes of Martin Ritt's film *Sounder* involve little dialogue and progress quite slowly. Because of this we wondered how the students would react. We were pleasantly surprised. The students were interested and attentive. They leaned toward the screen without being restless or talkative. Some of them were taking notes to use later in their response journal entry about the film. As we read the journal entries later, we became aware of the connections being made by the students between the film and their previous explorations. The journal entries also gave students the opportunity to investigate and clarify their responses to the film without the inhibiting influence of their peers or the teachers. It also provided a confident foundation for the groups' concluding assignment.

As a final activity, we gave the students an assignment titled "Clashing Critics." In it, we asked each group to produce and present a "Siskel and Ebert" type programme on *Sounder*. On the day of the presentations, students arrived with theme music, costumes, make up, props, scripts, and cue cards. The camcorder was ready to roll.

When our journey with the novel, screenplay, and film of *Sounder* began, we had a sense of our general direction, but were uncertain about the nature of the final destination. Although we chose the texts and assignments, content for the discussions, journals, letters, and presentations was derived from the students themselves. Because of this, we had real conversations about *Sounder*. We were co-explorers and co-creators. We discovered much about our students' engagement with literature, their ability to cooperate, and the nature of their learning. Our journey continues.

→ See: Kroll, p. 113; Literature Reference List, p. 429; Short, p. 18.

References

Armstrong, W. H. 1969. *Sounder*. New York: Harper & Row.

Baldwin, J. 1974. "My childhood." In *Man in the expository mode 2*, ed. Sarah Solotaroff. Agincourt, Ontario: Book Society of Canada.

Corcoran, B. 1988. "Spiders, surgeon, and anxious aliens: Three classroom allies." *English Journal* 77(1).

Elder III, L. 1986. "Sounder." *Best American screenplays: First series, complete screenplays*, ed. Sam Thomas. New York: Crown.

Horan, D. 1964. *My childhood: James Baldwin's Harlem*. Metromedia.

Probst, R. E. 1988. *Response and analysis: Teaching literature in junior and senior high school*. Portsmouth, NH: Boynton/Cook.

Ritt, M. 1972. *Sounder*. Twentieth Century-Fox.

Rosenblatt, L. M. 1976. *Literature as exploration*. New York: Noble & Noble.

Weinberger, R. 1972. "Talk in the classroom." In *How porcupines make love: Notes on a response-centered curriculum*, ed. Alan C. Purves. Lexington, MA: Xerox College Publishing.

Adapted from a revised version of "Exploring *Sounder*: The Novel, the Screenplay, and the Film," *English Journal*, National Council of Teachers of English, December 1989.

Heinz Senger is a teacher at Earl Marriott Secondary School, Surrey, British Columbia. B. M. Lynn Archer is an English helping teacher in Surrey School District.

Classroom Demonstrations

by Susan S. Abel

How Much Is a Million?

After reading all the books written or illustrated by Steven Kellogg and discusing Kellogg's pen and watercolor drawings, children chose their favorite book and drew an illustration using pen and watercolors. Our reading specialist took slides of each illustration. They read their sentence on the tape recorder. Now, we have a traveling show. We have shown our slides for a school asssembly and PTA. The illustrations look wonderful up on the screen. We named our traveling show "How Much Is a Million?" after the book written by Davik Schwartz and illustrated by Stevern Kellogg.

➔ See: Burns, p. 330

Susan S. Abel is a reading specialist at Dollahan Elementary School, Rialto, CA.

Classroom Demonstrations

by Peter Hasselriis

Try a Whole Author!

Here's a variation on reading all of an author's works that you and your students might enjoy. I read Mark Schorer's biography *Sinclair Lewis: An American Life* and stopped every time one of Lewis's works was mentioned. I found whatever work Schorer had referred to and read it. Carlos Baker's *Ernest Hemingway: A Life Story* came along, and again, while I was reading it, I stopped every time a work was mentioned and read it. I stayed with my goal of reading Hemingway's entire output by also reading *A Moveable Feast*, which was published years after Baker's biography and Hemingway's death.

The enjoyable thing about reading a biography along with an author's work is that you learn exactly what was going on in the author's life as the work was being conceived and written.

My friend and UMC colleague Nancy Knipping found kindergartners in literature study groups who noticed that two books they read were illustrated by the same author. I see no reason why they might not enjoy reading a full selection of one author's books. How about Tomie de Paola? Stephen Kellogg? Ezra Jack Keats? Maurice Sendak?

William Sheldon, who was for years the director of the Reading and Language Arts Center at Syracuse University, was an avid collector and reader of the works of Carl Carmer, a writer of historical fiction set in the Genesee region of New York State. I mention Sheldon's affinity for Carmer as a suggestion you might like to explore: Find authors who have focused on your part of the world and encourage students to read those authors. You might do this as a class project. Round up everything that is available and divide the volume of reading among the students in your class.

➔ See: Hasselriis, p. 178; Literature Reference List, p. 429.

Peter Hasselriis is a professor in the College of Education at the University of Missouri, Columbia, MO.

Resource: Bibliographies

Books for You: A Booklist for Senior High School Students

Richard F. Abrahamson and Betty Carter, editors 1988; 507 pp.; $12.95, NCTE members $9.95 Urbana, IL: NCTE

The NCTE Committee on the Senior High School Booklist took three years to review over 4,000 books written for young adults. The result is this listing of nearly 1,200 fiction and nonfiction titles published from 1985 to 1987. The books are organized alphabetically in sections that cover a range of topics from dating and sexual awareness to archaeology and anthropology. Each book is described in a paragraph, with all relevant information to help you find the books you want.

The Junior High School Paperback Collection

John T. Gillespie 1985; 312 pp.; $17.50 Chicago: American Library Association

Gillespie lists 2,833 recommended fiction and nonfiction titles arranged by popular interest categories, followed by an author and title index.

Junior High School Library Catalog, 5th ed.

Richard H. Isaacson, editor 1985; 835 pp.; $80 New York: H. W. Wilson

This catalog is arranged in three parts: (1) annotated titles arranged in Dewey decimal order for nonfiction and in alphabetical order by author for fiction; (2) author, title, subject, and analytical indexes; and (3) a directory of publishers and distributors. It is very useful as a purchasing and cataloging guide, and as a reference tool for title discarding and replacement.

Your Reading: A Booklist for Junior High and Middle School Students

James E. Davis and Hazel K. Davis, editors 1988; 494 pp.; $12.95, NCTE members $9.95 Urbana, IL: NCTE

The NCTE committee that selected the 2,000 books (published in the last five years) in this annotated bibliography was looking for books to interest students "for pleasure, for school assignments, or merely to satisfy curiosity." Fiction and nonfiction books are grouped by 61 categories that reflect contemporary concerns and interests, such as ethnic experiences, divorce and single parents, and ecology, as well as the more traditional interests of sports, science fiction and the future, and fine arts. Each annotation includes all the information needed to find the book.

Literature for Today's Young Adults, 3d ed.

Kenneth L. Donelson and Alleen Pace Nilsen 1989; 640 pp.; $26.25 Glenview, IL: Scott Foresman

Donelson and Nilsen discuss all aspects of young adults' reading needs in this edition for teachers and librarians. Chapters on the history of young adult literature from 1800 to the present day are useful for providing background and historical perspective. In addition to an expanded examination of literary forms, there are new sections covering censorship and the relationship between books and big business. Another new feature is the annotated booklists included for all genres discussed—realism, romanticism, suspense, science fiction, and life models.

Frances Christie/Katy Obringer

Breakthroughs

by Lois S. Vandagriff

Our Room Is a House for Ideas

One day, with only a few minutes to spare before lunch, I picked up the big book *A House Is a House for Me*. The students gathered around and listened, chiming in as they began to recognize the refrain. Quietly, after the reading, they lined up to go to lunch. As we sorted out a lunch or two, and waited for a few to wash their hands, one child said to himself, "A lunchbox is a house for a sandwich." I drew a breath and held it as another child said, "A thermos is a house for milk." The line was quiet, the children seemed to be thinking. I asked with some urgency if they could hold onto these wonderful ideas until we returned to the room and I could write them down. A small, soft voice said, "You could write: A heart is a house for love." During lunch, I kept overhearing them talking, exchanging ideas of what was home to what . . .

As we sat around the chart paper after lunch, ideas flowed freely. We collected two pages of ideas. Here are some of my favorites:

Shoes are a house for feet.
A lamp is a house for a bulb.
Lines on a paper is a house for writing.
Our room is a house for ideas!

The children then worked hard at making wonderful illustrations for their ideas and we plastered them all over the hallway walls outside our classroom. They were rewarded with many positive comments from teachers and students.

Lois S. Vandagriff is a primary teacher at Woodland Elementary School, Oak Ridge, TN.

Cornerstone: Kathy Gnagey Short

Exploring Connections through Text Sets

When readers read two or more texts that are related in some way, they are encouraged to share and extend their understanding of each text differently than if they had read and discussed only one text. Learning and understanding are processes of searching for and making connections. We can understand what we read only because of the connections we make between our current reading and our past experiences, which include previous books we have read or written. Text Sets highlight the cognitive and social strategy of searching for connections as we read (Harste and Short, with Burke 1988).

As a curricular strategy, Text Sets involves pulling together a variety of written materials that are related in some way, having students each read from different sources within that set, and coming together to share and make comparisons across these different sources in discussion groups. I began exploring texts while working with several teachers who were using literature groups in their classrooms. Because we were just starting, we did not have enough multiple copies of single books to keep the groups going. We realized that if we took a topic or a theme, we could go to the school library and pull single titles of books on that topic to create a set. A small group of students could then read from the various books in the set and discuss the connections across the books.

Once we became involved in using Text Sets in the classroom, we realized that their potential went far beyond solving our need for more books for literature circles. Text Sets highlight reading as a process of searching for and making connections. Looking at books in terms of how they connect, compare, and contrast to other literature and life experiences becomes a more conscious strategy that students use as they try to understand what they read.

Because students read different materials, there is a real reason for retellings in Text Set discussions. Each student has something different to contribute to the discussion. We found that Text Set discussions encourage students to really talk with each other and to feel that they are valued members of a group.

Most of the Text Set groups begin with each person reading one or two books. The group then shares retellings and looks for similarities and differences among the books. There are many variations, however, in the strategies they use in reading and discussing the books. In some groups each person is an expert on several books during the discussions. In other groups, everyone keeps reading until each person has read all or most of the books in a set. Some groups decide to read one book within the set at a time so that they can share the reading of a book, discuss it, and then go on to the next book. Some groups take their set and divide it into subsets from which they read and discuss each day. In all groups, some books are read in entirety and other books are used as reference sources.

Most groups make lists of possible comparisons after their sharing and then spend each day looking at one or two of these comparisons before going on to another comparison the next day. However, some spend their time closely examining only one or two comparisons or one

Kathy Gnagey Short teaches children's literature at the University of Arizona where she is an assistant professor in Language, Reading, and Culture. She has worked extensively with elementary teachers in their efforts to develop curricula that actively involve students in using reading and writing to learn. Much of her work has centered around integrating children's literature into the curriculum.

general theme. Some make a list of questions about their books and use them for discussion. All of these groups highlight strategies that support readers in making connections as they read and talk with others.

A wide range of types of sets can be developed. These types of Text Sets include (1) folktale variant and version sets such as Cinderella stories from different countries; (2) theme sets such as war and peace, family relationships, or valuing individuality; (3) topic sets such as pigs, volcanoes, or World War II; (4) text type sets such as mysteries, tall tales, or fables; (5) character sets such as a set of Beverly Cleary's books about Ramona; (6) author sets such as sets of books written by Betsy Byars, Chris Van Allsburg, or Eric Carle; (7) cultural sets such as books reflecting Japanese or Native American cultures; (8) same book sets where the same text is illustrated by different illustrators, such as *I Know an Old Lady Who Swallowed a Fly* or *The Night Before Christmas;* and (9) literary element sets, such as books that all have a cause-and-effect cumulative plot line.

We realized that we could create sets to feature almost any concept or theme that was important within the school curriculum and children's interests. We wanted to make connections between literature circles and the broader units of study going on in the classroom. Instead of literature circles being a separate experience, they became integrated into focusing studies on topics growing out of content fields such as science, social studies, mathematics, or literature.

As we worked with the sets, we observed that some sets were better than others in terms of children's responses and thinking. The critical factor seemed to be that within each set we needed to have reading materials that offered different *perspectives* on the same topic. When readers are forced to take different perspectives on the same topic, anomalies or unexpected ideas are encountered that make readers stop and reexamine their own beliefs and predictions.

One way to introduce multiple perspectives is to mix books coming from a variety of genres. Whenever possible we had fiction, nonfiction, and poetry within the same set. This literature included both professionally authored and student-authored texts. We also put in reading materials other than literature, such as maps, songbooks, magazine and newspaper articles, and pamphlets. We added books written at different levels so that some were lengthy and comprehensive and others were short overviews. We used authors who wrote from their own personal experiences, as well as from a particular knowledge domain such as history, science, or economics.

We also searched out materials that came from a variety of cultural perspectives. If we put together a set of books on cats, we wanted stories that came out of many different cultural traditions, because we knew this would encourage readers to go beyond their own viewpoints and experiences with cats. We wanted materials highly familiar to children that would meet their expectations about the topic so that they could easily make personal connections. We also wanted materials that would take them beyond their own current knowledge and expectations.

We have begun to add other sign systems such as music, art, movement, and mathematics to our sets. Tapes of native speakers or music, instruments, art prints, videotapes of dances or scenery, and objects and artifacts are some of the additions we have made to our sets. Text Sets now are stored in plastic tubs or baskets to keep everything together as students work with them.

Text Sets highlight the process of intertextuality; the making of connections between past and current texts. These discussions have made readers aware of the importance of searching for connections and patterns among books, and have helped them develop strategies for making this search more productive and wide-ranging. This search supports their learning as authors and creators of their own understandings about the world.

➔ See: Baxter, p. 203; Cain, p. 299; Kitagawa, p. 299; Literature Reference List, p. 429; Short, p. 18.

Reference
Harste, J., and K. Short with C. Burke. 1988. *Creating classrooms for authors*. Portsmouth, NH: Heinemann.

Further Reading by Kathy Gnagey Short
◆ *Creating Classrooms for Authors,* with J. Harste and C. Burke. Heinemann, 1988.
◆ "New Potentials for Teacher Education: Teaching and Learning as Inquiry," with C. Burke. *Elementary School Journal* 90(2), January 1990.
◆ *Talking About Books: Creating Literate Classrooms,* with K. M. Pierce. Heinemann, 1990.
◆ "Teachers and Students as Decision-Makers," with G. Kauffman. In *Portraits of Whole Language Classrooms,* ed. H. Mills and J. A. Clyde. 1990.

📷 **WHOLE LANGUAGE CAMERA**

Waiting in the wings . . . a classroom production of "Greyling," Cynthia Motsinger's fifth grade, San Ramon Elementary School, Novato, CA.

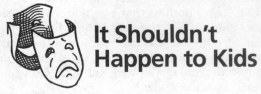

It Shouldn't Happen to Kids

That Dangerous Literature

A student teacher who had spent the first semester in a fifth-grade whole language classroom was assigned, for her second semester, to a traditional skills class where literature books were stored in a cupboard. Missing the rich literature experience she had shared with the children in the first classroom, she got up her nerve one day to ask her new supervising teacher if she could display books on the countertop. "Oh no!" the teacher said. "Then the children will read those instead of their textbooks."

—LBB

Cornerstone: Jacqueline L. Gmuca

Images of the South in Children's Literature

Among the regions of our country, the South has always been one of the most intriguing. Images from Margaret Mitchell's *Gone with the Wind*, replete with magnolia trees, charming belles, and a code of honor, fill our imaginations. However, this view is highly stereotypical and reflects little of the present-day South and its diversity. Regional literature for children and adolescents portrays a multifaceted view of the South, its values and concerns. Picture books, folktales, and realistic novels set in the South describe an area where the land is treasured, the oral tradition valued, and the past remembered.

The emphasis on land is evident in a number of works, among them Ianthe Thomas's *Lordy, Aunt Hattie* (1973), one of the finest for the preschool and early elementary child. In this picture book Aunt Hattie's vivid descriptions and Thomas Di Grazia's full-color illustrations celebrate summertime in the Southeast. In Aunt Hattie's words, it is time for Jeppa Lee, her niece, to get out of bed, for the "sun done shined and whistled to the crocuses." A world of big, juicy huckleberries, jumping catfish, hot sun, and cool lemonade await Jeppa Lee's enjoyment.

In Stella Gentry Sharpe's *Tobe*, enjoyment of the land is witnessed through Tobe and his brothers riding a mule, hunting for wild grapes, and wading in a brook. On their working farm, tobacco and cotton are grown, eggs gathered and cows milked, wheat and sweet potatoes harvested. Published in 1939, *Tobe* was among the first books to highlight and present black characters in a nonstereotypical way.

These books often show a strong sense of family, whether it be Tobe's traditional family or the nontraditional one of Cynthia Rylant's *When I Was Young in the Mountains*. Winner of the 1982 Caldecott Award for its illustrations by Diane Goode, this picture book opens with a sense of love and caring as sister and brother wait for their grandfather to come home from the coal mine. Security is evoked by a scene at the supper table and a meal of corn bread, pinto beans, and fried okra. The last illustration portrays closeness as Grandfather sharpens pencils, Grandmother shells beans, and all sit on the porch swing.

The Southern concept of family recognizes ties to aunts, uncles, first and second cousins. In Cynthia Rylant's *The Relatives Came* (1985), both families meet and hug for hours. Stephen Gammell's illustrations highlight the humor of these hugs as family members are squeezed, lifted off the ground, and playfully punched in the stomach. Good food and quiet talk fill the house that evening; heavy breathing and snoring are heard at night as the relatives sleep everywhere.

Another theme is a sense of independence, a feeling gained from the reliance on land and family. The last page of *When I Was Young in the Mountains* captures this independence as a girl, now grown, reflects on her childhood: "When I was young in the mountains, I never wanted to

Dr. Jacqueline L. Gmuca currently teaches children's and adolescent literature as well as composition and advanced British literature courses at the University of South Carolina–Coastal Carolina College. She is an active member of the Children's Literature Association, serving on the scholarship committee, and has frequently presented papers on the local and national levels. Her article on Arnold Lobel appears in the *Dictionary of Literary Biography;* assessments of the work of Anita Lobel, Arnold Lobel, and Cynthia Rylant in *Twentieth Century Children's Writers.* "Images of the South in Children's Literature" has grown out of her comprehensive study of children's books set in the Carolinas.

go to the ocean, and I never wanted to go to the desert. I never wanted to go anywhere else in the world, for I was in the mountains. And that was always enough."

At times this sense of independence becomes too fierce and stubborn. Mary Call Luther, of Vera and Bill Cleaver's novel *Where the Lilies Bloom* (1969), portrays this extreme. Independence turns into overwhelming isolation as she strives to keep the family together after the death of their father. Mary Call hardens into a cruel person but in the end accepts that she can receive help and still be independent.

These values of the land are the means by which this literature is connected to regional books of the Midwest or New England. All regional literature, wherever it is set, conveys agrarian values, recognizing that a life lived close to the land is fruitful, emotionally and morally.

The preservation of the past is distinctive to children's literature of the South through the prominence of folktales and storytelling. In the Carolinas, for instance, the oral tradition is represented by Cherokee Indian folklore, Appalachian Mountain variations of British folktales, and black folk literature reflecting the Gullah dialect. Folktales embody the cultural values and environment of the region in which they are told; they become a vital part of the literature from that region. In Richard Chase's *The Grandfather Tales* (1948, p. 115), the Appalachian Mountains are evoked through references to the economic necessity of having a "bound out" girl or boy apprenticed to a family in exchange for room and board.

> One time there was a woman had two daughters, and they kept a hired girl. They treated this girl mean. She was bound out to 'em, had to do all the hard work, little as she was. They wouldn't buy her any pretty clothes or nothin', made her sleep right up against the fireplace and the ashes got all over her, so they called her Ashpet.

Language is yet another way in which the life of a region is captured. The passage above conveys the flavor of mountain speech just as the Gullah dialect, spoken on the islands off the South Carolina and Georgia coast, is reflected in the word choice and syntax of the Br'er Rabbit stories. Gullah clearly rings out in Virginia Hamilton's (1985, p. 35) opening paragraphs for "Bruh Alligator Meets Trouble" from *The People Could Fly:*

> Bruh Rabbit has words with Bruh Gator on account Bruh Gator can't keep he mouth shut. He tell Bruh Rabbit one day, t'cause of that. Bruh Rabbit, I can't see how *oonuh* can live *pontop* the hard land. Can't stand the land, myself." Say all that to Bruh Rabbit, and the rabbit dint think much of the gator for it.

These dialects are necessary to express and capture the lives and environment of people from various areas and ethnic backgrounds.

Language is certainly instrumental in Eleanora Tate's *The Secret of Gumbo Grove* (1987, pp. 27, 163). In one scene, Raisin, her main character, helps a church elder in weeding an old graveyard. Her voice rises from the page to inform us of the rigors of yardwork: "She [Miss Effie] turned back to the tombstone and with her hoe pulled at the ropes of brown and green. Not knowing what else to do, I pulled at a tiny pine tree with my hands. Tree wouldn't budge. I pulled again. Finally I got down on my knees and fought with it."

Eleanora Tate's highly realistic novel is part of a growing trend of works that echo the internal conflicts faced by Southerners because of their culture. Books like Suzanne Newton's *What Are You Are up To, William Thomas?* and Cynthia Rylant's *A Fine White Dust* respectively present the class consciousness of Southern society and the power of an evangelical preacher to affect a young boy's religious development.

"We need to know our country better. We need to know not only our own region, where our roots are firmly put down, but other regions where live people different from ourselves—people of different races, faiths, cultures and backgrounds" (Lenski, p. 35). These words, written in 1946, are even more true today in our highly mobile society of the late 20th century. Since most people do not expect to live and work in the same area in which they grew up, they need this knowledge of our country and its varied regions to prepare for the future. More important, they need to recognize and celebrate the uniqueness of a particular region whether it is a Slovene church hall in western Pennsylvania or a tobacco auction in Horry County, South Carolina. Equally important is their understanding of the values and behavior of people who grew up in a totally different area. Through this celebration and understanding, the quality of our lives is enhanced.

→ See: Beatty, p. 298; Cain, p. 299; Literature Reference List, p. 429.

References

Chase, R., ed. 1948. "Ashpet." In *The grandfather tales.* Boston: Houghton Mifflin.

Cleaver, V. and B. 1969. *Where the lilies bloom.* New York: J. B. Lippincott.

Hamilton, V. 1985. "Bruh Alligator meets trouble." In *The people could fly.* New York: Alfred A. Knopf.

Lenski, L. 1968. "Seeing others as ourselves." In *Adventure in understanding.* Tallahassee: Friends of the Florida State University Library.

Rylant, C. 1982. *When I was young in the mountains,* illus. Diane Goode. New York: E. P. Dutton.

———. 1985. *The relatives came,* illus. Stephen Grammell. New York: Bradbury.

Sharpe, S. G. 1939. *Tobe.* Chapel Hill: UNC Press.

Tate, E. 1987. *The secret of Gumbo Grove.* New York: Franklin Watts.

Thomas, I. 1973. *Lordy, Aunt Hattie,* illus. Thomas Di Grazia. New York: Harper & Row.

Classroom Demonstrations

by Lois Bridges Bird

Literature Study: Discovering Real Reading

Imagine walking into a schoolroom and finding the whole class deeply absorbed in books. The students are reading a variety of original works in children's literature. Some read at their desks, others sprawl across big pillows on the floor. Some write in literature logs, or leaf through their books, applying notes on colored Post-its to selected pages. Suddenly you hear a voice exclaim, "No, I disagree! Katherine Paterson means for Louise to be a sympathetic character." You move closer to a group of six students seated at a round table, all holding Katherine Paterson's *Jacob Have I Loved* (1980), and engaged in a heated discussion. Two students have found the main character, Louise, whiny and unsympathetic. The other four disagree. As they argue they refer to their books, reading passages aloud to support their various viewpoints. The classroom teacher is a member of the group. He waits for an opening in the conversation before interjecting his own opinion. Some students agree with him, but others voice contradictory opinions. He holds a notebook and takes notes on what the students say.

Is this just a fantasy? No! You can prove its reality by entering almost any classroom at Fair Oaks Elementary School, in Redwood City, California, during a literature study. It's a scene made possible through the pioneering work of Karen Smith, a talented sixth-grade whole language teacher in Phoenix, Arizona, and Carole Edelsky of Arizona State University, who has spent hours observing Smith share literature with her students. Edelsky refined and defined the model Smith uses and introduced it to Fair Oaks in 1986.

The theory behind the practice is simple. As Edelsky explains, we don't directly teach young children to talk. We do show them how to live as members of their families and communities, and we use language to do much of that teaching. Thus, as they learn to be family members, they also learn what language is and what language can do. Likewise, we don't have to directly teach children to read. We do need to show them what it means to live in the worlds authors create in their books. We show them by immersing them in literature, reading it aloud, and inviting them to read on their own. We help them further by talking about literature, sharing our experiences in the literary worlds we've entered as readers, revealing and describing the almost limitless range of experiences that is possible within the pages of a book. With younger readers, this demonstration is especially important. In fact, in a primary classroom, literature study is initially centered around whole group discussions after a read-aloud. Later, kids can break into small groups and, with teacher guidance, carry a discussion on their own.

Just as we trust that our youngsters will learn our ways of living in households and communities and become proficient language users in the process, so we must trust that our students will become sensitive, critical readers as they enter and explore, with our help, the worlds of books. It is this trust that is, perhaps, the most significant point of contrast between what Edelsky calls a "reading comprehension group" approach to literature and literature study. In the reading comprehension approach, teachers

check up on their students' comprehension of the book they are reading. In effect, teachers become "gentle inquisitors," rather than participants in a "grand conversation" (Higgins 1986) with their students about the book. The following is a chart that Edelsky (1986) developed to illustrate the differences between literature study and a reading comprehension group approach:

Contrast Between Literature Study and a Reading Comprehension Group	
Literature Study	**Reading Comprehension Group Approach Session**
General Characterization	**General Characterization**
• Grand conversation	• Gentle inquisition
• More like an adult book group	• More like a classroom reading group
• Community of learners	• Individual learners
Teacher Activity	**Teacher Activity**
• Teacher participates	• Teacher facilitates.
• Teacher asks questions to increase own comprehension of text.	• Teacher asks questions to check up on students' comprehension.
Role of Text	**Role of Text**
• Open the book (and let's investigate).	• Close the book (and see what's remembered).

In literature study, then, we *assume* comprehension. We realize that initially our students may not understand everything they read. They may miss the finer points of meaning or even misinterpret, and if they do so, we don't hesitate to tactfully bring it to their attention. But we trust that with repeated readings of books they have chosen themselves and care about, and through further explorations of the books in writing and discussion sessions, their abilities as critical readers will grow. We respect them as capable readers right from the beginning; we do not reduce the literary experience to a reading exercise by quizzing them on lists of questions to which we already know the answers.

Literature study is often launched with a teacher-given book talk. Teachers have six to eight copies of each book (Fair Oaks teachers have collected sets of approximately 50 different titles). Initially, they choose four or five titles and talk informally to the class about each book, briefly describing its contents. They then invite students to choose a book. Of course not all students will get their first choice, but before the year is over they are usually able to read all the titles that most appeal to them. Groups form around the books and the teacher meets briefly with each to negotiate the date by which they will complete their reading and be ready to meet for the first discussion session. Students may sign contracts that their parents countersign, promising to read the book on time (Yencho 1989).

In some classrooms, students keep daily literature logs in which they simply reflect on their experience with the book. What do they find surprising? Confusing? Captivating? What are their thoughts about the author's style? How does this author compare to others they've read? These daily entries reveal their understanding of the book as their reading progresses. Generally, students have a week or two to complete the book. If they finish before the date of the first discussion session, they begin reading another book. At any given time, students usually have two books going: one they are reading for literature study and another they read as time allows.

As Edelsky (1988) explains, there are two purposes for reading in literature study. The first is aesthetic—to simply revel in the world the author has created, "to feel it, sense it, smell the smells, taste the tastes . . ." The second purpose is analytical, and entails exploring and examining the literary elements (plot, setting, characterization, theme, symbolism) that authors use to create and craft their literature. The first discussion is always centered around the aesthetic purpose; subsequent discussions are analytical. After the teacher and the students have met to discuss the aesthetic impact of the book (what did you think and feel as you lived inside its world?), the teacher makes an assignment. The assignment evolves from the discussion (this is one reason for taking notes during the discussion; the notes also help teachers evaluate their students' participation and progress) and from the teacher's own knowledge of the literary strengths of the book. The assignment challenges the students to do a more analytical reading of the book. For example, in response to the students' discussion about Louise, the teacher may suggest that they find the places in the text where they come to know Louise; additionally, he will ask them to explore the ways in which K. Paterson enables them to know Louise. They must return to the book and identify where Louise is revealed, and then read and reread to ascertain what literary devices Paterson uses (e.g., description, character's actions, conversation, and character relationships) to create Louise.

The ability to understand books and discuss them in this way develops gradually over time and requires that teachers be readers of literature too. Teachers must demonstrate—in the discussion sessions in which they participate as full-fledged, equal members of the group, and after all-class read-alouds—both the aesthetic and analytical reading of literature.

The results of all this are most satisfying. As the students enjoy good literature and develop their appreciation of it, they improve their reading ability; and through participation in open-ended discussions, they reveal more about their understanding of books than one could ever pull out of them with lists of questions. The less proficient readers, often paired with more proficient readers and surrounded by meaningful discussion, can also participate in literature studies. The teacher may give them additional support by meeting with them daily and "setting the scene" for the reading they will do that day. Thus they too are drawn into the rich, exciting realm of books. They and their classmates discover what it means to be a real reader.

➜ See: Bird, p. 92; Edelsky, pp. 72, 77; Literature Reference List, p. 429.

References

Edelsky, C. 1986. Literature Study Workshop, inservice for Redwood City School District, Redwood City, CA.

———. 1988. "Living in the author's world: Analyzing the author's craft." *The California Reader* 21(3), March/April.

Higgins, J. 1986. Quoted by Carole Edelsky in the Literature Study Workshop, inservice for Redwood City School District, Redwood City, CA.

Paterson, K. 1980. *Jacob have I loved.* New York: Avon.

Yencho, P. 1989. "My escape from basals." *Becoming a whole language school—The Fair Oaks story,* ed. L. B. Bird. Katonah, NY: Richard C. Owen.

Carole Edelsky informs me of two other contributors. Ralph Peterson of Arizona State University helped Smith develop some of her ideas, and Chris Boyd, a whole language kindergarten teacher in Phoenix, Arizona, adapted the model for primary age children.
—LBB

Breakthroughs

by Nancy Wildermuth

From the Mouths of Babes

One of the things I try to impress on my students in the classroom communications course I teach at the University of Missouri-Columbia is that management and discipline problems begin to evaporate when students are involved in activities that are inherently meaningful and personally satisfying. While substituting in a kindergarten class, I had an experience I could swear was Providence providing me with a personal corroboration of this strongly felt belief. I wish I had it on videotape!

Though I am not certified for kindergarten, I was substituting for a kindergarten aide, where my duties included the "slow" reading groups. I was given the basal manual to "study" and workbook pages for the students to complete. I was also given a stack of small books—miniature copies of *The Very Hungry Caterpillar*—which I was told I could use as a time filler if necessary. As I gathered the afternoon group of six or seven and settled them in the hallway where we were to conduct our group, there was a constant air of dissonance. "Teacher, teacher! . . ." rang in my ears as child after child pointed out minor infractions of apparent rules and complained of being bumped, crowded, or otherwise disturbed. Before we began, one boy quietly got up and moved to the other side of our circle, and a peer reported with horror, "Teacher, he moved!"

We settled finally to the task of underlining pictures of objects that began with the same sound that begins "sock." When a pencil lead broke, rather than have the owner trek back into the room for another, I suggested she and a peer share. They managed to do so with long sighs, grumpy looks, and constant reminders from me. Two other girls obviously had our underlining task well in hand and asked to work ahead. When I said yes, they promptly finished with loud exclamations of who had finished ahead of whom and then engaged in private conversation while others worked. Several other students seemed to understand what to do but

waited patiently until I told them to do it. One girl was adamant that she did not hear the similarity in the beginning sounds of "sock" and "sun," which was either the truth or an effort to rattle my chain.

A little fellow to my left watched patiently until he had underlined each proper picture. Then, while I engaged in discussion with my disbeliever, he would entertain himself by scooting backward, pulling his legs in and quietly spinning around on his bottom. After each discussion with my disbeliever, I called the wandering minds and bodies back to the task, and we laboriously worked our way through rows of pictures that began with the same sound that began "sock."

The required work finished, I brought out the stack of little books, and asked the class to scoot close together so they could hear me read over the noise down the hall. I also wanted them to watch me model turning pages as I read, since I had discovered that in an earlier group one child didn't know where the front of the book was or how to turn through it as it was read. When all had located the first page, I turned through the book and read with relish. After one reading, a girl asked if she could collect them—obviously assuming that since it had been read once, we were finished with it—but I said I wanted to read it again. Again they turned pages with me, and I paused to let them chime in on ". . . but he was still hungry!"

As we read this second time, the teacher stuck her head out to announce recess. I nodded my acknowledgment, and we went on with our second reading. As we finished, a child asked (remember, recess has been announced) if we could read it again! So we read it a third time. There were several spontaneous questions and comments about caterpillars and butterflies, and as we read again, the children chimed in more and more, eager to get to the part where the caterpillar turned into a beautiful butterfly. I actually had a request to read it a fourth time, but I told them we really had to go to recess.

Though we were elbow to elbow, not one grumble surfaced about being crowded or bumped. The complainers had stopped complaining, the spinner had stopped spinning,

and no one worried about who was first—we were all together, and all eyes and ears were tuned into the delightful story. A sense of peace and unity had settled on this group in a matter of minutes.

→ See: Edelsky, p. 72; Literature Reference List, p. 429; Mooney, p. 120.

Nancy Wildermuth is a professor in the College of Education at the University of Missouri, Columbia, MO.

Book Note

A Critical Handbook of Children's Literature, 4th ed.

Rebecca J. Lukens
1990; 264 pp.; $11.96
Glenview, IL:
Scott Foresman

English Lit majors may not need this book, but for the rest of us it's a lifesaver. When I first began teaching, my experience with analyzing literature was almost nil, and I certainly didn't know how to help children do it. Thank goodness for Rebecca Lukens's *Handbook*! In clear, readable chapters organized around the major literary elements of plot, setting, characterization, and symbolism, she demystifies literary analysis. How did E. B. White make us care so passionately about Charlotte and Wilbur—a spider and a pig? What are foreshadowing and inevitability, and how are they used in *Charlotte's Web*? Lukens answers these questions and many more. Without this book, I couldn't have shared literature with students in the way in which I am now able. Lists of award-winning books found in the back are an added bonus.
LBB

❝ Conflict and an unknown outcome keep us reading *Charlotte's Web*. Wilbur's struggle is serious: life and death. Although we may define the struggle as a person-against-society conflict, the child knows it simply as 'Will Wilbur live? Will Charlotte save him from being made into bacon?' In this case we may regard society as the farming business, which, after all, is based on profit. A runt pig is not worth keeping. Although the child reading *Charlotte's Web* gets involved in the conflict of Wilbur-versus-dinner table, the conflict is actually Wilbur against good business. The conflict begins immediately, page one, line one: 'Where's Papa going with the ax?' Whether or not Wilbur will be saved from death commands our interest. This conflict of Wilbur against the business of farming keeps our interest from start to finish. ❞ (p. 57)

❝ Whether the story is meant for the young child being read to, or for the older child reading alone, it is possible for character to be well developed. Why does a child demand that *The Tale of Peter Rabbit* be read again and again? Short as the tale is, Peter is a developed or round character. ❞ (p. 42)

❝ By White's use of the device called foreshadowing, we are well prepared for Wilbur's salvation and Charlotte's death. Her life is complete, and her mission accomplished. She has saved her dearest friend and produced her egg sac to carry on another spider generation. There is no other way for the story to end. Although there may be a shadow of sadness, there is a more profound sense of the quality called inevitability, or 'it had to be.' 'It was inevitable' is high praise for a writer's skill in bringing plot to conclusion. ❞ (p. 69)

What Is Reading?

Last year Javier was sent home at least once a week for behavior problems. Asked to define reading, he had a ready answer: "Holding a book in front of you and being quiet." One year later, a year in which he has explored many books through literature study, he now gives a very different answer to the same question, "What is reading?"

The author is an inventor of another world. You get into that world and you wonder and you get worried. You feel like it's happening to you, and when the tension builds and goes down, and builds and goes down . . . like I was reading *Cracker Jackson,* and the tension built so high that I jumped when the teacher said to put your books away . . . I just couldn't right then.

→ See: Literature Reference List, p. 429.

—Gloria Norton, staff development teacher, Redwood City School District, Redwood City, CA

Resource: Videotape

Literature Study: One Classroom, One Session

Available for $45/individual copy from:
CED
325 E. Southern, Ste. 14
Tempe, AZ 85282
1-602-894-1333

In this useful half-hour videotape, Karen Smith conducts a literature study session from start to finish in her combination fifth- and sixth-grade classroom. The Center for Establishing Dialogue in Teaching and Learning (CED), a nonprofit corporation organized by teachers in the Phoenix area, is the producer. Carole Edelsky introduces the session on tape. You should allow six to eight weeks for delivery.

Classroom Demonstrations

by Laura S. Robb

Understanding Complex Issues:
The Island of the Skog Revisited

I briskly walked into my eighth-grade humanities class, my arm cradling a dozen copies of Steven Kellogg's *The Island of the Skog*. Five years ago Mr. Kellogg spent a day at Powhatan, an independent elementary school in the Shenandoah Valley. These young adults were third-graders five years ago, and I recall them watching breathlessly as Mr. Kellogg integrated the melodies of story and picture while he told and illustrated the adventures of Bouncer and the Rowdies. That year the story of the mice and the Skog became an all-time favorite at Powhatan, and most youngsters acquired their own autographed copy.

The title of my humanities class is "Peaceful Resolutions to Conflicts." For me, teaching this class was the realization of a dream conceived at the Everychild Conference in New York City in August 1985. Hearing Whitley Streiber, Katherine Paterson, and Nancy Larrick talk about nuclear war made me determined to bring these issues before my eighth-graders. Our learning began with an intensive study of propaganda using *The Wave* by Morton Rhue as the core book. The students were about to initiate their own propaganda campaigns, attempting to change the dress code and a snack rule at school. At this point in the course the students and I had completed a study of *The War Prayer* by Mark Twain and *My Brother Sam Is Dead* by James Lincoln Collier and Christopher Collier. As we explored and wrote about issues together, I hoped the students would grow to understand that, yes, conflicts are a part of living, but how we elect to resolve conflicts will determine whether or not this planet and its inhabitants will survive.

I brought *The Island of the Skog* into my classroom to introduce several concepts: patriotism, decision-making models, and different types of leadership. How simple it would have been for me to list information on the blackboard and require the students to dutifully copy all this wisdom in their journals. But they would have learned nothing. I believe it is crucial that students begin to comprehend how decision-making relates to the tone of leadership and politics of a country. Since we had been listening to patriotic music around the world, and were ready to work in groups on propaganda campaigns that required leadership and decision-making, I chose *The Island of the Skog* to stimulate student discussions about these issues. I am convinced this book deepened students' awareness of the problems leaders face while it aided them in their own process of group interaction, leadership, and decision-making. I also wanted these students to see that books they had come to believe were a nostalgic remembrance from their childhood had much to teach them as young adults.

Before reading we opened our journals and worked on a clustering activity relating to patriotism and different kinds of leadership. Students each shared one idea from their journals which I recorded on a transparency. For patriotism the ideas ranged from faith in and love of country to disregard for others' beliefs and lack of individuality. The class was familiar with the name tags of different types of leaders and could automatically paraphrase a definition, but I believed they needed this story to acquire a thinking knowledge of leadership and power. In our final discussion of *The Island of the Skog*, these collec-

tive thoughts would help students begin to formulate and measure the ideas they could claim as reasonable to hold.

Anxiously watching the students, I passed out the books asking them to share and read in pairs. I felt my body stiffen, waiting for one or two eighth-graders to make negative comments about using a "kid's" book. None. Inwardly I shouted hurrah! And what some began to do as they read was tune into the small, often satirical signs sprinkled throughout the illustrations. There were shouts of "Look at this one!" and "I never noticed these when I was little!" They approached the book with anticipation and respect because they knew and loved Mr. Kellogg personally and through his books. Not one student let adolescence interfere with enjoyment and learning.

I divided the class into two groups and each group had one of these tasks: (1) to discuss the leadership styles of Bouncer and Jenny; (2) to discuss the decision-making processes of Bouncer and Jenny. Each group made a formal presentation using story and pictures to back up statements.

The class quickly characterized Bouncer as aggressive and impulsive—a self-appointed leader who loved the idea of leadership as long as things rolled along smoothly. When rough times arrived, Bouncer left. Opposing views surfaced here. A few students believed that the mice were justified in blazing their way to the island with twelve cannonballs, for how did the mice know what the Skog was? Immediately, a student countered with a question that I hope will haunt this class forever: "But do the means justify the end?" This quickly led to close scrutiny of the general population of mice, "the people," who mindlessly follow Bouncer and Jenny like lemmings marching to the sea. Politically and socially, the entire group felt that following without question and thinking could destroy democracy and individuality. Because my students could discuss these issues through this book, I believe they have begun to develop inner resolve to not follow blindly, but to pause and think before acting.

When we compared the decision-making models of the two mice, Jenny and Bouncer, the class labeled Bouncer the dictator and Jenny the more democratic leader. The students readily agreed that listening and communicating were the most important characteristics of the democratic decision-making model. However, one student pointed out that listening was not enough, for what if you only heard one point of view. Therefore, consideration of all options became part of our definition of the democratic decision-making model. Moreover, we all agreed that careful consideration of all options was necessary for an individual or group to arrive at fair and just decisions. The class also observed that a fear of the unknown, symbolized by the mice and Skog, often precipitated hasty actions. Students noted that propaganda techniques preyed upon human fears, and this story illustrated that most fears were irrational and unfounded. We ended our study by discussing why the last action of mice and Skog was the singing of a new national anthem. Working in small groups, students compared the ideas that surfaced in the clustering activity with their present thinking and recorded their reactions in journals.

Resource: Books

Focus Units in Literature: A Handbook for Elementary School Teachers

Joy F. Moss
1984; 240 pp.; $15.50,
    NCTE members $11.95
Urbana, IL: NCTE

The author gives concrete examples of how to introduce literature into the classroom through the medium of her own instructional model, the Focus Unit. The activities in the 13 units are clustered around a theme, such as Giants or Toy Animals. For each unit, objectives are given, followed by a bibliography for group and independent reading, detailed descriptions of group story sessions, and suggestions for creative writing or other extension activities. An introduction gives some theoretical background and suggests general strategies for guiding discussions, so you can create your own focus units.

Adventuring with Books: A Booklist for Pre-K–Grade 6, 9th ed.

Mary Jett-Simpson, editor
1989; 550 pp.; $16.50,
    NCTE members $12.95
Urbana, IL: NCTE

The latest edition of this annotated bibliography covers children's books published between 1984 and 1988. Categories include genres, social studies, sciences, fine arts, sports and games, professional books, and more. A description and full ordering information is given for each book. A subject index is included, in addition to the author and title indexes given in previous editions. Like the other NCTE booklists, this should serve as a valuable reference tool for anyone involved in choosing and using children's books.

This year 24 first-graders at Powhatan also studied *The Island of the Skog*, using the story to better understand why people emigrate to a new land. The children painted a grand mural depicting the pilgrims and the Indians on one side and the mice and Skog on the other. Their bold, colorful strokes spoke of enjoyment in thinking about a story and comparing it to their history. These first-graders also compared the Rowdies to Columbus looking for the New World.

How exciting the study of history and ideas becomes when teachers use trade books in the classroom that celebrate the joys, adventures, and difficulties life presents. The *Island of the Skog* is a picture book that tells a complex and powerful story, speaking to all ages and offering students the opportunity to use their imagination to think and talk about issues that enable them to better understand themselves. Such books help guide students to see more clearly the ideals they must maintain to keep the democratic process alive and our planet safe from destructive fears.

➜See: Carter, p. 292; Doerr, p. 290; Literature Reference List, p. 429.

From *Language Arts* 65(3), National Council of Teachers of English, March 1988.

Laura S. Robb is a junior high teacher at Powhatan School, Boyce, VA.

Resource: Book Talk Series

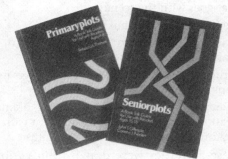

Primary Plots: A Book Talk Guide for Use with Readers Ages 4–8

Rebecca L. Thomas
1989; 392 pp.; $39.95
New York: R. R. Bowker

Introducing Bookplots 3: A Book Talk Guide for Use with Readers Ages 8–12

Diana L. Spirit
1988; 352 pp.; $39.95
New York: R. R. Bowker

Juniorplots: A Book Talk Manual for Teachers and Librarians

John T. Gillespie and Diana L. Lembo
1967; 222 pp.; $24.95
New York: R. R. Bowker

Seniorplots: A Book Talk Guide for Use with Readers Ages 15–18

John T. Gillespie and Corinne J. Naden
1989; 386 pp.; $39.95
New York: R. R. Bowker

If you are new to the world of literature, you may find the literature guides available from R. R. Bowker useful. Although there is no substitute for reading on your own the books you are sharing with your students, a plot synopsis can help jog your memory if it's been a while since you've read a particular book. Whole language educators need to be careful about packaged discussion questions, but certainly the background bibliographic and biographical information about authors that the guides provide is most helpful.

LBB

Resource: Book

A to Zoo: Subject Access to Children's Picture Books, 3d ed.

Carolyn W. Lima and John W. Lima
1989; 896 pp.; $44.95
New York: R. R. Bowker

An invaluable reference tool in locating picture books on a specific subject for children ages three to seven, more than 11,500 fiction and nonfiction titles are listed alphabetically under 600 subject headings. Author, title, and illustrator indexes are provided, as are ISBN numbers and review citations for all new titles. Caldecott award-winners are noted.

Katy Obringer

Classroom Demonstrations

by Howard M. Miller

Getting Started with Literature Sets in the Junior High Reading Class

I began using literature sets with seventh-grade students who possessed a wide range of interests and abilities. This literature-based approach to reading instruction brings together elements of self-selected, sustained silent reading, response journals, and discussion groups in such a way that students are encouraged to be responsible for much of their own learning.

The Classroom Library. The backbone of the reading program is the classroom library. In order to start with literature sets, I put together groups of four or five copies of 10 different books. From these, I selected seven to offer at the start of the new school year, holding back some to be added later; it is important to keep the classroom library alive and interesting by changing titles on a regular basis.

Student Selection of Books. I discussed the concept of self-selected, sustained silent reading and gave students a week to look through the books during silent reading time. We called this "trying it on for size." During the course of the week, almost all students selected and stuck with one book.

Forming Groups. After the first week, I typed a list of the seven books and had students select their first and second choices. If there weren't enough copies of a particular book, I asked for volunteers to accept their second choice. There were cases when someone picked a book that no one else in the class had picked. Here, too, I sought compromise, and with one exception, a second choice was made so that all students could have partners. Eventually, this book selection process became too time-consuming. Now my students practice true self-selection and self-pacing and pick any available book they want to read.

Scheduling. The curriculum, based on Dewey's concept of "learning by doing," demands time for reading, writing, listening, speaking, and strategy lessons. The schedule that evolved provides silent reading for 15 minutes for each of four days, writing for 10 minutes each of three days, and discussion groups for 15 minutes one day per week. I also read aloud as often as possible.

Response Journals. Students are required to write about the book they are reading every writing period. Students add a "postscript" if they have anything else they want to talk about. They may respond to the book I am reading to them, or they may write on a topic of their own.

One of my concerns with journal writing in the past was what I could say to students that would guide them to become better writers. What I have been doing now—and, yes, it has been a lot of work—is to write weekly a longer response to their journals.

Discussion Group. At first the groups comprised students reading the same book; later I encouraged students who were reading different titles to share with one another. The discussion groups are self-selected, but in most instances they remain the same throughout the year. The best discussions occur between students who are reading different books. They tell each other about their respective books and try to "sell" the other group members on reading it. Students challenge each other with questions about their books and learn from each other. I make the rounds of all the groups during discussion time, but I do not feel it necessary to sit with every group.

Evaluation

• I read the journals and comment on them as outlined above. After the discussions, students return to their seats to fill out an evaluation form, consisting of five questions: What good things happened in today's discussion? Were there any problems with the discussion today? What did you do to help the group? What do you need to work on to help improve the discussions? Based on your comments, what grade do you think you should get for your discussion today?

• As for that eternal problem of assigning grades, one-half of the students' reading grades is based on their work in silent reading, journals, and discussions. I give five points per day for reading, a letter grade for their week's journal entries based on how much they wrote and how clear they were in showing what they are getting from their book, and a letter grade (which they give themselves) for their discussion group. I honor their discussion-grade decision unless I have clear proof based on my direct observations that they did not earn that grade. When it comes time to average grades, I average the silent reading/journal writing, discussion grades separately and weigh them as 50 percent of their grade.

Samples. These are verbatim quotes, spelling intact, from journals. This first set shows how students are making connections. *Trapped* is the story of a young man who is imprisoned in his car after an automobile accident in a remote area. Here is what the student wrote:

> The book I'm reading now is *Trapped*. The reason I picked the book is because I had a experience from 1974, January 22. I was born in the Seattle Washington State hospital and when my father was comming to pick us up he crashed and went of a bridge. They say he survived 12 hours then he died. Thats the main reason I picked this book.

Obviously, this student will read that book like no one else in the world.

Other students choose—without a hint from me—to write about the processes they go through while reading or writing:

> I wish every book written by Paula Danziger would be like a sequal to each other. That way you could just reading and read and read her books til your eyes popped out.

One student chose her next book based on what she heard about it in her discussion group:

> It was a good *discussion* and I think that I want to read *Trapped* next because Mirvat is Reading it and she doesnt like it, but the way she was talking about it, it seems like a good book.

Following a discussion in which the students shared their predictions on what would happen to the main character in *Ace Hits the Big Time*, one student wrote:

> I like to shar peoleos idas about Ace hit the big time. Me and Peter have almost the same prudishon [prediction].

When a child like this can write about making predictions in reading, regardless of the spelling, we're making tremendous progress. All in all, I'm quite pleased with the program so far and anticipate continued success as students assume greater control over their own learning.

→See: Literature Reference List, p. 429.

Howard M. Miller is a reading and English teacher at Jefferson Junior High School, Jefferson City, MO.

Classroom Demonstrations
by Melissa Cain

Book-related Activities for Literature Classrooms

1. Write a play based upon a book. Plan to act it out with some classmates. Find appropriate costumes and props.
2. Make a poster advertising a book. Use an appropriate medium. Display the poster in the classroom.
3. Research the life of an author. Point out to classmates any similarities between the author's life and the author's fictional characters.
4. Write a book review for a newspaper or magazine. Limit yourself to 300 words. Compile reviews in a class book review journal. Compare this journal to professional ones like *The Horn Book* or *Perspectives*.
5. Draw a map of the setting of a story. Calculate distances characters must travel in the story. Determine what mode of transportation would be most efficient. If the story takes place in a real city, acquire a map of that city and trace the action of the book on it.
6. List five interesting facts you learned from a book. Verify or amplify them and list the sources you used to do so.
7. Prepare a short speech telling why you liked or disliked a book. Back yourself up with quotations or examples.
8. Illustrate two of the characters you liked. Make full-length portraits showing the clothing appropriate for the time and setting.
9. Develop a timeline of the events of a story.
10. Record your impressions about each day's reading in a journal.

11. Compare a character from a book with someone you know or with a character from another story.
12. Write a letter recommending a book to a friend or relative. Explain how it would particularly interest that person.
13. Write or tell a story to go with a wordless picture book.
14. Write a letter to a living author. Compliment the author, ask questions, or share a project or insight related to the author's book(s).
15. Write about why one of the characters in a book would make a poor or a good friend.
16. Write a poem based upon a story or ideas from it.
17. Discuss with a classmate how your personal experiences have been similar to or different from those of a character in a book.
18. Explain orally or in writing how a book could be made into a continuing TV series.
19. Find a friend who read another book by the same author and discuss similarities and differences between the two books.
20. Create a mobile from characters or events from a book.
21. Pretend you are a newspaper reporter on the scene of one of the major plot events. Write a 200- to 300-word story in newspaper style.
22. Decide what the theme(s) of a story are and tell what you think about them.
23. Write a play-by-play broadcast of the action in a story. This may or may not be for a sports book.
24. Design a game based on a book that could be played by two or more people. This could be a question game like Trivial Pursuit or a board game that uses setting or events.
25. Compare and contrast two books with the same theme, setting, or subject.
26. Cut a "window" in a box. On a roll of paper create a "movie" of a book. Attach the movie to rollers and insert into the box to create a show.
27. Make a comic strip out of a book.
28. Create a book jacket that you think would sell a book. Laminate the jacket and put it on the book. This can jazz up books in the school library that have dull covers.
29. Share books on how to do things by giving a demonstration.
30. Think about the emotion of a story. What feelings did the author evoke, and how? Talk about words that evoke emotion.
31. Create or find musical accompaniment for an oral reading of a story.
32. Check comprehension of a story with a friend by writing questions to ask each other.
33. If food is mentioned, find out how to prepare it and make some for the class.
34. Broadcast a book review or advertisement over the school PA system.
35. Dress up as one of the characters in a book. Describe that character or take on his or her personality for a day. This is a good all-school project.
36. Create a sculpture out of wood, clay, soap, plaster, etc., of some facet of a book.
37. Use a lap board and 3-D props to tell a story to others, perhaps younger children.
38. Make a series of dolls to represent characters in a book. Dress them appropriately.

39. Create a mural representing a story.
40. Create a living book with students dressing as the characters and freezing into position in a tableau. A narrator could tell the story that goes with the scenes.
41. Rewrite a story in rebus form.
42. Make a bulletin board from a story. Try to make it interactive.
43. Write a new adventure for the characters in a book.
44. Share poetry through choral reading, dramatization, illustration, accompaniment with rhythm instruments, clapping, or music.

These activities were drawn from various sources, now unknown.

→ See: Cain, pp. 299, 357.

Melissa Cain is the editor of *Perspectives,* a journal published by the University of Toledo.

Resource: Publisher

Harper Trophy Books

Catalog free from:
Harper & Row,
    Publishers, Inc.
10 E. 53rd St.
New York, NY 10022
1-800-242-7737

The Harper & Row Junior Books Group publishes quality fiction and nonfiction for readers from early childhood to adolescence: Special attention is given to beginning readers with the I Can Read Series and award-winning picture books, to awakening scientific minds with the Let's Read and Find Out Science Books, and to older readers with many award-winning works of fiction and nonfiction.

Harper also offers free lesson guides to 37 picture books. The guides vary in quality but, in general, they are more open-ended than typical guides and forgo vocabulary lists or comprehension questions.

Arrietta Chakos

Resource: Activity Books

Exciting, Funny, Scary, Short, Different, and Sad Books Kids Like About Animals, Science, Sports, Families, Songs, and Other Things

Frances Laverne Carroll and Mary Meacham, editors
1984; 192 pp.; $10.00
Chicago: American Library Association

This is an annotated bibliography for all the categories mentioned in the title and much, much more. The emphasis here is on books for second- to fifth-graders, with the maximum upper range being eighth grade. The titles are listed by subject.

Creative Uses of Children's Literature

Mary Ann Paulin
1982; 730 pp.; $49.50 hardcover, $29.50 paper
Hamden, CT: Library Professional Publications, an imprint of The Shoe String Press, Inc.

Paulin's rich resource includes chapters on introducing books in a variety of ways, experiencing art through picture books, enhancing books through music, acting out stories, and playing with riddles. Aimed primarily at the serious librarian or teacher, the book has title listings and practical information on techniques.

Katy Obringer

The Funny Side
Shh!

It was a rainy Friday afternoon. My sixth-graders were hard at work, making papier-mâché puppets for their production of *The Elves and the Shoemaker*. I sat on a chair in the middle of the room simply taking it all in, enjoying their obvious enthusiasm as they designed their puppets. In spite of all the activity, I must have dozed off. Moments later, I awoke with a start to find a sign pinned to my chest. It read: DO NOT DISTURB!

—As told to LBB by Gloria Norton, staff development teacher, Redwood City School District, Redwood City, CA

Cornerstone: Trevor H. Cairney

Developing Literature-based Programmes: Getting Kids "Inside" Books

The Lived-through Experience of Literature

Recently, after sharing John Burningham's book *Granpa* with a group of librarians, I asked them to tell me the things they liked and disliked about it and the things that puzzled them. As is always the case when I share this book, the comments varied greatly.

Several people said, "We hate the way the book's just a collection of incidents; it doesn't have a story." They were quickly contradicted by others who said, "We really liked the way it is written, because that's the way dialogue between adults and children often unfolds." Some hated the ending while others liked it. "But it was too close to my world," said one librarian. "I lost my grandfather several years ago, and I have never quite gotten over it." For all these readers, the "reading" of the text reflected who they were, what they had experienced, their relationships with other people, and so on. The sharing of this text was a lived-through experience, culminating in the creation of quite different texts for each reader.

Readers who see books as an important part of their lives do more than read words and "extract meaning"; they create their own worlds as they read. The way readers create these worlds is extremely varied and individualistic. The following incident, which occurred recently while I was reading *The Quinkins* (Trezise and Roughsey 1987), illustrates this point. This is a story about the legendary Imjin Quinkins, creatures that steal children and take them back to their mountain homes. I was reading it to a group of second-year early childhood students and had reached a part of the text describing the beginnings of a search for two children who had disappeared.

> Warenby said to Margara, "Here are the tracks of the hunting party. We will look about for the tracks of our children." They searched and searched but found nothing. The two willy-wag-tails sat and watched. After a long search Margara said, "Now we are certain the Imjin are trying to steal our children."

Trevor H. Cairney is an associate professor at the University of Western Sydney, Nepean. He is a former elementary school teacher with 10 years' experience in a variety of settings ranging from a one-teacher rural school to a large city school. He also worked for three years as a language consultant before commencing tertiary teaching. He taught at two universities before his current appointment, including three and a half years as head of the Riverina Literary Centre. His publications and research have been primarily concerned with the reading and writing processes, comprehension, children's literature, early literacy development, and the social context of literacy.

At this stage I stopped reading, showed the illustration, turned to the group, and started to say, "Isn't that interesting. I wonder if that's where we get the saying 'a little bird told me'?" Before I got to "interesting," a student said, "Yeah, it's just like *Picnic at Hanging Rock*."

At that exact moment I inferred that the wagtails had told the children's parents what had happened. This in itself is interesting, because it is not stated at any stage in the text. As the children were lured away by the Imjin we were told that two "willy-wagtails were watching him. . . ." The extract above tells the reader once more that "the willy-wagtails sat and watched." My inference that the birds had told the children's parents was perhaps deeply rooted in my memories of a primary school teacher who constantly told me (30 years prior to the reading of the story) that he knew special secrets because "little birds told him."

While I was off on my own literary tangent, at least one listener was more concerned with the illustrations of the Australian landscape, and had connected this, and perhaps other parts of the text, with the movie *Picnic at Hanging Rock*. It should be obvious that the lived-through experience of this text, at this moment in time, was quite different for each of us.

A Transactional View of Reading

Rather than viewing reading as a process of meaning transfer, we need to recognise it as a transactional and constructive process (Cairney 1986). Such a conceptualisation of reading recognises that

1. Readers create meaning as a result of transactions with texts;
2. The meaning readers create as they read is "greater than" the written text's potential meaning, and the reader's prior knowledge;
3. No two readers ever read the same text in the same way; nor do they arrive at the same meaning;
4. Repeated encounters with the same text results in the creation of different meaning for each reading;

5. Above all, meaning is relative—there is no meaning for any one text.

If one accepts this, and the arguments I have developed so far, then there are a number of important implications for classroom teachers. As teachers of reading, our priorities should be to

1. Help children create more elaborate texts as they read;
2. Support readers as they make meaning, not provide isolated skills lessons;
3. Invite responses to texts, not set "closed" reading activities;
4. Encourage children to make connections between what they know and what they discover as a result of a new textual experience.

If these children are to discover the world of literature, we need to make changes to our classroom reading environments. I believe that five important steps are necessary.

1. Provide time for children to read books of their choice.
2. Read quality literature without expecting a response.
3. Provide time for your students to share their reading with you. Listen and respond, if appropriate.
4. Provide time for children to respond creatively to their individual reading.
5. Read literature to your students that can be analyzed, criticized, assessed, interpreted, compared, and linked with their own knowledge and experiences.

➔ See: Cairney, pp. 116, 345; Goodman, p. 98; Literature Reference List, p. 429.

References

Cairney, T. H. 1986. *Helping children to make meaning: 10 literature-based activities for literacy development.* Wagga Wagga, Australia: Riverina Centre Publications.

Trezise, P., and D. Roughsey. 1978. *The Quinkins.* Sydney: Collins.

Adapted from *Developing Literature-based Literacy Programmes: Getting Kids 'Inside' Books,* Riverina Literacy Centre, 1987.

Further Reading by Trevor H. Cairney

◆ "Reading Comprehension: To teach or test? That Is the Question." In *Reading-Canada-Lecture* 6(1), 1988.
◆ "Building Communities of Readers and Writers," with S. Langbien. In *The Reading Teacher* 42(8), 1989.
◆ "Intertextuality: Hidden Echoes from the Past." In *The Reading Teacher* 43(7), 1990.
◆ *Other Worlds: The Endless Possibilities of Literature.* Heinemann. Melbourne: Nelson, 1990.
◆ *Teaching Reading Comprehension: Meaning Makers at Work.* Milton Keynes, UK: Open University Press, 1990.

Classroom Demonstrations
by Beverly DeCarlo Beauvais

Celebrating Books

During our book party we celebrated all the stories we had read and listened to during the school year. Children were asked to come to the party dressed as a story character. They kept their identity a secret. We tried to guess who or what each child represented—the character and the title of the book and sometimes even the author. We had great fun doing this, and as we identified each character, children were given a name tag to wear during the party. Those children who stumped us after many guesses received a small reward. We had Cinderellas, cats, a lobster, Puss 'n Boots, a comic-book character, Wilbur from *Charlotte's*

Web, a witch from a Halloween story of course, and many, many others. Oh yes, and Amelia Bedelia!

We took time out from our treats, music, and songs to tally the number of books children read aloud that year. We had kept a record of these books by writing each child's name and the title and author of the book he or she read on a circle of paper, and then adding this circle to the body of our "hungry caterpillar" that was growing across the walls of our classroom. We had also recorded on chart paper the number of books each child had read at home. The title and date were written on a story form

for a parent to sign. The ohs and ahs were music to my ears as the children rejoiced in their success. They couldn't get over the number of books they had read.

Throughout the party the children talked about the books and characters—recalling when that story was read, by whom, and what it was all about. They hadn't forgotten a detail. As the party came to an end we talked about ourselves as readers and writers.

Did I have a good year? Do you have to ask?

Beverly DeCarlo Beauvais is a primary teacher at John F. Kennedy School, Chomedey, Laval, Quebec.

Classroom Demonstrations

The Virginia Young Readers Program

by Suzanne F. Sprenger

The Virginia State Reading Association (VSRA) has developed a program to encourage reading for pleasure in all grades. Over 38,000 students received a certificate for completing the requirements in 1988–89, a 300 percent increase over the previous year.

The program offers schools and libraries a list of 10 books (selected by specialists in the field of reading and children's literature) from which students read or hear and then select their favorite. Lists are provided for four levels: primary, elementary, middle school, and high school.

The program seeks to (1) encourage young readers to become better acquainted with contemporary books of outstanding literary appeal, (2) broaden students' awareness of literature as a lifelong pleasure, (3) encourage teachers to read aloud in the classroom as a means of introducing reading for pleasure, and (4) honor favorite books and their authors.

The winning authors are announced at the VSRA conference in late February or early March. Enclosed with the certificates for the schools and libraries is an announcement of the winners and the new lists and guidelines for the

upcoming school year. This enables teachers and librarians to budget for and acquire the books before the start of the school year and to read them over the summer.

Funding for the program is provided through the Virginia State Reading Association on a year-to-year basis. Participation growth has required funding to rise from $200 the first year to $2,000 for the current year. Major expenses include printing the 8 1/2-by-11-inch certificate for each qualifying student and mailing costs for all requested informational packets. Various educational organizations across the state include information about the program in their newsletters, generating numerous requests for ballots, information, and so on. One additional expense is an engraved pewter Virginia Cup for each winning author.

The Virginia Young Readers Program encourages reading for the sheer fun of it—reading that continues for lifelong pleasure.

Suzanne F. Sprenger is a media specialist with the Roanoke County Public Schools in Virginia. She is on the Board of the Virginia State Reading Association, state chairman of the Virginia Young Readers Program, and reviewer for *School Library Journal*.

A Summer Reading Booklist

by Alicia Rivera

In May my students and I compile a summer reading booklist. We select favorite books from our classroom and school libraries, books we have read in groups or all together during the year. Each child chooses only two (not easy!), and records title and author on small filing cards. We classify the titles into several categories. When the final list is typed, children volunteer to make small pencil drawings of story characters on separate paper. We cut out the drawings and mount them on the original with clear tape. Then to the copy machine!

The children are very proud of our completed booklist, and so am I. We give the booklist to several other classes and to each member of the

school staff. The children take home two copies, one to keep and the other to send to a relative or friend. I distribute my own copies far and wide, advertising the joy my students and I find in the world of books.

Additionally, I keep a folder of booklists created year after year. Each list has its own personality and brings special memories of the children who made it. The lists serves as a valuable record for me of my work with children and books.

➔ See: Huck, p. 188; Rivera, p. 166.

Alicia Rivera is a primary teacher at Hillcrest School, Oakland, CA.

📷 WHOLE LANGUAGE CAMERA

Kristy Ann Blackhorse, author of *St. Patrick's Day*, discusses writing with British author Lynne Reid Banks, at the Northern Arizona Young Readers' Conference on March 17, 1988. Kristy Ann is the student of Louise Lockard, Pinon Elementary School, Pinon, AZ.

➔ See: Kasten, p. 161; Lockard, p. 238.

Resource: Video Newsletter

Children's Video Review Newsletter

$36/year (6 issues) from:
E. P. Carsman, Ph.D., editor/publisher
110 Lena Ct.
Grass Valley, CA 95949
1-916-273-7471

This bimonthly newsletter reviews between 15 and 20 selected videotapes for children, describing the contents and giving age suitability, awards when applicable, length, price, distributor, and other ordering information. Only reviews of new releases are published, and the last issue of each year has an annual cumulative index of all videos reviewed, organized by age and subject matter.

Katy Obringer

Resource: Mail Order Book Service

Chinaberry Book Service

Catalog and information from:
2830 Via Orange Wy, Ste. B
Spring Valley, CA 92078-1521
1-800-777-5205

Chinaberry Book Service has an excellent, detailed 100-page catalog offering a wide range of children's books, books for parents, and video- and audio-cassettes. The emphasis is on books for children through the third grade, though titles for older readers are available.

The book descriptions contain personal accounts of children's and adults' reactions to the books and are written by someone who obviously has a love of great books. There is also a subject index, helpful for locating certain types of books.

Though it is impossible to have a comprehensive offering of children's books, Chinaberry does a great job of including books of social awareness and those dealing with real problems and fears that children have. Catalogs are sent out four times a year.

David Hartle-Schutte

Resource: Mail Order Video Program

The Children's Circle Video Reading Program

Information from:
47 Richards Ave.
Norwalk, CT 06857
1-800-243-5160

Morton Shindel, the founder and director of Children's Circle, turns children's literature into children's video movies. Program members receive two videocassettes and two books every other month. One video offered recently included *Doctor DeSoto, Curious George Rides a Bike, The Hat,* and *Patrick,* with accompanying softcover edition of *Curious George Rides a Bike.* Subscription rate is $24.50 a month (the price of one tape and book).

Children learn and are stimulated in different ways. These quality videos bring another dimension of literature into the child's overall experience. (They are also useful in ESL programs.)

Katy Obringer

Classroom Demonstrations

A Fourth-Grade Literature Reading Program

by Edith Baker

I use literature to teach reading, writing, and social studies. Literature provides a forum for integrating children's experiences and points of view into the classroom program. The experiences are available to all children. Close examination of literature helps children acquire the ability to read critically. It also helps them develop analytical skills to better understand what writers do in creating successful, sustaining texts.

We start the year with a single text. Together, we read the book and share our reactions. As we read, we discuss characters, action, setting. Having read the book once, we reread it and, through rereading, come to understand the elements that went into its construction. Thus, children are introduced to new ways of looking at and experiencing books.

We continue to explore four or five books together. This year we read *Castle in the Attic* by Elizabeth Winthrop; *Sarah, Plain and Tall* by Patricia MacLachlan; *The Egypt Game* by Zilpha Snyder; *Stone Fox* by John Gardiner; and *The Big Wave* by Pearl Buck.

The books deal with themes such as grandparents, stepmothers, loss, growth, moving, fantasy, medieval adventures, transformations, special relationships with animals, death and dying, life cycles, catastrophes, family stories, neighborhood stories. They offer opportunities to share with children a wide range of picture books, novels, and poems. Many titles are shared through class read-aloud sessions. Children also meet regularly and share with classmates titles and excerpts from other books they are reading.

Children are encouraged to read widely. They keep a record of the books they read in a journal, which I read and comment on regularly. I use the journal to note student interests, and to suggest titles for future consideration. I ask students to respond orally and in writing to their reading. The act of writing encourages them to make connections, and to form opinions about their reading that they perhaps would not have made otherwise.

Questions are posted in the classroom for students to think about as they write in their journals: As you read, did you think of your own life and experiences? Did the book remind you of another book you have read or listened to? Do you like the way the book was written? Are there parts you found particularly exciting? slow? boring? Is there something you read you would like to share with someone else? Why?

How to Begin?

Start with a topic or book that intrigues you. Start slowly, build. Web and connect. Make the connections that appeal to you. Children will help you see others. Make connections to your life, to the lives of others, to books.

Once a book has been chosen, I like to have a copy for each student. For durability I cover books with contact paper, adding an extra one-inch strip inside the front and back covers to prevent the text and binding from coming apart.

Students make folders in which to keep their ongoing work. At the end of the unit their folders are full of activities, writings, drawings, and interpretive and comparative charts to share with parents and siblings.

Our first group activity is to read the cover. We discuss what the cover indicates about the characters and content of the story. Information is charted for students to see and refer to as the class continues its investigation of the text.

Using an overhead projector, we develop character profiles as children share their feelings about a particular character. Often I will invite children to return to the text to look for the particular way the author has developed and described a character. Student and class responses are recorded on a class chart. When charts are completed, students write several sentences describing their character at a particular point in the book.

Discussion

1. We talk about how the author convinces us, the readers, of the singularity of the adventure being described. Students look for descriptive words that help set the scene.

2. Children take note of significant ideas.

3. I make an outline of each major character. I attach the outline to chart paper. Together we brainstorm and make a collection of words that describe the personalities of the important characters. The charts are displayed and the children continue to add to them.

4. Children work in pairs exploring the text for ways the author develops the reader's understanding of the characters. Children look for the ways in which the author describes the characters, what the characters say about one another, and what can be inferred from text and illustration. Children work in small teams to devise displays of their own findings, which they present to the class.

5. In pairs, children reread sections of the text in preparation for discussion. Then pairs meet in foursomes to discuss the section.

Follow-up

- Children are asked to select favorite passages to interpret through illustration.

- They participate in readers theater. I post suggested passages for children in small groups to act out with book in hand. They frequently find their own scenes to dramatize. Sometimes a group will add a scene that might have been in the book but isn't.

- Literature provides children with models to frame their own writing. Children are encouraged to imitate the forms and structures noted in the text. For example, in reading *Stone Fox* by John Gardiner, children like the loving, teasing scenes depicted in the opening pages of the book. They enjoy writing these scenes in their own words and in inventing new situations based on similar situations in their own lives.

- I feel it is important to tell children that what they do in literature study matters. I comment on their journals. I type writing selections and help children with editing and revision. Final pieces are bound, published, and added to the class library.

I am excited about the literature reading program. Not only does it provide learning opportunities for all students, but it enables children to experience authentic language learning.

➜ See: Literature Reference List, p. 429.

References
Buck, P. 1947. *The big wave.* Curtis Publishing.
Gardiner, J. 1980. *Stone fox.* New York: Crowell.
MacLachlan, P. 1985. *Sarah, plain and tall.* New York: Harper & Row.
Snyder, Z. 1967. *The Egypt game.* New York: Atheneum.
Winthrop, E. 1985. *Castle in the attic.* New York: Holiday House.

Edith Baxter is a primary teacher at Hartwell School, Lincoln, MA.

Literature Board Game

by Patricia Paige

After reading *Abel's Island* by William Steig, my students worked in groups to make board games based on the story. The boys in this photo are (left to right) Haijii Allal, Joshua Bowlin, Ronald Curtright, and Daniel Valenzuela. In their game, a player draws a card with a question about the story. For example, "Do you think Abel thought it was worth rescuing Amanda's scarf after all?" or "Why do you think Abel made statues of his family?" If the player's answer is accepted by a majority of the other players he may spin and advance his mouse marker the number of spaces indicated. There are several places on the track where the player is directed to take a special yellow card with additional instructions. For example, "You didn't gather enough food. Lose your turn." The first player to arrive home is the winner.

I felt this was a valuable activity for my students because it required them to work cooperatively to produce the game, and to read critically to write interpretive-level questions. Best of all, it helped them enjoy a good piece of children's literature in an innovative way.

➜ See: Literature Reference List, p. 429.

Patricia Paige is an elementary teacher at Westside Elementary School, Thermal, CA.

Resource: Book

Sequences: An Annotated Guide to Children's Fiction in Series

Susan Roman
1985; 116 pp.; $17.50
Chicago: American Library Association

This guide is a selected list of fiction in series and sequels written for third-graders through young adults. Brief introductions for each series describe the quality of writing and explain the reasons for inclusion.

Continued from page 243

From the Civil War to the New Century:
Colonel Parker

Even though she had left teaching, Elizabeth Stokes kept up on things happening in education. One experiment that she followed with particular interest was initiated in 1873 by Francis Wayland Parker, superintendent of schools in Quincy, Massachusetts.

Parker, known to everyone as Colonel Parker ever since his service in the Civil War, had been a schoolteacher before the war. In 1871, after his wife died unexpectedly, Parker, instead of continuing teaching, went to Europe where he met with Froebelians, visited Pestalozzi's school, and talked with educators throughout the continent. Upon returning to the United States he was hired by the Quincy, Massachusetts, school board as superintendent.

In Quincy, Colonel Parker made drastic changes. The set curriculum was abandoned and with it spelling books, readers, and formal grammar. Children were started on whole words and sentences, rather than memorizing letters by rote. Magazines, newspapers, and materials created by the teachers were used instead of textbooks. Arithmetic was taught through experimenting with objects rather than through learning rules. The emphasis of Parker's curriculum was on observing, describing, questioning, and understanding.

Elizabeth was intrigued by Colonel Parker's work and felt that Parker's (1894) description of himself described her feelings about her own life and work perfectly:

> I had a small garden . . . that I used to tend and hoe, morning and night; beans and corn and so on. Always it seems to me when I was hoeing I was dreaming and thinking of school. I remember one day I was hoeing beans. I remember just where I stood when I said to myself, "Why do I love to teach school?" And then I looked around on the growing plants and said, "It is because I love to see things grow." If I should tell the secret of my life, it is the intense desire I have to see growth and improvement in all living things, and most of all human beings.

Elizabeth read that quote often and dreamed of knowing more about Parker who had left Quincy in 1882 to become a director of the Cook County Normal School in Chicago. When Elizabeth finally got the courage to tell her daughter, Alice, about Parker's work, Alice was already getting her teaching credentials, which were becoming a requirement in common schools.

Reference

Parker, F. W. 1969. *Talks on pedagogics* (1894). New York: Arno/New York Times.

Continued on page 245

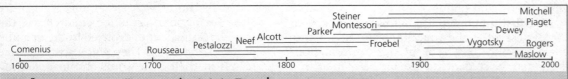

			Steiner					Mitchell	
			Montessori					Piaget	
			Parker					Dewey	
		Neef Alcott							
Comenius			Pestalozzi			Froebel		Vygotsky	Rogers
	Rousseau								Maslow
1600	1700		1800			1900			2000

Pioneers: Francis W. Parker (1837-1902)   by Ron Miller

John Dewey called Parker the "father of progressive education." Francis W. Parker was a colonel in the Civil War whose army experience apparently inspired him to think hard about regimentation and authority in education. In 1872 he went to Germany and studied the work of Pestalozzi and Froebel, and returned to the United States to become superintendent of schools in Quincy, Massachusetts. His "Quincy system"—also called "the new education"—was the most significant school reform of its time. During the 1880s and 1890s he headed a teacher-training institute in Chicago (where he met and worked with Dewey), and further advocated his methods.

Parker explained his approach forcefully in an 1894 book, *Talks on Pedagogics*. His central theme was that true education is not the authoritative curriculum handed down by the teacher, but the student's self-initiated activity that is sustained and focused. Parker asserted that education is nothing less than "the realization of all the possibilities of human growth and developments"; he insisted that intellectual growth must be integrated with moral, social, and physical development. He discussed the importance of the arts, manual skills, emotional nurturing, and the school as a community. Furthermore, Parker argued that learning should be a joyful experience, motivated by the student's own interests and desire to know the world; he severely attacked the use of prizes, punishments, and grades in education as corrupting influences.

One chapter of Parker's book was titled "Democracy and Education," the name of Dewey's classic published more than 20 years later. Parker contrasted democracy—the principle that society can rule itself—with aristocracy—the rule of the many by the few who disparage the common person's ability to make his or her own decisions. Parker despised aristocracy because it thwarts human freedom and self-development; he argued that traditional education practices, in their authoritarian control over students, perpetuated aristocratic rather than democratic attitudes.

Parker was more successful than most such educational reformers. His work came at a time when American society was receptive to "progressive" criticisms of its institutions; the age of the robber barons, social Darwinism, and unchecked industrial enterprise was beginning to trouble the American conscience; and the horrible conditions of the immigrant working class—especially its children—had become a national disgrace. For a time, "progressive" education seemed like a solution to major social problems. Parker's educational ideas are still very much alive and deserve further study today.

Reference

Parker, F. W. 1969. *Talks on pedagogics* (1894). New York: Arno/New York Times.

As kids see it

What Literature Means
by Christy

If life were without literature, I think the world would be lost. Nobody would be able to read other's thoughts, ideas, or messages.

Books and magazines are like a place you can go, where you are not bothered by anyone. All literature is a learning experience. You learn how to spell a word, you learn about a new subject, a new language, or even a part of yourself you never knew before.

Literature opens up new ideas, thoughts, and challenges. It is very important to me.

➔ See: Dalrymple, pp. 63, 108, 204, 210, 426.

Christy is a fifth-grader. Contributed by Karen Sabers Dalrymple, teacher at Eagle Valley Middle School, Eagle, CO.

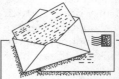

In the Mail

When I visit with Ken and Yetta in Tucson, they always send me home with books for my three children. After one visit, Aislinn, age six at the time, wrote this thank-you note.

—LBB

> DeAR Kin and ytae,
> I RAD ox CARte MAN
> at My Skool. Theis is
> the tee they gat the
> MAPR SRAP from.
> TAnke you
> for the Book's.
> Love, Aislinn

"We need revalued teachers to achieve revalued students."

—Kenneth S. Goodman

PAULINE LUBENS

Teaching

Contents

A Metaphor for Teaching

by Lucy McCormick Calkins

Three summers ago I took my newborn son Miles to the lakeside cabin in northern Michigan where I had spent my childhood summers. While we were there, at Barking Waters, as the place is called, I lay back in a rope hammock with Miles against my chest, the giant pines forming a canopy overhead, and I thought about all the summers that stretched ahead for Miles and me.

I told Miles that someday I'd take him on the Indian trail that skirts the lake and we'd pick blackberries together. I know just the place. I told him that someday I'd show him how to catch the wind in such a way that we could sail all around Fox Island.

Afterward I thought to myself that what I was doing with Miles in that hammock was a metaphor for what we as teachers of reading and writing do. I was inviting Miles to share a world and ways of living in that world.

In another few weeks, John, Miles, baby Evan, and I will return to that lakeside cabin in northern Michigan. But this time when we lie back in the rope hammock and look up at the pine canopy overhead, I won't tell my boys that someday I'll show them how to catch the wind just right so that we can sail all the way around Fox Island. Instead, we'll listen to the wind and I'll feel Evan's soft hair against my cheek and I'll wiggle my toes against Miles's toes, knowing that in the summers to come, my boys will teach me that it doesn't matter if we catch the wind just right and make it around the island, but look, when you drag a stick from your boat it leaves a trail of splashes, and listen, the gull is talking to us. They'll teach me too that it doesn't matter whether we ever quite reach the blackberry patch; there are trails to explore and forts to build and stories to tell along the way.

As I look up into the giant pine canopy overhead and think of the summers that stretch ahead for Miles and Evan and me, I know that my boys will teach me about making sand castles for little toads, and about using the extra lump of pie dough to make tiny blackberry tarts.

This, of course, is the real metaphor for our teaching. If we listen well, our youngsters will invite us to share a world and ways of living in that world.

➜ See: The Art of Teaching Writing, p. 141; Learning from Children, p. 137; The Writing Workshop—A World of Difference, p. 399.

Lucy McCormick Calkins grew up as one of nine children on a farm in western New York State. Her education came not only from a flock of chickens and a cherished place alongside a creek but also from Williams College and from being a co-researcher with Donald Graves. Now a professor at Teachers College, Columbia University, Calkins and her colleagues are joining teachers throughout New York City in establishing and learning from writing workshops.

Further Reading by Lucy McCormick Calkins
◆ Lessons from a Child. Heinemann, 1983.
◆ The Art of Teaching Writing. Heinemann, 1986.
◆ The Writing Workshop—A World of Difference,
    with S. Harwayne. Heinemann, 1987.

As I See It:
Kenneth S. Goodman

Whole Language Teachers

The whole language movement is unique in the history of American education in that it is led by teachers. American teachers have come of age as a profession and they have done so in the face, often, of repressive opposition from school authorities and administrators. In choosing to move to whole language, teachers have rejected their being made subservient to tests, textbooks, and tight administrative mandates. They have rejected being treated as indifferent incompetents who must be controlled through teachers' manuals and checklists of behavioral objectives. They have asserted their professional authority and taken professional responsibility for knowing what to do and doing what they need to do for the maximum good of the pupils in their classrooms.

But whole language teaching isn't simply negative—a rejection of demeaning and deprofessionalizing teacher roles. Whole language teachers have recreated teaching and redefined their own roles. They've found that they must rely more on their professional judgment, that they must know more about their pupils, that they must be informed decision-makers, and that they must be advocates for their pupils. And they have found that, with their newfound power and confidence, they can remove themselves from center stage in their classrooms, creating the necessary conditions for learning and then giving learners all the room they need to learn. Out of this new professionalism new teacher roles are emerging.

The Teacher Is a *Kidwatcher*

Effective teachers have always realized that they must know their pupils well. Whole language teachers are becoming skilled at observing kids at play and at work, knowing where they are developmentally and seeing directions in which they are ready to grow and learn with a little support and guidance. They are kidwatchers: They are always observing their pupils, watching for learning and growth and signs of need and potential.

Vygotsky (1978) talked about "zones of proximal development," naturally occurring points in children's development where they can learn easily if they get a little help. Whole language teachers understand that they must observe their pupils carefully, through informal and formal means to know them well. So teachers create authentic contexts in their classrooms and participate with their students in order to stimulate learners to engage in solving problems and answering their own needs. These teachers know how to create conditions that will cause learners to exhibit and make the most of their zones of proximal development. And they know how to detect the evidence of what learners are ready to do with and without the teacher's support.

The Teacher Is a *Mediator*

Vygotsky's (1978) concept of *mediation* is a third element in the learning context. The learner is in a situational context in which problems need to be solved or experience understood. The teacher is present also as the learning transaction takes place but in the role of *mediator*—supporting the learning but neither causing it to happen in any direct sense nor controlling it. This gives learners room for creativity and invention, necessary parts of their learning. The

teacher is there to help the learners discover the social conventions and physical relationships of the real world and to help the learners to achieve an equilibrium between their own constructions and the world around them.

In defining themselves as *mediators* whole language teachers understand that less can be more. They realize that helping a learner solve a problem is better than giving him or her an algorithm or a solution. In reading and writing teachers interfere as little as possible between the text and the reader. Teachers mediate by asking a question here, offering a useful hint there, directing attention at an anomaly, calling attention to overlooked information, or suggesting a strategy.

There is a vital difference between mediation and intervention. In intervention the teacher takes control of learning, knows with great certainty in advance what learning will be acceptable, and thus undermines the learners' confidence in themselves as learners; the teacher becomes the determiner of social conventions. Invention is inhibited, risk-taking is limited, and zones of proximal development are unlikely to be revealed. Whole language teachers keep learning going without taking it over or controlling it.

The Teacher Is a *Liberator*

Paulo Freire (1970) contrasts "banking" views of pedagogy with liberating views. The banking view deposits bits of learning into students' heads. They have no control over the process nor are their needs or interests considered. Liberating pedagogy sees learners in a power relationship to society. The learners must own the process of their learning. They must see learning, including literacy and language development, as part of a process of liberation.

Freire was successful in helping Brazilian peasants to become literate by using the ideas and concepts of their political movement in the texts they used in learning to read. In a broader sense Freire was recognizing that learners learn best when they are freed to control their own learning.

This liberation is neither romantic nor abstract. Teachers cannot liberate pupils from society or from the constraints of social transactions. They cannot liberate their pupils from their responsibilities to themselves or to others. But they can free them to be what they are capable of being. They can free them to think for themselves and take ownership over their own learning.

Teachers can remove the artificial controls of traditional schooling. They can encourage pupils to enter freely into speech and literacy events, and authentic social transactions in which language is a tool for communication. In whole language classrooms a full range of language genres occur naturally, and the full range of the pupils' language and the language of their home cultures are completely accepted.

Teachers can make their classrooms democratic communities of learners. Freedom in democracy is not anarchy; it is achieved through cooperation and common consent. In such a community pupils are free to invent ways of dealing with their functional needs and free to discover the conventions in the authentic social language transactions. They are free to become citizens of a democratic society.

Freeing pupils to take risks is a major concern of whole language classrooms. In traditional classrooms, not only are pupils required to stay within

arbitrary conventions in their oral and written expression, but they are penalized for their errors. Whole language classrooms liberate pupils to try new things, to invent spellings, to experiment with a new genre, to guess at meanings in their reading, or to read and write imperfectly.

Our research on reading and writing has strongly supported the importance of error in language development. Miscues represent the tension between invention and convention in reading. They show the reader's use of existing schema in attempting to comprehend texts. They also show how the text itself mediates learning. In whole language classrooms risk-taking is not simply tolerated, it is celebrated. Learners have always been free to fail. In whole language classrooms they are free to learn from their failures with the support of their teachers.

The Teacher Is an *Initiator*

Perhaps the characteristic of whole language teachers that has impressed skeptical colleagues and administrators the most is their creative energy. Cutting themselves loose from the bonds of tests, texts, and mandates, teachers can utilize their professional knowledge, their personal strengths, and their inventive intuitions to create exciting and inviting situations and contexts for their pupils' growth. This may take the form of stimulating interest in a thematic unit that has its roots in a current news event or a well-chosen field trip. It may take the form of putting in the right child's hand just the right book to "turn on" a sense of personal ownership in reading. It may show in an atmosphere created through great care over a long period of time that makes even shy and fearful pupils willing to take risks. It may show in the wisdom of the teacher in bringing pupils together in social groups for particular purposes.

Whole language teachers use materials, they attend to the objectives of their school's curriculum, and they play close attention to their pupils needs and interests, but they are constantly exercising their professional initiative. They do what they think is best for a given pupil or group of pupils. By carefully evaluating what they do and how their pupils respond, they become very good at knowing what will succeed.

There are other roles that whole language teachers are developing in the course of their own empowerment. They are sharing them with other teachers, now, and thus whole language grows—teacher to teacher.

➔ See: Goodman, pp. 215, 252, 390; Moll, p. 413; Rigg, p. 239; Slotter, p. 14; Weaver, p. 382.

References

Freire, P. 1970. *Pedagogy of the oppressed.* New York: Herder and Herder.
Vygotsky, L. S. 1978. *Mind in society.* Cambridge: Harvard University Press.

📷 WHOLE LANGUAGE CAMERA

Six year old Kristy reads to her first grade teacher, Annette Maggitti, Desert Winds School, Tucson, AZ.

Kidwatching
Yetta M. Goodman

Kidwatching Includes Kidlistening As Well

When we listen closely to children, we are sometimes taken aback by their adherence to taking schooling and teacher's statements so literally. I want to tell two short stories and then suggest that although there is little we can do to avoid having students misinterpret the meaning structures that take place in school, at least by always kidlistening we may be able to help them avoid becoming too dependent on the exactness of our statements.

Billy was working with the reading resource teacher. He was in a classroom with a whole language teacher for the first time. He did not have a background for the type of reading and writing that was now an expected part of his school experience. In seventh grade Billy was unable to complete much of his class work. He could read self-selected narratives with few miscues and retell the story with good understanding. But now in seventh grade it became apparent that his understanding of the concepts being discussed in class was limited. After seven years in school Billy had learned to function in traditional school settings. He knew how to answer questions at the end of chapters, he could fill out worksheets, and he could get most of the spelling words right on the end-of-the-week test. But in the whole language classroom he was lost. "You know," he said to the reading resource teacher after they had worked on writing a response to a social studies report he had chosen, "my teacher says that we have to put everything we read in our own words. But these aren't my own words. I used some of the words from the article" (Goodman 1989).

Aaron is younger than Billy. At seven he is just beginning to be involved in doing reports and other kinds of inquiries. He decided to do a report on different kinds of soil. He asked his mother to read him a section in the encyclopedia that he thought would give him some information and that he couldn't read by himself. Suddenly as she was reading, Aaron hit his forehead with his hand and called out, "Oh, my God!" His mom asked him what the problem was, and Aaron said, "I can't do this report any longer. You just read the answers to some of my questions and the teacher said that we could only do a report on something that we do not know the answers to."

These stories have the same issue in common. Kids often think that teacher's words are law. If a teacher says that the kids have to have a red notebook, then it becomes a problem if a parent suggests that a blue one might do as well. We can't always avoid such misconceptions on the part of children. On the other hand, as we give assignments and make suggestions for materials and resources, we should let students know of alternative ways to go about what they are doing. This helps them to see the power of alternative methods, and to become flexible in their problem solving. We also need to "kidlisten" carefully as our students respond to our suggestions, ideas, and invitations—to make sure we haven't helped them back themselves into a corner. It may save kids from being so concerned about there being only one way to respond to their teachers.

➜ See: Goodman, pp. 32, 101, 356; Newman, p. 211.

Reference
Goodman, D. 1989. "Why don't I feel good about myself?" In *The whole language evaluation book*, ed. K. Goodman, Y. Goodman, and W. Hood. Portsmouth, NH: Heinemann.

I Used to Be...But Now I...

I used to think there was one teacher and 27 learners in my classroom,
But now I know there are 28 teachers and 28 learners.

—Anonymous

As Teachers See It

A Success Story

by Leslie Mangiola

I can't seem to separate my successes from those of the children I teach. It's a lot like being a parent. I won't take credit for the good nature and generosity of one child, but I tend to take the responsibility for the lapses of good judgement in another. As teachers, I think we tend to do the same.

Watching my sixth-grade student Pablo fills me with pride. I've never seen a child so euphoric about his success in the classroom. He is articulate, loves being involved in collaborative writing, and enjoys experimenting with new ways to work with his kindergarten tutee. His smile could not be wider, his self-confidence more apparent. Everyone who sees him surely observes the happiness he feels in learning.

I wish I knew what part I played in his joy. Maybe none. Maybe his genetic makeup, his supportive parents, his previous teachers, etc., are what fashioned him into the scholar he is. But I have so many Pablo stories. I remember his trials and errors in learning, his writing blocks (and his genius at writing his way out of them), his ability to analyze and revise his tutorial strategies. I remember the six months when he did nothing but read, bootlegging books into writers' workshop, thinking I'd never notice. I always figured he was storing up authors' writing strategies and would some day burst out, a talented author himself. And darned if he didn't!

And so I'll go ahead, throw caution to the wind, deny modesty, and take a small bit of credit for some of Pablo's success in his pursuit of knowledge.

➜ See: Mangiola, p. 381.

Leslie Mangiola is an elementary teacher at Fair Oaks School, Redwood City, CA.

writers

Create an Adventure
by Sigmund A. Boloz

Create an adventure,
Exhilarating and wild,
By issuing an invitation
For listening to a child.

Speak of real topics
As they seem of import
Then negotiate your distance
With challenging support.

Respond to the meaning
And see where it leads,
You can't kill a discussion
If it meets a child's needs.

So create an adventure,
It's easy if you try.
Listen to their stories
And you'll understand why.

➜ See: Boloz, p. 208.

Sigmund A. Boloz is the principal of Ganado Primary School, Ganado, AZ.

MarVELous INVENTIONS
Invented Words

Children's use of language has often been a source of amusement for me. When we moved into our new house a few years ago I encountered a problem with our heavy, roll-up garage door. As the mother of three I was constantly going in and out of the garage to take care of the laundry, not to mention the many times I needed to use the car to run errands or to chauffeur the family. Being pregnant with my fourth and having a babe in arms made gaining access to the garage difficult. My husband finally agreed to install an automatic door opener. The task took a good part of the day and the neighborhood kids, as well as our own, were constantly "checking out" the job site. Finally, the time came for the trial run. Lo and behold the door rolled smoothly down. To share in the jubilation my five-year-old son called his older sister out of the house. "Come, look!" he shouted. "The door is automagic now!"

—Gail Sakagawa, primary and elementary teacher, Wilson Elementary School, Honolulu, HI

📷 WHOLE LANGUAGE CAMERA

Sharon Markell watches as her kindergarten students share their writing, East Aurora, N.Y.

I've learned much from my teachers; I've learned more from my colleagues; I've learned most from my students.

WELL-SAID
—Maimonides

Viewpoint: Glenda L. Bissex

The Listening That Makes Us Whole

The tables are being turned: Teachers are listening to students—through dialogue journals, through writing conferences on papers generated from student interests, and through teacher research. "Listening skills" used to mean obedience training for students: following directions, being able to repeat back accurately what has been said, inevitably by an adult. That is not whole language listening. But another kind of listening—or, I should say, hearing and its accompanying experience of being heard—is essential to our wholeness as teachers, learners, and persons.

Obedient listening is a power game: The weak must listen to the strong, the ignorant must listen to the knowing. Our society has trained us to listen to those who have power, and not to take seriously the words of the powerless—the poor, women, minorities, and children.

While silence may be commanded, listening and hearing cannot be. They arise from caring respect. Hearing connects us to others and to ourselves as well. When we truly hear another or ourselves, the experience of being heard is empowering. Coming from trust instead of submission, it liberates us rather than subjecting us to authority as obedient listening does.

Teacher-researcher Pat Fox (1988) was trying to understand the conditions that led to both good and poor writing from her seventh-graders. Enlisting their help as her research collaborators, she asked the class what kinds of writing they did best and worst. "Best and worst according to whose standards, yours or ours?" questioned a student. Possessing the courage to listen, Pat asked, "You mean there's a difference?" And her students told her. Pat found they had a strong sense of their own strengths and weaknesses as writers, they had their own criteria for valuing "based on both moral and intellectual rigor and integrity" (p. 35).

Judith Boyce (1987) was also hearing what her students had to say, not just what she wanted or expected to hear. She was in for a surprise when she asked for her sixth-grader's reactions to the comments she wrote in their logs. Elizabeth responded: "I think that some of your comments in my book are bad and wrong, but I realize that you must do them quickly. I cannot answer your questions by the side anyway, so why do you write them?"

"Once I had recovered from my initial defense posture," writes Judith, "I began to wonder about Elizabeth's negative reaction to question comments. . . . It was time to ask my experts"—her students, that is—"how they felt about comments on their ideas" (pp. 130–133).

The most successful comments, the ones students liked best, were those in which I was just another human being rather than the teacher. Amy said, "I like the comments where you tell what you did or what you think." The example she pointed out was a comment I wrote on an entry about Amy cleaning her room. She told of dusting and packing old books she plans to save "for my own kids." I wrote, "I have an attic full of old books I am saving for my grandchildren. Some I had when I was twelve and my children read them. They are like old friends."

It took time for Judith to hear what her students had to tell her. True listening is not an instantaneous occurrence; it is a process. Sometimes I know I do not fully hear what a student says in a conference or through a paper. My expectations or my pride may interfere. I may wake up the next morning knowing I have not heard, as happened to me several times this past year while I read case studies by the teacher researchers with whom I work. Then I would try again to listen by rereading and by writing in my teaching journal.

By the third reading of Tilly's paper I felt I could hear and appreciate her experiences and her interpretation of them, as well as grasp what gave me trouble as a reader, both in her writing and in my own expectations. How do we teachers get the academic forms and ideals out of our heads long enough to listen to what our students write? And if we get them out, how do we grade without a model paper or a 100 answer in our heads? We struggle nobly to shift the basis for grading to include more of the individual's progress through writing folders or portfolios, for example. Is this anything more than a compromise with traditional standards? I honestly don't know. What are the reader's responsibilities? How can we read with respect for the writer and the writing?

Through listening to my students as writers, I came to listen to myself as a reader. And I came to articulate a conflict I avoided confronting until then.

Our students are empowered by being heard. Our listening helps them to speak and to write in their own voices. The dialogue of learning flows and they usually listen to us in response, as well as hear themselves better. We teachers become whole when we listen to ourselves, to the intuitions and wisdom that the pressures of our work may cut us off from.

Lolly Ockerstrom set out to study (1989, pp. 3–4) the experiences of the new teachers of writing she supervised.

I had no idea I would study gender differences when I began this case study. But the nature of the verbal interactions between the men and women in the group struck me immediately, and the more I noticed men speaking and women not speaking, the more I realized this was important to look at. As I focused on gender and language, I realized that I was looking at issues in my own teaching and learning—why I felt blocked from speaking out in groups, why I doubted my own authority, and most importantly, how I could change self-defeating behavior into action that allowed me to speak when I needed to speak.

By listening, Lolly found what was important or, as she puts it, it found her.

"The writer only does half the job," writes novelist Ursula K. Le Guin. "It takes two to make a book" (1989, p. 177). A story needs a reader to be completed just as a conversation or dialogue or discussion depends as much upon our listening as our speaking. Thus listening makes other language acts whole.

→ See: Dalrymple, p. 210; Goodman, p. 208; Kamler, p. 140; Shor, p. 223.

References

Boyce, J. 1987. "Vision of communication: The use of commonplace books in the English class." In *Seeing for ourselves: Case-study research by teachers of writing,* ed. G. L. Bissex and R. H. Bullock. Portsmouth, NH: Heinemann.

Fox, P. S. 1988. "Conditions, contexts, and competencies: Seventh-graders look at their own writing across the curriculum." Case study, Northeastern University.

Le Guin, U. K. 1989. *Dancing at the edge of the world.* New York: Grove Press.

Ockerstrom, L. 1989. "Gender and authority: Who am I in the classroom?" Case study, Northeastern University.

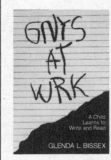

Glenda L. Bissex has been a teacher most of her life in one form or another—of high school English students, of readers and writers from first grade through college who were experiencing difficulties, and of beginning as well as veteran teachers. Interest in her own child's literacy development helped her become a more careful observer of other learners, a researcher with the Vermont Writing Program, and a mentor to other teacher researchers from whom she has learned much about listening.

Book Note

GNYS AT WRK: A Child Learns to Write and Read

Glenda L. Bissex
1980; 235 pp.; $22
Cambridge: Harvard
University Press

The "GNYS" (genius) is the author's own son, Paul, and the work, the process in which he engaged as he learned to read and write. This remarkable chronicle of Paul's journey into literacy from ages 5 to 11 was one of the first to provide an in-depth account of written language development. What was true for Paul can be true for all children provided we, like Bissex, invite them to explore literacy, and then trust and respect them as learners.

LBB

❝ Five-year-old Paul was in the house. I was outside on the deck reading. After he had tried unsatisfactorily to talk with me, he decided to get my attention a new way—to break through print with print. Selecting the rubber letter stamps he needed from his set, Paul printed and delivered this message: RUDF (Are you deaf?!). Of course, I put down my book.❞ (p. 3)

❝ When he was five-and-a-half years old, Paul wrote and posted this sign over his workbench-desk: DO NAT DSTRB GNYS AT WRK. The GNYS (genius) at work is our human capacity for language. DO NAT DSTRB is a caution to observe how it works, for the logic by which we teach is not always the logic by which children learn.❞ (p. 199)

📷 WHOLE LANGUAGE CAMERA

Michael Caff and his kindergarten students study the emerging creation on the computer, Palo Alto, CA.

Further Reading by Glenda L. Bissex

◆ *GNYS AT WRK: A Child Learns to Write and Read.* Harvard University Press, 1985.

◆ "The Beginnings of Writing." In *Home and School: Early Language and Reading.* Ablex, 1987.

◆ *Seeing for Ourselves: Case Study Research by Teachers of Writing,* ed. with R. H. Bullock. Heinemann, 1987.

◆ *Encouraging the Skills of Good Writing,* School Success Series. The Hume Companies, 1988.

◆ *Writing for Everyday Success,* School Success Series. The Hume Companies, 1989.

As Teachers See It

Teaching as Improvisational Theater

by Marty Morgenbesser

When you come right down to it, teaching is improvisational theater. Unfortunately, most of us are trained in classical acting. We learn our lines to the letter, plan the blocking precisely, don our masks, and deliver our soliloquies. We might as well be Hamlet talking to poor Yorick's skull.

Real teaching occurs the moment we stop delivering our lines and listen to the other. As in improvisational acting (and in life, for that matter), we have a general idea of the scene, but we don't know the lines until they leave our lips. What we say depends as much on what the other says as it does on what we think we're going to say. So we'd better damn well listen.

Last year I was teaching a group of seven- and eight-year-olds to build two-digit numbers with base-ten blocks. I remember asking Anna to construct the number 96. This would normally be accomplished by placing nine ten-sticks to the left of six ones.

Anna reached for a hundred block. I reached for my teacher mask.
Teacher: Are you *sure* you need a hundred block?
Student: I want to do it a different way.
Fortunately my mask was loosely fastened. "Okay," I said tentatively.

Anna proceeded to place a hundred block in the middle, flanked by one ten on the left and six ones on the right.

She beamed, "See, it's like a roman numeral!"

I was floored. This same child, earlier that day, had appeared to be totally confused by roman numerals. Now she not only demonstrated an understanding of the concept, she was able to apply her knowledge, rather creatively, to a different situation. Incidentally, upon completing her Romanesque construction, Anna announced that she could also build the number "the regular way" and did so, with no difficulty whatsoever.

My teacher's mask, dangling just below the chin, slipped off and shattered. Without that mask, I find that I hear much better.

➜ See: Goodman, p. 249; Morgenbesser, p. 149; Newman, p. 211.

Marty Morgenbesser is a primary teacher at San Miguel School, Santa Rosa, CA.

Parents' Perspective

by Nancy Knipping

"She's Reasonable": Learning from Children

It was my son's first day of school in a new town. I had been reassured by new colleagues at the university that although the woman who was to be Jonathan's second-grade teacher did not hold a whole language perspective, she enjoyed an excellent reputation. I had heard her described as intelligent, thoughtful, good-humored, sensitive, and warm. Eager for Jonathan's first impression, I asked how he liked Mrs. McGruder as he settled in the car for the drive home from school. He told me that a boy in his class had said that she was the best teacher in the school, but that he was going to see how things went and make up his own mind.

A week or so later, he gave me his opinion: "I don't know whether she's the best teacher in the school, because I don't know all the teachers, but I do think she's really good because she's reasonable." As I questioned him further, Jonathan expanded his description: "She's fair. She listens to us. She asks us what we're doing, and she thinks about what we say. When there's a problem, she lets us explain what happened. And she usually lets us talk to a friend while we're working." I thought, what a compliment from a child who, like his peers, prizes fairness and friendship!

Since that time, as I have come to know Sheryl McGruder better, I have realized the accuracy of Jonathan's description and the importance of those abilities in her development as a whole language teacher. The year Jonathan was in third grade, Sheryl took a course from Dorothy Watson and began to change the way she did things in her classroom. As she examined her beliefs about language and learning, Sheryl tried some of the whole language strategies that Dorothy proposed. In the four years since she was introduced to whole language, Sheryl has become well known as an excellent whole language teacher. Other teachers often observe in her classroom and she frequently presents at whole language conferences on a variety of topics including writing, drama, and literature study groups.

Sheryl's transition to whole language was eased because she was already in the habit of

trying to understand how children understand something. She was already trying to see the sense in a child's comment or question. She was, in Eleanor Duckworth's words (1987), "giving children reason." If children are to be curricular informants (Harste, Woodward, and Burke 1984), teachers must understand and appreciate child logic. Jonathan valued the respect Sheryl demonstrated when she asked him to explain his actions or his thinking. Duckworth (pp. 96–97) reminds us that trying to understand a child's thinking is important for other reasons as well. Teachers' questions, such as, "I'm afraid I don't understand; could you say it another way?" "Are you saying . . . ?" "What do you mean?" "Could you give an example?" "Why do you say that?" "How does that fit with what she just said?" not only aim to clarify for the teacher what children are thinking, but additionally encourage the children to go further with their ideas. Reasonable teachers affirm the unspoken contract Vivian Paley (1981, p. 223) has with her students: "If you keep trying to explain yourselves I will keep showing you how to think about the problems you need to solve."

Honoring Paley's contract is not easy. It requires helping children see connections between things they know. "My task is to keep the inquiry open long enough for the consequences of their ideas to become apparent to them" (p. 213). That task requires an ability to carefully observe and critically consider the meaning of an individual child's response to a classroom experience, based on the teacher's understanding of learning and learners. Sheryl McGruder, like Paley and Duckworth, is a master at listening to, understanding, and appreciating child logic.

➜ See: Goodman, p. 24; Paley, p. 31; Wilde, p. 240.

References
Duckworth, E. 1987. *"The having of wonderful ideas" and other essays on teaching and learning.* New York: Teachers College Press.
Harste, J. C., V. A. Woodward, and C. L. Burke. 1984. *Language stories and literacy lessons.* Portsmouth, NH: Heinemann.
Paley, V. 1981. *Wally's stories.* Cambridge: Harvard University Press.

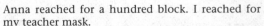

As Teachers See It

Listening as a Vital Teaching Tool

by Karen Sabers Dalrymple

I asked a parent of a former student to ask her son this question: "If there was any one thing that Karen Dalrymple did that made you a better thinker, what was it?"

The boy, now a fifth-grader, said, "She was a good listener. That made me think more. And she read my writings and asked me questions that made me think more about my thinking. She was a good listener."

After analyzing Orion's comments I realized that teachers' listening is demonstrated in their responses to the student's oral and written communication, drawings, and other artwork. Thus, I want to discuss the strategy of listening and the many ways listening encourages thinking.

On the last day of school last June, several of my third-graders were visibly upset when they came in from noon recess. These were four girls who were generally very well behaved but on this last day in the lunchroom had joined a group of students in throwing food. We gathered as a whole class and they shared what had happened. I asked, "Have you heard of peer pressure?" They hadn't. One of the boys told what he knew of it and several children shared their experiences in similar situations. By this time, Erin was sobbing less and Elaine looked less morose. Jeremy said, "You remember Digory and Jill in that book . . . uh . . . (Jessica interjected, "*The Magician's Nephew* by C. S. Lewis.") Yea, well, this is like that. If Digory had not hit the bell, he would never know some of the world. You guys would never know about peer pressure if you hadn't been copy-catting each other in the lunch room."

I wasn't very active during the discussion. I had noticed the girls were upset and commented on that. After several of the children had spoken, I asked the question about peer pressure. These eight- and nine-year-old children were able to discuss the issue and comfort their peers with little obvious control from an adult. My control was that of a listener—someone who sensed a wrong and pointed it out, then asked a question that allowed the children to view the problem in a broader perspective. The children's discussion exemplified compassionate and critical thought.

Another Way to Listen . . .

While there are times when we can capitalize upon and respond to the thoughts of our students while they are in the act of creating, there are not enough minutes in an hour for us to "listen" to every student in this way. Thus it becomes important for us to be good "listeners" when we are reading our students' writings and looking at their illustrations. When I read my fifth- through eighth-graders' papers, I find that I can easily write a quick response to the content of their writing.

> The theme of your work extends the universal idea of youth being careless. When I read your essay I felt it was almost poetic. You might enjoy writing the same ideas into another form. Let me know if you want to talk about this.
>
> I especially enjoy your description of the New Orleans' coast . . . when I read of your vacation I realized how important it was that you went on the trip with your father. You learned so much. Thanks for sharing. Is there anything more you'd like to do to share your new knowledge and impressions?

Writing is an obvious means of gathering information about student thinking. As a math and science teacher of sixth- through eighth-graders, I ask my students to write for ten min-

Cornerstone: Judith M. Newman

Learning in Our Own Classrooms

At a recent workshop a teacher asked me, "When I'm publishing my first-graders' writing, how much should I worry about spelling and punctuation?" I sensed her hidden request: "Tell me the right thing to do." If I give her tips, I thought, if I tell her what I might do in her situation, the next time she has questions she may go looking for authoritative answers and not take the time to reflect on her own about the choices she has and what each might convey to her students.

So I asked a question. "What are your reasons for wanting to publish your students' work?" She explained how she believed writing was important enough for the children's writing to be read by readers other than herself. She wanted an opportunity to create a little pressure for the children to be concerned about spelling, punctuation, layout, and the like. Also, by publishing some of her students' writing, she would be able to draw their attention to published books and the conventions authors and publishers use. She could help the children see connections between the writing of professional authors and their own.

"How much writing are you wanting to publish?" I inquired. "Who is the audience?" "How much writing have the children done to this point?" "What different kinds of writing are they doing?" "What have they been reading?" The teacher began to see that I couldn't give her a single right answer to the question. How much attention to revising and editing depends on a number of factors. Her judgment about what level of pressure for conventional writing is appropriate is going to be different for each child and for each piece of writing.

This incident demonstrates the dilemma facing teachers. We want to do a credible job. We're concerned about the kinds of learning opportunities we offer our students. We want the products of that learning to be competent, and to meet high standards.

So how should we be helping our students? The answer to this question comes not from the assurances and suggestions of outside experts, but from our students.

In a social learning context, students are continually commenting on procedures, making connections, questioning decisions, asking for information. These questions and comments have potential for turning us into learners. To learn from my students, however, I have to

Judith M. Newman is professor of education at Mount Saint Vincent University in Halifax, Nova Scotia. She consults with teachers about literacy development, about writing and reading instruction, and about computers and their use in the classroom. Committed to inservice education, she has devoted considerable effort to helping teachers become reflective learners in their own classrooms. Her support for teachers includes five half-hour videotapes on reading, several journal articles, a number of monographs, and a computer column ONLINE in Language Arts.

change how I function in the classroom. Instead of transmitting information, I must discover how to invite students into the learning arena, and how to create situations in which they see other people doing what they imagine doing themselves. I have to learn how to sustain their participation in the group enterprise, how to keep conversations going, and how to respond to what they are trying to do.

Through students' engagement I learn about their interests, their strategies, and their difficulties. By following where students lead, I allow them to show me new directions to pursue, and I discover their potential for learning. Every teaching encounter becomes an opportunity for me to discover new things both about learning and about how to assist individual learners. When we change from teacher-driven learning to learning-focused teaching, we become learners, too.

Trying to be learning-focused involves opting for risk, not security. While I have a general sense of what I might try with my students, I have no carefully scripted lesson plans. Instead, I have had to learn how to suggest we try something and then, based on students' interests, offer suggestions to extend their engagement with literacy. That means I have to follow their lead as well as know what researchers believe about how reading and writing are learned. I also have to have some sense of how to create an open learning environment. I have to be on the alert for opportunities to collaborate with students as well as encourage them to collaborate with one another. I have to try and make the students feel as comfortable as possible so they will be willing to take some risks.

Let me describe an instance in which I was able to follow a student's lead. In class, I asked the teachers I was working with to list a couple of things they were good at and enjoyed doing. Then I invited them to "freewrite" about one of their accomplishments.

After we had done the freewrite and discussed what we could learn from our accounts, one of the teachers returned to her focal agenda. She wanted to know what any of this had to do with writing and teaching children about spelling, punctuation, and grammar. As we discussed possible connections it occurred to me that we could use these learning experiences to craft stories and accomplish two ends at the same time: We could explore learning in more depth, and simultaneously discover something about where a concern for conventions becomes important. As another teacher later wrote in her journal:

> The writing of learning stories wasn't a part of your original agenda but when Trish suggested we write a story, you picked up on this as a learning opportunity. I saw you use Trish's demand to meet your own agenda. I am reminded once again how important it is to negotiate the curriculum with students.

Changing from a transmission way of teaching to creating an open, learning-focused environment isn't easy. It involves recognizing that what we'd like to have happen in our classroom and our ability to make sense of what students are trying to do will be in need of continuous revision. No sooner will some aspect of our instructional program be sorted out when something will happen to raise new questions.

There is no single right way, no one right answer to any question about teaching. Every question can, and perhaps should, be answered with "It depends." It depends on what has gone before, on what the students seem to know, on the strategies they currently have at their disposal, on how ready they seem to be to forge ahead, and on how far we think we can push the conventional expectations of the wider context of the school and community.

Transforming teaching into a learning enterprise is a journey without end. A profound philosophical shift is necessary, a shift supported by constantly updating our theoretical understanding, by learning more about what is involved in how language is learned and used, and by always questioning our instructional objectives and practices. Becoming a learning-focused teacher means learning to be receptive to the unexpected. Like our students, we have to be willing to take risks. That doesn't mean abandoning objectives or working without a curricular framework. It means offering students an invitation to explore in some specific direction and then following the leads they present us. To allow learners to direct us, we have to be prepared to learn from them.

→ See: Craft of Children's Writing, p. 32; Goodman, pp. 249, 252, 253; Manicom, p. 384; Torbe, p. 232; Weaver, p. 382; Whole Language: Theory in Use, p. 385.

Further Reading by Judith M. Newman
◆ *What About Reading?* Education Media Services, Department of Education, Province of Nova Scotia, 1978.
◆ *The Craft of Children's Writing.* Scholastic, 1984.
◆ *Whole Language: Theory in Use.* Heinemann, 1985.
◆ *Finding Our Own Way: Teachers Learning.* Heinemann, 1990.

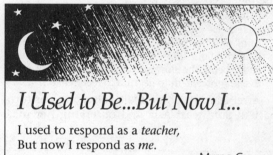

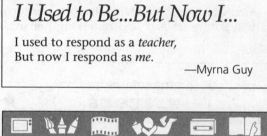

I Used to Be...But Now I...

I used to respond as a *teacher*,
But now I respond as *me*.

—Myrna Guy

Resource: Publisher

Workman Publishing Company

WORKMAN
THE NEW BASICS

FALL 1989

780 Broadway
New York, NY 10003
1-800-722-7202

Workman publishes a variety of nonfiction children's books, including a series of creative activity books (Steven Caney's *Invention Book, Play Book,* and *Kids' America*) and an excellent series of hands-on science books (*The Bug Book and the Bug Bottle,* and *The Bird Book and the Bird-feeder*). Two useful beginning cookbooks, *My First Baking Book* and *My First Cookbook,* with child-tested recipes and pleasing illustrations, are listed. Both series offer a variety of up-close, do-it-themselves projects for children. Another interesting title is *The Kids' Book of Questions,* which offers 260 questions that deal with moral, ethical, and even fanciful issues.

utes about a math concept, a new set of scientific tools I have introduced, or an experiment they are designing or completing. Ten minutes offer the students an opportunity to share their thinking. That allows for retelling, paraphrasing, summarizing, analyzing, synthesizing, and evaluating. When teachers listen, wonderful things happen.

→ See: Bissex, p. 209; Dalrymple, pp. 63, 426; Goodman, p. 208; Kamler, p. 140; Literature Reference List, p. 429.

Karen Sabers Dalrymple is a teacher at Eagle Valley Middle School, Eagle, CO.

Cornerstone:
Yvonne S. Freeman & David E. Freeman

Case Studies

Many schools have been inundated in recent years with immigrant students. In trying to deal with this influx, districts and teachers have tended to lump all the second-language learners together and have tried to develop methods that will work with all of them. Often, districts and teachers see bilingual students as a kind of unified "problem" that must be dealt with.

We believe that kids aren't problems, and we have found that when teachers look carefully at one second-language student, they begin to see all their students as individuals. One way to help teachers in our classes to become what Yetta Goodman calls "kidwatchers" is to have them do a simple case study of one second-language learner.

As they do their case studies, teachers often begin to see for themselves that bilingual learners are individuals with different needs and strengths. Teachers become more sensitive to the needs of all their language minority students. The following examples from the case studies of three teachers give an idea of the insights teachers get from doing case studies.

As she did her "kidwatching," Blanca, a student teacher in a Spanish/English bilingual classroom, came to some important conclusions. She closely observed José, a sixth-grader, over several months in the classroom to which she had been assigned:

> It is obvious to me that José has a very low self-esteem. He is convinced that he is not smart. I also think that his misbehavior has a lot to do with how he feels about himself and the frustration he feels about being the slowest. . . . He needs lots of positive reinforcement to get him to feel free to risk.

After learning about Mai's traumatic war-torn past in Southeast Asia and observing her in a

> Yvonne (Bonnie) S. Freeman is the director of Bilingual Education and the codirector of the Language Development Program at Fresno Pacific College, Fresno, CA. David E. Freeman is codirector of the Language Development Program and director of the Secondary Teaching Program at Fresno Pacific College, Fresno, CA.

special education classroom, another student teacher, Kathy, also formed some strong opinions about ways to work with this Hmong child. Kathy realized that the boring, repetitive lessons Mai was given were not helping her learn:

> Mai needs to be read to from literary works that would be of interest to her. . . . I feel she can go far to meet success in acquiring a second-language if emphasis is put on using more meaningful, real-life situations, and challenging her.

Over a period of three months, Katie worked with Mony, a Cambodian kindergartner who had been in class for only a few weeks and was then transferred to another school. Katie was not satisfied with what she had learned about Mony in the brief time she had been in class and decided to work with her to learn more. After reading to Mony, writing in an interactive journal with her, and talking to her at length, Katie reflected on how her case study would affect her teaching in the future:

> In terms of the influence this case study will have on my teaching, I plan to . . . (1) expend more effort in getting to know my students personally, (2) provide individual time for each student . . . , (3) never again assume that "what I hear" is "what they know," (4) arrange my classroom/curriculum around whole, real, purposeful, meaning-filled experiences, (5) find, value, and exploit each student's contributions and talents.

By observing one student carefully during a case study, Blanca, Kathy, Katie, and other teachers have gained new understanding that will guide them as they work with second-language students.

➔ See: Bausche-Ude, p. 26; Freeman, pp. 87, 110, 184, 294, 368; Goodman, pp. 247, 249, 252, 253; Urzúa, p. 42; Wallace, p. 88.

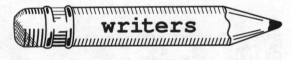

Strange Mathfellows

by Mary M. Kitagawa

Four students were working as math buddies on some thought-provoking problems. Their styles were different, yet all reasonably successful.

Anna, the spider, keeps her eyes on her own work, builds and revises patterns to organize her thinking. She is so quietly self-reliant that the others would be loudly insisting to me they were all stumped, then Anna's little voice would say, "I think I'm getting it," and the others would finally notice that she was.

Sara, the hare, bounds to possibilities and moves her body in the same hither and thither way. She uses stacks of scratch paper and sometimes abandons possibilities that later turn out to be good ones.

Elisha, the lizard, reads and rereads problems. You don't see anything happening until she knows exactly what will work.

Niles, the thoroughbred, works standing up. He relies on past formulas, looking for something familiar to latch on to. He is too quick to complain or ask for help, and it seems as though he's

desperate to be the first to solve the problems. He is also the least likely to consult others, although he's a great mathematician in the making.

> A spider, a hare, a lizard and
> A thoroughbred racehorse, one day,
> Gathered to seek some solutions
> Each in a particular way.
>
> The spider started right in to weave,
> Quietly confident that as she wove
> The design itself would reveal
> Something to share with her friends.
>
> The hare made the most of her speed
> Hopping here, bounding there,
> Rejecting this, tasting that,
> Until she judged which choice was best.
>
> The lizard observed, pondered,
> Reconsidered, studied details,
> No movement could be seen until,
> Suddenly, out darted a solution.
>
> The racehorse chomped and stamped,
> Recalling past triumphs, he was
> Impatient to overcome obstacles set,
> Knowing well the sweet taste of victory.
>
> Who contributed most, you ask?
> Did they get in each other's way?
> I only know that, in the end,
> The conclusions they reached were perfect.

➔ See: Goodman, p. 249; Kitagawa, pp. 132, 420.

Mary M. Kitagawa is an elementary teacher at Mark's Meadow School, Amherst, MA.

Reflections
by Jay Sugarman

Having taught elementary school for the past 14 years, Jay Sugarman is interested in providing forums for teachers and administrators to discuss their roles as educators. Jay founded *Reflections,* Brookline's school-system-based educational journal, in 1984. Since 1986, he has also produced and hosted a local cable television show entitled *Video Open House: Teaching in Brookline.* These programs feature the work of both individual teachers and special programs in the school system.

Despite all the recent national reports and recommendations for improving schools, we have had little input from teachers and administrators, the people who are responsible for implementing school change. In order to facilitate this input, I initiated and coordinated the production of an educational journal entitled *Reflections,* which is written by teachers and administrators of the Brookline, Massachusetts, Public School System. It is a way for teachers and administrators to comment on their practice, to respond to educational issues, to evaluate recent research findings, to share poetry, and to be able to reflect about pedagogical matters.

Produced twice a year, this school-system-based publication is a unique way to encourage and value the opinions and professional growth of the staff. Since its inception in 1984, more than 125 teachers and administrators have contributed to this venture which is funded by the Brookline Foundation, a nonprofit group of parents and other concerned citizens who support a variety of teacher projects in the school district.

The value of a school-system-based educational journal is outlined in the following points:

(1) It encourages teachers and administrators to be reflective, helping them foster student reflection.

(2) When teachers are supported in their writing, they obtain a better understanding of the writing process; they develop their own abilities as writers, and appreciate what their students are experiencing when they write.

(3) The publication helps alleviate isolation among teachers, and enhances collegial communication.

(4) It improves the status of teachers in both their own eyes and the eyes of the public. Copies of the journal are found in the town and school libraries, and are sent to various members of the community as well as to educators throughout the country.

(5) *Reflections* helps bridge the theory-research-practice "gap." Practitioners are provided with the opportunity to read and react to research and theory in the field.

The positive outcomes of a school-system-based educational journal can only be achieved when both the school administration and the school community support, encourage, and value teachers reflecting and commenting on their role as educators.

➔ See: Curry, p. 352; Goodman, p. 390; Rhodes, p. 405.

Resource: Periodical

Reflections: The Brookline Educational Journal

Free (2 issues/year) from:
Jay Sugarman
Runkle School
50 Druce St.
Brookline, MA 02146
1-617-730-2590

I Used to Be...But Now I...

I used to know all the answers,
But now I ask questions.

—Kathy Waner

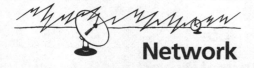

Network

LLIMY TIMES
LITERACY AND LEARNING IN THE MIDDLE YEARS

A Course Where Teachers Learn from Their Students:
Learner as Informant I

Edited by Phil Cormack & Kevin Comber

This year, the concept of teachers learning from their students has emerged as a central theme in the work of the LLIMY teacher/tutors in South Australia. One of the units of study in the Graduate Diploma—*Learner as Informant I*—has been the catalyst for this development. The unit aims to help teachers to discover more about literacy learning by close observation of one of their students. Teachers become researchers in their own classrooms and practise strategies for observing, recording, analysing, and describing the literacy behaviour of their "informants." Teachers have investigated many aspects of their learner's language and literacy experience, including:

- Their informant's attitude to literacy, schooling, books, etc.;
- Their informant's assessment of her or his own performance;
- Their informant's understandings and/or misunderstandings of tasks;
- Their informant's strengths, preferences, choices, and aspirations;
- The way their informant operates with peers;
- The kinds of literacy tasks their informant can do well;
- The way their informant sees the curriculum and the classroom context;
- How to respond to their informant by watching, listening, and talking; and
- How the informant's cultural background may affect his or her interactions with peers and teachers.

Gathering the Information

A variety of strategies was trialled for gathering this information. Many suggested them-

As Teachers See It:

by Laura Harwood

A Perspective on a Child Study Group

For almost four years now, a group of teachers has been meeting at each other's houses about once a month. We call ourselves the Boston Laboratory for Teachers, or BLT for short, and come together from Brookline, Cambridge, Wenham, and several other communities. Although we teach different grade levels, we share a belief that all children are unique and have strengths that need to be recognized.

Each meeting has an agenda that is planned during the previous meeting. Usually a participant volunteers to give a presentation of a child's artwork or writing, or possibly a full description of a child for a staff review. Occasionally, we discuss a topic such as poetry, science, classroom management, or educational issues.

The format we use for our meetings was developed by Patricia Carini and others at the Prospect School in North Bennington, Vermont. These group processes for studying children and their work call for a chairperson and a notetaker (we rotate these responsibilities), and a way of systematically giving each person a chance to contribute ideas and insights.

Although only one child or his/her work is discussed, the ramifications benefit others. Looking at the work or at a child in depth gives me a perspective on how to see all my students and their work more clearly. The group process is amazingly enriching. Each person's comments are valued, and periodically the chairperson summarizes. This helps keep me stimulated and reflecting on what was said, and can help me reach a deeper level of understanding.

During one of our meetings, the letters of a seven-year-old boy were studied. His teacher was concerned about him, and letter writing seemed to be the way he best expressed himself. We started the meeting by reflecting on the words "letter writing." This exercise usually helps to get a fuller perspective on the focusing word. Some of the group's responses were communication, and making oneself known to others. Letters can be a dialogue with oneself. Some emotional letters are never sent.

The child had sent eight letters to the teacher and principal. Here is an example of one sent to the latter.

> Dear Mr. ____,
> I hope you read my first note that M. and J. were bad at recess. But now that you mention it, most of it is not true. The part when T. was bad at recess is not true. But that M. & P. & J. and his gang is very bad to

everybody is true. I have heard many complaints about the gang. Would you do something about it? I want this nasty gang to stop once and for all.

> I hope this note comes in time. If they get me in trouble I will get the gang problem. Please help me. Help, Help! I hope this gang stops I hope. Please help me get rid of it.
> From,
> H.

As the group looked carefully at the words, tone, style, rhythm, and content of the series of letters written by this child, we began to understand more about what these communications might have meant to him. There were clear indications of fear, urgency, and a sense of helplessness in a child who had previously not expressed his feelings so directly. We also noted that the letters reflected changes over the year toward a greater sense of power and responsibility for himself. We all felt that it was extraordinary for such a young child to write such a letter, and it was evidently important for him to be able to continue to use writing to express strong feelings and obtain a sympathetic response to his appeals for adult help.

Within each child's work, there is so much to notice. These letters made me realize that every child does work that can be studied. Every child has a way of communicating, whether it be through stories, art work, or letters. When we look at children and their work, our guidelines are to examine the work without criticizing it.

As long as I work with children, I want to be able to clearly look at each child psychologically, emotionally, and intellectually and be aware of the group dynamics. So many times I get bogged down and anxious about a child's behavior or learning problem. This group helps me to have a clearer perspective of what my role as a teacher is and could be.

Although I have supportive colleagues in school, I find that our group has professional support built into the structure of it. I come to listen to teachers and feel nourished by what is shared. Over time, trust and compassion for each other have developed. Teaching is a difficult profession, but I find it can be extremely rewarding if I can continue to see unique possibilities in young children.

➔ See: Goodman, pp. 249, 390; Newman, p. 211; Stevenson, p. 411.

From *Reflections* 4(2), Spring 1987.

selves as potentially useful for language groups and the whole class. They included:

- Talking with children (interviews, conferences, group conferences);
- Observing children (watching and listening to them engaged in classroom literacy tasks);
- Asking children to write to the teacher (dialogue journals, written self-evaluation);
- Monitoring students' questions and requests for help;
- Analysing students' writing (error analysis, noting features in writing); and
- Seeking students' perceptions of their own work (self-evaluation, confessions).

What the Teachers Learned

Many teachers have reported being surprised by what they have discovered—often assumptions about students were called into question and richer understanding of students' perceptions of the classroom and task demands was made possible by the investigations.

I found several things that were totally unexpected. I thought "M" was disinterested in shared book experience and did nothing but wriggle. This was not the case. I asked a fellow teacher to take the ses-

sion so I could observe. To my absolute surprise she was totally and actively involved and absorbed . . . She responded to every question but not loud enough for anyone to hear.

There was also a spin-off effect with teachers starting to watch other learners in their class in closer ways.

Each teacher produced a written profile of his or her informant as a literacy learner. These profiles were combined into a booklet and make exhilarating reading.

➔ See: Goodman, pp. 247, 249, 252; Newman, p. 211.

From *LLIMY Times*, no. 2, October 1987.

Periodical Information: *LLIMY Times* is an occasional publication designed to provide up-to-date information about Literacy and Learning in the Middle Years Project (LLIMY) to the people involved in its development, trialling, administration, and support. It also provides an in-house forum for informal sharing of ideas on the possible directions for the project. Contributions are welcome from any person involved in LLIMY. Send them to English Language Arts Project, Wattle Park Teachers Centre, 424 Kensington Road, Wattle Park, 5066, South Australia.

As Teachers See It

The Whole Language Experiment
by Lauren Hoyt

None of us start out as whole language teachers. No matter how we try to convince ourselves, when we take a careful look at our beginnings, we see that we've all come out of a traditional model. Looking back at myself as a language learner, I have gained some interesting insights into my emergence as a whole language teacher.

As a child I was taught to read by the "see-it/say-it" method. I was asked to memorize stacks of cards, each with a single word printed on it. Reading was memorization, a game for a six-year-old. But oh, how frustrating it was! As soon as I'd memorized one set of cards I'd be asked to begin on the next. Occasionally I'd see these words as they appeared in "real" books. But the books themselves used such controlled vocabulary that they were as dull and removed from my life as those endless stacks of word cards. Reading was a laborious process, and it wasn't until I was 13 years old that I finally began to read books because I wanted to.

When I was 33 years old, I took a risk that profoundly affected my teaching. I moved to South Korea and became a language learner. Unlike my high school experience memorizing lists of French words on little flashcards, I studied Korean because I had to. I was adrift in a sea of language, desperately reaching out to survive. I learned the language of bargaining in the marketplace. My teachers were farm women and fishmongers eager to sell their wares. Laughing faces wrinkled in delight each time I learned a new phrase.

In restaurants I strained to grasp strings of sounds, that if repeated carefully enough, would produce a bowl of steaming noodles and a hot cup of barley tea. I also learned to decode the Korean alphabet and to recognize the shapes of Chinese characters so that I could independently roam the city and return home safely.

I realized that listening carefully and using language worked much better for me than memorizing wordlists or dialogues. I needed to use language within the context of a real situation, and I had to use it every day. Before I came into contact with theories such as whole language and the Natural Approach, I had experienced them and had internalized what worked for me as a language learner.

After three years as a language learner, I returned to the United States. My reentry was far from smooth. I wasn't the same person who had set blithely forth. My appearance hadn't changed, but on the inside I felt like a different person. I had made substantial adjustments in order to survive. Now I had to readjust all over again. I was often angry and depressed. Why couldn't anyone understand my feelings of frustration as I struggled to recall an English word I had forgotten? Why didn't anyone want to hear about my experiences? Why was I now limited to expressing myself in just one language? I began to search for someone who could understand, a community of newcomers who, like myself, were adjusting and in need of support. I found that community in an ESL classroom.

My first experiences were in rural Oregon teaching English to Hispanics, Vietnamese, and Laotians. I taught by the "seat-of-the-pants" method, which meant that the students and I were always exploring new possibilities and learning from each other.

We soon abandoned the textbook series purchased by the previous teacher. Our classroom became a supermarket or a restaurant, because that was how I had learned Korean.

All of us, myself included, were suffering from culture shock. I'd forgotten a lot of things! When I took the class to a nearby Dairy Queen, we all made mistakes. I wasn't sure if we needed to clear our own tables or how much we needed to tip. But we laughed at our mistakes and we learned from each other.

Our classes were laboratories where we cooked up language learning schemes. We made lists of questions, went out to observe and ask, came back ready to compare what we'd gathered, and prepared to try again. We worked on this new language together.

Some people made little lists of words to memorize, using their dictionaries constantly. They wanted their oral and written language to be perfect. Their language learning strategies were very different from mine, but somehow I learned to allow for and appreciate the difference.

Whole language . . . I didn't even know the term four years ago. But when I did there was a realization, an ah ha! Now I had words to describe the way I learned and taught language.

➜ See: Caprio, p. 226; Chen, p. 26; Kagawa, p. 353; Krashen, p. 86; Urzúa, p. 42; Wallace, p. 88.

Lauren Hoyt is director of instruction at the Preparing Refugees for Elementary Programs (PREP), Philippine Refugee Processing Center, Morong, Bataan, the Philippines.

Resource: Organization

The Centre for Teaching and Research in Literacy

Charles Sturt University—Riverina
P.O. Box 588
Wagga Wagga 2650
New South Wales, Australia
(069)22-2000

If every institution of teacher education were modeled after The Centre for Teaching and Research in Literacy, we would be light-years ahead in our classroom application of sociopsycholinguistic research. Staffed by some of Australia's leading educational researchers, the Centre provides preservice and inservice teacher education, conducts research across a wide range of subjects, and publishes an impressive list of professional books, articles, and videotapes. *Literacy, Literature and Learning,* the Centre newsletter, is sent free of charge to everyone on the Centre mailing list.   *LBB*

➜ See: Brennan, p. 228; Cairney, p. 201; Gollasch p. 233; Kamler, p. 140.

Book Note

Portraits of Whole Language Classrooms

Heidi Mills and Jean Ann Clyde
1990; 307 pp.; $18.50
Portsmouth, NH: Heinemann

In *Portraits of Whole Language Classrooms,* Mills and Clyde travel from a home day-care setting through preschool programs, elementary classrooms, junior and senior high schools, special education sites, and an English as a second language class, all run by whole language teachers. The journey ends in an education laboratory staffed by graduate students in a reading methods course. The authors illustrate that the curricula discussed are united by a universal theory of learning (whole language) that cuts across grade levels.

Teachers and those who educate teachers will find this book useful as they consider how various teachers have translated their educational beliefs into classroom practice. Descriptions of classroom life and teachers' personal reflections encourage readers to examine the beliefs that underlie their own practices. In so doing, readers are invited to expand and refine their vision of whole language.

➜ See: Clyde, pp. 26, 49; Mills, p. 325.

Letter Writing and Glenn
by Denise Ogren

Letter writing between my kindergartners and me begins before school starts when I send postcards welcoming them to Stinesville Elementary School. Our message board is loaded with letters I have written to the children on a regular basis and those the children have written back. If I read their letters in front of the class and make comments like "I'll write you back tonight, and tomorrow there will be a message on the board for you," then the amount of mail I receive will increase remarkably. Usually I have the child who has written the letter to me read it in front of the class.

Glenn was one of my more prolific letter writers. I had taught his sister the year before and he was ready to write from day one. His mother understood my reasoning for encouraging children to write, and she let the children write by themselves.

Joey was very cautious and quiet and liked to do everything right. He wrote to me on lined primary paper with all the words spelled correctly. I could tell someone at home was giving him lots of help. When I received a letter from Joey, I would usually read it myself to the class to save time.

One day Glenn's mother came in to help out in class. She said, "Mrs. Ogren, Glenn seems to think that he has to spell every word correctly. I don't understand this since I know you don't teach that way." I was surprised and confused. Glenn had told her that if all the words were spelled correctly, then I would read his letter in front of the class; but if he spelled the words his own way, then he would have to come up and read it in front of the class. What a revelation! That was the last thing I wanted the children to think.

I changed my ways the next day. Joey was asked to come up and read his letter and sure enough he said, "I can't read it because my mother helped me with it." Joey then understood why I kept telling the children to do their own spelling and not ask their mothers, and I learned about teaching from my children.

➜ See: Goodman, p. 208; Newman, p. 211; Ogren, pp. 155, 376.

Denise Ogren is a primary teacher at Stinesville Elementary School, Stinesville, IN.

Teachers as Mediators

As I See It:
Kenneth S. Goodman

The Relationship of Teaching to Learning and the Role of the Teacher

Consider these classroom episodes:

- A group of black inner-city fourth-grade pupils have read Langston Hughes's poem "Mother to Son" (Bontemps 1963, p. 67). The pupils discuss the poem. The teacher is a codiscussant. The classroom procedure involves a pupil leading the discussion. The teacher wonders what the pupils think about the mother's saying, "Life for me ain't been no crystal stair." Some pupils point out other references to stairs in the poem. The teacher shares with them her knowledge of the author's life and political beliefs. She suggests that the stairs represent the author's view of this woman's attempt to raise herself up from her difficult conditions. One boy asks, "She talkin' 'bout climbin' up to heaven?" They decide that the mother is contrasting her hard life to the biblical idea of a beautiful crystal stair leading to heaven. In doing so they draw on their own knowledge of the likely experiences and religious beliefs of the mother. They share stories of their own mothers. "I never thought of this poem in quite that way," says the teacher.

- An eighth-grade group in a working class suburb plans a unit on evolution. As pupils discuss and web their knowledge of the concept they are introduced to the controversy over the biblical view of creation. Two weeks after the unit begins, one boy tells the teacher his minister would like to come in and debate evolution with the teacher. The teacher declines, explaining that studying a theory is different from advocating it. The class discusses the situation and reaffirms that they are studying evolution as a theory. They decide to explore the role of theory in science and the difference between established fact and theory. The teacher encourages the boy and his classmates to bring in literature on evolution from creationists. The ensuing study is enlivened. The pupils search avidly, not only for resources on evolution but also for the history of the theory and the controversy over it. One group reads Irving Stone's adult biography of Charles Darwin.

- A third-grade class enjoys playing Hangman. In an informal conversation pupils comment that some people are better players than others. They relate this to the idea of strategies. One comments that it pays to know which letters are most common. The teacher suggests they prepare a manual, *Rules for Hangman Players*. During the course of preparing the manual the pupils decide on studies they need to do of letter frequency, of letter sequence, and of common patterns.

In all these examples, the teachers play crucial but not controlling roles. The teacher is not intervening in the learning but is mediating it. He or she is a colearner, a resource, a guide, and a monitor. The teacher's role as mediator is an active one, but the teacher understands that teaching supports learning—it can't force learning to happen. In building comprehension, the teacher knows that the pupils' development of their own strategies is more important than whether they agree with the teacher's view of the meaning of a text. So the teacher helps the pupils to examine the available facts, to evaluate their hypotheses and their own beliefs, and to find more information as they need it. Asking a good question is better than prematurely sup-

plying an answer. Pushing pupils to explore where an idea is leading them is better than telling them it's not going to work. Helping pupils think through a problem to come up with potential solutions is better than presenting a ready-made solution.

Teaching as Mediating and Supporting Learning

Putting the learner at the center of education necessarily means that classrooms can't be teacher centered. That doesn't mean less of a role for the teacher. But it means that the teacher plays a more subtle, supporting role. The teacher is not abdicating authority—rather the teacher is using the authority on behalf of the learners, assuring them of the optimal conditions for learning. The teacher is not giving up power. The teacher is enabling learners to develop and use the power they have: power to learn, to think, to use language, to make decisions, to collaborate with others. There is no one-to-one correspondence between each act of teaching and each act of learning—there never was. But if there is more learning going on in the classroom, then surely there is more effective teaching going on.

Good teaching involves a delicate balance: knowing how much support to give without taking control of learning from the learner. That's why intervention is an inappropriate term for any kind of teaching strategy. The teacher should be aiming to give enough support to involve learners and to keep them involved in useful learning.

It is important for teachers to expect learning and not to be satisfied until it is happening. But it is also necessary for the pupils to expect to learn and to come to feel comfortable with the risks that learning involves. They have to see themselves ultimately as capable of learning and in control of their own learning.

→ See: Goodman, p. 207; Torbe, p. 232; Wigginton, p. 220.

Reference
Hughes, L. 1963. "Mother to son." In *American Negro poetry*, ed. Arna Bontemps. New York: Hill and Wang.

Resource: Periodical

Teaching & Learning: The Journal of Natural Inquiry

$12/year (3 issues) from:
Center for Teaching and Learning
Box 8158, University Station
University of North Dakota
Grand Forks, ND 58202
1-701-777-2764

Promoted as a journal that wants "to define teaching and learning as broadly as possible," *Teaching & Learning* invites contributors to "stretch or dissolve traditional categories of education." The complimentary copy we received was a refreshing mix of scholarly yet readable articles, personal narrative and poetry. It looks like a potential rival of *Language Arts*.

LBB

Book Note

Whole Language: Inquiring Voices

Dorothy Watson, Carolyn Burke, and Jerome Harste
1989; 72 pp.; $6.75
New York: Scholastic

What does it mean to be a whole language teacher? This delightful book explains through thought-provoking commentary, deft descriptions of teachers and students involved in classroom inquiry, and challenging invitations to the reader to engage in professional self-evaluation and reflection.

The slim, easy-to-read volume captures the excitement teachers feel when they shed the restrictive role of teacher-as-imparter-of-information and emerge as teacher-as-inquirer: They are free to listen to and learn from their own intuition, their theoretical understanding of language and learning, their collaborations with colleagues, and their students.

The book is one of Scholastic's Bright Idea Series, conceived and edited by Adrian Peetoom, in which leading authorities in the field share "the hearts of their professional lives." Other titles in the series include K. Goodman's *What's Whole in Whole Language?* and David B. Doake's *Reading Begins at Birth*.

LBB

❝ Well, as you know I've been a strong supporter of the notion of using children as informants. Essentially I want teachers to understand inquiry as a way of understanding children in classrooms, and the teaching-learning relationship as one in which children act as informants. I also think that perceiving teaching as inquiry is the direction whole language has to take.

"When I was at a conference this summer a teacher said to me she was 'doing Graves.' That scares me. It means teachers are seeing whole language as an orthodoxy rather than a vehicle for self-renewal and learning. I think there's some real urgency to change these perceptions if we don't want whole language to stagnate. ❞ (Jerome Harste, p. 5)

❝ We love errors and invite you to love them too. Nothing should scare you more than groups or persons who think they know all the answers. Good learners always encounter errors that make them itch professionally.

"On the theoretical level, 'error' means that at least one of the tenets of a particular theory doesn't wash, and we've talked about this as a thrust towards inquiry. In fact, we'd say that good inquirers know an important reality: that wallowing in correctness, being hell-bent for 'mastery,' stops learning. Messes are the fodder of creativity. Thinking through what is initially seen as an error makes new insights possible. The longer you involve yourself in inquiry, the more you'll cherish messes. They'll become signs that you're about to grow. Under the best conditions, anomalies force you to develop a new perspective on the world. ❞ (p. 69)

→ See: Peetoom, p. 415; What's Whole in Whole Language?, p. 380.

📷 **WHOLE LANGUAGE CAMERA**

Sarah Costello works with a seventh-grade writer, William J. Pistor Junior High, Tucson, AZ.

Whole Language Teachers Do Teach

"How can you claim that you teach when all that you do is watch kids try to teach themselves?"

Whole language teachers know how vulnerable they are to this question. It may come, subtly or bluntly, from an advocate of traditional education. It may even raise doubts in the mind of a new whole language teacher. Yet it is invalid. We can take full measure of its invalidity by considering three false dichotomies from which it arises: (1) learning versus teaching; (2) unstructured versus structured; and (3) process versus product.

Learning Versus Teaching

Once teachers understand that reading and writing are language processes and not a set of skills listed at the back of a language arts textbook, they can begin to respect literacy learning as a developmental process that follows a course similar to oral language learning. Supporting developmental literacy learning does not mean, however, that we simply create a "garden of print" (Goodman and Goodman 1979), plant our students in it, and then retreat behind the garden gate, peering expectantly through a knothole while we wait for them to blossom into readers and writers. Whole language teachers are not passive observers of their students' developmental progress. They are active, creative supporters of that process who have developed three qualities essential for effective teaching: (1) a theoretical understanding of language and learning; (2) an ability to observe and learn from children; and (3) an instructional vision.

Theory

We now understand how children learn, what language is, how language develops, and what we can do as educators to best support the language learning process. The challenge for whole language teachers is clear: They must read the professional literature and keep abreast of the latest findings in educational research. But good teaching is much more than just knowing the research and putting theory into practice.

Observing and Learning from Students

As Angela Jaggar (1985) explains, "Observation plays a critical role in teaching. . . . It is the link between theory and practice." Observing students is but one aspect of a general "teacher-researcher" trend that promises to place classroom teachers in their rightful position as professional educators and curriculum decision makers. Glenda Bissex (1987) defines teacher researchers as not only observers but as questioners, learners, and more complete teachers who use a range of ethnographic methodologies, such as formal and informal interviews with students, anecdotal record-keeping, and analysis of oral and written discourse. Thus, they can determine what their students know, what they still need to learn, and what they as teachers can do to support and extend the learning process. Whole language teachers study the "culture of the classroom," and the answers they find to their questions become the basis of their curriculum.

Instructional Vision

The instructional agenda that whole language teachers outline from the records they keep of their students' progress, is guided by an overarching instructional vision. They have specific goals for their students and a clear sense of how they are going to help their students achieve these goals.

Little is left to chance in a whole language classroom. Although whole language teachers are delighted daily, they are seldom surprised. They carefully create and craft an environment that allows and supports optimal learning. Students are encouraged to take the lead in the content-rich, literate environment of the whole language classroom, controlling and monitoring their own learning, but their teachers take the lead when

their skilled observation and assessment informs them a student is in need of some specific help. Demonstrating and sharing information, however, in response to student needs or interests is very different from traditional instruction that centers around a body of knowledge that teachers impart to their students regardless of whether it is needed or of interest to them.

As much as possible, whole language teachers make kids responsible for every aspect of classroom living. This includes everything from organizational concerns to teaching and learning. In whole language classrooms every child is a teacher and every child claims an area of expertise. Donald Graves (1983) remarks that most American classrooms are highly centralized. "The teacher sets up every activity and takes it down, almost in fifteen to twenty minute intervals or sometimes less. So the children don't move unless the teacher makes the first move." In sharp contrast, whole language classrooms are not teacher-directed, but student-centered.

Structured Versus Unstructured

Because there is so much movement and interaction in a whole language classroom, initiates might jump to the conclusion that whole language is "unstructured." Nothing could be further from the truth. While you generally won't find the physical structure of the traditional classroom—desks arranged in straight rows, all facing the teacher's desk up front—there is indeed a highly organized structure. To enable 30 different students to function as both independent and interdependent learners and teachers demands both finely honed organizational abilities and strategic planning. Graves's analogy of the classroom as workshop or laboratory is apt. Everything has its place, everything has its routine, and every child knows his or her way around this carefully organized learning environment.

Contrary to some misinformed thinking, whole language teaching does not mean letting everyone do what "feels good." There are rules, there are expectations, there are deadlines, there are standards. There is, in fact, no dichotomy between:

Process Versus Product

While whole language teaching/learning deliberately rejects programmed instruction and its product-oriented obsession, this doesn't mean that product doesn't count in whole language classrooms. Effective whole language teachers expect and demand high-quality work. There is a significant difference, however, in the work students do in whole language classrooms and the work they are subjected to in traditional rooms. The difference is authenticity (Edelsky and Smith 1984, pp. 55–59) and the resultant pride of ownership. Few children can maintain a high level of interest and commitment to top-level work when every morning they confront a stack of stapled worksheets. But the desire to learn burns bright when, like 11-year-old Dewayne, you are on your way to becoming the school's resident expert on poisonous snakes, a topic you have chosen yourself to research, interview experts on, and finally present to other students and teachers, telling them all you know about cobras, anacondas, and rattlers. Learning experiences that arise from the student's own needs and interests, that are shared with an audience that extends beyond the teacher result in pride of ownership and a natural desire to do high-quality work.

The temptation to take the easy way out occasionally is a very human trait, and sometimes students prefer to slide by with less than rigorous standards. Also, some students hesitate even to try lest they fail. This is where the role of the whole language teacher again becomes critical.

Look, for instance, at the sequence of events between whole language resource teacher, Gloria

Norton, and a second-grader who needed some encouragement. When Gloria first met with Paul on November 20, his writing consisted of nonsensical letter strings.

Nonetheless, Gloria engaged Paul in a written conversation and responded to each of his entries on the basis of what he explained it said.

This continued for several weeks, until Gloria, having watched Paul at work on several occasions, knew that he could do more. On December 7 she said, "Paul, I want you to write so that I can read it."

The results were dramatic and instantaneous. Paul became a writer, able to use written language to communicate with others.

[I want to go to the park]

[Yes, maybe I will go to the park.]

In 17 days, Paul changed from a child with no confidence in his ability to write to a child who knew he could write—and did. Gloria Norton's informed and sensitive mediation made the difference. Paul's next entry read:

[We have to catch the kids before they get under the table.]

[So they won't get tagged.]

This is the critical "zone of proximal development" that Vygotsky (1964) writes of, the prime teachable moment when the child, on the edge of a developmental leap, needs only a gentle nudge from the teacher to make the transition into a new realm of knowing. Frank Smith (1983) instructs us, "Respond to what the child is trying to do." Donald Murray (1985) concurs: "Effective teaching is responsive."

Responsive teaching begins with creating a literate, content-rich environment into which we invite our students. Inside, they explore with our careful guidance and support, and they share with us and with each other what they know and what they are coming to know. We watch, we listen, we question, we assess, and then we respond. This is the joy and challenge of real teaching, and this is what educators who embrace whole language do—they teach.

➜ See: Bissex, p. 209; Cormack, p. 213; Freeman, p. 212; Harwood, p. 213; Wigginton, p. 220.

(Continued on next page)

Viewpoint: Thomas Newkirk

Notes from a Worrier: The Vulnerability of the Whole Language Movement

We have a curious attitude toward history in the United States. We spend vacations walking the Freedom Trail, standing in awe before the Lincoln Memorial. But at a basic level we are like the characters in Joan Didion's essays for whom "time past is not believed to have any bearing on time present or future."

A sense of history, after all, threatens three basic beliefs that we would like to hold about ourselves. First, we want to believe in our own radical freedom—we can be whatever we want, unlimited by family background, social conventions, or even our own prior experience. Second, it threatens the sense of our uniqueness; just as adolescents imagine that no one—particularly not parents—has ever experienced what they have experienced. And third, history threatens our sense of stability; we don't like to think that our present situation may change for the worse.

The whole language approach is, of course, not new. It has strong similarities to the New Education of the 1880s—the Progressive Education of the 1920s and 1930s, and the open classroom movement that had a short life in the late 1960s and early 1970s. In tracing the lineage of the whole language movement we are reminded, uncomfortably, that each of these previous movements lost public support—and that the whole language movement runs the same risk.

These movements lost support because the public perceived them as lacking intellectual rigor, as more concerned with social development than academic excellence, as denying the legitimate authority of the teacher and the school. At worst, these approaches were criticized as naive, based on a sentimental, romanticized view of the child—just provide freedom and opportunity and the child will choose for himself or herself the most beneficial path of development.

Anyone who advocates the writing process or the whole language approach—no matter how carefully—meets some of this criticism. No matter how many times I explain that grammar can be taught as part of the writing process, there are some who want, perhaps need, to believe that correctness does not matter to me. No matter how many times we explain that phonics is

Thomas Newkirk is associate professor of English at the University of New Hampshire, where he directs the freshman English program and the New Hampshire Writing Program, an annual summer institute for teachers. He has written and edited widely in the areas of teaching reading and writing.

part of a whole language approach to reading, there are some who want, perhaps need, to believe that we are depriving children of all tools of word analysis.

We explain our position and still get nowhere because the resistance we meet—this almost religious belief in phonics or grammar—is a coded argument for something else. A culture that fears its own disorderliness, and doubts its own capacity to check that disorderliness, naturally looks to schools to provide an institutional check on the chaos we feel in our own lives. Joe Clark, patrolling the halls with his bat, becomes a hero. Creativity or self-expression, from this standpoint, indulges rather than checks the disorderliness that some critics project onto schoolchildren. By contrast grammar instruction and phonics drills make for a regimented and depersonalized environment, one that holds anarchy at bay. Little wonder then that our explanations make no difference.

But we also meet objections from more sympathetic critics, objections which we may invite. Even John Dewey felt a need to criticize the extremes of progressive education in *Experience and Education* (1963). He objected to the way in which the progressive movement took "its clew in practice from that which is rejected instead of from the constructive development of its own philosophy":

> To imposition from above is opposed expression and cultivation of individuality; to external discipline is opposed free activity; to learning from texts and teachers, learning from experience . . . (p. 19)

The result is a polarized set of good/bad terms which fail to clarify the complexity of the progressive classroom as he saw it. And we can see the same polarization going on today. Two examples:

Process Versus Product. One of the rallying cries of the writing process movement was "teach writing as a process not a product." To the extent that this appeal caused teachers to attend to the ways students went about writing, it was undoubtedly healthy. But why should we have to choose? Don't we want students to write good products? Doesn't a knowledge of products (gained from reading) help guide our processes? Do we really want to suggest that writers can engage in a process and not take responsibility for a product?

Freedom Versus Teacher Control. Many teacher accounts take the form of conversion narratives. For a long time the teacher controlled the classroom until the point of conversion when authority was passed to the students. The problem here is that control is often treated as a zero-sum game; there is a fixed amount of control to be distributed—so if the student gains more control that is because the teacher gives up some.

I think we're kidding ourselves when we phrase the issue this way. Teachers in whole language classrooms still exert great control; in fact the individualization that goes on in the one-to-one conferences and increased teacher-student talk may make the teacher an even more influential person in the student's life. But this influence does enhance children's freedom by inviting them to make choices within a range defined by the teacher.

If we insist on choosing process over product, we can be accused of an indifference toward

standards. If we insist that the freedom of the child is paramount, we can seem to abandon our responsibility to pass on a common literary, historical, and scientific culture.

The excellent whole language classes that I have visited convince me that teachers are not making these either/or choices; rather, they are working in the best tradition of progressive education. They recognize that the choice is not between teacher direction and student choice—rather it is how teacher and community expectations can draw on student interests. I believe that we diminish the effort of these teachers when we suggest that they are giving up traditional values for "progressive" ones.

Should the public become convinced that whole language education means a rejection of traditional values and standards, what support we have will vanish.

It's happened before.

➡ See: Breaking Ground: Teachers Relate Reading and Writing in the Elementary School, p. 392; Heath, p. 422; Miller, p. 219; Weaver, p. 382; Wigginton, p. 220.

Reference
Dewey, J. 1963. *Experience and education* (1938). New York: Macmillan.

Further Reading by Thomas Newkirk

◆ *Breaking Ground: Teachers Relate Reading and Writing in the Elementary School*, ed. with J. Hansen and D. Graves. Heinemann, 1985.
◆ *Only Connect: Uniting Reading and Writing*, ed. Boynton/Cook, 1986.
◆ *To Compose: Teaching Writing in the High School.* Heinemann, 1986.
◆ *Understanding Writing: Ways of Observing, Learning, and Teaching*, ed. with N. Atwell. Heinemann, 1988.
◆ *More Than Stories: The Range of Children's Writings.* Heinemann, 1989.

For Now
by Natasha L. Osborn

For now
Be my friend
Accept me
As the person
I am
Don't force me
To shut you out

For now
Please understand
No lies
For they
Only confuse me

For now
Be patient
Inside
You'll see
A person
Give me time

For now
Let me know
You care
Meet me halfway
Walk with me
From there

➡ See: Treasures, p. 162.

From Treasures 2: Stories & Art by Students in Oregon, comp. by Chris Weber (Portland, OR: Oregon Students Writing and Art Foundation, 1988).

Natasha L. Osborn lives in Eugene, OR, and was 16 years old when she wrote this poem.

(Continued from previous page)

References

Bissex, G., and R. Bullock, eds. 1987. *Seeing for ourselves: Case-study research by teachers of writing.* Portsmouth, NH: Heinemann.

Edelsky, C., and K. Smith. 1984. "Is that writing—or are those marks just figments of your curriculum?" *Language Arts* 58(3).

Goodman, K. S., and Y. M. Goodman. 1979. "Learning to read is natural." In *Theory and Practice of Early Reading*, ed. L. Resnick and P. Weaver. Hillsdale, NJ: Lawrence Erlbaum Associates.

Graves, D. 1983. *Writing: Teachers and children at work.* Portsmouth, NH: Heinemann.

Jaggar, A. 1985. "On observing the language learner: Introduction and overview." In *Observing the Language Learner*, ed. A. Jaggar and M. T. Smith-Burke. Newark, DE, and Urbana, IL: International Reading Association and National Council of Teachers of English.

Murray, D. 1985. *A writer teaches writing*, 2d ed. Boston: Houghton Mifflin.

Cornerstone:
Barbara M. Flores & Eddie Hernandez

A Bilingual Kindergartner's Sociopsychogenesis of Literacy and Biliteracy

In 1985 Dool Elementary primary teachers in Calexico, California, began to transform their beliefs, theories, and practices related to emergent literacy and biliteracy. . . . In kindergarten, the teachers only expected the children to learn how to write the alphabet and their names. First-grade children were expected only to perfectly copy sentences from the blackboard. Bilingual children, especially those from very poor families, were not expected to do anything more than know the alphabet, their name, how to copy from the board, and how to decode syllabically in Spanish if that was their dominant language.

The teachers taught letter names and some phonics in kindergarten. Phonics were always taught in isolation using worksheets and basal readers. In first grade the children were grouped by reading ability. Bilingual teachers grouped their children into six groups: high, middle, and low in English, and high, middle, and low in Spanish. Copying was considered writing. Not many bilingual children learned to read and write proficiently in spite of the teachers' dedication.

In 1985 the teachers began to shift their focus from a skill-based approach to a whole language approach. They had agreed, as part of their staff development efforts, to collaborate with us in action research, teaching, and learning using the new praxis (theory-in-action and action-guided-by-theory) about literacy learning and teaching in two languages. They also agreed to a three-year commitment to monthly staff development that focused on the critical pedagogy of coming to know.

Dialogue journal writing was the first social context that they organized for the teaching and learning of written language (Staton et al. 1988; Peyton and Staton 1990). The program set up was based on an earlier study (Flores and García 1984). From the first day of school, the children, the majority of whom were bilingual and from low socioeconomic families, were asked to draw and write in their journals on a daily basis. Many children said they could not write, but when they were told it was okay to pretend to write, to write their way, or to write like five- and six-year-olds, they did. The teachers were absolutely incredulous because they had assumed that the children did not know anything about written language.

The following is a case study of one kindergartner's cognitive and linguistic evolution of knowledge about writing. Jesús comes from a bilingual family that speaks both Spanish and English. His acquisition of literacy in both languages is a living testimony that we cannot continue to underestimate the cognitive and linguistic potential of our language-minority (soon to be majority) children.

His first journal entry demonstrates that Jesús had a knowledge about left-to-right directionality, letter formation, linearity, and the arbitrariness of letter/symbols, and an adequate repertoire of letters. (figure 1)

His October entry shows more sophisticated letter formations, refinement, and better control of the pencil. He was using a presyllabic conceptual interpretation (Ferreiro and Teberosky 1982) of alphabetic writing systems in Spanish and English. His teacher, Mr. Hernandez, genuinely responded to Jesús' rendition of having spiders at home. Even though Mr. Hernandez could not

figure 1

read what Jesús had written, he encouraged the children to write "their way." Each child orally read his message and therefore mediated meaning (Vygotsky 1978) with an alternate sign system. Since the children could not read Mr. Hernandez's written message either, he also mediated his meaning by orally reading it as he wrote it with each child watching.

figure 2

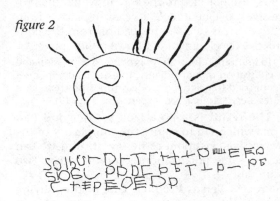

I have a lot of spiders at home. I don't know what to do.

Mr. Hernandez and the children were engaged in more than just dialogue journal writing. They were engaged in a meaningful exchange of personal and academic cultural knowledge. As Jesús wrote, he shared his evolving knowledge about written language. As his teacher wrote and mediated his writing, he shared the adult cultural expectation of written language in this particular context. He also demonstrated how all the cuing systems (pragmatic, semantic, syntactic, graphophonemic, and orthographic) (Goodman 1982) are simultaneously used to represent meaning in writing. Finally, he deliberately organized a zone of proximal development (Vygotsky 1978) each time he wrote to Jesús.

By the end of the year Jesús was a balanced bilingual, writing alphabetically in both Spanish and English. His invented spellings, both in English and in Spanish, approximated adult expectancy. In Spanish he wrote: "LA CHAKA TBO I GATO" (Chaka had one cat). His teacher responded authentically: "Tú abuelita me dijó

que la chaca estaba muy triste y no quería comer" (Your grandma told me that Chaca was really sad and didn't want to eat). (figure 3)

figure 3

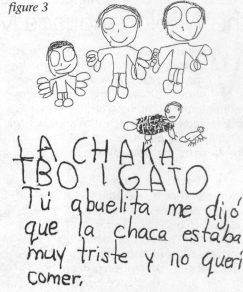

In English he wrote: "AI HAV A WALE AV RABO" (I have a wallet of Rambo). His teacher responded authentically: "Cesar has a wallet too. So do I, but it's not of Rambo." (figure 4)

figure 4

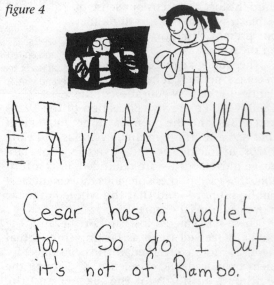

From his teacher's daily transactions within the communicative context of dialogue journals, Jesús learned to read and write alphabetically in both Spanish and English. Both his teacher and parents were amazed. Yes, it is amazing what children can learn if we teachers know how to socially organize the learning and teaching. It is important for us to learn more about how children learn language, oral or written, first or second, so that we can not only organize, but deliberately facilitate, monitor, and document our children's sociopsychogenesis of literacy and biliteracy.

→ See: Altwerger and Flores, p. 418; Flores, p. 412; Kalman, p. 34.

References

Ferreiro, E., and A. Teberosky. 1982. *Literacy before schooling*. Portsmouth, NH: Heinemann.

Flores, B., and E. García. 1984. "A collaborative learning and teaching experience using journal writing." *Journal of the National Association for Bilingual Education* 8(2).

Goodman, K. 1982. *Language & literacy: The selected writings of Kenneth S. Goodman*. London: Routledge & Kegan Paul.

Peyton, J. K., and J. Staton, eds. 1990. *Dialogue writing: Analysis of student-teacher interactive writing in the learning of English as a second language*. Norwood, NJ: Ablex.

Staton, J., R. W. Shuy, J. Kreeft Peyton, and L. Reed. 1988. *Dialogue journal communication: Classroom, linguistic, social and cognitive views*. Norwood, NJ: Ablex.

Vygotsky, L. S. 1978. *Mind in society*. Cambridge: Harvard University Press.

From *Dialogue* 5(3), Handbook Press, December 1988.

								Mitchell	
				Steiner				Piaget	
				Montessori			Dewey		
			Parker						
		Pestalozzi	Neef Alcott				Vygotsky	Rogers	
Comenius	Rousseau				Froebel			Maslow	
1600	1700	1800				1900		2000	

Pioneers: John Dewey (1859–1952) — by Ron Miller

No single thinker has stimulated as much debate and innovation in American education as John Dewey. He was a gifted and versatile scholar who wrote on philosophical, moral, social, and political problems as well as education. Along with Francis Parker, he was a leading figure in the progressive education movement and was its most important theorist. His Laboratory School at the University of Chicago (which he codirected with his wife from 1896 to 1904) was a prototype for many of the private progressive schools that were founded in the first decades of this century. His writings—especially *The School and Society* and *The Child and the Curriculum* (1900), *Schools of Tomorrow* (1915), *Democracy and Education* (1916), and *Experience and Education* (1938)—are classics in educational philosophy.

One way to understand Dewey's approach is to recognize his consistent emphasis on life *experience*. In *Democracy and Education*, Dewey (1966, p. 144) stated that "an ounce of experience is better than a ton of theory simply because it is only in experience that any theory has vital and verifiable significance." This emphasis on experience over theoretical, conceptual knowledge is the basis for Dewey's criticism of traditional education, and in order to appreciate his educational approach, it is important to understand what he meant by "experience." Dewey did not (as many of his critics have charged) advocate a "do-your-own-thing" style of education. His concept of experience is much more subtle and sophisticated than this.

Dewey observed that experience is "habitual"—that is, we are attuned to our surroundings in unconscious, nonverbal ways; we derive certain meanings from the world before stopping to think about them. For example, we absorb many assumptions about the world through our cultural conditioning. In addition, experience is whole and organic; all living beings are in an ongoing relationship with their environment and their every action affects the quality of this relationship. Thus, experience evolves. Dewey frequently emphasized the *reconstruction* of experience, the further development or growth of an organism through its intelligent interaction with the environment.

What does all this mean for education? Dewey argued that education is not the mere presentation of curriculum, knowledge, facts, or the "great books"; knowledge and facts are not purely objective but are always *experienced* from a learner's perspective. The real task of education is the reconstruction of experience; education must *expand a person's perspective* so that he or she can engage the world with a wider range of meanings—that is, with greater intelligence. Subject matter and the great books are important, but they must be incorporated into the world that is experienced by the learner, or else they lack true meaning. Dewey argued that education should focus on the present needs of the learner, that education is most truly the growth and enrichment of current experience, not preparation for some anticipated future. With the dramatic acceleration of social and technological change, Dewey recognized, the future can no longer be so confidently planned for.

Dewey stated that the *logical* organization of the curriculum must be balanced with the *psychological* needs of the student. Dewey did not hold a radical child-centered position; he strongly emphasized that intelligence is cultural and social; in other words, the reconstruction of experience depends upon acquiring socially useful knowledge. Still, he argued that a democratic society must encourage diversity and initiative among individuals, and must recognize their diverse needs and ideas. He criticized traditional education for suppressing curiosity and demanding conformity and docility.

For Dewey, academic learning is an aid to, not a substitute for, first-hand experience of the world. As early as 1898, in an essay titled "The Primary-Education Fetish" (1940, p. 26), he wrote that "a premature demand upon the abstract intellectual capacity stands in its own way. It cripples rather than furthers later intellectual development." Forty years later Dewey (1938, p. 50) made the same point in arguing against the overemphasis on "basic" skills:

> What avail is it to win prescribed amounts of information . . . to win ability to read and write, if in the process the individual loses his own soul: loses his appreciation of things worth while, of the values to which things are relative, if he loses desire to apply what he has learned and, above all, loses the ability to extract meaning from his future experiences as they occur?

Education should develop "reflective habits" that are useful in any situation, said Dewey, and should not be seen as a convenient way to inculcate established facts and ideas.

Dewey recognized that in modern culture people have increasing access to *information*. What they really need is a greater ability to judge information critically and use it effectively. In an information age, the role of education has changed from dispensing knowledge to developing thinking and problem-solving skills. Dewey argued that the curriculum should revolve around social problems that are universal to all cultures, and should involve young people in exploring these problems in active and democratic ways. In his later writings especially, Dewey emphasized *aesthetic* experience—appreciation of the deepest possible meanings—as a primary goal of human life; consequently, progressive education came to emphasize creative self-expression through the arts.

It has been argued by many critics (e.g., E. D. Hirsch in his best-selling book *Cultural Literacy*) that the incorporation of Dewey's ideas into American public educational practice has led to a decline in academic rigor and excellence. But this argument rests on two questionable premises. First, Dewey's ideas were not adopted by mainstream education in any significant way. School practices may not be as rigid as they were in the 19th century, but in many ways they are still a long way from fostering an authentic "reconstruction of experience" through reflective intelligence. Second, genuine Deweyan progressive education does *not* cause a decline in academic excellence, as the famous Eight Year Study of progressive high schools in the 1930s clearly demonstrated; rather, it achieves excellence in ways that respect students' natural learning processes and inherent curiosity.

Book Note

From Communication to Curriculum

Douglas Barnes
1976; 304 pp.; $11.50
New York: Penguin (distributed by Heinemann)

Douglas Barnes's book is a classic that is not nearly as widely known as it deserves to be. The basic premise is a simple one: Talking is an important mode of learning. The book begins with transcripts of several classroom discussions, some with and some without teachers; Barnes then broadens the focus to look at how teacher control of knowledge and discourse subtly (or not-so-subtly) works against true learning. This book is a wonderful example of theory that is grounded in classroom reality. His discussion also reflects concern with the broader social context, as he discusses how classroom discourse has been used to disenfranchise poor and minority students.

Sandra Wilde

66 Some years ago I saw a lesson which illustrated this all too well. A geography teacher in a rural secondary school had prepared a lesson for his fourth-year mixed-ability class. He distributed copies of an excellent aerial photograph of the area around the school. Most of the pupils came from farms in the area: the photograph reflected their world to them, the patterns of settlement, the communication systems, the distribution of cultivation and pasture. I expected a fine discussion, for the photograph would enable them to reflect upon their everyday knowledge and to see it more schematically. But the teacher wrote three words on the blackboard, 'shape,' 'tone,' and 'texture,' and asked for definitions. In the end he himself had to provide a definition of 'shape.' Then he asked, 'What can you learn from the *shapes* in the photograph about this area?' He was met with silence. By insisting that the pupils talked about the photograph in his terms he detached them from what they knew best, their everyday lives. They could not join in the discussion on his terms, and the teacher had prevented them from starting on their terms—which would have enabled him to introduce his own more abstract analytical categories during the discussion. He was asking them to arrive without having traveled, and this is often the effect of demands for final drafts. 99 (p. 118)

Progressive education, as it was practiced in a variety of experimental private schools (especially during the 1920s), explored new ways to develop children's creativity, self-reliance, and social awareness as well as intellectual skills. William Heard Kilpatrick (1871–1965), a popular and influential professor at Teachers College, Columbia University, developed the "project method"—a Deweyan approach that actively involves students in the learning process. Because he dealt with the fundamental problems of education in modern society, most serious rethinking of American education is influenced in some way by the work of John Dewey.

➜ See: Dewey, pp. 270, 285, 286, 335.

References

Dewey, J. 1938. *Experience and education*. New York: Macmillan.

———. 1940. "The primary-education fetish." In *Education today*, ed. J. Ratner. New York: Putnam.

———. 1966. *Democracy and education* (1916). New York: Free Press.

Viewpoint: Eliot Wigginton

Get the Radio Man!

"This little booger," exclaims Linda Oxendine, a second-grade teacher in eastern Kentucky, brandishing her district-mandated basal reader, "about did me in. It almost ruined my teaching career."

Linda, like thousands of her peers, myself included, have turned away from a style of instruction we know is bankrupt. We have rejected forever those teaching materials that have sucked all the life from our language arts classes and have destroyed our students' enthusiasm for the work. And it is right that we have done so. We have passed a mile marker in our careers, and we will never return to materials and activities that anesthetize our students as surely as a surgeon's drugs. We will quit teaching first.

It is much too early, however, to be too self-congratulatory. As John Dewey reminded us in 1938, if we adopt a new philosophy of education that is based on opposition to and rejection of an old one, we may land ourselves in even deeper water by going to the opposite extreme. In rejecting the basal, for example, do we also reject all published readers from all text manufacturers, and all assigned readings? In rejecting our workbooks, do we ban all such drills and exercises forever from our rooms? In rejecting what we perceive as excessive, stupid direction of our students from outside sources, do we reject all direction of our kids as authoritarian and wrongheaded?

Rejection of a style of instruction that does not work well demands that we replace it with one that is *demonstrably* better—one more carefully and thoughtfully worked out and shaped and tailor-made to our kids in our specific circumstances. For the issue here is the development of literacy; and if we do not understand the meaning of that word, and we are not sure how to nourish and evaluate its development in specific, concrete ways, we may do our students an even greater disservice than we did when we drove them like mules through directed silent readings provided by anonymous sources from on high.

We begin, in short, by rereading and carefully considering the implications of the first chapter of Dewey's *Experience and Education*. Then, if we're not sure where we're going, we simply have to do some homework. Our kids deserve that.

I know. I know. Many of you are saying to yourselves, "Of course we're going to do better than that. We wouldn't be that irresponsible."

Well, let me tell you a story. Once upon a time, I assumed that all of my high school students who were involved in the production of our magazine, *Foxfire*, were learning far more about writing through that project than through any of the other activities we had ever tried together. The topics they chose to work on were their own, they were conferencing in small groups and collaborating with each other, there was a real audience for their work—all the right ingredients were in place for a successful experience. We proceeded. I knew what I was doing. I had been trained at Cornell, for heaven's sake.

Then the graduates began to show up during their freshman year in various colleges bemoaning the fact that they apparently did not know how to write essays or research papers. Again

Eliot Wigginton teaches high school English in Rabun County, Georgia. *Foxfire* magazine, which he started with his ninth- and tenth-graders in 1966, is still produced quarterly. Articles from the magazine make up the contents of the *Foxfire* book series published by Doubleday. Wigginton has served, or is serving, on some two dozen boards and advisory councils including the National Endowment for the Humanities. He is a member of the National Faculty of Humanities, Arts, and Sciences. He lives in Rabun County, on the side of Black Rock Mountain, in a two-story log house that he built with the help of his students.

and again came the same lament: "We're getting hammered out there. We're all failing 101." With permission from my high school administrators, I designed and began to teach two new courses for college-bound seniors, one to get them ready for 101 and one to help them understand how to put a research paper together. In a separate course, tenth- and eleventh-graders continued to produce *Foxfire* under my direction. And I swear, as seniors, those students who had produced *Foxfire* were absolutely no better at writing well-organized, grammatically correct essays or pieces of research in my college prep classes than their peers who had not had that experience, but had gone instead through a completely traditional grammar-to-composition offering. There was no difference that I could see in their skills levels at all. The *Foxfire* veterans were more self-confident in some ways, it seemed, and they knew a bit more about their traditions and their communities, but the point of publishing had been to build their writing skills—the other benefits being supplementary icing on the cake—and the answer to the simple, stark question, "Are they writing better than their peers now as a result of the publishing experience, yes or no?" was simply, starkly, "No."

Looking at my own *Foxfire* class, and then looking at classes around the country where other teachers and their students were publishing similar kinds of oral history/folklore magazines, a scary pattern began to emerge. Inordinate amounts of precious classroom time were being wasted in the rather automatic exercise of transcribing tapes. Some students were spending entire semesters hiding behind cameras and in darkrooms and never writing a word except on hall passes. Students who were already comfortable with writing were producing introductions to the articles that were no more sophisticated than anything they had ever written previously; students who were reasonably proficient at grammar and mechanics were proofreading and correcting the work of those who were not; in short, nobody was learning anything. All had simply fallen into the old pattern of doing what they already knew how to do.

A look at the end products flowing from many "whole language" classrooms persuades me that if the practices going on inside those rooms were similarly scrutinized, the same patterns of malpractice would emerge. If the kids aren't being stretched far beyond existing competencies, then what's the point? That they feel better about themselves and about the time they're spending in school? Fine. Just don't claim that their writing is improving unless clear, reliable evidence is present to support that fact.

And when it's not, we redesign. We have to, *if* one of the major goals is writing competence.

Thankfully, there are patterns to go by. Here and there across the country, sensitive colleagues are taking their students through a brainstorming process where those students discover how writing and reading surface in the real world, from the trayliners at McDonald's to the videos they rent. They then vote as to what they'd like to produce, determine the specific audience, plan the specific processes they'll use

to get the job done, begin, and check their progress and redesign at every stage. And as the students are about their work, they, with their teacher, build in whatever activities are necessary to increase the language proficiencies of all—activities which are sometimes quite traditional, built in, now, as part of a meaningful *context* where the point is not so much the production of an end product as the utilization of that production process in the service of far higher ends. In some such classes, in fact, in what will seem to many like the ultimate paradox, the end product becomes almost irrelevant, for long before it appears, the students have bled from its design all there is to be learned, and they are ready to move on.

Look, for example, at Amy Rogers's second-graders in Harlan, Kentucky. Her original idea was to have the students collect traditional folktales, write them down, and then dramatize them for other classes in the school. Knowing that the students might have a better idea, however, and knowing the importance of student ownership, and confident enough of her abilities to know that no matter what they chose to do, she could integrate all the needed literacy skills, she took them through the brainstorming, decision-making process. Their final choice? A half-hour video about environmental pollution in their county for which they wrote four original plays, created posters and slogans, and interviewed and filmed community residents—the man who operated the local landfill, for instance—about the issue.

At this point, they *could* have stopped, a narrower academic agenda having been memorably and powerfully served. In this case, the kids would have none of it, however; they voted to continue, practiced, performed, and filmed the plays, filmed the posters, and, with the help of an adult who knew how to edit video, put it all together into a finished tape. Amy allowed the process to continue, knowing that there were other related literacy skills that could be directly served, documented, and evaluated, and knowing the importance to these particular rural students of seeing *their* project—not *hers*—brought to a conclusion. There were compelling reasons, in other words, for continuing the process.

The result? The finished tape won a "Take Pride in America" award, and students and their parents journeyed to the White House to receive it. Each of the students received a personal copy of the video. The last word I had from Kentucky was that each played it over and over on his or her home VCR, awed by what had been accomplished. Had Amy imposed her original idea upon the students, she would have stolen from them what became the most memorable educational experience of their lives—an experience that stretched them far beyond what any of them, Amy included, had known how to do.

In the face of such an example, the more typical student projects—students writing and illustrating little stories individually and having them "published" and put into a classroom library, to name one—seem rather pale and toothless. That's not to say that I am opposed to that particular activity. Rather, everything has to do with intensity and quality. Back to Linda Oxendine. On Mondays, she and her second-graders deal with the required basal reader. For the rest of the week, her students, half of whom cannot write at all in the beginning of the year, work in small groups using invented spelling to create stories out of their own experiences. Those who cannot write dictate them as Linda, or one of the other students, transcribes. Each student has a folder of his or her work; each has a "story speller" or personal dictionary. When Linda asks, "What are the words you *want* to learn how to spell today?" students call out words from their stories and others help them find them in a dictionary and add them to their spellers. (On a recent visit, a group was wrestling with the spelling of the word "navigator.") As stories are completed, they are shared out loud with the whole class during story time. "Without the sharing, the whole thing's a flop. That's what makes them feel like a family."

Fairly standard procedure so far. But as the year goes on, the stories become increasingly sophisticated. Students begin to write to other schools requesting students to share stories they have written. Out of this comes a weekly radio show, broadcast to the entire community. When the students voted to start it, and Linda admitted she didn't know how, they said, "Well, get the radio man in here." He came. On the first show, they requested letters from their listeners, and the show's format evolved to one where, for the first five minutes, the team of announcers for that week reads mail their class has received. For the next five minutes, they read stories—both theirs and ones received from other schools. For the last five minutes, the entire class sings mountain songs they have learned and practiced that week with the help of a visiting folk artist.

Behind the scenes, Linda constantly monitors the growth of every child. At the end of the year, the best of their work, including stories and illustrations from every student, is published in their own fat, bound volume—their class answer to the basal reader. And at state testing time, "They don't have trouble with it [Iowa Test of Basic Skills]. They zip through it. They think it's stupid." Every student progresses at least two grade levels, and without the destruction of their enthusiasm for the work. As Linda said recently to a group of Kentucky teachers, "They don't ever miss school, and the reason is they have ownership. . . . Honey, they even take their stories with them to the bathroom and sit on the pot and write. They don't want to turn them loose until they're done."

Patterns to go by. My classes have been redesigned. In the *Foxfire* class, students will spend the 1989–1990 school year creating the manuscript for a book which will be published by Doubleday to commemorate our twenty-fifth birthday. In the summer of 1990, a group of them will be hired to complete the manuscript and deliver it to New York. As seniors, these students will help teach my 101 and research classes. Most will be exempted from the college 101 requirement entirely, testing out of it. I know they will.

And then I, like many of you, will redesign my classes yet again. For all of us who care about our kids and the craft of teaching have declared that we will not spend the remainder of our lives in repetition. We have embarked on a long journey, the conclusion of which we cannot see—do not want to see. We want only for ourselves the same thing we want for our students: to be involved in a process of continual, intriguing, satisfying growth as knowing human beings.

➜ See: Dedicated Teachers Bring Change to State Classrooms, p. 286; Miller, p. 219; Newkirk, p. 217; Weaver, p. 382.

Further Reading by Eliot Wigginton
◆ *Aunt Arie: A Foxfire Portrait,* ed. Dutton, 1983.
◆ *Sometimes a Shining Moment: The Foxfire Experience.* Doubleday, 1985.
◆ *"Foxfire Grows Up." Harvard Educational Review* 59(1), February 1989.

Book Note

Sometimes a Shining Moment: The Foxfire Experience

Eliot Wigginton
1986; 456 pp.; $10.95
Garden City, NY: Anchor
Press/Doubleday

Sometimes a Shining Moment is ostensibly about high school students learning to write, but it is really about both students and teachers learning how to be learners. Wigginton is best known for the *Foxfire* books and magazines, but it is wrong to assume that he is actually responsible for these publications. His students are the ones who do it all: interviewing, writing, revising, photographing, marketing, and bookkeeping. This sounds like a remarkable feat for high school students, and one at first assumes that these students must be exceptionally bright, talented, motivated, and responsible. Reading the book makes you realize this is not the case. Wigginton's description of his first year of teaching sounds like every teacher's worst nightmare. These southern, rural students appeared to have no interest in education and even less interest in English. Wigginton imagined them spending the rest of their lives happily pumping gas.

Many teachers have experienced this kind of frustration. There is a great temptation, in the face of such problems, to blame the students. Wigginton took a different approach. He assumed that, at the very least, part of the problem lay with him and with the traditional teaching methods used in high school English classes. He brought the lives and culture of his students into the classroom. His students found purpose in education as they began to write a magazine about their own community. They developed responsibility as learners because Wigginton believed they could be responsible. Like all success stories Wigginton's is full of frustrations, hard work, and setbacks. The success came, I believe, because Wigginton realized that "shining moments" can happen in education only when we are willing to take a hard look at what we believe and what we do.

Janice Henson

As kids see it

Our Radio Show

by Jason Garland

We like our radio show. It's called "Knox County Kids." We talk to you listeners on our show. We write stories through the week to put on the show. Every week we have a new host. The host begins the show and ends the show. We sing songs at the end of the show. When we hear ourselves we hide our faces and giggle. Sometimes Mrs. Bonnie Carr plays her banjo and sings with us on the radio.

From *Great Mountain Tales,* written by Linda Oxendine's second-grade class, G. R. Hampton School, Barbourville, KY, 1989.

I am Jason Garland. I am 8 years old. I like to ride my bike because it is fun. I was named after my Daddy. I live up Winn Hollow. When I grow up I want to be a fireman so I can put fires out. My Mommy and Daddy and my little brother means the most to me. I wish I had a race car so I could get to places fast.

Resource Essay

Foxfire Teacher Outreach Programs

Foxfire's success as an approach to classroom instruction attracts teachers and educationists interested in implementing similar programs. In the past, we responded by conducting cultural journalism workshops that resulted in over 200 spin-off programs around the nation.

We now also provide graduate-level instruction and staff development programs for teachers of all grades and all subjects—at nine institutions of high learning: Berea College (Berea, Kentucky), North Georgia College (Dahlonega, Georgia), SUNY-Cortland (New York State), Georgia State University (Atlanta, Georgia), University of Idaho (Moscow, Idaho), Carson-Newman College (Jefferson City, Tennessee), University of Washington (Seattle, Washington), West Virginia University (Morgantown, West Virginia), and Southern Maine University (Gorham, Maine).

Eastern Kentucky Teachers Network visiting the Foxfire Center, Rabun County, GA.

Teachers participating in those courses develop hands-on units of instruction to implement in their classrooms. We also provide grants for teachers to conduct research, primarily classroom-based, that adds to the body of knowledge about this approach to education and the pedagogical principles on which this approach is based. The results of those products and that research are captured in the teachers' case studies published in *Hands On,* our journal for teachers.

Jason and Erin interview Mac McGaffee about life during the Great Depression.

Teachers in those nine regions formed networks as a means of working together to enhance their successes and to deal with problems as they arise. Each network now has a coordinator responsible for managing the network's development. The Teacher Outreach Office at Foxfire coordinates the network's ventures and evaluates the overall efficacy of our outreach initiatives.

For additional information about Foxfire's Teacher Outreach initiatives and *Hands On: A Journal for Teachers,* contact Foxfire Teacher Outreach, Box B, Rabun Gap, GA 30568, (404) 746-5319.

From *Hands On: A Journal for Teachers,* Foxfire Fund, Inc., Rabun, GA.

Teachers as Liberators

 Viewpoint: Patrick Shannon

Whole Language and Critical Literacy

You must look beyond the linguistic principles of whole language to see the possible connections between it and critical literacy. Whole language linguistic principles help us to understand what language is, how it is supposed to work, and under what conditions it is easiest to learn. Critical literacy suggests how language can be used to identify the problems in our lives and to act collectively to promote a just, democratic society. I think both whole language (broadly interpreted) and critical literacy are part of the American educational tradition.

The Whole Earth Catalog was an expression of revolt against puritanism and commercialism in America. Along with Charles Reich's *The Greening of America* and Herman Hesse's *Steppenwolf*, it offered readers a different way to look at themselves, to think about the environment, and to live with others by developing personal creativity and authenticity. Many read these and other similar texts during the 1960s and early 1970s, hoping to escape the competitive, destructive forces that had worn their parents into the tired routine of consumption, complacency, and television. Others, at that time, read Michael Harrington's *The Other America*, the Students for a Democratic Society's *Port Huron Statement*, Malcolm X's *Autobiography*, and Herbert Marcuse's *One Dimensional Man*, trying to understand why that parental routine existed, who benefited from its existence, how it was maintained and reproduced, and what barriers existed to freedom and justice. These books and readers were also expressions against traditional America.

Patrick Shannon has taught and worked with teachers and children in New York, Minnesota, Texas, Indiana, and Ontario, Canada. He studies societal effects on how literacy is defined, who is considered literate, what is read and written, and how literacy is taught.

Perhaps you can see what I'm leading to here. The metaphor of *The Whole Earth Catalog* pushes whole language beyond linguistic theory to include assumptions concerning our social, political, and economic relations. The metaphor places whole language within a historical context of protest. Shortly after the Great War, a similar split occurred in progressivism, when "bohemians" placed the free, unrepressed individual and self-expression at the center and radicals sought social action to correct societal inequalities. (Cowley 1934) These different interpretations of what was important in changing America carried over into conceptions of schooling, dividing the experienced-based wing within the progressive education movement into child-centered and community-centered perspectives.

Child-centered educators (e.g., William Kilpatrick, Caroline Pratt, Margaret Naumburg, Hughes Mearns, etc.) sought to develop school environments and practices that would allow and enable each individual child to realize his or her uniquely creative essence. This was both a revolt against the mechanical education of the past and a positive response to liberalism and self-expression. Its purpose was to allow the learner to expand, to discover his or her latent capacities, to break through the artificial barriers of conformity, and to reveal fresh, creative possibilities in his or her relationship to the environment.

Because creativity and self-expression were possible in many forms—music, drama, painting, etc.—child-centered schools did not need to make a fetish of literacy. Rather languages (the symbols systems, logic, and pragmatics of all the creative arts) were to be learned incidentally as the students pursued their interests—building a boat, finding out whether or not dew falls, helping a family discover the reasons for recurring infections of typhoid in the community, and ascertaining how New York outgrew Philadelphia (Shannon 1990). The goal of these schools was to have these languages become "ways of behaving" rather than just learned skills.

Community-centered educators (e.g., John Dewey, Eleanor Clapp, Elizabeth Irwin, George Counts) placed the individual within society, arguing the absurdity of trying to define the good individual or the good education without a conception of the nature of the good society. Social action toward a better society, not self-expression, was the goal of community-centered schools. Although lessons and projects always began with children's interests, the object of each activity was to connect these interests and the students' lives with the matters of the world outside the home and school as well as to consider the academic principles which were embedded in or could be extended from these chosen activities.

Community-centered teachers encouraged readers and writers to see the ideological basis of any text. No longer was it sufficient for the literate to read accurately or to write clearly and expressively; what was needed to reconstruct society was the ability to read beyond the text to understand how the author and the ideas connected with the various political, economic, and social arguments concerning the future of America. In short, community-centered educators (or social reconstructionists as they were called) were less concerned with how students learned to be literate than they were concerned with how citizens used their literacy after they learned to read and write.

Although both these conceptions of schooling were based on students' experience, the goals for how students were to reflect on that experience were quite different. In a similar manner, whole language and critical literacy advocates hold differing goals for language use. Whole language advocates seek purposeful, meaningful uses of language in which students can learn about themselves, their history, and their culture, but they do not necessarily seek to help students make connections between their language and lives and those of others, nor do they promote action beyond the classroom door to assure that everyone enjoys the rights implied in the basic tenets of whole language. Critical literacy advocates (just like their community-centered predecessors) are often unclear concerning how people can use language to learn about themselves, but they are explicit and articulate concerning the needed connections and social action (Freire and Macedo 1987).

For those whole language teachers who see or would like to see the political and sociological implications of their work, critical literacy may be the catalyst that helps them to ground their work in a developed theory of the nature of the good society and to act in conjunction with their students and community in order to build a just and equitable democracy.

→ See: Apple, p. 416; Broken Promises, p. 171; Giroux, p. 417; Horton, p. 74; Literature Reference List, p. 429; Peterson, p. 348; Shannon, p. 170; Sherman School Story, p. 342.

References

Cowley, M. 1934. *Exile's return.* New York: Norton.
Freire, P., and D. Macedo. 1987. *Literacy: Reading the word and the world.* South Hadley, MA: Bergin & Garvey.

WELL-SAID This is a great discovery, education is politics! When a teacher discovers that he or she is a politician, too, the teacher has to ask, What kind of politics am I doing in the classroom? That is, in favor of whom am I being a teacher? The teacher works in favor of something and against something. Because of that, he or she will have another great question, How to be consistent in my teaching practice with my political choice? I cannot proclaim my liberating dream and in the next day be authoritarian in my relationship with the students.

—Paulo Freire, *Freire for the Classroom: A Sourcebook for Liberatory Teaching*

Ira Shor and Paulo Freire

 **writers**

Impressions
by Carol Maytag Christine

words
spewing
splat!
on deaf ears

of teachers who
in turn
spew
their own
splat!

on students
seeking
meaning
from their
ideas and
questions
smothered by their
teachers'
noise.

→ See: Christine, pp. 379, 411.

Carol Maytag Christine is a doctoral student at the University of Arizona, Tucson, AZ.

Shannon, P. 1990. *A struggle to continue: Progressive reading instruction in America.* Portsmouth, NH: Heinemann.

Further Reading by Patrick Shannon

◆ *Report Card on Basal Readers*, with K. Goodman, B. Freeman, and S. Murphy. Richard C. Owen, 1988.
◆ *Broken Promises: Reading Instruction in 20th Century America.* Bergin & Garvey, 1989.
◆ *A Struggle to Continue: Progressive Reading Instruction in America.* Heinemann, 1990.

Viewpoint: Ira Shor

Overcoming Teacher-Talk and Student Silence: Freirean Dialogue for Critical Education

Many teachers want lively student participation in their classes. They also want students to think critically. Some who apply Paulo Freire's ideas even hope that education can empower students. Yet teachers often complain of motivation and discipline problems. Students are routinely silent or respond in monosyllables. What I want to argue here is that the first obstacle to dialogue, to critical learning, and to student participation is the teacher-talk that now pervades the classroom. Only by transforming teacher-talk into critical dialogue can we hope to offer empowering education.

I want to focus on the large part of teacher-talk known as the didactic lecture, sometimes called "frontal" pedagogy because the teacher stands up at the front of the room and talks nonstop about some material, and sometimes called "direct" instruction because the teacher speaks directly about a specific content in the hope of transferring it from the teacher's mind to the students.

Didactic and Sedating:
The Transfer-of-Information Lecture

The didactic lecture imposes silence on students and denies them a thinking and speaking role. It diminishes critical dialogue on any material because the subject matter is already worked out and delivered whole. It is a one-way funnel of information for students to swallow. Such a narrative transfer of information has a sedating effect on student attention. Their brains are invited to sleep.

This sedating discourse includes some other silencing habits such as:

- Preempting student discussion with fast summaries
- Doing analyses ahead of and without the students
- Asking questions requiring only short answers from students
- Restricting student questions and discussion of student experience
- Rejecting the students' native idiom in class discussion and writing
- Denying students peer-discussion groups in which they work on material without supervision
- Giving safe answers to questions instead of critical ones

The entrenchment of teacher-talk in the classroom greatly preoccupied John Goodlad. In an eight-year study of public schools, Goodlad (1984, pp. 108–109) concluded in *A Place Called School* that

> No matter how we approach the classroom in an effort to understand what goes on, the teacher comes through as coach, quarterback, referee, and even rule-maker. But there the analogy must stop because there is no team. . . . On one hand, many teachers verbalize the importance of students increasingly becoming independent learners; on the other, most view themselves as needing to be in control of the decision-making process. The classroom is a constrained and constraining environment. The prospect of this setting slipping from their control is frightening for many teachers, not surprisingly.

Goodlad's research (p. 229) into teacher-talk in a thousand classrooms revealed the absence of student response:

> We observed that, on the average, about 75% of class time was spent on instruction and that nearly

Ira Shor is professor of English at Staten Island College. For the past two decades, he has been adapting Paulo Freire's ideas for his classes. Shor was a Guggenheim Fellow in 1983 and Chancellor's Scholar-in-Residence at City University of New York in 1986. He speaks extensively and offers workshops for teachers on Freirean methods for critical literacy.

70% of this was "talk"—usually teacher to students. Teachers out-talked the entire class of students by a ratio of three to one . . . These findings are so consistent in the schools of our sample that I have difficulty assuming that things are much different in schools elsewhere. Clearly, the bulk of this teacher-talk was instructing in the sense of telling. Barely 5% of this instructional time was designed to create students' anticipation of needing to respond. Not even 1% required some kind of open response involving reasoning or perhaps an opinion from students.

The sad absence of dialogue Goodlad found in the 1980s repeated the results of his earlier survey of some 260 classrooms in the 1960s, where Goodlad concluded that "teaching was predominantly telling and questioning by the teacher, with children responding one by one or occasionally in chorus" (Silberman 1970, p. 159).

In another report on American schools in 1984, Theodore Sizer saw the same problem of anti-dialogue. He said in *Horace's Compromise* (1984, p. 82) that

> Save in extracurricular or coaching situations, such as athletics, drama, or shop classes, there is little opportunity for sustained conversation between student and teacher. The mode is a one-sentence or two-sentence exchange . . . Dialogue is strikingly absent, and as a result the opportunity of teachers to challenge students' ideas in a systematic and logical way is limited . . . One must infer that careful probing of students' thinking is not a high priority.

Those minimal responses are imposed by the discourse in the classroom, according to studies of language in school by Shirley Brice Heath (1978, 1982), by Michele Sola and Adrian Bennett (1985), and by Michelle Fine (1987). These anthropologists see silencing as an institutional problem, not an individual one of student mediocrity. Fine (p. 157), for example, wrote that teacher-talk and the official curriculum "obscure the very social, economic, and therefore experiential conditions of students' daily lives . . . and expel critical 'talk' about these conditions." Heath found that school language conflicted with the speech habits learned by working-class schoolchildren at home, favoring the children from the middle class. Teacher-talk and official curricula deny students critical contact with their immediate experience and with society at large, thus retarding their opportunities to change both.

Education for Social Change:
Paulo Freire's Transformative Pedagogy

Transforming teachers into dialogic educators preoccupies Paulo Freire, for whom dialogue means cultural empowerment, not merely conversation in the classroom. In *Education for Critical Consciousness* (1973, p. 52) he states:

> A major problem in setting up the program is instructing the teams of coordinators. Teaching the purely technical aspects of the procedure is not difficult. The difficulty lies rather in the creation of a new attitude—that of dialogue, so absent in our upbringing and education. The coordinators must be converted to dialogue in order to carry out education rather than domestication. Dialogue is an I-Thou relationship, and thus necessarily a relationship between two subjects. Each time the "Thou" is changed into an object, an "It," dialogue is subverted and education is changed to deformation.

Here, anti-dialogue means treating students as vacant receptacles who receive lectures on official knowledge but do not challenge it.

In *Pedagogy of the Oppressed* (1970) Freire wrote that when members of the elite decide to work for popular empowerment they show a "lack of confidence in the people's ability to think, to want, and to know . . . They talk about the people but do not trust them" (p. 46). This concern reappeared in Freire's report of his work with the new government in Guinea-Bissau, *Pedagogy in Process* (1978, p. 104). Freire suggests the prolonged transformation teachers need to shake off the habits of traditional culture, including the dominant lecture habits of traditional schooling.

Doing Dialogue in the Classroom:
Contradictions and Options

By engaging students in dialogue, we face some interesting contradictions of dialogic practice (Shor and Freire 1987). For one thing, the dialogic teacher has to be restrained and assertive *at the same time,* holding back from providing quick answers while posing challenging problems, intervening to present issues and material hidden by dominant culture while creating open space for student voices, not lecturing students on what to believe and not narrating passive scholastic information to memorize, yet leading the dialogue forward into consciousness change with value judgments and some expert knowledge, opening the classroom to student speech while integrating a critical study of standard usage (the language of power). Not the least of the delicate contradictions is leading the class while inviting students to take the lead themselves.

For the transforming teacher, this means being authoritative without being authoritarian, being expert without being arrogantly professional. This creative balance is learned in-process over a span of years, as an experiment in remaking our teaching role. The future of this experiment is a creative new terrain for language—where we reinvent classroom discourse *with* the students, in the hope of reinventing society as well.

→ See: Apple, p. 416; Bissex, p. 209; Giroux, p. 417; Goodman, p. 338; Lindfors, p. 79; Weber, p. 78.

References

Fine, M. 1987. "Silencing in public schools." *Language Arts* 64(2), February.

Freire, P. 1970. *Pedagogy of the oppressed*. New York: Continuum.

———. 1973. *Education for critical consciousness*. New York: Continuum.

———. 1978. *Pedagogy in process: Letters from Guinea-Bissau*. New York: Continuum.

Goodlad, J. 1984. *A place called school*. New York: McGraw-Hill.

Heath, S. B. 1978. "Teacher-talk: Language in the classroom." *Language and Education: Theory and Practice* 9. Washington, DC: Center for Applied Linguistics.

———. 1982. "What no bedtime story means: Narrative skills at home and school." *Language in Society* 11(2).

Shor I., and P. Freire. 1987. *A pedagogy for liberation: Dialogues on transforming education*. South Hadley, MA: Bergin & Garvey.

Silberman, C. 1970. *Crisis in the classroom: The remaking of American education*. New York: Vintage.

Sizer, T. 1984. *Horace's compromise: The dilemma of the American high school*. Boston: Houghton Mifflin.

Sola, M., and A. Bennett. 1985. "The struggle for voice: Narrative, literacy, and consciousness in an East Harlem school." *Journal of Education* 167(1).

Further Reading by Ira Shor

◆ *Critical Teaching and Everyday Life,* 4th ed. University of Chicago Press, 1988.

◆ *Culture Wars: School and Society in the Conservative Restoration, 1964–1984,* 3d ed. Methuen-Routledge, 1989.

◆ *Freire for the Classroom,* 2d ed. Heinemann, Boynton/Cook, 1989.

◆ *A Pedagogy for Liberation,* 3d ed., with P. Freire. Bergin & Garvey, 1989.

by Debra Goodman

Utopia Town: Organizing a Classroom by Committee

Town Rap
My name is Sweet V. and I work in this town.
I like it so much that I don't frown.
I am the head of the General Store . . .
And you better believe me cause I'm telling you more.
I tell you the rest of the town is cool.
The only thing missing is a swimming pool.
We got a library where you can find a book
Why don't you come and take a look.
We got a rec center if you want something to do,
And the post office is holding your mail for you.
I just told you something that was very down
And it's all about our Utopia Town.
So chill

—Verneisa Mangham, fifth-grader

On the day that I brought the mailboxes (old liquor boxes covered with contact paper) into my fifth-grade classroom, the kids got very excited.

"Ms. Goodman," Cassie waved her hand in the air , "can we make a post office? Can we sort the mail, and have mail carriers, and . . . can we have a store... and we already have a library... Ms. Goodman, could we have a town?" And that's how our fifth-grade town got started.

Simulation is to social studies as plants and animals in the classroom are to science. We're not living the actual experience, but we are able to experience the situations, problems, and feelings firsthand.

All town decisions were made using consensus (allowing me to introduce the kids to alternate forms of democratic processes). With consensus, each student has a strong say in town decisions. No one can be overruled by the majority. Students who make proposals must think of reasonable and convincing arguments to support their proposal. They learn to argue without insulting put-downs, since their goal is to convince opponents of the value of their own ideas. Consensus also helps kids learn to compromise. The kids who object to a proposal must voice their specific objections.

The consensus process also equalizes my role as a member of the classroom. Every year kids come up with outlandish or objectionable proposals such as a town candy shop or a police force. Usually a wise and brave student will speak out against the idea. If I do have to veto a suggestion, I exercise the same right as any other town citizen.

The town areas always include the library, museum (a sort of thematic unit center), publishing house, and post office. Cassie's mother built us a small stand that has been used as a general store. We sell pencils, pens, erasers, paper clips, stickers, and anything else that I can pick up inexpensively and resell for less than 20 cents. The post office has also sold stationery and envelopes. Profit is used to buy supplies and games for the town. Committees vary each year. We have had a maintenance crew, a recreation center, a studio theater group, an art committee, and a courthouse. Students usually suggest a town hall, but I encourage them to make it a representative body.

This decision-making process, which I have used each year I have had a classroom town, takes several weeks. During that time, students have a chance to circulate in the established areas and decide which committee they would like to work on. I have a chance to observe student interests, abilities, and social interactions. When we have selected seven or eight town areas, I ask each student to identify his or her first, second, and third choices for town committees. I organize the town committees carefully: I consider the academic and social strengths of each student and male/female and ethnic mixtures. I try to honor the requests of the students themselves.

The committees follow the same consensus process for planning activities, work schedules, and so on. They brainstorm ideas, prioritize, and select two or three projects to start with. Committee members are assigned jobs as needed. During committee meetings, I circulate and try to assist committees that are having difficulties. I encourage students to be sensitive during discussion. Everyone should take turns talking. In small groups, consensus means asking each student whether he or she agrees to an idea. Every activity must be agreed to by the entire group. Schedules must be fair. Everyone takes turns doing unpopular activities such as cleanup.

Students learn many things about planning and organizing, and (more important) how to work with other people. In addition, they truly feel that the classroom belongs to them. In attempting to organize my room into seven town areas, I was always stuck for a place for my bulky and non-functional teacher's desk. I finally placed it near the door and gave it to rotating town receptionists. The receptionist greets visitors, hands out supplies, takes attendance, returns papers, monitors hall privileges, and so on.

The opportunities for language learning in our fifth-grade town are endless. Students have made lists, charts, signs, posters, books, newspapers, price tags, library cards, checkout forms, sign-in sheets, schedules, displays, and so forth. They learn to make announcements, share ideas in groups, argue, convince, listen, question, perform, and organize. They read books, instructions, rules, charts, signs, announcements, and newspapers. They write stories, poems, articles, reports, plans, and proposals. They also use math strategies.

As citizens of a fifth-grade town, the kids become concerned with many issues, including things that are typically teacher concerns such as class behavior and cleanliness. In weekly town meetings, they raise issues and address problems. They don't always come up with the same solutions that I would have suggested, but typical classroom problems have led to lively discussions.

In organizing town clubs we have discussed inclusive and exclusive groups. We have dealt openly with cliques, gender-based roles, and prejudice. This often extends to a discussion of the civil rights movement. Decisions about how our town should be run have encouraged discussions of different economic and political systems. We have talked about cooperative versus competitive systems. Some students spent one hour a week at the neighborhood food coop as a result.

I encourage the students to consider their image of an ideal society, rather than design a mini-Detroit. This is why Cassie's class called our town "Utopia Town." The Utopia committee was selected to construct a sign for the classroom door:

Welcome to Utopia
pop. 63

- Utopia is a town where you can be yourself. You can do what you want as long as it is not insulting, cruel, or disobedient to other people.
- Utopia is a town where people share with other people.
- Utopia is a town where people are allowed to think about what they want to think.
- Utopia is a town where *you* have the freedom what *you* think is right, and make the friends you want to make.

Utopia Committee
on behalf of town citizens

➜ See: Apple, p. 416; Giroux, p. 417; Goodman, pp. 236, 252; Hagan, p. 246.

Debra Goodman is a teacher at Dewey Center for Urban Education, Detroit, MI.

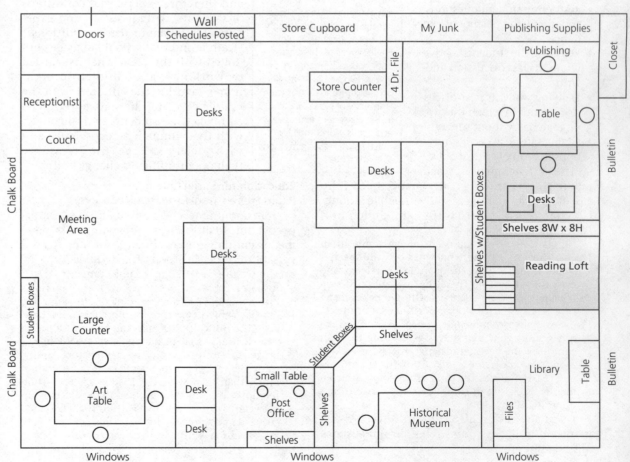

Book Note

The Way It Spozed to Be

James Herndon
1968; out of print
New York: Simon & Schuster

How to Survive in Your Native Land

James Herndon
1971; out of print
New York: Simon & Schuster

Both of these books are currently out of print, but are such classics that they are well worth borrowing from libraries or searching for in secondhand bookstores. Some of us decided to become teachers after reading James Herndon's books. In both *The Way It Spozed to Be,* in which he describes his year teaching in an inner-city school (from which he was fired) and in *How to Survive in Your Native Land,* the story of his ongoing life in a suburban school, he struggles with the question of how to be a teacher and still remain an authentic human being. Although he was writing before the days of whole language, his instincts were those of a whole language teacher, as he worked at finding out what his students really needed to learn rather than what he was "spozed to" teach them.

Herndon's writing is very funny. In my opinion, his comments about flax in *How to Survive* are the best metaphor yet of traditional schooling's stultifying distance from real life: "I think you could live your entire life in America and never see or even hear of flax, never know about it or need to know about it. Only in the school, only from the geography book, only from the teacher could you learn about flax." (p. 107)

Around 1970, several books were published that inspired a new generation of idealists to go into teaching with the hope that schooling could be different from what it had been. A professor of mine once referred condescendingly to the authors of these books—Herbert Kohl, John Holt, Jonathan Kozol, and George Dennison—as "our romantic critics." I still reread *How to Survive* regularly.

Sandra Wilde

❝ And while teachers are complaining they haven't any time you see that you have all the time in the world, time to spend with Lucy and Sally telling them they got glue on their heads and threatening them about what you're going to do if they get on the hood of your car again until they are satisfied, time with Eileen and Rosa, who have discovered that if they get caught a couple of times smoking in the bathroom their mothers will reach most satisfactorily, time to talk with Howard, who has discovered simultaneously a real woods out in back of the drive-in and The Byrds and is trying to make sense out of of both (the woods have foxes and a skunk and a red-tailed hawk flying overhead and some kind of marvelous purple moss which the Museum of Science don't know about and who would have thought that right here in this prototype [his word] of suburban developments there would be a real woods, and here too that is just what The Byrds are singing about)—every day there are going to be kids who want to spend some time talking to you as adult, as teacher, as whatever you are, wanting to relate their adventures and troubles and excitements and miseries and aspirations and confusions or hoping perhaps to get some clear idea of the world they live in through you.❞ (*How to Survive in Your Native Land,* p. 63)

Book Note

36 Children

Herbert Kohl
1968; 224 pp.; $8.95
New York: Penguin

Respect—that's what I remember about this book, which I first read 20 years ago when I was in high school, and that's what hit home as I read it again, this time as a classroom veteran myself. Herbert Kohl respected his students; they weren't kids who had to be controlled, made to sit in silence, and taught a curriculum that had no bearing on their lives. Kohl respected them as human beings— driven by curiosity about their world and the ones beyond their Harlem neighborhood— and he responded. He filled the classroom with books and invited them to choose the books they needed. He encouraged them to explore in writing, unfettered by assigned topics and red-inked corrections, and they learned together. Kohl could respect his students as learners because he respected himself as one.

LBB

❝ Later that year my supervisor told me I was running a very effective individualized reading program. That may have been it, but the truth seemed simpler and less structured. I overwhelmed the class with books, many of which I loved, and let them discover for themselves what they liked. There were no reports to be written, no requirements about numbers of pages to be read. Some children hardly read at all, other devoured whatever was in the room. The same is true of my friends. ❞ (pp. 39-40)

❝ I promised to bring Maurice a binder (having the symbol of being sanctioned to write privately and as one pleased was very important) and the next morning brought a dozen to school. I explained to the entire class that some children wanted to write their own books and that the binders were available for anybody who cared to write. I also explained that though I was available to help or to read their work for pleasure, still the books were their private property—the author's control over his work would be respected completely. There was no mention of grading or grammar as it never occurred to me then even to bother with a disclaimer. ❞ (p. 61)

Resource: Organization

Renaissance Educational Associates

4817 North
Country Rd. 29
Loveland, CO
80538
1-303-679-4309

This international membership association of educators and parents knows that their example of creative living invites others into meaningful and purposeful lives. The group publishes a quarterly newsletter, *The Renaissance Educator,* sponsors an annual membership conference, hosts local activities in 30 places around the world, and offers a professional leadership institute each summer.

Book Note

Whole Language Sourcebook

Jane Baskwill and
Paulette Whitman
Two Sourcebooks: K–2
and 3–4
1988; 236 pp. each; $70
each
Toronto: Scholastic

The aptly named *Sourcebook* is a rich source, indeed, of information about creating a primary whole language classroom. Written by two Canadian whole language teachers with thirty-some years of classroom experience between them, it provides both the theory and the sort of practical details teachers crave: instructional strategies, plans for classroom organization, lists of needed materials, scheduling tips, and so on. Particularly helpful for teachers new to whole language are the complete plans for several month-long thematic units; the authors map out daily learning experiences across the curriculum, all structured around a theme. Having the *Sourcebook* is the next best thing to having Baskwill and Whitman with you in the classroom.

LBB

The Glass Teacher

by Julia A.

When she thinks
it's like you can see
through her.
Looking for the
correct answers.
Giving right answers.
Seeing through to
her mind. Glass
teacher. It's like
you can see right
through her.

➔ See: Chock, p. 226; small kid time hawaii p.157.

From *small kid time hawaii,* ed. Eric Chock (Honolulu: Bamboo Ridge Press, 1981, 1989).

📷 **WHOLE LANGUAGE CAMERA**

Students from Annette Maggitti's first grade class pay careful attention as a Tucson Desert Museum volunteer shows them the talons of a great horned owl, Desert Winds School, Tucson, AZ.

Whole Language Internacional
by Mark Caprio

Hey Teach, When Ya Gonna Start Teaching

Thirty Japanese junior and senior high school teachers solemnly filed into the classroom. They ranged from the hard-core veteran with over 20 years' teaching experience to the new recruit with only a few years' experience. They had come to take part in a summer intensive English-language training session sponsored by the prefectural government. In one week, these teachers would devote over 35 hours to improving their language skills. Although they did not expect the class to be as demanding as the classes they taught during the school year, they did expect to work. After all, there was a test scheduled for the last day.

They took their seats in order and waited for me, the teacher, to open the class. I began to talk. What came from my mouth, though, was not what they had anticipated hearing. "I have never met any of you until today," I began. "I don't know anything about you so I do not feel qualified to teach you. For this reason, you will decide how you want to study English this week." They heard. They understood. But they did not comprehend. Puzzled looks crossed their faces. Mr. Y. sat in the back of the room, arms folded, with a this-is-ridiculous look on his face.

I handed the students a sheet of paper with 23 blocks and asked them to create their ideal schedule for studying English. I organized them into groups of four or five students and asked them to agree on one schedule, keeping in mind our class goal: "To inquire about things that are meaningful to us. To gain knowledge about ourselves and others through reading, writing, listening, and speaking in English."

The younger students quickly got involved, which helped to draw in some of the hard-core veterans. Mr. Y. sat on the periphery of one group and sulked. Each group then made its proposal, and through class discussion, brainstorming, and compromising, the following schedule evolved:

The class could not decide on what to do during one of the periods (each period was 90 min-

	Period 1	Period 2	Period 3	Period 4
Day 1	Introduction	Schedule planning	Discussion	Group project
Day 2	Lecture	Discussion	Games	Video pt. 1
Day 3	Lecture	"60 Minutes"	Discussion	Video pt. 2
Day 4	Lecture	Debate	Games	Video pt. 3
Day 5	Open	Individual project	Ind. proj.	Video pt. 4
Day 6	Discussion	Test	Beer party	

utes) and so they left it as an open class. This allowed students time to study English as they felt best. Some students used this time to read; others chose to listen to tapes in the carrels on the floor above us.

Students had five responsibilities for the class:
1. To participate;
2. To do some kind of reading during the week;
3. To keep a journal;
4. To listen actively; and
5. To make a 10- to 15-minute presentation to the class.

It was important that students engage in reading, writing, speaking, and listening during the week we were together. But, it was also important that their language experiences in school be such that they could use the experiences outside school. In fact, on Day 6, we discussed how one could improve one's English without a teacher present.

The activities that took place over the course of the week can be divided into four groups: discussions, videos, lectures, and projects.

Discussions

Many of the students mentioned that they hoped to learn new teaching techniques from fellow classmates. The free discussion periods were very popular and dynamic. With the exception of the discussion scheduled for Day 6, group members decided on the topics to discuss such as illiteracy in America, their individual teaching situations, students, and language-learning techniques.

Videos

We watched two different videos: a news video, "60 Minutes," and a popular movie, *Kramer vs. Kramer*. After viewing the three stories on the "60 Minutes" video, students formed groups and talked about the story they found most interesting. I noted in my journal that the students were now using English as a tool for learning other things.

During the last period of every day, we viewed a 20-minute segment from *Kramer vs. Kramer*. Students discussed each segment and then wrote their thoughts and impressions in their journals. The movie script was provided to help them understand the dialogue. When they devised the schedule for the week, students felt that this activity would be less stressful and a good way to end the day.

Lectures

Most of the students belonged to one or more professional language-teaching organizations in Japan and attended the annual conferences.

Although they wanted to take an active role at these conferences, they lacked the confidence to question presenters in English. By simulating a professional lecture in a nonthreatening environment, they hoped to gain confidence in using English at these meetings. During the week, I gave lectures on topics that I was researching at the time. After the lectures, students asked questions that were helpful to me and improved my presentation.

Projects

We had group and individual projects. On the first day of the class, students viewed American television commercials. After discussing the differences they saw in American and Japanese commercials, students formed groups and wrote a script for one of the commercials. Then the groups acted out the commercial before the rest of the class.

Another group activity was the debate that took place on the fourth day. The topics for the debate were chosen by the students. After brainstorming a wide array of topics, students voted to debate "divorce" and "exam English." Since I was not familiar with the proceedings of a debate, one of the students, who had been on a debate team in college, organized our debate and helped to make it a smashing success, one of the highlights of the week.

To fulfill the fifth responsibility, students had to give an individual presentation in front of the class. Students were free to talk about anything

I Used to Be...But Now I...

I used to think teaching meant telling,
But now I know it means enabling.

—Pat Pollock

writers

From the Front of the Class
by Eric Chock

And you, silly fool,
do you realize
you're standing there
with your hands folded,
sneaking a prayer at them
every once in a while
begging for
I don't know whose sake
they'll write a poem
from the heart
of a good local kid
everyone would want
to claim as one
of their own?
Do you really think
they see the prayer
in your eyes
everytime you smile
into theirs, checking
to make sure
they got good
souls in there?
Is the gospel beginning
to come through?
All it needs now
is to be said
as clear
as a clear Hawaiian
day can be.
And then, I think,
everyone who looks
will see
who we all are!

➡ See: small kid time hawaii, p. 157.

From *small kid time hawaii*, ed. Eric Chock (Honolulu: Bamboo Ridge Press, 1981, 1989).

that they were interested in and present it to the class in any way they wished. Some students chose to make a speech, while others demonstrated something. Many students could not finish in the time allotted and had to be stopped.

I kept an eye on Mr. Y. as the week progressed, and noticed a change in his attitude. He had slowly moved to the front of the class and was actively participating. He was even smiling on occasion. I noticed a similar change in the students who had grumbled about having to make the schedule. I did not realize why this change had occurred until I read the students' self-evaluations. Perhaps it is best summarized by the student who wrote: "We [the students] thought that it [creating the schedule] was just an activity and that after it was over, you would begin to teach us English. When this didn't happen, we realized that this was our responsibility."

➡ See: Caprio, p. 94; Hoyt, p. 214; Krashen, p. 86.

Mark Caprio is a professor at Nanzan University, Nagoya, Japan.

The Funny Side
The Ultimate Authority

A second-grade girl in a whole language classroom in Ottawa wrote a sign in invented spelling: "Do Not Move This Chair." Before taping it to the chair, she signed the note "God." Her teacher couldn't resist asking, "Why did you sign it that way?"

"Because if I signed my own name no one would pay attention."

—As told to LBB by YMG

Teachers as Initiators

Great Teachers:
David Bloome
by Toby Kahn Curry

➜ See: Bloome, pp. 229, 359; Bloome and Solsken, p. 82; Curry, pp. 251, 314, 352; Writing: Teachers and Children at Work, p. 131.

Toby Kahn Curry is a teacher at Dewey Center for Urban Education, Detroit, MI.

Five years ago, when I first welcomed David into my classroom, he said he wanted to see how the kids at our school learn. He made it clear to me that he was there as an observer, a researcher, and a learner, and *not* as an evaluator. Sensitive to my fears and trepidations, since I viewed myself as the bottom rung in a huge bureaucratic hierarchy (just above the kids), David tread lightly into my classroom, his notebook in hand.

Soon the notebook was accompanied by a tape recorder as David began making audio tapes of our classroom lessons, discussions, and small group conversations that took place daily.

Before I knew it, video cameras were perched in two corners of our room. David has taped and saved for posterity some of my worst and best days in my classroom.

During the second year of our relationship, David gave me a copy of Don Graves's book *Writing: Teachers and Children at Work,* and once again he was part of my classroom: observing and interviewing my kids and steadily sharing with me what was going on beneath the surface. It was then that David became a participant in *my* learning, subtly teaching me how to step back and take a look at what my students were doing. He helped me recognize the conspiracy I was engaged in with my students by showing me how, unconsciously, we plotted to teach and learn around the mandated curriculum of skills, drills, and lower- and higher-order thinking skills.

Reflecting on that time, I'd like to believe that *I* was part of what Ken Goodman might call David's dual curriculum or agenda. On one level, David was there in our building to find out how kids from different cultural groups learn to read and write in an American school setting, and what relationship the kids' own cultural backgrounds had to their school learning. On *another* level, David was there to empower me with knowledge about my own classroom and the success of my own teaching. Through David's research with parents, I learned that some students had been enrolled at our school in fourth grade because the parents had heard about the teacher in seventh grade. Suddenly my rung on the bureaucratic ladder began to get higher, *not* with a pay raise, not with a promotion, but with the self-confidence and self-esteem that came from my collaborative relationship with David. Since then he has quietly and consistently functioned as a catalyst for my change and growth as a teacher.

Two years ago David involved me in yet another dimension of his work as a researcher. He suggested we pilot a writing program for my seventh-graders. From David's research in our school, we had come to understand that most of our kids couldn't take ownership of their writing. Our students could easily reproduce text, but often their writing had no voice. How were we to get reluctant writers to produce their *own* text when writing in the Social Studies content area? David suggested that we have the students examine and write about their own cultures and communities. His proposal sounded intriguing, but the thought of teaching writing still overwhelmed me. Like many teachers, I had never been instructed in how to teach writing. But David soon allayed my fears.

During the project, David suggested we switch roles. David planned and taught the lessons and I took the role of the teacher-researcher. So, for the first time since we'd worked together I was the one watching, listening, and taking notes in a notebook, while David planned the lessons, presented the material, and responded to the students' writing.

The writing research project was a huge success. David and I presented our findings at NCTE in 1988 and at IRA in 1989. For my 30 kids the writing project was of tremendous benefit. It taught them how to be researchers in their own communities, acknowledged the information they had about their own lives and the people around them, taught them how to conference with one another about their own writing, and helped them to discover their own writing voices. All of the kids were able to produce their own original text.

But the real success of our collaborative research project began after the project ended. The real success was the impact it had on me as a writing teacher. The following year I published two books with my students: *Murals,* a collection of 30 family histories, and *Imagination Is the Key,* a 60-page anthology of short stories. In the spring of 1989, my next class worked on completing their anthology titled *Kaleidoscope,* a mixed collection of fiction and nonfiction that is being published for us by a generous department of teacher-educators at the University of Michigan (professors that David had introduced me to before his move to Massachusetts).

David has done for me as a learner what I now try to do for my students: He has helped me understand the impact of the community outside the classroom and the community of the classroom itself. David has helped me to empower my kids to become the independent readers and writers I always wanted them to be, because he empowered me with the knowledge of how real learning evolves in the classroom. Through David's teaching I have come closer to being the teacher I've always wanted to be. He has taught me how to value myself as a reader and writer, and shown me the impact those values have on my students. David has helped me take research out of some lofty ivory tower and put it where it belongs: in my classroom with real kids and real teachers. More than anyone else, David has taught me to be a "kidwatcher." I haven't written or given a content-area test in my classroom in five years. I don't have to use tests to evaluate my kids' learning, because through David's teaching and research I have learned a hundred other ways to evaluate my teaching and my students' learning.

WELL-SAID

Teachers can have the satisfactions of both scientists and artists in their professional lives. They can have the scientific approach to teaching: careful observations of their children, which is gathering evidence; experimental attitude in planning programs for their children, which is testing their data; flexibility in changing plans according to their findings. Teachers can function as artists in building a curriculum. They can be creative, not slavishly bound to a pattern in thinking and planning for and with their children.
—Lucy Sprague Mitchell

➜ See: Goodman, p. 376.

Excerpted from *Our Children and Our Schools,* by Lucy Sprague Mitchell (New York: Simon & Schuster, 1950).

Resource: Publisher

Zephyr Press
3865 E. 34th St. #101
P.O. Box 13448-A,
Dept. 60
Tucson, AZ 85732-3448
1-602-745-9199

Zephyr is a wind that blows from the west. It's also the name of an educational publishing company that features a wide variety of materials from the innovative, holistic, hands-on side of education. Browsing through their lively catalog is like having Mary Poppins blow into your house—their materials offer the same excitement and anything-is-possible optimism that Mary offered Jane and Michael. Zephyr Press also publishes a biannual newsletter, *Reaching Their Highest Potential,* on issues at the forefront of education. Joel Brown reviews some of the Zephyr Press publications below.
LBB

Picture This: Teaching Reading Through Visualization

Laura Rose
1988; 176 pp.; $17.95
Tucson, AZ: Zephyr Press

A book that will stimulate imagination in both teachers and students. It's appropriate for all classrooms, but especially helpful for kids who have the notion they cannot read and who experience anxiety in the process.

Inventors: A Source Guide for Self-Directed Units

Sally J. Patton and Margaret Maletis
1989; 72 pp.; $12.95
Tucson, AZ: Zephyr Press

Zephyr Press has a number of these self-guided units that do an amazing job of synthesizing information about various topics for teachers and kids. I think they could prove to be a real time saver!

Smart Art: Learning to Classify and Critique Art

Patricia Hollingsworth and Stephen F. Hollingsworth
1989; 112 pp.; $12.95
Tucson, AZ: Zephyr Press

A book of fun and creative ways to look at and explore art; it would add nicely to a learning center in the Art Corner.
Joel Brown

Becoming Literate

by Mark Brennan and Brian

Never Let a Chance Go By

Talking, responding, recording, and reviewing are all parts of the process of writing. Many people write just *anything* but want to write *something*. Finding out how to do this is a learning experience. This publication outlines Brian's learning. He could be a primary school child, a secondary student, or an adult client. He is in fact a prisoner, controlled by constraints of time, space, relationships, and resources. In all situations, but especially this, you never let a chance go by.

Brian is in prison. He is 25 and has been in institutions since he was 14. He has some suspicions that writing and reading are a kind of release from his depressing and violent surroundings. He says, "When you're reading you're learning, as well as imagining." And of writing poetry he says, "It's an achievement when you get something down that upsets you. . . . you write about things that worry you. When I write poetry I put it all down in my own words; words that I understand; words that other people might just skip over."

Brian can write and read. Because he is in prison he needs more than ever to express himself clearly—to himself as well as others. He feels disabled and would like to "write better descriptions." The time to prepare was nil. He could be transferred anytime. His request was urgent and so the time was now. As I had an hour before the gates were closed, I suggested we start immediately.

I asked Brian to think of a place that meant something special to him, and to write it down. Then I asked him to write some words, straight off the top of his head, that he associated with the place. He wrote the first couple and then started to gaze and think. I suggested that if we were going to get going then we'd better get a move on. And the best way to do this was just to grab what was passing through his mind—put it down—and worry about what to do with it later. He complied—a little disbelievingly.

He had said he wanted to write "better descriptions" and "things that mean more to myself." As we had to start somewhere, we started with five minutes of *forced writing*—stimulated by his word association. I stressed that he should write and not stop writing. That he should let in whatever thoughts arose and get them down by *writing*—and NOT *thinking about what he was going to write*. No one need see it. It was for himself. Anyway we were looking for *something new*, which meant wandering off the beaten track.

Brian was convinced by this kind of explanation and encouragement, so he started in on the journey, which began with his need and finished with his satisfaction.

At the start we decided to find a way together to do what he wanted. He would write and I would respond for as long as either of us thought it worth persisting. He was preoccupied with his parole and release by the third session and that is where we finished together. I am very glad not to have let the chance go by.

(Session 1)
Learmonth
Home, Love, Family, Friends

Being brought up in a country town, I was unaware of what the world was like outside it. We were a very close family especially so when I was young. We lived less than 200 yards from a faily large lake, and on hot nights we all use to go down to our usuall swiminspot for a swim. Dad use to come, but he very rarely went in the water if he did, it was only up to his knees. For such a big man, I thought it was funny that he was afraid of water. Or thats the way it appeared to me. My brothers are all older than me, and they were out of primary school, before I started. So I only had my big sister to help me out of any trouble I would get into. Most of the time I was in the trouble in the first place because of her! She was temramental when she was yougk, as most of the boys would tell you.

We've got something on paper that he can see. "Is that alright?" he said.

I said, "Have you said what you want?"

"Sort of."

(I think he was waiting for me to mark his work and do corrections.)

He was also waiting to see whether I'd stick to my word to help him with his writing, or simply take it over and get him to write—like I thought he should.

"Is there anything that you're either pleased or not pleased with?"

"I could have said more about the family—how everyone was related and so on."

"Okay. Is there anything that you're a little bit surprised about—something you haven't seen in 'quite that way' before?"

"Well yeah. The bit about my father being afraid of the water."

"Well we can talk about it but if it's something new—and that's what we're looking for—why don't you carry on and write about it. And see what else comes up."

"Okay."

Large as my father is I felt, at this moment, much biger. I felt as though this idole of a man who I hero worship for as long as I could remember, was just as human as I was. He to expirinces fear I'd never seen in him before that, to me, seemed as though it had no right being their.

Fear was for week people I thought, not for brave people like my father. Maybe theirs something about the water that I should be afraid of. Were my parents hiding some dark secret about water that they never disclosed to me. But my mother wasn't afraid and my big brother went out much further than I even could. So it must be that dad was scared. All at once is seemed funny to me. I felt glad that I had conquered something my father couldn't. So I'm not so small after all, and I'm not such a baby. My father had shown me that even the strongest men have fears. And its not a falt, to be afraid.

At the end of this piece he, without any prompting, started to tell how his first line meant most and could he go on and do another piece using this as the take-off.

"Let's go" I said, as I also continued my writing in a journal I was keeping at the time.

When he finished this piece our hour was up.

He said, "I didn't know those things were in my head."

"Do you want to go again in a couple of days?"

"Sure—if you're game."

(Session 2)

By the time we worked together again a format and technique had been established. We'd have a bit of a chat and get right down to work. The content of the "lesson" wasn't in my talk or in our conversation but in his head. We started as before. He chose "Lenny" as his important person and "Friend, Laughter, Close, Confide, Trust" as the associated words.

Then he wrote . . .

The first time I met Lenny was in prison. We were both undergoing a sentence.

I first noticed him in the exercise yard in "B" Division. He sat alone in a distant corner of the rough ashfelt yard. As I was walking back and forth across the yard, as I often did, to help me to think, Lenny got up and started racing beside me. He is roughly my height around 5-8.

And he picked a line and wrote more.

He sat alone in a distant corner of the rough ashfelt yard. Stareing across the yard, with eyes that saw nothing except his iner thoughts. I could understand how he must feel at that moment. For I had often sat alone in the same yard, just as he did now. Deep in thought, unaware of what was happening around him. Lost within his mind, asking question after question and each question being answered with confusion. Although I'd never met him, at the moment I felt very close to him. I wanted to go and sit by him, and tell him that what he was feeling, as I could understand that. I had been through the same experience, and felt as alone and confused as he was.

And . . .

I had often sat alone in the same yard, gazeing up at the high, rough blue stone wall. Trying to rid my mind of all the confusion, all the problems, that had engulfed my mind. I wanted to run at the wall with all the speed and anger I had in my body, and try one last attempt at freedom. But I new it to be a futile attempt. I had resigned to the fact that I was in prison, now the hardest part seemed to be controlling my emotions.

A hundred thoughts would race through my mind. All at once. Creating furies of emotions that I couldn't deal with. Lost within in myself, I was fighting a battle. My emotions were like soldiers of war, that I had to restrain. Fighting them back, left me excusted, I felt drained, the energy witherd from my body.

Brian was tired and pleased and happy. We made arrangements for our next session and left it there for the day.

(Session 3)
Ballarat School—Growing up, Friends, Learning

He just wrote, starting with the warm-up we knew worked. And I carried on with my own writing on the other side of the desk. Close enough to respond and occupied enough not to be just "checking" or "waiting."

The first time I saw Ballarat was out a window of my parents car. We had lived in the country for so long as I could remember, and Ballarat was home to me. As we travelled along the smooth flowing traffic lanes, I marvelled at the amount of buildings. They seem to go on forever, house after house, they all looked the same to me.

The thought of living in Ballarat suddenly frightened me. How could anyone remember all those streets, they were like a maze, twisting and turning, never seeming to go anywhere, just street after street.

What would happen if I was to get lost, how would I get home. I'd be roming around those strange roads for ever. At first the thought of moveing to Ballarat had thrilled me. The idea of living in a different house promised adventure. Now the idea wasn't so exciting. In fact, I was beginning to wish we had never left our old house. With its familiar rooms, and garden. Its beautiful flower beds that I had watched Mum create into splender with her own hand. Flowers which she was so proud of. Now all of this is gone forever.

He didn't think that sounded quite right—so he gave it another go.

. . . flower beds that I had watched my mother create into splender with her own hands, now were nothing but chared remains.

Everything seemed forein to me, this useless pile of powdered ash couldn't be my parents home. My eyes wondered over the ashes, to the place that the lounge room once was. I could almost hear the laughter that we had once shared. I could hear my fathers deep kind voice floating up to me. Telling me how I was too young to leave home, "Wait", he had said, "Wait until you've finished school, then you will be old enough to make decisions". If only I had listened I might have been here when the fire started. I might have been able to stop it, or at least been able to die with them.

At the end of this our third hour, seven days from our first, Brian, somewhat exhausted, said, "I think I'd like to write on my own now."

"Mm."

"There's a thread running through all the stuff I've got here. I'd like to put them all together. I'd like to do that before I write any new stuff."

That sounded like a fair idea to me and I told him so. I also told him I'd be available if he wanted us to do any more work together.

He said thanks but that he just wanted to get on with his larger piece and added "Some bits still don't sound like me—but I know the ones that do now."

→ See: The Centre for Teaching and Research in Literacy, p. 214; Life in Prison, p. 185.

Adapted from *Never Let a Chance Go By,* The Centre for Teaching and Research in Literacy, Charles Sturt University—Riverina.

Mark Brennan is the director of The Centre for Teaching and Research in Literacy, Charles Sturt University—Riverina, Wagga Wagga, New South Wales, Australia.

Resource: Publisher

Creative Publications

Order Dept.
5040 W. 111th St.
Oak Lawn, IL 60453
1-800-624-0822

Teacher room copies of the Creative Publications catalog generally look pretty ragged and worn, a clear indication of the excellent materials this company offers. Long appreciated for their outstanding hands-on materials that promote problem-solving, Creative Publications is now producing thematic units built around literature that encourage student involvement through discussions, dramatic play, flannel board stories, puppetry, cooking, drawing, roller movies, story-writing, and singing.

LBB

YOUNG ARTISTS

—Brenda McConathy, 13, Vale, OR
(from *Treasures 2,* see p. 162)

Great Teachers:
Toby Kahn Curry
by David Bloome

Tom doesn't look like the other children in his class. His father is black, raised in Appalachia. His mother was born in the Philippines but raised in Hawaii. On Tom's face you can see the beauty of both his parents' heritages, and in his actions you can see both his parents' heritages. When you talk with Tom you can hear his parents' love of family and learning. But because Tom did not look like anyone else—neither black, white nor Hispanic—he had a hard time with his peers in elementary school. To his parents, his teachers seemed preoccupied with control and management. Tom became quiet and learned little in school.

I got to know Tom and his family because I had been interviewing children and their families from Burton International School as part of a study on cultural diversity and reading and writing development. Burton International School is a K–8 Detroit Public School that serves a local community and students throughout Detroit. I had asked Tom's mother why they transferred Tom to Burton International School. She told me about the difficulties that Tom had in elementary school and that they had no faith that junior high school would be better. Indeed, they feared that things would get worse. They had heard that there was a good seventh-grade teacher at Burton and decided to transfer Tom while he was still in elementary school.

It was after talking with Tom's parents that I began to understand the importance of a good teacher. We think of teachers as facilitating learning, helping children become readers and writers. We think of teachers in the school context. But here was a teacher who had a reputation throughout many different and distant parts of the city. Not only did I hear about Toby Curry from Tom's parents but also from other parents. Only a few of them knew her name. When I asked them what they had heard about why the teacher was so good, some parents told me that she got students to like school. So often, I was told, no one cares. Children get lost.

Toby was extremely surprised when I told her about the interviews. She hadn't seen herself as a teacher deserving such a reputation. She had doubts about her own teaching, about whether she was really helping students learn and grow. She wanted to try new things. She wanted her students to be well prepared for high school, whether they chose an academically competitive high school, a comprehensive high school, or a vocational school. But she wanted more. She wanted her class and what students did in her class to matter, to have meaning for the students. She demanded it of herself and of her students.

Toby teaches a combination social studies and English seventh grade. When you walk into Toby's classroom you immediately pass by the student mailboxes. Students leave notes to each other and for Toby. Later, as I became a regular member of the class, I had a box too. In the corner is a computer where students communicate with other schools, playing a simulation game of Middle East conflict. They are the only junior high class playing against high school classes all over North America. In the center of the classroom is a table called the writing center with writing supplies, mostly paper. The table serves primarily as a place for students to get away from each other. The students sit in groups. If they need quiet, they can move to the writing table. Frequently, there are so many books, folders, and other materials on the table, that students can easily hide. The rest of the room is crowded with desks and chairs; 35 students, and they usually all come.

I spent three years studying the students in Toby's classes, so I know Toby mostly through her students. I've seen Toby engage students in brilliant lessons on the revolutionary war, geography, and mythology. I've seen students argue with each other about whether Israel should attack Syria or make a deal with the United States. I've also seen lessons bomb and students at their silliest. I've seen traditional-looking lessons and innovative ones, teacher-directed instruction and indirect instruction. I've seen some students get interested in a topic and spend nearly every waking moment learning about the topic while other students resisted. But what characterizes Toby's class is her demand that you care about what you do. If you want to resist, that's okay, but you have to be serious about it and provide alternatives. You have to seriously engage Toby in your resistance. If what happens in class excites you, fine, but you still have to be serious about it and know why what you are doing is important. If you read a good book you are expected to have an opinion and share it because what you think matters. If you write an essay or a story, what you write should matter to you.

In many ways Toby's classrooms are a conspiracy between her and her students. In a school district emphasizing isolated skills and competencies, test scores, and standardized curricula, there is little room for demanding importance. I remember one incident when the district monitor was coming to check whether students had been using the seventh-grade basal reader and mastering the designated competencies. Neither Toby nor her students had any time for such nonsense. They were busy reading myths and making up myths of their own. So Toby passed out the reading skills competency checklist to her students and told them to check off the ones they were able to do, including all those that had been checked off in previous years. For Toby, schooling was not going to get in the way of learning, and it was not going to get in the way of the important work they were doing.

Tom is now in high school and doing well, the last I heard. In Toby's class he was able to use his family heritage as a strength, as a foundation for growth. His parents told me that he talked with them about what he wrote and about what he was studying. He complained to them about all the work that Mrs. Curry gave him, but I don't think his parents sympathized. He also told them about the social doings, friends and girls, and sports.

I know Toby often wondered how Tom was doing since he tended to be quiet in school. There were times when Tom would sit and think while others were busy writing or getting books or reading. I don't know whether that ever bothered Toby for she let him be at such times, respecting how he needed to approach what he was doing. After all, when you are doing something important you approach it with care and respect, whether you're the student or the teacher.

→ See: Bloome, pp. 82, 359; Curry, p. 227.

David Bloome is an associate professor in the School of Education, University of Massachusetts, Amherst, MA.

Questioning Effective Teaching

As I See It:
Kenneth S. Goodman

Is Whole Language Compatible with Narrow Models of Effective Teaching?

Many administrators have been impressed recently with staff development programs that promise to make effective teachers out of all teachers by presenting them with a single teaching model and requiring them to follow it. In this staff development, teachers are rehearsed in a series of steps to follow in each act of teaching. They are even provided with gestures to use to get and keep the attention of learners. One such model is Madeline Hunter's EEEI program. Some school districts have spent many thousands of dollars "training" their entire professional staff in this model.

But a remarkable thing is happening in school districts all over North America. Many whole language teachers are telling their administrators that these narrow views of teaching are incompatible with their professional teaching criteria. That shocks a lot of the administrators: first because they are not used to thinking of teachers as having professional belief systems, and second because they aren't used to teachers asserting their professional right to decide how they will teach. When they recover from their shock, they may respond by saying, "It's just a way to be sure you're an effective teacher. You can do Madeline Hunter and whole language, too." "No, we can't!" say these teachers. "That's too narrow a view of teaching for whole language."

The problem is that the administrators are still following the idea that teachers are basically incapable of conducting themselves as professionals and that the way to assure effective teaching is to tightly control the teachers. We tried that through explicit, controlling teacher's manuals and even "teacher-proof materials." Now we're trying to control teachers by putting them into a narrow mold and requiring them to follow explicit steps and use explicit gestures in every act of teaching.

These whole language teachers understand some basic facts: If you can force teachers to do it, it isn't whole language. If it gets teachers to all look and act and sound the same, it isn't whole language. Whole language requires a commitment based on understanding and belief from each teacher. Whole language teachers are professionals who make their own professional decisions. They are the ones who implement curriculum and turn it into learning experiences for their pupils. Whole language is the belief system that provides the criteria for making their decisions and that they draw on in their interactions with their pupils. It's the knowledge base that they use in getting to know their pupils, planning authentic experiences for them, and mediating their learning.

Whole language forms the basis for teachers taking power in their own classrooms and in turn empowering their pupils. A teacher can't take power while surrendering to the control of the narrow "effective teaching" model. New roles for teachers are emerging in whole language classrooms as they put aside mandated texts, tests, and skill sequences and reject the subservient roles of the past.

Any approach to effective teaching that can be delineated as a series of invariant steps that must always be included by *every* teacher in *every* act of teaching is incompatible with whole language. Any model of teaching that eliminates, prohibits, or cannot accommodate any of the teacher roles that are emerging in whole language classrooms is not acceptable to whole language teachers. Effective teaching is far more than a series of overt behaviors that can be easily observed in any lesson and checked off by an occasional evaluator.

In whole language classrooms the relationships between teachers and learners are complex and subtle. They are built carefully, over time. They depend on achieving a level of trust, understanding, and mutual respect between teachers and pupils.

The teacher in the whole language classroom may occasionally be seen in front of the class, but more often the teacher is somewhere in the room observing, mediating, inquiring, initiating, liberating, supporting, and always transacting with the pupils.

The teacher may be sitting in on a group discussion of a novel the members of the group are all reading. Or the teacher may be moving from group to group as pupils carry on a research study as part of a science unit. Here the teacher is reading a story to a group or to the class; there the teacher is crouched next to two pupils as they work through an arithmetic problem together; now the teacher is standing aside writing anecdotal notes while observing pupils; later the teacher is sitting in the midst of the pupils while they conduct a class meeting or share their writing or reading. Or the teacher may not be in the room at all, leaving for a few minutes to chat with a group in the hall while the class goes right on busily and productively.

In every situation, effective teaching is happening. In every instant the teacher is supporting learning and acting like a professional. Effective teaching is also happening when the teacher is rounding up resources for a unit, reading pupils' response logs, visiting a pupil's home, or meeting with other teachers in a support group.

If all this teaching can't be evaluated on a checklist based on a narrow model of teaching, then it's the model that's at fault and not whole language teaching. What makes this effective teaching is much more than a memorized sequence of behaviors, a collection of attention-getting devices, a few ways of manipulating kids and focusing their attention, or some games to keep pupils engaged in arbitrary and irrelevant school tasks. It's effective teaching because the teacher is an informed professional who demonstrates that in creative and inspiring teaching.

Administrators who have had high hopes for teaching their teachers a narrow way of acting the role of teacher must ask themselves who they really want in their classrooms working with their pupils: the teachers whose behavior always fits the checklist; or the dynamic, informed, and confident professionals who always seem to be inventing new ways to get kids involved and excited about learning.

→ See: Freeman, p. 212; Goodman, p. 207; Newman, p. 211; Shor, p. 222.

Book Note

Language, the Learner and the School, 4th ed.

Douglas Barnes, James Britton, and Mike Torbe
1989; 166 pp.; $14
Portsmouth, NH: Boynton/Cook

We have the old classics, the teachings of John Dewey and Lev Vygotsky; we also have the new classics, one of which is *Language, the Learner and the School.*

LBB

66 We teach and teach and they learn and learn: if they didn't, we wouldn't. But of course the relation between their learning and our teaching isn't by any means a constant one. From any given bit of teaching some learn more than others: we teach some lessons when everybody seems to learn something, and other lessons when nobody seems to learn anything—at all events, not anything of what we are 'teaching.' As the syllabus grows longer we teach more—but do they learn more? And if we get three lessons a week when we ought to have five, presumably we teach more to the minute than we would otherwise: but again, do they learn any quicker? How *do* we judge how much is being learnt, in any case? 99 (p. 91)

66 The commonest theory of learning is modeled on the way a book works: it is about uniformity, continuity and lineality, to use McLuhan's formulation. Learning is seen as a logical and rational process, because 'rational' has for a long time also meant uniform, continuous and sequential. But 'logic,' as Susanne Langer points out, is not a mode of thinking but a technique for evaluation or checking a thought. Understanding, which ought to be the purpose and the outcome of the educational process, entails simultaneity, a grasp of a field of knowledge and a perception of the interconnections, and is likely to be reached not by following someone else's logical presentation but by creating one's own pathways. A part of the politics of language across the curriculum was an assertion of the right of an individual to learning. 99 (p. 136)

I Used to Be...But Now I...

I used to think I had to stand up in front of the class and lecture to my students for the whole hour in order to be a good teacher, But now I step back from center stage and let them actively grow and learn under my more invisible facilitating.

—Susana de la Peña

YOUNG ARTISTS

David Montgomery, age 5, wrote his name on the computer, Palo Alto, CA

Viewpoint: Katharine Davies Samway

A Response to the Effective Teaching Movement

One day a few years ago I saw examples of two opposing trends in education, one focusing on mechanistic effective teaching (Hunter 1969, 1982) and the other emphasizing a meaning-based process approach to learning and teaching (Goodman 1986; Graves 1983; Calkins 1986). Each Monday I visited two classrooms. In the mornings I volunteered in Ms. Armstrong's suburban kindergarten class, helping the children with their writing. In the afternoons I gathered research data in Ms. Olson's inner-city elementary ESOL (English to Speakers of Other Languages) classes. I would like to share my impressions.

Ms. Armstrong

At 8:50 A.M., while Ms. Armstrong was checking attendance, a visitor quietly entered the classroom, sat down, and took out a pad and pen. For 20 minutes or so she watched the activity that the teacher was leading and then left as inconspicuously as she had entered. Later, Ms. Armstrong remarked that the visitor was a teacher from another building, a member of her effective teacher cohort group. She had been recording the incidence of two teacher behaviors: (1) the frequency with which Ms. Armstrong physically approached individual children, and (2) the frequency with which she acknowledged children's responses to her requests and questions.

All the children sat in a circle on the area rug and manipulated colored blocks according to Ms. Armstrong's directions (e.g., "Put one blue block to the right of the yellow blocks"). Her singsong voice dominated the activity. The children were attentive and engaged. The majority of them had no apparent difficulty though they were confused by the mirror image of their teacher as she demonstrated left and right. They rarely spoke.

Ms. Armstrong conscientiously responded to the children by name and moved closer to them when reinforcing or clarifying particular concepts. She should have been judged as quite effective by her visitor. She was an approachable, personable, caring teacher who handled a subskills, teacher-oriented curriculum well. She did not have discipline problems, and the class operated with a pleasant hum as children moved from one activity to another.

Each day children completed several ditto sheets that gave them plenty of practice in cutting and pasting, matching, coloring in, and tracing letters. Ms. Armstrong read stories to them, but she did not make connections to the children's own rapidly growing capacities as users and consumers of written language.

Except for Monday mornings when I was working with them, the children were not expected to write for authentic purposes. When I first visited the classroom the only pencils in the room were tied together, unsharpened, and stored in Ms. Armstrong's desk, "until they are ready for them." The class spent the whole year tracing and printing letters of the alphabet and practicing writing their names, but they rarely wrote stories or letters or reports, the kinds of challenging and authentic writing activities that researchers have documented (and parents have noticed) that children are capable of and eager to do (Bissex 1980; Harste, Woodward, and Burke 1984). Some of Ms. Armstrong's kinder-

gartners would say to me, "I don't know how to read or write," convinced already that they could not do what they almost certainly did freely before coming to school.

Ms. Olson

At lunchtime I drove across town to another classroom in another district that did not have an effective teaching program. As I entered this ESOL class I noticed that the kindergarten children were huddled in a tight semicircle around their teacher, Ms. Olson. Their bodies and faces reflected intense involvement as they discussed a story she had read them. It was filled with new concepts and exquisite, but comprehensible, language—not usual fare in programs for nonnative English-speaking youngsters. At the conclusion of the storytelling and discussion the children scattered to draw pictures and write stories to accompany them. Despite their nonnative English speaking status, these kindergartners were challenged by an authentic, student-centered activity. They were not limited by a skills-based curriculum.

In the large group activity Ms. Olson did not move from her seat at the entrance to the semicircle of chairs, except to bring over materials. Neither did she respond in any consistent way to the children's comments or answers to her questions. If the teacher effectiveness profile had been applied to Ms. Olson, she would not have done well. But it appeared to me that, unlike Ms. Armstrong's class, this one was geared to the development of each child's language and intellect. This became even more evident when Ms. Olson's overage fifth- and sixth-grade students came to class after the kindergartners had left. The older youngsters had not lost the enthusiasm for learning that so many children lose as they progress through the grades. They became immersed in their work with the same enthusiasm and confidence as the kindergartners; they too were being challenged, and the classroom had a sense that the children would actually enjoy learning.

Ms. Olson would probably be a better teacher if she were better organized, if her directions were clearer, if she would respond to the children more consistently, and if she would move around the classroom making sure that she attended to all the children. In contrast with Ms. Armstrong, a ten-year veteran, Ms. Olson was relatively inexperienced. However, she had a clearly defined view of her role in children's learning, one that was influenced by an understanding of what it means to be a reader and writer, rather than by lists of decontextualized skills that had been written by unknown school and textbook committees.

The Dilemma

I am sure that proximity and response to students are both important. However, I was dismayed by the importance that Ms. Armstrong's district attached to them. Considerable time and money had been devoted to isolating and improving quantifiable behaviors, but virtually no emphasis had been placed on discussing issues of content or methodology. I was not convinced that the effective teaching training would make a substantial difference to her teaching if it failed to encourage her to critically

analyze her curriculum, and her role and the role of her students in the learning process.

We must not dismember the practical *how to's* from the *why* and *what* of teaching. Effective teaching models such as Hunter's offer the prospect of a quick, efficient, and mechanical method of improving surface features, and districts have responded with alacrity, but not with vision.

Successful teaching is much more complicated than replicating quantifiable teacher and student behaviors. Teachers and administrators must ask themselves and others, "What are my goals?" "Why am I doing this?" "How will it develop students' potential to think critically in academic and real life situations?" If we ignore the content, we must ask the price that we are paying for focusing on the strategies.

➔ See: Goodman, p. 274; Krause, p. 396; Stevenson, p. 271; Weaver, p. 382.

References

Bissex, G. 1980. *GNYS AT WRK: A child learns to read and write.* Cambridge: Harvard University Press.

Calkins, L. M. 1986. *The art of teaching writing.* Portsmouth, NH: Heinemann.

Goodman, K. 1986. *What's whole in whole language?* Portsmouth, NH: Heinemann.

Graves, D. H. 1983. *Writing: Teachers and children at work.* Portsmouth, NH: Heinemann.

Harste, J., V. A. Woodward, and C. L. Burke. 1984. *Language stories and literacy lessons.* Portsmouth, NH: Heinemann.

Hunter, M. 1969. *Teach more-faster!* El Segundo, CA: TIP Publications.

————. 1982. *Mastery teaching: Increasing instructional effectiveness in secondary schools, colleges and universities.* El Segundo, CA: TIP Publications.

Katharine Davies Samway is a teacher-educator with ARC Associates, Oakland, California, and specializes in the language and literacy development of nonnative English speakers. Together with teachers, she is investigating the role of response in child-adult literacy correspondence. She has published articles and is editing a book on innovative literacy practices for nonnative speakers of English.

It Shouldn't Happen to Kids

Essential Elements and Whole Language

With the wide adoption of an approach to lesson planning named after a certain lady from California, teaching in many school districts has been reduced to a seven-step (or five- or four-step depending on the administrators' short-term memory abilities) procedure for all-purpose "instruction" in every area from prekindergarten music to advanced placement physics. As one result several whole language teachers have reported incidents similar to this one:

> It was writing workshop time in my class; some students were also reading. Linda had just finished the first draft of her piece about her grandmother, and we were having a conference. Billy and Samuel were taking turns reading to one another from the class book on spiders that we had made last month. Others, alone mostly but talking with partners from time to time, were at various stages of work on their current efforts. Three were busy at the bookmaking table.
>
> Everyone seemed productively occupied, and I was feeling pretty good about the scheduled evaluation visit. In came the principal, right on time with clipboard in hand. After glancing around the room, he backed out through the doorway, whispering across the room, "I'll come back later when you're teaching."

➔ See: Salzer, pp. 119, 409.

—Dick Salzer, professor, State University of New York at Buffalo

Classroom Environment: Literate and Content-Rich

 ## Viewpoint: Mike Torbe

Learning About Language: A Thoughtful Panic

Language Events

Watch Lisa. She is eight. She's writing a story, sitting at the table with five of her friends, who are also writing. While she writes, she twists a strand of her long fair hair around a finger of her left hand. She writes seven words, pauses; her friend asks her how to spell a word, she tells her. She writes three more words, then pauses for a long time, looking at nothing in particular. Then she starts again. Five more words. She leans back, chats to the girl on her left. When she returns to her work, she rereads what she has written. She carefully writes over the last two words and then writes another four words. During the 25 minutes we watch her, she writes 59 words, 30 of them in the last seven minutes. Her story fills three-quarters of the sheet of paper she was using.

Martin is seven. He too is writing, but he is stuck on the spelling of the word *how*. He says to himself, "How," then again, drawing it out, "H-ow-w." He frowns and says, "Ow, ow," then with exaggerated mouth movements, listening to the sounds, he says, "Ow-a-oo—aa-oo." His face lightens, and he writes down *au*, his spelling for *how: au*.

These three girls are older, about 13. They are using a book in a science lesson, trying to find the answer to a question on a worksheet.

Tracy opens the book she has brought back from the bookshelf and begins reading at page one. Sarah impatiently takes the book, turns to the contents page, and reads down the chapter headings. Not finding what she wants, she rereads the contents list. I point out that she can use the index. She turns to it, but instead of looking up *leg of housefly* under *F* for *fly*, she looks under *L* for *leg*. Eventually we discover that Tracy has brought back a book called *The Physiology of Plants*.

Michael is six and new to the school. It is a PE lesson. The teacher speaks to him, and the conversation goes like this:

Teacher: Have you got some gym shoes?
Michael: No.
Teacher: No *what*?
Michael: (remains silent)
Teacher: No *what*?
Michael: (remains silent, but goes red)
Teacher: "No, Miss Wilkinson." Don't you know that?
Michael: No.
Teacher: NO, WHAT?

Mrs. Jones sees three of her ten-year-old boys in the carpeted quiet area. They are grouped in the corner, with their backs to her. She frowns: They shouldn't be in there, for three reasons. First, they should be in the math area now; second, they're not supposed to go in there now because it's the infants' turn; and third, she suspects them of being up to no good. She opens her mouth to shout, but then walks across to tell them. As she gets there, Darren turns round, sees her, and says, "Miss! You tell him! I can't explain it."

"Tell him what?" she says, taken aback.

"About how a helicopter works, like you told us when he was away." She joins them and helps Paul to understand the principles she had explained to the class two weeks ago.

Craig has always had difficulty with reading. Now that he's nine, he and his teachers are worried about it. An advisory teacher works with him, and makes a tape of Craig and himself walking in some woods near the school. He extracts from the tape enough of Craig's words to produce a little book called "The Den." Craig is able

Mike Torbe has taught in schools and at a teacher-training college, and has worked as an English adviser and a general education adviser for Coventry Local Education Authority in the United Kingdom. For many years he was on the executive committee for the National Association for the Teaching of English, and was NATE's publications officer for five years. He has written extensively about language and learning in relation to learners of all ages, and has lectured and run workshops in Australia, Canada, Switzerland, the United States, and throughout the United Kingdom.

to read it easily. The advisory teacher and Craig's teacher meet Craig's mother: She tells them she reads to Craig every night and that Craig has a lot of books of his own. Later, the two teachers confess to each other that they both assumed that Craig had no experience of reading, and that the mother's information had surprised them.

William, who is nine, is alone in the stockroom with a tape recorder. His teacher is on a course at the Teachers' Centre, and has to have a tape of a child. She has chosen William, because he is inarticulate, and she suspects he has speech problems and may need therapy. She leaves him alone with the tape recorder and tells him to say anything he likes to the tape, and to come back when he's finished. She expects him to come back very quickly with a blank tape. When he returns, half an hour later, she finds that there is at least half of a C60 tape used. He explains that he couldn't think of what to say at first, but then decided to interview himself. She listens to the tape. In a feigned deep voice he asks himself questions, and in his ordinary voice answers them. He speaks fluently about his hobby, fishing, and explains to the "interviewer" how to catch his favorite fish.

Making Events Significant

There is nothing unusual about any of these experiences. Each one, or something like it, happens in classrooms everywhere, every day. The only unusual thing is to have them brought together like this, in a context that makes it clear that I, the writer, think they are significant.

Their significance lies in the way we might look at them, the meanings we derive from them, and the effect those observations have on our understanding. I want to look at them as language events, and to interpret them through what we know of language processes and their connections with learning. When we do, what is illuminated is not just those events but teaching and learning in general. That will take us on to the question—what do we need to know about language to be successful teachers?

From Lisa, we can learn something about the complexity of the process by which words make their way onto paper, and particularly how an eight-year-old copes. Like all writers, she has to find ways of starting the thoughts on their way—rereading what's there, the measured tracing over of words that all writers do when they plan what's coming next. We can see clearly the sporadic movement of the writing, the short burst, the rest, the longer burst, the thinking and planning time, and the final surge as the shape becomes clearer. None of this would be visible if we looked only at the final piece of writing, because the final piece of writing shows nothing of the processes that generated and sustained it.

Martin teaches us many things. He is uncannily accurate in his analysis of the diphthong: Indeed, the phonetic symbol for the sound he is trying to spell is /au/—exactly what he has written. What he doesn't know, and what he needs to be taught, is best expressed in the sentence: "Yes, that's the way we say it, but we spell it like this." That is, he has to learn the conventions by which sounds are presented in English orthography. He shows us how informative "errors" can be if they are seen not as mistakes but as determined attempts by the learner to solve problems. What he does also raises interesting and difficult questions about the relationship between phonics and learning to spell; the phonics he has been taught do not help him to grasp the notion of spelling convention.

We take so much for granted about reading; but our assumptions are shaken by Sarah and Tracy. Unless they have been taught it, few 13-year-olds (or indeed, much older people) will know how to search for information or use indexes. The girls use the index as though it were a dictionary, looking up *leg of housefly* under *L;* whereas we know that an index is organised conceptually, under the overall concept of fly, with its subsets *housefly* and *leg of housefly*.

The teacher who talks to Michael illustrates another way of taking things for granted. She assumes that Michael knows all the ground rules for behavior in the school, including linguistic behaviour, and that his omission of the courtesy address means he is deliberately testing the rules. She uses language herself as a form of social control. What she communicates, and what Michael will learn from the exchange, is that there are approved forms of behavior that are far more important than Michael's shoes, or whether he does PE or not. The most important element in the exchange becomes the establishment by one partner of dominance over the other.

Mrs. Jones could easily have made the same mistake, if she had acted on her first instinct and told the boys off. If she had, she would not have discovered that learning does not take place simultaneously with the first encounter with something; that if something is interesting, children will mull it over and talk about it, perhaps a long time later; and that explaining something to someone, as Darren tries to do, is a good way of finding out what you yourself do and don't understand. She has also learnt, on reflection, that it is best not to immediately interpret outward behavior as representing insolence or naughtiness, although that was her first reaction.

The question of assumptions, and of what people do as a result of them, is acutely present in Craig's story. So many cherished and comforting beliefs are destroyed by Craig and his mother. Craig, who "can't read," *can* read when the language structures are familiar and when he has himself constructed the text. The questions this raises about the reading materials he has been offered previously are obvious. Would he be a reader now if the language and structures of the reading programme in the school had been consistently closer to the rhythms of speech? Or was it the sustained contact with one adult who took an interest in him as a person that helped him most? Why did the professionals automatically assume that if a child cannot read, his parents don't read to him? More to the point, they are now faced with the uncomfortable suspicion that the source of Craig's problem is not Craig himself, or at home, but in the school, and in the materials and strategies the school uses to teach reading.

William epitomises all that we know and do not know about children and their language. We might know from all the work on the effects of context upon performance that what this teacher did would unlock William's locked-in words. But who would expect such an overperformance? We might predict he would do *something*, that he would see the tape recorder as representing an ever-patient, ever-attentive absent teacher; but would we be able to predict the startling and complex form he devises to cope with the situation? Above all, though, as Craig was a "failure" in reading, so William is a "failure" in talk. Both, when the context is supportive and relaxed, show they can achieve success. What was it, we must ask, that turned William, a fluent and inventive speaker, into someone labeled "inarticulate?" What were the contexts that made it hard, almost impossible, for him to speak?

Asking Questions

The glimpses of children seen engaged in the normal flux of classroom life sketch out some of the key questions about the nature of language and its relationship with teaching and learning. The questions have to do with the process of writing, and how writers plan, generate ideas, get started, and sustain their ideas. With the effects upon novice readers of the materials they read; and the importance of those materials being

(Continued on page 265)

Cornerstone:
Fred Gollasch & Chris Weckert

Quality Classrooms

The following are eight features of quality literacy classrooms. Each feature is based on a principle derived from the successful learning environments naturally provided in the home by parents as their young children learn to handle the complexities of oral language. This broadsheet can be used by teachers in a number of ways: as a checklist on the type of literacy environment they provide; as a basis for programming; or as a resource for ideas and activities. However you use it, remember, it is not meant to be prescriptive. It is not expected that you will incorporate all of these features in any one day, but rather that you will strive to understand the principles and how best you can apply them to facilitate your children's development.

From The Centre for Teaching & Research in Literacy, Charles Sturt University–Riverina, Wagga Wagga, New South Wales.

Principle	At Home	Quality Features (At School)	Notes for the Teacher (At School)
1 There is an immersion in language.	When young children are learning to talk they are surrounded by and immersed in oral language. They are exposed to millions of demonstrations of how human beings talk in many varied situations	**READ DAILY** • Silent, personal reading for enjoyment and information—the teacher too! • A variety of shared reading aloud by the teacher and children in the whole class or small groups. **WRITE DAILY** • In a variety of registers and genres for a variety of purposes and audiences—the teacher too! **CREATE A PRINT-FILLED ENVIRONMENT** • Saturate the classroom environment with functional print. • Ensure the children have ready access to a wide variety of written material.	1. Display meaningful signs, labels, directions, instructions, suggestions, message boards, children's drafts, and finished products. 2. Hold stocks of fiction, nonfiction, magazines, newspapers, atlases, directories, reports, poems, etc. 3. Share the joys and sorrows of your personal experiences with books—be honest! 4. Write in front of your children. Show them how you take risks, revise, and edit your writing. Let them see you reach for the dictionary to check spelling during proofreading. Share the agony and the joy of writing. Model writing in a variety of registers and genres. 5. Involve your children in making charts, labels, and signs. Encourage them to use these as sources of help and ideas. 6. Discuss the purposes of the range of printed material in the classroom. Show your children how to use printed resources, e.g., atlases, dictionaries, the thesaurus, when needed.
2 The language is whole & children learn from whole to part.	Parents don't teach their children how to talk in highly structured, sequential steps using initial consonants and blends. They use whole language in context. Children, through exposure to the enormous complexity of the language in meaningful situations, take what they can handle and begin to develop hypotheses about how language works. The complexity and richness of the language enables the hypotheses to be tested and the meaning sorted out through context.	• Reading schemes and writing activities that break language up into artificial, decontextualised pieces are avoided. • Children of all ages are exposed to literature that is rich and complex. • Skills and strategies are learnt in the context of whole language activities, e.g., spelling through writing. • Teaching is approached from whole to part, i.e., environments and activities draw children into active involvement and teach specifics within that context.	7. Select reading materials carefully. Use rich, natural, whole, interesting material for group or class activities. Avoid reading schemes with passages that are decontextualised, unnatural, and shallow in context. 8. Teach spelling when there is a purpose for learning about words—during writing and prior to publishing.
3 The primary concern is meaning.	The home language environment is driven by a preoccupation with meaning. It always remains central.	• Reading and writing activities and materials are selected with meaning in mind, e.g., "Is the primary focus of a particular reading activity creating meaning, or is it something less worthwhile?" • The making of meaning is the main focus when interacting with children and when helping them interact with each other. • Strategies are taught that help children make meaning. They are helped to discard strategies that prevent them from making meaning.	9. Use literacy activities that focus on meaning, such as: never-ending stories; reorganising familiar text cut into pieces; activities relating to quality children's literature. 10. In reading look for children who do not predict well, who do not monitor meaning by self-correcting. Help them to learn to predict. If they are happy to produce a nonsense word, ask them, "Does that make sense?" "Could it be that?" 11. When discussing a piece of writing attempted by a child, respond to the content before responding to any surface features. 12. Show your class what joys and sorrows can come from getting meaning from the pages of good books.
4 The language (& activity) is relevant to the child's world.	The language used is relevant to the child's world, as is the activity in which the language is embedded (e.g., bedtime stories).	• Language is used that is relevant and appropriate for the children, without oversimplifying it. • Children are treated as individuals. Teachers try to get to know them, to get inside their heads, to discover how they operate and what their interests are. • Classroom activities that are relevant to children's interests. • Children are given opportunities to choose their own reading and write about what is important to them.	13. Organise time each day for your children to read something of their own choosing and to write about something that interests them. Help them make choices about their audience, the intended outcome, and the purpose for writing.
5 The language is functional.	Language in the home is centred in the life, the actions, and the interests of the family. If mother asks father to pass the milk at the breakfast table, the child sees language in action. In learning oral language, function usually precedes form. When the child asks for a "gink," the function of language takes precedence over the "correctness" of the language.	• Reading and writing are for learning about ourselves, about others, and about the wonderful world in which we live. • Classrooms are built around the three R's: Real Reading; Real Writing; Responding to each other's attempts at communicating through written language. • Teachers ask themselves "What can we learn together, through reading and writing?" rather than, "What can I teach my children about reading and writing?"	14. Focus on the importance of the social aspects of communicating through written language, how reading and writing to and with real people can draw reluctant learners into wanting to read and write. 15. Use message boards or post boxes in your classroom to get notes and letters flowing between classmembers. 16. Write to your children (particularly those who don't see a great need to write). Send personal letters or begin dialogue journals. 17. Beware of any activities that you only ever do in schools and never anywhere else—busy-type activities done only to please the teacher. Avoid them; they are destructive to development.
6 Risk-taking is encouraged.	Parents encourage their children to respond from a very early age. If they respond in non-standard form, they are not reprimanded but are usually replied to in a meaningful way with the parent modelling the standard form. The encouragement to take risks while making meaning which involves giving ownership to the child is a powerful factor in learning.	• Children are given ownership and control of their own learning, but teachers still seek the right moment and the best way to teach in context. • Teachers show their children that they believe that taking risks and making mistakes is an important part of the learning process.	18. Be a risk-taker yourself. Be honest, open, and willing to admit your own weaknesses and mistakes. Seek your children's help during your own attempts to make meaning. 19. Use/adapt literacy activities in ways that allow risk-taking. Remember, though, that the key to risk-taking amongst your children is you. Your attitudes, your modelling, your relationship to them will be the most powerful factor.
7 Strengths rather than weaknesses are emphasised.	Parents react positively to their children's early attempts to talk. They offer positive reinforcement and usually overlook weaknesses in production. They are preoccupied with the children and their attempts to communicate.	• Teachers respond first to what the children can do (state specifically what it is they have done well), before discussing any needs or possible weaknesses. • They build on what each child already knows.	20. Build individual profiles on each child, focussing particularly on what they can do and have recently learnt to do as developing readers and writers. 21. In reading and writing conferences, tell the children exactly what it is they have done well. 22. Celebrate with the whole class any obvious achievement by an individual, e.g., read to the class a strong piece, passage, or sentence written by an individual. Let the writer hear their peers' congratulations.
8 The child is a member of the larger community.	Parents usually do a good job of involving their children in the family community. It is the community interaction that produces talk that is real, useful, relevant, and meaningful. It is in the web of this community involvement that most learning takes place.	• Teachers share their own successes, and frustrations when reading and writing with and in front of the children. • They encourage their children to share with each other and with the teacher. • They encourage their children to use each other as sources of help, e.g., reading a word, spelling, listening to the effectiveness of a piece of writing, etc.	23. Use activities or techniques that allow children to learn from each other, e.g., cooperative cloze; written conversation; authors circles; small group work; cooperative writing on a word processor. 24. Set up your classroom to facilitate small group work and interaction.

Viewpoint: Moira G. McKenzie

"But Wait! Everything Was Upside Down!"

Many teachers see a lifeline within whole language offering them and their students welcome relief from the narrow restrictive reading programs and prescriptive packaged learning that has threatened to engulf real education. Reading researchers offer support for broader learning opportunities that draw upon and develop critical readers and creative thinkers (Harste 1989). The basic assumption is that the focus must be on whole, integrated learning, with reading and writing as the tools of learning, not ends in themselves. This was the assumption underlying integrated or informal education that was so successful in the British primary schools in the sixties and seventies.

> Moira G. McKenzie has been a classroom teacher and a headmistress in two primary schools in London. From 1974 to 1986 she was director of the Centre for Language in Primary Education (CLPE), part of Inner London Education Authority's provision for inservice education in language and literacy. McKenzie has contributed to journals and books. Her major publications include *The Challenge of Informal Education* (coauthor), *Reading Matters: Selecting and Using Books in the Classroom* (coeditor), *Journeys into Literacy* (1986), and *Extending Literacy* (1989).

Outstanding teachers on both sides of the Atlantic, from whom I have learned and continue to learn, set up their classrooms to be rich in learning possibilities, highly relevant to their pupils and to the curriculum. Children are actively engaged in thinking and learning as they choose, within themes, the particular interests they wish to follow. They take responsibility for their own learning. They are encouraged to collaborate with their peers, to share their ideas, feelings, and concerns. The teacher provides time, space, and opportunity to read and explore a range of literature, information books, poetry, reference materials. Children become aware of language: They are fascinated with words, how they are used, how they relate to each other, how to use them for special effect, and how to play with them.

Children explore ideas in talk and drama, and represent them in art forms and diagrams as well as writing. There is no problem in knowing what to write about, though there may be some struggle to say what they mean. Their writing serves a real purpose in learning. It is a significant way of reflecting, organizing, and representing current concerns of understanding oneself and others. When whole language is unrestricted by work books, story prompts, comprehension exercises, and other distractions, they will then have something to say, talk, and write about.

Katharine, in Jean Sperling's kindergarten class, has been observing the caterpillars in the classroom vivarium. She has seen the eggs hatch, the caterpillars grow and shed their skins, wondered at the chrysalis that formed, and shared the delight as the butterfly emerged. I was there when one of the butterflies began to emerge and I shared the wonder and excitement. The children commented on the butterfly's struggle, the limpness of its damp wings, and its gradual strengthening. They said their final goodbyes when they set it free. Soon afterwards I found Katharine busily making the following book, called BDRFLIYBOOK BY KATHARINE.

Katharine has recalled, reflected on, and organized the experiences she has enjoyed, incorporating all four levels of Wells' proposed

taxonomy (1987). It provides the teacher with information about Katharine's grasp of this particular knowledge: It gives the teacher detailed information about how Katharine is grasping the language system; it tells her much about Katharine's attitudes to learning and her ability to select a task and follow it through.

Michael is a student in Marlene Harbert's third- and fourth-grade class where he and his classmates have been studying light and color. The teacher provided books and materials and a range of experiences, and helped children read and set up their chosen experiments. The youngsters work collaboratively—in pairs or small groups. Opportunities for shared reading, questioning the text, forming hypotheses, discussing and checking abounded. The youngsters were aware of experiments other children were doing. They asked questions, checked back to see how the experiments were going, and often offered advice from their own experience. Each child was expected to report his or her own work in some way and the work was displayed; their writing plus diagrams, charts, and pictures gave evidence of their opportunities to be involved in several experiments related to light and color, fiber optics, and the particular functions of light bulbs, magnification and more.

Their teacher moved among them listening and talking with them, sharing their interest and delight, asking for evidence of their statements, focusing their attention when necessary, referring them to books, other children's work, and so on.

Here is a portion of Michael's report:

First I found a partner (His name was Jasper.) He held a ruler and piece of paper. He held the paper about five feet from the window and I held the magnifying glass in the middle of them. An image of the trees and scenery outside the window appeared on the paper! But wait, everything was upside down! As I moved the magnifying glass up and down—back and forth—the image would become more distinct, although after a while it would become fuzzy again. Then I tried moving the magnifying glass and the paper far back. To my surprise the image got smaller but also more distinct! Now I will explain what focal length is: When I held the magnifying glass up to the window I took the ruler and when I got the clearest picture I measured the distance between the paper and the magnifying glass. That distance is the focal length, my focal length was 4 in.

In Michael's writing we hear his voice clearly sharing his thinking and feelings. He and his partner have taken their early experience with magnifying a step further towards understanding underlying scientific principles. The transactional voice appears when Michael states some particular scientific fact, e.g., "focal length is . . . ."

As they reach the end of elementary school, children are often asked to write about their learning in a particular form. Rosen (1971) criticizes this and says in our zeal to get "correct" form we often "price children out of the market." Most of the learning a school tries to inculcate is couched in very particular kinds of language. Rosen reminds us that most information and text books have been written by scholars eminent in their fields. Their discourse has shifted from "its specific context to a very general one" giving little clue to the thinking and talking from which it arose. "The personal hinterland," says Rosen, "is populated with memories, attitudes, feelings and fancies which color our thinking." In making demands for particular kinds of language we may well limit children's thinking because they tend to focus on the form rather than the content. It is all too easy to have children imitate learning by copy-

ing and replicating rather than by transforming information and experience and constructing their own knowledge.

Children's growing interests and purposes will take them into a variety of reading. Literature contains not just unfamiliar words but everyday words that are used metaphorically. Teachers who plan a good program of stories and poems to read aloud can extend children's language and open up a whole range of literature for them. Children enjoy hearing and exploring stories. They soon begin to feel the symbolic power of language to create worlds, or to make their own world more vivid and more comprehensible. "Who goes trip-trap over my bridge!" demands John, standing guard at the end of a plank over an imaginary stream. He has a strong image of the stories he has heard and enjoys the power of language.

Older children may demonstrate high levels of thinking and feeling in their writing. Kristi's writing arises from a class experience with Mollie Hunter's *A Stranger Came Ashore* (1975). The children enjoyed the story, but they were particularly moved by the part where twelve-year-old Robbie rows out to count the newborn seal pups.

Kristi called her story, "Discovering the Young Selkies." She put herself in Robbie's shoes when she wrote, "I, twelve-year-old Robbie, couldn't wait to see the little selkies." She vividly described rowing the boat towards the pups, and continued:

When I finally reached the geo, I found myself surrounded by tiny young sleeping selkies. I stared at them without saying a word. I never had seen anything like what I was seeing right now. I stopped rowing the boat and drifted in a little until the pale green water brought me to a young selkie that was lounging around on a rock but very wide awake. His little eyes were like shining pearls and his expression made him look disappointed like he had lost something very important to him. . .

Kristi captures the intense feeling of the text. She controls the language she uses consciously to achieve a particular literary effect that expresses deep feeling, and builds an atmosphere of beauty and of tension.

Readers learn to look beyond "what happens next"; "why did that happen"; "where will that action lead"; and "what was the character thinking and feeling?" They look at other possibilities, asking, "What would I have done had I been there?" Returning to the text, discussing it, and reading it again enables readers to penetrate its secrets, to discover deeper layers of meaning. When reading, children enter a possible world; when writing they create—or recreate one.

Katharine is five and both Michael and Kristi are ten years old. Their work is representative of good learning experiences anywhere. They are accustomed to having some choice in what they wish to pursue and taking responsibility for following through with it.

The current focus on whole language may well have its roots in a growing realization by teachers that excessive concern with the surface features of literacy, its rightness and wrongness, means that many children who can read and write choose not to and too many of those fail to become critical readers and thinkers. There is a real need for schools to reconsider the learning opportunities they offer children and to make it possible for youngsters to be involved and excited by learning.

Whole language teachers are poised, ready to give evidence from their classrooms that language growth and understanding is embedded in rich learning opportunities.

→ See: Literature Reference List, p. 429.

References

Harste, J. C. 1989. *New policy guidelines for reading, connecting research and practice*. NCTE.

Hunter, M. 1975. *A stranger came ashore*. New York: Harper & Row.

Rosen, H. 1971. "Towards a language policy across the curriculum." In *Language, the learner and the school*, ed. D. Barnes, J. Britton, H. Rosen, and LATE. England: Penguin Papers in Education.

Wells, G. 1987. "Apprenticeship in literacy." *Interchange* 18(1, 2), Spring/Summer.

BDRFLIY BOOK
BY KATHERINE
1. First the eggs are laid
2. Soon a baby caterpillar hatches
3. Soon a baby caterpillar is grown up.
4. Now he's asleep on the branch. Now he's a chrysalis. Soon the chrysalis breaks.

Viewpoint: Jeanette Veatch

Whole Language as I See It

A democracy is more than a form of government. It is primarily a mode of associated living: of conjoint communicated experience . . . (Dewey 1916, p. 101)

So it is with whole language in the classroom. It is but the newest manifestation of progressive education, which is far from dead, alive and indestructible, based upon the "humanitarian effort to apply the promise of American life—the ideal government of, by and for the people" (Dewey 1916). It is the current epitome of democratic life in the classroom. I believe that whole language learning

1. Is based upon pupil choice of ideas, thoughts, or experiences, for content acquired through a process framework, on a one-to-one, group, or class basis;
2. Has unpredictable and unexpected outcomes;
3. Requires no extrinsic rewards for success;
4. Utilizes the expertise of many persons, regardless of their age or status;
5. Respects the physical, psychological, and intellectual rights of people;
6. Has an organized plan or system necessary for success.

To understand the implications of these criteria, let us view education as a continuum, with laissez-faire at one end, authoritarianism at the other, and democracy at midpoint.

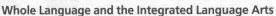

Jeannette Veatch, Ph.D., professor emerita at Arizona State University, is well known for her work in the movements called *individualized reading* and the *language experience approach*, early forms of what is now being called whole language. In 1956 she became the program development director for the Girl Scouts of America. She then returned to teaching at Pennsylvania State University, Jersey City State College, and Arizona State University.

Whole Language and the Integrated Language Arts

Whole language cuts across all the language arts. It has developed a support system for teachers to help and encourage one another: "Go ahead. *Try* it! Take risks!" Where success has come (Edelsky 1988, p. 396) this teacher cooperation can only be described as electrifying. It certainly is unparalleled in my experience.

The integrated language arts emphasizes the identical curricular areas of concern to whole language proponents, but it lacks this unique cooperative networking—the warm personal interaction between teachers on the job—that gives whole language a truly revolutionary quality.

Neglected Antecedents to Whole Language

Unfortunately, despite the extensive writing on whole language, there is a puzzling lack of consideration of what has gone before. Three activities in particular are missing from current literature: (1) Sylvia Ashton-Warner's Key Vocabulary; (2) Class Experience Charts; and (3) Individualized Reading. Each of these enjoyed as significant a popularity in its day as does whole language at the moment, and each threatened the publisher/professor/ psychology complex behind the pervasive traditionalist textbook commercialization.

Yet surprisingly not only are these activities largely missing from current literature, but also, when they *are* mentioned, there is little *understanding* of their characteristics and how they worked. For example, Key Vocabulary is considered by prominent educators to be a gimmicky, sight word drill operation. When talking about experience charts some educators insist that teachers take *verbatim* dictation when children tell experiences. If teachers had ever tried to do that in a classroom, they would know that it is an impossible task. As for Individualized Reading, a major text refers to me as advocating job cards, of all things!

These three activities were selected because of (1) their effectiveness in the classroom, (2) their clear relationship to whole language, and (3) their inexplicable omission from current writings in the field.

Key Vocabulary

In 1958 Sylvia Ashton-Warner presented her unique and effective practice that is part of the Language Experience approach. By means of a specific plan of action, teachers elicit, from their four, five, and six-year-old pupils, highly charged, dynamic words of *their own*. These words explode in an instantaneous, unplanned action on the part of the child, unpredictable and unexpected on the part of the teacher. They are "one-look" words, never needing drill, that lead directly into spontaneous writing and reading. These words are diametrically opposed to "sight word lists." They internalize the alphabet along Piagetian lines, as no rote parroting of the alphabet is needed. Most important, they produce the self-recognition in the learner that "I have words in my head."

Is Key Vocabulary whole language? Check it out with our six criteria:

1. Pupil choice: No words are given—all are the learner's;
2. Unpredictability: The words are different;
3. Rewards: Satisfaction is reward enough for all action—no extrinsic rewards to learn are needed;
4. Expertise: Expert teachers record and promote language;
5. Respect: Children's rights to their own ideas, action, and place of operation are honored and developed; and
6. Plan or system: The process to get a Key Word is structured, so if you do it wrong, the words are wrong.

Class Experience Charts

Recording the daily newsworthy experiences of the members present is another practice as misunderstood and malpracticed as Key Vocabulary. Teacher-pupil interaction, originating from the spoken language of the pupils, is highly conducive to later capabilities of writing, spelling, and reading. Being a part of the language experience arena, it starts with children's spoken language.

The teacher encourages the children to tell about an interesting, exciting life experience, preferably of the day before. The teacher probes, questions, and clarifies the dimensions of the report. After several incidents have been shared, the teacher chooses one to use for that day's newspaper (on chart paper, the chalkboard, whatever). The teacher records much of the language used by the child, but rewrites the material for ease in reading back.

Is this activity whole language? Look again at the six criteria:

1. Pupil choice: Only pupils' experiences are recorded;
2. Unpredictability: No one knows prior to the session what has happened to any one of the pupils;
3. Rewards: The quality of the experience and the need to record makes grades (or other extrinsic rewards) unnecessary;
4. Expertise: The teacher's expertise is used to record spoken language and to judge which experience makes the activity worthwhile;
5. Respect: Children have a right to tell their own experiences;
6. Plan or system: The teacher's wisdom in editing the talk is essential, along with his or her choice of offering for the most dramatic and newsworthy effect.

Individualized Reading

This approach is the most frightening of the three to the publishing world, as it is the simplest, the cheapest, the most effective methodology to produce high-ability readers eliminating basal readers. Each pupil chooses his or her own material for reading instruction from a wide variety of trade books. Children read at their own rate regardless of the progress of the rest of the class. They participate in groups organized on bases *other* than ability, have frequent one-to-one instructional conferences with the teacher, and are taught skills when they are needed. There are no reading assignments in the traditional sense; instead, readers follow their own interests and broaden their exploration in that chosen direction.

The research on this approach emphasizes the promotion of the love of reading, as well as significantly improving achievement.

Is Individualized Reading whole language? Indubitably so:

1. Pupil choice: All material read is pupil chosen;
2. Unpredictability: As no one mandates choice, individual choices are unexpected, as is the learning of needed skills;
3. Rewards: Reading their own chosen material uarantees high interest, so grades are not needed;
4. Expertise: Teacher expertise is needed to help during individual conferences, and peer experts are consulted in content areas;
5. Respect: As personal choices are respected, so the choices of others are similarly respected;
6. Organization: Without an adequate supply of trade books, or a teacher who follows a system allowing the activity to occur, chaos will result.

Whole language is a healthy, exciting, and promising development. That it will prevail over the current stultifying, commercial, authoritarian educational practice is to be profoundly desired.

➔ See: Goodman, p. 386; Huck, p. 188; Ohanian, p. 176; Van Allen, p. 307.

References
Dewey, J. 1916. *Democracy and education.* New York: Macmillan.
Edelsky, C. 1988. "Research currents: Resisting (professional) arrest." *Language Arts* 65(4), April.

Further Reading by Jeannette Veatch
◆ *How to Teach Reading with Children's Books,* 2d ed. Richard C. Owen, 1984.
◆ *Reading in the Elementary School,* 2d ed. Richard C. Owen, 1984.
◆ "The Effect of Teacher Selection on Reading Achievement." *Language Arts* 63(4), April 1986.
◆ "Individualized Reading: A Personal Memoir." *Language Arts* 63(6), October 1986.
◆ *Showing Teachers How.* Videotape series. Jan V. Productions, 1986–1989.

Resource: Publisher

Lerner Publications
Carolrhoda Books

241 First Ave. N.
Minneapolis, MN 55401
1-800-328-4929

Lerner Publications focuses on readers from grade three up; this press specializes in nonfiction trade books. Among their publications are award-winning series in the natural and physical sciences and social studies, in formats ideal for the whole language classroom. Carolrhoda Books focuses primarily on the younger reader, from preschool to grade six, with highly acclaimed series in biography and science, supplemented by a strong list of picture books and beginning readers.

Fifth-grade teacher, Debra Goodman, and seventh-grade teacher, Toby Kahn Curry, teach at the Dewey Center for Urban Education in Detroit, MI. Pauline Lubens, a *Detroit Free Press* photographer, spent a day in each classroom.

Inside Two Whole Language Classrooms

Debra Goodman's Fifth-Grade Classroom

My fifth-grade room is organized into a town. This year the town was named Terabithia. We try to create our own ideal society (see Goodman, p. 224). This is a view of the room from the reading loft. Desks are arranged in groups because we don't have tables. The store booth was made by one of the parents. We sell pencils, pens, etc. for small amounts. The money is used to purchase supplies and games.

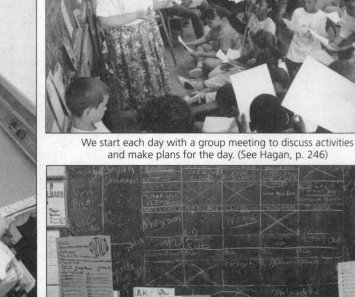

We start each day with a group meeting to discuss activities and make plans for the day. (See Hagan, p. 246)

The students plan their own clubs and activities. This week, there is a working schedule on the chalkboard so we can coordinate activities. Scheduling can get very complicated as students work in the kindergarten, visit the school library, plant flowers, etc. Clubs are advertised on the chalkboard and students invited to sign up. The fifth-graders spend a lot of time making signs and charts for their clubs.

After quiet reading, we have a general work time. I have helped students to plan and schedule their work (see Goodman, p. 254). Omari and I go over the layout and paste-up of his pages for "My Place".

After the class meeting, we have twenty minutes of quiet reading. The quiet reading precedes the general work time so that students can continue reading if they like. Jennifer reads "Ghost Cat" while I look through final drafts of our class book, "My Place".

Omari admires his finished pages. In this book, each student has mapped and written about their family and community. (See Goodman, p. 315)

Students keep their folders and books organized in boxes and turn in or pick up work from these baskets.

Meanwhile Michael and Walter proofread the rap they are composing with the help of a word processor.

As I meet with some students, others are involved in a variety of activities. The loft, a reading-only area, is available for quiet reading almost any time of the day. It was built by parent, Paul Weertz. Students sign up for a turn.

In the museum (Our Social Studies Center) Shani consults with Marie about ideas for the end-of-the-year program. The room is divided into small areas by shelves and cabinets. This creates space for 33 students to work and move around. The walls are covered with print, and students feel free to add their own.

In the library, staff members are organizing the books. This large bookshelf supports the loft and creates a library on one side and publishing area on the other side.

After the work time, we meet back in the large group again. The kids and I are interpreting the poem *America, I Know You*, by Bill Martin Jr. I invite the students to write their own metaphors about America for the class program. We have had a busy day.

Toby Curry's Seventh-Grade Classroom

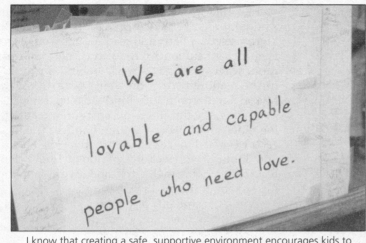

> We are all lovable and capable people who need love.

I know that creating a safe, supportive environment encourages kids to make approximations, take risks, and accept my invitations for learning.

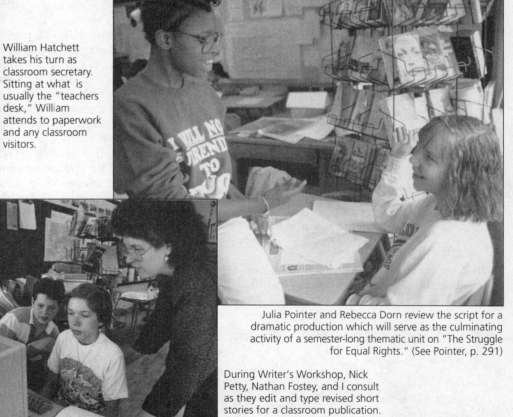

Numerous activities occur simultaneously during open work time. Students write about current events, discuss sports news, look for a good book to read, or peruse the classroom news board.

William Hatchett takes his turn as classroom secretary. Sitting at what is usually the "teachers desk," William attends to paperwork and any classroom visitors.

Astere Asaka, Thadd McGaffrey, Ben Atkinson and Timothy Robinson enjoy a role-playing game similar to *Dungeons and Dragons* during club time. The students roll dice to create complex characters and bizarre scenarios.

Julia Pointer and Rebecca Dorn review the script for a dramatic production which will serve as the culminating activity of a semester-long thematic unit on "The Struggle for Equal Rights." (See Pointer, p. 291)

During Writer's Workshop, Nick Petty, Nathan Fostey, and I consult as they edit and type revised short stories for a classroom publication.

7th-grader Titiena Swan shares with me a draft of her short story which will later be published in the classroom anthology, *Kaleidoscope*.

Kids always have so much to say. Derf Jackson enjoys his conference time with me. Most students look forward to having their teacher's undivided attention.

As Teachers See It

by Louise Lockard

Myron Elthie Has a Story to Tell

Myron Elthie is an author in my second-grade classroom. What do I expect Myron to say? What does he expect me to say? What kind of a conversation can we have?

Myron is the captain of our class softball team. He's not a good hitter and he doesn't run very fast because he wears cowboy boots, not tennis shoes. When I went on a home visit, Myron's dad was standing in front of their hogan helping Myron hold a bat. His older brother Harry was pitching, and his mother and his younger brother were waiting to catch the ball. Myron writes about his dad because his dad works with him and teaches him.

> My dad fixes the truck. And I helped my dad to give him a screwdriver. It is fun to help your dad. I like to help my dad.

In his "About the Author" section Myron writes:

> Myron Elthie is a Navajo Indian boy from Whipoorwill, Arizona. He is 8 years old. He is in the second grade at Pinon Public School. Myron likes to help his dad.

Myron speaks Navajo at home. I speak English. There are two languages and 24 people in one classroom. There are many separate conversations. My job as a teacher is to use these conversations to enhance learning.

In *Classroom Discourse* (1988, p. 67), Courtney Cazden says:

> One of the most important influences on all talk (some say the most important influence) is the participants themselves—their expectations about interactions and their perceptions of each other.

She quotes the poem of an Apache girl (1988, p. 67):

> Have you ever hurt about baskets?
> I have, seeing my grandmother weaving
>   for a long time.
> Have you ever hurt about work?
> I have, because my father works too hard
>   And he tells me how he works.
> Have you ever hurt about cattle?
> I have, because my grandfather has been
>   working
>   on the cattle for a long time.
> Have you ever hurt about school?
> I have because I learned a lot of words
>   from school.
> And they are not my words.

In my classroom Myron expects to be heard. Myron published 15 books this year. His titles, *I Like to Herd Sheep, My Dog Lonzo, My Little Brother, My Friend Donavan, About the Horse,* use Myron's own words. Myron writes every day. He decides what he will write about. He edits and publishes his own books and reads them with his classmates. The writing classroom is a place to be heard.

It's also a very busy place. Myron wrote over 300 pages this year. Many of his false starts ended in the trash can. Many of his stories were rehearsed in conversations with his friends, not written. Multiply this talk by 22, the number of students in my class. Think about the diversity of talk and multiply this talk by 175 days, the length of the school year. Myron expects to be busy talking and writing every day.

I structure my classroom to meet Myron's expectations. I structure my classroom so that Myron will talk and read and I will listen to him. This structure includes time: a full hour every day for writing; a scheduled weekly conference when Myron reads me what he has written and we discuss how he will continue; a group sharing time for Myron to read what he has written. This structure includes materials: paper and pencils for writing, staplers and staple removers to experiment with layouts, a variety of bookmaking materials, including felt-tipped pens, colored pencils, and crayons.

More important than time or materials is my ability as a teacher to engage Myron in conversation. I read his scrawled handwriting and run-on sentences. I read the invented spellings and repetitious patterns. Sometimes Myron may be reading only marks scribbled on a paper. Sometimes he looks at me during a writing conference with a puzzled, "What say, Teacher?" I am listening for a story. It is this engagement between teacher and student that lets learning happen.

As I listen to Myron I ask Donald Murray's question, "How can we see in our students what they see in themselves?"

How do I set up a classroom where Myron expects to be heard? I provide a variety of books for him to read: trade books, magazines, science books, books with tapes, and newspapers. In the fall Myron and his friends read *Curious George.* Myron said to his friend Timothy, "He was a good little monkey but he was too curious." The stories and the characters in the stories become Myron's own. Timothy brought Conan books from home and shared them with his friends. Timothy, Myron, and Donavan wrote Conan stories.

I set aside a shelf of 25 to 30 books for partner reading. I change these books every two weeks. Myron selects a book and reads it with a partner. Each pair of students has a special place in the room where they go to read—behind my desk, in the reading corner, on chairs near the sink. Myron and Aaron read behind the filing cabinet. Every day Myron makes an entry in a reading log when he finishes reading. I collect the log each week and make comments about the books and about Myron's choice of books. I send the reading log home each week, and Myron talks to his dad about the books he has read.

While the students read with a partner, I read with Myron and we talk about the book. Myron read *The Hungry Giant*. He retold the story:

> The Giant. They gave bread to the Giant. The bread was so dry. The Giant said, "Give me some butter!" And he tried to get some honey. And the people found the bees house. The Giant said, "This is not a honey!" And the Giant hit a gummy knocker and the bees come out. And the Giant ran home.

I asked Myron, "Who would like to read *The Hungry Giant?*" He answered, "Timothy." I asked, "Why did you pick this book?" He answered, "Read it before."

Every day the students write in their journals and read what they have written to me. The next day they start again by reading my comment or question. Some students use their journals as a very safe place to recite what they know. Thomelissa drew the same blue house and wrote about it for most of the year. Other students introduce topics like the lights of a jet plane at night that are unique. Each student can expect a story to be heard and responded to every day. Myron wrote, "I like to ride bull at rodeo." I responded, "I like to watch calf-roping too." The next day he wrote, "I see jet plane at night. I see five jet plane. It have lights the tail. I see big dipper." I responded, "Do you know the names of the stars in the Big Dipper?"

Group sharing time is a time when the children come together to read their stories. Myron reads:

> ### I Like to Herd Sheep
> I Like to herd sheep.
> I herd sheep.
> The little lambs are cold.
> When they drink milk they are not cold.
> They are hot.
> I like little lambs.
> I milk the mother.
> They drink three bottles.

Here again I'd like to ask my questions. What do I expect Myron to say? What does he expect me to say? As Myron's teacher I am asking these questions so that in the words of British sociolinguists Connie and Harold Rosen, Myron may "speak more powerfully and act more effectively."

→ See: Lindfors, p. 79; Literature Reference List, p. 429; Mestnik, p. 241; Van Allen, p. 307; Watson, p. 40; Weber, p. 78.

Reference
Cazden, C. 1988. *Classroom discourse: The language of teaching and learning.* Portsmouth, NH: Heinemann.

Louise Lockard is a teacher at Pinon Elementary School, Pinon, AZ.

YOUNG ARTISTS

—Bryan Peterson, 18, Enterprise, OR
(from *Treasures 2,* See p. 162)

YOUNG ARTISTS

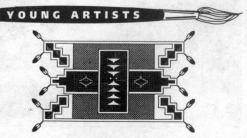

—Nelson G. Begay, Nazlini Boarding School, Chinle, AZ

Great Teachers:
Wendy Hood

by Pat Rigg

Wendy Hood's faith in her students shows from the first day. When her kindergartners arrive, she meets them at the door, offering a basket of new crayons and gesturing toward a large easel covered with paper. "Sign your name, please," she says in English and in Spanish. Some children grab a crayon, turn to the easel, and print their names. Some carefully draw the first letter of their first name. Others balk, saying they don't know how to write, but Wendy won't accept that. "Pretend you can," she urges. "If you can write it, I can read it." That sign-up sheet serves more than one purpose (as most of her activities do): It tells the students that they are literate and that their teacher knows it, and it gives Wendy a daily record of each student's progress in name writing.

After signing in, the students pull their journals from their mailboxes, find comfortable places to sit, and write and draw whatever they want. As they finish, they take the journal to Wendy and talk about it; Wendy writes her response on the same page, reading it to the youngster at the same time. As the students finish the daily journal entry, they find something to read while others are still writing. After a period in which everyone reads their self-selected books, Wendy gathers the class together on the rug. They sing songs in Spanish, English, and sometimes Yiddish. Students move the cardboard cutouts with their names on them to show they're here today. Wendy reads a story to the students and then demonstrates how to do the activities that expand on this piece of literature.

The youngsters move into one of four committees to carry out the activities. Wendy uses four geometric shapes—a red circle, a yellow triangle, a blue rectangle, a green square—to mark the different committees. In four plastic baskets, each marked with one of the shapes, are the materials the committee will need. Each of the four working tables also has a colored shape. The youngsters know what committee they are in by finding their names and seeing which geometric shape the names are under, and they go to the corresponding table and get the corresponding basket of materials.

As the students complete the assigned task, they put away the baskets, clean their area, and begin playing. Some students play house, pretending to be grown-ups with grown-up concerns. Two climb into the loft to whisper secrets. Three boys pull out giant wooden blocks and build a highway that extends halfway across the room; then they zoom their cars and trucks back and forth, occasionally crashing into each other with appropriate sound effects. One plays with an old Royal typewriter and decides to write a real letter to her father, getting Wendy's help. Wendy thinks it's vital that kindergartners have at least one hour of free time daily in the rich classroom environment, time to select not only activities and materials but playmates.

Each child is free to move into an activity and to move out again. No one is forced to play with anyone else or to participate in an activity. If one child starts to bully another, Wendy puts her arm around him and says, "I don't want you to hurt my friend." If someone tattles, Wendy says, "Tell him how you feel when he does that." I've only once before seen such a peaceful kindergarten that at the same time is so full of activity. Part of this comes from the appropriateness of the activities and materials offered to the children. Part of it comes from Wendy's respect for her students, which shines through in so many ways: When she invites the students to do something, it's a real invitation, not an assignment couched in current jargon; when she assigns a task, she wants the task to help her learn about the students at the same time that the students learn from the task.

Before they go home, the students again gather on the rug for songs and group games. This is also a time for reflection: What did I learn today? What did I do well? In a variety of ways Wendy has demonstrated her faith in these youngsters, helping them to value themselves. Tomorrow they will play more games, read more books, sing more songs, and without noticing it, become more proficient at language, literacy, and life.

➡ See: Goodman and Hood, p. 102; Goodman, p. 207; The Whole Language Evaluation Book, p. 252.

Pat Rigg is a consultant with American Language and Literacy, Tucson, AZ.

WELL-SAID I have been teaching for 20-plus years and it still makes the adrenaline pump when one of those magic moments happens in my classroom. As you might guess, none has ever occurred around a workbook or ditto sheet!

—Lois S. Vandagriff, primary teacher, Woodland Elementary School, Oak Ridge, TN

I Used to Be...But Now I...

I used to say *my* bulletin board, *my* books, *my* room,
But now I say *our* bulletin board, *our* books, *our* room.

—Anonymous

Towards a Reading-Writing Classroom

Andrea Butler and Jan Turbill
1984; 96 pp.; $11.50
Portsmouth, NH: Heinemann

A practical book to help teachers integrate writing with reading in the elementary classroom. It gives theoretical background, offers insights into classroom practice via vignettes of real teachers, and explains with examples how to immerse children in reading, involve them in writing, and help them make the links between the two. It includes lots of adaptable ideas and schedules so that teachers can essentially put themselves into another teacher's classroom. A good book for teachers with some background in whole language who are now trying to put that philosophy into practice.

Lois Mather

❝ The control and responsibility for the writing and the reading should generally be left with the children. In the main, they should be allowed to choose the topics they want to write about and the books they want to read. These choices will stem mainly from their own experiences and interests. Unknown spellings may be "guessed" or "invented" as a piece is written; punctuation, too, is often ignored in the early stages. Similarly, when they encounter unfamiliar words in their reading, children may make reasonable guesses about them, based on their prior knowledge and the context of the piece they are reading. Sometimes an unknown word will be skipped if it does not affect the overall meaning for the reader.❞ (p.22)

➡ See: Turbill, p. 424.

Resource: Book

Everyday Circle Times

Liz and Dick Wilmes
1983; 216 pp.; $12.95
Elgin, IL: Building Blocks (distributed by Gryphon House)

This book has over 900 ideas for circle times, including finger plays, recipes, field trips, suggestions for classroom visitors, language games, active games, and ideas for thematic units on self-awareness, animals, foods, science, occupations, and recreation, along with numerous subthemes.

Katy Obringer

Circle Time Book for Holidays & Seasons

Liz and Dick Wilmes
1982; 126 pp.; $8.95
Elgin, IL: Building Blocks (distributed by Gryphon House)

The *Circle Time Book* contains more than 400 circle time activities for preschoolers. A list of 39 seasons and holidays are included, as well as games, songs, and lists of related books.

Arrietta Chakos

Cornerstone: David Hartle-Schutte

Literate Environment Evaluation

Evidence from an increasing number of investigators indicates that children growing up in literate home environments acquire much knowledge about written language prior to school and with little or no formal teaching (Goodman and Altwerger 1981; Harste, Woodward, and Burke 1984; Ferreiro and Teberosky 1982; Teale and Sulzby 1986; Durkin 1966, 1984; Heath 1983; Taylor 1983; and Taylor and Dorsey-Gaines 1988). In these literate home environments reading and writing are done for various functional purposes, a wide variety of reading and writing materials are available, and literate siblings or elders answer questions asked by children emerging into literacy.

As part of a study investigating the extent to which schools capitalize on preschool literacy knowledge, and create literate and literacy-encouraging environments, I developed the following observation sheet. Readers may find it useful in evaluating their own classrooms or in developing grade-level guidelines for appropriate learning environments.

The observation sheet is not all-inclusive, nor is it meant to be used in formal teacher evaluations by administrators. The observation sheet shows a variety of options that can be useful in promoting the development of literacy. The presence of all or most of these items in the classroom does not guarantee a literate or literacy-encouraging environment. Nor does the absence of any single item or group of items indicate a poor literate environment. What is more important than any of these items or groups of items is the quality of the interactions among students and between teachers and students. Therefore, establishing criterion levels (e.g., "Teachers will have a minimum of 80 percent of these items evident in their classroom.") for teachers and classrooms is totally inappropriate.

→ See: Edelsky, p. 72; Hartle-Schutte, pp. 106, 260, 264, 265.

References
Durkin, D. 1966. *Children who read early*. New York: Teachers College Press.
———. 1984. "Poor black children who are successful readers: An investigation." *Urban Education* 19(1).
Ferreiro, E., and A. Teberosky. 1982. *Literacy before schooling*, trans. Karen Castro. Portsmouth, NH: Heinemann.
Goodman, Y., and B. Altwerger. 1981. *Print awareness in pre-school children: A working paper*. Tucson: University of Arizona, Program in Language and Literacy.
Harste, J., V. Woodward, and C. Burke. 1984. *Language stories & literacy lessons*. Portsmouth, NH: Heinemann.
Heath, S. 1983. *Ways with words: Language, life, and work in communities and classrooms*. New York: Cambridge University Press.
Taylor, D. 1983. *Family literacy: Young children learning to read and write*. Portsmouth, NH: Heinemann.
Taylor, D., and C. Dorsey-Gaines. 1988. *Growing up literate: Learning from inner-city families*. Portsmouth, NH: Heinemann.
Teale, W., and E. Sulzby, eds. 1986. *Emergent literacy: Writing and reading*. Norwood, NJ: Ablex.

David Hartle-Schutte is an assistant professor at the University of Hawaii, Hilo, HI.

Literacy Environment Observation Sheet

Teacher: _____   School: _____

Is the functional use of print for entire classroom observed in:
Daily messages, schedules, assignments, notices (chalkboard, bulletin board, or charts) _____
Labels (on cabinets, containers, equipment) to identify needed materials and storage areas _____
Current child-written messages, labels, etc. _____
Bulletin boards, etc., related to class activities _____
Sign-up, sign-in, sign-out sheets _____
Different charts _____
Classroom rules _____
Songs _____
Nursery rhymes _____
Class or group original stories _____
Calendar _____
Class log or diary _____
Recipes _____
Project directions _____
Instructions for pet care, etc. _____
Physical arrangement of classroom and materials conducive to literacy development _____

Is the functional use of print on an individual basis observable in:
Students labeling of own work (including but not limited to name) _____
Individual journals or log books _____
Student-published materials _____
Physical and temporal access to a variety of writing materials and equipment (markers, pencils, pens, chalk, paper, chalkboard, etc.) _____
Letter writing or pen pals _____
Individual messages to parents _____
Teacher notes to students _____
Students have opportunity and encouragement to write _____

Is a variety of printed material available/accessible?
Children's literature _____
References (dictionaries, encyclopedias, lists, charts, pictures, etc.) _____
Nonfiction information books _____
Miscellaneous print (comics, newspapers, maps, globes, student-authored books, magazines) _____
Students have frequent opportunities to read self-selected material _____

Is the modeling of literacy behaviors by the teacher observable?
Writing _____
Notes to parents _____
Notes to students _____
Notes to other adults _____
Notes to self _____
Lists, signs, etc., for classroom _____
Revises and edits _____
Reading _____
Communications from others _____
Books to children _____
Notices, announcements, etc., to kids _____
Other materials to self _____
Attitudes _____
Tries new things _____
Makes and points out own errors _____
Refers to books or other references _____
Models enjoyment of reading and writing _____
Responds to message over form _____
Encourages child to attempt reading and writing _____

Areas to avoid:
Is there a reliance on basals and other textbooks? _____
Is there a heavy use of ditto masters and workbooks? _____
Is there emphasis on sequential skills and "mastery"? _____
Is there an emphasis on immediate error correction? _____
Are all students engaged in identical activities? _____

Comments:

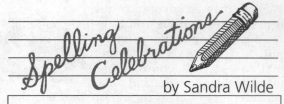

by Sandra Wilde

Invented Spellings: Homophones

It was bring (brighting) in *ARE* (our) eyes. . . . We almots (almost) went of (off) the *RODE* (road).
Elaine, 4th grade

Homophones are words that are pronounced the same but spelled differently. Spelling textbooks usually devote at least one lesson a year to studying homophone pairs, with the idea that if students' attention is drawn to them they are less likely to confuse them. I wonder about this, though. Frank Smith (1982) has said that often we misspell words not because we can't remember the right spelling but because we can't forget the wrong one. Before I became a teacher, I never confused the words *their* and *there*, but after a year or so of seeing one substituted for the other in student writing, I began to occasionally switch them myself. (I still knew the difference between them, but my pen would produce the wrong one.) Maybe we'd be better off not associating homophones with each other at all. Homophones that we don't think of as homophones (such as *prize* and *pries*) are probably not confused very often. As for Elaine, her class had studied homophones the week that she wrote these lines. (In her dialect, as in many, the words *are* and *our* are homophones.) I can't prove that there's a connection, but this is certainly something for teachers to think about!

Reference
Smith, F. 1982. *Writing and the writer*. New York: Holt, Rinehart & Winston.

Classroom Demonstrations

by Alyce E. Dalzell

Books—and Readers and Writers—Everywhere!

Baskets of books began filling my kindergarten classroom as I built our class library. In the past, the book rack held 25 books on the current theme and sat in my library corner. I soon had 12 baskets containing over 200 books covering pet care, space exploration, biographies, quality children's literature, and much more.

I moved the book baskets into every corner and onto every table in the classroom. I surrounded the children with books, shared happy memories of my childhood and current favorites, and read them a minimum of six books a morning!

My reading corner turned into a reading classroom. Children became book consumers. They could be found reading in the block corner, refrigerator box spaceship, or under tables on their magic carpet rugs. The children learned from each other as they listened, questioned, challenged, and shared their thoughts, books, and writing.

While immersing the children in print, I was immersing myself in research written by Yetta and Ken Goodman, Andrea Butler, Jan Turbill, Marie Clay, Donald Graves, and Judith Newman. I enrolled in a class taught by Yetta Goodman: Written Language Development. I was definitely becoming "whole" and felt good!

Attending Dr. Goodman's class and reading the books *Reading, Writing and Caring* (1988), and *Towards a Reading-Writing Classroom* (1984), drastically changed the environment and methods of my teaching. I found myself dreaming thematically, catching the children's excitement and traveling the wave.

A dinosaur unit evolved into building a dinosaur cave on the playground, complete with papier-mâché dinosaur eggs. Inventive spelling was used in writing stories, which were read into the tape recorder so the two-year-old's class could hear about the kindergartner's archaeological adventures. Plaster fossils were poured and bread-dough dinosaurs were formed. As the classroom began filling with dinosaur artifacts, a group of children brought me a poster they had made. "DNSR MOOZM." They wanted to change their classroom into a Dinosaur Museum and invite the school and their parents! I knew then that they had captured the energy of a whole language classroom. One five-year-old student wrote this sign and taped it to a telephone pole.

[Dinosaur museum parking lot and go through hallway to the kindergarten room]

The enthusiasm for meaningful writing opportunities grew. The children began composing and illustrating posters and writing invitations to opening ceremonies. Signs were made stating the museum hours, tickets were printed, and a ribbon-cutting ceremony held! The children beamed as they filled their new roles as tour guides, explaining in explicit detail the sizes and different species of dinosaurs, and performed science experiments of erupting volcanoes to explain one theory of dinosaur extinction.

I had watched my kindergarten class evolve into reading and writing children. Committee or large-group story-writing was no longer satisfying their great appetite and urge to write. They wanted more time to experiment with the written word and to enjoy discovering that they could write joke books, stories about princesses, and bumblebee finger plays! I was exhilarated when I found that I could actually read their inventive spelling!

The children and I decided to make a change in our morning program. We began to devote a block of 45 minutes to reading and writing about topics the children chose and were interested in.

I had some reservations about our change. My kindergarten class consisted of 16 very verbal and active boys and 5 enthusiastic girls. Although I had made the decision in the fall to let the children guide my teaching, I was unsure that they would be able to handle the responsibility of daily reading and writing tasks for an extended amount of time.

My children surprised me. Their on-task behavior increased, and writing filled the walls, folders, and cubbies. Our Author's Chair had a constant line of children waiting to read their creations or classroom books.

The physical layout of the classroom also began changing. Writing areas were no longer confined to one corner of the room. Baskets containing personal writing folders, assorted sizes and colors of lined and unlined paper, wallpaper book covers, pens, pencils, and markers were all made available to the children. A desk, typewriter, telephone, telephone book, paper, stamps, and envelopes were added to our home center.

Paper in the block center allowed the children to label their creations or post "save" signs.

Daily conferencing with the children gave them an opportunity to share their ideas and writing. Conferencing allowed me to give personal attention and guidance to my authors. Anecdotal records were kept on each child, so that I was able to reflect and share their growth with them and their parents.

A reading of Eric Carle's *The Mixed-Up Chameleon* multiplied into a two-week unit that included insect and reptile joke books, a class big book on mixed-up people, an anatomy mural of lizards, measuring and observing the developmental stages of mealworms (a source of food for the chameleon), published books on lizards, snakes, and insects, and the purchase of a chameleon for the classroom.

The interest in Eric Carle was so great that we decided to continue reading some of his other books. *A House for Hermit Crab* brought us a gentle pair of crabs, and units incorporating gardening and insects evolved from *Tiny Seed, The Grouchy Ladybug,* and *The Very Busy Spider.*

There was no stopping the children's enthusiasm for learning, reading, and writing. My kidwatching had paid off; we were growing together.

Through my readings and observations I had become aware of the rich reading and writing classroom environment needed to allow children and teachers to grow as readers and writers. I am looking forward to expanding my knowledge in the growing and positive field of whole language.

➜ See: Boyd, p. 19; Literature Reference List, p. 429.

References
Butler, A., and J. Turbill. 1984. *Towards a reading-writing classroom.* Portsmouth, NH: Heinemann.
Cochrane, O. and D., S. Scalena, and E. Buchanan. 1988. *Reading, writing and caring.* CEL.

Alyce E. Dalzell is a primary teacher at St. Mark's School, Tucson, AZ.

As Teachers See It

by Kathy Mestnik

Wanted: User-Friendly Classrooms

The popular terminology in the business world today is "user-friendly." Executives prefer computers that fit this description. I began to wonder whether my classroom was user-friendly. Were my students interacting with a literate environment? Were they relating their experiences in school to their learning experiences outside school? I carefully examined my classroom activities and concluded that yes, indeed, my classroom is user-friendly. The following experiences were my proof:

The first day of school I stepped out of my classroom for just a few moments. I returned to discover that all of my second-graders had taken books off the shelf and were reading. I didn't need to invite them; they were readers.

One day after school I found a piece of paper left on the floor. It read, "1-17-89 I need to remember my book." One of my students had discovered that writing actually served a purpose; it was functional.

James was reading *The King's Pudding* during Reader's Workshop and shared that the end of the story reminded him of the time that he had been stung by a bee. He was connecting literature to his own life.

Brandi read a big book and she wasn't pleased. She said the words were too easy and requested that the class rewrite the story. After all, she said, we wrote better! She saw herself and her classmates as authors.

Gretchen told me one day during Writer's Workshop that she really liked Mercer Mayer's *Just Me and My Dad.* She thought she might try writing a story similar to *it.* Gretchen had made the connection between reading and writing.

During DEAR (Drop Everything And Read) one day, Jeff asked me for a book I had read during DEAR the previous day. I told him *Misery* by Stephen King and asked him why he wanted to know. He replied that the cover looked interesting and that he wanted to read it. Jeff was in tune to what other people in our classroom were reading.

These anecdotes indicate to me that my students are making connections in their learning. They are transferring their experiences from one situation to another. Their environment is rich with literature and the students are making literature their own. My classroom is user-friendly. I challenge all teachers to step back and carefully examine their classrooms to see whether they are also user-friendly.

➜ See: Literature Reference List, p. 429; Lockard, p. 238.

References
Cowley, J. 1987. *The king's pudding.* New York: Modern Publishing.
King, S. 1987. *Misery.* New York: Viking.
Mayer, M. 1977. *Just me and my dad.* New York: Golden Books.

Kathy Mestnik is a primary bilingual teacher in Denver public schools, Denver, CO.

Questioning Homework

 Viewpoint: Ann M. Marek

The Research on the Benefits of Homework

The effect of homework on academic achievement has been of interest to educators throughout the 20th century; it is one of the most researched topics in the current educational reform movement.

During the 1920s and 1930s, educators began to question the utility of what was then assigned as homework: rote memorization tasks requiring hours of attention, drill and practice exercises inviting inordinate amounts of assistance from peers or parents, and homework assigned as punishment. The limited experimental and survey data on homework by Otto (1950) concluded that compulsory homework was not consistently shown to improve academic performance, that voluntary homework was about as valuable as required homework, and that there were many disadvantages to the whole concept of homework.

Di Napoli did a key study in 1937 of approximately 1,200 fifth- and seventh-graders from six schools in New York City. He paired students on the basis of age, mental ability, and achievement test scores. Within each school, some classes were designated as the compulsory homework group, and others as the voluntary homework group. At the end of the spring semester, the achievement tests were again administered. The fifth-graders who were assigned compulsory homework performed better than the voluntary group in eight of nine subjects. However, for seventh-graders, the overall gains slightly favored the voluntary homework group. Di Napoli recommended the "abolition of compulsory homework in favor of voluntary homework."

Swenson, Cost, and Taylor (1955) reviewed homework studies from 1950 to 1955, including an experimental study by McGill (1950) that showed that the assignment of homework in high school social studies did not produce statistically significant improvements. They concluded "certainly there is no conclusive evidence . . . to justify the persisting faith of many persons in the merits of routine homework" (p. 22).

Goldstein's (1960) review of the homework literature reflected his view that "the consensus among educators is swinging back toward the desirability of regular homework assignments" (p. 222).

Goldstein agreed with Di Napoli's findings that the results favored compulsory homework for fifth-graders and slightly favored voluntary homework for seventh-graders. But Goldstein interpreted these findings quite differently than did Di Napoli.

Goldstein (p. 212) stated that the answer to whether regularly assigned homework contributes to academic achievement "may well depend on the subject, the grade level, the type of assignment, and the amount of homework." He also pointed out that "no statements whatsoever can be justified about the value of homework in grades one through four, since no research studies have dealt with these grades" (p. 221). Studies beyond grade four "tend to show positive effects of homework on academic achievement and certainly do not disprove such effects" (p. 222). Goldstein recommended:

> The homework program should stress regularity and continuity. It should be smoothly graduated, from a token daily assignment (perhaps five minutes) in first grade to two or three hours in high school. It should be required and not optional. It should be worthwhile and varied, including recreational reading, assigned reading for information, written composition, creative manual arts, research problems, practice in problem-solving and other basic skills, and drill when appropriate.

Goldstein seems to have ignored his own warnings that the efficacy of homework may depend on individual situations, and that no evidence supports the value of homework in grades one through four. Goldstein's recommendation was that homework should be "worthwhile and

varied," a statement that echoes the concerns expressed by educators in the 1940s and 1950s.

Rickards (1982) pointed out that "there is virtually no experimental evidence to support these . . . recommendations" (p. 832), and suggested, "What is needed is more well-designed and well-executed experimental research aimed at systematically examining different kinds of homework under different sorts of conditions" (p. 833). Rickards also raised the issue of "worthwhile" homework, citing surveys showing that parents, students, and teachers tend to "strongly favor homework . . . and feel that homework is necessary. However, parents, teachers, and students are all concerned about the type of homework assignments being given" (p. 831).

Throughout major shifts in opinion about the value of homework, one researcher seems to have captured the relevant issues in the homework debate. In 1955, Strang wrote a monograph published by the NEA entitled *Guided Study and Homework.* Her interpretation of the research prompted this tentative conclusion: "In the elementary school the observed values of a traditional type of homework do not justify assigning it. Homework done voluntarily produced about as good achievement as compulsory homework" (p. 20). Strang's conclusion remained essentially unchanged in 1966 and 1978 revisions of her work, even though her review of the literature was updated.

Despite decades of controversy, the homework debate can be easily summarized. Taken as a whole, the experimental research proves only that the effect of homework on academic achievement is extremely variable: For every study producing positive results another can be found producing

negative results. Those who oppose homework object strenuously to the routine assignment of drills and other exercises unsuited to the individual needs of students. Even those who advocate compulsory homework emphasize the need for worthwhile assignments tailored to individual needs, a challenge that the survey research indicates has not been met in the past.

What we can expect from mandates for regularly assigned homework is a plethora of assignments that are neither imaginative nor individualized (since those take the kind of time not always available on a daily basis)—precisely the kind of "busywork" that both proponents and opponents of compulsory homework have cautioned against for decades.

References

Di Napoli, P. 1937. "Homework in the New York City elementary schools." In *Teachers College, Columbia University, Contributions to Education* 719. New York: Columbia University.

Goldstein, A. 1960. "Does homework help? A review of research." *Elementary School Journal* 2.

McGill, V. J. 1950. "How valuable is homework?" *High Points* 32.

Otto, H. J. 1950. "Elementary education." In *Encyclopedia of Educational Research.*

Rickards, J. P. 1982. "Homework." In *Encyclopedia of Educational Research.*

Strang, R. S. 1955. *Guided study and homework: What research says to the teacher* 8. Washington DC: Department of Classroom Teachers, American Educational Research Association, National Education Association.

Swenson, E. J., J. C. Cost, and G. Y. Taylor. 1955. "Research on homework." *Journal of Education,* March.

Ann M. Marek is an educational consultant working for the state of Nevada.

As kids see it

Busywork: A Teacher's Easy Way Out
by Tmirah Haselkorn

There is a widespread notion that if the U.S. high school system were successful in cutting back the number of student dropouts, the crisis in the country's educational system would be undone. Unfortunately there are other problem areas that are no less damaging; one of these is the distribution of busywork: assigning classwork or homework for other than purely academic grounds, often with no apparent benefit for the students.

There are several kinds of busywork. One type is designed to keep the students occupied because the teacher either is ill-prepared that day or simply does not feel like teaching. For example, last year the first day in an English class was spent listing the students' favorite books on a piece of paper. The next day was spent listing favorite movies. The third day the students ranked the books in order of preference, a procedure repeated with the movies as well. Each student shared with the class his or her favorite books and movies on the fifth day. The week after, the students were told to draw a picture of the devil. The pictures were never collected, and their purpose remains unexplained. In fact, the aim of all of these bizarre assignments is still shrouded in a deep mystery.

An even more humiliating experience involved an absurd assignment, unfit for a six-year-old, given to high-school sophomores. The students were told to imagine themselves as fire hydrants and write a composition about it. There was a universal feeling in the class of disbelief and shock.

Busywork is also used to shift the responsibility of teaching from the teacher to the students. For example, last year an enormous amount of time was spent in my biology class on study guides. These were lists of important subjects covered in the 1,300-page biology book. In essence, it meant hour after hour of copying sentences from the book onto paper, without the teacher ever discussing them. These study guides simply substituted for lectures, in effect forcing the students to take responsibility for a crucial course.

One of the most dubious assignments given to the class was writing (fabricating) lab reports that were never even performed. These were invented essays, containing up to five sections, additional drawings, and conclusions.

By using this method, the students are forced involuntarily into teaching the material to themselves. The result is invariably an extra load on the students, a weight that ordinarily would have been the teacher's responsibility. Often the shift is made on the presumption that the students can handle the material alone, and that handling it will be a sign of maturity.

The question of quantity over quality is a problem in today's educational system. Busywork is no substitute for actual lessons, lectures, and overall teaching. Teachers are required to make a student's crucial learning years worthwhile and beneficial. There is no easy way out.

Tmirah Haselkorn is a senior at Palo Alto High School, Palo Alto, CA.

Education in Turin: A Romance by Herbert Kohl

Continued from page 204

From the Civil War to the New Century:
Education in an Industrial Society

Alice decided to attend the Cook County Normal School and arrived in Chicago in the fall of 1883. This letter, which she wrote to her fiance, Ralph Burns, describes a few of her impressions there:

Chicago, March 1, 1883

Dearest Ralph,

I do not know what is more remarkable, the public school we work at or the course of study at the Cook County Normal School. Colonel Parker said in a talk to new students that a course of study must be flexible if he is to train flexible teachers. We are all to do manual labor, to study the history of education, and to learn how to teach reading and arithmetic without the use of textbooks or workbooks. Colonel Parker said that textbooks are the work of the devil.

Today I was introduced to printing. Learning to operate a press is part of my instruction in the teaching of reading. The press is used to print our reading lessons, which consist of our children's poems and stories as well as the remarkable writings on scientific observations students make in Mr. Jackman's class and upon class trips. The press is also used to prepare material for the Chicago Normal School Envelope, which is written by Colonel Parker and the rest of the staff. The envelopes contain stories of the work at the school and I have learned much from them.

All this is the more astonishing in that Colonel Parker is under constant attack from the *Chicago Tribune* and certain members of the Chicago school board. They simply do not or will not understand what we are doing.

I look forward to resting and spending the summer being with you in Turin. Please share this with mother as I have no time to write.

Alice finished her training at the Cook County Normal School the next year and in 1885 she married Ralph Burns. She was fortunate enough to get a job at the Turin Common School, which kept on growing as Turin and the United States became industrialized. Alice's work was encouraged. A modern America entering the 20th century would need modern schools that stressed flexibility, invention, and the ability to adjust to the social demands of progress.

Progressivism grew as industry grew. In Turin, attacks were mounted on fundamentalist education from two groups, both in the name of progress. One group felt that it was basic that school prepare students to take their roles in a growing industrial world. The other group agreed that students should be prepared for industrial society, but it added to that preparation for a socially progressive democratic society.

Alice discussed educational issues with her mother, Elizabeth, right up until Elizabeth passed away in 1893. In 1896 Alice decided to return to Chicago for renewal. She had taken a leave from teaching in 1894 when her first child, Phillip, was born.

Continued on page 245

In the Mail

Karen Goodman is a doctoral student in epidemiology in the School of Public Health, Univeristy of California, Los Angeles, CA.

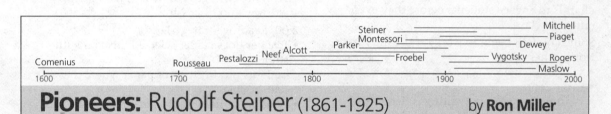

							Steiner				Mitchell
							Montessori				Piaget
						Parker				Dewey	
Comenius			Rousseau	Pestalozzi	Neef Alcott				Froebel		Vygotsky	Rogers
												Maslow
1600		1700			1800				1900			2000

Pioneers: Rudolf Steiner (1861-1925)   by **Ron Miller**

Around the turn of the 20th century, when the industrial age and scientific worldview were at their peak, a number of European and American philosophers began to wonder about the social and human consequences of scientific/technological civilization. Henri Bergson, Alfred North Whitehead, John Dewey, William James, Edmund Husserl, and other serious thinkers began to question the mechanistic tendencies that had developed during the 19th century. Rudolf Steiner, an Austrian scientist/philosopher as well as a mystic, was among this group. He probed deeply into problems of politics, theology, agriculture, medicine, and education in a civilization he viewed as lopsidedly materialistic. In 1919 he founded the first Waldorf school—a model that has been adopted by over 400 schools in more than 20 countries.

Like Montessori, Steiner believed that human development occurs in stages, with each six- or seven-year phase marked by its own developmental needs. Steiner asserted that very young children need their life energy to construct their physical being, and should not be led into academic work before their being is truly ready. In Waldorf education, young children are encouraged to play and explore the world through activity, imagination, and creativity. As they grow toward adolescence and beyond, intellectual and social concerns become more appropriate and are nurtured through close relationships between adults and children. In a Waldorf school, for example, the elementary teacher moves up a grade with his or her class each year. Steiner saw education as an art and the educator as a highly sensitive and creative artist, attuned to the unfolding personality of each student.

Like whole language, Waldorf education views learning as the forming of meaningful connections between the child and the world. Academic skills are not taught as isolated subjects, but are integrated into a comprehensive curriculum grounded in the great myths and legends of human history and in the creative arts; it is a curriculum meant to spark the child's imagination and appreciation for the whole scope of human endeavor.

Further Reading

Richards, M. C. 1980. *Toward Wholeness: Rudolf Steiner Education in America.* Middletown, CT: Wesleyan University Press.
Steiner, Rudolf. 1982. *The Roots of Education* (1924). London: Rudolf Steiner Press.

📷 WHOLE LANGUAGE CAMERA

The Boucher family works together at a Math Fair, West Stockbridge, MA.

Classroom Demonstrations

A Day in Two Whole Language Classrooms

As whole language has evolved, it has moved considerably beyond traditional classroom schedules. These schedules were compiled by Ken Goodman and Myna Matlin from classroom observations that they made six years ago. We include them because they have proved useful in teacher workshops. The reader should realize that the linear progression of classroom events as shown in the schedules is somewhat outmoded. Today, kids deal not so much with compartmentalized segments of classroom time as with continuous problem-solving. Every day is a little different.

—LBB

Fourth-Grade Developmental Reading Class

by Kenneth S. Goodman

A.M.

8:30

As students enter the classroom, they stop to read door charts on the outside of the room. The charts are invitations to create a pantomime, dance, etc. Some interpretation of Byrd Baylor's books.

The teacher's purpose in putting up the door chart is to engage students before they even enter the class.

Some children begin to work on the interpretations; others go to
• Science Center
• Book Center
• Writing Center/Logs (writing is tied to the current unit of study, "America Before the Settlers")
• Message Board (where they can leave notes for friends and their teacher)

Morning business—roll, lunch count, etc., is done by the students.

Songs on charts (popular songs and those tied to thematic unit too).

Sharing (even with older students) to encourage development of composition. Children talk through the composing, revising, and editing processes while engaged in oral discourse.

9:30 Math Center—three groups:
• Real world problems—algorithms
• Mean temperatures
• Division

10:45 Morning Recess

11:00 Byrd Baylor Group Presents:
• Dancing—*I Dance Mountains*
• Dramatizing—*And It Is Still That Way*—*Hawk, I Am Your Brother*

Teacher shares—*Everybody Needs a Rock*

11:30 U.S.S.W.
• Writing
• Book binding
• Revising and editing with other students and with the teacher

P.M.

12:30 Lunch

1:00 Social Studies Groups
• Murals of animal life in early America
• Dioramas of Native American villages
• Library trip for resource materials
• Working with groups with much reading, writing, and discussing

2:00 Reading Strategy Lesson
• Teacher does reader-selected miscues with students.
Students put in strips of paper where they had trouble.
• Working at helping students realize the can figure out their own strategies and that everyone makes mistakes, not just poorer readers.
• <u>Names</u> are a common problem for most readers:

How did you know it was a name?

Why are we having trouble with names?

Varied, not repeated; authors tend to deliberately vary names.

What do you know about foreign words and phrases?

2:30 Physical Education

3:00 "Get-Yourself-Together Time"
• Write in personal journals
• Finish up anything from the day

Kindergarten

by Myna Matlin

A.M.

8:30 Enter classroom—read letters from pen pals.

8:35 Put name on chart rack to show child is here—put notes on teacher's rocking chair.

8:37 Get books to begin SSR (Sustained Silent Reading) or get writing paper to start writing to pen pals.

8:55 Classroom Business:
• Child reads names of children who are not in school so teacher can mark absences.
• Lunch money, etc., business.
• Singing—using song chart.
• Explanation review of centers or activities for the day.

9:15 Work activities/centers/committees. Centers on weekly rotation based on thematic units, such as Thanksgiving:
• Working with adult (aide or parent) to find factual information about holiday adult reading from books and charts.

Map reading—where pilgrims came from.

Homework—to find out where family is from—to put on map.

Experience chart of remembered feasts.
• Writing recipe for cooking a turkey—to be published and given to parents, write and illustrate.
• Review of basic food groups for Thanksgiving feast—cutting out foods from magazines to make food group charts—each does a different food group.
• The block printing of cards—which will be eventual invitation to the feast.

Send to family.

Some children do extra for principal—custodian—other guests.
• Begin writing Thanksgiving books to be illustrated and published—most based on brown bears, red turkey.

9:45 Finish Centers—write in journals.

10:00 Free Choice:
• Grocery store
• Clay
• Puzzles/games
• Reading/writing

10:30 Work on pen pal letters (all finished by two days from now).

11:15 Discuss morning's work—wash hands, get lunch.

P.M.

12:00 Child reads to class—he prepared something special.

12:10 Math centers—coin identification for shopping trip.

1:10 Discussion of foods needed for feast—make shopping list, categorize by basic foods group.

1:50 Movement or lie on floor for quiet rest.

2:15 Come to meeting—teacher reads "Chapter book," ends at interesting or suspenseful part.

Myna Matlin is the principal of Warren Elementary School, Tucson, AZ.

Resource: Publisher

Raintree Publishers

310 W. Wisconsin Ave.
Milwaukee, WI 53203
1-800-558-7264

Trying to evaluate materials from a catalog alone is like trying to buy a pair of jeans through the mail—the jeans may be your size and look great in the mail-order catalog, but when you actually try them on, you find they are too tight to zip up. We can't promise that the materials offered by Raintree Publishers will really fit a whole language classroom, but as I scanned their glossy photographs and promotional copy, I thought, "Okay!" Their science and social studies materials, especially, look promising. *A Portrait of the Soviet Union*, in particular, caught my eye. It's a seven-volume set, illustrated with spectacular photographs, that examines the people, geography, economy, and history of this country we are so eager to know more about. Have any of you ordered from Raintree? Did their "jeans" fit? Write us and let us know.

LBB

As kids see it

Baptized
by April Kay Smith

One day my Mom got a letter from her sister. Her name is Pam. The letter said come to my church I am getting baptized Saturday. It was the next week. We went the next week at night and we saw Pam get baptized. I was scared. They turn all of the lights out except two of them. She put a cloth over her mouth. She went down in the water and she came back up. Then they turned the lights back on.

My name is April Kay Smith. I am 8 years old. I live up in Little Poplar Creek. When I grow up I want to be a babysitter because I like little children. The persons that I love the most is Mommy and Dad and Brother. I wish I could have a car so I could drive it and go places.

From *Great Mountain Tales,* written by Linda Oxendine's second-grade class, G. R. Hampton School, Barbourville, KY, 1989.

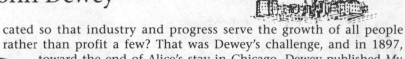

Education in Turin: A Romance by Herbert Kohl

Continued from page 243

From the Civil War to the New Century:
Alice Meets John Dewey

During the time of Alice's second stay in Chicago, from late spring 1896 to early spring 1897, the following events were held at the University of Chicago campus: the annual institute of the Cook County Teacher's; a meeting of the Illinois Society for Child Study; conferences on teaching English, mathematics, reading, the arts; a celebration of Horace Mann's Centennial; a celebration of the 150th anniversary of the birth of Pestalozzi; and most important for Alice, a series of public lectures on the science of art and teaching by Colonel Parker, and a seminar on education conducted by Professor John Dewey, who had arrived in Chicago in 1894.

Dewey was in many ways the opposite of Colonel Parker. He was dry and a bit wry, given to rambling. However, his students recognized that, involuted and complex as his words were, they had substance. Dewey in his early work tried to reconcile the free individual, the natural person, with the citizen in an industrial state. How can children be edu-

cated so that industry and progress serve the growth of all people rather than profit a few? That was Dewey's challenge, and in 1897, toward the end of Alice's stay in Chicago, Dewey published *My Pedagogical Creed*, which proclaimed:

> I believe that education is a regulation of the process of coming to share in the social consciousness; and that the adjustment of individual activity on the basis of this social consciousness is the only sure method of social reconstruction.
>
> I believe that this conception has due regard for both the individualistic and socialist ideals.

At the turn of the century Alice was a Deweyite, a socialist who did not believe in violent revolution but who did believe that education could produce fundamental social change.

Reference
Dewey, J. 1897. *My pedagogical creed.* Chicago: A. Flanagan.

Continued on page 303

As Teachers See It

by Judith Kalman

On Scheduling

When I started teaching in September, I didn't clearly distinguish between smaller routines and scheduling events in the classroom. I thought that a routine was a structured set of activities that you do repeatedly and insert between other, bigger activities, regardless of what they might be. I don't believe that anymore. I have come to think of a schedule as a framework that allows one activity to flow into another.

The period I have worked with the most is the 90-minute reading/math time. At first I devised a schedule of small group work, followed by an individual activity that was to be "meaningful" (i.e., not just dittos or coloring) and would keep the kids involved in their group while I worked with another one. Then we would come together for a large group activity and switch. It was great on paper, but there were several serious problems. One was making sure that the activities lasted approximately the same time; another was keeping the gears going, so to speak. If the group of kids who were working on their own lost interest or had a problem or just plain fell apart (as kindergarten students do at times) before I was free to direct what was next, I had half the kids wandering around or coming up to me and asking, "What do I do now, Teacher?"

So a couple of months later I tried another approach. When the kids first came in, they had a job to do. When they finished they were supposed to sign in and get a book. Then we had circle time; everybody did an activity together at the same time. As they finished they got their journals and worked in them, found a partner for journal sharing, and then they could choose something from the "choose table." This worked okay, but I still felt like a traffic cop, telling people where to go and what to do.

I seemed to be the one who was choosing the time span of the activities; either I was trying to push the kids through it when they wanted to continue with something, or I was entertaining kids who finished first so that the other kids could get done and the next thing could start. They all depended on *me*.

While I am still convinced that a schedule is important, I think that it must be structured enough to give a sense of organization, and at

the same time be flexible enough to give all the students the possibility of using their time most constructively. I am trying to find a way to put this concept into practice. As a starting point, I decided that I would first try to pinpoint what I want out of a new framework:

- I want everybody to be engaged in what they are doing.
- I want the children in my class to work independently, to know what to do without depending on me to tell them.
- I want the children to be responsible for selecting activities and materials, as well as cleaning up after themselves.
- I want the students in my classroom to be exposed to and try new things.

With these things in mind I have reshaped the 90-minute reading/math time for both the early bird and late bird shifts. My most recent attempt at trying to organize this time differs only subtly from my previous schedules when written on paper. The main difference is that I have let go of directing and coordinating every movement that takes place and have allowed the students to make some choices on their own. Our morning (and afternoon) sessions now feel something like this:

When the kids arrive, they help take down the chairs and get books. They sit at the tables and look at their books either by themselves or together. When this activity comes to an end, I meet on the rug with the children who have finished and begin to work on our newspaper, a sorting activity, a guessing game, or a story. The other children usually join us shortly, and if someone is still looking at their book, that's okay too. The children are then divided into groups and do

a series of activities that will be repeated throughout the week, so that by the end of the week they will have done them all. When they finish what they are doing, they sign the sign-in sheet at their table, put their things away, and get their journals. When they are done with writing, they choose an activity until it is time to go to recess.

During this one-and-a-half-hour period, the children have the opportunity to do five different things or stick with any one of them as long as they like. There are some days when nobody gets to the free choice at the end because they are so involved in other activities. There are other days when everyone seems to race through their journals or group work because what they really want is to get to the sorting tubs. They will settle into sorting and stay with it for perhaps 30 minutes. They are involved and hard at work, learning.

→ See: Kalman, pp. 34, 148.

Judith Kalman is a Ph.D. candidate at the University of California, Berkeley, CA.

Resource: Organization

North Dakota Study Group

c/o Vito Perrone
Center for Teaching and Learning
Box 8158, University Sation
Grand Forks, ND 58202

In November 1982, a distinguished group of educators, led by Vito Perrone, met at the University of North Dakota to discuss the problems with narrow measures of accountability and evaluation, and to see if they could generate more sensible ways of evaluating children's thinking and learning. The result was the founding of the Center for Teaching and Learning designed to support government policy makers, administrators, parents, and teachers on the hard issues of testing and evaluation. Most notable is a series of monographs that address children's thinking and language, teacher support systems, staff development, and the schools' relationship to the larger community. The papers are not to be "taken as final statement—new ideology, but working papers, written by people who are acting on, not just thinking about these problems, whose implications need an active and considered response."

I Used to Be...But Now I...

I used to be a child commander,
But now I'm a kidwatcher.

—Trifona Andres

Cornerstone: Michael Hagan

Social Learning: Discipline in Whole Language Classrooms

"Mista Hagan, I seen that book before!" For the fifth time Michael stood up in the middle of the reading circle waving his arms, a broad smile on his face. The mood so carefully cultivated for this story was shattered, and Michael once more demonstrated why he had been kicked out of two preschools before he set foot in my door as a kindergartner.

Helping children develop self-discipline is much too complex to be resolved by the "Rambo" mentality of assertive discipline. Discipline is at the core of classroom practice facilitated by both a well-planned curriculum and some fundamental attention to positive classroom management.

Curriculum and Classroom Environment

Children are less likely to become "problems" in classrooms that encourage their movement within the room, action on objects, and interaction with people. In traditional educational environments, these activities are often restricted if not prohibited. Whole language teachers are well aware of the educational importance of children constructing knowledge through their own actions. It is when this act of construction is denied to children that they are more likely to "act out."

The very way in which our rooms are arranged has a significant effect on children's behavior. Child-centered classrooms facilitate movement if unnecessary furniture is removed. Materials are available and accessible. Private spaces are provided, as well as large open areas in which the whole class can meet for class meetings and other shared experiences.

A whole language teacher is fundamentally concerned about children's successes, both academic and social. When learners are engaged they don't want to waste time in behavior that distracts them from an enjoyable activity. A whole language classroom is a productive room; a healthy buzz of activity is pervasive.

A Collaborative Community

In whole language classrooms children are repeatedly encouraged to support each other. In

Michael Hagan travels around the country working with teachers and school districts as a consultant in whole language learning. His current work includes a half-time position as staff development resource teacher at Horace Mann Elementary Magnet, a whole language school in San Jose, California, which was recently recognized by NCTE as a Center of Excellence in Language Arts. Michael is a part-time instructor at San Jose State University, and is currently participating in a federal grant for adult literacy through literature for limited-English and non-English speakers. He has published articles in *Arithmetic Teacher, Teachers Networking,* and *The Whole Idea*. Michael and his wife, Joan, were recently invited to visit New Zealand classrooms as guests of the New Zealand Ministry of Education.

the writers workshop children learn how to point out what they like in a classmate's writing. They learn how to listen to and honor each other as authors. Mostly, they learn to respect each other in the process of communicating meanings.

We lessen discipline problems when we lead the class in shared reading experiences, cocreating an environment in which everyone's ideas are honored, and when we discover that "*all* of us are better thinkers than *one* of us." A community of learners is also built up through songs, chants, poems, and whole class involvement in themes.

Perhaps most significantly, we bond with each other. The room is our common space, a place in which children may choose to spend time during recess or after school. We celebrate the publishing of a child's writing, share a favorite story, and just plain laugh together. We work together to cocreate a joyful environment in which solidarity triumphs over self-righteousness. Children learn that the least desirable outcome of their misbehavior is to break that bond.

Bonding is facilitated by older children who are regularly responsible for being tutors or pals to younger ones, and all the children benefit academically as well as socially. Caring is also fostered by children being responsible for classroom pets. Even more basic, children want their teachers to care for them.

Children actively create their understanding of the social world by observing and approximating what they see around them. As they internalize a predictable and stable environment, they feel free to interact in ways that seem appropriate. By beginning with a more apparent structure and gradually loosening up, teachers help children internalize what may be an unfamiliar school environment.

Whole language teachers are active, not passive. They see themselves as neither authoritarian nor permissive but rather as authorities with final responsibility for maintaining a learning environment. However, their dealings with social learning, as with cognitive learning, are formed by a unique set of values. Extrinsic rewards are replaced by intrinsic motivation. Praise and punishment are replaced by encouragement. Most important, a whole language teacher is constantly on the lookout for opportunities to interact positively with children.

Recognizing the one time during the day when a child does well is many times more powerful than constantly recognizing failure. This was powerfully demonstrated to me by Michael, my impulsive kindergartner. Michael was talking so constantly that I finally realized I would have to catch him taking a breath in order to acknowledge his silence during story time. When I did so he straightened up and stopped talking instantly! The more I got to know Michael, the more I realized that he had received attention only for misbehavior. He needed adults to tell him when he was doing what he *should* be doing more often. To begin to ignore some of that negative behavior is not to be ignorant of it.

Problems are best solved when and with whom they occur. Just as I expect a child to

have attempted a spelling before I will give advice, I expect an honest attempt at a solution to a disagreement. Should that attempt fail, another child or I can be called in to mediate. The final step in conflict resolution is to bring an item to a class meeting.

During daily class meetings, which last about 20 minutes, children are provided an opportunity to get to know each other, solve problems, set routines, and establish rules. In these meetings we learn to support and listen to each other, to discuss possible solutions and vote on them, and to build more consciously the solidarity necessary for a positive learning environment. Even very young children quickly learn to listen to contrasting points of view and make decisions that positively affect the class as a whole (Nelson 1987).

Facts, Meanings, Values

As teachers, we are constantly evaluating and responding to situations. As we do so we respond to three levels of reality: facts, meanings, or values. Suppose that a child pushes another child. If we react at the level of facts, we may think that punishment is in order. However, if we take time to ask about the situation, we may find out that the first child was defending a friend from a bully. At the level of values, we would focus more on getting the two children to resolve future situations without force. All too often, we find it more expedient to deal with the surface of a situation. Yet, just as we are learning that reading for meaning is more important than reading for facts, we need to begin to search social situations for deeper levels and respond appropriately.

All of this is a tall order for an educational system that is more often based on the morality of constraint than on the morality of cooperation. Social education was once based on the motto "Do as I say, not as I do." What we failed to accomplish by example we could always restore by verbal wisdom. Children will be more impressed by our performance than by our admonitions. As we develop environments that place a high premium on mutual respect and self-respect, we will enlist children's commitment to a lifelong process of social as well as academic learning.

→ See: Bird, p. 271; Goodman, pp. 207, 224.

Reference
Nelson, J. 1987. *Positive discipline.* New York: Ballantine.

Language Stories

Assertive Discipline

As she did every morning the kindergarten teacher began to write the day of the week and the date on the chalkboard. When she finished the *T* for Thursday, Thomas, sitting at his seat, began to look agitated. When she wrote the *H*, he burst into tears, jumped from his seat, ran out of the door, and started to run home. He didn't know what he had done, but he knew the teacher only wrote your name on the board if you'd been naughty.

—KSG

Resource: Organization

End Violence Against the Next Generation

THE LAST ? RESORT

977 Keeler Ave.
Berkeley, CA 94708-1498
1-415-527-0454

One would like to believe that this organization is not necessary, but the sad truth is that corporal punishment in schools is still legal in 31 of the United States. Let's hope that one outcome of whole language and empowered teachers and students will be the abolition of this medieval approach to discipline. The organization, also known as EVAN-G, offers a newsletter titled *The Last ? Resort* as well as a variety of booklets that emphasize alternatives to physical punishment.

LBB

Principals Speak Out

by JoAnn C. Shaheen

Children Speak Up for Fairness

What can teachers and principals do when a student acts cruelly or unfairly? Can we allow the child's peers to take responsibility for seeing that justice is done? How can we set up systems that will help students deal thoughtfully with unfair and harmful behavior?

At Schaefer School, which serves children from kindergarten to fourth grade, the children take the initiative to identify interpersonal problems—sometimes quite serious ones—and work out fair and just solutions. We have one Due Process Board drawn from third-graders and one drawn from fourth-graders. All children, kindergarten through fourth grade, can appeal to the Due Process Boards.

At 12:10 P.M. a knock on my door from one of the third-graders reminded me that our Due Process meeting was ready to begin.

When we entered the library, the third-grade board members were arriving with their lunches and choosing their places at one end of the table. Four other third-grade children also entered the room, but rather hesitantly: Blanche, a black girl; Sara and Lisa, both white; and Joe, a white boy who was accompanied by Mrs. Almquist, a teacher of the learning disabled.

The three girls were there to question Joe's actions. I asked them to sit to the left of me. I placed Joe to my immediate right. Even though he had an adult friend with him, it is customary for me to place next to me the child in question, in case he or she needs protection, understanding, advocacy, encouragement, or approval.

When everyone was sitting and having their lunch, I introduced Mrs. Almquist to the children and explained that she was there as Joe's friend because he was rather new to our school. The children agreed that this was fair.

I asked the girls to speak about what they believed was Joe's unfair behavior, reminding them that they had five minutes to tell their story. After that, they were not allowed to speak unless a member of the board called upon them and until Joe and his friend had five minutes to tell their side of the story.

Blanche's friend began. "He said terrible things to Blanche. He called her bad names." She told us that she could not say them aloud, and was obviously embarrassed. She ended with, "He said that he would take care of Blanche when he goes to the bathroom."

No one understood what it meant, and Blanche jumped in angrily, "He makes fun of me because I am a different color."

Pam, a black member of the third-grade board, stood up, sandwich in hand. Waving it, she screamed at him, "I know what he means. He means that when he goes to the bathroom and does doo-doo, it is brown, just like us."

Everyone at the table was stunned.

Joe spoke very quietly, in almost a hushed voice, "No. I really didn't mean it." All four girls confronted him until he finally admitted that he had called them "chocolate cake," "chocolate cookie," "brownie," and "chocolate ice cream."

Boyd, a third-grade board member, rose to address Joe. "Now listen, Joe, you've got to understand. When the blacks were brought to this country, they were brought here as slaves. We didn't give them enough food. We didn't give them good housing. Their clothes were terrible. We let them work and work and work, and we didn't even teach them to read. Now lately, we're making some changes. We're starting to do what is right. This just can't happen again. You can't take us back. You just can't take us back to those days. We have got to learn to live together. *You must help!*"

Joe fumbled and mumbled, saying he'd try to help. I stepped in and said that it was clear Joe

had said unfair things to Blanche, and I asked Joe if people did this in his other school. He said that nobody there seemed to care too much about what people said to each other on the playground. I asked the board to remember that Joe had had experiences where people did not care about fairness.

The board members were asked to caucus—to choose a leader and go to the front of the room to discuss what the consequences for Joe's actions should be. In a few minutes the board returned and recommended that Joe should write a "sorry" note to Blanche and that they wanted Mrs. Almquist to help him.

I asked Blanche if this would be satisfactory with her and her friends and they agreed that it was fair. Joe agreed that it was fair, but the Due Process Board members continued to feel righteous indignation.

Several of the board members started saying that Joe was always misbehaving—that he didn't treat anyone right and that he was a troublemaker. Blanche stood up and quietly declared, "That is not true. Joe is a nice boy, and I will be his friend."

The whole table melted. Boyd closed the meeting with, "Aw, it's all right, Joe. We just don't do that here. We will teach you how to help."

Our Due Process Board members are selected, not elected. Working from class rosters, the principal, special area teachers, and classroom teachers select a representative from each of the third- and fourth-grade homerooms. Experience has taught us that we function most effectively if there are at least five board members present at a meeting; so to allow for absences, we select at least seven children for each board.

If something doesn't seem fair to our students, they direct the steps to be taken to reach a solution or alternative. The school staff has a commitment to being the advocates of children. We help them to take active roles of leadership, to identify and solve problems, to think, to argue, to take positions—and to approach and question authority.

➔ See: Shor, p. 223.

Excerpted from *Democracy and Education: The Bulletin of the Institute for Democracy in Education* 2(4), June 1987.

JoAnn C. Shaheen is the principal of William O. Schaefer School, Tappan, NY.

Resource: Book and Audiocassette Kit

Getting Along: A Fun-filled Set of Stories, Songs and Activities to Help Kids Work and Play Together

Children's Television Resource and Education Center
1988; 63 pp.; $12.95
JTG of Nashville
1024C 18th Ave. S
Nashville, TN 37212
1-800-222-2584

Getting Along: A Social Development Curriculum

From:
American Guidance Service
Box 99
Circle Pines, MN 55014-1796
1-800-328-2560; in MN, 1-800-247-5053

Remember the old Hollywood musicals like *Seven Brides for Seven Brothers* in which the characters would inexplicably break into song? If you share with your students the tape and book kit *Getting Along,* don't be surprised if they suddenly belt out a heart-rending version of "Bully, Don't You Push Me Around," or any of the other 10 great songs designed to help kids work and play together. My friend and fourth-grade teacher Elizabeth Doerr says that her students beg for this tape over and over again, and sing along with it with gusto. Besides great tunes, these songs give kids strategies for working things out and can serve as openers for class discussions. In the book you'll find 10 stories that deal with the same issues as the songs, and also activities. The creators of the stories and songs kit, Children's Television Resource and Education Center, tell us they have developed a whole K to 4 curriculum that helps kids learn cooperation, caring for others, and positive conflict resolution in a structure that promotes self-esteem. This program will be published by American Guidance Service in fall of 1990.

LBB

Assertive discipline is already an admission of failure.

—Kenneth S. Goodman

WELL-SAID

Resource: Workshop

Creative Response to Conflict

American Friends Service Committee (AFSC)
931 N. Fifth Ave.
Tucson, AZ 85705
1-602-623-9141
Newsletter $3/year from:
CCRC/FOR
Box 271
Nyack, NY 10960

American Friends Service Committee has a centuries-old commitment to peaceful nonconfrontation. They have now brought that commitment and expertise into the classroom and are helping teachers find creative alternatives for problem-solving and conflict resolution. They offer workshops, a handbook, *The Friendly Classroom for a Small Planet,* and a newsletter, *Sharing Space,* in which readers and CRC staff share new ideas and techniques they've discovered through their work in classrooms. Conflict resolution CRC-style centers on four themes: affirmation, communication, cooperation, and problem-solving.

LBB

Resource: Book

Tribes: A Process for Social Development and Cooperative Learning

Jeanne Gibbs
1989; 248 pp.; $19.95
Center Source Publications
P.O. Box 436
Santa Rosa, CA 95402
1-707-578-0223

Are you a teacher who feels the need for more structure in your classroom, but can't abide the mindless control of assertive discipline? *Tribes* may be the program for you. Stressing social development and cooperative learning, *Tribes* offers a management process that new teachers in particular may find reassuring. The handbook provides detailed instructions and theory to help teachers create positive learning environments and cooperative learning groups. It promises that kids will learn genuine mutual regard, interaction skills, and responsibility.

LBB

Breakthroughs

by Elizabeth D. Nelms

Stephen

Meet Stephen, alias Big Daddy Kane. A fellow teacher once described him as the perfect character for one to write into a sitcom. He sits very quietly in the seat farthest from the teacher. A thin, bespectacled, young man, he reminds me of a daddy longlegs—much too light and airy to be restricted to a school desk. Behind this quiet facade hides an imaginative, clever, humorous man-child who often seems to suppress some inner turbulence. The days he is angry, Stephen will produce little and say nothing. On the good days he comes in the room with a teasing "Hi, Beth" as he slides into his seat before I can show my shocked amusement at his impertinence.

And I let him get by with it because Stephen, I discovered several weeks into the school year, can weave magic with words, but he has to weave on his own time, in his own space. He spends a whole class period producing a sentence or two, acting angry at the blaring green of the intimidating computer screen, and quietly asks if he can bring in something tomorrow. The next day, without fail, a beautifully printed full page of writing appears in my hand as he enters. I smile, put it aside to read, and then later run to him with delight; his writing is truly rich.

Stephen loves to be loved but sends out all the signals that say *do not touch.* His humor is the under-the-breath kind that usually gets a sharp look from a busy teacher. But now I know to call on him and ask him to share with us all. His comments are astute and seldom disruptive.

Stephen is hard to stimulate because his first strategy from the old days is to think, "I can't do that." He will sit dejected until I can ease over and try to help him make an idea his own, find his own way to meet the challenge. If his spirits droop, he throws in the towel. My concern for Stephen boils down to two questions: How can I help him take responsibility for his own actions? and How can I encourage high achievement in a student who seems stuck in a rut of underachievement?

In an effort to help Stephen take responsibility for his own actions, I began with a written conversation, hoping to establish a personal, caring relationship with him. Stephen seemed to enjoy this time, especially since we were sharing french fries dipped in catsup. He was at ease, respectful, involved in this one-on-one meeting. I wanted the written conversation so that he could see his ideas in print. He is very verbal, as am I, and I did not want in any way to step on his words or interrupt the flow of his thought. I also think that words in print have a special kind of power of conviction. We both enjoyed this time.

The next day I asked him how he felt about being in the basic class and whether he would consider visiting one of the college-bound classes that I thought he might like to consider for next year. His face brightened, he swaggered a bit, and he spoke very much like a gray-suited businessman who knew he had life by the tail.

When Stephen visited my class we were involved in an energetic discussion about poetry. It was fast paced, ideas flowing from one student to the next. Out of the corner of my eye, I saw Stephen taking it all in. I wondered what he was thinking, but I didn't pay any special attention to him, nor did the others. Later Stephen told his language arts specialist, "There are just a bunch of smart kids in there. They were all talking about books!" I am convinced that Stephen too would talk about books and become a more serious student if he could be among such models.

The next two weeks took me absolutely by surprise. Stephen reverted to misbehaving in the basic class. He called attention to himself, almost as he had at the beginning of school. I pondered the situation and wondered if I had pushed him too fast toward thinking of himself in terms other than a "basic" student. Had I cornered him into taking on more than he was emotionally ready for? He assured me, "No, no, Mrs. Nelms, I want to take the more challenging class next year." I told him that I would approve such a move, but expected his behavior to improve.

Stephen did not improve. In fact, I had to march him and eight of the students in his seventh-hour class down the hall to the principal for "a little talk." I told the principal that I was not able to have a discussion or sharing of any kind with this many students who showed absolutely no self-control. I also told him that he would have to search hard to find eight students more interesting and energetic. What could we do to help them? He laid down the law. They had two choices: to remain in my class or to be taken out of English and given study hall. They all chose to remain and knew that any additional offense would get them bounced out for good.

The next strategy involved a special roundtable meeting with Stephen and his language arts specialist. She too had become concerned about Stephen's habit of putting the blame elsewhere. His smile and charming ways had helped him out of many a close scrape. She too saw that he needed to confront his problems and assume some responsibility for their solution. We scheduled a meeting during which I agreed to bring a contract for Stephen to consider if we were to continue to work together.

The conference was good. When he had had his say ("Teachers always pick on me; nobody gives me a chance," etc.), I read the contract and left him with the specialist. I was especially concerned that he be able to restate to her his perception of the meeting we had just had. He was uncomfortable. He had no one with whom to argue. He had been given the responsibility and had to stand on his own and consider the facts as seen by someone else.

The puzzle is falling into place. I helped that seventh hour by making a seating chart, even though it was a real struggle to shift eight people around so that their immediate seat buddies would not invite trouble. Stephen seems to respect my need to do that, and his behavior is 100 percent better. He is involved with our discussions. I truly believe that Stephen is creating a new self-image as he redefines himself in his own eyes and in those of his classmates.

➔ See: Dalrymple, p. 63; Meier, p. 50; Nelms, p. 62.

Elizabeth D. Nelms is an English teacher at Hickman High School, Columbia, MO.

YOUNG ARTISTS

"Soaring", Lili Pang, 15, Portland, OR
(From *Treasures 2*, see p. 162)

Resource: Publisher

Reader's Digest Books

American School Publishers/
  Macmillan-McGraw Hill
Princeton Rd.
P.O. Box 408
Hightstown, NJ 08520
1-800-843-8855

"Dentist office" used to be the first thing I thought of when I encountered *Reader's Digest.* Not anymore. The five hardbound books that arrived in the mail from *Reader's Digest* has forever changed the way I think about this publisher. Richly illustrated with colored photographs, scientific diagrams, and on almost every page offset boxes highlighting interesting facts, these books are a delight to read. We all know how kids spend hours poring over the *Guinness Book of World Records.* These books: *Story of the Great American West, Reader's Digest Book of Facts, ABC's of the Human Body, ABC's of Nature,* and *North American Wildlife,* invite the same sort of perusal. By the way, did you know that, if your blood vessels were laid end to end, they would encircle the globe twice? I learned that from the *ABC's of the Human Body.*

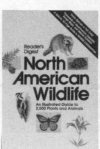

LBB

Breakthroughs

by Kathryn M. Krauskopf

Growing Pains

Personality conflicts between teachers and students are probably more prevalent in the junior high school grades than anywhere else in the elementary or secondary years. This happened to me once: A very pretty, very bright, very aggressive girl was in my journalism class, and with one look we immediately locked horns. This bothered me because I could foresee the disturbing friction the situation would almost certainly generate, to the detriment of a smooth-running class. So one day soon I asked Betty to stay after class for a few minutes and she complied, eyes snapping and chin thrust well forward.

"I suppose you've noticed that you and I have a personality conflict," I started right in.

Shocked, surprised, and interested, she admitted that this had crossed her mind.

"Well, when two people sort of instinctively dislike one another, there isn't very much to do about it except to take extra pains to be polite and not tread on one another's toes. I suggest we try to do this—is that all right with you?"

Betty agreed enthusiastically and we maintained a good businesslike relationship for the entire semester. Halfway through high school the girl came back to visit me and tell me how she was getting along. I think we both learned a good lesson in tolerance from the experience.

➜ See: Krauskopf, p. 288.

Kathryn M. Krauskopf is a counselor and teacher at Jordan Junior High School, Palo Alto, CA.

Principals Speak Out

by Bob Wortman

Working With Children

Put this checklist in a place where you will run across it again (and again):

- Do I remember to say (both in action and in words) "I like who you are"?
- When I don't like what you do, do I remember to say "I don't like what you are doing" but clearly have it understood that "I still like you"?
- Do I make sure that I am not doing things for the children that they can do for themselves?
- Do I allow the children to work problems out for themselves?
- Do I give the children choices (the ones I am willing to live with)?
- Am I able to say "I've changed my mind" or "I was wrong"?
- Am I observing what the children like to do and are interested in? Do I follow their lead occasionally?

- Do I make an effort to get inside their minds for a while? To see things from their point of view?
- Do we brainstorm options, evaluate, and make choices together?
- Do I say "I like you," "I feel happy to share this with you," "How special our time together is," "I learn from you"?
- Do I build on strengths?
- Do we play together?
- Do we laugh together?
- Do I say, "I appreciate . . ."?
- How many times did we touch today? Keep track one day—especially for older children.
- Do we sit and talk one on one, eye to eye, heart to heart?

➜ See: Hagan, p. 246; Matlin, p. 47.

Bob Wortman is the principal of Borton Primary Magnet School, Tucson, AZ.

I was toKeng
w and the tehsb
stop and was
steoll toKcn
and wud the
tcch wns toKcn
I was toKcn.

[I was talking when the teacher said stop and (I) was still talking and when the teacher was talking I was talking.]

MarvELous INVENTIONS

Writing Away Trouble

Before second-grade teacher Pam Adair meets with her students to discuss problems they are having in class, she often asks them to write about the difficulties. Besides the quiet time for reflection the writing affords, it also provides both the students and Pam with helpful insights into possible reasons for the trouble. Here is one student's analysis of his classroom transgression.

—LBB

➜ See: Bird, p. 92.

—Contributed by Pam Adair, second grade teacher, Fair Oaks School, Redwood City, CA

It Shouldn't Happen to Kids

Not Worth the Wait

Once upon a time there was a little boy who was so eager to go to school, he just couldn't wait. He waited and he waited . . . finally, the great day arrived. He kissed his mother goodbye, skipped out the front door, and went off to school singing merrily. Two hours later he came home looking very dejected. His mother said, "What are you doing home? I thought you were so eager to be at school!"

"Well, the teacher told me that I can't read, I can't write, and I'm not allowed to talk, so I came home. There's nothing to do at school."

—KSG

Resource: Organizations

National Association for Mediation in Education (NAME)

425 Amity St.
Amherst, MA 01002
1-413-545-2462

NAME promotes the teaching of conflict resolution skills, and offers programs for peer mediation. Serving as a national clearinghouse for publications, curriculum guides, and information on conflict resolution programs already in action, it publishes a bibliography, directory, a newsletter, and various reports.

Holistic Education Review

ABC Distribution Company

Capital Cities/ABC Video Enterprises
825 Seventh Ave.
New York, NY 10019-6001
1-212-887-1731
FAX 1-212-887-1708

Educators can purchase video copies of ABC TV's educational and nontheatrical (nonfiction) programs. ABC Distribution Company will send you a list of all programs available. Programs are organized by topic and cover everything from health, substance abuse, safety, science and the environment (the contents of one division) to children's programs and literature, sports, the arts, and miscellaneous. For an educational, nonprofit organization's use, prices range from $160 for a 30-minute program to $210 for 60 minutes of airtime. Bulk order discounts for quantities of five or more units can be arranged.

WHOLE LANGUAGE CAMERA

Book discussion, Nancy Moyer's class, Amphitheater Junior High, Tucson, AZ

Beginning the Year

Classroom Demonstrations

by Robin Myers

A Strategy for Starting the School Year

It is nothing short of a miracle that modern methods of instruction have not yet entirely strangled the holy curiosity of inquiry.

—Albert Einstein

After my first year of teaching high school, I spent the summer wondering, "What did I just do?" I was proud of myself for just making it through that grueling first year, teaching 160 ninth- and tenth-graders. But my missionary zeal of turning teenagers into people who all of a sudden would rather read or write than watch "Riptide" was deflated. Why, after all I had learned in college, did I so easily succumb to the boring units and lessons in the Scope and Sequence curricular guide? Yes, I voiced my opinions, but how loudly should a first-year teacher rebel? Still, I wanted my second year (now that I'd decided that there would be a second year) to be more like my original vision.

Day One

This year I would teach all seniors—various tracked levels, but all graduating (hopefully) seniors. All had stuck out 12 years of school and 12 years of "English." What did they think about it all? Could this last year provide them with anything that had been missing?

The first day of school I put a single question on the board: "What is English?" As the kids filed in, I smiled, said hello, answered questions, listened to gossip and stories, and waited until they stopped talking. Then the questions began: "I heard we have to read *Beowulf* and lots of Shakespeare. Do we have to memorize stuff from that old poetry?" "Do we have to do those stupid plays for the freshmen?" "Why do they make us do the most boring stuff (English literature) when we're seniors?" Interested, I smiled, acknowledged their questions, and then (for a reason yet unknown to me) started writing their questions on the board, around mine. After a few minutes, the questioning stopped and discussion raged. I told them they were raising very good questions; they looked at me quizzically, as if I was supposed to be offended by their questions and responses. I passed out a sheet of blank paper to each student.

They got quiet, waiting to see what I was going to say. "Tell me what you think of all this—about 'English class.' What should be the purpose of it? Why is it the only subject you're required to take for four years? Answer any of the questions on the board if they appeal to you. I spent the summer, not to mention the past five years, with these ideas in mind, and they're still not clear to me. You help me decide what this—your senior year—is about and what you want to get from the class. The only rule is don't use any names of former teachers."

I've never seen such frantic writing. There was the occasional "Remember last year when . . ." whispered across the room, accompanied by various facial expressions and bodily noises. To my amazement, they wrote until the end of the period. I had thought we would discuss their ideas when they finished, but the bell stopped at least half of them. Several students left the classroom telling animated stories and discussing what they wrote.

As the next class filed in, I was eager to read first period's papers, but I knew I had to wait. My curiosity probably accounted for the changed course of second period, who did not write at all but discussed the same ideas. They wanted to tell stories of their worst experiences—how worthless and boring certain exercises and teachers were. A few remembered some good units or books or papers. Finally, one student asked me what I thought, and the others quieted, as if they hadn't considered that I might have an opinion. I explained that I wasn't quite sure what it was all about; that I enjoyed reading, writing, communicating, and the arts, and I thought I could help

others find the same pleasures I did; that I thought reading and writing were important for getting jobs and getting into good colleges, but for more important, personal reasons too, which I couldn't quite define. I explained that at the end of my last year, I felt a bit let down, as if I hadn't accomplished what I had intended, although I wasn't even sure what that was. And, most of all, I told them I wanted to start the year, and continue it, with their needs and interests in mind, rather than a prescribed set of literary works, writing assignments, and grammar rules as a guide. Some looked pleased, others skeptical, some almost shocked.

As soon as I paused, hands went up, offering suggestions, until it seemed like a million conversations were going right past me. "Homework," I wrote on the board. They groaned. "Optional," I added. They cheered. I then said, "In writing, tell me what you'd like to get out of English class this year and what I can do to make the class worthwhile to you." This class left, again talking excitedly as they walked out of my room. For my other three classes that day, I continued the same way—sometimes only discussing, sometimes writing in class as well. The students were eager to share with each other, some more so than with me. Still a few in each class came to me to pour out their ideas before they left, hoping this discussion would continue.

The results and the suggestions varied tremendously. Some were asking to be allowed to chew gum or drink sodas, others wanted to be forced to read aloud. Some focused on grading, others on assignments, tests, books, late policies. Some wanted to be prepared for college English classes; others wanted to be allowed to read Stephen King. A few even said they wanted to have discussions like the one on that first day, about "real" things.

Day Two

After reading their responses and thinking about what they had said already in class, I knew I was on to something important, not only to me but to the students also. I honestly believe there was not one student who wasn't actively involved, whether orally or in writing. I made a list of their suggestions and dittoed them for all the students to have. I made copies of Langston Hughes's "Theme from English B" and a cassette tape including Pink Floyd's "We Don't Need No Education" (or whatever it's really called), Lou Reed's "Teach the Gifted Children," and Crosby, Stills, and Nash's "Teach Your Children."

Before day two began in each class, I already had a written response from each student. So many

students wrote about how they "can't write well," then proceeded to write wonderful, two- to six-page papers full of rich, authentic voices and thoughtful ideas. In the classes in which I had already read the papers, I asked if they would be willing to share what they wrote. In some classes individuals read aloud to us all; in other classes they read to each other in small groups. They were as interested in each other's papers as they were in their own.

For the second half of the period, I played the tape of the three songs, letting them move into a group, some sprawled comfortably on the floor. Everyone listened intently. Some took notes. (I had told them I was going to ask them to respond.) When the helicopter sounds of Pink Floyd's song started, some eyes lit up, and feet tapped. Pencils beat in rhythm on desks and knees. A few lip-synced entire songs. But they listened. "Can we write now, or do we have to wait till the end?" I shrugged and said, "Whenever you want."

When I turned off the tape, there were a few animated comments, a few questions like, "Do you listen to that kind of music?" but mostly intense gazes. They wrote. And wrote. And wrote. The bell rang. They finished their writings and left almost silently. Surprising me, more than one uttered a quiet "Thanks."

Day Three

For the first half of the period, again they shared what they wrote. I suspected that the topic might already be getting stale, but they assured me that it wasn't. But it was time to focus a little more and try to wind down—to get a mind-set and a plan for the year. Yes, there was certain material we had to cover. But in the scheme of things, I was realizing, that was minor.

We went through the lists of what they wanted, what they wanted to learn, what they wanted from me as their teacher. Those that I could agree to, I did. Those that were unacceptable to me, I gave reasons for. Actually, I changed my mind on a couple of things overnight, and told them the next day. But I had reasons that, even if they didn't agree with, they could understand. I am convinced that no one left dissatisfied. Their final assignment for this unit was to make me a list of what I could and should expect of them in return.

I compiled lists of what we could and should expect of each other and dittoed them for everyone to have. We discussed them, agreed to them, and began the year on the right foot—as a community of learners who think, share ideas, and listen to and respect each other.

→ See: Blynt, p. 134; Crafts, p. 136; Edelsky, p. 72; Shor, p. 223.

Robin Myers is an instructor at the University of Missouri, Columbia, MO.

Breakthroughs

by Bonnie Laster

Conflict "Rugolution"

What a difference a day makes!" Last fall this quip in a popular teacher magazine caught my eye. The author suggested letting kids who were having trouble getting along sit down on a small rug, talk over their difficulties, and see if they could come up with a solution to everyone's liking. As the referee for many a fight and disagreement in my kindergarten room, I thought the idea was worth a try, but I decided I'd give it two weeks—max!

Twenty years ago, my sister had given my infant son a Winnie-the-Pooh rug. I gave it to her when her children were born, and then she returned it to me when they outgrew it. It's tiny—just five by seven—and I wondered how it could possibly serve the needs of 29 children.

I brought the rug to school and showed my kids how to use it. It then took its place of honor behind my desk. When two students bumped heads, they would take the rug to an unused corner of the classroom, sit cross-legged facing each other, and hash out their problem.

Those few precious moments together on the little rug never fail to produce miracles. Inevitably, within two to five minutes, the conflict is resolved. The former "enemies" can often be seen walking back to their seats arm in arm or holding hands.

After months of successful conflict "rugolution," my instructional aide, who has three teenagers, turned to me and asked, "Where did you get that Winnie-the-Pooh rug anyway? I've got to have one for home!"

→ See: Smullin, p. 45.

Bonnie Laster is a primary teacher at Brentwood Oaks School, East Palo Alto, CA.

Classroom Demonstrations
by Toby Kahn Curry

As kids see it

Beginning the School Year

The first writing assignment I give every fall is one in which I ask my new students to write me a letter about their expectations, hopes, wishes, or goals for seventh grade. It's a great way to meet the kids. I try to answer the letters as soon as possible. Here are two examples.

Dear Mrs. Curry,

You have changed my whole attitude about seventh grade. Last year I thought that the seventh grade would be nothing but work, and that it would be really boring. But by you being so creative with the work that you have, my feelings about seventh grade have changed. The work that you assign us is very challenging, but it is fun. I admire the way that you treat your pupils like young ladies and gentelmen instead of just children. (Which is more than I can say for some teachers.) . . .

The library books that you have in your class are much better than the ones in other teacher's rooms. I think that the books are far more interesting than the others. Another thing that I like about your seventh grade class is the 50 book club. It is very good to have that kind of reading experience. Some kids hardly ever pick up a single book unless they're practically forced. . . .

I think that I like your class better than the rest because it calls for more responsibility, and will make the class a lot more mature than they were last year. All in all I enjoyed my first day of school and I enjoyed the activities that we were allowed to participate in and I think that I am going to enjoy my seventh grade better than I thought that I was going to in the beginning.

Sincerely,
Your Pupil, Shirley P.

Dear Mrs. Curry,

All I expect is for you to be fair to me & my classmates. I think that your class is going to be very interesting and exciting. I'm eager to participate in the "50 book club" because I like to read a lot. It may sound like someone is dictating this to me, but don't worry.

I've never used a computer so it'll be fun to learn. I like your ideas about spelling. My previous teacher only concentrated on the words in spelling books—which don't have the same effect on everyone. Someone may think the words are easy while someone else has trouble.

I also like your ideas about groups. These are two people I'd like to sit with: Tony and Aaron.

They are two of my best friends and we wouldn't talk (very much). That's about it. I think this years going to be fun for me and I hope its fun for you, too.

Sincerely,
Polly W.

Suggestions for Working in a Group

1. Come to the Group with Something
   - An idea, a suggestion, a question
   - Bring writing tools
2. Know the Group's Purpose
   - Sharing ideas
   - Weaving ideas
   - Building an end product
3. Accept All Ideas Somehow
   - All good, all help
   - Incorporate somehow
   - Agree on use, adjustments
   - Say something
4. Trust in the Process
   - You don't know how it will turn out
   - Allow time to listen, time to talk
   - Respect each member and their suggestions
5. Keep Attention on Project
6. Record Ideas and Suggestions
7. Work Toward a Goal
   - End product
   - Consider who it is from, where it goes
8. Congratulate Each Other for Getting Together and Completing Project

—Developed by Rich Thompson's sixth-grade class, Columbia Falls Elementary, Columbia Falls, MT

Debra Goodman begins the new year by asking her students to write an essay called "The Real Me." Here is one example.

The Real Me
by Janelle Toles

I'm real outgoing. If something goes wrong I try to sort it out. If someone asked me if I liked sports it would be a definite yes. If there's spare time I usually use the telephone, read, play tennis, piano, violin, or go shopping but I'd prefer shopping. But when I draw I'd draw fashion. I love looking at sick things in my microscope. I would say I'm an active person.

Toby Kahn Curry and Debra Goodman are teachers at Dewey Center for Urban Education, Detroit, MI.

Resource: Poster/Cards

The Peaceable Kingdom Press

Catalog from:
2980 College Ave., Ste. 2
Berkeley, CA 94705
1-415-654-9989

Peaceable Kingdom is a wonderful source for quality posters and greeting cards for classroom or home use. The press, started in 1983 by the Hurd family, a name long associated with children's books (Clement Hurd and Thatcher Hurd), is dedicated to publishing fine reproductions of great children's book illustrations.

Resource: Posters

Free posters are available from many publishers and generally advertise the company's newest title. Write directly to publishers for posters (check for addresses in *Literary Market Place* or *Books in Print*, available at most bookstores and public libraries). Publishers also set up display booths at the following events and give away numerous things—books, posters, mobiles, friezes, bookmarks.

- American Library Association conventions (one-day passes are generally available to the public)
- State Library Association conventions
- Reading Association conventions
- American Booksellers Association conventions
- Local Booksellers Association gatherings
- Whole language conferences

Also ask your local children's bookstores or public libraries for free surplus posters.

—*Katy Obringer*

Book Note

Understanding Direct Writing Assessments: Reflections on a South Carolina Writing Study

Arthur N. Applebee, Judith A. Langer, and Ina V. S. Mullis
1989; 40 pp.; $6.50
Princeton, NJ: Educational Testing Service

Using observations from a South Carolina study, A. Applebee, J. Langer, and I. Mullis provide an informative and pithy document for anyone seriously undertaking direct writing assessments.

The pamphlet *Understanding Direct Writing Assessments* critiques direct writing assessments (including holistic evaluation) and analytic and primary trait scoring, with consideration of how the assessment measures are related to the tasks student writers are asked to perform.

The South Carolina study was motivated by a concern that there actually be a time to write during writing assessment. The authors caution that "developers have to make a number of difficult choices that involve trade-offs in the breadth and depth of the assessment and the extent to which it corresponds with curriculum." They go on to say that assessments "give strong signals as to the kinds of learnings that are valued."

—*YMG*

YOUNG ARTISTS

—Bill Conklin, 16, Springfield, OR
(from *Treasures 2,* see p. 162)

WHOLE LANGUAGE CAMERA

A whole language classroom is a democratic community of learners. Eighth-grade teacher Nancy Moyer knows that a sense of community begins with mutual respect, understanding, and friendship.
Ampitheater Junior High, Tucson, AZ

As I See It:
Kenneth S. Goodman

Evaluation in Whole Language

Adapted from the preface of *The Whole Language Evaluation Book*, ed. K. S. Goodman, Y. M. Goodman, and W. J. Hood (Portsmouth, NH: Heinemann, 1989): pp. xi–xv.

To understand whole language evaluation one must understand the basis of whole language as a grass-roots movement among teachers. Partly it has been motivated by a positive view of teaching and learning and an attempt by informed teachers to use new knowledge about language development and learning to build more effective, and more satisfying, experiences for their pupils and themselves.

Whole language teachers have rebelled against behavioral objectives, textbooks, mastery learning, and narrow curricula. And they have rebelled against standardized tests because they find them synthetic, contrived, confining, controlling, and out of touch with modern theory and research. The tests reduce reading and writing to trivial, decontextualized abstract skills to be tested with multiple-choice questions.

In their curriculum planning, whole language teachers create opportunities for pupils to use language in authentic, richly contextualized, and functional ways. The language is kept whole so that all the necessary data for language learning will be present. Evaluation can be useful only if it is also taking place in these whole and richly contextualized learning experiences.

An increasing number of principals, central curriculum supervisors, and state personnel are supporting and actively encouraging whole language teachers to move away from textbook and test-dominated teaching and to make their evaluation fit the principles and requirements of whole language.

Like the curriculum, evaluation must be consistent with the principles on which whole language is based.

All forms of evaluation are consistent with principles of whole language if:

1 • They are holistic and do not fragment language.
 • They employ natural language in authentic contexts.
 • They are meaningful and relevant to learners.
 • They are interesting and functional.
 • They treat language difference with accuracy and respect.
 • They integrate oral and written language

development with development of thinking and knowledge.

2 • They treat both teachers and learners with respect.
 • They do not control teachers.
 • They draw on what pupils can do and reveal their competence.
 • They allow for variations in background and development.
 • They are designed to encourage independence.

3 • They are consistent with the best scholarship on language, learning, teaching, and curriculum.

4 • They are innovative, creative, and dynamic.
 • Whole language teachers don't want old wine in new bottles.
 • Whole language plumbs the limits of the potential of both teachers and learners.
 • They reflect or are ahead of the best practice in the field.

5 • They are open-ended.
 • They allow for modification and change.
 • They are never permitted to be closed and completely self-contained.

Keep these points in mind about whole language evaluation:

In whole language, evaluation is mostly ongoing; it happens in the course of the teaching-learning. It is therefore an integral part of the curriculum and not something separate.

Self-evaluation is the most significant kind of evaluation; pupils and teachers need to have a sense of their own success and growth. Reporting progress to parents is an important but secondary purpose of evaluation. It is most successful when it helps parents to evaluate growth themselves. Marks or grades on report cards are only the outgrowth of evaluation for improving teaching and learning.

Whole language is not simply concerned with measuring changes in behavior. It uses behavior as indications of developing knowledge and underlying competence.

Informal—and even formal—evaluation measures may be used in whole language classrooms. But when they are used, it is because they add to the information available, and there always is a learning function as well as an evaluation function: Readers may discuss their own miscues; peer-editing conferences may offer constructive criticism; a test over concepts involved in a unit on chickens may refocus discussion and stimulate reflective thinking; and a group project may distill knowledge gained from reading and discussion.

When whole language teachers reject traditional evaluating techniques such as standardized tests or multiple choice tests over lectures and textbooks, it is because the content, nature, and uses of such devices are in direct conflict with the whole language teacher's view of teaching, learning, and curriculum. That's why we can't provide one-to-one substitutes that meet behavioristic criteria. It's also why whole language evaluation can't be reduced to precise right or wrong scores.

The contrast between objective and subjective evaluation is inappropriate for whole language classrooms. Whole language teachers are professionals who accept all pupils—their language and culture. They are careful not to let personal feelings or prejudices get in the way of their judgment, but they are not detached or impersonal when they teach and when they evaluate. They view all evaluative information,

whether incidental, informal, or formal in the context of the personal and social goals of the learners and the school. Whole language teachers trust their professional judgment, but they're constantly open to new insights.

The curriculum in a whole language classroom is an integrated dual curriculum. Language and thought are developed through using them to build knowledge. So whole language teachers are always evaluating linguistic and cognitive growth in context.

Coping with Pressures

In the United States whole language teachers have had to cope with the standardized tests and pressure by administrators and local and state authorities to evaluate by gains in scores on these tests. Whole language teachers work out their own ways to cope with, resist, ignore, or get around these pressures and help their pupils to do the same.

Rather than be defensive, teachers should keep a positive focus in their evaluation: How do we, as whole language teachers, judge how well we're doing, and even more important, how do we help our kids to do so?

Super Teachers?

Every diligent teacher spends a professional lifetime learning how to teach. Ironically, one attack on whole language is that it requires super teachers to do it. Whole language teachers are caring, informed professionals. What we do is hard work, but any competent teacher who wants to do so can become a whole language teacher.

Self-evaluation is an important part of becoming a whole language teacher. Whole language teachers evaluate themselves as they evaluate their pupils. Because whole language teachers have liberated themselves from the constraints of textbooks and mandated programs, they are free to grow. We may not all become super teachers, but through self-evaluation we will become better teachers.

➜ See: Cerny, p. 258; Goodman, pp. 251, 252; Vincent, p. 253.

YOUNG ARTISTS

"No hurting other people."
—Rachel Arnow, 5, Palo Alto, CA

Book Note

The Whole Language Evaluation Book

Kenneth S. Goodman, Yetta Goodman, and Wendy J. Hood, editors
1988; 296 pp.; $16.50
Portsmouth, NH: Heinemann

A very usable collection of evaluation techniques for whole language educators and inservice directors. All forms of evaluation are discussed, including incidental, informal, and formal, and are adaptable to most school settings. Especially meaningful for me is Lois Bird's article, "The Art of Teaching: Evaluation and Revision."

—Lois Mather

I Used to Be...But Now I...

I used to teach children and evaluate their progress,
But now I kidwatch, facilitate the learning of children, and try to discover why learners do what they do. I have learned to celebrate children's strengths as language users.

—Lorraine Gillmeister-Krause

As I See It:
Yetta M. Goodman

The Double Agenda of Evaluation

Adapted from "Evaluation of Students: Evaluation of Teachers," in *The Whole Language Evaluation Book,* ed. K. S. Goodman, Y.M. Goodman, and W.J. Hood (Portsmouth, NH: Heinemann, 1989) pp. 7-8.

Evaluation is part of the double agenda in the whole language classroom. As shown below, the right side of the agenda, Students Are Learning, indicates where students and the teacher are busily and actively involved: in reading to solve problems, to add to their scientific knowledge and their aesthetic pleasure; in writing to express their meanings, to discover what they know, to create artistically, and to take care of everyday business; and in using oral and written language to learn about the world. The left side of the agenda shows that while the classroom community is engaged in learning, the Teacher's Evaluation is monitoring the goals of language learning and conceptual development.

The Double Agenda

Teacher's evaluation	Students are learning
Teacher is involved	Kids & teacher are involved
Evaluation of language development	Learning about their world
Cognitive development	Answering their questions
Curriculum	Solving their problems
	Evaluating their own learning through language use
A continuous ongoing integral process	
	Reading
	Writing
	Speaking
	Listening

Evaluation doesn't get in the way of the kids' learning. At the same time that the students are involved in learning as one part of the double agenda, evaluation is a continuing part of the other aspect of the double agenda. Teachers are involved in evaluation during all aspects of the curriculum. It is a continuous, integral process.

Whole language teachers don't decide to think about evaluation in June; they don't start to focus on evaluation in order to get ready for report card time or for parent conferences. Whole language teachers know that evaluation is going on all the time; it is built into the plans of every day. It is integral to the process of teaching and learning and not a separate, discrete activity. As the kids and the teacher are involved in learning about their world, answering their questions and solving their problems, another part of that ongoing learning is to answer other kinds of questions. What am I learning? How are things going? Who is getting things done? How are students' concepts and hypotheses changing? Who seems confused? How did things go in our discussion group? Did we do an adequate job of cleaning up after our art activity today? Did I organize the writing area so those who wanted to continue to write could do so?

➜ See: Freeman, p. 212; Harwood, p. 213; Kitagawa, p. 212; Morgenbesser, p. 210; Newman, p. 211.

📷 **WHOLE LANGUAGE CAMERA**

Sheilah Nicholas assists her first grade student as he participates in Show and Tell at Butterfield School, Tucson, AZ.

Book Note

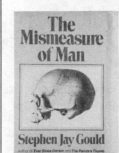

The Mismeasure of Man

Stephen J. Gould
1983; 352 pp.; $7.95
New York: Norton

For teachers who are concerned about the impact of standardized testing on schools and learning, there is no better book than this one for understanding the checkered history and theoretical flaws of intelligence testing. Gould, the distinguished Harvard geneticist, examines the history of attempts to measure human intelligence from the 19th century, when one's skull size was thought to be an indication of intelligence, up to the 1970s, when Arthur Jensen argued that blacks are innately less intelligent than whites. In many cases, Gould reexamined original data and administered old IQ tests following the original procedures. Throughout, he describes how intelligence testing has often been used, consciously or not, in the service of social prejudices, namely racism and sexism. Although the book is technical in spots, it is intended for a general rather than a scientific audience; and Gould's excellent writing, sense of humor, and humane values make reading it a rewarding experience. Although many books have been written about standardized testing, this one is unique.

Sandra Wilde

❝ Terman also included this item from Binet's original: 'My neighbor has been having queer visitors. First a doctor came to his house, then a lawyer, then a minister. What do you think happened there?' Terman permitted little latitude beyond 'a death,' though he did allow 'a marriage' from a boy he described as 'an enlightened young eugenist' who replied that the doctor came to see if the partners were fit, the lawyer to arrange, and the minister to tie the knot. He did not accept the combination 'divorce and remarriage,' though he reports that a colleague in Reno, Nevada, had found the response 'very, very common.' He also did not permit plausible but uncomplicated solutions (a dinner or an entertainment), or such original responses as: 'someone is dying and is getting married and making his will before he dies.' ❞ (p. 176)

As Teachers See It
by Patty Vincent

Confidently Evaluating Students

One of the most difficult tasks initially for me in implementing whole language in my first-grade classroom was to develop some method for evaluating my students. My traditional classroom background had led me to believe that there must always be a test instrument, developed by "experts," to evaluate my students. But through my reading and experience with whole language I have been liberated from the traditional modes of evaluation and have developed a trust in my ability to evaluate my students.

Jane Baskwill and Paulette Whitman have been instrumental in the development of my classroom evaluation process. I have attended their lectures, read their books, and learned to evaluate students by observing and listening to them. I keep a journal of daily events, making notes on activities I have used: Was the activity successful? What things worked or didn't work? What might I add, cut, or do differently next time? I also keep an anecdotal journal on students, recording noteworthy impressions as they occur. It was difficult at first to get into the habit of observing and then recording information, and I had to train myself to observe particular children at specific times.

I also keep a reading conference sheet. Each day or every other day I meet individually with students and conference with them about the book or story they have read. I make notes about their comprehension abilities, oral reading, and the kinds of strategies they are using. I note the date and what they have read. In this way, I get to know my students academically and socially. It is a safe, risk-free experience for them, and gives me valuable information about my students. At conference time I can give parents a detailed account of their child's capabilities and accomplishments.

Because writing has been such an integral part of my program this year, I also collect a monthly sample of each child's writing. It is exciting to compare the samples from each month, and to see the growth. At conference time, parents are pleased to see how their children are progressing as writers. These writing collections are one of my most effective evaluation tools.

Through observation and record keeping, I have also learned I can do a better job of evaluating my teaching. By documenting and evaluating data, I am making important decisions about each child's learning.

The process of change is not an easy one, but I have found getting out of the comfort zone is the only way I can grow as an educator. Whole language and the holistic process of evaluation are both challenging and rewarding. I am better able to meet the needs of my children, because I have a broader range of information about each student. I have the confidence that I am the expert in my classroom and can confidently evaluate my students.

➜ See: Baskwill, p. 168; Evaluation: Whole Language, Whole Child, p. 257; Vincent, p. 329; The Whole Language Sourcebook, p. 225.

Patty Vincent is a teacher and consultant with Park County District #1, Powell, WY.

Involving Parents and Students

Classroom Demonstrations

by Debra Goodman

Planning and Evaluation: Involving Students and Parents Right from the Start

As a teacher, I have always involved students in planning classroom activities and in evaluating their own progress. When students are involved in developing classroom experiences, centers, and evaluation, they have a much greater understanding of what is expected of them and what is possible for them. They feel ownership in the classroom and want things to go well. I, in turn, have a greater opportunity to get to know their expertise and preferences.

Setting Goals for the Year

I teach language arts and social studies to two groups of fifth-graders, one group in the morning and the other in the afternoon. One of the first things I do with my fifth-graders is to set some personal goals for the year. We discuss some of the possibilities for the year and what we would like to accomplish in our classroom and in our personal lives. I ask each student to write four or five goals for the school year. After students have written their goals, we proofread and edit, and the goals are rewritten on the bottom of a sheet where I have written my goals for students. Both sets of goals are sent home; parents are asked to sign the sheet and are invited to write goals of their own.

The kids' goals reflect the concerns of fifth-graders. While they want to do well in school, they also hope to make friends, grow their hair long, and generally become better people. Parents will write goals for their child, parenting goals, or personal goals for themselves. Besides revealing the actual concerns and interests of my students and their parents, the goals reflect many other things, including level of self-confidence and attitude toward school. In most cases, the goals can be grouped into three areas of concern: acquisition of knowledge, development of learning strategies, and social/personal growth. I feel that these three areas are the business of schooling.

Some of My September Goals for Fifth-Graders:
1. Learn to work together and help others.
2. Learn to solve problems and think for themselves.
3. Learn to organize work and take responsibility for their own work.
4. Improve their communication in speaking and writing.
5. Learn some steps in doing research.
6. Find books and authors they *love*.
7. Have an idea what history is.
8. Learn about many different cultures.
9. Learn more about their own family history and culture.

Student Goals

My goals for 5th grade:
1. To work in groups.
2. Learn together.
3. Be independent.
4. Have my own choices and opinions.
5. Be what I want to be.
6. Work hard.

—Athena B.

Parents: Please comment and return.

I approve wholeheartedly of Athena's goals as well as those set by you (the teacher). I know she will strive to achieve whatever goals she sets for herself, with our help as well as the help of her teacher.

—Jeannette B.

Writing Checks

I use one sample of each child's writing as a "writing check" about four times a year. I usually use a classroom writing project, rather than assigning writing strictly for this purpose. For the writing check, I look at the overall quality of the piece, the improvement from rough draft to final draft, the number of words written, and the percentage of words spelled correctly. (At the fifth grade, the average percentage of words spelled correctly is 95 percent, and the lowest percentage is 75 percent.) This evaluation allows kids to see that I am focusing on strength and growth rather than on perfection.

The first writing sample is sent home to parents with a cover letter that explains my writing program and gives a personal critique of each child's writing. The letter explains that the English and spelling grades on the child's report card are based on the writing. But more important, the letter helps parents understand my philosophy and why they may see pieces of writing that are not edited or corrected. Although personalizing these letters is time consuming, it invites parents to join in celebrating the positive aspects of their child's writing and to support a process approach when they work with the child at home.

Program Description

I have a five-page description of my fifth-grade program that I hand out at the open house at the beginning of the year. Although it is on the long side, I find it useful for parents who have questions about the whole language approach and want a more detailed explanation. In addition, I work in a district where we are expected to give regular homework. The final page, describing my homework policy, is a response to that requirement as well as an effort to encourage some supportive literacy activities for kids.

Homework

While students focus on their class assignments, I am concerned about the learning process as much as the final product that a student turns in. I want to help students learn how to study, read, write, and think. In order to do this, I need to see their ideas developing as discussion, notes, and rough drafts. For this reason, I will provide time for students to do most of their work during the school day.

Homework assignments will be those that are most appropriately done at home, or those that extend upon the work done in school. Reading logs and writing folders can be taken home, but this is not required. However, there are some things I would like to see students doing on a regular basis after school hours:

1. Going to the library every week or two to look for independent reading books, and for materials for the social studies unit.
2. Reading for 15 or 20 minutes each day, perhaps before going to bed.
3. Keeping a home journal or diary.
4. Stretching their minds by reading a newspaper, taking a trip, going to a play, or watching an educational film.

These activities should be done for enjoyment and practice, and need not be monitored by parents. Fifth-graders will probably do better with a journal if it is private.

Ongoing Progress Reports and Self-Evaluation

Students are frequently reminded of current assignments, available choices, and personal progress in a number of ways. Assignments and due dates are listed on a small poster board for student review. Current assignments are discussed during planning time and often listed on the chalkboard. Major assignments are also listed on a small class chart, and students can check off the work they have completed. When I have reviewed the assignment, the check is covered by a sticker or my initials.

In many center areas, there are places for students to record their participation in choice activities as well.

I have also used a variety of record-keeping systems for students to organize and record their classwork. I usually have a record-keeping package that goes along with each unit or card-marking period. I will list the general assignments for that unit or time period, and leave spaces for students to record their own choices as well. I recently included a planning sheet on the cover of the student records. An outline of our weekly schedule allows students to plan their own activity and work schedule in the open work times. The "to do" list allows students to prioritize their immediate assignments. Sometimes I use a daily log to record actual activities.

For many students, the record-keeping form is invaluable. They can see exactly what they have to do and what choices they have. It is especially exciting for kids who are hardworking but have never been very successful in school. They go through their checklists and finish all their assignments with a great sense of accomplishment. When assignments are turned in, I write my own comments on the student records, and they know if a particular assignment is completed or needs more attention.

My fifth-graders need a lot of initial supervision and reminders to use their record-keeping. The type of record-keeping I use varies according to the amount of direction and supervision needed by a particular group of kids. But the record-keeping allows me to do a quick check of student progress and find out who is working well independently, who needs encouragement to get to work, and who may be confused and need special attention.

The records also demonstrate my own values to students and eventually their parents. They can see that I assign the reading grade based on actual reading, reflection in their response log, discussion in literature groups, use of the school library, and so on.

By the end of a marking period, most of the record-keeping sheets have been filled in. Work is checked off, assignments are evaluated and commented on. The child and I take a look at ongoing assignments, such as the independent writing folder or the reading response log, and make comments about general progress. The student looks over the records of his or her work, and requests a grade for each subject, with reasons for requesting this particular grade.

Date:
READING AND LITERATURE
Books Read:
Reading Log:
Library Experience:
Listening Enjoyment:
Participation:
Other:
My favorite book this card-marking was:
My goal for next card-marking is:
My Reading grade should be __ because:
My Literature grade should be __ because:

ENGLISH
Writing Progress:
Extra Writing Activities:
Folder Check:
Conferences and Progress:
Teacher Comment:
My English grade should be __ because:

SPELLING
Writing Check: __% words spelling correctly in own writing
Spelling Check: __% words spelled correctly in dictation
Writing + Spelling Check / 2 = __%
Spelling Grade:

CITIZENSHIP AND RESPONSIBILITY

Fifth-graders are learning to work together and get along well with the other members of our class. They are learning to take responsibility for their own work. They are expected to be helpful and cooperative and participate fully in all activities. How have they done this card-marking?

Citizenship Grade:

WORK PROGRESS

Date: Activity

What are the most important or interesting things you've learned this card-marking?

Teacher's comments:

Parent's comments:

I have a lot of problems with the grading system in general. I am required to give the fifth-graders a grade in reading, English, spelling, and social studies. The report card also lists handwriting and literature. Since most of the teachers in my school leave the literature slot blank, I feel I can ignore the handwriting slot instead. So I have given over 60 kids five letter grades six times a year for the last three years. Next to administering standardized tests, I find report card marking the most distasteful aspect of my teaching job.

However, with the record-keeping system, the kids take home a self-evaluation that reflects the work the student has done and the reason for the report card grade. I invite parents to sign the self-evaluation and write comments of their own.

Student's Name: *Joshua D.*

Dear Parents,

We have completed our fall social studies unit —Cultures in Contact in America—and we are beginning our second unit—Childhood in America. Assignments will include interviewing an adult about his or her childhood, reading a second historical fiction book, and a research project.

We will also be working on our publishing program, and each child will "publish" at least one original piece of writing. We will publish a class anthology in the spring.

The following pages detail your child's progress for the first semester. Please look them over carefully.

Sincerely yours,
Debra Goodman

Dear Parents,

Here's what I'm most proud of this semester: *I am most proud of my writing folder and reading literature book.*

Here's what I'd like to improve: *My reading log because I haven't written in it 3 times a week.*

My Social Studies grade should be B because: *I did pretty good on my review and read a literature book.*

My Reading grade should be A- because: *I turned in my reading lists and my log book but it was late.*

My Literature grade should be A because: *I read two and 3 quarters Literature Books and got an A on my family tree.*

My English grade should be A because: *I did the amount of pages needed in my writing folder and am finished with my story for publication.*

Joshua D.

Teacher Comment: *Fine Work!*

Student and Parent Assistants

It's easy to spread yourself thin when you're trying to reach each child in a creative and expansive language program. I ask kids and parents to help in every way they can. At the door of my classroom the student receptionist sits at the "teacher's desk" ready to take attendance, write hall passes, distribute special supplies, pass out papers, answer questions, and so on. All areas of the classroom are organized and run by a student committee.

In addition, I have found great success in using small groups and peer tutors to help kids complete major and minor assignments. During each class unit, I ask the students to do a research project to answer their personal questions related to the unit. I had little success with

this until I organized the kids into research groups. Although they are working on their own questions, the groups form a support base for finding and using materials, getting information, making progress, and so on.

I have also had great success with peer assistants when kids are having difficulty completing an assignment. When most of the class is done with an assignment, I will ask who would like to assist students who are not through, and I will quickly match up assistants with kids needing help. I have also paired kids up for reading, log writing, and any number of other activities. There is no stigma attached, since the "difficulty" can stem from any number of reasons, and the kids enjoy working together.

My fifth-graders have also served as class assistants in kindergarten and first-grade classes. With partners, they will do everything from art activities or reading a book, to writing and making a joint-authored book. Fifth-graders can help make book covers, respond to journals, supervise centers, and so on.

I ask parents to do the usual activities, helping out in the room or supervising field trips. Working parents have difficulties with these activities, but are often happy to buy supplies for the room, make book covers at home, type, come in as a guest speaker, and so on. At the beginning of the year, I send home a note listing class supplies needed and possible parent activities, and I ask parents to fill it out and send it back. This year one parent volunteered to coordinate the other parents for me. Volunteer parents have built me a small store stand and a reading loft, brought in scrap cardboard from frame shops and a variety of other giveaways, typed for many class anthologies and other productions, come in to make a presentation on their own area of expertise, written and received grants for artists in residence, and many other things at my request or their initiative. I have no preconceived expectations for parents, but invite them to share their talents and expertise with us as they are able.

End-of-Year Program

At the end of the year, I have always had a culminating program in the auditorium, usually related to a theme we have explored for social studies. With a committee of students, we write a script that includes a number of reports, poems, and other writings that students have done over the year. I have had great success starting with a skeleton script that presents the general outline and focus, and inviting students to "write themselves into the program" by writing a short part for themselves. We also include songs and dances that relate to our topic. I am a fan of folk music and dance, and I always include folk songs in my social studies units. I invite kids to bring in songs from their own heritage, and sometimes the kids will write a "rap" or song of their own.

Parents are notified of the upcoming program and get involved in costumes, writing, typing, or supervision. On the night of the program, the families attend and share in their child's learning. The programs are a tremendous amount of work for everyone, but the results make it worthwhile. Every student feels a sense of success and accomplishment. Their understanding of the content we are presenting increases as we rehearse the songs and speeches. They become more serious about expressing their ideas as they think of their parents sitting in the audience.

The parents are impressed with the information presented in the program and touched by the children's speeches. It is often hard for them to believe their child has written a particular poem or report. By placing these children, their ideas and writings in the limelight, I invite parents to rekindle the pride they felt as they

watched their child's first steps or listened for their child's first words.

Final Evaluation

At the end of the year, we reflect on our goals and evaluate our progress for the year. I ask students to evaluate their own learning and my teaching. I invite parents to write their responses to the year, and to evaluate my classroom in terms of their child's growth. The evaluation gives the student and the parent an opportunity to think about the high and low points of the year and reflect on their own growth and change. Some of these letters represent the culmination of a year of close contact between a student and myself, or a parent and myself. But sometimes these letters are the first time I have realized the impact I have had on a child or his or her parents. Here are some of the responses I have received.

Dear Ms. Goodman,

Every since I walked into this room and found out you were going to be our teacher I knew this was going to be a fun year. My opinion is the program we did June 4th put all the fun in it. This hole entire school year has been just perfect, or, shall I say fantastic year. I worked hard on everything we had to do. I liked when we had writer's club and did special activities. I did not like it when we had to decide what grades we wanted. I think a teacher should decide grades. By. Have A GOOD SUMMER!!!

Love,
Dena

P.S. I'm so glad we made it though the program. I loved it!

Dear Debra,

Looking back at Kasia's fifth grade year we both agree that it has been her best. We recall the goals you requested we set at the beginning of the school year and can definitely say that they have been met.

Kasia is well on her way to becoming an independent, self-directed learner. Under your creative guidance, her reading and writing skills have flourished. She enjoys writing stories of her own creation and we often find her reading for enjoyment, sharing what she's read with us.

The family history project was one in which we all became involved and enjoyed. We've made several copies and are giving them to both sets of grandparents, who became as involved in the research as we did.

Thank you for giving our daughter your very best. I'm sure it will stay with her for the rest of her life.

Sincerely,
Linda & Bob Kolnowski

➜ See: Bonfils, p. 135; Goodman, pp. 224, 236; Loveless, p. 263; Manning, p. 258.

Debra Goodman is a teacher at Dewey Center for Urban Education, Detroit, MI.

YOUNG ARTISTS

Camela Davis, Palm Harbor, FL, kindergarten, Sutherland Elementary School, Mrs. Elizabeth Ziecheck, Teacher, Motts Apple Award Winner

As I See It:
Yetta M. Goodman

Evaluation of Students — ƨʇuǝpnʇS ʇo uoıʇɒnןɒʌƎ

Adapted from *The Whole Language Evaluation Book,*
ed. K. S. Goodman, Y. M. Goodman, and W. J. Hood
(Portsmouth, NH: Heinemann, 1989): pp. 3–7.

The power of evaluation in whole language classrooms lies in the process of becoming—the changes or moves that people make from what they are to what they come to be. To examine these moves let us consider the concept of reflection and mirror image as a metaphor. In our classrooms as we critically examine what students do in order to help them grow as educated human beings, we become consciously aware that at the same time we are seeing a reflection of ourselves. Our planning and organization influences the classroom environment in so many ways that the evaluation of students becomes an evaluation of ourselves and the curriculum. As we see ourselves reflected in our classrooms and in the responses of our students, it helps us become consciously aware of our influence on that learning and on the relationship between teaching and learning.

The dynamic transaction between teachers and students results in change in all the actors and actions involved in the teaching-learning experience. Evaluation—the examination of that change—reveals the development of the learning, the teacher, and the curriculum. At the same time that we look in the mirror to see the reflection of our teaching in the students and their learning, we also take advantage of what we see to reflect on our own professional development as teachers.

Evaluation: An Integral Part of Curriculum

Evaluation is part of curriculum: It cannot be divorced from classroom organization, from the relationship between teachers and students, or from the ongoing and continuous learning experiences and activities. To think about and plan for evaluation, it is necessary to keep in mind the classroom community and its organization.

Respect for all the members of the learning community suggests that each plays a role in teaching, each is involved in continuous learning, and, therefore, each has a role in the evaluation process. The classroom belongs to the community that lives there, with the teacher providing the major leadership role but respecting the students' ideas about how the classroom should be organized as an effective place in which to live and to learn. The classroom community is part of the larger community in which teachers and students live and communicate daily. It is, therefore, important to involve other teachers, administrators, and parents in the evaluation process.

Whole language classrooms are rich in resources and opportunities. Students are enabled to use language in all its forms. Students are trusted to care for the variety of resources that are available and accessible. The social community in the classroom is organized and planned by both teachers and students. That means that students see the potential in their experiences to solve their problems and to gain the knowledge they believe they need as citizens in a democracy. As members of the learning community plan together, they include opportunities for the evaluation of their own experiences.

Building a Professional Sense

As parents, we know when our kids have grown physically, intellectually, and emotionally. I remember having to buy them new, larger-sized clothes. The doctor would measure and weigh my children, but the figures simply confirmed what I already knew as an observant parent and what the children knew about themselves. The weight and height measurements were only additional bits of statistical information. All the other subtle, nonstatistical, but important information let me know that my kids were growing up, how they were changing, what they knew, and how much they cared.

When children begin to ask questions about people's health, or their economic condition, we begin to see growth in their empathy for others. When they join in conversations about current events, we realize that their interests and knowledge base have changed. As parents, we use our common sense to make decisions about the growth of our children.

Teachers build similar senses that I call *professional senses*. Teachers build these senses through their interactions with and reflections about students. They professionalize their senses by confirming their judgments through their reading and continued scholarship in areas such as human development, language learning, and practices of effective schooling.

Initially, professional senses are intuitive. Beginning teachers are often unaware that they are thinking intuitively, using their background knowledge whenever they have to make decisions such as whether a student is a good reader, which are the appropriate ways to make presentations to the class, and what their students understand about scientific or mathematical concepts. However, as teachers take account of what they know about learning, language, and conceptual development, they then build confidence in their ability to make judgments about their students' growth. Their reflective thinking grows and takes on new dimensions.

The professional intuition of teachers has largely been ignored for at least two reasons. The first is lack of respect for teachers as thinkers and decision-makers. Scholars like John Dewey (Archambault 1964) and Elliot Eisner (1976) explore the significance of reflective thinking, educational connoisseurship, and criticism for teachers, but the educational establishment does not seem to respect the thinking ability of teachers to give the concept of a developing professional sense legitimacy. Eisner (p. 140) states:

> What I believe we need to do with respect to educational evaluation is not to seek recipes to control and measure practice but rather to enhance whatever artistry the teacher can achieve. . . . Good theory in education . . . helps us to see more; . . . theory provides some of the windows through which intelligence can look out into the world.

The second reason that the professional sense of teachers has been neglected is the unexamined belief in statistical information. Because numbers take on an aura of objectivity, *which they do not intrinsically deserve,* statistical test data are equated with the development of knowledge and are valued more highly than the sense of an informed, committed professional teacher who

uses knowledge about the students, the community, and the context to make judgments.

Educators need to know the limitations of their professional sense and discover a variety of ways to confirm their intuitions. But when the power of professional intuitions are denigrated with comments such as "It's just subjective" or "Test scores are better than nothing," then the power of professional judgment and the legitimate uses of the professional sense of teachers are canceled. Whole language teachers are willing to assume responsibility for their judgments and have no problem being accountable to their students, their students' parents, and the other professionals in their schools and districts.

Professional sense comes from the interplay of what teachers know about language and learning, what they observe in their relationships with students, and the knowledge that builds from those relationships.

Building a Knowledge Base

In order to evaluate language and conceptual development as well as the physical and emotional growth of students, it is necessary for teachers to be lifelong learners. Whole language teachers learn from their students through the evaluation process; they learn from their interactions with other teachers as they share ideas and problems, and they learn from child-study groups organized within the school by resource teachers or principals. They attend classes and become active in professional organizations. They attend workshops and conferences not only to hear from other knowledgeable professionals but to present their ideas in order to think them through and get responses from others. They read the latest scholarly articles in professional journals and books about their subject matter specialties, about the kinds of kids they work with, and about language and learning. They critique research about language and cognitive development and relate it to their classroom setting, and they participate in action research in their own classes to learn more and to see if certain ideas may have merit for their own kids.

The knowledge base becomes the foundation on which professional sense grows. John Dewey suggested (Archambault 1964, pp. 258–259) that genuine freedom comes from reflective thinking that interacts with an ever-developing knowledge base.

> . . . the power of thought, an ability to turn things over, to look at matters deliberately, to judge whether the amount and kind of evidence requisite for decision is at hand, and if not, to tell where and how to seek such evidence. If . . . actions are not guided by thoughtful conclusions, then they are guided by inconsiderate impulse, unbalanced appetite, caprice of the circumstances of the moment.

The ability to think reflectively about a knowledge base in order to build a professional sense develops over a professional lifetime. We can't hurry learning in kids and we can't hurry learning in ourselves as teachers. Whole language teachers have to be as patient with themselves as learners as they are with their own students. Self-evaluation is an important contribution to the growth of both teachers and learners.

➜ See: Bissex, p. 209; Freeman, p. 212; Goodman, pp. 207, 208, 215, 252; Newman, p. 211.

References

Archambault, R. D., ed. 1964. *John Dewey on education.* Chicago: University of Chicago Press.

Eisner, E. W. 1976. "Educational connoisseurship and criticism: Their form and functions in educational evaluation." *Journal of Aesthetic Education* 10.

Classroom Demonstrations
by Marilyn Burns

Assessing Students' Understanding
Open-ended Questions for Twelfth-Graders: A Report from the California Assessment Program

A Question of Thinking was recently released by the California Assessment Program (CAP) of the California State Department of Education. Responding to the reality that what is tested is what gets taught in schools, CAP is committed to aligning assessment with state and national goals that call for developing students' abilities to think and reason mathematically. The document reports students' responses to open-ended questions, describes what was learned from students' work, and includes suggestions for improving classroom instruction. Though focused specifically on twelfth-graders, the book's message is valuable for teachers of all grades.

The 1987–1988 statewide mathematics test for twelfth-graders included some test items that depart from standard multiple-choice questions. Students were asked to give written responses to open-ended problems. In this way, they had to construct and communicate their mathematical reasoning.

The following is one of the open-ended questions from the test. This item asks students to use logic and diagrams to make sense of a situation.

James knows that half of the students from his school are accepted at the public university nearby. Also, half are accepted at the local private college. James thinks that this adds up to 100 percent, so he will surely be accepted at one or the other institution. Explain why James may be wrong. If possible, use a diagram in your explanation.

The students who were successful in solving this problem explained that some students may be accepted at both schools. Their responses, however, differed both in the statements they wrote and the types of diagrams they used. The following are examples of successful responses.

People accepted by the public Universtity ⊙

People accepted by both ⊕

People accepted by the private college ⊕

People not accepted ○

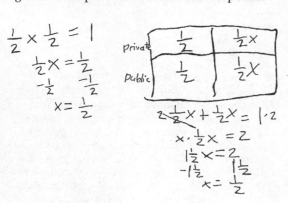

AS MUCH AS 50% MIGHT NOT BE ACCEPTED.

Some students who wrote inadequate responses focused on extraneous factors, such as grades or graduation requirements. Some were unable to make sense of the problem and gave inappropriate answers. Others resorted to using symbols in a meaningless way. Some were not able to provide an appropriate diagram. Following is an example of an unsuccessful response.

$$\frac{1}{2} \times \frac{1}{2} = 1$$
$$\frac{1}{2}X = \frac{1}{2}$$
$$-\frac{1}{2} \quad -\frac{1}{2}$$
$$x = \frac{1}{2}$$

Private	$\frac{1}{2}$	$\frac{1}{2}X$
Public	$\frac{1}{2}$	$\frac{1}{2}X$

$$2\frac{1}{2}X + \frac{1}{2}X = 1 \cdot 2$$
$$X \cdot \frac{1}{2}X = 2$$
$$\frac{1\frac{1}{2}X = 2}{-1\frac{1}{2}} \quad \frac{}{-1\frac{1}{2}}$$
$$X = \frac{1}{2}$$

Approximately 500 solutions were evaluated and sorted into four categories. (The report explains the procedures used for scoring responses.) The results were disappointing:

Demonstrated competence	20%
Satisfactory	12%
Inadequate	65%
No response	3%

The large number of inadequate responses indicate that students may not be familiar with open-ended problems nor accustomed to writing about mathematics. The report presents teaching implications for each category of misconception and encourages classroom teachers to consider incorporating open-ended questions and writing into instruction. A section of problems for this purpose is included.

This report makes a substantial contribution. Buy it, read it, discuss it with your colleagues. The issues are timely and important.

→ See: Burns, p. 330; Mills, p. 325.

From *The Math Solution*, no. 8, Fall/Winter 1989–1990.

Note: To purchase the report, send $5 (plus sales tax for California residents) to Bureau of Publications, Sales Unit, California State Department of Education, P.O. Box 271, Sacramento, CA 95802-0271. Indicate with your order that the book is ISBN 0-8011-0815-2.

I think that one's art is growth inside one. I do not think one can explain growth. It is silent and subtle. One does not keep digging up a plant to see how it grows.

WELL-SAID

—Emily Carr, *A Writer's Notebook*

writers

When I Was Born
by Diane Ochoa

When I was born
I was held by
these cold hands.
And I was floating
across, toward a
beautiful lady.
I was held by her
soft and warm hands.
And here comes my father
with a big smile and
his teeth showing a
sparkling against the
bright light.

→ See: ArtsReach, p. 22.

From *Dancing with the Wind: ArtsReach Literary Magazine*.

Diane Ochoa was in sixth grade when she wrote this poem.

Social Studies Simulation: One Student's Evaluation
by Rachel Y.

Here is a junior high student's evaluation of a social studies project in which she participated.

I have thoroughly enjoyed every ICS simulation I have been involved in. Having participated in four different countries, I have viewed the Mideast conflict through a variety of perspectives. I believe that before one states their opinion on the Arab-Israeli conflict, they should study every angle of the issue. This way, they can weigh the differences according to their own principles. This is very important. The simulation is really a great aid in doing this. It is also a lot of fun. It is great to be given the opportunity of putting on the shoes of a government leader of a foreign country, trying to solve their problems. I've met some neat people and always have fun in Ann Arbor when we go for the debriefings. When you get right down to it, I have really learned a lot. The simulation is totally worthy of the time and energy I have put into it because of the fun and knowledge I have gotten out of it. Thank you for including me.

—Contributed by Toby Kahn Curry, teacher, Dewey Center for Urban Education, Detroit, MI

Classroom Demonstrations
by Judith Oliver

Young Evaluators

Kindergarten is not too soon to help students engage in self-evaluation. Here is a form that Judith Oliver gives her five-year-old students to help them evaluate their "paired reading" experiences (two students reading and discussing a book together).

I Did not Sue Fn

I was a good listener. (Yes) no

I talked about the story. Yes (no)

My friends were good listeners. (Yes) no

My friends talked about the story. (Yes) no

This is a copy of the self-evaluation after discussing the book.

Judith Oliver is a kindergarten teacher in Huntsville, MO.

As kids see it

What I Have Learned

by Deborah A. Manning

At the end of the school year, as part of my students' evaluations, I asked the children to reflect on what they had learned. I also asked them why learning these things was important, what they were going to do this summer to help them to continue to grow, and finally, what they would change in the classroom. Below are excerpts from some of the responses written by second-graders in the Dailey Elementary School of the Fresno Unified School District. (I have typed these in conventional spelling, but I have not changed the students' syntax or punctuation.)

I learned you cannot get your way all the time and reading and writing is very inviting. I think learning is important because it will help you get a education.

—Erika Wilson

This year I have learned that some people think dissecting is gross, but once you try it is not gross it is fun. So you can't judge things until you do it.

—Barbara Sue Ayers

One thing I learned this year important is you don't judge people on their looks. This is important cause you may have a kid who looks like a whimp but can kick a home run on kickball or hit a home run on baseball.

I will try to work on a chapter book during the summer. This chapter book will help me get better on spelling and on handwriting. I think the best thing is coming in the class at recess. I would change nothing.

—John-Michael De La Cerda

I have learned that books are special things to have and that school is a fun thing.

I guess I'm going to work on my reading because I sometimes stumble over words. I'm going to do it by reading the whole summer and I think that could work.

—Greg Ferguson

I have learned that kids that I don't like are really nice and that I have really wrote better. I think learning is important because when you grow up you want to know a lot of stuff. I will work on my writing every day for one hour. Then I will get better. I like the pen pals the best. I would change my writing and my reading. One more thing—drawing.

—Andrew Rutledge

One of the most important things that I have learned this year is how to read and write. I used to take up five finger spaces just to put things. But now it only takes up two finger spaces. And when I read a book and I didn't know what a word meant or what it was I would skip a page. But now I just skip the word. One more thing I learned is to make new friends.

—Meghan Quinn

I have learned lots of things this year. I have learned science this year. I have learned where to put my periods, question marks and exclamation points after my words.

—Gregory Gonzales

This year I have learned that a book is the best present you could ever give to someone in the whole world, another thing I learned was there are different kinds of math in this world, and one more thing I learned was penguins do not fly.

—Alana Shapazian

Deborah A. Manning is an elementary teacher at Dailey Elementary School, Fresno, CA.

Classroom Demonstrations

by Catherine Howard

Self-Evaluation Form

Whole language educators continually strive to get their students to reflect on their own learning. Here's a simple yet effective form Catherine Howard gives to her first- and second-graders at the end of the school year to help them evaluate their completed year and begin to plan for the next (she allows more space for student writing than we were able to show).

—LBB

My Accomplishments

_____

_____

_____

My Goals

_____

_____

_____

→ See: Howard, pp. 159, 303

Catherine Howard is a primary teacher at Ohlone School, Palo Alto, CA.

📷 WHOLE LANGUAGE CAMERA

Three-hole binder notebooks stored on a shelf in a kindergarten classroom contain student writing samples, artwork, and notes about the students' reading. Principal Ron Hutchinson wrote us that the kindergartners read and share their notebooks with each other and evaluate the growth reflected in their work, Yaquina View School, Newport, OR.

At "Beetle-Mania", a science exhibit created by high school teacher Dan Gapp, older students introduce younger ones to the wonders of insects, Tucson, AZ.

Network

The Granite State Integrated Language Network — NETWORK NEWS — International Reading Association · Volume 1 • Number 3 • Summer 1989

Anecdotal Recording: Writing to Learn

by Donna Cerny

Brandon accomplishes magical mental revisions on his first story, shuffling pages in his mind, leaving gaps for two days' worth of writing yet to come, and planning alternate endings while fielding questions from his fellow first-graders. Michelle's writing, rich with sentiment and sensitivity, moves us to tears as she tells of her cat's death. Jimmy finally lets go of his spelling worries, unlocking a wealth of words he's now willing to risk using. Darren begins writing workshop with a picture rather than his usual text. And quiet Christen finds a voice.

As a new practitioner of writing process, I found myself wondering, as I read student writing, What am I seeing? How do I share what I'm not sure I know with others who care about this child? All the reading, the information that I thought I had synthesized, seemed a jumble as I pondered the wealth of information (often in wobbly letters, vowels missing) at my fingertips.

Reaching for pen and paper, I began making notes on anything that came to mind, each observation clearing away a bit of the fog. Forms gradually emerged and my own thoughts began to take shape. Donald Murray (1987) notes, "We don't write what we know, we write to know—to learn." With writing we also begin to define our questions and, as learners ourselves, we seek answers. Reading, observing, thinking, writing, confirming, questioning—the cycle draws us in.

Hours later, I knew each child a little better and reflected on the many ways and reasons we keep records. Test scores, checklists, report cards, permanent files—each meant to tell us (or colleagues, parents, administrators) about the child. But what? Do we see in [these records] Bridget's unique humor as she approaches a topic? Jolee's mastery of periods and capitals after a single editing conference? The expanding complexity of Erica's sentences? Jason's blending of two stories and his willingness to push through five drafts to please himself?

As whole language practitioners, we are obliged to find meaningful ways to communicate to others not only what our students can do as writers (or readers), but their growth in the process and strategies they employ. The usual recording and reporting systems are inadequate and inappropriate for what we have to say. The anecdotal summaries we may choose to add can achieve what no checklist can and, in their doing, bring us knowledge of our students and their history as learners. As Murray observes, "We write first to understand, and if that understanding is clear to us, it may be clear to others."

→ See: Goodman, p. 248.

Reference

Murray, D. 1987. *Write to learn*. New York: Holt, Rinehart & Winston.

From *Network News* 1(3), Summer 1989.

Membership Information: The Granite State Integrated Language Network is an association dedicated to supporting teachers who share a holistic philosophy about literacy, literature, and learning. Members of the Network receive *Network News,* notification of upcoming events, event and book discounts, and automatic affiliation with the Whole Language Umbrella. For more information, contact Debbie Boisvert, Old Center Road, Deerfield, NH 03037.

Perhaps nowhere is the revolutionary nature of whole language more apparent than in the realm of evaluation. In a radical break from traditional evaluative measures, whole language teachers value the developmental process of learning as well as the product, appreciate rather than red-circle "mistakes" as invaluable indicators of their students' thinking, involve students in self-evaluation rather than impose external evaluative criteria, and use evaluation continually to guide instruction and build curriculum, rather than to judge students. Grounded in theory, sensitive observers of their students, whole language educators are continually pushing the frontiers of stu-dent-centered, holistic evaluation. The measures they use today change tomorrow as they grow in their understanding of learning and what they can do to best support that process. What you will see in this section is a sampling of forms for a variety of evaluative purposes, all developed by teachers, working alone or with consultants, for use school-wide or in their own classrooms. The forms are meant to be adapted to fit your and your students' needs. There is no one right way to organize for whole language evaluation; let us know what works for you.

—LBB and YMG

Classroom Demonstrations

by Jacqueline Finn

Monitoring Writing

I have developed this form to monitor growth in spelling and to assess and guide instructional decisions. I note, in my own short-hand, some aspects of the child's process, including writing and drawing. I also note talk, though I did not do so in this instance. "Writes narrative (b, m, e)" indicates that the child has a beginning, middle, and end to a narrative piece. "Chaining" refers to a piece of writing threaded by a central idea. "Front-rear view" and "bird's-eye view" refer to the graphics on the page. "Voice and feelings" denote remarkable authenticity—I hear the writer's voice. In the "can" column, "exper. w. ." means that the child is approximating the use of the period.

In the code at the upper right, the R (Record) is a cue that I need to be available, to record the meaning generated by these children if need be. Since their spelling is prephonetic, they sometimes do not remember what they wrote earlier. E and F can help me to confer with the children, though the agenda always belongs to the child. This simple record provides me with insights into my students' growth and guides my instructional planning; most of my mini-lessons arise from this record.

Jacqueline Finn is an adjunct professor at Fitchburg State College, Fitchburg, MA, and a language arts specialist in Milford, MA.

Name	John	Michelle	Laura	Danny M.
Process	narrative has beginning, middle, end, illus: bird's eye view, 2 pp. R	narrative—sequences ideas	literary language—generates several sentences	much voice & feelings
Spelling				
Random				
Pre-Phonetic				
Phonetic	X	X	X	X
Transitional	X			X
Conventional				
Can:	Use upper, lower case	experiments with	choose topic, sequence ideas	(use for mini-lesson)
Needs:	E	mixes upper/ lower case	ck	

KEY:
R: May need to record child's message.
E: Expand
F: Focus

YOUNG ARTISTS

"Molly"- Liesel Jung, 16, Dexter, OR
(From *Treasures 2*, see p. 162)

MarVELous INVENTIONS

Priorities

Pat, i LICITRID MIY BIC BUT MOST OF AL·LILIICSCHOOL

[Pat I like to ride my bike but most of all I like school.]
—Contributed by Pat Robinson, kindergarten teacher, Ohlone School, Palo Alto, CA

WHOLE LANGUAGE CAMERA

Nancy Buscaglia's sixth grade students write at the computer, Clarence, N.Y.

Classroom Demonstrations

by David Hartle-Schutte

Cumulative Writing Folders, K–5

Purpose: To maintain representative samples of each student's writing for grades K–5, and to provide a systematic means of documenting student development in writing. These folders will provide teachers with useful and meaningful information about students' strengths and weaknesses. The folders also provide teachers with a very broad outline of the types of things emphasized in the writing program at each grade level. This will help to develop more coordination within and between grade levels.

How to Use Them: The folders are intended primarily as observation checklists for teachers to use as students engage in the writing process. Since writing is a developmental process, there is much overlap between the grade levels. The majority of the items are never "mastered" once and for all, but become more complex each year.

Thus, the observations by the teachers must be considered within the context of each particular grade level. For example, the expectations for the use of descriptive language at fifth grade would be more complex than for kindergarten or first grade. An effective beginning for a story written by a second-grader would not necessarily be an effective beginning for a story written by an older child. In other words, teacher judgment plays a big role in these evaluations.

There will also be great variation between different pieces of writing done by the same child. For this reason, the initial idea of a simple check mark was replaced with the letters S, M, and W, to tell whether or not the child has a consistent strength in an area, or only displayed that ability once. A child who consistently demonstrates an item on the check sheet in most or all writing is given an S (for a definite

strength). A student who shows the capability in some but not most writing receives M (for moderate ability). A student rarely showing the capability is given a W (for definite weakness). If an item on the list is never demonstrated by the student, the space is left blank.

Cautions: The use of letters rather than check marks may unfortunately carry the connotation of grades. This is *not* intended, nor do folders represent lists of "minimum competencies," "exit requirements," "promotion/retention criteria," nor any other such traditional evaluative measures. The items listed for each grade level are not expected to be "mastered" by each student. Some may be accomplished by only the more proficient writers. Students will demonstrate a wide range of abilities. The folders may be useful in identifying areas needing more teaching emphasis.

The items listed on the folder are not intended to be tested, but rather are guidelines for what to observe and evaluate in student writing. Passing an item on a test does not mean students can apply it to their own writing.

A lack of space prevented us from including the entire K–5 continuum; shown here are the checklists for kindergarten and fifth grade.

Student_____ Year_____

Kindergarten

S = definite strength
M = moderate ability
W = definite weakness
(leave blank if never accomplished)

	Date 1st qtr.	Date 2nd qtr.	Date 3rd qtr.	Date 4th qtr.
Recognizes name in limited contexts (name tags, personal items)				
Recognizes name in many contexts (on lists, etc., throughout class)				
Writes first/last name (indicate F/L)				
Involves in prewriting activities (brainstorming, sharing, drawing, etc.)				
Uses letters to represent meaning (may be random use of letters)				
Systematic use of letters/words to represent meaning (beg. & end letters)				
Labels pictures with words/sentences (own writing/dictation to teacher)				
Uses approximate & standard spelling				
Selects writing as a choice				
Uses writing spontaneously				
Reads some environmental print				
Reads patterns/predictable books				
Chooses own writing topics				
Reads back own writing				
Shares own writing				
Revises own writing				
Writing expresses complete ideas				
Writing has logical sequence (time, cause & effect, etc.)				
Handwriting legible				
Published final draft				

Comments, strengths/weaknesses
(include references to writing samples in folder):

Student_____ Year_____

Fifth Grade

S = definite strength
M = moderate ability
W = definite weakness
(leave blank if never accomplished)

	Date 1st qtr.	Date 2nd qtr.	Date 3rd qtr.	Date 4th qtr.
Involves in prewriting activities (brainstorm, discuss, draw, list . . .)				
Chooses writing topics, narrows topic appropriate				
Shares own writing (first and later drafts) (in small/large groups)				
Revises own writing for meaning				
Revises own writing for sentence structure (independently, w/others)				
Expresses complete ideas within sentence & story as whole (in final draft)				
Writing has logical sequence				
Uses descriptive language				
Writes effective beginnings				
Middle of text well integrated with beginning and end				
Writes effective endings				
Develops characters well				
Uses dialogue effectively				
Uses other literacy techniques (metaphor, flashback, foreshadowing)				
Edits for mechanics (spelling, caps., punctuation, grammar, handwriting)				
Published final draft:				
personal experience narrative				
imaginative story				
report				
communication (letter, note, etc.)				
poem				
summary				

Comments, strengths/weaknesses
(include references to writing samples in folder):

David Hartle-Schutte is an assistant professor at the University of Hawaii, Hilo, HI.

Classroom Demonstrations

by Helen B. Slaughter

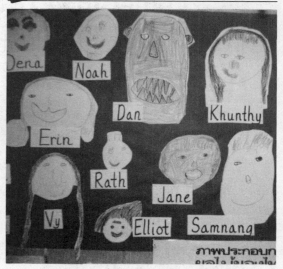

Self-portraits of Janice Stradford's first-graders, many of whom are recent immigrants from Cambodia, peer out from class bulletin board, Santa Rosa, CA.

A Whole Language Approach to Assessing Beginning Reading

Margaret Meek Spencer (1989, p. 45) has said that reading cannot "be satisfactorily tested before, or even by, the age of eight. It can, however, be clearly demonstrated and recorded." A study by Bussis, Chittenden, Amarel, and Klausner (1985) showed that the poor performance of some first-graders on tests was caused by the short comprehension paragraphs used on standardized tests. This was especially true for holistic, meaning-focused readers. The researchers recommended that first-graders should read in a naturalistic context using real books instead of tests.

We developed *K–2 Reading Stages: Independent/Self-Directed Reading* as a guide to teachers and evaluators for a more developmentally appropriate approach to assessment.

It is divided into two sections: "Form A: Emergent Readers," and "Form B: Beginning Readers." Although individual differences override any notion of "stages" as fixed categories, for convenience it is usually practical to use different assessment procedures for *emergent readers,* who cannot independently read unfamiliar texts, and *beginning readers,* who have developed some reading strategies for texts they have not previously read.

The assessment begins by asking the child to select and read a favorite or familiar book. If the child selects a book that is too difficult to read, the teacher or evaluator provides a few books within the child's expected reading range. Next, the student is asked to read an unfamiliar book at his or her instructional level. The student is asked to make a prediction before reading and to retell the story after reading.

After the assessment is finished, the miscues are analyzed in terms of strategies used or not yet evident, and the retelling is evaluated as a measure of reading comprehension (Goodman, Watson and Burke 1988; Clay 1985). The forms also encourage using narrative comments to document other pertinent information about students' individual reading performances.

In order to systematically use these procedures for program evaluation, a collection of well-written children's stories of graduated reading levels must be available. The Ohio State Reading Recovery Program Evaluation (Pinnell, Deford, and Lyons 1985) uses such a collection. These stories are best identified through experience by having children read and retell them, rather than through readability formulas.

This approach provides a high level of information about individual students' reading development. Unlike conventional testing, children enjoy the process, which resembles one-to-one instruction. The procedures are readily applied to evaluating bilingual programs, and were successfully used in evaluating reading in the Hawaiian Language Immersion Program (Slaughter, Warner, and Palmiera 1989).

➜ See: Hartle-Schutte, p. 106.

References

Bussis, A. M., E. Chittenden, M. Amarel, and E. Klausner. 1985. *Inquiry into meaning: An investigation of learning to read.* Hillsdale, NJ: Lawrence Erlbaum.

Clay, M. M. 1985. *The early detection of reading difficulties.* 3d ed. Auckland: Heinemann.

Goodman, Y. M., D. J. Watson, and C. L. Burke. 1988. *Reading miscue inventory: Alternative procedures.* Katonah, N Y: Richard C. Owen.

Pinnell, G. S., D. E. Deford, and C. A. Lyons. 1985. *Reading recovery: Early intervention for at-risk first graders.* Arlington, VA: Educational Research Service.

Slaughter, H., S. N. Warner, and W. K. Palmeira. 1989. Evaluation report for the second year of the Hawaiian Language Immersion Program. Honolulu: Hawaii State Department of Education.

Spencer, M. M. 1989. *Important reading lessons.*

Helen B. Slaughter is a professor in the curriculum and instruction department, College of Education, University of Hawaii, Manoa, Honolulu, HI.

Form A: Emergent Reader
K-2 Reading Stages: Independent Self-Directed Reading

Student Name _____ Age _____ Grade _____

Date of this Report _____ Assessor _____ School _____

Language Observed _____ Teacher(s) _____

I. Storybook Reading: Reading-like Behavior

    A. Independent *Reenactment* of Favorite Story Books (books that have been previously read to the student): Title of book and comments: _____

    B. Constructing Text for Unfamiliar Texts _____

        1. Looks at Print _____

        2. Does not produce/create text for pictures on pages having no print _____

        3. Creates/uses book-like language _____

        4. Creates/uses dialogue for characters _____

        5. Produces text that is *appropriate* to pictures or produces *superior* meaning for the storyline (if narrative) or expository text _____

        6. Other observations _____

II. Storybook Reading of Highly Predictable Books

    A. When given the first line or two of predictable text, can read rest of book (i.e., remembers the exact pattern and words of the repeated text): Title of books and comments: _____

        1. Uses picture cues, rhyming, graphophonics to identify new words in the predictable text _____

        2. Other reading behaviors _____

    B. Partial grasp of reading predictable text; describe briefly:

III. If student is unable to do the above, use a language experience approach. Print the student's dictated story. Describe the extent of which student attends to print, reads his/her Language Experience Story:

IV. Other information or assessment information, e.g., word recognition, ability to write a sentence, etc.

Titles of Other Books "Read" by Student: (Give several examples observed)

Additional comments:

© Helen Slaughter

Questioning Grading

Cornerstone: Diane Stephens

Learning-centered Evaluation

Whole language teachers often feel there is no room for the concept of grades. We talk instead about supporting the learning of our students and helping them to *progress as readers, writers, learners*. We refer to assessment as *continuous*, use our knowledge base to make *informed observations*, and consider students *curricular informants*. Grades seem to exist on the periphery as something that someone else requires us to give. As Lee Gunderson (1989) notes, "Whole language teachers generally believe that grades are not useful for indicating student growth, and try to avoid giving them."

I would argue, however, that grades do not have to be a "terrible, horrible, very bad" anti-whole language burden. Grades do become problematic when they reflect an external judgment relative to an imposed standard.

In my college classes, I ask students to take responsibility for their learning: to set goals for themselves relative to the course and to evaluate themselves relative to their goals. I believe that individuals continuously self-assess and that learning can best be assessed by the learner. We know when we have done well or have had a bad day.

Diane Stephens is currently visiting assistant professor at the Center for the Study of Reading, University of Illinois, where she conducts research on teacher decision-making, teacher-researcher collaboration, and the influence of Reading Recovery training on teaching. Before coming to Illinois, she was the director of a whole language clinic at the University of North Carolina at Wilmington. Diane has worked with learners ages 5 through 63, and has a particular interest in individuals who find reading difficult.

I have other reasons for asking students to self-assess. First, engagement, critical to learning, can't be mandated. Self-evaluation puts students in charge of their learning, and when students are in charge, they choose to engage. I've yet to have a student chose to spend a semester doing nothing.

Second, good teachers understand learning and learners, and self-evaluation helps students gain those understandings. Third, good teachers are reflective practitioners. They reflect on themselves, their goals, their students, their teaching, their classrooms. Education at all levels has the potential to provide individuals with opportunities to develop and hone their skills as reflective practitioners. Learning-centered evaluation is one means toward that end.

How It Works

Self-evaluation begins on the first day of class. When students introduce themselves, I ask them why they are taking the course and what they expect to get out of it. I then explain a bit about the course, go over the course outline, and discuss requirements. I note that students will be writing a learning-centered evaluation (LCE) and that this plan will be used to determine their grade in the course.

I've learned through experience that students often have difficulty establishing criteria that they consider quality, and so I talk about this with students on that first day. I use one of the course requirements as an example: What constitutes doing an excellent job of reading texts as opposed to a mediocre job? As I most often teach "reading" courses, these discussions also provide an opportunity for students to consider what it means to be a reader and to address the relationship between reader and text.

For the next class meeting, I ask students to think about what they want to accomplish in the course, how the course requirements will help them reach those goals, and how they want to assess themselves as learners. On the second day of class, students meet in small groups to share their ideas with their peers. They prepare a first draft for the third day and confer with each other about content. Drafts are revised and edited on the fourth day. Plans are given to me on the fifth.

I read the LCEs and respond to students in dialogue journals. If I understand their goals for the course and how they are going to evaluate themselves relative to those goals, the plan is accepted. If the plan is not clear, I respond to the students and ask them to elaborate.

Accepted LCE plans are filed away until two weeks before the end of the semester. Occasionally, however, I refer to the plans in my correspondence with the student: "John, I looked over your LCE this morning and it seems to me that, according to your criteria, you have a C so far in this course. Are you comfortable with that?"

Two weeks before the end of the semester, students begin writing their evaluation documents. Again, students confer with one another. Plans are submitted to me one week before the semester ends. This gives me time to read and respond to each before class ends. If the class size has been reasonable—30 students as opposed to 60—I hold individual conferences to discuss the grade.

Evaluation documents that are logical and consistent with original or revised evaluation plans are accepted. Students are asked to revise if there are inconsistencies. Grades are thus collaboratively determined.

I have been asking college students to prepare LCEs since 1983. I have also asked them to evaluate the process. At one point, I researched learning-centered evaluation. The results have been consistent: Students say that (1) it is harder to devise an evaluation plan than they first thought; (2) they work harder when they self-evaluate; and (3) they learn more.

Learning-centered evaluation takes me out of the judge-evaluator role and frees me to spend my time helping students learn. Rather than spending my time grading, I spend my time responding. It enables me to move closer to "practicing what I preach," to "living my model."

➔ See: Goodman, pp. 252, 253, 254; Stephens, p. 361.

Reference
Gunderson, L. 1989. *A whole language primer* (*most likely an oxymoron*). Ontario: Scholastic-TAB.

Classroom Demonstrations

by Lois Bridges Bird

Anatomy of a Student Portfolio

Ten years ago, as the faculty of Fair Oaks School in Redwood City, California, moved into whole language, they wanted a method of evaluation that reflected their student-centered educational philosophy. Working with Jeanne Blake, a whole language middle school teacher, the Fair Oaks resource teacher, Gloria Norton, developed a student portfolio that includes a variety of holistic evaluative measures:

Semimonthly Anecdotal Records

Teachers include notes from their anecdotal records on a semimonthly basis; they try to capture a variety of information that will be helpful to successive teachers.

Quarterly Writing Samples

Writing samples from across genre: journal writing, personal narrative, fiction, nonfiction, poetry, and so on are collected in September, December, March, and May. Teachers may attach notes to each sample explaining its significance.

Retellings

Students are asked to retell a literature story in September and again in May, which are scored according to procedures outlined in the *Reading Miscue Inventory: Alternatives* (1987).

Invented Spelling/Developmental Evaluation

In September and again in May, primary students are given 14 words to spell; the students' spellings are evaluated on a four-part scale: pretend writing, pre-phonetic, phonetic (initial, final consonants, short and long vowels), and conventional.

Environmental Print

Entering kindergarten students are given the Goodman Print Awareness Inventory. Both English and Spanish print are used depending on the child's home background; items are chosen that reflect the print present in the environment around the school, such as K Mart and McDonald's.

Sampling of Books Read

Each year, a sampling of the literature books each child has read is listed.

Burke Reading and Writing Inventory

Developed by Carolyn Burke of the University of Indiana (Goodman, Watson, and Burke 1987, p. 219), the inventory is administered if there is some cause for concern with a particular student.

Miscue Analysis

If a child is experiencing difficulty, a full-scale miscue analysis is done; the results are included in the portfolio.

➔ See: Bird, p. 92; Goodman, pp. 98, 100; Print Awareness in Preschool Children, p. 39; Reading Miscue Inventory, p. 101.

Reference
Goodman, Y., D. Watson, and C. Burke. 1987. *Reading miscue inventory: Alternatives*. Katonah, NY: Richard C. Owen.

YOUNG ARTISTS

—Debbie Smith, 16, Salem, OR
(from *Treasures 2*, See p. 162)

As Teachers See It

by Jan B. Loveless

From "Going Gradeless" to a "Learning Club": High School Writing Research in Evaluation and Atmosphere

Last year I was pleased with the results of a portfolio-grading experiment with accelerated, college-bound seniors. This year I wanted to repeat the research with the average-to-remedial students who populate general writing. I taught the course as a Nancie Atwell-style workshop, beginning each class with a minilesson and status-of-the-class roll check; then offering 30 minutes or so of workshop time in which students write and I circulate and confer. The class ends with a 10- to 15-minute sharing time. Students choose their own topics. Evaluation includes student self-evaluations and evaluation conferences with me. I grade holistically on volume of writing; use of workshop time; progress toward jointly set goals; risk-taking; participation in the community of writers through sharing critiques, and so on; and use of revision strategies (as opposed to recopying only).

Students received grades and comment sheets in their cumulative folders once per six-week marking period.

We also settled on a semester-long class project to write a book about the experience of being a teenager in Midland, Michigan, in 1989.

After an initial period of uncertainty about their lack of books and worksheets and my unwillingness to assign topics, students settled down to writing, learning ways to generate topics and getting ideas from one another. They quickly got over their shyness about sharing and began to demand sharing time—even whole sharing days.

I was, however, disappointed in their sketchy self-evaluations and minilesson logs during the first marking period, and I found the class hard to keep on track during my individual evaluation conferences, which I held in a glass-enclosed room that adjoins the classroom. They also tended to select seats in "caste" groups—the jean-jacketed auto lab crowd (primarily male), the punks, the "intellects," and the quiet girls. When I assigned seats and "homogenized" the class, they worked more steadily. I solved the evaluation problem by teaching them more specifically what I expected on self-evaluations and by conducting evaluation conferences in the classroom.

As time went by, my 27 students began to produce more writing. The average number of pieces completed in six weeks rose from three to four in the second marking period. One student, an "at risk" boy, completed 11 pieces and wrote about how quickly the hour passed for him. Students also seemed more comfortable with the grading method. Two students protested their first grades, even though they both received B's, a grade higher than normal. They said that they had been fooled by my positive comments into thinking they would receive A's. Neither had ever received positive comments on their papers before.

By the second marking period, no students complained about their grades. Seventy-four percent received A's or B's. None failed. This represents, I believe, the kind of grade improvement Donald Murray talks about in *A Writer Teaches Writing*.

My students are overwhelmingly enthusiastic about the grading system. Most are convinced they have learned more than they would have if they had been graded conventionally.

They are also very proud of their class book, *The Way We See It*, a collection of their favorite writing and illustrations they edited, typed, and laid out themselves. My contribution was to provide materials for the illustrators and arrange for the computer lab for the typists, then get the book to the printer.

I believe that my class has an esprit de corps now that fits Frank Smith's description of a "learning club." We meet his four criteria: (1) no grades except on portfolios at the end of the marking periods, (2) no coercion, (3) no restrictions, and (4) no status. I tried very hard to function as a "more experienced member of the club" and not as an authority figure.

My students' enthusiasm and growth in confidence as writers convince me that the best way to teach writing, at least in an introductory course, is through a workshop in which students begin right away with writing whole pieces, choosing their own topics, and learning grammar through communicating with real audiences rather than from exercises in workbooks. When students are treated as real writers, they begin to function as writers.

➔ See: Crafts, p. 136; Edelsky, p. 72; Goodman, p. 252; Graves, p. 129.

Jan B. Loveless is an instructional designer for the Learning Center, Dow Chemical Company, Pittsburg, CA.

Resource: Catalog

Educational Resources

2360 Hassell Rd.
Hoffman Estates, IL 60195
1-800-624-2926
1-312-884-7040 (Illinois)
$14.95 for 5,000 address labels

Address labels are very handy for keeping track of an active classroom. Teachers, for example, use the labels to write their observations of students' activities throughout the day. At the end of the day, they stick the labels in the appropriate section of a regular notebook. In this way anecdotal records (a major concern of whole language teachers) are easily kept. By checking to see how many "stickers" a child has, a teacher can see who is in need of attention.

Joel Brown

I Used to Be...But Now I...

I used to send all the students' work home with parents on Open House night,
But now we keep the work and review it to mark our progress.

—Linda Tsubata

I used to think I would buckle under the drudgery of circling and correcting,
But now I don't even own a red pen.

—Anonymous

 ## Book Note

The Primary Language Record: Handbook for Teachers

Centre for Language in Primary Education, London
1989; 64 pp.; $20
Portsmouth, NH: Heinemann

Some of the top authorities in the field worked for two and a half years creating this remarkable document, the primary evaluation component of the Inner London Education Authority in Great Britain. Its focus is observation-based assessment and anecdotal record-keeping that involve not only the child's teacher, but the parent and other support staff who work with the child. The *Record* is a compendium of sociopsycholinguistic theory coupled with theoretically sound strategies for gathering information about language and literacy development in English, as well as in other languages.

LBB

❝ The new record offers a coherent view of what constitutes progress and development in language. It encourages teachers to identify children's strengths and note growth points, to regard errors as information, and to analyse patterns of error in a constructive way. It will be particularly helpful to teachers who are interested in informal methods of assessment, based on observation and on teacher judgement. ❞(p. 8)

➔ See: Hall, p. 282; McKenzie, p. 234.

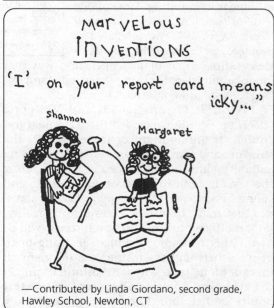

—Contributed by Linda Giordano, second grade, Hawley School, Newton, CT

Resource: Pamphlet

Building a Home Language Portfolio

Coal Creek Elementary School
801 W. Tamarisk
Lewisville, CO 80027
1-303-666-4863

This small pamphlet is given to students at Coal Creek Elementary School to take home to their parents, so that parents can work with their children as readers and writers. The pamphlet has space for both parent and child to record the child's skills in language development. Also included is general information about learning (taken from the Brian Cambourne Model of Literature Learning), spelling, and reading. Coal Creek also offers a taped session, led by educators, on ways for parents and volunteers to work with students.

The Tyranny of Testing

 Viewpoint: David Hartle-Schutte

Standardized Tests as Measures of Success

It has been estimated that 200 million achievement tests are given in the United States each year, and this represents only about 65 percent of all the educational and psychological testing that is conducted (Mehrens and Lehmann 1987).

Test results are increasingly used to evaluate not only students, but also their teachers and their programs. The majority of these tests are based upon a normal curve, which means that half the population scores below the mean and half is above the average. If scoring above average is considered a criterion for success, then only half the population can be successful. Likewise, half the population is considered unsuccessful. As an example, Goodson (1973), in his study of factors relating to success in "disadvantaged" children, defined a successful reader as one with a score higher than one deviation below the mean on the Sequential Test of Educational Progress. A "failure" (his word) in reading was defined as one with a score lower than one deviation below the mean. By his definitions, an error on one item on the test could distinguish between success and failure.

Numerous critics have examined the content and the consequences of standardized testing. Most of one issue of the NEA's *Today's Education* (March/April 1977) was devoted to problems associated with standardized testing. Their major conclusion was that group-administered, norm-referenced standardized tests should not be used in schools.

Taylor (1977, pp. 39–43) and McKenna (1977, pp. 35–38) concluded that (1) much test content is unimportant or irrelevant; (2) the structure and formats of the tests are confusing and misleading; (3) the process of administering the tests is demeaning, wasteful of time, and counterproductive; (4) the application of statistics that result from test scores distorts reality; (5) it is difficult to ensure that test results will be used either to improve student learning or to help teachers improve instruction; (6) many of the questions represent false information; (7) the reporting, interpretation, and use of test results are harmful; (8) the tests are culturally and linguistically biased; and (9) the language used in the test is language not commonly used in the real world.

Much of the current content of IQ tests is indistinguishable from achievement tests, aptitude tests, and even developmental screening tests (Selden 1983; Meisels 1987). As Meisels points out, though many people subscribe to the use of standardized tests for assessing achievement and developmental readiness, few would be comfortable using IQ tests for the same purposes. IQ and aptitude tests supposedly reflect innate, stable mental characteristics that are relatively unaffected by learning or coaching, while achievement tests are supposed to reflect learning (Williams 1983, p. 193).

However, Cole, Sharp, and Lave (1976, p. 119) describe the genesis of Alfred Binet's IQ tests:

The inspiration for their content came from an examination of the school curriculum, combined with Binet's sage guesses about the fundamental principles that underlie success in mastering that curriculum. The correlation between successful performance on Binet's tasks and success in school

David Hartle-Schutte is currently associate professor in the Education Department at the University of Hawaii at Hilo, where he teaches courses in reading, language arts, language development, and children's literature. For 14 years, David taught elementary children on a Navajo reservation, where he worked as a classroom teacher, an ESL instructor, and a reading specialist. He has also served as a language arts consultant for numerous school districts. David earned his doctorate in elementary education from the University of Arizona. He, his wife, and two children reside happily in Hilo, Hawaii.

was a tautology; the items were picked because they discriminated between children at various levels of academic achievement.

Williams says (p. 184): "The early testing movement was inextricably interwoven with belief in the superiority of the Anglo-Saxon Culture." The consequences of the racist and elitist roots of testing and student classification have great social impact. Tests that were designed to *demonstrate* racial and social class differences are the predecessors of the tests currently used to judge success. According to *Issues in Testing: Coaching, Disclosure and Ethnic Bias* (1981), ethnic bias occurs in individual items and in "unfairness of use" of tests as a whole.

Besides the content of the tests, there are a number of other crucial variables in testing. Labov (1973, 1982) demonstrated the importance of pragmatic and social-interactional considerations in determining performance in a particular setting. Philips (1972, 1983) and Riner (1979) identify cultural and communicative patterns in different Native American communities that are fundamentally different from the expectations of a typical public school classroom. They suggest that those differences account for differences in tests.

Another major factor in test performance besides cultural background is language differences. Goodman and Buck (1973, p. 197) state:

The only special disadvantage which speakers of low-status dialects suffer in learning to read is one imposed by teachers and schools . . . Simply speaking, the disadvantage of the divergent speaker, Black or White, comes from linguistic discrimination.

Responding to criticism of the misuse of testing and the cultural bias in testing, AERA, APA, and NCME (1985, p. 73) acknowledge in a joint statement:

For a nonnative English speaker and for a speaker of some dialects of English, every test given in English becomes, in part, a language or literacy test. . . . Test results may not reflect accurately the abilities and competencies being measured if test performance depends on these test takers' knowledge of English.

They also caution that local validity of a specific test must be verified for a particular local population (p. 16). These two cautions are frequently ignored, as standardized tests are often used to compare minority performance with norms. But using local norms wouldn't eliminate all the problems, because half the students would still score below average.

One further difficulty results from using "grade level," "reading level," or "grade equivalent" scores for reporting scores. Test publishers caution that these scores are the least accurate and the most subject to misinterpretation. Identical grade equivalents earned on different tests do not necessarily represent equally good performance" (Iowa Test of Basic Skills, *Technical Manual*, 1983, p. 27).

The International Reading Association passed a resolution in 1981 "advocating the abandonment of the practice of using grade equivalents to report performance of either individuals or groups of test-takers" (Cadenhead 1987, p. 438). The practice still continues.

As a result, the process of curriculum development is becoming narrower and narrower,

with more time being spent testing and preparing for testing. The tests have come to define what is taught and valued in classrooms (Cadenhead 1987; and Mayher and Brause 1986). Published programs are aimed specifically at teaching the skills that are tested. In some schools, teachers are evaluated and promoted on the basis of student achievement test scores.

Paradoxically, studies show that in schools where teachers had choice and flexibility in implementing reading instruction, children's achievement increased. In the schools where teachers were excluded from decision-making, achievement declined (Veatch and Cooter 1986).

➔ See: Ahlmann, p. 267; Hartle-Schutte, pp. 106, 240, 260, 265; Howard, p. 266.

References

AERA, APA, and NCME. 1985. *Standards for educational and psychological testing.* Washington, DC: American Psychological Association.

Cadenhead, K. 1987. "Reading level: A metaphor that shapes practice." *Phi Delta Kappan* 68(6).

Cole, M., D. Sharp, and C. Lave. 1976. "The cognitive consequences of education: Some empirical evidence and theoretical misgivings." *Urban Review* 9(4).

Goodman, K., and C. Buck. 1973. "Dialect barriers to reading comprehension revisited." In *Language and literacy: The selected writings of Kenneth S. Goodman, vol. 2,* ed. F. Gollasch. Boston: Routledge & Kegan Paul.

Goodson, F. 1973. "Factors relating to success in reading by disadvantaged children." Ph.D. diss., University of Arizona.

Green, B. 1981. *Issues in testing: Coaching, disclosure, and ethnic bias.* Washington, DC: Jossey-Bass.

Iowa Test of Basic Skills. 1983. *Technical manual.* Chicago: Riverside Publishing.

Labov, W. 1973. "The linguistic consequences of being a lame." *Language in Society* 2(1).

———. 1982. "Competing value systems in the inner-city schools." In *Children in and out of school: Ethnography and education,* eds. P. Gilmore and A. Glatthorn. Washington, DC: Center for Applied Linguistics.

Mayher, J. and R. Brause. 1986. "Learning through teaching: Is testing crippling integrated language education?" *Language Arts* 63(4).

McKenna, B. 1977. "What's wrong with standardized testing?" *Today's Education,* March/April.

Mehrens, W., and I. Lehmann. 1987. *Using standardized tests in education.* 4th ed. New York: Longman.

Meisels, S. 1987. "Uses and abuses of developmental screening and school readiness testing." *Young Children* 42(1).

Philips, S. 1972. "Participant structures and communicative competence: Warm Springs children in community and classroom." In *Functions of language in the classroom,* ed. C. Cazden, V. John, and D. Hymes. New York: Teachers College Press.

———. 1983. *The invisible culture: Communications in classroom and community on the Warm Springs Indian reservation.* New York: Longman.

Riner, R. 1979. "American Indian education: A rite that fails." *Anthropology and Education Quarterly* 10(4).

Selden, S. 1983. "Biological determinism and the ideological roots of student classification." *Journal of Education* 165(2).

Taylor, E. 1977. "The looking-glass world of testing." *Today's Education,* March/April.

Veatch, J., and R. Cooter. 1986. "The effect of teacher selection on reading achievement." *Language Arts* 63(4).

Williams, T. 1983. "Some issues in the standardized testing of minority students." *Journal of Education* 165(2).

📷 **WHOLE LANGUAGE CAMERA**

Free reading time in John Moran's second grade, Mary Dill School, Tucson AZ

(Continued from page 232)

written in a language that is at least end-on with the natural language of talk. With the realisation that research skills and reference work are not natural processes, acquired simply by some kind of intellectual osmosis, but must be taught and learned. With the effects of teacher and adult talk upon children, and the kinds of relationship that different forms of talk establish and maintain. And, above all, with the question of how a teacher can construct contexts that foster and support kinds of language that are rewarding and purposeful for the children.

Once teachers begin to ask questions about their teaching, and to look for answers, they have started themselves on the long and difficult road of change. Change is uncomfortable, sometimes painful; but it is also, perhaps, essential if we are to keep pace with the constant demands of teaching.

I return now to my first question—what do we need to know about language to be successful teachers? Well, we need to know something about the way in which individual people use and receive language, what the processes of reading, writing, and talking are, and how teachers can help them to take place efficiently and successfully. But what we do as teachers must not cut across the human dimensions of teaching and learning. That is to say, the business of teaching should not fracture the sort of relationship we would, in all humanity, want to see between any child and any adult. So the teacher has the professional responsibility to learn how to do the difficult job of teaching while at the same time coping with the quite unfair demands of being one adult among too many small children.

We need to know something about how people learn, and the ways their own language helps them to do that. We need to know when it's best for them to learn alone, or together with their peers, or with the help of an older or better-informed person. We may well need a professional knowledge of the nature of language itself, an understanding of how children acquire their native language and of what it is precisely they are acquiring. We need constant, shared discussion about what it is that helps teachers to learn—to learn about teaching, about language, and about how their colleagues and peers do their job. And we need some understanding of what circumstances will enable us to take a deep breath and immerse ourselves in the thoughtful panic out of which will emerge new learning. The model of learning that we present as right for children in classrooms is also the model of learning for the profession as a whole—collaborative, functional, supported by the full structure of the system, and enabling each individual to realise his or her full potential.

➜ See: Britton, p. 69; Moffett, p. 70; Weaver, p. 382.

An early form of this paper appeared in *Education 3–13* 10(2), Autumn 1982.

Further Reading by Mike Torbe
◆ *Language Across the Curriculum: Guidelines for Schools.* Ward Lock Education, 1976.
◆ *Teaching Spelling.* Ward Lock Education, 1978.
◆ *The Climate for Learning,* with P. Medway. Boynton/Cook, 1982.
◆ *A Framework for Reading: Creating a Policy in the Elementary School,* with M. Somerfield and C. Ward. Heinemann, 1985.
◆ *Language, the Learner and the School,* with D. Barnes and J. Britton. Boynton/Cook, 1989.

YOUNG ARTISTS

"Cheeta"—LaNae Hull, 7, Umatilla, OR
(from *Treasures 2*, see p. 162)

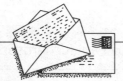

In the Mail

Although educators may have an obligation to administer standardized tests as employees of a school, they do not abrogate their parental rights because of their employment. As a teacher in a school with more than 95 percent Navajo children, I was outraged to be required to administer these totally inappropriate measures. I also recognized that there was little hope that schools or local administrators would reduce the quantity of testing merely upon the recommendation of an individual teacher. Since schools are often somewhat more responsive to parents than they are to their own employees, I wrote letters as a concerned parent to the principal, the local superintendent, and the state superintendent of education. I also provided copies of my letters to a statewide organization that was lobbying against excessive testing, and to numerous parents in the local school district.

Although dramatic reductions in testing did not occur, the Arizona state legislature did eliminate mandatory standardized testing for grades one and twelve. The local school district also rescinded the link between teacher merit pay and scores on locally administered criterion-referenced tests.

Since the schools were unwilling to provide alternative educational activities for my two children in lieu of the three sets of standardized tests administered each year, we have chosen to keep our children out of school during the testing sessions. The teachers have been very supportive of our decisions. Perhaps with their growing awareness, support can be generated for further reductions in testing. Teachers need to educate parents, administrators, school boards, and state officials about the detrimental effects of excessive testing, and to offer alternative means of evaluating students and programs. Only then can we begin to be free of the tyranny of testing.

—David Hartle-Schutte

March 8, 1988
C. Diane Bishop
Superintndent of Public Instruction
Arizona Department of Education
Phoenix, AZ 85007

Dear Ms. Bishop:

As a parent and an educator, I am extremely concerned about the use of standardized testing in our schools. For my doctoral dissertation, I have investigated the testing issue quite extensively. My research has convinced me that we need to work toward the elimination of most standardized testing now used in our schools.

Toward that end, I am requesting our local school to exempt my two children from both the Iowa Test of Basic Skills and the locally developed Criterion Referenced Tests. I am requesting that they be provided with educationally appropriate activities in lieu of these tests.

Attached is a copy of a number of pages of my research, for your information. These pages identify many of the technical problems that these tests have. I believe that these technical problems alone easily provide enough justification for the elimination of standardized testing. I would be happy to provide a full bibliography, if you would like one.

Although my children have consistently done extremely well on these tests, I believe that they are detrimental to them, but even more detrimental to their Navajo classmates and other minority students.

Below are a few of my more personal major objections (any one of which I believe is reason enough to eliminate the testing).

1. Testing wastes valuable educational time. With the ITBS testing and the local CRT testing, my son would be deprived of more than 3 weeks of instructional/learning time. For my daughter, the time involved is about 2 1/2 weeks.

2. The classroom teacher has the professional expertise and the personal long-term contact to determine what my children's weaknesses and strengths are, and how best to help them improve. Test results do not provide accurate or timely information.

3. Testing situations create unnecessary anxiety on the part of many students, and provide a boring, negative experience that becomes associated with school. All this is achieved while gathering notoriously incorrect and useless information on student abilities.

4. Curriculum is altered to reflect the tests, even by teachers who know that the tests and the reporting of the results are severely flawed. All children lose because of this.

5. Language and culturally different children are at a disadvantage when taking these tests. Professional organizations recognize this and caution against using the tests, results, or norms to draw conclusions if the local population is different from the norming population.

6. By definition, half of those taking the test will be "below average." In fact, the norms and the tests themselves will be adjusted to assure this. The tests are constructed to show that half the students do poorly. This is extremely poor educational policy and is very difficult to explain to parents.

7. The concept of "grade equivalent" is such a false notion, subject to great misinterpretation (partially because it is defined by the median score) that it should not be used at all. Yet this score is reported to parents, to the legislature, and to the media.

I will be sharing a copy of this letter with my principal, my fellow teachers, and parents in the area. At this point, I feel that I can only protect my children from these testing abuses, but I strongly believe that this protection should be given to all students in this state. I understand that these tests are mandated by the legislature, and that you may have limited power to address these problems.

I look forward to receiving a response.

Sincerely,
David Hartle-Schutte

As Teachers See It

by Paul Richardson

American Classrooms

The papers I read by Kenneth S. Goodman on the report on basal readers and the one by James Moffett were significant in articulating the unease I felt in visiting classrooms and talking to teachers in Philadelphia, Tucson, San Francisco, and particularly Los Angeles. The unified school district tests and the California Test of Basic Skills both fascinated and horrified me. My colleagues here at Gippsland IAE (in Victoria, Australia) were also a little taken aback by the intrusiveness of the tests and the assumptions they make about children's learning, teacher competence, and professionalism; not to mention the underground curriculum of conformity and regimentation.

Parents' Perspective

by Pam Howard

One Parent's Fight Against Standardized Testing

My interest in standardized testing began in April 1986. While living in Phoenix, I had the opportunity to observe my son's first-grade class during the administration of the Iowa Test for Basic Skills. As I walked around the classroom, I could see the anxiety and uncertainty on many of the children's faces . . . including my own son. The teacher had done her best to prepare the children for the test. However, it was impossible for first-grade children to take a test that contained ambiguous questions, and questions that were well beyond a first-grader's comprehension level. As I watched some of the children crying with frustration, I knew that I had to voice my concerns about the effects of standardized testing on first-grade children.

My first step was to attend a local school board meeting. Some of the members were sympathetic and understanding. However, they quickly pointed out that I should talk to our Arizona legislators since they were responsible for mandating annual standardized testing for all children, grades 1 through 12.

I contacted legislators who were on the Arizona House and Senate Education Committees. Some of the legislators were concerned, and said they would look into the problem, but unfortunately most of the legislators, since they had not heard from other people, did not share my concerns. Frustrated, I tried unsuccessfully to involve other parents.

From April to June of 1986, I wrote letters to several Arizona newspapers explaining my concerns about standardized testing for first-graders. The *Arizona Republic* printed my letter, as well as a letter from a first-grade teacher who also shared my views.

In January 1987, the Arizona State Board of Education recommended to the Arizona legislature that annual standardized testing for grades 1 and 2 be eliminated. Surprisingly, Rep. Jim Green, chairman of the House Education Committee, sponsored a bill that would require testing in grades 3, 6, 8, and 11 only. I testified before the House Education Committee in support of the bill, as did members of the State Board of Education and Arizona Education Association (AEA). Unfortunately, the committee also heard testimony from an Arizona State University professor who said testing should be fun and if the kids were stressed out, it was due to the teacher—not the test. Consequently, Rep. Jim Green, lacking the support of his committee, killed the bill.

From January to June 1987, I continued to write and call Arizona legislators. Most of the legislators listened politely, but they were not really interested in what I had to say. However, Rep. Bev Hermon (Tempe) of the House Education Committee agreed with me that standardized testing for young children was unnecessary and unproductive. She agreed to sponsor a bill in the next Arizona legislative session (1988) that would eliminate the annual statewide standardized testing for grades 1 and 2.

During the summer of 1987, I had the good fortune of meeting a group of teachers and educators from the Phoenix area who were also interested in the elimination of standardized testing. We had several meetings to discuss our philosophy and goals. Our group became known as Community for Effective Student Evaluation (CESE). Our short-range goal was to push for the elimination of the statewide standardized testing in grades 1, 2, and 12. We felt that testing children in grades 1 and 2 was unnecessary since these children did not have the abilities or experience to undergo a strenuous standardized test. We also felt that testing twelfth-graders was a waste of money since these children graduated before the results were ever known. Rep. Hermon agreed to include grade 12 in her bill.

In January 1988, speakers from CESE (including myself), AEA, and the Arizona State Board of Education testified in support of the bill before the House Education Committee. Several members of the House Education Committee did not feel that second grade should be eliminated from the statewide testing. Therefore, in order to save the bill, second grade was deleted. The bill passed the House Education Committee and the full House. The bill stated that all grades would be given the annual statewide standardized test, except grades 1 and 12.

After the bill passed, with an amendment that allowed school districts to determine if they wanted to give the standardized tests in grades 1 and 12, CESE realized that most of our lobbying efforts had been directed at the House Education Committee. Due to a lack of time and volunteers, we were not able to lobby the Senate Education Committee as well. Experience has now taught us that both education committees need to be contacted constantly in order for a bill to have a fighting chance.

My involvement with CESE and standardized testing came to an end after the bill passed. I had been fighting standardized testing for two years, and I felt good about the progress we had made. My suggestion to other parents in a similar situation would be to "hang in there." There were so many times that I was so frustrated that I wanted to quit. But then I would remember the crying six-year-olds in my son's first-grade class and I knew I had to keep going.

→ See: Goodman, p. 360; Hartle-Schutte, p. 265; NAEYC, p. 266.

Pam Howard is an elementary teacher, Marana School District, Tucson, AZ.

It Shouldn't Happen to Kids

Iowa Test of Basic Skills

Dorothy Watson tells the story of a teacher who found a little girl crying in the hallway.

"My goodness, what's wrong, dear?" she asked, stooping down to comfort the child.

"I have to take the Iowa Test of Basic Skills," she stammered, catching her breath between sobs.

"There now, that's okay. I'm sure you'll do just fine."

"But," sobbed the child, "I don't know anything about Iowa!"

—LBB

YOUNG ARTISTS

"Ring around the rosy"
—Rachel Arnow, 6, Palo Alto, CA

MarveLous InvenTions

Double Duty

It's about an hour's drive from our home in Half Moon Bay to Stanford where I work and where my five-year-old, Brooke, attends preschool. One morning Brooke was unusually quiet in the back seat of the car when she suddenly piped up, "You know what, Mom? I guess I have two brains."

"What makes you think that?"

"Because I can think about two things at once!"

—As told to LBB by Catherine Gardner, Half Moon Bay, CA

As Teachers See It

by Martha Ahlmann

Thoughts on CTBS

The children are agitated. One complains of an upset stomach. Two others come up and tell me of a third who did something wrong. The normal calming routine of listening to a story is an exercise in futility—it is not calming, and the children can't settle down. As soon as the story seems to be ending, half are already on their feet, wandering without purpose. A mother comes in to check on her child who woke up suddenly during the previous night in a panic. What kind of nightmare is this? Quite simply, it is the second day of the CTBS testing in a whole language first-grade class.

Children who have spent eight months learning to work with and help each other have been instructed to work silently, not to copy, and not to let anyone see their papers. Children who have spent eight months learning to express themselves and give thoughtful opinions must now choose one of three answers—quickly. Children who have learned the sounds of language, who delight in repeating "terrible, horrible, no good, very bad day" must listen for beginning sounds, ending sounds, and vowel

sounds totally out of context. Children who have experienced language and literature as part of a whole theme must decide about unrelated pieces of language—sounds, capital letters, meaning of words. Children who pick up books much beyond their "grade level," and who are thrilled with picking out new words such as *extinct* simply by using context clues and their own interest, must decide if the right meaning for the word *end* is fence, finish, or whatever.

Why do we do this? I have yet to hear an answer that satisfies me. The theme of whole language is *trust*. Trust in the learner. This should also include trust in the teacher. We do not need CTBS to tell us if our children are learning, because it can't do that. It has no validity in a whole language classroom. We teach these children to reason and to think and to respond; we then frustrate them by demanding answers they aren't equipped to give.

➜ See: Hartle-Schutte, p. 264; Howard, p. 266; Wegner, p. 269.

Martha Ahlmann is a primary teacher at Chuska School, Tohatchi, NM.

As kids see it

Testing in Arizona Schools

Dear State Comm,   4/24/87
I thought the Iowa Teast was trash. Cus I dint lean any thing It we dint do the Iowa Teast I would lean more. I dint lean any thing cus my teacher said I can't tell you the anwes. And on ragler work my teacher comes around and looks at it and sais wats rong.

2nd grade

From "Testing in Arizona Schools," *Centerspace* 1(5), May/June 1987.

It Shouldn't Happen to Kids

Testing of Young Children: Concerns and Cautions

The National Association for the Education of Young Children (NAEYC) believes that placement decisions such as enrollment in school, retention in grade, or assignment to remedial or special classes—decisions that have a major impact on children's lives—should be based on multiple sources of information and should *never* be based on a single test score. Sources of information to consider include careful observations of qualified teachers; observations of parents and family members; and samples of children's drawings, paintings, dictated stories, and other activities of school and at home.

Is Standardized Testing Harmful for Young Children?

Mass standardized testing of young children is potentially harmful to children educationally. Testing narrows the curriculum. Inevitably teachers teach to the test. Many of the important skills that children need to acquire in early childhood—self-esteem, social competence, desire to learn, self-discipline—are not easily measured by standardized tests. As a result, social, emotional, moral, and physical development and learning are virtually ignored or given minor importance in schools with mandated testing programs.

Testing programs also harm children intellectually. Where test scores are stressed, the curriculum is often designed to ensure that children memorize facts and figures that can be easily addressed by a multiple-choice test. More challenging intellectual pursuits such as reading for information, composing stories, problem solving, and creative thinking are given less emphasis. But these abilities will be even more important in the future. Children need to learn how to learn, so that they are prepared to func-

tion in an ever-changing American society.

The potential psychological harm of testing is well documented. Testing puts undue stress on young children at a time when they are adjusting to new people and unfamiliar surroundings. Even children who perform well on tests are found to suffer from the stress of preparing for and taking a test.

Testing leads to labeling and mislabeling. Children are labeled as "smart" or "dumb" on the basis of test scores. Too often test scores are used to determine if children should be held back, assigned to a special class, or told to wait a year before entering kindergarten. Despite the fact that adults never say the words, children know if they are in "the dummy class" or if they "have flunked." Such labels harm children's feelings about themselves and also influence teachers' and parents' feelings about children's learning ability. These expectations about what children are capable of doing almost always influence how children are treated in school and at home. Parents' and teachers' expectations are one reason why self-fulfilling prophecies almost always come true.

Why Is Standardized Testing Inappropriate for Young Children?

Mass standardized testing of young children is inappropriate for several reasons.

- **Young children are not good test takers.** The younger the child, the more difficult it is to obtain reliable (consistent over time) and valid (accurate) results from tests. Results are easily influenced by a young child's test-taking skills: the ability to sit down, be quiet, and make a mark in the correct place. Such behavior does not necessarily reflect children's level of learning.

- **Young children are growing and learning rapidly.** Just how quickly children grow and learn is reflected in the fact that a school year constitutes one-fourth of the lifetime of a four-year-old. With any group of young children, there is wide variation in what may be considered normal. This means that the potential for obtaining inaccurate test results, and thus misdiagnosing or mislabeling, is particularly great with young children. Just as young children of four or five vary widely in height and weight, they also vary in other

areas of development that are not as apparent.

- **There is no such thing as a culture-free test.** Test bias has been well-documented. Test developers ignore language and culture variations too often. Any test in English given to nonnative English speakers, or children who speak a dialect of English, is first and foremost a language test, regardless of its intent. With young children, language and culture are essential aspects of children's learning and development. For example, when asked on a test, "Where do lions live?" a child who had spent his early years in Kenya might answer "in the park." From his experience, the answer is correct; however, the test manual says that the correct answer is "in the zoo," and the teacher would record his answer as an error.

Without Testing, How Can Schools Assess If Children Are Learning?

A more important question to ask is—Do we gain any new information about children from testing? Standardized testing seldom provides information beyond what teachers and parents already know. The systematic observations of trained teachers and other professionals, in conjunction with information obtained from parents and other family members, are the best sources of information. Most teachers and parents know that paper-and-pencil tests are not accurate measures of young children's development and learning. Teachers should be trained to observe and assess young children in general. But parents know their own children better than anyone else and should be active participants in the assessment process.

➜ See: NAEYC, p. 23.

More Resources: You can order the following resources from NAEYC, 1834 Connecticut Ave., NW, Washington, DC 20009; 1-800-424-2460.
Appropriate Education in the Primary Grades. #578.
Developmentally Appropriate Practice in Early Childhood Programs Serving Children from Birth through Age 8, ed. S. Bredekamp, #224.
Good Teaching Practices for 4- and 5-Year-Olds. #522.
"NAEYC Position Statement on Standardized Testing of Young Children 3 through 8 Years of Age." 1988. Published in *Young Children* 43(3): pp. 42–47.

Excerpted from NAEYC brochure, no. 582.

Coping with Tests

In the Mail

NTE
Educational Testing Service
Princeton, NJ 08541-6051

November 12, 1988
To Whom It May Concern:

Today I took one of the NTE exams: 30-Reading Specialist at site 4630, the University of Maine, Orono, ME. My registration number was 587072, and my test booklet was numbered 0435. I think I was the only person there taking that particular exam.

I would like to sit down with someone and discuss the exam. Having read the sample items and accompanying answers, I concluded that the exam was written by those whose theory of reading is word recognition. That puts people who have studied psycholinguistic theory in the position of Galileo's students when they were tested on the flat-earth theory—knowing better, but giving the answers considered "correct" by the testers.

I request that you unearth booklet 0435 and look for specific comments I made during the test period. One question that I remember shaking my head over was somewhere around the midpoint of the exam. It went something like this:

According to Kenneth Goodman, miscues are
a. incorrect hints
b. reading errors
c. blah
d. blah
e. blah

None of the answers were correct. Had it said that what word recognitionists consider reading errors, Ken calls miscues, that would be one thing. The question caused me to try to guess whether the test makers used the term incorrect hints (or something to that effect) as a distractor meaning mis = incorrect and cues = hints; or if they were actually picking up on the knowledge that syntactic and semantic cues do suggest certain possibilities for words in context. More likely, I decided on the basis of their orientation, they consider miscues to be reading errors. Did you, by the way, check with Dr. Goodman on the wording of this item?

As someone who has spent much of the past 15 years working with children who have been disabled by methods and materials based on a word recognition theory of reading, and as someone who has studied reading and writing in great depth, I feel insulted by your test. I realize that my experience in taking many a standardized test over the years helped, but, as I pointed out in the test booklet, many of the questions were loaded in favor of the behavioristic, word recognition theory tradition rather than in knowledge of the reading process. I read recently in Education Week that this test will be trashed by 1992 or so, but is it soon enough?

I do hope that someone at ETS will have the courage and integrity to unearth my test booklet and respond to me.

Yours truly,

Pamela Perkins

March 1, 1989
Dear Ms. Perkins:

Thank you for your letter of November 12 concerning the NTE Reading Specialist Exam. I apologize for our slow response to your comments. After receiving your letter, we retrieved your test booklet and conducted multiple reviews of the items you questioned. These reviews took some time.

Concerning the question on Kenneth Goodman's definition of "miscues," we agree that none of the options could be selected as a correct answer. All tests that contain this question are being rescored. Thank you for calling our attention to this question.

Concerning the comments you wrote in your test booklet on other questions, after an in-depth review of each of the questions about which you expressed concern, our test specialists and reading specialists are still of the opinion that there is one single best answer.

The questions you cited do represent a behavioristic/word recognition theory of reading. When these questions were written and reviewed, theories of reading based on behaviorism and word recognition skills were dominant in the field and these theories continue to dominate many reading programs.

Each new edition of a Specialty Area Test (such as the Reading Specialist Test) is developed by a committee of examiners made up of elementary and secondary practitioners (in this case, reading specialists), as well as professors who teach the subject in colleges and universities in different regions of the United States. In selecting members for each committee of examiners, the NTE Program staff seeks the advice of the appropriate professional associations in the subject (such as the International Reading Association). The content and scope of each test are specified and reviewed periodically by the committee of examiners who, with other subject-matter specialists, write the test questions.

In the fall of 1989, a new committee of examiners of the Reading Specialist Test will assemble to set new specifications reflecting current theory and practice in the field and begin the development of new forms of the test. I will see that your concerns about the current nature of the test and its questions are brought to the attention of this committee.

Thank you for writing to us and calling attention to the remarks in your test booklet. We always appreciate comments that help improve the quality of our tests.
Sincerely yours,

Claudia A. Gentile
Associate Test Examiner

Pamela Perkins is an assistant professor at Chapman College, Orange, CA.

It Shouldn't Happen to Kids

Reason to Boast?

The principal of a Texas school that had received a federal citation for excellence based on its high test scores boasted on a radio show that when his students missed items on standardized tests, they cried.

—LBB

CAT Test

by Debra Goodman

Oh my noisy,
enthusiastic, argumentative
energetic, mischievous
and sometimes obnoxious
fifth-graders—
I have put you in rows
for the California Achievement Test.
The straight lines silenced you
bound and gagged
working in a small box—

by yourself—

you are all the same.
Is Linda sad today?
Is Jenny thinking of her next story?
Is Bert hatching up some wild prank?
Is Lawrence worrying about his dad?
And Ellen, who asked me just this morning
if I was in a good mood . . .
Does she still care?
We all bow before the god of mystical choice.

➜ See: Goodman, pp. 24, 25, 224, 236, 252, 274.

Debra Goodman is a teacher at Dewey Center for Urban Education, Detroit, MI.

ETS granted us permission to print Claudia Gentile's response to Pamela Perkins provided we included the follow-up note from Charlotte Solomon.

LBB

March 15, 1990

ETS's response to Pamela Perkins's inquiry regarding the NTE Reading Specialist Test and specifically the error in the question of Kenneth Goodman's Miscue Analysis clearly demonstrates ETS's commitment to fairness and our determination to prepare and review our tests under the most exacting of standards. Note that every test question challenged by a test taker is carefully reexamined for accuracy, and ETS responds to each inquiry. When a test question is found to be inaccurate, we rescore those tests in which the item appeared. While we strive to have 100 percent accuracy on our tests, it is noteworthy that 99.7 percent of the questions on NTE tests are accurate. Readers interested in knowing more about ETS's test quality control process should contact Charlotte Solomon, ETS, Rosedale Road, Princeton, NJ 08541.

➜ See: Goodman, pp. 98, 101, 102.

Classroom Demonstrations

by Angela Wegner

Testing My Patience: A Kindergarten Teacher's Diary

5-17-88

The idea of giving kids the required standardized tests has long been abhorrent to me. My attitude was reinforced when I looked over the new "revised" Metropolitan Readiness test and couldn't for the life of me decipher how it could tell me anything about the kids I didn't already know—especially since I was giving it at the end of the year so it couldn't possibly be diagnostic.

Why, then, was I giving up a whole week of education for this nonsense? How much money is this kindergarten testing costing anyway: the test booklets, the substitute time needed, the cost of collating the results?

And this business of breaking "pre-reading skills" down into meaningless bits of unconnected tasks like matching nonsense symbols is so contradictory to the current research on emergent literacy! In the end does it tell anybody—teachers, principals, parents, *the kids themselves*—anything really useful?

But I tried to approach it as positively as I could with the kids.

We began our introduction to testing by reading *First Grade Takes a Test* by Miriam Cohen. In this story the children come up with creative and thoughtful test answers, but when Anna-Maria is moved to a special class because she "did a good test," the other children react with a feeling of self-denigration. They begin to call each other "Dummy." Jim says softly to *himself,* "Dummy!" Their teacher reacts strongly, pointing out that a test can't show how kind or cooperative or creative they are.

We talked about the book for a long time, and the children demanded to hear it again.

"Now," I said, "there are some very different things about taking a test we need to talk about. The most different thing is this: You know how we always help each other?"

"Yes!" they said. "We always help our friends."

"Well, when we take a test we don't help each other because we want to see what we can do all by ourselves."

They just sat and looked at me.

I couldn't help feeling immoral at this point. We'd spent nine months building a cooperative ethic, and here I was telling them they couldn't help their friends.

"Just for this test . . ." I said defensively.

In the end they came up with four "test rules" that we wrote on a sign. It read:

No talking
No helping
Don't worry
You're smart

Then we did our practice test.

"Oh, that was easy!" they said when we'd finished.

"Of course it was," I reassured them. "You're smart."

I made sure to explain to them all the details of the upcoming week: The test was pretty long; we'd need a couple of days to do it; we'd go to the nurse's room.

They left that day feeling comfortable, pleasantly anticipatory and with some sense of power over the test process.

Even though I was feeling angry and resentful about the absurdity of giving them this "standardized mess," I tried to give the kids a way to handle the tests.

5-18-88

And it worked! It worked!

The first day of testing left me buoyant . . . not because of the test itself but because of the opportunity it gave me for kidwatching.

Once settled, we reviewed the test booklet format and our test rules sign—especially "Don't worry, you're smart!"

And then the magic moment.

"When I ask you the questions, what are you going to do?" I asked. And waited.

They thought.

Finally little Quentin (the youngest and tiniest member of our literacy club, the one who can barely peer over the top of his desk), little *Quentin* piped up. "We think the answer in our heads," he lisped in his little voice.

"Tell me more about how you're going to think it in your head," I urged.

He paused thoughtfully and replied, "I'm gonna look over the *whole* thing and then I gonna think the answer and then I gonna look at it real careful."

Now if that isn't a whole-to-part strategy, I don't know what is! I could have fallen off my chair in pride.

5-25-88

I just scored and normed Quentin's test. His "prereading composite" puts him at a percentile rank of 17 percent and at the third stanine.

Ha!

The norm takes no account of the fact that Quentin is chronologically much younger than his classmates. It also completely ignores Quentin's individual personal developmental growth patterns and rate, as well as his individual life experiences. It measures Quentin against some absolute measuring stick, completely missing the fact that Quentin has shown phenomenal individual growth and progress since he began school. Standardized testing in general misses the essential point that *we are all on a continuum of growth and learning* and that it usually isn't particularly helpful to compare ourselves to anyone else.

If you define reading as meaning-making, Quentin has the concept of reading well in hand. He retells stories using picture clues. He retells them in sequence using a combination of remembered phrasing and improvised but logical language. He "reads" expressively and fluently, if not yet word-perfect.

Quentin is also working at making sense of the process of writing. He does understand that writing is a symbolic representation of language. As yet his writing consists of mostly alphabet-like scribbles with occasional standard letters—considerable growth from his pure scribbles at the beginning of the school year.

During a writing conference with Quentin one day, I was impressed to see the letters "B-E-C-H" scrawled semi-recognizably in his journal as he read, "One day my auntie gonna take me to the beach."

"Quentin," I exclaimed, "tell me how you knew how to write beach!"

"I asked Tony and Torie and they helped me."

And his stories! How they've grown as his confidence and familiarity with story format and "book language" has increased. He enjoys sharing his stories with his friends and is proud when they respond.

Tell me: Do I need standardized tests to tell me about Quentin?

Angela Wegner is a primary teacher at Lloyd Elementary School, Milwaukee, WI.

Language Stories

The No-Nonsense Teacher

Let me tell you about my contacts with Sister Mary Rose, a fifth-grade teacher in El Cajon, California. She was part of a team of teachers Carolyn Burke and I were working with, helping them understand the power of miscue analysis. I spent a number of days in Sister's classroom, observing and interacting with both her and her students. Sister Mary Rose had a special relationship with her group of fifth-graders. She helped them understand what she was learning about reading as part of our project. She told the students that she now believed that if readers have some knowledge or ideas about what they are reading, then it is easier to read. However, if what they are reading is nonsense to them—that is, they don't know anything about it, and it just doesn't make sense—then they really shouldn't even try to read it. She and her students began to use a slogan in class whenever they read something they did not understand. They would say, "We will not tolerate nonsense."

She worked with her students to help them reject reading that they did not understand and to discover ways to build their background if they needed to read something. Sister Mary Rose told me about this understanding that she and the students were working out together. She thought it was working quite well and was making a real difference in the confidence with which students would accept or reject what they were reading. The students discussed a number of strategies they would use when something was nonsense and that included, among other possibilities, just closing up the reading material and putting it away. Not tolerating nonsense also became part of their criteria for choosing what to read.

Toward the end of the school year, Sister Mary Rose's beliefs were tested. She was giving her class the California Test of Basic Skills. Jerry came up to her a few minutes after the test began and whispered, "Sister, I can't tolerate this nonsense. I really don't understand any of it."

Sister responded: "Well, Jerry, what are you going to do about it?"

Jerry: "We're not to tolerate nonsense so I think I just won't read this test."

Sister Mary Rose: "Could you put it quietly in your desk and just not say anything to anyone else about this?"

"Fortunately," Sister Mary Rose said, as she related this incident to me, "none of the others came up to tell me that so I just marked Jerry absent. I had to be true to him. We'd made the decision together as a group and I had to honor his belief in himself to make such decisions. I'm not sure if what I did was right, but it did help Jerry out."

—YMG

➔ See: Ahlmann, p. 267; Literature Reference List, p. 429.

Excerpted from *Rethinking Schools* 3(3), May 1989.

Resource: Organization

The National Center for Fair & Open Testing

342 Broadway
Cambridge, MA
02134-1802

Want to join the fight against standardized testing? Join the Center for Fair and Open Testing, a national nonprofit research and advocacy organization working to eliminate the abuse and misuse of standardized tests. A $15 fee buys you membership and the newsletter *Fair Test*.

LBB

I Used to Be...But Now I...

Yesterday I tested more and understood less,
Today I observe more and perceive more.

—Jo Glaser

As kids see it

Strategies for Taking a Test

by Carol and Liz Gilles

As a former teacher for children labeled learning disabled, I know how devastating testing can be for children who have trouble in school. The tests are usually timed, and children panic when the clock starts ticking. The questions are often poorly worded, and there is little continuity from one set of questions to the next. If the child thinks deeply about the question, many of the answers seem plausible! For kids having trouble, testing serves only to accentuate what the child already believes: I'm just not good enough.

But what about those children who are good students? How do they deal with testing in the curriculum? My daughter, Elizabeth (age 10), had just finished the mandated week-long state competency testing, as well as some end-of-unit math testing. She wrote this in her home diary:

Dear Diary,

Today I had to take a test in math. I used to hate taking tests but I made it fun for my self when I take computer tests with a, b, c and d. I pretend that there on a game show and I keep a tally. Every time I have that letter for an answer I give them a point. B usually wins. I pretend that he's an orphan and his parents are looking down from heaven and cheering.

Liz Gilles

Carol Gilles is a research/teaching assistant at the University of Missouri, Columbia, MO.

Resource: Pamphlet

What Does My Child's Reading Score Mean?

H. Donald Jacobs, D.Ed.
Arizona State
    Reading Council
    of the International
    Reading Association
College of Education
Arizona State University
Tempe, AZ 85287-0311
1-602-965-7766

Whole language educators are fighting to do away with invalid and inhumane standardized testing, but until our goal is achieved, it helps to know exactly what we're dealing with. Parents, especially, can find the numbers on a scorecard confusing. Help is here in the form of a clear, easy-to-read, four-page pamphlet, available in English and Spanish, written by Reading Clinic Coordinator Dr. H. Donald Jacobs of Arizona State University and the Arizona State Reading Council. Through a question and answer format, the pamphlet explains the difference between a grade equivalent score and a percentile score. Most notably, it describes why listening to a child read and asking questions about the material being read provides a more accurate assessment of a child's reading ability than a test. The pamphlet also provides a helpful list of testing strategies (do the easy questions first) that parents can share with their children. After reading this pamphlet, parents will be able to interpret their children's reading scores, and most important, understand that score as just one measure of reading ability, and not a very accurate one at that.

LBB

Resource: Book

Assessment Alternatives in Mathematics: An Overview of Assessment Techniques That Promote Learning

EQUALS/California
    Mathematics Council
1989; 35 pp.; $4

Available from:
EQUALS
Lawrence Hall of Science
University of California
Berkeley, CA 94720
1-415-642-1823

Teachers who believe that math is best learned by students working in small groups or individually, solving real problems, using tools such as manipulatives, calculators, textbooks, and computers, displaying their results in journals, graphs, and other written reports, have a big problem when it comes to traditional assessment methods. Current assessment instruments are failing if the purpose of assessment is to provide information for teachers to make instructional decisions. Tests should measure what is of value, not just what is easy to test.

The premise of this brand-new book, a joint project of EQUALS and the California Math Council, is that assessment should promote learning. It is filled with a wealth of suggestions to expand our ideas of how students can demonstrate what they have learned and how teachers can gain better information about their students.

The book contains two sections on assessing both students' mathematical products and processes used to gain mathematical understanding. There are numerous valuable and creative suggestions for alternate ways to measure progress in both these areas that will delight whole language teachers. Included under students' mathematical products are student-generated questions, videotapes, computer demonstrations, dramatic performances, debates, mathematical art, and physical constructions. Mathematical process assessments include observations, interviews, and questions that focus on whether a student usually works alone or with others, how their information is organized and recorded, whether estimation techniques are used, and how diligently problems are pursued.

The book concludes with a summary of some of the major issues in assessment. These issues include standardized and timed tests, learning modes, closed response tests, and the difficult correlation of standardized tests with state and local math frameworks.

Doug Haner

At all events, *quality* of activity and of consequence is more important for the teacher than any quantitative element. . . .

WELL-SAID The educator cannot sit down and wait till there are methods by which quality may be reduced to quantity; he must operate here and now. If he can organize his qualitative processes and results into some connected intellectual form, he is really advancing scientific method much more than if, ignoring what is actually most important, he devotes his energies to such unimportant by-products as may now be measured.

Moreover, even if it be true that everything which exists can be measured—if only we knew how—that which does *not* exist cannot be measured. And it is no paradox to say that the teacher is deeply concerned with what does not exist. For a progressive school is primarily concerned with growth, with a moving and changing process, with *transforming* existing capabilities and experiences; what already exists by way of native endowment and past achievement is subordinate to what may become. Possibilities are more important than what already exists . . . The place of measurement of achievements as a theory of education is very different in a static educational system from what it is in one which is dynamic, or in which the ongoing process of growing is the important thing.

—John Dewey, *Progressive Education and the Science of Education*

➜ See: Miller, p. 219.

Leadership

Cornerstone: Margaret T. Stevenson

From Grass Roots to School Language Policies: Institutionalizing Change

For ten years teachers in Edmonton have met together in professional groups to support each other as they introduced programs that treated language as basic to all learning. They were encouraged that their point of view about the role of language in learning had support from research and practice in the United Kingdom, New Zealand, Australia, the United States, and Canada. Some of the teachers worked alone in their schools to implement their beliefs; others had the active support of their principals and other teachers. With the consultants the language arts supervisor organized workshops, brought in authorities from outside the district, assisted with the development of material, and generally facilitated the work of the teachers. A great deal was accomplished over the years, from organizing the first Young Author's Conference for 200 district students, grades two through six, to developing informational brochures for parents and producing a videotape with the University of Alberta. Whatever their focus, the teacher support groups thrived because teachers see other teachers as their most influential source of ideas (Watson and Stevenson 1989).

A basic change came in the fall of 1986 with the appointment of a new associate superintendent who had previously been a teacher, consultant, assistant principal, and then principal in the Edmonton Public School District. In these positions he showed great understanding and respect for children, their language and their learning. His most recent assignment had been to staff and administer a new elementary (K–6) school, Tipaskan. The focus at Tipaskan was on children's active experiences and language development. The library with all its resources was literally in the centre of the school, and central to the school's programs. Primary children were organized in groups that cut across grades, enabling teachers to work with children for two years. Reading series (basal readers) were available but were never used. Children achieved beyond expectations. Tipaskan was named a Centre for Excellence in Language Arts in the first NCTE competition in 1985–86. When this concerned and enterprising principal was appointed one of six associate superintendents and placed in charge of over 30 schools, his first action was to require that each school principal, along with the teachers, develop a language policy for their school—elementary, junior high, and senior high.

Principals had a full year to do this, followed by a year in which they and their staffs developed an action plan. During the third year they were expected to be involved in implementing their plan. Throughout these years—this is the beginning of the fourth year—a series of workshops was provided for the principals and key staff members. The associate superintendent works with the planning committee, is present at the sessions, and takes part in the discussions.

Now the cause of a grass-roots movement has been taken up by a senior administrator who not only supports and facilitates it, but has mandated that his 30 school principals and

After several years teaching at elementary and secondary levels, Margaret T. Stevenson worked as elementary consultant and then as supervisor, language arts (K–12) with Edmonton Public Schools. During these years Margaret worked extensively on Alberta education committees that provided guidelines and coordinated language programs across elementary and secondary levels for the province, and was also a member of the Reading Commission, NCTE, 1983–1986. Presently, as a retirement project, she has undertaken studies toward a Ph.D. in education, and is documenting the process of facilitating educational change.

their teachers understand and implement it. That is a strong position to take, but one that is not without precedent in the field of language learning. Rutledge (1988) describes a language policy that was officially adopted in Toronto and, after 25 years, is still in the process of being implemented. In contrast, McKenzie (1986) discusses ways in which clear, general policy at the national level in England is elaborated on through an organizational network that supports and assists teachers. School language policies are a "given" and courses are provided to assist teachers revise their practices based on current circumstances and needs.

The 30 Edmonton elementary school principals report that the mandate supports what they were attempting to do in their schools. In fact, a few of the schools were already well on their way. It will be no surprise that the extent to which they are succeeding depends on the principals' growing understanding of the language learning of children and the role of language in learning, as well as on their leadership ability. Any real change takes a very long time, and three years are the minimum in which you can expect change to begin to be evident. Inservice and on-going support for the principals are imperative, with regular sessions comprised of both content and process.

Developing and implementing a school language policy in the junior and senior high schools is more difficult than in an elementary school, even when the principal is convinced. This is probably due partly to the specialized nature of secondary teacher training and school organization.

A preliminary examination of the data reveals at least two themes—consistency and emergence. Principals and teachers are striving for consistency between and among their beliefs, the strategies and approaches they use with children, the materials and other resources they draw from, and the ways in which student progress is assessed and reported to parents. As school staffs deal with the variables individually and in combination, "things come together" and their policy emerges.

Operating between the grass-roots movement of the teachers and the mandate of central administration is another group that supports and collaborates with both. Language Arts Services is a group of dedicated Edmonton public consultants and a supervisor. The group has no administrative power, but has had a great deal of influence over the years. Their influence is based on their knowledge of language theory, their years of experience in the classroom, and their expertise in working closely with teachers and principals in translating theory into practice.

What has this process of institutionalizing change meant to the teacher support groups? We have seen some decline in numbers because the need is not perceived as great. Many teachers find support in their own schools now, as they work with the principal and their colleagues in developing and implementing their school language policy. We must not forget, too, that our teacher support groups recently celebrated their tenth anniversary. Many original

Book Note

The Administrator's Guide to Whole Language

Gail Heald-Taylor
1989; 196 pp.; $14.95
Katonah, NY:
Richard C. Owen

This is a comprehensive guide for implementing the whole language philosophy within a school. Topics covered include philosophy, principles, common questions, strategies, building parent support, student evaluation and report cards, research, an implementation process, an assessment checklist to monitor continuous growth of whole language, and a resource list. A very helpful book for the school that is trying to grow into whole language. Much of it is quite adaptable; its charts can be used by the whole staff.

❝ Whole language is governed by some important principles that are quite different from skills-based approaches. In whole language it is believed that youngsters acquire language rather than learn through direct teaching; that language learning is child-centered, not teacher-dominated; that language is integrated rather than fragmented; that children learn by talking and doing rather than through passive listening; that they learn to read and write by engaging in experiences with literature and writing, as opposed to drills and workbook exercises; and that children learn best in interactive problem-solving situations rather than in isolated individual tasks. ❞ (p. 15)

Lois Mather

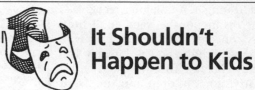

It Shouldn't Happen to Kids

Kennel Philosophy

"Good education," the administrator explained to the teacher he was observing and evaluating, "is knowing how long—or how short—to make the leash."

—LBB

members are now principals, consultants or curriculum coordinators who are busy encouraging and implementing change in their own schools.

Yes, you can make a difference, but it takes time.

→ See: Easton, p. 272; Heath, p. 422; Krause, p. 396; Stevenson, p. 411.

References

McKenzie, M. 1986. "Cultivating teacher power." In *Roles in literacy learning: A new perspective*, ed. D. R. Tovey and J. E. Kerber. Newark, DE: International Reading Association.

Rutledge, D. 1988. "Institutionalizing change: The problem of system belief." In *The word for teaching is learning: Essays for James Britton*, ed. M. Lightfoot and N. Martin. London: Heinemann.

Watson, D., and M. Stevenson. 1989. "Teacher support groups: Why and how." In *Teachers and research: Language learning in the classroom*, ed. G. S. Pinnell and M. L. Matlin. Newark, DE: International Reading Association.

Further Reading by Margaret T. Stevenson

◆ "An Alternative Assessment Program in Language Arts," with D. Searle. *Language Arts* 64(3), 1987.

◆ "Teacher Support Groups: Why and How," with D. Watson. In *Teachers and Research: Language Learning in the Classroom*, ed. G. S. Pinnell and M. L. Matlin. International Reading Association, 1989.

Cornerstone: Lois E. Easton

Turning on the Power: The Arizona Literacy Initiative Connects Exemplary & Emerging Literacy Classrooms

What does electricity have to do with literacy? One answer may be that they both carry a powerful "charge." Another might be that both fuel possibilities. A third might be that the light comes on, realistically and metaphorically, with electricity and literacy.

The Literacy Team at the Arizona Department of Education had none of these answers in mind when it decided to use a "conduit" approach to activate our Literacy Initiative for Children. We visualized the Department of Education as a conduit, conducting power from teachers and library media specialists to educators all over the state. This conduit would "power up" literacy for K–3 students in all classrooms in Arizona.

The Literacy Team could have chosen a mandatory approach. Instead, the five specialists who made up the team decided that the function of the department would be to recognize good literacy practices all over the state and provide access to them.

Some Background

In February 1987, C. Diane Bishop, superintendent of Public Instruction in Arizona, enacted the Literacy Initiative and directed staff members to devise literacy programs addressing it. A task force recognized the distinction between adult literacy concerns and those that apply to younger children. The Literacy Initiative became two: the Literacy Initiative for Children and the Adult Literacy Initiative.

The team dedicated to the Literacy Initiative for Children decided to target children in grades K–3 because of the belief that if you "catch them young," you'll never lose them as readers and writers. They subscribed to Frank Smith's description of reading as a social phenomenon, reading as belonging to a club of readers and writers. The team worried that because of current reading practices, students might not want to join that club. Thus the team's goal was to make sure that by the end of third grade, children would want to read and write, and become literate, so that they would never drop out of the club of literate people in the world. The target group, then, became children from the first day they enter public school.

Here are some examples of how the "conduit" approach has worked for the Arizona Literacy Initiative for Children.

Bookstarts

The team decided that a list of books that work with kids might become too prescriptive, too definitive. They felt that an ongoing list would work better, a list of books recommended by teachers and library media specialists. In the fall of 1988, *Bookstarts* was published. It consisted of a folder with a pocket. Inside the pocket were six lists of recommended books, each annotated, some indicating how to use the books with children. Also in the pocket was a very important card on which were solicited additional recommendations of books.

Teachers and library media specialists began mailing in the postcards, and each month an additional list was published. The team grouped

After teaching 15 years in junior high/middle schools and thwarting current practice by teaching through integrated units, Lois E. Easton joined the Arizona Department of Education as its first writing specialist. She worked throughout the state to spread the word about writing, reading, and learning language through language use. Later she became director of curriculum and instruction and is currently working as director of curriculum and assessment planning. Her present position involves her in Arizona's new assessment plan, a plan that incorporates integrated performance-based assessments. She is also director of Arizona's Literacy Initiative for Children.

the recommendations into categories by theme, topic, or type of literature. At the end of the year, 14 lists had been published.

Bookstarts will continue during the 1989–90 school year and after if interest is high. Teachers reading *Bookstarts* know that the books had been used successfully by practicing teachers and library media specialists. The Department of Education simply spread the good news.

Literacy Sites

Perhaps the biggest success of the "conduit" approach is the identification of literacy sites. In April 1988, applications were sent to all public school superintendents and principals. The applications were very simple—just a list of possible descriptors of a literacy site, with room at the end for the applicant to add additional descriptors. The application required a 15-minute videotape of the literacy site, and it was these videotapes that made possible identification of the literacy sites.

The videotapes were to be a "slice of classroom life." The team did not expect the tapes to be polished or professionally done, but it did expect them to allow the viewer a peek into the classroom. Views of the walls and the areas of the room revealed the teacher's attitude toward children's literacy. Focus on what the children were doing allowed viewers to decide who was in charge of literacy in the classroom. The team could usually tell within the first two minutes if the site promoted literacy the way it was described on the application. The signs of a literacy site were subtle but clear. For example, a literacy site usually

- Displayed children's work throughout the classroom at children's eye-level, not adults';

- Showed children pursuing literacy activities independently (although it was clear that the teachers had worked hard to set up these activities and structure the classroom to make them accessible, the focus wasn't on the teacher directing the class but on the children going about their business of reading and writing);

- Did not show a "lesson" unless that lesson was of a teacher sharing a big book with children or reading aloud to children;

- Showed various groupings, often selected by the children (in other words, some children read to each other, others read by themselves in a reading loft, still others shared their reading with a teacher and a larger group);

- Featured children not the least bit bothered by the presence of the videocamera (these children were so intent on reading or writing that they were not interested in the taping);

- Showed activities that made sense or seemed purposeful, activities that were connected or meaningful.

The videotape and the completed application were all that it took for an individual teacher to have her classroom declared a literacy site. Schools could be declared literacy sites with a videotape and an application completed by at least two-thirds of the K–3 teachers, plus a short

description of the school's philosophy about literacy and how that philosophy has been implemented schoolwide and a description of how the library media center is used.

Twelve applications were selected following the May 1988 deadline from among 25. Three of those selected were schools; the rest were individual classrooms. Another 15 were selected following the October 1988 deadline from among 27 applications. Five more were selected in January 1989 from among 8 applications, and 20 more following the May 1989 deadline from among 25 applications.

The *Directory of Arizona Literacy Sites* was published in the spring of 1989 and distributed to all K–3 schools. This directory lists and describes the initial 27 literacy sites. At the end of each description, those at the site indicate what they are willing to do to advance literacy in Arizona, such as visiting schools or classrooms to discuss what they've done, welcoming others to their site, sharing materials, or producing and sending another videotape. Supplements to the directory listing the sites selected since October 1988 will be published regularly.

The directory also gives information for ordering the application videotapes for the sites listed within. This videotape library is the most powerful way of spreading the news about classroom practices that enhance literacy.

The Literacy Cadre

Teachers and library media specialists from the initial 27 literacy sites were invited to join the Literacy Cadre to produce materials that can be published by the Department of Education and made available to all educators in the state. Working in committees in 1988–89, they produced brochures, posters, integrated teaching units, curriculum materials, and guides for a variety of audiences, including administrators, school-board members, teachers, and the public.

They also planned staff development activities and, during the 1989–90 school year, will be taking their staff development modules and materials to schools and districts around the state. Funding for their travel is a joint project of their own school districts, the districts wanting their services, and the Department of Education.

A Little Conclusion

What does electricity have to do with literacy? The Literacy Team at the Arizona Department of Education answered this question with its decision on how to go about promoting literacy in Arizona. It decided that a "conduit" approach would be better than a "top down" approach. However, it is clear that the conduit approach carries a powerful "charge" and has fueled possibilities. It definitely has helped the literacy light shine in Arizona.

➔ See: Graham, p. 426; Heath, p. 422; Stevenson, p. 271.

📷 WHOLE LANGUAGE CAMERA

First grade authors in Ardith Cole's class read their books to their school principal, Lockport, NY.

Great Teachers:
Lois E. Easton

by Saundra Bryn Harmon

"My earliest remembrance of a book? *The Little Engine That Could*—a terrible book for a compulsive person." Golden eyes sparkling, Lois Easton leaned back and chuckled softly. "All my life I've been saying, 'I think I can, I think I can.'"

A preadolescent Lois wanted to teach creative dramatics. "I think I can get the YMCA to let us teach," she told her friend, "especially if I tell them we'll do it for free."

And she did.

"I think I can teach better than this," an annoyed first-year teacher said to herself during her second month of using traditional methods to teach her junior high students. "I'm bored; the kids are dispassionate. Can these kids be the same ones who entered kindergarten eager and full of self-expectations? There must be some other way to teach."

And there was.

During the past five years, Lois has provided statewide leadership in Arizona's quest for literacy. Lois entered the Arizona State Department of Education's newly formed School Improvement Unit as writing/language arts specialist. Almost immediately she accepted her first impossible task: to coordinate the effort of a State Board of Education–appointed committee and write the Language Arts Essential Skills (LAES), a K–12 curriculum framework of reading, writing, speaking, listening, and language concepts for Arizona schools.

Working closely with the board-appointed chairperson of the committee, Lois provided speakers, numerous readings, and extensive opportunities for discussion, so that the committee—composed of professional and laypeople with different backgrounds, knowledge bases, educational beliefs, and reasons for serving —could, after much wrangling, come to a consensus and be satisfied and proud that their work represented the process and products that were current and solidly research-based.

Once the framework was written, Lois developed inservices, a videotape, and a management system related to the LAES, which she presented in districts throughout the state.

Lois invited school districts to volunteer to serve as lighthouse sites—places that would examine their existing curriculum and compare it with LAES, develop action plans for modifying their curriculum, train a trainers' cadre to work with all the district's teachers, and implement a curriculum-based assessment plan.

She conducted extensive training sessions in which she guided participants through cooperative activities to analyze the LAES and compare them with their existing scope and sequences. She involved participants by having them role-play students in two diverse language arts classrooms. Just as she always does, Lois questioned, probed, and forced the participants to examine their beliefs about language and learning and

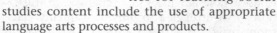

Lois E. Easton

teaching. Modeling strategies she wanted the teachers to use in their classroom, Lois did what she does so well—she taught.

Lois also facilitated statewide student writing contests and directed the Arizona Teachers' Academy, weeklong sessions that focused on the effective use of integrated units in math and science. She also served as president of the Arizona English Teachers Association and as a board member of the Center for Establishing Dialogue in Teaching and Learning.

For a time after Lois was appointed director of curriculum and instruction, she continued to serve as writing/language arts specialist. Not only did she continue to provide the types of services to which the language arts educators in the state had become accustomed, but Lois also designed and supervised the implementation of a format for delivering staff development in schools, including regional inservices that featured the trainer of trainers model. She supervised seven subject area specialists and curriculum development in six subject areas, as well as directing the Leadership Academy.

In both the staff development and curriculum development planning, she insisted that the concepts always be correlated and, wherever possible, integrated. As a committee was developing the Social Studies Essential Skills document, they included the use of study skills, problem-solving, and decision-making that was already in the LAES, and the suggested activities for learning social studies content include the use of appropriate language arts processes and products.

During Lois's tenure as director of curriculum and instruction, the legislature formed a K–12 curriculum committee, which set specific, measurable goals for educational excellence. The goals read: "By 1990, 80 percent of the students will . . ." The legislature also passed a second piece of legislation which mandated that the Department of Education must provide a statewide student assessment plan.

State Superintendent of Public Instruction C. Diane Bishop selected Lois to spearhead the superintendent's Literacy Initiative for Children, an attempt to identify exemplary practices throughout the state, publicize them, and provide other schools access to the sites.

After watching the goals and literacy initiative burgeon and take on life, next Superintendent Bishop created the position of director of curriculum and assessment planning specifically for Lois. Lois began to work with developing the comprehensive K–12 assessment plan mandated by the state legislature. The legislature would not be satisfied to have a single essential skills document ready each year. All of them needed to be ready by 1990. Yet she knew that the traditional kind of norm-referenced assessment did not truly measure students' learning. She also knew that districts and media generated abuses

of the every-kid-every-year test and that students and schools are judged by a single indicator: their performance on a single test.

The way standardized tests are used is obscene. Our recommendation will be to reduce substantially norm-referenced testing; students in grades 2 through 12 will take a reading subtest each fall so that the results can be used for diagnosis. All other subtests will be administered on a revolving basis. Currently some districts spend a tremendous time preparing; others do not. We want to cut down on the pollution.

In addition, we will add new ingredients. Performance-based, curriculum-referenced tests based on the essential skills documents will be administered at grades three, eight, and twelve. These tests will be the 'real stuff'—instructionally valid, what we really believe kids should know. All tests will be distributed a year ahead of time; they are not meant to be secure. We want it to be a compliment to say, "Teach to the test."

The goals project is a mammoth undertaking. Not only must the essential skills for each area be completed, but so must the assessment plan, the assessments, and the reporting system be developed. Again, Lois's philosophy about teaching and learning is evident.

Reports will be presented in a number of ways with many comparisons. After each school receives its baseline data, it will follow a goal-setting process so that the competition to improve is with itself. The goal for the school will be published, and when the next year's report is published, the school will complete a self-assessment to see how well it is progressing toward its goal. Goal-setting and self-analysis are critical components of the assessment plan.

Again, the manner in which Lois attacked the goals and literacy initiative reflects her philosophy of teaching and learning: "I'm very goal driven. I simply think of the end product, then work backward. The way I approach any task must fit my values—although I also need to get to the outcome in the most expedient way."

Seemingly impossible tasks—achieved through diligence and skill, knowledge, and wit. Lois always believes she can accomplish the impossible tasks. "Sometimes people are appalled at the lengths I go to satisfy myself," she smiles. "All I know is . . . it can be done."

➜ See: Hartle-Schutte, p. 264; Heath, p. 422.

Saundra Bryn Harmon is the principal of Dysart Junior High School, Peoria, AZ.

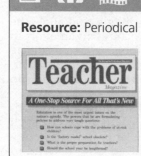

Resource: Periodical

Teacher Magazine

$18/year (12 issues)
from:
Suite 250
4301 Connecticut Ave., NW
Washington, DC 20008
1-202-686-0800

Jay Sugarman, editor and creator of *Reflections: Brookline Educational Journal* is also an editor of this recently created magazine. *Teacher* provides a forum for issues such as research, classroom concerns, and working relationships with administrators and parents from the perspective of teachers as professionals. A refreshing break from teacher magazines that feature a bag-of-tricks approach to teaching, these articles, written largely by teachers for teachers, reflect the exciting changes that are occurring within our profession.

LBB

➜ See: Sugarman, p. 213.

As Teachers See It

by Debra Goodman

Whole Language and the Myth of the Super Teacher

When George Rosato first considered publishing the *Whole Language Catalog*, he visited the Detroit school where Toby Curry and I taught. Although he was impressed with both our classrooms, he was concerned about the amount of time and work Toby and I put into them. He wondered if whole language required a "super teacher."

It's true that sometimes I have had to work much harder in order to be a whole language teacher. But this was not because I use a whole language approach. Whole language teaching does not require more work than any other kind of teaching. Every teacher has to plan, organize, teach, and evaluate. Organizing centers or thematic units may take a lot of creativity and effort at first, but this initial planning provides weeks or months of class experiences. Students and parents usually help plan and gather materials. Individual conferences, small group lessons, journals, independent reading, and writing folders require time and organization to keep up with, but the whole language teacher does not have stacks of workbooks and ditto sheets to check. And again, students are usually involved in recording and evaluating their own progress.

It's true that whole language teachers tend to work hard. But most of the teachers I have known work hard. Whole language requires only a super teacher in rigid and nonsupportive settings.

In some cases teachers must fulfill traditional requirements *and* provide holistic experiences "as enrichment." Many teachers have worn themselves out with this sort of split personality. In other cases, teachers are forced to justify whole language with elaborately detailed plans and records. As a beginning whole language teacher, I was subjected to intense scrutiny of all my plans and records. I was also observed more frequently and attacked on several occasions. Traditional documentation, such as standardized tests and report cards, also requires more time and effort if a teacher wants to use whole language evaluation strategies.

There are some situations in which whole language teaching is nearly impossible. One principal told me that first-graders could not handle sharpening their own pencils or visiting the library corner by themselves. I could not use journals, even as "enrichment," because the size of paper and invented spelling would allow the children to develop "bad habits." In an effort to meet her requirements, I found I was a mediocre (at best) teacher of skills. I left the position, determined not to work where I could not do my best teaching.

It takes a seasoned, hard-nosed and hardworking teacher to successfully negotiate such pitfalls and bring a whole language philosophy into the classroom. These constraints tend to preclude beginners. But several years ago, I heard a Canadian teacher speak of her first fumbling years of teaching. Teachers from the United States were struck by the way she was "allowed" to be a beginning teacher, and to learn and grow while taking a whole language approach. I became convinced that any teacher could be a whole language teacher if they were given two things: professional autonomy and support.

The teacher must be allowed to be the decision-maker in the classroom. Teachers who are encouraged to use their own knowledge and insights in the classroom often feel excited and energized. Last year, in a staff development session, we discussed alternatives to basal readers and workbooks. One second-grade teacher informed the assistant principal that she would

not be needing the workbooks for the next level. The assistant principal consulted with the principal and decided that the teacher *would* use the workbooks. The teacher complied, but she felt excited and empowered simply because she had taken a stand. Good teachers are being held back by mandates and restrictions.

Whole language doesn't make good teachers out of bad teachers or hardworking teachers out of lazy teachers. Whole language involves the kind of close observation of learners and their learning that only the classroom teacher can have. We believe students must take ownership of their own learning. This can occur only when teachers have ownership over their own teaching. This means that no one program or approach (including whole language) should be mandated and imposed on teachers. Whole language district, state, or provincial policies can be very supportive and progressive. Scheduling and school organization can be established to support whole language, but the teacher must be allowed to decide when and how changes in that classroom will take place.

Whole language teachers require a different, more supportive, form of administration. For the past several years, I have been "allowed" to make decisions about what went on in my classroom. However, I was never given time to talk or plan with other teachers. I was on my own to gather materials, raise funds, organize volunteer assistance, and schedule special events or projects. Rather than receive praise or recognition following a publication or performance, I was sometimes admonished not to ask for any special consideration (such as secretarial help or use of the copying machine) as these activities were undertaken by my own choice.

In addition, Toby Curry and I (as the only whole language teachers in the building) were constantly challenged through little memos and articles. At one staff meeting, the assistant principal suggested we wouldn't be allowed to use whole language if our test scores weren't adequate. Our initial elation over being "allowed" to use whole language soon changed to frustration as we struggled to provide a quality classroom program without support. Each parent challenge, each attack by another staff member, each district policy decision was endured alone. If it hadn't been for Toby, the situation would have been impossible. Many whole language teachers have survived only as a result of the teacher support groups that have spread throughout Canada and the United States.

Teachers deserve the encouragement and support of administration. They need opportunities to talk and plan with other teachers, to attend meetings and conferences, to visit other schools. Teachers should be encouraged to take a chance and try something new; to be unsure of themselves and ask their own questions. Teachers can be supported by being provided with any available assistance, materials, time, and funds for classroom experiences and projects.

In many settings, the administrator has the role of weeding out weak teachers and dealing with problems. Teachers never admit to being insecure or unknowledgeable. This is especially true if the teacher is using strategies that differ from those the administrator expects. Our staff was recently trained in "effective education." I had to search hard to find a time when I could be observed "teaching a lesson." The principal observed the "lesson," left without observing the student activity, and praised me for "extrinsic motivation by raising and lowering the level of student concern" during the lesson. All of the

exciting student work and experiences going on in my room were ignored.

Where does this sort of supervision leave whole language teachers with problems and questions: How can I encourage kids to work independently? What do I do with kids who play traditional teacher/student games and refuse to take ownership in the classroom? How do I cope with 31 kids?

Do you have to be a "super administrator" to deal with teachers who ask questions involving kids in elaborate projects and demand encouragement and support? I don't think so. We have just started a whole language school in Detroit with an administrator who was unfamiliar with whole language just two years ago. She can't answer all our questions, but she is willing to provide us with the time and the encouragement to find our own answers. She's willing to give us the right to make decisions about our own classrooms. She's willing to give us ownership of our classrooms, listen to our suggestions, and support us in any way she can.

You do have to be a super teacher to adopt whole language in a setting based on mandates and restrictions. At this time, whole language beliefs and practices are much more widely accepted, and even the super teachers are considering moving to jobs where their strengths are valued and welcomed. A student teacher who worked with me last winter was rejected for a Detroit job because he couldn't respond to questions about three reading groups. Creativity has it's place, he was told, but what about the skills? The next week, in an interview in a Detroit suburb, administrators were visibly excited by his talents and expertise. They were eager to accept a whole language beginning teacher and encourage him to learn and grow.

Any teacher can be a whole language teacher. The only requirements are willingness, the right to learn and act like a professional—and a little encouragement and support.

→ See: Goodman, p. 24; Hutchison, p. 275; Matlin, p. 398.

Debra Goodman is a teacher at Dewey Center for Urban Education, Detroit, MI.

(Continued from page 275)

received constant support and confirmation from each other, our principal, and Dr. Pierce at these meetings. But not all of us attended those meetings at first. We all change at different rates. One teacher explains:

I didn't ever attend those first meetings. I was so overwhelmed with all the readings and changes that I felt I didn't have time for them. But then after I took a summer study course from Dr. Pierce, I felt I had internalized it all enough to take time out for the weekly meetings. I found that they absolutely kept me afloat that first full year I implemented my program, and the meetings have continued to help me to this day.

Because the program is philosophy-based, we have all implemented it to suit our personal styles. We all have some form of sustained silent reading and we all facilitate writing in its many forms. Each of us uses methods we are most comfortable with to achieve the common goal of providing child-centered (as opposed to teacher-directed) classrooms.

Mary Bertun and Julia Craig are primary teachers at Yaquina View School, Newport, OR.

Publishing Information: If you care to know more about the Yaquina View story and the school's publishing house, Dolphin Publishing, you may request a copy of *Through the Eyes of a Child* by sending $4 to Yaquina View School, 351 SE Harney, Newport, OR 97365.

Great Schools — Yaquina View School

by Mary Bertun & Julia Craig

Yaquina View School is located in Newport, on the central Oregon coast. It is one of 17 schools in the Lincoln County School District. Our school's natural language arts program, "Through the Eyes of a Child," originated in the spring of 1985 and is now in full operation throughout our 16 first- through fifth-grade classrooms. Today, the teachers are committed to a reading and language arts program that supports the natural language learning of children and focuses on meaningful and purposeful written and oral literacy.

We believe children learn best from the whole to the part. We believe that literacy develops naturally from a child's need to communicate. Given a risk-free nurturing environment with good modeling techniques, children will succeed in reading and writing at their own rate.

Modeling is one of the most important elements of our program. We inundate our children with the sounds of literature —stories, poetry, plays, personal teacher writing, and children's own writings. We fill our rooms with all kinds of books. We immerse ourselves in reading literature, writing plays, presenting choral readings of poetry or stories, reading our own stories to each other, writing letters, and developing reports. With so much literature in our environment, we watch the reading and writing process become a part of our children. One parent related this story:

Fifth- and first-graders share books and stories.

> It was in the afternoon. We had been moving for four days to a different house. My tired husband and I were both sitting with our feet up, trying to recoup for one more load. In the lull of activity, our first-grade daughter found a scrap of paper and a pencil and proceeded to write a poem, followed by a story that she immediately read to us all. Our fifth-grade son used this same spare time to read a favorite book. To think that they both turned to reading and writing as a form of personal entertainment overwhelmed us.

Today we are totally involved in the reading and writing and putting together of literature, the thinking and analyzing and enjoying of written and oral expressions. But it wasn't always this way. For several years there had been growing discontent with the adopted district language arts program. One of the first seeds of change was planted in January 1985, when Dr. Virginia Pierce, on sabbatical leave from Austin College, came to our school to do some research and share literacy research with us.

This seed could not have been planted in more fertile ground as we were all ready for a change. Our basal reading program worked with precision, a precision built around a tightly structured management system. As one teacher put it, we all felt

> . . . like a ringmaster keeping three reading groups busy. I had become increasingly dissatisfied with the management system because all instruction was direct instruction and students are dependent on the teacher for everything.

With our full encouragement, two teachers began a collaborative relationship with Dr. Pierce, who not only provided them with endless research-based information in books and articles, but also provided support and encouragement to implement changes. After we had been involved for a month, several other teachers expressed interest and requested Dr. Pierce's advice and support. By May, the entire school was beginning to change.

The change from traditional teaching to a whole language philosophy was not a simple change. We were embroiled in emotions and complexities. The teachers (who first tried) started with a few changes—message boards, journal writing, reading more stories aloud—without changing the bigger, more obvious traditional components, such as formal basal reading groups and workbook assignments. These first changes had such an impact on the children that the teachers who tried them were compelled to add more and more whole language strategies and to drop major elements to which they had been accustomed. They had read extensively, so they had a beginning philosophical base; they had Dr. Pierce's able guidance and their principal's support. With a classroom of suddenly animated, enthusiastic children, one teacher wrote in her journal:

> Today was super! First I explained to the class all that we were doing. Then we sat down and compared Preya's book, *My Mom Went to Denver*, with Carolyn Feller Baur's book, *My Mom Travels Alot*. I have never seen children so animated and excited. They wanted to comment on everything. I think that will settle down once we get into a routine. Then we read our dinosaur poem and a book about digging up dinosaurs. The interest level went from 5 to 95. I could hardly contain them!

Even amidst all the excitement, dropping the old structures was difficult. After changing her entire classroom environment one teacher wrote, "We changed my room around today. I am scared and uncertain. It's as if I don't know how to teach, and have nothing to offer." Once her program was in full swing, she wrote:

> I have realized a very important thing, mainly, that my momentum is giving out. I had started this whole thing out thinking that one fix would do it. The "fixes" keep coming apart. I can progress in my course. But things don't seem to stay the same. I feel like I've built this magnificent new bridge, parts of which keep falling down, and I am losing my strength to keep it up.

The Tuesday afternoon literacy meetings were the one saving grace to this teacher and others. We found we absolutely needed a time to hash over our anxiety attacks and to discuss articles Dr. Pierce had put in our mailboxes. We

(Continued on page 274)

There is always lots of activity at Yaquina View... even the Coast Guard landed.

Principals Speak Out
by Ron Hutchison

Through The Eyes of a Child

When the teachers of Yaquina View School and I first started to examine our past reading practices, we naturally changed our attitude about the reading/writing process as we gained more information and knowledge. We had no idea our school would become a whole language school. We did believe, however, that children learn naturally enjoy reading and writing. We also wanted to celebrate literacy in a supportive environment where children were encouraged to actively participate in their learning.

A first-grader at Yaquina View said, "If you're doing something you like, it happens easy. If you don't like it, it usually is harder to learn." Whole language learning

values relevant and meaningful experiences that are taught with care and understanding. These experiences are not packaged and programmed—children are not programmable! When we take time to listen to children's ideas, thoughts, problems, writings, and readings, we are taking the first steps in becoming a whole language teacher.

The learning process requires change, and some changes will be easier than others. When our traditional practices are challenged or even changed, some people will have difficulty accepting a different approach. But the school is one place where we should be able to question and examine old practices, exchange ideas, and create new successful strategies for learning.

Changing our teaching is bound to cause some concern for parents. We must remind ourselves that we have an obligation to educate them as well as their children, as we help them to understand the changes that are occurring in their children's education. Schools should communicate weekly with parents, not just quarterly with report cards.

It has taken too many years for research to have an impact on our classrooms. In this age of ever-increasing information, we cannot afford a five- or ten-year informational lag in our schools. Our classrooms should be the hallmark of research—where teachers and administrators are listening, watching, interacting, and recording student feedback and observations. We should listen to students, like first-grader Clayton Smith, who shared his view of the learning process: "I like to find out what other people know, too. Each person is different. If someone helps you with your work, then you might know more than one way to do something. Your way and their way." Insightful comments like Clayton's can aid teachers in successful lesson planning. For too long we have believed that the reading-writing process should be systematically taught to children rather than experienced with children. Children will provide us the cues if we only watch and listen.

The change to a whole language school is a road that will hold many rewards and successes; but it is also one that is very difficult and not without some tension. In our commitment to grow and change we have to remind ourselves to be patient, and to rely on open dialogue as the main vehicle for staff growth and school improvement. We must also remember that we all will become better learners and teachers if we take the time to look through the eyes of a child.

➡ See: Bird, p. 92; Boloz, p. 277; Fearn, p. 372; Gulseth, p. 310.

Ron Hutchison is currently the principal of Jackson School, Hillsboro, OR.

Principals Speak Out

by Lois Bridges Bird

An Interview with Whole Language Principal Mary Maxwell

Mary Maxwell was the principal of Horace Mann School, a whole language school in San Jose, California, at the time I interviewed her on December 4, 1988.

Lois: Mary, how do you see your role as the principal of a whole language school?

Mary: Management is a part of it, and so are curriculum and instruction. It's like a triangle. Supporting teachers is key; when I see a well-run school I see teachers who have autonomy to make professional decisions, supported in their interest of doing what's best for their students. A really good teacher is one who continues to grow, who continues to revise and develop those strategies that are most effective with his or her students. Simply stated, if I let the teachers run with it, I'll get more from them rather than telling them "do this, do that."

Lois: So you're really trusting them as professional educators.

Mary: Yes, that's a must. I'd like to see us move toward a situation where we have shared decision-making. I'm not advocating a school without a principal; a school must have a principal—the buck has got to stop somewhere—but I do favor a system where teachers could be more involved in the decisions that affect them. I tend not to make decisions for teachers who don't have any effect on the whole organization of the school; if they want to move the coatrack to the other side of the room, that has no effect on anyone else. If it does affect the whole school (not taking afternoon recess, for instance), then it's got to be a shared responsibility.

Lois: Your school is unique because, as I understand, everyone made a commitment to whole language before they joined the Horace Mann faculty.

Mary: Actually, teachers came to Horace Mann with a commitment to using literature as a big part of their program and getting kids to be actively involved in their education—not to doing whole language. They gradually decided that whole language was the most effective way to accomplish those goals.

Lois: Some districts are mandating whole language. How is your faculty developing as professional whole language educators, and what role do you have in that process?

Mary: A district that is mandating—you will do this tomorrow—is looking for lots of trouble because, as with anything new, even if you don't consider the change issues, and the inevitable resistance to change, you have to know how to do it. Our district went into *Math Their Way*, but didn't plan out a strong training model so you had teachers saying, "But we need workbook pages!" The same thing will happen with whole language if you say to teachers, "Throw that basal away and read good literature!" They are then left with a bunch of trade books and no idea how to use them.

Some districts are supporting a literature-based curriculum with these tomes of nifty activities to do with each book; book extensions have their place but there's so much more to whole language. What I'm doing to encourage people is to help them to be continual learners. What we say here at Horace Mann is that we are lifelong learners, and we want to help our kids to become lifelong learners. To teach a whole language program you have to know more about children and how they learn than just that there's research that shows that if you read to kids they'll learn to read. You have to have an underpinning of knowledge about how children progress developmentally.

So I encourage people to take classes. We have a full-time staff development person [Michael Hagan] who has a dialogue going about that all the time. One direction we're going into is assessment. We're trying to develop a combination of things: records of skill development we see in kids; records of pre- and post-holistically scored writing samples; attitudinal surveys are also a part of it. My role in this is to nudge quietly. My style—and this, of course, varies from person to person—is to plant the seed, nurture it, and watch it grow.

The role of the principal is to support continual staff development, offer continual encouragement; for example, provide opportunities to observe in other classrooms. I hire subs so the teachers are free to do this or Mike Hagan can relieve them.

All-day planning days during the school year are very, very important. We go off campus to plan; that's our time to say, "Okay, what's going on? Why isn't this working?" It's not just curriculum planning; it may be social interaction stuff and getting along with each other.

Lois: How do you organize for your staff meetings?

Mary: On a monthly basis we have four days planned for staff development—every Tuesday morning. The first Tuesday of the month is a business meeting, just your basic, boring, boilerplate, principal-led, bang, bang, bang meeting. The agenda is set by the group; I collect agenda items throughout the month. Any major issues are set aside for committee work. We meet between eight and nine in the morning; school doesn't start until nine.

The second Tuesday is set aside for inservice; that is, when we have specific people from the district (or wherever) sharing information about second-language learners or on cooperative learning, or it might be a staff member talking about how to use the resource room. The third Tuesday is devoted to team building; I don't attend unless invited. The fourth Tuesday is for extra things that come along. An artist might come in and show the various ways to bind books, or a staff member might share what she or he learned at a recent conference.

Lois: So there's constant attention paid to staff development. One thing that is unique about Horace Mann is that you have a full-time staff development person, Mike, on campus.

Mary: I feel very strongly that principals need to be out in the classroom, but I also have this desk and you can't do everything. So, to be able to do continuous, quality work with the teachers is just not in the realm of the principal anymore. I can talk about the kind of things we want to do, the direction we want to do go in, and then Mike can go in and work with the teacher on that, spend all day if he wants, or work an hour and get their reaction. He's also not an evaluator and even though I don't think my staff sees me as a particularly scary person, even when I'm observing a lesson in a nonevaluative situation, there is still an evaluative quality to it. Michael is able to be a colleague and to have a running dialogue with teachers and be in and out of their classrooms. He's also part of the planning group of the school. He meets with me and the other resource people monthly, and so we can integrate the various strands that are going on in the school.

Lois: So you have weekly meetings set up with him?

Mary: Yes, and with the other resource people; ESL, for instance.

Lois: How do you handle teacher evaluation?

Mary: The mainstay of my evaluation process is lots of informal walking through—almost daily—in classrooms; looking and observing without being intrusive. You've got to spend a lot of time in a classroom over a long period of time to know what's really going on.

As far as formal evaluation goes, I schedule two formal observations per week with two different teachers. We follow a set format for the observation. They use a little form to explain in writing what lesson they want me to see. I ask them to explain what the student outcome will be; that is, what children will get out of it and what they want me to watch for.

After my observation, we meet and talk. My main goal is to help teachers engage in self-analysis. I try to provide lots of meaningful feedback on *specifics*—not just give empty praise. I ask them to write down a goal or two and then we discuss how best their goals might be achieved. At the end of the semester, they write again about the progress they've made toward achieving their goals. I engage in this process with them.

Lois: How do you work with teachers who don't seem to be making progress?

Mary: I provide more support, more time to talk. If I have a concern I express it up-front. Unless the teacher refuses to discuss it or doesn't respond in some way, I don't file negative observations. Professional growth takes time. And again, Mike is working with them constantly in a nonjudgmental way.

Lois: How is Horace Mann involved with disseminating whole language?

Mary: We're into subversive dissemination! Mike and Joan [Hagan] did a little presentation, "What Is Whole Language," for the school board. We like to share with people in that way whenever possible, but actually we get more visitors from outside the district than we do inside. They'll say, "Oh, this is wonderful! But . . ." then have five reasons why they can't do it.

I do speak up at district meetings when I hear that we're planning to buy 40 copies of some obsolete textbook for every class. I do speak up and say it's inappropriate, and I do get lots of contact with the district coordinators about the kinds of things we're doing here.

The other way I evangelize is to argue for the professional autonomy of the teachers. So often what I hear from the district—and I was the former district language coordinator so I'm allowed to talk like this—is that teachers can't do that, teachers won't do that. I think that we don't give teachers enough credit. There are teachers who veer away from trying new things but that's not the norm.

Lois: What have you done to acquaint yourself with the research underlying whole language?

Mary: To begin with I started teaching in the sixties with learning centers and individualized instruction and contracts. Literature was important to me, and language experience was a big part of my program. Roach Van Allen was very big, so I started with that background. Then I've attended workshops and conferences. I can't stay on top of all the professional literature, but I'm a good listener. I've taught in the graduate department at San Jose State, and I had to be prepared for that—that was Early Childhood. Plus the state department has sent out a wealth of information about the [English-Language Arts] Framework. Really and perhaps most important, whole language just makes sense to me. It's easy to support something that makes so much sense.

➜ See: Boloz, p. 277; Hagan, p. 246; Krause, p. 396; Matlin, p. 398.

Cornerstone: Alexa Lindquist-Sandmann

Let's Teach Real Reading and Writing

Why can't Johnny read? Why can't Johnny write? For the past decade these questions have become symbols of public outcry against education and educators. Have we as educators addressed these issues?

Politicians, superintendents, curriculum supervisors, and principals have. They decide on a curriculum based on perceived community wishes. Readers first, then writers. Removed from the classroom and current research, the decision-makers choose ready-made programs. Is there a problem? When the program materials become the curriculum, there certainly is.

Why are these programs so tempting? Because they dissect reading and writing into artificial parts, their very nature makes pretest and posttest measurement a breeze. Because superintendents and principals are accountable for the curriculum in their schools, it is easy to understand their need for the "hard numbers" these materials give to support the programs.

The problem is that what is being tested and measured as reading and writing is probably not what the public means by "reading and writing." Reading is gaining meaning from print; it is not pronouncing words correctly—that is word identification. Writing is creating an essay, a short story, a play, or a poem from what one

Alexa Lindquist-Sandmann has shared literature and writing with students from the sixth grade through freshman year in college. She has also shared her love of education with teachers-in-training. Believing that a teacher's most important challenge is to create independent learners by helping students learn how to learn, she has published articles on reading strategies and metacognitive study strategies in the *Journal of Reading*. She has also coedited an issue of *Education and Urban Society* on ethnography. She has participated in the national meetings of IRA, NCTE, and NRC. She is currently finishing her dissertation on the social nature of writing.

knows of the world. Writing is not filling in the blanks of workbook pages or answering questions "in a complete sentence." Unfortunately, the tests measure word identification and editing skills. Though both are valuable, neither is important without content.

Students taught in a classroom organized to support reading and writing will become readers and writers. They learn to read carefully and write effectively because both processes have a purpose in the "real world" of their own classroom. No slick commercial program filled with writing topics can do that. Students who have control over their own learning, those who choose their own reading materials and writing topics, will become lifelong refiners of reading and writing because they understand there is a reason for becoming proficient at each.

If Johnny can't read or write, it is because we educators have not been allowed to let him do so. Just as reading is not learned by dividing words, and writing, by dividing sentences, change does not come from a divided contingency of educators. As professionals we have to know what is most effective in helping students learn to read and write and then do it. We cannot permit others who know less about students to undermine our efforts.

➔ See: Goodman, pp. 272, 389; Mooney, p. 416; Owen, p. 414.

As kids see it

I Don't Know Which Road to Take!
by Adam Sidaway

When I was little and before I could read, I used to make stunt ramps and roads with my books. Then I'd race my Hot Wheel cars on them. But now that I can *read*, I found out that *my books are still* roads. I travel on my roads all over the globe. I can visit koala bears in Australia, whales in Alaska and pandas in China (my favorite). But my most favorite are my dinosaur books that take me way back to prehistoric times.

There are so many good books in our school library that sometimes I don't know which road to take!

Adam Sidaway is a second-grader. This essay, which won a National 1989 Mott's Apple Award, appears exactly as he wrote it.

"Books Keep Dinosaurs Alive!" —Mike Roeters is the student of Mrs. Ernestine Van Asselt, first grade, Grant Primary Center, Grant, MI.

The Mott's Apple Awards are a national public service program designed to encourage children to value reading as a lifelong skill and pleasure, and to focus national attention on the importance of reading in children's lives.

Principals Speak Out
by Sigmund A. Boloz

The Blue-Eyed, Fire-Breathing Dragon: One Principal Tamed

Ten years ago, at the end of my first year as principal of Ganado Primary School, I was surprised to learn that some of my staff viewed me as a blue-eyed, fire-breathing dragon. I had begun the year believing that, in order to be an effective administrator, I had to assert my control. Perhaps I had seen my role as a manager rather than a leader of others. Looking back over the past decade, I have learned some valuable lessons.

I learned that I must continually monitor my own growth, which I do primarily within the pages of a daybook. I capture not only what I think or plan but also the interesting situations in which I find myself. Within its pages, I am able to think through options or reactions to situations.

It is not enough to say that I believe in whole language. I find that I must understand what this means from the different points of view of my many audiences: students, parents, fellow administrators, researchers, and so on. More important, I must be able to recognize when others are confused about whole language issues, and I must be prepared to address their concerns.

I try to balance reading the latest research and theory with involvement. I attend the workshops that are provided for my staff. I team-teach with them and provide demonstration lessons in classrooms, and I am alert to the exciting breakthroughs of others.

My early training in risk-taking and in trusting myself and others has carried over, and I know that I need not be afraid of change. It takes planning and understanding of how certain tasks may enhance our mission. I have learned that I cannot carry everyone's problems and that I cannot solve all the problems myself. As I have given up the responsibility of simply managing people, I have turned to working with them toward a common end. I delegate decision-making and I encourage the staff to share ideas and to help solve problems.

My primary task has been to build a cushion of support around teachers. We have worked with universities and teacher support groups to provide appropriate coursework and workshops in the form of preservice beginning the school year and continuous inservice throughout the year. We rewrote position descriptions to reflect an implementation of our meaning-based curriculum. Staff evaluations were modified to mirror that implementation, and self-evaluations comprising holistic checklists further helped teachers to assess their own growth.

The staff are encouraged to visit each other's classrooms, and we use one of our two monthly staff meetings for sharing strong classroom practices. During frequent curriculum dialogue groups, teachers can share successes and concerns. We have early release days and "eight-o'clock-to-whenever meetings," when classrooms are covered by teacher assistants until topics are explored. Lastly, a full-time instructional resource teacher, supported by an expanding 800-book professional library, often facilitates meetings and serves as staff consultant.

We network staff with other successful teachers and schools that share their views. We budget funds for visits to other schools and for attending state and national conferences. Our staff has joined with a teacher network support group called GRIN (Greater Reservation Interdisciplinary Network), which now includes members from many of the surrounding districts and supports two local yearly conferences. We also have a local writers circle for teachers.

In the past few years we have implemented a "success" classroom model, which teams special education teachers with regular teaching staff within self-contained classrooms at each grade level, rather than scheduling pull-out programs. This year we are implementing "schools-within-a-school" teams and "uninterrupted block time" concepts. Within the teams, two teachers from each grade (kindergarten through second grade) work closely together to coordinate the curriculum for their team's students. In the block concept, most of the support staff work directly within the classrooms during the first hour of each morning to assist implementation of the curriculum.

The principal who chooses to be a manager of programs can probably do so without entering a classroom. An instructional leader, on the other hand, accepts the idea that education is exciting, that it must be exciting for everyone involved, and that it is hard work.

➔ See: Hickman, p. 410.

Sigmund A. Boloz is the principal of Ganado Primary School, Ganado, AZ.

Classroom Demonstrations

by Nancy Hyland Areglado

Sharing Whole Language with Administrators

Many administrators like to see proof that whole language works before they will allow their schools to move away from traditional basal programs. The two most convincing books to lend administrators are *Report Card on Basal Readers* and *The Administrators' Guide to Whole Language*. Share examples of local credibility from surrounding school systems. Also, keep impeccably accurate anecdotal records and other assessment information, and share your own success stories.

If your administrator is hesitant about whole language, begin by using whole language as a supplement to the current program. Reassure your administrator that all skills will be covered but that they will be taught differently. Invite him or her weekly or biweekly to your class to see how your children have progressed using whole language. Share assessment results on a continual basis. Send children to the office periodically to read published books, or to demonstrate how well they're reading with this program.

Invite your administrator to all the programs you invite parents to. If parents tell you how happy they are with your whole language program, ask them to tell your administrator too.

Find model whole language classes in your county and ask your administrator to observe them with you. Always accompany a person who is unfamiliar with whole language in case any questions arise that are left unanswered after the visit. Try to arrange a meeting between your administrator and the principal of the school you are visiting.

Attend conferences on whole language to sharpen your knowledge and skill base, and ask your principal and colleagues to accompany you. You will be considered the "whole language expert" in your school. Join networking groups, subscribe to research journals and networking newsletters and develop a whole language resource library for yourself.

Obtain funding from your school to hire a whole language consultant to come and speak to your staff and parent group. If this is impossible, try writing a grant proposal, or asking the parent group for funding. Investigate other ways to fund the speaker, such as joining another school system and pooling smaller amounts of money. Discuss ideas with your administrator.

➜ See: Areglado, pp. 369, 412; Bird, p. 271; Goodman, p. 274; Hutchison, p. 275; Stevenson, p. 271.

Further Reading About Sharing Whole Language With Administrators

Epstein, Joyce. 1987. "What Principals Should Know About Parent Involvement." *Principal* (January): pp. 6–10. Five basic ways are presented for getting parents involved in schools.

Goodman, Kenneth S., Patrick Shannon, Yvonne Freeman, and Sharon Murphy. 1988. *Report Card on Basal Readers.* Katonah, NY: Richard C. Owen. An important book for all administrators and teachers now using basals.

Heald-Taylor, Gail. 1989. *The Administrators' Guide to Whole Language.* Katonah, NY: Richard C. Owen. Excellent research and many useful ideas for implementing whole language.

Nancy Hyland Areglado is a language arts coordinator and primary teacher at Berkshire Hills Regional Schools District, West Stockbridge, MA.

The Funny Side

Doing What Comes Naturally

We had just come in from an hour's romp in the pool. While the weather was warm, I'd been taking my second-graders swimming twice a week. The kids had thrown T-shirts and shorts over their wet suits. I suggested they find a comfortable spot on the rug and I'd read aloud from a class favorite, *Morris and Boris*.

I had just opened the book when in walked Mr. Warren, the principal. He pulled up a chair and joined our circle. That meant he was going to stay and observe me. This was only the second week of my second year of teaching and I felt my pulse quicken and my hands go clammy.

Avoiding his gaze, I threw myself into reading *Morris and Boris*, changing voices for the different characters, gesturing whenever possible, and in general, putting on quite a show. I hoped I'd captivate the children—and Mr. Warren. Much to my delight, shrieks of laughter rose from the back of the circle. Encouraged, I read on, heightening my performance. More wild laughter. Boy, was I into it now! I couldn't resist a peek at Mr. Warren. I glanced over at him and saw that he was doubled up in laughter. At the same instant, I finally saw what all the hilarity was about. Avery Brown was standing in the back of the room, stark naked, methodically pulling on one sock and then the other.

"Avery!" I gasped.

"It's okay, Mrs. Mayo, I'm just changing out of my wet suit."

➜ See: Literature Reference List, p. 429.

—As told to LBB by Robin Mayo, primary teacher, Columbia School, Columbia, CA

In the Mail

Dear Principal,

I appreciate your concern about the quality of my teaching. It is also a major concern of mine. Throughout my first two years at this school, I have worked very hard to provide a nurturing learning environment for my students. I have a clear picture in my mind of the teacher I want to become. I envision a classroom in which children are excited about learning, they are engaged in productive activity, they are able to articulate their needs and their feelings to each other, and they feel good about themselves as complete human beings. I am happy that there have already been many times when my classroom has been such a place.

Teaching is a developmental process. I am a better teacher now than I was last year. I will be a much better teacher five years from now. *This year I am as good a teacher as I can be.* I deal with this inherent limitation in two ways: One is by being patient with myself and the other is by seeking help from other educators. Many times over the last two years I have invited other staff members to my classroom to observe me. I do this because I know that people who have more experience than I do can help me become the excellent teacher I want to be.

During my implementation of F.O./D. this year, I have been observed seven times by Stanford University and district staff. The supportive evaluators use an objective observation tool with which you are familiar; this form, used to help me improve my teaching, is given only to me. I welcome these supportive evaluators into my classroom, because I too am concerned with improving my teaching.

During your informal walk-throughs, you observed children who were off-task. You consider this to be primarily a discipline problem. I have learned that off-task behavior is sometimes a discipline problem, and sometimes it is a curriculum or classroom management problem. Sometimes it indicates a lack of motivation, proper work habits, or self-control. Sometimes it is caused by a problem the child is having at home, and *sometimes it is not a problem.* Looking for a pencil and thinking about what to write are appropriate behaviors for Writers' Workshop, unless, of course, a child is spending more time with these activities than with writing, in which case I have to intervene. I have watched, guided, and taught my students for 150 days of Writers' Workshop this year, and I see literacy development in every student.

I am concerned with the whole child in my classroom, i.e., 27 whole children, and I chose to work at this school because the teachers here share my philosophy. So when a child appears to be off-task, I have to consider *all* aspects of my teaching: discipline, curriculum, presentation, motivation, and classroom management. I have to remember to listen to my students, to be patient, to give them choices, and to let them know that I have high expectations and won't settle for less than they are capable of. Furthermore, I have to allow for individual differences and learning styles.

Just as I always try to consider *children* as whole people, I would like you to consider *me* as a whole person. If you feel that I am an asset to the district and to this school, I would like you to encourage me and help me in my professional growth. I appreciate the support you have given me so far, and I would like to continue to feel free to ask you for support and advice. I realize that your position allows you to make an addendum to my evaluation stating your concerns about my teaching, but when I read the addendum I was hurt. I felt misjudged and betrayed. If the purpose is to improve my teaching, you would be more effective by simply talking to me or writing me a note. That way I might be able to help clear up the confusion you have about what you have seen, and to ask for your advice about concerns we *share.*

Thank you again for taking the time to talk to me about your concerns and to listen to mine. I truly hope that we can establish the kind of professional relationship that won't require my having to write letters to defend myself.

Sincerely,

Carlen Luke

➜ See: Bird, pp. 92, 271; Luke, p. 321.

Carlen Luke is a primary teacher at Fair Oaks School, Redwood City, CA.

JOEL BROWN

"Tacit knowing is the fundamental power of the mind, which creates explicit knowing, lends meaning to it, and controls its uses."

—Michael Polyani
Knowing and Being

Curriculum

Contents

How I'm Different from the Rest of the Kids

by Juana Arcelia Sainez

I dedicate this to my high school English teacher, Art Peterson, who discovered the writer in me.

If I were to become a world famous heart surgeon, or if I were to drop out of school to marry Mr. Wonderful, either way my parents would still consider me their perfect baby girl. My parents never judge me by my literacy nor my success in school. Because my parents, raised on a farm in Mexico, never attended a school, they haven't found reading and writing an essential part of their lives. Growing up, my dad planted corn seeds in the field with other men in the family; my mom cooked tortillas, like all Mexican peasant women.

Now, in California, my dad, a laborer, stirs cement for a living; my mom shows me, the youngest girl, how to cook refried beans using her secret spicy recipe. They've managed by scribbling their signatures on documents, but they depend on me to write out their checks, read important mail, translate for them when they confront an English-speaking individual, and make phone calls.

Although my parents can neither read nor write, they live happy, traditional lives. My parents enjoy monthly get-togethers for a family member's birthday. The 20 or more relatives devour my mom's homemade tamales;

When she's not at school attending classes, or at home studying, Juana works in a local lab, good training for her chosen profession as a physician.

the stereo plays Mexican rancheras; the women in the family gather in the kitchen, gossiping about a relative in Mexico; the men, discussing living costs in Mexico, sit around the dining room table playing poker; the grandchildren play house in the family room. The action begins when everyone dances to salsa music while the very young clap their hands to the beat. The party ends the next morning after the guests eat breakfast and head homeward. During all this time, no one has talked about a book.

Because my sister and brother like my parents' traditional lives, they consider my parents their ideal role models. My sister, who never learned to read beyond the fourth-grade level, graduated from a San Francisco public high school, deciding to work as a file clerk, a job demanding little reading. At 19, she was married and gave birth to her first child. Presently, she still works, but she sees her role as [that of] a mother, not a cosmopolitan businesswoman. Oftentimes, she calls me up to help her spell words such as "necessary." Recently, I had to correct her grammar in a letter she had written to her daughter's principal. When the principal wrote back I had to translate the letter into spoken English because my sister couldn't understand the formal content of the letter. She depends on me for all these reading and writing tasks.

Now an English major at the University of California, Berkeley, Juana browses in the library.

My brother, who reached high school not knowing how to read, dropped out because he wanted to earn money working as a laborer. At 25, he hated not knowing how to fill out a job application when necessary. I tried to teach him to read and write by sounding out the letters of the alphabet. I have no teaching skills and had the feeling I was leading him into a black hole—a feeling that was confirmed. Writing a Christmas card, he asked me if he [had] spelled "from" correctly, when in fact he had spelled it "furm." He still doesn't have a hold on reading and writing. My other brothers and sisters, more or less, fit the same pattern I've described. Why am I different? I think it's because I've had different school experiences that have encouraged me to find out my interests through reading and writing.

In elementary school, my teachers convinced me that reading was fun. When the teacher announced "We are walking down to the library to get a free book from the Reading Is Fundamental program (RIF)," my classmates and I ran to form a single line, folded our hands in front of us, and shushed the noisy kids so we could be the first class down there. On the way, we whispered about our favorite Curious George book we hoped to find in the gold mine of books we saw in a RIF pamphlet. After reading my free book, I swapped with my friends so I could read another of Snoopy's adventures. The books were like healthy, sugary lollipops, and no one took them away.

In the middle school, my reading became related to my future goals. I remember the day I decided to become a doctor. In science class, my classmates and I were dissecting a frog. I didn't close my eyes and say, "gross"; instead I was fascinated. Recognizing the frog's heart, I thought, "Wow, here's a real heart that looked nothing like a Valentine heart!" Since that day, I've been reading everything I can get my hands on about science and medicine.

In high school, my teachers indirectly help me reveal my individuality through reading and writing. In my English class, my teacher inspires my classmates and me to use writing to discover who we are. That's why, when I wrote my college essay, I was easily able to discuss my own experience in terms of that quote from *The Breakfast Club;* "What we learned today is that each one of us is a brain, an athlete, a basket case, a criminal, and a princess." Writing has helped me become my own person.

Unfortunately, my sister and brother never encountered the pleasure of writing, nor any of the other positive school experiences I've had with reading and writing. But, examining these experiences, we can get some clues toward a solution to the problem of illiteracy. We can see what would have helped my sister and brother. If schools make reading and writing fun, if they use reading and writing to help students find future goals,

and if they encourage students to read and write as a way of finding out about themselves, more students will grow up with ambitions to be world-famous surgeons, and fewer will be dropouts and illiterates.

1987 Winning Essay of the San Francisco Branch English-Speaking Union Essay Contest, reprinted in the *San Francisco Chronicle*, Spring 1987.

Juana Arcelia Sainez was a senior at Lowell High School when she wrote this essay. It won first prize in an English-Speaking Union's essay contest in honor of "The Year of the Reader." She is now an English major at the University of California, Berkeley, and plans to attend medical school.

Juana chats with student friends on the Berkeley campus.

School as Life

As I See It:
Kenneth S. Goodman

Whole Language at the Chalk-Face

The concept of whole language requires an examined view of curriculum because it is in the curriculum that everything else comes together. No great theory or innovative idea, no inspired research or brilliant insight can make a bit of difference unless it becomes reality at the chalk-face (as the British say), the place where kids and teachers come together in the classroom.

In the first half of this century in the United States, considerable headway was made in building a holistic curriculum theory. During that period, *progressive education* and the philosophy of John Dewey caused many people to think about what curriculum must be and how it should be implemented. Here are some key concepts of that progressive view of curriculum:

- The curriculum must start where the learner is. So it is important to know the learners and build on their strengths.
- Experiences in school must be relevant to the learner. They must satisfy the felt needs of the learner.
- Children learn by doing. So there must be active involvement of children in activities that are real or simulate the real world. Play is an important way to involve pupils in learning.
- School is not preparation for life; it *is* life. So school experiences must be functional and useful for children while they are learning.
- In school, as in life, experiences should be integrated around problem-solving and inquiry. So thematic units should be used to integrate language, thinking, science, social studies, mathematics, physical education, the arts, and humanities.
- The classroom must be democratic so that children will learn how to participate in a democracy and to work with others in social groupings.
- The curriculum of a school must satisfy the personal needs of all learners while it serves the needs of society. It must provide for diversity while it provides common and unifying experiences. Curriculum is a transaction between the child's knowledge and experience and that of society as organized into content.

As Dewey said in 1902:

Abandon the notion of subject-matter as something fixed and ready-made in itself, outside the child's experience; cease thinking of the child's experience as also something hard and fast; see it as something fluent, embryonic, vital; and we realize that the child and the curriculum are simply two limits which define a single process. Just as two points define a straight line, so the present standpoint of the child and the facts and truths of studies define instruction. It is continuous reconstruction, moving from the child's present experience out into that represented by the organized bodies of truth that we call studies.

In response to this progressive view of curriculum, two more traditional views were articulated in the thirties and forties.

The perennialists argued that education must concern itself less with the mundane and more with eternal truths and loftier concerns. For the progressives, truth was relative and pragmatic; for the perennialists it was unchanging, and so was the curriculum.

Also responding negatively to the tenets of progressivism, the essentialists believed that schools should provide learners with the basics, the essential skills of reading, writing, and arithmetic, the minimum knowledge necessary to build further learning and survive in modern society. Their back-to-basics argument was that children must be taught the skills that everyone must know.

For several decades this debate over curriculum was set aside. Partly this was due to the post-Sputnik preoccupation with competition and achievement of academic excellence. Partly it was caused by the domination of curriculum by simplistic concepts of behavioral psychology. Curriculum in a behavioral view is taking learners through a tightly planned sequence of skill and subskill drill. Learning is demonstrating "behaviors" that can be measured through performance on paper-and-pencil "objective" tests.

Schools became preoccupied with behavioral objectives. In this they confused what we ask pupils to do with why we ask them to do it.

"The pupil shall spell correctly ten words on a list." Yes, but why should the pupil do that? And why those words and not others?

"The pupil shall successfully answer 80 percent of the questions on the end-of-level test in the basal." Yes, but what if they're bad questions? What if the basal is dull and uninteresting? What if the pupils are from a minority culture or are divergent thinkers?

And what if reading and spelling aren't learned that way?

Whole language picks up where the progressives left off. It recognizes that a school curriculum is a dynamic way of organizing experiences to meet the needs of learners and of their cultures and communities. It brings content alive and builds bridges from the learners' experiences.

Whole language takes the philosophy and positive, child-centered view of the progressive educators and adds the knowledge of language, of learning, of child development, and of teaching, and builds a strong scientific base under them. It is this combination of science and humanistic educational and social philosophy that forms the foundation for whole language curriculum.

We take the concept of integration as represented in thematic units. And we add to it the concept of dual curriculum: language and thinking are learned best while they are being used to learn, to build knowledge, to solve problems. So we don't teach isolated skills; we build reading and writing while we read and write to learn.

The curriculum in reading and writing starts with pupils reading and being read whole, meaningful, relevant texts. It starts with pupils inventing the writing system and discovering the conventions of writing as they use writing to write journals, keep records, take notes, and perform other real language functions. We take the knowledge from research on the reading and writing processes and use it to build authentic experiences for learners. We involve learners from the beginning in predictable and meaningful print in a wide range of contexts, including but not limited to books. We read to our pupils at all ages to help them build a sense of each language genre and to expand on the written language functions they already control.

We take the concepts of learning through experience and add from modern language theory the concept of authentic speech acts and literacy events. We can invite pupils to engage in these authentic events and then evaluate their language development as we mediate their learning. We use the psychological concepts of Piaget and Vygotsky to underscore Dewey's concept of learning as transaction: pupils making sense of their world and being changed themselves in the transactions.

And some new concepts and key ideas are emerging:

Choice: In whole language classrooms there is always choice. Learners help to set their own objectives; they choose how they will participate and fulfill their goals. They choose what they will read, what they will write about, what problems they will study, and how they will get the information they need.

Ownership: The whole language curriculum incorporates the concept that pupils must feel in charge of their own learning. They own their language processes, their thoughts, and their purposes. Within social limits, they make their own personal decisions.

Process Goals: Whole language is concerned with process as well as product. We're concerned not only with correct answers but with how the problems are solved. The research report is less important than the process of planning the study, framing the questions, finding information sources, organizing information, building schema, and presenting the results. In Dewey's pragmatic philosophy, ends become means and means become ends. So the product of a process (reading a book for example) stimulates more reading, develops new interests and strategies, and builds a sense of style and story useful in future reading. Thus there is a unity between process and product in the curriculum. There are no exits goals, no terminal objectives—only more doing and more learning.

Authenticity: Whole language builds a curriculum in which the experiences in school have the characteristics of those outside of school: they are authentic. In authentic experiences the participants have real, personal purposes for participation. The language used is real, relevant to the purposes and context, and comprehensible. That doesn't mean that nothing new and different happens to learners in school. The very fact that schools are places explicitly dedicated to learning gives experiences in schools distinctive characteristics, not the least of which is that there is a professional teacher present dedicated to supporting learning. Experiences in school must have *all* the characteristics of authentic experiences outside of school and additional characteristics that are authentic within the social-educational context of the school.

Invention: In whole language we build on the constructivism of Piaget. People construct their world. They invent it; that is, they continually expect to find order in it and they keep inventing ways of organizing it. They keep their inventions, their schemas, as long as they are useful. Language is invented too. Each individual creates language and moves toward social conventions. So the whole language curriculum encourages invention. It encourages children to invent the spelling system, to invent reading and writing strategies, and to invent schemas of the world around them.

Convention: Whole language redefines what convention means and places new value on the importance of conventions in the curriculum. Conventions are socially and culturally determined ways of doing things or viewing things. They are not static or invariant. They change as people, societies, and circumstances change. Only in authentic social experiences can learners test their inventions and discover the conventions. Rarely are these conventions created by experts and handed down in books. They are part of the social world. Dictionaries do not create definitions for words, for example; they record the conventional meanings society has assigned them. Our personal meanings come from using language in social contexts. Dictionaries can confirm or sharpen a personal meaning but not assure one.

It is in trying to achieve equilibrium between the conventions and their own inventions that conventions are eventually internalized by learners. Teachers build activities that provide

(Continued on page 282)

Whole Language Internacional
by Nigel Hall

Whole Language in Great Britain:
Whole Language Made Legal?

Relatively few teachers in Great Britain are familiar with the term *whole language*. The phrase has only very recently appeared in books and articles, and, except among those British teachers familiar with American journals, has little general currency within the teaching profession. However, paradoxically, the concepts that lie at the heart of whole language may be better understood by British teachers than they are by most American teachers. The resolution of this paradox is partly historical and, more recently, partly political. Indeed it is probably fair to say that Britain is likely to be the first country in the world to have enshrined many whole language principles in national law.

Britain has for long been recognised as having a child-centred stance towards the education of elementary children. British elementary school teachers have never been slaves of textbooks, basals, word lists, ditto sheets, and tests. There is a rich tradition of practice and research relating to the child-centred curriculum. British teachers have resisted hard any pull away from their freedom to put the child at the centre of the educational process. This has been particularly true where literacy is concerned. The public face of education has promoted the notion that children should have freedom of expression and that creative processes are more important than repetitious instructional practices.

More recently, however, political developments, deriving mostly from dissatisfaction with the quality of education in this country, have given a huge boost to *more holistic* approaches to literacy education.

From September 1989, every child starting school at age 5 will be taught the National Curriculum. This is a centrally imposed 10-subject curriculum (9 subjects up to the age of 11), with math, science, and English as core curriculum subjects. For each of the subjects a government committee has set out attainment targets and programmes of study, although the manner in which each subject will be taught is still left to

Nigel Hall is senior lecturer in the School of Education at Manchester Polytechnic, England. He taught young children for several years before becoming a college educator. For the last 14 years he has worked with hundreds of teachers in developing authentic, meaningful, and purposeful situations in young children's classrooms. He has written extensively in the field of early literacy education, presented papers at conferences throughout the world, and written books for young children. He is currently serving on the editorial board of *Language Arts*.

the discretion of teachers. All children will be tested in each of these subject areas at ages 7, 11, and 16. The panel that was set up to produce the details for English has finished its work, and their proposals (with some modifications) for the first Key Stage (up to age 7) have now become law. Their proposals for the later stages are, at the time of writing, still being debated, but are likely (again with some modifications) to become law very shortly.

Despite the intentions of the government (which would have liked nothing quite so much as a version of mastery learning) the English curriculum that has resulted is, in fact, quite a radical one. Radical, that is, for everyone except supporters of whole language, who will recognise instantly many of the central precepts. For those of us promoting ideas similar to those of whole language, the significant point is that not only are the attainment targets law but also the programmes of study. It becomes possible for the first time in Great Britain to say with force to a teacher, "You must allow children to do . . ."

Allow them to do what? That is inevitably the central question and can only be effectively answered by offering some examples. The English curriculum is divided into three main areas: speaking and listening, reading, and writing.

Amongst detailed and lengthy programmes of study, the law now says that during Key Stage One (up to seven years) reading "should build on the oral language and experiences which pupils bring from home. Teaching should cover a range of rich and stimulating texts, both fiction and nonfiction, and should ensure that pupils regularly hear stories, told or read aloud, and hear and share poetry read by the teacher and each other." And that children should "read in the context of role-play and dramatic play, for example, in the home play corner, class shop, or other dramatic play setting such as cafe, hospital, or post office. Such reading might include a menu, a sign on a door, a label on a packet, or a sign above a counter."

Where writing is concerned, the law says, "Pupils should have frequent opportunities to write in different contexts and for a variety of purposes and audiences, including for themselves," and "Pupils should write in a wide range of activities. Early 'play' writing, e.g., in a play house, class shop, office, hospital, should be encouraged and respected."

Where speaking and listening are concerned, the law now says that children should be "working with other pupils and adults—involving discussion with others; listening to, and giving weight to, the opinions of others; perceiving the relevance of contributions; timing contributions, adjusting and adapting to views expressed," and "Pupils should therefore be encouraged to reflect on and evaluate their use of spoken language and to reformulate it to help the listener."

There are some persistent whole language themes running through the documentation. These include respect for the child's efforts, the provision for diversity of experience, the use of authentic experiences, the potential of collaborative work, access to and use of all the genres of written and oral language, the importance of play as a learning experience, the need for experiences meaningful to the children, and the realisation that speaking, reading, and writing are related activities that complement each other in a multitude of ways.

When the idea that a National Curriculum might be imposed upon schools was first announced, those of us who had struggled hard over the last decade to develop holistic approaches to literacy imagined that our efforts were about to disappear under a right-wing government's narrowly constructed views of what counted as good literacy education. The government's views have not, I believe, changed, but the government has had to recognise the sheer weight of evidence that recent developments in literacy education have more to offer than ritualistic, mechanical skill instruction.

Of course everything in the garden is not all rosy. How all this is to be assessed is still not known, and the manner of assessment could make or break all the efforts of teachers. However, the word so far is that assessment is likely to recognise the interdisciplinary nature of elementary education, and instead of being based on narrow testlike elements, it will be based around projects or medium-term tasks.

At the end of the day it is an *English* curriculum, not a language or literacy curriculum, and all assessment will be in English. Thus it is unclear whether this will seriously disadvantage children from other language backgrounds. It is also the case that the attainment targets are rather less inspirational than the programmes of study. However, given all the possible alternatives, it is a wonderful relief to know that children in Great Britain will experience an English curriculum based on ideas that are also an intrinsic part of whole language. We may not call it whole language, but it would be difficult to argue that it is anything else.

Note: The orders relating to the Key Stage One of the English curriculum are published by Her Majesty's Stationery Office in a document "English in the National Curriculum," and were laid before Parliament in May 1989. This article was written in July, 1989.

→ See: Britton, p. 69; The Emergence of Literacy, p. 38; McKenzie, p. 234; Torbe, p. 232.

Further Reading by Nigel Hall
◆ *The Emergence of Literacy.* Heinemann, 1987.
◆ *Literacy in Action.* Falmer Press, 1989.
◆ *Writing with Reason: The Emergence of Authorship in Young Children.* Heinemann, 1989.
◆ *Keeping in Touch: Interactive Writing with Young Children.* Mary Glasgow Publications, 1990.
◆ "Some Day You'll No All About Me": *Young Children's Investigations with Letter Writing.* Mary Glasgow Publications, 1990.

(Continued from page 281)

for invention to thrive and convention to be found and controlled.

Invitation: The progressives helped educators understand the importance of motivation, the purpose and desire the learner must bring to an experience for learning to take place. Whole language teachers are learning how to invite learners to participate in useful learning experiences. They understand that teachers can't compel learning, that ultimately motivation must be intrinsic, and that learners must feel that they have chosen to participate. If learners do not respond to our invitations, we must examine the relevance and value of the experiences for the learners. The teacher can never give up on a learner—but neither can the teacher cop out by

using force or bribes to coerce participation. Nor is it sufficient to issue only easily accepted invitations. The teacher must be able to invite pupils to take risks involved in moving beyond what is easy and comfortable.

The whole language curriculum provides knowledge goals, language and thinking process goals, and social goals. It supports and encourages self-evaluation. And it makes evaluation an ongoing activity, integrated with the learning experiences.

In traditional schools the high achievers get a rich fare of expanding experiences and the low achievers get an intellectual starvation diet of skill, drill, and remediation. In whole language classrooms all pupils participate in rich

(Continued on page 283)

WELL-SAID

September on Cape Cod can be a glory of late summer: crisp, cool, brilliant. And 1959 was one such year. At Woods Hole we gathered at the old Whitney estate, . . . that could take all thirty of us. And it was a curious thirty. There were the curriculum-makers—biologists, mathematicians, physicists—plus a sprinkling of psychologists and several professional educators. We had invited a couple of historians and a classicist, to leaven the mix. . . .

Historians of education now say that Woods Hole was "seminal," that it "revolutionized" education, etc. But education is an enterprise whose ways and whose knowledge base are still much too unorganized to revolutionize. Insofar as there was anything revolutionary, it grew out of the . . . "cognitive revolution." . . . There were three aspects of that upheaval that expressed themselves in our discussions.

The first, I think, was a point I trace to the philosopher Gilbert Ryle. It is a conception of mind. Mind, as he colorfully proclaims, is in the lorry driver's hands, in the moves on the chessboard, in the strategies on a football field; it is not just in your head. Mind is method applied to tasks. You don't think about physics, you think physics. . . .

Piaget was the origin of the second emphasis. The vulgar way of presenting him in educational clothing is to make the argument . . . that certain subjects can only be taught to children after they have reached a certain level of maturity. What Barbel Inhelder emphasized was not that. Rather, it was that the child's understanding of any mathematical or scientific idea would be framed by the level of intellectual operations that he had achieved. There are ways of framing ideas that are appropriate to the level of development or abstraction that the child has reached. Lower levels of understanding are routes to higher ones. The lower level is not a degraded version of the higher level. Each has a logic of its own. Each is to be respected.

The third emphasis was on the "generativeness" of knowledge. Knowledge is not a storehouse. You already "know" most of what you "learn" in science and mathematics. "Learning" is, most often, figuring out how to use what you already know in order to go beyond what you currently think. There are many ways of doing that. Some are more intuitive; others are more derivational. But they all depend on knowing something "structural" about what you are contemplating—how it is put together. Knowing how something is put together is worth a thousand facts about it. It permits you to go beyond it.

—Jerome Bruner

➔ See: Moffett, p. 70; Whitmore, p. 311.

From *In Search of Mind*, by Jerome Bruner (New York: Harper & Row, 1983).

As Teachers See It

by Dorothy F. King

A Curriculum of Trust

"What," I was asked, "would you say most characterizes a whole language teacher?" Confidently, I opened my mouth. Thoughtfully, I closed it.

"I have to say it depends on the individual teacher," I said. "That's one of the strengths of whole language. But there are commonalities."

One of the commonalities I find most gratifying and affirming is demonstrated belief in children, the trust in children to be capable human beings.

As I visit classrooms, I am continually struck with what teachers say and do, and what these words and actions mean to students.

Some teachers communicate that teachers and students are vastly different species, that decisions must be made for students, and that children are constantly on the brink of self (and teacher and school) destruction. Other teachers communicate that they are in the learning adventure with their students, that they are glad to have their students as friends and fellow beings, and that they trust children.

D. Barnes (1969) tells us that communication is the most important factor in shaping the actual curriculum of a classroom.

Following are two excerpts from classroom observations that demonstrate trust in students. Children are trusted to know what academic activities are useful to them; they are trusted to accept and deal with life's tragedies; they are trusted as competent decision-makers about their own use of time and the running of their lives.

The teacher has just assigned the daily penmanship exercise in the writing workbook—copying and recopying the same letter(s), words, and phrases.

Child: Why do we have to do this?

Teacher: (Pauses) I don't know. (Pauses.) I wanted to say "because we're supposed to," but I don't know. (Pauses.) Let's all think about this. Let me know what you think. I'll get back to you on this. (Pauses.) Put your books away. Let's do something else.

This particular teacher was a first-year, full-time teacher. He had worked very hard to set up an atmosphere of partnership in his classroom. He treated the students with respect and always assumed that they were asking genuine questions. (Hence, he never had to worry about threats to his "authority.") Later the teacher told the young questioner's parents, "I'm glad he asked that question. Doing those exercises always bored me, but the kids never said anything, so I guessed it wasn't a problem. The school pays enough for those workbooks. Now we have a time each day when we focus on our handwriting by copying poems and phrases we want to keep. Some kids copy things other kids have written, or they copy their own work over. It seems to meet the intent of the school requirement."

The teacher has been reading *Wilfrid Gordon McDonald Partridge* by Mem Fox to her third-grade class. She is overcome with emotion at Miss Nancy's memory, inspired by a military medal.

> **Teacher:** "She touched the medal and talked sadly of the big brother she had loved who had gone to war and never returned." (Silence. Teacher's eyes fill with tears. She eventually looks up at the children, her eyes traveling to each one. The children sit quietly. Some get tears in their eyes; some look at the teacher; some look down. After about two minutes, the teacher is able to speak again.) This reminds me of something very sad for me. Perhaps I'll tell you about it later; it might help me. (The teacher continues reading.)

The teacher offered no apology, nor did she make excuses. She trusted in the students to accept her pain, and her comment said that she invited them to help her deal with her grief.

Frank Smith (1981) says that children are always apt to learn what is demonstrated to them. These students get the message that they are competent, capable, respected, and trusted human beings. That's quite a curriculum. May these be the learnings these young people hold with them throughout their lives.

➔ See: King, p. 28; Literature Reference List, p. 429; Wilde, pp. 32, 406.

References

Barnes, D., et al. 1969. *Language, the learner and the school*. Harmondsworth, England: Penguin.

Fox, M. 1985. *Wilfrid Gordon McDonald Partridge*. Brooklyn: Kane/Miller.

Smith, F. 1981. "Demonstrations, engagement and sensitivity: The choice between people and programs." *Language Arts* 58(6).

Dorothy F. King is an educational consultant in Chinle, AZ.

Resource: Periodical

Penny Power

$11.95/year (6 issues) individual from:
P.O. Box 54861
Boulder, CO 80322-4861

Consumer's Union, the publisher of the enormously popular *Consumer Reports*, also publishes a consumer magazine for children and young adults entitled *Penny Power*.

The articles in *Penny Power* are as appealing to kids as are the product reviews. There are tips on doing homework, shopping for clothes, strategies for earning money, advice on using 900 telephone numbers, and an analysis of buying baseball cards as an investment. I particularly enjoyed the ratings on books, TV shows, and movies.

My only criticisms of *Penny Power* are that the product reviews are not very extensive and there is no listing of products from best to worst. This is probably because the tests are not as rigorous and complete as those in *Consumer Reports*—oftentimes only two or three kids review a board game or science kit. The positive side is that kids are writing the reviews. This recipient of the Parents' Choice Gold Seal Award is a good buy.

Doug Haner

(Continued from page 282)

experiences. There are no pupils who are held back until they are ready. They all frame questions, solve problems, pursue knowledge; they all expand on their experiences; they all grow and learn.

Out of this bringing of new knowledge into a renewed concern for curriculum comes a dynamic and developing whole language curriculum which is exciting for both the learners and the teachers. No longer is curriculum bound within the covers of the basal readers and the other dry and sterile text series. No longer are learners kept endlessly climbing a behavioral stairway to nowhere. Curriculum is alive and well in the whole language classroom.

➔ See: Britton, p. 69; Crites, p. 308; Edelsky, p. 72; Goodman, p. 308; Miller, p. 219; Moll, p. 413; Van Allen, p. 307; Whitmore, p. 311.

by Fiona O'Donoghue

The Baffin Divisional Board of Education, created in April 1985, has stated that its goal is the development of a relevant, effective, Inuit system of education. The Baffin, as it is usually called, includes all the communities on and close to Baffin Island, as well as the communities of Grise Fiord on Ellesmere Island, Resolute Bay on Cornwallis Island, and Sanikiluaq, which is perched on one of the Belcher Islands in Hudson's Bay. Travel between most Baffin communities is by air and geographically speaking, the Baffin is one of the largest educational jurisdictions in North America. In spite of its size, the feeling in the Baffin is one of cultural and linguistic unity. Eighty-five percent of the ten thousand people living in the Baffin Region are Inuit and speak Inuktitut as their mother tongue. A traditional way of life is only a generation away for most adult Inuit—the link with the elders is still very important to the people. The Inuit have dramatically felt the impact of "southern" culture over the last forty years. Previously, the harsh realities of the Arctic climate and terrain prevented all but the hardiest missionaries and explorers from moving into the far North and settling for any length of time. This is certainly not the case in 1989, with Ottawa, Toronto, and Montreal less than a three-hour plane ride away from Iqaluit, the regional centre of the Baffin. The developing tourist industry and the revolution in communications technology mean that the Baffin is fax time away from its communities and the business world in the South, and a satellite link away from almost every TV channel available in North America.

The first school opened in 1950. Since then the rapid change experienced by the Inuit has had profound impact on their environment and culture. In the past, Inuit children learned a great deal about the South while they were in school. Inuit tell stories of learning to make pig and cow noises, of having to draw trees and apartment buildings, and listening to Dick and Jane stories. For Baffin children the reading series and its content brought Canadian middle-class values into the daily life of young Inuit in the same way that TV does today. Inuit values and the rich Inuit way of life were not part of the curriculum, and were certainly not included in the stories children read in school.

Southern Canadians living in the North sometimes believed that Inuit should give up Inuktitut and their culture so they could survive in the new world which was coming so quickly north. They did not realise that an erosion of identity and pride could result in calamities such as suicide and family violence. The Inuit are now determined to maintain their language and culture, and to make significant changes in the school system. Baffin Inuit have not lost their language, their pride, sense of humour, and spirit of endurance and survival. Their ability to adapt will stand them in good stead as they build a school system that reflects their own contemporary society.

The Baffin Divisional Board of Education developed a school program called Piniaqtavut following an extensive survey of the Baffin public in November 1987. More than 400 responses were returned in Inuktitut and over 160 in English. The overwhelming demand for maintaining Inuktitut traditional values gave the board a clear mandate for change. The people requested that the school teach self-confidence, responsibility, a love of learning, traditional survival skills and bilingual literacy and problem-solving skills. The public stressed the importance of teaching civics, history, and geography with an emphasis on the northern environment.

A committee of Inuit and long-term southern Canadian teachers spent 18 months attending meetings to brainstorm topics that might be covered in schools in order to meet the expressed wishes of parents.

Keeping Inuit values and rich way of life at the heart of the school curriculum was the job of planning commitee members (from left to right) Lena Metuq, Leah Qaqqasiq-May, and Jukeepa Hainnu.

These educators also brainstormed with Inuit students at all grade levels to determine their interests, and used their own knowledge of the "favourite" northern topics chosen by students over the years.

The Committee designed a developmental framework that they believe reflects learning for Inuit children. Concrete, hands-on experience extends throughout the grades.

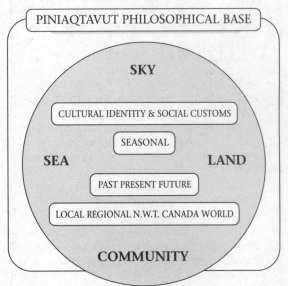

PINIAQTAVUT PHILOSOPHICAL BASE

SKY

CULTURAL IDENTITY & SOCIAL CUSTOMS

SEASONAL

SEA   LAND

PAST PRESENT FUTURE

LOCAL REGIONAL N.W.T. CANADA WORLD

COMMUNITY

In addition, the committee felt strongly that Piniaqtavut must be grounded in a worldview that is truly Inuit. The elements of land, sea, sky and community are fundamental to this worldview. Inuit values are the centre of the learning experiences for the children at all grade levels.

Resource kits are being developed across the Baffin. This will involve recording traditional knowledge. It will be necessary to gather stories, legends, myths, artifacts, and photographs, to write books about the wide range of topics suggested in Piniaqtavut. Until quite recently, there have been virtually no Inuktitut resources in science, social studies, health, or any other subject area. By gathering information about northern topics, it should be possible to build up libraries and resources over the next ten years. Piniaqtavut, which was completed in May 1989, should be a powerful step towards the development of a school system that is culturally relevant and meaningful. Past attempts to bring Inuit culture into the school have involved sewing and woodworking programs that took place outside the classroom. Known as "cultural inclusion," these activities helped children to maintain their cultural links and traditional skills.

Piniaqtavut Developmental Learning Framework

6-9 years Acquiring language proficiency, psychomotor skills, attitudes and behaviors.

PLAYING
Here & Now

What Is Our World?

Processes of exploring, observing, investigating, modelling, describing, and questioning developed through concrete and semi-concrete learning experiences. These experiences will extend throughout the program.

Kindergarten to Grade 6

10-12 years Acquiring knowledge and understanding of our world.

SHARING
Past & Present

Who Are We?

Developing independence through processes such as investigating, comparing, analysing, discussing, valuing, choosing, and applying.

Grades 7 to 9

12-16 years Extending and applying knowledge and skills.

INVESTIGATING
Historic, Present & Past

Where Do We Belong?

In-depth study of topics, which develops process skills such as synthesizing and evaluating, and encourages the ability to theorize and express concepts.

Grades 10 to 12

SENIOR HIGH SCHOOL

Who Am I?
Where Am I Going?

Choices of Lifestyles

An elder in Sanikiluaq demonstrates preparation of an animal skin as part of Piniaqtavut's goal of maintaining traditional skills.

Piniaqtavut, however, sets a cultural base for daily learning in all Baffin classrooms. The major goals of Piniaqtavut are the development of:

- Bilingual communication skills
- Pride in cultural identity
- Responsibility and independence

The approach recommended to Baffin teachers and taken from the work of Jim Cummins (1989) involves:

- Genuine dialogue between student-teacher in both oral and written modalities;
- Guidance and facilitation, rather than control of student learning by the teacher;
- Encouragement of student dialogue in a collaborative learning context;
- Encouragement of meaningful language usage by students rather than arbitrary adherence to form;
- Conscious integration of language use and development with all curricular content, rather than teaching language and other content as isolated subjects;
- A focus on developing higher-level cognitive skills rather than factual recall;
- Task presentation that generates intrinsic rather than extrinsic motivation.

Achieving literacy in Inuktitut means that literature in Inuktitut must be created for Baffin children. Over the last two years, Inuit educators and others have managed to write, edit, proofread, and organize the printing and distribution of over one hundred very beautiful books for their children. Students completing the Inuit Literature courses offered at the Eastern Arctic Teacher Education Program in Iqaluit have been responsible for writing many of the books which are usually in full colour and are truly professional and appealing. The books include biographies of well-known elders, traditional stories, pattern books, stories of loss and pain, as well as tales of adventures about young Inuit, and many wonderfully amusing stories.

This literature has made literacy in Inuktitut not just a dream but a joyful reality. Students of all ages read the Inuktitut books over and over again. Instead of the funny southern street scenes and stories of lions and gardens, Inuit children now read about polar bears, skidoos, spring camp, and a close family life. They enjoy pictures of children like themselves wearing parkas and playing in the snow. This literature is recording the past, capturing life as it is presently lived, reflecting Inuit values back to the children, and helping to explain the enormous cultural changes that are taking place in the Baffin.

Baffin educators are working very hard to help young Inuit become writers and authors themselves. The Baffin Writers' Project, sup-

Lizzie Vavik explains the dynamics of kayaks to kindergartners of Baffin Island, Northwest Territory, Canada.

ported by the Canadian Writers' Development Trust, is similar to a writer-in-residence program. The Project brings established writers to Baffin communities. Many of the visitors are aboriginal authors like Alice French, an Inuk who wrote *My Name is Masak,* and Minnie Aodla-Freeman, the Inuk author of *Life Among the Qallunaat.* The Apple Canada Education Foundation has supplied computer and desktop publishing facilities to four Baffin schools through the establishment of an Apple Centre for Innovation. Students in these communities are busy producing a bilingual quarterly magazine.

Leah Qaqqasiq-May helps a child in Arctic Bay to write his story.

Jeannie Alainga, Nanook School-Apex, writes on a computer in Inuktitut.

The implementation of Piniaqtavut has brought a considerable challenge to those educators who have chosen to teach in the Baffin. They are encouraged to incorporate Inuit content into their regular daily activities and, with the support of their Inuit colleagues and parents, to increase the classroom use of Inuktitut. They are expected to be involved with the community, to try to learn Inuktitut, and to make every effort to assist in the development of an Inuit school system. In addition, they are strongly encouraged to use interactive/experiential methodology and whole language. It can be an overwhelming task. There are too few Inuit teachers and classroom assistants, and funding is never sufficient. The midnight and weekend oil burns in many Baffin classrooms, yet there is a shared vision for the future of young Inuit.

➜ See: Edelsky, p. 72; Empowering Minority Students, p. 90; Goodman, p. 281; Literature Reference List, p. 429; Peterson, p. 348.

Reference
Cummins, J. 1989. *Empowering minority students.* CABE.

Fiona O'Donoghue is supervisor of Schools with the Baffin Divisional Board of Education, Iqualuit, Northwest Territory.

Books produced by students of Inuit Literature courses include tales of adventure.

Students can identify with literary characters who wear parkas like themselves and play in the snow.

WELL-SAID

We do not have a series of stratified earths, one of which is mathematical, another physical, another historical, and so on. . . . All studies grow out of relations in the one great common world. When the child lives in varied but concrete and active relationship to this common world, his studies are naturally unified. . . . Relate school to life, and all studies are of necessity correlated . . . if school is related as a whole to life as a whole, its various aims and ideals—culture, discipline, information, utility—cease to be variants . . .

—John Dewey, *Experience in Education*

Learning by Doing

Great Teachers:
Eliot Wigginton

From the *Lexington Herald-Leader*

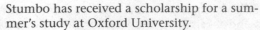

Dedicated Teachers Bring Change to State Classrooms

Learning begins with questions, and some kids in Floyd County had plenty of questions about the trains that passed through the Martin Coal Yard. Where does the coal come from? Where does it go? And what happens when it gets there?

These are not idle queries now for the students in Bud Reynolds' classroom. These students decided early in the year to study the world's environment through the coal that leaves Floyd County.

Their studies will follow the coal from the mine, down the railroad tracks and roads that lead out of Martin, to the plant where the fuel is burned. Along the way, students will learn about ozone depletion and acid rain, the price of coal and the cost of cleaning the air, how coal is mined, how it's shipped, and where it is burned. Its study will take the class from the coal mines of Eastern Kentucky to the polluted skies of Rome.

The kids are excited about the project and so is their teacher. Real learning is always exciting, and real learning is taking place in this Martin Elementary School classroom.

No test can quantify this learning. You can't put it in a workbook. You can't place a label on it and sell it to the legislature. But the education in Bud Reynolds' class is alive, nourished by a teacher who will listen to his kids and students willing to do real work.

It would be useful in the middle of the tumultuous debate over school reform to take a step back and look at what is happening in Bud Reynolds' classroom and others around Kentucky. If you look, you will find an innovative program helping students right now.

The program is the work of 65 teachers who call themselves the Eastern Kentucky Teachers Network. With a simple notion of learning and a commitment from some smart and daring teachers, the network has shifted the foundation of education in dozens of schools.

To find the beginnings of the network, one has to look south, to the hills of Georgia, to a man named Eliot Wigginton. Wigginton is best known as the originator of the series of Foxfire books. His philosophy of education is making a difference in Eastern Kentucky.

During a two-week seminar each summer, teachers from the fifth and seventh congressional districts come to Berea to study Wigginton's techniques. They learn a style of teaching that is cooperative, purposeful, and academically sound.

In a typical Wigginton project, teachers and students decide together on a project. Each project must satisfy academic requirements, be based in the local community and, ultimately, have an audience.

Bud Reynolds' coal project is a good example. His students are learning geography, science, economics, and social studies as they trace the path of coal out of Floyd County. And, to pass the knowledge on, they are preparing a slide show and radio spots on the dangers of waste and air pollution.

The same techniques can be found in the classrooms of other network members. In Anthony Ballou's Cumberland County High School classroom, students have put together a learning conglomerate.

Eliot Wigginton

They have produced a cassette tape of music played by local musicians featuring tunes from gospel to rock and roll. The kids researched and wrote a booklet to accompany the tape that tells something about each group. And they are now working on tray liners featuring snippets of local history. Barkesville residents will soon be able to learn about their county while they down burgers and fries at local fast food restaurants.

"We've done some things I didn't think we could do," a weary Anthony Ballou said early this year. Students, he said, had spent nights and weekends on the projects. "But you tell me," he challenged, "how else are you going to get a kid to work on an English project for 100 hours out of class?"

The answer is the teaching techniques he learned through the network. "Learning by doing teaches responsibility," Ballou says, echoing Wigginton, "and learning is the responsibility not just of the teachers or the school board, but of the students themselves."

While the governor, legislature, and the education lobby fight to lead a revolution in Kentucky's schools, they might be surprised to find the revolt has already begun—in the state's classrooms. The reformers, with all their talk of budget and structures, could take a lesson from the network.

Ultimately, the aim of education is a simple one. "What we really ought to be shooting for in the education field," Ballou, now worked up to his subject, says, "is instilling in these kids the burning desire to learn."

Like Anthony Ballou, we all need to keep our eyes on that target.

Minds at Work: Some Examples

The techniques of the Eastern Kentucky Teachers Network work across the school curriculum.

Most projects teach history, literature, languages, and social studies. Students in Doris Brown's Green Hills Elementary School class in Harlan County, however, have set up a recycling center and small store where they are learning math and business skills. Projects wait only for a spark between teachers and students to begin. Some other examples:

- Linda Oxendine, a teacher at G. R. Hampton Elementary school in Knox County, has her young students writing their own books. Replacing Dick and Jane (and their decidedly urban problems) with Papaw and stories of berry picking, Oxendine has taught her kids to read and write. She is now preparing a book of her students' stories.

- Winfrey Bates' fourth-graders at Mansville Elementary School in Taylor County have written and drawn a history of their town. They plan to produce a play based on that book.

- Students at Wheelwright High School have produced several issues of *Mantrip*, a journal of Floyd County literature and history. Because of her work on *Mantrip* and her skill at teaching rhetoric, teacher Carol

Stumbo has received a scholarship for a summer's study at Oxford University.

- Seventh- and eighth-graders at Crockett Elementary in Morgan County have written a history of their school, built by the Works Progress Administration. To end their study, led by teachers Nell Adkins and Ruth Yerian, the students will host a reunion of all the school's graduates.

- A video on solid waste entitled "Make Harlan a Better Place" won teacher Amy Rogers and her Harlan Elementary School students an award from then President Ronald Reagan.

→ See: Wigginton, p. 220.

From the *Lexington Herald-Leader*, Lexington, KY, 26 February 1989.

Resource: Publisher

Creative Education

Encyclopaedia Brittanica
P.O. Box 227
Mankato, MN 56002
1-800-445-6209

This intriguing catalog contains a wide variety of high-interest books that will appeal to elementary through high school students. The books are written at a fourth-grade level, which is especially helpful to older students who need material written at that level. The books are colorful, relevant, well written, and reasonably priced, and most have library bindings. The topics and genres include sports, animals, biographies, science fiction, classic short stories, fairy tales, living philosophies, amazing facts, and self-esteem.

Doug Haner

I Used to Be...But Now I...

I used to feel guilty about not reading the teachers manual,
But now I encourage others not to.

—Ward Cockrum

Education, therefore, is a process of living and not a preparation for future living. The school must represent life—life as real and vital to the child as that which carries on in the home, in the neighborhood, or on the playground.

WELL-SAID

—John Dewey, "My Pedagogic Creed"

YOUNG ARTISTS

The San Francisco-Oakland Bay Bridge after the October 17, 1989, earthquake
—as drawn by Juan Manuel Villa, 9, student of Elizabeth Doerr,
Fair Oaks Elementary, Redwood City, CA.

As Teachers See It

by Margaret A. Heath

Why Archaeology?

When students ages 10 to 18 were asked about what was the most important thing they had learned from a three- to five-day study of archaeology at Crow Canyon Archaeological Center, their answers varied. Some students enjoyed learning how to grind corn or start a fire with a fire drill or throw a spear with an *atlatl* (spear thrower). Others liked visiting actual places where the Anasazi, the prehistoric people of the Southwest, lived. Many were fascinated by the magic of watching a flint knapper (arrowhead maker) create a beautiful spear point out of a hunk of rock. Others enjoyed pretending to be a scientist during a mock dig, or working side by side with a real scientist at an actual archaeological site. Most mentioned that they were impressed by the patience required to be an archaeologist.

The school classroom can be a terribly regular, rather dull place in which to spend 13 years of one's life. Archaeology invites getting out of that room and stepping into experiential learning. The advantages of hunting with an *atlatl* over a spear can be read about, but will probably not have much meaning until students actually try throwing spears with and without the *atlatl*. Students can read about the patience required for science, but they will understand it better if they actually do a mock dig, from their own beginning research question to their own final report.

Besides social studies and science, the study of archaeology includes math skills such as measuring, making grids, and using the metric system; language arts such as journal, poetry, and story writing; drama and music; art; industrial arts; and physical education. Skills include spelling, reading, writing, computing, mapping, listening, and movement. Teamwork and cooperative problem-solving have always been a part of archaeology.

The goals of archaeology education are several.

1. It fosters an appreciation of other cultures.
2. It fosters an appreciation of the need to preserve and protect our cultural heritage.
3. It enhances students' understanding of the prehistory and history of their immediate area, and those of other areas of the country or world.

WHOLE LANGUAGE CAMERA

Angie Boloz sells cookies and chocolates at a Ganada Primary School concession sale to raise money to help starving Ethiopian children, Ganada, AZ.

4. It broadens students' understanding of science as a career.
5. It improves students' ability to imagine the future because it expands their ability to understand how people solved problems in the past.

Appreciation of Other Cultures. Our children need to be offered more than a cursory look at other ways of living. Intensively studying a past culture enables them to imagine what it would be like to be someone else.

Appreciation of the Need to Protect Our Heritage. Properly taught, archaeology demonstrates to students that evidence of the past is finite and is disappearing all too rapidly. Students learn that, rather than being a treasure hunt, archaeology is a painstaking effort to discover cultures of the past.

Appreciation of Prehistory and History. Many adults will tell you that they didn't like history much in school; small wonder, since it is so often reduced to names, dates, and places. Because archaeology relies on artifacts for clues, it forces an in-depth study that is far more interesting than the traditional history curriculum, especially when it includes a nearby area that students can visit.

Understanding Science as a Career Option. Many students have never been to work with their parents or anyone else. Yet we set up career fairs for middle schoolers and give large scholarships to high school seniors who presumably know what they want to do for the next 40 or 50 years of their lives. Working or talking with archaeologists in a nonschool setting at least exposes students to science.

Improved Ability to Imagine the Future. Before attempting to imagine the future, it may be best to investigate the past. As the past is explored experientially, it expands the mind's ability to imagine one's self in another time.

Resource: Network

The Artifact Box Exchange Network

First exchange and teachers guide for $35 from:
University of Connecticut
231 Glenbook Dr.
Storrs Hall, Rm. 28, U-7
Storrs, CT 06269-2007
1-203-486-4826

Imagine your students receiving a mystery box in the mail. The box contains items from an unknown location—a picture of a local landmark, a sample of a food item grown or produced in that region, a set of seasonal weather reports from the town newspaper, and a two-inch portion of a road map. These and other artifacts (25 altogether) come with suggestions on how to identify their origin. Your students become sleuths, analyzing clues and researching reference books and nonprint resources to determine the mystery location.

The Artifact Box Exchange Network is a biannual interschool project that uses hands-on simulation activity to help students develop advanced research, reference, and reasoning skills. Participating classes from grades 1 to 12 exchange artifact boxes, which contain 25 items students collected from their community. Only the participating teachers know the identities of the mystery locations.

Doug Haner

Why archaeology? Why *not* archaeology? It is interdisciplinary, kids enjoy and learn from it. It offers different ways of learning various subjects and skills in an atmosphere of exploration. It can be a way of getting students into new learning environments, and it might be just the spark to turn them on to school.

Margaret A. Heath is a director of education at Crow Canyon Archaeological Center, Cortez, CO.

Resource: Organization

Crow Canyon Archaeological Center

23390 County Road K
Cortez, CO 81321
1-800-422-8975

Crow Canyon Archaeological Center is a research and education center located near Cortez, Colorado. Students from fourth grade on are invited to spend three days or more learning experientially about the Anasazi people and archaeology. Activities include mock excavations and lab for elementary students, and real excavations and lab for older students, using Anasazi tools, making coil pottery, and touring Mesa Verde. Programs are available year round for elementary, middle, high school, and college groups. A four-week-long High School Field School and a Teachers Workshop are both offered for credit during the summer.

Margaret A. Heath

Resource: Organization

Association for Experiential Education (AEE)

Membership: $35 to $50 (individual); $50 (family); $125 (institutional)
CU Box 249
Boulder, CO 80309
1-303-492-1547

Resource: Periodical

The Journal of Experiential Education

Free to AEE members; nonmembers $18/year (3 issues) from AEE

I wasn't quite sure what to expect when I began reading the *Journal of Experiential Education*, but once I began, I found I couldn't put it down. The issue I read dealt with problem-solving and decision-making by groups, and included articles about making consensus decisions, judgment calls for outdoor leaders, and using fictional stories to teach problem-solving skills. I found it a fascinating collection of articles, and the inclusion of an index of titles from the last 10 years only fed my interest.

Membership fees are based on income, but I would recommend at least a year's subscription to the journal. With roots in outdoor adventure programming, this organization is committed to furthering experience-based teaching and learning in a culture that is increasingly information-rich but experience-poor. Members are united in a belief that learning and human development are best achieved from experience. They also share a belief that learning is further enhanced when socially, culturally, ethnically, and racially diverse populations are engaged together in the educational process.

Doug Haner

Resource: Book

Math for Girls and Other Problem Solvers

Diane Downie, Twila Slesnick, Jean Kerr Stenmark
Math/Science Network
Lawrence Hall of Science
University of California
Berkeley, CA 94720

This thoughtful and practical book has its roots in the spring of 1974, when a Math for Girls class began at the Lawrence Hall of Science. At that time, boys constituted more than 75 percent of the eager young people experimenting with motors, programming computers, and exploring mathematical puzzles and patterns at the popular after-school classes at the Hall. In response to this inequity, Dr. Diane Resek developed the original course curriculum that in six years helped double the number of women students enrolled in other Lawrence Hall classes.

Math for Girls and Other Problem Solvers is a collection of these hands-on activities, ideas, and strategies; its focus is more on problem-solving than traditional arithmetic skills. Teachers will appreciate the skillful blend of a research-based approach with practical, thoughtful, student-centered activities. The authors have identified the characteristics of good problem-solvers and have created content around four problem-solving skill areas: using logic, strategies, and patterns; breaking set, creative thinking; estimating and observing; and spatial visualizing, all of which are applied to cooperative, non-threatening, and supportive explorations that encourage success. The ultimate reward is developing the confidence and realization that problems can be solved through diligence, cooperation, and perseverance.

Doug Haner

Resource: Distributor

Creative Dimensions

P.O. Box 1393
Bellingham, WA 98227
1-206-733-5024

The day after the big one hit on October 17, 1989, teachers in San Francisco and the Bay Area were all scampering to find information on earthquakes and faults. If we had been aware of Creative Dimensions, a small educational supply house in Bellingham, Washington, we could have ordered their Seismograph Study Kit, and our secondary students would have been comparing our quake with the 1964 Alaskan earthquake. Follow-up activities from their earth science kit on fossils and plate tectonics for grades 6 to 12 will deepen students' understanding of how and why earthquakes occur.

Creative Dimensions' collection of science kits provides concrete materials on topics of interest to kids. It includes investigations and samples for studying of sand, beaches, rocks, and even has a unique unit on owl pellets. (Since owls swallow their prey whole, a pellet of a bird that had eaten two mice, three shrews, and one mole would be expected to contain six complete skeletons.) There are posters of animal skeletons, individual bone-sorting sheets, pellets, a teachers guide, and a poster that shows the food web in a typical barn-owl community.

A catalog item for those who want to deepen young children's fascination with dinosaurs is a set of 33 posters of dinosaurs and their relatives, including a teachers guide. And don't miss *A Book About Me*, which involves children in K through 3 in measurement, art, and recordkeeping activities about themselves—always a high-interest topic! It includes opportunities for interactions with others, and both reflective and manipulative activities.

Doug Haner

Resource: Publisher

INTERACT: Learning Through Involvement

P.O. Box 997
Lakeside, CA 92040
1-800-359-0961

INTERACT is a company dedicated to simulations. In one called "Who Really Discovered America?" seven explorers, including Hoel-Shin, a Chinese Buddhist monk who claims to have touched the shores of North America in 495, each try to convince the audience on a talk show that he or she was the one. What fun activities!

Cynthia McDermott

Resource: Publisher

Let's-Read-and-Find-Out Science Books

Harper Junior Books Group
Thomas Y. Crowell
Keystone Industrial Park
Scranton, PA 18512
1-800-242-7737

It's hard to find good books for kids that teach science concepts without being too long or too overwhelming. The Let's-Read-and-Find-Out Science Books are a refreshing and popular source of science information books written especially for children. The publisher does a thorough job of finding books that are informative but not overwhelming, and that are long enough to challenge but short enough to entice.

For over 25 years Harper's catalog has been a standard for children's books on redwoods, blood, dinosaurs, astronomy, rocks, weather, glaciers, sleep, and other science topics; their titles include 10 books by Aliki. Excellent and complete annotations include reading level, a listing of professional recommendations, and selected awards and honors.

Doug Haner

Westward Movement

Faced with the average eighth-grader's monumental disinterest in the history of their country, plus the large amount of material a long-suffering social studies teacher is expected to force down students' gullets, I decided to adopt a different approach. For the Westward Movement the kids paired up, and each pair was responsible for getting a covered wagon from the East Coast to California or Oregon. They had to decide what to take: (food, tools, nails, etc.) and how much of each item to take for the entire trip. There was a lot of agonizing over the amount of space in the interior of a prairie schooner! They then had to decide on a route and describe how they would traverse each section of the country. One enterprising pair of boys actually worked out a way to do the whole trip on water! I really hated to point out that some of their water wasn't navigable, but they got rewarded for effort.

Occasionally some background was needed, so the class would spend a period on a textbook exercise. They also watched suitable movies as well as spent a period in the library every two or three weeks. But they really enjoyed best working on their projects, and they *really worked*.

At the end of the year I let them make up their final exam. When their jaws had finished hitting the floor, they turned to with a will and worked out a very well-rounded test of the entire year. (I hadn't specified how much of the course the test should cover.) It was a much harder exam than I would have given, but surprisingly the grades were just about what they would have been on a test the kids hadn't seen. I think they all learned more making up the test than they did taking it. They had some wonderful knock-down drag-out arguments over what should or should not be included.

Kathryn M. Krauskopf is a counselor and teacher at Jordan Junior High School, Palo Alto, CA.

📷 WHOLE LANGUAGE CAMERA

Careful maneuvering of chopsticks pays off for a first-grader…his first delicious mouthful. Annette Maggitti's first grader's stir-fried vegetables they grew in their own class garden, Desert Winds School, Tucson, AZ.

The Funny Side
Breaking New Ground

My second- and third-graders had been investigating "things that float, things that don't." I then instructed them to think of their own projects—some phenomena they'd like to explore on their own. One morning, Brian called out to me, "Mr. Morgenbesser, I've decided on a project!"

"Great, Brian! What did you come up with?"

"Things that break, and things that don't!"

—As told to LBB by Marty Morgenbesser, primary teacher, San Miguel School, Santa Rosa, CA

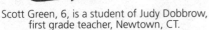

YOUNG ARTISTS

things that are huge
jiynt
[Giant]

Scott Green, 6, is a student of Judy Dobbrow, first grade teacher, Newtown, CT.

dinosaurs

Classroom Demonstrations

by Dot Muller

Classroom Demonstrations

by Tarà Ransom

Welcome to China

The sign on our door said "Welcome to China" because China was the theme in our first-grade whole language classroom for about five weeks. Our objective was to initiate in the children an interest in this country through books and hands-on, real-life experiences. Our focus was on China: its people, its festivals, its stories, and its famous architectural works.

Three high school students, who were in their fourth year of studying Chinese, visited our class. They read a story in Chinese, helped us learn Chinese charac-

ters, and brush-printed Chinese New Year greetings on the scrolls we had made.

Another highlight of our study was a trip to Chinatown, in New York City, just prior to the Chinese New Year. We visited a Buddhist temple, where a monk welcomed us and told us about the different Buddhas and about the symbols and artifacts around the room. Our next stop was at a Chinese restaurant for lunch, which the children ate with chopsticks—a skill we had practiced for days in our classroom. We visited a first-grade class in the public school in Chinatown. The Chinese children sang in Chinese and in English for us, and we sang in English for them. Between these stops we walked the streets of Chinatown, and all the books and pictures and pieces of information we had studied became a reality for the children.

From our school and public libraries we were able to find a considerable number of stories about China to read, and an ample supply of nonfiction material for the children to use for research. Parents and teachers were generous in their willingness to share pictures, Chinese clothing, and articles and slides from their trips to China.

We painted and constructed a colorful 12-foot dragon "kite" and shared it with other classrooms. The children wrote journals with charm and sensitivity. Our culminating activity was to write, print, and illustrate a big book entitled *China: The People, Places and Things*.

Not only have the children developed an interest in China, they seem to care about the Chinese people. That the children will forget this experience is hard to imagine. And perhaps they will be better world citizens because of it! Surely they will be better readers!

Dot Muller is a primary teacher at Huntington Elementary School, Huntington Station, NY.

Language Stories

Bring the Books

by Carol Hittleman

Our first-grade class was discussing our upcoming trip to Chinatown, New York, as part of our month-long theme—China.

Julia asked, "Can we take a book on the bus with us?"

A chorus of "Yes, yes" arose. I was surprised (never heard of this before). I was pleased (they're turned on to books). And I was doubtful (thinking of the possibility of motion sickness). So I told the children we would see.

Four days later, two days before the trip, Eddie (not forgetting) asked, "Are we going to take books on the bus with us?"

Playing innocent, I replied, "What for?" "To read, to read!" the multitude answered. I said yes! Who could argue with such enthusiasm?

The day of the trip, each child chose a book and carried it onto the bus. They read, they exchanged books, and they read to parents during the trip. Why do we ever doubt the wisdom of children?

Carol Hittleman, director of Language Arts, Huntington Public Schools, Huntington, NY

Resource: Organization

National Women's History Project

7738 Bell Rd.
Windsor, CA 95492
1-707-838-6000

As a resource teacher, I frequently get requests for materials on women's studies—posters, children's books, biographies, films, and curriculum ideas on the roles of women in history. There is a wonderful catalog of these materials now available from the National Women's History Project. All of the K through 12 curriculum materials they offer have been carefully screened to fit their four criteria: historically accurate, interesting to read, multicultural where appropriate for the subject, and a good buy for the money.

Doug Haner

Book-Learning at Its Best

Their book may never make the best-seller list, but almost 50 local high school students were acting like famous authors anyway.

English students from Saginaw and Arthur Hill [Michigan] high schools smiled graciously, blushed, and occasionally bragged as they celebrated the publication of their book *The Bridge—Linking Minds: Growing Up in Saginaw* during an autograph-signing party.

"I felt like a celebrity," said Melinda Thompson, an 18-year-old Saginaw High School senior.

Thompson is one of 48 students who contributed to the 152-page paperback book about "crossings from children toward adulthood."

The book grew out of a two-year assessment and writing project involving the Saginaw School District and the University of Michigan's Center for Educational Improvement through Collaboration, said Patricia L. Stock, a lecturer in the university's English department.

Publishing a book is an excellent way to teach students to write, Stock said.

When teenagers know the public is going to read their work, they take greater care about everything from punctuation to grammar to organization, she said.

And in this case, a University of Michigan professor will even require his students to read the book this semester, Stock said, adding that the students and their teachers are hoping the book eventually will grace the shelves of local bookstores.

Stock said students spent time before, during, and after school and on Saturdays typing their works into computers and critiquing each other's writing until it was "perfect."

"We had to do a lot of reviewing and proofreading," said Jason T. Marcoux, an 18-year-old Arthur Hill High School senior who wrote about how his uncle, Peter Caulfield, grew up in Saginaw.

Students often rewrote their essays 10 to 15 times, he said.

"It makes me feel proud to see the book published, but the best part is the recognition you receive," said Marcoux.

➜ See: Curry, p. 352; Treasures, p. 162; Wigginton, p. 220.

Excerpted from *The Saginaw News,* 9 June 1988.

Resource: Book

The Bridge—Linking Minds: Growing Up in Saginaw

1988; 124 pp.; $5
Instructional Staff Development Center
1505 Ottawa St.
Saginaw, MI 48602

Reading the World

As Teachers See It

by Elizabeth Doerr

Reading the World

Carole Edelsky writes, "The viewpoint of educators themselves is one of the challenges; 'we have met the enemy and they is us.' We don't read the world in Freire's sense—and we don't want to (or we're afraid to)."

I want to recount an experience I had last year that made me aware of my own silencing. I think sometimes, even while we brainstorm ideas and watch and listen to children, we maintain distance, hold issues on a certain level, and keep some information and experiences out. We prevent all voices from being heard.

One day I was passing out one of the typical mimeographed notes that we are barraged with in our school. This one announced a community meeting, to discuss the drug problems in the neighborhood of Fair Oaks. So I added some emphasis: "This meeting is very important. It's about guns and drugs in the neighborhood. Tell your parents about it." Their hands went up, anxious to speak. One by one they began to tell their stories. And I realized that this was a meeting about them; about violence, guns, and crack affecting them. Yet it was a meeting for adults. So I said that if they had any testimony, they could write it and I would bring it to the meeting.

What I got was 30 letters—30 voices describing their lives. Reading one letter was moving; reading 30 was an indictment.

We learned that one voice is powerful but collective voices have an even greater power. We continued to deal with drugs in the neighborhood as part of a community effort.

There were plenty of contradictions: undercover agents busting pushers, *la migra* busting their own families. When do you trust and when don't you? The sheriff visited the students to answer their letters; he ended up answering questions about trial by jury and about the district attorney. Others came, and talked about the coca trade, about where it comes from, who profits, and who pays.

To understand the drug problem, we had to look in our own backyards and talk about why someone would use a drug to feel powerful and competent. It was a safe place, actually the only place, where they could talk about problems of alcoholism, cocaine use, and teenagers they knew pushing drugs.

Since then I've tried to listen, pay attention, and provide opportunities to explore the students' agendas that might otherwise have gone unnoticed.

Here is a letter three students wrote to the family of Chico Mendes following his murder in the Amazon:

> Querida familia Mendes,
> Sentimos muito o que arontecie a vosso querido pai. Desejavios ajudar les mos estauvos taõ longe. Oremos tenter suportar les o quanto. Dodemos do. Estedes unidas.
> Vosso pai foi muito por selurar an arvore de burradie esperamos que vose sejamo taõ covejosos como fai pai
> con muito

They had the letter translated into Portuguese. Angie's father had also been murdered, by a death squad in El Salvador.

Here are the same three students writing to the president of the World Bank:

> Dear Mr. Barber J. Conoble Jr.
> President of the World Bank,
> We want to keep the Rainforest. We wanted to ask if you could pleas stop financing rainforest dams; We dont want the animals to die.
> We know this is not our business because we are not Brazilian but we feel sad for the animals and most of all the people that live in the rain forest.

How would you feel if some people would come and tear up your home? We know you wouldn't like that. Neither would the animals. If you will stop financing the rainforest every body will be thanfull.

> Love
> NANCY
> Angie
> Wendy

In studying the environment, we approached it as a complex social problem. For me, this meant viewing the students not just as future citizens, but as active members of a democratic society. We watched the Frontline presentation "Murder in the Amazon," and split up a loaf of bread to help us understand how wealth is divided among social groups in Brazil. We also role-played various interest groups. Over time, students began to look more carefully at other issues such as the roots of homelessness, the role of the church in society, and conflicting political interests.

When the Exxon Valdez oil spill occurred, we recreated it in our classroom to try to understand the problems of the cleanup. We looked at Exxon's role, what happened aboard the ship and the effects a spill like that would have on our own coastline and Bay Area life. One day, while we were making posters about the spill, Josh chimed in, "What about the planets?" I asked him to illustrate what he was thinking. Here is his poster.

THE Only Planet with Life

keep it alive!

This fall, there were several incidents of students putting each other down with racial slurs, sometimes directed against students of the same race, other times directed against other ethnic groups in the community. In a traditional classroom, a teacher might have dealt with this by telling the students involved that their behavior just wasn't nice, and putting it on hold until Martin Luther King's birthday. But in this classroom, the students themselves raised it as a question for discussion. Since then, we have been looking at the roots of our own prejudice, including its cultural, historical roots in the conquest of Mexico and the slave trade. So the students were again reflecting on their own experiences, which provided a basis for analysis and discussion.

Let me sum up some of what I've learned. We need to:

1. Recognize our students as already functioning members of society.
2. Remove the barriers that prevent our students from reflecting and acting on the social realities that shape their lives and futures.
3. Stop withholding or censoring information students need to make informed decisions.
4. Reflect and act ourselves on our students' lived experience, in the contexts of their communities and of the social, political, and economic forces that affect them.
5. Confront historical, political, and conceptual illiteracy, as well as the more traditionally defined illiteracy.

We're a long way, in Room 8 at Fair Oaks School, from reading the word and reading the world. But I feel now that I have a sense of where I need to go.

→ See: Apple, p. 416; Bird, p. 92; Edelsky, p. 72; Giroux, p. 417; Shannon, p. 222; Shor, p. 223.

Elizabeth Doerr is an elementary teacher at Fair Oaks School, Redwood City, CA.

Resource: Organization/Periodical

Network of Educators' Committees on Central America (NECCA)

Central America in the Classroom

$10/year (6 issues) individual; $25/year institution from:
P.O. Box 43509
Washington, DC
20010-9509
1-202-667-2618

With Central America making daily front-page news, this organization provides essential, accurate, and up-to-date resources for educators at all levels. The stated goals of NECCA are to provide information on Central America for teachers and students, and to support Central Americans' efforts for peace, human rights, and a negotiated settlement to the conflict in the region.

NECCA's resources include maps, classroom exercises, and readings for students on Central America, as well as a newsletter entitled *Central America in the Classroom*. If you are interested in learning about how other Spanish, social studies, English, ESL, and art teachers introduce Central America in the classroom, this newsletter tells you all you need to know. It will bring a wealth of ideas for hands-on activities, reviews of new materials, news from students and teachers in Central America, reports on innovative projects to promote cross-cultural understanding, and short stories by student authors. It will also provide you with information on summer educator tours to Central America and specific ways you can help get desperately needed school supplies to Nicaragua.

Consider adding *Wilfredo, the Story of a Boy from El Salvador* to your library, or using their slide show entitled *The Children of Nicaragua*.

Doug Haner

YOUNG ARTISTS

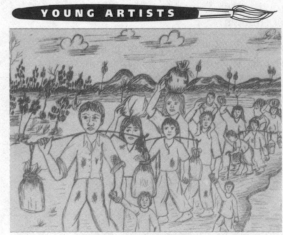

"Flight"—Moeun Mon, 17, Portland, OR (from *Treasures 2,* See p. 162)

Book Note

Cultural Literacy: What Every American Needs to Know

E. D. Hirsch
1987; 251 pp.; $18.95
Boston: Houghton Mifflin

Whole language teachers tend to dislike *Cultural Literacy,* which has gotten a lot of publicity for its list of 5,000 words, names, and concepts, ranging from "abominable snowman" to "Zeus," that every American should know. Hirsch's book has been seen in bad company, used by William Bennett and other members of the "back to basics" establishment to argue for a return to "content" and a uniform curriculum. Hirsch has also been attacked for his misinterpretations of John Dewey and the Eurocentric bias of his list.

However, *Cultural Literacy* has more than a grain of truth in it and in a sense can be used to make a very powerful argument for whole language. Hirsch would heartily agree with teachers who complain that time for their students to read has been usurped by endless worksheets on "skills," and that they're required to use basal readers that chop up and water down good children's literature. Hirsch

also feels that poor and minority children will be best served by a curriculum rich in meaning and content: "being taught to decode elementary reading materials and specific, job-related texts cannot constitute true literacy." (p. 11)

Where most of us would part company with Hirsch, however, is with his contention that rote learning (supported by his mini-industry of cultural literacy dictionaries and standardized tests) is the best way to acquire cultural literacy. If people who know most of the items on Hirsch's list were asked, "Hey, where did you learn that?", their answer would probably not be that it was through the rote learning that Hirsch recommends. In my case, I know most of what I know on that list because of wide reading and other life experiences, from incidental learning rather than formal instruction. So read Hirsch for his discussion of schema theory, his critiques of skills-based education, and his support for a broad conceptualization of literacy; mentally argue with some of his overly simplistic ideas; and use him as ammunition to advocate a rich curriculum based in literature and nonfiction trade books rather than "skills" and textbooks.

Sandra Wilde

Book Note

Multi-Cultural Literacy

Rick Simonson and Scott Walker, editors
1988; 188 pp.; $8.50
St. Paul, MN: Graywolf Press

Multi-Cultural Literacy is a much-needed response to two books published in 1987, *The Closing of the American Mind,* by Allan Bloom, and *Cultural Literacy,* by E. D. Hirsch, Jr. Both Bloom and Hirsch called attention to the need for an overhaul of American education; their respective guidelines for this overhaul, however, called for a back-to-basics curriculum that was sadly out of touch with the reality of pluralistic American life. Simonson and Walker felt these books did not go far enough as attempts to cure the ills of our schools. *Multi-Cultural Literacy* goes beyond the male, Eurocentric limits of mainstream curriculum, and suggests that our lives are fueled by knowledge and appreciation

of various cultural perspectives.

Many distinguished writers are featured in this book: James Baldwin, Paula Gunn Allen, Wendell Berry, and Carlos Fuentes, among others. Together the essays point to the sort of knowledge that truly literate people need in a complex world. The editors include a list meant to supplement one presented in Hirsch's book, called "What Literate Americans Know." The Graywolf list breaks the monocultural barriers we all too often encounter.

Arrietta Chakos

❝ When I heard a schoolteacher warn the other night about the invasion of the American educational system by foreign curriculums, I wanted to yell at the television set, 'Lady, they're already here.' It has already begun because the world is here. The world has been arriving at these shores for at least ten thousand years from Europe, Africa, and Asia.❞ (Ishmael Reed, p. 159)

Resource: Program

International Network for Global Educational Activities in Rural Schools (INGEAR)

Dr. Nancy L. Quisenberry,
Associate Dean for
  Academic Affairs
College of Education
Southern Illinois University
Carbondale, IL 62901
1-618-453-2415

INGEAR is a unique program that introduces international culture into kindergarten through 12th-grade classrooms in southern Illinois. It demonstrates how colleges can share resources with schools and local communities to create innovative educational opportunities.

Through this program, teachers request international college students to visit social studies, geography, home economics, or foreign language classes. In class, the college students wear the dress of their homeland, perform dances and rituals, bring artifacts to talk about, prepare food, demonstrate their language, teach songs, and answer questions about their country. The opportunities for developing whole language through these experiences are numerous.

Doug Haner

 **WHOLE LANGUAGE CAMERA**

Friends from Fratney, Milwaukee, WI
(See Peterson, pp. 336, 348)

Taste test, Palo Alto, CA

As kids see it

A Letter to President Bush

Julia is a teacher's dream. She brought this letter to me last spring and asked me to edit it with her. I had read the class Meltzer's book All Times, All People: A History of Slavery *and had brought back other titles that I had purchased at the 1988 NCTE where I was thrilled to have met the author in a nonfiction workshop. I love Julia's politics and how she incorporated our current events studies with the literature in the classroom.*

—Toby Kahn Curry

Burton International School
Detroit, Michigan
May 2, 1989

The White House
1600 Pennsylvania Avenue
Washington, DC 20510

Dear President Bush,

I am a black 13-year-old girl. I am in seventh grade at Burton International School in Detroit, Michigan. I have a B-plus average. In my class, reading is stressed thoroughly (even though I'm already fond of it).

I just finished a book called *Winnie Mandela: The Soul of South Africa.* The author is Milton Meltzer. Since my class is also studying the Struggle for Equal Rights throughout the years, I found the book very interesting and moving.

Back when you were campaigning in 1988, my friends and I thought that if you were elected, black Americans would suffer greatly because you were only interested in rich white Americans. I had hoped you would have changed our minds by now, but so far you haven't.

What are doing about drugs in Detroit? What are you doing about all the murders in Detroit, even Washington? What are you doing about our wasting environment? What are you doing about our school system? What are you doing to help all the people getting killed in South Africa?

Did you know that Milton Meltzer had to write his biography by using Winnie Mandela's autobiography as a source? Want to know why? Because Winnie was in jail and no one was allowed near her (writers, photographers, journalists, etc.). Do you know why she was in jail? Because she was trying to free her people from apartheid.

She wants to live in peace with the whites. You know, what's happening in South Africa right now is not very far from slavery. And what are you doing to help?

You could start by not giving South Africans as much political and economic support. I bet you a lot of people don't even know the basics of what's happening down there. I bet a lot of people don't know what apartheid means! I didn't. Stop sending arms there. Stop buying things from them. Condemn racism there as we condemn it here. Without our support, they'll be lost. Help change people's minds about you!

It's not that I'm prejudiced against anybody. Going to an international school prevents that. But I feel that these topics are important. Please respond.

Sincerely,
Julia Pointer

Julia Pointer is now in the eighth grade at Burton International School, Detroit, MI. Toby tells us that she is still waiting for a reply.

As Teachers See It
by Candy Heinsen Carter

The Vietnam War Era in the English Classroom

Where were you in 1969? My students were not even born then. For me, it was a pivotal year. I graduated from college. I started teaching. My fiancé was drafted. A high school friend was killed in Vietnam.

It was not just my memories of that time that started me squirreling around B. Dalton's for suitable material on Vietnam for my high school students, but also my students' unsatisfied curiosity about the war that their parents fought in, protested, or simply lived through. Many did not know where Vietnam was on the map. Most students had no grasp of the war's political and military complexities. Yet, with the coming of *Platoon* and "Tour of Duty," the old dialogue about the war surfaced again—in my classroom.

I discovered a tremendous body of literature—over 200 novels, many plays, and countless poems and short stories. Some are written in the "soldier of fortune" style. Other texts, especially the plays and poetry, are healing pieces for the veteran-authors. Some, though excellent, are too graphic in language and content for high school. But a great many excellent works remain.

My goal was not to spend a lot of time on the events of the war (although an interdisciplinary team approach with a social studies teacher is ideal for giving students a historical context). Rather, I decided that every name on the Wall in Washington, DC, and every Vietnamese casualty had a story to tell. I wanted to help students realize, through literature and language, what the war in Vietnam was like and what its legacy has been for all of us.

My search for suitable material and activities for students led me to strange places—Vet Centers, tobacco stands, bookstores (used, university, and chain), libraries, mail order catalogs, and ultimately, the Vietnam Memorial itself. The result is a six-week unit of study, "The Literature of War," with a heavy emphasis on Vietnam.

I begin with "The Minefield." I darken the classroom by covering windows and set up coffee cans across parts of the room, connecting them with thread and masking tape. The result is a labyrinth of "mines," which, when knocked over, crash on the linoleum floor. The students are brought into the room in "squads" and must make it from one end of the room to the other without tripping a mine. If they do knock over a can, they have "killed" their squad. About half the squads make it through.

If students suspend belief during this exercise, they have some idea of the real terror of combat. So many of them have either romanticized combat or intellectualized war to the point that they have no feeling for soldiers or their experiences. "The Minefield" has an impact on students.

Afterward, students write about and discuss issues. "The minefield . . . really made you put yourself in those men's shoes. You could understand what was really going on in their minds. I'm sure they must have been terrified all the time. And you really have to rely on all the other people to do their job, or your own life could be at stake. . . . People need to be reminded about war and all the things involved with it so they will make sure it will never happen again."

The centerpiece of the unit is the two novels I use, *In Country*, by Bobbie Ann Mason and *If I Die in a Combat Zone, Box Me Up and Ship Me Home*, by Tim O'Brien. Students select one to read. *In Country* tells the story of Sam Hughes, a teenage girl whose father was killed in Vietnam before she was born. She lives with her uncle, a Vietnam vet, and worries about his aimlessness and his poor health due to possible Agent Orange exposure. She seeks her own identity by trying to understand her father's Vietnam experience. The novel begins and ends at the Wall, as Sam and her uncle come to terms with the war that has been with them for so long. *If I Die In a Combat Zone* is a personal narrative written in a journalism style. The author describes his induction, struggle between his antiwar beliefs and his sense of duty, experiences in combat, and almost surrealistic journey home. The book depicts the ambiguity and complexity of the war.

I developed brief questions for each book. Students must keep a double-entry (dialectic) journal, and there is a group collaboration on a graphic depicting the theme of the novel. There are many other novels and personal narratives that are usable at the high school level; I have included them in a bibliography at the end of this article.

My students also read short stories and poetry. One excellent source of short works is *Lessons of the Vietnam War*, a modular textbook published and distributed by the Center for Social Studies Education. The collection contains 13 units, which can be bought individually, and one chapter alone is dedicated to "The Literature of the Vietnam War." Poems and other short works (such as excerpts from diaries and letters) are also interspersed throughout the entire textbook. Short story writers whose material is especially usable in high school are Tim O'Brien, Larry Rottman, Tobias Wolff, and Robin Moore. Poets to look for are William Ehrhardt, John Balaban, Larry Rottman, Bryan Alec Floyd, and Wendy Wilder Larsen and Tran Thi Nga in their collaborative poetry anthology, *Shallow Graves*. The film (available in video) and the book *"Dear America: Letters Home from Vietnam"* move students once again to look at the individual soldier, nurse, Red Cross worker, or girlfriend at home. The power of everyday language in their letters personalizes the legacy of the war and helps students understand the curious melange of courage and dishonor, confusion and sense of purpose, altruism and arrogance, that prevailed at the time. These short pieces from "real people" do more to demystify life in a combat zone than even the best history text or lecture.

There are many excellent oral history collections on the Vietnam War. Many are quite specialized, containing interviews with such specific groups as black veterans (*Bloods*), women who served in Vietnam (*Piece of My Heart* and *In a Combat Zone*), and midwestern veterans (*Vietnam: The Heartland Remembers*). After reading selected oral history interviews and analyzing the techniques of questioning needed to elicit good responses, my students interview veterans and transcribe the oral histories for a class collection. The impact of these interviews has been electric. Some interviewed their fathers, who in some cases had never discussed their war experiences. Others interviewed a person at a nearby Vet Center. I put the collection of transcribed interviews in a binder, and it was passed around the classroom and read with great interest. The interviews stand collectively as a call for peace. One vet said it all: " . . . I hope that by the time your kids have a say-so in the world, all this will be done with."

In the novel *Buffalo Afternoon*, by Susan Fromberg Schaeffer (1989), the central character, Pete, begins to keep a journal of his dreams and visions. He starts reading again, whereas at his lowest point he could not. He makes true human contact for the first time in years by talking—first to other vets, then to a counselor, next with a woman who will accept him, and finally with the next generation. At the end of the novel, Pete meets the ghost of his dead grandfather, who gives him a slender white box containing hundreds and thousands of small pieces of paper, each with a tiny black mark on them. His grandfather explains, "I'm giving you back the words you had as a child. Now you won't have to play things out. If you're angry, you don't have to hit the wall. You have the words. If you love something, you don't have to touch it or see it. You have the words. You can't lose anything anymore. You have the words" (p. 520). By giving students "the words" of the Vietnam experience, they are empowered to be peacemakers.

→ See: Robb, p. 198; Senger and Archer, p. 192.

Reference
Schaeffer, S. F. 1989. *Buffalo afternoon*. New York: Alfred A. Knopf.*

Bibliography of Books About Vietnam
The works cited below are specifically usable (in whole or in part) in the high school classroom. Those marked with an asterisk should be examined for possible problems caused by language or content.

Bloods: An Oral History of the Vietnam War by Blacks, by Wallace Terry (New York: Ballantine, 1985)

Born on the Fourth of July, by Ron Kovic (New York: Pocket Books, 1989)*

Dear America: Letters Home from Vietnam, edited by Bernard Edelman (New York: Pocket Books, 1987)

Dispatches, by Michael Herr (New York: Avon, 1978)*

Everything We Had: An Oral History of the Vietnam War, by Al Santoli (New York: Ballantine, 1985)

Fallen Angels, by Walter D. Myers (New York: Scholastic, 1989)*

Going After Cacciato, by Tim O'Brien (New York: Dell, 1987)*

If I Die in a Combat Zone, Box Me Up and Ship Me Home, by Tim O'Brien (New York: Dell, 1987)*

In Country, by Bobbie Ann Mason (New York: Harper & Row, 1989)*

In the Combat Zone: Vivid Personal Recollections of the Vietnam War from the Women Who Served There, by Kathryn Marshall (New York: Penguin, 1988)

Lessons of the Vietnam War: A Modular Textbook, edited by Jerold Starr (Pittsburgh, PA: Center for Social Studies Education, 1988)

Nam, by Mark Baker (New York: Berkley, 1987)

Piece of My Heart, by Keith Walker (New York: Ballantine, 1987)

Rumor of War, by Philip Caputo (New York: Ballantine, 1987)

Shallow Graves: Two Women and Vietnam, by Wendy Wilder Larsen and Tran Thi Nga (New York: Harper & Row, 1987)

Shrapnel in the Heart, by Laura Palmer (New York: Random House, 1988)

To Bear Any Burden, by Al Santoli (New York: Ballantine, 1986)

Touring Nam: The Vietnam War Reader, edited by Martin H. Greenberg and Augustus R. Norton (New York: Bantam, 1989)

Vietnam Anthology: American War Literature, edited by Nancy Anisfield (Bowling Green, OH: Bowling Green State University Press, 1987)

Vietnam: The Heartland Remembers, by Stanley W. Beesley (Norman, OK: University of Oklahoma Press, 1987)

When Heaven and Earth Changed Places: A Vietnam Woman's Journey from War to Peace, by Le Ly Hayslip and Jay Wurts (New York: Doubleday, 1989)

Candy Heinsen Carter is a secondary teacher at Tahoe Truckee High School, Truckee, CA.

Resource: Organization

American Forum for Global Education

45 John St., Ste. 1200
New York, NY 10038
1-212-732-8606
The American Forum for Global Education is the result of a merger of Global Perspectives in Education and The National Council on Foreign Language and International Studies. They provide consulting services, and a newsletter called *Access* ($25/year). They also have a catalog available with such resources as the *New Global Yellow Pages* and *Short Stories from Around the World: A Guide for Language Arts and Social Studies Teachers.*

Cynthia McDermott

Resource: Periodical

Skipping Stones: A Multi-ethnic Children's Forum

$15/year (4 issues) from:
80574 Hazelton Rd.
Cottage Grove, OR 97424
1-503-942-9434
Skipping Stones is an extraordinary multicultural quarterly journal for children that has featured India, Ethiopia, Nepal, the USSR, and Latin America. It includes striking black-and-white photographs of children from around the world, and the text, written and illustrated by children and adults, appears in the language of the authors. An English translation is provided. The editors suggest that students read the journal together, guess the meanings of words, compare the language of the text to the language of the readers, and explore cultures. A visual and literary delight, *Skipping Stones* links the hearts and minds of children from around the world.

YMG and LBB

Resource: Organization

Global Education Motivators

Chestnut Hill College
Germantown and Northwestern Aves.
Chestnut Hill, PA 19118-2695
1-215-248-1150

Global Education Motivators is an interesting group that uses a variety of media, such as videos and computers, to help people learn about the world they live in. At the yearly subscription rate of $400, they provide access to data bases such as UNISER, which contains daily press releases, speeches, and information about the United Nations.

Cynthia McDermott

Resource: Organization

Global Education Associates

475 Riverside Dr., Ste. 570
New York, NY 10115
1-212-870-3290/3291
Global Education Associates publishes a hefty, quarterly information journal called *Breakthrough.* Although fairly advanced for many school-age children, it has the potential of being an excellent resource for the classroom. The association is an international network of people who work to advance world peace by conducting research and educational programs. In addition to the magazine, they produce other resource materials, such as books, filmstrips, and audio and videocassettes.

Cynthia McDermott

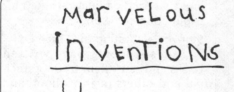

writers

Spring
by Hang Nguyen

Every morning of spring, when the sun is
  coming up,
a crowd of flowers bloom,
opening their pretty eyes.
Birds are singing.
All carry me to my dear country.
Remembering all the things I miss.
What a beautiful morning!
And all the garden is filled with long green grass
  and roses and flowers.
Flowers are a gift of love for friends.
They are the background of love.
But sometimes they carry a heart broken,
  a reminder of a lost land.

➜ See: Treasures, p. 162.

From *Treasures 2: Stories & Art by Students in Oregon,* comp. by Chris Weber (Portland, OR: Oregon Students Writing and Art Foundation, 1988).

Hang Nguyen lives in Portland, OR, and was 11 years old when this poem was written.

YOUNG ARTISTS

"Planting Rice"—Cam Luong Hua, 15, Gresham, OR

writers

Boats
by Chau Vu

I don't think you understand—
All the time people talk about boats.
It reminds me about the awful night
We got in the center of the ocean.
It was a darkness night.
It was a scary night.
A killing night.
A missing person night.
It was a most terrible night I ever had.
That night I almost went crazy.
People remind me about the boat—
I try to forget that night
But I can't.

➜ See: Treasures, p. 162.

From *Treasures 2: Stories & Art by Students in Oregon,* comp. by Chris Weber (Portland, OR: Oregon Students Writing and Art Foundation, 1988).

Chau Vu lives in Portland, OR, and was 16 years old when this poem was written.

Shea Shocat is a 6-year-old living in Tucson, AZ.

—Contributed by Joel Brown and Gene Hanson

"Veteran"—Diana Peterson, 17, Enterprise, OR
(from *Treasures 2,* see p. 162)

Language Stories

Joyful Literacy

I walked into a whole language primary class and asked the kids, "Are you going to have fun in here today?"

"Yes!" was their enthusiastic response. "We're going to do lots of reading and lots of writing!"

—*YMG*

Cornerstone: Yvonne S. Freeman & Bobbi Jentes Mason

Organizing Units Around Powerful Contrasts, Concepts, and Content

One of the most difficult aspects of developing thematic units is building in choice and drawing on students' background knowledge and interests. It is also difficult to do long-term planning that does not consist of lists of activities that have no discernible connections. As we worked with teachers to help them develop meaningful integrated units, we looked for other ways to organize long-term plans. After reading Kieran Egan's book, *Teaching as Story Telling: An Alternative Approach to Teaching and Curriculum in the Elementary School*, we became intrigued with the idea of binary opposites. Egan believes that students of all ages are able to explore deep issues and values and that one way to do this is to look at the contrasts within a theme.

Drawing on what we believe about whole language and learning, we took the idea of contrasts and tried to give teachers a way to conceptualize units that would challenge students and capitalize on their interests. The following chart shows how teachers might go about organizing units using contrasts, concepts, and content:

Step 1: Identifying the Three C's: Contrasts, Concepts, Content

What is most important about them?

Why should they matter to students?

How can we "hook students in"?

Step 2: Finding Contrasts

What powerful contrasts develop the concepts?

   Freedom/Tyranny

   Inequality/Freedom

   Reality/Fantasy

   Knowledge/Ignorance

   Civilization/Barbarism

   Change/Stability

   Good and Poor Uses of Time

   Positive and Negative Changes

Step 3: Organizing Content Around Contrasts

What content supports the concepts and contrasts?

What activities give students the chance for choices/ownership in developing the theme?

Step 4: Celebrating the Three C's

What kind of culminating activities demonstrate depth of students' understanding of the contrasts, concepts, and content?

An example of what one teacher is trying to do might help explain this chart. In his combined bilingual first- and second-grade classroom, Sam decided to move from fragmenting content areas to integrating his curriculum.

Step 1: Identifying the Three C's

Sam decided city and country would be an appropriate contrast theme for his classroom. Though we live in Fresno, a city, many of the students are migrant children whose parents work on farms. There are also children in the class who have lived in the city all their lives. Sam began the unit by reading *El campo* (The country)

Yvonne (Bonnie) S. Freeman is the director of Bilingual Education and the co-director of Language Development at Fresno Pacific College in Fresno, California. She has presented at local, state, and national conferences and worked with teachers in school districts in several states. She also works with Hispanic parents helping them to see the important roles they have in their children's school success.

Bobbi Jentes Mason has spent over 15 years helping junior high and high school students develop effective reading and study strategies. She has presented these strategies to teachers throughout California and to business professionals as well. She presently teaches at Fresno Pacific College in Fresno, California, where she specializes in working with underprepared college freshmen and preservice high school content area teachers. Her special interest is applying whole language at the secondary level in all the content areas.

and *La ciudad* (The city) by María Rius and Josep M. Parramón (1987). He asked children to tell all that they noticed in the books. This led to lively discussions in both Spanish and English on what they had seen and experienced. Other literature stories that related to city and country were also read in both languages, and poems and songs were chanted and sung.

Step 2: Finding Contrasts

Sam attached butcher paper on a wall and had students list contrasting characteristics of the city and the country. Students then brainstormed other contrasts: the advantages and disadvantages of living in the city and the country, and the effects of the city's pollution and water waste on the country.

Step 3: Organizing Content Around Contrasts

Sam did several things to bring the content areas into the unit on contrasts. For example, he did map work with the students. He made a huge atlas of the world available. Small groups would take the atlas and point out things they discovered on their own. They studied the markings for cities and rivers. Several children became interested in the symbols for airports and parks.

Sam had the students tour the school and draw maps of it. He also had them draw maps of their neighborhood and of Fresno itself. They discussed stores and shopping, including the advantages and disadvantages of shopping at certain places. Sam found that there are many possible directions for social studies, math, art, and music and that each day new avenues for exploration come up.

Step 4: Celebrating the Three C's

Sam's students have written books and sent them to the principal and others in the school, and written about what they are learning in pen pal letters to teacher education students at a nearby college. They took field trips to several shopping centers in town, drew maps of what they saw, and wrote about their experiences.

Other Teachers Use Contrasts

Valerie, an eighth-grade teacher, decided that working on the contrasts of prejudice and tolerance would provide the framework for discussing slavery in American history. The students read different pieces of literature about slavery, and then compared and contrasted prejudice and tolerance in the past and present. Contrasts have provided a base for exploring different topics in her curriculum.

At the graduate level Bobbi, in her Content Area Reading/Writing course, helped teachers explore a theme together using contrast. She had them look at technology and determine whether it has affected our culture negatively or positively. Students brought newspaper and magazine articles relating to the theme for a weekly class discussion. Students then chose topics that interested them, such as computer dating, stomach stapling, and fax machines.

At different levels, the idea of contrasts has challenged teachers and students to explore content and concepts in new ways.

➜ See: Freeman, p. 87, 184, 189, 212, 368; Literature Reference List, p. 429.

References

Egan, K. 1986. *Teaching as story telling: An alternative approach to teaching and curriculum in the elementary school.* London, Ontario: Althouse Press, University of Western Ontario.

Rius, M., and J. M. Parramón. 1987. *El campo.* Woodbury, NY: Barron's Educational Series.

———. 1987. *La ciudad.* Woodbury, NY: Barron's Educational Series.

📷 WHOLE LANGUAGE CAMERA

Two students in Anne Henderson and Elizabeth Walen's kindergarten use an old-fashioned apple press to make cider. (See Henderson and Walen, p. 301)

Resource: Book

Learning and Loving It: Theme Studies in the Classroom

Ruth Gamberg, Winniefred Kwak, Meredith Hutchings, and Judy Altheim with Gail Edwards
1988; 256 pp.; $17.50
Portsmouth, NH: Heinemann

After constructing a seven by five foot playhouse on the playground, a class of 6-, 7-, and 8-year olds at the award-winning University of Dalhousie School in Nova Scotia turned enthusiastically to a theme study on "Houses of the World." Weeks of brainstorming research questions, researching a variety of reference materials, and categorizing and charting the information led to the construction of accurately detailed models. As a culmination of the study, the models were displayed along with descriptive student-written books and posters at a fair to which parents and friends were invited. The proud researchers stood by their displays, explaining what they had learned to the interested visitors. This theme study, one of six which are described in inspiring detail, help readers understand the critical difference between a traditional thematic unit with paste-on activities and a core-of-the-curriculum theme study from which flows multiple opportunities for authentic reading, writing, researching and presenting. This is a book I wouldn't want to be without.

LBB

➜ See: Manicom, p 384.

Cornerstone: Bess Altwerger and Barbara Flores

The Theme Cycle: An Overview

The theme cycle is an approach to the study of content that is consistent with the theory and practice of whole language. It differs sharply from the more traditional thematic unit or integrated curriculum in a number of fundamental ways. (See table below.) Students are fully involved in developing the themes, and therefore negotiate topics, engage in problem-posing, and learn how to participate in critical inquiry. In a theme cycle study, topics are not exploited for the purpose of fulfilling literacy and subject area objectives (as in more traditional themes). Rather, oral and written language, as well as the various content fields, are regarded as vehicles for studying and researching the topic. The theme cycle leads to authentic uses of literacy, genuine learning experiences (instead of superficial activities), and student-teacher collaboration.

Theme Units Versus Theme Cycles

Theme Unit	Theme Cycle
Teacher-oriented, predetermined	Student-oriented, topic negotiated
Teacher responsible for planning, organizing, materials	Student and teacher share responsibility
Based on teacher's learning goals	Based on students' and teacher's knowledge, questions, interests
Theme used as tool for learning subject areas, reading, writing	Subject areas, reading, writing used as tools for learning
Activities are focus	Learning process, critical thinking, problem-solving are focus

From this perspective, topic study takes the form of a cycle in which learning issues, problems, and questions lead to learning experiences and literacy uses. Initial questions are answered and problems solved, and new learning issues, problems, and questions are posed, leading to further learning. (See rectangles in figure below.) This cycle is actualized in the classroom through (1) negotiating topics, webbing known information, and posing issues and questions for study; (2) collaboratively planning appropriate experiences, finding resources, and developing an organization for the study; (3) identifying functional and purposeful literacy uses related to the learning experiences; (4) reflecting upon and sharing new knowledge; and (5) evaluating learning, and posing new topics and questions for study (see ovals in figure).

The theme cycle is a process that the teacher and students must gradually learn and implement. Teachers must learn to trust students, trade control for collaboration, and resist efforts to plan the theme in advance. Students must learn to trust the teacher as colearner, believe in their own competence as problem-solvers and learners, and resist efforts to take a passive role in the process. The following are guidelines for developing theme cycles:

1. Children and teacher need to be active participants in the joint development of the theme cycle.
2. Children's interests and curiosities need to be incorporated into the selection process.
3. Children and teacher need to share their collective knowledge once the topic has been selected.
4. Questions or learning issues upon which learning experiences or events are based should be collaboratively generated by teachers and students.
5. Activities should be authentic learning experiences that focus on exploring problems and questions.
6. Reading and writing should be used naturally for a variety of purposes and functions in order to facilitate learning.
7. The teacher should serve as a guide and facilitator for developing appropriate social and physical environments for learning.
8. The learning events should naturally incorporate any or all of the subject areas such as math, science, art, music, or social studies.
9. Evaluation of the theme cycle should be in terms of how successfully the theoretical position is actualized into practice, how engaged students were in the process, how many new questions and learning issues the theme generated, and how enthusiastically students approached the next theme.

➜ See: Altwerger, pp. 407, 418; Flores, pp. 218, 412, 418.

Note: Charts and graphs in this article appear in Edelsky, Altwerger and Flores, *Whole Language: What's the Difference?* (Heinemann, in press).

Bess Altwerger is an associate professor at Towson State University, Baltimore MD.
Barbara Flores is an associate professor at the California State University at San Bernardino.

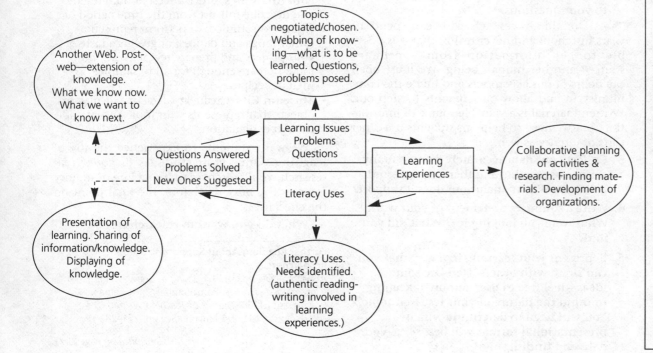

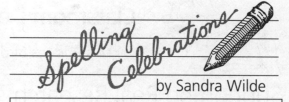

by Sandra Wilde

Patterns and Strategies: Avoiding Hard Words

The mountains USE TO BE volcanoes.

Gordon, 4th grade

Gordon had been reading about Hawaii and decided to write about the intriguing fact that many of the mountains there were once volcanoes. He was temporarily stumped when he couldn't figure out how to spell *used to be,* and considered writing, "The mountains were volcanoes a long time ago but they aren't now." Finally, with the help of the dictionary, he came up with a spelling that made sense to him.

Gordon was a confident speller who recognized how silly it would be to write a much longer and more convoluted sentence just because he didn't know how to spell a word. Yet consider all the children in classrooms who are expected to use only correct spellings when they write. Children will consult resources like the dictionary and other people comfortably when it's a matter of choice, but if they feel they need to do so for every word they don't know, they'll begin limiting their expression to words they do know how to spell. Wouldn't you?

I Used to Be...But Now I...

I used to set the curriculum,
But now the students' needs and interests dictate it.

—*Barbara Reid*

Resource: Book

The Pocket Book: Integrating the Primary Curriculum Through Themes

Lynn Taylor and David Cooper
$66; assorted individual theme packets $6 each from:
P.O. Box 3143
Livermore, CA 94550
1-415-373-7390

Although whole language educators often explore serious social issues with their students, they may still find a place in their curriculum for more lighthearted subjects such as those available in *The Pocket Book*—a big looseleaf notebook divided into six primary themes. Within each theme, the authors have collected a delightful array of songs, stories, and poetry plus a variety of activities across the content areas. The book also includes patterns for special shape books, board games, flannel board stories, and puppets. Primary teachers new to whole language will find the organizational format helpful, and may use *The Pocket Book* as a point of departure for creating their own thematic units.

LBB

Classroom Demonstrations

by Lois Bridges Bird

Supporting Real Research

As I recall my school experiences from elementary to junior high, it was always just before spring vacation when we were assigned the dreaded annual research report. I would worry about it all week long, and then on the Sunday night before we had to go back to school, I'd look up my assigned topic in the encyclopedia and attempt to rewrite the information in my own words. I thought that this was true research; no teacher told me otherwise. Often in conjunction with the assignment, we were handed a list of directions, which we were to use as a guide. There was never anything on the list about exploring our own ideas or pursuing any real questions we might have. The emphasis was always on the form of the research report; I remember feeling anxious lest I misnumber my outline, or incorrectly insert my footnotes. My bibliography rarely consisted of more than two sources from the family library: *The World Book* and *The Golden Book* encyclopedias. Sometimes the teacher would take us to the school library and give us 20 minutes to find one reference book related to our topic.

Sadly, this sterile textbook version of research doesn't begin to match the way real research is conducted. Real researchers are driven by a passionate desire to learn; they've stumbled across a puzzle, and they can hardly sleep until they've solved it (whereas students struggling with the traditional research paper often have trouble staying awake). And though real researchers certainly spend time in the library and read everything they can get their hands on related to their topic, including newspapers, magazines, journals from historical archives, and so on, they also talk to people who might know something about their chosen topic. Real researchers interview, conduct surveys, spend time observing the phenomenon they are researching, and, depending on the nature of the topic, conduct a variety of experiments. There are a lot of ways to find out about things, and real researchers use them all.

If we're really serious about supporting our students as learners and helping them develop the tools for exploring the world on their own, we should abandon the contrived textbook version of research and take our cues from the professionals. The first order of business is letting kids choose their own topics. As Donald Graves asks: On what topics do they wish to become expert? Or to put it more dramatically, what wakes them up at three in the morning with the intrigue of the unknown? We have to accept, of course, that what intrigues them may be very different from what piques our interest. Fifth-grade teacher Leslie Mangiola, who routinely allows kids to pursue their own research interests, has had reports on everything from poisonous snakes to how rock star promoters work. The "what" of what is studied is often less important than the "how" of the research process. That's not to say that there aren't specific facts that we want our students to know, nor that we mustn't ever assign a topic; but in general kids learn the research process best by exploring topics that they choose themselves. Personal inquiry leads to more formal academic searches.

We must also understand that students cannot absorb the skills of a researcher through osmosis; these skills develop over time with practice and careful guidance from us. Fifth-grade teacher Betty Doerr leads her class through a group research project first before guiding her students through their own individual or small group projects. Beginning each research session with a mini-lesson on some aspect of the research process, she demonstrates on an overhead projector how to use learning logs to spark and expand thinking, how to skim material and take notes, how to ask effective interview questions, and so on. In this way she prepares her students to use basic research strategies on their own.

Bringing real researchers into the classroom to talk about their work provides students with an exciting firsthand look into the world of research. First- and second-grade teacher Cathy Howard invited my husband, Dennis, a geochemist who spends summers in Arctic Greenland exploring continental rifting, to talk to her class about how he conducts research: He brought in some of his tools, including his rock hammer, compass, and map book. Students must learn that researchers use different methods depending on the nature of their research: My father, a historian, spent hours poring over documents in libraries and historical archives. Students must also learn that published research necessarily takes different forms: Dennis's findings often appear as detailed maps and chemical flowcharts; my father's research as narrative and expository prose in books and journal articles. Children can publish their research in a variety of ways depending on their audience and the nature of their topic.

So, to aid my students as they pursue their research interests, I would give them a checklist, very different from the kind I received as a student, and I would serve as their diligent guide in the exciting process of learning and discovery.

1. **Once you have chosen your research topic, list everything you know about your topic. Then list everything you don't know and formulate a list of questions to which you would like to find answers. Review the questions, drop the ones that don't fit, clarify the ones that do.**

   In this way students learn how to narrow a topic and learn what kinds of questions relate to each other. Knowing how to ask the right question is just as important as finding the answer. Kids need to discover what questions are appropriate for the kind of research they want to do. And as they become involved in their research, they will discover that some questions are more effective than others.

2. **Brainstorm ways you can find the answers to your questions.**

   As Donald Graves says, kids can spend 12 years in school and never realize that it is possible to get information from a primary source—another human being. We must open the doors of our classrooms and invite the community in and allow our students to step out. Written material is a valuable source of information, but we need to help our students use other sorts of inquiry as well.

3. **Collect your data accurately from as many sources as possible and then organize and collate it. What conclusions does it support?**

4. **Write a summary statement of your work: What were you looking for? What did you find?**

5. **Represent your learning in a way that you can share with others. Here are some ideas—feel free to use your own, keeping in mind the nature of your research topic. You will need to determine which presentational format will best serve your data and findings.**

Learning how to transfer information from one format to another as they represent their learning to themselves and to others is invaluable as is the process they need to engage in as they determine which format is appropriate for their data and findings. These suggestions may be adapted to various grade levels.

- **Letters to the Editor.** If you have some new information or have developed a unique perspective on a particular issue that you would like to share with the public, consider writing to the editor of your local newspaper or to the editor of an appropriate magazine or journal. Explain what you did and what you found and why you have assumed your particular stance.

- **Poster Sessions, Bulletin Board.** Create a poster or bulletin board display with headlines and captions, charts, diagrams, and so on, and explain it to the class. Be prepared to answer questions.

- **Scrapbook or Photo Album.** Arrange your notes, pictures, graphs, or articles in a scrapbook or photo album and write a description of your research process and findings.

- **Oral Histories and Interviews.** In keeping with the Foxfire tradition, transcribe tapes from your interviews and present with photographs, artwork, artifacts, and background information.

- **Newspaper.** Do an edition that is related to a historical time period—every article, editorial, advertisement, and so on should reflect the time period you studied.

- **Surveys, Interviews, Questionnaires.** Design tools for collecting further information.

- **Slide or Video Presentation.** Represent your findings through a video or slide presentation. Write an accompanying script.

- **Debate or Panel Discussion.** If you worked with a partner or as part of a group, and you reached different conclusions, present and debate your different positions. Or present your findings as a panel; be prepared to field questions from the audience. One member should serve as the moderator.

- **Models and Maps.** Life size or to scale, cross-sections, dioramas, shadow boxes, mobiles; relief; trace routes on road maps.

- **Diagrams, Tables, Graphs, Flowcharts, Time Lines.** Chart the sequential steps involved in making something; if you conducted an experiment, the steps you followed; or represent the chronology of a historical event you studied. Can also capture this information in a how-to book, written so someone else can follow your procedure.

- **Role-playing, Socio-Drama.** Role-playing is an effective way to present a biography; try socio-drama for a dramatic presentation of a historical or current sociopolitical event.

- **Folk Art, Songs and Dances, Food.** Present and describe folk art from the time period or region you studied; or perform representational songs and dances; or give us a taste of your project and prepare regional or ethnic food; prepare enough for all to sample! Include recipes.

- **Museum Kits.** Create an attractive display of objects that represents your topic and provide written explanations.

We want students to experience the joy of learning. Once your students discover real research, you'll discover that one line of inquiry leads to the next. Therefore, the final point on the checklist is:

6. **What do you want to research next?**

Further Readiing About Supporting Student Researchers
Atwell, Nancie, ed. 1989. *Coming to Know: Writing in the Intermediate Grades.* Portsmouth, NH: Heinemann.
Calkins, Lucy. 1986. *The Art of Teaching Writing.* Portsmouth, NH: Heinemann. (See pp. 271–283.)

(Continued on page 297)

(Continued from page 296)

Gamberg, Ruth, Winniefred Kwak, Meredith Hutchings, and Judy Altheim, with Gail Edwards. 1988. *Learning and Loving It: Theme Studies in the Classroom.* Portsmouth, NH: Heinemann.

Goodman, Kenneth S., E. Brooks Smith, Robert Meredith, and Yetta M. Goodman. 1987. *Learning and Thinking in Schools.* Katonah, NY: Richard C. Owen.

Graves, Donald. 1983. *Writing: Teachers and Children at Work.* Portsmouth, NH: Heinemann.

———. 1989. *Investigate Nonfiction.* Portsmouth, NH: Heinemann.

Martin, Nancy, ed. 1984. *Writing Across the Curriculum Pamphlets.* Portsmouth, NH: Heinemann.

Martin, Nancy, et al. 1976. *Writing and Learning Across the Curriculum 11–16.* Portsmouth, NH: Heinemann.

Mayher John S., Nancy B. Lester, and Gordon M. Pradl. 1983. *Learning to Write, Writing to Learn.* Portsmouth, NH: Boynton/Cook.

📷 **WHOLE LANGUAGE CAMERA**

Jane, a fifth-grader in Cynthia Motsinger's class, cooks on her homemade stove as part of a science experiment involving alternative fuels, San Ramon Elementary School, Novato, CA.

Classroom Demonstrations
by Cindy Elliot

Thematic Journals

I have found thematic journals useful in providing an opportunity for writing in the science center. Working like real scientists, students use a hands-on approach to discovery by observing, questioning, classifying, and predicting. The science journal focuses on the topic we are currently investigating. Students use the process skills in exploring and write their thoughts in the journal. With my first-graders, we make a class science journal by compiling our individual writings on a daily basis. *The Hamster, The Beta Fish, Mealworms,* and *Caterpillars, Chrysalises,* and *Butterflies* are examples of the science thematic journals we've made.

The only rule for this journal is that each time a student writes an entry it should be dated.

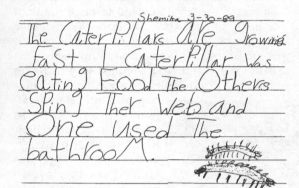

📷 **WHOLE LANGUAGE CAMERA**

Entering a new world…a first-grader peers into a microscope.

Caterpillars and Butterflies

I like to look at caterpillars.
I see them in the spring.
Most of them are fun to play with.
But some of them can sting
Caterpillars do not spin cocoons
I really don't know why
Instead they spin a chrysalis.
Then they become a butterfly.
Butterflies fly around flowers.
Butterflies fly around trees.
I think butterflies are beautiful.
Don't you agree with me?

by Kacee

Cindy Elliot is a primary teacher at Audubon Elementary School, Baton Rouge, LA.

Book Note

Coming to Know: Writing to Learn in the Intermediate Grades

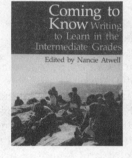

Nancie Atwell, editor
1989; 248 pp.; $16
Portsmouth, NH: Heinemann

Anything written or edited by Nancie Atwell is well worth owning, and this book is no exception. Fourteen classroom teachers detail the strategies and materials they use to support their students' research across the curriculum. Includes four valuable appendices: a list of different genres kids can explore for research publishing, guiding questions for learning logs, lists of thematically related, fiction and nonfiction books and professional and commercial resources for both teachers and students that support reading and writing to learn.

LBB

❝ In the best of all possible worlds, language study might no longer be isolated as a separate subject in our curricula. Writing and reading workshop would become redundant because students and teachers would be writing and reading everything all day long: poems, plays, stories, essays, lists, articles, autobiographical sketches, and journals about math, literature, history, the sciences, *life.* In the best of all possible worlds, teachers of all subjects might become not English teachers but experts about the processes of reading and writing, about literature appropriate to the various disciplines, and about students—who they are, what they can do, what they know and need to know. Then the child's day might become a *learning* workshop in which writing and reading are learned in the richest possible context and appreciated as tools of the highest quality for helping children come to know about the world. ❞ (p. *xxi*)

Marvelous Inventions

Keegan, a 6-year old researcher in Beth Huntzinger's first grade, created this semantic map to represent his study of the fox.

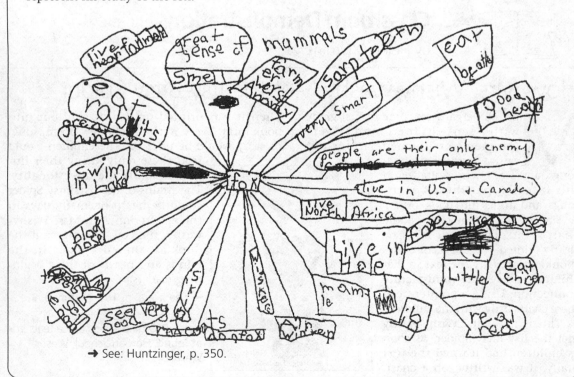

➜ See: Huntzinger, p. 350.

Literature

 Viewpoint: Patricia Beatty

My Life with a Capital "E"

"**E**" stands for "education" because this is what my life has been for the most part, a continual progression of being educated and educating in one fashion or another—first as a student, then as a teacher, and now as a writer.

My own education has been quite strange for one Oregon-born in 1922, and therefore a 20th-century person. By the time I was 22 I had run the absolute gamut of available public educational institutions from the Abe Lincoln-type one-room cabin school for grades one through eight to what was and probably still is the most academically rigorous private liberal arts college on the West Coast, Reed College in Portland, Oregon, from which I graduated in 1944. Between these educational polarities I attended a typical small-town elementary school in Washington State, an elementary school in a tiny hamlet in Oregon, another country school to which I was "bused" 40 miles a day, a big-city junior high school, and a very large urban high school that quite confounded me by its frightening size and brutal social distinctions.

How did I happen to have such an unusual educational career? My father's unusual occupation. He was a U.S. Coast Guard officer stationed in very out-of-the-way places on the ocean or navigable rivers. I'd lived in Coast Guard stations on three Indian reservations in two states by the time I was 13. Though the school for Indian children was but a stone's throw from the Quileute River Station, as a white child I could not go there. I had to walk a mile to that one-room cabin school off the reservation.

All this varied experience made me a careful observer, I like to think, of schools, teaching, and teachers. It led me in the 1940s to becoming a teacher—to get on the other side of the desk, that is. I taught English and American history for five years in Oregon and Idaho high schools. In the 1950s I worked in university and public libraries first as a clerk, then as a librarian, though my credential was in teaching.

I had not planned to become a writer. I fell into that career via boredom with a library job where I sat expectantly waiting for scientific reference questions that seldom came my way. In 1960 I decided to write a book for children about the Quileute Indians. To my joy and amazement I sold it at once. Since then I have written and coauthored 48 more books for young readers, and have won 14 prizes for specific books.

Where does this imagination come from? How can a person who never entered a public library until she was 13 get such a burning passion for the writing of book after book? From other books! I was a ferocious reader from the first grade on. I still am. I average three books a week, big ones. My mother purchased books for us to read on our isolated reservations. By the time I was 11, I had read all of Victor Hugo's works at home as well as the Bible. I read everything from cereal-box labels to *True Confessions*.

In school I read my textbooks, of course, but found those weak fare for a word-hungry child. I recall a steady diet of "he said," "she said," dull child characters with dull parents, and a very dull dog. What I liked best about my classroom

elementary readers each September was their sharp scent of newness and the sleekness of their pages but not their contents. I cannot remember a single story from my readers from those late 1920s and early 1930s days, though I do recall one teacher reading aloud from children's literature classics to a rapt audience as a "treat for good behavior."

I well remember at home and classroom readings from the literary classics as a high school student, though. As a major in English history at Reed I read several college-level texts on the Industrial Revolution, but *Silas Marner* from my high school days will never represent that era as Hugo's *Les Miserables* will represent revolutionary mid-19th-century France. Ivanhoe means medieval England to me more than the many other texts I ever read. *Gone with the Wind* is the touchstone of the Civil War—not the movie, but the book I read in my teens.

It is my belief that the best way to bring something to a durable and vivid life is by anecdote and by literary treatment—never by arid paragraphs of facts, lists, historical happenings, and legislative milestones. For the last 30 years I have written historical fiction for the 9- to 14-year old reader. I stress accuracy. I specialize in the Civil War. I write of battles as they were. I describe real people, and if and when they speak, I try to have them say what I am sure they would have said in the 1860s. I append author's notes to each book to distinguish fact from fiction.

Some reviewers have accused me of the "sin of educating" while I write fiction. I do that. I know that what I write will often be the only material a child will ever read or have read to him or her about that particular era or person. That's a responsibility for me!

I try to write books a word-hungry, knowledge-hungry child can sink his or her teeth into and come away with something to stick in the memory as part of mental provender for a lifetime. I think children deserve meat in their readers, not watered-down, written-to-a-word-list gruel. I use large words and I define them in the text.

What else can I say of myself? In the late 1960s I taught creative writing at the University of California, Los Angeles, and the University of California at Riverside, where I still live today.

My husband and I still read aloud one hour per night—mostly social history, classic literature, and biography. Together we have studied the Russian language for nine years. Embarking on this was an experiment to learn if aging minds can learn not only a new language but a new alphabet. Reading our first Chekhov play in the original tongue proved this to be possible. And to me Chekhov's ineffectual characters will always be the distillation of Russia's prerevolutionary bourgeoisie I could savor in one play but never in a stack of pure sociological histories. We are still "learning," and living with a capital "E."

→ See: Huck, p. 188; Larrick, p. 173; Literature Reference List, p. 429.

A sampling of the many books by Patricia Beatty

- ◆ *At the Seven Stars,* with J. L. Beatty. Macmillan,1963.
- ◆ *The Nickel-Plated Beauty.* Morrow, 1964.
- ◆ *Campion Towers,* with J. L. Beatty. Macmillan, 1965.
- ◆ *Hail Columbia.* Morrow, 1970.
- ◆ *A Long Way to Whiskey Creek.* Morrow, 1971.
- ◆ *Holdfast,* with J. L. Beatty. Morrow, 1972.
- ◆ *Lupita Mañana.* Morrow, 1981.
- ◆ *Turn Homeward Hannalee.* Morrow, 1984.
- ◆ *Charley Skedaddle.* Morrow, 1987.
- ◆ *Eben Tyne, Powdermonkey,* with Col. P. Robbins, USA. Morrow, 1990.

 **WHOLE LANGUAGE CAMERA**

A boy and a book, Palo Alto, CA

 **Classroom Demonstrations**
by Helen D'Ordine

How Mrs. Wishy-washy Met the Itsy-Bitsy Spider

Most kindergartners come to first grade with a sense of the sound system (phoneme-grapheme relationship) and a love of poems, songs, and stories. To capitalize on this interest, put these poems, songs, and stories into book form.

Start by using large charts and a chart stand. The words must be clearly printed. A lot of picture cues should accompany the text so that children can see the word-picture connection. Using a pointer, read these charts daily with the children.

This is how Mrs. Wishy-washy met the Itsy-Bitsy Spider. As soon as children had learned the text orally, it was written on a chart.

A read-together book

Then it was printed on a ditto and put into book form. Every week or so a new poem, song, or story would be inserted. The children would read these daily, using their fingers to show the directionality. The strains of the Itsy-Bitsy Spider could be heard on many days in the classroom. And Mrs. Wishy-washy, the cow, the pig, and the duck all shared a place in the minds and hearts of these beginning readers.

→ See: Hara, p. 105; Martin, p. 96.

Helen D'Ordine is a resource teacher at John F. Horgan School, West Warwick, RI.

Classroom Demonstrations

Thematic Teaching through Books: A Sampling

Recommended by Melissa Cain

Here is a sampling of the ways in which literature can form the heart of a thematic learning experience. Melissa Cain suggests books to develop three units: architecture, dragons, and peace. Mary Kitagawa recommends books for an in-depth study of the Holocaust.

—LBB

Architecture. These books are sure to provoke interest in the built environment.

• *Castle,* by David Macaulay (Boston: Houghton Mifflin, 1977). In this book David Macaulay uses detailed pen-and-ink drawings to show how castles were built. Also of interest are Macaulay's *Cathedral (1973)* and *Unbuilding (1980).*

• *City Safaris: A Sierra Club Explorer's Guide to Urban Adventures for Grownups and Kids,* by Carolyn Shaffer and Erica Fielder (San Francisco: Sierra Club, 1987). This nonfiction book contains a wide variety of activities for urban explorers that can be adapted to any city or town.

• *The House on Maple Street,* by Bonnie Pryor. Illustrated by Beth Peck (New York: William Morrow, 1987). Three hundred years ago, there was no house and no street at 107 Maple Street. This book shows what happened to the site over time and how an arrowhead ended up in a china teacup in the backyard.

• *The Inside-Outside Book of Washington, D. C.,* by Roxie Munro (New York: E. P. Dutton, 1987). Roxie Munro takes her reader on a visual tour of the major buildings in Washington, DC.

• *New Providence: A Changing Cityscape,* by Renata von Tscharner and Ronald Lee Fleming (Washington, DC: Gulliver, 1987). This shows a made-up town, New Providence, as it changes over the decades. Text and illustrations highlight typical architectural elements of the time periods.

• *The Room,* by Mordecai Gerstein (New York: Harper & Row, 1984). This look at a single room over a long period of time invites children to think about what changes might be going on around them over the years.

• *Round Buildings, Square Buildings, & Buildings that Wiggle like a Fish,* by Phillip M. Isaacson (New York: Alfred A. Knopf, 1988). This nonfiction work describes a wide variety of architecture through beautifully textured photographs and an interesting, well-written text.

Dragons. What is more appealing to the imagination than dragons? These books are sure to stimulate writing and drawing projects.

• *The Book of Dragons,* by E. Nesbit (New York: Dell Yearling, 1986). E. Nesbit wrote these wonderful short stories about dragons in the late 1800s; they are as appealing today as they were then.

• *Dragondrums,* by Anne McCaffrey (New York: Atheneum, 1979). This is one of a whole series of dragon-oriented fantasies for grades nine and up.

• *Dragon's Blood,* by Jane Yolen (New York: Delacorte, 1982). This is part of a series for grades seven and up that takes place on another planet where dragons are bred for fighting. Yolen is a masterful storyteller.

• *The Dragons of Blueland,* by Ruth Stiles Gannett. Illustrated by Ruth Chrisman Gannett (New York: Alfred A. Knopf, 1987). Written in 1951, this delightful fantasy makes good reading for younger intermediate readers.

• *Dragon Steel,* by Laurence Yep (New York: Harper & Row, 1985). The sequel to *Dragons of the Lost Sea, Dragon Steel* is a fantasy for ages 12 and up that provokes wonderful images of a strange undersea world.

• *The Secret in the Matchbox,* by Val Willis. Illustrated by John Shelley (New York: Farrar, Straus & Giroux, 1988). No one takes the secret in Bobby's matchbox seriously until the dragon inside it grows to enormous proportions.

• *Sky Dragon,* by Ron Wegen (New York: Greenwillow). This picture storybook encourages children to use their imaginations to find pictures in the clouds.

Peace. As we look to the future, such books as these may shape the way we deal with our problems. They will at least stimulate students to think about and discuss the complex issues related to peace.

• *The Butter Battle Book,* by Dr. Seuss (New York: Random House, 1984). Through the Zooks, who eat their bread with the butter side down, and the Yooks, who eat theirs "the right honest way," Dr. Seuss explores the arms race.

• *Global Rivals,* by Seweryn Bialer and Michael Mandelbaum (New York: Alfred A. Knopf, 1988). This nonfiction book for more sophisticated readers explores the relationship between the Soviet Union and the United States, including current changes.

• *The Gold Cadillac,* by Mildred Taylor. Illustrated by Michael Hays (New York: Dial, 1987). In this short book for intermediate readers, Taylor describes race relations in the 1950s from a black child's perspective. The story is poignant and promotes racial understanding.

• *Potatoes, Potatoes,* by Anita Lobel (New York: Harper & Row, 1967). This picture storybook illustrates a mother who builds a wall around her house to keep out the war that rages around her. Her sons, however, join opposite sides and eventually battle over their mother's potatoes.

• *Voices of Northern Ireland: Growing Up in a Troubled Land,* by Carolyn Meyer (Washington, DC: Gulliver, 1987). When Carolyn Meyer writes nonfiction, she researches, goes to the country, and tries to be as impartial as possible. She has also taken a look at the troubles in South Africa and, in 1988, the culture of Japan. Her books are for ages 12 and up.

➜ See: Cain, pp. 200, 357.

Melissa Cain is the editor of *Perspectives,* a journal published by the University of Toledo, Toledo, OH.

Books on WWII and Holocaust for Upper Elementary and Junior High

Recommended by Mary M. Kitagawa

• *Alan and Naomi,* by Myron Levoy (New York: Harper & Row Junior Books, 1977). Through his friendship, Alan helps Naomi recover from the psychological devastation of seeing her father murdered during the Nazi occupation of France. The story takes place in New York.

• *The Boys Who Saved the Children,* by Margaret Baldwin. This easy-to-read book is about survival in a Polish ghetto.

• *The Devil in Vienna,* by Doris Orgel. This is a story about a friendship between a Jewish girl and a daughter of a storm trooper. Flashbacks make the first half hard to follow.

• *The Devil's Arithmetic,* by Jane Yolen (New York: Viking Kestrel, 1988). In this time-travel book, a modern girl finds herself in a Nazi concentration camp.

• *Diary of Anne Frank,* by Anne Frank. This famous diary describes how a young Dutch girl and her family hid from the Nazis in Holland.

• *Friedrich,* by Hans Peter Richter (New York: Dell, 1970). This largely autobiographical account describes the friendship between two boys in Germany, one Jewish and the other the son of a Nazi Party member.

• *Great Escapes of World War II,* by George Sullivan (New York: Scholastic, 1988). A collection of short stories.

• *I Was There,* by Hans Peter Richter (New York: Holt, Rinehart & Winston, 1972). This fairly hard-to-read account is about a boy involved with Hitler's youth movement.

• *Night,* by Elie Wiesel (New York: Bantam Books, 1983). Written for adults, but not too long or hard to read for adolescents, this graphic account of Wiesel's own experiences in a concentration camp is extremely haunting and thought provoking.

• *Number the Stars,* by Lois Lowry (Boston: Houghton Mifflin, 1989). A Danish family helps Jewish friends escape to Sweden.

• *Promise of a New Spring,* by Gerda Weissmann Klein. A picture book on the Holocaust.

• *Refugee,* by Anne Rose. A Belgian girl is allowed to emigrate to New York before her parents; the rest of the war is seen through her eyes via news and letters from those left behind.

• *The Upstairs Room,* by Joanna Reiss (New York: Thomas Crowell, 1972). This largely autobiographical account (though told in third person) is about a Jewish girl who hides from the Nazis in a Gentile home in Holland. *The Journey Home,* sequel to *The Upstairs Room,* tells the story of readjustment after World War II.

• *When Hitler Stole Pink Rabbit,* by Judith Kerr (New York: Dell, 1971). This largely autobiographical (though told in the third person) account is about a Jewish refugee from Germany living in Switzerland and France.

• *World War II Resistance Stories,* by Arthur Prager and Emily Prager (New York: Watts, 1979). A collection of short stories.

➜ See: Kitagawa, pp. 132, 212, 420.

Mary M. Kitagawa is a junior high teacher at Mark's Meadow School, Amherst, MA.

WHOLE LANGUAGE CAMERA

Cathy Crockett's fourth graders follow the steps for checking books out of their classroom library, Coronado School, Tuscon, AZ.

Classroom Demonstrations

The Media Specialist as a Basketball

by Sharon Wetherell

With a bit of imagination, the media specialist (librarian) can perceive herself as a basketball. To do this, she recognizes that the school is like a well-practiced team, led by a skillful coach (the principal), that uses the media specialist's knowledge, her time, the IMC (library) collection, and the IMC space in a flexible game plan, passing the media specialist from player (teacher) to player, maximizing strengths, scoring frequent three-pointers, and an occasional free throw.

The media specialist knows IMC services extend far beyond the storing and circulating of books and materials. The media specialist allows all students to come to the IMC when they need to and teaches the search skills needed in the context of the regular curriculum and the students' personal needs. She sees the IMC not as a released-time or free-time place but as a vital, functional, active instructional place and set of services.

The media specialist employs a number of strategies to ensure her effectiveness and the effectiveness of the IMC services:

1. The media specialist makes a conscious effort to contact every staff person on a regular basis and keeps a record of these contacts lest anyone be omitted. If teachers do not approach her, she approaches them on "rounds," during which she asks, "What are you working on? How can I help?"

2. The "How can I help?" consultation may result in brainstorming, searches for materials, adapting instructional materials, designing instructional activities, team teaching, class presentations, working with a small group of students, or being prepared for helping individual students as they come into the IMC.

3. The media specialist maintains a basically unscheduled IMC space. Teachers may send students at any time. She encourages "teach-able moment" reference activities and uses those moments to model and teach problem-solving and search strategies. She asks wonderful questions.

4. The media specialist schedules her activities (stories or whole-class instruction) in classrooms, leaving the IMC space available to others. Good communication, a very capable secretary, and the assistance of many staff members make the IMC function without her constant presence.

5. The media specialist is a storyteller rather than a story-reader. Stories have action, props, and participation. Her instruction is organized, varied, and well planned.

6. The media specialist participates in child study teams and mini-staffings that assess the educational needs of all students on an individual basis. She is well suited for this activity as she sees students in a nonclassroom setting on a regular basis.

The media specialist begins each day with a game plan, which is modified by the new interruptions and the creation of an electric learning atmosphere.

Basically, the media specialist practices the philosophy of Peter Drucker: "What can I contribute that, if done well, will make a difference?" When the IMC is a service rather than just a depository for books, the media specialist can contribute much more to the elementary school program. A service style IMC requires greater energy expenditures and creativity on the part of the media specialist, but she can also honestly answer the question "How was your day?" with "I feel like a basketball—passed around, occasionally bounced, and well dribbled, but very seldom deflated."

➜ See: Obringer, p. 179; Yowell, p. 178.

Sharon Wetherell is a media specialist at Johnson Elementary School, Cedar Rapids, IA.

A Book Revolution

by Susan E. Davis

For more than 40 years, scientists and computer specialists have dreamed of "electronic books," or whole worlds of computerized information for readers to explore. These books are more than text. They include sounds, photos, and moving pictures—everything you need to fully understand your subject.

But it wasn't until this summer, when doctors and programmers at Stanford's Advanced Media Research Group finished their Electric Cadaver, that anyone brought the idea of an "electronic book" fully to life. Their work shows that our ideas of learning and communication may be in for the most radical change in centuries.

The Cadaver is a computer program for teaching human anatomy to medical students. It provides an "electronic atlas" of the human body, with thousands of drawings and photographs, in which students move from one part to another, zooming rapidly from region to subregion to microscopic detail and back again, rotating some parts here and activating other parts there.

In the future, all the information in the world could be digitized, interlinked, and accessible. "Readers" could peruse the world's libraries at their leisure, linking into texts cited in bibliographies, bringing them to life with sounds, pictures, even simulated films, collecting the information via associative links for presentations, reports, and personal entertainment. Instead of clawing through card catalogs, tramping up and down library stackstairs, and ordering videotapes and slide shows, users would select a word, phrase, or object on screen, and watch hidden worlds unfold before them.

Teacher Patricia Hanlon and librarian Robert Campbell of San Francisco's Lowell High School have developed a multimedia version of John Steinbeck's *The Grapes of Wrath*. In it, you can move from the novel's text, to Depression-era radio programs, photographs, and magazine articles, to information on crop yields, the Dust Bowl, and economic conditions—even fireside chats by then-president Franklin Roosevelt.

What's different about hypermedia is that it encourages active engagement, which some researchers believe facilitates learning. "Most computer education is passive," says Martin Zagari, a third-year student and collaborator. "You log in and it teaches you. You're bound into the creator's structure and hierarchy. With electronic books, people get in and have fun playing with it. It sticks in the memory more."

➜ See: Literature Reference List, p. 429.

Excerpted from the *San Francisco Sunday Examiner*, 17 September 1989.

Story Stretchers: Activities to Expand Children's Favorite Books

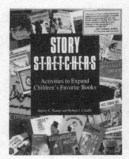

Shirley C. Raines and Robert J. Canady
1989; 251 pp.; $14.95
Mt. Rainier, MD: Gryphon House

Story Stretchers provides activities to stretch 90 outstanding picture books. Each book is featured in a photograph, with an accompanying synopsis to remind the familiar reader of that selection. In the "Circle Time" section, the authors suggest ways in which children can participate in the story, topics for discussion or visualization, and ideas for rereading. Each book is then stretched into different centers of the classroom: art, block building, cooking or snacking, housekeeping, science and nature, music, and water/sand.

Organized with the busy teacher in mind, *Story Stretchers* groups the children's books into 18 common preschool and kindergarten themes such as families, friends, and feelings. Also included are four helpful appendices for teachers to further enhance and expand classroom centers.

Marcy Guddemi

Focus on Literature: A Context for Literacy Learning

Joy F. Moss
1990; 221 pp.; $16.95
Katonah, NY: Richard C. Owen

Moss aims to provide her readers with "a starting point for creating new ideas for bringing children and books together." She achieves her goal. Moss is an expert in children's literature and an experienced classroom teacher. What I most like about the book is its open-ended nature. It should appeal to both elementary and middle school teachers as well as parents. They will find well-developed theoretical and practical frameworks for sharing literature with students rather than "this-is-the-way-to-do-it" formulas. The frameworks are developed around nine thematic units, each of which includes a comprehensive bibliography of children's literature. Also included are two detailed appendices: "Focus on Literature: Resources" and "Literacy Learning: Resources."

LBB

📷 WHOLE LANGUAGE CAMERA

Convenient wall storage makes getting lost in a book easy for these third grade boys in Terrianne Jacobson's class, Manzanita School, Tucson, AZ.

Hands On

Classroom Demonstrations
by Anne Henderson and Elizabeth Walen

The Good Old Days

Holding an antique coffee grinder in his chubby hands, five-year-old Raymond, dressed in a storekeeper's white apron, greeted his first "customer": "Would you like to buy some freshly ground coffee?"

"Nope," replied Jennifer as she reached for the tape measure and a bolt of cloth, "I just came to the General Store to buy a couple of yards of calico for a new dress."

Our five-week whole language unit on "The Good Old Days" seemed to gather steam and momentum as it rolled along. We brainstormed and webbed ideas about social studies, science, reading/writing, math, music, and art. Our goal was to create a hands-on learning environment as children discovered what life was like in the late 1800s.

With the help of marking pens and brown butcher paper our classroom walls took on the appearance of a log cabin. We sectioned off the room into a town of long ago, complete with a schoolhouse, livery stable, and general store. Aided by our imaginations, we had the beginnings of something Great-Grandma and Great-Grandpa might have experienced.

Each day we discussed such topics as pioneer customs, dress, games, activities, music, and life-style. Following our discussion, the children participated in some hands-on experiences related to the topics at various centers.

The children could hardly wait to get to the "General Store," where they could browse to their hearts' content. They could examine a wide array of antiques, from bellows to crocks to chamberpots. They could purchase a lantern or a cowbell from the storekeeper, or weigh out enough flour to make tomorrow's bread. To encourage writing there were plenty of colorful markers to make shopping lists and mark weights on muslin bags. Some children measured calico for dresses or tried on coonskin hats. Using an antique scale, they counted and weighed bushels of apples fresh from the orchard, and weighed and charted the circumference of pumpkins in preparation for the end-of-unit activity, the "Country Hoedown." It was great fun to sequence these orange giants in pumpkin pie or jack-o-lantern shapes, but if a child felt tired, he or she could always rest a spell and read in the old rocker next to the wood-burning stove.

The post office was well stocked with pens, pencils, multicolored paper, and envelopes— everything a young author might need to write a letter to his cousin Nancy in St. Louis. The storekeeper would take the letter and save it for the pony express rider, who was due to arrive sometime later that week.

The livery stable was located across from the post office and general store. Here our kinders could examine a real saddle, halter, and bridle, and try on chaps and cowboy boots. There was always a bale of hay on hand for the horses. And children made their own stick ponies— from socks and broom handles—to ride in the Country Hoedown. Outside the stable a Conestoga wagon, fashioned from chicken wire,

Father and son enjoy "Country Hoedown" festivities in Henderson and Walen's kindergarten classroom, Aurora, CO.

muslin, and a four-by-four wooden box, was filled with fiction and nonfiction books on cowboys and the olden days.

In the one-room schoolhouse the schoolmaster rang the bell to call class together. Here, our students relived the schools of yesteryear: They sat on rough wooden benches and pretended to keep the wood-burning stove stoked. Those who forgot to bring an armload of wood to school experienced a dose of old-fashioned punishment: a dunce cap and banishment to the stool in the corner. Children "toed the line," a way of reciting in unison, and wrote the alphabet on chalkboard slates. Anyone who was thirsty could dip into the water pail.

During the unit, we also tried our hand at quilt-making. Using fabric crayons, each child decorated one square cut from a white sheet. A mother volunteer helped the children tie off their squares and sew them together. The result was a beautiful quilt, sure to keep its owner warm on a cold winter night. It was given away to one lucky child the night of the Hoedown.

The Country Hoedown, the culmination of our whole language unit, finally arrived. The kinders designed invitations for parents and family members. Everyone arrived in their best jeans, shirts, and cowboy hats. Guitar music and bales of hay helped transform our gymnasium into the best old barn west of the Mississippi. With the help of several parent volunteers, the children prepared a barbecue dinner: We had plenty of beef, baked beans, rolls, and juice. The apples from the General Store made a delicious apple pan dowdy.

After the last plate was cleaned, we moseyed down the hall to six different classrooms in which we had set up hands-on learning experiences for both parents and children. Volunteers we had found through a community search helped the Hoedowners churn butter, pull taffy, knead bread, make jelly, and press apples for cider. There was also a chance to dip candles, and weave the hair of an angora rabbit into yarn. Children milked goats, brushed the curly wool of a baby lamb, and gave oats to a frisky colt.

Returning to the gymnasium for a sing-along around a tissue-paper campfire, children taught their parents the songs we had learned during the unit. Then we "raised the roof," as 84 children delighted spectators with their square-dancing ability. There was enough knee slapping and hollering to be heard all the way to the Rio Grande.

In sum, the kindergartners entered Great-Grandma's world through all five senses, and in the learning process interacted with their peers, parents, and community members. This unit of study incorporated all aspects of the curriculum. It provided a beginning sense of history while encouraging reading, writing, science, social studies, music, art, and more fun than you can shake a stick at.

Anne Henderson and Elizabeth Walen are primary teachers at Summit Elementary School, Aurora, CO.

Resource: Catalog
Marcy Cook Math Materials

P.O. Box 5840
Balboa Island, CA 92662
1-714-673-5912

These inexpensive, hands-on, easy-to-use materials are a nice supplement to an existing math program, and are most useful for reinforcing particular math concepts. Individual packets include instruction in whole numbers, decimals, percentages, and tangrams for grades K to 8.

I have also heard good things about the Marcy Cook Think About It series, which has math and language arts problems of the day for primary and intermediate students.

Doug Haner

Classroom Demonstrations
by Annette Maggitti and Joel Brown

Exchanges: Video Pen Pals and Museum Kits

In the interest of expanding my class's awareness of other places in the world, I've always been an advocate of a pen pal writing project. This past year, however, looking at all the books and poems we'd written, and the pictures we drew and things we talked about, we decided that those friends of ours at the other end just had to get more information about us than our letters would handle.

We continued writing, to be sure, but we added two important elements, the first of which was video. Now we could write, and on camera, we could read our letters, special books and poems about our homes, and favorite trade books. We could also present puppet shows and plays, and introduce friends and neighboring classes. Second, we began collecting things around us. As young anthropologists, we created "museum kits" that we could present on tape and then send to our pen pals to show them what a cactus looked like, what a snake skin felt like, and what prickly pear jelly tasted like! We made cue cards to help the kids present the more complex items.

Our Alaskan friends sent us fur mittens, different kinds of rocks, an Eskimo dance fan, and a dress parka. We taped a walk in the desert, and the kids pointed out things and talked about their experiences in the desert and what they loved to do. Our Alaskan friends took us to a dogsled race! And they showed us the snow drifts that buried their playground, the tops of the swings barely visible.

Some of the Alaskan materials were on "museum loan," of course. But others have become permanent artifacts in the classroom, reminders for students of the places and people with whom they've been in touch.

It is fun to see different things and have friends who know the things as a matter of their daily life, friends who can answer your questions. Whether it be about Alaska, or the city, or the coast of Georgia, there's so much to exchange!

Annette Maggitti teaches developmental first grade at Desert Winds Elementary School, Tucson, AZ. Joel Brown is a graduate student at the University of Arizona, Tucson, AZ.

Classroom Demonstrations

by Lois Bridges Bird

Learning Ohlone Ways

Curiosity about the origin of their school's name led Arlene Malkin and her second- and third-grade students at Ohlone School into a three-month study of the Ohlone Indians of the San Francisco Peninsula. Students participated in a variety of learning experiences that replicated the village life of the Ohlone. After reading a wide range of reference materials and noting the information in their journals, students learned how to write with Ohlone symbols, tried their hand at tool making and stringing abalone shells, ground acorns, made grass skirts, examined beautiful Ohlone baskets that Arlene borrowed from a local museum, and as the culminating experience, built an Ohlone hut using reeds and saplings they collected themselves. They also invited parents to a performance of Ohlone dances followed by a feast of chicken, roasted in outdoor fire pits, much as the Ohlone did it 100 years ago.

(Above) Bending the saplings for the framework.

The walls go up.

Breaking ground.

Arlene tries it out.

As the Egyptians Did It

Did you know that Senet is an ancient Egyptian board game that is still popular throughout much of Africa? Cathy Howard's first- and second-graders do. Making and playing this game was just one of many activities in which they participated as they explored the games, folktales and myths, food, clothing, and mathematical and written language systems of ancient Egypt. Here they are with the full-size mummy case they made from papier-mâché, complete with authentic inscriptions and clay artifacts such as those they saw at the Egyptian Museum in San Jose, California.

—LBB

Catherine Howard's students pose with mummy case, Palo Alto, CA.

Serving the feast to parents.

—Photos contributed by Arlene Malkin, primary teacher, Ohlone School, Palo Alto, CA

Resource: Catalog

1001 Things You Can Get Free

$1.98 from:
Jetco Publications
P.O. Box 1225
Newark, NJ 07101-1225

I guarantee the *1001 Things You Can Get Free* catalog will start an avalanche of reading, writing, planning, and scheming on the part of elementary and middle school students. You can imagine how many letters kids will write when there are possibilities of getting a skateboard bumper sticker, animal bookmarks, the official rules of baseball, paper money, samples of seeds or suntan lotion, stamps, recipes, a roll of film, iron-on decals, maps, posters, or information about any state in the union—all for free! Bulk quantities at discount prices are available to schools.

Doug Haner

Resource: Book

Kid Vid: Fun-damentals of Video Instruction

Kaye Black
$13.95 from:
Zephyr Press
P.O. Box 13448
Tucson, AZ
85732-9448

Are you interested in using video in your classroom? While we've always had a pretty good sense of what video is for, we've struggled with figuring out what to do, how to work it, and what was missing. Over time, in our hit-and-miss manner, we worked out how to use our equipment reasonably well. Then we discovered something that told us everything we already knew, plus some. *Kid Vid* is not only a great "what it is" and "how to" manual for kids and teachers; but it also offers examples and blank forms that kids can use for storyboarding and editing. There is even a production proposal guide, which asks students to do things like consider budget and analyze their intended audience. The hints and cautions are very welcome reminders, even to us veterans. A highly recommended resource for any class with a camera.

Annette Maggitti and Joel Brown

READING
Reading, telling & listening to Egyptian folktales & myths.

Reading & listening to non-fiction books about mummies, pharoahs & pyramids.

SOCIAL STUDIES
Looking at slides, pictures & posters of ancient & modern Egypt.

WRITING
Writing hieroglyphics on name cartouches & as inscriptions on the mummy case.

GAMES
Making & playing Senet, an ancient Egyptian board game/Playing Seega & Mancala (all three games were & are popular throughout much of Africa).

COOKING
Baking & eating date crescents & pita bread.

Ancient Egypt

ART
Looking at slides & pictures of treasures from King Tut's tomb. Making a full-size mummy & mummy case out of papier maché. Making clay artifacts like those we saw at the Egyptian museum.

CULMINATIONS
Taking a field trip to the Egyptian Museum in San Jose Having a procession with our mummy & "artifacts" to a nearby nursery school.

MATH
Measuring in digits, palms & cubits Writing & figuring out Egyptian numerals.

Resources: Adler, Irving, *Giant Golden Book of Mathematics*; Aliki, *Mummies Made in Egypt*; Purdy, Susan, *Ancient Egypt* (a "civilization project book"—source for nearly all the crafts & projects); Zagloyul, Ahmed, *The Black Prince and Other Folktales*; Materials from a workshop on Ancient Egypt sponsored by the S.F. World Affairs Council and Bay Area Global Education Project (recipes, slides, background information, hieroglyphics, Senet game)

—Semantic map contributed by Catherine Howard, primary teacher, Ohlone School, Palo Alto, CA

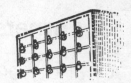

Education in Turin: A Romance by Herbert Kohl

Continued from page 245

Education in the New Century:
Straining to be Scientific

During the first decades of the 20th century, the "science of education" was developing. IQ and achievement tests were being tried out for the first time on a fairly large scale. A number of educators at teacher-training institutions (many of which were now colleges instead of normal schools) became involved in planning programs for local school districts. Often these educators (many of whom considered themselves scientific progressives) were not schoolteachers but trained psychologists and statisticians. They believed that the schools, especially in large districts, needed rational planning and scientific management. Many of the plans they made laid the groundwork for the development of non-teaching school bureaucracies whose function was to implement programs and evaluate progress.

In 1904, at the request of the local business community, the school board in Turin turned to the state teachers college for advice. A professor from the state university in Canton visited Turin and recommended that the district hire a professional principal/superintendent, an educational expert, who could develop a unified program for the community and retrain teachers in current methods. He also recommended that the school for black students be closed and the children in the expanded plant be grouped by ability, with two classes in each grade. One would be for high-ability students, the other for the rest. That way, he implied in his report to the school board, blacks and immigrants could be separated from "native" children on a scientific basis.

The recommendations were accepted with the specific promise, insisted upon by the business community, that an Americanization program be instituted as soon as the new principal/superintendent took over.

John Dorfman, who had big city teaching experience, was hired. He had been a principal in a small city high school, and had done several semesters of graduate work at Teachers College, Columbia, with Edward Thorndike on the measurement of teacher effectiveness and pupil achievement.

Dorfman puzzled Alice. He considered himself an educational progressive and supported her work. At the same time, he disassociated himself from progressive political ideas, which to Alice were the basis of progressive educational practice. He also worried her with his talk of testing.

Dorfman appeased the Deweyites by integrating community learning and activity methods in the curriculum. He quieted the fundamentalists by instituting achievement tests in reading, writing, and arithmetic, and persuaded the business community to raise a bond issue in order to build a new modern wing for the school. In his first few years he seemed to incorporate all the different views in the community into the school,

but there was a vague sense that by incorporating everything, nothing of substance was happening.

In 1910, after five years in Turin, Dorfman presented a comprehensive plan for the school. The boldness of the plan shocked even Alice. It was based on the Gary Model, which was a plan for the reorganization of the Gary, Indiana, public schools that was being put into effect by William Wert, the superintendent there.

The Gary Plan was an attempt to translate many of John Dewey's ideas into practice in an urban, industrialized community. The school was to become the center of social, artistic, and intellectual life in the community. It would be open all day, every day of the year. This way it could provide adult education classes, especially in English, as well as citizenship classes for the immigrant community. The school would also provide community services, have a nursery and a health clinic, teach nutrition and vocational education. The school itself would be organized into four centers: the shops, the labs and classrooms, the auditorium, and the playground. Students would rotate from one center to another on a "platoon system," or what we now call departmentalized learning.

Teachers would specialize in subject areas and students would no longer have their own classrooms for the whole day but move from teacher to teacher. Instead of having their own desks, students would be given lockers in the hall. Perhaps the major lasting effects of the Gary Plan initiated in 1907 were these lockers and the departmental system, which now symbolize, ironically enough, dehumanizing aspects of school life.

Two components of the plan made sense to Dorfman's school board. One was the departmental system, which would save the school from building new classrooms even if the student population grew. The other was adult classes in English and citizenship. The board instructed Dorfman to proceed with those aspects of his plan and forget about those notions of the school as a social and community center.

The teachers resisted the reorganization. After many heated battles at faculty meetings, it was decided that the plan would be modified so that an upper division would use the platoon system and a lower division would remain in single classrooms. The dividing point would be between the sixth and seventh grades.

Alice volunteered to be an English and social studies teacher, and she always felt that the years from 1911 to 1917 were the most creative of her teaching career. The reorganization put her in more contact with immigrant and black children than she had ever been. She was appalled at how badly taught these children had been and resolved to compensate for their educational neglect.

THE GARY PLAN
ACHIEVEMENT TESTING

Continued on page 311

Resource: Mail-Order Company

Creative Educational Surplus

1588 S. Victoria Rd.
Mendota Heights, MN 55118
1-612-454-7499

Good teachers have always sought out sources for free and inexpensive surplus materials. Now, a group of preschool teachers has formed a small mail-order company, Creative Educational Surplus, that combs surplus outlets to find basic, low-cost materials for teachers. Their goal is to help teachers create an environment where children's imaginations can run free, using materials that suit their educational needs and interests.

The selection changes, but currently they are offering such materials as magnets and magnetic strips, magnifiers, clear plastic containers, soft velour storage sacks, aprons, plastic bowls, beakers, colored masking tape, and Velcro. Each material comes with an activity card suggesting potential uses—the cards are surprisingly complete and well done.

Doug Haner

📷 WHOLE LANGUAGE CAMERA

A Navajo rug provides inspiration for first-grade weavers in Annette Maggitti's class, Desert Winds School, Tucson, AZ.

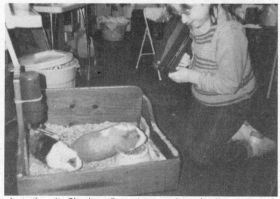

A student in Charlene Roger's second-grade class captures the guinea pig act on on video, East Aurora, NY.

Resource: Curriculum Unit

The Duck Unit: Activities and Ideas

Holland-Dalby
Educational Consulting
P.O. Box 327
LaRonge, Saskatchewan,
S0J 1L0, Canada
1-306-425-2858
1-306-425-3231 (FAX)

This 40-page unit on ducks is part of a series and serves as a model for developing theme-based curriculum units. Inspired by two whole language teachers working with Year 1 and 2 students at the Saskatchewan Urban Native Teacher Education Project, The Duck Unit illustrates how to develop themes sensitive to students' interests, experiences, and environment. Other units in the series cover fish, water, rocks, transportation, and winter festivals.

Doug Haner

A Classroom Without Walls

Cornerstone: Oliver Patterson

Literacy and Community Resources

During my early years of teaching I took my classes on field trips. However, these field trips were little more than diversions from the real work in which the children and I were engaged behind the walls of the school—mastery of the content of the textbook. To a very limited degree, I am ashamed to report, the trips served to enrich the classroom, but conceptually, from both my perspective and the children's, they were a day off from school, a pleasant outing. Whatever was learned was purely incidental. And, in fact, several negative things may have been learned.

A week or two before the trip, I would give the students a form letter telling their parents about the upcoming trip to, let's say, the Museum of Modern Art. They were told that the children would have to bring lunch and a couple of dollars for snacks. At the end of the letter was a consent slip to be signed and returned, apparently to relieve the school of any lawsuits resulting from loss, injury, or damage committed by the children.

On the day of the trip, my 30 children and I would board the overcrowded subway, and if looks could kill, the passengers certainly would have slain my charges then and there. After departing the train, I would gather them up and form straight lines and, as if we were an invading brigade from Bedford-Stuyvesant, we would surge through the pristine halls of the galleries. In a stern voice the security guard would intone: "You are not to touch any of the paintings or sculpture and at all times you are to stand behind that red line."

Properly forewarned, intimidated, and somewhat angered, we would go from gallery to gallery. Usually, we were the only African-Americans in the museum. My task was one of law and order: "Stay in line! Don't speak so loudly!" I felt every eye was on us, judging our every movement, waiting for some misconduct to occur. Certainly, I was not encouraging any dialogue. I wanted silence.

The trip would end at Central Park, eating lunch there, and playing some form of baseball—punchball, running bases, or catch.

The next day I was usually disappointed. Although there were always a few who were excited about a particular painting, most of the children not only did not enjoy the trip but could remember little about it. The vast majority did enjoy playing in Central Park and that is what they vividly recalled.

In summary, my use of community resources through field trips to extend the language, knowledge, and aesthetics of the children was of very limited success. In fact, the children learned that museums were not places of either learning or enjoyment. They felt uncomfortable. They could not make sense of all the data entering their senses. "Those paintings were stupid" was a favorite retort. How could the paintings make sense to them when I had done nothing to provide a knowledge, linguistic, or cultural context for their experiences?

Young Communicators Club

For the past two years I have conducted a program for children in grades four through six called the Young Communicators Club. The objective of the program is to extend children's language knowledge and aesthetics through field trips to community resources.

The program is inquiry-based in that the young people are intellectually engaged in discovering the relationships between the artist, the artwork produced, the cultural community from which the art emerged, and the relationship of art to themselves and their community. The program is intentionally and consciously multicultural. We want our children to appreciate and respect not only their culture, but also the diversity of cultural expressions extant in the world.

The City College is located in Harlem, New York, and our student population reflects this largely African-American and Hispanic community. Fortunately, the Harlem community is replete with institutions that celebrate the arts: Schomberg Library, Davis Theatre of City College, Studio Museum of Harlem, Dance Theatre of Harlem, Children's Art Carnival, Harlem School of the Arts, El Museo del Barrio, Museum of the American Indian, and National Black Theatre. In addition, extensive use has been made of Museum of Modern Art, Hayden Planetarium, Museum of Natural History, and Cathedral of St. John the Divine.

In writing about his metaphorical literacy club, Frank Smith (1986, p. 38) expresses the attitude we attempt to engender among our children: "From the beginning the child is a reader or writer, a member of the guild, who takes learning for granted and who will learn."

Pre-trip Activities. The purpose of the pre-trip activities is to ready the children for the field trip. All the language arts are used. Children listen to the teacher who provides background information.They share their experiences and information with each other. They listen to music related to the experience. They read about the artists, their form of expression, and their culture. They are shown samples of the artwork they will be viewing. They are encouraged to trace, copy, or generate that artwork. Their work is kept in a notebook we call the Field Trip Journal.

During the Trip. Armed with their journals, pencils, and pens, the children could, in fact, be mistaken for journalists. They engage in a variety of group tasks: answering questions, sketching paintings they particularly enjoy, and asking questions of the tour guide and teacher.

After the Trip. Normally, the children go home and return to the college the next week. Five types of activities typically ensue: discussion, writing, reading, drawing, and presentation. The teachers engage the children by having them brainstorm everything that happened before and during the trip. The children are divided into writing groups. They select a topic from the semantic map to write about. Following a snack, the groups make their presentations. The presentations are critiqued by the entire club as well as by the teacher. Revisions are made, and the completed text is kept in the field journal.

Often an art activity follows. During one such activity, a colleague of mine came upon a group of the children sketching a cluster of maple trees. "That's lovely, " she remarked to one of the children. The youngster replied, "I'm doing it in the style of Claude Monet, the French painter." Of course, I was very proud, for it was evidence that we had developed a curriculum that was both thought- and language-centered. We certainly agree with Kenneth Goodman and his colleagues (1987, p. 6):

> Each serves the other and that both have to be planned and monitored for either to be successful. We need to be concerned for the thought and language structures that should be developing and then consider the kinds of life situations that rely on knowledge from the arts, sciences, mathematics, or social studies that should become the matrix for their development.

To be sure, our small program is not perfect, for none of the program participants are perfect humans—children, teachers, myself. Yet, given all the imperfections, we believe we have created an environment that supports the intellectual, linguistic, and cognitive growth of children.

→ See: Foxfire, p. 221; Goodman, p. 281; Harwayne, p. 337.

The author wishes to acknowledge New York Community School District 5, which provided the funds and teachers for this program.

References

Goodman, K. S., E. B. Smith, R. Meredith, Y. M. Goodman. 1987. *Language and thinking in school.* New York: Richard C. Owen.

Smith, F. 1986. *Insult to intelligence.* New York: Arbor House.

Further Reading by Oliver Patterson

◆ *Strategies for Reading,* with H. A. Robinson et al. Allyn & Bacon, 1978.

◆ "Functional Adult Literacy." In *Projections for Reading: Preschool through Adulthood,* ed. F. Hesser. U.S. Department of Health, Education, and Welfare, 1979.

◆ "Critical Issues in Adult Literacy." In *Outlook for the 80s: Adult Literacy,* ed. L. Mercier. U.S. Department of Education, Basic Skills Improvement Program, 1981.

◆ *Learning from Textbooks,* with I. Lynch. Kendall-Hunt, 1988.

◆ "Strategies for Teaching Reading Comprehension." In *Teacher to Teacher.* Video series. New Readers Press, 1989.

Book Note

Ideas and Insights: Language Arts in the Elementary School

Dorothy J. Watson, editor
1987; 244 pp.; $16.50
Urbana, IL: National Council of Teachers of English

This book is a teacher's dream—a compilation of whole language ideas and strategies, all written by experienced K through 6 whole language teachers. Teachers new to whole language can experience immediate success with *Ideas and Insights*—all the ideas, which explain the *why* of what to do as well as the *how,* can be adapted to fit teachers' needs.

Sandra Patton

Dr. Oliver Patterson is professor of education at City College, CUNY, where he teaches in the graduate reading program. He has published over 20 articles in professional journals. His research interests include readability and effective adult literacy instruction. Patterson has been principal investigator on a number of grants, including the Young Communicators Club, GED and Pre-GED Instruction, and Characteristics of Effective Adult Literacy Instruction.

Parents' Perspective

by Judith Larner Lowry

There Are Field Trips and There Are Field Trips

I would like to describe two contrasting field trips that our field-trip-oriented multilevel classroom took, both to the same place—the world-famous Muir Woods. The home of increasingly rare old-growth redwood trees, Muir Woods, in Marin County, is visited by something like five million people a year. Parking can be difficult, and solitude is not to be found on most days. With such quantities of people, rules tend to be strict, of necessity.

Our first field trip was led by a park ranger. She was well informed and fairly experienced in leading tours with children. Each child was given a junior ranger pack equipped with notebooks and guidebooks, pens and pencils. Our group set off into the trees, following the asphalt paths, staying on the path side of the fences that kept visitors from getting too close to the trees. For the roots of redwood trees are vulnerable to soil compaction, which is a clear danger with visitors of such great numbers.

The ranger began presenting information to us in small, digestible doses, and the children were mildly interested. Around us were trees sometimes 200 feet tall, with sunlight drifting through the dark leaves and brooks still running. Also around us were literally hundreds of other groups of visitors, chain link fences, and asphalt. As attention began to wander, the parents in attendance found themselves working hard to keep the group focused on the ranger. Numerous admonitions to stay off the fences, to stay off the roots, and basically "not to touch except when given permission" were necessary but exhausting. A lot of facts were floating around; I know that I retained few of them.

I was glad when that field trip was over, and I usually love to be in the ancient fogbound forests of redwoods, ferns, and alders.

Consider our next visit, the same year, to the same place. This trip is led by our teacher, Cathy Niccolini, and it is to coincide with John Muir's birthday. Our teacher is passionately interested in John Muir.

We get out of the cars and hit the asphalt, but this time we march right on through the fenced and cemented part of the park, out onto a trail. As the kids' feet feel earth under them, they start to lope and are soon stretched out along the trail leading up into the hills. Our group is alone. We find ourselves following a creek winding into the coastal scrub. We stop at a place along the creek and sit in a circle. The teacher brings out a loaf of bread and tells the children how John Muir would set off into the mountains with only a loaf of bread. Then she tears off a hunk of bread and eats it. The loaf is passed around, and each child tears off a bit and eats it. We are celebrating John Muir's birthday.

Later they find a streak of clay in the bank and she shows them how to make little pots out of the clay. Some of the children smooth clay on their faces, which we wash off just before we re-enter the paved part of the forest.

The most moving look I ever saw from a child in the woods was on a mud bar by the footprints of a heron. We were on our knees, making handprints beside the footprints. You could feel the creek vibrating in the silt and sand. The sun beat heavily on our hair. Our shoes were soaking wet. The look said: I did not know until now that I needed someone much older to confirm this, the feeling I have of life here. I can now grow older, knowing it need never be lost. . . . The quickest door to open in the woods for a child is the one that leads to the smallest room, by knowing the name each thing is called. The door that leads to the cathedral is marked by a hesitancy to speak at all, rather to encourage by example a sharpness of the senses. If one speaks it

should only be to say, as well as one can, how wonderfully all this fits together, to indicate what a long, fierce peace can derive from this knowledge.
—Barry Lopez, *Crossing Open Ground*
New York: Charles Scribner Sons, 1988

One Other Thing About Field Trips

I want to say one other thing about field trips. Anything can seem boring to kids; have you noticed? I remember one of the first trips I was involved with. Out at the Marin Headlands, there is a place called Hawk Hill. There, because of the way the land masses rise out of the San Francisco Bay, a great concentration of hawks can be seen at certain times. The movements and numbers of these hawks are charted daily by a retired 70-year-old man. With some trepidation, I asked him if we could bring the Pine Gulch classroom there for a field trip. He somewhat unenthusiastically assented.

The day of the field trip was cloudy and windy, which is not at all unusual for that area or time of year. We met at the top of Hawk Hill, where the hawk expert discoursed knowledgeably about hawks and raptors in general. He said that on his best day ever, he had counted 3,000 hawks, that the sky had been dark with them. But on this particular day, we saw not a single hawk. And the wind blew relentlessly.

The next day in the classroom, I happened to be there when the field trip was discussed. Some comments were not so favorable: "It was boring." "It was cold." "We didn't even see any hawks." Undeniably, the field trip had fallen short of that particular goal.

"But," said the teacher, Kathy Sweeney, "this field trip would be a success if we hadn't seen a single bird. You met a man with an interest. And that is what will get you through your life. That's what makes life worth living."

I had never heard a teacher tell a classroom what made life worth living before.

I recently attended a lecture for laypeople by an entomologist. It was about insects, but as an aside he mentioned the beginnings of his lifelong study of insects. He told about his encounter, in the first grade, with a caterpillar that his teacher had brought in. So gripped by this encounter was he that he couldn't rest until she had told him exactly how he could catch and observe one of his own. After that, school was a mere vehicle through which he could gather the tools to pursue his fascination with insects. "A central interest," he said, "is the best educational tool."

You never know, of course, when or how a child will encounter that which grips him. In the meantime, it can't hurt to let the child know you expect it to happen, and that when it does, you'll be there waiting and ready.

➔ See: Lowry, p. 374.

Judith Larner Lowry is the owner of Larner Seeds, Bolinas, CA.

 WHOLE LANGUAGE CAMERA

Off for a hike through the desert, Signal Hill, Tucson, AZ

MARVELOUS INVENTIONS

Bird Watching

We wat to see the Birds We sa dFrt Kes af Birds the Birds dfit cars I hd a god tem.

I bet you did !!

[We went to see the birds. We saw different kinds of birds. The birds were different colors. I had a good time.]

—Contributed by Pat Robinson, primary teacher, Ohlone School, Palo Alto, CA

Resource: Organization

The Experiment in International Living

School for International Training

Kipling Rd.
P.O. Box 676
Brattleboro, VT 05302
1-802-257-7751
For the past 25 years, the Experiment in International Living has been combining academic content with field experience. Their mission is to promote peace by living and working with people from other cultures. Undergraduate and graduate students from the school have studied and worked on every continent: They have taught Japanese in Indonesia, worked for a feminist organization in Cairo, artificially inseminated cows in Bolivia, and studied rain forest ecology in the Amazon. *Odyssey,* their semiannual publication, features articles on their various programs worldwide. "The Experiment" is a leader in defining the concepts of global education.

Doug Haner

The Funny Side

Car Years

I was taking Markaya and Rosa to the pet store after school to buy crickets for our class lizards. As I opened the door of my venerable blue Volvo, I mentioned that the car was 12 years old. "That's older than you," I told the girls.

Markaya looked puzzled for a moment, then asked, "Well, how old is that in car years?"

—Carlen Luke, primary teacher, Fair Oaks School, Redwood City, CA

Questioning Skills

As I See It:
Kenneth S. Goodman

The Part-Language Curriculum

Look at any common elementary school report card in the United States and you have a sense of what parents, pupils, teachers, school authorities, and the general public believe is the school curriculum. They have a right to believe that something must be pretty important to have its own place on the report card. Most commonly you'll find separate grades for spelling, handwriting, reading, English or language arts, and sometimes literature. But the other subjects will be arithmetic (or mathematics), social studies, and perhaps art, music, and physical education.

So it must be that the typical school language curriculum is a *part-language curriculum*, one in which parts of language are isolated and treated as ends in themselves, separate from the rest of language and separate from the use of language in learning.

In fact, historically speaking "subjects" earned their place on the report card, their own textbooks, and their own time in the teachers' plan book without a lot of thought given to how they fit in the whole picture. Spelling as a separate subject is unknown outside the English-writing world. That doesn't mean schools in other language cultures don't care about spelling. It means they treat it as part of writing, part of written language development. In America spelling probably got enough status as a school subject to get a spot on the report card in the middle of the last century when it was commonly believed that it was necessary to learn to spell words before one could read them. Noah Webster's *Blue-backed Speller* was the most important school textbook of its time.

Handwriting used to be called *penmanship*, a term that passed into obsolescence when inkwells disappeared. Handwriting doesn't enjoy much status as a separate subject beyond primary grades, but it still is entitled to its own spot on many upper-grade report cards.

Around the turn of the century, school curricula and report cards had accumulated so many parts, so many separate subjects, that something had to be done. There just wasn't enough time in the day. So a national Committee on the Economy of Time was formed. From about 1905 to 1925 it worked on deciding which parts belonged in the curriculum and which could be fit together. Out of this came language arts, social studies, and general science as broad subjects that could unify some of the parts. The trouble was that at the same time the committee was working on how to teach reading, spelling, and handwriting as separate subjects. By the time they were done, we had language arts (or English), spelling, reading, and handwriting. And we've had a *part-language* report card and a *part-language* curriculum ever since.

The idea of getting straight the difference between ends and means, and between parts and wholes is not a new one. Educators have been saying for a long time that spelling is only important in the context of writing and reading; and both old and new research show that spelling and handwriting, like grammar and usage, develop best when pupils are doing lots of reading and writing. *Whole language* puts all the old and new knowledge together and sensibly says that the focus should be on whole functional, meaningful language. We need to put the parts in the proper perspective of how they fit into the functional whole. That doesn't mean whole language advocates are against spelling or handwriting or grammar. And we're certainly not against reading and writing. What we're trying to do is to put things in proper perspective: to stop letting the spelling tail wag the language dog. What's the good of attractive handwriting for someone who never writes? And how important is handwriting anyway in an era of type-writers and computers?

How can grammar be studied in any useful way outside of how the system works in real language, written or oral?

Several years ago Linus was shown in a "Peanuts" comic strip coming home from school with his report card. "I got an A in spelling," he said. "When I grow up I'm going to be a speller." Kids will rightly believe that spelling is an end in itself as long as we have a *part-language* curriculum.

Of all the *parts* of language, reading has had the most time and attention. In fact, parts of reading like phonics, vocabulary, word-attack skills, and comprehension are sometimes given separate grades on report cards. That's because in *part-language* curricula, reading is isolated from its use and taught and tested piece by piece. With so much focus on bits and pieces in classrooms it's natural for kids, teachers, and parents to see reading as learning skills and words and not as making sense of print. They may believe that reading basal stories and even real books is only practice for words and skills. And many children are barred from reading real books because they can't *master the parts*.

The parts of writing got so much special attention in the *part-language* curriculum that in many schools there was no connected writing at all except on workbook pages. We had the ironic situation that children learned writing skills without ever writing. And far more report cards still show grades for spelling and handwriting than for writing or composition.

Whole language doesn't ignore the aspects of language that *part language* makes central. *Whole language* keeps everything integrated in authentic language contexts and focuses on the function of the parts in the whole: legible handwriting, functional spelling, comprehensible writing.

In a whole language curriculum maybe we'll reach the point where we'll get rid of letter and number grades altogether and have report cards with sections that deal with how well the pupils are using oral and written language to comprehend, to express themselves, and to learn in a wide range of ways. But we won't get rid of the *part-language* report cards until we get rid of the *part-language* curriculum.

➜ See: Britton, p. 69; Goodman, p. 308; Moffett, p. 70; Van Allen, p. 307.

As Teachers See It
by Carol Gilles

Signs of Whole Language

In March and April my three children and I go on long walks to look for signs of spring. The ribbons of crocus, hesitant sprigs of green grass, even moss beginning to grow again on cold tree trunks, assure us that those long, hot days of summer aren't far off.

Recently I've noticed some other "signs" in and out of schools. Teachers who have gripped their spelling books tightly and dictated word lists religiously all year are abandoning them for spelling words that come from children's writing. Kids like my son Andrew, who never used to comment about spelling except to complain, has begun to talk to me about his spelling words on the personal word list: "Here's a funny one, *were:* You know, I always want to add an *h* after the *w*. I'm working on that."

In one third-grade classroom a student aide from the university has suggested that kids can self-select books and read uninterrupted. Although the teacher was dubious that children would select appropriate books and really read,

she went along with this idea, and the children are reading enthusiastically.

Fifth-grade girls in another school are begging their mothers to take them to the public library to work on research reports. They have selected an era on which they want to work, chosen coinvestigators, interviewed informants, read and digested more materials than I would have dreamed possible, and called one another often to collaborate. Other children are busy planning news shows, which will be presented to their class on Fridays. Of course all the scripts, staging, and acting will be planned and carried out by students.

One class of third-graders is visiting restaurants and preparing meals for large numbers of people. When one boy found 100 grams of pepperoni made the tastiest personal-size pizzas, metric measurement finally made sense to him.

What has prompted these "signs of whole language"?

Teachers and students have completed the basal, the state-mandated testing, and the standardized paper curriculum for this year. Springtime signals a readiness for the "extras." Whole language is dessert.

One side of me is joyful; at least these children get to taste child-centered, meaning-centered, whole learning. Maybe these activities foreshadow a time when learning and process is more important than testing and product.

But another side of me is angry. In our town, the paper curriculum is so strong that even committed, knowledgeable teachers feel they can only use whole language activities and strategies as the "extras." If the mandators could only see the faces of these children, freed from endless practice pages, drill sheets, and tests, involved in learning because it is important to them, they might realize the power of literacy and learning.

If we want children to become lifelong learners, we can't relegate real learning to the last month before school is over. Children need a steady diet of real learning opportunities. It must be the stuff from which the curriculum is made, not just dessert.

➜ See: Edelsky, p. 72; Gilles, pp. 154, 270.

Carol Gilles is a research/teaching assistant at the University of Missouri, Columbia, MO.

Viewpoint: Roach Van Allen

Whole Language Is Holistic

Language in its natural form has always been holistic. That is, the whole of language is greater than the sum of its parts. The only places where "parts" seem to be more important than the "whole" is in school programs. There, in too many places, language is fragmented into phonics, spelling, reading, writing, listening, and literature. These parts are viewed as separate subjects to be taught. Children are organized and drilled on parts of language and are expected to conceptualize the wholeness with a great deal of independence. This is not to say that children might not, at times, need to know some of the parts, especially when they are exploring spelling; but such parts need to be introduced in a meaningful setting—in a whole language format.

Ease in conceptualizing language as a meaningful experience is fostered in many ways that do not require a study of the parts as prerequisites to understanding.

Roach Van Allen, Ed.D. has been a teacher, school administrator, author, consultant, and lecturer for more than 50 years. Responding to the great need for effective ways of working with children who could not profit from basal reader instruction, he developed the first descriptive materials of what came to be called a language experience approach. In all his research and study, first at the Department of Education, San Diego County, California, and then at the University of Arizona, Van Allen has focused on keeping language study meaningful to learners—*to keep it whole.*

- Children can echo the language of literature as adults read and then pause for children to try on and try out language that they have never said before.

- They can assume the roles of characters in literature that are impossible for them to experience in real life and say new things in new ways as drama experiences.

- They can paint pictures and use materials in creative ways, and in so doing, develop ideas that they can share with others.

- They can sing songs and play singing games that give them a chance to repeat language patterns that they never use at home.

- They can learn to say whole books that are written with language that is so predictable that they do not need to see the print in order to participate successfully.

With the influence of new language and new language patterns they can begin their ideas—real and imaginary—through writing. Experiences like these assure children a degree of understanding about the processes involved in reading and writing. They permit them, from the beginning, to communicate with authors in meaningful ways. Language, for them, is whole regardless of the parts they might look at carefully as they refine their skills and abilities. They do not need to analyze parts in order to learn how to read and write. They already know how. No one taught them. These abilities emerged as artists, teachers, and supportive parents, using a whole language approach, trusted them to possess the basic ingredients necessary for literacy. These teachers and parents empowered the students to use and make useful in ever maturing ways their abilities to communicate with others. Each child is exposed to artful ways of communicating ideas. Each child learns to use many resources that will continue as influences throughout life. Normative scores are minimized in assessing progress. Personal responses in many forms are maximized.

Teachers who love the language of literature demonstrate that love through the choices they make in their oral reading with children—but they reflect the feeling that the best books are yet to be written.

They share art objects and art prints that are meaningful and that, to them, demonstrate the great art of the past—but they imply in their interaction with children that the greatest paintings are yet to be painted.

Inventions of great scientists are shared with enthusiasm and appreciation—but there is always the real possibility that the greatest inventions for the benefit of humanity are to be made in the future.

Music is a continuing part of the school program, and teachers bring children in contact with the greatest masters of classical and modern music—but they reserve the idea that the greatest music will be composed in the future.

Reading in the content fields of the school curriculum is important and is used as a base for understanding places and people and a few of the reasons they act as they do—but teachers who are responsive to children and their potential remain convinced that

- The greatest explorations are in the future;
- The greatest governments are yet to be formed;
- The greatest structures are yet to be built;
- The most important ideas for the benefit of humanity are ahead of us.

And, perhaps, by some chance, some of those who will bring it all about are in our schools today.

Can we offer these potential leaders less than an opportunity to respond in personal ways to literacy programs that

- Generate productive thinking?
- Allow freedom of expression?
- Stimulate individuality with pride?
- Value ingenuity?
- Satisfy curiosity?

Whatever else might be done in literacy programs to achieve the complex skills and knowledge that permit reading and writing processes to be a part of life and living, a whole language philosophy suggests that there are at least three major ideas for teachers to hold. These ideas, when implemented, assure a measure of success for each child.

- Idea 1: The natural language of each child must remain useful and be used throughout the period when the refined skills required for literacy are being developed. Personal language is the power that is *whole.*

- Idea 2: The natural language of each child must be influenced by many sources and by many people. Each child deserves to try out new forms of communication under the influence of successful practitioners. These influences culminate in personal responses that seek ever higher levels of quality, greater fluency, and increased flexibility in communication.

- Idea 3: Teachers do not attempt to force student's language into uncharacteristic forms. They respond to language that is natural and normal. From natural language they progress continually through influences related to phonology, syntax, morphology, and semantics. But through all of this, teachers let the child's own language and personal meanings remain in central focus.

The implementation of these three ideas, along with others that might be developed, will assure that language growth will remain in a setting of wholeness. The whole will always be greater than the sum of the parts. Whole language is holistic!

Further Reading by Roach Van Allen

◆ *Language Experiences in Communication.* Houghton Mifflin, 1976. A major treatment of a language experience approach.

◆ *Language Experience Activities,* with C. Allen. Houghton Mifflin, 1982. A worktext for teachers. Basic language concepts that are useful in writing and reading are illustrated in multiple learning centers.

◆ *Predictable Storybooks,* with C. Allen, E. Robinson, and T. Allen. DLM Teaching Resources, 1985–1987. Three sets of six books each with teachers guides. A collection of books that students can say along with a reader without having to see the print.

◆ *Read-Aloud Storybooks.* DLM Teaching Resources, 1988. A series of 10 storybooks with language like that found in reading literature, but with enough dependability of language that children can say them without having to read.

◆ *Experiences for Literacy.* DLM Teaching Resources, 1989. A series of whole language units for young children. *Dinosaur Land,* one of the units, includes a comprehensive teacher guide, a big book, eight dinosaur posters, a cassette of original songs, and blackline masters for duplication.

◆ *Pathways to Literacy,* with M. B. Sampson and M. Sampson. Holt, Rinehart & Winston, 1990.

Resource: Book

Science Predictable Storybooks

DLM Teaching Resources
One DLM Park
Allen, TX 75002

What a find: *Science Predictable Storybooks* for elementary school students, with Roach Van Allen as the educational consultant! These beautifully photographed, oversized books are both a superb supplement and a vivid contrast to traditional science books. Written in large type with predictable patterns, the books are a natural progression for the class making its own big books. Skilled teachers will find these books valuable in building interest in the natural world. Currently available in this series are books on birds, butterflies, the five senses, and nocturnal animals.

Doug Haner

YOUNG ARTISTS

"Birthday Party!"
Rebecca Arnow, 5, Palo Alto, CA

As I See It:
Yetta M. Goodman with Annabel Crites and Kathryn F. Whitmore

Teaching Skills in Whole Language Classrooms

There are those who believe that whole language teachers sacrifice the teaching of "skills." On the contrary, students in whole language classrooms learn the "skills" of language and other subject areas by actively using language as part of real experiences.

Whole language teachers take their cues for skills instruction from their students. They realize, however, that the environment they create is crucial to inviting learners to participate in reading and writing. It is through immersion in literacy that children learn the skills they need. The greater the opportunities for students to read and write for a wide range of functions of importance and interest to them, the more knowledge they have about the "skills" they need.

Whole language teachers do not usually use the term *skills*. In traditional reading and writing instruction, the word *skills* has come to mean the isolated study of units of language (phonics, grammar, vocabulary, punctuation), with little concern for helping students understand the relationship of the skill to its proper place in the greater context of language. We prefer to use the term *strategies* because it provides a more appropriate label for the complex intellectual functioning learners develop as they come to understand language and language use.

Let's follow up on this idea by taking as an example learning the alphabet in kindergarten. Whole language teachers know that kids use their knowledge about the alphabet for a variety of reasons. Most important, children use knowledge of letters and letter sounds to make choices for inventive spelling in the composing process. They also learn to use the names of letters to retrieve information from encyclopedias, dictionaries, and libraries and to categorize, alphabetize, and file as they function in the classroom environment.

Whole language kindergarten teachers don't teach one letter a week, as a separate *skill*. They don't use worksheets with stylized letters repeated over and over. Practice with letters, letter names, and letter sounds out of context does not help children understand the reasons for knowing and using the alphabet.

Instead, whole language teachers embed attention to the alphabet in daily experiences so that the children learn the alphabet without being consciously aware that they are doing so. The teacher monitors what the children know as she watches how they respond to the alphabet in a variety of settings. Additionally, the teacher discusses with parents the many opportunities the children will have to learn the alphabet at school, helps the parents learn how to observe alphabet knowledge development in their children, and suggests activities for expanding that development at home.

Annabel Crites's Kindergarten

Annabel's classroom environment exposes the children to many different alphabet forms. There are magnetic letters stuck to the filing cabinet, large 18" hand-colored letters across the top of the wall (the children color them the first week of school and know that . . . "I did the *g*"), laminated alphabets on the wall beneath the chalkboard that the children can touch, an alphabet pocket wall hanging with objects of each letter stuffed into the pockets, and a typewriter or computer with typical keyboards.

The alphabet frieze on the wall changes over the year from commercially made alphabets to teacher-made alphabets from pages of ABC books, to class-produced alphabets based on units of study. For example, when the class studies clothing, the children make an alphabet from the items they are studying (*z* is made from zippers, *b* from buttons, *f* from fur, etc.) and the children have access to the alphabet for touching and as a reference for content and letter information.

The alphabet corner contains alphabet templates for tracing, plastic alphabet pieces that can be sorted or used for building names and words, alphabet stamps of all kinds, alphabet picture cards, alphabet stepping-stones, and a library of alphabet books. The children have access to this corner when they need to use letters for their own purposes or when they are looking for information about letters.

In the game and puzzle area children may choose from commercial and teacher-made games, which include alphabet puzzles as well as a Bingo and other matchup games with letters. Annabel often makes board games to go with specific units of study. The children make name puzzles, which are added to the game and puzzle area throughout the year.

Each child has a cubby clearly marked with the child's name. These labels change from time to time. At the beginning of the year they may include the child's picture next to the name and later in the year be changed to reflect children's nicknames or family names. The labels not only mark each child's place and belongings, but frequently serve as a resource or reference for other children in need of information about the alphabet or their classmates' names.

Children are involved in organizing the classroom environment. They move their name cards or sign in to take attendance. They label artwork and other creations with their names and often leave instructions for the rest of the class when their work is in progress: "Please don't touch" or "Save this." They sign up to participate in popular activities or to reserve special books. Children's writing portfolios are labeled and filed alphabetically, and children get their folders and refile them as necessary.

Alphabet books are identified by a colored dot and kept in a labeled dishpan. Other collections of books are also so identified and organized, and as each new unit of study begins, a new collection is started. These collections are added to the large classroom library, which is housed in bookshelves and organized alphabetically. Children are responsible for re-shelving books, and an appointed and rotating classroom librarian checks to see that they are in order. Library books are checked out for use at home and are displayed so the children see the covers. The children maintain the system by filling out the cards and checking the books in and out. Throughout the year, they assume greater responsibilities for all of the reading and writing it takes to keep the system going.

Instructional Uses of the Alphabet

Children are given a good deal of opportunity to write in Annabel's classroom before there is a focus on letter formation. Only those children who need help are shown how to form the particular letters that are difficult for them. The focus is on the communicative aspect of writing, not on the form.

From the first day of school, children are encouraged to label block buildings and other constructions with their names so everyone knows who made them. Children are also encouraged to write down interesting oral sharings. Annabel will often ask, "Would you like to put that into a book so we can remember it later?"

The classroom is connected to the total school through a schoolwide post office. Children write letters to friends and siblings throughout the school community. In the playhouse lists are made for the grocery store, charts are kept when the playhouse becomes a doctor's office, and menus and orders are written when it turns into a restaurant. Memo pads are kept near the phone and taped on the refrigerator for writing shopping lists. Books of all varieties (literature, the phone book, content appropriate books, etc.), magazines, and newspapers are standard.

Language about the alphabet is used whenever appropriate and may include such examples as: "Look at the beautiful *o* the artist made at the beginning of the story" when reading children's literature; "This recipe says we need m-i-l-k" when cooking; "My goodness, there are three children here whose name begins with *b*" when entering a dramatic play area. Annabel may spell aloud as she writes a child's dictation or refer to a wall chart to answer a child's question and show the child how to use accessible resources.

Often art activities are built around the alphabet letters. Children's drawings are used to illustrate alphabet friezes, or they may make personal alphabet books by cutting pictures from magazines. Children may be involved in finger painting, crayon resist, paper batik, paper cutting, and making collages while working on specific letters or the whole alphabet.

Poetry, rhymes, and songs are put on charts for shared reading experiences. Often the words to songs like "Bingo" are changed so that children can sing and spell about a new topic. After the children become very familiar with the song or rhyme and it maintains the children's interest, the charts are used for reference to focus on different aspects of the alphabet.

In Annabel's classroom the environment is rich with written language in both English and Spanish. Alphabet wall friezes, class-made and commercial alphabet books, and bulletin board captions appear in both languages. Annabel uses both alphabets naturally and as appropriate to a particular situation while working with the children. Strong consonant sounds in English provide a focus for their letter-sound relationships, while stable vowel sounds in Spanish are the focus of initial attention to those letter-sound relationships. Books are available in both languages and are clearly marked. It does not take long for the children to discriminate easily between the Spanish and English books and help sort them appropriately.

This description is not exhaustive. Building alphabet strategies does not require an inordinate amount of time during each day. It is simply a part of the purposeful activities that take place continually in a whole language kindergarten. Immersed in written language, the children develop the strategies they need to know the functions and purposes that the alphabet serves in their literate world. The alphabet is one small part of the whole which is written language with all its richness and variety.

➡ See: Boyd, p. 19; Dalzell, p. 241; Fennacy, p. 309; Goodman, p. 308; Watson, p. 40.

Annabel Crites is a bilingual kindergarten teacher at the Borton Primary Magnet School, Tucson, AZ. Kathryn F. Whitmore is a doctoral student at the University of Arizona, Tucson, AZ.

Cornerstone: Jean W. Fennacy

Teaching and Learning Literacy in Two Kindergarten Classrooms

During the past 20 years increasing evidence from all over the world has shown that children in literate societies learn a great deal more about reading and writing before they reach school age than was previously recognized. Moreover, the way they learn differs substantially from what educators have believed. When children reach school, they encounter a curriculum that often conflicts with the way they learn in the real world as well as with their understanding of reading and writing.

The more I read about such evidence, the more fascinated I became. I decided to explore the understanding kindergartners develop before entry, the literacy curriculum they encounter in school that conflicts with understandings, and their literacy development by the end of their first year in school. I was interested not only in what the children were learning but also in the assumptions of teachers as evidenced by their teaching practices.

I chose two kindergarten classrooms. One teacher was selected on the basis of her commitment to whole language philosophy. She encouraged her students to engage in a great deal of reading and writing that focused on the construction of meaning. She relied extensively on children's literature rather than on commercial materials. The other teacher followed a skill-based literacy curriculum. In this classroom students focused on mastering letters and sounds to prepare for first grade.

There were three overlapping phases in this naturalistic study. The first involved selecting 10 representative students from each classroom, engaging them in a series of literacy tasks, and interviewing them early in the school term.

The second phase involved documenting and describing the classroom literacy instruction as well as the students' responses to the curriculum. Field notes, interviews, and a compilation of student work were the primary means of data collection in this phase. I spent one day per month in each classroom and also made a second monthly visit of at least one hour.

The third phase of the study consisted of repeating the initial literacy tasks and interviewing the 10 students.

Jean W. Fennacy has lived most of her life in Fresno, where she is currently director of the Graduate Reading Program at Fresno Pacific College. She teaches graduate as well as teacher education courses in reading and writing. She has taught primary and intermediate grades and has served as resource teacher, reading specialist, and curriculum specialist in a large school district. She regularly spends time in an elementary school classroom where she enjoys reading and writing and learning with students.

Children in both classrooms entered kindergarten at the beginning of the school year with a great deal of knowledge about written language. All demonstrated an awareness that written language serves to sign meaning. All of them knew a good deal about the function and form of written language.

The school literacy curriculum the children encountered in the two classrooms differed dramatically. In the skill-based classroom, all children were expected to follow the same path to literacy, regardless of the knowledge they had when they entered. They were expected to learn letters and sounds, master recognition of words in books designed to instruct novice readers, and learn particular words by copying them into books they were assigned to make so that they would be ready for first grade. The perceptions children brought with them were rarely acknowledged. Only children with more refined understanding of reading and writing were able to demonstrate knowledge of the surface structure and features of written language. On most days the teacher read a book to the class, but this book-sharing time was not a focus in the classroom. Although children on occasion did select their own books from a limited supply, and although they had opportunities and materials for writing, the texts they produced during these free-choice times were seldom acknowledged by the teacher.

In contrast, the whole language classroom focused on engaging the students in reading and writing. Whenever children read or wrote, their efforts were celebrated and responded to as meaning focused. From the first day of school they were treated as readers and writers. They had many experiences to engage in reading and writing. Children were not expected to master certain aspects of written language in a particular order or fashion but were expected to read and write as best they could. The teacher read extensively to children, provided them with ample time and a wide range of trade books to enjoy, and responded to their work as meaningful text. Letters and sounds were never discussed in isolation from whole text, nor were children ever asked to fill in worksheets on sounds and letters or master particular words.

The differences between the literacy curricula reflected the teachers' differing assumptions on how literacy develops. In the skill-based classroom, the teacher rarely took advantage of the children's previously developed understandings of reading and writing. There were limited acts and artifacts of literacy as well as few opportunities for children to engage in authentic literacy events. Errors were often viewed as needing correction, especially when children did directed writing, worked on their phonic worksheets, and read to the teacher. Learners were expected to follow a predetermined agenda of mastering skills in order to become literate, and that agenda went from specific to general, from part to whole. Finally, learning was not viewed as a social activity. Instead, children were reprimanded for talking while they were working.

In the whole language classroom, each child's previously developed understanding of reading and writing was accepted and built upon. The classroom was awash with print as well as demonstrations of written language in use by the teacher and other adults who were invited in. There was much opportunity, encouragement, and time for children to engage in real literacy events. Errors were viewed as part of the learning process, not as things to be stamped out, and children seemed to be able to follow their own particular path toward conventional literacy. The focus remained on meaning, and parts of language were never isolated. As a result, children's development could move from whole to part, from global to specific, as they were individually ready to do so. Children were free, even encouraged, to collaborate on their work.

At the end of the year, the 10 children from each class repeated the literacy tasks they had engaged in at the beginning of the school year and showed that they knew more about reading and writing than they did in the fall. However, the following differences were evident:

1. Considerably more children from the whole language classroom had moved closer to conventional writing than had children from the skill-based classroom.

2. Children from the whole language classroom indicated a greater awareness of themselves as being instrumental in their own literacy learning than did the children from the skill-based classroom.

3. Children from the whole language classroom revised and edited independently more frequently that did those from the skill-based classroom.

4. More children from the skill-based classroom sought help in spelling than did children from the whole language classroom.

At the end of the school year, children who had been immersed in meaningful reading and writing were more self-sufficient as they wrote, took more risks in their writing, and applied sound/symbol correspondence to a far greater degree in their writing than did the children from the skill-based classroom. What teachers do makes a difference for students in their classrooms. Their curricular decisions affect not only how and what children learn, but also how they view themselves, others, and learning.

➔ See: Dalzell, p. 241; Goodman, p. 308; Manning, p. 401; Watson, p. 40.

Further Reading by Jean Fennacy
◆ "Teaching and Learning Literacy in Two Kindergarten Classrooms." Ph.D. diss., University of Southern California, 1988.

WELL-SAID

It's easy to convince people that children need to learn the alphabet and numbers ...How do we help people to realize that what really matters...is how a person's inner life finally puts together the alphabet and numbers of his outer life. What really matters is whether he uses the alphabet for a declaration of war or for the description of a sunrise, his numbers for the final count at Buchenwald or for the specifics of a brand new bridge.

—Neil Postman and Charles Wingartner, *The School Book for People Who Want to Know What All the Hollering Is About*

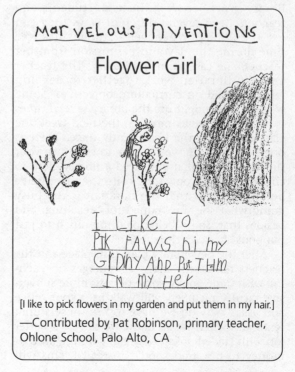

[I like to pick flowers in my garden and put them in my hair.]

—Contributed by Pat Robinson, primary teacher, Ohlone School, Palo Alto, CA

Principals Speak Out

by Gordon Gulseth

"Creating" a Whole Language School

A small voice in the back of your mind keeps telling you that with change comes confusion, and just for a moment you have second thoughts about moving toward whole language. But then you remember visiting with some whole language teachers who talked as if they had just rediscovered the joys of teaching. After carefully considering the pros and cons, you decide that if whole language is the Rubicon, then you'll just have to be Caesar.

Before you can begin, though, there are three things you must do as the instructional leader of your school: (1) read everything you can get your hands on that deals with whole language, (2) talk with anyone who knows anything at all about whole language, and (3) check to see if you are on good terms with your superintendent.

Start educating your superintendent by sending articles and books to his or her office. But don't just limit yourself to educating the superintendent. Send whole language articles and books to directors and other administrators. Leave copies of articles in the school mailboxes and loan the books out to teachers.

At some point in your efforts to encourage whole language, you will encounter resistance, both overt and covert, from some teachers in your building. If you practice shared decision-making, these teachers need not feel alienated as they will have a say in this all-important decision. By focusing attention on the successes of the whole language teachers in your school, you will be able to convince the other teachers that whole language is worth considering. With the support of your superintendent, you might develop some appropriate building-level workshops, or perhaps take your teachers to a whole language conference. Staff development can help teachers explore the promise and excitement of whole language. If they don't like or agree with whole language, it's probably because they don't completely realize the potential it has to transform education.

After a decision has been made to move toward whole language, one of the goals will be to get kids and books together—as often as possible. One program that will help you accomplish this is the integrated or collaborative library plan, which provides a more flexible library schedule and encourages a working relationship between the librarian and the classroom teacher. It abolishes the two 30-minute library visits per week. Instead, students and teachers have several different ways they can use the library. Whenever a student has free time during the day and permission from her teacher, she can go to the library. The teacher and the librarian work together to develop lessons based on curriculum objectives. Some weeks a class might use the library several times to work on various projects; the next week the class might use the library only once. There is one catch though; you'll have to convince your superintendent that you need a library clerk to check in, check out, sort, collect, and reshelve books. Tell him that the librarian is too busy doing what she was trained for—teaching; and besides that, she is being paid too much to just put books back on the shelf.

After the new library plan is in place and the teachers realize the many advantages of teaching with trade books, some of your more subversive faculty members will walk into your office and ask, "Why do we have to use those stupid textbooks when we all know we can do a better job with trade books? Why can't we use all that money to buy trade books instead?" This will

not be a rhetorical question. By the way they clench their fists and set their jaws you will know they expect an answer. Now, if you're still on good terms with your superintendent . . .

Regardless of how you get the trade books, get them—have a fund-raiser, ask the PTA for money to buy books, have parents donate books, apply for grants. Get the best, the most interesting books you can. Get big books, little books, books that shout with bright pictures, and books that whisper secrets. Get books that are so good that students will want to share them with each other (and maybe even with the principal).

Along with this celebration of reading, you'll also want to give emphasis to the writing process. Through staff development activities your teachers will begin to see the personal, social, process-oriented activity that writing is, and will begin to help students understand this process and feel good about themselves as writers.

The whole language school, just like the whole language classroom, will have many places to display students' writings. Hallways and bulletin boards will provide young authors opportunities to be "read" and will give young readers opportunities to read. A weekly writers fair in the gym can give students, parents, and teachers a chance to see what is being published. Self-confidence will soar as the authors see their books picked up and read. Proud parents will tell their neighbors what a great school their children attend. All of these activities will celebrate reading and writing and show students, parents, and the community how much you value literacy.

When the students bring home their "published" books and insist on reading them to everyone, parents are going to wonder not only why Johnny can read and write, but why he is so excited about it. Parent newsletters, PTA programs, brochures, releases to the media, and one-on-one visits will all be useful vehicles for informing the parents and the community of the whole language activities at your school. Educated and informed parents can provide a powerful base of support.

In addition to parental support, assistance can come from a well-developed whole language network. Contact everyone in your area who is interested in whole language. Find out if there are any local college professors who advocate whole language. Become a member of professional organizations that support the whole language movement.

Start a support group for teachers in your district who are using whole language. Find out if there are any whole language conferences or conventions that you and your teachers could attend. Subscribe to every whole language newsletter you can find (there are several). In short, become the whole language resource person for your school.

With patience, persistence, and good planning, your school will change from a place where students study textbooks to a place where teachers and students study their world. No longer will it be a place where students are isolated and alone, always competing against one another. Rather, it will be a community of learners where cooperation is a common objective. And finally, it will be a place where students and teachers rediscover the joy of learning.

→ See: Bird, p. 90; Boloz, p. 208; Fearn, p. 372; Hutchinson, p. 275; Krause, p. 396; Obringer, p. 179; Pessah, p. 347; Wetherell, p. 300.

Gordon Gulseth is the principal of Franklin Elementary School, Junction City, KS.

Network

The Literacy Connection

A Kinder, Gentler Curriculum

by James Allen

Partnerships. Collaboration. Cooperative Learning. Empowerment. Whole Language. Whole Learning. Individualized Education Plan. Increasingly these terms are entering the jargon of educational reform. Finally, we are reevaluating the "bits-and-pieces" learning that has for so long dominated American schools and schooling. We now are talking of teaching children *how* to learn, not *what* to learn. For too long, the "what" has been the focus of American education at the expense of the "how." In Upper Arlington, Ohio, we are trying to design "education for the 21st century." We are trying to make education special for every child.

Our school district is in the implementation phase of the new language arts curriculum. Never has a curriculum initiative drawn more attention—both positive and negative—than this one. This process has been both riveting and revealing. Suddenly, educators in every building are being confronted with a design for the future. As its theoretical core, the new curriculum emphasizes two basic assumptions: Education should be personalized and individualized, and teachers should be empowered to make instructional choices that honor their full

professionalism. Unfortunately, too many teachers in the regular classroom remain grounded on a model of learning that requires skill-and-drill instruction, textbook dependence, and error-hunting assessment.

But how can we prepare students for the information age on a model designed more for behavior modification than lifelong learning? Do we want students to know how to write a sentence or to list the names of its parts? Do we want students to learn spelling rules or self-monitoring strategies to edit and correct? In other words, do we want a curriculum that is adult- rather than child-centered?

The controversy surrounding the new language arts curriculum will become much more commonplace in school districts throughout the nation. We are ahead of our time. This curriculum has redefined knowledge, redefined teaching. Education in the 21st century requires this redefinition. Lauren Resnick, professor of psychology at the University of Pittsburgh, puts it this way: "Just as knowledge is not a collection of separate facts, so learning competence is not a collection of separate skills." Good teaching should be honored by good curriculums. Our new curriculum celebrates real learners and whole teaching.

Excerpted from *The Literacy Connection* 7(1), September 1989.

James Allen is a language arts coordinator for the Upper Arlington City Schools, Upper Arlington, OH.

Subscription Information: To subscribe to *The Literacy Connection,* contact Kathleen Taps, 1018 Bricker Blvd., Columbus, OH 43221.

Education in Turin: A Romance by Herbert Kohl

Continued from page 308

Education in the New Century:

War and Its Aftermath

World War I was traumatic for the people in Turin as for the rest of the nation. There were fights between the German immigrant community and the Anglo-Saxon community. Many men died or were wounded in Europe. And the Russian Revolution led to more red fear and red baiting than Alice had ever experienced. People treated her with suspicion because she was a member of the Socialist party. During the last years of her teaching career, from 1919 to 1925, Alice spent most of her time trying to heal wounds the war exacerbated. She also became more active in the National Education Association and the Progressive Education Association.

Alice retired in 1925 and her two children didn't follow her into teaching. Her son, Phillip, became a dentist. He remained in Turin, where he became a member of the school board. Her daughter, Elizabeth Ann, received an M.A. in social work from Columbia and remained in New York, working at the Henry Street Settlement House.

The main educational issue in Turin after World War I was consolidation. The town was growing. It annexed two small unincorporated townships on its borders. John Dorfman led the

fight to build a new comprehensive high school and to combine the Turin Common School with the elementary schools from the newly annexed towns. Consolidation passed and John Dorfman became the first superintendent of the Turin Unified School District. Walter Johnson, the new principal of the common school (renamed the Turin Elementary School), was chosen by the superintendent without community input. There was considerable grumbling in town about an outsider choosing the new principal, and rumors circulated about Johnson being a communist and having a perverted sex life. The Russian Revolution and bohemian life in Greenwich Village were in the news those days, and there were constant allusions to progressives being communists or libertines. Of course, there were socialist progressive educators, child-centered progressives, and scientific progressives like the former principal/superintendent. There were probably some progressives who were communists and some who had complicated sex lives. However, the progressive education movement was not unified, though John Dewey's name and the leadership he provided gave that impression of unity from without.

Continued on page 366

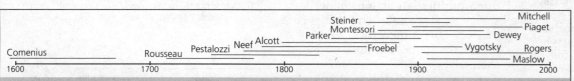

					Steiner				Mitchell	
					Montessori				Piaget	
				Parker				Dewey		
			Neef Alcott							
Comenius		Rousseau Pestalozzi				Froebel		Vygotsky	Rogers	
									Maslow	
1600	1700		1800			1900			2000	

Pioneers: Jean Piaget (1896–1980)   by Kathryn F. Whitmore

Jean Piaget began his intellectual career as a young student studying biology and epistemology. His professional career originated in the Binet Laboratory in Paris where he was involved in the standardized testing of intelligence. His dissatisfaction with this work led him to formulate his own theories about intelligence and the testing of intelligence. Three major observations guided Piaget's early thinking.

1. He noticed young children's thought was qualitatively different than older children's, not just quantitatively different.
2. He rejected the standardized test procedure in favor of a less structured method, which gave him more freedom to question children and allowed children to manipulate materials during testing.
3. He considered the role of logic in the psychology of intelligence.

These initial observations inspired Piaget's lifelong curiosity and research regarding the nature of intelligence and its structure and functions. One of Piaget's legacies is the clinical method that educators and researchers use to observe children as they explore specific problems; in this way, adults gain insight into young children's thinking.

Piaget's work revolutionized the field of psychology and has had lasting impact on educational theory and practice, as well as on research methodology. His view of children influenced areas of cognition, moral development, thought and language, memory, causality and reasoning. Educators and social scientists, in describing and analyzing children's cognitive development, still use Piagetian terms such as *scheme* (knowledge structures that develop through the adaptive processes of assimilation and accom-

modation); *assimilation* (the taking in of information through the senses and incorporating it into existing structures of knowledge); *accommodation* (modifications of existing knowledge structures to fit with the reality of the environment); and *semiotic function* (the ability to make something represent something else that is not present, manifested in language, symbolic play and deferred imitation).

Piaget's influence on education was indirect but powerful in that he presented new data about children that held implications for teaching, education, and schools. In 1964 (p. 5) he wrote specifically about his goals for education:

The principal goal of education is to create people . . . who are capable of doing new things, not simply of repeating what other generations have done—people . . . who are creative, inventive, and discoverers. The second goal of education is to form minds which can be critical, can verify, and not accept everything they are offered. The great danger today is of slogans, collective opinions, ready-made trends of thought. We have to be able to resist individually, to criticize, to distinguish between what is proven and what is not. So we need pupils who are active, who learn early to find out by themselves, partly by their own spontaneous activity and partly through material we set up for them; who learn early to tell what is verifiable and what is simply the first idea to come to them.

Whole language teachers—educators who respect children, who value what children know, and who care how children think—strive to reach these goals.

➔ See: Bruner, p. 283.

References

Piaget, J. 1964. "Development and learning." In *Piaget rediscovered*, ed. R. E. Ripple and V. N. Rockcastle. Ithaca, NY: Cornell University.

Further Reading

Ginsburg, H., and S. Opper. 1979. *Piaget's Theory of Intellectual Development*. Englewood Cliffs, NJ: Prentice-Hall.

Morrison, G. S. 1976. *Early Childhood Education Today*. Columbus, OH: Charles E. Merrill.

Kathryn F. Whitmore is a doctoral student at the University of Arizona, Tucson, AZ.

Book Note

Whole Language Strategies for Secondary Students

WHOLE LANGUAGE STRATEGIES FOR SECONDARY STUDENTS
Edited by Carol Gilles, Mary Bixby, Paul Crowley, Shirley R. Crenshaw, Margaret Henrichs, Frances E. Reynolds, Donelle Pyle

Carol Gilles, Mary Bixby, Paul Crowley, Shirley R. Crenshaw, Margaret Henrichs, Frances E. Reynolds, and Donelle Pyle, editors
1988; 208 pp.; $18.95
Katonah, NY:
Richard C. Owen

Although this oversized book is chockful of detailed explanations of holistic learning experiences for secondary students, don't look for quick-fix, instructional recipes that can be dished up Monday morning. The author-editors, seven experienced whole language teachers, open their book with theory, and theory prevails throughout. There is an excellent theoretical overview by Dorothy Watson and another chapter devoted to issues and answers. They also begin each strategy lesson with a theoretical rationale to further emphasize that these lessons are not blueprints for instruction, but points of departure for learning experiences that you can create with your own students. Well worth owning, it is a book for the experienced whole language teacher and initiate alike, elementary as well as secondary.

LBB

It Shouldn't Happen to Kids
Ditto-less Teaching

A kindergarten teacher who had recently visited a whole language school was sharing her experience with a visitor to her school. "So how was it?" the visitor questioned her.

"Well," the teacher explained, "they told us that they don't use *any* dittos, but you know and *I* know that you can't teach kindergarten without dittos."

—LBB

Social Studies

Cornerstone: Cynthia McDermott

Whole Language Social Studies

Most of us remember our years in social studies as times of memorization and rote recall. Can you still sing the song: "In fourteen hundred and ninety two Columbus sailed the ocean blue"? Or remember the days of memorizing the states and their capitals in alphabetical order? Well, the good news is that things are changing. Just as whole language offers a process approach to language, social studies offers a way of learning that is action oriented. Shelly Berman, president of Educators for Social Responsibility, reminds us that schools provide opportunity for practicing math skills and for doing reading, but kids merely study democracy. Yetta Goodman tells us that we can't expect kids to come out of 13 years of an autocratic environment able and ready to be practitioners of democratic principles. So what should we do?

If we want children to grow into responsible adults, we need to provide opportunities and materials that will encourage them. The social studies class provides a place where values and ethics can be evaluated and discussed. Within the disciplines (economics, anthropology, sociology, history, ethics, geography, political science), responsibility can be nurtured. And because social studies teaches us so much about life, when presented as an action process, it is respectful of the learner.

As we watch the changes in our global community and see old enemies as new comrades, it

After Dr. McDermott began her career as a high school teacher in Philadelphia, she quickly learned that students most enjoy experiential learning. A curriculum consultant with the Department of Education in Pennsylvania for 10 years, she recently moved to California to be close to the strategic reform of the language arts and social studies curriculum. Last year she taught whole language strategies in an inner-city, bilingual kindergarten and is currently teaching social studies and reading methods at California State University-Dominguez Hills. She will publish two books this year; the first is a scholarly work on gender models for boys in literature and the second, cowritten with Kathy O'Brien, is a strategy guide for the thematization through literature of the elementary curriculum.

becomes increasingly important to help students develop sensitivity to and respect for differing views and perspectives. In addition, we want students to learn about the relationships among societies, cultures, and individuals. Since social studies is the study of our social relationships, what better way than through a holistic approach that is child-centered, literature-based and meaning-centered?

The new social studies provides students with literature that shows the past; with primary sources that take students into another person's experience; with action tasks that require them to think for themselves and determine their own answers; and with cooperative methodology that provides for collaboration, networking, and responsibility for their own learning. Just as whole language can provide for dramatic learning opportunities, an action model in social studies can encourage students to direct their own learning and make social studies a part of themselves.

Good, action-oriented social studies has happened in classrooms for years. As Ken Goodman says, there have always been whole language teachers but they did not have the *tag*. The same is true for social studies. It is easier to teach social studies with materials that support a meaning-centered classroom. From a large collection of possibilities I have chosen a small sampling that supports a whole language, meaning-centered social studies class.

California is in the midst of a curriculum reform, and among those things changing is the social studies. The state's recently adopted *History/Social Science Framework* addresses the concerns raised above and encourages an integrated approach that incorporates literature into the entire curriculum.

The *Framework* is available from the State Department of Education, Bureau of Publication Sales, P.O. Box 271, Sacramento, CA 95802-0271 (916-445-1260). The price is $6.

📷 WHOLE LANGUAGE CAMERA

Butter or bust! Two young westerners make butter the old fashioned way, Palo Alto, CA.

by Sandra Wilde

Patterns and Strategies: Big Words

The *MAT-ATAR-SE'S* (metatarsus) is co-nec-ted to *TIB-E-A* (tibia)...
the *PA-TAL-A'S* (patella's) co-nec-ted to the *FIMER* (femur)...
the skil's (skull's) co-nec-ted to the *MAN-DA-BUIL* (mandible).

Mike, 1st grade

First-graders aren't usually expected to spell big words like *metatarsus* and *mandible!* Mike's class had been learning about the human body, and he was inspired to write this piece when he wondered why the song "Dem Bones" didn't use the scientific names of bones. All of Mike's spellings for bones were his own (rather than being copied from reference materials), but at one point he did look at a chart of the human skeleton to find out the names of some of the bones. His spellings of these big words are surprisingly good, particularly the consonants. When children are exposed to interesting information like the names of bones, they may very well choose to write about it if they feel comfortable using their own spellings. So often schools are afraid to expose children to challenging material, because they feel that curriculum is a matter of "mastering objectives," that time shouldn't be wasted on content that children won't be tested on. Curriculum *has* been watered down—into simplistic "skills." It's perfectly appropriate to expose first-graders to the scientific names of bones—if it's seen as enrichment, knowledge about the world that children might be interested in. Encouraging children to use their own spellings as they include such knowledge in their writing is just a small part of the process.

Resource Essay

Social Studies Books *en español* for Whole Language Classrooms

Recommended by Yvonne S. Freeman and Carolina Cervantes

For Emerging Readers

◆ *Primera biblioteca de los niños* (Children's first library), by Josep M. Parramón (Woodbury, NY: Barron's Educational Series, 1987). This collection of book sets includes teacher guides for generating discussion and research on six themes. Though vocabulary is sometimes more typical of Spain, illustrations and large print make this collection very predictable. The sets are very well suited for work with the following units: *Las cuatro estaciones* (The four seasons), *Los cuatro elementos* (The four elements), *Un día en . . .* (A day in . . .), *Los cinco sentidos* (The five senses), *La familia* (The family), *La vida* (Life).

For Independent Readers

◆ *Nico y Ana quieren ser médicos* (Nico and Ana want to be doctors), by Juan Capdevila (Barcelona: Editorial Timun Mas, S. A., 1986). This hardcover book centers around the medical profession and includes detailed drawings of a hospital and respective medical items, as well as numerous pictures. The setting is more European than American, and the story line is a bit simplistic.

For More Proficient Readers

◆ *Los niños de La Pacanda* (The children of the Pacanda), by Ulf Lofgren (Mexico City: Sistemas Técnicos de Edición, 1989). This well-researched text tells about the Tarasco people who live on the largest isle of Mexico's largest lake, Patzcuaro.

◆ *El Tornaviaje* (The return voyage), by Armida de la Vara (Mexico City: SEP and Libros de Rincón, 1986). This softcover text with black-and-white illustrations is a short historical novel set in the later half of the 1500s. Without his parents' permission, young Andrés stows away on a ship headed from Mexico toward the Philippines. The voyage is a dangerous one since no Spanish ship had yet completed a safe route from these islands to the American continent.

➜ See: Freeman and Cervantes, pp. 87, 184, 320

Yvonne S. Freeman is a professor and Carolina Cervantes is a graduate student at Fresno Pacific College, Fresno, CA.

Social Studies Resources
Reviewed by Cynthia McDermott

Resource: Books

The Changing City

Jorg Muller
1977; $14.95

The Changing Countryside

Jorg Muller
1977; $17.95..
New York: Atheneum

For use in geography with any age and in any language are two resources, *The Changing City* and *The Changing Countryside*. Both books by Jorg Muller comprise wordless oversized drawings that show how a city and a farm area change over 20 years. It is a truly remarkable resource.

K–6 Geography, Themes, Key Ideas and Learning Opportunities

$6 from:
National Council for Geographic Education
16A Leonard Hall
Indiana University of Pennsylvania
Indiana, PA 15705
1-412-357-6290

The National Council for Geographic Education has produced *K–6 Geography, Themes, Key Ideas and Learning Opportunities*. Written in simple language for those of us who need help with teaching geography, this publication is immensely useful.

Resource: Catalog

Resources for Educational Equity

Women's Educational Equity Act Publishing Center
U.S. Dept. of Education
Washington, DC
1-800-225-3088

From the government comes *Resources for Educational Equity*, a catalog that contains a wide variety of resources related to gender-equity issues. Call for your copy today!

Resource: Distributors

Social Studies School Service

10200 Jefferson Blvd.
P.O. Box 802
Culver City, CA 90232-0802
1-213-839-2436 (CA)
1-800-421-4246

One of the most comprehensive collections of social studies materials in the nation is housed by Social Studies School Service. They produce catalogs on a variety of subjects, but unlike most other distribution companies, Social Studies School Service only sells materials they have carefully reviewed. Catalog descriptions are written by the reviewers and not by the producers of the materials. And the reviewers are teachers with expertise in the area. You won't find a more helpful staff, and they are available for advice.

Spectrum Books

P.O. Box 3463
Glendale, CA 91201
1-818-545-3934

In various parts of the country there is a greater need for multicultural titles than in other parts. In California teachers search for books written in the many languages spoken in our classrooms. Spectrum Books specializes in Spanish books. Give Bud Fish of Spectrum a call; he's eager to catch your business.

Resource: Organizations

The Council for Indian Education

517 Rimrock Rd.
P.O. Box 31215
Billings, MT 59107

The Council for Indian Education produces a one-page list of what it describes as "authentic, interesting books for children depicting the true life of the American Indian." In their wide assortment of books, you will find humor, mystery, and adventure.

National Council for the Social Studies (NCSS)

Membership: $50 (comprehensive);
$40 (regular); $20 (student/retired)
3501 Newark St., NW
Washington, DC 20016
1-202-966-7840
FAX 1-202-966-2061

Social Studies and the Young Learner

$25/year (4 issues);
$15/year NCSS members
from NCSS

The National Council for the Social Studies is the oldest organization for social studies educators. Over 60 years old, and international in scope, its members receive a variety of benefits. These include the journal *Social Education*, the newsletter *The Social Studies Professional*, books, information and crisis intervention services, and travel and study programs. NCSS also publishes *Social Studies and the Young Learner*.

National Geographic Society

17th and M Streets, NW
Washington, DC 20036

The National Geographic Society continues to encourage a love of geography in children. Yearly fellowships provide selected teachers with the opportunity to have fun with geography. Children can subscribe to *World*, a monthly social science magazine.

Resource: Periodicals

The Daybreak Star Indian Reader

$24/year (8 issues) library rate;
$16/year teacher and gift rate from:
1945 Yale Pl. E.
Seattle, WA 98102
1-206-325-0070

The Daybreak Star Indian Reader is a 24-page children's learning resource, published monthly throughout the school year by Native American students and an adult staff. Although the newsprint magazine includes some typical basic skills activities, the stories compiled by students are interesting. For large orders, subscription rates are based on a sliding scale.

Images of Excellence

Images of Excellence
Foundation, Inc.
215 W. College Ave.
P.O. Box 1131
Boiling Springs, NC 28017

Four years ago, a group of adults decided to encourage young people to look to role models such as Thomas Jefferson or Mother Teresa, rather than Rocky or Prince. As a result, *Images of Excellence* was born. This unique company is staffed entirely by volunteers. Each issue of this magazine presents facts, stories, photos, or drawings of one significant person, and a teacher's supplement. Excellent for junior and senior high.

Resource: Mail-Order Company

California Kids History Catalog

P.O. Box 1521
Sonoma, CA 95476
1-707-996-0121

Jim Silverman is really interested in kids, particularly California kids, who supply part of the name of his mail-order company offering books, videotapes, maps, posters, puppets, and other interesting materials for sale. They all help teachers explore California history with children. Jim himself wrote and published the primary resource, *California Kids: An Indian Girl, a Mexican Boy, and a Yankee Girl Born in California Before 1850 Book 1*. He is also available to lead special school programs and teacher workshops. Starting in Spring 1990, the *California Kids History Newsletter* will be available semiannually from the catalog for $5 an issue.

Resource: Publishers

Childrens Press

5440 N. Cumberland Ave.
Chicago, IL 60656
1-312-693-0800

Childrens Press produces a variety of supplemental social studies books for grades two to eight, on subjects such as Vietnam, black studies, and civil rights. One of their series, *Encyclopedia of Presidents*, presents facts, pictures, and primary dialogue.

Cobblestone Publishing Company

20 Grove St.
Peterborough, NH 13458
1-603-924-7209

Cobblestone Publishing produces three magazines for kids. *Faces*, a black and white magazine about kids in other cultures; *Cobblestone*, a wonderful history magazine with lots of primary sources and beautiful pictures; and *Calliope*, an ancient history magazine, from which you might even learn that *hoi polloi* is Greek for "the many."

Lucent Books, Inc.

P.O. Box 289011
San Diego, CA 92128-9011
1-619-485-7424
1-800-231-5163
FAX 1-619-485-9549

Lucent Books publishes wonderful titles on a variety of topics, some as far ranging as pyramids and poltergeists. The most challenging series for kids is the Opposing Viewpoints series, which presents a variety of opinions on issues such as immigration and animal rights, and asks students to make up their own minds.

Great Teachers:
Debra Goodman
by Toby Kahn Curry

Walking into Debra Goodman's fifth-grade class is like diving into a sea of kids alive with language. There are kids talking, writing at desks, reading on the floor, conferring in groups, writing in pairs, giggling over books, listening to tapes, and quite possibly one or two kids having a conference with Debra.

Probably the only one who'll notice there's a visitor in the room will be Debra's class secretary, a student who gets to sit at a big desk (in most classrooms, it's the teacher's desk) and takes care of all of the small paperwork tasks that can consume some teachers for hours. Since you usually can't spot Debra, the class secretary will tell you where she can be found.

As a frequent visitor to Debra's classroom, I've learned never to go in empty-handed. I always have a notebook handy, ready to take notes and jot down some of her superb activities and organizational strategies. Each corner of Debra's room houses a different center, and each center is run and operated by the students. The kids run the classroom museum, operate their town (classroom) general store, elect to join the class theater, take turns using the library (located mainly in a parent-built loft), feel free to use the art center, and meet individually and in small groups at the writing conference table. Books can be found all over the room. Hundreds of selections are in the loft, while special reference books and literature sets are found in various bookcases especially placed to help organize the different work areas.

Last year, Debra's classes named their room "The Land of Teribithia" after listening to the first of many stories that Debra read to them, Katherine Paterson's *Bridge to Teribithia*. This naming was the first of many literature-to-life connections that Debra's students would make throughout the new school year.

Debra is a master at teaching history through historical fiction and exploring feelings and moods through poetry. She helps her students become researchers of their own families by interviewing family members and presenting their family histories. Students are taught a wide scope of American and world history through two year-long thematic units: "Cultures in Contact" and "Childhood in America." In Debra's class you can meet a fifth-grader who feels that she is an expert on the Great Depression and one who knows what it was like to grow up a slave in the pre-Civil War American south. Debra's kids are immersed in language and emerge as independent readers and writers with a strong sense of self and an understanding of the community that surrounds them.

These classroom accomplishments would be enough to strive toward for most teachers, but not for Debra. She is not just a teacher for children, she is a teacher for teachers. She has always encouraged and supported her peers, helping coworkers deal with an unrealistic mandated curriculum or brainstorming methods for real evaluation in the face of archaic grading systems. Debra has also been the driving force in maintaining the Detroit TAWL group.

Though many teachers are satisfied with making an impact in their own classrooms and often close their doors to the inadequacies of the systems that surround them, Debra, to the good fortune of hundreds of Detroit kids, has helped to encourage meaningful literacy instruction by consulting and collaborating with other teachers in the birthing of a new whole language school. For Debra, it's not enough to have a classroom where literacy is "dripping off the walls," she plans to live in a city where literacy is resounding off the rooftops.

➜ See: Bloome, p. 229; Goodman, pp. 24, 25, 107, 224, 236, 268, 274, 283, 400; Literature Reference List, p. 429.

Toby Kahn Curry is a middle school teacher at the Dewey Center for Urban Education, Detroit, MI.

MarVELous INVENTIONS

The First Speech Ever Written

After listening to her father, a history teacher, praise Lincoln's Gettysburg Address, this first-grader sat down at her desk in school the next day and wrote her own version: —*LBB*

[The first speech ever written...Four score and seven years ago, our fathers brought forth on this continent, a new nation, conceived in...the proposition that all men are created equal]

—Contributed by Marsha Umland, primary teacher, Albany, CA

The first four scor speech AndseveN ever write Years ago our fathers Brout fourth on this continent ol new nas inon. consed in To The Proprasish n thatALL men are created eqeL

Becoming Literate
by Arlene Lecours

We've Got *World Book* in Our Hands

My intentions were pure and simple (and of course "whole"): Get folks to look at what's been printed about Detroit and, after milling through the travelogues and various "What's What About Detroit," get folks to write their own guide to Detroit. Oh, me of little faith.

I collected a variety of materials from sources published within the city and nationally—newspaper articles saying good and bad things about Detroit; locally produced brochures detailing restaurants, museums, historical and current statistical information; and the Detroit pages from the *World Book Encyclopedia*, including a map.

And that's when all the fun began. I noted that several elements fairly important to the city were missing from the map and the resources. Through my open-ended questioning (What would you add to the map? What would you say about———? Why do you think they left those things out?), my students opened fire. How can they say that? Don't they know anything? This was published in 1989? They vented their anger toward the source of their frustration: *World Book Encyclopedia*.

I modified my previous plan, excited by their changing focus. The crux of their investigations and presentations became an in-depth comparison of encyclopedias and critique of their worth in general.

The encyclopedia project involved answering such questions as: What do other encyclopedias say about us? How can we get accurate information about the city of Detroit (and why didn't the research staff from the encyclopedia get that information)? How much information changes from year to year in encyclopedias? What is the value of an encyclopedia? To whom should we direct our questions? How do we write a good business letter? How long must we wait for answers?

The project lasted about three months (meeting three hours per week). The city of Detroit responded to a list of our questions and *World Book* wrote, thanking us for our interest and explaining their procedures.

As this project was winding down and we were waiting for the responses from *World Book*, my eager students began to wonder, "What next?" The most exciting element of our research was not what we found out but what we were able to ask. In many ways it supported the motto, "It's not the answer that enlightens, but the question."

➜ See: Edelsky, p. 72; Lecours, p. 346.

Arlene Lecours teaches adult education at the Rouge Academy (UAW-Ford National Education, Development & Training Center), Dearborn Stamping Plant, Dearborn, MI.

YOUNG ARTISTS

—Nelson G. Begay, Nazlini Boarding School, Navaho Nation, AZ

Classroom Demonstrations

by Debra Goodman

Community Study: A Focus for Social Studies and Language Learning

I want to look at the writing of two students, Lisa and Shanda. Both are products of my fifth-grade classroom. Lisa's Family Tree Project is impressive, the type of thing you'd read to other students for inspiration:

Family Tree Project
by Lisa Rousseau-Clark

I was thinking the other day about Culture, What is it? Culture is a word we use to describe our life: our clothes, what we do for a living, what we eat, our background.

My background is made up of many cultures. My Dad's side of the family is Italian on his Mother's side and Appalachian on his father's side. My Mother's side of the family is German on her Mother's side and French-Canadian on her Father's side.

My Grandfather on my Father's side was named Paul Clark. He was from Virginia. He came from a family of Farmers who were called sharecroppers. That means that the person who is the sharecropper does not own his own land but he farms somebody else's land in return for some of the crop. My grandfather was in the Army for 26 years and went all over the world. I never met my grandfather because he died before I was born.

My Grandmother came from an Italian family in Brooklyn, New York. Her Mother and Father came from Italy, but she was born here. My mother worked in a factory to make doll dresses. And her father put in safes. My Grandmother worked at Hudson's for twenty-five years. She first came to Detroit when my Grandfather was sent to Fort Wayne to be at the Army base. . . .

When I started this project I felt kind of bad because we don't speak any other language, we don't have any customs from another country, but now I have learned a lot about my relatives. Now I want to do more research to find out more about my relatives. Who they were, where they came from, why they came here.

I found out a lot of interesting things about my families that I never knew before. It's interesting that people end up living wherever their jobs are. Like my Great-Grandfather Rousseau ended up in Saginaw because that's where the lumber industry was. My Great-Grandfather Krauss ended up in Freeland because that is where there was good farm land.

I think my culture is an interesting one because I have four different ones . . . Italian, Appalachian, French-Canadian and German. I want to find out more about each of the cultures and how my family has changed with each generation. I like learning about old cultures and traditions. My Mom and Dad and I try to make our own traditions. We go to Nowel Night every year, and we have tried to have a traditional Italian Christmas Eve dinner. We always buy a real tree for Christmas. We decorate the house real spooky every Halloween. Every Sunday we try to go to Belle Isle with our dogs. I like our traditions and I hope that we can make them better each year.

Shanda, on the other hand, copied her report out of an encyclopedia. The fact that she mistook "slavs" for "slaves" serves only to demonstrate the lack of personal involvement or any integration with past experience in this type of writing.

Although Shanda produced her piece in my classroom, it can also be seen as the result of four years of traditional schooling. Shanda was working on a personal research project. She was asked to select a topic that interested her. She selected slavery. She was asked to make a list of questions about the topic and read selectively for the answers to her questions. I asked her to hand in her notes, not a completed formal paper. But Shanda approached this whole language assignment in a traditional way. She looked up the topic in an encyclopedia and copied down what she saw, disregarding the fact that she didn't understand what she was reading and copying.

But just as I can't really accept the blame for Shanda's traditional response to my assignment, I can't take credit for Lisa's work. Lisa has also had traditional schooling for the past four years, but she has parents who have encouraged her to be creative, artistic, and thoughtful. They spent a great deal of time discussing her family history with her, and I picture them standing behind her as she sat at the computer to write her report.

Some colleagues have wondered how much of Lisa's project she "wrote herself." I'm not sure what difference it makes. No writer writes in a vacuum, without the influence and assistance of friends, editors, and the strong background of literary works the writer has read. The real question is: What has Lisa learned from this project? Will she ever forget that Michigan has a history of farmers, lumberjacks, and miners? That soldiers were stationed at Fort Wayne, that German prisoners were held in Michigan during World War II? She will listen differently when someone mentions Appalachian, Italian, German, or French-Canadian history and culture.

Lisa has learned that she has a rich culture and that she can learn about many things from members of her own family. And she leaves her Family Tree Project eager to learn more. I started asking fifth-graders to look at their family histories as a way of bringing their own background and experiences into the classroom. I wanted to introduce history by having my students make connections to their own lives.

As I worked on this project with my students, David Bloom was involved in ethnographic research in my building. He found that community study has far-reaching effects. When kids begin to recognize the expertise within their families and their communities they tend to draw on that expertise in other areas of research. They see authors of history texts and encyclopedias as people, experts on par with the members of their own family. They tend to integrate new information into their own experiences and this is reflected in their reading and writing.

I now include community study in all of my social studies units. Combined with historical fiction books, discussion, and group inquiry projects, the community study gives social studies the human quality that often gets left out of textbooks. In addition, it helps children to see connections between themselves, their community, and the fiction and nonfiction texts in the classroom.

➜ See: Goodman, pp. 24, 25, 224, 254, 274.

My Place: A Community Study

The fifth-grade students at Burton International School have described and mapped their neighborhoods in a book that is a presentation of their community research. We got the idea for this book from one called *My Place*, by Nadia Wheatley and Donna Rawlins, published by Collins Dove in Melbourne, Australia.

Here is Brian Greer's description of his neighborhood:

This is a very interesting neighborhood. A lady who lives down the street is named Rosa Parks. She is famous because she would not give up her seat for a white person a long time ago on the bus. She knew Martin Luther King, Jr. and worked with him for civil rights. There's 90% senior citizens on our block. A neighbor, who we call Luther, helps the older people by cutting their grass and helping out inside. He has the best lawn on the block. The school in our neighborhood is Brady Elementary. My brother goes to Brady Elementary and my sister goes to the preschool there. Behind Brady is W.D.T.R. radio station for Detroit Public Schools.

➜ See: Literature Reference List, p. 429.

Debra Goodman is an elementary teacher at Dewey Center for Urban Education, Detroit, MI.
Brian Greer is a fifth-grader at Burton International School, Detroit, MI.

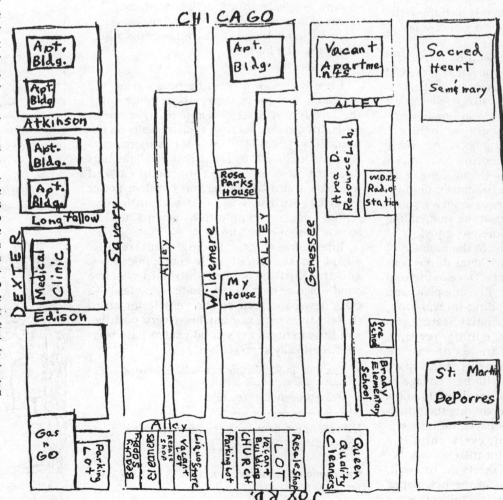

Network

New Ways to Use the News? Tying Your Teaching Together with a Class Newspaper!

by Jeff LaBenz

One summer as the school year was approaching, I began to get a little anxious regarding the myriad of little pieces of curriculum in our scope and sequence book. I wanted to come up with some sort of grand unifying idea, an "elegant solution" to tie all of the loose ends of curriculum together. While in the shower one day, I came up with this idea.

I realized that other teachers have done newspapers in their classrooms, but I envisioned this as something different: not just as a unit on newspapers, or a newspaper as an aside to all the other aspects of the curriculum, but a newspaper as carrier and unifier of the curriculum—to be used even as "metacognition," in order to get the children to think about what they had learned.

My first task was to get the children to plan their newspaper and to feel ownership of it as well. The first homework of the year was to do research as follows:

"Talk with your mom or dad about newspapers. We want to find out a few things to help us publish our own class newspaper, the *Colina Columns*. If you receive a newspaper at your home, look through it a minute with your mom or dad. If not, just ask Mom or Dad. Here are some things you want to find out:

1. Who writes a newspaper? Just one person? Many? What are these people called?
2. What are some sections of features in the newspaper (hint: like the sports section, or the food section)? Find as many as you can. List them here.

We discussed each of the contributions and tried to figure out ways to convert commercial newspaper ideas for use in our own class newspaper. For instance, questions like "How can we make an entertainment section in our newspaper?" and "What could/should we include?" brought up answers like doing book and movie reviews. Instead of writing boring *book reports* (which often end up boring because the "purpose" and "audience" are vague and/or unmotivating), children write *book reviews* to be published for everyone to read, recommending exciting books for other children to enjoy!

There are similar solutions to the problem of seemingly unpurposeful curriculum throughout all content and process areas. Developing oral language and listening skills, devising plans and outlines for writing, compiling information, writing rough drafts, cooperative learning in child-to-child conferences, editing, revising, exploring varied forms/formats of written expression, identifying statements versus questions, and so much more—children engage in *all* of these things when they are allowed to do a simple (but fun!) task of interviewing the principal for a write-up in the newspaper, for instance.

Regarding management, every child is a reporter—everybody writes for the *Columns*. We have 11 laminated sign-up sheets on the wall, one for each of the sections of the newspaper. Using nonpermanent Pentels, children write

their "possible story lead," name, and date under the appropriate section, and begin work on their stories. I can see at a glance who is working on what, and for how long. Limiting the number of sign-up spaces on each list limits the number of children working on stories within a certain section. It also ensures that *each* section gets in *each* issue (in case 21 people want to do an *interview*), and lets the children know if someone else is already covering a story topic they wanted to choose. Nonpermanent Pentels are used on laminated lists so that entries can be wiped clean with a wet paper towel as the stories get published.

Here is a list of the sections included in our newspaper:

- **Current Events** (reports about items taken from our whole-class journal, i.e., class activities, units being studied);
- **TV and Movie Reviews;**
- **Travel Section** (field trips we've gone on, trips the kids have taken);
- **Sports Section** (what we're doing in PE, recess, after-school sports);
- **Food Section** (One child recommended ravioli in the cafeteria! Others have written recipes for foods that they can make themselves. Also reviews of restaurants they've visited);
- **Book Reviews** (instead of book reports);
- **Art and Leisure** (art projects, music class reports, reports about free-time activities);
- **Features and Interviews** (articles focusing on how we do various things in the classroom, interviews of teachers or students);
- **Science and Technology** (science experiments results);
- **Want Ads** (notices that the kids write for parents to save things we need for projects in the room, e.g., egg cartons, milk cartons, etc.! One child wrote a description of his lost cat and included his telephone number for other kids to call if found!);
- **Weather/Statistics**.

I use the word-processing program on my own computer to do the printing, while doing the layout and pasteup manually. (Numerous programs can be used with similar results on the Apple IIe.) Photos of all sorts of classroom activities are included, as are occasional drawings done by the children (photocopied and reduced). I also have a section entitled: **Letter from the Editor.** I use this section for my school-home communications when I need to send a "parent-letter" home.

Integrating writing, reading, math, science, art, PE, music, school-home communications, and the thrill of being published (with the child's picture next to the headline, no less!)—a class newspaper can be the vehicle for all of these! My experience has been very positive, and the parents of my second-graders have been enthusiastically appreciative!

➔ See: Bird, p. 92; Christine, p. 410; Edelsky, p. 72.

From *Newsletter IV s.m.i.l.e.*, 1988.

Jeff LaBenz is a primary teacher at Kyrene de la Colina, Kyrene District, AZ.

Subscription Information: *s.m.i.l.e.*, P.O. Box 25170, Tempe, AZ 85282.

Resource: Publisher

Newspower

12 Highland Ave.
P.O. Box 203
Northfield, MA 01360
1-413-498-2133
1-800-346-8330

This is one of those "why didn't I think of that idea?" resources! Newspower produces "Make-Your-Own-Newspaper" templates that allow students to become newspaper reporters and to use real newspaper layout. These versatile teaching tools promote creativity and originality in writing; in addition, students learn that editing is a necessary part of the writing process.

Students in grades two through eight write articles on leisure, sports, school, food, travel, special events, and local and world news; they also conduct interviews, review books, and place classified ads. All materials are printed on large, sturdy paper stock that stands up to erasures and gives a quality feel to students' work. Teaching Idea Booklets are provided for each "Make-Your-Own-Newspaper" template.

Doug Haner

Resource: Program

Newspaper in Education (NIE)

American Newspaper Publishers Association (ANPA) Foundation
The Newspaper Center
Box 17407, Dulles International Airport
Washington, DC 20041
1-703-648-1000

My son discovered the newspaper, the sports page I should say, when he was seven years old and an avid baseball fan. Now we have a contest each morning to see who gets to the paper first. Students who read the newspaper daily are knowledgeable about local and world events and have more to talk and write about because they are better informed.

Newspaper in Education is a program that provides ideas and materials for utilizing newspapers in classrooms. NIE materials are packed with such ideas as using the weather page to plan an imaginary vacation, developing math problems or devising a household food budget from supermarket ads, and analyzing sports statistics.

Doug Haner

YOUNG ARTISTS

Fifth-grade reporters in Don Penthal's class work at publishing a weekly newspaper, often written around a particular theme. Here's a cartoon from their environmental edition. Harry Hopkins School, Mentor, OH.

Science

Cornerstone: Mike McGuffee

Hands-on Science

Where Do I Begin?

Across the country there seems to be a renewed interest in elementary science education. With the renewal of this interest come many questions of when, where, and how to extend elementary science beyond the traditional textbook-centered approach. Fortunately, help is near, and the perfect place to begin is with *Science for Children*. Prepared by a joint effort of the National Academy of Sciences and the Smithsonian Institution, this guide describes curriculum materials and sources of information that can provide excellent support for effective, hands-on, inquiry-based programs. Copies have been sent to the nation's school superintendents.

The guide is divided into three major sections: curriculum materials, supplementary resources, and sources of information and assistance. The section on curriculum materials offers an annotated bibliography of most of the major science curriculum projects. Each entry includes citation, appropriate grade level, sources for kits or materials, and price. The supplementary resource section includes annotated listings of science activity books, methods books, and magazines for children and teachers. The third section offers institutional resources such as museums, technology centers, professional organizations, publishers, and suppliers. The introductory remarks in the guide could have just as easily been written for the introduction to a whole language guide:

> We at the NSRC believe that children begin to learn science from the moment they start to perceive their environment. They have an innate need to make sense of what happens. They make assumptions based on their perceptions, and they begin to predict what will happen and to test their predictions. Bit by bit, they form a useful model of the world around them.
>
> Before children go to school, they exercise their natural curiosity daily. School can expand their universe and open new areas of inquiry for them.

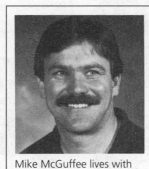

Mike McGuffee lives with his wife, Phoebe, and two sons, Jordan and Nicholas, in Stillwater, Oklahoma. He teaches fourth grade at Skyline Elementary School. In 1988 he was recognized as a Christa McAuliffe Fellow by the U.S. Department of Education. His fellowship enabled him to work with various school districts to assist in the development of a hands-on science program. He continues to work with other elementary schools through inservice education on the role of science in whole language classrooms.

Or, it can close off their search for knowledge by presenting science as a set of words and rules to be memorized from the pages of a textbook.

Sound familiar? Hands-on science is a natural in the whole language classroom, and this guide can be an important resource for taking that first step.

"Hey, This Is Fun"

"Hey, this is fun! We're not learning anything, but it's fun!" Ten-year-old Jeremy just *had* to add that second sentence. His comment left me speechless, which proved to be fortunate, because it wasn't until later that I understood its meaning.

It was early in the school year, and our fourth grade was involved in a hands-on science activity on astronomy. The previous two weeks had been filled with the children busily making models, observing the night sky, recording their observations, and experimenting with predictions gleaned from their data. Jeremy's comment didn't stir much of a response from the class, but it did cause me to stop and reflect.

What was Jeremy communicating? Unfortunately, he was echoing feelings I suspect many children in our schools share—first, you're not learning science unless you are answering questions at the end of a chapter, and second (and maybe worse), you can't be learning if you're having fun. These sentiments shouldn't be surprising. After all, a quick survey of an elementary science textbook will provoke many thoughts, but I doubt if fun and excitement immediately come to mind.

Typically we teach children, "This is the moon. It orbits the earth. It goes through phases." The children respond, "That is the moon. It orbits the earth. It goes through phases." Yawn.

Wouldn't it be great if we could evoke other responses like "Wow, look at that! It's like a big ball. I wonder why sometimes it's lit on one side and at other times lit on the opposite side." These responses can be achieved by following the simple advice given by child-centered educators like the Goodmans. The advice? "Take your cues from children."

The "cues" children are giving us are an invitation—an invitation to join them in their world of a thousand questions. In the child's world, every question leads to another question. Therefore, to accept their invitation is not to answer all the questions, but to share in the fun of exploring the universe.

Children seem to be born asking the question "Why?" We can be forever trying

to find all the answers, or we can try other responses such as "Let's explore and see what we find."

Teaching in this manner wakes us from the sleepy world of traditional science. It adds a dimension of playfulness to school that follows the natural course of childhood. Leaving behind the familiar, it allows us to risk, not always knowing our destination. Taking this journey can inspire excitement and a renewed sense of wonder about our universe.

Participating with children in the world of a thousand questions might cause other children like Jeremy some misunderstandings. They might not realize that learning can be fun. Even some parents and teachers might need convincing. But it will be worth our effort. We have only to watch the faces of our children to know that it is the right thing to do.

Evaluating Hands-on Science

Like whole language, one of the challenges for hands-on science is evaluation. In science, we are so accustomed to measuring the content that we overlook other ways children might be learning. During a hands-on activity, it's especially important to evaluate the *processes* of science as well as the content. Let me give an example.

My fourth-grade class completed a unit of activities called Clay Boats. In this unit, they were given a ball of clay and a beaker of water and were asked to drop the clay into the water and record their observations. The clay sank to the bottom and a discussion followed.

Next, students were asked to try to make the clay float. They eventually realized that a boat or saucer shape would float, and the class took off. After a few sessions exploring with their boats, students were challenged to see how much "cargo" their boats could carry. They used paper clips, pennies, and washers as cargo, and made many comparisons between the shapes of the boats and their cargo-carrying capacities.

After completing a dozen activities, I asked a question that I had saved, "What happened to make the clay float when you reshaped it?" The most common response was "When you reshape it, it weighs less!"

If the objective of the lesson had been to teach the scientific reason for why clay floats, most of the class would have failed. The children's answers revealed that they were having trouble with the concept of conservation of mass. According to Piaget, fourth grade is right on the border developmentally for learning such a concept. Therefore, if my only interest was content, this activity would be better saved for older children. What were the children learning?

In this activity, the processes of observing, measuring, classifying, recording data, predicting outcomes, as well as cooperative learning and problem-solving, are some of the kinds of learning that took place. Teachers need a solid understanding of these processes in order to effectively evaluate hands-on science. If these processes are unfamiliar, there are many good methods books cited in the resource guide *Science for Children*. If we are armed with a knowledge of these processes, our evaluation of elementary science can then follow many of the principles of evaluation outlined in the *Whole Language Evaluation Book* (1988), such as observing, interacting, and analyzing.

The content of science, such as the law of buoyancy, *is* extremely important. However, we must keep in mind that there can be many other types of learning occurring in a good science lesson. Observing the process as well as the content of science can provide the teacher with a richer, broader base for evaluation.

(Continued on page 318)

Hands-on science can expand the child's universe and open new areas of inquiry.

(Continued from page 317)

Taking the Plunge:
Water in the Classroom

Imagine 25 elementary students totally captivated by a science activity. Not too hard to picture, right? Would it seem more difficult to imagine if I told you that the only thing they were doing was dropping water from a medicine dropper onto a sheet of wax paper and then recording their observations? Imagine another 25 students bubbling with excitement, this time captivated by experimenting with colored water mixing in clear water. Pure and simple science, revolving around one theme—water.

Mention studying water to most elementary science teachers and they usually begin talking about oceanography. "Okay, but have your students ever observed a drop of water?" I ask.

"Well, not exactly," they respond.

Could we be overlooking something? What we might be overlooking is some great science. And there is no better place to take a second look than many of the units developed by the Elementary Science Study (ESS). ESS was a major elementary science project funded by the National Science Foundation during the sixties and seventies.

The program philosophy was designed to build on the natural curiosity of children while overcoming the common obstacles that prevent teachers from doing more hands-on science. Units such as Colored Solutions, Drops, Streams and Containers, Ice Cubes, Sink or Float, and Clay Boats offer weeks of activities with minimal equipment lists.

Teachers interested in obtaining guides for these units can find them in two primary sources. First, the original activities are now part of the public domain and many are available through ERIC. Another source is Delta Education. Delta has revised the teacher's guides and markets them commercially. Equipment for these units can be found locally, bought through Delta or through major science equipment distributors like Frey Scientific.

I have found it worthwhile to purchase teacher's guides first, then figure out my own equipment needs. Science kits just seem to naturally flow from order to disorder. Our school has been more successful with ordering general science equipment such as classroom sets of beakers, graduated cylinders, medicine droppers, thermometers, balances, magnifiers, and so on, then sharing them as needed while classrooms work through different units.

Hands-on science does require some planning and preparation, but the benefits are worth it. By keeping the focus simple, we can all be captivated by science. Water is an often overlooked source for some exciting science lessons and is a great way for teachers just beginning a hands-on science program to get their feet wet.

References

Goodman, K. S., Y. M. Goodman, and W. J. Hood, eds. 1988. *The whole language evaluation book*. Portsmouth, NH: Heinemann.

Children exploring the world of a thousand questions.

Students captivated by investigating a drop of water.

During a hands-on activity, it's especially important to evaluate the processes of science as well as the content.

Resource: Organization

National Audubon Society Expedition Institute

Northeast Audubon
 Center
Sharon, CT 06069
1-203-364-0522

I opened the National Audubon Society Expedition Institute booklet and 15 minutes later I was ready to spend my upcoming sabbatical year being a part of this program.

Imagine learning environmental education by traveling through the U.S. and Canada for a year, and studying the impact societal patterns of behavior have on our fragile ecosystems! For those in the field of environmental education who are ready for in-depth field studies, or for those wanting a quality college degree in Environmental Education at Lesley College, Cambridge, Massachusetts, this is definitely a program to investigate.

Doug Haner

Resource: Organization

National Science Resource Center (NSRC)

National Academy
 of Sciences
Arts and Industries Bldg.
Smithsonian Institution
Washington, DC 20560
1-202-357-2555

Resource: Book

Science for Children:
Resources for Teachers

$7.95 from:
National Academy Press
2102 Constitution Ave.,
 NW
Washington, DC 20418

In response to national concerns about science illiteracy, the Smithsonian's National Science Resource Center is getting involved in elementary-level science curriculum. Its Science and Technology for Children Program (STC) is in charge of finding immediate and practical ways to develop high-quality hands-on science programs.

Field testing is now under way on the first 3 of 24 proposed units for grades one to six. These units include inexpensive apparatus, teachers guides, and student activity books on such topics as electric currents, plant growth, and magnifiers and microscopes. All units integrate science with art, mathematics, and language development.

The NSRC's *Science for Children* is an excellent annotated sourcebook of science curriculum materials, supplements, and pertinent information.

Doug Haner

Marvelous Inventions

Knot Know-How

I. Wat to Naw haw to toay a fesh noat naw I olred noaw hew to tay a fesh in noat

You goa ren maran then you lek it to wet down then you pl it in Wen you kesh a big cra py and bigr xesh in kas Your fesh intes lok Bres.

[I want to know how to tie a fish knot now I already know how to tie a fishing knot You go around then you lick it to wet it down then you pull it When you catch a big crappie and bigger fish in case your fishing line breaks.]

—Contributed by Diane Gammon, primary teacher, Westran Elementary, Huntsville, MO

Science Resources

Reviewed by Doug Haner

Resource: Organization

National Science Teachers Association (NSTA)

1742 Connecticut Ave., NW
Washington, DC 20009
1-202-328-5800

With over 50,000 members worldwide, the National Science Teachers Association is the largest professional organization that is dedicated to improving the teaching of science at all levels. It provides a typical range of services: conventions, a publications catalog, journals, and so on. The association's position statements address such issues as creationism in the science classroom, teaching human sexuality, and using animals in science laboratories. It is currently working on a program designed to change the scope, sequence, and coordination of U.S. science classes.

NSTA's 30-page publications catalog is surprisingly refreshing. In place of esoteric books and pamphlets, the catalog authors pride themselves on making the best science education resource books available to teachers at all levels. The catalog truly brings together an interesting assortment of hard-to-find, practical books.

Resource: Book

Science on a Shoestring

Herb Strongin
1976; 187 pp.; $16
Reading, MA:
Addison-Wesley

I first met Herb Strongin in 1974 when I was director of the Park South Teacher Center in San Francisco. One of the teachers on our advisory council had heard about Herb and suggested I contact him to teach a workshop. We were looking for inexpensive, alternative, hands-on methods of teaching science to elementary school students that involved a discovery approach.

Herb arrived for the workshop with 20 Science on a Shoestring kits that he had assembled from inexpensive materials, and proceeded to involve us in investigating solids, liquids, earthworms, musical instruments, flashlights, and magnets. He had a sincere and infectious enthusiasm for teaching and learning, and a belief that science should be discovered through handling real materials.

After successful field tests by over 700 elementary teachers in San Francisco and the Bay Area, Herb wrote *Science on a Shoestring,* which was published in 1976. Teachers will recognize immediately that a classroom teacher wrote this book. Each activity clearly and simply states the specific concept or skill to be taught and the materials needed, and gives an excellent, fail-safe, step-by-step script for those who may approach teaching science hesitantly.

Resource: Book

Mudpies to Magnets: A Preschool Science Curriculum

Robert A. Williams, Robert E. Rockwell, and Elizabeth A. Sherwood
1987; 157 pp.; $12.95
Mt. Rainier, MD:
Gryphon House

Finally—a science book for preschoolers that builds on a child's curiosity and natural sense of wonder. When science begins with such a child-directed approach, it becomes alive and vibrant, and sets a tone that makes science an enjoyable part of learning about life.

The authors demonstrate their years of experience with preschoolers by packing the book with simple suggestions to make the activities successful for young children. The activities are organized by theme and by grade level. Each activity begins with a section suggesting ways for teachers to elicit oral language from children. There is a list of easy-to-find materials, instruction guidelines, and then a "want to do more" section that will help extend an activity for weeks. The authors begin with simple, easily accessible materials and suggest questions that lead to the early stages of the scientific method.

Resource: Book

The Whole Cosmos Catalog of Science Activities

Joe Abruscato and Jack Hassard
1977; 134 pp.; $12.95
Glenview, IL:
Scott, Foresman

This is one of those books that seems intriguing at first glance and then gets better and better with each chapter. The authors know that true learning begins with a sense of joy and wonder, and have selected their activities on that basis. If you are one of the "kids of all ages" mentioned on the front cover, then you will enjoy this book.

Learning becomes an adventure as you wander through the enticing selections and illustrations of this oversized catalog. The authors have skillfully blended four types of activities through this book: science, puzzles and games, creative arts, and biographies. Don't miss the last two chapters, which have science fiction stories to read and create, ESP experiments, guided fantasy five original board games, magic tricks, and a one-act play.

Resource: Periodical

Science Is Happening Here

Valerie Stieg, coordinator
Elementary Science Network
York University
Faculty of Education
4700 Keele St.
North York, Ontario, M3J 1P3 Canada
1-416-736-5004

The science curriculum of the Province of Ontario is based on *Science Is Happening Here.* I have never seen better thematic units that integrate literature with science. Activities include making a web of the unit and working in small groups in science centers to record the results. The activities detailed in this periodical are always open-ended and stimulate problem-solving and inquiry skills. I especially enjoyed the special weather issue, which suggested ways for building a weather vane with a cork and a feather and discussed weather folklore. The focus on hands-on science, suggestions for recording observations, and lists of related children's literature are extremely useful.

Resource: Organization

National Association of Biology Teachers

Membership: $35 (active, US); $75 (active, outside US); $12 (spouse); $18 (student/retired)
11250 Roger Bacon Dr., No. 19
Reston, VA 22090
1-703-471-1134

The National Association of Biology Teachers is a professional organization with over 10,000 members. Their official journal, *The American Biology Teacher,* which is published eight times each year, contains an extensive "How-to-Do-It" section with many practical ideas for teaching biological concepts. A newsletter entitled *News and Views* lists available grants, workshop and conference opportunities, new resources, policy statements, and news from the various affiliates.

Membership includes a subscription to the journal and newsletter, discounts on publications, and the opportunity to participate in national education and curriculum projects. There is an optional subscription to an electronic bulletin board that provides a link to other biology educators.

📷 **WHOLE LANGUAGE CAMERA**

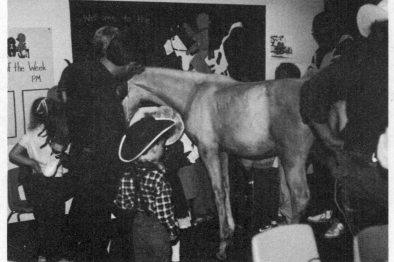

"A horse in the classroom?!" asked Summit Elementary School principal. Of course! (See Henderson & Walen, p. 301)

The Funny Side
Scientific Criticism

While visiting in a kindergarten classroom I began chatting with one of the five-year-old students whose father I knew was an oceanographer. "So what sorts of things do you do in here?" I asked. "Do you do science?"

She shook her head and sighed, "Well, they call it science, but all we do is draw pictures."

—As told to LBB by Suzanne Gespass, Princeton, NJ

Language Stories

What Keeps Our Bodies from Falling Apart?

I should have known that the question Chris was asking me was not really what he meant. It hadn't been long since he had asked me, "Mom, where do farmers get their seeds?"

After a short discussion, it was apparent that what he really wanted to know was, which came first, the plant or the seed, and how the first one came to be. Now he was seriously asking, "Mom, what keeps our bodies from falling apart?"

I felt the answer was a simple one. "Everything is attached. Our bones are attached by joints, and our muscles are attached to our bones, and the skin helps to hold everything inside."

I saw frustration developing in Chris, and he responded, "That's not what I mean. I want to know what keeps our bodies from falling apart."

Knowing that I understood the question, I felt that my explanation, although very simple, was not simple enough for a five-year-old. I tried again. This time my explanation was met with whining, and tears were beginning to form. Since it was our bedtime talk, I felt that Chris was tired and no answer would be right, but as we continued to talk, we finally communicated.

"What keeps our cells together?"

The light came on for me. We had been talking earlier in the week about our bodies being a mass of cells and about how dead skin cells come off your body when you take a bath. He wanted to know how cells stuck together. I didn't have the answer but assured him that we would find it. He seemed even more frustrated, and the tears rolled.

"Chris, it is something we can find out, but we'll have to do it tomorrow."

"But I need to know now."

"Why now? It's late and you need to get your sleep."

"But I'm scared."

"Scared of what? Oh, are you scared your body will fall apart?"

"Um-hmm."

"Chris, cells stay stuck together. No one's cells have come apart and their body fallen apart."

"No one?"

"No one. Do you understand what I'm saying?"

"Um-hmm."

"Do you think you'll be okay now? I'll stay here until you go to sleep."

Later that weekend we were able to find the answer to Chris's question from our high school biology teacher. Cells are basically held together by small fibers that exist in the walls of the cells and by a jellylike substance that acts like glue. They work together to keep our bodies from falling apart. Chris was impressed—and so was I.

—Marilyn Richardson, instructor, Lincoln University, Jefferson City, MO

Resource: Periodical

Chem Matters

$5.50/year (4 issues) individual; $2.25/year student group rate (10 subscriptions minimum) from: American Chemical Society 1156 16th St., NW Washington, DC 20036

I knew these magazines were scientifically accurate—they are published by the prestigious American Chemical Society—but I wondered if they would be interesting to junior and senior high school students. One look at an issue with "Dyeing for Blue Jeans" on the cover set me straight. All teachers know that young people, especially at middle and senior high level, need to be interested in a topic before they can be expected to want to learn more about it. So let's deal with something close to home: stone-washed blue jeans. This issue deals with dyes (derived from snails and insects!) and their chemical properties, and covers the history of denim from the gold-rush times. Interesting experiments are suggested, such as using dandelion greens or coffee grounds to re-dye an old sweater, or describing how to stone-wash your own pair of jeans and save $10 in the process! Other issues deal with chocolate, whales, beach pollution, and caring for your skin—interesting topics for adolescents. As one student wrote, "I think it is great that articles are about things that are happening and have an effect on us in the present."

Doug Haner

Resource: Organization

NASA Teacher Resource Center Network

NASA CORE
Lorain County JVS
15181 Route 58 South
Oberlin, OH, 44074
216-774-1051

Teachers need immediate access to the information that is generated by NASA programs, technologies, and discoveries, so they can bring that excitement into their classrooms. NASA educational materials are related to art, mathematics, energy, physics, careers, spaceflight, aeronautics, technology utilization, physical science, and social science.

To help disseminate these materials to elementary and secondary educators, the NASA Educational Affairs Division has established the NASA Teacher Resource Center Network (TRCN). The Network comprises Teacher Resource Centers (TRCs), Regional Teacher Resource Centers (RTRCs), and the Central Operation of Resources for Educators (CORE).

NASA's Central Operation of Resources for Educators is a non-profit organization. Minimal fees represent the cost of operation and production of additional educational materials.

Christina Reski

YOUNG ARTISTS

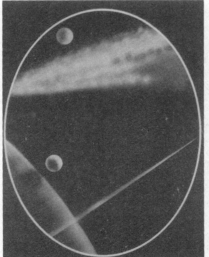

"Saturn and Beyond"
—Erik Sanchez, 18, Portland, OR, from *Treasures 2*
(See p. 162)

Resource Essay

Science Books *en español* for Whole Language Classrooms

Recommended by Yvonne S. Freeman and Carolina Cervantes

For Emerging Readers

◆ *Soy el sol* (I am the sun), by Miguel Angel Pacheco and José Luis García Sánchez (Madrid: Ediciones Attea, 1974). A high-quality, small, soft-cover book that would be ideal *if* it were available in a larger size. Well-researched content and supplemental illustrations center around the various roles of the sun. Could be used for discovery learning and problem-solving activities.

For Independent Readers

◆ *Rollito* (Little roll), by Eduardo Robles Boza (Mexico City: Editorial Trillas, 1983). This high-quality softcover book presents learning in a natural setting, and offers the possibility of studying a butterfly's stages of growth. Allegory about freedom makes this story a powerful one. Colorful illustrations and natural language make the extensive text more predictable.

For More Proficient Readers

◆ *¿De quién es este rabo?* (Whose tail is this?), by Barberis (Valladolid, Spain: Miñón, 1985). A high-quality hardcover book. Text is amusing and highly predictable. Despite its technical language, the vivid illustrations of animal tails help readers predict what the animal on the next page might be. Personified animals are described in silly and fun ways.

◆ *La seda* (Silk), by Pascuala Corona (Mexico City: Editorial Patria, 1985). A book with colorful illustrations from Collección Piñata. The content includes a historical account of the migration of silk, from its Japanese origins to its transportation by the Spanish Dominican friars to the Mexican state of Oaxaca. Though the text is not very extensive, the content is rich with scientific and historical detail. Some suggested activities are included at the end of the text. Ideal for unit work with silkworms.

➔ See: Freeman and Cervantes, pp. 87, 184, 312

Yvonne S. Freeman is a professor and Carolina Cervantes is a graduate student at Fresno Pacific College, Fresno, CA.

It Shouldn't Happen to Kids

Squelched

One afternoon Paul, age five, caught a grasshopper and put it in a pickle jar. Excited by his catch, he pleaded with his mother to let him bring it to his kindergarten class. His mother, assuming that Paul's teacher and the other students would find it interesting, agreed. The next day Paul, hugging the pickle jar to his chest, proudly carried it into his class and waved a cheerful good-bye to his mother. After school his mother was waiting outside the room to pick him up. Taking him by the hand, she asked eagerly, "What did your teacher say about the grasshopper?"

"Don't bring glass jars to school anymore."

—LBB

Resource: Program

Finding Out/Descubrimiento

Dr. Elizabeth Cohen, Director
School of Education
Stanford University
Stanford, CA 94305
(415) 723-4661

Finding Out/Descubrimiento is a hands-on science and math program that emphasizes multiple learning strategies, open-ended problem solving and cooperative learning. Materials are available in Spanish and English.

Resource Essay

Finding Out/*Descubrimiento:* Program for Complex Instruction

by Carlen Luke

It was reporting time after F.O.D. (Finding Out/*Descubrimiento*), and Humberto was in the reporter's chair. He spoke:

"I'm not going to start until I have everyone's attention. I see Maria's ready, and Arnoldo, and Pedro. OK. It looks like everyone's ready." Each time Humberto made one of these teacher remarks he'd look over at me and give a self-conscious yet proud grin.

"OK. I am going to make a circuit. But before I hook this up, I want you to predict if the light is going to turn on. Who thinks it's going to turn on? Raise your hand. Who thinks it won't turn on?"

Humberto then proceeded to lead the class in a series of collaborative group experiments for the next 15 minutes. I could feel the class getting excited as they realized they were controlling themselves.

Mele said, "Hey, it's so quiet!"

They all scooted in and observed intently as Humberto added another battery to the circuit to see whether the light would get brighter.

Maria suggested they try three batteries. The magic continued. Tears were coming to my eyes and I hoped the kids wouldn't notice.

I then told them I had a huge battery we could use. I helped hook it up. The light didn't go on. I asked who had suggestions about what was wrong and how we could make it work. Then Pablo had an idea.

Pablo had arrived from Mexico a few months ago. He was very bright, but had trouble being accepted by the other children because he spoke no English and he poked them a lot. During this F.O.D. unit, a few kids had commented that Pablo knew a

lot about electricity. David later told me that the reason Pablo knew so much is that in Mexico he had worked with his uncle, who was an electrician.

Now David said, "Let Pablo try it. He has an idea about how to make it work." Pablo came up front and started connecting the wires a different way.

Humberto, who was still sitting in front of the class, said, "No, wait. Like this."

David gently insisted, "Let him try what he was thinking." Humberto agreed and sat back. The cooperative mood was overwhelming.

Then Arnoldo, intuitive Arnoldo, said with a smile, "Humberto, you feel envious because Pablo is taking over your experiment."

Humberto replied, "No, I'm proud of Pablo."

That was about all I could stand. I almost broke down and cried. It was my best moment as a teacher to date.

So that's F.O.D. Or that's what can happen with F.O.D. By using a cooperative learning model, the teacher gives what are traditionally her or his roles to the students. This then frees the teacher up to observe the children (kidwatch) and to recognize them publicly for their intelligence. The children also start to recognize and value each other's abilities, because the group needs these abilities in order to do the experiments and to learn about measuring, change, shapes, crystals, structures, balance, maps, light, sound, and electricity, and so on (each of these is a unit).

There are several aspects of F.O.D. that are whole language: social and intellectual development are equally important; the child's strengths, abilities, and strategies are highly valued; and students take on the traditional teacher roles of facilitating, reporting, explaining what to do, helping, and problem-solving.

For me, the greatest strength of F.O.D. is that it makes you take a hard look at your role as teacher and analyze your interactions with children to see whether you are taking control of the learning away from your students or leaving it with them where it belongs. As I become more sophisticated as a teacher, I am going to give my students even more responsibility for their learning than they currently have in F.O.D. This year I'm going to have them keep learning logs in which they can reflect on what *they* get out of the experiments in F.O.D. I will continue, as I would with any instructional program, to look at it closely in the light of my philosophy of teaching and learning, and omit some things, and add others so that what I'm doing matches what I believe and what I see that my students need.

→ See: Bird, p. 92; Luke, pp. 278, 305.

Carlen Luke is a primary teacher at Fair Oaks School, Redwood City, CA.

Resource: Organization

Astronomical Society of the Pacific (ASP)

390 Ashton Ave.
San Francisco, CA 94112
1-415-337-1100

Astronomy is not only inherently interesting, but it also lends itself naturally to an integrated curriculum. As one of the world's leading astronomical organizations, the Astronomical Society of the Pacific is dedicated to sharing the excitement of astronomy and science with the public, and especially with educators. One way the society accomplishes this mission is by producing an interesting and extremely readable newsletter on teaching astronomy, *The Universe in the Classroom,* which is free to educators who request a subscription on school stationery.

The society's catalog includes videotapes, from PBS's "Nova" series and from NASA archives, of planets and lunar landings. It also offers audiocassettes for stargazing, software selections, stunning color posters, a moon-phase calendar, slide sets, videodiscs of the planets and the space shuttle, and recommended books.

Doug Haner

Resource: Mail-Order Company

Educational Images

P.O. Box 3456,
   West Side Station
Elmira, NY 14901
1-607-732-1090
1-800-527-4264
FAX 1-607-732-1183

This catalog of media materials—videocassettes, computer programs, filmstrips, and slide sets—is particularly suited for high school and college/adult audiences. Titles are mostly science related; topics range from oil spills, earthquakes, and drugs to acid rain, energy, and the greenhouse effect. There are also a number of extremely specialized books for science professionals as well—*Skeletomuscular Systems* and *Vibrations of Bent Triatomic Molecules,* to name a few! In addition, the company carries titles in comparative cultures, environmental and social issues, and career education. Don't miss the visual stimuli kit for slides that invite student viewer response.

Doug Haner

Resource: Organization

Challenger Center for Space Science Education

Membership:
   from $25 to $35
1101 King St., Ste. 190
Alexandria, VA 22314
1-703-683-9740
FAX 1-703-683-7546

The Challenger Center for Space Science Education was founded by the families of the seven crew members who perished on *Challenger* Flight 51-L. In their honor, the center continues the *Challenger* mission through innova-

tive science programs for upper elementary to high school students and teachers that promote analytical thinking and problem-solving skills.

A growing network of Challenger Learning Centers, which provide a simulated working space laboratory, is truly unique. Students enter a novel and realistic educational environment, and become engaged in a wide variety of math, science, and problem-solving situations. Teacher workshops across the country are an integral part of the Challenger Center program.

Membership for educators includes the quarterly newsletter, *The Challenger Log,* and a professional journal, *Educators Today Touching Tomorrow,* which contains book reviews, news, feature articles, interviews, and updates on the Challenger Learning Center activities.

Doug Haner

The Funny Side

Right Concept, Wrong Word

Erin and Jennifer, both age four, were discussing their future marriage plans in the back seat of the car as I drove them home from their morning preschool class. "Are you going to marry your brother?" Erin asked Jennifer.

"Oh, no, I can't marry *him!* We have the same *germs!*"

—LBB

Resource Essay

Family Science

by Madeline Moore

Imagine one of your students telling you that a giraffe's heart weighs 25 times that of a human, or that a yagi is a type of shortwave antenna. Or imagine a parent who felt unable to help his daughter and her friends explore the world of science, but who now comfortably makes predictions with them while dissolving salt and sugar crystals in the kitchen.

All this can happen as a result of Family Science, a series of classes for children and their parents that emphasizes the enjoyable and ongoing nature of science. Family Science, funded by Chevron USA and developed by Northwest Equals of Portland State University, is targeted toward families of female and minority students. The goal of Family Science is to involve families in their children's science education by showing its relevance and making science less intimidating.

Modeled after the successful Family Math program, which was developed by Equals of the Lawrence Hall of Science, Family Science offers such interdisciplinary themes as measurement, investigations, words and principles, and patterns and relationships. The program emphasizes the process of learning science that involves cooperation, questioning, and easily accessible materials. In an effort to make the subject appealing to diverse families, Family Science activities incorporate a multicultural approach to science.

Family Science is in the development stage. More than 70 pilot sites across the country (and in Costa Rica and Australia) are currently field-testing the materials. *The Family Science Book*, a resource for parents, community members, and educators, will be published in the fall of 1991.

For more information, contact: Peggy Noone, director, Family Science, Northwest Equals, Portland State University/Division of Continuing Education, P.O. Box 1491, Portland, OR 97201-1491.

➜ See: Stenmark, p. 328.

Madeline Moore is the former director of the Family Science program, Portland, OR.

Resource: Organization

The Institute for Earth Education (IEE)

Membership:
$20 (personal);
$35 (professional);
$50 (affiliate);
$100 (sponsor)
Box 288
Warrenville, IL 60555
1-312-393-3096

The Institute for Earth Education is an international, nonprofit organization committed to developing a serious educational response to the environmental crisis of the earth. I was intrigued by their catalog, *The Earth Education Sourcebook,* which features complete environmental education programs, supplementary student materials, cassettes, T-shirts, a slide show, conservation-oriented books, posters, and props, such as hand lenses and dental mirrors to see in tight places. IEE also sponsors workshops, hosts conferences, supports regional branches, and publishes books and program materials. IEE members also receive the provocative seasonal journal entitled *Talking Leaves.*

Doug Haner

Resource: Organization

Audubon Naturalist Society of the Central Atlantic States

Membership: from $10 (student) to $600 (life)
8940 Jones Mill Rd.
Chevy Chase, MD 20815
1-301-652-9188

Local Audubon societies can often be a valuable free resource for the science educator. They are usually very happy to help teachers. With a little scouting, you can find members of a local group who will volunteer information and possibly slides—they may even visit your class. The Audubon Naturalist Society of the Central Atlantic States provides year-round classes, weekend programs, and junior naturalist programs for children. There are college-accredited courses for teachers, in addition to workshops, field trips, and special travel programs.

Doug Haner

Resource: Organization

Vermont Institute of Natural Science (VINS)

Membership: from $15
(individual or library)
to $1,000 (benefactor)
P.O. Box 86
Woodstock, VT 05091
1-802-457-2779

Resource: Book

Hands-On Nature: Information and Activities for Exploring the Environment with Children

Jenepher Lingelbach, editor
$16.95 from VINS

Many teachers don't think they know enough to do science and nature activities with their students —and they may be right! *Hands-On Nature* is a book from the Vermont Institute of Natural Science that prefaces each section of activities with background science information for teachers. It may provide you with the confidence to jump in and try some of these activities with your students.

The book is divided into the major themes of adaptation, habitat, cycles, and designs of nature, which could form the basis of an outdoor education curriculum. The book also contains ideas for puppet shows, sharing circles, poems, pantomimes, and writing. Each activity concludes with a list of suggested reading for children.

Doug Haner

Resource: Publisher

Ruwanga Trading

Books $7.95 each;
puppet $7.95

P.O. Box 1027
Puunene, HI 96784
1-808-244-0986

Ruwanga Trading, run by a husband-and-wife team of teacher naturalists from Hawaii, has produced a wonderful collection of five nature books for children in preschool through third grade. My favorite is *The Whale Who Wanted to Be Small,* a delightful story that weaves together concepts of animal habitat and survival. The print is large and the illustrations colorful, which make this a good read-aloud book. Another book, *The Wonderful Journey,* describes the migration of a baby whale from her birthplace in Hawaii to the summer feeding grounds of Alaska. A baby whale hand puppet is also now available, developed at the request of teachers and librarians.

Doug Haner

Resource: Periodical

Science Weekly

Minimum order of 20 subscriptions: $3.95/year (18 issues); $2.80/semester
Individual: $8/year;
$5.50/semester from:
Subscription Dept.
2141 Industrial Pkwy.,
Ste. 202
Silver Spring, MD 20904
1-301-680-8804

Using the byline "Put a little science in your week," *Science Weekly* tries to do just that for K to 8 students. This four-page newsletter is packed with activities to keep kids current in the science world. Each issue has a feature article, an activity or an experiment, a problem to figure out, a suggestion for writing, and a nice section called "Home Base," which describes an activity to do at home, usually involving parents or other family members.

There is a different version for each grade level—a nice idea that helps to make this especially appropriate for the wide K to 8 range. I liked the lower-grade versions the most, as the grade 6 to 8 levels tend to focus more on vocabulary. All versions have excellent suggestions for activities that integrate reading, writing, science, and mathematics.

Doug Haner

📷 WHOLE LANGUAGE CAMERA

A world in her hands, Palo Alto, CA

Environmental Education

Environmental Education Resources

Reviewed by Doug Haner

Resource: Book

Hug a Tree and Other Things to Do Outdoors with Young Children

Robert E. Rockwell, Elizabeth A. Sherwood, and Robert A. Williams 1983; 106 pp.; $8.95 Mt. Rainier, MD: Gryphon House

The real value of this book is not so much the more than 50 nature activities to do with children, but the 30 introductory pages, where you will find suggestions for getting kids to talk and write down observations about their experiences in nature. Listed are ideas for using graphs, charts, sketches, and tallies as starting points for extending written language; places students can write for more information, such as the U.S. Forest Service and the National Audubon Society; science books and nature magazines for parents and teachers; and nature-related literature books for children.

Resource: Organization

National Wildlife Federation (NWF)

1412 16th St., NW Washington, DC 20036-2266 1-202-797-6800

Resource: Periodicals

National Wildlife International Wildlife

$15/year (6 issues) each; $20/year (12 issues) for both from NWF

Ranger Rick

$14/year (12 issues) from NWF

Your Big Backyard

$10/year (12 issues) from NWF

You've probably heard of *Ranger Rick* magazine, the popular periodical published by the National Wildlife Federation. My nine-year-old son can't wait for his copy to come in the mail each month. Elegant color pictures are sprinkled liberally throughout this classic children's magazine, stimulating interest in the adventure stories about nature's mysteries and the world of animals.

Elementary and middle school teachers will be particularly interested in another NWF publication, the Naturescope series. This series contains detailed articles and suggested activities for students, on topics from birds and insects to weather and the ocean. We used the wetlands issue during our Oceans Week at school and found the information and activities wonderful.

Preschool educators shouldn't miss *Your Big Backyard*, a magazine for three- to five- year-olds. A subscription to either of the bimonthly periodicals, *National Wildlife* or *International Wildlife*, or to both, buys you membership in the NWF.

Resource: Organization

Concerned Educators Allied for a Safe Environment (CEASE)

Membership: $5 17 Gerry St. Cambridge, MA 02138 1-617-864-0999

A number of organizations are concerned with the relationship between world peace and environmental preservation. CEASE is one of these groups—a national network of parents, teachers, and other youth advocates who have a special interest in preserving a safe world for children. They have a small list of books for purchase, a slide-tape presentation called *Children of Hiroshima,* and the newsletter *CEASE NEWS,* published three times a year.

Resource: Periodical

Dolphin Log

$10/year (6 issues) from: Cousteau Society Membership Center 930 W. 21st St. Norfolk, VA 23517 1-804-627-1144

Conservationists will appreciate the strong environmental ethic that is woven through this excellent bimonthly educational magazine for children in upper elementary and middle schools. The issue we previewed included easy-to-read features on coral polyps and reef formations, the symbiotic relationship between small goby fish and shrimp, and sea-snakes. Other sections include fun-filled activities such as making a tornado in a two-liter soda container and deciphering a secret message from a ship's flags. Stunning color photographs make this publication a visual delight for children of all ages. The *Dolphin Log* is available either separately, or as part of a family membership in the Cousteau Society, for which you also receive the *Calypso Log.*

Resource: Periodical

Greenpeace

1436 U St., NW Washington, DC 20009 1-202-462-4507 FAX 1-202-462-4507

Leave it to Greenpeace to develop an international, action-oriented environmental education curriculum. Teams of students from schools in the Soviet Union, North America, and Europe are piloting the East/West Project materials in 1989–90. Using a multidisciplinary/ multimedia approach, each school identifies a local environmental issue to research. Students then develop an action strategy, which culminates in a community action project. Results in each country are shared by satellite. Summer camps allow students from all countries to network and further discuss results.

The bimonthly magazine *Greenpeace,* yours with a $20 donation, has timely, well-written articles on topics ranging from whales and ivory to unilateral disarmament and big business's assault on the earth. Another resource, the Greenpeace catalog, won't do much to support your need for curriculum and teaching tools, but it does offer a wealth of tote bags, posters, and coffee mugs, all with environmental motifs.

Resource: Organization

Earthwatch

Membership: $25 680 Mt. Auburn St. Box 403N Watertown, MA 02272 1-617-926-8200 FAX 1-617-926-8532

What better way for teachers to learn about the environment than to be a part of a research project spending hours digging, observing, tagging animals, or interviewing native peoples? Sound too good to be true? The only catch is that you pay for part of the project.

As a teacher from Boston said, "An Earthwatch expedition is a crash course in what science really is: puzzlement, frustration, tedium, and eventual wonder. The energizing effect of this experience is revolutionary."

Earthwatch matches paying volunteers with scientific research projects for two to three weeks of total involvement. They sponsor 106 projects in 27 states and 46 countries, in disciplines as diverse as archaeology, marine biology, animal behavior, and rain forest study. It is open to anyone 16 years of age or older, with scholarships available to high school students and fellowships to K to 12 teachers.

📷 WHOLE LANGUAGE CAMERA

Third-grader Katie Post helps Erin Bird, a student in Lisa D'hollande's kindergarten, plant a "space seed," a special tomato plant that has been exposed to the harsh environment of outer space, Ohlone School, Palo Alto, CA.

Resource: Books

Sharing Nature with Children

Joseph Cornell
1979; 143 pp.; $6.95

Sharing the Joy of Nature

Joseph Cornell
1989; 165 pp.; $9.95
Both books from:
Dawn Publications
14618 Tyler Foote Rd.
Nevada City, CA 95959
1-916-292-3484 (CA)
1-800-545-7475

If sharing a love of the natural world with children is your goal, then *Sharing Nature with Children* and *Sharing the Joy of Nature* from Dawn Publications will provide a continuing stimulus and source of ideas. The suggested activities convey the sense that it is not as important to know as it is to feel; they help children develop awareness of the world around them and feel the satisfaction of being in touch with the earth. Blind walks, role-playing, night hikes, scavenger hunts, barefoot walks, and all varieties of games make this an intriguing guide to enjoying nature.

Doug Haner

Resource: Curriculum Guide

Earth Day 1990: Lesson Plan and Home Survey

$5 each volume from:
Earth Day 1990 K–12 Program
P.O. Box AA
Stanford, CA 94309
1-415-321-1990

Although Earth Day 1990 is now history, the importance of Earth Day will continue to be relevant as environmental pressures on the planet become greater each year. In response to this, Earth Day 1990 K–12 Program at Stanford University created lesson plans and home surveys for teachers of both K to 6 and 7 to 12 levels. These excellent guides provide background for understanding the issues of energy, solid waste, toxics, water, and transportation. Using a model similar to the California State Environmental Education Guides (which were written by the same authors), these activities integrate environmental themes with language, math, reading, art, and writing.

The authors are masters at choosing topics and activities that children truly enjoy. How about an ecological picnic using only recyclable materials? Or inviting local elected officials to explain how they are helping the environment? Or making reusable canvas grocery bags as an art project? The teaching methods involve discovery, rather than direct teaching; students collect, organize, and interpret data, while developing an understanding and awareness of ecological issues.

Doug Haner

Resource: Book

The California State Environmental Education Guide: K–6

$17.95 from:
Alameda Co. Office of Education
313 W. Winton Ave.
Hayward, CA 94544-1198
1-415-887-0152

The State of California has pushed the environmental education movement a giant step forward with the recent publication of *The California State Environmental Education Guide: K–6*. I recommend this guide to any school—our school has made it the framework of our outdoor education program this year. The activity-based units integrate math, reading, writing, and science around projects that kids truly enjoy. With coordinated grade-level teaching at an elementary or middle school, students will learn about diversity of life, homes and habitats, communities and cultures, adaptation and variation, and energy issues. Sections on Extension Ideas and Home Learning Suggestions allow students and teachers to go as deeply into a theme as their interest takes them. The suggested Action Projects turn environmental learning into hands-on environmental-protection activities for kids.

A supplement entitled *Toxics: Taking Charge* is also available, with activities for grades 4 to 6; a unit on water will be available in the summer of 1990.

Doug Haner

YOUNG ARTISTS

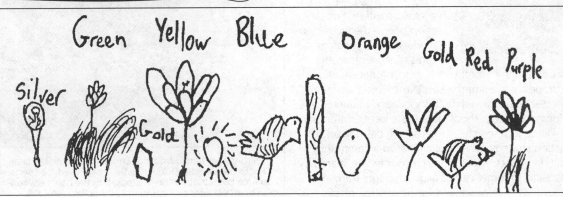

Ryan was in Catherine Howard's primary class at Ohlone School,
Palo Alto, CA, when he created this garden of delights.

Resource: Organization

Project Ocean

San Francisco Bay Chapter
Oceanic Society
Building E,
 Fort Mason Ctr.
San Francisco, CA 94123
1-415-441-5970

For one week each year, our typical, inner-city elementary school in San Francisco becomes unrecognizable. The bottom floor is completely transformed into an underwater marine science environment, with sharks, deep-sea fish, squid, and marine mammals dangling from the walls and ceilings. Avocets, long-billed curlews, willets, and other shore birds adorn the first floor, with beaks of varying sizes probing sand and mud murals for clams, worms, shrimp, and various crustaceans, neatly hidden in burrows. The kindergarten and first-grade wing shows the differing splash zones of the tide and the various tidepool creatures that live at the different depths. Project Ocean has helped our staff develop a schoolwide, interdisciplinary marine science program that awes our students and parents.

The Project Ocean team has truly developed a curriculum model that makes the term "interdisciplinary learning" a reality. As a result of three years with Project Ocean, our teachers work more cooperatively, articulate thematic instruction across grade levels, and are enthusiastic learners about the ocean and adamant protectors of the marine environment.

Doug Haner

Resource: Periodicals

Chickadee
Owl

$17/year (10 issues) from:
Young Naturalist Foundation
56 The Esplanade, Ste. 306
Toronto, Ontario, M5E 1A7 Canada
1-416-868-6001

Chickadee and *Owl* are two award-winning children's nature magazines that have it all—dazzling photography, readability, and a superb variety of activities. They are full of games, puzzles, crafts, stories, and contests that will engage children in quality activities related to nature.

Designed especially for preschoolers and beginning readers, *Chickadee* mixes a hands-on approach to learning with vivid illustrations that capture the imagination. *Owl* is intended for 9- to 12-year-old children and regularly features pull-out animal posters, science activities from Dr. Zed, and the Mighty Mites—a hilarious comic-style troupe of, yes, mites, who get you to see life from their perspective.

Doug Haner

Math

Cornerstone: Heidi Mills, David J. Whitin, & Timothy O'Keefe

Supporting Mathematical Understanding

The children in our transition first-grade classroom were quite familiar with the counting song "Ten in the Bed" (1986). When we shared an illustrated version of this song with the class one morning, the children all chimed in and sang it together:

There were ten in the bed
And the little one said,
"Roll over,
roll over."
So they all rolled over
And one fell out.

We invited the children to create their own version of this story. Tray composed the following variation:

The baby said, "Go cook breakfast."
And three babies in the bed.

Tray's story is interesting for several reasons. First, he highlighted the subtraction process by drawing a line down one side of the bed to separate the three babies from the fourth one, who was being asked to leave and cook breakfast. Since the fourth baby had not yet left, Tray's drawing nicely conveyed the inverse relationship between addition and subtraction. The line he drew indicated the total set of babies (four), as well as the two subsets of one cook and three sleepy babies. Tray also used space to demonstrate his understanding of the subtraction process. He drew the fourth baby in the kitchen, standing by the stove, busily preparing breakfast for his friends. "He's cooking ham and eggs," said Tray, pointing to the ham bone boiling in a kettle on top of the stove. Thus, Tray cleverly used space and line to designate this process of separation.

His inclusion of the kitchen scene is important because it represents a dimension to mathematical stories that is rarely reflected in mathematical textbooks, i.e., life really does exist after subtraction! In most textbook problems the reader never learns about what happens to those children, or animals, who are separated from the original group. They merely disappear. But where do they go, and what do they do? Traditional textbook publishers perceive such details as irrelevant to the mathematical intent of the problem. However, mathematics should not be separated from the natural context in which it operates. When we do, we distort it. The complexity of events that surround mathematical stories actually supports its use. To claim that cooking in the kitchen is an irrelevant detail is a value judgment. When children are given regular opportunities to compose their own mathematical stories, they will create ones that are placed in richer and broader contexts.

Sheree responded to the same invitation by drawing a bed with six little ones lying on top. Then she turned her paper over and began singing her number pattern aloud as she wrote a sequence of subtraction problems that directly corresponded to the tune: "There were six in the bed and one fell off. There were five in the bed and one fell off . . ." Sheree continued this pattern until they all met their destiny.

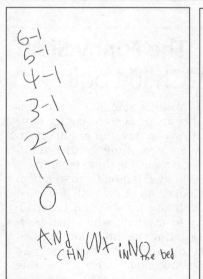

"And wasn't no children in the bed."

Sheree completed her piece using mathematics and written language. She used the numeral zero to indicate that there were no more children left on the bed and then composed a written message to finalize the sequence of events. She wrote, "And wasn't no children in the bed."

Though Sheree did not write complete equations for each step, the difference for each subtraction problem is implied in the minuend of the equation that follows. Sheree's strategy may not appear to be completely conventional, yet it allowed her to communicate her ideas clearly and concisely. Uncovering patterns and discovering relationships is part of the order and

David Whitin, Heidi Mills, & Timothy O'Keefe

Heidi Mills is an assistant professor in elementary education at the University of South Carolina. As an undergraduate, Heidi embraced whole language as a most promising perspective for both teachers and learners. Since then she has had the good fortune to use the theory in various classroom settings. She was hired by the Grand Rapids Public School system to work collaboratively with the teachers to develop a whole language curriculum for the Child Development Centers, where her belief in the process was confirmed. She continued her work in whole language with Drs. Harste and Burke while pursuing her doctorate at Indiana University. Her colleagues, David Whitin and Timothy O'Keefe, have helped extend her understanding of the literacy learning process by exploring how children develop mathematical literacy.

David J. Whitin is currently an assistant professor of elementary education at the University of South Carolina. He is a former elementary school teacher and principal. He enjoys reciting poetry, investigating mathematical patterns, and telling stories; he has written articles for journals in the fields of language arts and mathematics. He is proudest of his family, with whom he has read aloud stories and kept a family journal for many years. He is working with his wife, Phyllis, currently a middle school teacher, on a book about family literacy.

Timothy O'Keefe teaches transition first grade in South Carolina. He has taught preschool through sixth grade in public schools in Indiana, Michigan, and South Carolina. His interests include reading, writing, and performing and writing music. He has presented at state and national conferences, and he is currently pursuing an Ed.S. degree in public school administration from the University of South Carolina. Of all the teachers Tim has had, he feels that his students have taught him the most about life and learning.

structure of the mathematical system; Sheree has latched onto this pattern and represented it in her own way.

It is important to encourage learners to draw upon multiple forms of communication such as art, music, mathematics, and written language to construct and share meaning. Such forms of expression naturally complement one another when used in concert. Children learn to select the form of communication that most closely conveys their intentions. Tray wanted to address what happened to the little one after he rolled out of bed. Art was his medium of choice. Sheree, on the other hand, used art, mathematics, and writing in a complementary fashion.

But there is much more to their stories than what simply appears on paper. Through discussion we discovered Tray's full intentions. Through our observation of Sheree singing we realized that she was making connections with the original text and re-presenting the story in her own way. Sheree certainly wasn't a soloist, however. Lovely six-year-old voices filled the room as the children pursued their enterprises.

After completing the projects, the class met to share their stories and reflect upon the strategies they used. By sharing their work, they crystallized their thoughts and perhaps learned new ways of making and recording information.

Characteristics of Learning Experiences That Promote Mathematical Literacy

When we began working together as a teacher-researcher team, we were united by our beliefs about how children learn language, and we brought a variety of teaching experiences to this classroom. We found ourselves concentrating on how children were learning to read and write. Once we were willing to venture beyond reading and writing to consider how children develop mathematical literacy, we began to ask ourselves some new questions:

- How is learning mathematics like learning language?
- What are characteristics of learning experiences that promote mathematical literacy?
- How can we create a balanced, integrated curriculum that encourages children to explore their own interests while providing experiences for development of mathematical literacy?

Because of space limitations, we will only address the second question.

We (1990) believe that some salient features of authentic mathematical experiences are:

1. They are open-ended; they invite children to solve a given problem in a variety of ways. These experiences encourage learners to interpret them from a variety of perspectives. Another aspect of an open-ended activity is that it requires no preentry qualifications before children can engage in it and demands no criterion level before they can exit.
2. They can be adapted and changed by the children. When provided the opportunity, children often devise their own variations and extensions to instructional invitations. Their ideas are usually quite ingenious.
3. They are multimodal; they encourage children to access a variety of communication systems—art, music, writing, reading, and mathematics—to convey their observations. It is important that children see that numbers do not operate in a vacuum but gain meaning as they work in conjunction with other communication systems.
4. They promote risk-taking. Children grow in mathematical literacy when they are willing

(Continued on page 326)

(Continued from page 325)

to take some risks, stepping outside the sphere of what they know by testing out a new hunch or a current hypothesis about how numbers work.

5. They encourage social interaction. Children learn from each other as they share observations and insights about how to construct and share meaning in mathematics.

Final Reflection

We have found that we can apply much of what we have learned about curriculum development from whole language to create an authentically rich mathematics curriculum. We must work collaboratively with the children to fashion learning experiences that allow them to explore the purposes, processes, and content of the mathematics system.

➜ See: Burns, p. 330; Edelsky, p. 72; Larson, p. 327; Stenmark, p. 328; Whitin, pp. 41, 354.

References
Rees, M. 1988. *Ten in the bed.* Boston: Little, Brown.
Whitin, D., H. Mills, and T. O'Keefe. 1990. *Living and learning mathematics: Stories and strategies for supporting mathematical literacy.* Portsmouth, NH: Heinemann.

Further Reading by Heidi Mills
◆ "Empowering Teachers as Researchers Through a Collaborative Model of Inquiry." *Carolina English Teacher,* SCCTE, 1988.
◆ "Children's Success as Readers and Writers: It's the Teacher's Beliefs that Make the Difference." *Young Children,* NAEYC, in press.
◆ *Portraits of Whole Language Classrooms,* ed. with J.A. Clyde. Heinemann, in press.

Further Reading by David J. Whitin
◆ "Good, Now Try Some Sentences! A Fluent Writer Enters First Grade." *Educational Horizon,* Spring 1988.
◆ "Bring on the Buttons." *Arithmetic Teacher,* January 1989.
◆ "Number Sense and the Importance of Asking 'Why'." *Arithmetic Teacher,* February 1989.
◆ "The Power of Mathematical Investigation," In *New Directions for Elementary School Mathematics.* NCTM, 1989.
◆ "Literacy Learning in a Home Day Care Setting," with Phyllis Whitin. *Portraits of Whole Language Classrooms,* ed. H. Mills and J. A. Clyde. Heinemann, in press.

Further Reading by Timothy O'Keefe
◆ "Empowering Teachers as Researchers Through a Collaborative Model of Inquiry," with T. O'Keefe. *Carolina English Teacher,* SCCTE, 1988.
◆ "A Day with Dinosaurs." In *Portraits of Whole Language Classrooms,* ed. H. Mills and J. A. Clyde. Heinemann, in press.

Resource: Math Program

Curriculum Development Associates

737 Foam St. Monterey, CA 93940 1-408-649-3992

The late Robert Wirtz was a pioneer in using manipulatives to develop reasoning abilities. He left a 25-year career in research and engineering in private industry because he wanted to devote time to developing his own theories of math teaching. His focus was unique at the time, for it centered on language development as the key to promoting problem-solving skills in mathematics. He once said, "Whenever you pick up a pencil, thinking stops." He advocated visual models to help children learn how to compute using a tenframe of beans.

Robert Wirtz's work is being continued through the Curriculum Development Associates. Their catalog includes student books, classroom activity centers, teacher resource books, and parent materials.

Doug Haner

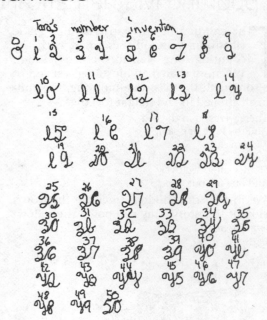

MarVELous INVENTIONS
Cursive Numbers

My name is Tara Nickel. And as you see I have invented cursive numbers. I have been working on them for a long time ever since before Nov. 1988. I told my mom about it and she said that there was no such thing as cursive numbers. But on Feb. 15, 1989 I asked my mom if I could invent cursive numbers and she said I could.

—Contributed by Dorothy Watson, Columbia, MO

Book Note

Living and Learning Mathematics: Stories and Strategies for Supporting Mathematical Literacy

David J. Whitin, Heidi Mills, and Timothy O'Keefe 1990; 176 pp.; $17 Portsmouth, NH: Heinemann

Here's a book that supports what veteran whole language teachers have always known: Learning mathematics is a process much like learning to read and write. The book identifies strategies that children use as they construct their own mathematical stories and investigations, lists characteristics of learning experiences that promote mathematical literacy, and provides a framework for making curricular decisions. The authors' whole language recommendations, well documented through numerous photographs and examples of children's work, emphasize interdisciplinary themes of study and children's interests as a framework for curriculum development.

The Funny Side
Child Logic

An understanding of the concepts of age and aging have long been known to develop gradually in children. Here are two of my favorite examples of child logic regarding those topics.

As he stood in line waiting to go to lunch, a first-grader looked up at me with a startled expression. Noticing for the first time the streaks of gray in my hair, which had been there all along during the three months I had been observing in his classroom, he exclaimed, "Dr. Knipping, your hair is getting old!"

Several years ago the children in my kindergarten class were discussing the age of their parents. One child reported that his father was 26 and his mother was 25. Another child said, "My father is 31 and my mother is 155, but she's going to Weight Watchers and pretty soon she'll only be 120."

➜ See: Knipping, p. 210.

—Nancy Knipping, assistant professor, University of Missouri, Columbia, MO

Resource: Organization

National Council of Teachers of Mathematics (NCTM)

Membership: from $40 (individual with one periodical) to $75 (individual with three periodicals) 1906 Association Dr. Reston, VA 22091 1-703-620-9840

With a reputation for quality publications, excellent conferences, and engaging and informative newsletters and periodicals, NCTM is *the* organization for math teachers. Unlike many other professional membership organizations for educators, NCTM publishes materials that are highly creative and extremely useful for classroom teachers at all levels. At NCTM's regional and national conferences, there are always thought-provoking speakers as well as hundreds of workshops stressing hands-on, field-tested, creative mathematical explorations. NCTM's periodicals include *The Arithmetic Teacher, The Mathematics Teacher,* and *The Journal for Research in Mathematics Education.*

Doug Haner

Classroom Demonstrations

by Carol Novillis Larson

Reading in Mathematics Education for the Whole Language Teacher

In March 1989, the National Council of Teachers of Mathematics (NCTM) published the *Curriculum and Evaluation Standards for School Mathematics*. This document presents a broad framework to guide reform in school mathematics (K–12) in the 1990s. One of the five major goals (p. 6) for students at all grade levels is "learning to communicate mathematically . . . [which] is best accomplished in problem situations in which students have an opportunity to read, write, and discuss ideas in which the use of the language of mathematics becomes natural."

Stage 1: Child's Language
The natural language a child uses to describe the concept in a familiar situation, often a real-world story.

Modeling	Creating	Sharing

Stage 2: Material Language
The new language that might be used with concrete or pictorial materials as a child acts out or represents the real-world story.

Modeling	Creating	Sharing

Stage 3: Mathematical Language
The use of a few words to record the language that describes the action of the materials. This stage leads to using more specific mathematical language.

Modeling	Creating	Sharing

Stage 4: Symbolic Language
The use of mathematical symbols as an even shorter way of recording action.

Modeling	Creating	Sharing

This and the other goals, which focus on problem-solving, reasoning, and connecting mathematics with other content areas, should interest whole language teachers.

NCTM's 1989 yearbook, *New Directions for Elementary School Mathematics*, examines in more detail the changes for the K–6 mathematics program outlined in the *Standards*. Many of the chapters include practical suggestions for teachers as well as specific activities and examples of children's work. For instance, in chapter 7, "Language Experience: A Base for Problem Solving," Rosemary and Calvin Irons provide a model for helping children develop oral and symbolic mathematical language (see fig.).

For years Marilyn Burns has been advocating the approach to teaching mathematics that is described in the *Standards*. Her two recent books, *A Collection of Math Lessons from Grades 3 through 6* (1987) and *A Collection of Math Lessons from Grades 1 through 3*, coauthored with Bonnie Tank (1988), contain detailed descriptions of about 15 excellent mathematics lessons, including children's responses and writing samples. Each lesson incorporates a problem-solving experience for students; explores important mathematics concepts using concrete materials in a cooperative group setting; and includes an opportunity for students to describe their thoughts and procedures in writing. The lessons focus on mathematics topics from the strands of number, geometry, measurement, probability, and statistics. They contain enough detail so that you can successfully try them with your students.

Children's Arithmetic: How They Learn It and How You Teach It (1989, p. xv) "is based on the belief that an understanding of children's learning and thinking can lead to vital improvements in mathematics education." This theme is developed in "Part One: Informal Arithmetic," which describes young children's development of

mathematical concepts and language from birth until they begin formal schooling. "Part Two: School Learning" shows that the traditional practices used in teaching mathematics do not foster the cognitive strengths and strategies that children use in learning mathematics. Suggestions are made on how to revise teaching practices so that they are more in line with children's cognitive development.

One of the NCTM's goals, as discussed in the *Standards,* is to connect mathematics with other curriculum areas and investigate the role of mathematics in culture and society. *Africa Counts*, by Claudia Zaslavsky, is a unique book that looks at the rich diversity of mathematics found in African culture. The following topics, which are covered in the book, would enrich both mathematics and social science classes: 1) numeration systems, including spoken and gesture counting; (2) numbers in daily life as related to time, money, and measurement; (3) mathematical recreations—networks, games, and magic squares; and (4) geometry in art and architecture.

Two effective and interesting how-to books address the important topics of gender and mathematics anxiety. No curriculum change in mathematics can be successful unless it addresses the affective domain. Past teaching practices have discouraged girls and ethnic minorities from continuing their study of mathematics beyond required courses. *How to Encourage Girls in Math and Science* (1982) describes how girls' avoidance of math and science is a result of attitudes, parenting and teaching practices, stereotyped play activities and books, and other variables. This book includes effective strategies and specific activities that can assist girls in overcoming negative influences. *Mind Over Math* (1987) is a self-help book for decreasing math anxiety. The book examines "math myths" and contains exercises that have helped many students who attended the authors' workshops.

➜ See: Burns, p. 330; Cuisenaire Company of America, p. 327; Stenmark, p. 328.

Math Books for Whole Language Teachers

Burns, M. 1987. *A Collection of Math Lessons from Grades 3 through 6.* New Rochelle, NY: Cuisenaire.

Burns, M., and B. Tank. 1988. *A Collection of Math Lessons from Grades 1 through 3.* New Rochelle, NY: Cuisenaire.

Ginsburg, H. P. 1989. *Children's Arithmetic: How They Learn It and How You Teach It* (2d ed.). Austin, TX: Pro-ed.

Kogelmann, S., and J. Warren. 1987. *Mind Over Math.* New York: McGraw-Hill/Dale Seymour.

National Council of Teachers of Mathematics. 1989. *Curriculum and Evaluation Standards for School Mathematics.* Reston, VA: NCTM.

Skolnick, J., C. Langbort, and L. Day. 1982. *How to Encourage Girls in Math and Science.* Palo Alto, CA: Dale Seymour.

Trafton, P. R., and A. P. Shulte. 1989. *New Directions for Elementary School Mathematics.* Reston, VA: NCTM.

Zaslavsky, C. 1973. *Africa Counts.* Boston: Prindle, Weber & Schmidt.

Carol Novillis Larson is an associate professor at the University of Arizona, Tucson, AZ.

Resource: Organization/Periodical

AIMS Education Foundation
AIMS Newsletter

$22.50/year (10 issues) from:
P.O. Box 7766
Fresno, CA 93747
1-209-291-1766

Project AIMS has what most teachers like—a nice selection of hands-on activities in math and science for grades K to 9, workshops, a catalog of materials, and a newsletter with suggestions for creative, teacher-tested activities. Kids like their materials too—teddy bear counters, interesting graphics, and the bananas they can eat after taking samples and measurement. Also, AIMS does a good job linking language and literature through annotated bibliographies that correlate with their activities.

This program is best used as a supplement to an established curriculum. I'd go easy on their blackline masters and focus more on the process skills they suggest. The *AIMS Newsletter* keeps math and science ideas coming to you throughout the school year.

Doug Haner

Resource: Catalog

Cuisenaire Company of America

12 Church St., Box D
New Rochelle, NY 10802
1-800-237-3142

What began as a single-product organization selling Cuisenaire Rods 30 years ago now boasts a 115-page catalog that sells thousands of math manipulatives and hands-on science materials. Cuisenaire prides itself on the fact that it responds to teacher needs and suggestions; they provide the most complete math and science selection for teachers striving to create a materials-rich learning environment for their students.

The catalog lists a complete selection of science and math teacher resource materials, which includes Marilyn Burns's *A Collection of Math Lessons From Grades 1 through 3* (with Bonnie Tank), *From Grades 3 through 6*, and *From Grades 6 through 8* (with Cathy McLaughlin); they also carry *The Science Book* by Sara Stein.

Doug Haner

➜ See: Burns, p. 330.

📷 WHOLE LANGUAGE CAMERA

Two fifth-grade girls from Cynthia Motsinger's class use a self-made measuring tape to plot the perimeter of the four-square game on the playground of San Ramon Elementary School, Novato, CA.

Resource: Program/Book

EQUALS
FAMILY MATH

Lawrence Hall of Science
University of California
Berkeley, CA 94720
1-415-642-1823

Resource Essay

FAMILY MATH

by Jean Kerr Stenmark

When we want to help children with reading, there are lots of things we can do: read to them, look at picture books, go to the library—all fun and enjoyable. What about helping them with math? All most of us can think of is to help our children learn the multiplication tables by using flash cards or to insist that they do their math homework before they go out to play. These approaches don't create the same warm feelings!

—Virginia Thompson, Director of FAMILY MATH

Look in the door of Room 16 of the Sunshine School. There are colorful posters on the wall, each one with a mathematics problem. A couple of adults and two or three children are seated at each table. This is a Family Math class, the first of six classes. Mrs. Jones and her twins, Alice and Alan, walk in the door slowly, a little afraid of what they might find. Mrs. Jones never did like math in school, and while Alice is doing very well in the third grade, Alan seems to need more help and encouragement. So when a Family Math flyer came home from school, Mrs. Jones signed up.

The class will meet every Thursday at 6:30 P.M., taught by a parent and a teacher who learned how to present classes at the Lawrence Hall of Science at the University of California in Berkeley.

Mrs. Jones and Alice and Alan are welcomed and invited to sit at one of the tables with another family. There are colored blocks and some beans on the table, and Alan is soon moving them into a pattern. One of the teachers offers Mrs. Jones a cup of coffee.

In a few minutes, the teachers begin by introducing themselves and asking those in the group to introduce themselves too. Then a math game is started. There is a lot of talking and laughing as the game goes on. When families have played the game two or three times, the teachers explain why the game was included and what can be learned from it. Several other games and activities are just as interesting, and copies are given to the families to take home and play again. All three Joneses leave feeling good about the mathematics they had done.

The Jones family is imaginary, but the description is based on experiences of real families who have been in Family Math classes. The following are some of the things they say:

• "We haven't laughed like this together in a long time!"
• "You can't imagine what ten minutes a day can mean to your child—homework without frustration and tears! It enhances your child's and your own understanding. She gets math in an unthreatening, unpressured way—the same way that we read to her."
• "[Family Math] makes me feel I can do things I didn't think I could do."

Family Math is a way for parents and children to enjoy doing mathematics together. It usually starts with a Family Math class, which can happen in a school, a community center, church, or any other convenient place. Family Math can also happen at home when parents use some of the activities from the Family Math book with their children.

Parents and children can learn together. Parents don't have to know how to teach "new math" or be experts, but can be introduced to new ideas right along with their children. In classes, there is also a lot of sharing as families do activities with other families. Talking about mathematics with others is a good way to learn. Putting ideas into words helps clarify our thinking.

Parents are encouraged to let children work problems out for themselves rather than telling them how to proceed. Problems will often have many possible answers, so that continued thinking is fostered. Learning about strategies to solve problems becomes more important than getting a quick answer.

The mathematics is active and fun. There are nearly always parts to be moved around to help look at various aspects of the problem. Blocks, beans, pennies, and toothpicks are mathematical tools. There is usually a lot of moving around the room. No boring lectures!

Family Math is not just drill in arithmetic facts but also includes geometry, probability and statistics, measurement, estimation, logic, thinking, and a lot of problem-solving. Flash cards are not a part of Family Math!

Role models are often invited to talk to the class about careers that involve mathematics. They emphasize the importance of taking as much mathematics as possible in school. Almost every role model talks about the value of problem-solving and the need to learn to work in groups. Parents themselves become role models for their children as they are seen working on mathematics problems. Many parents are motivated to take other mathematics courses.

Family Math began in 1981 as part of the Equals program at the Lawrence Hall of Science, University of California at Berkeley. Equals is an equity and mathematics inservice for teachers of all levels, stressing a problem-solving approach to learning. Teachers who came to Equals asked what they could give to parents to help students learn math, and so they started Family Math.

Family Math has expanded to five other sites in California and to Arizona, Colorado, Idaho, Indiana, Maryland, Massachusetts, Minnesota, New Jersey, North Carolina, Oregon, Tennessee, Vermont, and Washington, DC. International sites are found in Australia, Canada, Costa Rica, New Zealand, Puerto Rico, and Sweden. The Family Math book has been translated into Spanish and Swedish, and some activities have been translated into other languages.

Other related courses have been or are being developed. Some classes have specialized in certain topics such as Family Geometry and Family Algebra to help prepare students for future classes. Family Science is being developed in Oregon and is now in its pilot phase.

It has been very rewarding to watch so many people around the world become excited about mathematics. We believe that the philosophy and methods of this program can make a real contribution to the quality of learning in many subject areas for both adults and children.

Advice for parents who want to set up a mathematical environment at home:

• Let your children know that you believe they can succeed. Let them see you enjoying mathematics activities.
• Be ready to listen to your children talk about mathematics, and have a few questions ready such as "What do you know so far?" "What does this part mean?" "Is there a pattern?" and "How would it look if we drew a diagram of it?"
• Be more concerned with the process of doing mathematics than with getting an answer quickly. The answer to any particular program has very little importance, but knowing *how* to find the answer is a lifetime skill.
• Try not to tell children how to solve the problem. Once they have been told how to do it, thinking usually stops. Better to ask them questions and help them find their own methods of working it through.
• Encourage talking together about how to solve a mathematics problem. Learn together and keep it fun!

Jean Kerr Stenmark works for the Equals and Family Math programs in Berkeley, CA.

Resource: Books

Mathematics Their Way

Mary Baratta-Lorton
1976; 416 pp.; $35.65
Reading, MA: Addison-Wesley

Last year when the California State Department of Education adopted math textbooks and approved the *Mathematics Their Way* materials for purchase last year, K to 2 teachers in my school who were familiar with this activity-centered math curriculum developed by the late Mary Baratta-Lorton were elated. Finally there was an alternative to the traditional paper-and-pencil-oriented textbooks for teaching primary math. *Mathematics Their Way,* is a collection of more than 200 innovative math experiences including patterns, measurement and weight, volume, time, graphs, counting, and adding and subtracting. Teachers can gather the required manipulative materials or purchase a companion manipulative kit.

Doug Haner

Resource Essay

Mathematics Their Way and Whole Language

by Patty Vincent

Mathematics Their Way and whole language have given me a fresh outlook on teaching and have given the children in my classroom an opportunity to experience learning in a stimulating, risk-free environment. Both *Mathematics Their Way* and whole language are developmentally based and incorporate many language experiences to express what has been learned. I have intertwined both so that a visitor, upon entering my classroom, would have difficulty distinguishing which discipline I was teaching.

Graphing is one example of how both can be tied together. After we read *Johnny Appleseed,* we graphed all the favorite ways to eat apples, and surrounded the graph with everything we had learned about apples. Another example is the pajama party we had after reading *Ira Sleeps Over*. We brought

our favorite toys that we sleep with, piled them together, and then sorted and graphed them according to ones that had fur and ones that didn't. We then wrote stories about how our toys must feel when being lain on, squished, and scrunched between the bed and the wall while sleeping with us.

Inspired by patterning activities in *Mathematics Their Way,* my children have created pattern books and then described these patterns in writing. The kids are consistently pointing out word patterns in stories, poems, and songs that we are working with. Number writing activities have encouraged my children to publish number books to share with their families. The book publishing opportunities for my children are numerous. Jewel books, Unifix cube books, and tiny number books are all possibilities when we begin to work with the number operations concepts.

The children are encouraged to tell a story about any math problem they encounter. When sorting they must describe orally the attributes they are sorting. Through whole language and *Mathematics Their Way* my children experience the concept, verbalize it, and then connect it to the written symbols. Print becomes meaningful, together with the mathematical concepts in which they are immersed.

Mathematics Their Way and whole language have allowed my children to learn in a way that is in tune with their own developmental time clocks, and have led to significant growth in both math and reading. The children are happier and more enthusiastic about reading and math and demonstrate a greater understanding than I have noticed in previous classes.

"Children aren't vases being filled but fires being lit." *Mathematics Their Way* and whole language give children the opportunity to learn in ways that are relevant to their world. It is rewarding as an educator to see such growth, and challenging to use methods that light learning fires.

→ See: Burns, p. 330; Literature Reference List, p. 429.

Patty Vincent is a teacher and consultant for Park County District #1, Powell, WY.

■ **WHOLE LANGUAGE CAMERA**

How much does it weigh? A student in John Moran's third-grade class performs a number of tests in his search for an answer. Mary Dill School, Tucson, AZ.

Resource: Publisher

Key Curriculum Press

2512 Martin Luther King
Jr. Way
P.O. Box 2304
Berkeley, CA 94702
1-800-338-7638
FAX 1-415-548-0755

Early in my teaching career, I discovered some mimeographed materials that a teacher had done in Berkeley, California. These successful classroom materials were informally distributed to a small group of people who happened to hear about them; I had used them for tutoring students in math. I was happy to see that 15 years later, this informal distribution circuit had grown into Key Curriculum Press, which developed the Miquon Math program and now distributes it. The program is based on cooperative learning, imagination, and discovery, and helps children explore mathematical concepts using concrete models. If you like to help children observe, investigate, and discover patterns for themselves, then these materials will offer you a unique approach that has been developed over the past three decades.

Doug Haner

Resource: Organization

Center for Innovation in Education

20665 4th St.
Saratoga, CA 95070-5800
1-408-867-3167

The Center for Innovation in Education was founded in 1975 by Mary and Bob Baratta-Lorton. This organization serves to develop, evaluate, and further the use of innovative methods, materials, and programs in elementary school education.

The center offers workshops, an annual conference, and seminars on using Baratta-Lorton materials—*Mathematics Their Way* and *Mathematics a Way of Thinking,* which are published by Addison-Wesley. The *Mathematics Their Way* primary workshop schedule for summer 1990 included week-long classes in 46 states. These workshops are run as model classrooms with teachers actively involved in the learning process, and focus on manipulative materials and activity-centered learning. Participants discover alternatives to using textbooks to teach mathematics. The annual conference is intended for people who participated in these workshops and who wish to learn more about integrating the Baratta-Lorton materials into their classrooms.

Doug Haner

Resource: Distributor

Dale Seymour Publications

P.O. Box 10888
Palo Alto, CA 94303
1-800-872-1100

For printed materials in mathematics, the Dale Seymour catalog is one of the most complete. Whether you have a penchant for Mathematics-Their-Way books, Marilyn Burns's concept-oriented materials, or mental math ideas this catalog will probably have it. You will also find posters, manipulatives, calculators, and offline computer activities interspersed in their catalogs for K–8 educational materials and secondary mathematics, or in their new catalog supplement on thinking skills.

Doug Haner

■ **WHOLE LANGUAGE CAMERA**

Your move. Two students play chess in Sarah Costello's seventh-grade class, William J. Pistor Junior High, Tucson, AZ.

Cornerstone: Marilyn Burns

Writing in the Math Class (K–8)

The movement in education for "writing across the curriculum" calls for writing to be an integral part of the teaching of all subjects. It calls for the end of sequestering writing solely to the language arts curriculum and instead using it as a tool to help students think about ideas in all content areas. This movement is not a newcomer to education. Yet progress has been slow.

Progress has been particularly slow in the area of mathematics. Mathematics is seen as a subject that communicates through the manipulation of symbols in orderly ways, rather than one that uses words to express ideas. To many people, mathematics and writing seem like oil and water, disciplines that have little in common.

The process of writing requires gathering, organizing, and clarifying thoughts. It demands finding out what you know and what you don't know. It calls for thinking clearly. Similarly, doing mathematics depends on gathering, organizing, and clarifying thoughts, finding out what you know and what you don't know, and thinking clearly. Though the final representation of a mathematical pursuit looks very different from the final product of a writing effort, the mental journey is, at its base, the same—making sense of an idea and presenting it effectively.

The top priorities for elementary mathematics instruction should be to develop children's understanding of mathematical ideas and to promote their ability to think and reason.

Traditionally, the primary goal for elementary school mathematics has been a narrow one—to develop children's arithmetic competency. Students spend the bulk of their instructional time in math class learning arithmetic procedures and practicing them on worksheets or textbook pages. Word problems are the usual vehicle for applying these skills, presenting situations that students translate into arithmetic sentences and then do the computation needed.

In June 1988, the Educational Testing Service released a document titled *The Mathematics Report Card—Are We Measuring Up?* The answer to the title question is a clear, resounding "No!" The findings document a critical lack of effective reasoning skills among the nation's students.

Another implication of this approach becomes evident when children's views of what is important in mathematics is examined. Cathy McLaughlin is a middle-school math teacher in San Jose, California. On the first day of class, she asked her seventh- and eighth-graders to write math autobiographies about their elementary school math experiences. Their papers provide views about mathematics from students who have received traditional math instruction in the elementary grades. The papers are typical of the more than 100 she received.

Jamie wrote: "So far in my math classes, I have learned addition, subtraction, multiplication, division, etc. . . . .all the basic things. For example, I remember 2d grade—Ms. Fraser's class. We had all come in from snack time. She was trying to teach us how to multiply. I remember getting so frustrated on learning what 9 × 9 equaled! I finally understood it. Then what

Marilyn Burns is the creator of *The Math Solution* in-service courses which focus on teaching mathematics through problem solving for K-8 and 9-12 teachers.

A former classroom teacher, Ms. Burns is the developer of two series of videotapes. *Mathematics with Manipulatives,* designed for K-6 teachers, and *Mathematics for Middle School,* designed for 6-8 teachers. Both series were produced for Cuisenaire Company of America.

Ms. Burns' most recent books are *A Collection of Math Lessons* and *The Good Time Math Event Book.*

She also continues to bring her messages directly to children. She is the author of ten books for children, including the best-selling *The I Hate Mathematics! Book, The Book of Think,* and *Math for Smarty Pants.* Her latest children's book is *The $1.00 Word Riddle Book.*

Ms. Burns lives in Sausalito, California.

hits us . . . division! That took longer to learn, but I got it after a lot of help from my dad."

From Ed: "When I first studied math I kind of liked it because it was very easy. All we had to do was add and subtract. But the numbers got bigger over the years and I didn't have enough fingers. But then it got easy again because I did multiplication tables up to twelve and I memorized them very quick and I was one of the best in the class. When fifth grade came I still was good because division was very easy too. But when I got to sixth grade and seventh grade, I was kind of in the middle because I was too afraid to ask questions, and I got C's and B minuses on my report card."

It is sad that these children equate learning math with learning how to do arithmetic exercises for which there is always one right method and one right answer. For these students, it seems that the quick right answer has been valued more than the thinking that leads to the answer.

Also missing from traditional instruction is the opportunity to involve children in the richness of what mathematics has to offer. Mathematics is more than arithmetic. The study of mathematics, even for young children, should encompass all strands of the math curriculum—geometry, measurement, functions, probability, statistics, logical reasoning, and algebra, as well as numbers. In contrast to traditional instruction, current practices for effective mathematics teaching call for actively engaging children with mathematical experiences that promote their thinking and reasoning processes.

The difference between math instruction that has as its goal "doing arithmetic" and math instruction that has as its goal "doing mathematics" is substantial. Theresa, a third-grader who had transferred to Mill Valley in March, described the contrast in her final paper.

She wrote: "When I first came to Park school I learned how to find the volume of things and more things in multiplication and division and measuring. Then I learned how to play the fraction game and learned shapes. Then I learned how to play pig. Pig was fun because you get to add and subtract. Then I learned how to find the area and use centimeters with a ruler. I learned about polygons then box filling and foot measuring.

"In Reno we learned easier things than here. Like easy multiplication and division in hard back math books and we didn't have any activities or measurement like there is here. We had our own desks and we did our math on our own."

Writing is a tool for children to use to explore mathematics and make sense of mathematics ideas and relationships. Writing gives children chances to tell what's on their minds. It gives you opportunities to examine their reasoning processes, to find out what they don't know. As you work to cover the math curriculum in your class, think about writing as a way for children to uncover the curriculum for themselves.

→ See: Mills, p. 325; Stenmark, p. 328.

Excerpted from *The Math Solution Publications,* 1988.

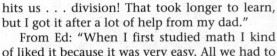

Music, Art, and Drama

Great Teachers:
Eddie Corona
by Elizabeth R. Saavedra

As I walked up the hallway to Eddie Corona's classroom, I could hear children singing. Eddie always begins his day with song. He teaches in a multi-aged classroom of first-, second-, and third-grade children at Alamosa Elementary in Albuquerque, New Mexico. Eddie loves to sing and always uses music and song to facilitate many activities throughout the day. He has the words to the songs on charts so the children can follow along during the singing events or even read them at other times during the day. The children use these charts to demonstrate what they know about language and writing. Many times they point out certain types of language or discuss the way language is used and the meaning it conveys.

Eddie's environment is built around the children and their activities. There were no desks in the room. There are centers and areas where the children can create their own spaces and decide on the function of the areas. There are designated areas such as the library and writers corner. Materials and equipment are organized and placed appropriately, so that the children can have access to whatever they need as they work on their different projects and activities. The children make decisions about their environment and the activities that they will pursue, and Eddie orchestrates these decisions.

Near the song chart is a sign-up sheet for reading conferences. The students sign up when they are ready for a conference with Eddie. These conferences last from 10 to 20 minutes and allow the children to read and discuss their books. Eddie sometimes asks them to read, then retell, which allows him to make an ongoing informal assessment of their progress. Eddie has a literature-based reading program. The children choose their own books and spend a portion of the day reading. Some children choose to group themselves and read the same book, while others read individually. Their choices sometimes reflect specific topics that are being studied in other content areas.

As you move about the room, you find children reading silently, in groups discussing their shared story, writing individually, or having writing conferences about their stories. The children move through their day, knowing that they will have time to read, write, pursue different topics of study, and share with their peers what they know and what they are learning. Eddie moves from conducting reading conferences to conducting writing conferences with small groups of children. Again students sign up for these sessions when they are ready to have their work edited or if they need assistance in moving forward with their writing. Together Eddie and the small group of children help the writer to develop his or her story.

Eddie and his students decide on the topic of study and through this topic draw in concepts and issues from the different content areas. Eddie creates committees around topic-related activities, questions, and observations that the children engage in as a group. It is wonderful to see Eddie and the children weaving literacy, never separating reading and writing. There is a blend of all the content areas into a learning day in which Eddie and his students are absorbed.

Eddie is a colearner as well as a guide.

Eddie has since taken a position supporting teaching interns with the University of New Mexico and the Albuquerque Public Schools. He is currently a Chapter 1 reading teacher and a Support for Instructional Development teacher. He works with teachers and students in their classrooms, focusing on developing strategies and innovations that promote literacy. He maintains his stance as a learner in his current endeavors.

➔ See: Saavedra, p. 111.

Elizabeth R. Saavedra is a doctoral student at the University of Arizona, Tucson, AZ.

📷 WHOLE LANGUAGE CAMERA

Sing out! Annette Maggitti's first-graders from Desert Winds School perform for Sheilah Nicholas's third-graders at Butterfield School, Tucson, AZ.

Cornerstone: Lois Blackburn

Whole Music

It is the first class meeting of the elementary-school band class. The children are handling their new instruments, squirming with eagerness to make music. And what happens? The teacher says, "The note on the first page of your book is B-flat. Watch me and put your fingers like this; this is a B-flat. Now let's all play B-flat." The book (and the teacher) introduces B-flat for three pages, first in quarter notes, then in half notes, and finally in whole notes. A few more notes are presented like this, in isolation and ad nauseum, with the goal of eventually combining them into a tune. There are plenty of exercises in "note naming," and the kids toot away earnestly, making single bleats in response to single, unrelated symbols. A few lessons hence, some of these would-be music-makers won't show up for class.

Whole language fans, does this sound familiar? What is needed is whole music. With considerable support from the wisdom of Ken and Yetta Goodman and Frank Smith, I developed a sequence of teaching that simultaneously develops musical thinking and efficient sight reading. My students first sing or play by rote as much whole, real music as possible before they approach music reading. I then introduce notation *in context:* notated phrases that students have played or sung (no exact pitches or note names; no clefs). They learn to recognize them immediately by their shape or contour; this recognition is later unconsciously generalized in recognizing similar patterns. Students then work as a group to notate other familiar phrases the same way, learning to "count up and down" the staff to get the intervals right.

Dr. Lois Blackburn is an assistant professor of music at Marshall University of Huntington, West Virginia, where her assignment includes the training and supervision of prospective public school music teachers. Her innovative methods of teaching music reading have proved highly successful in difficult learning environments. Her doctoral studies at the University of Arizona, including work with Dr. Yetta M. Goodman, focused on interdisciplinary notation and reading written language. She has presented workshops in music education techniques in California, New Mexico, Arizona, Wisconsin, and West Virginia.

Only then do we back up to learn to identify exact pitches, and these are used *only* as reference points, for a starting note or when the reader is stuck. Rhythmic patterns are also recognized in context, associated with how they sound in familiar music. By the time we discuss those awful mathematical charts of relative note values, their meanings are internalized already.

Music readers, like language readers, sample the available graphic cues and make guesses; then they predict a probable continuation. They construct meaning according to their experience with music, looking for something that makes musical sense. Any listener who has become familiar with a given musical idiom, say, Irish folksong or 18th-century classical symphony, can predict likely continuations after a certain point. Unlikely continuations can be very humorous, a phenomenon exploited by musical comedians like Victor Borge or Peter Schickele (PDQ Bach). So, in my teaching, I work to develop adventuresome musicians who sample the text for patterns, take risks, and make guesses and predictions. The result is a high level of musical literacy.

➔ See: Goodman, p. 98.

Further Reading by Lois Blackburn

◆ "Music Reading and Language Reading: Correlations in Processes and Instruction." *Bulletin of the Council for Research in Music Education,* Summer 1987.

◆ "Chaco Resolution: The Music of Michael Mauldin." *Proceedings of the 31st Annual Conference of the College Music Society,* October 1988.

◆ "Julie Rive-King, American Pianist." *Bulletin of the Council for Research in Music Education,* in press.

Classroom Demonstrations
by Paula Anderson

The Music Box

I covered a large box ($36'' \times 30'' \times 3''$) with colored sticky paper and used contrasting colors to decorate the cover and write THE MUSIC BOX on the attached cover flap. Another kindergarten teacher and I charted many favorite children's songs on individual sheets and illustrated each chart with a picture that cues the singing. All the song sheets are included in the box along with a teacher-made pointer. (Spray-paint a dowel. Glue a pencil eraser on one end and a colorful, small wooden cut-out on the other.) When propped appropriately, the flap cover acts as an easel or chart stand to hold the song sheet. I used magnetic tape at the two top corners of the charts and two roofing tins glued to the box cover to make the magnetic connection.

➔See: D'Ordine, p. 298; Martin, p.96.

Paula Anderson is a kindergarten teacher at Flagg St. School, Worcester, MA.

As Teachers See It

by Rick Gartner

Music for Children

It's fun; it's easy. And it might well be the key to unlocking your untapped potential. Don't pass up this golden opportunity to enrich your family's present and ensure a brighter future for your children. Act now; don't wait. This is the opportunity of a lifetime that can last a lifetime, and longer.

Does this sound like the opening pitch for another "nothing down" seminar? Well, that's exactly what it is. You've already paid for the seminar, so don't get your credit card ready. I don't want anything from you; I have some advice for you, writing as an admittedly biased journalist who also happens to be a music teacher and a parent.

I'm a "recovering" television addict. I got started with "American Bandstand," Beaver Cleaver, and chocolate-coated graham crackers after school. Then I got into the "Twilight Zone," and even lied to my parents about having my homework done. What relevance does my confession have? I'll answer that question with another question. What device really provides the impact behind the scenes and spoken words on virtually all TV shows (and movies), both past and present? Picture if you will a very starry night sky. Is that the least bit unsettling or ominous? But now add the dimension of sound—as Rod Serling used to say—a repeating dissonant tick-tock twang melody culminating with a cacophonic crescendo, and then you know: " ... you've just crossed over into the twilight zone." Music is a language, and it is indeed a powerful one.

Another example along the same lines is what I call the "mealtime theme" from the movie *Jaws*, a minimal tidbit that builds tension deep inside you, even though all you see is a shallow seascape passing by. An irritating horn enters the soundtrack. And then, that sure-fire cacophonic crescendo maximizes terror in you as a mechanical fish swallows yet another unsuspecting swimmer. I find it interesting that the moviemaker needed a ridiculously oversized shark, but nothing more than a musical half step to scare you three inches into your theater seat. This is all very formulaic to media manipulators—simple musical grammar—just Dick-and-Jane stuff. These are the same people that have planted hundreds of drippy commercial jingles deep into your brain circuitry. You know how music can get to you. Think of how much more it sinks into the psyche of your precious, impressionable children.

Don't leave your children as the passive prey for the commercial media's vulgar musical verbiage. Turn off the TV. Surround your home with the warm, harmonious ambience of art music. In a "highly scientific" study I've conducted—with no control group and a random sample of one (my own son)—I have established that children are both receptive to hearing music and capable of making music. Actually, as a music teacher with 20 years of experience, I can honestly tell you that *anyone* can learn to appreciate a wide variety of musical fare and can play a musical instrument. The main stumbling block seems to be the mystique that teen-idol marketeers have created, and the resulting "I have no musical talent" attitude. Don't buy that myth. I urge you to make music a part of your everyday home environment, for yourself and especially for your children.

Where do you start? At the beginning . . . Listen. That might sound like the credo of the Zenco school of music, but it's true. Listen to all kinds of music, especially the kinds you think you don't like. You might be shocked and disgusted with much of the heavy-metal you hear on a hard-rock radio station. But that will probably be a great motivation to find—dare I say it—some *good* music, when you stop to think that unless you take your parental responsibility as family-room DJ, your children will most likely dial into some very trashy stuff. Yes, I'm a total snob. I have a right to be. As a parent I have a *responsibility* to be selective.

I'll give you a short vignette from my parenting experience to help justify my judgmental feelings about the bulk of contemporary commercial music: When my son was still a cribster, and he was staying awake for the sake of staying awake, many were the nights that I took my guitar into his room and played soft, harmonious chord cycles, or warm, simple classical pieces, and he would usually drift off to sleep. I sincerely doubt that a heavy-metal tape would have done the job.

They don't show X-rated movies on commercial TV. But in my opinion, we are such a material culture that we recognize the harmful potential of certain visual images and control them more responsibly than we do the commercial music on the uncensored airwaves. I would no sooner allow some of that garbage to come pulsating through my home's stereo than I would feed my child from a shattered glass jar. I'm funny that way.

The good news is that I guarantee you will find some very pleasant, even inspiring music if you take the time to broaden your horizons. This is step one of your seminar: becoming a reasonably well-rounded listener so that you can be family-room DJ.

Greatest Hits or Best Of anthology-type albums do coat the coffers of record companies, but they usually offer the breadth of an artist's work. So I often recommend anthology albums to my music-appreciation students. I'll list a few of my favorites and provide a brief description of each one.

Gordon Lightfoot, *Gord's Gold*. This double LP is filled with some of the earliest and still finest recordings that blend folk songs with beautifully appropriate orchestrations—strings, percussion, and a variety of acoustic instruments.

Dan Fogelberg, *Greatest Hits*. Dan once told me that his music was very much inspired by the work of Gordon Lightfoot. This anthology showcases a profound and versatile singer/songwriter/producer, and there are no "fillers."

Doc Watson, *Doc and Merle Watson Live*. This double LP (Vanguard Records) contains flawless performances of American folk music, spiced with some of Doc's inimitable storytelling.

Muddy Waters, *Fathers and Sons*. This double LP is a "super session" of modern urban blues (Chess Records). (I found it on a CD the other day for $8.99 and walked out of the record store with a Cheshire-cat grin.)

Classical Guitarists. I'm listing this as a category because if you think you don't like classical music, this is the best way find out that you do. First, **Andres Segovia**, the grandfather of the genre. This gentleman from Spain is one of the greatest artists in the entire history of music. He set the stage for those who follow.

Julian Bream, *An Evening with Julian Bream*. This double LP includes both classical guitar and lute recordings. The lute is the Renaissance predecessor of the guitar, and its sound is spellbinding. Bream is the most versatile and accomplished guitarist of our time.

John Williams also deserves your attention. *John Williams Plays Spanish Music* contains brilliant performances of many core pieces in the repertoire for the classical guitar. *Julian Bream and John Williams Live* is a wonderful double LP of guitar duets. One other duet live album that is absolutely enchanting: *Rampal and Lagoya in Concert*. This double LP of **Jean Pierre Rampal** (flute) and **Alexandre Lagoya** (guitar) is chamber music at its finest.

Christopher Parkening, *Parkening and the Guitar*. This collection will amaze you with all the different sounds that a true master can elicit from an acoustic guitar. *Parkening Plays Bach* is also superb.

I promised you a short assignment list, so, just one more category, and then perhaps your own curiosity will take over. That's really the point of all this, both for yourself and for your kids.

Ragtime Piano Solos. This music was a raging hit in America at the turn of the 20th century. It is some of most delightful music ever written for any instrument. Tidbits of this music by the great composer Scott Joplin were frivolously cast about in the motion picture *The Sting*. My favorite recordings of ragtime are those of Joshua Rifkin (Nonesuch Records).

You and your family will love most of the music I've listed. It beats the (expletive deleted) out of video games. As I said earlier, let your curiosity be your guide. If you and your children want to play a musical instrument, go for it. Please believe me, it's not that difficult. I recommend the guitar (and of course my teaching method). But if you or your child have an interest in learning to play any instrument, follow your intuition. Go to a few music stores to inquire about teachers and instrument rentals or purchases. I think I'll go and play my guitar for a while to unwind . . .

Rick Gartner served as a writer/editor and music editor for 10 years with Guitar Player International, and was the Talent Director for the Strawberry Bluegrass Festival (Yosemite, CA). He completed his undergraduate studies in music and social science at the University of California, Riverside, and California State University, Chico, where he also taught guitar. He is currently giving seminars based on his multimedia First Lessons For Guitar method, which is available from Silver String Productions, Box 7327, Chico, CA 95927 (Telephone: 1-800-423-6147).

WHOLE LANGUAGE CAMERA

An outdoor concert, Los Altos, CA

Resource: Newsletter/Mail-Order Company

KidsArt

$8/year (4 issues) from:
P.O. Box 274
Mt. Shasta, CA 96067
1-916-926-5076

Bring the world of art and imagination into your home or classroom through the quarterly *KidsArt* newsletter. Its lively format, designed by kids, parents, and teachers, reflects its exciting, hands-on approach to all aspects of art: art history, art appreciation, and, of course, create-it-yourself art. Each newsletter includes

- A full-color print of a great work of art with the story of its artist and art media;
- Art techniques explained in-depth through easy-to-follow project instructions;
- Dozens of creative hands-on activities, open-ended so kids create their own art;
- International art contests for kids;

- Interviews and articles with young artists;
- Reviews of the best art toys, books, and materials;
- Ordering information for hard-to-find unique art resources like inexpensive rubber stamp alphabets and nontoxic tempera paint (including sparkling silver and gold metallics!).

Of particular interest to whole language educators may be the KidsArt Mail Art Project. Children are invited to design their own Mail Art envelopes. All entries mailed to KidsArt are paired with student artists from around the world. Each participant receives another child's entry and address: Artistic pen pals are the result!

LBB

Resource: Publisher

Theatre, Drama & Speech Resources Catalog

Contemporary Drama Service
Meriwether Publishing Ltd.
Box 7710-L4
Colorado Springs, CO 80933
1-719-594-4422
1-800-93PLAYS

In a letter we received from this company, the president

explained that they "publish theatre, drama and speech resources with special emphasis on comedy and student participation." They offer over 500 one-act plays and musicals on contemporary student concerns as well as adaptations from classic literature. Included in their offerings are the original comedy scripts from *The Carol Burnett Comedy Hour* and *Saturday Night Live*. They also feature how-to books and videotapes on acting, staging, clowning, and mime. I found Readers Theatre scripts for younger children, but most of the entries are appropriate for middle, high school, and college-level students.

LBB

Resource: Mail-Order Company

The Children's Art Collection

Hello Studio, Inc.
587 Third Ave.
New York, NY 10016
1-212-679-1444

"An inspiration for the artists in our classroom," said fourth-grade teacher Elizabeth Doerr, after reviewing the materials we received from this company. Original children's art in brilliant crayon colors is available on posters, greeting cards, and

stationery, often accompanied by a funny, clever, or poignant thought. On the back of each card is an invitation to all young artists to send in original works for possible publication.

LBB

Resource: Organizations

The Touchstone Center for Children

141 E. 88th St.
New York, NY 10028
1-212-831-7717

Recipient of the 1988 Schools and Culture Award, the Touchstone Center for Children guided by director Richard Lewis has a 20-plus-year tradition of linking children in New York City schools with an innovative array of visual and performing arts. Touchstone also produces a series of thematically based workshops in museums and community and environmental centers for children and their families. The center's publications brochure features posters and intriguing titles ("Sing We of Creeping and Crawling Things") by children and adult artists and authors.

LBB

National Art Education Association (NAEA)

1916 Association Dr.
Reston, VA 22091
1-703-860-8000

A professional organization for art educators from elementary through university as well as for those involved in museums and continuing and adult education, NAEA publishes a bimonthly, *Art Education;* a research quarterly, *Studies in Art Education;* a newsletter, *NAEA News;* and many other publications on a wide variety of topics concerning art education. An annual five-day national conference focuses on an array of issues of concern to art educators across grade levels and affiliations.

LBB

American Indian Artists (AMERINDA)

P.O. Box 4352
New York, NY 10185-0037
1-212-598-4757

Founded in New York in 1987, AMERINDA uses the performing arts to preserve and present the seldom-told stories of this country's Native American roots. Through theater, film, and television productions, the group's goal is to "share the truth of our history as Americans." In so doing, they serve to promote and foster the work of Native American artists.

📷 WHOLE LANGUAGE CAMERA

Jared, a recent immigrant from India, tries his hand at watercolors in Annette Maggitti's first grade, Desert Winds School, Tucson, AZ.

I feel good! Young artist from Palo Alto, CA

Self-portrait with a twist, Palo Alto, CA

As Teachers See It
by Sheryl McGruder and LeeAnn Sinclair

Making Literacy Connections with Creative Dramatics

Creative dramatics and other dramatic arts complement the goals of a whole language classroom. According to Purves and Monson (1984), literacy has a broader definition than reading and writing and includes drama, art, film, and music. Early cultures shared ideas through dramatic presentations, such as storytelling, puppet plays, and performances by masked actors.

Based on the understanding that the language arts are interrelated, creative dramatics techniques, which promote the use of body, voice, imagination, and emotion, enhance a child's ability to use the other language arts forms. When a teacher includes dramatic arts in the curriculum, the skills the children develop carry over into reading and writing. If children plan a story for a puppet play, they better understand the structures of stories they write and of those written by others. As with other forms of literacy, children learn to understand themselves, others, and their culture.

In *Creative Drama for the Classroom Teacher*, Heinig and Stillwell (1981) explain how a teacher incorporates creative drama into an already full curriculum.

> Many educators feel that creative drama provides an essential style of learning for children. Since children naturally dramatize, the teacher who uses creative drama is actually capitalizing on what the children already inherently know how to do. . . . Through dramatization children are provided an opportunity to use a wealth of information in a more concrete and meaningful way. When children play out an idea, they become an integral part of it. They become kinesthetically involved in experiences that might otherwise remain only words on a printed page.

In creative dramatics a leader guides the group in three major ways. The first is through example followed by an invitation to play. In order for the children to receive the maximum benefit from creative drama, the teacher must ignore her own inhibitions and jump right in, thereby demonstrating the value of the activity.

Second, it is important for the teacher to move through the group, offering encouragement and honest praise for the children's efforts to express themselves. While it is important to be honest, the leader should be accepting and supportive of all ideas. When the children have gained self-confidence, the leader and the other children can offer constructive suggestions to one another.

Third, the teacher encourages risk-taking and collaboration by fostering a secure environment. In the beginning everyone works at once because the children and the teacher feel safer, more willing to try out a voice or movement, more willing to show an emotion. When the children and the teacher have developed a sense of trust, the teacher can work with half the group at a time, while the rest of the children are watching. In this way the children can begin to value the differences in others' opinions and approaches to problem-solving. While the fundamental purpose of creative dramatics is to promote the personal growth and educational development of the participant, rather than to entertain an audience, it does help children become more comfortable when they are before an audience.

Creative drama techniques can be used effectively to dramatize a piece of literature. After everyone is familiar with the story, the group discusses the voice, movement, and motivation of the various characters. If the teacher, when reading aloud to the class, has used different voices, the children will quickly try some of their own.

There is a time and place for scripts, but drama without scripts is fun and more freeing. If the children know the story, the characters, and the sequence of action, whether or not they say the exact words each time will not matter as they act out the tale. Every child will know what is needed and what must be done to move the story along. The children's ideas are valued and accepted, so they develop a real sense of ownership of the story.

Creative dramatics is an excellent way to extend literature and bring children back to the text. This technique encourages the children to engage in repeated readings of the text; to interpret and make personal connections with the text, the author, and/or illustrator; and to adapt the text for their own purposes. Besides these academic advantages, children gain pleasure, improve self-concept, learn group skills, and develop confidence in their own abilities.

➔ See: Martin, p. 96.

References

Heinig, R., and L. Stillwell. 1981. *Creative drama for the classroom teacher.* Englewood Cliffs, NJ: Prentice-Hall.

Purves, A. C., and D. L. Monson. 1984. *Experiencing children's literature.* Glenview, IL: Scott, Foresman.

Sheryl McGruder is a primary teacher at Fairview Elementary School, Columbia, MO. LeeAnn Sinclair is an instructor at the University of Missouri, Columbia, MO.

📷 WHOLE LANGUAGE CAMERA

Homa Arvin, star of "The Adventures of Paddington Bear," belts out an operatic marvel, flanked by Phuong Bui, left, and Paul Choi. Students from Sutro Elementary School wrote and staged the opera, San Francisco,CA. (Carolyn Cole/*San Francisco Examiner*)

Book Note

Classroom Drama: Act It Out

Gare Thompson
1988; 29 pp.; $6.28
New York: Scholastic

If classroom drama brings to mind expensive sets and props and elaborate costumes and lighting, think again. It need not be (nor should it be) a Broadway production. Gare Thompson, who has a background in professional theater, shows how children's natural love of language and action, coupled with their vivid imaginations, is all that's needed to make drama an exciting part of your classroom. He suggests how to dramatize favorite literature, help children write their own plays, introduce music and sound effects, and critique dramatic efforts. Get this book and break a leg!

LBB

Resource: Periodical

Plays: The Drama Magazine for Young People

$23/year (8 issues) from:
120 Boylston St.
Boston, MA 02116
1-617-423-3157

Capture your reluctant and enthusiastic readers alike through the magic of drama with the help of *Plays: The Drama Magazine for Young People*. A subscription to this monthly magazine gives teachers and drama directors one-act plays and programs for use in classrooms and on special occasions throughout the school year. Each issue contains 8 to 12 exciting plays including skits, comedies, mysteries, melodramas, science fiction, dramatized classics, fairy tales, and more. Flexible casts adapt to all program needs, and production notes give suggestions for simple settings and costumes. Active subscribers to *Plays* may use all plays from current or past issues without payment of a royalty fee, provided the performance is part of the regular school or dramatic club activity.

LBB

Resource: Distributor

The Dramatic Publishing Company

P.O. Box 109
Woodstock, IL 60098
1-815-338-7170
FAX 1-815-338-8981

Publishers of the 272-page catalog *Plays and Musicals*, the Dramatic Publishing Company takes you out of the classroom and onto the stage. For the serious drama director of a school drama department or children's theater, the catalog includes old standbys (*Annie, Get Your Gun*) and new classics (*Marat-Sade*), adaptations of children's literature (*Charlotte's Web*), and dramatic biographical presentations (*The Amazing Einstein*). Most entries include royalty fees.

LBB

Book Note

Creative Dramatics: An Art for Children

Geraldine Siks
1958; 472 pp.; out of print
New York: Harper & Row

What caught my attention at the beginning of this book was this quote from Dwight D. Eisenhower: "As you encourage the growth of artistic achievement through the medium of creative drama, you strengthen the cultural life of our nation and all nations. The inclusion of the arts in the education of children contributes to the enrichment of mankind."

This book will help you foster the artistic growth of your students. It gives many excellent suggestions for using creative drama in the class. The social/affective/cognitive needs of all age groups, primary through intermediate elementary grades, are carefully discussed by the author.

Kathy M. Whalen

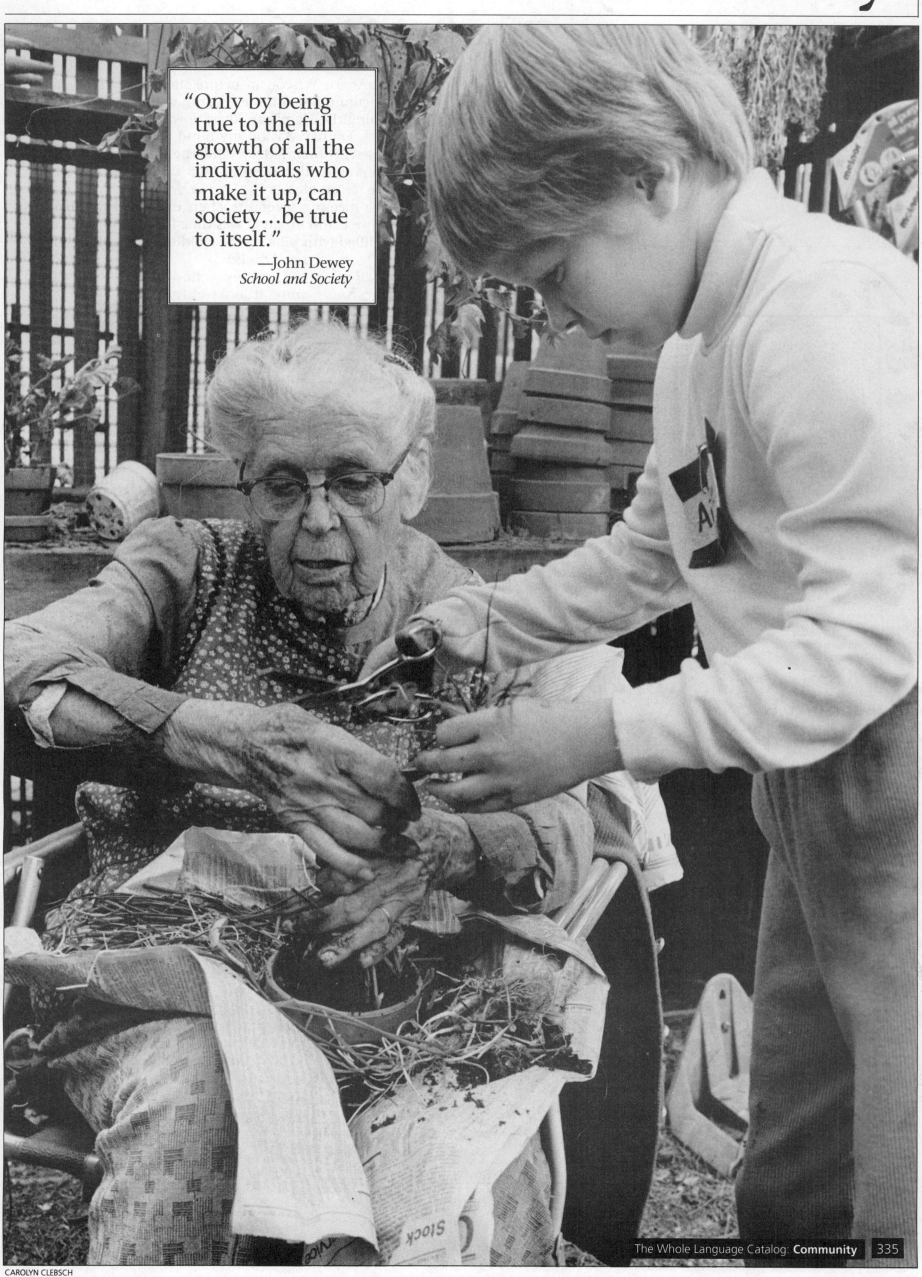

"Only by being true to the full growth of all the individuals who make it up, can society…be true to itself."

—John Dewey
School and Society

CAROLYN CLEBSCH

Community

Contents

The Pine Cone Story

by Robert Peterson

I sought refuge in northern Wisconsin before starting work on the Fratney School curriculum last summer. Sitting under a large white pine tree and watching the Flambeau River flow by, I focused on a pine cone at my side. Fratney was on my mind and the upcoming meeting with parents who planned to send their children to our school. I was to explain multicultural education.

The small cone gave me an idea.

On the night of the meeting several teachers explained the main components of our school, and finally it was time for me to speak.

I took up a big bag filled with pine cones. Holding one up for all to see, I said:

"Fratney School is like this pine cone. It looks only like an empty shell, a vacant structure. And yet what is on the inside is marvelous and full of potential. For this cone, the marvelous potential is hundreds of seeds; for Fratney, it is us—the students, teachers, and parents who are going to become this school community. We have the potential to grow into a school as strong and beautiful as a pine forest.

"But Fratney is unlike this pine cone in one important way. While this pine cone contains seeds from only one tree—a white pine, our school contains people of all colors and nationalities. Our school, if we all work together, will be even more beautiful than a pine forest; it will be a diverse and spectacular place of many people and cultures. It is for this reason we call our school multicultural and why our curriculum will be multicultural and antiracist. All of us will learn to live and work together with respect and commitment to build a world as beautiful as any forest.

"Finally, one thing we are going to stress at Fratney School is responsibility. We will expect students to be responsible for their own behavior, to have a stake in their education. Tonight we will start. I am going to give each child here a pine cone, and if you can hold onto it until the first day of school I will reward you with a book."

(Thirty-four children held onto their pine cones, and within the first week of school I had given away over $100 worth of new books.)

→ See Peterson, p. 348.

From *La Escuela Fratney: Year One*, Milwaukee Public Schools, Duplication Department, 1989.

Robert Peterson is a teacher at the Fratney School, Milwaukee, WI. He is also an associate editor of *Rethinking Schools*.

© CATHY BLACKI LINTACK '91

Connections: Home, School, Community

 Viewpoint: Shelley Harwayne

Reading and Writing for Real-World Reasons

"Gramma said when you come on something good, first thing you do is share it with whomever you can find; that way, the good spreads out where no telling it will go. Which is right." So begins *The Education of Little Tree* by Forest Carter and so describes what's happening in reading and writing workshops in and around New York City.

The good hard work that teachers and children are doing is leaving the four walls of the classroom, and making a difference up and down the corridors and throughout the community. Whole language is extending to whole communities. The work of the classroom is becoming the work of the community. Which is right.

The signs are everywhere. Quite literally, the signs are everywhere. A wooden sign is propped up against the curb in Riverside, Connecticut. "Sandy Squirrel Died Here—In Vain—Please Drive Slowly— Thanks," and four young children signed their names.

A group of primary youngsters in a Queens neighborhood offered to make signs for all the shopkeepers in their neighborhood: "Push," "Pull," "Open," "Closed," "Be Back in Five Minutes," and even "Credit Cards Accepted." The children wrote them with bright markers, complete with stick-figure merchants and rays of sun in the corners.

Fourth graders in Brooklyn protested when the 100-year-old trees on their block were to be cut down for a sewer project. Huge signs were hung on each tree: "Save Our Trees." "Don't Kill the Trees." "Don't Kill Nature."

Not too long ago, I received a letter from a 12-year-old boy asking me what I thought of his writing. He had sent along a three-page piece he had written about his sister who has Down's syndrome. I wrote back to the young writer, telling him how powerful and important I thought his writing was. I also told him that his words could make a difference in a lot of people's lives. I suggested he send it off to a few special education journals as well as the National Down's Syndrome Society. Writing is not for decorating bulletin boards and filing folders. Writing is for the real world.

Marcella, a fifth-grader, wrote the following entry in a notebook she carries with her everywhere:

> Everywhere I go I see homeless people, in alleys, corners, and on the street. I get the shivers all over, and I start to think how do they go through winter, most of them die, and the ones that survive usually get very bad diseases.
>
> They eat out of garbage cans because they're hungry. They sleep in subway stations because they're cold. The ones that have some kind of instrument play for money.
>
> Some dig in the garbage for cans to get money. Most of them carry carts or garbage bags with them. They keep their stuff in there. Only a few of them have clothes that are a bit decent. Most of them wear old rags that are given to them by kind people or that they find in the street.

Her teacher encouraged her to turn her thoughts into a letter to the editor and send it off to the local newspaper.

Teachers have come to trust Valerie Martin's advice, "Teaching people to write requires, first of all . . . they be forced to open their eyes and ears, to take off the blinders and let the images

Shelley Harwayne codirects the Teachers College Writing Project, a staff development effort jointly sponsored by Columbia University and the New York City Board of Education. She also works as a consultant to school districts throughout Canada and the United States. For the past few summers she has led writing institutes in Vermont, Colorado, Oregon, Washington, Sweden, Norway, and the Philippines. In the fall, she will be doing literacy work in the black townships of South Africa.

pour in—a necessary first step toward taking life seriously and even, I suspect, a good way to start taking responsibility for themselves and for the world they can finally see."

A young Long Island boy wrote a letter to Yukio Tsuchiya after his teacher read aloud *Faithful Elephants*, a heart-wrenching story of Japanese zookeepers forced to kill their animals for fear that a bomb dropped on the city would allow them to roam free.

The 85-year-old author wrote back, explaining to the young boy that he puts his heart into writing books for children in the hopes of banishing wars forever. The child then told the story of the Faithful Elephants and shared the author's letter at a Holocaust Memorial Service in his town.

Of course, it is not just the writing that is leaving the classroom, the reading is going out as well. Junior high school students in the Bronx loved Katherine Paterson's *Bridge to Terabithia* so much, they wanted to share it. Their teacher, Liz Dolon, sent the following note home:

> Starting April seventh, and every Thursday thereafter, Academy students will be sharing this beloved book with the Senior Citizens at Notre Dame residence on 183 Street. We are taking our literature group into the community because we want to share the joy of *Bridge to Terabithia* with the elderly.

Her seventh-graders each hosted a small cluster of senior citizens. They read aloud to their new friends and they invited the seniors to keep reading logs and join in book talks.

Children all over the city are making it easier for others to fall in love with reading. The older students are hosting read-aloud hours at local libraries and running escort services for younger children who are unable to walk to the library alone. They're performing their own poetry at store-front libraries and preparing read-along tapes as gifts for beginning readers.

And the community is welcoming these children who love reading. Just this past June, the Museum of Natural History invited a group of fifth-graders to spend an overnight in the whale room. "Bring your bedroll and your favorite nonfiction book!"

Of course, it's not just the students who are spreading the joy of literacy into the community. Throughout New York City, teachers are leading book talks. They're hosting small reading circles made up of parents, paraprofessionals, principals, and school secretaries. They're gathering weekly to respond to *Beloved* and *Ironweed* and *The Woman Warrior.* They're gathering weekly to respond to *Breathing Lessons* and *The Counterlife* and *Love in the Time of Cholera.* They're gathering because they love to read and "when you come on something good, first thing you do is share it with whomever you can find . . . "

Children and teachers are reaching out into the community and the community is entering the schools.

- A fifth-grade teacher in the Bronx launched a study of poetry by inviting every adult in and around the school building to share a poem that has made a difference in their lives. A kitchen worker read the Greek national anthem, a crossing guard read her favorite Hebrew poem.

Resource: Organization

 **Schools Reaching Out**

Institute for Responsive Education (IRE)

605 Commonwealth Ave.
Boston, MA 02215
1-617-353-3309

IRE offers a wealth of resources and information for parents, educators, community members, and policymakers pioneering educational equity. The institute has conducted research studies, organized conferences, carried out advocacy projects, provided consultation and technical assistance to state and local education agencies, and more. Their catalog describes these services and provides how-to guides and other publications promoting citizen participation in educational decision-making and school improvement. A journal called *Equity and Choice* is published three times a year ($15 yearly subscription).

Debbie Montgomery

- Paula Bower and her first-graders turned a littered lot in front of their school into a fruit and vegetable garden. The community cares for the blossoms over the weekend and joins the annual garden party, a feast filled with original songs and poems and paintings.

- New York middle schools and high schools are filling with Adopt-A-Class sponsors. The city's business, government, and arts leaders are adopting classrooms and helping the students take on big challenges and big projects. The mayor's office recently helped a group of seventh-graders publish their memoirs, *Pages of Our Lives.*

Whole language is extending to whole communities. The work of the classroom is becoming the work of the community. Which is right.

→ See: Archey, p. 351; Literature Reference List, p. 429; Patterson, p. 304; Pessah, p. 347; Peterson, p. 348; Shannon, p. 222; Sherman School Story, p. 342; The Writing Workshop— A World of Difference, p. 399.

Further Reading by Shelley Harwayne
- *The Writing Workshop—A World of Difference,* with L. Calkins. Video. Staff development book with same title.

Resource: Pamphlet

Helping Your Child to Read

Garry Carter
From:
Auckland Teachers
College
60 Ipsom Ave.
Auckland, New Zealand
686-179

Carter's pamphlet is a good brief description of the reading process. He draws an excellent analogy between the ways parents help a child learn to speak and the way they can help their children learn to read. This small publication is filled with practical instructional tips and good titles to use for various ages and reading levels.

Arrietta Chakos

As I See It:
Kenneth S. Goodman

A Time for Sharing

The tall ceilings of my second-floor class-room echoed and magnified the tumult of my 36 eighth-graders as they tumbled, bounced, slumped, strolled, and shuffled in from lunch. Dennis, 5' 9" and 115 pounds, staggered in, shoes in one hand and eyes on a book he was holding in the other hand. The boys took their shoes off to play football so that they wouldn't mar the high gloss. Soon, shoes back on, they were in their seats, each one combing the hair of the boy in front of him, carefully shaping the Bryl-creemed ducktails and one-inch flattops.

The girls in midcalf, tight, narrow skirts folded themselves carefully to slide into their seats. A week earlier, during a state mandated "drop drill," Janice's skirt had split halfway down the seam as she scrambled to get under the desk to protect herself from potential falling debris and radiation from a hypothetical atomic bomb attack.

Now Skippy, a compactly built, athletic young man, was up in front leading cheers for "Good-man's Warriors." Peggy took over to lead the class in songs beginning with "I Had a Little Chicken" and ending with "White Choral Bells" in which the dominant soprano voices blended with the deepening voices of a few of the boys to achieve a near harmony.

I winced a little when Faran got up to lead our sharing time. But I shouldn't have worried. The usually sullen boy handled the routine comfort-ably and the class responded positively. (Men-tally I congratulated myself on the undeserved C's I'd given him to forestall the beating a poor report card always brought at home.)

Sharing began with the usual movies, Uncle Miltie's antics on TV, and weekend trips. Then it was Tony's turn. He was a good-natured and pop-ular boy. Maura, his studious older sister, had recently dropped out of high school to work in the tiny grocery their family owned in La Rana.

Tony began: "Me and Paco and Gordo barely got away from the cops yesterday. We threw some rocks and broke some windows at the new factory they're building in La Rana. Then we saw the cops coming and we took off. They chased us

Magic Bird

by Madeline Friedman

One day I saw a blue bird
and the blue bird sang
to me and the blue bird
flew away and then I was
happy for the rest of my life.

From *A Book of Fantasy and Adventure*, by 100 students from Alternative Community Schools (Summertown, TN: National Coalition of Alternative Community Schools, 1982)

into the oil fields but we hid out behind the pumps. We didn't go home until it was dark. Man, we had fun."

The burst of response was more than poor Faran could handle. "Remember our rules," I reminded them. "One at a time and wait for Faran to call on you." Initially the responses ranged from disbelief—"You just made that up"—to open admiration. They wanted to hear more about the chase, about the window-break-ing, and about how they hid themselves.

I noticed Margaret's agitation before her turn came. Her teacher-mother had been working with her to control her temper—which wasn't all that bad—in fact, she was the kind of student teachers loved to have: socially poised, enthusi-astic, and productive. The struggle to control her emotions caused her to sound cold and hostile: "Why did you break those windows? You had no right! You shouldn't have done that."

Tony's mood changed. "They shouldn't have built that factory there. They're the ones who aren't right."

Now a dialogue ensued that bypassed Faran.

Margaret: That was private property. You were trespassing. Somebody has to pay to fix those windows.

Tony: Private property! That was our soccer field they took away. The men from the church cleared all the junk and garbage away. They made a nice level soccer field for us. And then one afternoon we come home from school and there's a fence up and signs that say "Keep Out." Man, that was our field. And now it's a factory.

Margaret: They needed that land. Lots of towns wanted that factory. But we got it because that was the best place to put it.

Tony: How come you know so much?

Margaret: My dad's the construction superinten-dent. He's got to get the windows fixed now.

Tony: (whistles) Oh, man! Well, they shouldn't have taken our soccer field.

Margaret: Play somewhere else. What's the big deal?

Tony: Where? The nearest park is way over across the freeway. There ain't no place for kids from La Rana to play except the street. We were here before anybody, before the rest of the town. Now nobody cares about a few poor Mexicans. No need to ask us if we want a factory or not.

Margaret: But the factory will bring jobs. My dad says you should all be grateful.

Tony: Then why didn't they build it where you live? Then you'd get all the noise and traffic. We'd come and work there and still have our soccer field.

Margaret: There's no room for a factory in our neighborhood.

Tony: You had room for the new mall they built two years ago.

Margaret retreated to her moral position: "It's just wrong. You can't go around breaking windows every time you think you're not treated right."

And Tony summed up his moral position: "Lots of things ain't right."

I didn't think of my classroom, so many years ago, as a whole language classroom. But I knew that if I wanted my kids to learn to live as citi-zens in a democracy, I had to involve them in the governance of their own classroom. I knew that my classroom had to be a place where they could share their experiences, their triumphs, and their defeats. I knew that they had to feel comfortable taking risks, speaking out, and trans-acting with each other. I knew that if they didn't

I wish more kids I knew as a teenager had access to a magazine like *Listen*. Celebrating positive choices, it presents the values of a contemporary lifestyle that is drug-free. Its portraits of positive role models concentrate on prevention and aim to improve the self-image of youth, "who are daily bombarded by the multi-million-dollar promotions of the drink, drug, and tobacco industries." Edited by Narcotics Educa-tion, this educational journal also offers a teacher's guide published monthly September through May.

Debbie Montgomery

For Parents

Interpersonal Communi-cation Services
$14.95/year (5 issues)
from:
7052 West Ln.
Eden, NY 14057
1-800-992-9147

This organization offers the newsletter *For Par-ents,* which aims to improve family communica-tion and to help parents create a stimulating environment for their children's social, intellec-tual, emotional, and moral development. Pub-lished five times a year, it offers practical suggestions and in-depth articles on sensitive top-ics like drugs, teen sexuality, sibling rivalry, living with stepchildren, single parenting, death, and separation. Reviews of relevant resources are included in each issue. In addition, family "together time" exercises are suggested as ways to build family closeness and strengthen family communication. The editor of the newsletter, Carolyn Shadle, has also developed the Building Communication Skills game, which she recom-mends to families and schools.

Debbie Montgomery

Networking: Empowerment & Family Support Bulletin

Free from:
Cornell Empowerment Project
G19A Martha Van Rensselaer Hall
Cornell University
Ithaca, NY 14855

Designed as a network-building tool, this new bulletin reports on practical applications of empowerment in local communities. The pub-lisher, Cornell Empowerment Group, hopes that it will "spark a dialogue between readers interested in empowerment approaches to community development and those involved with the family supports movement … "

Debbie Montgomery

learn to accept each other in the sheltered social environment of our classroom, they were not likely to do so outside in the larger community.

So much of what I know I learned from what my students shared with me.

→ See: Bissex, p. 209; Goodman, p. 207; Newman, p. 211; Shannon, p. 222; Shor, p. 223.

Viewpoint: Bill Moyers

An Interview with Sara Lawrence Lightfoot

Sara Lawrence Lightfoot: Part of the process of education is beginning to, in some sense, expand one's ways of being in the world.

Bill Moyers: (voice-over) Sara Lawrence Lightfoot knows the importance of telling stories. In her writings and her classes at Harvard's Graduate School of Education, she teaches by example and from experience. Her newest book, *Balm in Gilead*, tells of her mother's extraordinary personal and educational journey to a career as a child psychoanalyst. And in *The Good High School*, through stories of real people at six American high schools visited often by Professor Lightfoot, she describes what makes some good schools good and some teachers memorable. At her home in Boston, we talked about the problems and promise of school today.

(interviewing) You talk about good schools, but every time I mention the word *high school*, I can see people's eyes reflecting back to me truancy, dropouts, violence, alcohol and drug addiction, illiteracy, racial conflict. The image of schools today in the mind of the public, I think, is very negative. Do you think it is?

Lightfoot: There are too many schools that look like the school that you are describing with all of those terrible things going on inside. But there are many more good schools, it seems to me, than we imagine, many more good teachers than we imagine.

Part of what I want to do in my work is to begin to describe things that work and not merely describe things that don't work.

Moyers: Are there certain things that good schools have in common?

Lightfoot: I think good schools have a sense of mission that kids and adults can all articulate. We know what we're about, this is who we are, and adults will echo those same kinds of values and notions. I do call it, in my book, ideology. I mean, there is a kind of ideological stance that brings coherence to the school.

Moyers: What else?

Lightfoot: Good schools tend to be a chemistry of extraordinary teachers, relatively good teachers, and mediocre teachers. We can't expect in any profession that we'll have goodness throughout, but there has to be this chemistry of wonderful people who are rewarded for being wonderful—rather than denigrated for being wonderful—good people who continue to be good, and relatively mediocre folks who are inspired or nudged or supported into becoming better. I also think that good schools are disciplined places, and I don't mean by that just behavioral discipline, but a place where people set goals and set standards and hold each other to them.

Moyers: What about the role of the leader, the principal?

Lightfoot: In all of these schools it happened that the six principals were male. All of them in various ways described the feminine sides of their natures when they talked about leadership in schools.

Moyers: And those qualities are?

Lightfoot: Listening, building a sense of community, sustaining relationships, supporting people through failure, all of those.

Sara Lawrence Lightfoot is professor of education at the Harvard Graduate School of Education. Since joining the faculty at Harvard in 1972, she has been interested in studying the schools as social systems, the patterns and structures of classroom life, the relationships between adult developmental themes and teachers' work, and socialization within families, communities, and schools. Besides numerous articles, monographs, and chapters, she has written four books: *Worlds Apart: Relationships Between Families and Schools* (1978), *Beyond Bias: Perspectives on Classrooms* (1979) (with Jean Carew), and *The Good High School: Portraits of Character and Culture* (1983), which received the 1984 Outstanding Book Award from the American Educational Research Association. Her most recent book, *Balm in Gilead: Journey of a Healer* (1988), a biographical and historical narrative, won the 1988 Christopher Award, given for literary merit and humanitarian achievement.

Moyers: Do you agree with the general lament that our schools are in crisis?

Lightfoot: My feeling is that we have expected far too much of schools, that we have had very high aspirations for the ways in which schools will in some sense solve all of our cultural and social crises, and economic crises.

Moyers: I know a lot of teachers, and they say, "I'm expected to play every role."

Lightfoot: In some sense schools have been our most visible and vulnerable institution in society. I mean, in other words, they are the stage on which a lot of cultural crises get played out, and so we see in schools most vividly the inequities, most vividly the hypocrisy. And we tend to blame the teachers, the primary adult actors there, or the system, if we don't want to blame individuals, rather than in some sense seeing the ways schools are connected to other institutions of learning and development, and also without sort of recognizing what might we ask realistically of schools, and hold them accountable for.

Moyers: And you say they should be held accountable; there are certain things professionally that they ought to do.

Lightfoot: I really do think that anyone who graduates from high school should be literate.

Moyers: What is it that makes a good teacher?

Lightfoot: I think one thing is that teachers who are good do regard themselves as thinkers, do regard themselves as intellectuals. In schools where teachers do not see their own destinies in the eyes of their children, it's unlikely that good teaching is going on. In some sense, you have to see yourself reflected in the eyes of those you teach, or at least see your destiny reflected in that.

Moyers: You talk in your book about how a school takes on the personality of its community.

Lightfoot: Yes. It's terribly important to recognize that there is a culture alive and throbbing in a school. And it takes on, really, the character and color and vitality of those who live inside, students and teachers.

Moyers: Do you find a lot of burnout in teachers today, or is that a cliché?

Lightfoot: I would call it boredom. I would call it the need for, in some sense, renewal, change, inspiration, rewards.

Moyers: Do you think there really is a negative attachment to teaching today?

Lightfoot: Oh, absolutely. For the most part I think teachers are denigrated.

Moyers: If a president-elect called you and said, "Professor Lightfoot, how in my inaugural address should I address the school crisis?" What would you tell him?

Lightfoot: I think I would really ask them to focus on teaching and learning, I mean, really on the essence of the enterprise, rather than on how to restructure the institution. Somehow the American public has to get back to the great richness and mystery of learning, where we began, the playfulness and the seriousness of learning, and how that can be nurtured and supported in schools by teachers in classrooms. So I would really hope that they would focus

The Funny Side

The Real Thing

A Texas grandfather laughed at the memory. His daughter brought her 16-month-old son Leonard for a Sunday afternoon visit. While she sipped coffee with her mother in the kitchen, Leonard, a tireless imitator of adults, amused himself with a flyswatter, whacking imaginary flies around the back screen door. Unnoticed, he pushed open the door and walked out on the back porch, where he found grandpa dozing on a comfortable couch. Leonard also found a real, live fly—on grandpa's bushy moustache.

Whap!

—Hal Bridges, professor emeritus of history, University of California, Riverside, CA

on, first of all, how do we begin to attract good people back into this profession, who have these commitments, who have these values, who can develop skills; and how can we continue to support them once they have entered the profession, how can we support them so that they can sustain themselves at times of adversity, you know, which are always there, even in the best of schools.

→ See: Goodman, p. 274, 389; Heath, p. 422; Stevenson, p. 271; Watson, p. 427.

Excerpted from *Bill Moyers' World of Ideas*, 12 October 1988, © 1988 Public Affairs Television, Inc. A book based on the series, *A World of Ideas*, has been published by Doubleday and is available at bookstores everywhere.

 ### WHOLE LANGUAGE CAMERA

Sunnyside High School teacher Vicci Fox confers with her student Bertha Gamboa, Tucson, AZ.

As kids see it

Through the Looking Glass

by Jude McClain

I was born in San Francisco, but my earliest memories are of Detroit. I have lived in the inner city since infancy with my parents and sister, and with our adopted menagerie of pets. I attended elementary school at Burton International from kindergarten through eighth grade. The teachers were inventive and caring, and my schoolmates were of every ethnic and social background, each person more interesting than the next. When I graduated and began my career at Cass Tech, my strong sense of identity, which I had developed at Burton, enabled me to adjust and make new friends quickly, and my high school experience thus far has been quite good. My most important job at this point is to build a solid foundation for the future through good grades and valuable experience.

The future does not frighten me, but I often feel that I need more room to spread my wings. Success, to me, is as simple as being content and proud of what I have done, but this can be much more difficult than it sounds. The motivation for being successful can come only from the heart, and once that motivation is found, it must be steadily nourished with work and persistence. The distance between wanting a dream to come true and actually going out to make it happen is great.

The people who have influenced me the most during my life are my parents. My parents have always supported me in whatever I have wanted to do, from figure skating to voice lessons. We have always shared an enormous amount of love, the most basic of human needs. They have helped me find myself and have taught me what to look for in others. Our good relationship stems from mutual respect and desire to please each other; they have many fine qualities I hope to see in myself someday. Most important, they taught me how to care and not to fall into the trap of apathy. Every day I see many of my peers becoming more and more oblivious to the world, aware only of their own self-pity, insensitive to others. Too much negative energy inside a person is ultimately self-destructive.

The biggest problem among teens today is pressure. It comes from everywhere, and the only way to fight it is to have a solid support system of friends, family, and faith in oneself. In these years of confusion, boredom can become dangerous and harmful, and depression, though normal, can be deadly. Young adults must take it upon themselves to become the most complete persons they can be, and to learn to relate well with others. A closed mind gets nowhere, while an open one can go to the limits of imagination and back. Education, communication, and motivation are the most invincible weapons this world has ever seen, but people must learn to use them carefully. Once mastered, the future is an open door.

Jude McClain is a high school student at Cass Technical High, Detroit, MI. This essay was contributed by Toby Kahn Curry, a junior high teacher at Dewey Center, Detroit, MI.

Resource: Organization

Office for Substance Abuse Prevention (OSAP)

5600 Fishers Ln., Rm. 9A54
Rockville, MD 20857
1-301-443-0365

National Clearinghouse for Alcohol and Drug Information (NCADI)

P.O. Box 2345
Rockville, MD 20852
1-301-468-2600

OSAP offers a variety of services: the operation of demonstration grant programs targeting high-risk populations; management of the National Clearinghouse for Alcohol and Drug Information (NCADI); support of community-based comprehensive prevention programs; development and dissemination of prevention-related materials and media programs; and development of a National Prevention Training System for professionals, parents, and youth. The National Clearinghouse offers a catalog of free publications as well as a bimonthly information service; *Prevention Pipeline* (available for $15 a year), which gives the latest information about prevention research, resources, and activities in the field.

Debbie Montgomery

Child Welfare League of America (CWLA)

440 First St., NW, Ste. 310
Washington, DC
20001- 2085
1-202-638-2952

Working to improve practices and policies on behalf of needy and troubled children, this organization offers in its catalog timely and cutting-edge books, monographs, newsletters, and journals on a wide variety of vital topics. The publishing program and marketing/distribution system are second to none in the child welfare field. Several newsletters report on the activities of federal agencies that affect children.

Debbie Montgomery

📷 **WHOLE LANGUAGE CAMERA**

Playground antics, Palo Alto, CA

As kids see it

Your Room Can Wait

by Timothy Cooper

It's late afternoon. My little sister is napping peacefully. My homework is done and so are my chores (sort of).

I'm curled up on the couch, reading. I'm helping the Hardy boys solve an especially complicated mystery. Right now they're dodging bullets from the KGB. It's very exciting!

"Timothy, clean your room!" calls my mother from the kitchen.

"Just a second, Mom!" I reply. I hope she'll let me read a little more. It's my favorite thing to do.

Through my reading, I've made scrambled eggs super with Peter T. Hooper and eaten cake in the bathtub with the Cat in the Hat. I've gotten into trouble with Curious George and made friends with a beautiful spider named Charlotte.

I've enjoyed Toad's ridiculous adventures with his car. I've shared Ellen Tebbit's embarrassment about her woolen underwear. And I've stayed for years on a lonely island with an Indian girl named Karana.

Reading has taken me on fantastic adventures. It has introduced me to many people and places. I have even gone to outer space!

My mother enters the room. "Timothy, your room is a disaster area!"

Then she sees that I'm reading.

"I guess your room can wait," she says.

Timothy Cooper is a fourth-grader. This essay, which won a 1989 National Mott's Apple Award, appears exactly as he wrote it.

The Mott's Apple Awards are a national public service reading program designed to encourage children to value reading as a lifelong skill and pleasure, and to focus national attention on the importance of reading in children's lives.

Resource: Distributor

Kidsrights

3700 Progress Blvd.
P.O. Box 851
Mount Dora, FL 32757
1-904-483-1100

Kidsrights is a clearinghouse for prevention and education materials, from preschool to professional, in print and film, in the fields of children's and family issues. Children's moral and legal rights are supported in a wide range of resources. Their catalog offers not only books, but also videotapes, games, activity books, anatomically correct dolls, play therapy toys, and a variety of curriculum materials.

Debbie Montgomery

If a child lives with tolerance, he learns to be patient.
If a child lives with encouragement, he learns confidence.
If a child lives with praise, he learns to appreciate.
If a child lives with fairness, he learns justice.
If a child lives with security, he learns to have faith.
If a child lives with approval, he learns to like himself.
If a child lives with acceptance, he learns to find love in the world.

Kidsrights 1990 Catalog

Resource: Book

I Have Something to Say About This Big Trouble: Children of the Tenderloin Speak Out

Collected by
Reverend Cecil Williams
and Janice Mirikitani
$9.95 plus tax and shipping from:
Glide World Press
Glide Memorial Church
330 Ellis St.
San Francisco, CA 94102

For booksellers and librarians from:
Publisher's Group West
4065 Hollis St.
Emeryville, CA 94608

Foreword to *I Have Something to Say About This Big Trouble*

by Maya Angelou

❝ Where do children fit on the adult landscape? What hands do they have in the creation of an earth reeling with misery, weakened by hate?

They do not hurl explosives into the houses of the helpless. Rather, they inhabit those blazing infernos. Children do not poison the morning air with pollutants nor choke our rivers and streams with defecation, hospital waste, and chemical detritus. No, they simply breathe the air, drink the water, and play upon the obscene beaches.

They did not invent the buying of souls nor the selling of dreams. Rather, too often, they themselves are the commodities sold and bought by their own community.

Children do not flood neighborhoods with crack and smack and cocaine, but rather their infant bodies are invaded with the fanatic drugs before they leave the wombs and struggle for their first breaths of air.

It is amazing that our children do not hate us, do not gather together as one strongly knit and righteously indignant group and turn their backs on us and this decrepit world we offer them.

This compilation of poetry, prose, and drawings by children living on the ledge of life humbles me. I am humbled by the mysterious information in its contents; despite our society's malignant neglect, they, the children, still reach their arms out searching for our love. Despite the many ways we have abandoned them, their poems still dance with hope for our acceptance.

Thanks to Reverend Cecil Williams, Janice Mirikitani, and the Mary Agatha Furth Children's Program, we are given another assurance that our crimes against the children can be erased if we will only act with love, and responsibility, and promptness.

Read this book. The children have already forgiven us, and while children may prevaricate, exaggerate, and fib, they do not lie. They must wait until we teach them that unhealthy action. ❞

Community clean-up in Palo Alto, CA

Resource Essay

Children's Poems from Tenderloin Streets

Glide Church Hosts Festive Book Debut

by Perry Lang

From the altar at Glide Memorial Church yesterday, the children of San Francisco's Tenderloin took center stage.

The youngsters, most of whom live in the city's most impoverished neighborhood, were introduced to the standing-room-only congregation as the proud authors of a book entitled *I Have Something to Say About This Big Trouble.*

The 124-page paperback is a collection of poems, essays, and hand-drawn pictures from the imaginations and realities of about 30 Tenderloin young people, most of them daily witnesses to crime, drug abuse, and poverty.

The world as seen by these children, who range in age from 5 to 15, is filled with both hope and despair.

"We're all very proud of our book," said 10-year-old Tianah Awezi Maji, who happily autographed copies of her work yesterday for enthusiastic members of the Glide congregation.

"These are their stories," said the Rev. Cecil Williams, pastor of Glide Church. Williams and his wife, Janice Mirikitani, collected and compiled the stories, which nearly a dozen of the children

shared with the congregation during yesterday's morning worship service.

The book, 13-year-old poet Rashanda Struggs told the audience, is "about the trouble we have and see; it's about the things we dream to be."

"Every child dreams of their own career, not walking the streets drinking beer; with a job, a future or hope, we don't want to be doomed to dope," she said.

Drugs, particularly crack, are a recurring theme of the book, whose young authors span a rainbow of ethnic groups and nationalities.

One essay by a 14-year-old girl tells of a woman caught in a crack war and how she gets shot to death. A poem by a 15-year-old boy tells of a man who sold his Caddy to get drugs to shoot up and now has contracted AIDS. Other stories warn about the dangers of crack, including a rap by James and Johnnie Mar Fairbanks that warns: "Stop the rock, Hubbas in troubba."

Although laced with the sad realities of drugs, poverty, and crime, the book is also full of stories, poems, and pictures of magic, rainbows, and love.

"Despite the many ways we have abandoned them, their poems still dance with hope for our acceptance," novelist Maya Angelou wrote in an introduction to the book. The book can be purchased for $9.95 at Glide Church.

➜ See: Corridors, p. 352; The Sherman School Story, p. 342.

From *San Francisco Chronicle,* 11 September 1989.

As kids see it

Glide Church

by Matt Dudley

Glide is a church and a community too
It offers love for me and you
It gives you hope and thrill of life
Makes you love your kids, your husband and wife
There's crack meetings for the needy
First Aid if they bleed
And if you're illiterate they'll teach you to read
They give the homeless food
They're never rude
And Cecil Williams is a real nice dude
This is what I wanted to say
I'm gonna say goodbye the Glide way:
I love you

Matt Dudley is 15 years old.

From *I Have Something to Say About This Big Trouble,* Glide World Press, 1989.

YOUNG ARTISTS

Israel Mendoza, 9, Brentwood School, East Palo Alto, CA

Resource: Organizations

Children's Defense Fund

122 C St., NW
Washington, DC 20001
1-202-628-8787

The Children's Defense Fund is a private organization that exists to provide a strong and effective voice for the children of America who cannot vote, lobby, or speak for themselves. The Fund's goal is to educate the nation about children's needs and to encourage preventive investment in children. A monthly newsletter, *CDF Reports,* covers current developments in children's issues on local, state, and federal levels.

National Committee for Prevention of Child Abuse (NCPCA)

332 S. Michigan Ave., Ste. 1600
Chicago, IL 60604-4357
1-312-663-3520

The NCPCA Catalog includes brochures, pamphlets, and booklets for parents, children, and teachers on child abuse prevention. Offerings for parents range from practical hints on discipline and communication skills to foster-parenting abused children. Some materials are available in Spanish.

The Sherman School Story

Sherman Elementary School in downtown San Diego is a success story. Two years ago, this school, with an enrollment of over 1,100 students, most from poor immigrant families, was struggling. The neighborhood was overrun with drug dealers and crime. The school's principal, Cecilia Estrada, and the former vice-principal, Maria Garcia, worked with community agencies to gather the support of teachers, parents, and community leaders, and Sherman—and the community—were transformed. Dennis Doyle, the vice-principal, who stepped in after Garcia, joined their effort.

—Democratic Schools

The school and the community have become a coalition, and it has to be that way because the school doesn't exist independently of the community. Currently, we are very involved in bringing together people from the neighborhood to work with administrators, teachers, and students.

One of our first projects was a campaign organized by the student council to clean up the neighborhood around the school. The students teamed up to work with various city and community officials. They got trash bags donated by a city agency. They got a garbage truck to come on the school playground and park during the cleanup. They contacted another city agency to get out street sweepers to clean the streets. They also arranged for tow trucks to haul away burned-out, abandoned cars. The cleanup teams put cards on the front doors of all the homes, which said, "The area in front of your house was cleaned by students at Sherman School." It's important to realize that the kids did most of this entirely on their own. We helped with some of the organization of it, but they ran it.

Through our close work with the community, vandalism is down 50 to 70 percent of what it was a year ago. Drug dealers no longer hang around the corners of the school. Now in the evening next to the school parking lot, which used to be deserted except for gang members, you'll find 40 neighborhood kids playing basketball in pickup games. Dozens of kids are on the playground after school with a recreation leader who supervises games until 5:00 P.M. Where drugs were being sold now there are community gardens. Kids work in the gardens every evening after school.

This occurred because about 200 parents of our students got together at our school and demanded—and got—better police cooperation. The police responded by bringing in a walking beat called WECAN, Walking Enforcement Campaign Against Narcotics. The neighborhood is very appreciative that the police are there to eliminate the drug dealers. The school has a direct role in the WECAN program. It serves as a go-between for people in the community who want to contact the police but might hesitate because they fear immigration checks or retaliation from criminals. They feel comfortable contacting the school and asking us to report any drug dealing they see going on. The police have become involved in our school in other ways as well. We instituted a program in which officers come in regularly to tutor the kids at all levels, in all subjects. The Spanish-speaking officers have skills that are especially needed.

Some may call our projects to clean up trash and eliminate drug dealers extracurricular. But at Sherman, learning doesn't stop at 3:00 p.m. Our curriculum evolves in a very dynamic way from what is happening in our community. When the students become involved in community projects, they gain a great deal in terms of responsibility, cooperation, and analytical skills—as well as the basic skills of reading, writing, speaking, and arithmetic. They look at the reality of what is happening. They learn to work with others and to develop ideas with others about how to build the kind of community everyone wants.

Another way our students learn from community action is through meetings about community issues held on the school site. When we teach about government at Sherman, we do not say to our students, "This is how government operates, study it and give us back facts." We say, "Here are some of the ways government serves and some of the ways it falls short—let's develop ways to *impact* that system."

Recently we had a community meeting at the school. About 75 parents and kids attended. We invited the city council representative for our district, the city managers' representative, someone from the parks and recreation department, the planning department, the police department, and representatives from the social services agencies that work in the community. Many people expressed frustration with the lack of adequate police services and with the absentee landlords who are raising the rents sky-high and leaving buildings in decrepit condition. Our students testified on their own about what they wanted to see changed. People complained that we don't have Little League, soccer leagues, proper street lighting, or child-care centers. The people asked for another meeting at which they would give the city a report card evaluating how well it was addressing their concerns.

Later we talked with the city planner about working directly with our students. She agreed to work with the students at all levels to create a community plan. We discussed how teachers can help all grade levels—kindergarten through sixth grade understand how the government works. People from city government will work with our students.

We work hard to get parents involved in the school. We offer parent institute classes in which parents get help with things they can do at home that support what's happening in the school. These things make a world of difference. The teachers, the students, the parents, will all tell you what a difference there is.

Another way we support parents is by developing positive home contacts. We know from the research that most contact with the home from the school administration is negative, particularly for black and Hispanic kids. Dennis Doyle, the vice-principal, has been reading to kids in their homes once a week in an effort to build positive school-home relations. In three of our classrooms we are using literature instead of basal readers to teach reading. With the parents' approval, Dennis goes to the home and reads aloud chapters that the kids have picked as their favorites. They get to invite a certain number of their friends and neighbors to come and listen. He has had some wonderful readings with a mixture of preschoolers, high schoolers, and grandmothers. They usually have milk and cookies together afterward. It is fun, but it also helps us learn more about what is happening in the home.

We have become known throughout the school system as a school that's doing some interesting and productive things within the community. We constantly publicize what we are doing. Not a week passes that we don't get some kind of media attention, because we make sure the press knows about events at our school. For example, at the beginning of the school year, we had the students register to vote for student council members. We had 98 percent registration. We gained media attention because we held the election on the same day as the city primary. We were a polling place for the city, and you would walk into the auditorium and see adults voting on one side and kids voting on the other.

We must empower people to take control over their lives and to create the kind of future they want—and to do this in a democratic way. We keep learning that the more people are involved in making decisions about their own lives, the better the outcome for everyone. It doesn't work for somebody to come in and say, "Here is what should be." That is what Joe Clark did and real, lasting change did not happen in his school.

We must get people involved in deciding together what they want. If at Sherman we simply teach our kids about the economy and the world of business and government as it is, they will be frustrated. Our schools have been reflections of what the socioeconomic condition is in our country—with tracking, and reading groups that reflect the upper, middle, and lower classes—and we must restructure that. We want to work toward a future with socioeconomic justice. The only way to achieve that is through democratic means—by working closely with parents and young people as they take responsibility for their own communities and destinies.

→ See: Apple, p. 416; Giroux, p. 417; Horton, p. 74; Peterson, p. 348; Shannon, p. 232.

Adapted from *Democratic Schools* 3(3), June/July/August 1988.

Resource: Periodicals

Growing Child Research Review

$36/year (12 issues) from:
22 N. Second St.
P.O. Box 620
Lafayette, IN 47902
1-317-423-2624

This review periodical is a great way to keep up with current research in child development. Brief summaries of research findings are published monthly, representing a full range of viewpoints. A very readable way to sift through what would otherwise be mountains of journals and professional publications.

Debbie Montgomery

Growing Child

$14.95/year (12 issues) from:
22 N. Second St.
P.O. Box 620
Lafayette, IN 47902
1-317-423-2624

This monthly child development newsletter is written to correspond with the child's age; that is, if the child is six months old, parents receive the newsletter written about children of that age. Parents are informed of what to expect at each age of development. A supplement, *Growing Parent*, is included with each issue, and has topical articles on handling stress or dealing with the demands of a busy lifestyle. Each quarter *Growing Child* offers a selection of age-appropriate playthings, all traditional toys with educational value.

Arrietta Chakos

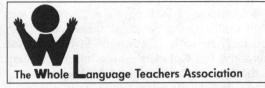

Network

The Whole Language Teachers Association

A School in Transition

by Barbara Siaki

Over the past two years an exciting metamorphosis has taken place at the E. J. Harrington School in Lynn, Massachusetts. Harrington, a large urban elementary school serving nearly four hundred fifty students, is making the transition from traditional instruction to a more innovative, developmentally oriented whole language approach. Many of the key players in Harrington's process of change were discovered through the Whole Language Teachers Association. This network has proven to be an extremely valuable support system. I hope that by sharing our staff's process of change, it may help others to establish whole language classrooms or programs.

In the spring of 1987, Harrington, along with six other Lynn schools, was designated as a "magnet" school. Our goal, defined by the State Department of Education, was to develop a unique theme which could set our school apart from others in Lynn by offering distinctive educational opportunities. As program facilitator, I felt strongly that the key to successful, meaningful change was comprehensive staff development. No truly innovative curriculum can be successfully instituted without the involvement of those who are responsible for its implementation. Teachers in transition must be afforded professional regard. The gifts of time, ownership, and response that Mary Ellen Giacobbe extends to her student writers provided an excellent model for effective staff development.

From the outset, staff development aimed for inclusivity. During the summer of 1987 the entire staff was invited to participate in the planning and development of our magnet theme. As a result of engaging all staff members in this initial planning stage, we concluded our summer session with a sense of ownership and a shared mission. We developed a written statement of philosophy and a commitment to exploring new, more effective methods of teaching language and promoting literacy.

In the fall, a subcommittee of teachers visited numerous Boston-area schools featuring specialized language arts programs. In December we previewed a "new" approach to teaching reading and writing. Whole language was in concert with our developmental philosophy and offered promising concepts and methods relative to literacy learning. Still, our staff was cautious. Many had reservations. Wasn't this just another name for open education or language experience? What about basals, phonics, structure? Resistance had begun to rear its ugly head. It was apparent that the teachers needed time. However, in order to make intelligent decisions they also needed information. Armed with a briefcase full of articles and notes from my meetings with whole language proponents, I attempted to define and describe what I had learned. "Whole Language: What's New?" (Altwerger, Edelsky, and Flores, *Reading Teacher*, November 1987) was particularly helpful. Comparing and contrasting whole language with the language experience approach, the open classroom and the whole word approach, the authors presented a description of whole language theory and practice. As teachers became informed, their resistance waned. Our staff, though still somewhat cautious, decided to pursue whole language.

➜See: Bird, p. 92; DeLawter, p. 389; Gillam, p. 56; Goodman, p. 379.

Excerpted from the Fall 1989 newsletter of the Whole Language Teachers Association, Sudbury, MA.

Barbara Siaki is the Magnet Program coordinator of E. J. Harrington School, Lynn, MA.

Membership Information: Membership dues for the WLTA are $20.00 for two years. To become a member, send a check payable to The Whole Language Teachers Association, c/o Carol FitzPatrick, 47 Whitewood Road, Westwood, MA 02090. The WLTA cannot accept purchase orders.

Resource: Games

Family Pastimes

R.R. 4
Perth, Ontario,
K7H 3C6
Canada
1-613-267-4819

Maker and distributor of cooperative board games, Family Pastimes advocates playing together, not against each other. Players of Harvest Time, for example, work together to bring in the harvest before the winter weather spoils everyone's crops. This and other games provide the opportunity to experience sharing and caring behavior in a noncompetitive group effort. "We won" replaces "I won" and "you lost." Cooperative games enable people of different ages and abilities to play side by side, each making his or her best contribution. A catalog describes the many games; several are available in languages other than English.

Debbie Montgomery

Resource: Organization

National Peer Helpers Association (NPHA)

P.O. Box 335
Mountain View, CA
94042
1-415-965-4011

The NPHA is a professional organization that sponsors peer helping programs for young people. Trained and supervised by counseling professionals, peer helpers offer a variety of supportive services to those in need. Services include substance abuse prevention, gender support groups, dealing with divorce and loss, suicide awareness, conflict resolution, and more. NPHA publishes a quarterly newsletter, *The Peer Facilitator Quarterly,* for association members and organizes national conferences for peer helping professionals. The association plans to publish a resource catalog for peer helping programs and professionals.

Arrietta Chakos

Parents' Perspective

by Mandy MacCalla

A Lot Is Cooking at Ohlone

When it's noon at Ohlone School, there's more cooking than hot lunch. Students may choose from a wide range of activities, thanks to suggestions from the Student Council that were made reality by parent volunteers. Old standbys and new offerings such as photography and chess keep lunchtime blahs at bay.

Noon Art is a venerable tradition at Ohlone and a favorite activity for students. Every Thursday children may enjoy a variety of art experiences. Each week students may choose from four or five different art projects. Participants in Noon Art are working to decorate the auditorium for the Ohlone production of *Jack and the Beanstalk*. Parent volunteer Dayle Dodds said of the Noon Arts program, "We have a lot of parental help and more donations than storage space—everything from egg cartons to tiles."

On Mondays, the Storytelling Club meets with Cathe Wright, an instructional aide at Ohlone. Participants hear stories from around the world and learn how to tell stories themselves while meeting local authors.

Chess enthusiasts meet every Friday in the Ohlone library. Under the guidance of parent volunteer Red McCalley, Chess Club members may benefit from beginner sessions with rule explanations, demonstration, and problem-solving.

Music is yet another noontime offering at Ohlone. Parents coordinate the noon music program that encompasses miniconcerts, guest artists, and films. The miniconcerts feature student performers and provide a valuable opportunity for learning to be a good audience. Guest artists scheduled this year include a percussionist, who will demonstrate a sophisticated computerized keyboard, and a harpsichordist.

On rainy days, the Ohlone library is a popular spot for those who wish to play games, use computers, read, or even study. The library is kept open four noontimes a week by instructional aides and volunteers.

For the back-to-earthers, the Ohlone Farm is kept open three noontimes a week. Supervised by Ohlone parents, the young naturalists work in their classroom plots, collect eggs, and play with the ducks and rabbits.

Two new noon activities at Ohlone this year are Photography Club and Yearbook. Joan Swanson heads both. Children may bring their camera or use one donated to the Photography Club.

Nothing to do at the noon recess? Not at Ohlone School.

➜ See: Fearn, p. 372; Pessah, p. 347.

Mandy MacCalla is a parent volunteer at Ohlone Elementary School, Palo Alto, CA.

WHOLE LANGUAGE CAMERA

First-graders picnic in the park after a trip to Tucson Zoo with Annette Maggitti and Gayle Power, primary teachers, Tucson, AZ.

Whole Language Internacional
by Yetta M. Goodman

Glimpses of Whole Language in Australia and New Zealand

In Melbourne we entered the staff room of Eltham East Primary School. There were large sheets of butcher paper covering the walls on which the staff had listed their agreed upon whole language principles they had developed over the past few years. They were examining whether their practices were consistent with their principles.

Every classroom we walked into was alive with students writing together, solving math problems, doing science projects, and working on the editing of many different kinds of both fiction and nonfiction publications. Literacy events were dripping from the walls and ceilings. Often we walked through curtains of material strips or yarn hanging from the ceiling or the tops of doors with signs, messages, or graffiti stapled to them. These hangings were used to establish temporary separate work areas in the classroom.

In one of the sixth-grade classrooms we were introduced to Paul, who was author of the week. According to the teacher, Paul had come to the school recently, reluctant to read and write. Paul was eager to talk to me about his "writing process"—how he wrote his story first; how he discussed it with the other students and the teacher; how he produced the dummy; and how he kept his personal dictionary. He was serious, proud, and intent about the importance of his work, and showed me the "author of the week" bulletin board with his picture, writing he had selected to be displayed there, and an interview done by other students who had discovered what he liked to write about, the kinds of things he thought about, and the way he went about his writing. He told me that when he wanted to use some hard words he wasn't sure of, or when he wanted to say something in a particular way, that he would just "have a go" (Australian for "take a risk").

Paul solicited serious criticism from me. "Do you like the words I used here? Do you think this line belongs here or would it be better at the beginning?" Paul was receiving strong support from the teacher and the other students. The other students wanted to talk to me about their writing too, but they stood patiently, slightly back from where Paul and I were, so that Paul could have the limelight.

We also visited Melbourne's Moonie Ponds West Primary School. The principal introduced himself as the real Frank Smith. This school has been influenced for a number of years by Lorraine Wilson, a language experience advocate. Literacy events were strongly in evidence once again: writing, drawings, and reports were on walls, hanging from ceilings, on charts and easels, and surrounding door entries. Children were working on projects on the floors, on tables in hallways, as well as in the classrooms. Parents, often mothers with their babies, were reading to and with students, listening to them read, and helping them find resources.

Frank said that they can't do things two years in a row because they are always trying something new. "Everything revolves around the children and the children know it. They're loved, they feel secure, and there is tremendous rapport between children and teachers. You only come in here (the principal's office) when you have something good to show me. The discipline policy is developed by the school and adapted and updated each year. The teachers and I read a great deal and look for new ways and new understandings. This is an ethnic working class area with many Italian families."

When I entered one fifth- and sixth-grade

team-teaching situation, the teachers were not visible. Eventually I found one teacher sitting in a low armchair. Students were sitting on the arms of the chair and on the floor deep in talk about some problems they were having interacting with each other. Other students were busy writing, reading, and working on various projects. The class was working on a human body unit. Students had drawn their bodies on large sheets of paper. They had labeled the anatomical parts using the language most familiar to each student. In the middle of the room hung large illustrations of the male and female human body. As the students studied the anatomical systems, they labeled the illustrations with scientific terminology.

South of Sydney we visited Worrawong School. With a group of teachers visiting from the United States, we participated in a program presented by the staff and the students. The principal, Roy Williams, said, "It is necessary to lose time to gain time." He explained that the school needed to take the necessary time for the professional staff to work with parents to change attitudes and develop strategies for continuous learning. As this begins to happen, they all participate in the dynamic process of moving toward an integrated curriculum. "Language is the basis of the curriculum. The child learns through language whilst he learns language." The kids greeted us with songs about Native Americans and then welcomed us in Macedonian, East Indian, and Vietnamese—languages which, among others, are spoken by the children and their parents. These children were involved in poetry, report writing, or narrative. Teachers and children spent a lot of time discussing their reading and their writing using the terminology of the genre they were studying. In the computer lab the kids were collaborating with each other on their writing.

In New Zealand we saw a unique kind of bilingual education occurring at Titahi Bay School outside of Wellington. We were greeted by the children, the principal of the school, and their teachers with a traditional Maori welcome ceremony. Piti Nohotima, an advisor on Maori for the New Zealand schools who took us to the school, helped us with our roles in the ceremony. The kids danced and sang and we responded appropriately. Ken made a statement of welcome and friendship. We touched noses with the school staff and the children. The first grade has a Maori immersion program. Kids are reading in both Maori and English. They read aloud in English from children's books written in Maori. When the teacher and the students read English books, they often translate them directly into written Maori.

We also visited Richmond Road School, a wonderful Samoan and Maori neighborhood school in Auckland. The children are in family clusters from kindergarten to fifth grade. The school is organized to teach English as a second language to the Samoan students and to provide a Maori language immersion program. The principal was a revered Maori educator, Jim Laughton (who died in 1988, a few months after our return to the United States). The assistant principal, Joy Glasson, leads the staff in writing their own social studies and science materials that focus on the ethnic and linguistic riches of the community and build on the strengths the children bring to school. A good deal of the material is translated into Maori and Samoan. Don Holdaway pioneered big books at this school years ago. No two Australian or New Zealand schools are quite the same. We have much to learn from both countries.

➔ See: Cambourne, p. 17; Holdaway, p. 44; Pigdon, p. 152; Wallace, p. 88; White, p. 395.

Resource: Magazines/Periodicals

Magazines can be an important classroom tool, but choosing the best publications on your own is a tricky business. Teachers can use their public libraries to look at various magazines before purchasing; because quality varies, this preliminary evaluation is essential. Most libraries circulate the magazines in their collection. Teachers may want to borrow a variety of magazines from the library to expose students to many formats and varied information.

Magazines for Children: A Guide for Parents, Teachers, and Librarians

Selma K. Richardson
1983; 147 pp.; $12.50
Chicago: American Library Association

With periodic updates, the ALA publishes this useful guide that reviews magazines, gives grade level suggestions, and provides subscription information.

Children's Magazine List

Free from:
Educational Press Association of America
Glassboro State College
Glassboro, NJ 08028

This is a comprehensive list of children's publications for readers from 2 to 18. The list is furnished as a public service and comprises publications that are home delivered or bought through schools.

Great Teachers:
Inta Gollasch
by Trevor Cairney

It's All Relative

Though I had known Inta Gollasch for almost five years, I had not spent long periods of time in her classroom until June 1987, when I began visiting her classroom as part of a research project that was concerned with the links children make between the texts they read and write. Inta was teaching a grade-one class in a small independent Christian school.

Inta has over 20 years' teaching experience in infants classes. She has completed studies through the Riverina Literacy Centre and is committed to whole language principles. As a practitioner, she has long been recognised as an outstanding teacher with progressive and innovative ideas. She is a teacher with an amazing warmth and love for children, parents, and other staff.

When I first walked into Inta's classroom, I was struck by the "busyness" of it, both physically and in terms of pupil behaviour. It was also at times messy and noisy, but there was always an atmosphere of work and engagement in a variety of tasks. The figure below is a floor plan of Inta's classroom:

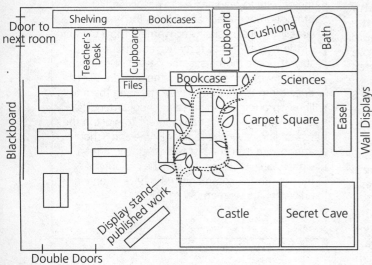

I recorded my first impressions of Inta's classroom in my field notes:

My arrival in the classroom has hardly been noticed by the children. There is activity everywhere. Children are sitting at desks writing, writing folders are lying open revealing masses of twisted trampled paper—drafts as yet unpublished. Several children are sitting discussing something, perhaps their stories. Inta has just realised that I've arrived. A bright six-year-old has caught her attention, and mentioned that I am here.

As I wandered around the room on the first day, it was clear that these five- and six-year-old children were remarkably self directed. Two children were lying on the floor writing, two more were inside the magic cave, another three were in a "castle" (both were constructed by the class). Several boys were searching for information on snakes and lizards in encyclopaedias. Everywhere there was a gentle hum of noise, rising to a roar at times, only to be gently lulled by Inta.

The children continued to work in spite of my watching and peering. No one asked what I was doing there. Everyone seemed prepared to let me observe them. They would write a word, look up to smile, write another, and so on. Their independence is reflected in the following field note entry:

10:20 A.M.—A visitor arrives from next door asking if the class will be coming for the regular television program. Inta announces, "If you'd like to go next door for TV, put your folders away and go on through. If you'd like to keep writing, then just keep on going." Several children drop everything

and run, others finish the work or sentence they're on and make their way next door. About 10 students keep working on, while the rest leave over a period of 10 minutes.

On my first day in Inta's classroom I stayed for approximately 90 minutes, circulating around the room at will, talking to specific students, making notes, chatting, helping those who wanted assistance, and so on. At the end of the session, I talked briefly with Inta and left.

This was a pattern that was to be repeated weekly for almost a year. During this time a picture began to emerge not only of the classroom environment and the students, but also of Inta Gollasch. I was challenged by what I saw and kept asking myself what it was that made Inta such a special teacher. I concluded that Inta was assuming a rather special role as a teacher and that she had created a sense of literary community in her room.

Inta was not simply a giver of knowledge or a controller of children, she was an observer and a learner, acting as:

- A sensitive information giver, if her students needed her knowledge;
- An interested listener, when students wanted to share the excitement of their reading and writing;
- A strategy suggester, if the existing reading strategies of her children were not working;
  - A sharer of insights, successes, and problems she experienced from personal reading and writing;
  - A willing opinion sharer who was prepared to give an interpretation or opinion of a specific text;
  - A skilled introducer to new language forms, new authors, new uses for reading, new literary genres;
  - A demonstrator of real and purposeful reading; and
  - A committed member of the "Literacy Club."

Inta had also managed to create a special type of learning environment. Her classroom was a place where:

- Students learned as extensions of social relationships—partner sharing, response groups, whole class sharing;
- Spontaneous talk about the books they were reading and the texts they were writing was encouraged;
- Students pursued reading and writing without the pressure of competition or the fear of failure;
- Students saw lessons they completed as relevant to their needs and purposes;
- Students were given varied and frequent opportunities to read and write for a range of purposes;
- Students were given help in interpreting their reading;
- Movement around the classroom was encouraged;
- Students were frequently engaged in many different reading and writing tasks at any one time;
- Students were treated like fellow learners and the role of expert was shared depending upon specific areas of learning; and
- The teacher supported and responded to student needs for help as part of "real" literacy tasks.

In short, Inta Gollasch is a teacher who considers the needs of students as central to all that she does and who sees her main task as one of support for an active and self-directed community of readers and writers.

→ See: Cairney, pp. 116, 201; Cambourne, p. 17; Gollasch, p. 233; Pigdon, p. 152.

Trevor Cairney is an associate professor at the University of Western Sydney, Nepean, Kingswood, New South Wales, Australia.

The day was tough... Hien cried in school today. He said he misses his mother in Vietnam. Kim Hang peed on the floor again. Trung and Bao scratched at each other, fighting over a small book. Phuong came to school late, her chest and neck showing violet and reddish marks of "coining." It made me wince inside as I imagined the process. Today the kids were unusually noisy, and I was grumpy because of the scorching summer heat. I hate April and May—some months are fine, but April and May...

"Teacher, I have list today," Tan, my AT, excitedly beamed as he reported to work.

"That's great, Tan." I was sincerely happy for Tan, who waited four months to get a sponsor. And I was glad he was here today to help me quiet my restless class.

"Teacher, I go now. I need to go to JVA [Joint Voluntary Agency] and Warehouse. I go America tomorrow."

"Oh." My jaw dropped. "God bless you, Tan. I wish you a good life in America." I managed a faint smile and had the kids say thank you and good-bye to Tan.

I guess I just have to face this day on my own, I thought. As I sat back on my chair to check their journals, Phuong approached me gingerly, wide-eyed, with guilt written all over her face. She was hiding something behind her back.

"What is it, Phuong?" I calmly asked. She handed me a broken drumstick. I mentally calculated the fine I would pay to the materials room. I asked Phuong what happened, and in her struggling English, she said Bao grabbed it from her as she pulled it back, dividing the stick in two.

What else could go wrong today? I was beginning to lose my patience. I just hoped Mang Armand would deliver lunch today, or that Mang Ben would fetch us on time. I resignedly told Phuong to take her seat and, feeling spent, fetched for their math books.

As the kids worked on their addition, I had a chance to catch my breath. I looked at those small heads buried in their math books. I began to think of the other kids just like them—still in their country—probably barefoot and hungry and without a chance to write in a math book. And then I thought how thankful I should be for these kids in my class. Even if they are noisy, they are special. They, too, have a struggle of their own.

The empty gurgling of my stomach cut off my reverie. I was glad when I looked at the clock. I told the cleaners of the day to sweep the floor and close the windows.

As I gathered my things I noticed Kim Hang stayed after all her classmates had left. Now what is it this time? I wondered. Mang Ben's on time today and honking his horn for the last time. I'll be left behind again. I had to stay and see what Kim Hang was up to.

"Yes... " I raised my brow questioningly. With an impish grin she handed me a paper with her scribblings on it. On the other side of the paper she drew the classroom and her classmates and me. It was far from artistic, but there was pride in her eyes as she looked at me. Below the drawing, she wrote down the words "Miss Boiser I love, very good... class very noisy, Miss Boiser no get angry. Good-bye Miss Boiser. Kim Hang."

I chuckled. It had not been a tough day after all. I smiled at Kim Hang and then thought again of the kids just like her and Bao and Phuong... still in Vietnam, barefoot and hungry. Their days are tougher than mine.

I looked outside the window and noticed that the bus had left without me. I thought it would be nice to walk home with Kim Hang today.

→ See: Urzúa, p. 42.

Yvonne Boiser is an elementary ESL teacher for Preparing Refugees for Elementary Program (PREP), World Relief Corporation, Morong Bataan, the Philippines.

Becoming Literate

by Arlene Lecours

"It's Hot! Hot! Hot!" or You've Lived the Life; Now Write the Play!

Henry reluctantly picks up a pencil and begins to write. He looks at me and says, "You're the teacher." I hate when he says that. I am, as a good whole language teacher, trying to get him to take responsibility for his own learning. I hate being "the teacher."

And of course, I hate calling them "students." They are so much more than just "students." They are parents and grandparents, union representatives and church leaders. They have mortgages and car notes. (They drink the same beer I do.)

I am an adult education teacher in a very nontraditional learning environment. My "students" work eight to ten hours a day and then come to class or put in their schoolwork time before their afternoon shift. Some have finished high school and have taken college-level classes. Some have not made it through the third grade. Some want to get their GED. Some just want to write a letter to their mother in Alabama.

In the historic Ford Rouge Complex in Dearborn, Michigan, our "Rouge Academy" uses whole language to teach reading and writing improvement classes. The participants, UAW hourly workers, come voluntarily to the learning center on their own time, but through educational contract agreements with the UAW and Ford, there is no out-of-the-pocket charge to the auto workers for this program.

After an atypical 10-week session, I ask my students to write their feelings about the class. Henry, as always, hesitates. The next session he arrives with a piece of paper in his pocket. He unfolds the paper and says, "I wrote something for you." I ask him to read it. He clears his throat and reads, "The class has helped me to understand the world around me better."

I can go on.

One of the themes that seemed a natural for my students is work and, in particular, factory work. Living in Detroit and being raised the daughter of a factory worker, I have always scanned for materials on this theme. By the time I learned what whole language was about and began *my* work in the plants, I had already collected a sizable trunk of materials associated with this theme.

Included in this bundle were poems; short stories; articles about training, shifts, boss/worker relations; historical accounts of strikes and working conditions. They came from magazines, books, newspapers—all the usual places!

One of the articles I shared with a group was entitled "Workers Take the Stage," and was taken from *Solidarity* magazine (a UAW publication). The article highlighted acting groups started in UAW locals throughout the United States who either wrote their own plays or worked with professionals expressing their ideas about the workplace. My students had never heard of such a thing and were excited about the concept and jokingly agreed, "We should write a play about this place." I agreed. And again, they agreed with a nod and a wink.

Several weeks later, one of the students came up to me very seriously and said, "Arlene, I think we should write a play. And you know what? It would be really good for us. We'd have to organize our thoughts. We'd each check each other's spelling. We'd have to write strong words and we'd learn to speak better." I continuously shook my head at his rationale (as if I'd disagree!) "You're absolutely right," I said and ran (very professionally) to the women's room and jumped up and down in excitement.

It was not difficult to convince the others, especially because Jimmie (the play originator) had been updating our group on his work situation, which gave us the foundation for our play. Now, when Jimmie would come in disgusted about something at work, I would say, "Write this down, it could be good dialogue!"

We agreed on a purpose: to show unity between workers and how safety affects the workplace. We outlined characters, plot, and settings. We wrote a skeleton to help us get from the first act to the finale. And then we started over and over again.

We went to plays. As a group we went to see a musical version of Studs Terkel's book *Working* at the local university, and individually we went to see plays and brought back suggestions and ideas.

We read plays (even though some authors say this is the worst thing to do while writing a piece) and listened to radio dramas. We read about playwrights.

We wrote back and forth. Someone being one character and someone being another. We kept dialogue journals. We taped and then transcribed. We changed our minds about what happens when. We criticized each other when something didn't sound right. We wrote a climactic scene. And then threw it away. We wrote an ending. And threw it away. But in the end, we wrote a two-act play called "It's Hot! Hot! Hot!" (Choosing the title was a story in itself.)

Long before the play was finished, the word had spread through the plant that we were writing a play. Students from my other classes would walk into the center and overhear our discussions (and laughter). "What is going on?" And, of course, no one could hide their excitement about the play. Certainly, I couldn't.

What next? We discussed production and decided nothing could be done until we found actors for the roles. We wrote an ad for the plant newspaper and displayed the ads in washrooms and cafeterias announcing auditions for the play. Several strangers made it up to the center to try out. (One man had done USO shows in World War II and boomed a voice so spectacular, the audition committee almost cried!) We've got a minor role or two left, but because of summer plant shutdown, the play has been put on hold. But we will be back, because, as we say to each other, "The play must go on!"

→ See: Lecours, p. 314; Literature Reference List, p. 429; Voices, p. 128.

Arlene Lecours teaches adult education at the Rouge Academy (UAW—Ford National Education, Development and Training Center), Dearborn Stamping Plant, Dearborn, MI.

The Funny Side

I Lost It

Four-year-old Caitlin, returning to her nursery school after several days' absence, bounded into the classroom and rushed over to greet her teacher, Marcy Davies.

"You know what, Marcy? I was sick."

"You were, Caitlin?" Marcy bent down to give her a sympathetic hug. "I'm so sorry. Did you have a temperature?"

"Well, I had one once but I lost it."

—As told to LBB by Marcy Davies

Book Note

Literacy and Living: The Literate Lives of Three Adults

Lorri Neilsen
1989; 164 pp.; $14.95
Portsmouth, NH: Heinemann

Literacy and illiteracy, in their many forms, have been publicly debated, ignored, exploited, and researched. Much of the inquiry into literacy and its effects has been ill informed or poorly documented, or both. Public information about literacy stems from superficial surveys, impersonal experimental designs, or conventional wisdom.

Lorri Neilsen, who lives and works near Halifax, Nova Scotia, makes scientific research in literacy accessible to us all. Her book is an anthropological study that documents the role literacy plays in the lives of normal, functioning citizens. Teachers, especially those who are acquainted with whole language, will be enthralled with these stories of adults and their families who make authentic use of what they've learned from books and schools.

Robert F. Carey

66 Literacy in Hubbards is the province of women. Although men and women alike seem to use their ability to read and write equivalently, the promotion of literacy activities in the home is largely the responsibility of women. Most women of the twenty-five to forty-five age group are stay-at-home mothers; some have part-time jobs. It is the women who read to their children, introduce them to paper and crayons, bring them to library programs and nursery school, attend Christmas concerts, and volunteer to work in the school library. Of the regular Home and School attendance over the last two years, more than eighty percent were women. The majority of those from the community who have attended university are women. 99 (p. 27)

WELL-SAID

I always saw teaching adults to read and write as a political act, an act of knowledge, and therefore a creative act. I would find it impossible to be engaged in a work of mechanically memorizing vowel sounds, as in the exercise "ba-be-bi-bo-bu, la-le-li-lo-lu." Nor could I reduce learning to read and write merely to learning words, syllables, or letters, a process of teaching in which the teacher *fills* the supposedly *empty* heads of learners with his or her words. On the contrary, the student is the subject of the process of learning to read and write as an act of knowing and of creating. The fact that he or she needs the teacher's help, as in any pedagogical situation, does not mean that the teacher's help nullifies the student's creativity and responsibility for constructing his or her own written language and for reading this language.

—Paulo Freire and Donaldo Macedo

Excerpted from *Literacy: Reading the Word and the World,* by Paulo Freire and Donaldo Macedo (New York: Bergin & Garvey/Praeger, 1987).

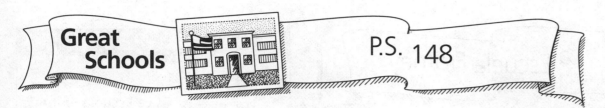

Great Schools

P.S. 148

Classroom Demonstrations
by Anita Castañeda

Package the Energy

by Laurie Pessah

Last November, John Block, producer of the "NBC Nightly News," visited our school for two days to videotape children in reading and writing workshops. As the last of the equipment was being packed away, John told the principal, "I've been in many schools across the country, but there's an energy here that feels as though teachers like to come to work and kids like to come to school. Wouldn't it be great if that energy could be packaged?"

Package the energy! As we begin our sixth year studying reading and writing workshops, I can't help but wonder about the sources of energy that keep P.S. 148 alive.

Energy sources come from projects that teachers and students initiate in their classrooms. This past year, some of our upper-grade classes began a study in nonfiction writing. In Eileen Braghieri's fourth-grade class, children chose to study deafness. "Information Wanted" posters were taped all around the school and in windows of neighborhood stores. A woman from the community spoke to children about what it's like to have a deaf child. Children gathered information in their notebooks. Tricia wrote, "I saw how hard it was for her to talk about it. I wanted to tell her that it was OK and I understood. She told us how, when her son was little, children (that went to our school) wouldn't play with him. When she was leaving, I hugged her."

Children toured the audiology department at Schneiders Children Hospital. They interviewed audiologists and learned sign language. Lexington School for the Deaf opened its doors to us. Children asked questions like "How do they have fire drills here?" "Do you have to know sign language in order to teach here?"

Sara Hadfield, a teacher at Lexington, visited with one of her high school students, Yakov. He spoke to the children about what it feels like to be deaf. Vincent's piece, "The Heart of a Non-Hearing Person," was dedicated to Yakov. You should never judge a book by its cover, he wrote. Some of the most caring people in the world have different ways of expressing themselves.

Energy sources also come from schoolwide projects on reading and writing. Last November, we initiated what will be an annual event—a "Bed 'n' Books" Slumber Party. The gymnasium became a communal bedroom for 35 girls and their moms. They brought their favorite books as well as their teddy bears. Parents and teachers read aloud while the girls rolled out their sleeping bags and got into their pajamas. As the lights were dimmed, flashlights were turned on, and all around were mothers and daughters reading together.

Pat Valenzano initiated a schoolwide writing process magazine. Children in writing workshops submitted pieces for publication. Fourth- and fifth-graders applied for jobs as editors, illustrators, and publishers. Each afternoon from 2:00 to 3:00 the magazine staff would meet with Pat. When the magazine was finally distributed in June, it became an instant best-seller. Children throughout the school sent messages to the authors. A parent sent the magazine to a local publishing company who called us and offered to make our 1990 edition a joint venture.

Our Authors' Gallery across from the principal's office displays pieces from each of the 20 writing classes. Dangling from the side of the bulletin board are pencils with which children, teachers, and parents write messages to the authors on comment sheets that are taped below the pieces. "Please come to my class. I'm in 3-315. I also write poetry," one young poet writes to another.

P.S. 148 celebrates young authors on Authors' Night. A child chooses a favorite piece and then takes time to publish it in a beautiful way. Stapled to the back of the book is a blank sheet where readers can write and tell the author why they liked the book. Attendance at PTA meetings rarely exceeds 30, yet this year we held two Authors' Nights—one for primary grades and one for upper grades—in order to accommodate the 400 guests.

But it's not only the schoolwide celebrations that keep the energy high. It's also the celebrations between the classrooms. It's one class inviting another for a notebook celebration. It's fifth-graders reading their own picture books to kindergartners, often with the older child's arm draped over the shoulder of the younger one. It's upper-grade children making tapes of favorite picture books and giving the tape along with the book as a gift to first graders.

Ten teachers created a lunchtime writing group, keeping writing notebooks alongside their students. In response groups of threes and fours, we listened to Rose Calabro struggle with the question of whether or not she was a good enough granddaughter. We heard newlywed Anne Gianatiempo's view of modern marriage, and we listened as Antoinette Ciano's piece about her childhood turned into a love letter to her father.

A group of primary teachers met another day of the week to study teaching reading without a basal. We brought articles to share with one another. We took field trips to other schools to see alternative ways of teaching reading. We went picture book shopping to Barnes & Noble and searched for the best books for our classrooms.

Next year, we plan to form an adult reading group composed of teachers, paraprofessionals, and parents. We hope to learn more about the process of reading and study the implications for our own teaching.

Package the energy? I'm not sure that we could! I'm not sure that we should! Rather, it's the projects that take us outside our classroom into the community. It's the celebrations that give our students a sense of authorship. And it's finding new ways to care for our own learning.

➜ See: Fearn, p. 372; Harwayne, p. 337; MacCalla, p. 343.

Laurie Pessah is a reading/writing teacher at P.S. 148, District 30, Queens, NY.

WHOLE LANGUAGE CAMERA

Students from Lamberton Middle School share conversation and their yearbook with a resident of the Alliance House, a nursing home across the street from the school, Carlisle, PA. (See Leverson, p. 350)

Adopt a School

The majority of the schools in our district have been adopted by a business, a community, or civic organization. When a business adopts a school, they usually provide materials such as computer hardware and software, books, and funds for field trips; however, they also may become personally involved in the school and serve as tutors, crossing guards, playground supervisors, and so forth. Tandy Corporation, one of the district's largest contributors, also provides generous scholarships for graduating high school seniors.

Community and civic organizations provide a variety of services: Texas Wesleyan College contributes volunteer tutors and Christmas parties and gifts. Local nursing home residents are paired with middle school students; they write to each other, exchange gifts, and eat together at least twice a month. Officers from a police substation serve as crossing guards; they also read to students and eat with them so as to free the teachers during the lunch hour.

➜ See: Bird, p. 92.

Anita Castañeda is a curriculum specialist at Fort Worth Ind. School District, Fort Worth, TX.

Resource: Catalog

Family Travel Guides Catalogue

$1 from:
Carousel Press
P.O. Box 6061
Albany, CA 94706
1-415-527-5849

Family travel authority Carole Terwilliger Meyers publishes this unique catalog to help parents plan family vacations. Over 200 family-oriented travel guides, game books, and related articles are included. Meyers calls them "the best of the lot"; she has personally reviewed and selected each title. Many of the items are not easy to find elsewhere, and all promise to make family vacation planning easier.

Arrietta Chakos

The Funny Side
You Can't Escape!

A harried mother of four young children arranged for a sitter so that she could take a much-needed day off and treat herself to a shopping excursion in San Francisco. Waiting on the commuter platform, she caught sight of the train. "Look!" she exclaimed to the businessman standing next to her. "Here comes choo-choo!"

—As told to LBB by Gloria Norton, resource teacher, Fair Oaks School, Redwood City, CA

Great Schools

La Escuela Fratney

Resource: Book

La Escuela Fratney: Year One

Staff, Parents, and Students of La Escuela Fratney
$10 from:
La Escuela Fratney
3255 N. Fratney St.
Milwaukee, WI 53212
Attn: Robert Peterson

La Escuela Fratney: Year Two is now also available.

Constructing a Special School, La Escuela Fratney

by Robert Peterson

A parent's dream: A decent school that children want to attend in an integrated neighborhood, teaching children to be bilingual in Spanish and English, using cooperative and innovative methods, governed by a council of parents and teachers. That was the goal of Neighbors for a New Fratney as 1988 began.

This small, multiracial neighborhood organization, made up of parents, teachers, and community activists, is based in one of the few integrated neighborhoods in Milwaukee. The neighborhood, known as Riverwest, is wedged between the nearly all-black inner city and the more affluent nearly all-white east side.

In the space of just a few months, the group of parents and teachers mobilized the immediate community and built city wide support. The objective was to take control of an elementary school in the neighborhood and create for the school both its own educational program and structure of governance.

The Proposal

The proposal called for the creation of a kindergarten through fifth-grade school that was a two-way bilingual, multicultural, whole language, site-based managed school. A two-way bilingual program is one in which instruction is in both English and Spanish, with students from both language groups. While each student learns to read first in their mother language, they are also learning a second language. The goal is that by the end of the fifth-grade the children will be bilingual and biliterate.

Whole language means the emphasis will be placed on using language skills—reading, writing, speaking, and listening—as the means to learn and acquire language as well as to learn about the real world. This real use will be valued over drills and practice exercises, not only because such use provides integrated practice in phonics, spelling, semantics, and so on, but also because it shows children that language is for making meaning, for accomplishing something.

The multicultural curriculum stresses the history and culture of several nationalities and ethnic groups. The curriculum is organized around school wide themes: Our Roots in the Community; Native American Experience; Hispanic American Experience; Asian American/Pacific Islander Experience; and We Are a Multicultural Nation. The school plans on drawing on the cultural diversity of the Fratney neighborhood and the city as a whole. The plan called for the school to be explicitly antiracist and antisexist, teaching children that racism is unscientific, unhealthy, and something to be fought against.

Cooperative learning and democratic discipline are two other aspects of the curriculum. Children are taught and encouraged to cooperate and learn from one another. Discipline is to be conducted in a way that is humane and places responsibility onto the student and the class.

Support from *Rethinking Schools*

Part of the success of the project has been due to the progressive trend in educational circles in Milwaukee centered on an innovative quarterly newspaper called *Rethinking Schools*. Started in the fall of 1986 by a group of progressive teachers and area educators, the newspaper has grown in circulation from 6,000 to 20,000 with 750 paid subscriptions. The newspaper/journal, which is linked to a number of organizing projects, deals with both the theory and practice of educational reform and has had a major impact on several key curriculum policy questions including the blocking of the Outcomes Based Curriculum initiative and the granting of a whole language and literature option to teachers and schools in place of the traditional basal reading program.

The winning of the school and the continued success of *Rethinking Schools* has raised many more questions for activist educators in Milwaukee. For the school, the first question was what kind of governing structure should be established. After much debate, a council was established with five parents, nine teachers, one community representative, the principal and a representative from the other school staff. The key issue in the debate was the relative importance of the workers at the school versus the community it serves. The council meets monthly and discusses a broad range of school issues. A parent/teacher curriculum committee also meets regularly to discuss questions of what is being taught at school, special projects, and assessment.

The Future

A key issue is how to sustain parent involvement and to involve those parents—many of whom are quite poor—who don't regularly come out to school events. One particularly positive effort was made in January during our first school year when the parent curriculum committee organized a "Fratney Family Day" with workshops, performances, and a potluck in our third-floor gym. The parents organized a phone bank and called every family in the school who had a phone. The resultant turnout of over 275 people on a cold Saturday morning was deemed a great success.

Another key question is how to find time, money, and energy to help the staff develop their teaching abilities. Like most elementary schools, there is so little planning time built into the day that teachers rarely get a chance to collaborate. A final question is how to deal with the children, many of whom have spent years in traditional schools and classrooms, influenced by peers and television. As one of the children put in a letter to a local peace education center prior to a visit, "I want you to explain why I should give up my war toys!" Despite our boldest dreams, the realities of society profoundly limit what can be done at school.

But perhaps the largest dilemma of all, particularly for the organizers, is how to build a progressive, popularly governed, antiracist institution, while simultaneously finding the time and energy to educate the children and to work for the changes that must occur on a system wide level in order for this experiment to flourish.

→ See: Apple, p. 416; Giroux, p. 417; Harwayne p. 337; Rethinking Schools, p. 425; Shannon, p. 222; Sherman School Story, p. 342.

Excerpted from *La Escuela Fratney: Year One,* Milwaukee Public Schools, Duplication Department, 1989.

Robert Peterson is a teacher at the Fratney School, Milwaukee, WI. He is also an associate editor of *Rethinking Schools.*

Parents' Perspective

by Barbara Miner

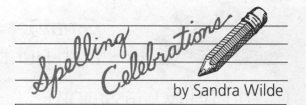
by Sandra Wilde

"Right On, Fratney"

When I ask my four-year-old daughter, Caitlin, what she did in kindergarten that day, she always has the same answer. "Nothing."

Sometimes she says it with an air of defiance, as if to add: "And I dare you to ask me again." Other times it's said with authority, as if there couldn't be any other answer. Then there are times it's said with utter indifference.

After several weeks of "nothing" in its various forms, I got the message. I stopped quizzing her about school, even though I was intensely curious. After all, having children in school is a new event in my life. And, like many parents, I wanted to know what Fratney's bilingual, multicultural philosophy meant in practice.

In her own way, however, Caitlin slipped me a few clues about school. One day, for example, she said: "I know what Spanish for blue is, *azul*." Or she would say, "I want a glass of agua. *Agua* is Spanish for water."

Before long, we had an unspoken agreement. I would never directly ask her about school, and in exchange she would toss me tidbits of information. But none of her brief remarks prepared me for the following:

It happened while we were on our way to day care one morning. I was listening to the news when I heard, "At President-elect George Bush's inauguration today . . ." Suddenly I remembered, today was inauguration day.

"Girls, I want to watch the television news tonight because the new president is going to take his job," I said to Caitlin and my two-year-old daughter, Mahalia.

"Is it Ronald Reagan?" Caitlin asked.

Hmmm, I thought to myself, I didn't realize that Reagan's name had sunk in. Funny what those little minds squirrel away.

"No," I answered. "Ronald Reagan is the man who was president. The new president will be George Bush. And even though I don't particularly like George Bush, I think we should watch him take his new job."

"Why don't you like George Bush, Mom?" Caitlin asked.

Oh great, I thought. At least grown-ups don't ask such direct questions. Or at least I could answer with something vague like, He's a Republican.

"Because," I answered, trying to come up with a response I felt she could understand, "because I don't think he's very nice to poor people and black people."

"Oh," Caitlin answered.

Silence. I waited for the next question. So far, so good, I thought.

"I know someone else who was mean to black people," Caitlin answered. "I learned it in kindergarten. A long time ago, black people were slaves,

and they couldn't do what they wanted. And then they were mean on the buses."

Mean on the buses? Heaven knows where she's going with this story, I thought.

"What do you mean, mean on the buses?" I asked.

"Well, after they were slaves, they wouldn't let the black people sit on the buses. They had to go to the back," Caitlin said.

Ah, I thought, there is some logic to this story.

"But one day a lady got on the bus and she was real tired," Caitlin continued. "She was so tired that she just sat down and fell asleep in the front."

Before I knew it, Caitlin was telling me the entire story of Rosa Parks and the Montgomery bus boycott. She didn't use the name Rosa Parks. But she had it all down, even how the police came to arrest the lady and there was a preacher who came to help her.

"And that preacher was Martin Luther King, Mom," Caitlin said.

At this point the two-year-old— eager to show off what she had learned from Caitlin—chimed in: "Martin Luther King. He died, Mom."

"Yeah. He was at work and a mean man shot him," Caitlin elaborated.

I wondered where this conversation would lead. Unfortunately, by this time we were at day care. The story abruptly ended. But as I turned off the car, I sat back in amazement. This is wonderful, I thought. My four-year-old is learning about Rosa Parks. Martin Luther King is one thing, but Rosa Parks? How many adults even know her story? What's more, she's teaching it all to her two-year-old sister.

Amanda's "only" picture

"When I was little I could only make one picture. My mother said that it was great! Now I can make a lot of pictures; sun, water, plants and people."
by Amanda Warr

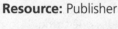

Invented Spellings: Permutations

We AET (ate) some POPCONR (popcorn)
Elaine, 4th grade

Sometimes writers will produce a spelling that seems more visual than phonetic: one that has all the right letters but in the wrong order. I call these permutations. In my study of six elementary school children (Wilde 1988), eight percent of *all* their invented spellings were permutations. Producing a permutation is likely to involve a fair amount of knowledge about a word's spelling; for instance, a child who spells *clothes* as *COLTHES* is probably more familiar with the word than a child who spells it phonetically as *KLOZ*. An interesting historical comparison: Masters (1927, pp. 113–116) listed 221 invented spellings of *pneumonia* written by students from eighth grade through college age. Eighteen of the spellings (eight percent) were permutations. Many of the typographical errors that touch typists make are permutations; some permutations of handwritten words may even be "typos of the pencil" of words that the writer knows how to spell.

References

Masters, H. 1927. "A study of errors in common difficult words." *Elementary English Review* 4.

Wilde, S. 1988. "Learning to spell and punctuate: A study of eight- and nine-year-old children." *Language and Education: An International* 2.

Resource: Publisher

Chronicle Books

275 Fifth St.
San Francisco, CA 94103
1-800-722-6657
1-800-445-7577 (CA)

A diverse mix of children's books (picture and activity books), family travel titles, and a beautiful nature series makes Chronicle Books a good resource for parents and teachers. Their edition of *A Child's Garden of Verses* by Robert Louis Stevenson is distinctive.
Arrietta Chakos

I felt proud. Not just of my daughter, but of Fratney. The kids should be learning these things, I said to myself. After all, isn't one of the purposes of school to teach children how to live in society. And aren't racism and inequality some of society's biggest problems?

"Come on, girls," I said as we got out of the car and I launched into my usual monologue of instructions. "Grab your lunch boxes, don't forget your hats and scarves, and make sure you have your mittens."

And then I mumbled to myself, "Right on, Fratney."

➔ See: Doerr, p. 290.

From *La Escuela Fratney: Year One*, Milwaukee Public Schools, Duplication Department, 1989.

Barbara Miner is the parent of two daughters who attend the Fratney School, Milwaukee, WI.

Great Teachers:
Beth Huntzinger

Community Classroom

by Mandy MacCalla

When the community becomes the classroom, many possibilities open up for the enrichment of children in literacy and literature. Beth Huntzinger, a first-grade teacher at Columbia School in Sunnyvale, California, took her students out into the community on a voyage of discovery that pulled together many components of learning: reading, writing, observation, history, math, and geography.

Beth designed a thematic unit on aging, focusing on relationships between the young and old. Though she used it with first-graders, the activities can be adapted to any grade level. Beth and her students invited their own grandparents into the classroom to tell their stories, interviewed elderly people at nursing homes, instituted an adopt-a-grandparent program, and ultimately became so involved with the lives of elderly people in the community that they put in a stint working in a soup kitchen.

The unit includes a literature-based reading list, embracing a wide variety of thought-provoking writing, from poetry to Eudora Welty's short story "A Visit of Charity." Many projects were spawned from this single theme. Children collected antiques and artifacts from home and shared their history. They created a map of the United States, recording where their grandparents and other elderly relatives lived. They described personal experiences with older people in their journals.

Another inspiring program instituted by Beth involved other classes besides her own. For two years running, she adapted and produced the plays *Teaser and the Firecat* and *The Mountain*, both dealing with environmental issues. The first play was acted by her own class, but the second used students from grades one through four. Once again, Beth made community concerns a focus of classroom learning. One of the plays even found a spot on the local TV news station.

Beth Huntzinger brings excitement to her curriculum by involving the students with their community. As a fellow teacher reports: "Beth is like a breath of fresh air. Her enthusiasm toward the profession and especially toward her students is a joy to see. She helped bring back my desire to try new and innovative ideas with my children."

➔ See: Literature Reference List, p. 429.

Mandy MacCalla is a parent volunteer at Ohlone School, Palo Alto, CA.

Nature Gets Top Billing

by Phyllis Lee

School Play Dramatizes Environmental Issues

Protecting the environment was the theme of a play at Columbia Community School in Sunnyvale, California, on Thursday. About 75 children from the first and fourth grades starred in the production, which featured a musical performance by Kermit the Frog and a stirring finale using a Carly Simon song called "The Turn of the Tide."

Major roles in the production, titled *The Mountain*, include the park ranger, the Teaser, and the Firecat. Other children played bears, squirrels, banana slugs, and flora.

The play, adapted by first-grade teacher Beth Huntzinger from the book *The Mountain*, was performed in conjunction with Arbor Day festivities planned at the elementary school.

Students were scheduled to plant seven trees at the school to mark the occasion.

"The book and play are about what happens when too many people come to the National Park," Huntzinger said. "How the animals have to find other homes. Birds fly away, deer have to move on...."

The action in the play picks up on Huntzinger's adaptation of former rock star Cat Stevens's story *Teaser and the Firecat*, which the children performed last year.

The plot centers around Teaser's return to the mountain to find her brother, Firecat. There the pair are joined by a city-weary Kermit, who has come back to the mountain looking for respite.

Kermit's solo, performed by seven-year-old Brian Reyes, laments the effects of water pollution in his song, "On My Pond." "We are the turn of the tide," Huntzinger said. "As an environmentalist, I think it's really important to get to kids early and get them to think about taking care of their environment."

➔ See: Environmental Education Resources, p. 323; Literature Reference List, p. 429.

From Times.Tribune, Palo Alto, CA, 31 March 1989.

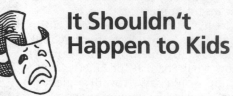

It Shouldn't Happen to Kids

Damaged Reasoning

From the very first day of school, Beth Huntzinger encourages her first-graders to write. Using invented spelling, they record their thoughts and feelings in personal journals, document their research findings in semantic maps, and write letters to friends they've made in nursing homes. By the end of the school year, the children are fluent writers, able to use this powerful medium for a wide range of purposes. One day her principal surprised and shocked her by harshly criticizing the use of invented spelling. His reason? He asserted that Beth was "damaging the students' self-esteem" by sending their work home "uncorrected."

—LBB

Classroom Demonstrations

by Ed Levenson

Students Get New Perspective

When Geane Hanson first came to Lamberton Middle School, she noticed the Alliance Home across the street.

"I thought it was a waste that the home was here but the children (from the school) were not visiting," she says.

Ms. Hanson, a sixth-grade English teacher, decided to do something to link the school, 777 S. Hanover St., Carlisle, and the home, 770 S. Hanover St.

Last December, she started the Youth Action Club at Lamberton.

The purpose of the club is to get students involved in the community, to make them aware of other age groups and to give them a new perspective, she says.

The club, a voluntary activity, meets for 35 minutes during a school activity period once every six days. Each student is assigned someone to visit at the Alliance Home, a combined old-age and nursing home. The membership of the club, limited to 15 students, changes each semester, Ms. Hanson says.

On their first visit, the students are required to write something about themselves to present to their "partners" at the home. Subsequently, students are encouraged, but not required, to have something planned each time they visit. . . .

Students interviewed say they joined the club because they wanted to provide company for the elderly residents, many of whom are women.

"A lot [of the residents] don't have relatives," says Brenda Fox, an eighth-grader. "They just want to talk."

Popular topics of conversation, according to the students, include schoolwork, after-school activities, holidays, weather and what the students want to do when they grow up. The residents occasionally talk about their past.

Students have brought presents for the residents. For example, Brenda made ceramic mushrooms for 10 persons; Angie Mountz, an eighth-grader, gave her partner a plant; and Christie Loy, a sixth-grader, brought a ceramic mouse for the woman she visits.

"I like being able to share," Christie says.

Ms. Hanson says she feels "good that the students are using their initiative" on the visits. "I don't have to encourage them to be thoughtful," she adds.

Some students even visit the home on their own after school, Ms. Hanson says.

She believes the Youth Action Club has helped to bridge the gap between the two different age groups and the two institutions. It also has helped students to gain an awareness of the community outside the school.

"It's important [for students] to be involved," she says.

[Ms. Hanson] would like to expand the program to other institutions but there is not enough time in a club period to take students elsewhere.

The students interviewed say they have benefited from visiting the home.

Roger Stephens, an eighth-grader, says the club has helped him "know about senior citizens."

Angie says she has "learned how the [elderly] people feel."

One girl has improved a skill that can be useful anywhere. Brenda says she is now "able to listen more."

➔ See: Amarelo, p. 351; Archey, p. 351; Hanson, p. 22; Whole Language Camera, p 347.

From The Evening Sentinel, Carlisle, PA.

In the Mail

"War Is Hell"

June 20, 1989
Dear Ken and Yetta:

I decided to use *Faithful Elephants* to start our study about the war. We developed its theme: "No more war—no more war!"

We felt our students needed to learn to stop being physical and sometimes even violent.

As part of our study, students wrote to their grandparents to learn about their experiences. Their replies (as you can see) have been very emotional and helpful.

When we were reading the letter from a grandfather who said, "War is hell," one of my most physically overreactive students said "That's what you wanted us to learn, isn't it?"

I hope you are well and not too busy.

Affectionately,
Janine Archey

5-17-89
Dear Amy,

We received your lovely letter yesterday, and since school will soon be out we are going to try and answer some of your questions quickly.

I had a group of ladies over for lunch today and they helped me on some things. Here at home we had some problems getting these items—

Nylons, housing materials, permits for gas furnaces, did not make refrigerators, ice boxes, no automobiles; there were rations on coffee, sugar, meats, shoes, tires, gasoline, etc. Prices were high—

We had car pools to get to work, we all had victory vegetable gardens and traded our ration coupons with each other. If more coupons were needed you had to go to a ration board and ask for them, they in turn made out forms and decided if you could have them. We also sent many care packages over seas—lots of them never received. The Germans kept them.

Our entertainment was mostly bowling, movies or home parties. Most people were working long hours—I worked 60 hours per week.

I'll never forget the day when it was announced the war was over! Bells were ringing all over and people flocked to churches to pray. What a relief.

Amy, I worked for four years at the bomber plant in Willow Run. I got there in a car pool with 6 people in it—the drivers took turns.

Henry Ford took on this project in 1940, when his company agreed to manufacture the nose-landing gear for the B24 bomber being produced by San Diego's Consolidated Vultee. H. Ford boasted that his company could eventually turn out a B24 an hour using assembly line methods. Contract was approved Dec. 4, 1941. A huge plant was built, each of its two assembly lines spanned more than a mile, and when the plant was in full production, it would house 20,000 workers a shift.

People came from all over to work here—men and women. Even short men—then called dwarfs were used in small places—like a pin setter. In all, 15,000 women flocked to W.R., where they donned overalls, put their hair up in scarves and learned to wield acetylene torches and operate rivet guns. The pay, for them, was better than any other jobs they could get. Most of the men were engineers whose expertise exempted them from the draft.

There were also a lot of men and women that worked in offices, which is what I did. That was great as you got away from the noisy, dirty assembly lines. We all had to wear blue uniforms and white blouses.

All in all, it was quite an experience and the pay helped to save our new home and keep me busy until my husband came home. You felt you were doing something for the war effort.

When the men came home it was an adjustment for a while. Many were ill, nerves shot and, of course, had to get their jobs back and get into a daily routine again.
Amy, I hope this will help you a little. I'll let Grandpa Jack tell you some more.

Lots of love,
Grandma Grace

P.S. I forgot one big item during the war. We learned to make oleo from white to yellow to look like butter. It tasted the same but looked better. Do let us know how you make out on your assignment. Good luck.

May 16, 1989
Dear Megan:

The Pacific Ocean side of World War II affected us greatly and in many ways. Japan bombed Hawaii on December 7, 1941! Grandpa was born in Hawaii. Grandma was born in Chico, California, and grew up there. Our parents had come from Japan and we looked Japanese. The two countries were at war!

We will never forget the last days of March 1942. We both worked at the produce market owned by Grandma's uncle. Grandma's people had a farm nearby. The Army Order came saying that all of us of Japanese ancestry would have to go to the concentration camp. If we wanted to leave, we had three days to do so. We wanted to stay free, so we left.

Grandma had relatives in Colorado. They had a large beet farm. We, and Grandma's family drove all day and night to Salt Lake City. We were so tired we slept all day and night. We then drove across the Rocky Mountains to the plains of Colorado. We each had only our bedding and one suitcase. We became beet farm laborers for two seasons! It was a back-breaking hard time for us!

We were glad to move to the city of Denver. Grandpa worked in the factory making army skis. Grandma worked in the factory sewing jackets for the soldiers. When the war was over we moved to Cleveland. We are happy here.

We went to Hiroshima, Japan, several times after the war. Grandpa's family and relatives live in the suburbs. We are very lucky that they were not all killed by the atomic bomb on August 6, 1945. They all worry that they could become ill any day. Several have died early.

The city of Hiroshima is a beautiful new city built over the ashes. The big attraction is the Peace Memorial Park on the site of the bombing. Many people died there. Some day we will take you there, Megan.

Love,
Grandpa and Grandma

➜ See: Cain, p. 299; Harwayne, p. 337; Literature Reference List, p. 429.

Janine Archey is an elementary teacher at the Starr School, Royal Oak, MI.

Classroom Demonstrations
by Odete Amarelo

Portuguese Grandmother Shares Stories

Our classroom of four- and five-year-olds comprises new arrivals from Portuguese-speaking territories, children who have been here for one or two years, and children who were born in the United States.

We are whole language learners. We read and write everything; we read to write and we write to read.

Ninety-nine percent of these children have little "print" at home. Some have never seen a children's book. We Portuguese are "oral language people." We invite our parents and our grandparents to come to our classroom for storytime. Most of our children left their grandparents behind, and the children miss them very much. My goal is to deal with the issues of family, self, and community, and, through social interaction, help children identify their experiences and articulate them.

During storytime, I have noticed the great value of stories told by grandparents. Children listen and they are relaxed. An intimate bond is formed. Isn't this what whole language is all about? The grandmother pictured here has shared story experiences and story patterns, themes, and characters that are culturally relevant. Students retold this grandmother's stories in books they wrote. We are developing language and experiencing success in a natural way.

Odete Amarelo is a bilingual educator at Lincoln School, Fall River, MA.

Teller of Tales
by Laurie M. Brown

I slowly unwound the thick, coarse hair. Her braids loosened, unfolding past her hips.

Brushing my grandmother's hair was an intimate, loving moment. The yellowing hair reflected her wisdom, age, and mystical intrigue. I felt the dirt and oil on her hair and acknowledged the paisley dress she'd worn three days in a row.

I stroked her hair, feeling the resistance of each snarl. Fairies began dancing in my ears. Grandmother's personified animals rumbled, bellowed, and sang. Voices that will forever twirl and leap within me.

Her hair quickly filled my brush. Again, I'm brought back to her decaying body. And I wonder, are the fairies still leaping in her soul?

➜ See: Brown, p. 133.

Laurie M. Brown is an elementary teacher at Landis Elementary School, Alief ISD, Houston, TX.

Principals Speak Out
by Norman Sherman

The Double Mitzvah

Lucy Calkins says that writing is life work, not desk work. I have learned from Norman Sherman that being a principal is life work too. He brings his life to P.S. 201 and has created a special learning environment for every person who enters his building.

—*Kathleen O'Connell Cunningham, Writing Process coordinator, District 25, Queens, NY*

It was five o'clock, and there was still no parent. Little Cory lay curled and asleep on the stuffed chair in my office. This was the fourth time that Cory had not been picked up after school. The last time he was picked up late, his Dad had said, "We had things to do and I knew you'd take care of him." On that day, Cory had been left with me until 4:15.

I gently roused Cory. I helped bundle him into his winter jacket. He was happy to hear that I was walking him home. He knew the way. He kept up a constant chatter as he pointed out his special route for going home—across the school yard, through the hole in the fence, and down the winding path into the project. He excitedly pointed out his building, which was straight ahead.

We quickly climbed the three flights of steps to his floor. He pointed out his apartment. "That's where I live!" I rang the bell. We waited. No answer. I rang again. No answer. I asked Cory if he knew his next-door neighbor. He replied, "Yes."

I rang the neighbor's bell. A gentle, neatly dressed gray-haired woman answered the door. Her face appeared quietly dignified and she smiled when she saw Cory.

"Hello, Cory. Please come in."

I quickly explained the problem to her. "No one picked up Cory. His phone has been disconnected. I decided to walk Cory home in hopes that I'd find someone there. My only other choice is to take him to the police station."

Looking down at Cory, her face brightened. "Of course I'll take care of him. I've known him since he was born."

As she talked I noticed that her demeanor was more than just quietly dignified; it was sad. I looked at the woman's neat apartment. A yellow cellophane wrapped basket of fruit attracted my eye. Hesitantly I asked, "I hope the basket of fruit was given to you for a nice event in your life?"

"No. I buried my husband on Monday. We were married for forty-five years. I'm sitting shiva. I'm not Jewish, but I wanted to respect his customs."

Stunned, I replied, "Oh, I'm sorry to hear that."

I was silent as I dealt with this new revelation. Finally, I said, "You have enough problems right now. I'll try to find someone else to take care of Cory until his parents come home."

"No, Cory can stay with me. Come, Cory, let's go into the kitchen and get something to eat."

With that, she helped Cory out of his coat. She gently placed her arm around his shoulder and led him into the kitchen. I looked at their retreating figures—a small woman with her own sadness taking care of a no longer frightened little black child. Cory was almost home.

Norman Sherman is the principal of P.S. 201, Queens, NY.

Corridors: Stories from Inner-City Detroit
by Toby Kahn Curry

As fate would have it, the naming of this book, though late in coming and long in debate, could not have been more perfectly titled. We could have toiled and raged for another month, our 36 personalities all searching out in 36 directions, but no other one word could best describe this collection of writing. Physically, the writings in this book took place at the west end of the Cass Corridor, a wounded, healing, infamous neighborhood in Detroit's inner-city. The young authors published here come from numerous parts of Detroit, but many reside in the immediate neighborhood, including the Jeffries Homes. *Corridors* functioned, in one sense, as a gallery for bringing together children from a variety of backgrounds and cultures, many of whom felt distant and apart from one another.

In the process of living this community writing project, we were blessed with the life stories of many long time residents and volunteers in Detroit's inner-city. Their interviews and experiences gave us our inspiration as writers and taught us a history of the community that can't be found in any textbook. Rose Bell and Dorothy Miles opened our eyes and hearts to truly understand the meaning of "born to serve." Manatee Smith and Fannie Jones taught us their own living histories of a community that has gone through life-threatening changes as it struggles for survival. George McMahon

and Molly Rubino escorted us down the passageway of commitment and hope when they defined for us their work and missions of humanity that are a part of their everyday lives. Dr. Bob Feldman, a trusted friend to many students in the Burton International School community, showed us the true meaning of voluntary service by the many deeds he performed during the project.

The writing of *Corridors* has served in many ways as the connecting pathway or link between the separated lives of students, teachers, community residents, and the life force of inner-city Detroit.

➜ See: Bloome, p. 229; Curry, pp. 236; 251; 314; Glide Church, p. 341.

From *Corridors: Stories from Inner-City Detroit,* The Dewey Center Community Writing Project, 1989.

Toby Kahn Curry is a teacher at Dewey Center for Urban Education, Detroit, MI.

📷 WHOLE LANGUAGE CAMERA

Kristen Cummings reads her original story to her pen pal, Rose Breda, at the Willowood Nursing Home, North Adams, MA.

A Giving Woman
by Mianne Adufutse

Mrs. Rose Bell lived in a small town called Oil City until she was 19. She lived with her parents, grandparents, ten brothers and sisters, plus her sister's husband and three kids. Mrs. Bell explains that Oil City was a small, cozy town nestled between the mountains just like God set it down there. It was divided in the middle by a river. The city is so small it's not shown on maps because you wouldn't be able to see it there.

When Mrs. Bell was young she liked to skate and play basketball and was raised strongly in the Bible and giving. She said even though her house was filled with people, if a needy person came to their door for food they had enough to give to them.

When Mrs. Bell was 19, she moved to Detroit and later moved to the Jeffries projects. Even though people might say it's a bad neighborhood, she says it has its good and bad times. She gives tours of the projects to visitors, city officials and people like that. Once she gave a tour to a minister and she told him, "Go ye into the vineyards and reap the harvest. This is a vineyard."

She has been living there for 17 years and beautifies the projects by planting flowers for peace. As a young girl, flowers amazed her. She stated, "To be able to put a few seeds in the ground and have a little sunlight and rain and see what God can do; it turns into a little flower."

Mrs. Bell also started a nursery school before it was in the other cities, because she loved people and babies. She loves volunteering work and likes to help young women and their children get food and have clothing. But they have to earn what they get by working. As she stated, "No work, no food."

Mrs. Bell never complained about her job and enjoys it and helps people when they need her. She plans to start her own school and teach volunteers how to get next to people and how to be loving through volunteer work. She ends this statement by saying, "What a thrilling life it is."

From *Corridors: Stories from Inner-City Detroit,* The Dewey Center Community Writing Project, 1989.

📺 ✂️ 🎞️ 👐 📼 📖

Resource: Book

Corridors: Stories from Inner-City Detroit

The Dewey Center Community Writing Project
From:
The Dewey Center
3550 John C. Lodge
Detroit, MI 48201; or
The Center for Educational Improvement through Collaboration
2018 School of Education Building
University of Michigan
Ann Arbor, MI 48103

Parents' Perspective

by Masako Kagawa

Acculturation and Language Learning

Amish Literacy: What and How It Means

Andrea Fishman
1988; 240 pp.; $18
Portsmouth, NH: Heinemann

Based on an important study on the meanings of literacy for one group of Americans in modern times, Andrea Fishman comes to the following insight.

YMG

Many people told me before we left Japan that, since kids were good at learning languages, my daughters would become fluent English speakers after one year's stay in America. However, it wasn't true in my daughters' case. By watching them this past year, I realized that acquiring a language is not merely acquiring some skill like cooking or sewing, but it is a more complicated process deeply intertwined with psychological factors, such as how they regard the people and the culture of the target language, or how they locate themselves between their native language culture and target language culture.

My elder daughter was 11 and my younger daughter was 9 when we came to America in April 1988. The elder one had been protesting my decision to come to America, since she didn't want to miss her last year at elementary school in Japan; she complained even after we arrived here. The younger one didn't say anything explicitly, but she also seemed to miss her friends in Japan.

A week after we arrived in San Francisco, they began to go to school. The elder one was in the sixth grade in middle school, and the younger one was in the third grade. Both were the only Japanese at each school, which made their adaptation to the new life more difficult. Every day they came back from school frustrated because most of the time they couldn't figure out what was going on around them. In addition to the language barrier, the American school system is entirely different from the Japanese—the differences include the way to take lunch or the way to interact with teachers.

For the first several months, the girls spent a lot of time inside after they came back from school eating snacks and sweets while reading Japanese comic books. I just let them do it because I knew they were releasing their frustration. Although I wanted them to watch television so that they could learn English faster, they never watched English programs. They seemed to refuse everything that had anything to do with English. They never showed up when my American friend visited me, nor did they ever answer the telephone.

On the other hand, they seemed to stick to Japanese firmly. They watched Japanese TV programs all through the evening on Saturday and Sunday. The rest of the time they spent reading Japanese books or writing letters to friends in Japan. It is ironic that my daughters' Japanese seemed to become stronger after we came to America.

In the fall, about one month after the new school year had begun, I noticed a change in my elder daughter. She made friends with a girl from Hong Kong. They began to spend a lot of time together; my daughter also received telephone calls from other friends, all of whom were ESL students like my daughter. These new friendships indicated her growing willingness to use English.

The situation seemed to be harder for my younger daughter. She seemed to be happy and enjoyed her school life for the first two months of her schooling here, because everyone was kind to her and overlooked her silence. However, when she started school the following year, a new teacher came to her class and expected my daughter to express herself in English. Even though five months had passed since we had arrived here, because of her negative attitude toward English, she had made little progress with her new language. She continued to be silent at school, and this time her silence was regarded as negative. She was reluctant to go to school, and one day she refused to get out of the car. There didn't seem to be any change in my daughter throughout the fall.

The turning point came at the beginning of the spring semester. One day, she told me when she came back from school that a new boy from Korea came to her class and she was assigned to take care of him. After that I heard stories about this boy almost every day; my daughter talked about how little English he knew, how funny his pronunciation was, how he was eager to answer the question even if he wasn't sure of it, and so on. At the same time I noticed that my daughter was becoming more confident about her English as she learned from this boy that people could communicate with limited English. Thus my daughter gradually began to speak out in class. After we had been here one year, the teacher told me that my daughter had begun to initiate conversation at school. When her class studied Japan, she was willing to contribute by showing and explaining the pictures we had brought from Japan. Thus, by the end of the 1989 school year, both my daughters seemed to be comfortable in American culture. They were not afraid to go out and interact with people anymore.

In retrospect, the progress in second language learning and acculturation came along side by side. As my daughters came to understand English, their hostility toward American people and culture gradually disappeared; the more open they became to the American people and culture, the more opportunities they had to hear and use English. It was not easy to help them get involved in this cycle at first, because they sheltered themselves in their native language. Clearly, providing a nonthreatening environment is crucial for second language learners.

➜ See: Bird, p. 93; Chen, p. 26; Cress, p. 85; Hoyt, p. 214.

Masako Kagawa is a graduate student at San Francisco State University, San Francisco, CA.

> ❝Before I became involved with literacy as a theoretical, philosophical, dissertation-research issue, I never thought about "meaning." I never wondered where meaning is found or how meaning is made; in fact, I never even knew those were things to wonder about. To me, the notion of meaning was simple: if I wanted to know what a book meant, I read it. If I didn't understand the meaning on first reading, I read it again. If I continued to miss the meaning on second reading, I knew I was not smart enough to understand that text, so I either asked someone smarter to explain what it meant or I gave up, leaving the meaning in that book for someone else to find. This process served me well all through school, for my teachers were usually both willing and able to tell me what books meant. Especially my English teachers. They always knew.
>
> Then, when I became an English teacher, somehow I always seemed to know what books (and poems and stories and plays and essays) meant, too. I could tell my students when they had the right meaning and when their interpretations were wrong, and I could tell them what to think if they didn't know. If anyone asked me how I knew what a particular text meant—how I figured out a certain verse or passage—I pointed to the words themselves. There was the meaning, I said, in that word, that line, available to anyone who knew how to read. It never occurred to me that I was reading in one particular way, reading as my teachers had read. It never occurred to me that the academic community in which I grew up had taught me what meanings to ascribe to words and what views to take of different kinds of writers and different kinds of texts; so it also never occurred to me that there might be other meanings or other views. In other words, that I was putting the meaning in through what I brought to a text, not taking the meaning out only from what I found there; never crossed my mind. Instead, I believed in and perpetuated the myth that a single meaning is bound in every text and that a single way exists to discover and understand the meaning hidden there.
>
> I no longer subscribe to that myth, however, for I no longer understand reading, writing, and meaning that way.❞ (p. 157)

George McMahon: Life Stew

by Toby Kahn Curry

4 cups of hope in the human spirit
3 cups of faith in Christianity
2 quiet summers in Harlem, New York
1 full year of migrant life
from Michigan to Texas
3 days in jail, eating green bologna
1 tablespoon of tolerance
A dash of curiosity
21 years of matrimony

Mix thoroughly. Simmer inside a struggling, inner-city neighborhood for at least 24 years. Serves hundreds of troubled, first fired, last hired people.

From *Corridors: Stories from Inner-City Detroit,* The Dewey Center Community Writing Project, 1989.

Toby Kahn Curry is a teacher at Dewey Center for Urban Education, Detroit, MI.

I Make My Little Puddings

by Christine Wright

I make my littel puddings
with mushrooms and moss
thay are so good with toppings
like cocoa and rice.

From *A Book of Fantasy and Adventures,* by 100 students from Alternative Community Schools (Summertown, TN: National Coalition of Alternative Community Schools, 1982).

Family Literacy

Parents' Perspective

by David J. Whitin and Phyllis E. Whitin

Writing and Growing Together as a Family

For seven years our family maintained a tradition of writing together. Almost every Sunday evening we sat down to write for about 15 minutes on whatever topic we wished. Then there was time for each writer to share his or her piece and to allow others to tell what they enjoyed about it. At the conclusion of each year we bound our writings into a large family journal and placed it beside our photograph albums as a testimony of our life together.

We began this writing time because we were disappointed in the kind of writing instruction some of our children were receiving in school. They spent many hours learning the alphabet, punctuation, and grammar, but no time actually writing. We wanted to switch the focus from correct spelling and neat handwriting to discovering topics and refining ideas.

Lessons Learned

The more we wrote, the more we learned about ourselves and about the writing process. When Rebecca was six years old, she wrote the following piece:

as I wocht of the car I sow a Hous it was a shagee Hous with sagd widos An old womin wos siring on Hr sowfnut porch ow sere.

[As I watched out the car window I saw a house. It was a shaggy house with shagged windows. An old woman was sitting on her front porch sewing a blanket. How sweet.]

Rebecca was helping us see that writing topics are to be found everywhere; brief glimpses and casual observations are important parts of the stories we wish to tell. Writing helped us all become better observers of the world around us. Rebecca also showed us that being a writer causes one to view the world from a different perspective. Very often during the week one of the children would remark to us, "Oh, I know what I'm going to be writing about on Sunday!" The children began to look at the world through the lens of a writer. They knew that Sunday would be a time for sharing stories, and so they became more aware during the week of how they could use writing as a frame for reflecting and recording their experiences. The descriptive

language that Becca used to tell her story also highlighted for us the value of reciting poetry, reading aloud, and telling stories as a family. We suspected that her choice of words was influenced by her continued immersion into children's literature.

David, 11 years old, showed us some other benefits of writing together as a family when he shared his piece on cross-country skiing:

Today we rented some skis and went skiing on the lake. Brett used Becca's skis because she was at Jaime's house. We made a path, Brett, Dad, Mom and I, that went straight and then turned around to where we started. At the end Dad stayed on shore with Brett, and Mom and I went around the loop once. I tried my hardest to keep up with Mom. When we got back to shore, I was pooped, but as I saw Dad take off I wanted to go one more time with him. So I went my fastest, and I almost got real frustrated because I couldn't keep up with Dad, but I told myself, "Don't get mad. Dad is faster than you, and you just went around while he was taking a break." So I didn't get mad, and I just went as fast as I could. When we got back to the house, Mom said, "That was the fastest I've ever skied in my life." I couldn't believe it. I didn't know that I could go THAT fast! It really made me feel good when Mom said that because I knew I must be skiing well. Dad also said that I would have cried about not being able to catch up with him if I was a few years younger. That made me feel good, too. It made me feel like I WAS growing up. Dad says that we will get skis of our own next year. I hope so.

As David read his piece aloud, and came to his description of the skiing race with his father, he broke down and cried. He was sharing an important step he took in growing up; his reflection on this momentous event made it difficult for him to continue. We huddled together as a family, surrounded him with our arms, and

cried along with him. Writing time had provided him the opportunity to reflect on his own growing up and to come closer to knowing who he was as a person. Writing helps us discover what we do not know. In David's case, he really did not know how deeply the incident affected him until he wrote it down and shared it. He also showed that writing time can build a sense of trust among family members. David knew that we would give him support if he shared a sensitive piece of writing. A supportive community of writers can help all members take risks and grow.

When Brett was nine years old, he wrote a piece that highlighted the humorous side of family living. He described the antics of himself and his brother as they tried on new clothes in a department store.

Brett helped us see that writing time was a way to preserve the funny experiences that we encounter as a family. The episode itself may have been transitory, but by writing about it Brett froze that moment in time for all of us to remember again and again. Brett loved to draw, and his illustration helped to emphasize the importance of having an artistic representation of family events as well. Brett's use of descriptive words, such as *whizzed, waddled, flung,* and *crumpled up,* helped us all focus on the need for writers to show, and not tell, about their experiences. We talked often about the power of strong verbs in our family meetings and would brainstorm other words to use as we discussed certain pieces. Writing time helped us all become more sensitive to the choice of words.

A Final Reflection

Writing time helped to bind us closer as a family. It provided a time for us to be physically together, even though our lives during the week could be quite busy. It forced each one of us to adopt the stance of a writer, and we began to view our daily experiences through the eyes of a writer. We developed a greater appreciation for the minutiae in our daily living because we found that in small happenings came rich stories. We found that writing was risky business, but we continued to learn and grow because we realized that we were members of a supportive and caring community of writers. Lastly, we came to view writing as a valuable tool for recording and preserving our family history.

→ See: Mills, p. 325; Whitin, pp. 21, 41.

David J. Whitin is a professor at the College of Education, University of South Carolina, Columbia, SC. Phyllis E. Whitin is a middle grade teacher at Irmo Middle School/Campus R, Columbia, SC.

How I Learned to Read and Write

by Barbara Ingram

I don't remember learning to read. I remember my grandmother teaching me the letters on my blocks as we built towers on the living-room floor. When did I begin to recognize groups of these letters as I followed her finger in the storybooks she read me?

Nana took care of me all day before I started school in 1932. After that, I got home about the same time as my mother, a first-grade teacher in another school district. In those days "sight" reading was the vogue, but Mother sabotaged the system by teaching phonics to her first-

graders. I had already been trained in phonics by those alphabet blocks.

At bedtime Mother read or recited poems to me by James Whitcomb Riley and Robert Louis Stevenson. From downstairs I could hear the peck, peck, peck of Daddy's typewriter. The combined rhythms lulled me to sleep.

My father worked by day administering relief for the city of Columbus, Ohio. In the evenings he worked at his typewriter, writing and revising his own historical fiction and typing my mother's poetry. He typed my first poem for me (imperiously dictated at age four from the sofa where I lay with the chickenpox):

Hot are the covers,
Itchy are the chickens.
If you want to have some
Come and catch the dickens.

In a few years I was pecking out my own words on his Corona portable. My fictive efforts in those years were strongly influenced by what-

ever series of children's books I was reading at the time. During the Bobbsey Twins era, I often addressed my reader directly. When I was a fan of Nancy Drew, my stories spoke of "chums" and "sporty roadsters."

Even though I could read for myself by then, my parents kept up the bedtime reading as a ritual that I think they enjoyed, too. I remember my father reading *Oliver Twist* to me at night when I was in third grade. Dickens's vocabulary may have been too hard for me to tackle on my own, but in Daddy's voice the story unfolded thrillingly.

Reading and writing have remained lifelong pleasures and resources for me, born very early in my life because the grown-ups who surrounded me so obviously enjoyed words.

→ See: Parkes, p. 36; Watson, p. 40, Literature Reference List, p. 429.

Barbara Ingram is the owner and publisher of Terrace Press, Palo Alto, CA.

Parents' Perspective

by Janet Sloatman Files

"bEmAmbr MY ALF to dAu MOM"

As I threaded my way through the tourist-clogged streets, my eye caught the note my five-year-old Mikey had taped to the dashboard: "bEmAmbr MY ALF to dAu MOM" (Remember my Alf today Mom).

I turned into Burger King just in time to purchase the Alf, knowing my efforts would help Mikey learn the power of the printed word. A recent course in children's writing had led me to invite my children to engage in a variety of writing activities. What amazed me was how such simple "invitations" had generated an explosion of written language from Mikey.

One morning I said to my three children, "Let's talk on paper this morning. The rule is, no one can talk—we have to write down everything we say."

Janet Sloatman Files, her husband and their four children.

Mikey arrived at the breakfast table and I presented him with the following note: "Come and eat your breakfast. Here is your cantaloupe. Do you like it?"

Mikey seemed delighted with the game. He had a little trouble reading the word *Come*, but once I helped him with that he had no further trouble until the word *Here* and then the rest flowed for him. It was easy for Mikey to read long words such as *breakfast* and *cantaloupe* because of the enhanced context. The cantaloupe sat in front of him. He wrote back *Yas*, took a bite of the fruit, crossed out *Yas*, and wrote *NO*.

I was impressed with how easily Mikey read the message. I thought I had high expectations of Mikey's literacy abilities, but my surprise on this occasion and others to follow made me realize that I had underestimated Mikey's knowledge of reading and writing.

Early reading material in basal readers often eliminates long words, assuming they are too difficult for children to read. But Mikey's ability to read *breakfast* and *cantaloupe* demonstrated that when the language is whole and occurs in a meaningful context, long words can be easier to read than short ones.

Further into our breakfast, Mikey mentioned that he wanted to get an Alf at Burger King. I wrote back: "I will try to get it tomorrow." Mikey only needed help reading *try*. He replied on paper: "OK PEZZ WOod you Gitt MY it tomorrow" (OK. Please would you get me it tomorrow?).

I was impressed with his fluency and his approaches to conventionality in spacing and spelling. Most of all, I was struck by his ability to access my conventional spelling of *tomorrow*. Children learn the complex constructions of oral language from implicit demonstrations of their form and function in meaningful contexts. Mikey showed me that he could learn written conventions in the same way. Mikey needed the word "tomorrow" to express a meaning. Therefore, he used the conventional spelling.

Normally, I would have written myself a reminder to buy Mikey his Alf, thereby robbing him of a chance to discover the power of print. This morning I asked Mikey, "Would you write me

a note so I won't forget and I'll tape it to my dashboard." Mikey had shown me his potential for learning literacy strategies—my new awareness helped me to reveal and maximize that potential. Mikey discovered that night that his carefully penciled reminder, "bEmAmbr MY ALF", had the power to detour my homeward journey, but the note he received from me said: "Dear Mikey, I am sorry but Burger King had no more Alfs. They said to call them up Thursday morning and they might have more in. XXOO Mommy."

Mikey understood the note halfway through as was evidenced by his wails of dismay. He was somewhat reassured by the idea of a phone call. Later that evening, while shopping for a Father's Day gift, Mikey spied a big Alf and a little Alf puppet, similar to those available at Burger King, but six dollars more. Not being noted for his patience, Mikey was not easily persuaded to give me another chance to find a less expensive Alf at Burger King.

The next morning as we were driving to swimming lessons, Mikey noticed his old reminder on the dashboard and spontaneously added on so that it now read: "bEmAmbr MY ALF to dAu MOM NOt it BorgrKiNG ROzis BOt Noot a BiG wooN" (Remember my Alf today Mom. Not at Burger King Roses but not a big one).

Another trip to swimming lessons produced this new reminder in the car:

[Remember for me to watch Alf tonight and get me Alf at Burger King.]

I had to respond one more time that there were no Alfs. They had sold out again. My note lead to a family discussion that evening of the dangers of false advertising which in turn generated a family letter writing session with each person writing their own "letter of indignation". Mikey's "voice of disgust" is loud and clear in the letter which follows:

Dear Burger King,
You keep saying tomorrow you have Alfs but its not true so I say you should send me a Alf. My address is 3 South Gate Road and my name is Mikey.

The following correspondence between a friend of mine named Floyd and Mikey tells the end of the Alf literacy story.

Dear Mikey,
Janet told me how much you wanted an Alf from Burger King so last night while I was in Marion at Food Lion I went to Burger King. I asked if they had Alfs and the lady said "Yes." So I got one for you. Hope you enjoy it.
Sincerely,

Mikey typed his response on my typewriter:

dear Floyd,
thak you for the alf. i love him wil you git me somting es

woin
we r chien to git soting?
from
Michael
ilov you

[Thank you for the Alf. I love him. Will you get me something else when we are trying to get something?]

Mikey not only found his Alf, but his own personal "elf"—he saw Floyd as possessing wonderful wish-fulfilling potential. Mikey had learned to extend himself to a larger community through the power of literacy and his empowerment with literacy.

My literacy relationship will continue to expand and grow with Mikey as a natural extension of our social and environmental interaction—transaction would be a better word, because from interacting with Mikey I have changed and learned as much as he has. I see how limited my former assumptions were about his literacy abilities and I look for natural instances to enhance that learning now.

➜ See: Files, p. 94; Kalman, p. 34; King, p. 28; Sudol, p. 44; Written Conversation, p. 145.

Janet Sloatman Files is a consultant and graduate instructor at USC Coastal College, Myrtle Beach, SC.

Book Note

Home: Where Reading and Writing Begin

Mary Hill
1989; 120 pp.; $8.95
Portsmouth, NH: Heinemann

Parents and teachers often ask me for books that will illuminate the role of parents as the child's first teacher. Mary Hill has done just this in her insightful book *Home: Where Reading and Writing Begin*. Admitting that parents rarely go to school to learn how to become a parent, Hill explores ways in which parents are their children's first literacy-learning partners.

Hill highlights the literacy environment that children live in and discusses ways to invite children to explore and reflect on their literate world. She has

gentle advice for ways to read and write with children; she talks about organizing for reading and writing experiences at home; and she helps parents know what to expect and how to understand the meanings of what they will see in their children's reading and writing.

Based on my own experiences with grandchildren during the last eight years, I know that grandmothers and grandfathers will find this book useful as well.

YMG

❝ Another go-ahead signal we can give children is to tell them to spell the word the way they think it might be spelled and we'll talk about it later. Telling children to spell the word the best way they can and keep on writing helps them retain a focus on what they are saying. In other words, they don't lose their train of thought. Telling children that we will talk about the word later helps them to know we are not abandoning them. ❞ (p. 60)

Kidwatching
Yetta M. Goodman

Reversals — ƨlɒƨɿɘvɘЯ

Whenever I am shown a student's reversal, I usually can provide a rationale explaining the conceptualizations that occurred during the production of the reversal. I received the following example from a pre-first-grade teacher in Fresno, California. Andy Lopez, a six-year-old, came up to his teacher, Katie Udie, to get a response to his journal. As she looked at his entry she noticed the right to left directionality and the reversals in both *Mayflower* and his name.

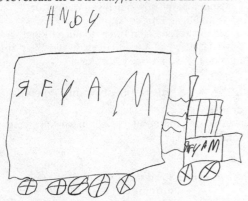

Ms. Udie asked, "Andy, when you wrote *Mayflower*, where did you start?"

He explained, "I started *Mayflower* here" (pointing to the *M* on both the trailer and the truck body) "and my own name here" (pointing to the *A* in Andy).

"Why did you write your name starting here and going this way" (pointing to the *A* in Andy and moving her finger from left to right), "but *Mayflower* going this way" (moving her finger from right to left below *Mayflower*)?

Andy replied, "Well, you know Ms. Udie, when a truck is going down the road, you have to read it this way" (eyes/head scanning quickly right to left).

I wonder if creative thinkers like Andy invented the way *ecnalubmA* is presented on emergency vehicles or the way signs are written on streets for drivers to read as they approach intersections. Regardless, what is important is that Andy is not writing backward because he has a perceptual or cognitive deficit. In fact, the opposite is true. Andy is using his developing perceptual and cognitive strategies to make sense of the graphic information of the world and to work out concepts of directionality. Consider Andy's reversal of the *d* in his name (which he can read regardless of its orientation). Is it possible that Andy is developing a generalization that most English printed letters are made in a left to right direction. Most capital letters tend to be produced in a left to right direction like the capital letters *B* and *D*. But in their minuscule forms, *b* faces to the right while *d* faces to the left. Andy may have generalized that all letters are made facing to the right and experimented with the *d* in his own name.

The system of directionality in English writing is not very old historically and has its roots in systems of languages that were first written from right to left; then for a time from right to left on one line and from left to right on the next line. It is interesting to read about how, when, and why changes were made in the directionality of writing over the centuries and to realize that the standardization of directionality for the human race has been as complicated and experimental as it is for young children as they come to understand their own cultural writing forms.

Let's examine a few other examples of reversals and explore the children's intellectual experimentation.

Barbara Flores's niece, Melanie, wrote her a letter saying that she had been sick and that her younger brother was crawling all over the place. Melanie represented herself and her aunt facing each other and verbally sharing their love. As she wrote their speech with talking balloons, she had to show the person facing to the left with the language coming out of the mouth backward since the word *I* had to come first. Note the control that Melanie has as she writes each individual letter conventionally in the reversed string. Younger children will often reverse letters if they start writing on the right-hand side of the paper.

One of my graduate students was invited to a parent-teacher conference to discuss the teacher's concerns with her six-year-old daughter's reversals. The graduate student knew a good bit about literacy development in young children as well as about the history of written English. Since her daughter was waiting outside, she called to her, showed her the writing, and asked why she had reversed specific letters and underlined others. The six-year-old responded: "I knew I wouldn't have enough room to get it all on the line, so I scrunched all the letters together but I wanted to show where the words ended. If I could turn them around, I did but if I couldn't, I just put a line under the last letter."

The six-year-old's mother told the teacher that before English writing had spaces between words,

word endings were often shown by underlining the last letter and that Hebrew has different forms of letters in the ending positions of words than those same letters in initial or medial positions. Her daughter did not have a serious problem. She was experimenting with written language just as society at large has experimented with written language over centuries.

Most research on letter and word reversals has only examined instances of reversals in isolation: That is, the writing and reading of letters are presented out of the context of words, and the writing and reading of words are out of the context of a whole text. As soon as reversals are placed in the larger context of written language, different patterns appear. In the context of a story or a note, reversals of a letter always constitute a small percentage of the total times that particular letter is written. There is even a difference in the percentage of reversals of a particular letter depending on whether it occurs at the beginning, in the middle, or in the final position of the word, indicating the strong influence context has on reversing tendencies.

In reading also, amount and type of reversals change drastically, depending on the written context. For example, children who reverse *no* for *on* in an isolated list almost never read *no* for *on* in a story where *on* occurs in its common position introducing a prepositional phrase.

We can scare parents into believing that their children have serious problems. We can continue to use unrelated and perhaps dangerous remedies such as creeping, walking balance beams, tracing and eating letter forms, colored lenses, and so on. Or we can collaborate with children, find out what they are doing and why, and celebrate their intellectual abilities as they experiment with written language.

→ See: Goodman, pp. 32, 101; Harlow, p. 51; Kalman, p. 34; Torbe, p. 232.

Book Note

Growing Up Literate: Learning from Inner-City Families

Denny Taylor and Catherine Dorsey-Gaines 1988; 256 pp.; $16 Portsmouth, NH: Heinemann

Denny Taylor and Catherine Dorsey-Gaines looked at literacy and literacy learning in poor black families in inner-city Chicago. They learned that literacy was used for a wide variety of purposes and that sociopolitical connotations of literacy were not always liberating. The myths and stereotypes perpetuated by the mass media have little relevance when we stop counting and start observing and working with people; and it is important for each individual to examine his or her assumptions. These families—the parents and their children— were both smart and literate.

Carol Christine

❝'Dear Sunshine,' the letter began. It was lying on the floor in the bedroom. It must have fallen as the children played, since there were pens and paper scattered on one of the beds. Tanya had written the letter, either to her brother, who was then in jail, or to her friend, with whom she had once lived. Without easy access to a telephone and with no money to call, Tanya wrote letters to both of them. She also wrote to some of the men she had met when visiting her brother. 'No one writes to them,' she said. For Tanya, letters written meant letters read. Her brother wrote to her, and so did her friend. She also received many letters from men serving time. ❞ (p. 131)

Book Note

Reading Begins at Home

Dorothy Butler and Marie Clay 1987; 48 pp.; $8 Portsmouth, NH: Heinemann

Useful for parents, the suggestions and information in this book are equally valuable for teachers of young children. The authors show the way for children to have real and meaningful experiences with books at home and at school.

Kathryn F. Whitmore

❝ Ideas about reading are more readily caught than taught in the very early years. A youngster who grows up in a family where people read will come to feel that books and papers are worth attention. They certainly take attention away from him! Perhaps he will try to get into the scene by crawling into Dad's lap, putting himself between the paper and his father. ❞ (p.8)

❝ And when reading begins at school, well, imagine a child who has never heard fairy tales read aloud trying to decipher 'Once upon a time'! ❞ (p. 21)

Resource: Booklet

A Collection of Letters About Books, Children and the Joys of Sharing

Ann Pulvertaft
1987; 220 pp.
From:
Centre for Teaching &
Research in Literacy
Charles Sturt University–
Riverina
P. O. Box 588
Wagga Wagga, NSW
Australia 2650

❝ These letters were originally written as quarterly newsletters for the Picture Puffin Earlybird Bookclub. The club, which operates in pre-schools throughout Australia, was formed in 1982 by Penguin to meet a perceived need for parents of young children to have access to high quality picture storybooks. Here is an example of one of our newsletters:

Dear Parent:

This newsletter is about helping your child to read.

You've been led to believe that teaching reading is best left to the "experts." I'd like to suggest that you forget all about so called methods of teaching reading. The very best preparation you can give your child can be written in three words—the bedtime story.

Of course children love stories, they love picture books, they love to be snuggled up with you while you read to them. Of course all this encourages them to want to read for themselves. I think we have all known these things for quite a while. Lately, however, we've been taking a closer look at all the other things children learn about stories and books when their parents read to them.

Children are active, busy learners. They are always picking up bits and pieces which no one has actually taught them. ("Where did Jimmy learn that swear word!") When your child is on your knee and you are sharing a book together, he or she is not only listening to the story but also learning all sorts of useful information about how a book "works" and how print "works." Here are just some of the things we have found that children who are really familiar with books know when they start school—without ever having a "lesson." They know that—

- Stories have names (titles).
- Books have covers and pages.
- You read left hand pages before right hand pages.
- You start to read each page at the top left.
- The black squiggles (print), not the pictures, carry the actual message.
- You read along the line from left to right, and then go back to the start of the next line. (You could show your child how to do this as you go along, but they usually notice it anyway.)
- Unlike conversation, the printed story comes out exactly the same each time. (This fascinates young children—they love you to read and re-read a favourite story! You know what happens if you try to skip a bit!)

When you add these "book experience" skills to all the other hidden messages which children learn—such as books are friends, books are fun, my parents enjoy sharing books with me—you can see how important it is to find that extra time to read to your children.

You could look at this from another angle by imagining how far away from reading a child is whose parents say, "Well, we don't bother with books much, as they get all the stories they need from television these days." Just as children learn to talk by listening to language, by joining in, by playing with language, so they learn to read by being involved with books and print. Those who have plenty of opportunities to do just this will have been given a head-start in learning to read. Happy book sharing. ❞

➔ See: Parkes, p. 36; Martin, p. 96; Watson, p. 40.

Resource: Periodical

Mothering

$18/year (4 issues) from:
P.O. Box 1690
Santa Fe, NM 87504
1-505-984-8116

Progressive educational philosophy has long been a tradition with *Mothering* magazine, which serves an international community of parents and explores a wide range of parenting issues. I have always looked forward to *Mothering*'s fresh ideas and dare-to-be-different approaches to child-rearing, education, and social policy. Articles on invented spelling and "whole reading" were published in *Mothering* long before they appeared in other parenting magazines.

Debbie Montgomery

❝ **The Journey Book by Anna Joyce**

The Journey Book was first described to me by Strephon Kaplan Williams, founder of the Jungian Dreamwork Institute in Berkeley, California. He had made one for each of his two daughters to chronicle their passage through life. Much more elaborate and choreographed than a scrapbook, the Journey Book attempts to show a person's passage through time, change, and growth in both inner and outer ways. Because its contents can be expanded infinitely and portrayed aesthetically, it is a genuinely creative keepsake.

What you place inside is entirely up to you. Ideally, entries should reflect the movement of your child's life—the various stages of growth and many changing emotions. Some pages might recast day-to-day events; others might share a deeper, underlying theme of meaning and purpose.

Some of our family's favorite Journey Book items include the following:

- *Christmas wish stars.* On the glitter-covered points of these stars, we write what each family member hopes will be born in him or her during the coming year. Concretizing our wishes helps them come true.
- *Transcribed baby tapes.* Over the years, I have made each of my children a cassette containing the child's own "baby songs," songs that I sang as we nursed and rocked, and songs that we later sang together. In the Journey Book, the words and music to these songs are transcribed in simple form, along with additional childhood favorites.
- *Games we created and played.* "Bathtub Restaurant," "Honey Bears," "Chocolate Fairy," and other invented games are described and illustrated by both the children and myself.
- *Birthday passages.* Each year I compose a letter to the birthday child, recounting growth and change as well as favorite memories of the year.

Other entries include flyers and photos from talent shows, choir performances, and school plays, as well as campfires, badges and activity articles, newspaper clippings of gymnastic meets, programs from recitals, artwork, stories of favorite animals, dreams and sometimes nightmares, photos of special gifts along with pictures of the givers, baby

teeth and hair wrapped in cellophane, zany anecdotes of babyhood and toddler years, and hand prints and footprints made at various ages.

Include whatever you and your child want to remember. What gives the Journey Book its special magic is the conscious act of choosing what is important, deciding what warrants remembrance, and then portraying it visually and artistically. Choose entries that reflect who your child is. ❞

➔ See: Jacobson, p. 365.

Excerpted from "Journey Books and Memory Quilts," *Mothering,* Fall 1988.

MARVELOUS INVENTIONS

Clunker Bike

Melissa Cain's seven-year-old son, Bennett, had repeatedly asked his parents for a new bicycle, but had been denied. As a last resort, he asked his "Clunker Bike" to write a note on his behalf.

—LBB

[Kick me, hit me, throw me away. I can't outrun a garden slug. My chain fell off. I'm 10; I'm older than Ben. My paint's peeling. I'm rusty. I'm missing bolts and screws. Either get and buy Ben a new bike, or make him embarrassed whenever he rides me. Signed, Clunker Bike]

—Contributed by Melissa Cain, editor, *Perspectives,* University of Toledo, Toledo, OH

Kick Me hitMe throw me away I can't out run a garden Slug My chain fell off I 10 I'm older then Ben my paints peeling I'm rusty I'm missing bolts and screw eiter get and by Ben a newbike or make him inbarrassewen-ever. He rides Me.

Sighned, Clunkerbike

Book Note

Family Literacy: Young Children Learning to Read and Write

Denny Taylor
1983; 144 pp.; $13.50
Portsmouth, NH:
Heinemann

Denny Taylor spent three years studying the literacy experiences of six different families. Through her documentation she supports the view that literacy learning is most successful in relational contexts which are meaningful to young children. Schools rarely provide this context and instead "reading and writing are lifted out of context in schools and become the focus of specific, culturally remote pedagogical attention. Literacy becomes an end in itself, reduced to a hierarchy of interrelated skills."

Carol Christine

Resource: Periodical

Parents' Choice: A Review of Children's Media

$15/year (12 issues) from:
Diana Huss Green, editor
Parents' Choice Foundation
Box 185
Newton, MA 02168
1-617-965-5913

Parents' Choice reviews books, television shows, movies, home video, recordings, toys, games, computer programs, and rock 'n' roll. This periodical is a useful source for selecting a variety of material. Parents and teachers will be pleased by the high caliber reviewers and quality writing.

Katy Obringer

❝ There are essentially two categories of videos for children—those that sire couch potatoes and those that don't. The do's make mush of body and brain. The don'ts are harder to define. In general they have commercial and substantive appeal, i.e., they entertain and teach and they do both professionally. The information they provide is respectful of the child's intelligence. Above all they present values that inspire courage and common sense. ❞ (Vol. 10, no. 3, p. 5)

Building Blocks

$15/year (10 issues) from:
Liz and Dick Wilmes,
  editors
38W567 Brindlewood
Elgin, IL 60123
1-800-233-2448

This important resource for parents and teachers of young children is filled with numerous activities that could be adapted for use as extensions of literature. Activities for every occasion are included: inside and outside active games, inside quiet games, language games, art activities, suggestions for field trips, finger plays, and just plain fun activities that foster children's creativity. The editors, Liz and Dick Wilmes, also produce other publications (such as *Circle Time Books*), loaded with great ideas for cooking projects, tips on fostering a love of reading, and reminders on improving time spent with children.

Katy Obringer

Classroom Demonstrations

by Alicia Rivera

Friends of the Hillcrest Library

Beginnings

Friends of the Hillcrest Library (FHL) was begun in April 1985. Its goals were to raise money to purchase books for the school library as well as to foster greater interest in books and in reading. By purchasing a bookplate to be attached to a selected book, a donor would become a Friend of the Hillcrest Library.

Before the Friends' drive was initiated, care was taken to identify areas in the collection that were most wanting. A logo was chosen. Next came the designs for a membership form, letter of acknowledgment, and bookplate. Finally, when we received permission from Maurice Sendak to use his drawing, we were ready to start.

Procedures

FHL is open to participation all year long; additionally, there are two annual campaigns, one in late fall (before the holidays) and one in spring (commencing with the annual auction evening). Publicity consists of announcements in the school's weekly newsletter for parents, including a complete list of all the books we hope to acquire. Another copy of the list is handwritten on large manila sheets and posted in the school hallway. Titles are arranged in categories such as Books by Aliki, Picture Books, Nature, and Old Favorites. Attention is given to balancing the number of books for younger and older children. Donors select a title from among those listed, complete a FHL membership form (available from the office), address an envelope to their honoree, and include a check made to the Hillcrest PTA. Bookplates cost $10 for one, $50 for six, and $100 for thirteen. Once the application form is received, the following steps are taken:

- A colored dot is placed before the selected title on the list posted in the hall so that no one else will choose the same book;
- A letter of acknowledgment is written and sent to the honoree;
- A bookplate is filled out and clipped to the form (or attached to the book, if the book is already available);
- The form is kept in an appropriate binder for future reference; and
- Monies are recorded and sent to the PTA treasurer.

Outcomes

The success of FHL has exceeded our expectations. In just over two years, we have raised

Resource: Periodical

The Kobrin Letter

$12/year (7 issues) from:
Dr. Beverly Kobrin,
  publisher
732 Greer Rd.
Palo Alto, CA 94303
1-415-856-6658

This is a review letter for parents and educators concerning children's books about real people, places, and things. It's a very good source for nonfiction book reviews. Dr. Kobrin is the author of *Eyeopeners!*

Katy Obringer

➜ See: Eyeopeners!, p. 361.

---

more than $5,400. We have improved our collection in tangible ways, adding new and notable titles, replacing worn copies of old favorites, expanding and updating our science, history, and biography sections, adding titles by authors formerly unrepresented, and increasing the number of titles by various authors of special merit. Just as real, though perhaps less tangible, has been the growing interest, enthusiasm, and support for books and reading shown by our students, staff, and parents. At Hillcrest, everyone talks about books.

Advice

The FHL plan has worked for us, but there are many other possibilities that might be more appropriate for your school. Create a program that suits your own needs and tastes and those of your community. Take time to select specific goals, then think your plan through, looking for ways to keep procedures as simple as possible. Be prepared to be successful. A good deal of work is involved in selecting book titles, publicizing lists, sending off acknowledgment letters, and attaching bookplates. You might find one dedicated volunteer who will oversee all the steps, or you might want to share the tasks within a committee. In any case, you can expect to work hard and have fun, to experience satisfactions that you can already anticipate and others that you will only discover once your fund raising is underway.

If you have any questions about FHL, write to Friends of the Hillcrest Library, Hillcrest School, 30 Marguerite Dr., Oakland, CA 94618.

➜ See: Obringer, p. 179; Rivera, pp. 166, 202.

Alicia Rivera is a primary teacher at Hillcrest Elementary, Oakland, CA.

Resource: Book

For the Love of Reading: A Parent's Guide to Encouraging Young Readers from Infancy through Age Five

Marsha Kabakow Rudman
  and Anna Markus Pearce
1988; 399 pp.; $14.95 paper; $21.95 cloth
Mt. Vernon, NY: Consumers Union

This book focuses on a young child's developmental level and the role that books can play toward encouraging not only the love of reading, but also the love of thinking and learning.

Katy Obringer

YOUNG ARTISTS

Bobby Swartz, Mott's Apple Award Winner, kindergarten, Holly Hills Elementary School, Mt. Holly, NJ, Sandra Danziger, teacher

Parents Fight the System

Parents' Perspective
by David Bloome and Joshua Bloomekatz

The Monster's Friend

Prologue

At the end of second grade, Joshua wrote a story titled "The Monster's Friend." To understand the story, and what it has to say to educators and parents, you first need to know the background of the story.

Joshua had just moved to a new city and had no friends. He tried to make friends at school, but he was small for his age and also the youngest. Bigger kids cut in line in front of him, kept him from getting a chance on the monkey bars, punched him, and called him names.

Things weren't good academically either. Joshua entered first grade reading books like *Nate the Great* and *Frog and Toad,* but he hadn't learned anything about vowels or phonic rules. His teacher praised his comprehension, she worried about his word attack skills. She placed Joshua in a low-reading group. Joshua knew he was in a low-reading group and wanted to be in a higher group with his one friend, Aaron.

When Joshua's music teacher was preparing the class for a Thanksgiving concert, she gave the students a song to sing, but they had to finish the lyrics. The lyrics were, "We give thanks for _____." The students had to fill in the blank. According to Joshua, they offered many different suggestions: the world, peace, our parents, and so forth. One suggestion was Jesus Christ. The teacher listed the suggestions on the blackboard and had the students vote on the one to use in the concert. The majority voted for Jesus Christ. Joshua, being Jewish, told his parents he didn't want to sing such a song. Not believing Joshua had accurately reported what had gone on in the music class, they contacted the principal. They were sure no teacher in a public school would have allowed such a situation to occur. The principal investigated and found that Joshua was right about what had happened. The teacher had to select another song, explain to the class why they could not use the song they had selected, and apologize to Joshua and his parents. She did so reluctantly, making her reluctance clear to both Joshua and his parents.

At midyear, Joshua was transferred to the district's open education school. There Joshua spent the mornings reading and writing whatever he wanted, prompted by his teacher who encouraged him to choose interesting books and write reports about animals, knights, and other things that interested him. He spent the afternoons learning math, music, and physical education. Although still uptight and unable to relax, Joshua was able to pursue his interests and enjoy reading and writing reports. Making friends was still hard. It took nearly the rest of the year before Joshua made a friend with whom he could play on a regular basis.

At midyear, just as Joshua was transferring schools, the school district administered a standardized reading test to all first-graders. Joshua scored in the lowest 10 percent. The scores were sent home with his report card five months later, on the last day of school. Although the teacher sent a note with the test scores asking parents not to take the test scores too seriously, Joshua was devastated.

The family decided to move again. During the summer, Joshua read 30 books and got buttons, certificates, and free movie passes from the library reading program. He read *The Mouse and the Motorcycle* and all the other Beverly Cleary books (as long as they weren't about Ramona). He read science fiction and mysteries.

In the new city, Joshua and his parents were anxious about school. They met with and talked with principals and teachers. They told potential teachers that if the teacher would leave Joshua alone, he would do all right. He was a self-motivated kid. They had Joshua tell his new teacher about the books he had read over the summer; they didn't mention the test scores. They delayed having Joshua's old school records forwarded. And so, Joshua entered second grade.

In his second-grade classroom, Joshua wrote books and had them bound. He conducted science projects and wrote reports on a wide range of topics. He participated in two plays. Friendships developed slowly, but Joshua did make a small number of friends. At the end of second grade, Joshua wrote:

The Monster's Friend

One night a big storm broke. It came and picked me off to a place that was scary. / I saw a monster. He did not know that I was a person. / So he put me in his dinner. When he ate his dinner, suddenly I stood up. The monster was surprised. / "What's your name," said the monster. "My name is Joshua." "What's you [*sic*] name," I asked. "My name is Max." / The monster said, "Do you want to play hide-and-seek." "No thanks." "I am hungry." "Do you have an orange?" / "Sure," said Max, "here." "Thank you" Then Max ate his dinner. / We chatted for a long time. Then Max said, "Will you be my friend?" "Yes," I said. Then Max said, "Do you want to go on a trip around the universe." "Sure," I said. / We went to Venus. We saw the Sun; it almost exploded. Then we went to Jupiter.

Chapter Two The Emperor of the Universe. When we got back, I said, "Do you have a friend?" "No," said Max, "except my cat." / "I would like a friend," said Max, "but I cannot." "Why not?" / "The Emperor won't let me," said Max. "Why not?" I said, "The Emperor does not like me." / "Why not," I said. "He thinks I am ugly." / "I will be your friend." "OK," Max said. / They were friends forever. / The End.

Epilogue

At the beginning of "The Monster's Friend," Joshua dedicated the book "To my class who helped me write my first fantasy." But "The Monster's Friend" is only a fantasy on one level. The story is all too real. Joshua, as both author and protagonist, lives in a world of monsters. Monsters that do not see him, that try to eat him up. The monster is school, the whole of school: teachers, classmates, parents, friends, bullies, work, activities, tests, reading groups, grades, competition, emotions, and more. To the monster, Joshua is invisible: He does not count as a Jew and as a child. As a reader of stories he did not count. In each case, he did assert himself, even though it was painful.

Interestingly, Joshua is not the only one facing hardship. The emperor of the universe will not let the monster have friends because the monster is ugly. By becoming visible, by standing up and offering friendship, Joshua transforms not only himself but also the monster: school. They go on a trip around the universe together, sharing, exploring, and learning exciting things. Joshua offers friendship and the monster accepts the friendship. The monster stops being ugly, Joshua becomes visible, and together they grow.

In part, Joshua is writing about friendship among children, and his struggle to find friends. But there seems to be another sense of friendship in "The Monster's Friend," a friendship between school and the children in the school.

"The Monster's Friend" ends with "And they were friends forever." It would be nice, not only for Joshua but for all children, if that were not a fantasy.

➔ See: Bell, p. 48; Bloome, p. 82; Curry, p. 229; Goodman, p. 24; Literature Reference List, p. 429.

David Bloome is a professor in the School of Education, University of Massachusetts, Amherst, MA. Joshua Bloomekatz is now in the third grade.

Book Note

Family Storybook Reading

Denny Taylor and Dorothy S. Strickland
1986; 116 pp.; $11
Portsmouth, NH: Heinemann

Taylor and Strickland provide telling accounts of parents sharing storybooks with their children. Through colorful vignettes of different families with varied lives, readers begin to see the critical connection between storybook reading and the acquisition of language and literacy. In addition to the informative real-life examples of reading aloud in the home, the authors give general guidelines for sharing stories and suggest specific books and activities.

Katy Obringer

66 New words, new concepts, and new connections are all part of family storybook sharing. It is one way that parents have of making meaning to the infant and child, and a way that they can help their children to learn the whys and wherefores of everyday life. Connections are made between books and between lives so that eventually real-life experiences can be related to stories that have been read and new understandings can develop. 99 (p. 38)

Resource: Book

The New York Times Parent's Guide to the Best Books for Children

Eden Ross Lipson
1988; 421 pp; $12.95
New York: Times Books

Eden Ross Lipson, the children's book editor at *The New York Times Book Review,* has compiled an annotated selection of nearly one thousand titles from first-grade level through young adult. Helpful indexes guide users in book selection by offering different categories, such as age appropriateness, subject, and listening levels.

Katy Obringer

In the Mail

Dear Mrs. T.:

I hereby contest the grade of Needs Improvement received by my daughter, Shoshana Castro, in the area of reading on the first grading period of her school career in the kindergarten class of the year 2000, academic year 1987-88.

I am a certified elementary school teacher with classroom experience, extensive knowledge of literacy development in early childhood, and sufficient professional judgment to know that this grade was based on inappropriate expectations regarding the average kindergarten child and a misguided interpretation of the goals of kindergarten.

I understand that Shoshana's performance in reading was not judged satisfactory because she was not sufficiently good at sounding out letter patterns that had been introduced to her during the preceding 10 weeks. I submit that children who can perform to such a standard are those who arrive at kindergarten with the inclination, advanced level of cognitive development, and perhaps previous coaching necessary to be successful at phonic analysis of written language. A program based on such expectations confers success on only those students who begin school having nearly completed the job that kindergarten teachers should attempt to facilitate over the course of the year. These are standards geared toward students who have precociously tuned in to the alphabetic nature of written language and who have the disposition to sit for extended periods of time attending to phonics drill. Even if a school population has large numbers of such students, this is no excuse for judging as deficient other normal children whose development takes different paths. In addition, this type of program places at a serious disadvantage the younger kindergartners, such as Shoshana who turned five in August.

The criteria used to judge satisfactory performance in reading, in addition to being inappropriate for the average kindergarten child, also have questionable relevance to the learning of reading. Experts in reading instruction believe that the initial focus should be on the function of written language rather than on its form. The form of language is learned as the child explores its function. At the time Shoshana received the N for reading she knew a lot about the function and was beginning to learn about the form of written language. She could:

· Identify print in the environment and in books as carrying a message;
· Narrate storybooks coherently using appropriate literary style;
· Explain who the author and illustrator of a book are;
· Learn a story by memory after having it read to her two or three times;
· "Read" storybooks to her little brother;
· Read and write her name;
· Distinguish numbers from letters;
· Call friends on the telephone reading from a list of names and numbers;
· Compose and dictate stories and letters to relatives;
· Form letters and numbers legibly;
· Recite the alphabet;
· Follow print and write with appropriate directionality;
· Identify most letters and numbers both in and out of context;
· Copy written texts legibly;
· Write words dictated to her letter by letter;
· Form strings of letters to represent a message; and
· Generate spellings for words using a beginning knowledge of the alphabetic representation of oral language.

I have no doubt that my daughter will become a proficient reader and writer over the next few years. There is no need for her to do it any faster than that. Furthermore, I resent a kindergarten curriculum that requires parents to spend an inordinate amount of time coaching their children at pointless and *developmentally inappropriate* skills exercises (flash cards, worksheets, reading books void of meaningful language) that they shouldn't even waste their time on in school. I have little time to be with my daughter and I refuse to spend it in this fashion.

It may be said, as Shoshana's teacher did to me, that the grades are not important; they are required by the district. That may be the case. But why use them, then, to make parents feel that their children are inadequate? And why use them to establish a permanent record indicating that at the very beginning of her school career this child was not off to a good start? I must contest the grade of N both as unacceptable educational practice and as unfair to a child who has struggled to do her best at the unreasonable tasks she has been directed to do.

My objections to this grade are not just based on my own personal opinions. I would be happy to furnish documentation supporting my position, including published works of the leading authorities on beginning literacy as well as policy statements by the major professional organizations, the National Association for the Education of Young Children, the National Council of Teachers of English, and the International Reading Association. In addition, I can furnish examples of Shoshana's work.

I request that the grade of Needs Improvement that Shoshana received in Reading for the first grading period of her kindergarten year be changed to Satisfactory. And I strongly urge your school to reevaluate the goals of its kindergarten reading program. It represents an arbitrary and narrow view of excellence based on ignorance of the current state of knowledge regarding early childhood education and literacy development. Instead, it should be a celebration of a new beginning for children that instills in them a positive view of themselves and their language learning.

Sincerely,
Karen Goodman

➜See: Goodman, pp. 24, 32, 314; Watson, p. 40; Whitin, p. 41.

Karen Goodman is a doctoral student in epidemiology in the School of Public Health, University of California, Los Angeles, CA.

Parents' Perspective
by Ruth Ann Blynt

Who's Getting the Blynt Kids?

"Want to tell stories?" he'll ask. And a yes will draw my son from "Sesame Street," G.I. Joe, and floating boats in the bathtub. We lie together flat on our backs on the blue cotton sofa and begin. The stories are about pirates, storms at sea, treasure chests, and little boys. I tell one and then Mike tells one. Or the other way around. I know enough about stories to be sure that even when we're finished, the stories are not. And I hope the stories are good enough to last him when he goes to school next year.

I want him to have the stories if his teacher says, "Slow down," "Do it neatly," or "Draw as the other kids draw." I want him to remember the stories if his teacher insists, "Sound it out first," "Do these workbook pages again," or "You can read only after you finish your seatwork." I especially want him to feel the stories if his teacher hands back papers that say "minus one" in big red numbers at the top, if she writes on his report card that his penguin story is too short, or if, especially if, he ever writes one of his stories and she fails to give it the applause it deserves.

What else can a whole language mom do when her kids go to a traditional elementary school? I could (and do) sit in the kitchen and complain. I can (and do) drool with envy over the whole language classroom slides Nancie Atwell shows at conferences. I will (and must) keep reading to them (good books); let them stay up (too late) making journals; and assure them that it's okay if different people think different things are necessary. As long as *we* recognize the most important things—the stories.

Otherwise, we whole language moms with kids in traditional classrooms can be quietly disruptive, I guess. We can provide extras in the way of open-ended art or dance classes where the teachers encourage free expression; we can send in Christmas gifts marked "To a Child" rather than "A Girl Gift" or "A Boy Gift"; we can cringe and collect the hundreds of worksheets filled with correctly done problems that come home marked "minus two," and send back work done by chicken-pocked kids at home marked "plus seventeen," and hope. We can gently disagree at parent conferences, explaining, "She's not concerned about neatness because I tell her as long as she has something interesting to say, that's what really matters." We can lend books, not so subtly, "Say, have you read Lucy Calkins?" and we can let ourselves, I'm certain, be the brunt of teachers-room bantering, "Who's getting the Blynt kids next year?"

Or, I suppose, we could pretend we don't know what we know. But that won't work. Because our kids already know it, too. And it's awfully hard to ignore a four-year-old who balances his spoon partway across a bowl of vegetable soup and says, "This bridge will only take you halfway there . . ."

➜ See: Bell, p. 48; Blynt, pp. p. 134, 379; Goodman, pp. 24, 360.

Ruth Ann Blynt is a writing instructor at Utica College, Utica, NY.

YOUNG ARTISTS

—Ben Geislinger, 9, Portland OR
(from *Treasures 2*, See p. 162)

Parents' Perspective

by Diane Stephens

Calling Home

Kris was 18, a freshman attending college in North Carolina. We'd dropped her off there last August on our way to new jobs and a new home—a home Kris wouldn't see for the first time until December.

The calls were frequent that first semester—calls for money, for advice, for comfort. I heard about classes, professors, roommates, jobs, boys, concerts, and, again, money—or her lack of.

Some calls were general ("Hi, Mom, just wanted to touch base"); some specific ("If I don't get tickets to the Bon Jovi concert, I'll just die"); sometimes she needed advice ("Do you think I should sign up for a double major in psychology?"); sometimes she gave it to me ("Yes, Mom, I think you should go to California and see Jenny"). A lot of our calls were about writing. Kris is a writer and I am a writer, and we'd been responding to each other's texts for almost as many years as she is old: notes in lunches, on refrigerators; notes and poems and stories; texts that tied us to events—real and imagined; texts that wove our lives together and had helped us learn to live apart.

For years, writing had been a joyous part of life outside school—as well as one of the more tedious parts of "English" homework. So far, her freshman writing class was disappointing: assigned topics, red-marked papers, no opportu-nity for conferencing. (I asked Kris, "You mean you *never* meet in groups to discuss your writing?") She met the requirements, wrote dull, lifeless themes, got A's and B's.

In October Kris called:

Mom? I just *have* to read you this. Mom, are you there? It's about you. I cried when I was writing it and then I read it to Emily and I cried again. Mom? Listen.

Kris had written not only about me, but about the two of us, of how unique and wonderful she thought our relationship was. I listened, touched by what she was saying and impressed with the writing.

Now, do you think it's good? Think I should turn it in? It's for my freshman writing class. We were supposed to write a descriptive paper about a person, place, or thing. Do you think it sounds okay? What about the way it begins? And when I said "the first time I met this woman," do you think I should have said that? And what about that last part, do you think it ends okay?

I dried my tears, told Kris I loved her, and then responded to her text—writer to writer.

In November Kris called again:

Mom! Mom! I got my paper back. She thinks I cheated! Mom, she thinks I can't really write like that, feel like that. She says those aren't my own words. She says that I either take an F or redo the paper on an entirely different topic. She doesn't even want me to write about you! Mom, I tried talking to her, I tried telling her. She won't believe me! What am I gonna do? It's the best thing I've ever written.

Kris rewrote her paper, on an "entirely different topic." She got an A. I wrote the professor a letter, but asked Kris for permission to send it. Kris asked me not to. I tried again—what if I send it after the semester is over? Kris asked me not to. I filed the letter.

I tell this story in response to hearing a similar story about a seventh-grade, inner-city, minority child, and her teacher. Later that day, Carolyn Burke suggests I write the story up for *The Whole Language Catalog*. She feels it is a powerful story and should be shared.

I fly home, thinking about what Carolyn has suggested. It's a sad story. It haunts me. Hardly seems like it should be in a book that celebrates whole language.

But maybe . . .

Maybe sharing sad stories enables us to see ourselves and others more clearly. It's easy to see myself in Kris—to take her side. Maybe, in the telling, I will be able to see myself in the teacher, see how I judge, evaluate, decide.

Maybe others will do likewise.

Maybe that is reason enough to tell sad stories.

Kris was 18, a freshman attending college in North Carolina . . .

➔ See: Stephens, p. 262.

Diane Stephens is a visiting professor at the Center for the Study of Reading, University of Illinois, Urbana, IL.

Parents' Perspective

by Jerline Quintal-Finell

Helping Camille and Melanie Cope

We have two daughters, Camille, seven, and Melanie, twelve. Both girls attended whole language schools in a remote northern Saskatchewan Native Indian community. Camille's experience with whole language took her from nursery school to grade two; Melanie's, from grade three to grade six. When my husband, Jeff Finell, and I went back for a formal education at the University of Saskatchewan in the city of Saskatoon, the girls were placed in the public school system.

Their public school did not favour whole language. Pedagogy centered on competency-based learning, which included positivistic evaluation instead of process-oriented, natural evaluation. The girls were forced to learn literacy by rote and math by precise application. The girls were required to memorize textbook words; any deviation from the text was considered wrong. For example, Melanie had to memorize facts in her grade-six social studies class. She had to copy word-for-word out of the textbook to answer assigned questions at the end of the chapter. Melanie became turned off to learning about different parts of the world. She stopped writing and researching on her own. We helped Melanie deal with her studies by suggesting that she

- Read the assigned work;
- Rewrite what she understood in her own words;
- Choose her own genre, register, and format when relating the information to her own experience (Melanie chose poetry written in verses);
- Reread her own creation to help remember the salient points;
- Reread the assignment and answer the questions using the textbook words; and
- Keep all personal writings in a log and reread them for her enjoyment.

Both girls had teachers who splintered language and who segregated children into ability groups based on standardized test results. This was especially evident in the teaching of reading. The reading tests required children to recognize words in isolation, race against the clock to spell words from word lists, and guess the meanings of words in a sentence.

At the beginning of the year, the emphasis of the reading program for Camille was on remedying her weaknesses, primarily her ability to identify blends. At home Camille was able to read words with these blends in context. Unfortunately, at school these same words were to be read in isolation. Camille's teacher perceived her as a remedial reader, while we saw Camille as a developmental reader who was especially adept at using syntactic and semantic cues.

We communicated our surprise to the teacher that Camille was placed in a remedial reading program. Although the teacher was somewhat sympathetic, we realized that it would be futile to buck the system. Consequently, we decided to help both girls survive the system as best we could.

We helped Camille deal with her reading frustrations by discussing these points:

- The difference between reading words in isolation and in context and how we felt in each situation;
- How we make sense of what we read by relying on our knowledge of how language works, and by using our experiences of the world;
- What happens when we write; and
- How we may use invented spelling for draft writing.

We encouraged the girls to continue reading and writing for their own enjoyment. We encouraged them to take risks in school, and to ask questions when they became confused about what the teachers expected of them. Although the teachers at this school never did learn to value the girls' strengths as readers, in time they stopped viewing them as remedial readers.

Both Camille and Melanie benefited from our discussions and our strategies for dealing with competency-based learning. Together, as a family, we figured out a way to retain our confidence in our natural abilities to learn new things. The girls are continuing to experiment. We all learned when we could compromise and when we could not. We must question schools when our children begin to doubt their own abilities to read and write, and when they come to view literacy as a threat rather than a fascinating and enjoyable process.

➔ See: Whitin, p. 41.

Jerline Quintal-Finell is a middle-year resource teacher at Opawikoscikan School, Pelican Narrows, Saskatchewan.

Resource: Book

Eyeopeners! How to Choose and Use Children's Books About Real People, Places, and Things

Beverly Kobrin
1988; 317 pp.; $7.95 paper;
$16.95 cloth
New York: Penguin Viking

This handbook offers adults the chance to enjoy and share nonfiction books with children. Helpful to parent and teacher alike, it includes hints for picking the right book and has ideas for exciting book-based activities. It features a complete guide to 500 current nonfiction books arranged by subject. *Eyeopeners* is a great way to encourage reading to learn, rather than learning to read.

Lynne Griffiths

Resource: Publisher

We believe strongly in public education. Our children and grandchildren attend public schools. We believe that it gives them an ability to appreciate others. But we recognize that home schooling is an alternative some parents prefer, so we include these resources.

—KSG, YMG, LBB

Home Education Press

Catalog from:
P.O. Box 1083
Tonasket, WA 98855
1-509-486-1351

The Press is one of the largest publishers of home schooling books and special publications in the United States. Their main publications are *Home Education Magazine,* which appears bimonthly; *The Home School Reader,* which is an annual guide to home schooling; and *The Home School Primer,* a yearly resource guide for home schoolers. All these publications support the publisher's belief that education should begin in the home. *Alternatives in Education,* edited by publishers Mark and Helen Hegener, is a comprehensive guide for families who wish to explore the current choices available to them in the education of their children. A historical perspective summarizes the alternative education movement.

Arrietta Chakos/Debbie Montgomery

Resource: Organizations

National Coalition of Alternative Community Schools (NCACS)

Membership: from $6 (subscription to one publication) to $75 (super voting membership)
58 Schoolhouse Rd.
Summertown, TN 38483
1-615-964-3670

The NCACS is a nonprofit national coalition of schools, groups, and individuals dedicated to provid ing people (and adults) with a personalized, yet globally oriented, education. Member schools mostly have low student/teacher ratios and a good deal of freedom for students; NCACS supports and promotes these educational experiments. The coalition produces several publications: *National Coalition News,* published quarterly; *Skole,* a biannual journal with articles about educational innovation; the *National Directory of Alternative Schools,* a comprehensive list of alternative schools and resources; the *Book of Fantasy and Adventure,* writings and drawings by students; and the *Alternative School Sampler,* a two-hour video about alternative schools.

Arrietta Chakos

National Home-school Association

Membership: $5 (individual or family); $25 (group)
P.O. Box 167
Rodeo, NM 88056
1-505-557-2250

The National Home-school Association is a grass-roots service organization that believes parents have the right to educate their children. The NHA sponsors an annual homeschool conference, publishes a quarterly newsletter, and provides a networking/resource service. Other services include a Family Travel program, a Homeschool Travel Directory, and an Apprentice/Mentor program.

Arrietta Chakos

Parents' Perspective

by Anita Shaw

The Tree House Club

From the time that Ben and Matthew were seven and four, respectively, to the time that they were ten and seven, the tree house in the backyard of our home in Honolulu was the center of their creative play activities. Soon after the boys and their father constructed the tree house, the Tree House Club came into existence. Ben named himself president, and Matthew served as vice-president.

Among the many activities of the Tree House Club was designating each part of the tree house. Ben and Matthew used old wood, paint, and invented spelling to make signs that labeled each part of the tree house according to function. The boys made signs for the Garden Shop, Workshop, fire escapes, fire detectors and sprinklers, burglar alarms and traps, and lookout tower. In addition, they wrote a list of instructions for each part. For example, the list of instructions for the Garden Shop explained the proper use and care of garden tools; the list for the Workshop explained the use and care of hammers, nails, and other tools. Of course, the boys posted a sign outside the tree house that read "Tree House Club, property of Ben and Matthew Shaw." Their keep-out signs showed skull and crossbones!

The writing activities associated with the Tree House Club grew in complexity as the boys matured. Though Ben did most of the actual writing during this time, Matthew contributed many of the creative ideas and suggestions that inspired Ben's developing literary skills. The boys drew an elaborate map of the tree house and the backyard that showed all of the best hiding places. They duplicated this map by hand on several pieces of paper and reproduced it in larger form on a piece of wood, which they placed in the tree house. Another writing activity was publishing the *Tree House Magazine.* The magazine included a map of the tree house, conditions for membership in the club, a schedule of upcoming activities, and some advertisements. Ben's father duplicated the magazine at his office and the boys sold it for five cents a copy.

Matthew found the tree house an ideal place to explore the mysteries of machinery and electrical wiring. Knowing of his interest in such things, many of our friends donated their "dead" machines, household appliances, and machine parts to Matthew so that he could build his projects. Matthew "invented" various machines to "air condition" the tree house and wired it to provide electricity for lights, burglar alarms, and so on. He could describe in detail what his machines and inventions were meant to accomplish, and supervised Ben as he labeled their parts and functions.

For a brief time, the Tree House Club went into business, forming the Tree House Real Estate Corporation. This involved publishing a new magazine, *The Tree House Real Estate Magazine;* creating advertising leaflets and posters; "subdividing" the backyard and nearby empty field into land parcels, each with boundaries marked by flags made by the boys; and developing a map to show the location of each land parcel.

From time to time, the Tree House Club would hold activity days, such as the Backyard Fair and exercise days. Friends were often invited to join in the fun, as were Mom and Dad. Ben and Matthew developed games and prizes, and made signs and advertising posters for these activity days.

On other occasions the boys used the tree house as a stage for puppet shows. The audience sat below the tree and the puppeteers would perform from the top story of the tree house.

Finally, the top story of the tree house often served as a favorite get-away-from-it-all nook for the quiet reading of books. Mom or Dad might read aloud to the boys, or they might go up alone with a good book.

We bid a sad farewell to the tree house this summer when we moved from Honolulu to Kealakekua. But we will always remember it as a very special place in our sons' development as creative individuals who love learning and expressing ideas.

Anita Shaw is an elementary teacher at Kahakai Elementary School, Kailua-Kona, HI.

📷 WHOLE LANGUAGE CAMERA

Parent Gene Hanson responds with interest as a student in Annette Maggitti's first grade reads aloud to him, Desert Winds School, Tucson, AZ.

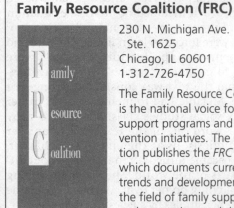

Resource: Organization

Family Resource Coalition (FRC)

230 N. Michigan Ave.
Ste. 1625
Chicago, IL 60601
1-312-726-4750

The Family Resource Coalition is the national voice for family support programs and prevention intiatives. The Coalition publishes the *FRC Report,* which documents current trends and developments in the field of family support and prevention, and the bimonthly *FRC Connection,* a networking newsletter of current information, research, and initiatives. The FRC maintains the only national information and referral service for parents seeking information about programs close to their homes. A new division, Parent Action, represents a national voice for parents who together are fighting for laws and policies that will help families.

Debbie Montgomery

Helping Parents Know Whole Language

As I See It:
Kenneth S. Goodman

A Letter to Parents

Dear Parents,

Before your children started school, they had accomplished, in the context of your family and community, a remarkable feat. We usually call it learning to talk, but that doesn't half cover it. They learned language, or more precisely, they learned the language of the home and the community. They came to understand you and speak to you in your own language. And they learned to do that at a very tender age without professional help. Some of your children learned more than one language—in fact, they easily learned as many languages as they needed to communicate comfortably with the people most important to them.

You and your children's other relatives and acquaintances played a vital role in this learning. You talked to and about and around them. They were immersed in whole, functioning language. They experienced language with virtually every transaction with significant others. And the language always was whole, always had a purpose, and always made sense. There were no skill drills, no vocabulary exercises, and no blending of sounds to produce nonsense syllables.

But the miracle would not have been accomplished without the genius of the children. All geniuses? Yes, all—because all children have this ability to learn language when it is whole, functional, and meaningful. They need to learn language to survive and participate in human society. They can and they do learn language: useful language—a lot like yours.

Furthermore, we now understand that children have made a good beginning, often a very good beginning, at developing written language before school. They pay attention to the print in your home and community. They have a sense of what you use reading and writing for, and they play at using it in the same way. If you read to them, they quickly learn the stories so well they can read themselves as they turn the pages. Just memorized? Try getting them to memorize a list of words. It's because they have a sense of the whole story—what it means, how it sounds, and what its sequence is—that they can remember whole pages of the story.

Well before they start school, children are picking up pencils, crayons, pens, and markers, and experimenting with writing. They play at writing shopping lists and messages, writing notes and letters, and writing their names. Many kids have some kind of recognizable signature before they start school. They write mostly in capital letters because most of the environmental print is in capital letters. They're keen observers of their world; they expect it to make sense, and they work at making sense of it.

Whole language education continues this language immersion in school. Language development, and all learning, in school is put in this same holistic context. We make it possible for these linguistic geniuses to put the same ability to work in learning written language in school that they used before they came to school. And we provide rich, authentic experiences in school to expand their oral language(s) and written language while they are using them to learn.

That's the essential reason why your children need whole language experiences in school. Traditional school programs were based on the notion that language and learning are hard. That's wrong. They're only hard if we work at cross-purposes with the learners instead of with them. Whole language accepts their language and supports them as they expand their competence in all directions. It invites them to take the risks that learning involves, confidently, because they know they have learned and can continue to learn when things are whole and make sense.

At every stage of development, people learn language best as they use it to think, to communicate, and to express their wonder about their world. So whole language classrooms for students of all ages don't use workbooks, skill practice sheets, flash cards, and controlled vocabulary. School is a rich array of challenging, authentic learning experiences in which reading and writing, speaking and listening, become more and more effective and powerful as they are used to build concepts, solve problems, and frame and answer important questions.

The kids learn more and produce more in whole language classrooms because their genius for learning is not limited and hobbled by artificial, meaningless drills on decontextualized bits and pieces of language.

Most kids go off to school with eager anticipation. It is not the natural course of events that this enthusiasm is lost and school becomes drudgery. Learning in school should continue to be exciting, involving, and uplifting.

How can you tell if your children are in whole language classrooms? Here's what to look for: Students in elementary grades will be involved in thematic units. They will be involved in learning about chickens, or weather, or their family history, or why there are wars. They'll be bringing home school activities to continue at home, but it will be voluntary because they can't wait to find the information they need for their projects and group presentations. They'll be reading real literature and not graded, basal readers. You'll discover that they have favorite authors like Judy Blume or Katherine Paterson, Bill Peet, or Bill Martin Jr. And you'll discover their delight when for their birthday presents they get books. They'll share their laughter over Tomie dePaola's *Strega Nona* and their tears over the death of the sled dog in *Stone Fox*. And they'll ask you if it really was like that when you were young when they read Mildred Taylor's *Roll of Thunder, Hear My Cry* or Patricia MacLachlan's *Sarah, Plain and Tall*.

If your kids are in whole language classrooms, then they'll proudly share the stories they've written. The papers they bring home will be rich in invented spellings, wonderful evidence of their developing control over the complexities of English spellings and wonderful evidence of their willingness to take risks and use words they're not sure they can spell in standard ways.

And most likely the kids will involve you in their search for information, in their projects, and in their joy of learning. Visit your kid's school to see for yourselves.

What should you do if they're not getting whole language? Ask the teacher and the principal why not. Donate a copy of *The Whole Language Catalog* to the school. Get together with other parents. Get involved in the PTA and offer to raise money for a library of real books in every classroom. Send books to the classroom for your child's birthday. Go to the school board and ask them to consider moving toward whole language. Or ask for an alternative magnet program in your community where informed parents like you can work with teachers to produce a whole language school.

And in all cases provide supportive experiences at home to keep your children enthusiastic about language and learning.
Sincerely,
Kenneth S. Goodman

➜ See: Areglado, p. 369; Freeman, p. 368; Jacobson, p. 365; Kaczmarek, p. 368; Literature Reference List, p. 429; Robb, p. 369.

As kids see it

Reading Is Even Better
by Reena Maria Ghosh

The other day my mom asked me why I loved ice-cream so much. I said "that's simple—because it tasted so good." Reading is even better. The taste of ice-cream goes away after it melts in my tongue. But reading stories and ideas stay in my mind for long. I love to read because I get to know about famous people and about the world around us.

I go to places where my mom and dad can't take me to. In a book I can go anywhere and stop anytime. When I DREAM I can dream of interesting places—a little like Oz, a little like Wonderland, like the Wind and Willows. Animals can be there, children and grown-ups can be there. Also I love to read because my mom and dad love to read and there are books all over our house.

But there is one thing I love more. I love my mom to read to me.

Reena Maria Ghosh is a second-grader. This essay, which won a 1989 National Mott's Apple Award, appears exactly as she wrote it.

📷 WHOLE LANGUAGE CAMERA

Gardening partners, Palo Alto, CA

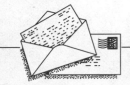

In the Mail

Open Letter to Administrators, Parents, and Students

Dear Friends:

According to recent research and practice, young people learn to read and write just as they once learned to talk — through practice. No one sits down with a baby and has her go through formal "talking exercises" to teach her to talk — rather the baby learns to talk through constant exposure to language, supported by her parents' absolute faith that she will indeed learn to talk. Similarly, young people learn to read, write, speak, and listen to English through reading, writing, speaking, and listening. They need to practice these activities in real-life ways rather than through isolated drills on bits and pieces of language.

All activities my classes engage in are based on research showing that language is learned when it is relevant to the student's own experience and when it has a real-life purpose. Students in my classes are learning to be writers, and like professional writers, they write every day and have *ownership* over their writing; that is, they choose their own topics or story ideas in their area of interest and expertise. They may write how-to manuals for their cars or letters to a newspaper editor rather than dry assignments given by the teacher, and they may interview real people for research papers rather than paraphrase unoriginal reports out of the encyclopedia. Like professional writers, their stories are published in magazines and their letters are mailed to grandparents or girlfriends, their advice columns are read by business people and teenagers, and their plays are performed. The same premise holds in reading. Students have many interests and *will read* if they are allowed to choose their own reading material. It is absolutely essential that young people's experience with language be *meaningful* and *purposeful* if they are going to learn to read and write well.

Writing is not simply an activity done in order to put down on paper what we already know; rather, it is a process through which we learn new information and find connections and patterns in what we already know. It is more important that students write and read *to learn* and *to create meaning* than to use language *perfectly*. My classes focus on students' abilities, not their disabilities. Rather than stopping students each time they make a spelling mistake or use a word incorrectly, thus creating a climate that is not conducive to students taking risks that are essential to learning, I encourage students to keep on using language. This is not to say that mistakes aren't addressed. Each day we talk about a troublesome area as it comes up naturally. My classes prepare students to use standard English, but not at the expense of their self-confidence or their creativity. My classroom is a cooperative one in which students learn together rather than compete against one another. Whole class discussions are not a time for students to try to prove to Teacher what they know and how smart they are, but rather for them to develop their ideas through discussion with *each other*. Students have a wealth of experience to share with one another—the teacher is not the only authority. In my classroom students often form small groups to work on writing projects or to read together. Research on cooperative learning shows that students are often each other's best teachers. We are not "playing school" in my classroom; we are making learning a joyful and interesting pursuit.

In our ever-changing world it is critical that students learn *strategies* for learning rather than learning isolated bits of information or rules. They must learn to learn on their own. The most basic purpose of my class is to teach my students to be writers, readers, thinkers, researchers, learners, cooperators, and finally, believers in themselves. It is my hope that through the use of meaningful, purposeful language that students have taken the responsibility for choosing, students will grow in these areas.

Beth Cohen

Beth Cohen is a former high school English teacher now working as a freelance writer and photographer in Somerville, MA.

Classroom Demonstrations

Ideas for Parents to Use at Home with Junior High and High School Students

1. Talk about the books, journals, magazines, and newspapers that you are reading. Share your reading experiences with your teenagers, and let them know what reading means to you.

2. Read aloud to your teenagers. The bedtime story is a wonderful tradition to establish when your children are young, and is important to maintain throughout adolescence.

3. If your teenagers have not developed into fluent and eager readers, continue to help them find high-interest books that are not too long or difficult. (S. E. Hinton is an author who has turned on many a turned-off adolescent. Her most popular books are *The Outsiders, Tex,* and *Rumble Fish*.)

4. Read the books your teenagers are reading. Much fiction deals with the common problems of young people: how to be attractive, how to handle physical maturity and sex, how to get along with friends, and how to be part of the crowd when socially acceptable behavior is put down. Discuss these problems with your teenagers as they relate to the characters in the book.

5. Talk about the role writing plays in your personal life, on your job. Share your writing with your teenagers. Some families not only read together, they also write together.

6. Encourage your teenagers to write away for interesting samples, travel brochures, and catalogs. Give them junk mail to read and critique.

7. Help your young people develop an interest in current affairs by watching worthwhile TV news programs together. Invite comments and discussion. Provide newspapers and news magazines to follow up on what was seen on TV.

8. Introduce teenagers, as well as younger children, to new sights and experiences. Help them note significant details, even in the everyday things that we take for granted. Take a bus ride or tour your job site; visit places that interest your teenagers.

Resource: Organization

The Home and School Institute

Special Projects Office
1201 16th St., NW
Washington, DC 20036
1-202-466-3633

Resource Essay

Helping Parents Help Their Children Learn

by Dorothy Rich

The National Commission on Excellence in Education (1983) addressed parents in a postscript: "As surely as you are your children's most important teachers, your children's ideas about education and its significance begin with you . . . Moreover, you bear a responsibility to participate actively in your children's education." Good words. But what does that responsibility include? And what is expected of schools in working with parents?

(Continued on next page)

---

9. Quiet and comfortable surroundings are as necessary for reading as they are for studying. Make sure that your teenagers can read in their rooms without being disturbed by younger siblings. Regulate the volume of TV and stereo, if necessary, and the times they may be used. Limit the amount of television your family watches and encourage selective viewing. Discuss program content, especially if your teenagers seem confused or frightened.

10. Parents should be aware that they may disrupt reading by poorly timing household chores. Be sure that these chores are scheduled for particular time periods, not staggered throughout the day or evening. Your teenagers should be able to read and concentrate without interruption.

11. High school is a time for joining clubs, attending or participating in sports, dances, and other social activities, and working at part-time jobs. No one would debate these are valuable parts of adolescence, but too many activities can crowd a teenager's schedule and cut out time for reading. Guide your teenagers in devising a well-balanced schedule so that there is sufficient time for studying, reading, and pursuing other interests and activities.

12. Ask your teenagers questions that require more than a "yes-no-I-don't-know" answer.

13. Make books special by often giving them as gifts.

Brochures for Parents

How Can I Get My Teenager to Read? (#871, $.50) and *Studying: A Key to Success/Ways Parents Can Help* (free with self-addressed, stamped 10" envelope): International Reading Association, 800 Barksdale Rd., P.O. Box 8139, Newark, DE 19711.

How to Help Your Child Become a Better Writer (free) and *All About Letters* ($1.50, U.S. Postal Service booklet): National Council of Teachers of English, Order Dept., 1111 Kenyon Rd., Urbana, IL 61801.

➔ See: 1001 Things You Can Get Free, p. 302; Literature Reference List, p. 429; Whitin, p. 354.

Author unknown—please let us know if you recognize this work.

Classroom Demonstrations

by Debra Jacobson

(Continued from previous page)

After 20 years of experience the home and School Institute has developed four rules for successful parent involvement programs.

1. Link parents' involvement directly to the learning of their own children. An important reward for parents is their children's school success.

2. Provide ways for families to teach academic skills at home. The Home and School Institute has initiated a number of successful home-teaching projects with school systems in California, Michigan, South Carolina, and the District of Columbia. These projects, which do not duplicate schoolwork, involve sending home learning activities as "recipes" for parents and children to do together. As a result, student test scores have improved, as have attitudes about schools. This experience indicates that all parents, even those with limited formal education, can help teach children.

Easy techniques are used to foster learning: young children use the TV schedule to keep to time limits and dial and read telephone numbers; older students make "best buy" purchases at the grocery store and use maps to plan family trips.

The hurried parent, in just a few minutes a day, can teach science, reading, math, or writing in a relaxed, informal manner. The material is presented in such a way that parents know exactly what to do. This approach has the added advantage of being nonthreatening because the assignments are not traditional school work.

3. Link the school's work to the community. Schools must share the responsibility of teaching. Distribute home learning activities at workplaces, churches, gas stations, and grocery stores. Set up family learning centers in schools and storefronts. These demonstration rooms show how real home items and household furniture are used for home learning. And use senior citizens or teenagers to staff these rooms and share the teaching materials.

4. Provide for parent involvement at all levels of schooling. Research and parent programs have primarily centered on early childhood, but continuing support is needed as children move through school. Teens need help from home to get the best from the secondary years.

A successful home involvement program can begin with one parent, one teacher, one administrator. But it will not continue unless there is support from groups of parents, teachers, and administrators. To ensure its acceptance, parent involvement must be viewed as a legitimate activity of the school, and reaching the family must be considered as important as reaching the child.

Reference

National Commission on Excellence in Education. 1983. *A nation at risk.* Washington, DC: U.S. Department of Education.

From *Educational Leadership,* 1984. Copyright 1984 by The Home and School Institute, Inc.

Dr. Dorothy Rich is the founder and president of the Home and School Institute, Washington, DC.

Information for Parents About Whole Language Teaching and Learning

Whole Language

- Is a way of teaching and learning where language is kept whole, meaningful, and purposeful;
- Is child-centered, based on student interests and strengths;
- Recognizes that reading and writing are related language processes;
- Allows students to play an active role in their learning;
- Encourages students to take risks and to appreciate their "mistakes" as a necessary part of the learning process;
- Believes that language conventions (such as punctuation or spelling) are learned in context and through authentic use, not through isolated drills.

Some Things You Might See in a Whole Language Classroom

- Thematic unit study in which students explore subjects in-depth;
- The publication of student writing; students write rough drafts, revise and edit, and experience the writing process just as professional writers do;
- Writing across function and content area; students write letters, publish class newspapers, keep journals, and experience the full range of functional writing;
- Thoughtful discussions in which students are challenged to ask questions;
- Hands-on, problem-solving learning experiences;
- Reading experienced as a source of pleasure and information.

Some Things You Probably Won't See in a Whole Language Classroom

- Use of workbooks or worksheets where students spend their time filling in the blanks;
- Lots of copying from the board and little writing by students of their own thoughts;
- Phonics taught in isolation;
- Reading word lists;
- Emphasis on a finished product;
- Reading only a basal reader.

Some Points to Keep in Mind

- Children need a lot of support; we need to help them see themselves as capable learners.
- Since we want to help children become independent learners, it is best to ask an open-ended question such as "What do you think?" rather than to give them the answer.
- Learning to read and write like adults takes time and a lot of experimenting.
- It is easier to read things in context than out of context. It is not a good idea for children to read word lists.
- Children become fluent readers and writers at different times. Be patient with your children.
- Children learn a lot about reading and writing from everyday experiences.
- Children like to try to do the things they see adults do. When you read, encourage your children to read.
- Talking is important for children. It helps them to feel good about themselves, and promotes academic as well as personal success.
- You can contact your child's teacher if you feel any concern about your child's progress or attitude.
- Educational research has shown that sometimes when children make progress in one area, they might regress in others. Be patient.

Suggested Activities

- Set aside 15 minutes or more each day to read to your children.
- Encourage them to take an active part in your reading time. They can hold the book, turn the pages, read along with you, talk about the story, pretend to read the book to you, predict what will happen next at different parts of the story, talk about how this story relates to their lives. Share your favorite books and stories.

- Talk to your children about the environmental print that is present in everyday experiences, e.g., street signs, posters, cereal boxes, movie and TV schedules, letters, bills, notes, grocery lists, cooking.
- Provide materials for your children to explore and experiment with writing, for example, bank slips, applications, mail order catalogs.
- Read the newspaper with your children. Check the ads, clip coupons, and read interesting headlines, photo captions, stories, and comics together.
- Leave notes around the house for your children. Encourage them to write notes to you.
- Enter contests that require filling out entry forms and addressing envelopes.
- Post a "Helpers Chart" for your children to refer to when it is time for chores.
- Share the cooking with your children. Plan and write out menus, read and follow cookbook directions, and measure the ingredients together.
- Encourage your children to explore their interests and help them find books and other materials on these subjects.
- Teach your children how to use the telephone book. Help them look up the names and numbers of friends they want to call, and show them how to use the yellow pages.
- Provide quiet times for homework, reading, and writing away from the television.
- Write labels on things your children use each day.
- Encourage your children to label and write their names on their possessions.
- Leave toys and food in original containers that have pictures and print on them. Encourage your children to find groceries, unwrap household items, make choices based on the print or pictures.
- Place books on your children's level for easy and *continuous* access.
- Write down your children's stories and observations so that later you can read and share them together.
- Make books about important events in your children's lives.
- Share the mail with your children; read cards and letters to them; give them the junk mail to explore and play with.

→ See: Areglado, p. 369; Freeman, p. 368; Goodman, p. 363; Jacobson, p. 118, 160; Joyce, p. 357; Kaczmarek, p. 368; Kitagawa, p. 420.

Debra Jacobson is an elementary teacher at Coronado Elementary School, Tucson, AZ.

Resource: Pamphlet

I'm Still Learning to Read

Nancy Weber and Chris Hein
For $1.50 from:
Edmonton Public Schools
Warehouse
and Distribution
10515 100 St.
Edmonton
Alberta, T5H 2R4
Canada

Written for the parents of students at Caernarvon School in Edmonton, Canada, this pamphlet is an excellent description of the process of learning to read. It is simply written and filled with information parents and teachers need to know. (Edmonton Public Schools offer for sale a variety of other language arts curriculum materials.)

Arrietta Chakos

Continued from page 311

Education in the New Century:
Walter Johnson and the Project Method

Walter Johnson was an energetic man in his late fifties who loved working with students. His main educational interest was the "project method," and he persuaded Alice to come out of retirement and train the teachers in it. Walter Johnson and Alice became closer friends and worked together until Alice died of emphysema in 1933.

The curriculum at the Turin Grammar School was reorganized so that subject areas were replaced by projects. This method was an outgrowth of Colonel Parker, John Dewey, and Williams Heard Kilpatrick's emphasis on learning by doing. Each project was meant to relate to life in the community and be based on subjects that interested the students. The projects were to integrate reading, writing, math, science, the arts, and social studies. Some of the projects studied in Turin were

- Planning, building, and planting a student-run vegetable garden and food cooperative;
- Studying the post office and setting up a student post office in the school; and
- Studying machinery and building an assembly line to make metal toys for the lower grades.

There were parents and teachers in Turin who were angry at having the project method forced into the curriculum. They felt it represented a neglect of the three Rs. They were also angry about questions children were dealing with at school. There was no place, they claimed, for students raising social issues or questioning authority.

The Depression hit Turin in the middle of the project method. Money for the school was cut and some teachers had to leave. A new school board put pressure on the superintendent to cut programs, to eliminate anything that could be considered a frill. The principle's response was that his program was basic, that he didn't allow frills in his district.

Ever since he had been appointed principal of the Turin Grammar School, Walter Johnson had been vowing to spend part of his day teaching his favorite subject, American history. In 1937, a few years after Alice died, he decided to teach history to the upper grades of his school "for Alice," as he said to his staff. He requested and got approval to buy a new social studies curriculum developed by Harold Rugg entitled *Man and His Changing Society*. The curriculum was designed to assist students in thinking about social problems and speculating on ways to solve them. At that time almost a million sets of the books were being used throughout the country.

Rugg's books tried to analyze problems associated with developing democracy in the United States. For example, in one of the texts, Rugg (1937) summarized the making of the United States Constitution in this way:

THE CONSTITUTIONAL CONVENTION SET UP A GOVERNMENT BY WHICH CHANGES WERE MADE DIFFICULT
The fathers of the Constitution feared "too much democracy." They were afraid of what the majority of people, who did not possess property, would do to the minority, who did. They were afraid of what they regarded as the ignorance and rashness of the lower classes.
The spoken and written words of the men in the Convention show very clearly that they regarded democracy as a dangerous thing. Gerry, for example, said that the unsettled condition of the country "came from the excess of democracy."

In 1940 the National Association of Manufacturers (NAM) announced that it would investigate school textbooks that were supporting communism and undermining the American way of life. NAM joined the American Legion and a coalition of conservative organizations called the American Coalition. They claimed that the spectre of collectivism was sneaking into the schools and that they had to be "sentinels" to protect capitalist America. The target these groups selected for their most violent attacks were the Rugg textbooks.

Turin was not immune from the attacks on Rugg's texts. The county office of the American Legion as well as some business organizations banded together to eliminate not merely the textbooks, but Walter Johnson as well from the Turin school. Walter defended his use of the books and cited a study by leading historians from Harvard and Dartmouth that affirmed that the texts did not distort the primary documents of American history in any way. He had depended upon this study to quiet this opposition, but the opposition was political, not "scientific." The battle was won in the name of patriotism, fundamentalism, and, as one school board member said, "back to basics." Walter Johnson resigned in early 1941. His resignation was accepted by the school board with only one dissenting vote, that of Dr. Phillip Burns, Alice's son.

Reference: Rugg, H. 1937. *America's march toward democracy*. Boston: Ginn & Company.

Continued on page 375

Resource: Organization

The Elisabeth Kubler-Ross Center

Membership: from $15 (limited income) to $500 (lifetime); includes newsletter
South Rte. 616
Headwaters, VA 24442
1-703-396-3441

The Elisabeth Kubler-Ross Center/Shanti Nilaya is a nonprofit organization that offers workshops to help participants overcome the effects of major trauma in their lives. Dr. Kubler-Ross is an internationally recognized authority in the field of death, dying, and transition. She has worked extensively with terminally ill patients and families with terminally ill children. *On Death and Dying,* her first book, is a seminal work, as are *On Children and Death* and *The Dougy Letter (Letter to a child with cancer).* Dr. Kubler-Ross sponsors experiential workshops for those confronting death or illness. The newsletter includes a mail-order catalog for reading materials, videotapes, and audiocassettes. You'll also find listings for support groups all over the world.

Arrietta Chakos

Should you shield the
 canyons from the windstorms
you would never see the
 beauty of their carvings...

Elisabeth Kubler-Ross, M.D.

writers

Obituary for Libby

by Kathryn Elizabeth Mullarkey

Person: Elizabeth (Libby) Jacobson
Born: February 11, 1989
Died: February 15, 1989

Elizabeth was born at Tucson Medical Center. She has two sisters named April and Jamie. She was loved very much by her family and friends. She was put in a coffin and buried at East Lawn cemetery. Elizabeth's death was caused by an underdeveloped heart. Her father was African. Her mother's name is Terrianne. She is my teacher. I was interested in Elizabeth. I care about my teacher and her baby. So I write about what I feel and care about.

Elizabeth loved all people. It was shocking when her death happened. When Mrs. Shaw and Mrs. Goettl told us about Libby, we were silent for at least five minutes. I like babies and that's not the only reason why I LOVE Libby. I love her because I love her mother.

Libby was twenty-one inches long and weighed eight pounds and six ounces. She was born at 3:00 P.M. People could not believe that they released her from the hospital, but even the doctors did not know about her heart. She had spent two nights at home. Ms. Jacobson thought it was o.k. for Libby to die because she could not live a good life. She held her while she was dying.

She was very, very sad. At the beginning we thought that Elizabeth was very healthy. But she unfortunately was not. Everyone I saw at the funeral felt miserable, including me. So remember, Libby will "KISS YOU IN YOUR DREAMS."

Kathryn Elizabeth Mullarkey is a third-grader at Manzanita School, Tucson, AZ.

This was contributed by Terrianne Jacobson, primary teacher at Manzanita School, Tucson, AZ.

Resource: Book

Helping Children Cope

Joan Fassler
1978; 162 pp.; $26.95
New York: The Free Press, a division of Macmillan

The emphasis here is on books for children from four to eight years old that deal with potential stress such as illness, moving, hospitalization, death, separation, adoption, divorce, or the birth of a baby in the family. Each chapter contains a discussion of the topic and a listing of books that might be useful.

Katy Obringer

Pioneers: Maria Montessori (1870–1953)   by Ron Miller

Montessori was the first woman to enter an Italian medical school and, after winning high honors, graduated in 1896. As a physician, she treated children who were institutionalized for a variety of mental and emotional problems, and eventually concluded that many of their problems were fundamentally *educational*; these children were not receiving the intellectual stimulation or emotional nurturing vital to healthy development. After engaging in intensive studies of psychiatry, anthropology, and educational theory (including the work of Pestalozzi and Froebel), Montessori devised a new educational system that has been adopted by thousands of educators in all parts of the world.

The Montessori method is primarily a sensorial approach. Young children, she discovered, engage the world through intensive tactile, visual, and auditory exploration, not at first through adult logic or language. She studied the methods that Jean Itard (teacher of the "wild boy of Aveyron") and his student Edouard Seguin had used to treat deaf-mute and retarded children earlier in the 19th century, and devised extensive "didactic apparatus" that would gratify the young child's sensorial exploration. In 1907 she opened a classroom filled with these materials in a housing project in Rome. The results were spectacular. Young children who had been listless or destructive in their tenement environment became active, inquisitive students and "exploded" into writing and reading by the age of five. Language for them was a tool for expanding their exploration of the world, rather than an academic exercise commanded by the teacher.

Montessori believed that the child naturally progresses through developmental stages of approximately six years each, and more specifically through "sensitive periods"—times of

exceptional receptivity to events in the natural and social environments. If this natural unfolding of intelligence and personality is served, she argued, then children are enabled to learn independently, enthusiastically, and with surprising concentration. She called this unfolding process "normalization," a term that suggests that intellectual development is intimately related to emotional and psychological development. Indeed, for Montessori, education was not merely a program to make children learn a predetermined curriculum, but the provision of a "prepared environment" that would answer the organic needs of human development.

In the Montessori classroom, children work with the didactic materials independently or in small groups. The teacher is present to *observe* the needs and achievements of each child in order to demonstrate the appropriate materials to each individual. This unusual educational atmosphere—more like a buzzing laboratory than a typical classroom—was later adapted (by Montessori herself) to the elementary grades, and has been applied in other settings as well. Children of mixed ages—generally between three and six, six and nine, nine and twelve—help each other and learn from each other in a genuine community.

Montessori was a passionate defender of the dignity of childhood. She believed that every child is the builder of his or her adult personality, and that consequently the young generation is the creator of society's future possibilities. The purpose of education, for her, was not to maintain the present culture with all its injustices and imperfections, but to nurture the inner resources of every child so that the new generation might create a new world of brotherhood and peace.

Further Reading

Montessori, Maria. 1965. *Spontaneous Activity in Education* (1917). New York: Schocken.
———. 1978. *The Absorbent Mind* (1949). Madras, India: Kalakshetra.

Resource: Periodical

Public School Montessorian

$12/year (4 issues) individual; $20/year (20 copies of 4 issues) parents group from: Jola Publications 230 10th Ave. S. Minneapolis, MN 55415

This journal examines the application of Montessori education in public school settings. It addresses issues of child development, teacher preparation, public education policies, and more. A good resource for non-Montessori-trained parents and educators who want to understand Montessori principles.

Resource: Organizations

American Montessori Society

150 Fifth Ave.
New York, NY 10011

Association Montessori Internationale

170 W. Scholfield Rd.
Rochester, NY 14617

International Montessori Society

912 Thayer Ave.
Silver Spring, MD 20910

Resource: Organization

The Quality Education Project (QEP)

2110 Scott St.
San Francisco, CA 94115
Contact: Nancy Honig
1-415-921-8673

Founded in 1982 as a non-profit staff development program, QEP focuses on improving student achievement through engaged parent involvement, particularly in school districts where students are at risk due to poverty or limited English proficiency. Individualized district needs assessment, effective home-school communication, and home-reading activities are hallmarks of the program, which currently serves over 150,000 students in 32 school districts in California and Mississippi.

Resource: Book

Books to Help Children Cope with Separation and Loss: An Annotated Bibliography, Vol. 3

Joanne E. Bernstein and Masha Kabakow Rudman 1988; 532 pp.; $39.95 New York: R. R. Bowker

This is a bibliographic guide to fiction and non-fiction books for children ages 3 to 16. Essays, recent theories and research, bibliotherapy, and an annotated bibliography of 606 books relating to separation and loss are included. Bernstein and Rudman cover topics such as losing a pet, getting lost, leaving home, divorce, kidnapping, serious illness, and abuse.

Katy Obringer

Resource: Books

Little Tan Books

$3 each from:
Dorothy Gehres Fraembs
10758 Chelmsford Rd.
Cincinnati, OH 45240
1-513-825-3831

Four titles are available: *When My Mother Died; When My Father Died; My Mother Told Me...*; and *My Father Told Me ...* Use them to help a child with the thoughts and feelings that are natural in the months following the loss of a parent. These books are also intended for a surviving parent to read with a child when the demands of survival often tend to keep them apart; they deal simply and effectively with a child's grief.

Arrietta Chakos

❝ As a widow, as a mother, as a teacher, as a volunteer with a widowed persons' group, I became aware that people often misinterpret children's words and actions concerning the loss of a loved one.❞ (Little Tan Books brochure)

Communicating with Parents

Cornerstone: Yvonne S. Freeman

Communicating Whole Language to Parents in English and Spanish

"The parents can't read or write themselves, or they just don't care. They often don't even speak English. How can we expect anything from those kids when they come from homes like that? We can't expect the kids to read and write at home." I have heard words like these many times from educators while doing whole language inservices at schools with large Hispanic populations. I cannot accept their conclusions. I taught English as a Second Language to adults for nine years and never met parents from any language or cultural background who did not care about their children's success in school.

My convictions have been put to the test in the past few years as I have been asked to speak to parents about whole language and the important role parents play in their children's success at school. Because many parents are monolingual Spanish speakers, I have prepared presentations in both English and Spanish. Even though parents can communicate fairly well in English, they appreciate someone making an effort to talk to them in the language they are most comfortable speaking.

It is necessary, however, to do more than speak Spanish to successfully communicate with Hispanic parents.

1. I give concrete examples of points I am making about learning and whole language. I tell stories.
2. I make a few basic points with examples rather than present long lists.
3. I suggest things parents can do to support their children's success.
4. I joke with parents and admit my own parenting has been far from perfect at times.
5. I encourage questions and always allow time for parents to come up to me with individual questions at the end.
6. I use music and poetry in Spanish and English that are well known and fun.

Since most parents believe that their children's school is like the school of their own childhood, I find it necessary to give parents a new view of learning and teaching in whole language class-

	Three Keys to School Success
Talking	Parents who play with their children and have conversations with them are helping them to think and to explore their world.
Reading	Parents who read with their children and take them to the library are giving their children experiences with books that they need for school success.
Writing	Parents who encourage their children to draw and write are beginning to teach their children to express themselves in writing.

	Tres claves para lograr el éxito escolar
Hablar	Los padres que juegan con sus hijos y que conversan con ellos estan ayudandoles a pensar y a explorar el mundo.
Leer	Los padres que leen juntos con sus hijos y que los llevan a la biblioteca estan ofreciéndoles experiencias con libros, las cuales necesitan para tener éxito escolar.
Escribir	Los padres que animan a sus hijos a dibujar y a escribir les estan enseñando a expresarse con palabras escritas.

rooms. I begin by emphasizing that even the little things parents do with their children are important to learning. I go over, in Spanish and English, how parents can help children believe in themselves and take risks. I stress the importance of positive feedback. I tell stories of my own learning experiences and those of my children. I discuss things I learned while living in Mexico.

After I have talked about learning, I present the **Three Keys to School Success/Tres claves para lograr el exito escolar**, which parents can follow to support their children's activities in school.

To discuss the first key, **Talking/Hablar**, I bring in nursery rhymes, songs, and poems in both Spanish and English. I talk about games that help children develop language and participate in family conversations. I suggest going over each child's day at mealtime. I point out that research has shown that children need to have meaningful conversations with their parents in the language that both children and parents are most comfortable using.

For the second key, **Reading/Leer**, I stress the importance of exposing children to books. I realize that some Hispanic parents are not confident of their own literacy, so I encourage them to have relatives and older brothers or sisters read to children. I suggest that children read to their parents and that they take trips to the library together so that children can see how their parents value reading. I read big books that are predictable in Spanish and English to show parents that prediction and rereadings are not only beneficial but also fun.

Finally, I talk about the necessity of encouraging **Writing/Escribir**, the third key. I mention having writing implements and scratch paper around the house. I encourage parents to let children make lists and play games like "store" and "office" where writing is part of the play. I show samples of scribbles and invented spelling and point out that conventional spelling comes with practice and lots of reading.

Giving talks to Hispanic parents has proved to be the most rewarding type of inservice I have done. Administrators and teachers are happy to see that parents do care and will support the school when they are empowered with information.

➜ See: Cress, p. 371; Freeman, pp. 87, 184, 189, 212; Goodman, p. 363.

Yvonne (Bonnie) S. Freeman is the director of Bilingual Education and the codirector of the Language Development Program at Fresno Pacific College, Fresno, CA.

📷 WHOLE LANGUAGE CAMERA

Kindergarten teacher Nancy Areglado of Berkshire Hills Regional School District explains her program to an audience of parents and students, Stockbridge, MA.

Classroom Demonstrations
by Kitty Kaczmarek

Collaboration Between School and Home: Helping Parents "Come to Know"

Mrs. Johnson plopped the heavy cardboard box down on the table. It was filled to the brim with phonics dittos, skills workbooks, and Lippincott Letter Books.

"My children are *not* bringing these worksheets home this year!" she stated, grabbing a ditto and waving it in the air. "I used to be able to help them with their homework. Now I don't know *what* they're working on! I feel that ties have been severed between the school and the home!"

This scenario reflects one parent's concerns as her children shift from an integrated skills environment to a whole language envir Phonics drills, skills workbooks, and flashcards are gradually being replaced by big books, author chairs, and literature study groups. These dittos, basals, and workbooks represent the familiar aspects of school to parents, who will continue to value these materials until exposed to a new perspective on reading and writing. As teachers and children gradually shift from an integrated skills view of reading to a holistic perspective, it is important to help parents "come to know" as well.

How can we help parents value *Charlotte's Web* and *The Tenth Good Thing About Barney* over circling schwas and coloring in the long-o pictures? How can we help them understand how children acquire written language?

Different parent education strategies need to be utilized in order to invite parents to grow along with us. We need to support parents in their *journey to know*. Here are several strategies:

- Literacy meetings can be held at night to allow teachers to discuss materials and strategies they use in their classrooms. Three teachers speak for 15 minutes each and then answer questions. The usage of predictable books or literature study groups are possible topics. The role of the parent in a child's literacy development should be addressed.

- Literacy breakfasts can be held in individual classrooms. Over fruit salad and coffee, parents and the teacher look at writing samples and discuss student growth in interactive journal writing. Other literacy events can be highlighted. Videos of students in action can be utilized.

- Family literacy classes can be held at the school level where one teacher works with 15 parents for four night sessions. Issues range from usage of invented spelling in the writing process to the role of prediction in reading.

- Student-authored class newsletters can be created bimonthly and sent home to inform parents of class research projects, upcoming trips, events, and so on. The role of the parent in these projects should be clearly delineated.

- Parents can observe/volunteer their time in the classroom. They learn the reading/writing process by doing!

Mrs. Johnson will soon be filling a second cardboard box with student-authored books, science projects, and tradebooks. She will come to value both process as well as product, *if* we support her on the journey to know.

➜ See: Goodman, p. 363; Literature Reference List, p. 429.

Kitty Kaczmarek is director of staff development for Glendale Elementary School District, Glendale, AZ.

Classroom Demonstrations

by Nancy Hyland Areglado

Sharing Whole Language with Parents

In an article published in *Phi Delta Kappan,* Herbert Walberg (1984, pp. 397–400) stated that children spend only about 13 percent of their waking hours in school, and only 3 percent to 6 percent of those hours effectively engaged in learning. Walberg also reported that parents controlled 87 percent of the out-of-school time. The question he posed is, "Can educators and parents cooperate to use this out-of-school time more efficiently for the welfare of students and of the nation?" Evidence exists that home/school partnerships, which can dramatically raise educational productivity, have declined in past decades.

As the U.S. Department of Education (1986) reported, "Parent involvement helps children learn more effectively. Teachers who are more successful at involving parents in their children's schoolwork are successful because they work at it." Research has shown that "most parents *want* to be involved with their children's schoolwork but are unsure of what to do or how to do it. Many say they would welcome more guidance and ideas from teachers."

What better time to educate parents about our whole language programs than now, when the research on parent/school partnerships is so encouraging? And what better way to strengthen student learning than by having supportive parents help at home? And finally, what better way to publicize how well our program is working than by engaging parents as our "publicity agents"?

Ways to Strengthen Parent Involvement

Newsletters. Send home an introductory newsletter on the first day of school and subsequently on a regular basis. Share samples of students' work and success stories. In every issue, interweave whole language in meaningful ways, explaining what children did during the past week or month, or what they will do in the next week or month.

Parent Questionnaires. Design a questionnaire for parents to list their skills and interests. Ask if they would be willing to speak to the class. Find out who would be willing to help out with field trips or with snacks for large student programs. Also ask for classroom volunteers.

Student Performances. Plan plenty of student performances. Most parents love to see their children perform. The more you invite parents into your classroom, the better the communication will be between home and school. Plan programs that center around the exhibition of whole language activities, such as big books that children have created; songs, chants, and poems that they have learned; plays they have written; and so on.

Newspaper Publicity. Give the local paper advance notice whenever your class is about to do something newsworthy. Send a press release that includes key ideas about the program you'd like to see printed. Parents will be excited and will take pride in their child's class, especially if their child's picture is in the paper.

Volunteer Programs. Begin this program as soon as children are ready for visitors. Always have projects ready for parents so that they will feel useful. Give working parents the option of helping you in their homes. Be sure to thank each parent personally and in the newsletter.

Letters Celebrating Accomplishments. As you take anecdotal records of each child over the course of a day or a week, you will notice a number of accomplishments. Design a form on which to jot down a quick note to parents acknowledging these accomplishments.

Providing Whole Language Information. If you read an article about whole language that you think parents would enjoy, copy it and send it home.

Authors' Days. Invite parents to join you for an authors' day party to celebrate the books that children have written and published themselves. At the party, show a video or slides of children at work during writers' workshops. Then present each child with his or her published book. To encourage attendance, allow children to make the invitations. Be sure to leave room for a response slip. Give parents plenty of notice so that they can make arrangements to come.

Informative Parent/Teacher Conferences. Have information about invented spelling or whole language reading available for parents to read before they meet with you. Whatever it is that you want parents to understand, mirror the learning in the child's work samples. Talk to parents about how they can reinforce important whole language strategies at home.

Welcome Mat. If parents have an occasional day off from work, make sure they know that they are always welcome to come in and help you.

References

U.S. Department of Education. 1986. *What works: Research about teaching and learning.*

Walberg, H. J. 1984. "Families as partners in educational productivity." *Phi Delta Kappan* 65 (February).

Further Reading About Parent Involvement

California State Department of Education. 1979. *Putting It Together with Parents: A Guide to Parent Involvement in Education Programs.* Sacramento, CA. General ideas for parent involvement plus parent forms.

Fredericks, Anthony D. 1989. "A Far-Reaching Effort." *Teaching K–8* 19 (February): p. 23. Excellent suggestions for "no show" parents.

Henderson, Anne, et al. 1987. "Building a Family-School Relationship." *Principal* (January): pp. 12–15. Practical examples of how schools can build bridges to parents.

Language Arts 66, (January 1989), "Home-School Relationship" issue. Many interesting articles.

Massachusetts Department of Education, Office of Community Education. 1988. *A Handbook on Home-School Collaboration.* Quincy, MA. Helpful booklet on parent involvement.

Rich, Dorothy. 1988. *Megaskills.* Boston: Houghton Mifflin. Excellent book about how families can help children succeed in school and beyond.

Rich, Dorothy, and Beverly Mattox. 1976. *101 Activities for Building More Effective School-Community Involvement.* Rockville, MD: Home and School Institute. A wealth of proven ideas for teachers and administrators.

Robinson, Norman, and Juleen Cattermole. 1985. "Effective Home/School Communication: From the Parents' Perspective." *Phi Delta Kappan* 67 (September): pp. 48–50. Interesting article about the parents' perspective on involvement.

The Reading Teacher 41 (May 1988), "Parents and Children as Co-Learners" issue. Informative articles about parents as colearners and also about parent involvement.

Suggested Books for Parents

Books for Sharing the Pleasures of Reading

Family Storybook Reading, by Denny Taylor and Dorothy S. Strickland (Portsmouth, NH: Heinemann, 1986).

Growing Up Reading, by Linda Leonard Lamme (Washington, DC: Acropolis Books, 1985) and

Growing Up Writing, by Linda Leonard Lamme (Washington, DC: Acropolis Books, 1987). These books are informative, easy to read, and full of practical suggestions on how to foster the development of reading and writing in your home. They are most appropriate for parents of one- to twelve-year-olds.

Leading to Reading, by Masha Kabakow Rudman and Barbara Lee (New York: Berkley Books, 1986). Recommended by both Bill Cosby and Jim Trelease, this books explains how to "turn kids onto reading and writing through TV, comics, cereal boxes, and other surprising sources that speak their language!" It is particularly appropriate for a more mature reader.

Make Your Child a Lifelong Reader, by Jacquelyn Gross, in collaboration with Leonard Gross (Los Angeles: Jeremy Tarcher, 1986). The authors offer new hope for parents concerned with improving their children's literacy skills. Many suggestions, games, and activities are provided to help turn on the reluctant reader. Ages infancy through 17 are addressed.

A Parent's Guide to Children's Reading, by Nancy Larrick (Philadelphia: Westminster Press, 1982). Well received by parents throughout the United States, this classic book is in its fifth edition. It is often cited as being a helpful resource for parents.

The Read-Aloud Handbook, by Jim Trelease (New York: Penguin Books, 1985). A best-seller, this book shows how every child can become a book-lover. Appropriate for all readers, it contains wise advice on how to begin reading aloud to your child.

The RIF Guide to Encouraging Young Readers, edited by Ruth Graves (New York: Doubleday Books, 1987). A tremendous resource for encouraging your reader, the *RIF Guide* explains hundreds of child-tested activities that engage kids from babies to 11-year-olds in the fun of words and reading. A recommended reading list is also included.

Books for Parents of Children in Whole Language Classrooms

The Craft of Children's Writing, by Judith Newman (Portsmouth, NH: Heinemann, 1985). This clearly written book explains the beginning of writing development in young children. It also clarifies the many ways parents can look at their children's writing as a mirror of their development.

Spel . . . Is a Four-Letter Word, by J. Richard Gentry (Portsmouth, NH: Heinemann, 1987). This brief book answers many questions about a parent's role in helping children with beginning spelling.

What Did I Write? by Marie Clay (Portsmouth, NH: Heinemann, 1975). This book is incredibly helpful for parents in understanding children's beginning writing skills. It is especially valuable in clearly depicting the different levels children flow through in writing skill development.

What's Whole in Whole Language?, by Ken Goodman (Portsmouth, NH: Heinemann, 1987). This book answers many parents' questions about whole language, giving them a clear idea about what whole language is and isn't.

Writing Begins at Home, by Marie Clay (Portsmouth, NH: Heinemann, 1988) and *Reading Begins at Home,* by Dorothy Butler and Marie Clay (Portsmouth, NH: Heinemann, 1987).

➜ See: Areglado, pp. 278, 412; The Craft of Children's Writing, p. 32; Family Storybook Reading, p. 359; Goodman, p. 363; A Parent's Guide to Children's Reading, p. 173; Reading Begins at Home, p. 356; Spel . . . Is a Four-Letter Word, p. 149; What Did I Write?, p. 44; What's Whole in Whole Language?, p. 380.

Nancy Hyland Areglado is a language arts coordinator and primary teacher at Berkshire Hills Regional School District, West Stockbridge, MA.

Classroom Demonstrations

by Laura Robb

The Lunch Hour Workshop:
Parents and Children Learning Together

"Yes," I said to the chairperson of our library's Booked for Lunch Committee. Moments after I agreed to share thoughts about reading and storytelling with a group of men and women on their lunch hour, I began to regret my decision. More comfortable with a workshop format than with a lecture, I wondered how people would rustle lunch bags and actively participate at the same time. My telling stories while they ate lunch worked well, however, and we used the remaining time for workshop activities. The large turnout and the enthusiastic response gave birth to The Lunch Hour Workshop, which I adopted in my sixth-grade English class.

At my elementary school, more that 80 percent of both parents work full time. Therefore, getting parents involved in their children's education posed a problem. Moreover, our school had recently adopted the writing workshop and literature across the curriculum. At the parents' night program there was not enough time to respond to parents' questions. And our parents had many questions, for the writing workshop and literature across the curriculum departed dramatically from the textbook-workbook approach they had experienced as children.

My students and I worked on plans for our first lunch-hour workshop. Students wrote invitations asking parents to spend their lunch hour at school, eating and learning with their children. Most of my students liked the idea; some were a bit nervous, thinking parents would "watch" rather than participate. When students understood that parents would be part of their response groups, and that they would prepare parents for the lessons, attitudes became positive. They loved the thought of helping parents get ready to read and work in class.

I suggested that we work on the same story for our first workshop. The class agreed and unanimously chose "I Don't See George Anymore" by Philip Oakes, a story about two boys whose friendship breaks apart forever.

Students worked in small response groups to brainstorm ideas about preparing parents to read this story. Their suggestions mirrored the types of prereading activities we had done together: using the title to make predictions about the content of the story; asking a concept question like "Why wouldn't the storyteller see his friend George anymore?"; or asking an open-ended question like "What might cause a friendship to break up?" Students selected one prereading activity to do with parents at home. They would record what they discussed in their journals.

The next day I found my students eager to compare journal entries and discuss their role as teacher-facilitator. Most of the parents wanted to read the story immediately—a reaction my students have when they do an activity that creates a driving sense of anticipation. As I circulated among the groups, I heard students talk about sharing the reading of the story with parents. The I'll-read-to-you/you-read-to-me of paired reading emerged, and I realized that reading as a social experience came so naturally. One young man said, "My mom was amazed that one of her ideas about why friendships end was actually part of the story. It made her feel great." Several students said that their moms and dads were a bit nervous about joining our response groups. And I clearly heard my own voice as students responded in the teacher mode: "It's okay. Discussions are to find out what you know and understand about the story."

During the next English class groups created interpretive and evaluative questions. Each group elected a spokesperson to explain to parents the guidelines for discussion. This was important because students wanted parents to keep the "no risk" atmosphere of their response groups, to be good listeners, to respect divergent opinions, and to support ideas by using facts and inferences from the story.

Nervous parents, lunches and notebooks in hand, joined the sixth grade shortly after noon. After 15 minutes of chatting and eating, the serious business of learning began. Groups dated their journals and recorded the title of the story. Each spokesperson carefully explained the guidelines for discussion and the function of the journal. Meanwhile, I circulated and listened to discussions. Bravo, I said to myself as I heard my most timorous student tell her mother, "You need to support that point by going back to the story."

One group argued about watching movies with violence. Students said such shows had no influence on their lives; parents pointed to the boys' pretend game in the story to prove the opposite point of view. Discussions were so intense and lively that no one noticed my slipping in and out of groups.

Too soon, I had to ask everyone to take a few minutes to record important issues in their journals. Then parents and the entire class discussed the meaning of the title and the last line of the story. What emerged was a passionate exchange about guilt as a destructive force in relationships. Parents and children agreed that the act of wounding and then killing the innocent cat created a lifelong barrier between these youngsters.

During the last 10 minutes we evaluated the workshop. Parents claimed that group and class discussions were more beneficial than filling in a workbook. Not having enough time to talk about all the ideas that surfaced was their only complaint. However, many looked forward to continuing the dialogue with their children at home. All saw the merit of using the journal to explore ideas. Writing, they observed, gave them time to think, evaluate, and change. My class and I inwardly cheered when every parent voted for more lunchtime workshops.

Students observed that their parents brought different perspectives to the story. "Because they're older," said one astute youngster. What a powerful lesson for us all—that our views on stories change as we grow and gain more experience. A wonderful reason for returning to stories again and again.

Our workshops continue, but from my point of view, the best benefit is that many students now read and discuss unassigned material with their parents. "It's fun and challenging," they tell me. "We even do it with movies and TV programs." Such activities foster positive and productive interaction among parents and children. When parents actively participate in their children's learning, they come to appreciate and understand departures from their own learning traditions. Moreover, each group quickly learns to value diversity and respect one another's opinions.

➡ See: Cress, p. 371; Kaczmarek, p. 368; Robb, p. 198.

Reference

Oakes, P. 1973. "I don't see George anymore." In *Strange fish and other stories,* ed. Leon Garfield. New York: Lothrop, Lee & Shepard.

Laura Robb is a middle school teacher at Powhatan School, Boyce, VA.

Classroom Demonstrations

Kinderbulletin

Reading Pat Robinson's weekly newsletter is the next best thing to being in her kindergarten classroom yourself. My daughter Erin, age five and a student of Pat's, loves to help me catch up on her week at school as we read the newsletter together.

—LBB

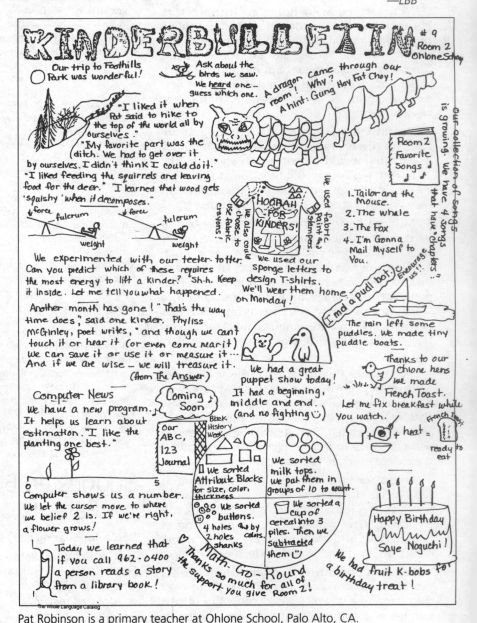

Pat Robinson is a primary teacher at Ohlone School, Palo Alto, CA.

As Teachers See It

by Laurel Cress

Shall We Point Fingers or Play Ball?
A Plan for Improving Parent-Teacher Relationships

Unfortunately, this cartoon is more sad than funny because it is so often true. These days, parents and teachers seem to spend more time pointing fingers than they do clasping hands in friendship. Children learn from their adult models. There is a lot of talk in education about cooperative learning, but if we want children to learn to cooperate we must begin by cooperating ourselves.

During the previous school year I had the privilege of playing on a softball team with the parents of one of the children in my kindergarten class. Because I saw Cathi and Harry every week, I regularly heard how their child was responding at home to what we were doing at school. Even after the season ended, Cathi would frequently step inside the classroom to share a funny story or discuss a concern. I enjoyed telling her about what her daughter was doing in the classroom and sharing with her the new things I was learning, particularly the research I was reading about literacy development. Cathi and Harry became strong supporters of my beginning whole language program.

Though I can't play softball with the parents of all the children in my class, I know there must be other ways to get to know them better in order to share with them, learn from them, and bond with them. I'd like to share with you two ideas I have for building relationships with parents:

Parent-Teacher Dialogue Journals

Through parent-teacher dialogue journals I hope to create the kind of ongoing communication I had with Cathi and Harry on the softball field. I plan to send composition books home on the very first day of school with a letter summarizing my philosophy of how children learn. I will invite the parents to write back to me, and to question or comment on my educational philosophy. I will also encourage them to write about anything they choose.

Will the parents write? I'm sure that some will and some won't. I hope that the journals will open the door of communication for working parents whom I don't see outside the classroom door when I say good-bye to the kids, and for parents who might be shy about speaking to me in person.

Monthly Parent Meetings

There are many practical issues teachers must consider in preparing for monthly parent meetings—how to help parents find the time to attend, what to do with their children while they are at the meeting, what to say and do once they've arrived. In fact, it's tempting to ask, why bother at all?

My answer is that once parents understand the underlying whole language philosophy, they can further their child's learning at home. It is my experience that parents care about what I do in the classroom and want to be informed. And the most effective way to communicate with parents is to contact them personally and directly.

In the book *Breaking Ground* (Hansen, Newkirk, and Graves 1985), Winnifred Braun describes how parents, who were initially critical of her whole language program, became supportive after she took the time to explain her philosophy and respond to their concerns in a parent meeting. She concludes:

> My communication with parents provided a valuable learning experience—for them and also for me. I learned the importance of explaining to parents what I do in school, particularly those aspects which are foreign to parents' own school experiences. The effort I put forth in explanation has been valuable for my own professional growth.

➔ See: Cress, p. 90.

Reference

Hansen, J., R. Newkirk, and D. Graves, eds. 1985. *Breaking ground: Teachers relate reading and writing in the elementary school.* Portsmouth, NH: Heinemann.

Laurel Cress is a bilingual primary teacher at Longwood School, Hayward, CA.

Resource: Book

Kids Can Cook: Vegetarian Recipes Kitchen-Tested by Kids for Kids

Dorothy R. Bates
1987; 119 pp.; $8.95
Summertown, TN: Book Publishing Co.

This basic cookbook for young chefs is filled with recipes for vegetarian foods children like to eat and cook themselves. There are sections on menu ideas, kitchen safety rules, and helpful cooking hints, as well as plenty of illustrations. Lots of tasty sweet treats and wholesome entrées to tempt the budding cook in your family are included.

Kids Cooking: A Very Slightly Messy Manual

The editors of Klutz Press
1987; 77 pp.; $9.95
Palo Alto, CA: Klutz Press

What a great cookbook! Who could resist a book filled with recipes like Not-So-Sloppy Joes, Frozen Bananoids, and Darrell's Forget-the-Cookies-Just-Give-Me-That-Batter Chocolate Chip Cookie Recipe? The book is filled with playful, imaginative, color illustrations in the Klutz tradition and even comes with its own set of measuring spoons.

Arrietta Chakos

Whole Language Internacional

by Nan Bonfils

A Malaysian Classroom In Transition—Take Parents with You

I see our classrooms here at the International School of Kuala Lumpur in the flux of change—waves of enthusiasm tempered with stalls of doubt. We are, at best, in transition.

I would like to share a strategy I used for taking parents with you, an essential component for any teacher in transition. This one worked.

When I met parents at an early back-to-school night, I spoke only generally and innocuously about a more integrated language arts program. I continued to maintain a low profile of change until first quarter conferences. There I distributed two items—an NCTE pamphlet for promoting writing at home and an invitation for a genuine open classroom visit about three weeks later.

This open house took place during the school day and was totally designed by the students. With a genuine audience in mind (Mom and Dad) and a real purpose (to explain what is going on in this room), students had no trouble putting together a program.

They brainstormed topics that needed to be covered (e.g., journals, writing folders, reading logs, new format of spelling tests, homework, etc.). They drafted speeches for each topic, tried them out on their peers who role-played unenlightened parents, and revised accordingly. Then they practiced delivery and listening.

On the day of the actual event, my role was small. I directed a vocabulary game for parents to play as latecomers straggled in. I scheduled the speakers and sat in the back with a big smile. I made a video to share with the administration and parents who were unable to attend.

My concluding remarks were brief indeed. I didn't have to do much explaining of integrated listening, speaking, writing, and reading. My audience was *in* it. I did offer to share a few books (Hansen, Calkins, and Routman, etc.) from my personal collection.

The session wrapped up with an invitation to parents to come back at any time and to leave an entry in their child's journal for us to read. "Please write in responses to these two questions: 'How has your understanding of our language arts program been modified by this morning's visit? What questions would you like to ask?'" I said. Reluctant parents were coached and coaxed by eager children. "It's okay. You can just write what you think. The spelling doesn't matter," they said.

Taking parents with me really paid off. The most common question I got was, "How can I help?" So our special open house left me with a flock of parents eager to read, respond, transcribe, and type. It also saved me a lot of potential transition trouble and kept the door open all year.

➔ See: Bonfils, p. 135.

Nan Bonfils is an elementary teacher at the International School of Kuala Lumpur, Kuala Lumpur, Malaysia.

Great Teachers:
R. F. Whitlow

by Richard D. McCallum

Master Teacher

The question what makes a master teacher may be difficult to answer in concrete terms but, as the expression goes, you know one when you see one. To many of those who have come to know him over the last 15 years, R. F. (Bob) Whitlow is the genuine article. Over the course of the last seven years I have had the opportunity to observe the impact of a teacher and a program on children's literacy development. This experience has directly shaped my views on teaching and learning. To understand the professional development of Bob Whitlow and to gain a sense of the type of teacher he is today, one needs to know some of the history and development of Charquin, where he has been teaching for 15 years.

Parents are an integral part of Charquin, and were instrumental in developing the program. Parents and teachers of Charquin share a common set of beliefs about the best way to educate their children. A parent handbook, developed in 1983–84, articulates the basic goals of the program:

1. To facilitate learning in an environment that respects the individual dignity of every child;
2. To allow children to share in the planning of their education;
3. To maximize the development of their feelings of self-worth and positive self-image;
4. To allow children to learn according to their own developmental timetable;
5. To encourage respect for our natural environment and all its inhabitants; and
6. To allow parents a maximum of participation in the education of their children.

Realizing the goals of Charquin requires alternative management decisions. Charquin differs from traditional classrooms in several important ways. First, Charquin is a parent

cooperative. Parent participation, in some form, is required for entry into the program. Second, students are heterogeneously grouped. Students between the ages of five and twelve may find themselves in the same classroom working on the same projects. Third, students can enter kindergarten and remain in the program until the sixth grade. Such continuity creates a sense of family and community, which is characteristic of the program.

At Charquin decisions are made in the context of the goals of the program and an unstated "Bill of Rights" for all participants:

- Article 1: The right to be a kid
- Article 2: The right to make mistakes
- Article 3: The right to be treated fairly
- Article 4: The right to be heard

At the heart of Charquin and central to Bob's beliefs about education lies a concern for the "whole" person—whether student, parent, or teacher. Such concern is evident in the goals of the program, the management decisions made, the "Bill of Rights," and the day-to-day operation of the classroom.

Bob's attention to the affective dimension of learning makes school fun. Concern for students' interests and motivation can be seen in the basic layout and day-to-day operation at Charquin. Currently, Charquin is housed in four adjacent rooms. All of the rooms are characterized by an "information explosion." The hallway is a gallery of student art and other work. Cartoons, newspa-

per articles, messages, maps, photographs, thematic posters, and other paraphernalia adorn almost every exposed surface.

There are no student desks in Charquin. Instruction occurs at various centers located throughout the rooms. Students can be found in all work areas as well as in the hallway and school yard. Groups also meet "around the rug," the area where most large group activities take place. Students must attend the centers at some point, but when they do so is up to them.

Charquin students like school. As one parent noted, "My son loves school. The idea of not liking school has never crossed his mind. He was shocked by his friends who constantly talk about hating school."

Teachers, like children and parents, change. A holistic approach to literacy instruction and, more specifically, a meaning-based focus in reading, evident in Bob's instruction, developed over a period of years. After several years of working with basal materials and developing a general orientation to reading instruction (what would today be considered child-centered and meaning-based), Bob was confronted by a parent who insisted that DISTAR (a direct instruction phonics-based program) be taught during reading class. Although Bob knew intuitively that his approach was preferable for the majority of students, he found himself unable to show the parent that DISTAR may undermine rather than reinforce comprehension.

This confrontation was a turning point: It provided an impetus for Bob to reapply himself to the study of reading and literacy development. He went back to school, attended workshops and summer institutes, talked to people, borrowed ideas, and resolved questions of their

Great Schools

Charquin

A Family in the Classroom
by Gloria Wilber Fearn

Charquin, 1988 winner of the California School Board Association's Golden Bell Award in reading and language arts, has been an innovator in all curriculum areas.

Surprisingly, it is not the progressive teaching methods that bring dozens of observers to Charquin, a parent cooperative K–6 alternative program at Markham Elementary School in Hayward, California. It is Charquin's parent participation that most impresses people. Charquin has approximately ninety students, three teachers in four classrooms. Seventy-five to eighty percent of participating families provide an adult (mother, father, grandparent) who works with children in the classroom one day per week. The expertise and enthusiasm with which these parents pursue classroom activities is remarkable.

Fifteen to twenty parents are present in the classrooms every day. They run centers in gardening, art, science, drama, puppetry, language arts, math, quilting, needle craft, and so on.

They bring instructional materials from home and work, and share their lives with children. For example, Shakespearean productions are directed by one parent who used to be a drama coach. Another parent, a chiropractor, does an outstanding unit on the human body. Props for stage plays, giant papier-mâché animals, and murals are other projects that parents supervise.

Whereas some parents are experts in their field, most parents spend several weeks in the classroom before finally seeing a need or developing a new interest. These parents may find materials and talk with other parents, teachers, and students. They grow, learn, and teach at the same time. In Charquin's multiage-grouped, team-teaching environment these parents may stick with the same theme for six or seven years. As their skills

and interests grow, parents may evolve into teachers of other parents.

So, how is it that Charquin has been successful in encouraging so many parents to participate so competently? Part of the answer is tradition. Charquin was started by parents in 1973. Since that time parents have exercised real ownership. Charquin belongs to the parents and children.

All parents are members of the Charquin Parent Committee, which is the policy-making body for the program. Parent Committee decisions are made through open debate, fact finding, and much soul searching.

Charquin classrooms are set up in a way that makes parent participation a requirement. They are loosely arranged "centers," staffed by parents who guide the day's activities. This arrangement offers many choices to parents. Every year a number of parents start new projects. Charquin's award-winning garden was started by one parent. The tradition of a major yearly musical production was started by another. Two parents developed a fantastic science program. Then one moved on and teamed up with her husband to start "Land of Blue Sky," a center

Great Schools

Pre-School Family

respective worth by trying them in the classroom.

Sensing the inevitability of change for everyone involved in education is both practical and personal for Bob. As Charquin grew from a class of 24 kids, K–4, and one teacher to its current size, there were two choices for Bob: Accept change as a natural process or fight against it. Bob chose the former.

Bob is a diplomat's diplomat. Meeting the needs and desires of parents, kids, and fellow teachers requires finely tuned "people skills": empathy, listening, and communicating often difficult and painful messages in a sensitive manner. Without these abilities Bob would not have achieved the same amount of success at Charquin.

You learn more from listening than from talking. Working with people and getting things done requires an ability to listen. Listening is the central element in sound communication characteristic of all of Bob's interactions.

Laughter is the tonic for the spirit. Everyone laughs at some point during the day at Charquin, and Bob sets the tempo. Whether it results from a silly joke or an offhand remark, laughter can be found in Charquin, and a safe bet is that it will be coming from Bob's room.

Bob Whitlow is a master teacher. He combines solid teaching methodology with a developmental perspective that is sensitive to the whole child. He has shown that parent participation and education are not mutually exclusive. There is a common ground which benefits everyone. He has reminded us that there are alternatives to current management practices. And finally, Bob has shown that diplomacy, tact, and a sense of humor are essential tools for teachers.

Richard D. McCallum is a professor of education at St. Mary's College of California, Moraga, CA.

A Historical Overview
by Eleanora Jadwin

It was in 1946 when a small group of mothers and children met and called themselves Pre-School Family. Little did they know what they were beginning or how it would grow to its present size in 4 years. They knew the idea was unique, but they never could have guessed how many parents then and in the future would be drawn to this notion of parent education.

Very few people, educators among them, considered that preschoolers might go to school. The idea that parents would or should be involved in their child's education was a revolutionary idea. Parenting skills and expertise were taken for granted, acquired with the birth of a child. These first Pre-School Family parents wanted a place to observe their children, to see their uniqueness, to learn what was typical behavior for their children's age.

The idea and force behind Pre-School Family was a petite, soft-spoken, woman named Besse Bolton. The character of the program is due mainly to the vision and determination of Besse. She conceived the idea of Pre-School Family after being a successful wife, mother of four children, and an experienced educator. When her youngest child was in kindergarten, Besse placed her in school on the San Jose State campus and went back to school herself, choosing early childhood education as her field of interest. Commenting on this choice, she said, "My life was absorbed with young children. I knew I wanted to know more about the little children I was rearing."

As a kindergarten teacher at Addison School in Palo Alto, California, Besse invited parents, mostly mothers, to observe her classroom and help with snacks, wraps, and other simple things. She began to realize that parents had different expectations for their children. She found herself wanting to help parents accept the feelings and emotions of their children, treat them as individuals, allow them to be open and honest, and make the family an accepting place. At this time Besse took a leave from teaching for a year, went to Stanford University, and tried to learn how to work with families as families.

When she returned to Addison the next year, she was told she could not teach half a day and counsel parents the other half. Her idea would not fly. She was so convinced of her idea that she resigned from her teaching job, gathered a group of interested parents, and went to Palo Alto Adult Education to sell the idea there. It sold and Pre-School Family was born.

The first class opened mainly because of the work and sweat of those first parents. The program moved almost yearly for the next 20 years—from schools, to churches, to cottages, to basements, to wherever space could be found. It was a lesson in tenacity and flexibility.

The program, then as now, was built around the idea of parents observing and writing about their children and then discussing child development at evening or lunchtime discussions. Besse Bolton guided the program until 1962. She died in 1985 at the age of 89. When Betty Rogaway, a teacher in the program, became director, there were one-day classes for two- and three-year-olds and two-day classes for four-year-olds. Adult discussions were held every week. Under Betty's leadership, days were increased. Young Fives was born in 1975 and parent support groups with infants and toddlers began in 1978. During her tenure the program also housed a state preschool program for disadvantaged preschoolers and saw the placement on site of a special-education class for preschoolers to enable mainstreaming.

In 1983 I became the third director of Pre-School Family. During the last five years our school has grown to 18 classes and involves close to 300 families. We run two 17-week semesters, and classes for children vary from 1 1/2 hours to 3 hours, 20 minutes. Single-day classes meet twice a month for adult discussions and multiple-day classes meet three times per month. Because we are a parent education program, the State of California reimburses us for adult attendance. That enables us to offer reasonable tuition for materials and teacher salaries. It also makes our program available to a broader spectrum of the public.

The original intent of Pre-School Family, to provide a place for parents to observe and learn about their children, is still the integral part of the program, 43 years later. We are a parent education program, where parenting is validated and its joys and tribulations are shared. We adamantly believe that our program must be developmentally appropriate for young children—emotionally, physically, socially, and cognitively. And we believe we must enable parents to know and understand the development and needs of young children. We hope we are knowledgeable facilitators. We know that parenting can be honed by experts and books, but we also know that daily living and learning with children constantly raises questions for us all. We hope to provide counsel, advice, encouragement, and, most of all, support. We hope to give parents an opportunity, in a nurturing environment, to learn about their unique child and to help them understand and appreciate who that child is becoming.

Eleanora Jadwin is the program supervisor of Pre-School Family, Palo Alto, CA.

that teaches science concepts and Charquin values through a peaceful and constructive game of fantasy.

During the 1970s many programs tried to do what Charquin does and failed. What makes Charquin such a notable success? Most parents would probably say "our teachers." I'd second that. Bob Whitlow has been with the program since 1974. Norma Oden came in 1984. Karen McCutcheon is new this year. The program has had only five teachers since it opened with one classroom in 1973. Three of the five teachers are currently on staff. The longevity, commitment, and talents of Charquin's teachers have given the program continuity and helped it develop tradition and stability. Charquin's teachers are open, supportive, and professional people who are dedicated to teaching children and convinced of the value of parents as educators.

Information is freely shared among parents, children and teachers. This free flow of information is a major characteristic of Charquin. A Parent Committee meets every five weeks. There are Steering Committee and Parent-Teacher Liaison Club meetings, and curriculum committees for the various centers. The parent newsletter is sent out monthly, and memos from teachers and parents are sent home frequently.

Charquin teachers and parents are constantly involved in adult education. Over the years teacher/parent interest in changing instructional methods has presented many opportunities for adult education curriculum. Developing this curriculum is, as always, a cooperative process between teachers and parents. Teachers often serve as the catalysts, taking courses, sharing what they learn, and inspiring parents to educate themselves and engage other parents in the pursuit of knowledge.

At Charquin parents, teachers, and children have developed tradition, built community, and learned to support each other. Teachers keep coming back with new ideas every year. Family members work together, argue together, eat lunch together, play together, and engage in sport, art, drama, and other cultural pleasures.

Family is the word that participants most often use when describing Charquin. *Caring* is probably the second most common word. Charquin is a place where members of the larger "Charquin family" are cared for, supported, and involved in shaping their own continuing education. It is a place where people work together to provide what today's children need: an empowering educational environment in which family, community, and school resources are brought together and shared.

→ See: MacCalla, p. 343; Pessah, p. 347; Peterson, p. 348.

Gloria Wilber Fearn is a freelance writer and a parent alumna at Charquin, Hayward, CA.

Parents' Perspective

by Judith Larner Lowry

Cats

Like every parent in our multigrade, project-oriented classroom, I am required to work in the classroom for one period a week. At the beginning of the year, I worked with a group of six or seven first- and second-graders who were somewhat overwhelmed by the vibrant and confident older kids who had been in the Pine Gulch classroom for years. I wanted to spend my time in the classroom working on a project just for them, one that would grab the kids with a subject dear to their hearts.

At home we had just become owners of a stray kitten, which was carrying every disease the vet could think of. My seven-year-old was entranced not only by the sweet purring nature of our new kitten, but also by the twice-daily applications of eye drops, nose drops, ear drops, and antibiotics. Thinking about the kids in the group before my next classroom visit, I realized that they all had cats too. So the idea of writing, reading, and learning about cats emerged.

That morning I asked children to fill out a Cat Information Sheet, indicating their cat's name, color, approximate weight, favorite food, favorite toy, and best friend. Children also drew a picture of their cat. We read the sheets to the class at large, thus announcing our project to the older kids.

We decided to use invented spelling, since the children's frequent requests for "the right way to spell words" were ruining my enjoyment of the writing process. So, freed from the need to spell correctly, we began to write true stories about adventures our cats had had. Most were quite grim, involving various kinds of accidents where "the insides came out." We also wrote fantasy stories about adventures our cats might have had, which proved much tamer than reality.

As time went along, we kept thinking of more cat-related endeavors. We wrote a continuing story of a cat's adventure: Each child wrote and illustrated one page of the story. I went to each child's house and took slides of his or her cat, alone and in the arms of its owner. The children were thrilled to present the continuing story and the slides to the entire class.

We read *Millions of Cats, Dick Whittington and His Cat*, numerous reference books on training and owning cats, and many picture books with irresistible illustrations of kittens and cats. The volume of cat literature surprised me, as I delved into the history of the domesticated cat and the nature of the cat-lover.

We kept planning various finales to the project, such as interviewing the local vet on the subject of cats, but new ideas kept coming to the fore. Much to our surprise, the project lasted for an entire school year. The visit to the vet was definitely a highlight. We wrote down appropriate questions to ask such as: Do cats have knees? Do cats get married? Do cats blink? Will it hurt cats to eat dog food or dogs to eat cat food? How far can a cat fall without getting hurt? How can you keep a cat alive a long time? (The vet knew an 80-year-old woman who brushed her 26-year-old cat's teeth every day and watched its favorite TV programs.) We made a group drawing called "The Cats of Pine Gulch" as a thank-you to the vet. (It still resides on the bulletin board, something for the kids to be proud of when they take their pet to the vet.)

For our finale, we went on a field trip to my house for "cat observation." The rules for cat observation are: Write down everything the cat does for a specified amount of time and do not interact with the cat in any way. We set the timer for 10 minutes and became so engrossed in the doings of this relatively inactive cat that we unanimously decided to set the timer again for another 10 minutes. Then we conceived the more ambitious project of sharing this procedure with the entire class by bringing the cat into the classroom. We talked about how differently the cat might behave in a strange environment.

On Cat Observation Day, we put chairs in a circle, explained the rules, and handed out Cat Observation Sheets for recording observations. I set the timer for 15 minutes, during which time not a sound was made. The cat obviously did not enjoy the situation and tried to escape. At the end, we read some of the observations aloud. Interestingly, the younger kids recorded their observations without editorializing, while some of the older kids turned their observations into intense dramas of cat longings and fears.

What I most enjoyed about Cat Observation Day, the conclusion of a year-long project, was the utter silence and absorption in the classroom as the children tuned into and lost themselves in the strange unknowable world of the cat.

→ See: Literature Reference List, p. 429; Lowry, p. 305.

Judith Larner Lowry is the owner of Larner Seeds, Bolinas, CA.

Great Teachers:
Yvonne Siu-Runyan

by Dale W. Vigil

There is discussion, if not insistence, that public schools need a revolution. Some educators are crying for different structures. Others are reminiscing about the success they had in the "good old days." The debate continues between educators who are uncomfortable with change and those who want to restructure public education. Systemic change needs to happen from the bottom up as well as from the top down.

Great teachers know how to provide opportunities for learning by coaching, observing, cheering, asking the right questions of their students, and teaching. These teachers provide a unique blend that visitors feel immediately when they step inside their classrooms. The teachers themselves are part of the community of learners. They instill in the students the idea of teamwork and encourage risk-taking.

Yvonne Siu-Runyan is this kind of learner/teacher. Always striving to improve the process, she creates a classroom environment that supports developmental learning. The students are self-starters and decision-makers in their daily quest for knowledge.

The learning opportunities Yvonne provides are organized through thematic units that have integrated the content into a meaningful context. Students respond naturally to the collective decision-making activities that are focused around concepts, strategies, and literacies. Yvonne orchestrates this ensemble. Young people learn to express their thoughts, ideas, and feelings as writers and orators. Their inquisitive nature is respected and encouraged as they investigate, probe, think, challenge, and draw their own conclusions. Yvonne nurtures this learning through status-of-the-class conferences, verbal contracts, and minilessons.

It is wonderful to see her students in action. They know how and where to seek information as they research topics of their own choosing. Yvonne's students understand that through collaboration, learning becomes more interesting and they become more productive. They use the computer to store their work and do their writing. Most important, these young students already know what literacy can bring them. They appreciate reading good literature. Some stu-

dents have sent the school librarian letters recommending titles by such authors as Richard Smith, R. A. Montgomery, and Edward Packerd. Through class surveys these students know what authors and themes are more popular in the classroom. They also are comfortable sharing their impressions of books. And they especially enjoy being writers. The standard that Yvonne has established is reflected in two of her students who received the Young Author Award given by the Colorado Council of the International Reading Association. One placed second and the other honorable mention.

Good teachers model sharing and writing with their colleagues the same way they want their students to model with their peers in their own classrooms. Yvonne has done this and more. She has worked with teachers and administrators in the district, state, and nation. Her classroom is a laboratory not only for young students but for adult students as well. Educators interested in effective change for students frequently observe and interact with Yvonne and her pupils. She has also reached educators and parents through her booklet *Supporting Your Child's Writing Development*, which has a circulation of over 40,000 copies. This booklet is being used throughout the United States and Canada as well as in several other countries.

Yvonne's classroom learning environment is thoughtfully and carefully shaped by her philosophy of learning and teaching. It is an example of the bottom-up changes that are dramatically influencing public education in a positive way. A teacher like Yvonne, who by design appears not to stand out in a classroom personally but who obviously stands out professionally through students' excitement and progress, is a great teacher.

Dale W. Vigil is the director of the Department of Bilingual/Second Language Education, Denver Public Schools, and a member of the Board of Education, Boulder Valley Public Schools.

Resource: Booklet

Supporting Your Child's Writing Development

Yvonne Siu-Runyan
For $1.95 from:
Curriculum Division
Boulder Valley Public Schools
6500 E. Arapahoe
Boulder, CO 80301
1-303-447-1010

This concise booklet addresses parents' questions and concerns about the writing development of children. Yvonne Siu-Runyan's clear explanations and hints make this a great resource to distribute to parents. Questions and comments to guide the child and a short bibliography are included.

Education in Turin: A Romance by Herbert Kohl

Continued from page 366

Beginning Again:
The Impact of Sputnik

From 1941 to the early 1950s, during and just after World War II, education was not a major public concern. During the early 1950s, Robert S. Rogers was made principal of the Turin Elementary School. He was supported by a large new middle class that had developed during the postwar economic boom. They wanted an efficient school that would pass students on so they could eventually get into the newly expanded state college system.

In addition, Rogers, who was a political moderate, had the job of keeping things quiet and not letting the unpleasantness associated with the departure of Walter Johnson, the former principal, recur. Discussion of socially progressive ideas was muted while Congress, led by the histrionics of Joseph McCarthy and James O. Eastland, conducted anticommunist hearings. Some people even whispered about Phillip Burns and remembered his mother's socialist ideas. In order to protect his children from unpleasantness, he decided not to stand for reelection to the Turin Unified School District school board.

Concern about the nature and quality of education became a national issue again only after the Russians launched Sputnik in 1957. The effect of Sputnik was to focus educational concern on the development of excellence, particularly in the areas of science and technol-

ogy. In 1961 President Kennedy established the Office of Science and Technology at the Executive Office of the White House and convened a series of meetings of physicists, mathematicians, biologists, chemists, and other scientists, and set them to work on what later became the new math, the new biology, the new physics. These curricula used "learning by doing" principles, and had many hands-on activities. But what chiefly characterized them was a systematic approach to subject matter based on current scientific knowledge and an emphasis on critical thinking and problem-solving. The goal was to produce many young scientists and engineers.

The principal in Turin was quick to adopt the new science and new math programs, especially since the material was purchased with federal money. When the material arrived at the school, there was excitement at first and then bewilderment. The teachers received elegant, beautifully packaged, scientifically sound material that ignored their teaching styles, the organization and structure of their classrooms, and the nature of children. They tried to use what little they understood of the materials, but they complained they didn't have enough time to teach the new program as well as all the other things expected of them. Most of the material remained in the closet, unopened.

Continued on page 393

Resource: Pamphlet

Parents . . . Partners in Education

The American Association of School Administrators
1801 North Moore St.
Arlington, VA
22209-9988
1-703-528-0700

Parents won't need convincing that they play a critical role in their children's learning after reading the small but cogent "Parents . . . Partners in Education," available in English, Spanish, Vietnamese, Lao, Cambodian, and Hmong—a real boon in our multicultural times. To order, write The American Association of School Administrators, which issues an excellent catalog with a wide variety of topics for school boards, administrators, and parents.

Resource: Organizations

The Center for Parent Education

Burton L White, Ph.D., director
55 Chapel St.
Newton, MA 02160
1-617-964-2442

The Center for Parent Education offers assistance to professionals concerned with the education of children in the first three years of life. Acknowledging the importance of parents as a child's very first teachers, the center initiated the New Parents As Teachers project in the state of Missouri, and now offers the program in Massachusetts. Trainers, who are experts in child development, make regular home visits to the family, starting during pregnancy and continuing until the child is three years old. The objective is to teach parents how to observe, stimulate, and oversee the development of their babies, in order to give them the best possible start in life. Independent evaluations of the program suggest that children in the program consistently demonstrate advanced

intellectual and language development. The Center for Parent Education publishes a bimonthly newsletter and offers consultation, professional training institutes and workshops, and audiovisual materials for training staff and parents. A bibliography of related readings is available.

Debbie Montgomery

National Association of Partners in Education, Inc. (NAPE)

601 Wythe St.,
Ste. 200
Alexandria, VA 22314
1-703-836-4880

NAPE represents schools, businesses, community groups, educators, and volunteers who work together as partners to enhance the education of children. It publishes monthly and quarterly newsletters for members and has a computer data base on school volunteer and partnership programs. NAPE publications cover a wide range of topics on volunteering and partnerships, including useful manuals to help guide program start-ups.

Arrieta Chakos

NWTC Nursery School Dinosaur Story

by Nathan Volz

A million years ago there was a father dinosaur (Tyrannosaurus Rex) and two baby dinosaurs, one named Eric and one named Emily. When they got hungry the father dinosaur put on his "knocking down" tail and knocked down some palm trees so they could eat. One was for lunch, one was for supper, and one was for dessert. Then the volcano exploded with red fire.

Nathan Volz is four years old. This was contributed by Barbara Dier, a nursery lab schoolteacher, Northeast Wisconsin Technical College, Green Bay, WI.

Resource: Periodical

News for Parents in *Reading Today*

From:
International Reading Association
800 Barksdale Rd.
P.O. Box 8139
Newark, DE 19714-8139

"News for Parents" appears six times a year in *Reading Today*, the membership newspaper of the IRA. The column, edited by John Micklos, brings items and ideas of interest to parents. Typical topics include book resources for parents and brief anecdotes about renowned children's authors. The IRA does not endorse the books mentioned in the column.

Arrietta Chakos

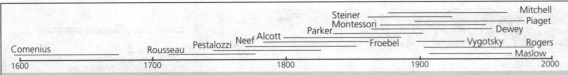

Pioneers: Lucy Sprague Mitchell (1878-1967)

by **Yetta M. Goodman**

Whole Language Teacher, Teacher Educator, Researcher

Lucy Sprague Mitchell is called a woman "before her time," but she was also a woman of her time. She was an educator, during the early part of this century, who was concerned with issues of humanism and science, concerns compatible with those that face whole language today. She provides an example for the active involvement of women in developing supportive, healthy educational lives for children and teachers.

Mitchell and her female colleagues wanted experiences for children that would capture their interests and expand their worlds. They studied children's language and conceptual development. They organized preschool and elementary school programs for children of all socioeconomic backgrounds in both private and public sectors. They wrote about social studies education, the teaching of geography, teacher education, and child language development. They wrote relevant reading materials. Joyce Antler captures this time period in a wonderful biography, *Lucy Sprague Mitchell: The Making of a Modern Woman* (1987), showing how Mitchell touched the lives of others, influencing their development as they influenced hers. Mitchell was a contemporary of and collaborated with

- Margaret Wise Brown, a children's author who started her writing in a Writer's Laboratory at Bank Street College;
- Caroline Pratt in developing the Play School Movement, which focused on preschool and early childhood education;
- Elizabeth Irwin in organizing the Little Red Schoolhouse;
- Harriet Johnson, who was concerned with scientific research on child development;
- Julia Richman, who contributed to public education and education of the "whole child";
- Evelyn Dewey in organizing progressive schools;
- Jesse Stanton, who was able to see the world through the eyes of children;
- Barbara Biber, who built bridges between the fields of psychology and education;
- and many of the women listed above and others in establishing Bank Street College to provide a supportive and cooperative working environment for teaching, writing, and research.

Jane Addams and Lillian Wald, the major social reformers of the day, also influenced Mitchell. It is sad that I had never been made aware of the influence these women had on progressive, humanistic, and holistic education. But I had been made very aware of John Dewey, G. Stanley Hall, William Kilpatrick, George Santayana, and Edward Thorndike who also influenced Mitchell.

Was I more aware of the males because of issues of sexism or the status between those considered "theorists and researchers" compared with those considered "practitioners"? Probably a bit of both. The politics of referencing is related to sexism and elitism (of supposed researchers over supposed practitioners—I say *supposed* because all of these women were involved in researching children in home, school, and play settings). As I examine the bibliographies of men in the field, there is a great tendency to reference each other and to ignore the work of women.

Things are similar today. Women are involved in classroom research and changing school practice. Teachers are also finding their voices and are writing for each other in newsletters, magazines, and books. It is possible that these modern women will also become invisible as the history of education is written. Perhaps more female historians such as Antler will help keep women educationists visible. Perhaps female teachers and researchers must think about the lesson to be learned and reference more carefully, keeping an eye on their own influences and stature.

This short essay introduces Mitchell's biography and suggests that it be read by whole language advocates. Vito Perrone, in a recent work, *Working Papers: Reflections on Teachers, Schools and Communities* (1989), especially recommends Mitchell's *Our Children and Our Schools*. Some direct quotes of Mitchell's work appear elsewhere in the catalog. Finally, this article is a backdrop for her article on the teaching of geography, which fits well with current concerns for geography and education and the interest of whole language teachers in integrating social studies with the language arts.

References

Antler, J. 1987. *Lucy Sprague Mitchell: The making of a modern woman.* New Haven, CT: Yale University Press.
Mitchell, L. S. 1950. *Our children and our schools.* New York: Simon & Schuster.
Perrone, V. 1989. *Working papers: Reflections on teachers, schools and communities.* New York: Teachers College Press.

Maps as Art Expression
by Lucy Sprague Mitchell

If a map means the representation of a part of the earth's surface with reference to the relative positions of certain factors, then it is fair to say that in the City and Country School, maps begin in block-building. The general floor play of "boats" on "water" or "elevated" on "streets" or "trains" on "land" early develops into ferries, ocean liners, barges in the Upper and Lower Bays or on the Hudson, the Sixth Avenue Elevated crossing the familiar streets around Twelfth Street, or the Pennsylvania Railroad. So that with five-year-olds a floor scheme will often represent true locational relationships actually observed by the children on their trips. Of course much practice in orientation of the children in their own immediate surroundings—their classroom in the building, their school in reference to their homes, and so on—precedes and determines such observation. These floor maps are incidental to play. They are simply the children's recall of particular aspects of their actual experiences.

From the early floor-scheme maps where water may appear as wavy chalk lines on the linoleum floor and four or five buildings important to the children appear as block constructions placed in their relative positions and where the block-constructed boats or the bench-made autos and trucks move along their respective highways—from these early floor maps there is a logical development to the decorative map of the world, or to a symbolic map of Indian tribes and their modes of life, or to a scientific map of the life of cows in the United States in relation to the kind of lands and kind of workers needed for their progress from the grassy plain to the table. The early orientation of the children facilitates the translation of geographic observations into symbols. This early use of symbols to record their own observations leads to an understanding of scientific maps of human or earth factors, and to consequent ability to use such scientific maps independently as tools in their own study.

But it is equally true that the maps originated as play—a reliving of an actual experience. This play element persists in the development of map-making in the school until it reaches a pitch of organization which ranks many of the maps as art. The children in the early stages make no distinction between science and art in their recalls of their experiences. With the older children—perhaps from ten to twelve—their keen analysis of all their own processes makes many of them distinguish between play-maps and real maps. There is no absolute or genuine distinction, however. It is merely a matter of emphasis. The play-map pretends to less accuracy than the real map. The real map on the other hand seldom appears in the school without some element which the child put there for the sake of form or beauty, rather than as a help to the understanding. It has, therefore, a play, an art, element. Maps as tools for study and maps as expressions of form do not conflict in the children's minds. Is it too much to hope that the children will never make the devastating divorces of these two elements which makes most adults feel that a scientist cannot be an artist or an artist a scientist?

From Progressive Education 3(2), April/May/June 1926.

Classroom Demonstrations
by Denise Ogren

Sharing with Parents

We write many class books in my kindergarten. Our first book is usually about our trip to the apple orchard. Each child writes about the trip and draws a picture on red paper shaped like an apple. Children read their messages to me, and I edit them, type them up, and glue them on the apple picture. The pages are glued back to front and then laminated and hooked together with metal rings. Children check the book out for the night. This year I included a message to the parents in the front of the book:

> Dear Readers,
> This book is a result of our trip to the apple orchard. The children drew their own pictures and wrote their own words. They then read me their messages and I edited them for our first class book. Please take some time to read this with your child. Return this book tomorrow so other children can have a chance to take it home. We would like your own comments about our book. Please add your words at the end of our book.

Here are some of the comments written by the parents:

> I think the book was cute and very imaginative. David read most of the book to me. I had to help him with a few of the names and words.

> I think this book is creative. Kassi likes to pretend to read making her own words, but still shows she's interested in reading or putting a story together that was made by her friends.

> I think this book helps the kids a lot because they can read what they wrote themselves.

Not only do the parents see what we are doing at school, but they can help us create our book and read the positive comments from other parents.

→ See: Ogren pp. 155, 214.

Denise Ogren is a primary teacher in Stinesville Elementary School, Stinesville, IN.

Understanding Whole Language

"A whole language world view empowers a new set of learners and creates a new social order."

—Jerome Harste
"Oh, I See You Whole Language Types Are Having Another Revival Meeting"
Teachers Networking

CAROLYN CLEBSCH, JOEL BROWN, PAULINE LUBENS, LOIS BIRD

Understanding Whole Language

Contents

On Taking Risks
by Oscar Arias Sánchez

To promote change, to work for a dream, means that we have to prepare to take risks. When in Costa Rica we abolished the army, most people thought we were wrong and that that was an impossible dream. Out of that risk we enjoy now a very different country in Central America.

When we proposed the peace plan for Central America, many people thought we were wrong and that that was an impossible dream. Out of that risk we now have a chance for peace, and guns have been silenced in Nicaragua for the first time in 20 years.

Don't ever fear the risks you will have to take to build a different world. Don't ever fear the risks when you are acting on your principles. You will soon learn that the accommodation with the old world, a world where you see violence and injustice, poverty and submission, offers no reward.

The dreams that you allow to die will not be replaced. Martin Luther King, Jr., said once that "Our scientific power has outrun our spiritual power. We have guided missiles and misguided men." I have seen many times men who abandoned their dreams. I have seen those misguided men who believe they can solve all problems with guided missiles. These are men without values and the world cannot afford their leadership into the 21st century.

The return of a life and a world dominated by values is urgent if we want peace to prevail. We should no longer be ashamed of feelings, of piety. It is not true that they degrade reason and science. Piety is no less than the intelligence of the soul and we need heart and brains to recover the world in our hands, for the values we cherish.

Nobody can ignore the problems of today, least of all intellectuals. Now, more than ever, my friends, you shall have to bear the loneliness of being leaders.... We require builders, men and women of vision and tenacity. We must commit ourselves to transform privileges into rights for all and never to convert the sweat of all into the privilege of the few.

Among all the values we have to restore in order to provide a new leadership, peace is the one we should never neglect even under the most desperate circumstances....

Peace is a never-ending process, the work of many decisions by many people in many countries. It is an attitude, a way of life, a way of solving problems and resolving conflicts. It cannot be forced on the smallest nation or be enforced by the largest. It cannot ignore our differences or overlook our common interests. It requires us to work and live together. Don't ever abandon your dreams. If you believe now that one poet has more vision than all the politicians, don't change that belief. Go out and take risks to achieve that vision. Together, we will be proven right!

Children greet the president, Oscar Arias as he arrives in his hometown of Heredia, Costa Rica. Arias is optimistic about the Peace Plan agreement.

From an address given at Harvard University. Reprinted in the *Christian Science Monitor, 27* July 1988.

Oscar Arias Sánchez is the former president of Costa Rica and was recipient of the 1987 Nobel Peace Prize.

The Whole Language Ethos

 As Teachers See It

by Rich Thompson

Spirit of the Emigrant

Do not emigrate in a fever, but consider the question in each and every aspect. The mother country must be left behind, the family ties, all old associations, broken. Be sure that you look at the dark side of the picture: the broad Atlantic, the dusty ride to the great West of America, the scorching sun, the cold winter—coldest ever you experienced!—and the hard work of the homestead.

In Ivan Doig's *Dancing at the Rascal Fair,* these words are found in a guidebook for emigrants facing the challenges of coming across the Atlantic to a new land. The fare was considerable, the gains unknown. The brave new world—what an intense dilemma for the wondering new emigrant!

How much of the emigrant's spirit still remains? As we change our teaching, we make an emigrant's voyage. As we gain ownership in decision-making and allow children's voices to be heard, we rekindle the emigrant's spirit.

We know the challenge in the search for meaning. True intentions and expectations meet to create new images. We take risks of not knowing how a shared project or dialogue session will work out until it has taken place. We come to revalue readers and writers and the risks taken with the understanding that capabilities increase through active involvement.

We exchange the eye of discipline for the ear of understanding. We affirm student efforts and growth. When conflicts arise, we conference. We recognize the importance of hearing frustrations and the reasons for them; not capping them under pressure, but growing from their release.

Children need a safe harbor for their voyages as well, a place where we celebrate personal meaning and personal stories on common ground. Let the spirit of the emigrant remain. A varied ancestry enriches our community. And as we journey, let us heed the final words to the emigrant in Ivan Doig's book: "But if you finally, with your eyes open, decide to emigrate, do it nobly. Do it with no divided heart."

➜ See: Literature Reference List, p. 429; Thompson, p. 251.

Rich Thompson is an elementary teacher at Columbia Falls Elementary, Columbia Falls, MT.

 As Teachers See It

by Carol Maytag Christine

Centering Teaching and Learning

Whole Language… Romantic? Academic?

The current International Reading Association president, Dale Johnson (1989), has publicly stated that "whole language is a romantic rather than an academic notion." So I've been thinking about romance . . . a heady, euphoric feeling that I can conquer anything, survive everything; a joyful, inner peace and harmony enveloping me with feeling good about being in the world . . . and wondering what role, if any, it's had in my personal commitment to whole language.

I do feel joyful and optimistic about being a teacher in this time. I do believe I can conquer and survive just about anything. My whole language way of thinking doesn't conform to the historic traditions and rules of the academic training I received as an undergraduate or as a teacher in the inservice training offered by my school districts. I learned and have been reminded in these institutions that learning is a product. It is exact and it can be measured and compared to a standard; it is fixed and it is established by someone outside of the learner with more autonomy, power, and authority who dispenses this product to the student.

Instead I respect language as a tool for constructing meaning with others and for myself about the world in which I live and work. I believe that students are learners with as much to offer me as the teacher, and also a learner, as I have to offer them. I recognize language as a mediator and I have rejected learning as fixed and given to a learner by someone else.

This is what I would call romantic—heroic and adventurous—about whole language. Peter Mosenthal describes the schism between academic and "romantic" approaches to literacy instruction in the April 1989 issue of *Reading Teacher* as "teachers between a rock and a hard place." By proclaiming whole language teachers and advocates as "romantics" replacing the open education movement, Mosenthal uses language as a device to create suspicion and doubt. When he describes the poor performance on standardized reading tests of the students from the open classrooms in the school where he taught he implies that (1) whole language teachers and thereby their students are the same as those from the open education movement, and that (2) therefore, they do poorly on standardized reading tests, and that (3) this failure can be eliminated by more effectively matching teaching to testing. He attempts to divert the discussion to a disagreement between academic and "romantic" approaches and contrasts them as two camps—the academic prepares "a uniformly knowledgeable citizenry" while the other "promote[s] individual differences." His discussion is about "the problem of placing teachers between a rock and a hard place." I also call it one of politics—achievement, measurement, and effectiveness—and status—an academic versus a nonacademic, "romantic" approach.

Whole language is not a new name for a previous concept of method (Altwerger, Edelsky, and Flores 1987). Whole language "romantics" are surrounded by (see note):

Linguists: Michael Halliday, in *Learning How to Mean* and Gordon Wells in *The Meaning Makers,* document and describe how children develop and learn about language through its use.

Ethnographers: Denny Taylor and Catherine Dorsey-Gaines in *Growing Up Literate* and Susan Philips in *The Invisible Culture,* dispel myths of language deficiencies by portraying the effectiveness and validity of language in cultures different from *the standard.* In *Ways with Words* Shirley Brice Heath describes the differences between home and school language and their impact on academic success and failure.

Psycholinguists: Vera John-Steiner reveals the power of our inner thoughts in *Notebooks of the Mind,* and Frank Smith exposes membership for what it denies in *Insult to Intelligence* and *Joining the Literacy Club.*

Psychologists: Emilia Ferreiro and Ana Teberosky successfully challenge classrooms as the place where literacy development begins in *Literacy Before Schooling.*

Whole language advocates like Ken Goodman, Yetta Goodman, Carole Edelsky, Jerome Harste, Carolyn Burke, Dorothy Watson, Judith Newman, and Ralph Peterson may be ruffling a few feathers but they certainly aren't in "nests of down" calling out to teachers in "rock canyons." Rather,

 As Teachers See It

Whole Language Whole

by Ruth Ann Blynt

Seventh-grade math theorems aside, we all know that the whole is not really equal to the sum of its parts. The whole has an indefinable something more. It has a soul.

That is maybe what the proponents of the philosophy were thinking when they dubbed their cause "whole" language. Unfortunately, as with anything else, giving the movement a name trivializes it. It also gives opponents something to attack. And whole language purists, I think, would object to much of what passes in its name these days: whole language workbooks, lesson plans, and so on, which are a contradiction in terms and a rabid disregard for the theories they presume to preach.

Whole language is more than a methodology. It borders on a life-style. It incorporates the tenets expressed by Donald Graves and others, that we should teach our kids to deal with the "big questions"; that "learning cannot and should not be divided into tiny components"; that literacy is "reading and writing because we need to, to live"; and that ultimately, "the student is the most important evaluator in the scheme," and "the student knows what the student thinks."

These ideas frighten educators. On the surface they smack of the seventies' misused drive toward relevancy, which cast aside educational practices that had benefited students for years and thus became misunderstood and much maligned. They open up a Pandora's box reminiscent of the "open classrooms" that, however valid in theory, often turned into "open chaos" in practice. But most of all they quietly, modestly assert an attitude that presents a monumental shift in responsibility. "I learned" becomes more important than "I taught." Providing the conditions for learning to occur is harder than teaching. But the rewards are immeasurable. They are also immediate, which is a rarity in this profession. I know. I had them bestowed on me last year.

➜ See: Blynt, pp. 134, 360; Van Allen, p. 307; Weaver, p. 382.

Ruth Ann Blynt is a writing instructor at Utica College, Utica, NY.

they are actively supporting and working with classroom teachers as together we are redefining education as teaching *and* learning. In the process, we are moving education away from a match between methodology and measurement. Whole language teachers have chosen their own place among these scholars and thinkers in a social, historical context shaped by Lev Vygotsky, Jean Piaget, Clifford Geertz, Paulo Freire, Gregory Bateson, John Dewey, Edward Sapir, Benjamin Whorf, Dell Hymes, and many others. We are not stuck...but we may be romantic!

Note: These names and titles are representative and not inclusive.

➜ See: Christine, pp. 222, 410.

References

Altwerger, B., C. Edelsky, and B. M. Flores. 1987. "Whole language: What's new." *Reading Teacher,* November.

Johnson, D. 1989. Quoted in *Reading Forecaster.* Portland Council of International Reading Association, Spring.

Mosenthal, P. 1989. "Research views—the whole language approach: Teachers between a rock and a hard place." *Reading Teacher,* April.

From *Centerspace* 3(6), July 1989.

Carol Maytag Christine is a doctoral student at the University of Arizona, Tucson, AZ. She is also a teacher advocate active in SMILE and the Center for Establishing Dialogue, whole language support groups.

As We See It:
Kenneth S. & Yetta M. Goodman

Teachers Describe Whole Language

Recently Ken and I did a two-day workshop on whole language for *Math Their Way* workshop leaders. They were mostly elementary school teachers knowledgeable about developing math concepts with children and interested in the relationship of math to language. In order to know something about the background of our workshop participants, we asked them to work together for a while and then brainstorm a list of ideas about what they considered to be important whole language ideas. The list we eventually posted looked as follows:

language of the child—> expand to learner—> humanness
teacher is facilitator
minimal text—> whole story, poem, song
systemic—internal—comes from the inside
time—to prepare, for kids to develop, for learning
no sequence of skills

writing	developmental
creative	literature
sorting and classifying	cooperative learning
immersion	active learning
literature based	communication
experiences	enjoyment
respect	self-expression
success	freedom
meaning	integration

We were impressed with the list and realized that we were working with a group of people who were not beginners with whole language concepts.

As Ken and I discussed this we remembered an old Jewish parable about Hillel, a beloved scholar and rabbi who had great influence on Jewish teaching and learning during the first century of the common era. Hillel was known for his patience and his tact. But often members from other groups would taunt him and try his patience. One such skeptic confronted Hillel one day: "If you can teach me all that you believe as I stand on one foot, then I will become a believer." Hillel responded, "Do not do unto others that which you would not have others do unto you. That is the essence of our philosophy. Now go and *study!*"

It is obvious that people for many centuries have been looking for simple ways to describe and discuss complex ideas. Any list of concepts, such as the one above, provides a sense of the insights and knowledge the teachers have, but it is thoughtful applications to the classroom and continued learning about what the concepts represent that deepen our understandings.

It is not surprising, therefore, that Ken and I are encountering more and more teachers who

make strong statements about whole language when the focus has been too much on the labels and not on the meanings they represent.

But whole language is not just big books. The quality of the language is important.

Some teachers think doing dialogue journals is whole language. It's how you respond to the journals and the meanings the kids give to them that needs to be understood. Cooperative learning alone is not whole language; it's what the kids are cooperating about and why they think they're doing it that makes the learning significant or not.

Such insightful concerns addressed by whole language teachers help us conclude that whole language represents a coming of age of teaching as a profession.

➜ See: Math Their Way, p. 329; Vincent, p. 329.

📷 WHOLE LANGUAGE CAMERA

Love, Palo Alto, CA

Book Note

Lives on the Boundary: The Struggles and Achievements of America's Underprepared

Mike Rose
1989; 272 pp.; $24.95
New York: Free Press

Mike Rose's inspiring book, which won the 1989 David H. Russell Award for Distinguished Research in the Teaching of English from the National Council of Teachers of English, tells the story of his journey from a poor, immigrant neighborhood of Los Angeles into the world of academia. One of the major themes that runs throughout the book is the often terrible mismatch between the schools and many of their students—a mismatch that's manifested in a consistent devaluing of students' backgrounds, abilities, and intentions when students present themselves in ways that don't fit the schools' expectations.

But such a summary statement only hints at the importance of this literate, deeply felt book. Unlike some other writers who have told how they learned to function in a wider domain than the world of their childhood culture, Mike Rose has not broken with his past. His thoughts on educating those who society has kept "on the boundary" grow directly out of his own life and the lives of the people he grew up with. He sees education in a multicultural society as helping to create a national community through providing an "encouraging, communal embrace" for everyone. Mike Rose's discussion of language and literacy provides an exciting vision of what truly democratic education could be like.

Sandra Wilde

❝ Growing up in South L.A. was certainly not a conscious misery. My neighborhood had its diversions and its mysteries, and I felt loved and needed at home.

"But all in all there was a dreary impotence to the years, and isolation, and a deep sadness about my father. I protected myself from the harsher side of it all through a life of the mind. And while that interior life included spaceships and pink chemicals and music and the planetary moons, it also held the myriad television images of the good life that were piped into my home: Robert Young sitting down to dinner, Ozzie Nelson tossing the football with his sons, the blond in a Prell commercial turning toward the camera.❞ (p. 44)

Book Note

What's Whole in Whole Language?

Ken Goodman
1986; 80 pp.; $7.50
Portsmouth, NH: Heinemann

Le pourquoi et le comment du langage intégré

1989; 88 pp.; $9.95 (Canadian)
New York: Scholastic
French edition

Lenguaje integral

1989; 88 pp.; $10.00
Merida, Venezuela: Editorial Venezolana
Spanish edition available from:
Program in Language and Literacy
University of Arizona
College of Education, Room 504
Tucson, AZ 85721

Japanese edition available from:
Ozora-Sha
2-36-12 Akabane
Kita-Ku, Tokyo
Japan 115 (2500 yen)

Unofficially recognized as the whole language bible, this is a slim book with a mighty message. More than 100,000 copies have sold and it's now available in Spanish, French, and Japanese. Teachers, parents, and administrators relate to the straightforward manner in which Goodman sets forth the principles of whole language teaching and learning. As he explains, whole language is both scientific (founded on more than 20 years of interdisciplinary research) and humanistic (trusting, respectful, and caring toward the learner). The same may be said for this indispensable book.

LBB

📺 🎨 🎞 🤿 📖 📋

Resource: Organization

Education Commission of the States (ECS)

1860 Lincoln St., Ste. 300
Denver, CO 80295-0301
1-303-830-3600
FAX 1-303-830-0558

Want to know what the latest recommendations are for helping at-risk youth or involving parents in the school? ECS and its publications may be your best bet. Founded in 1965, ECS is an "interstate compact that helps state leaders improve the quality of education." An ECS fact sheet says that ECS "conducts policy research, surveys, and special studies; maintains an information clearinghouse; organizes state, regional, and national forums; provides technical assistance to states; and fosters nationwide leadership and cooperation in education." Besides outreach and network programs, it publishes a quarterly review, the *State Education Leader,* and periodic reports. The organization also offers videos for purchase or rental.

LBB

Cornerstone: Philo T. Pritzkau

A Quest for Meaning

When I was teaching social studies in junior high school in Cheyenne, Wyoming, in 1927, we were supplied with the Rugg Materials, by author Harold Rugg of Columbia University. There was one big advantage to these materials: They did not consist of a compendium of facts with an ordered arrangement. What I could be and was determined to be was a first sharer of meanings. Let me caution here that this may be misunderstood. Being the first sharer does not mean that I "gave the word." Rather, I was a prober with ideas and questions as a learner—the first learner. My knowledge or learning was not complete but rather, in process. My behavior was an invitation to those around me to inquire into the questions, not just my questions, but all questions. This probing eliminated barriers between mathematics, English, science, arts, and other areas. Our quest for meaning drew us into all areas. There were no compartments, and all demarcation points disappeared as we dealt with the questions of food, hunger, scientific endeavors, abundance, need, mathematical relationships, arts, and other areas.

There was an interesting episode about this teaching experience. The social studies teacher in the next room felt that we should do something together, so we had a social studies "spelling-down" from time to time. The ground rules were that we should each have a turn at asking each other's class some questions. It was very interesting to note that my students were not as apt at answering simple questions about facts and events as hers, but my students were more responsive with questions that related to various areas. Also, my students were curious about extended meanings relative to problems and issues.

Language is the medium and center of one's aliveness. Social studies will extend to all areas. Actually the regularities of boundaries will vanish when the fulfillment of thoughtful encounter takes place.

To be effective with any subject, teachers should strive to become creatively articulate with it. They need to be the first learner with the subject. I have found that pupils become very interested even when staying with the area of mathematics by dealing with the relation of decimal to common fractions. For example, the whole question of estimation in number relationships leads to much occupation with language. As they approach numbers theory, they conceive of relationships in their individual ways. For example, in estimating the sum of 63 and 59 some will think of estimating in terms of 100 and others with ones or tens and so on. Then they will look at numbers such as .342 and try to evaluate the importance of the period as related to a whole and fractional number. We could go on and on to show how the rise of language in their reasoning takes them into other and intriguing ways in which numbers are used. In the pursuit of meanings regarding the nature of number relationships, many discoveries are made that can be articulated with real interest in economics, architecture, government, science, and other areas.

I believe one could safely hypothesize that language is equally involved and nourished in English, mathematics, science, art, and other areas. Each one of these used as a center can, through careful development, produce as articulate an ability with language as the other. Provided there exists a free flow of language, every student will achieve articulation and an understanding equally with every subject area encountered.

In conclusion let me reiterate that teachers and pupils must be first learners/scholars with ideas, thus producing the invitational setting where each helps produce the other. Actually each one becomes the question around whom knowledge revolves. Language is the vehicle through which each individual encounters knowledge.

Philo T. Pritzkau is a professor emeritus of education. Perhaps you've met aspects of him in the books of his daughter, Patricia McLaughlin.

Book Note

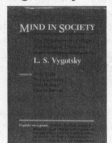

Mind in Society: The Development of Higher Psychological Processes

Michael Cole, Vera John-Steiner, Sylvia Scribner, and Ellen Souberman, editors
1978; 176 pp.; $7.95
Cambridge: Harvard University Press

Vygotsky's thoughts on play, the social nature of learning, and the zone of proximal development are part of the theoretical base for whole language. His comments hold much food for thought as educators reflect upon their ways of teaching. This book is a good one for a group of professional peers to read and discuss together.

Lois Mather

WELL-SAID

When confronted by those who suggest that school as it used to be did not do them any harm, that they hold jobs and are productive members of the community, whole language teachers do not react defensively. They simply ask, but what might you have become if you had been given the power to ask questions, to shape your own learning? Whole language teachers want to open doors to children so that the children can dream better dreams than we have ever known. Whole language teachers want to give children the power to become literate, the power to learn, the power to dream.

—Sharon Rich, "Restoring Power to Teachers: The Impact of 'Whole Language,'" *Whole Language: Beliefs and Practices, K-8*

➔ See: Rich, p. 27.

I Used to Be...But Now I...

I used to compromise,
But now I can afford not to.

—Kenneth S. Goodman

 ## As Teachers See It

What I Learned in School

by Leslie Mangiola

"Class, have any of you ever seen a mailman with a *green* uniform?"

She held Oliver's picture in front of her. His stick mailman was clothed in bright green.

"Nooo," we chorused. I looked at Oliver from the corner of my eye. He squirmed in his seat.

The rest of us sat there humiliated for Oliver but ever so grateful that she hadn't chosen one of our pictures to criticize. And we could always convince ourselves that Oliver wasn't the brightest star in the heavens anyway. Why, when he used scissors, he chewed on his tongue—obviously frustrated at not being able to cut along the line. Our teacher's tolerance for ignorance was severely limited—almost as limited as her compassion.

It was somewhat later in the year that she asked me what I had drawn (it was obviously an Easter basket—eggs and all). But I was one of the "good" students: top reader, always got my work done correctly, and on time. So how could she ask such a question? Hurt, I burst into tears. She was exasperated and sent me into the hall to gather myself together. Was I another Oliver? Of course not. My sin was a minor lapse of control. His was endemic. The year wasn't over, but I knew the difference. And, of course, so did Oliver.

What bothers me most now, 45 years later, is that I think I loved my teacher. And yet even then I knew what was happening to Oliver. I knew she was unfair and unkind.

There is always the danger that teachers will teach with the same kinds of attitudes with which they were taught. And it is frustrating to teach your best and see the children as unresponsive. It's easy to convince yourself they're just not trying, that they're deliberately resisting.

I think part of what saved me from that was becoming a whole language teacher. I have to look at children, not at products. I have to recognize where they are in the process of reading and writing. I can't determine where they *should* be. I can't criticize them for being slower than the others, but help them move as fast as they can through the process.

I know I have at least one Oliver in my class now. He's struggling with his writing—unsure of himself, afraid to take risks. I know that down the road a piece—not too far—he'll develop pride in what he's done. He'll risk and find out he's capable. His green mailman's uniform will be okay with him—and with me.

➔ See: Mangiola, p. 208

Leslie Mangiola is an elementary teacher at Fair Oaks School, Redwood City, CA.

📷 WHOLE LANGUAGE CAMERA

Veteran preschool teacher Virginia Deb shares stuffed animals and conversation with four-year-olds, Parents Nursery School, Palo Alto, CA.

Good Education

 Viewpoint: Connie Weaver

Whole Language as Good Education

Increasingly, I have come to realize that whole language educators need to emphasize the fact that "whole language" is not some esoteric philosophy, to be practiced by only a select few: It is simply one manifestation, with emphasis on language and literacy, of the broader philosophy and model of education that is being advocated across all the disciplines, and by diverse segments of the educational community. This model of education is what I and others have called a *transactional model*, in contrast to what might be called a *transmission model*. As the accompanying figure suggests, a transactional model emphasizes active learning, while the transmission model emphasizes passive "repeat-after-me" and "find-the-right-answer" kinds of behavior.

In order to make sound instructional and policy decisions, it is important for all segments of the educational community, including the public, to understand more fully the assumptions underlying the transmission model reflected in most of our educational practices and materials, in contrast with the transactional model that is supported by current research and theory converging from many disciplines.

For example: part of what concerns me is that even as prominent educators are attempting to help children develop active reading and learning strategies (the current buzzword is *metacognitive* strategies), teachers are doing so in a way that reflects a passive model of learning. This contradiction of paradigms is reflected in the following lesson frame, created by teachers in one school system in order to "teach" a metacognitive skill, namely the conscious use of context to "get" words and meaning:

1. "Today we are going to use the context to figure out the meaning of words." (Explain what "using the context" means, if necessary.)
2. "Let's talk about what the words in this column mean."
3. "The first word is _____."
4. "I'll read this sentence. You are to listen as I read it." Read the sentence in which the word appears.
5. "Now read this sentence with me." (Hand-drop

Connie Weaver is a professor of English at Western Michigan University. During the mid-1970s she was instrumental in developing an interdisciplinary and integrated language arts minor that reflected many of the principles that have come to characterize a whole language philosophy. Connie claims, however, that she is still very much in the process of "becoming" a whole language educator, as she continues to confront the contradictions between her philosophy and her educational practice.

signal orchestrates students to respond in unison to the sentence.) *Students read in unison.*
6. "Look at the words in the sentence around the unknown word. I'll name some of the words in the sentence that help determine the meaning of the unknown word. Underline each word in the sentence as you say it. Say each word with me." (Hand-drop signal.) *Students repeat the underlined words.*

Thus begins a lesson designed to teach an *active* reading strategy for determining the meaning of unknown words. What the lesson structure teaches, however, is passivity. And alas, the medium is all too often the message.

Nor is this conflict of learning models, of paradigms, confined to the public schools. For example, a teacher educator requires students in a beginning reading class to memorize the new Michigan definition of reading, which emphasizes the fact that readers actively interact (transact) with a text, in a variety of contexts that influence the nature and outcome of the reading transaction. Students who passively memorize this definition do not really understand it, and they can neither recite it nor paraphrase its essence a semester later, much less teach in a manner that reflects the definition.

The recognition that reading is an active cognitive process is spreading more rapidly than the recognition that learning in general is an active cognitive and social process, and that we are likely to be most successful in developing active, "strategic" readers if we assist students in developing reading strategies through means that are congruent with our ends.

As whole language educators, we need to expose the lack of congruence between the educational models underlying content and method wherever we encounter this incongruity. Our transactional model of education is now in the mainstream of current educational thinking, as reflected by recent statements and reports by the National Council of Teachers of Mathematics, the American Association for the Advancement of Science, the National Science Teachers Association, and, of course, the coalition of professional organizations concerned

with the teaching of English and language arts, as reflected in *The English Coalition Conference: Democracy Through Language* (Lloyd-Jones and Lunsford 1989). Similarly, the authors of several NAEP reports have concluded that the current passive concept of education must be replaced by an active view. Why? Because in all the disciplines, most students are demonstrating an inability to engage in any but the most simplistic kinds of reading, writing, and reasoning (Applebee, Langer, and Mullis 1989).

As whole language educators, we need to make people aware that teaching active learning strategies in a passive way can only convey the *illusion* that students have internalized those strategies. To promote active whole language education, we should emphasize the fact that what we know about how literacy develops and how teachers can foster the development of literacy is simply one particular manifestation of a broader model of learning and of education that is being advocated (if not yet practiced) almost universally within the educational community. "Whole language" teaching is indeed good education.

→ See: Cambourne, p. 17; McKenzie, p. 234; Moffett, p. 70; Reading Process and Practice, p. 103.

References
Applebee, A., J. Langer, and I. Mullis. 1989. *Crossroads in American education.* Princeton, NJ: National Assessment of Educational Progress.
Lloyd-Jones, R. and A. Lunsford. 1989. *The English coalition conference: Democracy through language.* Urbana, IL: National Council of Teachers of English.

Based on *Understanding Whole Language: From Principles to Practice,* chapter one, by Constance Weaver (Portsmouth, NH: Heinemann, 1990).

Further Reading by Constance Weaver
◆ *Grammar for Teachers.* NCTE, 1979.
◆ *Reading Progress and Practice: From Sociopsycholinguistics to Whole Language.* Heinemann, 1988.
◆ *Whole Language as Good Education: What Administrators Need to Know About Whole Language, Literacy, and Learning.* Heinemann, 1990.

Contrasting Models of Education

Transmission Model	Transactional Model
• Emphasis is on direct teaching, controlled by the program and secondly by the teacher.	• Emphasis is on learning, which is facilitated but not directly controlled by the teacher.
• Behaviorist model of learning (e.g., Skinner).	• Cognitive/social model of learning (e.g., Vygotsky, Halliday).
• Learning is viewed as a matter of building from simple to complex, from smaller to larger skills.	• Smaller "parts" of a task are seen as more readily learned within the context of a meaningful whole.
• Learning is viewed as habit formation; thus verbalizing/writing correct responses and avoiding incorrect responses is crucial.	• Learning is seen as the result of complex cognitive processes that can be facilitated by teachers and enhanced by peer interaction.
• Since correctness is valued, risk-taking is discouraged/penalized.	• Risk-taking, and hence "errors," is seen as absolutely essential for learning.
• All learners are expected to master what is taught, when it is taught; thus, most children experience varying degrees of failure.	• Learners are expected to be at different stages and to develop at their own pace, in their own ways; there is no concept of "failure."
• Ability to reproduce or verbalize a predetermined correct response is taken as evidence of learning.	• Ability to apply knowledge and to think in novel ways is considered evidence of learning, as is the ability to use general strategies across a wide range of tasks and contexts.

Viewpoint: Norma I. Mickelson

Joyful, Active Learning

When I was a little girl going to Quadra School in Victoria, British Columbia, my dad was out of work. We didn't have very much of this world's goods—the Depression assured us of that! We certainly did not have television. Nor did we have a car, a telephone, or money to spend on anything but the bare essentials—food, clothing, and shelter.

The opportunity to go to school was one thing we all had, however, and one day when I was in grade three, the classroom door opened and in walked Miss King with a big box in her arms. It looked heavy and as it turned out—it was! Miss King was from the public library and she had brought into our classroom (and for the first time into my world) a box of books.

She delved into her box and brought out a book about horses, *Black Beauty;* another about twins, *The Chinese Twins;* then came a book about some sisters, *Little Women;* followed by a story of a little orphan girl who was supposed to be a boy, *Anne of Green Gables.* Miss King showed us 50 books that day and then, wonder of wonders, she said she would leave them for a month! She also left us cards that we could get our parents to sign which would let us go to the public library and borrow all the books we wanted—for nothing! What a wonderful month that was for me. I still love Black Beauty, Ginger, Anne, Jo and Meg, among others, to this day. And I have an affinity for China, which ultimately led me there on five different occasions.

I never thanked Miss King—but I do so now! She could have had no inkling of the effect she was to have on my life and on the lives of all those with whom I have come in contact in my professional life. For she introduced me to the world through literature—a world which, to this day, I cannot imagine being without.

But somehow, over the years, this wonderful world became commercialized. Long after I was in elementary school, language learning (and teaching) in the classroom became centred on basal readers and workbooks. The more "professional" we became, the less literary we seemed to be. School became a place to keep quiet, complete your paper-and-pencil exercises, and do what you were told.

But now I have to say that, having been involved in education for almost half a century (student, teacher, supervisor, professor), things are once again changing. It is so very gratifying to see education being redefined and to watch the current transition from passivity to activity, from quiescence to empowerment for the children and teachers in our classrooms. Of course, there were always those ahead of their time—Froebel, Montessori, Dewey, Sylvia Ashton Warner—to name but four individuals who looked at children first and not subject matter, and who believed in the worthwhileness of childhood not as preparation for life, but as a time of life itself. In today's terms, this perspective is known as whole language.

Just what is whole language? It is a philosophy about teaching and learning that looks at education as an active, holistic exploration of life. No longer do we break the subject matter we teach and the language we use into bits and pieces for easy consumption. Rather, we focus on meaning and we accept children's attempts at discovering meaning as they listen, speak, read, write, and reflect across a wide range of activities. This does not mean that we ignore the structure of our language (skills), but it does

Norma I. Mickelson is a professor in the Faculty of Education at the University of Victoria in Victoria, British Columbia. She has been a teacher and a supervisor of instruction, and is the founder and director of the University of Victoria Whole Language Summer Institute. She has also been active in the past several years in North America and Australia in inservice work on whole language.

mean that the surface structure is not the end we are ultimately pursuing. Rather, it is the deep structure of language that interests us and for which we are attempting to find expression.

In our search for meaning, we focus on strategies or processes that enable children to solve their problems and assume responsibility for their actions. And how exciting teaching and learning become when classrooms resemble workshops rather than silent theatres. I don't mind using the words "fun," "excitement," "enthusiasm," and "love" because that's what holistic teaching engenders. Why should school be boring, tedious, and irrelevant?

One of the things that has become clear in education is that children do not develop into autonomous, responsible decision-makers by sitting quietly looking at the back of someone else's head for 12 years. Nor do they develop a sense of responsibility by always doing precisely what they are told, working with whom they are assigned, and focusing only on the "right answer."

This does not mean, however, that in whole language classrooms, children do not develop a sense of discipline. They do! When they are interested in what they are doing, they will persevere beyond anyone's expectations. Some wonderful teachers discovered this long ago—Elliot Wigginton, Nancie Atwell, Donald Graves, Lucy Calkins, Gail Heald Taylor, Margaret Reinhardt, and Susan Close, for example. In fact, we could fill pages with names of teachers who have rediscovered the wonderful world of learning as they themselves have become learners—participant observers in their own education and in that of the children whom they nurture.

As we restructure our educational systems in the 21st century, we need to realize that, as professionals, we must not deal with educational issues in a superficial way. We need to see, as do whole language teachers, that listening, speaking, reading, and writing are processes through which we learn about our world—not "subjects" to be taught. Together with problem-solving, monitoring, reflecting, decision-making, and evaluating, for example, the language arts become enabling and empowering.

Language is a uniquely human attribute. No other creatures have been endowed with this gift. As teachers, then, in a very real sense, we are "keepers of the flame." Because of us, the children in our classrooms and our schools can aspire to and reach undreamed-of accomplishment. There need be no limit if we free the potential within each one to grow and develop. This is what whole language is all about—the present—because in reality, it is all we have, but it is about the future, too, because as we empower children today, tomorrow will take care of itself!

➡ See: Britton, p. 69; Hasselriis, p. 178; Literature Reference List, p. 429; McKenzie, p. 234; Van Allen, p. 307.

Further Reading by Norma I. Mickelson

◆ *Whole Language.* Book and videotapes. University of Victoria, Department of Extension, 1988.
◆ "Point/Counterpoint: Basal Readers." *Reading Today,* August/September 1989.
◆ "Whole Language: Myths and Misconceptions." *Teacher* 1(5), March 1989.
◆ "A Whole Language Program in the Intermediate Grades," with A. Davies. *Reading Canada Lecture* 7(3), Fall 1989.

 **writers**

What Is a Whole Language Teacher?

by Norma I. Mickelson

A whole language teacher is a leader
along education's way,
but also is a learner
through every classroom day.

A whole language teacher is a friendly soul
to each student in the room;
is one who plays a helping role
as children grow and bloom.

A whole language teacher doesn't know it all,
nor frets about what's wrong.
But rather sees what's right and calls
from each a special song.

A whole language teacher has the power
in what is planned for every day.
To make a potential flower
in a special kind of way.

A whole language teacher's life is dedicated
to language growth for young and old;
and always it is predicated
on the inner person to unfold.

A whole language teacher is a person
whose work is blessed by love;
who risks, takes challenges, and who has fun
as though flying the clouds above.

A whole language teacher welcomes questions
and grasps the nettles as they come,
knowing that language is a blessing
given to humans—every one!

So wade right in—begin today,
just say "I can," you'll find the way;
you will grow as children do,
to unknown heights, scaled, yes, by you.

Norma I. Mickelson is a professor in the Faculty of Education at the Univeristy of Victoria, Victoria, British Columbia.

Resource: Bookstore

The Cornerstone

2548 Mangum
Commerce, TX 75428
1-214-886-8680

You can't judge a book by its cover, but you can judge a bookstore by its catalog. This bookstore offers the collections of two whole language favorites: Bill Martin Jr and Robert Munsch. *Jacque Wuertenberg Live!* is available on video or audiocassette.

LBB

Resource: Periodical

Substance

$15 year (12 issues) from:
161 W. Harrison St., 7th floor
Chicago, IL 60605
1-312-341-0977

From Substance, a group comprising substitute teachers who are affiliated with the Chicago Teachers Union, comes a monthly newsletter of the same name. Through investigative reporting, they tackle such substantive issues as educational reform and local school issues.

LBB

Cornerstone: Susan Church, Jim Rice, and Ruth Gamberg: An Interview by Ann Manicom

Whole Language in Nova Scotia: Benefits, Difficulties, and Potential

In late September, four of us—Susan Church, a curriculum supervisor, Jim Rice, a high school English teacher, Ruth Gamberg, an adult educator, and Ann Manicom, the interviewer—discussed the implementation in Nova Scotia of the whole language approach to learning. Nova Scotia has been in the forefront in Canada in mandating whole language as the approach to be taken in literacy instruction throughout the school system. However, long before the approach was mandated in the province, networks of Nova Scotian teachers, especially at the elementary level, began to study whole language theory, transforming their classrooms and teaching others about the theory and practice of whole language.

Whole Language as a Way of Learning

Ann: Whole language seems to be an overall approach to learning.

Susan: Right. Meaning is at the centre of everything. It's not a matter of transmitting knowledge from teacher to student. Every individual constructs knowledge based on his or her own experiences, and then in a social context tests out those ideas, thinks and rethinks them. This is what characterizes learning in general, not just learning to read and write. And with this view of learning, the classroom becomes very much a social learning environment. It's no longer a quiet place where people sit in their desks and work; it's a place where everybody's interacting. Whole language is based on the student assuming responsibility for his or her own learning and becoming independent.

Ann: So it's not only a change in the definition of what it is to learn, but a change in the definition of what it is to teach.

Susan: Yes. The entire notion of teaching is being redefined. Teaching is not a less active role, but a different kind of role than the traditional one. It means creating an environment within which learners are involved in exploring topics of interest, using talk, reading, and writing as tools for learning. It means serving as facilitator, mentor, and supporter rather than dispenser of information. It means demonstrating the value of literacy, mathematics, science, and all other aspects of the curriculum in the teacher's own life. It means being a learner as well as a teacher. I've seen more teachers who have felt burned out starting to say, "I'm really enjoying teaching again, I'm learning, the *kids* are learning."

Ann: From your perspective as a curriculum supervisor, what other good things are you noticing in whole language classrooms?

Susan: Well, in elementary classrooms (and increasingly in junior highs and in some senior high classrooms) there is increased involvement and engagement of the children in learning. They have opportunities to take control, assume responsibility, and become independent. There is a focus on problem-solving, with the learners actively involved rather than having curriculum delivered to them. The teacher and the learners jointly negotiate the curriculum.

The other thing I'm seeing has to do with the kinds of literacy experiences children are having. Certainly the move away from basal readers to real literature has made a big difference in how children learn to read. When they start with meaningful texts, reading becomes purposeful and enjoyable rather than a difficult task: Writing is the same way. When I go into classrooms now I find that all the students believe they're writers. From the beginning the focus is on conveying a message. Children are encouraged to use what they know at the time. Gradually they move toward more conventional punctuation, capitalization and spelling when representing these ideas on paper, to clarify meaning for an audience. This way of learning is very supportive.

Many of the books listed on the Provincial Department's authorized listing for *junior high* are now being read at the *elementary* level! The children really *are* becoming better readers and they *are* reading.

Ann: What does whole language mean to you, Jim, as a secondary English teacher? What difference does it make in your classroom?

Jim: One of the real advantages of whole language is that it might finally force us all away from a very traditional style of teaching: the teacher in possession of the knowledge standing at the front, disseminating it to students. It also, in its theory and its practice, stops us from making the artificial divisions that have plagued secondary English teachers (and junior high and perhaps even elementary teachers): that there are different periods for different aspects of language arts—literature, writing, comprehension, and skills.

Ann: Ruth, could you talk about whole language in terms of adult literacy? How is it valuable there?

Ruth: Well, most adults who are having problems with reading and writing are people who have been to school. Very often they went to school for a number of years, but still didn't catch on. If they're given more of the same approach that they got as kids, then they're really in trouble. Yet the traditional way of teaching reading and writing still dominates in adult literacy. It's a mechanical senseless process, especially to people who are not clear on what reading is all about or how to do it. So I think whole language becomes extremely important for adults. There's no point in doing more and more of the same things that people have failed at, that they are embarrassed about, that make them think they're stupid.

Reading and Writing for What?

Ruth: One of you mentioned earlier that people are going to end up doing a lot more reading for enjoyment as a result of this approach. The only thing that worries me—there's not nearly enough attention to content, to *what it is* that people are reading and writing.

Susan: The very best whole language teach-

ers I know are people who are voracious readers themselves, people who read a great variety of material, and share that interest with the kids. They convey a sense that it *does* matter what you are reading. They involve children in reflecting upon how they respond as readers, and this does involve value judgement.

Jim: But I think, Ruth, that you are saying that you want a progressive education that brings up issues—feminism or social justice or international issues—and you're asking how one does that in this context.

Ruth: Exactly. My feeling is that progressive content is not necessarily part and parcel of whole language. You can do work on Valentines and do it in a whole language way, but that's not exactly progressive content! The potential is there to do progressive teaching, but the potential is also there *not to;* someone can be a competent whole language teacher and not really touch the consciousness of the learner.

Jim: I agree with most of what you're saying, Ruth, but I think there is an important progressive dimension to whole language, which is built in, and which you haven't recognized here.

The teacher who has thought a lot about whole language starts realizing there are issues about control and empowerment that are central to what happens in the whole language classroom. A whole language classroom gives the responsibility to the learners, makes learning meaningful, allows them to shape what they learn, and then plays fair by them, not punishing them for the choices they make and the risks that they take. The whole language approach has the potential to provide a liberating experience for students, so that they see themselves as active participants in society.

Some Misunderstandings and Resistance

Ann: Earlier, Susan, you mentioned that teachers were having trouble seeing what their role was in whole language approaches to teaching. What are some of the problems?

Susan: A lot of teachers, particularly at the elementary level where we've been thinking about these issues for some time, are struggling with what their role is, what it is they're supposed to be doing. Some believe, "Well, I'm not supposed to interfere in this process. I'm supposed to have all this reading and writing going

(Continued on next page)

Network

The WHOLE Group

Membership Information: Members of WHOLE receive mailing about local whole language activities, advanced notice and priority registration for WHOLE group classes, a newsletter published three to four times a year, and the opportunity to network with others. To become a member, send a check for $10.00 to Debbie Elliot, ESD 112, 1313 NE 134th St., Vancouver, WA 98685.

Resource: Periodical

Our Schools/Our Selves: A Magazine for Canadian Education Activists

$32/year (8 issues) regular;
$40/year (8 issues)
organization from:
Our Schools/Our Selves
Education Fdn.
1698 Gerrard St. E.
Toronto, Ontario, M4L 9Z9
Canada

(Continued from previous page)

on but I'm not supposed to interfere." So we're seeing some situations where children aren't learning a range of effective strategies, aren't getting any further in their reading and writing because the right questions aren't being asked. The needed support isn't being given at the right time to move the children further along in their development.

Teachers don't do enough thinking about their own reading and writing strategies, reflecting upon what they do as readers and writers. The most successful teachers of writing are those who write themselves and have some sense of how you support someone who is trying to write. Teachers ask, "Well, what questions should I ask when conferring with a writer?" But you can't tell them what questions to ask. It depends on where the writer is and what the problems are.

Ann: Do students struggle with their new roles?

Jim: In my experience, yes. In a sense, the learners' ideas of their roles are an obstacle to their own learning. That's something I have difficulty with at the senior high level. Students pressure me to just take the thing that they've written and deal with it as a teacher "ought to." Instead, I push back and try to keep *them* in control of the writing that they're doing, keep it *theirs,* keep it something that has meaning to *them.* As long as teachers set the agenda for everything, the assignments and marking, teachers can do *anything* they want. They can fail a student, but the student's ego is not destroyed by that process, because the student knows it's a big game and that it's the teacher who sets the rules. But as soon as you start playing with things and saying, "No, this is yours, *you* take responsibility, this is meaningful to *you,*" they're afraid we're going to cheat them, they're afraid we're going to draw on their real commitments and then turn around and slap them down with the same old grading system that we used all the way through.

A person gets along in any institution by figuring out how the system works and then working it to their advantage. But then some of us teachers come in with an entirely different set of rules. We arrange the classroom differently; we tell the students that our expectations are different; we do so many things that are different from what they're used to.

Ann: What about misunderstandings and difficulties with whole language in adult education?

Ruth: At the adult level, everybody wants a "whole language textbook," because textbooks have beginnings, middles, and ends. This is a problem because textbooks don't pay attention to where the learner is and what the learner needs. Textbooks don't know the learner's strengths and interests. But these things are important for whole language, because they tell us where to begin and what to build on.

Whole Language: Its Future

Ann: What do you see in ten years? Is whole language a fad?

Susan: I don't think so. Even some conservative mainstream educational organizations are starting to support it, which gives whole language some sort of credibility. This might be a problem, of course—their version of it is not always our version of it!

Ann: But maybe their version instead of yours will prevail.

Susan: What I hope is that we can continue to move along in our own context. We are fortunate in having a fairly large support group; we have support from the universities and the Provincial Department of Education, which isn't the case in other places. More and more teachers coming out of masters programs are committed to this way of working. They understand that whole language is not just a new method for teaching reading and writing but a theoretical framework, a philosophical stance. If you get a critical mass of teachers and other educators with this sort of understanding, I'm not sure you can go back.

Jim: I suppose the real test of whether it will continue is whether people will find it satisfying to teach that way, so satisfying that they won't abandon it.

Susan: All the teachers I've been talking to over the last three weeks since school started are saying, "Gosh, this is hard." But there's not one of them saying, "I'm not going to do this." They're going to do it despite all the odds. We need more people in positions like mine supporting them, making it possible for them to do what they know. The interesting thing about these teachers is that they are so reflective. They don't say, "I've got all the answers"; they're the ones who have all the questions about what this theoretical framework means. They're constantly questioning what's going on with their students and learning from those situations.

Ruth: We're very fortunate to be working in literacy here because Nova Scotia leads the way in whole language, not just in Canada, but perhaps even in North America. In adult literacy work, though, this approach is just beginning to see the light of day. Locally, a number of people are trying it out and helping others to understand it. Still, in general, when people think of whole language, they tend to think about the education of young kids only. But as Jim and I have been saying, it's just as appropriate for older kids and adults. Considering there's already starting to be a bit of a backlash, it will be hard going to get it accepted in secondary schools and in adult literacy programs. But, as Susan said, teachers who learn about it are almost invariably enthusiastic. So our hope lies there.

→ See: Goodman, p. 390; Heath, p. 422; Newkirk, p. 217; Newman, p. 211; Voices, p. 128; Wigginton, p. 220.

Excerpted from *Our Schools/Our Selves* 1(2), January 1989.

Ann Manicom is on the faculty in the School of Education, Dalhousie University, Halifax, Nova Scotia. Susan Church is a curriculum supervisor for the Halifax County-Bedford School System. Jim Rice is a secondary school English teacher in Halifax. Ruth Gamberg is a faculty member at Dalhousie University.

What, then, is a good life for children? An active, a full, a rich life of meaningful experiences at each stage of their development. It is a sound humanitarian impulse to **WELL-SAID** give children such lives. But it is more than that. A good life is a life in which one keeps growing in interests, in breadth of emotions and powers of expression, in depth and extent of human relations. Growth in all one's powers . . . leads on to an adulthood which is not static, completed, but still retains the capacity and the eagerness to grow. Adults, for good or bad, retain in their very fiber the results of their childhood experiences. Children's best chance to be learners, doers, creative, constructive members in the society they live in as adults is to have lived lives which gave these qualities a chance to grow steadily. . . . A good life for children is, above all, a chance to keep growing as "whole children."

—Lucy Sprague Mitchell

→ See: Goodman, p. 376; Mitchell, pp. 19, 227, 248, 376, 385, 390.

From *Our Children and Our Schools,* by Lucy Sprague Mitchell (New York: Simon & Schuster, 1950).

Book Note

Whole Language: Theory in Use

Judith M. Newman, editor
1985; 224 pp.; $15
Portsmouth, NH:
 Heinemann

Reading this book is like a month of eavesdropping and observing in a whole language school, or like a year's worth of support-group sessions. But it has another important merit: Judith Newman offers precise descriptions of the theory that we can explain to administrators, fellow teachers, or parents to help them understand whole language. Each section is introduced with concise yet comprehensive essays on whole language written by the editor. That is the "theory" part of the subtitle; the kidwatching stance of the Nova Scotia teachers chapters provides the "use." There are references throughout the book to research in classroom con

texts. Reading the book once a year keeps one fluent in ways to promote whole language.

A simple quote will not do justice to one of the cleverest presentations of all, the chapter "Yes, They Can Learn." In it, teacher James Boyer uses dramatic narrative to show us contrastive experiences of "problematic" Billy in two learning environments. However, as an example of the usefulness of this book, here below is Newman herself on how children develop their writing through letters.

Mary Kitagawa

❝ The most useful thing about letters as a vehicle for helping children develop as writers is that they circumvent our compulsion as teachers to correct everything in sight. Whoever heard of returning a letter to its sender with the mistakes circled in red? Letters are to be answered; they highlight the importance of meaning. Maintaining that focus on meaning, more than anything else, is crucial for becoming a writer. ❞ (p. 81)

→ See: Newman, p. 211

Resource: Organization

Mount St. Vincent University's Summer Institute for Teachers

Jean Hartley, director
Centre for Continuing Education
Mount St. Vincent University
Halifax, Nova Scotia,
 B3M 2J6 Canada
1-902-443-4450, ext. 324

From Nova Scotia, which has led the way in holistic education, comes an offer by Mount Saint Vincent University of Halifax for a two-week summer institute for teachers and administrators "who want to expand their experiences as readers, writers, classroom leaders, and researchers." Through workshops, discussion, and independent study, participants "explore issues and practices in language and education." Participants choose from four themes; *Catalog* essayist Judith Newman leads the reading/writing connection theme.

LBB

The History of Whole Language

As I See It:
Yetta M. Goodman

History of Whole Language

The earliest reference to the term *whole language* that I have found to date is in the first picture book written for children by John Amos Comenius (1887, English edition) in the 17th century:

> It is a *little Book*, as you see, of no great bulk, yet a brief of the whole world, and a *whole language*: full of Pictures, Nomenclatures, and Descriptions of things [first italics in original, second mine] . . . we have filled this first book . . . with the chief of things and words, or with the grounds of the whole world, and the whole language, and of all our understanding about things.

Although Comenius did not have exactly the same concept of whole language as we do today, important characteristics in his concern for children and learning tie 17th-century pedagogy with whole language as we know it.

Comenius believed that children can discover new information by being introduced to what is familiar to them within their life's experiences; by being able to manipulate the concrete objects being studied; and by using the native language to talk about what is being learned.

Common Ties to Earlier Educational Movements

Many scholars between the 17th and 20th centuries have advocated whole language principles similar to those of Comenius. In this brief history of whole language I have selected only a few influential scholars and movements from the 20th century. No doubt I have left out many who made contributions. The common ties between whole language and its antecedents include views of the learner, views of the teacher, and views about language.

Whole Language: The Concept and the Term

The popular use of the term *whole language* probably came from teachers becoming aware of the knowledge explosion surrounding oral and written language development and the reading and writing processes. Teachers realized that students needed to use language to solve problems that were significant and meaningful to their daily lives in order to take charge of their own learning (Goodman, Smith, Meredith, and Goodman 1987). Teachers used the term casually in daily discussions about classroom practices where language was kept whole and relevant before the term was used in preservice or inservice programs, curriculum guides, newsletters, professional articles or books, and as a descriptor in reference guides.

Those of us who have been close to the present use of the term *whole language* are unsure of its origins. Jerome Harste and Carolyn Burke (1977, pp. 32–40) described how teachers develop a theoretical view of the reading process, and one of the paradigms was called a whole language view of reading. In 1978 Dorothy Watson and others in Columbia, Missouri, formed the first teacher support group called Teachers Applying Whole Language (TAWL). Ken Goodman and I wrote a paper in 1979 called "A Whole Language Comprehension-centered Reading Program." Orin Cochran, Ethel Buchanan, and others in Winnipeg, Canada, organized CEL (Child-centered, Experience-based Learning), and began to present workshops about whole language teaching and learning in 1980. The early users of the term were not consciously naming a new belief system or movement. We were talking about some new ideas about language, teaching, and learning and what these meant in terms of implementation, and we needed new language to express our new meanings.

Major Theorists

John Dewey (1938, 1943) provided a theoretical rationale from which came key ideas: the power of reflective teaching; learners being at the center of the process of curriculum development; and the integration of language with all other studies in the curriculum.

Piaget and his coresearchers showed how children are actively involved in understanding their world and in trying to answer their questions and solve the problems that the world poses for them (Ferreiro and Teberosky 1982).

Vygotsky (1978, 1986) explored the relation between the learning of the individual and the influences of the social context. His *zone of proximal development* emphasizes the important role teachers play in students' learning, even though learners are ultimately responsible for their own conceptual development. Vygotsky also emphasized the important social aspects of learning: the role of peers as well as activities such as play in the development of intellectual functioning.

Halliday (1975) helps us understand the power of the context of situation on learning and on language use. He has developed a system that relates the study of language to functional activity within the situational context and to the relationship of the people involved. Halliday contends that as learners are using language, they are learning language, learning through language, and learning about language.

The Field of Reading

Some of the beginnings of whole language come from research in the 1960s on the reading process, especially the work of Kenneth Goodman and Frank Smith (1971), and from the subsequent move to apply the research findings to reading instruction. Working from different perspectives they established the notion of a unified single reading process as an interaction between the reader, the text, and language.

Much earlier, Louise Rosenblatt applied Dewey's concept of transaction to reading and literature in her now classic book *Literature through Exploration* (1938, 1976). Influenced by Rosenblatt (1978), whole language incorporated the term transaction to represent the rich and complex relationship between the reader and the text.

The views of Goodman, Smith, and Rosenblatt provide a rationale for literature and language experience-based reading programs. Such reading programs were well developed and popular before the 1960s. Research and theoretical support explained much of the success of programs that immersed students in reading real books and why children who were read to at home tended to be successful in learning to read. They also help to explain why children are so successful in learning to read when they read materials in their own language based on experiences relevant to their daily lives. At the same time, the theory and the research raised some questions about the direction various programs were taking.

The language experience approach became part of the reading instruction literature when Dorris Lee and Lillian Lamoreaux (1943) wrote *Learning to Read through Experience*. The theory and approach was updated in 1963 by Lee and R. V. Allen, who were instrumental in popularizing language experience. Language experience emphasized involving learners in excursions; group experiences with science, social studies, or math; storytelling; drama; music; and art. The experi-

ences were accompanied by all kinds of language. Many whole language educators like me were initially advocates of language experience.

Some supporters of language experience see whole language as a natural extension of their views. However, for some advocates, the original philosophical beliefs about language learning and child development became secondary to the orthodoxy of the procedures. For others, taking dictation from children and then having them read it became a way to teach children words and other subskills. As language experience was popularized and often misapplied, the label *language experience* lost the power of its original conceptualization.

In addition, new knowledge about the composing process, including the discovery that children invented spellings (Read 1975), raised new questions about the relation between oral and written language. In whole language children are helped to understand the differences between written and oral language and they are encouraged to become independent writers by doing more of their own scribing.

In New Zealand, Don Holdaway (1979) developed the concept of shared book experience using teacher-produced big books (Department of Education 1972, 1985) and was supported by the research of Marie Clay (1972). Using the work of New Zealanders, Jeannette Veatch (1985), long an advocate of personal choice in reading, raised questions about the nature of packaged programs and basal readers and urged that reading instruction focus on trade books for children.

Leland Jacobs (1965) and Charlotte Huck (Huck and Kuhn 1968) wrote about the power of trade books in reading programs. These influences were supported by research on children being read to, on the nature of storytelling, and on narrative (Applebee 1978; Rosen 1984; Wells 1986).

Influences from the Field of Composition

Alvina Burrows in *They All Want to Write* (1939, 1984) urged that young children should express themselves in their own voices in writing. She informed elementary school teachers that kids had to write about their own experiences. Burrow's work was supported in the 1970s by the research of Don Graves (1983), who clearly documented that children learn to write, and their writing continues to develop, when they have opportunities to do so in a supportive environment.

Secondary English educators involved with the National Writing Project have been instrumental in encouraging teachers to become writers themselves, to share their writing with others, to discuss successful ways of teaching writing, and to learn about the theory and research in the field of composition.

British educators also inspired secondary English and writing; these include James Britton,

Nancy Martin, Harold Rosen, and others (1975) from the London Institute of Education in England. The concept of language across the curriculum was popularized by these British scholars and is reflected in *A Language for Life* (Bullock 1975), a report that influenced the teaching of the English/language arts in all English-speaking countries and explains the early development of holistic concepts in Canada, Australia, and New Zealand as well as Britain.

Influences from Other Curricular Areas

Early childhood education in North America was strongly influenced by the British Infant Schools, which were themselves influenced by John Dewey in the 1930s (Featherstone 1967, pp. 17–21; 1968, pp. 23–25; 1969, pp. 18–21). Following the child's lead in planning curriculum, encouraging problem-solving, and seeing play as the building blocks of intellectual development are all theoretical notions that whole language advocates and early childhood educators have in common. (Laughlin and Martin 1988).

Programs were developed during the 1940s and 1950s that integrated language arts and social studies, social studies and humanities, and often science and math subject areas. The artificial isolation of content, which seemed appropriate for the purposes of research and scholarship in tertiary education, did not seem appropriate for growing children and adolescents.

In the post-World War II years, the American Council on Education (ACE) and the Association for Supervision and Curriculum Development (ASCD) were actively involved in organizing integrated curricula. As students represented an ever-widening range of race, ethnicity, nationality, and linguistic and socioeconomic status, entering and staying in schools and moving on to higher education, educators began discussing ways of making education relevant to students from all walks of life. The ACE organized the development of integrated curriculum with a focus on intergroup education (Taba 1950; Taba, Brady, and Robinson 1952). Building on Kilpatrick's (1918, pp. 318–334; 1936) project method, teachers and curriculum specialists developed units of work or thematic strands of study to help students relate what they were learning to their own lives.

The ASCD commissioned an impressive and influential volume by Kelly, Rogers, Maslow, and Combs (1962) entitled *Perceiving, Behaving, Becoming,* concerning respect for the learner's experiences both inside and outside the school.

During the 1970s the civil rights movement shifted our concerns to equal educational opportunity for all students. The effects of curricular innovations during the 1940s and 1950s could be seen as groups of educators came together to discuss integrated, relevant curriculum, taking into consideration new research and insights from psycholinguistics and sociolinguistics.

The Development of a Community of Scholars

In the early 1970s a group of educators formed the Center for the Expansion of Language and Thinking (CELT), whose first president was Ken Goodman. Its main purpose was to develop a network of teacher educators and educational researchers to provide a forum for continuous discussion; to identify ways of informing and involving school practitioners to consider the new knowledge and its applications to education; and to work collaboratively in various research endeavors. CELT members are actively involved in disseminating knowledge to support whole language.

Lillian Weber called for expanding beyond the walls of the classroom to provide activity-oriented curriculum for all children, and to facilitate talk, problem-solving, role-playing, and simulations. Weber (1973) established the Workshop Center for Open Education to provide

opportunities for teachers, administrators, para-professionals, and parents to explore issues and discover ways to exist in schools where there was often little support.

In 1972 the North Dakota Study Group was formed "to discuss concerns about the narrow accountability ethos that had begun to dominate schools and to share what many believed to be more sensible means of both documenting and assessing children's learning" (Perrone 1977, frontmatter).

In the late 1970s small groups of teachers in local communities formed to discuss how to use the new insights about language and learning. This was the beginning of the whole language teacher support groups. These groups established communication networks in order to respond to their discontent with traditional education and to find ways to advocate and support alternative educational options that reflect the latest scientific knowledge. I believe it is from this need that the whole language movement grew.

Whole language is a new response to an old argument. John Dewey (1938, pp. 18–19) said of the movement variously called *the new education* or *progressive schools* that it was a "product of discontent with traditional education. In effect it is a criticism of the latter." Dewey expresses this discontent: "The traditional scheme is, in essence, one of imposition from above and from outside. It imposes adult standards, subject matter and methods upon those who are only growing slowly toward maturity."

In Conclusion

Influences on whole language include the traditions of humanism and science. We take from humanism a respect for all learners regardless of their ages, abilities, or backgrounds. We take from science the latest discoveries in psychology, linguistics, psycholinguistics, and sociolinguistics.

What advocates of whole language are saying now draws on what came before, but it is substantially different from what was said earlier. There is greater understanding of the power of language, active learning, and the importance of the social classroom community. As new concepts grow and develop, it is helpful to have new terminology to talk about these concepts. That's why the term *whole language* has grown. On the other hand, if the term *whole language* remains static and does not reflect the dynamic changes that emerge from the continuous dialogue, debate, and exploration taking place at the present time, then the label may be supplanted by another. The educational theories and beliefs that whole language represents today will be foundational to educational understandings and practices of the future. In the same way that those of us who call ourselves whole language proponents today discover our roots in the humanistic and scientific beliefs of those who came before, future humanistic and scientific beliefs will have their roots in the dynamic movement called whole language.

➜ See: Britton, p. 69; Buchanan, p. 409; Dewey, pp. 270, 285, 335; Graves, p. 129; Goodman, p. 98; Harste, p. 388; Holdaway, p. 44; Horton, p. 74; Huck, p. 188; King, p. 16; Larrick, p. 127; Miller, pp. 219, 427; Moll, 413; Van Allen, p. 307; Veatch, p. 235; Watson, pp. 40, 427; Weber, p. 78.

References

Applebee, A. 1978. *The child's concept of story.* Chicago: University of Chicago Press.

Britton, J., T. Burgess, N. Martin, A. McLeod, and H. Rosen. 1975. *The development of writing abilities.* London: Macmillan Education.

Bullock, A. 1975. *A language for life.* London: Her Majesty's Stationery Office.

Burrows, A., D. Jackson, and D. Saunders. 1939, 1984. *They all want to write.* Hamden, CT: Library Professional Publication.

Clay, M. 1972. *Reading: The patterning of complex behaviour.* Portsmouth, NH: Heinemann.

Comenius, J. A. 1887. *The orbis pictus.* Syracuse, NY: C. W. Bardeen.

Department of Education. 1972. *Reading: Suggestions for teaching reading in primary and secondary schools.* Wellington, New Zealand.

———. 1985. *Reading in junior classes.* Wellington, New Zealand.

Dewey, J. 1938. *Experience in education.* New York: Collier Books.

———. 1943. *The child and the curriculum and the school and society.* Chicago: University of Chicago Press.

Featherstone, J. 1967. "How children learn." *New Republic,* 2 September.

———. 1968. "Experiments in learning." *New Republic,* 14 December.

———. 1969. "Why so few good schools?" *New Republic,* 4 January.

Ferreiro, E., and A. Teberosky. 1982. *Literacy before schooling.* Portsmouth, NH: Heinemann.

Goodman, K., and Y. Goodman. 1979. "A whole language comprehension-centered reading program." Occasional Paper #1. Tucson, AZ: University of Arizona.

Goodman, K., E. B. Smith, R. Meredith, and Y. Goodman. 1987. *Language and thinking in school.* New York: Richard C. Owen.

Goodman, K., and F. Smith. 1971. "On the psycholinguistic method of teaching reading." *Elementary School Journal* 41(5).

Graves, D. 1983. *Writing: Teachers and children at work.* Portsmouth, NH: Heinemann.

Halliday, M. A. K. 1975. *Learning how to mean.* New York: Elsevier North-Holland.

Harste, J., and C. Burke. 1977. "Reading: Theory, research and practice." In *Twenty-sixth Yearbook of the National Reading Conference,* ed. P. D. Pearson. New York: Mason Publishing.

Holdaway, D. 1979. *Foundations of literacy.* Sydney: Ashton Scholastic.

Huck, C., and D. Kuhn. 1968. *Children's literature in the elementary classroom.* New York: Holt, Rinehart & Winston.

Jacobs, L. 1965. *Using literature with young children.* New York: Teachers College Press.

Kelly, E., C. Rogers, A. Maslow, and A. Combs. 1962. *Perceiving, behaving, becoming.* New York: Association of Supervision and Curriculum Development.

Kilpatrick, W. H. 1918. "The project method." *Teachers College Record* 19 (September).

———. 1936. *Foundations of method.* New York: Macmillan.

Laughlin, C., and M. Martin. 1988. *Organizing for literacy learning.* New York: Teachers College Press.

Lee, D., and L. Lamoreaux. 1943. *Learning to read through experience.* New York: D. Appleton-Century-Crofts.

Lee, D., and R. V. Allen. 1963. *Learning to read through experience.* New York: Appleton-Century-Crofts.

Perrone, V. 1977. *First California conference on education evaluation and public policy.* Grand Forks, ND: North Dakota Study Group on Evaluation.

Read, C. 1975. *Children's categorization of speech sounds in English.* Research Report No. 17. Urbana, IL: National Council of Teachers of English.

Rosen, H. 1984. *Stories and meanings.* Sheffield, England: National Association for the Teaching of English; Upper Montclair, NJ: Boynton/Cook.

Rosenblatt, L. 1938. *Literature through exploration.* New York: Appleton-Century-Crofts. 3d ed., 1976, New York: Noble and Noble.

———. 1978. *The reader, the text, the poem.* Carbondale, IL: Southern Illinois University Press.

Taba, H. 1950. *Elementary curriculum in intergroup relations.* Washington, DC: American Council on Education.

Taba, H., E. Brady, and J. Robinson. 1952. *Intergroup education in public schools.* Washington, DC: American Council on Education.

Veatch, J. 1985. *How to teach reading with children's books.* New York: Richard C. Owen.

Vygotsky, L. S. 1978. *Mind in society,* ed. M. Cole, V. John-Steiner, S. Scribner, and E. Souberman. Cambridge: Harvard University Press.

———. 1986. *Thought and language,* trans. A. Kozulin. Cambridge: MIT Press.

Weber, L. 1973. "Letter from the director." In *Notes from workshop center for open education* 2(2). New York: City College.

Wells, G. 1986. *The meaning makers.* Portsmouth, NH: Heinemann.

Viewpoint: Jerome C. Harste

How Whole Language Got Its Name

I want to tell a personal story; namely my role in how whole language got its name. Much to some people's surprise, whole language wasn't always the name of the movement, nor did I just hatch advocating whole language.

I completed my doctoral work at the University of Minnesota in 1971. I had 38 hours of statistics, knew how to crunch numbers, and wanted to become known as a researcher—someone who did better teacher education research than was currently out there. My dissertation was a discriminant function analysis of program variables that aligned themselves with effective teacher education (Harste 1971). I was delighted when Indiana University offered me a position to develop a competency-based teacher education program in reading and language arts.

RELATE (REading-Language Arts Teacher Education), the program I helped develop, asked prospective teachers to define reading and, in light of their definition, create objectives that operationalized these beliefs. As definitions changed so did objectives. Although I personally preferred some people's definitions of reading over others, RELATE treated all positions as equally valid. Tolerance was science, scholarship was innocent, and eclecticism not a bad position to hold.

After two years of work in classrooms codirecting and codeveloping this teacher education project, I decided the problem was not with the program's design but rather that various groups had various objectives for what a good reading and language arts program ought to be. Elementary teachers thought their job was to teach phonics, word recognition, and vocabulary. Secondary teachers were more interested in comprehension. College professors were interested in effect. They wanted readers who not only could read, but did read.

So I decided to do a statistical study that would lend credibility to the rationale underlying RELATE as well as explicate the fact that different groups defined reading differently.

A group in California called the IOX Exchange had reduced reading to 15 major sets of objectives—vocabulary, word recognition, comprehension, attitude, and so on. Using a Q-Sort procedure I typed the elaborated form of these objectives on 3" × 5" cards and asked various groups of educators (elementary teachers, secondary teachers, college professors of reading) to rank them in three groups (the five most important, the five least important, the five that fell in the middle).

All went well. My stratified sample of elementary and secondary teachers sorted the objectives just fine. So did most of the college professors—19 out of 20.

The 20th one was Dr. Carolyn Burke, a recent graduate of Wayne State University. Instead of taking my 15 cards and sorting them as I asked, she scrawled on my form, "You can't do this, Harste. Reading doesn't work this way. We need to talk!"

I found her comment maddening. I called to set up a meeting while the data were running. I was not interested in learning anything as much

Jerome C. Harste, professor of Language Education at Indiana University, has been an elementary school teacher, and a Peace Corps volunteer, and has chaired the Commission on Reading of the National Council of Teachers of English. Dr. Harste is president of the National Conference on Research in English, past president of the National Reading Conference, treasurer for the Center for the Expansion of Language and Thinking, and is currently on the board of directors of the International Reading Association (1988–1990). He was a cowinner of the 1988 David H. Russell Research Award for outstanding contributions for the teaching of English.

as in having a fuller explanation for her refusal to participate.

And talk about refusals to participate. Years later I was having breakfast at an IRA convention with Yetta Goodman when she saw Jack Cassidy, past president of IRA, enter the restaurant. She invited Jack to join us for breakfast and introduced me to him by saying, "Jack, do you know Jerry Harste?"

"Well," Jack replied, "I've never met him, but I know his work." And then turning to me, he said, "You know that Q-Sort procedure you developed for studying teacher beliefs? Well, I ran it on everyone in the state of Delaware and got the same results you did. It was very helpful. I think I talked New Jersey into doing it next."

"What study was that, Jerry?" Yetta asked.

"You wouldn't be interested," I said.

She would have been. She had never missed a teachable moment in her life, but at 8:00 A.M. on that day I wasn't up to getting a third doctorate. I had already earned a second. That had happened when I went to see Carolyn Burke.

"Well, look at this objective here—vocabulary. Words are not either known or unknown. It depends on the story. We had readers in our studies at Wayne State who recognized words in one story and then couldn't read the same word in another story. The word wasn't predictable to them in this new context. I think you need to get a tape recorder and go listen to a couple of readers. The process is much more complex than your simple set of objectives leads people to believe."

I took her bait and so began my understanding of the reading process. At Minnesota we had studied factors that affected reading, but never really looked at reading itself. I found early psycholinguistic explanations of the process powerful. Burke found my hypothesis about teacher beliefs and its effect on classroom behavior cogent.

Together we decided to look at theoretical orientation to reading. The results of our four-year program of research—her interest in the reading process and my interest in teacher education—were well received by the profession. Our 1977 article launched our collaborative careers.

In that article we argued that to change reading behavior is to change beliefs: helping teachers and students is never a simple process like adding a new strategy, but rather an altering of basic beliefs about the reading process itself.

We did one other thing. We drew three models of reading. After rereading all of Frank Smith and Kenneth Goodman's work we decided to take a phrase Ken had embedded in the middle of one of his sentences as the label for what we saw as a new model of reading evolving in the field. We thus collaboratively titled the model, "Whole Language."

The label we chose, "Whole Language," caught on as did our collaboration. Our studies of early literacy were initiated so that we could begin to understand what young children know about language before coming to school (Harste, Woodward, and Burke 1984). Our curricular studies were conducted to explore what a new

Book Note

The Tone of Teaching

Max van Manen
1986; 56 pp.; $6
Portsmouth, NH:
  Heinemann

"Thoughtfulness is a special kind of knowledge" and in this little book Max van Manen describes the influence of thoughtfulness on curriculum and how teachers and children participate in school settings. The atmosphere in a classroom is "the way a teacher is present to children, and the way children are present to themselves and to the teacher." The impact personal philosophy has on teaching is clearly presented and will be confirmed by all teachers striving to understand whole language.

Carol Christine

❝I offer you a new definition of pedagogue. Those who are inhabited by hope are true fathers, true mothers, true teachers to children. Pedagogic hope animates the way a parent or teacher lives with a child, and it gives meaning to the way an adult stands in the world, represents the world to the child, takes responsibility for the world, and embodies or stylizes the forms of knowledge through which the world is known and explained to children. ❞ (p. 26)

environment for language learning might look like in classrooms based on these insights (Harste, Short, and Burke 1988).

While our whole language conclusions continue to evolve, we tell this language story for its literacy lesson. Through the story we came to understand collaborative learning as a series of basic processes. To the extent that whole language is and always has been an attempt to get teachers and children in touch with the basic processes in literacy (rather than talk about reading, children really read; rather than talk about writing, children really write), the story of how whole language got its name is a lesson in collaborative learning and, hence, what the past as well as the future of whole language is all about.

→ See: Creating Classrooms for Authors, p. 24; Goodman, pp. 98, 386; Language Stories & Literacy Lessons, p. 29; Whole Language: Inquiring Voices, p. 215.

References

Harste, J. C. 1971. "A multivariate discriminant function analysis of program variables that affect teacher education." Ph.D. diss., University of Minnesota.

Harste, J. C., and C. L. Burke. 1977. "A new hypothesis for reading teacher education research: Both the teaching and the learning of reading are theoretically based." In *Reading: Research, theory, and practice*, ed. P. D. Pearson. Twenty-sixth yearbook of the National Reading Conference. Chicago: National Reading Conference.

Harste, J. C., K. G. Short, with C. A. Burke. 1988. *Creating classrooms for authors: The reading-writing connection.* Portsmouth, NH: Heinemann.

Harste, J. C., V. A. Woodward, and C. A. Burke. 1984. *Language stories and lessons.* Portsmouth, NH: Heinemann.

Further Reading by Jerome C. Harste

◆ *Language Stories and Literacy Lessons,* with C. Burke and V. Woodward. Heinemann, 1984.

◆ *Creating Classrooms for Authors: The Reading-Writing Connection,* with K. Short and C. Burke. Heinemann, 1988.

◆ *Whole Language: Inquiring Voices,* with D. Watson and C. Burke. Scholastic, 1989.

◆ "The Authoring Cycle: Read Better, Write Better, Reason Better." Videotape series. Heinemann.

◆ *New Policy Guidelines for Reading.* ERIC/NCTE.

Cornerstone: Jayne DeLawter

A New Educational Agenda:
From Skill Acquisition to Language Learning

On a recent trip with Bonnie, a third-grade teacher who had taught for three years, our conversation turned to teaching reading. Bonnie did not know of my background in literacy development nor, as I came to realize, about whole language as an alternative to other views of reading and language. She began describing her current instructional activities—exercises in guide words and apostrophes, assignments in workbooks and comprehension questions.

After listening carefully to Bonnie's remarks, I asked her when she thought she *truly* was teaching reading. Her response surprised me, given the context she had just created. "I feel I'm really teaching reading after lunch when I take out the library book and read to the kids for twenty minutes. I can tell everyone is interested. Some of them don't even bother to draw. That's when I know I am helping them develop a love for books and reading."

I pursued it. "Suppose that tomorrow you were notified that holding a separate reading period and using your basal and workbooks were against the law. What if you would be fined fifty dollars if you taught reading as you are now?"

"Then I'd have the kids read for their science projects and do some historical fiction. I'd have lots of library books around," she promptly replied. "I wouldn't miss much of my usual routine! I can't possibly do all the skills listed in the teacher's edition anyway." She paused, "If only someone would tell me which skills are the most important. Then I'd do them and forget the rest. Then there'd be time for reading books."

At first I was stunned. For Bonnie, a shift toward language learning might actually—and happily—occur in her classroom *if* reading instruction, as she now defined it, were illegal!

Of course, change in educational practice is not as simple or dramatic as this story might suggest. As we continued talking, Bonnie voiced concerns that if she did not follow the basal scope and sequence, "how would her kids do on the tests?" She also wondered about finding time to read children's books and to reconceptualize her teaching schedule. Bonnie was well aware of the many obstacles to change.

However, a new educational agenda is indeed possible. Teachers can shift from a preoccupation with skill acquisition to a commitment to language learning for their students. They can change from skills-based, teacher-oriented classrooms to meaning-based, child-oriented ones. They can discard trivial dry-run exercises in order to involve students in authentic language use. And they can do it without breaking the law!

Change requires a different perspective on instruction, a change of mind about what is important. This transformation affects much more than literacy instruction. It becomes a new philosophy of education.

From External to Internal

In Bonnie's situation, the basal series, the tests, and the administrators dominated her perspective and her practice. Bonnie tried hard to conform to all these authorities. She believed that she was acting most responsibly when she was most faithful to the teacher's edition and covered the basal lessons as thoroughly as possible to guarantee to her administrator, her community, and herself that she was doing her job. She con-

scientiously prepared her students for their tests and followed the prescribed curriculum.

To change, Bonnie needed a supportive environment to do what she intuitively knew would contribute to real literacy—reading and discussing trade books, using reading and writing projects, studying and responding to literature. She also needed to see herself as a valuable and knowledgeable professional—to revalue her own competence.

Teachers in transition from skills to language necessarily change their perspective. They evolve from relying primarily on external directives to valuing internal purposes and intentions. They begin to count more on themselves and their professional peers than on outside sources and authorities. They trust their professional judgment.

Coming to Know

Teachers who wish to encourage authentic language learning in their classrooms need opportunities to study about language and language development and to reconsider their beliefs about language learning in view of their new knowledge. They need to test out their emerging views about learning and about teaching literacy. They need to observe in their own classrooms to identify the particular interests and strengths among their students. They also need to read literature for children and young adults. They need to learn observation and reporting procedures so that they can confidently report about language learning to students themselves, as well as to parents and administrators.

As teachers learn more about language and language learning, they will seek to provide supportive meaning-centered environments, alternative expectations, and timely interactions. Their change of mind about teaching and learning is a theoretical commitment. It carries with it implications for different classroom actions.

Time

One aspect that needs reconceptualization is time. Bonnie lamented, "There just isn't enough time to meet each kid's needs in each of their seven curriculum areas each week. And I only have 28 kids!" From a skills perspective, the time issue is magnified because each skill is treated as a discrete entity which must be introduced, practiced, and evaluated separately.

But teachers acting from a language point of view do not expect to keep everything separate. The new role is to clarify, not simplify by reducing and distorting. Activities are designed to engage students in authentic language through projects and activities that make sense to them and fit into broad curriculum goals. Although still at a premium, time is not divided into unvarying segments, but instead is allocated in chunks appropriate to classroom goals. Time limits are established with language learning in mind.

Another issue of time that goes beyond classroom scheduling is the compulsion for teachers like Bonnie to do it all right—right now. For example, when I suggested that Bonnie consider giving herself a three-year period to change from where she was to a more authentic and satisfying role for both her and her students, her response was disbelief. "That's forever!" She wanted to have everything in place immediately.

However, change is both gradual and transformational. Early attempts may be irregular and tentative. Teachers may try a new method and realize that a larger structure in their teach-

ing then needs to be adapted. They make another shift—of timing, materials, grouping—and again realize that further adjustments seem to make sense.

Collaboration

Language-based teachers need and seek support among like-minded teachers to discuss matters of professional concern. At group meetings, teachers contribute and gain specific ideas for instruction and evaluation of student work. They come to know that they are learners as well as teachers and that both teaching and learning are social.

They also realize a solidarity with each other and build a strong sense of professionalism. They begin to see that issues in their classrooms are often related to forces beyond their individual control. They come to recognize the political nature of schooling as they place teaching in the larger context of social and political life. The support group serves as a source of professional rejuvenation.

The New Agenda

The comments from Bonnie, a competent skills-based teacher, personalize the shift from skills instruction to language learning. Teachers who wish to change will need to learn more about language and language learning. They will need time for reflection. They will need resources to grow toward autonomy and theoretically consistent practices. They will need support from others who have set the same agenda—one of meaning-centered, language-based teaching and learning.

→ See: Goodman, p. 274; Heath, p. 422; A Letter to Teachers New to Whole Language, p. 10; Torbe, p. 232; Watson, p. 427; Wells, p. 402.

Further Reading by Jayne DeLawter

◆ "Teaching Literature: From Clerk to Explorer." Paper prepared for the Center for Learning and Teaching of Literature. SUNY-Albany, 1988.

Jayne DeLawter currently teaches reading/language education at Sonoma State University and directs the North Coastal California Literature Project. Her research has centered on risk-taking, curriculum as response, and teacher roles in language learning for adults and children. She established the North Bay TAWL in 1978.

Insult to Intelligence: The Bureaucratic Invasion of Our Classrooms

Frank Smith
1986; 304 pp.; $19.95
New York: Arbor House

I first heard Frank Smith speak about three years ago at our local TAWL convention. I was immediately taken by the force of his arguments and the commonsense clarity with which he presented his points. I have since read several of his books, but in *Insult to Intelligence* Frank Smith is at his confrontational best. He takes on the misuse of computer technology in the classroom, profit-minded publishers who are apparently unconcerned about how their materials ultimately affect learners, and well-intentioned educators who may ultimately be doing more harm than good, simply because they don't understand the way humans learn. I especially enjoyed Smith's discussion on making the best use of computer technology in the whole language classroom.

Insult to Intelligence is a good starting place for those who wish to become more familiar with the political landscape surrounding whole language.

Alan Flurkey

❝ Computers can be productive, creative, facilitatory devices for experts and beginners alike. What is wrong is not the computer but the thinking of many of the people who want to flood schools with electronic teaching technology. Computers can help students apprentice themselves to more experienced writers, artists, engineers, explorers, and scientists; computers can dissolve the classroom walls. ❞ (p. 230)

Book Note

How Children Construct Literacy: Piagetian Perspectives

Yetta Goodman, editor
1990; 127 pp.; $9
Newark, DE: International Reading Association

In this welcome addition to our further understanding of children's early constructions of literacy, Yetta Goodman is joined by an international group of women scholars including the groundbreaking researcher, Emelia Ferreiro. As these researchers use Piagetian-inspired methodology to probe children's early encounters with print, they reveal the concepts individual children have about print and challenge us with new and fascinating insights into developing literacy. An eye-opening work for both researchers and teachers.

Geane Hanson

❝ The researchers do not tell children that they are wrong or inconsistent but leave the children's contradictions unresolved, believing that through future interactions with the same or similar objects and daily experiences with written language, the children will adapt their conceptualizations.❞ (Goodman, p.7)

Resource: Periodical

Educational Horizons

$18/year (4 issues) domestic;
$25/year foreign from:
4101 E. Third St.
Bloomington, IN 47401
1-812-339-3411

The theme of the fall 1985 issue of *Educational Horizons* was "The Writing Revolution," and it carried articles by some of the top researchers in the early literacy field: Anne Haas Dyson, Yetta Goodman, Elizabeth Sulzby, and William Teale. This issue confirmed the statement that appears on the inside cover of this fine journal: *Educational Horizons,* the official publication of Pi Lambda Theta, was "founded in the spirit of academic excellence in order to provide leadership in addressing educational, social, and cultural issues of national and international significance. . . ."

LBB

Kidwatching
Yetta M. Goodman

Sergio

Sergio is nine years old. He has been a student in a bilingual third-grade class in Tucson, Arizona, since September. He did not know any English when he started school in Tucson. He's a Spanish speaker from rural Mexico where he went to school sporadically for about three years. He is in a whole language classroom where they talk a lot about the city of Tucson and the kinds of people who live there. He visited the Desert Museum recently with his class where they saw a roadrunner and other animals from the Sonoran Desert. A Yaqui artist visited the school for three weeks and spent several days with the students in Sergio's classroom. The students have been reading and writing about these experiences. In December, Sergio wrote the following story, which has been translated into conventional English.

> On sopot a taem
> a liro Kanaroo was
> luquin for fur en he
> coren fan no fur
> en he sa a rotranr
> en he was ranin hafe
> the rotranr en he
> gat the rotranr
> yne he erem

[Once upon a time a little kangaroo was looking for food and he couldn't find no food and he saw a roadrunner and he was running after the roadrunner and he got the roadrunner and he ate him.]

Knowing about Sergio's background and his classroom, and how all children invent written language, I've learned the following literacy lesson from the language story I've just related.

Sergio knows the structure of an English narrative. He knows it has a beginning, a middle, and an end. He knows stories need a series of episodes in the middle with tension coming toward the end. He knows the specific kind of language with which an English story begins and how to resolve the tension at the end. He controls not only story structure but sentence structure in English as well. He overgeneralizes the connective *and,* and does not use any punctuation to segment his sentences, clauses, or phrases.

He knows how to use resources in the classroom. In the classroom he found a chart on which the students classified animals from different continents in order to spell the word *kangaroo. Roadrunner* was also on one of the lists, but Sergio had enough confidence to generate that spelling. He is a risk-taker.

His spelling patterns show important characteristics of developing writers. He shows control over high frequency words as he conventionally spells *a, was, for, he, no,* and *the.*

He applies his knowledge of the graphophonic and articulatory systems. These systems include using the letter *r* for the flap sound before vowels: *liro/little; fur en/food and; coren/couldn't; erem/ate him.* He hears vowel glides and employs English spelling rules to invent the spelling of *taem/time.* He uses the Spanish spelling of the sound represented by *k* in English: *luquin/lookin.* (If you want to know more about this relationship, see Charles Read's work listed in the references that accompany the article "History of Whole Language.") His use of *ranr* in the words *running* and *roadrunner* may be related to his use of phonics. But he also shows that he knows both words are related. In this case he uses the same spelling twice. On the other hand, his spelling of the word *and* shows that when he is not sure of a spelling he will make changes even in the same text. He uses *en* three times but spells *yne* the last time. This is a complex spelling. He uses three letters for the word, moving the *n* into its correct position. The initial letter *y* can be a vowel, but it is also the Spanish word for *and.*

It is possible to continue analyzing Sergio's invented spelling to see what he knows about English and Spanish spelling systems.

It is important in this language lesson to appreciate the complexity of Sergio's writing system. He does not write with abandon. He is developing control over all aspects of the composition process.

➜ See: Goodman, pp. 32, 100, 208, 356; Wilde, p. 32.

I Used to Be...But Now I...

We used to work in isolation from one another without ever having been nudged to examine our beliefs and practices,
But now we value our collaboration which compels us to articulate, refine, explore and challenge our thinking. These interactions empower us and our teacher candidates to the realization that there are no ready-made answers. Each one of us must define our own reality.

—June Gravel and Wendy McDonell, teacher educators, Faculty of Education, York University

---

Resource: Periodical

Education Week

$29.97 year (40 issues) from:
4301 Connecticut Ave., NW, Ste. 432
Washington, DC 20008
1-202-364-4114

Did you know that there is a weekly newspaper devoted entirely to education? *Education Week* follows the most important developments in American education and keeps you abreast of what's happening in our profession across the states. It's also a good way of keeping up with political developments in the United States. They accept articles for their commentary page.

LBB

WELL-SAID

Teachers, like their students, have to learn to love the questions, as they come to realize that there can be no final agreements or answers, no final commensurability. And we have been talking about stories that open perspectives on communities grounded in trust, flowering by means of dialogue, kept alive in open spaces where freedom can find a place.

—Maxine Green, *The Dialectic of Freedom*

As Teachers See It

by Barbara Means

Remembrance of Things Past

It was 1972. Expectant faces peered up at the rocking chair when I said, "Welcome to first grade. What will we learn this year?"

Twenty-four voices chimed. "We'll learn to read!"

"All right," I said. "Let's get started."

From my pocket, I pulled labels of Skippy peanut butter, Wonder Bread, Campbell's chicken noodle soup, Corn Flakes.

"You can already read some things . . ."

How does that classroom differ from a whole language classroom of today? Although I had a teaching certificate, I didn't want to teach as I had been taught. What should I do with 24 little people, five days a week, five hours a day? I read about Roach Van Allen's concept that "print is talk written down," Sylvia Ashton Warner's key vocabulary, and the British Open School movement. I banned the basal readers and set up what I hoped were conditions for learning. Rows of desks disappeared as I created a library area with rug and pillows, table with markers, blank books and paper, a plywood bus as a listening center with taped stories and books, shelves with games, and an art area over a drop cloth with paint, paste, crayons, and "junk."

As the weeks progressed, the environment became rich in print—words of the songs we sang daily, mail delivered to labeled shoeboxes, pictures of everyone with self write-ups on a bulletin board, child-authored books, and special words on shower hooks. Stories were read aloud and silently as USSR (Uninterrupted Sustained Silent Reading) increased from 5 to 25 minutes. The students learned, parents made blank books or listened to readers, the principal got us a stove, guinea pigs took up residence, a mother donated a sofa, and the other teachers left us alone.

By the second year, I experimented with sign-up sheets, name tags on pegboard, and finally abandoned the attempt to organize each child's options. Trust triumphed over control! I still did not know how to "teach" reading. I only knew that the combination of many story experiences, sharing the patterns of language in verse and song, writing with dictation, publishing, and self-selecting books to read resulted in everyone reading—eventually.

When a storyteller came to the room, David said proudly, "He can't read either; he has to *tell* his stories!" But even David, who showed no interest in books until February, was on grade level according to a standardized test in June. Two students were on sixth-grade level and five on fifth! Clearly something was working. For seven years I "taught" beginning reading, then left the classroom for other challenges.

My classroom "worked," but I never knew why. And it was lonely out there. There were no models, no experts to help. I only knew that I had to treat these children as individuals and could not impose a curriculum from Chicago upon them. I had no research-based theory of language, just an instinct that the basal approach was wrong. I set up an environment so that learning could happen. I trusted that students would learn if I filled the room with invitations.

How did my classroom in the 1970s differ from whole language classrooms of today? Clearly the activities in my classroom could be part of any whole language program. However, whole language is more than a series of activities. An overriding difference is that now there is a theoretical basis of language learning, grounded in research, that supports a literate environment where children are free to discover and to realize their intentions. Psycholinguistics, the relatively recent linking of cognitive psychology and linguistics, contributed the most to a learning theory that keeps language whole and understands that learning is the result of the learner's own activity.

Perhaps the most significant change for today's whole language teachers is that they are not alone. There are support groups, conferences, books, and resource people. Possibilities, growth, and strategies that succeed or fail can be shared. There is a safety net of support available to anyone who reaches out for it. No longer is it "lonely out there."

→ See: Christine, p. 410; Stevenson, p. 411; Watson, pp. 408, 427.

Barbara Means is the director of the Otsego–Northern Catskills School Library System, Stamford, NY.

Resource: Organization

THE ERIC CLEARINGHOUSE ON
HANDICAPPED AND GIFTED CHILDREN

Education Resources Information Center (ERIC)

Many educators have heard of ERIC, but may not know exactly what the acronym stands for: Educational Resources Information Center. The key word is "resources." ERIC is a federally funded education information system that features a data base of over 400,000 journal annotations and 300,000 education-related document abstracts. It is also a source of books and pamphlets about all aspects of education. The 16 ERIC clearinghouses are listed below.
LBB

Adult, Career, and Vocational Education
Ohio State University
Center on Education and Training for Employment
1900 Kenny Rd.
Columbus, OH 43210-1090
1-614-292-4353; 1-800-848-4815

Reading and Communication Skills
Indiana University
Smith Research Center
2805 E.10th St., Ste. 150
Bloomington, IN 47405-2373
1-812-855-5847

Counseling and Personnel Services
University of Michigan
School of Education, Rm. 2108
610 E. University St.
Ann Arbor, MI 48109-1259
1-313-764-9492

Rural Education and Small Schools
Appalachia Educational Laboratory, Inc.
1031 Quarrier St.
P.O. Box 1348
Charleston, WV 25325-1348
1-800-624-9120 (outside WV)
1-800-344-6646 (inside WV)

Educational Management
University of Oregon
1787 Agate St.
Eugene, OR 97403-5207
1-503-686-5043

Science, Mathematics, and Environmental Education
Ohio State University
1200 Chambers Rd., Rm. 310
Columbus, OH 43212-1792
1-614-292-6717

Elementary and Early Childhood Education
University of Illinois
College of Education
805 W. Pennsylvania Ave.
Urbana, IL 61801-4897
1-217-333-1386

Social Studies/Social Science Education
Indiana University
Social Studies Development Center
2805 E. Tenth St., Ste. 120
Bloomington, IN 47405-2373
1-812-855-3838

Handicapped and Gifted Children
Council for Exceptional Children
1920 Association Dr.
Reston, VA 22091-1589
1-703-620-3660

Teacher Education
American Association of Colleges
for Teacher Education
One Dupont Circle, NW, Ste. 610
Washington, DC 20036-2412
1-202-293-2450

Higher Education
George Washington University
One Dupont Circle, NW, Ste. 630
Washington, DC 20036-1183
1-202-296-2597

Tests, Measurement, and Evaluation
American Institutes for Research
Washington Research Center
3333 K St., NW
Washington, DC 20007-3893
1-202-342-5060

Information Resources
Syracuse University
School of Information Studies
Huntington Hall, Rm. 030
Syracuse, NY 13244-2340
1-315-443-3640

Urban Education
Teachers College
Columbia University
Institute for Urban and Minority Education
Main Hall, Rm. 300, Box 40
525 W. 120th St.
New York, NY 10027-9998
1-212-678-3433

Junior Colleges
University of California at Los Angeles
Mathematical Sciences Bldg., Rm. 8118
405 Hilgard Ave.
Los Angeles, CA 90024-1564
1-213-825-3931

Language and Linguistics
Center for Applied Linguistics
1118 22d St., NW
Washington, DC 20037-0037
1-202-429-9551

Cornerstone: Kathy O'Brien

How I Became a Whole Language Teacher

To understand how I became a whole language teacher, you have to go back to my first year of teaching. Everyone's first year of teaching is difficult, but mine seems to have been especially bad. Jack Prelutsky's *The New Kid on the Block* (1984, p. 67) reminds me of my first year:

> We each wore half a horse,
> and pranced in a parade,
> And you can guess, of course,
> which half of it *I* played.

My first year of teaching was one of the worst years of my life. I was in a first grade with 33 kids. Ronnie and Donnie were twins so identical their own mother couldn't tell them apart, and, of course, they were always dressed alike. Every 15 minutes one would come up and ask to go to the bathroom. I'd say, "No, you just went." He'd say, "That wasn't me, that was my brother."

I had a skinny girl named Ethel May Jones. She had a pint-size body and a 10-gallon voice. You could hear her talking way down in the principal's office. Ethel May didn't take nothing from nobody. And she had tons of energy. One day she came running into the room, slid halfway across the room on her knees, did a cartwheel, and finished up by jumping on top of someone's desk. When she was done, she gave me a big smile.

Ethel May used to wear her hair in cornrows. One day, just as we were doing all the stuff teachers and kids do before lunch, I thought, gee, Ethel May has been really quiet this morning; I'll go back and see what she's gotten done. I was pleased that Ethel May had been nondisruptive. I even thought that maybe I had something to do with it. When I reached Ethel May's desk, I found that she had indeed made excellent progress in her work: braiding her friend's hair into cornrows and spending a lot of time doing it. But Ethel May had run into a problem because her friend's hair was very fine and could not be braided into cornrows. Ethel May solved the problem with paste—an entire jar. She had generously applied it where the cornrows wouldn't stay.

So we struggled. They played in the restroom, got into fights, lost their pencils, did their skill sheets, practiced their handwriting and spelling. I worked long hours preparing lessons on short-*a* sounds, centers on alphabetizing, and dittos on the long-vowel sounds. I checked phonics pages on the schwa sound (which I was never able to recognize), devised handwriting exercises for the class to copy, and constructed sentences from the current spelling list that I thought would be funny or interesting.

And I hated my job. I lost my sense of humor, my sense of myself, and my sense of teaching. I hated my job because I wasn't being honest with myself and with the kids.

I was telling my students, through the way I taught and the kind of activities I had them do, that reading, writing, listening, and speaking are separate processes, separate subjects that don't have anything to do with each other or anything else. Because I didn't have a writing program, I was telling them that writing meant handwriting and practicing slants and circles and holding a fat pencil in the proper way. I was

Kathy O'Brien began her teaching career in a first-grade classroom in Pennsylvania and taught there for two years. Then, after adjusting to radical culture shock, she taught remedial reading to high school students for three years. She obtained her Ed.D. from West Virginia University and went on to teach at Columbia College in Columbia, Missouri. Kathy currently teaches at California State University San Bernardino and is president of the Inland Empire Teachers Applying Whole Language (TAWL) group. Her areas of interest are children's and adolescent literature with an emphasis on multicultural literature.

teaching them that reading meant learning vowel sounds and consonant blends and that real stories weren't important or related to learning to read. I wouldn't admit, to myself or to them, that the only good lessons I had, when both the kids and I felt good about what we had done, were those involving the reading and discussion of children's books. Or there were those rare instances when I'd take time out from the skill-and-drill period I called reading or language arts to do an art project, write a class story, or do something related to an upcoming holiday. Those lessons didn't count. We just did them for fun and they weren't really part of the curriculum. I had a curriculum that consisted of isolated skills taught for the sake of passing a proficiency test at the end of the book, as well as a district achievement test. It was a curriculum entirely prescribed by textbook publishers who didn't know my kids. And my students marched mindlessly through these programs, touched by nothing, including me.

I know now that this curriculum went against everything I knew and felt about the way kids learn. I was extremely unhappy with the basal reader and fragmented curriculum I was teaching, but I didn't know of any alternatives at the time and probably wouldn't have been confident enough to try them anyway.

In desperation, I enrolled in a master's degree program in reading and took my first class during the summer. There I began to hear about whole language and the theoretical tenets underlying whole language teaching. It sounded good in theory, but what did it mean in practice?

Luckily, I met a teacher who was willing to show me what it meant. She understood how kids learn and showed me what a supportive, risk-taking environment for learners was like. She showed me how real writing and real reading can be done in a classroom. And she understood how scary it is to let go of my basal, my skill lists, my spelling book, and my handwriting exercises and face an entire morning labeled "language." She gave me the same help and support that she gave her students as I learned how to be a risk-taker. She introduced me to other teachers who were trying some of the same things I was, and together we supported one another. My classroom began to change from a teacher-directed skill-and-drill classroom to a student-centered whole language classroom. The transition was slow, demanding, frustrating, and never easy. But the learning that I saw taking place, and the joy my students and I were sharing as we were involved in that learning, were so obvious to me that I felt the effort was worth it.

I have evolved slowly into a whole language teacher. I am confident that what I do is theoretically consistent with how people learn language, and I make no apologies for what I do in the classroom and how I do it. I believe learning and students, not basal readers and skill lists, should be at the heart of every classroom. Most important, I talk to other teachers about what I know about kids and learning and share my ideas of how to set up a whole language classroom.

I think that whole language teachers are like Bidemmi in Vera Williams's book *Cherries and Cherry Pits* (1986), who plants cherry pits in her yard. She nurtures them and protects them. Eventually the pits grow into trees that are strong and lush and feed Bidemmi's neighbors until they "all fall down laughing from eating so many cherries and spitting out the pits . . . and all the cherry pits start to grow until there is a whole forest of cherry trees right on our own block." Like Bidemmi, we whole language teachers need to plant the seeds of classroom change. Like Bidemmi, we have to nurture and support and protect those seeds. Eventually we will transform our "block," our community of learning and schooling, into one that respects and empowers all learners—teachers and students.

→ See: Goodman, p. 274; A Letter to Teachers New to Whole Language, p. 10; Literature Reference List, p. 429.

References

Prelutsky, J. 1984. *The new kid on the block.* New York: Scholastic.

Williams, V. B. 1986. *Cherries and cherry pits.* New York: Greenwillow.

Further Reading by Kathy O'Brien

◆ "Increasing Environmental Awareness through Children's Literature," with D. Stoner. *Reading Teacher,* October 1987.

◆ "Using Children's Literature in the History–Social Studies Curriculum." *Social Studies Review* 23(1), Fall 1988.

◆ "Integrated Language Arts and Whole Language Are Not Necessarily Synonymous." *California Reader* 23(2), Winter 1990.

Book Note

Breaking Ground: Teachers Relate Reading and Writing in the Elementary School

Jane Hansen, Thomas Newkirk, and Donald Graves, editors
1985; 224 pp.; $15
Portsmouth, NH: Heinemann

This collection of thoughtful, well-written classroom descriptions ranges from Alfreda Furnas's kindergarten class to Nancie Atwell's eighth-grade classroom. Exciting examples of student talk and writing illustrate the shared learning of teachers and students. Included are inspiring essays by the editors, as well as a brilliant piece by everyone's favorite writing mentor, Donald Murray.

Mary Kitagawa

❝I never really anticipated that these kindergarten children would learn to read without traditional teaching methods. Certainly we'd been learning how to write, but we'd had no reading books, no groups, no workbooks, no flashcards. As the year progressed and child after child, one third in all, spontaneously started reading, I had to admit that somehow the combination of their own writing and watching the writing and reading process go on day after day, must have somehow provided them access to the print around them. ❞ (Furnas, p. 43)

❝The student who was living one life becomes a writer and lives twice, thrice, a multiplication of lives, each life of words reassembling the lived life into new meanings. The text, moving away from the student's control, turns back to instruct the student, making meaning of what the student gathered, knowing and unknowing, living and studying. The evolving text, saying what it did not expect to say, passes back and forth over experience making new connections, contradictions, imaginings. ❞ (Murray, p. 201)

Education in Turin: A Romance by Herbert Kohl

Continued from page 375

Beginning Again:
The Progressive Legacy

The sixties and the civil rights movement took most people in Turin by surprise. They had conveniently forgotten that the black members of the community had been struggling to realize their share in the American dream for over 100 years. However, the Burnses were aware of the problems that existed in the school and in the economy. Alice's legacy wouldn't let them forget, and Phillip, and his wife, Susan, passed on that sense of decency to their children. In the summer of 1964, during his junior year at the University of Michigan in Ann Arbor, Robert Stokes Burns went to Mississippi with other whites to support black people's struggle for decency and justice. On returning from the Mississippi Freedom Summer, Robert decided that he had to become more fully involved in struggles for social and economic justice. One summer wasn't enough. Robert decided to teach in a poor community and build democracy through his work with the children. Robert chose the way of his grandmother and great-grandmother but didn't know it.

When he graduated from Michigan in 1965, Robert got a teaching credential. The open classroom was in the air, schools for democracy 1960s style. Robert took a job teaching in the Hough section of Cleveland. His students were mostly black and miseducated.

After several years of teaching he began to discover respectful, creative ways to reach his students, ways confirmed in books like *How Children Learn*, *Death at an Early Age*, *The Way It Spozed to Be*, *36 Children*, and *The Lives of Children*. Robert felt that he was part of a new movement that could change society through the schools. (He was part of a movement but not a new one.) Once again the democratic impulse surfaced in public education, cut off from its roots in the common school move-

ment, but with the same values and goals.

Robert met Joanna Berg in Hough. She was teaching third grade and he was the new sixth-grade teacher. They struggled together to undo their students' bitterness about schools, and to reach people in the community. However, as they felt they were about to succeed, they were fired when the parents they worked with lost a major battle with the district's central administration over minority hiring and local community control of schools.

After seven years in Cleveland, Robert asked Joanna if she was willing to go with him to Turin, his hometown, and settle for a while, take some rest and recreation. Robert had been offered a job teaching sixth grade by a friend of his family who was on the school board—and there was also talk of an opening teaching English at the high school that might interest Joanna.

Simply wanting to live quietly and do one's work well seemed like a moral failing, a betrayal of their friends' as well as of their deepest beliefs. Yet they were tired. They wanted to have a child and were afraid that since they were both over 30 it would soon be too late. They decided to return to Turin for six months, and stayed.

➡ See: 36 Children, p. 225; The Way It Spozed to Be, p. 225.

References

Dennison, G. 1968. *The lives of children.* New York: Bantam.
Herndon, J. 1969. *The way it spozed to be.* New York: Bantam.
Holt, J. 1967. *How children learn.* New York: Pitman.
Kohl, H. 1967. *36 children.* World.
Kozol, J. 1967. *Death at an early age.* Boston: Houghton Mifflin.

Continued on page 413

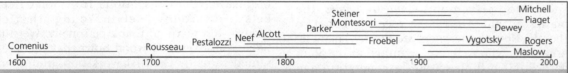

					Steiner			Mitchell	
					Montessori			Piaget	
				Parker			Dewey		
		Pestalozzi	Neef	Alcott		Froebel		Vygotsky	Rogers
Comenius	Rousseau							Maslow	
1600	1700		1800			1900			2000

Pioneers: Carl Rogers (1902–1987) & Abraham Maslow (1908–1970)

by Ron Miller

Carl Rogers

Rogers and Maslow are the key figures in the development of humanistic psychology in the 1950s and 1960s, which led in the following years to the popular human potential movement and various educational approaches known as "integrative," "person-centered," "affective," "confluent," and simply "humanistic" education. Rogers was a psychotherapist who developed his "client-centered" method as an alternative to psychoanalysis; Maslow was a researcher and theorist. Their work aimed to turn psychology's attention away from neurosis and animal behavior toward the innate human potentials for growth, healing, and insight. They sought to replace a mechanistic psychological science with a holistic understanding of human life.

Rogers made an explicit, and important, contribution to educational theory with his 1969 book *Freedom to Learn.* (It was reissued in 1983 under the title *Freedom to Learn for the Eighties.*) Drawing upon his long career as a distinguished psychotherapist, Rogers emphasized several themes that have appeared consistently in the holistic tradition: that true learning involves the whole person (including feelings, concerns, and creativity); that the human being aspires toward growth and personal integration, but needs an

Abraham Maslow

emotionally supportive environment that encourages self-discovery; and that every student—and every teacher—ought to be respected as a unique and precious person and not be treated according to social roles. For Rogers, these themes were extensions of his own central principles of client-centered therapy: trust and unconditional acceptance, empathy and understanding, and personal authenticity.

Rogers argued that the "dizzying changes" occurring in the modern world make traditional educational approaches obsolete; in a technologically advanced global culture, young people should not be expected merely to learn established answers, but to learn creative problem solving and empathic understanding of other people and cultures. In a nuclear age, Rogers warned, we must encourage new ways of relating to the world and each other, or else destruction will ensue. Still, Carl Rogers held an optimistic faith in the ability of human beings to grow in wisdom and compassion when given a nurturing, supporting environment.

Abraham Maslow, too, argued that human nature is intrinsically good, or at the very least it is neutral. He believed that "being needs"—the striving for identity, meaning, and

purpose in life—could be satisfied only if more basic physical and emotional needs were satisfied. Maslow stated that education must allow each person to "find out what's already in him" in order to facilitate personal growth.

The "human potential movement," which followed Rogers's and Maslow's work, led to many new approaches in education. The Association for Humanistic Psychology and the Association for Humanistic Education are international groups that sponsor publications, conferences, and professional collaboration. New educational techniques have been developed by these humanistic practitioners, including "encounter" groups, values clarification exercises, self-esteem enhancement programs, guided imagery and visualization practices, and many "integrative" and "whole-brain" techniques based on new understandings of how the brain actually works.

Further Reading

Maslow, Abraham. 1975. "Some Educational Implications of the Humanistic Psychologies." In *Four Psychologies Applied to Education*, ed. Thomas Roberts. Cambridge, MA: Schenkman.
Rogers, Carl. 1983. *Freedom to Learn for the Eighties.* Columbus, OH: Merrill.

YOUNG ARTISTS

"A Dog's Life is a Proud One"—Michael Blevens, 15, Gladstone, OR (from *Treasures 2*, See p. 162)

Professional Development

As I See It:
Kenneth S. Goodman

Hawaiian Memories:
Whole Language, Not *Haole* Language

On May 24, 1988, Yetta worked with a group of resource teachers led by Charlotte and Jo Miller and other professionals in Central District on Oahu in Hawaii. The district includes Pearl City and much of the military and naval bases in Honolulu. She met with a group of five women who are attempting to facilitate whole language in the district. The mentor is Ken Yamamoto, a sensitive and innovative educator whose path has crossed ours many times in the past. As a consultant, he did a great deal for education in American Samoa.

The first time we met, Ken saved us from considerable anguish. Yetta had arrived to do some advance setup for a research group I was bringing on the following Monday. We had made arrangements, we thought, to tape 60 kids reading two stories each as part of a major miscue research study. We would have just one week to accomplish this, so it seemed like a good idea for Yetta to go ahead to check things out with a research assistant.

When she arrived at the district office it became apparent that something was wrong. They didn't seem to want to give Yetta the information on the school we'd be working in. Finally on Friday morning she insisted on going out to the school. It turned out there was a problem. The teachers had been involved in a particularly unpleasant strike the year before and they were now balking at having their classrooms disrupted. Just when it looked really bad, one of the teachers showed Yetta a folder from a staff development conference. On the cover was a quote from me. After Yetta explained that it was indeed *that* Goodman who would be arriving Monday morning, the teacher quickly called Ken Yamamoto, who was heading the staff

development team. He arrived and in short order eased all hard feelings. When I arrived with the team, things went off without a hitch.

The reading I taped became part of a rich miscue data base that we've used in several studies. I've used the tapes often in presentations to teachers. A poster blowup of one Samoan second-grader still adorns my office wall. Her feet are bare, she has a Band-Aid on one heel, and she's reading.

I tell this story because it illustrates the long period of hard work that Ken Yamamoto and others like him have put in that is now bearing fruit in the whole language movement. Like us he must feel a sense of wonder as he sits with a group of teachers who are aware of the theory and research of whole language, who have read not only our work but that of Don Graves, Jerry Harste, Dorothy Watson, Judith Newman, and many others. The teachers themselves have gone as far as Nova Scotia, New Hampshire, and Toronto to expand their vision of whole language. These teachers sought Yetta's help so that they could help the teachers they work with move away from basal readers and integrate their curriculum.

There is a good deal more enlightenment now about the Hawaiian Pidgin (really a creole) that is spoken at home by many island children and on the playgrounds even by *haoles*, the mainland kids who have recently come to Hawaii. Now the teachers are mostly Japanese-Americans who were not permitted in the Standard English high schools a generation ago because they were pidgin speakers. A Hawaiian Standard has emerged that is not pidgin but not my midwestern dialect either. Hawaiian and pidgin words spice up the speech of islanders of all classes and ethnicity—words like *kapu* (it

means keep out, but in a special Hawaiian way—the *menehunes* will get you if you disregard a *kapu*) or *pau* (done, finished, over). Of course, thank you and hello don't at all carry the warmth of *mahalo* and *aloha*.

Yet even today there's a move afoot to legislate Standard English into the schools. One of the things we learned in our research is that pidgin-speaking children and those who speak other low-status dialects are not disadvantaged. They are able to understand the dialects of books and teachers as well as their own. Ironically it is children growing up in middle-class enclaves who understand only their own dialects.

The resource teachers Yetta worked with understand the importance of respecting the language of their pupils. They know each child must be encouraged to use and build on the language base he or she brings to school. They understand that Hawaiian Pidgin is not bad or useless in learning. And they understand that whole language programs make it possible for children to continue using their mother tongue, their home language, while expanding to include other genres, other dialects, even a second language as children feel the need and value of such expansion. All whole language classrooms are immersion programs. They immerse kids in rich linguistic and literate environments in which all forms of language are cherished. Kids emerge literate and linguistically empowered.

I went to Hawaii 20 years ago to teach the teachers about language. Yetta and I have returned many times to study island children reading, to do oral language workshops, to teach miscue analysis, to lecture, and, above all, to learn. We have learned from the kids, from the teachers in our workshops, and from many dedicated educators: Ken Yamamoto, Barbara Kim, Don Enoki, Frances Shimotsu, Stanley Murakawa, Gabriel I, Aloha Ho, Violet Hee, Betsy Fuji Young, Kelvin Young, Harriet Suzuki—too many to thank personally. We still have a monkey-pod wood bowl that was presented to us by the first workshop group. On the bottom, inscribed in pidgin is "Real good you wen' come" (We're glad you came). To them and all the others I respond, "*Aloha* and *mahalo: mahalo nui!*"

➜ See: Goodman, pp. 83, 98.

Classroom Demonstrations

by Donald Y. Enoki

Supporting Whole Language in Honolulu

As director of the Compensatory Education Section in the Honolulu School District, I am responsible for the planning, development, implementation, and evaluation of the ESEA Chapter 1, Students of Limited English Proficiency (SLEP), and the Gifted and Talented (G/T) programs. Based on the district's enrollment of 35,000 students, the three support programs combined provide instructional services to over 7,400 students, or approximately 21 percent of the population in grades K through 12.

In 1974 in the district's Chapter 1 program we began to develop and implement a holistic approach to language learning. Basic to our planning was the need to establish a philosophy, a set of beliefs stemming from research on language acquisition.

Curriculum and instructional strategies were developed and field-tested over the next several years incorporating whole language teaching and

concepts. Project teachers and principals were intensively inserviced by consultants from the Center for the Expansion of Language and Thinking (CELT). Drs. Kenneth S. Goodman, Yetta Goodman, Dorothy Watson, and Carolyn Burke provided much of the leadership and impetus for the staff to continue developing the theoretical framework, which gradually evolved into the Comprehensive Language Improvement Project plan (CLIP), a whole language approach based on the principles of sociopsycholinguistics.

In 1979, the heavy influx of refugee and immigrant students into the district created the need to provide bilingual, cultural, and English language assistance to these students. With the dedicated support and assistance from Dr. Dorothy Watson, the staff integrated the whole language concept and sociopsycholinguistic principles into the SLEP program. Intensive workshops were conducted for all bilingual and

ESL-trained teachers and administrators. Teachers' philosophical beliefs about language and reading changed significantly as they participated in the whole language workshops and applied the newly acquired teaching strategies in their classrooms. Based on DeFord's Theoretical Orientation of Reading Profile (TORP), the vast majority of SLEP teachers who were phonics or word-skills believers now became true believers and teachers of whole language teaching. They have created meaning-centered classrooms in which the students' natural language and experiences are emphasized.

Program results have been very positive for both Chapter 1 and SLEP. The curriculum and instructional integration through whole language have demonstrated the effectiveness of the approach. Positive student evaluation results since 1974 continue to confirm the soundness of principles and applications. In both programs, based on standardized measures, the average pretest mean scores in reading comprehension tests have shown significant and steady increases over the past 14 years. Presently, the district's CLIP model of whole language teaching is being piloted and implemented in the Gifted and Talented Program. The future for whole language in our district looks very promising.

Donald Y. Enoki is a district educational specialist in the Honolulu School District, Honolulu, HI.

 **As Teachers See It**

by Maureen C. White

Acquisition Learning with Don Holdaway in New Zealand

> Every time we teach a child something, we keep him from inventing it himself... that which we allow him to discover by himself, will remain with him.
>
> —*Jean Piaget*

Every summer, the Humanities Institute in Belmont, Massachusetts, organizes international travel tours for educators. Their 1988 New Zealand/Australia program, in cooperation with Lesley College, Cambridge, Massachusetts, was different from previous years in that it had classroom theory and practice as its focus and school observation as the major activity. Don Holdaway, the internationally acclaimed language theorist from Australia and previously a teacher in New Zealand, led 30 United States educators in an exploration of whole language learning in the New Zealand schools.

Two weeks of intense classroom observations and analytical group discussions finally made me see the whole picture—the connection between the whole language theory that is slowly but steadily creeping into our elementary schools, and the writing process philosophy that my school system in Haverhill, Massachusetts, has been zealously trying to implement for the past seven years. This New Zealand/Australia study tour gave me a framework to mesh these two natural models of learning. The measure of the trip's academic worth was being able to crystallize the role of process writing into a whole language setting, and to see how New Zealand's cooperative/collaborative method of teaching offers its students more permanent learning.

However, as Colin Turnbull (1986, p. 47) has written, "Each fresh discovery merely reveals more that is unknown; there is always another question to ask." This was happening to me as I observed classrooms and looked at the whole issue of literacy through the perspective of family learning. Harvard University's Courtney Cazden's (1988) superlatives for the "Kiwi schools as the world's best" piqued my curiosity as to what makes them stand out.

It only took our first warm Maori welcome at the Richmond Road School in Auckland for me to start challenging some of my teaching assumptions. Our introduction to this school started with an orientation and discussion of the school's philosophy by each staff member. Their system of cooperative/collaborative teaching and learning intrigued me. They stress unity, not individuality, and they distinguish between acquiring language literacy versus being instructed in it. As a reading and writing specialist, I was especially interested in their Reading Recovery Program, which boasts an unbelievably high success rate in remediating young children with reading problems; their emphasis on learning how good readers read, not how poor readers fail, also made sense to me.

I quickly learned that literacy learning in New Zealand has its roots in the home. Parents are truly perceived as children's first teachers, and beginning reading techniques are modeled on the bedtime story approach. A strong read-aloud program is pervasive in the schools. New Zealand does not use a basal reader; the teachers take pride in using quality literature from the very beginning to teach reading. Their focus is on meaning over skills; reading for them is a process of strategies—self-correction, prior knowledge, predicting, rereading—not an aggregation of discrete skills.

The New Zealand curriculum, which shifts the focus from the teacher as purveyor of information to teacher as facilitator and initiator of activities, merits more experimentation in our American schools. I've come home with a clearer understanding of what Thomas Carruthers (1987, p. 88) meant when he wrote, "A good teacher has been defined as one who makes himself progressively unnecessary."

→ See: Cairney, p. 345; Cambourne, p. 17; DeFord, p. 113; The Foundations of Literacy, p. 45; Goodman, p. 344; Holdaway, p. 44; Pinnell, p. 112.

References

Carruthers, T. 1987. *In the middle: Writing, reading, and learning with adolescents*, ed. N. Atwell. Portsmouth, NH: Heinemann.

Cazden, C. 1988. From a pamphlet distributed at Richmond Road School, Auckland, New Zealand, 19 July.

Turnbull, C. 1986. *Pursuit of literacy*, ed. M. Sampson. Dubuque, IA: Kendall Hunt.

Maureen C. White is a writing coordinator in the Haverhill Public Schools, Haverhill, MA.

 ## Classroom Demonstrations

by Shirley Kaltenbach

Alaska Hosts First Whole Language Institute

West Valley High School in Fairbanks, Alaska, was the setting for Alaska's first Whole Language Institute, June 5–23, 1989. During this three-week institute, 28 Alaskan teachers worked cooperatively to intensely explore whole language. Participants read and discussed texts by Constance Weaver, Denny Taylor, Nancie Atwell, Elizabeth Cohen, and Harste/Short/Burke, and heard noted guest speakers. In addition, participants read widely to research their own questions and wrote implementation plans for the coming school year. Facilitating the institute were Fairbanks teachers Terri Austin and Shirley Kaltenbach.

This graduate-level institute was a cooperative venture of the Fairbanks North Star Borough School District and the Alaska State Writing Consortium. Outstanding teachers, kindergarten through eighth grade, were selected statewide by an application process. Selections were based on the applicants' knowledge of process learning and their professional abilities. Teachers' applications were accompanied by letters of support from their principals or supervisors.

Teachers Learned by Doing

"Terri and I tried to model Vygotsky's theory of proximal development for the participants. Practice of this theory sets whole language classrooms apart from the more traditional educational setting. In the whole language classroom, students take charge of their learning and are allowed to struggle. Facilitators provide instruction when students have tried, struggled, and are primed to learn," stated Kaltenbach.

Teachers Experienced Group Dynamics

"We saw 28 teachers grow together as a family, a personal family and a professional family. We like each other as people and respect each other as professionals," added Austin.

Teachers' Learning Will Continue

These educators will continue to meet monthly with facilitators Austin and Kaltenbach for a one-credit class during the 1989–90 school year. In seven follow-up sessions, they will read professional publications, discuss their classroom observations, and prepare a case study of one student. Seven out-of-town teachers will participate through writing, use of audio and visual tapes, and an occasional audio-conference.

One Teacher's Evaluation

One participant's final institute evaluation reflected the positive feelings of many of the other members of the class. She wrote, "Twenty-eight teachers came together for three weeks to read, listen, discuss, argue, and write about literacy. This time came out of their precious summer vacation. Ask any member if this time was well spent."

→ See: Graham, p. 426.

Shirley Ann Kaltenbach is an elementary teacher at University Park Elementary School, Fairbanks, AK.

Resource: Organizations

Art Research and Curriculum Associates (ARC)

310 8th St., Ste. 220
Oakland, CA 94607
1-415-834-9455

ARC Associates, a private nonprofit organization, was founded in 1977 to address the needs of a rapidly growing Asian population. It has since expanded to serve the needs of all minority students. It carries out a range of activities including research, developing appropriate curriculum for second-language learners, encouraging and supporting community involvement in the schools, and disseminating information on exemplary education programs and practices for minority students. It also publishes a variety of educational materials.

One of ARC's major commitments is the operation of two federally funded agencies:

Multifunctional Resource Center (MRC)

310 8th St.,
Ste. 301
Oakland, CA
94607
1-415-834-9458

Two *Catalog* essayists, Katherine Samway and Carole Urzúa, help staff the MRC in Northern California; the other center is in Hawaii. The MRC supports teachers of second-language learners through an extensive inservice program and assists with the development of curriculum materials and the dissemination of information on effective educational programs for second-language learners. It also publishes a monthly newsletter for California educators.

Southwest Center for Educational Equity

4665 Lampson Ave.
Los Alamitos, CA 90720
1-213-598-7661

The center is a joint project sponsored by ARC and the Southwest Regional Laboratory in Los Alamitos, California. Its focus is the desegregation of public schools; it provides technical assistance and training for the preparation, adoption, and implementation of plans for desegregation based on sex, race, and national origin.

LBB

Cornerstone: Peter J. H. Krause

Do We Have Beliefs About Learning? You Bet!

As director general of the Lakeshore School Board (LSB) in Quebec, I work with board members to provide the best education possible. When I joined the LSB 14 years ago, it was already known for its outstanding educational services and leadership.

Three underlying principles account for our decision to embrace a whole language philosophy. Our first and perhaps most important principle is that students belong at the center of the learning process. We make all decisions about teachers, administrators, educational policies, budgets, personnel policies, collective agreements, facilities, and transportation with the children in mind.

Creating and maintaining a humanistic environment is our second principle. In negotiating with the various unions we stress problem-solving rather than confrontation. In this way we all come out winners. We look at problems as they arise from a global perspective and, as always, consider the children's interests first.

The third principle is that if we want our students to be learners, then we must be learners ourselves. The LSB spends a great deal of money each year on professional development, including teachers' salaries, replacement costs, and activity expenditures.

At a parents' meeting to discuss whole language and why the LSB believes in it, parents made these comments:

"I can really see how much my daughter enjoys coming to school since she has been registered here. It used to be a chore to get her ready for school; now she can't wait to get here."

Peter J.H. Krause is the director general of the Lakeshore School Board in Beaconsfield, Quebec. Located west of Montreal, the Lakeshore School Board has 13,500 elementary and secondary students. He has vigorously pursued his interest in whole language by studying the available literature, attending seminars and workshops, and participating in two 10-day seminars at the University of Arizona in Tucson as a student and a presenter. He belongs to a whole language support group (TAWL) in Montreal and has given many workshops and seminars over the last five years to teachers and administrators in Canada and the United States. In February 1989 he received the Administrator's Award from the Child-centred Experience-based Learning Group in Winnipeg, Manitoba, for improving the quality of education and for encouraging and supporting teachers in their quest for excellence in the classroom.

"I have never seen my child read so much; I wish I had had the experience when I went to school."

At the LSB we involve everyone in the learning process. Our nonacademic people, who do not deal directly with children, are involved as well so that they understand what we are trying to do for the children. For it is only by understanding that they can really help and support our efforts.

I receive a lot of mail every day. Some of it is very special because it comes from children in our schools. One day I received a letter from second-graders asking me questions about the school board and inviting me to their school to answer them.

Apparently the children had seen one of our trucks with the LSB logo in the school yard and asked their teacher about it. A discussion ensued and the class came up with a list of questions: Who owned it? Who ran the school board? What was a school board? Who was the boss? During my visit to the class, I answered these questions about the school board and its functions. I concluded my visit by reading to the children (which I do almost every time I go into a classroom). The visit was a very satisfying experience for me and, from what the teacher told me, for the children as well.

Perhaps the most exciting discussion that I had recently was with a couple of high school teachers at a whole language support group session. I believe whole language can mean a lot for high school students. High school is perhaps society's most rigid and unchanging institution. Over the last 50 years many attempts have been made to change the structure of the secondary curriculum but, unfortunately, all have failed. In my discussion with the two high school teachers we touched upon many ways to move away from this rigidity: language across the curriculum, integrated studies, thematic units covering all the subject areas for which high school teachers are responsible, and so on. Judging by the enthusiasm and the determination that these teachers demonstrated, I am very optimistic about change in our high schools.

Even though our high school dropout rate at the LSB is considerably lower than elsewhere, we still considered it necessary to create programs that try to address the problem. The underlying premise is that it is easier to adapt the school environment to some students than it is to adapt the students to the traditional school environment. Thus, one of our high schools has set up a program known as the "Inner Circle." This program basically reorganizes the school day for qualifying students by providing a flex-schedule. The result is that students who would probably drop out of school actually stay and graduate.

To establish the optimal learning community, we build on the three principles stated at the outset of this article: children at the center, a humanistic environment, and professional development. We try to:

- Offer a supportive environment for both students and teachers;
- Give students and teachers the freedom to risk and fail and pick themselves up again;
- Provide teachers with the right to exercise professional judgment and trust them to do it;
- Have principals accept their role as educational leaders in their schools and provide them with the wherewithal to carry it through;
- Support the people in the system who are dedicated to providing high-quality education;
- Create opportunities for releasing funds for attending conferences that support the philosophy of holistic learning;
- Purchase books about whole language, manipulatives in math teaching, holistic learning, and integrated studies and make them accessible to the people in the organization;
- Invite individuals to share their expertise with people in the organization but ensure that our people, the home-grown experts, are included;
- Encourage the establishment of the networks and support groups to allow people to discuss successes and failures; and
- Show that we are sincerely interested by active participation.

➔ See: Buchanan, p. 409; Goodman, p. 274; Heath, p. 422; Stevenson, p. 271.

Resource: Periodical

TIP: Theory into Practice

$20/year (4 issues) individual; $40/year institution from:
College of Education
Ohio State University
174 Arps Hall
1945 N. High St.
Columbus, OH 43210
1-614-292-2801

"Please skip the theory; just tell me how to do it." Teachers are often accused of not caring about the theory underlying practice. *TIP: Theory into Practice* puts that belief to rest. A quarterly journal published by the College of Education, Ohio State University, *TIP* is committed to the view that there is an "integral relationship between educational theory and practice." Each issue is related to a theme and is edited by a guest editor, highly respected in his or her field. A recent issue, edited by *Catalog* essayists Pat Shannon and Ken Goodman, presents alternative viewpoints of basal readers.

LBB

📷 **WHOLE LANGUAGE CAMERA**

"Say when, will we ever meet again?" Led by principal Bob Wortman, Borton School teachers end the school year with a musical flourish during a special performance for the students, Tucson, AZ.

MarvELous INVENTIONS

The Academic World

When I was in graduate school, action figures made by Mattel and other toy manufacturers were very popular, particularly with young boys. One of the most popular was the "Masters of the Universe" set, which included various muscle-bound warriors, made of different-colored, molded plastic.

Our son, who was two years old at the time, divided his days between playing with his action figures and adapting to his parents' college schedules. This was a time when his language was literally exploding. Since our lives revolved around the university, it is little wonder that he called his figures "Masters of the University."

➔ See: Hartle-Schutte, pp. 37, 87, 172.

—David Hartle-Schutte, assistant professor, University of Hawaii, Hilo, HI

As I See It:
Kenneth S. Goodman

Whole Language and Professional Organizations

William F. Jasper, writing in *The New American* (1989, p. 39), a magazine of the far-right, quotes the cover story of *Learn and Play* (1989), a trade magazine for toy and educational material retailers, as saying whole language is an "exciting grass-roots effort to change the way children are taught in schools."

Jasper, however, has his own view of whole language. To him whole language is not a grass-roots effort. It is a "'top-down' campaign devised and promoted by the professional 'reading wreckers' of the International Reading Association (IRA)." He goes on to say that "at its convention in New Orleans in May [1989], the IRA gave a hearty endorsement to the whole language movement."

Funny, I was there and I never heard such an endorsement. Perhaps Jasper looked at the program and noticed how many presentations dealt with whole language. Had he looked closer he would have been aware that most of these presentations were by classroom teachers for classroom teachers. The Program Committee for the IRA selects from hundreds of proposals they receive those that appear to be the best prepared and that are likely to hold the most interest for the ten to twelve thousand professionals who attend each year. Like all professional organizations, IRA regards itself as a platform for the discussion of

issues. Sometimes, as a board member and officer of IRA, I was frustrated by its essential neutrality on controversial issues and innovative practices. It strives to be representative and to provide interesting programs at its conventions and interesting articles in its journals. A full range of basal and trade book publishers exhibit at the conventions. Jasper would have found phonics programs at IRA that would have pleased even the most ardent "phonics-first" advocate.

If whole language is getting attention at IRA and other professional conferences, it is because of the strong grass-roots support it is generating and the whole language teachers who are articulate and enthusiastic about what their kids are accomplishing.

The National Council of Teachers of English (NCTE) is also an open forum for the discussion of professional issues and practices. Though it has more of a history of encouraging innovation in teaching English, like IRA it does not endorse movements or alternatives. When the Elementary Section Steering Committee realized it couldn't find room on the regular convention program, in Baltimore, November 1989, for all the excellent whole language programs proposed, it arranged for a "Whole Day of Whole Language" on the Monday following the main convention. More than 1,400 people attended despite space limitations. NCTE's professional journals have contained many fine articles about whole language, among other topics.

Besides IRA and NCTE, many other professional organizations have provided exposure for

whole language. The National Association for the Education of Young Children and the Association for Childhood Education International have been concerned about "developmentally appropriate experiences" and see whole language as compatible with this concern. Administrators' organizations are also showing interest.

Increasingly strong interest in whole language shows up in the National Association of Bilingual Educators (NABE) and Teachers of English to Speakers of Other Languages (TESOL) and their publications.These professional organizations have given me an audience for my ideas. They've put me in touch with teachers, authors of children's books, and other teacher educators. They've made me feel part of an extended, transacting professional community.

Whole language teachers are finding their voices as presenters and as writers. Having whole language support groups is important. But it is also important to reach out through the local, state, regional, national, and international conferences and publications of the major professional organizations to other teachers and professionals. Many whole language groups have been started by teachers coming home from IRA or NCTE conferences who were inspired by other teachers. IRA has a whole language special interest group. NCTE has a whole language assembly. A new independent Whole Language Umbrella has emerged to serve the common interests of the rapidly multiplying whole language teacher support groups.

So, Mr. Jasper, you've got it wrong. Whole language isn't a top-down conspiracy of IRA. IRA, NCTE, and the other professional organizations are fertile grounds in which strong shoots can come up from the grass roots. And their strength lies in the articulate, knowledgeable teachers who speak for whole language.

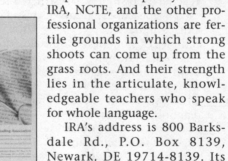

IRA's address is 800 Barksdale Rd., P.O. Box 8139, Newark, DE 19714-8139. Its annual convention is held at the beginning of May. IRA publishes *The Reading Teacher*, *Journal of Reading*, *Reading Research Quarterly*, and *Lectura y Vida*.

NCTE's address is 1111 Kenyon Rd., Urbana, IL 61801. Its annual convention is held in November the week before Thanksgiving. NCTE publishes *Language Arts*, *The English Journal*, and *Research in Teaching English*, among others.

→ See: A Declaration of Professional Conscience, inside front cover; Goodman, p. 400.

References

Indvik, K. 1989. "Where are you in the whole language revolution?" *Learn and Play,* April-June.

Jasper, W. F. 1989. "Half-taught with whole language." *New American,* 3 July.

Resource: Organizations

Whole language teachers need to be aware of what the major teacher unions are doing and their position in relation to whole language issues.
—KSG and YMG

American Federation of Teachers

555 New Jersey Ave., NW
Washington, DC 20001
1-800-238-1133

National Education Association (NEA)

1201 16th St., NW
Washington, DC
20036-3290
1-202-822-7200

NEA's position regarding whole language seems clear: They have published *Whole Language: Beliefs and Practices,* an excellent whole language anthology by Maryann and Gary Manning, and *Reading and Writing in the Primary Grades,* a book on early literacy by the Mannings, Roberta Long, and Bernice J. Wolfsan. NEA has two additional whole language volumes scheduled for publication in June 1990: *Reading and Writing in the Middle Grades*, by Maryann and Gary Manning, and *Reading and Writing in the High School*, by Eric Hobson and R. Baird Shuman.

LBB

→ See: Whole Language Beliefs and Practices, p. 406.

Within every professional there once was an amateur.
—Carolyn Burke

WELL-SAID

📷 **WHOLE LANGUAGE CAMERA**

Whole language teacher Debra Jacobson shares her professional expertise with the members of the Tucson, Arizona TAWL.

Principals Speak Out

by Myna L. Matlin

Yes, I Am a Whole Language Principal

Over the past 15 years I have studied children's learning and language development as a graduate student, a researcher-documenter, a teacher, and a staff developer. From these personal experiences and those of others documented in the vast body of emerging psycholinguistic and cognitive psychology research, I have incorporated knowledge and beliefs that contribute to my advocacy of whole language.

Last January I was selected to be an elementary school principal. My first week as principal saw me setting up an Essential Elements of Instruction (EEI) workshop for the intermediate teachers, which they had planned with their former administrator. "This is not something a whole language advocate would do," I was reminded by my conscience and my "friends."

The primary teachers at the school were all proponents of whole language and had worked long and hard to educate the parents and administration about their literacy goals for children. Yet as I looked around I saw a wide range of practices being called whole language, and it was hard to resist wanting to "show how it is really done."

Statewide achievement tests came next, and I found myself encouraging teachers to provide students with test-taking strategies and experiences for several months before the tests. Again I questioned whether I was "selling out."

Do I have a whole language school? No, not the kind that Goodman or Smith would recognize at first glance. Yet as one looks deeper into our plans for the school, the philosophical underpinnings of whole language are guiding the staff and principal, and I can say with confidence, "Yes, we have a whole language school." How can I as a new principal make this statement with confidence? As a staff, we have developed goals for our program. From these goals, I have pulled the essential components and developed a checklist to compare our stated beliefs with the daily school practices. This has become a practical way to keep whole language goals in front of us at all times and may be used with staff, parents and principal.

I offer other principals and teachers the use of our checklist (below) to see how whole language attitudes are visible in their schools, and to use in making any adjustments they may wish. This instrument provides one way to gauge staff involvement, student engagement, success in learning and communication, and assessment of the learning process. You may find other uses for it as well.

PRINCIPAL'S ASSESSMENT OF WHOLE LANGUAGE GOALS

Answer yes, no, partially, or not sure.

We are a community of learners.

____Principal and staff establish climate for learning.
____Students, teachers/staff, and principal are viewed as learners.
____It's okay to make mistakes.
____District curriculum is implemented.
____Team planning/grade level planning occurs regularly.
____Professional decisions are made by teachers.
____Staff development is planned by teachers and principal.
____Invitations are extended to parents to participate.
____PTA intergenerational program brings elderly into the school.

Everyone succeeds at our school.

____The potential of all students is revalued (Goodman).

____There are many experiences and opportunities for success.
____Alternative grouping strategies are employed.
____Rules for learning are developed jointly.
____Students are encouraged to help each other learn.
____All students' work is displayed publicly.
____Students and staff feel responsible for attractive learning environment.
____Special education students are mainstreamed.
____Learning is not fragmented—whole teachers teach whole students.
____Teachers start where learners are and enhance their knowledge.
____The principal starts where learners are and enhances their knowledge.
____The principal accepts the use of existing practices and helps expand the teachers' repertoire.

In our literate environment everyone learns to communicate.

____Reading occurs across the curriculum.
____Writing occurs across the curriculum.
____The focus of teachers is on the process of writing.
____The focus of teachers is on the process of reading.
____Students have access to a wide range of literacy materials.
____Literature is an important element of reading.
____There are many opportunities for conversations about curriculum in the classroom.
____There are many opportunities for informal conversations at school.
____Strong library support is available.
____Books are available all around the school.

Alternative assessment is used to support the learning process.

____Assessment provides information about the learning process.
____Informal and formal assessment and evaluation is used in classrooms.
____Teacher- and student-constructed tests are used to measure students' learning of specific content.
____Samples of student work provide documentation of learning.
____Written samples, as well as audio and video samples, are used.
____Observation and anecdotal records give diagnostic information.
____The place of standardized tests is acknowledged as public measures of achievement (even though we do not agree with their validity).

➜ See: Hartle-Schutte, p. 240; Matlin, p. 47; Teachers and Research, p. 402.

Myna L. Matlin is the principal of Warren Elementary School, Tucson, AZ.

YOUNG ARTISTS

"I wish I had a picture of this classroom. I could look at it every day." —Keyana, 6, student of Catherine Howard, primary teacher, Ohlone School, Palo Alto, CA

Resource: Organization

National Writing Project

James Gray, director
School of Education
University of California
Berkeley, CA 94720
1-415-642-0963

Resource Essay

The National Writing Project Approach

As for the character of the work, I have no hesitation in saying that the National Writing Project has been by far the most effective and "cost-effective" project in the history of the Endowment's support for elementary and secondary education programs.

—John Hale, National Endowment for the Humanities

The National Writing Project (NWP) is a program that is open to the best that is known about the teaching of writing from whatever source: from literature in the field, from research, and from the insights and experiences of successful teachers. The Writing Project proposes no packaged plans, no teacher-proof materials, no set formulas for teaching writing. We promote no single approach, though we favor a number of ideas that have emerged over the past decade, ideas now being adopted by more and more teachers. The National Writing Project remains open to discovery and open to qualification. This position is the sustaining strength of the Project.

I am convinced that the Writing Project effort, to put it mildly, is the most effective and widespread inservice effort I have seen in the course of my teaching career.
—NWP teacher

Basic Assumptions

Although each site in this network is autonomous, all NWP sites follow the same teachers-teaching-teachers model. Each site bases its programs on these assumptions:

1. Student writing can be improved by improving the teaching of writing, and the best teacher of teachers is another teacher.

2. Programs designed to improve the teaching of writing must involve teachers at all grade levels from all subject areas.

3. The writing problem can best be solved through cooperatively planned university-school programs.

4. Change can best be accomplished by those who work in the schools, not by transient consultants or by prepackaged systems.

5. Meaningful change can occur only over time. Staff development programs must be ongoing and systematic.

6. What is known about the teaching of writing comes not only from research but from the practice of those who teach writing.

7. Teachers of writing must write.

Most certainly the Writing Project experience has been the single most important influence on my professional behavior in 36 years of teaching. The experience has made over the way I teach writing.
—NWP teacher

Excerpted from a National Writing Project brochure published by California Writing Project, University of California at Berkeley.

Becoming Literate

by Mark McCue

Working with Peter

Because student/tutor writing often represents the earliest stages of writing and because it reflects how students feel and think, I strongly feel that it must have representations in *Voices*.

Sometimes learners who speak English well but do not know the letters of the alphabet come into our literacy programme. How can we most effectively help such learners? For us, as literacy instructors, the answer is the shared reading exercise, developed within the context of language experience. Through dialogue, the tutor either creates writing or the learner dictates writing. The writing becomes the reading text lesson. Tutor and student look at and talk about this short piece of writing. Through dialogue and shared reading, the learner can gain a positive reading experience resulting from a positive writing experience. The following notes and selected passages show the development of the shared reading/writing process with one student, Peter Harder.

The lady on the phone said, "I am calling for a friend, in his fifties, who wants to learn to read and write. Can you help him?"

We talked, exchanging information. I explained our programme, and she offered more information about her friend. He had been born in this country (Canada) and had attended school briefly. He truly wanted to know how to read and write, but he was very nervous about going back to school.

Like many learners, Peter showed anxiety during our first meeting. It had been almost 50 years since he had been to school, and he told me later that school had not been a good place for him. Although hesitant, Peter was able to talk about himself, and I was able to get enough information from him to determine that we could work together if Peter wanted to. He did, and we agreed to start right away.

When Peter came to his first class, we sat and talked. He had done hard physical work all his life and had not needed reading and writing. Peter did not know all the names of the letters of the alphabet and knew only a very few sounds. He wore a hearing aid, glasses, and did not always say his words correctly. Perhaps most important, through our conversation, I learned about Peter's hopes, concerns, and life experiences. I also came to understand and appreciate the extent of his determination. We would use these as a starting point.

During our first two meetings Peter talked about the long bus ride from his home to the school, and of how he had to transfer and was concerned about missing his bus, or getting on the wrong one. We decided that one of the first things we would write about for shared reading would be buses.

The following four passages were written by the tutor.

Story #1

I ride on the bus to school. It is fun on the bus. I see people on the bus.

As I wrote this story, I tried to use the same words that Peter had used in our discussion. I tried to imitate Peter's sentences, and use words more than once, when possible.

As I wrote the story I said the words aloud and Peter listened. Next, I read the story orally a few times and Peter listened and followed my reading with his eyes. We talked about the story, and then I asked if he wanted to read the story aloud together. Peter agreed, and we read the story together a few times. Next, I asked if he would like to read the story silently and put a line under any word he was unsure of. He did this and the reading problems he encountered, as well as possible solutions to these problems, were discussed. Peter continued to read his story silently until he

felt comfortable. Finally, Peter was given the opportunity to read his story aloud to the tutor, and he chose to do so. He read the story a number of times and felt very good about having had a positive reading experience.

Story #2

I have fun on the bus. There are many things to see on the bus. There are many people to see on the bus. It is fun on the bus to school.

Story #3

The bus ride home is fun. There are many people to see on the bus ride. There are many things to see on the bus ride home from school.

Story #4

I ride the bus to school and back home. It is fun on the bus. I like to see the people on the bus.

Stories 2, 3, and 4 are much like story #1. Notice that each story has one or two new words and the sentences are longer than the sentences in story #1. You can also see that although the stories tell us about the bus, they tell us about it in different orders. This was done to show the reader that in written language, words and sentences can be moved around and still make sense, and that in order to read properly, the reader must not only be able to say the words but must also understand what those words are saying.

Over the next few weeks we continued our shared readings and wrote longer stories about the buses. We added many new words including the names of the buses; soon Peter was riding the buses without fear of making a mistake. The following is a shared reading story dictated by Peter. They are his words, sentences, and ideas, and it was written about half a year after Peter started in the programme.

Story #5

It was April or May. I felt like I didn't know anything. Then I started to take notice. Little by little I started to learn. This made me feel happy. About five months ago I started to know how to read the signs on the bus, and I could read the names of the months.

We see Peter using many more words in his writing, and that one sentence is much longer than any in his first stories. Also, this story shows us that Peter is thinking about what he has been doing and understands how he has improved.

Peter dictated the following story a few months after story #5. It shows the kind of shared reading exercise Peter was doing after about one year in the programme.

Story #6

A long time ago I was in Prince Albert National Park. I was cooking for a trapper, Frank Reimer. One night after I finished washing the dishes, I opened the door and threw out the hot water. I heard a big noise. I told Frank about the noise. He got his big flashlight. We saw a big bear. Frank got his gun and shot the bear.

While purposeful and direct, the writing in stories 1 to 4 is, in a sense, flat, almost lifeless; it tells the reader little about the writer. It is the representation of a man for whom written communication has been mysterious and out of reach. In story #5 we begin to see change in Peter's writing; his confidence is increasing and with it, his desire to put the substance of his life into his stories. He writes about his feelings and his progress, and his writing legitimizes these for him and for the reader. We see a continuation of Peter's empowerment in story #6; he writes from his history and, in doing so, affirms its importance to himself and to those who share his writing.

For Peter, the process of writing, which at first was mechanical, has become more spontaneous, and the stories, which at first appeared on the page as indistinct and faceless, are now alive and individualized. He writes about his experience, and during the writing, this experience takes on heightened meaning, breathing life into his stories. Consequently, Peter, through the acts of

Resource: Professional Development Videos

Theory and Practice in Two Meaning-Centered Classrooms
Carole Edelsky
1984; $200 to purchase with manual;
 $40 rental fee/30 days from:
Katonah, NY: Richard C. Owen
1-800-336-5588

**The Writing Workshop:
A World of Difference**
Lucy Calkins and Shelley Harwayne
1988; $225 to purchase; $40 rental fee/5 days

**The Writing and Reading Process:
A New Approach to Literacy**

**The Writing and Reading Process:
A Closer Look**
Jane Hanson and Donald Graves
1986 and 1988; $175 each to purchase;
 $50 rental fee/5 days

**The Authoring Cycle: Read Better,
Write Better, Reason Better**
Jerome Harste
1987; $200 each to purchase; $1,450 for whole
 series; $50 rental fee/5 days
Portsmouth, NH: Heinemann
1-603-431-7894
FAX 1-603-431-7840

Unlike plug-into-this-program fads that have plagued education over the years, whole language is a philosophy that is built on more than 20 years of research across disciplines. Changing practice begins with changing beliefs about language and learning, a process that needs solid professional support. Unfortunately, teacher education classes in whole language are still not readily available in the states, and teachers cannot easily afford the cost of attending professional conferences or workshops. Videos are helping to fill the professional development void. There are excellent offerings from all the major whole language publishers, and most include guides with suggestions for viewing, workshop formats, and further reading. The videos are available for purchase or rental. Please let us know about others that you've seen and recommend. The videos listed above are some of our favorites.

LBB

Marvelous Inventions

The Secretary

While I was at my desk addressing envelopes, Brennan, 17 months, climbed into my lap, seized an envelope, took my pen, and addressed it as shown:

—LBB

concentrating and intensifying his experience in writing, is increasingly motivated to continue learning to read and write, and in doing so, is continuing to unlock the secrets of print.

➔ See: Calahan, p. 54; Pharness and Weinstein, pp. 128-129.

From *Voices: New Writers for New Readers* 1(2), Fall 1989.

Classroom Demonstrations
by Debra Goodman

Organizing a Presentation for Teachers and Parents

As whole language teachers, we create classrooms where children work together and share learning and knowledge; recognizing the value of this shared learning extends to staff development as well. I'd like to share some strategies I've developed for teachers and parents over the past few years.

Save Everything

Children's work or comments provide good illustrations for my presentations. I make good copies of interesting or amusing letters, writings, and other materials. Observations of student discussions or key moments during conferences are recorded in a journal or on a clipboard immediately. My anecdotal notes of conferences or overheard conversations have been invaluable for speaking and writing.

Select a Focus

I have found that to give a fairly decent *introduction* to my classroom takes at least a day and a half. In a half-day or day-long presentation, I can talk about several aspects of my classroom. For a short presentation I have to focus on a single topic or theme.

If I receive an open-ended request, I usually focus on one of my current concerns that I believe is shared by many teachers, not simply by whole language teachers.

Teachers who are new to whole language often come to sessions eager to learn everything at once. I usually state that moving toward a whole language classroom takes time, and that each teacher's whole language classroom is a unique expression of one teacher and one group of children.

Consider Audience and Time

The easiest presentation to make is the short talk to my own colleagues or TAWL group about a specific aspect of my classroom. If I know my audience, I can anticipate the type of understanding they bring to the talk. The hardest audience to speak to is one where teachers have come against their will. I don't recommend accepting such invitations.

I try to get to know the audience. I ask the person who invited me about the background and interests of the audience. If possible, I attend other sessions at the conference or meeting to see the audience response and hear the questions asked. Before I talk, I often survey the audience for the number of primary teachers, upper-grade teachers, and college educators.

I don't let the audience control my talk; however, sometimes teachers want me to stop talking about theory and just tell them "how to do it." I am careful to discuss the reasons for what I do, and offer examples that can be adapted (not adopted) to other classroom settings. Whole language is a view toward education. (If anything will kill the recent emergence of whole language, it's teachers who adopt practices without understanding the reasons behind them.)

I can best talk about my own area of expertise. My examples focus on my fifth-grade classroom experience, or my experience as a Chapter 1 reading specialist. I will offer suggestions for how my experiences might relate to a primary or middle school classroom, but too much emphasis outside my own area of expertise tends to lose authenticity. I treat teachers as experts in their own classrooms, capable of integrating meaningful points into their own current thinking and teaching.

In a 10- to 20-minute talk it's important to keep the focus limited to two or three points. I select examples for each point that illustrate a different aspect of my classroom. If I am giving a very short talk, I usually write it out completely so I can make the most effective use of my time. In a small group discussion, however, writing out the talk is often too formal. In this case, I find it best to make one or two points and allow the remaining time for questions.

A one- or two-hour talk seems long, but time goes by quickly. I used to find myself running out of time for the important examples I'd left for the end. Now I try to divide my presentation into 15-minute or half-hour segments. This way I know if I'm running behind and can cut some examples along the way. (It also helps to identify in advance which examples might be cut.) Dividing a talk into segments helps in planning too. It makes it easier to think about how many points I might have time to include.

For any talk over an hour, I try to involve the audience in the presentation. This can be done simply by asking those in attendance to reflect on their goals for the presentation at the beginning, and again at the end of the talk. Sometimes I will ask them to reflect on my focus: "What would you like your students to be able to do as readers and writers when they leave your room?" Other times I might ask them to consider and evaluate a sample of a student's work with me. Audience involvement makes a big difference in the effectiveness of the presentation.

Think About the Presentation

There is always a "precomposing" stage, when I am thinking about the talk I am going to make. Often, when I am driving to and from work, I will mentally brainstorm points I might make and examples I might include. (As the date of the talk approaches, I sometimes find myself several freeway exits past my house!) It often helps to sort through my box of students' examples, selecting any that I might use for the talk. I will read or reread good articles and books, as well as discuss my presentation with teachers, family members, and other interested people.

Prepare the Presentation

When I am ready to prepare a presentation, I take out my folder of ideas and favorite examples, look them over, and spread them out around me on my desk or table. Then I mentally put them out of my mind as I prepare an outline for the talk. I start by listing the major points I want to make. I then accumulate notes

for each point on the same sheet, and end up with a couple of pages crowded with ideas and examples. Eventually I write each general topic at the top of a separate sheet of paper, and list below them the points I want to make about those topics.

Once I have outlined a presentation, I try to provide examples (stories or students' work samples) to illustrate each point. It's usually more effective to limit the examples and spend more time on each one. Sometimes I will give a talk by telling the stories of three or four children, and making my point as a conclusion to each story. By using samples of various classroom experiences, I can refer to the activity within the discussion of a particular child's learning. David Bloom gave me the idea of keeping my written text or outline on the left side of a page, and listing my examples on the right side of a page.

I sometimes use slides or videotapes for a talk. Building a talk around slides can be very effective, but it involves a lot of work, as the slides have to be coordinated with the talk itself. It's easier to give a talk separately and use the slides as an introduction or conclusion. Audiences tend to enjoy slides, particularly if they are not familiar with whole language classrooms.

Giving the Presentation

What can I say about giving a presentation? I remember I'm a whole language teacher and I try to use good teaching when I present.

Many speakers engage the audience by starting out with a humorous story. I have tried this, but don't always get a laugh. (We can't all be Don Graves!) I am more successful with humorous stories in the middle of the presentation, when the audience is already engaged. Instead of humor, I will usually start with a classroom story that dramatically illustrates my major focus.

Often something will go wrong. The microphone won't work. A party will be going on in the next room. Only six people will show up. The overhead projector will be missing. No one will be there to make the introductions. People will get up and walk out in the middle of the talk. The main point is not to take anything personally. There are any number of reasons for what happens at a presentation.

I always go ahead with my talk, even if only a small group show up. The people who do attend are usually enthusiastic and appreciative. If I am talking to a small group, I will try to make the presentation more informal and interactive. If there is a break scheduled, I will use that time to review and revise my outline if necessary.

After the Presentation

I try to relax and not think too much. At some point I do reflect on the talk and consider what went well and what might be changed the next time. I try to keep all my written speeches and talk outlines in one place. At first I didn't get much opportunity to repeat a talk, but now that I am speaking more I find myself reusing outlines. Some talks are easily turned into articles.

Even if an outline is not reused, it can be a good starting point preparing for the next talk. I try to organize my samples and overheads into different categories and keep everything in a large box. Overheads fit nicely into plastic sheet protectors and can be organized into loose-leaf binders. (The sheet protector can go right on the overhead projector.)

Good luck! The first time I gave a presentation at a conference, I suddenly found myself nearly paralyzed with fear. The room felt hot, I felt faint, and I wasn't sure I would make it through without keeling over. I just stood up and started talking and everything went fine.

→ See: Goodman, pp. 24, 25, 224, 252, 274, 315.

Debra Goodman is an elementary teacher at Dewey Center for Urban Education, Detroit, MI.

Language Stories

The Absorbed Learner

During the course of the school day, at least 20 visitors had been in and out, whispering to each other and taking notes as they watched the goings on in a whole language classroom at Borton School in Tucson, Arizona. At the end of the day the principal, Bob Wortman, went into the room to thank the teacher and students for their cooperation with all the visitors.

As Bob finished expressing his appreciation, six-year-old Anna looked up from her writing, "We had visitors?"

—As told to LBB by Bob Wortman, principal, Borton School, Tucson, AZ

Classroom Demonstrations

by Deborah A. Manning & Jean W. Fennacy

Helping Classroom Visitors

When visitors come to spend time in a whole language classroom, they are often unfamiliar with the way such a classroom is structured. Without guidance, such visitors may focus on what they perceive to be chaos and fail to understand that there is a predictable structure or routine that helps the students and teacher work together. Since teachers in these settings are very involved with their students and want the visitors to see how the classroom operates normally, it is sometimes very difficult to spend time away from the children explaining how and why things are happening.

We have found that a combination of things helps visitors experience the classroom in a way we believe supports and encourages their understanding of whole language philosophy in practice. Four elements that are especially beneficial are hospitality, a visitor letter, a written class schedule, and a student-guided tour.

Making the visitor feel comfortable sets the tone for the visit. We have a small coffeepot going, and offering them a cup of coffee as they read the visitor letter establishes a homey touch. The visitor letter (following) not only explains to parents the philosophy undergirding the classroom curriculum but also calls their attention to the key elements we think are most important. The class schedule gives them an opportunity to get an overview of our day. The best part, however, involves students. Each time a visitor comes, two students serve as guides and take the visitor around the classroom, talking with them and answering their questions. Children do a wonderful job of explaining how the classroom works.

Dear Visitor,

This is a process-oriented whole language classroom. Within our classroom community, there are children from various cultural and linguistic backgrounds, who are learning to respond to and cope with real-world learning situations. Since children are the center of this community, there are certain inherent beliefs and philosophies that characterize our classroom. At the heart of this whole language philosophy is what we know about the way children learn to speak. This informs and supports our beliefs about the way children learn to read and write and, in fact, provides a basis for our learning theory.

Reading, writing, talking, and listening are interrelated. This can easily be observed as children select, interpret, and integrate information from their reading and writing. They make hypotheses and test these hypotheses. Inevitably there are times when contradictions occur between what they thought they were doing and what they in fact did. Therefore, their hypotheses do not work, they become puzzled, and they must refine their attempts. Through the excitement of self-discovery, children find out what they already know, what they want to know more about, and how and where to find out more information about meaningful subjects that are of importance to them. During the process of self-discovery, children use and learn language and, as a result, continue to become more proficient language users. This is a by-product of our learning community.

Below you will find four elements that are crucial to our structured, organized, child-centered classroom. These elements make possible the development of certain types of learning behaviors that emerge as children attempt to solve the written language puzzle. So I encourage you to take this opportunity to observe my students, my parents, and myself in action as we collaborate to understand and redefine the world around us.

- **Social Nature of Learning.** Since learning is enhanced as we share and interact with others, children are encouraged to talk with one another and to collaborate as they engage in activities. Students talk about books they are reading, share and respond to each other's writing, and work on projects together in the normal course of daily events.

- **Predictable Classroom Structure.** Certain routines provide the security needed to foster children's confidence to take the risks necessary for learning. In this classroom children can count on regularly structured large blocks of time for reading and writing. The major focus is consistently on meaning. The teacher supports them, but they are responsible for their own learning and are held accountable for their work.

- **Immersion in Print.** Crucial aspects in language learning are demonstrations of language in use. In order to learn to read and write, children must first become aware of the purposes that printed language serves. A concentrated effort has been made to make this classroom a rich, literate environment. Children are surrounded by and immersed in reading and writing stories, songs, poems, chants, and the like throughout every school day.

- **Evaluation.** In order for evaluation to be useful, it must assess each child's development with consideration for what the child was attempting to accomplish and the context within which the work was done. For the learner, this means focusing on what they can do today that they couldn't do yesterday. For the teacher, it means continually revising curricular decisions on the basis of student needs. Regular observations, anecdotal records, conferences, self-evaluation forms, writing and reading folders, and samples of children's work provide the basis for such meaningful and objective evaluation.

Sincerely,
Debbie Manning

→ See: Cambourne, p. 17; Fennacy, p. 309; Goodman, pp. 247, 249, 251; Manning, p. 258.

Deborah A. Manning is an elementary teacher at Dailey Elementary School, Fresno, CA. Jean W. Fennacy is the director of the Graduate Reading Program at Fresno Pacific College, Fresno, CA.

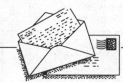

In the Mail

June 26, 1987
Dr. Bill Honig, Superintendent
California Dept. of Public Instruction
Sacramento, CA

Dear Dr. Honig,

I would like to share with you an experience that, in my opinion, manifests one of the major problems with education in California today. Allow me to explain.

At the _____ California School District Board Meeting, I heard the principal of _____ Elementary School make one of the most absurd statements I have ever heard an administrator make.

During the presentation of the CTBS test results of the first- and second-grade whole language students, the principal was discussing the growth made by the second-grade students on one of the CTBS subtests. It seems that the growth from the end of the first grade to the end of second amounted to 35 percentile points, or from the 33d percentile to the 68th, which is fantastic. The principal felt that this was too much. She felt that a growth of 15 to 16 percentile points per year would be more realistic.

Because of this "unacceptable amount of growth," the principal subsequently recommended to the board that only one third-grade class would be involved in the whole language program next year; the other two classes would be taught in the traditional manner. Never before in my 30 years as an educator have I heard an administrator recommend that a program be slowed down because the achievement test scores of the students were too high. The sad part about this whole fiasco is that the district superintendent supported the principal's recommendation.

Luckily three board members had the fortitude and intelligence to vote to extend the program to all three third-grade classes. These three board members are to be commended for supporting this viable and successful program. A negative decision could have presented some serious problems, e.g., how could the principal decide which third-grade students would continue in the whole language program and which would be in traditional classes? A parent who was in attendance stated that her son, who is a second-grader, achieved a CTBS test score in reading at the 4.5 grade level, and a 7.5 grade level in mathematics. She was very concerned that her son might not be able to continue in this program if the board followed the principal's recommendation. It seems to me that other parents would have the same concerns.

It is very difficult for me to comprehend the beliefs of the principal and the superintendent regarding this program. Surely they both want to see children achieve the optimum amount; however, their behavior seems to suggest otherwise. I suspect there are several reasons why this negative attitude is manifest, e.g.:

1. The program was made possible because of the teachers' interest and was teacher generated.

2. The teachers are in control of the classroom environments.

3. Whole language is not a mastery or skills program. The superintendent seems to favor programs that are skill based.

4. The whole language program develops a collaborative attitude among teachers, which may be a threat to the principal.

5. The principal feels that she is not in control.

6. The program is not her own child.

7. Who knows!

Dr. Honig, I think this scenario presents an example of one of the problems in education—the extreme rigidity of school administrators who are afraid of losing control of their position because teachers are breaking free of mechanistic and programmed curricula. I also feel very strongly that many administrators have little or no idea how children learn to read and write.

Sincerely,
George K. Parrish

George K. Parrish is a psychologist and counselor at Soulsbyville Elementary School, Soulsbyville, CA.

Teacher Education

Foreword to *Teachers and Research: Language Learning in the Classroom*

The past decade has seen a consolidation of research evidence and of classroom experience to support the image of children as active constructors of their own knowledge. Whether it be in the early stages of oral language development, in the behaviors that characterize emergent literacy, or in the use of spoken and written language as a means for learning about the world, what is most apparent to those who observe young children at work and at play is their drive to make sense of their experience and to develop the competence necessary to achieve their purposes.

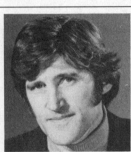

Dr. Gordon Wells is professor of education at the Ontario Institute for Studies in Education, Toronto, where he researches and teaches in the fields of language, literacy, and learning. Since arriving in Canada in 1984, Dr. Wells led a four-year longitudinal project of language and learning in schools serving multilingual communities. He and his colleagues also became involved in collaborative inquiries with some of the teachers in the project schools. He is currently serving as consultant to the Peel Board of Education's project, *Talk: A Medium for Learning and Change.*

To recognize the autonomous nature of the child's search for meaning is not to deny the important role of other people in this process. However, what has changed over the past decade is our understanding of the way in which this role can best be played. Although in the past we tended to assume that what the learner needed was sequentially structured input and strongly controlled direction, we now recognize that knowledge cannot be handed over ready-made but must be built up anew by individuals as they bring what they already know to the encounter with new information. In other words, the most helpful input is that which is contingently responsive to the learners' own efforts and which, in the context of a collaborative enterprise, enables learners to go further than they could have gone alone. The best teachers know likely routes to follow, but they lead from behind. We have come to see that the most effective model of the teaching-learning relationship is one not of transmission but of transaction.

To give widespread reality to this vision of education will require a major educational reform—one that will necessitate a change in beliefs, attitudes, and practices on the part of many teachers. The challenge is to find an effective way of bringing about this reform. In the past, attempts to bring about change in education typically have been carried out in a top-down manner. Experts outside the school have decided on the need for change and the form it should take and have handed their recommendations to the administrators. They, in turn, have drawn up guidelines for implementation and delivered them to the teachers who, after a few sessions of group inservice training, have been expected to put them into practice. Experience has shown, however, that this approach to change rarely is very successful. The reason, I think, is clear: A transmission concept of learning is no more effective in promoting learning in teachers than it is in the students they teach.

Perhaps the most important development of the past decade is the recognition that the insights about learning and teaching gained from close observation of children apply equally to learners at any stage of development. If teachers are to create classroom communities in which students learn through active, collaborative inquiry, they must have similar learning opportunities themselves. This means a major rethinking of teacher education, both preservice preparation and inservice professional development. New structures will need to be found within which teachers can take a more active role in their own learning and in shaping the curriculum for which they are responsible. And those outside the classroom—teacher educators, educational consultants, and administrators—will need to rethink their roles in order to be able to support this process.

➔ See: DeLawter, p. 389; Heath, p. 422; Teachers and Research: Language Learning in the Classroom, p. 403; Weaver, p. 382.

Excerpted from *Teachers and Research: Language Learning in the Classroom,* ed. Gay Su Pinnell and Myna Matlin

Further Reading by Dr. Gordon Wells
- *Learning Through Interaction: The Study of Language Development.* Cambridge University Press, 1981.
- *Language, Learning and Education.* Centre for the Study of Language and Communication, University of Bristol, 1982.
- *Explorations in the Development of Writing,* ed. with B. Kroll. Wiley, 1983.
- *Language and Learning: An Interactional Perspective,* ed. with J. Nicholls. Falmer Press, 1985.
- *Language Development in the Pre-School Years.* Cambridge University Press, 1985.
- *The Meaning Makers: Children Learning Language and Using Language to Learn.* Heinemann, 1986.
- *The Bristol Language Development Scales,* with M. Gutfreund and M. Harrison. NFER-Nelson, 1989.

Book Note

Among Schoolchildren

Tracy Kidder
1989; 340 pp.; $19.95
Boston: Houghton Mifflin

Author Tracy Kidder spent a year observing Chris Zajac, a dedicated, hardworking fifth-grade teacher who dreams and worries about her students and reads police reports in the newspaper, hoping she won't find the names of students from years past. As Kidder says, "the task of universal, public, elementary education is still usually being conducted by a woman alone in a little room," and Zajac is part of that brave army. *Among Schoolchildren* is a bestseller, described in reviews as indicative of either the pitiful or the intrepid state of teaching today.

Chris Zajac is a good traditional teacher, which is both her strength and her weakness. Throughout the book, the predominant metaphor she uses for the life going on in her classroom is "work": "You haven't done your work all year," "Art is only for the people who don't owe me any work," and so on. She handles about 150 pieces of paper a day, much of it her students' "work." She is a capable teacher whose intentions are good, but who has, like most teachers, internalized a model that implicitly sees school as an assembly line for producing worksheets.

Perhaps the major difference between a whole language teacher and one who has merely adopted some whole language techniques is that the former has achieved a paradigm shift about what learning is and how it works. Unfortunately, Tracy Kidder, while providing an engaging classroom portrait, has missed some of the real issues. Do read *Among Schoolchildren,* but provide your own interpretations.

Sandra Wilde

Stories from Preservice Teachers' Journal Keeping

Where do whole language teachers come from and how can we get more of them? We often assume that they are inservice teachers who have grown weary of prepackaged instructional systems that make no sense to them or to their students and who decide to move into a child- and meaning-centered curriculum.

However, student teachers may be brought into the world as fledgling whole language teachers through the careful guidance of empathetic and informed preservice education teachers. Such teacher educators practice their beliefs about learners and learning in their preservice methods courses and give teachers-to-be the room and comfort to decide to become whole language teachers well before they enter their first classrooms. Journal keeping is a powerful way to orient new teachers into whole language.

A remark to her teachers from one preservice student's (Jean's) journal (9/20/88) shows her reaction to journal keeping:

It must take hours and hours to read all the journals and comment on them as you did. I think it is a brilliant idea, though. It allows you to get to know each of your students better, and it also gives us a chance to know you a little better . . . I am now 100 percent sure that I am going to save this journal to refer back to when I am a teacher.

A glimpse into Sara's journal reveals the power of preservice students' writing and thinking about teaching when they are given support to wrestle with the issues and to evaluate new ideas. Sara carefully considered the ideas from her courses, and she tested them against her prior schooling experiences, her teacher-aide experiences, ideas she had heard at professional conferences and meetings, and the point of view of her mother, who was certified as a teacher but had never taught.

Sara clearly agonized over conflicting beliefs about basal readers. Several excerpts from her journal are presented to illustrate Sara's thinking over time and to show the power of the journal to promote and sustain inquiry into issues of reading instruction and, more globally, the world of teaching.

Read and listen to Sara as she takes ownership through her journal of a whole language model of teaching and learning.

9/6/88: Now that I've read this article (on basal readers) and I've had a chance to compare how I felt about basals when I was young to my neutral feeling about them recently, I can form a new conclusion. Basal readers should not be used as sole means of teaching reading. . . .

This year, I'm taking 21 hours of college classes. I thought at first this would be an almost impossible task. In contrast, however, these 21 hours are turning out to be fascinating! I had never before known what a "whole language" model of teaching was. Obviously, although I didn't know what it was called, I have been a student in a whole language classroom. . . .

10/4/88: I thought I had a definite opinion against the basal readers. I spoke with my mom, however, and she shed new light on the subject. . . . She said basal readers were very important to her as a child . . . All of my mother's positive experiences with basals made me really think about my views. I do think they have a place in the classroom, but not to the large extent that they are being used. . . .

10/12/88: It seems as if basals mechanize reading lessons. The teacher becomes the "robot" and the students are know-nothing learners. . . .

Viewpoint: Garth Boomer

Managers, Teachers, and Messes

Donald Schön (1983), in examining professions as seemingly disparate as architecture, psychiatry, teaching, engineering, medicine, and town planning, shows how a paradigm of Technical Rationality has dominated all professions, and he advances this as a major reason for the growing failure of the professions to cope with the world's problems. He asserts that the professions work from a base of "standardized knowledge" which is applied technically to problems. Says Schön, since World War II the limits of Technical Rationality have become increasingly apparent. Schön (p. 16) quotes Russell Ackoff to illustrate the dilemma:

> Managers [we might read teachers here] are not confronted with problems that are independent of each other, but with dynamic situations that consist of complex systems of changing problems that interact with each other. I call such situations *messes*. Problems are abstractions extracted from messes by analysis . . . Managers do not solve problems, they manage messes.

Schön's thesis is that while the professional is confronted with similar recurring cases, a technical/rational solution can be found, but that as soon as a unique case presents, Technical Rationality is inadequate. There is, he says, an element of art in professional practice. What he wants to explore is whether this art, sometimes called intuition, is irreducible or not amenable to conscious reflection. He asks a question which all of us in education need to keep asking: *What is the kind of knowing in which competent practitioners engage?*

Managing Mess

His project is crucial to the future of our society. If Technical Rationality is inadequate to the task, we need to replace it with a new explicit and rigorous paradigm. Unilluminated, mysterious intuition is not very helpful if we are trying to find ways of spreading a new view of problem solving. It is not enough for a competent manager/professional to demonstrate mastery of some problem if the sources of the performance remain mysterious.

Garth Boomer began life in a small country town in south Australia. He went to a one-teacher elementary school and finally found himself at Adelaide University studying English, Latin, and mathematics. He taught these subjects for some years before becoming a consultant in English. From 1980 to 1984 he worked at the national level as chair of the Commonwealth Schools Commission. He is now associate director-general of Education (Curriculum) in south Australia.

The notion of "messiness" should appeal to teachers. There is no doubt, I think, where most teachers would place themselves in Schön's world of professionalism. He says (p. 42):

> There is a high, hard ground where practitioners can make more effective use of research-based theory and technique, and there is a swampy lowland where situations are confusing messes, incapable of technical solution. The difficulty is that problems of the high ground, however great their technical interest, are often relatively unimportant to clients or to the larger society, while in the swamp are the problems of the greatest concern.

In the swampy lowland there is still necessity to act and this means that problems need to be extracted from the mess and addressed in the name of action. And yet the capacity to set and solve such problems, essentially a design capacity, according to Schön, is precisely what the professionals, including teachers, are not taught. With all our simplistic concentration on problem-solving, we have ignored the vital first stage of problem setting and design in complex situations.

In concentrating on the specific application of technique in identified cases, those who study professionals in action tend to lose sight of a rich penumbra of uncertainty and prior influence which attends the act. In the first place there is the overarching influence of what Schön calls *the appreciative system*. Someone trained in clinical psychology will design and solve problems quite differently from one who is a Rogerian. The act is also influenced by the actor's "role frame"; how he or she sees the relationship with the wider society, the institution and the clients, and by the actor's stance towards self and knowledge. All this has implications for how we educate/train and continue to "coach" managing professionals.

At the Crossroads

My reading of the international scene is that teaching is at the crossroads. Much of what I see in the United States provides the grimmest warnings about what can happen if teachers construe themselves, in response to political/societal conditioning, as functionaries and technicians. In Australia, teacher morale and self-esteem is falling in the face of an unremitting denigration of public schooling trumpeted in the media and reflected in education budgets. There are moves afoot to train our school principals as modern managers, but the kinds of management models I see around the place are firmly entrenched in a Technical Rationality mode. Both the heart and the art of teaching are being assailed and belittled. Narrow conceptions of skill seem to be squeezing out considerations of wisdom and judgement. High and dry commentators condescend to criticize teachers heroically managing messes in the swampy lowlands.

None of this is argument for us all to give up our own special toiling on behalf of teachers and children. It is a reminder that in our approaches to teachers and in the offering of what we know, we need to hold in mind both what is at stake and what is entailed in the art of teaching, beyond our specialism.

It is a particularly strong warning that in our pre-service preparation of teachers in most institutions, our packaging of disciplines is ludi-crously fragmented, partial and largely unrelated to the complex knowing-in-practice which must eventually be learnt. The picture I see is one of posturing on the periphery while the real business of teaching is learnt by contagion. Somehow, those in higher education have to convince their institutions that the life-blood and livelihood of teacher educators must be the grounded, intellectually rigorous study of *practice*, in collaboration with teachers as managing professionals adept at reflection upon their own knowing-in-practice.

Just as it behoves teachers to teach what they know with artistic passion as well as scientific know-how, having a deep understanding of the learners, their contexts and their problems, and without the condescension of helping the helpless, so it behoves those of us outside schools to teach teachers what we know that may be of use to them in their wider management tasks, with an empathy as all-embracing and as sensitive as possible. I have suggested here that in this teaching we need to find better ways of "coaching" based on our attempts to say to ourselves what it is we do when we are doing it. We will never finally push back all the frontiers of artistry, but it will be fun trying.

Given our understanding of the partiality of what we can offer, we need to be reasonably hospitable to, but not uncritical of, alternative appreciative systems. I do not advocate unbridled eclecticism (all of us need eventually to *stand* somewhere), but I do not see much to be gained from the kind of internecine skirmishing and chest-thumping that often goes on in the language field.

We need as much solidarity as we can get amongst all educators at this time, especially between teachers and teacher educators. A healthy, gutsy partnership is what is needed.

→ See: A Declaration of Professional Conscience, inside front cover; Heath, p. 422; Shanklin, p. 404; Torbe, p. 232; Wells, p. 402.

Reference

Schön, D. 1983. *The reflective practitioner: How professionals think in action.* New York: Basic Books.

Further Reading by Garth Boomer

◆ *Fair Dinkum Teaching and Learning.* Boynton/Cook, 1985.
◆ *Metaphors and Meanings.* AATE, 1988.

11/20/88: What a great article about standardized tests this was! . . . Tests are becoming much more important, scores are all-important, directing teachers as to which course to pursue next.

Let's get rid of standardized tests. Let teachers relax, motivate students, be creative, and do their jobs! Next, let's throw away the basals!

12/11/88: I've learned a lot about specific methods of teaching that I especially like, and I've also seen a lot of examples of methods that I don't like at all. . . . I think I've also learned a lot about my instructors. . . . I also think that for the first time my instructors know me. . . . If I can voice my views, refine them, and change some of them after hearing other people's experiences, I think I become a better professional and even a better individual.

I'm especially glad I've had this journal to write down how I feel.

→ See: Bissex, p. 209; Bixby, p. 53; Boomer, p. 403; Heath, p. 422; Kinzel, p. 155; Peetoom, p. 415; Wells, p. 402.

Mary K. Bixby is an assistant professor and learning resource specialist at the University of Missouri, Columbia, MO.

Book Note

Teachers and Research: Language Learning in the Classroom

Gay Su Pinnell and Myna L. Matlin, editors
1989; 177 pp.; $10.75
Newark, DE: International Reading Association

This exciting volume brings language research into a common discussion among educators at all levels and focuses on the element of change "in order to create the conditions under which learning can most effectively and constructively occur." Although children are at the center of the book, the authors devote particular attention to the issues of teacher research, teacher education, and teacher professionalism.

This, then, is the message of this book: a call for change. Let us hope that there will be many readers who, having gained a sense of what is possible, will be willing to join with the authors in extending and developing what they already have achieved.

Kathryn F. Whitmore

Cornerstone: Nancy L. Shanklin

Learning Something New

When teaching content area reading and writing, I offer an assignment option entitled "Learning Something New." My goal is for teachers to investigate learning in everyday life and then reflect upon how that experience relates to teaching students. The only restriction in the "Learning Something New" projects is that they must not be related to any other courses teachers are taking. I want them to experience structuring their own project, thus prompting discussions on how persons go about planning and revising their learning. Teachers keep learning logs documenting all reading, writing, speaking, and listening they do for their projects. Through their logs I hope they will discover new insights about how the four language systems inform and build upon one another.

Teachers have several weeks to work on their projects. At the end I ask them to use their log and any other documents they have written or gathered to write a paper reflecting on their own learning processes. As guides for the writing of these papers, teachers and I have generated several questions concerning the use of literacy as a tool for learning. The following are samples of our collaborative efforts:

Reading:
• What did you read?
• Why did you read each item?
• How did you adjust your reading process to learn this content?
• What did you do when you weren't sure you were comprehending?
• How did you handle new vocabulary you came across?
• What did you do to learn the material? In this case, what did *learn the material* mean? .

Writing:
• What kinds of writing did you do?
• What specific functions did each piece/kind of writing serve?
• Who was the audience for your writing?
• What was your writing process like?
• How did the writing help you to think?

Speaking and Listening:
• In what ways did you use speech to enhance your learning?
• In what ways was your learning social?
• Whom did you seek out? How did they add to your understanding of the topic?
• Who asked the questions? What was the nature of the questions?

Alternative Communication Systems:
• What other communication systems did you use to learn about this topic?
• How did each enhance your learning?

Ideation and Presentation:
• How did you go about mulling around and trying out ideas about your topic?
• In what ways did you present your learning?

Evaluation:
• How have you gone about evaluating your learning?
• What would you do differently next time?
• What do you plan to do next?

At first teachers react to this assignment with amazement. They find it hard to believe that I

> Nancy L. Shanklin is an assistant professor at the University of Colorado at Denver. She teaches courses on reading and writing processes, assessment of literacy, and content area reading and writing. She has been an active participant in elementary TAWL groups and helped to start the first secondary TAWL group in Denver. She was one of the founding members of Consultants/Coordinators Applying Whole Language (CAWL). She has worked extensively with Chapter 1 programs and on peer/technical coaching of teachers.

would give them credit for learning something they really want to know! Work on the projects has led to discussions of many significant principles about learning through language. For example, the presentation by one social studies teacher of his project on adoption (he and his wife were thinking of adopting) afforded teachers the opportunity to dialogue about the importance of positive models (other adoptive parents, in this case); the introspection caused by writing application forms, reading, talking and listening to others; the value of the collaborative learning; how good learners often read selectively to find answers to particular questions; and how learning can lead to further planning and other literacy events (buying a larger house; investigating ways to increase insurance).

Another project—training a dog—fostered discussion of the strategy of reading conceptually related materials: This teacher selected three books and then read them from easiest to hardest. She also kept a learning log and used the alternative communication system of observation (in this case, watching others interact with and train their dogs) and television programs as means of learning. This teacher's study led to exchanges concerning the use of visualization in reading and evaluation of learning in real life settings.

While I was confident that such discoveries would occur as outcomes of the projects, three additional unanticipated insights now seem significant. In writing papers and presenting them in class, teachers had difficulty focusing on their learning processes rather than on the content they had learned. I should have expected this: A focus on meaning is foremost in language learning and important to discuss! Teachers also developed a growing confidence in themselves as problem-solvers, critical thinkers, and independent learners as they worked on and presented their projects. Additionally, the sharing of these projects, all reflecting personal interests, contributed much to the creation of a close sense of community among class members.

The final question we discuss in "Learning Something New" is this: If this assignment puts teachers more in tune with how reading, writing, speaking, and listening contribute to learning in natural contexts, what happens in school to hinder students' use and development of the four language processes as tools for learning?

➔ See: Boomer, p. 403; Heath, p. 422; Wells, p. 402.

Further Reading by Nancy L. Shanklin

◆ *Relating Reading and Writing: Development of a Transactional Theory of the Writing Process.* Bloomington, IN: School of Education, Monographs in Language and Reading Studies, 1982.
◆ "Comprehension Instruction as Sharing and Extending," with L. K. Rhodes. In *Reading Teacher* 42, 1989.
◆ *A Research Base for Whole Language. LINK, 1989.*
◆ "Transforming Literacy Instruction: A University-Public School Collaboration," with L. K. Rhodes. *Educational Leadership* 46, 1989.
◆ "Improving the Comprehension of At-Risk Readers: An Ethnographic Study of Four Chapter I *Teachers*, Gr. 4–6." *Journal of Reading, Writing, and Learning Disabilities,* in press.

Approximately eight years ago, I was fortunate to be placed in a third-grade classroom next to Vera Milz's first-grade room. It didn't take me long to become aware that Vera's first-graders enjoyed reading and writing more than my third-graders did. Little by little the portable wall dividing our two rooms was opened, and I became not only a kidwatcher but a colleague-watcher.

Vera shows respect for each child as a reader, writer, and learner. Her classroom is a language-rich environment in which most of the children's "work" is displayed on bulletin boards, walls, doors, and windows, or hung from the ceiling. Her private collection of trade books that she has gathered over the years for her classroom guides other teachers who are starting or adding to their own classroom libraries. From day one children learn that the materials in Dr. Milz's classroom are to be shared and enjoyed by everyone. Vera introduces literature to children and then "makes way" for them to interact with the author, the story, and their own experiences.

To further describe this wonderful classroom environment, let me paraphrase one of Vera's descriptions. Print is found everywhere: on calendars, chalkboards, bulletin boards, charts, labels, published materials, and student-authored books. Vera's classroom allows for individual differences. As children enter, they become eager participants in the learning process. Their curiosity and enthusiasm are recognized and honored. They are involved in planning the learning activities for the classroom. This provides children with responsibility that, in turn, gives them ownership over learning. As children learn that their ideas are respected, they naturally become independent thinkers.

Parents are a very important support group in this classroom. They enjoy listening to children read, help to make blank books for young authors, and appreciate being a meaningful part of the classroom.

Over the years, numerous authors have corresponded with Vera and her children. She arranges for authors to visit her school and others in the district. How "alive" books become for readers who are afforded the wonderful opportunity to ask questions about stories face-to-face with the author.

Vera was involved in two videotape projects produced by Indiana University: The Reading Comprehension Videotape Series (*The Comprehension-centered Classroom: Making it Work,* and *The Teacher Variable: An Interview with Vera Milz,* 1980) and The Authoring Cycle: Read Better, Write Better, Reason Better Instructional Videotape Series, 1985.

Vera continues to participate in the International Reading Association, National Council for Teachers of English, Toronto Reading Association, and World Congress meetings along with the many workshops and inservices that she

Cornerstone: Lynn K. Rhodes

Helping Teachers to Publish (and to Experience the Writing Process)

"I've never worked harder on a piece of writing!" "I revised this piece of writing five times!" "Now I understand—from the author's viewpoint—what Authors Circle can contribute to writing."

These are a few of the comments from students (all teachers) in one of our final master's degree classes after they have written something for publication. The teachers usually choose to write a strategy lesson that they have adapted or invented and that they think other teachers would benefit from reading. Here are the steps I used most recently in the process of helping the teachers to ready their pieces for publication:

• I gave the teachers a packet of materials that listed examples of possible publication outlets. I also gave them an example of teacher's writing published in each outlet.

• By considering the grade levels taught, writing ability, and ability to reflect on teaching practices, I organized small heterogeneous groups (about four) to work together during the process of writing for publication.

• Each teacher was asked to generate a minimum of three topics. At their initial small group meetings, each author presented the topics and invited discussion regarding which one might be most helpful to other teachers.

• A week later, the teachers arrived with their first rough drafts. Before meeting in small groups, we talked about the author's responsibilities—helping the group understand what audience and journal the piece was intended for and what she or he wanted help with. We talked about the need for each author to listen carefully to the group's suggestions, take notes if helpful, and not be defensive or apologetic. We also considered the group's responsibilities—listening well, responding to the author's

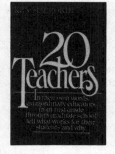

Lynn K. Rhodes, a former elementary school teacher, is an associate professor at the University of Colorado at Denver where she has been the coordinator of the graduate Reading and Writing Program for ten years. She was instrumental in founding the Denver TAWL group as well as Coordinators/Consultants Applying Whole Language, (CAWL), a group of Coloradan language arts, reading, and Chapter I coordinators and university faculty who support each other in developing whole language policies, philosophies, curriculum, and assessment instruments.

concerns, and being honestly constructive. The teachers decided that they couldn't be "too nice" and really be helpful to each other.

In the small groups, the teachers used the strategies they had talked about to provide each other feedback on content, clarity, organization and other meaning-based concerns.

• A week later, the teachers arrived in class with their revisions. I did a minilesson for the whole class in which we talked about capturing the reader's interest and about clearly relating the essay's purpose in the title or in the opening paragraphs.

Many teachers had done several revisions since the previous week. As in the previous meeting, the teachers responded to each other's meaning—clarity, detail, organization, and so on.

When the groups finished this third session together, they decided to bring what they considered their best "final" draft to class with enough copies for each group member if they wanted editing help from the group at next week's session.

• A week later, I did a minilesson on "clutter," a term borrowed from William Zinsser (1988). On an overhead, I showed them how I removed clutter from a piece I had written recently. I also gave them a copy of Zinsser's chapter to refer to in their own editing work at home. In the groups, each teacher declared his or her overall need—for more feedback on content or for feedback on conventions—and his or her specific concerns.

• In the final group meetings, the teachers were focused on editing concerns. They used me from time to time to answer questions about various matters.

• The following week, the teachers were rearranged in grade-level groups in order to read, appreciate, and celebrate each other's

final products. Some groups read and talked; others decided to read and write written comments to each other so they could save (and savor) the words of praise.

The teachers concluded the celebration by self-evaluating their efforts. They were asked to describe and evaluate the process used to construct meaning and to arrive at a conventional product, and to reflect on what they had learned from the experience.

• Following the celebration, each teacher submitted all previous drafts, the self-evaluation, and a final copy to me. After I read, reviewed, and commented on their work, I mailed their submissions to the designated publication outlet and quietly celebrated.

What do teachers learn from writing a piece for publication? First, they learn about the writing process and about their own writing:

I tend to repeat myself. I had to listen to others read my piece before I recognized a lot of it.

I learned the importance of including anecdotes and examples.

With every revision, I found myself both expanding and tightening—an interesting tension to deal with.

They also learn about the process of giving and getting feedback from others and the importance of that in their writing:

It helped so much to hear what parts were unclear to others. As I heard the same things over and over, I realized I had work to do!

They also become more confident about what they know and have to offer to their students and to other teachers:

I would never have done this on my own. I usually assume everyone knows what I know and forget I have unique knowledge.

Best of all, finishing a piece for publication may create a desire to write for similar purposes again. As one teacher commented about the piece she had written: "In my cover letter (to the editors of *The Whole Language Catalog*), I decided to suggest a few other pieces I could write."

Publication Outlets

The following outlets might be considered by teachers who want to publish brief articles about reading and writing:

• *The Reading Teacher,* in particular the "In the Classroom" section, published by the International Reading Association.

• *Notes Plus,* a newsletter of secondary ideas published by National Council of Teachers of English.

• *Teachers Networking,* a newsletter compiled by Richard C. Owen Publishers.

➜ See: LINK, p. 107; Readers and Writers With a Difference, p. 53.

Reference
Zinsser, W. 1988. *On writing well.* New York: Harper & Row.

Further Reading by Lynn K. Rhodes
◆ "I Can Read! Predictable Books as Resources for Reading and Writing Instruction." *The Reading Teacher* 34(5), 1981.
◆ *Readers and Writers with a Difference: A Holistic Approach to Learning -Disabled and Remedial Students,* with C. Dudley-Marling. Heinemann, 1988.
◆ "Comprehension Instruction as Sharing and Extending," with N. L. Shanklin. *Reading Teacher* 42(7), 1989.
◆ *A Research Base for Whole Language* with N. L. Shanklin, "Coordinators/Consultants Applying Whole Language, & CCIRA Studies and Research Committee," LINK, 1989.
◆ "Transforming Literacy Instruction: A University-Public School Collaboration," with N. L. Shanklin. *Educational Leadership* 46(6), 1989.

---

provides for parents, teachers, and administrators locally.

Permit me to close this feature with a few personal comments about my colleague and teacher Vera Milz. Vera, it was and is with you as a model and support that I was able to move from the bondage of basals to the wonderful world of whole language. You afforded me the opportunity to teacher watch eight years ago. You didn't lecture or preach. You just made what you and your children were doing look so natural, interesting, and fun, that I had to see its worth. You led me patiently and uncritically as I worked my way through the transition from basals to literature. You shared your experience, your time, and your expertise whenever I asked for it. You are still ready to come to my aid when I ask you to. When Angela Jaggar and Bernice Cullinan, professors at New York University, described you as one of the outstanding teachers in the United States, I knew what they meant!

Charlotte Haun is an elementary teacher at Conant Elementary School, Bloomfield Hills, MI.

Book Note

20 Teachers

Ken Macrorie
1984; 250 pp.; $7.95
New York: Oxford University Press

For more insight into the personal and professional beliefs of this remarkable educator see the interview with Vera Milz in chapter nine of *20 Teachers*. Each of the 20 chapters features an interview with an outstanding educator representing all subject areas and educational levels, primary through university. Particularly striking are the common beliefs and practices that unite these 20 teachers.

LBB

As Teachers See It

by Sandra Wilde

Tears in Teacher Education

I never cried in front of a college class until two summers ago.

That summer I was teaching a children's literature course for the first time. I decided to close the first day of class by reading *Love You Forever*. The first two-thirds of this picture-book story is funny, showing a mother singing her son to sleep through babyhood, childhood, his teens, and (by carrying a ladder across town on the roof of her car to climb in his window) adulthood. Then the story turns sad. The mother is old and sick, and her grown son goes across town to rock her in his own arms before returning home to sing the same lullaby to his baby daughter:

> I'll love you forever,
> I'll like you for always,
> As long as I'm living
> my baby you'll be.

I had just discovered this book and couldn't even read it through silently without crying. I nonetheless chose to read it aloud. After I finished, my voice having broken a few times, there were tears in my eyes and the eyes of many of the students. I closed the class by saying simply, "Isn't literature wonderful?"

I cried a few more times that summer. One of my students was a Chilean refugee. When she talked about how children's books about other countries often gloss over the realities of political repression, she told us that she had been tortured. After class that day, I cried and hugged her and said I was glad she had gotten out and was all right.

Another day I asked my students to reread a favorite children's book, write their response to it, and share their experiences in small groups. I also wrote about my favorite childhood book, a very personal piece of writing about how literature had helped me through a difficult time in my life (Wilde 1989, pp. 49–52). In an attack of cold feet, I gave it to my students pseudonymously. After we discussed it a little, I said "I'm the author," and was unable to hold back my tears.

It was by no means easy for me to cry in front of a class, although I cry fairly easily in other situations. My expectations about my own professionalism and a fear that my students would think I was weird had kept my teaching lively and involved but unemotional. That children's literature class, however, led me to rethink my assumptions about what a college professor should be like. That class was by far the most emotionally intense I had ever taught. In addition to the tears, we shared raucous laughter, heated discussions, and many personal experiences with literature in and out of class. I loved it, and many of the students said that they did too.

In my reading and language arts education classes now, I am no longer afraid of emotion. Every semester I guide students through their own writing process as a way of teaching them how to help children write. I encourage them to write a piece that will be meaningful enough for them to take through several revisions, yet not so private that they would be unwilling to share it in peer conferences. Every semester there is a mixture of light and serious pieces, and every semester there are tears during peer conferences as students share memories of recently deceased relatives, descriptions of their weddings that they will save for their children to read, and unsent letters to abusive parents. Every semester I also write a personally meaningful piece that I carry through conferences and revisions and then read to the whole class. Every semester I end up writing a piece that I can't read without crying. I usually start out planning to write something lighter, perhaps something academic,

procrastinate because my heart's not in it, and then sit down and write something real. I am usually nervous about revealing myself to students (although less nervous after I read their own often very private pieces), but I am always gratified by their responses.

Children's literature continues to be a source of emotional response in my classes. We were all moved when a group of students, responding to *Sadako and the Thousand Paper Cranes*, role-played the classmates of Sadako, reminiscing about her after her death from leukemia caused by the bombing of Hiroshima. Another group of students created a lightly mystical atmosphere, with a music box playing a haunting, elflike, "tinkling little melody" in the background, and shared the thoughts of characters from *Tuck Everlasting*.

I begin my language arts classes every day by reading a poem to my students. These are usually poems written for children. But on the 25th anniversary of John F. Kennedy's assassination, I chose an adult poem, the one that Robert Frost had written for Kennedy's inauguration. My reaction to it took me completely by surprise. I was overcome by emotion and had to stop reading for a few minutes, minutes of absolute silence in the classroom.

Why do I cry in class? Mainly because I feel most classrooms have, as John Goodlad (1984) described, a "flat" emotional tone. I feel that our classrooms need more laughter, more tears, more intensity, more feeling of all kinds. Not feeling just for the sake of feeling, but feeling that grows out of real experience with literature through reading, real interaction with others through oral and written conversation, and real exploration of one's own life through writing. It's not a matter of introducing emotions but rather one of allowing them to emerge, creating not only deeper learning but deeper personal relationships in the classroom. Carol Avery (1988, pp. 110–111) has written movingly of how a student's death was made more bearable because her classmates had really gotten to know her through her writing: "Laura will always be a part of us and none of us will ever be the same."

Not every teacher is comfortable with emotions or feels they are appropriate in the classroom. What I am trying to do is to provide a model of one way of being a teacher, let students know what an emotionally permissive classroom feels like for students, get them to think about one of the many ways there are to be a good teacher. (They certainly see many models of the alternative.) In addition to modeling, I talk about the role of emotion in the classroom. I suggest to prospective teachers that when they encourage their students to write about their own lives, their writing may reveal not only joy and fun but anger and sadness, since these are part of life. Discouraging the expression of some feelings can inhibit the expression of other feelings. I tell my students that if they read significant and meaningful children's literature aloud to their classes, they may cry along with their students at the sad parts, and that this can be a positive shared experience, rather than an embarrassment. I can't say that I'd be thrilled if my dean walked in while I was crying in class, but I'd sooner run that risk than shut off my tears.

→ See: Avery, p. 14; Crafts, p. 136; Heath, p. 422; Literature Reference List, p. 429; Wilde, pp. 32, 151.

References

Avery, C. 1988. "Laura's legacy." *Language Arts* 65.
Goodlad, J. 1984. *A place called school.* New York: McGraw-Hill.
Wilde, S. 1989. "The power of literature: Notes from a survivor." *New Advocate* 2.

It Shouldn't Happen to Kids

Who Is the *Real* Enemy

"Never forget, Martin," the supervising teacher told her student teacher, "the students are the enemy!"

—LBB

Book Note

Whole Language: Beliefs and Practices, K–8

Gary Manning and Maryann Manning, editors
1989; 240 pp.; $15.95
Washington, DC: National Education Association

This anthology offers relief from the bulging-file-cabinet syndrome: Instead of fighting overstuffed files, you can find your favorite whole language essays in one handy volume. There are classic offerings in this book from such leading authorities as Edelsky, the Goodmans, Graves, Harste, and Frank Smith. In addition, the editors have written several excellent essays that address such traditional concerns as phonics, reading comprehension, and spelling.

This is a good book to give an administrator or colleague who is new to whole language.

LBB

❝ First and foremost: Whole Language is *not* practice. It is a set of beliefs, a perspective. It must become practice but it is not the practice itself. Journals, book publishing, literature study, thematic science units and so forth do not make a classroom "Whole Language." Rather, these practices become Whole Language-like because the teacher has particular beliefs and intentions. ❞ (the editors, p. 10)

It Shouldn't Happen to Kids

Duck Soup

During my second week of student teaching, just as I was feeling exhausted and unsure of myself, I talked to a classmate who found herself in a most *unfortunate* position. It seems that she had been placed in a kindergarten classroom in a very traditional school setting, with a very traditional master teacher. My friend had been instructed to observe her mentor carefully, not merely for the purpose of learning classroom management and curriculum techniques, but to be able to mimic the regular classroom teacher in hand and body movement as well as in voice pattern and inflection. To achieve this cloning procedure, she had been advised to go home in the evening to practice in front of a full-length mirror. I gave her the additional suggestion that she watch the section of the Marx Brothers' *Duck Soup* when Harpo mimics Groucho's movements.

—Greg Chapnick, former filmmaker, now an elementary teacher, Fairview School, Hayward, CA

Network

WLSIG Newsletter
WHOLE LANGUAGE SPECIAL INTEREST GROUP OF I.R.A.   VOL 3 NO 1 FALL 1989

Five Tough Questions That Whole Language Teachers Ask

by Bess Altwerger

What happens to my students when they leave my whole language classroom and enter a basal reading program?

Although worrying about what will happen to your students who move on to a skills-based classroom may be natural, it would be a shame to change your marvelous language program because of next year's basal program. A literature rich program will give your students the basic strategies and comprehension focus that will carry them through future years at school. Furthermore, you will be nurturing a love for reading and literature that they might not have otherwise developed. It might be helpful for you to know that basal readers focus more on comprehension in the higher grade levels. The quality of the stories also improve through the grade levels. If you provide a good foundation in literature, chances are that your kids will shine when they move on to higher grades.

How do you explain to the children that sometimes it is all right not to spell words "correctly" and that other times it is necessary to get them just right?

There are several ways that you can ensure that your students achieve an understanding of the appropriateness of spelling conventionality.

Book Note

When Writers Read

Jane Hansen
1987; 256 pp.; $16
Portsmouth, NH:
Heinemann

Jane Hansen spent two years observing regularly in the Mast Way School of Stratham, NH. She shows us children's reading and writing primarily through what they did and what they said about it.

My favorite sections are those in which Hansen uses listening (and then talking) as the "lens through which to reexamine Time, Choice, Response, Structure, and Community," topics of earlier chapters. Since Hansen visited all over the school for a period of time, she also gives us portraits of the Chapter 1 teacher, the librarian, and the principal. She shows all of these, including the teachers and herself, as they developed over the two-year study.

Mary Kitagawa

❝John's notion of 'A Principal' was tested by the response method of leadership inherent in the way we work with writers and readers. As the teachers became a writing community and altered their ways of teaching, they made demands on John. They learned to listen to their students, to tell a student, 'This, specifically, is what you know,' to nudge, and to step back so the students relied on each other. In turn, the teachers expected John to treat them similarly, as teachers elsewhere will expect their principals to do. ❞ (p. 197)

Even as early as kindergarten and first grade, classroom environments and curricula should provide an abundance of opportunities to write for a wide variety of purposes. By fulfilling many communicative functions through writing, children will naturally encounter situations that vary in terms of their demand for conventionality and formality. Students will also have a wide range of audiences for their writing. This is an important factor in determining the appropriateness of conventionality in writing. Public relations demand that bulletin boards, and stories that go home or to the principal be somewhat polished (especially in the upper grades), and producing conventional yet meaningful writing will provide the children with a sense of pride and accomplishment. You'll feel pretty good about it too!

I have been using the language experience approach and we do creative writing several times a week. I also read aloud to the class every day. Does this make me a whole language teacher and if not, what do I have to add to my program?

Whole language is not a collection of activities and strategies. Although certain experiences are consistent with the view of learning and literacy underlying the whole language approach, these experiences alone do not define a classroom as whole language. The best way to determine if you are a whole language teacher is by examining your beliefs about language and learning. Teachers who are changing the way they deal with children's learning may be further ahead in their thinking than in making the practical changes to their curriculum. Conversely, teachers can provide many of the experiences associated with whole language without making the "paradigm shift" from a skills view of learning. The result is a classroom that appears whole language on the surface but is operating under a completely different set of assumptions.

Examining your own beliefs in light of what you learn from your students as they inform your practice is the best way to evaluate how far you've come and how far you still need to go.

How do I find the time to make big books, copy out charts, get the children's work published, keep anecdotal records, plan "hands-on activities," search through resource books for appropriate thematic materials, and so on?

It certainly feels at times that a good whole language teacher's job is never done. However, you must find a way to lessen your responsibilities in order not to fall victim to early burn-out. Organize your classroom environment and curriculum to guarantee your professional survival: planning theme topics, developing activities, gathering materials, creating charts, bulletin boards, and big books should be done collaboratively by teacher and students. Organize your classroom so that children are working as independently as possible; then you'll have the time to be a conscientious "kidwatcher."

Don't forget your community and parents as resources for your curriculum. Many teachers hold bookmaking and big-bookmaking parties for parents. Some schools have "grandparent" programs, where grandmas and grandpas read to children, listen to children read, and offer help as needed.

Finally, use commercial products that are consistent with your theoretical beliefs. Order big books and literature programs whenever possible. Whole language certainly cannot be packaged, but publishing companies have begun to respond to the needs of whole language teachers—take advantage of this, and demand more!

In what context should phonics be taught (if ever) by whole language teachers?

It will be helpful to define some terms and clear up some possible misconceptions before we attack this question head-on. The relationship between oral and written language for an alphabetic system such as ours is called the "graphophonic system." It is an indisputable fact that the graphophonic system exists, and that it is a vital aspect of our written orthography. *Phonics* refers to the direct teaching of the graphophonic system, most often in ways that are behavioristic in nature, and *linguistically inaccurate*.

Whole language teachers *do not* teach phonics per se, but we absolutely *do* concern ourselves with helping children learn how to use the graphophonic system. Every time your children write (and attempt to spell words), every time you read to them while they follow along, every time they listen to a tape as they read along in a book, every time they use charts to sing together, and every time they match what they know or can predict to print, they are learning how to use the graphophonic system.

At some point children will begin to ask questions and present their hypotheses about the graphophonic system to you. That is the time to discuss the matter directly, encourage, and offer new ideas to consider. Just be prepared to defend yourself to the whole language teacher next door when she hears you say, "Yes, Tom, when two vowels go walking the first one does the talking—sometimes!"

Excerpted from *WLSIG Newsletter* 2(1), Fall 1988.

Bess Altwerger is a professor at Towson State University, Baltimore, MD.

Subscription Information: The *WLSIG Newsletter* is published twice a year, in the fall and spring. A membership year runs from one IRA Annual Convention to the next (from May to May). To subscribe, send a check for $5.00 to Pat Jenkins, secretary-treasurer, WLSIG, 2801 West Broadway #F6, Columbia, MO 65203.

I Used to Be...But Now I...

I used to challenge the establishment accidentally,
But now I do it on purpose.

—Participant in the Tucson
Whole Language Institute

Resource: Organization

Educational Press Association of America

Donald R. Stoll, executive editor
Glassboro State College
Glassboro, NJ 08028-1773
1-609-863-7349

At the International Reading Association conference last year, Yetta and I visited the booth of the Educational Press Association of America and discovered what a valuable resource it can be for educators. It publishes a booklet that lists the names and addresses of 500 educational publishers. Membership in the association offers you a variety of services and publications, including *EdPress News*, a monthly update of educational issues and trends.

LBB

The Whole Language Umbrella

 **Network**

Whole Language Umbrella: A Confederation of Teacher Support Groups

The Whole Language Umbrella is open to any group or individual interested in whole language. The primary purpose of WLU is to provide a network for whole language support groups. There are more than 100 support groups in the United States and Canada.

As a confederation of groups, dues are set to favor group memberships. There are no requirements or restrictions placed on local groups by WLU other than the membership dues. Individual members have the same benefits as group members, with the exception of voting rights.

There are several good reasons for becoming a member of WLU. Membership allows you and your group to be more closely connected with other whole language groups. WLU offers networking and support services that include a newsletter that is published three times a year, contact lists of other member groups, and current information about available whole language activities. Future services and publications may include an information clearinghouse and a directory of support groups.

A large whole language organization can offer teachers a stronger voice and greater credibility. The WLU will actively support whole language teaching and teachers. Member groups may note affiliation with WLU on newsletters or conference brochures.

 **In the Mail**

Dear Whole Language Educators—Friends,

In her book *West with the Night* Beryl Markham wrote, "Africa is a continent on which you can feel the future under your feet." That same promise and excitement surrounds the whole language movement. The future is right here, right now, and not only can we feel it—we can do much more—we can shape it. But to do that we need a firm stand and a strong grasp. Our support groups along with our newly formed international Whole Language Umbrella can help us stand, reach, and mold the future.

February 18, 1989: The moment has passed, but the excitement and challenge haven't faded. It was on that day in Winnipeg that the dreams of educators across the continent became a reality, and the thoughtful work of the original steering committee of the North American Confederation of Whole Language Teacher Support Groups took on a life of its own. A life that needs our knowledge, hard work, and commitment.

In all our endeavors we have made some mistakes, and it's inevitable that we will stumble again, but like good whole language students, we will learn as much, maybe more, from getting it wrong as we will from getting it right. Bear with us, support us, make suggestions.

Our local support groups can help us create meaning. The WLU can help us come together to deepen our understanding and encourage even our most tentative and tenuous efforts. TAWL groups and WLU give us strength, but we have to provide the passion and the commitment to keep them alive.

What we do in our support groups, and the decisions and actions taken by our new Whole Language Umbrella can touch children, teachers, and curriculum right here and now, as well as into the future. The task is enormous; it appears to be worth the effort.

Thank you for making me your first Whole Language Umbrella president. Except for a few classroom experiences that I will never forget, this may be the most rewarding and humbling experience of my professional life. It's quite an honor.

Dorothy Watson

→ See: Literature Reference List, p. 429; Watson, pp. 40, 53, 427.

Dorothy Watson is a professor at the University of Missouri, Columbia, MO.

Dues

Groups: $25 plus $.25 per member up to 125 members—U.S. funds

$30 plus $.30 per member up to 125 members—Canadian funds

Individuals: $25 U.S. funds/$30 Canadian funds

In the U.S. send to:
Debbie Manning
4848 N. Fruit
Fresno, CA 93705

In Canada send to:
Lorraine Krause
257 Beaconsfield Blvd.
Beaconsfield, Quebec
H9W 4A5

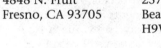 **In the Mail**

Sharon Zinke returned home inspired and excited from the 1989 CEL Conference in Winnipeg. Immediately following the conference, she attended a historic gathering of representatives of American and Canadian teacher support groups, who came together for the purpose of drafting a constitution that would serve as the basis of a new organization, the Whole Language Umbrella. Here is a letter that Sharon wrote to Professor Dorothy Watson, the first president of the Whole Language Umbrella, about the two meetings. —LBB

Dear Dorothy,

Someone said *empowerment* has been overused, but I don't care. I have been empowered. Hayward will never be the same after my weekend in Winnipeg. I don't know exactly what I'll do, but I know that the level of my commitment will cause nearly anything I do to make a difference.

What is it that empowered me in this way? It had something to do with the networking, the interactions, the hundred little conversations I had with people usually spread out all over North America who have the same fire inside and the same willingness to risk, to take whatever comes, and then to go out and risk it all over again. To be in the same room with so many of these warm people at once, an arctic chill standing guard outside. Our conversations built on each other like stalagmites, growing, making inner strength. And it had to do with being around a critical mass of people who are even more committed than I am, and having the opportunity to watch them: selfless people who don't worry about looking good or what anyone thinks, all their energy focused on getting our job done, changing the direction of a monster machine that has been moving with such force that no one knows how to turn it off. People who know that it will take a movement of individuals who come together and take a stand.

And finally, Dorothy, I had heard your name and had read one of your articles, but I was totally unprepared for who you are. There you were, taking responsibility for the whole event, and with such grace and quiet strength, and in the middle of this incredible historical moment for you and the Goodmans and all the rest of us, you still reached out to me, one person, to see who I was. I want you to know I'll never forget it, and I will think of you, standing up for all of us, whenever I feel that the challenge is too much.

Much love,

Sharon Zinke

→ See: Watson, p. 408; Zinke, p. 121.

Sharon Zinke is a language arts specialist at Fairview School, Hayward, CA.

Resource: Whole Language Conferences

FEBRUARY

CEL Conference
219 Garden Park Dr., Winnipeg, Manitoba, R2P 1Y3, Canada

New Mexico TAWL Regional Conference
P.O. Box 27651, Albuquerque, NM 87125-7651

APRIL

Springboards, Language Arts Conference
c/o McGill University, Department of Education Reading Centre, 3700 McTavish, Montreal, Quebec, H3A 1Y2, Canada

JUNE

California Whole Language Conference
3835 Perie Ln., San Jose, CA 95131

Summer Whole Language Institute at Myrtle Beach

Storytelling Conference

Writing Across the Curriculum Workshop

New Zealand/Australia Trip: "Whole Language Down Under"

Whole Language Conference
Graduate and Continuing Education, USC Coastal Carolina College, P.O. Box 1954, Myrtle Beach, SC 29578, 1-803-349-2671; 448-1481; 546-0234

AUGUST

Catskill Whole Language Council
Box 305, Oneonta, NY 13820

Northeast Whole Language Conference
Johnson State College, Johnson, VT 05656

OCTOBER

Mid-Missouri TAWL Renewal Conference
University of Missouri School of Education, 212 Townsend Hall, Columbia, MO 65211

DECEMBER EVERY OTHER YEAR

Whole Language Workshop with Ken and Yetta Goodman
Program in Language and Literacy, University of Arizona, Tucson, AZ 85721, 1-602-621-7868

This list is incomplete and may contain some errors; please send us your additions or corrections.
—LBB

Cornerstone: Ethel Buchanan

CEL: A Whole Language Teacher Support Group

The Child-centred Experience-based Learning (CEL) group was founded in Winnipeg in 1974, when five teachers were invited by Donna and Orin Cochrane to meet in their home to discuss teaching and classroom practice. This group held some beliefs in common:

- That all children are capable of learning to read;
- That the environment for learning must be safe and secure;
- That children must believe in themselves as being capable of learning;
- That each day in school, children must have successful learning experiences;
- That social interaction stimulates thinking and nurtures learning;
- That children learn language by using language for some meaningful purpose;
- That learners must be responsible for their own learning and must be free to have choices and make decisions; and
- That each learner is unique, and evaluation must take this into account.

Ethel Buchanan has worked in the Winnipeg School Division, Manitoba, as a teacher, primary supervisor, and elementary language arts consultant. She is one of the founders of the Child-centered Experience-based Learning Group, and an honorary lifetime member of CEL and the Reading Council of Greater Winnipeg.

All members of the group had experience in teaching reading without the use of basals and workbooks: They used a variety of trade books and encouraged all kinds of writing such as writing in connection with research and special projects, and personal writing.

Over the years some members have left the group and other teachers have been invited to join, but in every case the new members' views about teaching and learning have been consistent; and so the group has maintained continuity of purpose.

The group has been kept small, with an average of 28 members, in order to promote close relationships and to allow members to meet in each other's homes. It is completely independent of other institutions or organizations but has, on occasion, cooperated with school divisions, the University of Manitoba, and the local Reading Council in bringing speakers to Winnipeg. Members have been closely associated with other organizations and educational institutions, giving university courses in reading, serving as officers, members of executive boards of a number of professional organizations, and working on curriculum revision committees.

At first, the members really held no well-developed theory of reading; but they knew that children must be exposed to lots of good books, that whatever happens in the classroom should have a meaning and a purpose in the eyes of the child, and that joy could, and should, be a part of learning. But CEL members had gotten caught up in structured kits, skills lists, and phonics programs. Thus there was a dichotomy in their thinking: Children learn to read by reading, but you must teach phonics so that they can learn to read.

The period of using structured kits and phonics did not last very long. Members of the group heard Frank Smith and Ken and Yetta Goodman speak, and had a chance to talk to them and read some of their publications. These educators helped CEL members see learning as thinking and reading as a thinking process. At that point everything started to come together. They had found a philosophy of learning that could comfortably house their beliefs. They had to change some of their practices, which took time, discussion, reading, and thinking; but it was the work of the children themselves that convinced the members of the group that much was gained when the skills kits and structured phonics were abandoned.

Discovering together well-developed theories that supported what the group stood for provided its members with courage and the impetus to head more confidently in the direction they had chosen.

By June 1977, the CEL group was ready to share some things with other teachers. A notice was placed in the Winnipeg School Division bulletin. The response was far greater than had been anticipated. Participants had to be divided into two groups with one group commencing at 4:30 P.M. and the other group at 7:00 P.M. Workshops lasted two hours and were held once a week for six consecutive weeks. The same thing happened in November and again in February. The term ended with over a hundred people signed up for sessions beginning in April and ending in June. Since that time there has been a waiting list for every workshop.

Over the years, CEL members have planned and conducted approximately 40 series of sessions in Winnipeg, accepting no fees or expense money. Each session deals with some aspect of learning theory, the reading process, or the writing process. There are group participation activities or demonstrations and sharing periods. Participants are expected to turn up for all six sessions and to try out ideas in their classrooms between sessions. Certificates indicating attendance and participation are presented at the end. Some teachers proceed to a CEL Two series. At times CEL offers an advanced level.

CEL has also arranged a number of summer workshops, some presented by members, others by well-known experts. James Britton, Michael Halliday, and Harold Rosen were invited to conduct workshops on language development.

The first whole language conference arranged by the group was a one-day affair held in a school on a Saturday in the late winter of 1981. Because Dorothy Watson was the speaker, the conference was so well received that it became the forerunner of conferences held every year since that time in the Winnipeg Convention Centre. The conferences now last two days and feature some of the best-known proponents of whole language. Thousands of teachers and administrators from all over North America have attended.

CEL members have conducted numerous workshops throughout Manitoba and beyond. They published a journal, wrote *For the Love of Reading*, produced a script for a television science series, and contributed articles to professional journals and other publications. They now issue a newsletter, *Connections*, three times a year.

All these activities have stimulated the professional development of CEL members themselves. They have studied books together, they have taken time to share ideas and good literature for children, and they have encouraged professional reading and recommended books and articles to each other.

There are many reasons for having support groups such as CEL. Not long ago members were asked to write down what CEL had done for them. Their answers should inspire whole language teachers who are not already associated with a support group to form one of their own. Here are some typical comments:

"CEL put me in touch with world-renowned figures in the field of literacy development."

"CEL helped me view children differently."

"CEL helped me grow in my ability to make presentations."

"CEL helped me realize I was a writer with something to say."

"CEL showed me how I could improve."

"CEL put me in touch with new ideas and helped me use them."

"CEL gave me confidence in myself and my potential."

"CEL gave me knowledge to answer questions of parents and other teachers."

"CEL became my family."

→ See: Stevenson, p. 411; Watson, p. 40.

Further Reading by Ethel Buchanan
- ◆ *For the Love of Reading*, ed. CEL, 1980.
- ◆ *Where Butterflies Go.* CEL, 1982.
- ◆ *Reading, Writing and Caring.* CEL, 1984.
- ◆ *Spelling for Whole Language Classrooms.* 1989.

Network

C + C = WLR

by Dick Salzer

All one needs to start a revolution these days is a computer and a copy machine (hence, Computer plus Copier equals Whole Language Revolution). Our experience with a local support group (CLIC—Creative Literacy for Children) demonstrates that low-budget revolution is indeed possible. Certainly it's an advantage to start a whole language group with a sizable chunk of capital, but it isn't essential. CLIC grew substantially in a few years with only membership funds.

Clearly a computer is very useful when an organization is growing rapidly. Whole language is attractive to teachers and they are eager to associate themselves with like-minded professionals. We started with two dozen interested people and soon had 200—and this success produced logistical problems. Fortunately some of our members knew how to solve them. A computerized membership list, helpful in many ways, led to easy production of mailing labels—no small matter when everybody is busy.

With the aid of a word processor, creating an attractive newsletter to send to the membership becomes a manageable task. There are good programs for the various machines, and these are often complete with different typefaces and attractive graphics. Any computer enthusiast can provide the help required. A copy machine (or access to free or inexpensive copy service) completes the formula. All that is needed is notices of meetings and other content for the newsletter—and the revolutionaries should supply these!

→ See: Salzer, pp. 119, 231.

Dick Salzer is a professor at SUNY-Buffalo, Buffalo, NY.

Network

The History of SMILE and CED

by Carol Maytag Christine

In January of 1979 a small group of classroom and university teachers representing four different school districts in the Phoenix area and Arizona State University met for breakfast in Tempe, Arizona. We were interested in language experience and whole language, and we were aware of how the school curriculum and our teaching was influenced by our peers, as well as the general public and our district administration. In this first meeting we identified the following mutual needs: (1) communicating with other teachers, (2) identifying research to support what we do, (3) informing elementary principals, (4) communicating with our State Department, (5) watching legislation, and (6) identifying teachers and classrooms to visit.

By the end of the morning we had created our acronym, SMILE (Support and Maintenance for Implementing Language Expression), and we were making plans for our first workshop—less than two months away. We selected a school where we knew the administrator would support our work, and the first SMILE workshop was held on March 31, 1979. The 50 teachers who attended heard Wynn Wright of Washington School District applaud us for what we had accomplished. During the morning there were two workshop sessions; teachers selected from presentations on children's literature, bookbinding, puppetry, language experience resources for teachers, and learning center ideas. Other speakers donated their time at later workshops—Merri Schall, Ralph Peterson, Roach Van Allen, Jeannette Veatch, and Yetta M. Goodman. Attendance grew at successive conferences to more than one thousand.

Word spread quickly from our support group to other groups as teachers began to cluster to protect and to develop their work. Shortly after SMILE began meeting we learned of the Teachers Applying Whole Language (TAWL) groups in Tucson, Arizona, and Columbia, Missouri. In Arizona, WOW (Way Out West with Whole Language) and GRIN (Greater Reservation Interdisciplinary Network) asked SMILE for help in forming their groups.

In 1982 SMILE began selling selected titles of professional literature at workshops. We saw this as a way to raise money and as another opportunity to involve teachers in their professional growth. When Donald Graves's book on writing, called *Writing: Teachers and Children at Work*, was published in 1983, the volume of our sales tripled, and it continued to grow to a proportion that had to be protected by incorporation in the state of Arizona. In December 1985, the Center for Establishing Dialogue in Teaching and Learning (CED) was created to sell books and provide workshops on a more frequent basis.

The center is a direct result of the professional activities of classroom and university teachers working together to (1) support and develop educational practices that use children's experiences and their modes of expression as the means of learning, (2) encourage and support research and writing by teachers, (3) provide opportunities for teachers to link research and classroom practices in cooperation with public and private educational institutions, and (4) provide opportunities for individuals and groups to form coalitions to carry out common goals and purposes.

The center has been promoting dialogue through workshops and study groups. In 1989–90, we examined evaluation with Pat Carini from Bennington College in Vermont. Teachers from four different school districts met three times during the year to explore ways to observe, document, and evaluate classroom settings and children's growth and learning. At the final meeting, the participating teachers shared their work with other teachers and with administrators from their school districts.

This seminar was planned to complement and extend the activities that began in a seminar on student evaluation sponsored by CED in the spring of 1987. Out of that meeting the support group Community for Effective Student Evaluation (CESE) was organized. During the 1987–88 Arizona legislature, CESE was successful in changing legislation on standardized testing; mandatory testing of students in first and twelfth grades was made optional.

A writing support group meets monthly at the center and other teacher/writers have continued sharing work started during Don Murray's small group writing workshops in February 1989. Vivian Paley, the kindergarten teacher and author of *Wally's Stories*, provided a workshop in January 1990 for teachers to learn how to create literature from their classroom experiences. Activities recommended by Donald Graves when he spoke for SMILE in 1984 are beginning to take hold.

In our first two years, Shelley Harwayne and Mary Ellen Giacobbe worked with writing in classrooms, while a small group of teachers observed in addition to leading all-day workshops for a larger audience from all over the state. In some school districts these teachers have shared their experience during inservice workshops. In the networks that have developed, more and more teachers and administrators are asking questions about and encouraging understanding of whole language.

Yetta M. Goodman supported these workshops with her presentation on kidwatching and evaluation. Yetta's documentation of children's uses of environmental print, and her research on the roots of literacy, provided teachers with confirmation of their beliefs and practical resources to work with in their classrooms.

Ken Goodman was the first major speaker sponsored by the center. Ken's presentations on the pillars of whole language—teaching, learning, language, curriculum, and social context—provided an essential framework for teachers and administrators to take back to their schools.

All of the speakers from SMILE and CED workshops have played a crucial role in our development. Our opportunities for learning and collaborating have spread beyond our local boundaries, and I like to think of our groups as one thread of many, gently but persistently weaving change in and out of our classrooms throughout our nation's schools.

➡ See: Christine, pp. 222, 379; Graves, p. 129; Harwayne, p. 337; Howard, p. 266; Paley, p. 30.

Carol Maytag Christine is a doctoral student at the University of Arizona, Tucson, AZ.

More information: Center For Establishing Dialogue in Teaching and Learning, Inc. (CED), 325 E. Southern Ave., Ste. 14, Tempe, AZ 85282, (602) 894-1333.

Network

The Beginnings of the Greater Reservation Interdisciplinary Network: GRIN

by Debbie A. Hickman

"Maybe we could start a teacher support group here in Ganado that's something like SMILE in Phoenix."

"You mean get together with other teachers and talk about what's working and what's not?"

"Yes, a teacher support group for those of us who need to talk. We could share ideas for thematic units and problems with getting kids to write or whatever."

"Maybe we could focus on a topic or just share some good children's books or professional books. Who knows?"

"Why don't you bring it up, Debbie, at the next teachers meeting?"

And so in the fall of 1985 GRIN began . . . Ten teachers from Ganado Primary School showed up at our first meeting, including the principal, who was particularly enthusiastic about the possibilities of the gathering.

The meetings continued throughout the year at various teachers' homes. The most successful meetings seemed to be centered around a topic of interest, such as writing, art, or science. GRIN started making the school calendar, and teachers were asking about the next meeting.

Later we gathered at another reservation school to discuss with other interested folks some options for the organization, including the emergence of the name GRIN. After all we were inspired by SMILE, the whole language teacher support group in Phoenix. GRIN stands for Greater Reservation Interdisciplinary Network.

GRIN went on to orchestrate two workshops a year in various locations around the huge Navajo reservation with approximately 100 in attendance each time. Although attendance may seem small by most conference standards, we draw from a radius of more than 150 miles. Presentations at the workshops have engaged both local and big city talent with both theoretical and practical aspects of writing, science, songwriting, research, counseling, thematic units, art, literature, and drama.

In between all the conferences GRIN has been extensively involved in the Young Authors and Young Readers programs in northern Arizona.

GRIN is a survivor. But only after our seventh conference did GRIN take on a formal organizational status with officers and planning committees and business meetings. A newsletter will be forthcoming, and official GRIN stationery will carry our logo.

➡ See: Boloz, p. 277.

Debbie A. Hickman is an instructional resource teacher at Ganado Primary School, Ganado, AZ.

📷 WHOLE LANGUAGE CAMERA

"May we never cease to learn, to change, to grow."
—Ken Goodman (see p. 428)

Network

Ten Years of Children and Whole Language: CAWL

by Margaret T. Stevenson

In 1989 teachers in Edmonton celebrated the 10th anniversary of their teacher support groups at a dinner party with special guest Ethel Buchanan. We reminisced a lot—about our beginnings, what we felt we had accomplished, and how we as individuals had grown in our understanding of children and language.

Our beginning . . .

In 1979 a group of 30 teachers spent two precious weeks of their summer holidays at a workshop organized by the school district language arts supervisor, and conducted by Ethel Buchanan. It was our introduction to the term "whole language" and all that it implies. Excited and committed, but fearful of going back to their schools and trying to implement the ideas on their own, these 30 teachers decided to meet regularly and so became our first teacher support group. They were quickly followed by others until our groups numbered seven and our enrollment 250.

The groups carried out many exciting projects—the district's first Young Authors' Conference, a publication for parents titled *What Is the Whole Language Approach?*, and a videotape cooperatively developed with the University of Alberta. Heady stuff!

What makes our groups different from most is the strong support of the school district language arts supervisor and consultants who meet with the groups and facilitate the networking and the many projects.

But what about the individuals—how have they grown? They have developed into leaders who never stop learning. Their interest whetted, they have gone back to university to complete master's or doctoral studies. Most of the original members are now in a position to influence other teachers as principals, assistant principals, consultants, and curriculum coordinators. Those who have made a decision to stay in the classroom never let themselves get into a rut; they attend conferences and workshops, and move to a different school after a few years, thus broadening their sphere of influence. All our members present workshops for their own and other schools, for conferences, and other school districts. They have taken on the district IRA as a project, acting on the executive, planning exciting programs and a yearly conference for over 1,500 teachers.

"In 1979 we thought the only person in the room who knew what to do was the teacher. In 1989 it's the children who know what to do; the teacher is learning from them."

→ See: Stevenson, p. 271.

Margaret T. Stevenson is working toward a Ph.D. in education.

Further Information: For further information about CAWL contact Carol Anne Inglis, consultant, Student Assessment, Edmonton Public Schools, Centre for Education, One Kingsway, Edmonton, Alberta, T5H 4G9, Canada.

As Teachers See It

by Kittye Copeland

Mid-Missouri TAWL and the Education of Kittye Copeland

I was nearly burned out as a teacher in 1974, when I joined a group of teachers in Columbia, Missouri, to explore ideas about whole language. Our meetings kept me from quitting the field of education. With the encouragement of Dorothy Watson, six of us decided to meet regularly to share ideas, books, articles, and lots of support. Dorothy, who had come to the University of Missouri to teach college, was now also a member of our support group for Teachers Applying Whole Language (TAWL).

We all began to feel a new sense of growing professionalism. Our classrooms became communities of learners, and as we explored what was happening in our classrooms, we discovered support for our new developing theories.

In 1980, we went to the International Reading Association Conference in St. Louis, Missouri, to present our findings in support of whole language. The evening before we were to present I heard Bill Martin. As he spoke of my past skills-and-drill curriculum, I was reminded that I had moved in the right direction. Each time he told of an outdated drill practice he would cry, "How dare you do that to children." Wow, would they love our presentation the next day. We no longer practiced the methods to which Bill would say, "How dare you do that to children." But the next day, not many people came. Ken Goodman was there, sitting in the front row of my session. Would I live? He was the expert! What if I didn't explain things right? What if I said something wrong? After my speech, Dr. Goodman gave me a hug and said, "Every child in the United States should have a teacher like you." Talk about motivation.

I went to work with a new enthusiasm and professionalism that I had not felt earlier. In graduate classes I was relieved to discover that there were researchers validating my notions of how learning took place in classrooms. My teaching methods changed from textbook-controlled to child-centered, meaning-focused. With my students, I made curricular decisions that met our needs. My enthusiasm was contagious and the children responded, excited about becoming readers and writers. We learned together. I felt a new power. A few years later, when I was honored by the International Reading Association as the Nila Banton Smith award winner for teaching reading in the content areas (a first for a first-grade teacher), I realized that I represented a new kind of teacher, a whole language teacher. I was very proud of the headlines that hit the newspaper in the small town where I taught. Surely the community would be proud that one of their teachers had become a pioneer of an innovative, internationally recognized theory of teaching.

But the next headline read, "New Method of Teaching Reading Under Fire." After a substitute teacher had worked in my classroom and found that I was not following the basal reader manual, that teacher went to the board with 28 questions: "When did the board approve the whole language approach?" "The school did approve the basal series, Why isn't it being taught in the correct manner instead of supplementing it with the whole language approach?" "Doesn't a whole language program encourage laziness since children can write a word the way they want to and say 'blank' to a new word and not have to sound it out?"

An open meeting was called so that professors from the university could answer parents' questions. Even though I respect Dorothy Watson and Pete Hasselriis, and I realized that much of what I knew I learned from them, I wondered why I was not allowed to answer the parents' questions myself. I also wondered how anyone could explain in two hours all the knowledge I had acquired through all my years in the classroom and in a five-year graduate program.

I knew that I had come to a testing time in my career. Would I compromise my professional knowledge if they decided that I could no longer teach my own way, or would I resign? And could I find another job? Perhaps I would be fired.

I told a reporter that there was benefit to the controversy because it forced changes. However, I was sick with fear and I cried when the hate mail came. I had been a very passive play-it-safe, save-your-job employee. I now decided that regardless of the outcome I was *right*. I was a professional educator who knew what I was doing.

The final headline read, "Parents Flock to Support Whole Language Program." I wasn't fired, but somehow I didn't feel as valued as the professional I had become. I didn't return to that school. The night I was interviewed for my new job a story in the newspaper read "New Method Spells Controversy," with a picture of me reading a story to some children. In this new situation, I was immediately treated as a professional decision-maker. I work very hard to remain a professional. Never again will I allow other people to answer the questions that I know I can answer myself.

I continue to search for the best theories to guide my decisions by taking classes, reading articles and books, attending conventions, and being a member of professional organizations such as Teachers Applying Whole Language. As with all professionals, no teacher can practice alone. When I took the risk to become an innovative teacher I needed the support of others.

Our TAWL group has grown. We still meet monthly; however, we no longer meet in living rooms, but in schools with over 100 members. We continue to share our ideas and concerns. When we present at conferences, people no longer take chairs out of our sessions—they go to other rooms to get chairs for us. We have our own annual conference, which has grown to over 400 participants. I was privileged to be a delegate to the constitutional conference for the newly founded Whole Language Umbrella and to witness Dorothy Watson become the first president. For me TAWL remains the positive force that reminds me that I am a professional authority in my classroom.

→ See: A Declaration of Professional Conscience for Teachers, inside front cover; Altwerger and Flores, p. 418; Bell, p. 48; Copeland, p. 48; Swanda, p. 48; Watson, p. 408.

Excerpted from *Mid-Missouri TAWL Newsletter*, 25 September 1989.

Kittye Copeland is a primary and elementary teacher at Stephens Elementary Children's School, Columbia, MO.

Great Teachers:
Elena Castro
by Barbara Flores

Classroom Demonstrations
by Lillian Hentel

When I first walked into Elena Castro's classroom, I was immediately impressed with the *cariño* (genuine caring), the warmth, *el respeto* (the respect for others), and the social, physical, and political organization of the community of learners/teachers. She was not yet a whole language teacher, and she was not satisfied with how she was teaching. During one of our first talks (one of many to come), she told me that "something was missing." She lamented that she was unsuccessful at reaching all her children, even though she considered herself a dedicated and good teacher. "I want to make a difference in every child in my first grade. . . . I know that they can all learn even if they come from very poor, single-parent, or farmworker families."

Elena Castro presently works at Dool Elementary School in Calexico, California; she has been a whole language bilingual teacher since 1985. She has been instrumental in pioneering collaborative action research in literacy and biliteracy, conducting staff development within and outside her district and state. She has pioneered the development of theme cycles, literature studies, and interactive journals with Spanish/English bilingual children. She possesses energy, determination, and savvy about schooling. Because of her untiring leadership both within her school and in her district, she has been a mentor teacher and a literature project representative for the state language arts framework. In other words, her expertise is highly valued and rewarded.

She not only demonstrates her leadership in the areas of knowledge of curriculum, staff development, and research; she was also elected by her peers as the union president for her entire school district.

Elena is not afraid to take risks, to take stands, to make mistakes, to share successes, failures, to ask questions, to explore issues, to raise questions or concerns, to disagree, to be political, to care about kids, to talk to parents, to organize community action, to participate in the creation of new knowledge, to engage children in authentic learning and teaching, to share with others, to work, to dare to be intellectual enough, to say "I don't know," to teach, to grow.

In Spanish we have many *dichos* (proverbs); Elena admirably demonstrates *"querer es poder"* (love is power/to want to do something good is also powerful). *Ella misma muestra lo que deberíamos todos hacer y que la mayoría está haciendo* (She herself shows what we all should do and what most of us are doing).

→ See: Altwerger, pp. 295, 418; Flores, p. 218.

Barbara Flores is a professor at California State University at San Bernardino, CA.

How to Start Your Own Grass-Roots Whole Language Organization

Four years ago, several of us, all teaching on the west side of Phoenix, Arizona, attended a whole language conference on the east side of the Valley of the Sun, sponsored by SMILE—a grass-roots organization that had been in existence for several years. It was quite a distance for us to travel, but we felt it was worth the trip for the information and support it afforded those of us on the west side who were committed to whole language.

We met with Kris Jilbert, a former administrator at Dysart District who was now working on her doctorate and had left the district. We told her of our idea to form a west-side group. We felt many teachers would reach out to whole language if it reached out to them closer to home. With her support, we called our first meeting at my home in Glendale. We invited Dr. Ralph Peterson from Arizona State University.

The meeting was attended by about 15 teachers, one baby, whose mama put him snugly on the floor, and my deaf dog, who wandered in and out of the proceedings. We told Dr. Peterson that we really didn't know the first thing about starting up a whole language support group. His suggestion: "Have a conference! That will get you recognition for your organization."

We didn't know how to begin—we had never organized a conference, and we didn't even have a name or officers! We chose WOW—Way Out West with Language Expression. Officers were duly volunteered out of those 15 at the first meeting.

We started with a mailing list from SMILE. If we had been unable to get their list, we probably would have had the teachers start with other teachers in their district and asked them to send publicity to their friends in other districts. We would have obtained the lists of other teacher organizations, such as the Arizona Reading Association, the Arizona Education Association, and the English Teachers' Association. Money out of our own pockets paid for our mailings.

Our first conference was held as a "Back to School Conference" at Surprise School in the Dysart District. Dr. Peterson was our speaker. We gathered presenters from our own group, from people suggested by Dr. Peterson and Kris Jilbert. We wanted the material to be pertinent to the teachers on the west side, where there was a large Mexican-American population. The meeting was held on a hot August day, with only evaporative cooling; nonetheless, the meeting was attended by 175 people.

In addition to our conferences, we continued to have monthly meetings where we shared problems and ideas. We invited guest speakers. A new store opened in Glendale, called Primary Learning. It had meeting rooms in the back, and we were allowed to use one.

We decided to charge membership dues of $5 for a year, using this money to plan for our next conference. Our guest speaker was the wonderful children's poet, Jack Prelutsky. This second conference was attended by 350 teachers. It was hard work—the last days of the conference required almost round-the-clock phone calls and planning—attention to small details such as convenience of parking could not be overlooked.

From this second conference, we built up our membership list to more than 300, all teachers who, we hoped, would return to their classrooms fired up to try the things our presenters were suggesting. Little by little, the resistance in *some* of the western districts melted away as administra-

(Continued on page 413)

Classroom Demonstrations
by Nancy Hyland Areglado and Laurel Stevick

Suggestions for Organizing a Whole Language Networking Group

Many networking groups are organized informally. Teachers who are interested in sharing ideas about whole language get together in someone's living room or meet after school in someone's classroom. Participants range from seasoned professionals to student teachers and from experienced to novice whole language teachers. Responsibility for planning the meetings is shared. Discussions are held around questions such as: "What is whole language?" "How can we gather information about children's progress in ways that are consistent with a whole language philosophy?" and "What is being done with enlarged print in other languages?" Teachers bring samples of children's work to share, as well as favorite books, poems, chants, and songs. Sharing also includes ideas from professional books and articles, successful classroom practices and problem areas, and ideas gained from attending professional conferences. Other networking groups have chosen to invite a speaker to address a topic such as Writing Across the Curriculum. Meetings are advertised by word of mouth and through a contact person who contributes news to area newsletters such as the *Whole Language Teachers Association Newsletter*.

Nancy Areglado, networking chairperson for the Berkshires, prepared the following guidelines to assist networking team leaders in her area:

1. Form a core group of people who are interested in sharing ideas about whole language.
   a. Schedule the first networking meeting.
   b. Decide on the topic for the first meeting. Encourage each participant to bring materials and ideas to share.

c. Contact area schools and newspapers to publicize this meeting date.
2. During the first meeting:
   a. Provide a sign-in sheet. Ask for volunteers to be contact people to spread the news about the meetings in their schools.
   b. Decide on the locations and dates of future meetings.
   c. Choose a list of topics for future meetings.
3. Once various schools are represented, the group may wish to consider a team approach.
   a. Choose several convenient locations for holding meetings, rotating from one location to another.
   b. Choose one person from each location to be a team leader to take responsibility for the meetings held at that location.
   c. Team leader responsibilities might include the following:
   • Choose topics for meetings at your location based on suggestions from group members (for example, a literature-based theme such as "friendship" and a topic concerning whole language theory and practice, such as using the cloze technique.
   • Invite group members to bring materials and ideas to share or locate a speaker for that meeting.
   • Publicize your meeting by notifying area schools, contact persons, and newspapers.
   • Invite volunteers to provide refreshments.

From *Teachers Networking* 8(4), May 1988.

Nancy Hyland Areglado is a language arts coordinator and primary teacher at Berkshire Hills Regional School District, West Stockbridge, MA. Laurel Stevick is a member of the Whole Language Teachers Association.

Education in Turin: A Romance by Herbert Kohl

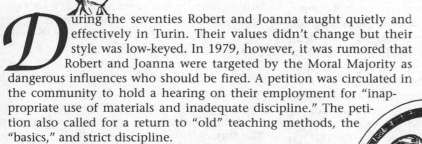

Continued from page 393

Beginning Again:
Making Democracy Work

During the seventies Robert and Joanna taught quietly and effectively in Turin. Their values didn't change but their style was low-keyed. In 1979, however, it was rumored that Robert and Joanna were targeted by the Moral Majority as dangerous influences who should be fired. A petition was circulated in the community to hold a hearing on their employment for "inappropriate use of materials and inadequate discipline." The petition also called for a return to "old" teaching methods, the "basics," and strict discipline.

Robert's parents had heard about the petition and, though they didn't enjoy controversy, they were proud of the decent and caring work their son and daughter-in-law did. One evening Robert visited with his parents and asked them how he should fight back. His father, an amazingly energetic and coherent 84, answered in a way that surprised him: "Your grandmother Burns would have known. There's a lot of her in you. Maybe you need to know more about her now. I'll show you her diaries and letters."

That was how Robert and Joanna got Alice's writings and began to learn about her and Elizabeth, and about Colonel Parker, John Dewey, and other educators who had struggled with similar problems. They learned that they were part of a nurturing tradition that is as old as our nation.

The petition never came to a hearing. Robert and Joanna had more allies and their ideas more advocates than they had realized. What emerged from the petition was a series of community forums on the shape of education in Turin during the 21st century.

Once again in Turin, as in many other places across the country, the public schools are the center of community conflict. People have to reaffirm what they believe should be basic in public education, remembering that what is basic in education cannot be separated from what kind of society they want their children to live in. All the strands of conflict that existed over the almost 200 years of public education in the United States are still present in Turin, and in just about every community across the land.

The struggle to find out what is basic in education is part of the struggle to find out what should be basic to life in the United States. Making democracy work is a problem and has always been a problem both in the schools and in our lives.

The End

An expanded version of "Education in Turin: A Romance" entitled *The Romance of Education* is available from Continuity Press, 40561 Eureka Hills Rd., Point Arena, CA 95468.

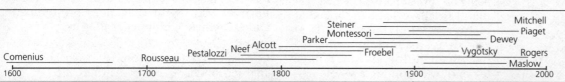

Pioneers: Lev S. Vygotsky (1896-1934)   by Luis Moll

Lev Semenovich Vygotsky (1896–1934) was born to a middle-class Jewish family in Orsha, a town located within the western limits of the European portion of the Soviet Union. A teacher throughout his life, Vygotsky developed his work in the context of the October Revolution. With his distinguished disciples and colleagues A. R. Luria and A. N. Leontiev, he founded the sociohistorical school of psychology. Inspired by the writings of Marx and Engels, the philosophy of Spinoza, and the work of several contemporaries, including Janet and Piaget, Vygotsky set out to develop a general approach to thinking that recognized how human beings and their social world are embedded in each other. He considered the capacity to teach and to benefit from instruction as the fundamental attribute of human beings. As such, human pedagogy, in all its forms, is the defining characteristic of his approach, the central concept in his system.

Vygotsky regarded education not only as central to cognitive development, but also as the quintessential sociocultural activity. Although he was clearly interested in how thought developed phylogenetically and socioculturally, his work focused primarily on the social origins and cultural bases of individual development. He argued that uniquely human psychological processes developed in children through social enculturation; through the acquisition of society's technology, its signs and tools; and through education in all its forms.

A central theme in Vygotsky's theory, the linchpin in his work, is that of mediation. He emphasized both social mediations (interpersonal activities and communications) and instrumental mediations (signs and symbols) for mediating between one's mental processes and one's environment and for assigning meaning to objects and activities. For Vygotsky, speech constituted the prototypical and most powerful mediating device, and much of his work was devoted to analyzing the complex interrelationships between speech and thinking, the link between social and cognitive functions of language.

Probably more than any other psychological theorist, Vygotsky assigned great prominence to formal education. He regarded schools (and other informal educational situations) not only as central contexts for enculturation and mastery of society's key tools and technology (such as written language and mathematics), but as the best "cultural laboratories" to study thinking: socially and historically created settings, characterized by special modes of discourse, and specifically designed to modify thinking. His central educational concept, that of the zone of proximal development, highlights this connection between social activity and individual thinking. Vygotsky emphasized the need to go beyond individual or static assessments of children's capabilities; he insisted that one could obtain a more dynamic and useful evaluation of children's capabilities by observing children in collaborative activities. The zone "is the distance between the actual developmental level as determined by independent problem-solving and the level of potential development as determined through problem-solving under adult guidance or in collaboration with more capable peers." The key point of the concept is the interdependence between children's thinking and the social and cultural resources provided to help develop (mediate) that thinking.

The power of Vygotsky's ideas is that they represent a theory of possibilities. The construct of the zone of proximal development reminds us there is nothing "natural" about educational settings and their practices (such as ability groupings, tracking, and other forms of stratification, and classroom lessons). These settings are social creations; they are socially constituted and can be socially changed. They warn us how easy it is to underestimate children's and teachers' abilities when we analyze them in isolation, in highly constrained environments, or in less than favorable circumstances. And they point to social and cultural resources that human beings use as primary tools for mediating and promoting change.

→ See: Bird, p. 216; Goodman, p. 207; Mind in the Society, p. 381; Vygotsky, pp. 37, 43.

Luis Moll is a professor at University of Arizona, Tucson, AZ.

(Continued from page 412)

tors and parents saw that their children were learning happily, excited about school.

After the second conference, we immediately began planning for the third one. Bill Martin Jr agreed to be our guest speaker. Grand Canyon University lent us their campus and any help they could give us. The halls were buzzing with the enthusiasm of 750 teachers from all over the valley, not just the west side. Teachers even attended from New Mexico and California.

If you think this is a success story, we do too! But we couldn't have done it without a team effort and a lot of hard work. If you are planning to start a grass roots organization in your area, you need a commitment to whole language, lots of publicity, teamwork, and the courage to take risks.

→ See: Graham, p. 426; Martin, pp. 96, 167.

Lillian Henteleff is a reading specialist with the Dysart District, Glendale, AZ, and president of Way Out West (WOW).

📷 WHOLE LANGUAGE CAMERA

Poolside meeting of the Tucson TAWL, Tucson, AZ

Publishers and Whole Language

 Viewpoint: Richard C. Owen

Whole Language from the Perspective of a Publisher

Let's talk about five-year plans. Teachers may not be familiar with such practices, but corporate publishers are. Five-year plans are annual rites at many companies. Editors are asked to define goals and objectives for the coming years and then to describe the steps they will take to get from where they are to where they are to go.

It sounds very logical, just as a mechanistic, skills-oriented model of reading sounds logical to folks who have little experience with introducing literacy to children. If we determine where we are, we can add to our base incrementally to reach a stated goal. Using that thinking, teachers can teach reading by adding selected skills until at last the child achieves literacy.

I admit to not having been good at preparing five-year plans. For one thing, the general goals were established by corporate managers and our job as editors was to figure out how to achieve the goals. Another problem was an inability to visualize how needs would change over a five-year period or to identify the opportunities that would occur.

When I incorporated my business in 1982, the first thing I did was write a five-year plan (ingrained habits of both teachers and publishers do not change easily). I tried to picture where I hoped my company would be by the late 1980s and what books I would publish to reach my goal. In my plan were book titles and estimated production costs, even list prices and unit sales. A well-prepared five-year plan is an impressive document.

But something happened along the way to creating a traditional college publishing company. I discovered whole language, or perhaps it discovered me. My plan had been to produce a list of college-level books in reading and language arts methods that helped teachers who endorse a skills orientation as well as teachers who support psycholinguistic views of literacy. The first book on my list was a reissued version of the *Reading Miscue Inventory* by Yetta Goodman and Carolyn Burke. Books that followed included reissued versions of Smith, Goodman, and Meredith's *Language and Thinking in School*, Frank Smith's *Comprehension and Learning*, and Jeannette Veatch's *Reading in the Elementary School*.

With one or two exceptions, the books we reissued promoted holistic thinking at a time when whole language was becoming more widely recognized among teachers dissatisfied with traditional models of teaching. The particular collection of books on our list attracted the attention of the New Zealand government, which was interested in finding a way to distribute their national reading program in the United States.

School publishing was not in my five-year plan, so I resisted getting involved. But the opportunity proved too enticing. After a period of exploration, we expanded our coverage to include books for use with children in the elementary school.

Further growth of interest in whole language made apparent the need for new lines of communication between people at the college level and people in the schools. Working with Debra Jacobson, a teacher in Tucson, Arizona, we developed a national newsletter called *Teachers Networking*, also not in the five-year plan. Another

The first lesson Richard C. Owen learned when he entered college publishing in the late 1960s was that publishers are in the business of selling books, not ideas. His belief in the ideas of whole language helped him conclude that the lesson needed rewriting. Richard C. Owen Publishers offers whole language experiences for children and teachers in the form of books, audiotapes, videos, posters, a periodical, and workshops. The company is located in Katonah, New York, a few miles from the 19th-century farmhouse he shares with his wife and young son.

deviation from the plan occurred when we began offering teachers a series of workshops based on the New Zealand model of literacy development.

By this time, the five-year plan that had looked so convincing on paper had become almost meaningless.

After a recent workshop one of the consultants with whom we work pointed out that we are not much like the publishers she has known (which she assured me was intended as a compliment). The comment reminded me that what we are trying to do as a company is not unlike what teachers are doing every day.

Each of us is in the process of redefining our role. Each of us is looking more closely at what we do and questioning the best way to achieve our goals. Each of us is trying to respond to the needs of our constituencies—children who are learning to read and write and the teachers who are helping them.

There is another way I see us as being on similar paths: The five-year plan I finally discarded looked at change as incremental and at growth as an addition to what we had been doing. What I have learned by becoming a whole language publisher is the necessity of reconceptualizing what I do. In the initial stages of building my business I was able to add on to the small base we established with the Reading Miscue Inventory. But soon enough the company

reached a point where we had to rethink the premise for our existence.

Whole language teaching demands a similar rethinking on the part of teachers. You can make small changes and incorporate whole language ideas into a traditional curriculum. But at some point it becomes necessary to take a broader view of teaching and children. At some point the teacher has to reconsider the whole process of achieving literacy.

There is a further comparison that can be made. At the heart of whole language is the belief that children read for meaning and that the curriculum needs to be structured to encourage meaningful interactions with print. The thoughtful teacher asks if there is meaning for the child in every action that she or he takes. Whole language publishers have to ask similar questions regarding their relationship with teachers. We serve well our audience to the extent that we are able to focus on developing meaningful experiences for teachers.

When I started my company, I selected reading and language arts because I believed there existed an intellectual ferment that was absent in other methods areas. Little did I know the extent of the unrest. From my perspective as a publisher, the exciting part of being involved in whole language is the knowledge that almost nothing is static. We have no rigid set of procedures that are applied to every teacher or child. Practice emerges from theory, and theory always seems to have new corners to explore and new layers to uncover. May the investigation and stimulation and excitement continue for all of us.

➜ See: Kitagawa, p. 420; Mooney, pp. 120, 416; Reading Miscue Inventory, p. 101; Language and Thinking in Schools, p. 67; Veatch, p. 235.

📷 WHOLE LANGUAGE CAMERA

Teachers discuss professional books during a Saturday morning meeting of the Tucson, Arizona Small TAWL. Here Debra Jacobson shares Margaret Meek's *How Texts Teach What Readers Learn*, London: The Thimble Press, 1988 (see p. 97).

🖥️ 🎨 🎞️ 🕊️ 📼 📖

Resource: Publisher

Richard C. Owen Publishers, Inc.

135 Katonah Ave.
Katonah, NY 10536
1-914-232-3903
1-800-336-5588
FAX 1-914-232-3904

The catalog from Richard C. Owen contains whole language resource books for teachers, including many that have been out of print for years.

The national reading program for elementary instruction in New Zealand, *Ready to Read*, a series of curriculum materials (audios, videos, big books), is now available in America through Richard C. Owen. This series contains consistently good titles and a well-thought-out format for developing a whole language reading program. The manual, *Reading in Junior Classes*, is valuable in and of itself.

The newsletter *Teachers Networking: The Whole Language Newsletter*, begun by whole language teachers, is now published by Richard C. Owen as a quarterly with articles by whole language leaders. Regular columns review books and help TAWL groups keep in contact with one another. The subscription rate is $15 a year. Last summer, Richard C. Owen also began sponsoring whole language courses throughout the United States. Participants commented on the solid grounding in whole language they received.

Michael Hagan

🖥️ 🎨 🎞️ 🕊️ 📼 📖

Resource: Publisher

Heinemann Boynton/Cook

70 Court St.
Portsmouth, NH 03801
1-603-431-7894
FAX 1-603-431-7840

Heinemann carries a multitude of books for the whole language teacher, including many seminal works on the reading/writing process. Titles such as *Writing: Teachers and Children at Work*, by Donald Graves, and *Lessons from a Child*, by Lucy Calkins, have launched many a teacher on a never-ending venture into the reading/writing process. Each year's catalog offers a dozen or more new books written by experts in the field. Catalog orders receive a 10 percent discount with no sales tax.

Michael Hagan

Viewpoint: Adrian Peetoom

Thoughts on Whole Language Publishing

The matter of what and how to publish for whole language classrooms has long occupied my mind.

How does one encourage and serve, with publishing, a set of relationships between schools and parents, relationships very different from traditional ones? What is (or ought to be) my model? I believe whole language is the answer if we understand its full meaning.

Whole language: Is it simply a refined technology?

Unfortunately, many teachers still believe that whole language is merely a new and interesting set of teaching techniques centred around trade books instead of basals and workbooks. I always sensed that, underneath the hoopla in California and many other jurisdictions, devotion to the traditional teaching model has remained intact. It assumes a body of skills and contents, a set of "somethings" to be defined, described, divided into bits, organized in a scope and sequence, published, taught, mastered in (mostly) invariant sequences, and finally assessed by means of standardized and/or criterion-referenced tests.

Adrian Peetoom is the director of Educational Research and Development, Scholastic Canada, Ltd. and editor of the *Bright Idea, New Directions*, and *Forum* series of professional books. He resides in Chatham, Ontario.

Even a cursory reading of recent educational wares that announce themselves as "whole language" makes clear that most of them are rooted in the model I have described. For one thing, this false view of whole language is in the interest of powerful basal publishers, who "purchase" the names of leading academics for inclusion on their title pages, and who, through powerful and often insidious marketing, totally overwhelm teachers. The basal boys will not let go easily. And neither will the existing (pyramidal) educational power structure the old model requires. A favourite ploy is to mandate implementation of whole language districtwide—within a time period—a sure way to destroy it!

But this is not the only available model, nor do we need to feel that changing the old model is a hopeless task. Rather, we should rejoice that over roughly the last two decades, diverse scholars in diverse places began to think alike about a range of diverse schooling problems—all at about the same time. I keep in mind Don Holdaway and Marie Clay in New Zealand; Michael Haliday, James Britton, Harold Rosen, the Barneses, and Margaret Spencer in the United Kingdom; Frank Smith and Johan Aitken in Canada; and the Goodmans in the United States. The questions they asked, each in their own unique circumstances, could not be answered within the bounds of the old model, and so a new model had to be developed.

The New Model: Whole Language Is a New Way of Being with Children

The significance of all this is not easy to put into simple terms. But this much seems clear to me: Seen together, these diverse and yet similar historical events indicate not a refinement of what has gone on before, but a new model of thinking about schooling-teaching. Whole language sees knowledge not as a definable object one can package, but as something that exists only when free people freely share what they already know within their learning communities.

The implications are quite staggering. Traditional educational hierarchies must disband, traditional educational publishing must be transformed, traditional antagonistic home-school relationships must be replaced by a peda-

gogical love affair, teacher training must be overhauled, professional development must abandon the guru model—fly the big names in for an hour or two—and textbooks and other traditional paraphernalia must be scrapped in favour of authentic print and other tools. And we've all been quite busy accomplishing all that.

Here home-school relationships become very important, with some of these crucial elements.

Parents: In the old model the work of parents as teachers is depreciated to such an extent that they almost always feel totally inadequate, educationally speaking, once their children enter school with its mystifying technologies.

Teachers: In the old model morale (and often actual performance) is dramatically inhibited by that model's low assessment of teachers:

• The contents of their teaching is packaged for them, in textbooks, for example.

• Their teaching practices are prescribed for them (in mandated scopes and sequences, and in ever more elaborate and detailed teaching guides).

• The evaluation of their teaching is determined by instruments they don't construct or always understand (standardized tests, to name but one).

No wonder burnout rate is high, pay low, initiative limited, and teacher bashing an always recurring sport of politicians and editorial newswriters.

The new model, on the other hand, suggests that the generation of curriculum, teaching practice, and evaluation is to be returned to the classroom to be shaped by the community of learners under the guidance of the classroom teacher.

Publishing: It Is Not Just Business, but Ethics

And here is where educational publishing is faced with an ethical decision. It must declare that it has understood the times and has sensed the grass-roots excitement of a new sort of classroom teacher. Also, it must give up believing that teachers, children, and parents aren't worth much, educationally speaking, and recognize instead that they can be trusted, that the knowledge and skills that already collectively reside in classrooms are the best possible base for building new knowledge.

In particular, new publishing must proclaim confidence in parents, by taking it for granted that learning begins at birth and that most parents are exceedingly accomplished teachers, who deliver to school children who have an extensive vocabulary, who have mastered 95 percent of the grammar they will ever need, and who know how "story" is constructed (this latter competence is especially crucial, for without it reading can never occur). It's simply foolish, shortsighted, and damaging to parents, their children, and teachers to freeze out such well-demonstrated expertise at the front doors of school buildings.

Whole Language: Part of It Is Politics

Schools have never been about education only, they have also been about power. After all, when knowledge is understood to be power, the shape, control, and delivery of it (schooling) is about power too. Parents, quite naturally, have always wanted some sort of control over their children in school. While some parents readily delegate their control to schools (especially new

immigrant parents), others, sometimes driven by religious or ideological motives, have wanted more direct control, to the point, at times, of demanding the right (and finances) to maintain nonpublic school alternatives. For us the crucial point is this: The old model invariably locates power in *administration* (*institution*).

As a result of the new research about learning I already alluded to, a very different understanding of where power resides, and how it ought to be shared, comes to the fore. It now appears that the control parents exercise over the educational destiny of their children resides not in how that power works its way through elections, boards, committees, and votes, *but in the model of learning that produces five-year-olds who exhibit amazing control over language as a result of the teaching their parents have already done*. Real power in schooling lies in the correct model of learning-teaching—in the essential model of whole language, that is!

So, the old model says to teachers, parents, and children alike: "We know it all. You don't know anything, but your children have a chance if you do what we tell you." But the new model says, again to all three: "We know how clever you have already demonstrated yourself to be, and we'll help you make even greater use of your insights." Educational publishers must learn to help teachers and parents discover the power they already have, and empower them to empower each other and their children even more. I think that means this: *They must begin to publish voices, instead of tomes of disembodied content requiring disembodied skills.* By "voices" I mean the narratives of the actual teaching/learning experiences of real teachers and parents, and children too! Some publishers have made small beginnings—this very book is part of the new mosaic. I only regret that these ideas have come to me when I'm only a few years away from retirement as a publisher.

➔ See: Bixby, p. 402; Goodman, p. 274; Krause, p. 396; Peterson, p. 348; What's Whole in Whole Language, p. 380; Whole Language: Inquiring Voices, p. 215.

Further Reading by Adrian Peetoom
◆ "Education Publishing: A Personal Perspective." *Language Arts* 64(4), 1987.

Resource: Publisher

Scholastic, Inc.

P.O. Box 7502
2931 E. McCarty St.
Jefferson, MO
65102-9968
1-800-325-6149
1-800-392-2179 (MO)
1-314-636-5271
(AK and HI)

Scholastic is providing more and more high-quality teacher resource books. Among their curriculum materials is "The Bookshelf," a program of well-written and finely illustrated books from Australia that features big books and tapes in a wide range of genres (literature, science, poetry, social studies). Scholastic's book clubs offer children an opportunity to buy affordable books and teachers a chance to establish classroom libraries. The *Whole Language Classroom* is Scholastic's excellent catalog for grades K–6; it features distinctive materials for holistic teaching and articles by whole language experts, including Ken Goodman, Don Holdaway, and Diane Snowball.

Michael Hagan

Political Action

 Viewpoint: Michael Apple

Teachers, Politics, and Whole Language Instruction

Given the emerging "conservative restoration" that is currently reconstructing both what education is for and who will benefit the most from it, the growing movement to emphasize whole language approaches in schools is, on the whole, definitely worthy of widespread support. Such a movement is important for teachers, not only students, today. There are some very real dangers in the movement, however, if it does not self-consciously connect itself to political, economic, and cultural issues in the larger society.

Educational institutions and especially the teachers who now work so hard in such uncertain conditions in them have come under concerted attack. The political right in the United States has been very successful in mobilizing support *against* the educational system, often exporting the crisis in the economy onto the schools. Thus, one of its major victories has been to shift the blame for unemployment and underemployment and for the supposed breakdown of "traditional" values and standards in the family, education, and the paid workplace *from* the economic, cultural, and social policies of business and industry *to* the school and other public agencies (Apple 1985, 1986).

This process is heightened by the federal and state governments, which literally bombard the public with a particular *selection* of statistical data about the well-being, or lack of it, of our society. The United States government sets up "great manufactories of 'facts' and 'figures'" that are distributed to the public. These are usually economic and serve to construct a view of reality as fundamentally revolving around the economics of profit and loss, of accumulation and profit (Horne 1986, pp. 189–190).

In the process, the value of education is reduced to economic utility (Apple 1986). Other goals that underlie the whole language movement such as critical understanding, political literacy, personal development, self-esteem, and shared respect are beside the point or "too expensive." The issues of care and connectedness, issues that, as feminists have so crucially reminded us, count so critically in building a society based on the common good, are disenfranchised as well (Gilligan 1982). Schools are to do one thing for society. They are to function primarily to supply "human capital," and to underwrite "the promise of individual success in competitive global markets" (Bastian, Fruchter, Gittell, Greer, and Haskins, 1986, p. 21).

At the same time, while the purpose of education is being drastically reduced, the schools have witnessed a steady increase internally in the use of procedures of standardization and rationalization. Increasingly, teaching methods, texts, tests, and outcomes are being taken out of the hands of the people, the teachers, who must put them into practice. Instead, they are being legislated by centralized authorities.

The effects have been widespread. The tendency for the curriculum to be rationalized and "industrialized" at a central level, largely focused on competencies measured by standardized tests

and dependent on predesigned commercial texts written specifically for those states that have the tightest centralized control and, thus, the largest guaranteed markets, is resulting in the *deskilling* of teachers. When individuals cease to plan and control a large portion of their work, the skills essential to doing these tasks reflectively and well atrophy and are forgotten. The skills that teachers have built up over decades of hard work—setting relevant curriculum goals, establishing content, designing lessons and instructional strategies that are responsive to students, individualizing instruction based on an intimate knowledge of students' desires and needs, and so on—are lost or are simply no longer needed (Apple 1985, 1986).

In the larger economy, this process has been called the degradation of labor. Importing these procedures into the school can have exactly the same effects as when they are employed in industry: a loss of commitment and respect, bitter battles over working conditions, a lowering not a raising of quality, and a loss of skill and imagination, not only on the part of teachers but students as well. Of fundamental import, it has also ultimately reduced the power of employees to have any significant say in the goals and procedures of the institutions in which they work. All of this runs directly counter to what is embodied in the whole language movement.

This process of deskilling needs to be seen in *gender* terms. It is not a historical accident that teaching, and especially elementary school teaching, is so often perceived as "women's work." Thus, as I document in *Teachers and Texts* (1986), this has had a powerful impact on the ways in which teachers have been and are treated.

Historically, when a job has been defined as mainly women's paid work, it is subject to greater external control, less respect, and lower salaries, and its autonomy tends to come under attack. This society unfortunately seems to care less about work that is done largely by women. This is in no way a good thing, but it clearly is an important dynamic in the struggle over control of curriculum and teaching.

All of this too, of course, has a long history. Conservative groups have nearly always attempted to control the daily lives of teachers and to blame them for serious problems in the larger society over which teachers usually have little control.

The increasing standardization, rationalization, and bureaucratization of pedagogy and curriculum signifies an attack on the skills and authority of teachers. Just as importantly it represents what is inherently the *masculinization* of the language of teaching and curriculum in which any concerns that are not encompassed by technical rules, efficiency, and cost effectiveness are made illegitimate. The accountant's infamous bottom line and the efficiency expert's standardized measures replace the human drama of classroom life (Apple 1986). The ability to place the principles that stand behind the whole language movement on the educational agenda withers here as anything that is human, that is grounded in caring, connectedness, and

the collective and individual *production*—not regurgitation—of meanings is marginalized.

In its very attempt to integrate conception and execution, to empower teachers and students to engage in more fluid and biographically significant activity in schools, the whole language movement—if connected to larger political sensibilities—can make a significant contribution to overcoming the deskilling and depowering of teachers that is rampant today. At the same time, at the level of the student, by emphasizing the organic connection between students' experiences and the acts of reading and writing, it is clear that the whole language movement can serve as an important alternative to the deadening emphasis on unconnected and reductive teaching and curricula in schooling.

Yet, we need to remember that there are *reasons* that our society stresses atomistic knowledge and skills. There are reasons that account for the current emphasis on employing schools for the creation of "human capital" in which education's primary goals are determined by business and industry and by the conservative alliance that has now taken center stage in educational rhetoric and debate. And there are reasons for the current emphasis on an educationally and politically problematic return to a curriculum based on the "western tradition" and "cultural literacy."

This means that—for all its meritorious goals—the whole language movement cannot insure that its own goals and methods will have a lasting and widespread impact unless it is willing to act not only within the school, but outside it as well. Its proponents need to join with others in the wider social movements that aim at democratizing our economy, politics, and culture, and that act against a society that is so unequal in gender, race, and class terms.

This does not mean that action in schools is unimportant. Such action is, indeed, utterly essential. However, there are socio-cultural preconditions for long term success in transforming education into something worthy of its name. And unless this is understood fully, the whole language movement may unfortunately remain isolated on the margins of "ordinary" educational activity. Or, perhaps even worse, small parts of it will be incorporated into classrooms in "safe" and very limited ways, thereby transforming it into one more set of techniques in the right's reconstruction of education (Willinsky 1990). We cannot afford to let that happen. The daily lives and futures of real students and teachers are at stake.

→ See: Horton, p. 74; Morduchowicz, p. 76; Peterson, pp. 336, 348; Shannon, p. 222; The Sherman School Story, p. 342; Shor, p. 223.

> Michael Apple is a professor of Curriculum and Instruction and Educational Policy Studies at the University of Wisconsin, Madison. He is a former elementary and secondary school teacher and past president of a teachers union. He has lectured widely in Europe, Latin America, and Asia and has worked with governments, teachers unions, and activist groups to democratize schooling. He has written extensively on the relationship between education and unequal power.

References

Apple, M. W. 1985. *Education and power.* New York: Routledge & Kegan Paul, Ark Edition.

____1986. *Teachers and texts: A political economy of class and gender relations in education.* New York: Routledge & Kegan Paul.

Bastian, A., N. Fruchter, M. Gittell, C. Greer, and K. Haskins. 1986. *Choosing equality: The case for democratic schooling.* Philadelphia: Temple University Press.

Gilligan, C. 1982. *In a different voice: Psychological theory and women's development.* Cambridge: Harvard University Press.

Horne, D. 1986. *The public culture.* Dover, NH: Pluto Press.

Willinsky, J. 1990. *The new literacy.* New York: Routledge & Kegan Paul.

Further Reading by Michael Apple

◆ *Education and Power*, rev. Ark ed. Routledge & Kegan Paul, 1985.
◆ *Teachers and Text.* Routledge & Kegan Paul, 1988.
◆ *Ideology and Curriculum*, rev. ed. Routledge & Kegan Paul, 1990.

Viewpoint: Henry A. Giroux

Literacy, Cultural Diversity, and Public Life

One cannot understand how literacy functions as a way of legitimating particular forms of life, authority, and culture unless one questions the particular interests, purposes, and values implicit in its meaning and social practices. In the most general sense, literacy can be defined in pedagogical terms that adapt people to existing configurations of power, as in the advocacy of functional literacy. It can also be defined as a set of practices that empower people by helping them to see the world and their lives in a critical way so as to change the material conditions that silence them. In the most emancipatory sense, literacy is a political and pedagogical process of naming the world, which is biographical, historical, and collective.

We do not learn how to be literate; we become literate in order to reclaim our voices, experiences, and histories, to interpret the world and to change it. Literacy always implies a particular relationship between knowledge and power, and always presupposes and legitimates particular forms of history, community, and authority. The question is, of course, whose history, community, knowledge, and voice prevails. Unless this question is addressed, the issue of how we should teach, function as intellectuals, or relate to our students and the wider society becomes removed from the wider principles that inform such issues. In short, literacy is about the issues of politics, power, and possibility.

One of the most important projects for teachers in the next decade will be the development of a critical literacy that incorporates the

Henry A. Giroux graduated with a master's degree in history from Appalachian State College, and then taught at the secondary level in Maryland and Rhode Island for eight years. He received his doctorate from Carnegie-Mellon University in 1977. He is currently a professor of Education, Renowned Scholar in Residence, and director of the Center for Education and Cultural Studies at Miami University (Ohio).

politics of cultural diversity with a view of pedagogy that recognizes the importance of democratic public life. Critical literacy must also find a language that articulates the shared political ends of a democratic society. Critical literacy means restoring to students and others that knowledge and those skills that provide the opportunity for creating unity around the principles of freedom, equality, and justice. This means recognizing the inadequacy of educational programs, public projects, and ideological calls for cultural literacy that merely affirm and express the interests and values of the Anglo, white, middle and upper classes. It means doing more than merely affirming the cultural capital of students who have been traditionally denied the benefits of a critical education.

Dominant views of reading and writing, with their emphasis on mastery learning, standardized testing, over-reliance on single texts, and their Eurocentric culturally dominated curricula must be rejected as resistant to seeing schools as places for educating students to be critical citizens in a vital, democratic society. On the other hand, progressive views of literacy must openly acknowledge their own politics and commitment to pedagogical practices that deepen the goals of democratic struggle and cultural justice.

A more holistic, liberated view of literacy can dignify and engage the different voices of students in ways that help them to redefine learning as a basis for affirming and engaging their communities and neighborhoods' sense of worth. This is not an argument against providing students with access to what some have called the foundations of disciplinary knowledge, but rather a call for focusing on what constitutes meaningful knowledge to expand rather than limit the potential to be literate in the language of the community, and also in the larger language of the state and world. Critical literacy must be fashioned around purpose and meaning and not merely on justifying one form of course content or pedagogy over another.

How students learn is as important as what they learn, but more important is the context of purpose and meaning that frames both the *what* and *how* of learning. Critical literacy must be conceived as a pedagogy that educates students to govern, that provides them with the history, knowledge, and skills they will need to effectively assert their role as citizens capable of exercising moral and public responsibility. This suggests a literacy that understands the books, ideas, and values that have played an important role in shaping this country's history but also affirms those histories, traditions, and stories that have been denied their rightful place. If literacy is linked to the imperatives of educating students for critical citizenship in a mass society, it will have to be concerned with the issue of how students become reflective in the process of learning. To be literate is not simply to know something, it also means knowing how to participate reflectively in the act of producing knowledge. Educators need to take seriously the ways in which students produce and mediate the categories that give meaning to their lives.

I am arguing for a holistic notion of critical literacy that shapes school curricula around democratic demands and traditions, that is attentive to critical knowledge that creates webs of possibility within shared conversations, and that encourages pedagogical practices that allow students to see the standpoint of others while recognizing the partial nature of all discourses. I believe that critical literacy should embrace a view of public service that gives students an opportunity to experience forms of solidarity and compassion aimed at alleviating the suffering of others. Literacy here is strategic interactions by students with those who are in dire need of public service. This might mean requiring every student to work for a semester or a short time in a community agency that provides services to the poor, elderly, disabled, the homeless, teen mothers, or other equally disadvantaged groups. In this context, literacy becomes synonymous with forms of experience that broaden the boundaries of citizenship and public responsibility.

The time has come for rethinking public education in terms of revitalized notions of diversity, democracy, and citizenship. Whole language has done much to provide educators with both a language of critique and possibility, particularly in terms of its emphasis on the necessity for teachers to incorporate into their teaching the voices that students bring with them to the classroom. As important as this contribution is, the time has come to extend its possibilities by linking the pedagogical practices of literacy to a sense of purpose and meaning that explicitly addresses how reading, writing, and literacy can contribute to the creation of critical citizens, democratic schools, and a more just society.

→ See: Horton, p. 74; Morduchowicz, p. 76; Peterson, pp. 336, 348; Shannon, p. 222; The Sherman School Story, p. 342; Shor, p. 223.

Further Reading by Henry A. Giroux
◆ *Critical Pedagogy, the State and Cultural Struggle*, ed. with P. McLaren. State University of New York Press, 1989.
◆ *Popular Culture, Schooling and Everyday Life*, ed. with R. Simon. Bergin & Garvey, 1989.
◆ *Schooling and the Struggle for Public Life*. University of Minnesota Press, 1988.
◆ *Teachers as Intellectuals*. Bergin & Garvey, 1988.
◆ *Critical Studies in Education Series*, ed. with P. Freire. Bergin & Garvey.

Book Note

Teachers as Intellectuals: Toward a Critical Pedagogy of Learning

Henry A. Giroux
1988; 288 pp.; $14.95
Granby, MA: Bergin & Garvey

Critical education theory examines the relations among knowledge, power, and domination, and Henry Giroux is one of its leading theorists and writers. He is critical of texts and materials that focus on mastery of techniques and transmitting knowledge, and says that schools are instructional sites rather than places for learning. Teachers as intellectuals will have to transform these conditions for time, space, activity, and knowledge in their schools and to see language for its possibilities.

When Giroux writes about pedagogy he addresses both teaching practices and the accompanying cultural politics. He suggests that the language used in a field of study (English, mathematics, drama) not only names but also transmits the dominant social view. Teachers' theories about curriculum can become a form of social theory that supports students' voices in defining their world rather than their performance in the institution.

Carol Christine

From *Centerspace* 3(5), May/June 1989

Resource: Periodical

Changing Schools

$10 year (3 issues) from:
Teachers College 1008
Ball State University
Muncie, IN 47306
1-317-285-5453 or
285-5452
FAX 1-317-285-5455

Changing Schools has served as the voice for a loose confederation of alternative educators across the United States. The publication provides information on programs, schools, and people advocating student choice and decision-making and instructional innovation. Though not directly tied to *Changing Schools*, a national alternative education conference is held each summer.

Roy A. Weaver

Viewpoint: Bess Altwerger and Barbara Flores

The Politics of Whole Language

Whole language teachers have a solid theoretical framework upon which to construct a common view of education, supported by research in learning, literacy development, and classroom instruction. We come together at local, state, and national meetings to share knowledge, experiences, and beliefs. But we also come together to feel the power and support from our numbers in order to assure ourselves that we're not alone, and to motivate ourselves to keep going.

We need this kind of support because every day whole language teachers not only expend endless energy on building environments of learning and literacy with their students, but also must wage a not-so-subtle battle for survival in the system. Whole language teachers engage daily in a political battle that threatens the foundations of traditional American schools. Whole language does so for two important reasons noted by Sharon Rich (1985, p. 722):

1. "It returns power where it belongs—to the children and the teacher in the classroom . . ."

2. "It assumes that everyone is a learner and everyone can become an expert."

The latter reason is truly threatening and radical because literacy has become a sorting instrument that effectively maintains the social stratification of society. Henry Giroux (1983) says literacy achievement has become a "new admission ticket for the lower class to an economy with limited seating."

The traditional approach to teaching reading works effectively as this sorting mechanism, virtually assuring that one group of children—usually the poor and minorities—don't win or earn that admission ticket. Whole language teaching is subversive, in the best sense of the word, because it seeks to restore equality and democracy to our schools, to our children, and, in essence, to our society.

Entering School

From the very beginning children are tracked on the basis of socioeconomic and cultural background. This is achieved initially by imposing expectations and criteria for the kinds of literacy experiences and abilities that will "count" as evidence for reading and writing development. The book-reading event is the most highly valued literacy experience prior to school. Academically related activities and abilities, such as displaying knowledge about print letters and the alphabet, are highly valued. These experiences are primarily associated with middle-class children.

Yet Heath (1983, pp. 198–199) and others indicate that poor and minority children are by no means lacking in literacy experiences prior to school. Heath has documented the variety and wealth of literacy experiences occurring in the poor black community of Trackton. The nature of these activities is very different from expected school experiences in the following ways:

1. Adults don't create reading events for children. Social situations such as shopping and delivering mail for the postal worker lead naturally to literacy events.

2. Reading is a public rather than a private affair. Heath (p. 190) states, "To read alone was frowned upon and individuals who did so were accused of being antisocial."

3. Reading and writing events are set within the context of immediate action, i.e., the social

and physical circumstances and reasons for the literacy event.

4. According to Heath (p. 195), print is not treated as "isolated bits and pieces of lines and circles, but messages with varying internal structures, purposes, and uses."

5. Authority in written words rests in meanings negotiated by the experiences in which the print is embedded.

Anderson and Stokes (1984) have studied home literacy events in low-income homes across ethnic groups. They found an abundance and variety of literacy events, all of which were meaningful and purposeful. They found literacy events across domains that included the use of print in activities related to daily living, entertainment, school, religion, general information, work, literacy techniques and skills, interpersonal communication, and storybook time.

So despite the fact that low-income and minority children have rich holistic literacy experiences prior to schooling, they are given little credit for these experiences. School systems and readiness tests disregard them. When their instruction is skill-based, these low-income and minority children look like failures early on because the view of literacy underlying instruction is totally foreign to them; for example, "circle the word with the same sound as the beginning of the word *ball.*" Shannon (1985) reports research indicating that in the absence of test information, children from low incomes or minorities end up in the "low-reading" group and that when test data are available, kindergarten teachers tend to ability group on the basis of sole criterion, and test scores are highly correlated with social class status.

Ability Grouping as an Instructional Device

In a skills view underlying basal programs, children are evaluated in terms of where in the hierarchy of skills they lie and where in the series they are placed. They are sorted into ability groups as an organizational device for the teacher and to gear teaching to the skills level of students. But ability grouping is a powerful social sorter as well, which by first grade can determine the course of a child's academic and social life. Research by McDermott and Gospodinoff (1979) indicates that minority children tend to stay in the same ability group throughout the grades.

In addition, lower groups receive very different instruction in terms of both quality and quantity.

1. Teachers tend to interrupt low-ability readers two to five times more frequently.

2. Teachers give students in low-ability groups less time to self-correct, and thus foster dependence on the teacher.

3. The teacher focuses much more on phonic characteristics of isolated words in the low group while the high group deals more with encouraging the students to use meaning and their sense of language to figure out troublesome words (Allington 1980, 1983; Gambrell, Wilson, and Gannt 1981).

Low-group students spend much less time on sustained reading during group time and students in high groups read three times as many words per

day in reading groups as poor readers do (Allington 1983). Thus, through the practice of ability grouping from a skills view, the rich get richer and the poor get poorer. Moll and Diaz (1987) also report differential treatment of bilingual students in reading groups according to the teacher's perception of students' ability in English and the native language with the low group getting the biggest dose of isolated skills instruction.

Testing

Standardized tests and reading tests in particular have replaced IQ tests as the most insidious form of social sorting in our schools, effecting discrimination practices in the guise of objectivity and neutrality. The literature repeatedly shows that the best predictor of scores on reading tests is socioeconomic status and this relationship remains throughout the school career.

As Meier (1981, p. 463) says, "The tests reflect the bias of reality . . . and this is a reality all children have to live with." The reality is unequal treatment in standardized testing.

If we do not begin to confront the eradication of built-in inequity in the educational process, at stake are our children's lives and our democratic rights. And, if we do not act, low-income and minority children will continue to think and act as if powerless. They will continue to do poorly on standardized tests. They will continue to receive a meager diet of isolated phonics and skills instruction. They will continue to "fail," to drop out (to be forced out), and to have unequal opportunity to advance in the system.

How Does Whole Language Change the Power Structure and Social Relations in Schools?

In whole language all children's literacy experiences prior to school are accepted, prized, and valued. Children are encouraged to use their literacy and language background in school. The focus of whole language on meaningful and purposeful literacy experiences is very consistent with the literacy experiences of low-income and minority families reported in Heath (1983) and Anderson and Stokes (1984).

In a whole language classroom there is no ability grouping; therefore, the children are not placed in the low group or tracked. All children are given the chance to read for meaning, to interact with good literature, and to critically engage in dialogue.

This potential for equalizing and democratizing the schools leads to the issue of how whole language changes the power base of traditional schools as well as society. Paolo Freire (1970) points out that traditional approaches to learning and literacy create a group of passive objects in which knowledge is deposited, instead of a group of active subjects capable of transcending and transforming their sociopolitical reality. In a skills approach the learners, especially low-income and minority students, are treated as passive objects who aren't expected to act on their environment.

Teachers are also treated as passive objects and expected to willingly accept any published program imposed upon them. Program management systems and discipline systems strip power away from both children and teachers. The school system creates a population trained for passivity and submission to authority. This sets the stage for the *de*democratizing of democratic countries.

Whole language puts power for learning, decision-making, and problem-solving back into the hands of teachers and students. It creates active learners; it empowers all of us to act upon and transform our environments and society in general. We are not just asking for a change in the teaching of reading, but a radical change in the social and political structure of schooling and society (Giroux and McLaren 1986).

(Continued on page 419)

Bess Altwerger began her career as a public school teacher in New York City. From 1980 to 1988, while she was a faculty member at the University of New Mexico, she taught courses in reading and language arts and worked extensively with the Albuquerque Public Schools. She provided on-site collaborative staff development on the implementation of whole language. She is currently an associate professor at Towson State University in Baltimore, Maryland.

Barbara Flores is currently an associate professor in the School of Education at California State University, San Bernardino, California. Her areas of expertise are in language and literacy/biliteracy. She has worked with culturally and linguistically diverse children and teachers throughout the United States.

Network

A Message from Kittye Copeland to TAWL Members

I hope you feel the excitement that I feel being a whole language teacher. This summer in my travels around the United States, I saw the importance of TAWL in helping professionals grow. I also became aware of the strength growing in TAWL because of the new enthusiasm for and acceptance of whole language.

In Fresno, California, I found a group of teachers who wanted to change their literacy programs. The enthusiasm was so catching that Paul Crowley and I thought we could take on any phonics advocates in the nation. I would like to share a part of a letter I received from one of those advocates after the conference which demonstrates her change of theory and risk in going back home to change her program. "My principal has been very supportive. I told him I wished I could put a hold on my basal workbooks and the teacher's manuals and the phonics books and he said that was great, it wasn't too late. So I'll get that money to spend on literature and other appropriate whole language materials. Isn't that fantastic!" I sure think so.

In Alief, Texas, I found a group of administrators who not only supported their teachers but wanted to learn and work with them, so they too came to the workshops. When a question came up about spelling books, I explained that children learn to spell by being involved in many authentic writing and editing experi-

ences. One teacher said, "But we don't have time. They make us use the books." The principals responded that they really didn't want spelling books either. The staff began to communicate in that meeting about new options for spelling instruction which they planned to continue in building study groups.

A group of teachers in Spencerport, New York, had been forced by their principal to attend a whole language workshop. However, by the end of the week, we saw them change because we asked them to be open, study, think it over, and then as professionals, make their own decisions. I'm not saying they ran to burn their basals, but they were excited to choose things *they* wanted to try. One teacher did say that two weeks of running off worksheets had been a waste of time because they were staying in the box.

I could tell you many stories like these which indicate that educators are willing to change and to give whole language a chance. More books and articles about whole language, more research to quote, more press about the failing basal methods, more companies publishing good literature, more conferences and a major factor, an international whole language umbrella group has given whole language the visibility and authority we have been working to develop.

As the WLU board met in Columbia, Missouri I was amazed at the energy. To think only 10 years ago we were only six people meeting in a living room. No wonder I'm so excited.

→ See: Bell, p. 48; Copeland, pp. 48, 411; Graham, p. 426; Swanda, p. 48.

Kittye Copeland is a primary and elementary teacher at Stephens Elementary School, Columbia, MO.

Subscription Information: For a year's subscription to the Mid-Missouri TAWL newsletter, send $10 to Dorothy Watson, 225 Townsend Hall, University of Missouri, Columbia, MO 65211.

(Continued from page 418)

Political Action

Whole language teachers need to become ever more politically aware and active. We need to support groups like the Whole Language Umbrella, bring issues to our unions and other professional organizations, and form political issues committees within such organizations. We need to influence lawmakers and policymakers about educational issues. We need to write letters to editors, be on radio talk shows, and write articles for popular magazines. We need to reach out to parents and the community through forums, parent education nights, and conferences.

We have a difficult struggle ahead. But we have each other, and most important, the children and their excitement for learning give us energy, determination, and a passionate commitment to move forward.

References

Allington, R. 1980. "Teacher interruption behaviors during primary grade oral reading." *Journal of Education Psychology* 72.

———. 1983. "The reading instruction provided readers of different reading abilities." *Elementary School Journal* 83.

Anderson, A., and S. Stokes. 1984. "Social and institutional influences on the development and practice of literacy." In *Awakening to Literacy*, eds. H. Goelman, A. Oberg, and F. Smith. Portsmouth, NH: Heinemann.

Freire, P. 1970. *Pedagogy of the oppressed*. New York: Seabury.

Gambrell, L., R. Wilson, and W. Gantt. 1981. "Classroom observations of tasks attending behaviors of good and poor readers." *Journal of Educational Research* 74.

Giroux, H. 1983. *Theory and resistance in education*. South Hadley, MA: Bergin & Garvey.

Giroux, H., and P. McLaren. 1986. "Teacher education and the politics of engagement: The case for democratic schooling." *Harvard Educational Review* 56(3).

Heath, S. 1983. *Ways with words*. Cambridge: Cambridge University Press.

McDermott, R., and K. Gospodinoff. 1979. "Social contexts for ethnic borders and school failures." In *Nonverbal Behavior*, ed. A. Wolfgang. New York: Academic Press.

Meier, D. 1981. "Why reading tests don't test reading." *Dissent* 28(4).

Moll, L., and S. Diaz. 1987. "Change as the goal of educational research." *Anthropology and Education Quarterly* 18(4).

Rich, S. 1985. "Restoring power to teachers: The impact of whole language." *Language Arts* 62(7), November.

Shannon, P. 1985. "Reading instruction and social class." *Language Arts* 62(6), October.

→ See: Altwerger, pp. 295, 407, 418; Apple, p. 416; Copeland, p. 411; Flores, pp. 218, 412; Freire, pp. 100, 222, 346; Giroux, p. 417; Hartle-Schutte, p. 265; Meier, p. 50; Shor, p. 223; Smith and Shepard, p. 58; Watson, pp. 408, 427.

Adapted from the newsletter of the Albuquerque Teachers Applying Whole Language, 1989.

Further Reading by Bess Altwerger

◆ *The Theme Cycle: Creating Contexts for Whole Language Strategies*, with V. Resta and G. Kilarr. Richard C. Owen, in press.

◆ *Whole Language: What's the Difference?*, with C. Edelsky and B. Flores. Heinemann, 1990.

Further Reading by Barbara Flores

◆ *Whole Language: What's the Difference?*, with B. Altwerger and C. Edelsky. Heinemann, 1990.

◆ *Language Interference or Influence: Toward a Hispanic Theory of Bilingualism*. State University of New York Press, forthcoming.

 ## As Teachers See It

Critical Pedagogy in a Whole Language Bilingual Classroom
by Samuel D. Nofziger, Jr.

To empower students, James Cummins says that teachers need to (1) validate the identity of each student, (2) assure each student that their language and culture are valid, and (3) actively challenge the status quo. "If the language and culture are validated," states Dr. Cummins, "then, in turn, the students will be validated."

In our whole language bilingual classroom of first- and second-grade learners, validating the cultures and languages of all the students is important. It seems that the more I understand the bases for whole language in a bilingual setting, the more we seem to utilize critical pedagogy in our classroom.

Validating the Identity of Each Student

Andres came to me one day and said, "Mr. Nofziger, someone stole my pencils!" He was saddened by his loss, so we decided together to ask the rest of the class to help us solve the problem. After discussing the matter, we decided that if someone knew where the pencils were, he or she should put them on the table in the back of the room. By the end of the day, Andres's pencils were on the table. Andres felt validated and secure enough to bring me the problem. Together, as a class, we solved it.

Validating the Language and Culture of Each Student

As a bilingual teacher, I have witnessed the importance of the development of the primary language of each student. Cummins states in his book *Empowering Minority Students* that "*All* the research data on bilingual programs, international and U.S., show this consistent pattern," and that "there is either no relationship or a negative relationship between amount of exposure to English for minority students in elementary schools and their academic success" (Cummins 1989).

The principles of a whole language classroom seem to lend themselves naturally to this idea. If we allow the students to use the language they feel most comfortable with or, as the Freemans (1989) say, to "have faith in the learner," students feel that they have power over their learning.

Challenging the Status Quo

Benny occasionally asks, "Why do we have to do this, Mr. Nofziger?" Is this simply defying authority? I don't think so. Benny is "challenging the status quo" in our classroom. To better understand the activity, Benny needs to know how it all fits together. Benny is becoming empowered.

As teachers, how do we become empowered without threatening fellow teachers and/or our administration? I have found that showing the positive results of our classroom seems to work. When the results of our reading basal tests came in, I shared them with my colleagues. Though we use literature in our classroom instead of the basal, our test results were very pleasing. My colleagues were curious about what we do in the classroom, and I was able to share our philosophy in a nonthreatening atmosphere.

Within the framework of a whole language bilingual classroom, critical pedagogy seems to be a natural outcome as we accept each student, including their language and their culture. The wonderful thing about a whole language environment is that *everyone* is valued.

→ See: Empowering Minority Students, p. 91.

References

Cummins, J. 1989. *Empowering minority students.* Sacramento, CA: California Association for Bilingual Education.

Freeman, D., and Y. Freeman. 1989. "Bilingual assumptions." *Holistic Education Review* 2(4).

Samuel D. Nofziger, Jr., is a primary bilingual teacher at Lane Elementary School, Fresno, CA.

Working for Peace

Great Teachers:
Debra Jacobson
by Mary M. Kitagawa

More than anyone I know, Debra Jacobson models by her relationship with other teachers, personally and by publication, an ideal learning community for educators, both as people and as professionals. And then she takes that same attitude into the learning communities of her classrooms.

For the past few years she has worked as a Chapter 1 teacher at Helen Keeling Elementary School, Amphitheater School District, Tucson, Arizona. But she doesn't limit herself to the 50-plus students on her Chapter 1 roll. Instead of a pull-out program, she teams with the teachers of those students in reading and writing workshops in their own classrooms.

Debra Jacobson and student.

Debra consults with the classroom teachers after school and on weekends and summer vacations to establish a comfortable rapport. Debra tailor-makes her role to fit the preferences of each teacher. Little by little Debra and the teacher develop more and more holistic ways for children to relate to language.

Debra started and runs the school "publishing company," where students publish their writing in either handmade books or the semi-annual literary magazine they compile. Debra models writing as well as teaching it, so her own stories and poems appear after the students help her with the composing process.

She launched a schoolwide post office that now runs itself. Classes take weekly turns with the postal operations, which gives everyone a chance to send and receive letters throughout the building.

Years ago Debra realized that whole language teachers need extensive support systems and that we should be closely connected with other dedicated proponents of the philosophy. She launched a regular newsletter that she called *Another Good Start*. Its circulation spread from coast to coast and provided the original network that grew into the present *Teachers Networking*, now published by Richard C. Owen, Publishers. Debra still promotes teacher exchanges by means of her regular columns in *Teachers Networking*. She is a mainstay in our Small TAWL writing support group; her insight has solved many a writing problem for the rest of our members. Debra helped form another Small TAWL study group, this one on educational theory. One summer we met regularly to read and discuss Vera John-Steiner's *Notebooks of the Mind*.

In *The Whole Language Evaluation Book*, her chapter, "The Whole Language Process—In Process," is an apt title for Debra herself. She is always in the midst of evolving a better way to do a better job.

Debra has the persistence to always ask questions of her colleagues, sometimes as gentle nudges toward rethinking an idea and sometimes as flat-out roadblocks. It all comes from the sort of honest questioning that whole language grew out of in the first place. She seems constantly to wave her "antennae" before new possibilities, open to them, but not as a bandwagon jumper. She constantly checks the grounding of theory with her experiences and her theory base with realities in the classroom.

Debra Jackson is a promoter. She promotes the whole language philosophy, teacher professionalism, and children. With all those promotional responsibilities that she has taken on, it is not surprising that she operates as well with teachers as with pupils.

→ See: Jacobson, pp. 118, 160; Kitagawa, pp. 132, 212, 299; Owen, p. 414.

Mary M. Kitagawa is an elementary teacher at Mark's Meadow School, Amherst, MA.

> If we are to reach real peace in this world . . . we shall have to begin with the children.
> —Mahatma Gandhi

WELL-SAID

Pieces of our World

An anthology of poetry and prose Written by the Children of the Riverina

Edited by Trevor H. Cairney

writers

Peace

by Nicole Black

No more war, let us be,
Let there be peace for you and me,
Happiness on Earth, what is it worth?
The lovely flowers and bees,
The cool wind and the trees,
If we could start all over again,
Maybe the world would not be in PAIN.

From *Pieces of Our World: An Anthology of Poetry and Prose Written by the Children of the Riverina*, edited by Trevor H. Cairney (Wagga Wagga, New South Wales: Centre for Teaching & Research in Literacy, 1988).

Nicole Black is a fifth-year student at the Cootamundra Primary School, New South Wales, Australia.

Resource: Publisher

New Society Publishers

BOOKS TO BUILD A NEW SOCIETY

Catalog $1 from:
P.O. Box 582
Santa Cruz, CA 95061
1-408-458-1191

New Society Publishers is "connected to a growing network of peace, feminist, environmental, and human rights activists," and is "committed to publishing books and other resources which promote fundamental social change through nonviolent action." Of special interest to whole language educators are New Society's books on peaceful conflict resolution and peace education.

LBB

My hope is to remind people of what it means to be alive among others, to achieve freedom in dialogue with others for the sake of personal fulfillment and the emergence of a democracy dedicated to life and decency.

—Maxine Green, *The Dialectic of Freedom*

WELL-SAID

Resource: Publisher

Aslan Publishing/
University of the Trees Press

JOY IN THE CLASSROOM
STEPHANIE HERZOG

310 Blue Ridge Dr.
Boulder Creek, CA 95006
1-800-372-3100
1-800-423-5784 (CA)

Aslan publishes books about meditating with children. At first thought this practice may not appeal to you, but Stephanie Herzog's sensitive *Joy in the Classroom* might change your mind. The glowing letters from public school administrators and parents at the back of the book offer further evidence (and reassurance for the uninitiated) that meditation is a powerful, life-affirming strategy that we might do well to explore in our classrooms. Other titles from Aslan devoted to helping children develop their full potential include *The Ultimate Kid* by Jeffrey Goelitz and two books by Deborah Rozeman, *Meditation for Children* and *Meditating with Children*.

LBB

Meditation for Children — by Deborah Rozman, Ph.D.

THE ULTIMATE KID — Levels of Learning That Make a Difference — Jeffrey Goelitz

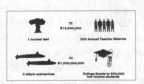

Resource: Organizations

Women's International League for Peace and Freedom (WILPF)

Membership:
$35 individual;
free resource list from:
1213 Race St.
Philadelphia, PA
19107-1691
1-215-563-7110

WILPF, one of the oldest peace organizations in the world, seeks an end to all war, oppression, and injustice. Its current program priorities include Undoing Racism, Disarmament by the Year 2000, and Ending U. S. Global Intervention. WILPF provides a series of Undoing Racism workshops held all across the United States. The organization's Literature Department distributes three publications: the U.S. section's bimonthly *Peace and Freedom,* the bimonthly *Program and Legislative Action,* and the quarterly *Pax et Libertas,* published in English. WILPF's famous poster showing children climbing on a play structure has the following words:

It will be a great day when our schools get all the money they need and the air force has to hold a bake sale to buy a bomber.

Arrietta Chakos

Educators for Social Responsibility (ESR)

Membership: $35 annual ($42 with journal); $50 family/couple ($57 with journal); $10 limited income ($17 with journal) from:
23 Garden St.
Cambridge, MA 02138
1-617-492-1764

Bertrand Russell, quoted on the brochure we received from Educators for Social Responsibility, said, "Teachers more than any other class are the guardians of civilization." This organization of educators, parents, and others committed to helping students "face the challenges of living in the nuclear age" is founded on that belief. ESR provides

Holocaust

by Alicia Brashear

The Holocaust was a dreadful fright,
It happened for years every day and night.
Thousands of Jews died horrible
Deaths,
The Nazis didn't even give them
A decent rest.
One of the voices that remains
With us,
Was a girl that had to learn
To trust.
To a girl named Anne Frank
This was a terrible must,
She had to trust so many times,
But someone betrayed,
Her that faithful night.
The Nazis came and took her away,
She hasn't been seen to this day.
Her father found her Diary,
And through that she became known to me.

From *Reflections* 8(2), June 1989

Alicia Brashear is from Hamilton, Ohio. She was 12 years old when she wrote this poem.

a wide range of professional development and curricular materials, sponsors local and national conferences, and publishes local chapter and national newsletters. The *ESR Journal* develops the theory and practice of educating for social responsibility.

LBB

Anti-Defamation League of B'nai B'rith (ADL)

Dept. JW
823 United Nations Plaza
New York, NY 10017
1-212-490-2525
FAX 1-212-867-0779

Most educators face instances of prejudice and discrimination in their classrooms during their careers. Whether it happens occasionally or on a daily basis, the time to act is immediately—it is not something to pass over lightly or ignore. As educators, we are not usually trained in how to deal with such issues, nor are materials readily available.

If you anticipate these issues surfacing in your teaching situation, the resources of the Anti-Defamation League of B'nai B'rith could be very valuable to you, whether you teach at kindergarten or university level. Their catalog includes student and teacher books, films, filmstrips, videocassettes, posters and whole curriculum packages. Topics include prejudice, discrimination, intergroup relations, multicultural education, political and social issues, and philosophy. The multicultural section includes specific materials for all Americans—Asian, Black, Hispanic, Italian, Jewish, and Native Americans, among others. In addition, there are sections on Israel and the Middle East and teaching about the Holocaust.

This catalog is a valuable resource for educators at all levels.

Doug Haner

The Martin Luther King, Jr. Center for Nonviolent Social Change

449 Auburn Ave., NE
Atlanta, GA 30312
1-404-524-1956

This is the place to find the most complete collection of the writings by and about Martin Luther King, Jr. Here you will find the four classic books he wrote, plus *Ebony* magazine's in-depth biography of Dr. King, Coretta Scott King's commentary on her experiences as the wife of the slain leader, and a textbook series written by Dr. King's only sister, Mrs. Christine King Farris. You can also order photographs of Dr. King and his family, teaching units for elementary and intermediate grades, videotapes, a kit on observing Martin Luther King, Jr.'s birthday, and records and tapes of Dr. King's speeches and sermons.

The center also has a Scholars Internship Program for graduate and undergraduate students, an annual summer workshop on nonviolence, a library, archives, and a museum that attracts over one million visitors annually.

Doug Haner

Nuclear Age Peace Foundation

Membership: from $35 (contributing member) to $1,000 (patron)
1187 Coast Village Rd., Ste. 123
Santa Barbara, CA 93108
1-805-965-3443
FAX 1-805-969-1725

For high school and college educators who are concerned about the threat

of nuclear war and an escalating arms race, this organization provides several valuable and free resources. A series of booklets entitled "Waging Peace" explores the nuclear weapons dilemma from different viewpoints, providing a catalyst for discussing this sensitive and critical issue. These well-written and informative booklets have helped create a dialogue for community discussions and conferences. A rather frightening newsletter entitled *Nuclear Alert: International Accidental War Prevention Newsletter* is published quarterly.

Doug Haner

Little Friends for Peace

4405 29th St.
Mount Rainier, MD 20712
1-301-699-0042

Here is one of those small grass-roots organizations created by concerned teachers that warms the heart. "My dream is to equip children with peacemaking skills," said Mary Joan Park. She identifies a constant problem for many educators—children having conflicts with each other and not knowing what to do about them.

Mary Joan and her husband have created two valuable booklets, *Peacemaking for Little Friends* and *Creating a Peace Experience,* to help educators and parents equip children with the skills of building self-esteem, affirming communication, resolving conflicts, and learning cooperative play. They are packed with ideas that work for solving the persistent and complex problems young people have of getting along with each other. What I like most are the numerous suggestions for integrating oral language, role-playing, photographs, art activities, writing projects, and children's literature as techniques for interdisciplinary and multisensory learning. I can't say enough about these two books.

Doug Haner

The Peace Garden Project

P.O. Box 5282 Elmwood Station
Berkeley, CA 94705
1-415-652-6351

One person *can* make a difference, as Elizabeth Ratcliff of Berkeley has proven. In 1985, after walking around the Capitol in Washington and realizing that most of the monuments are to wars or war heroes, she began to envision a peace garden. Now, through her vision and diligence, the national Peace Garden Project is selecting the winning design for a six-acre site at Hains Point in Washington, DC, at the confluence of the Potomac and Anacostia rivers.

By contemplating three main questions about peace (What is peace? How can peace be achieved? How can a national garden help create peace?), students from elementary through university levels are translating their abstract concepts into horticultural designs. A copy of the curricula for elementary school children can be gotten from Catherine Crawford at the address above. This short four-page brief integrates *Sadako and the Thousand Cranes* with cooperative learning projects for children. There is also an address for linking up with pen pals from foreign countries.

Doug Haner

Challenges: Present and Future

Viewpoint: Shirley Brice Heath

Whole Language: Promise and Challenge

Whole language makes so much sense and seems so overwhelmingly obvious that attempts to justify it or to point it out as positive seem unnecessary. But then we can think of many other features of contemporary human life that seem equally obvious and yet have relatively little active support—clean air and water and a drug-free society, for example.

Whole language differs from many other obvious positives in one critical respect. To get clean air and water, we have to work to undo long-standing pollution and to change established habits of industrial growth. To rid society of drugs, we have to challenge formidable international economic linkages as well as solve the individual and community problems that lead to drug traffic and use.

But whole language is there within every neurologically sound language learner. Whole language celebrates the full range of forms of language that people develop throughout childhood—creative stories, detailed accounts of everyday activities, and rapid-fire conversations about life experiences. As children learn to engage others to help them get what they need, to express their hopes and fears, and to become accepted members of their families and communities, they naturally use language in a holistic way. Thus youngsters enter school with "a whole language" for the environment from which they have come. The catch comes when the school takes on the task of expanding children's language to the written word and acknowledges

Shirley Brice Heath is professor of Linguistics and English, and by courtesy of Anthropology and Education, at Stanford University. Her research interests include spoken and written language, first- and second-language acquisition, and ethnography of communication. Named a MacArthur Fellow in 1984, she has also been an NEH and a Guggenheim fellow, a special fellow for research and development at the Stanford Humanities Center, and a fellow at the Center for Advanced Study in the Behavioral Sciences.

only a limited range of oral language uses as legitimate ways to display knowledge.

This task has seemed for centuries to spur teachers to reduce language to something less than its whole—to cut language into parts and to separate the pieces for instruction. Methods that follow from this simplification and reduction of language tend to limit time for talk, focus on specific ways of giving answers, oral and written, and place the highest values on answering rather than asking questions.

Whole language proponents urge that teaching methods and materials allow, encourage, and model language as rich in substance and style as everyday language. They urge teachers to use their imaginative powers to stimulate children to create and critique with their language, rather than merely feed back known answers. Whole language proponents also urge the full integration of written language with spoken language. They also argue that *all* children need to *add* to their repertoire the language forms most frequently acknowledged in academic life, but that such an addition cannot replace the full range of language forms individuals need in their lives outside the school.

The strengths—and indeed the obvious good sense—that whole language represents has been for many teachers and educators its greatest weakness. Whole language teaching does not offer quick-and-easy packages ready for opening on Monday morning; it does not stress narrow forms of assessment that give immediate (albeit unreliable) indications of student performance. Whole language instead depends on teachers who have learned a substantial amount about language, how it is learned, used, and reshaped by topics, listeners, style, and situations. Whole language expects teachers to think and create with language and to value wide-ranging efforts by students to use spoken and written language to learn.

Those who oppose whole language do so because they see it as pushing out other established methods of teaching reading. They argue that most teachers need packages and prescribed lessons for teaching their students; otherwise, textbook publishers would not think they have to provide "teacher-proof" curricula. They stress the fact that whole language proponents talk too easily of "wonderful" language gains, "beautiful" creations, and "inspiring" teachers—outcomes or results that do not stand up against the objectivity of standardized tests. They argue that whole language proponents tend to "stick together" and to have a quasi-missionary spirit about the merits of their approaches to reading. Perhaps most often, critics point to the absence of long-term studies of the effects of such teaching or the power of whole language to sustain itself as an approach when one or more of its committed proponents is no longer on-site to help keep the creative juices flowing for other teachers.

Whole language proponents need to take these criticisms seriously. There are studies that show the long-term effects of whole language environments on students, but these need greater dissemination. Younger scholars and teachers who support whole language approaches need to invite both doubting and neutral colleagues into collaborative evaluation efforts. The appearance of "opposing camps"—whole language versus

phonics or any other set of methods—will fall away when teachers and researchers have opportunities to find out where their agreements and disagreements really begin and end.

The most critical challenge whole language faces is that of teacher preparation. Teachers currently preparing to enter the classroom must have greater access to unbiased information about whole language. They must have instructors who can let them know of the support that whole language receives from the theories and research findings of a broad array of scholars in different fields—child language, cross-cultural learning, cognitive psychology, and literary studies. This challenge may be helped by the increasing emphasis in the late 20th century on promoting alternative and multiple forms of learning and valuing open-ended performance-based assessment.

Anthropologist Clifford Geertz (1983) tells us that common sense is more than just what anyone and everyone knows:

> When we say someone shows common sense we mean to suggest more than that he is just using his eyes and ears, but is, as we say, keeping them open, using them judiciously, intelligently, perceptively, reflectively, or trying to, and that he is capable of coping with everyday problems in an everyday way with some effectiveness.

These words speak then of the greatest challenge for whole language—to find and support those willing to *consider* it and to use it as *common* sense.

→ See: Bell, p. 48; Boomer, p. 403; Easton, p. 272; Goodman, pp. 390, 397; Stevenson, p. 271; Watson, p. 427; Ways with Words, p. 422.

Reference

Geertz, C. 1983. "Common sense as a cultural system." In *Local knowledge.* New York: Basic Books.

Further Reading by Shirley Brice Heath

◆ *Ways with Words: Language, Life, and Work in Communities and Classrooms.* Cambridge University Press, 1983.

Book Note

Ways with Words: Language, Life, and Work in Communities and Classrooms

Shirley Brice Heath
1983; 422 pp.; $22.95
New York: Cambridge University Press

In the winter of 1983, I had the good fortune to sit in on "The Ethnography of Communication," a seminar taught by Professor Shirley Brice Heath at Stanford University. During one class, a student arrived with a large cardboard box—it was the first shipment of *Ways with Words*. With intense interest we all watched as Shirley opened, for the first time, the covers of her just-published book.

Since then, thousands of educators and social scientists have experienced the excitement of intellectual discovery as they've read what is now viewed as a seminal work. It is difficult to find a professional book or journal in the field that doesn't reference *Ways with Words*. Drawn from an extensive nine-year ethnographic study, the book details the ways in which language and literacy shape the lives of the residents of two socially, economically, and politically different communities, just a few miles apart in the Piedmont Carolinas.

LBB

Book Note

The Web of Meaning: Essays on Writing, Teaching, Learning, and Thinking

Janet Emig
1983; 192 pp.; $13.50
Portsmouth, NH: Boynton/Cook

I've just finished reading, for the first time, Janet Emig's *The Web of Meaning: Essays on Writing, Teaching, Learning, and Thinking.* Two years ago a colleague suggested I read the book. I purchased it and placed it on my "to read" shelf. This morning, in an attempt to take myself away from the pressures of working in the local school district, I approached the shelf. I selected Emig's text thinking I ought to know something about her work before I heard her speak. Now, four hours later, I can't wait to hear Janet Emig. I also have a clearer perspective on our district issues. Her discussions are wise; I appreciate her intelligence and her knowledge of our work. Emig's essays offer me a broader base for my beliefs and an explanation for discoveries I've made and the strategies I use. Emig's ideas about metaphors and cognition might help us restructure our beliefs about the work of teachers. Her final essay on literacy and freedom is, and I apologize for the already overused word, empowering.

K. S. Dalrymple

In the Mail

November 30, 1988

Elm Street School
Rockport Elementary School
Rockport, ME

Dear Dr. Goodman:

I am the principal of a 600 pupil K-5 school. We have been involved with whole language thinking and teaching for about five years in the lower grades and two years in grades four and five. Our teachers have had a good background through courses, conferences, reading, TAWL group, and various other means. Our school is highly regarded among elementary schools in Maine. Many teachers visit us each year from other districts. As a staff, we feel terrific about what we are doing and the way we are doing it. We are still growing and learning in many ways.

The past few months we have seen our Board of Directors begin to receive verbally, and in writing, a series of statements critical to our whole language program and to the movement, in general. This is fueled to considerable degree by Jeanne Chall's research articles.

Our Board of Directors wants to look at the success or failure of the program in terms of (1) achievement test scores and (2) through identifying schools where whole language has been the direction for at least five years.

Can you help me by:

1. Providing standardized test score information from schools using a whole language program.

2. Provide the names of schools who have successfully used whole language for five years or more.

These are difficult grounds on which to analyze the program, I realize. The standardized tests don't measure much of what our programs are doing and attempt to measure reading success on isolated factors which are not the prime focus of our teaching.

Thank you very much for your assistance. I've heard your presentations on two occasions in the Northeast and have the highest regard for your work. Thank you for what you are doing, and have done, for the sake of children.

Sincerely,
Marvin Higgins
Principal

December 6, 1988

Dear Mr. Higgins,

I sympathize with your problem. But you need to remember that the best evidence of the success of your whole language program is in your kids and your classrooms. We've recently produced, with a group of teachers, *The Whole Language Evaluation* Book to document the rich innovative ways that whole language teachers have found to evaluate the full range of learning that takes place in their classrooms while it happens. We need to show the doubters not just scores on questionable tests but how much, how widely, and with what understanding and pleasure the children are reading. We need to have portfolios of their writing to show them how their expressive range is expanding at the same time that their spelling and mechanics are moving toward social norms. We need to show how thematic units build knowledge while they build problem-solving, cognitive strategies, and self-confidence as learners. We need to remind them how much the children enjoy school, how proud they are of the achievements of their classmates as well as themselves. We need to help them appreciate the energy and creativity the kids are capable of if they have supportive, empowered teachers.

Marie Carbo has done a devastating point-by-refutation of Jeanne Chall's conclusions and the research she summarized. She was wrong about phonics and how to teach reading and she has no right to make condemnations of whole language which she has not studied at all. I'm enclosing a copy of Carbo's study.

There is a growing body of research which shows the tremendous achievements of whole language. This even includes some experimental studies. Although I myself feel these controlled studies that compare whole language classrooms with traditional ones are the least interesting because they reduce what is measured to what happens in both sets of classrooms, the results again strongly favor whole language. Carol Stice and Nancy Bertrand are doing primary grade studies in Nashville, Tennessee. They presented at NCTE and NRC. Write them at Tennessee State University. They show the whole language pupils at least equivalent on norm-referenced standardized tests and far ahead on the range of achievement not emphasized in conventional classrooms, such as volume and quality of reading and writing. Wendy Kasten at the University of South Florida, Sarasota, Florida, has done similar comparative studies with

preschool and kindergarten pupils, with much the same results. Last week at NRC, Elfrieda Heibert and some colleagues presented the results of an extensive multigrade study done in a suburb in Denver. This is an interesting study because the researchers have no whole language connections and kept commenting on how surprised they were with the striking superiority of the whole language pupils in their studies. They found for example that the whole language pupils read far more outside of school as well as in school. Another finding was that whole language pupils took far longer to select books in libraries than other pupils and that the whole language pupils seemed to have developed perceptive criteria for making their selections. The pupils who were not in whole language classes seemed to be much more random in their choices.

New Zealand has a history of holistic education that goes back half a century though only recently have they applied the term whole language to their curriculum and school practice. Margaret Mooney coordinates the production of materials in their curriculum division (NZ Department of Education, Wellington, New Zealand). She was largely responsible for writing *Reading in Junior Classes*, published in the United States by Richard C. Owen. Recently, in a national poll, 14-year-olds in New Zealand listed reading as their second choice among leisure activities. To me, that's the best evidence of all. Quebec and Nova Scotia have had whole language curriculum policies for several years. Pat Barnes, in the Nova Scotia department of education, Halifax, can provide you with information on their success. The David Livingston School in Winnipeg, Manitoba has had a whole language program for over 10 years. In Edmonton, Alberta there are several whole language schools. Whole language schools with long standing we've visited include the Warrawong School in Warrawong, New South Wales, Australia where Jan Turbill has done a lot of work and Richmond Road School in Auckland, New Zealand. Don Holdaway began work with big books there and recently Courtney Cazden of Harvard has done research there. Carbo in a footnote to her article cites test results from the Portland, Oregon schools after a year of using Canadian *Impressions* reading program that are impressive for all ability groups. In private conversations, the Portland school people told me they were unhappy with the release of that data because they feel that they have much better evidence that gets more to the program than the materials.

I'm hearing every day of schools like yours with successful whole language programs but few in the United States have five years or more of experience. One is Fair Oaks School in Redwood City, California, a working-class suburb of San Francisco. It was featured on a recent PBS broadcast. Herrera school in Phoenix and Borton School in Tucson have also had extended histories but not always with strong school board support. The lab schools at Stevens College in Columbia, Missouri and at Lehman College in New York City also have whole language programs though I haven't personally visited them.

I'm completing an article on research on whole language which will be in a special issue of the *Elementary School Journal* next year. Its main point is that whole language has a strong research base in Piaget, Vygotsky, and Bruner from psychology, in linguistics from Halliday and Chomsky, in psycholingustics from George Miller, Jerome Bruner, and Frank Smith, in literature from Louise Rosenblatt, in the writing development work of Don Murray and Don Graves, in our own reading research as well as that of the Anderson schema group at Illinois. And there is a growing group of classroom teachers who are doing their own research including Nancie Atwell from Boothbay, Maine. Her book, *In the Middle*, is an excellent one to give your Board of Directors to get a sense of how middle-grade whole language rooms operate.

Please stay in touch. Keep your resolve and your confidence in your professional judgment.

Cordially,
Kenneth S. Goodman

In a telephone conversation May 17, 1990, Marvin Higgins told me that after several public forums, the Board of Directors voted in January of this year to renew their support for whole language. The two articles that Ken refers to in his letter are: Marie Carbo, "Debunking the Great Phonics Myth," Phi Delta Kappa, *November 1988, pp. 226–40, and Ken Goodman, "Whole Language Research: Foundations and Development,"* Elementary School Journal 90(2), *November 1989, pp. 207–222.*

—LBB

➔ See: Becoming a Whole Language School: The Fair Oaks Story, p. 92; Bell, p. 48 ; Bird, p. 92; Christine, p. 379; Crafts, p. 136; Edelsky, p. 72; Fennacy, p. 309; Goodman, pp. 24, 249, 252, 386; Graves, p. 129; Manicom, p. 384; In the Middle, p. 139; Mooney, p. 120; Owen, p. 414; Swanda, p. 48; The Whole Language Evaluation Book, p. 252.

The Whole Language Movement: A Warning

Frank Smith announced whilst talking to my masters students at Wollongong University that *whole language* was dead. Many would claim that Smith was simply being provocative, but I believe we should take heed and view his statement as a warning. He could well be right. Let me explain.

In the last year or so many writers have tried to define what whole language is and what this means for the classroom. Cambourne (1988) has written a book called *The Whole Story.* Goodman (1986) has written one called *What's Whole in Whole Language?;* Newman (1985) edited *Whole Language: Theory in Use,* and the journals are replete with articles on effective whole language classroom practices. Try reading these and doing what I asked my masters students to do: Define the term *whole language.* They found they couldn't do it. There appears to be no clear definition that can be synthesized from these writings. They did find, however, that there are several common characteristics emanating from all the writers, characteristics that appear to underpin whole language philosophy. These they identified as something to do with

Like many of us, Jan Turbill began her professional career in the classroom. After working as a consultant with the New South Wales Department of Education, she accepted a faculty position at the University of Wollongong.

- The beliefs or values teachers have about the purpose of literacy education, about the role literacy plays in learning;
- The notion of "making connections," i.e., learning is a process of making connections;
- The "connectedness" of reading, writing, talking, and listening, which is best explained by Linguistic Data Pool (the visual metaphor first discussed by Carolyn Burke), the metaphor that helps us to understand how language and the language components interact and support each other;
- The concept of "naturalistic" learning, learning that should be authentic, purposeful, and durable;
- The notion of child-centered learning and a focus on "kidwatching";
- The conditions existing in the classroom, which create the supportive, nonthreatening environment for learning;
- A focus on the process and the purpose of learning, which means that teaching, therefore, is a process of helping learners make connections;
- The notion that language is a social process learned for social purposes through social interaction.

Whole language, therefore, is a view of learning that encompasses the above (and possibly more) key characteristics. Furthermore, whole language classrooms are learning environments in which these characteristics are clearly evident. But this doesn't mean that all such classrooms will look identical and be organised in the same way. When teachers understand these characteristics, they become inherent in their belief and value systems. Thus, the way each teacher translates them into practice will differ according to the context in which she or he teaches. This context is affected by the teacher's personality, the children, the culture, the resources, and so on. No two classrooms, therefore, can ever be exactly the same, although there must be similarities. These similarities are most evident in the way teachers organise, use

time, space, and resources, select strategies, plan, and evaluate, and they are related to those characteristics mentioned above. My research is also showing me that there are similarities in the way whole language teachers use language.

To better explain what I mean, let me draw an analogy from the biological world. Let me liken this "view of learning" to that of a class or genus of animals such as birds. Birds have many common characteristics that are related to the class *birds* and underpin its very reason for being, characteristics such as having feathers, wings, beaks, and two legs, and being warm-blooded, egg-laying, and so on. These characteristics exist for the purpose of the class to survive, propagate, and thrive. It is a class of animals whose characteristics are quite distinct from those of the class *fish.* Thus, although they are living animals whose purpose it is to strive towards maintaining life, the class is based on a whole different set of principles from other animals, which is evident in the different set of characteristics pertaining to that class. However, the class of birds realise these characteristics differently within certain contexts. These different groups within the class are known as *species.* Species of birds look and act differently in response or adaptation to their contexts. There are some quite distinct differences, such as that some swim and some don't, but in the main, although species of birds nest differently, are different colours, act differently, and so on, the common characteristics of the class and purpose for their existence are evident and, in fact, shape the differences. All these differences are adaptations to the ecology, to the environment, to the availability of resources, and so on.

Drawing from this analogy, whole language teachers and their classrooms can be viewed as a species within the class of "the whole language view of learning." They too have a common purpose (or set of beliefs) for the teaching of language and literacy. They too have a common set of characteristics, which they take and adapt to their personality, to the children, to the contexts in which they find themselves. If the context changes (i.e., the teacher moves to another class or to another school) the teacher will adapt and change again according to how his or her overall belief system interacts with this context, just as a species of birds will adapt when its environment changes.

Thus, if we try to formalise whole language practice, if we try to make it the same for all, the movement will eventually die, as Frank Smith declared. It will die because, just as a species needs to interact with its environment to thrive, so does the whole language teacher.

So where is this all leading me? It means that those of us who believe in the whole language view of learning must be careful not to create orthodoxies. It means we cannot say *this* is what a whole language classroom looks like; *this* is how to organise a whole language classroom. We can demonstrate how the teachers with whom we work organise their classrooms and describe what these classrooms look like. But we must also be careful to clearly identify the context within which these teachers teach. We must warn those to whom we present that they cannot go away with this information as being *the way.* If they do, then whole language will not work in their classrooms. It will eventually die.

WELL-SAID

I think the lesson of the curriculum reform movement is that you cannot accomplish the deeper ends of education by altering only the content and spirit of the courses you teach. Schools as now constituted are not so much the solution to the problem of education as they are part of the problem. If I had it all to do over again, and if I knew how, I would put my energies into reexamining how the schools express the agenda of the society and how that agenda is formulated and how translated by the schools. That, it seems to me, would be the properly subversive way to proceed.

—Jerome Bruner

From *In Search of Mind,* by Jerome Bruner (New York: Harper & Row, 1983).

Resource: Organization/ Periodical

Center for Democratic Alternatives
Forward Motion: A Socialist Magazine

$12 year (6 issues) from:
P.O. Box 1884
Jamaica Plain, MA 02130

The motion of this group may be too radical for some, but if you are serious about effecting political change within our schools, you should take a look at *Forward Motion,* a journal published six times a year by the Center for Democratic Alternatives.

LBB

We must ask teachers to listen to what we have to offer but warn them that, when they try to adopt what we demonstrate, they must be ready to adapt it to suit their own contexts. Teachers can do this as long as they understand what the class of whole language is all about and understand the philosophy that underpins the practice.

Finally, we in the whole language movement must be aware of the responsibility we have in keeping the movement alive. We must assist teachers in understanding the philosophy that underpins the movement so that teachers and their children can thrive as learners in their whole language classrooms.

➔ See: Cambourne, p. 17; Goodman, p. 390; Newman, p. 211; Towards a Reading-Writing Classroom, p. 239.

References

Cambourne, B. 1988. *The whole story: Natural learning and the acquisition of literacy in the classroom.* Auckland, New Zealand: Ashton Scholastic.
Goodman, K. S. 1986. *What's whole in whole language?* Portsmouth, NH: Heinemann.
Newman, J. M., ed. 1985. *Whole language: Theory in use.* Portsmouth, NH: Heinemann.

Further Reading by Jan Turbill

◆ *No Better Way to Teach Writing.* Australia: Primary English Teaching Association, 1982.
◆ *Now We Want to Write.* Australia: Primary English Teaching Association, 1983.
◆ *Towards a Reading-Writing Classroom,* with A. Butler. Australia: Primary English Teaching Association, 1984.
◆ *Coping with Chaos,* with B. Cambourne. Australia: Primary English Teaching Association, 1987.

Viewpoint: Margaret Yatsevitch Phinney

Whole Language: Beware of Procrustes

Procrustes was the legendary Greek robber who "sized up" his captives by tying them in his special iron bed. Those who fit exactly were freed; those who didn't were either stretched or pared down till they did. We use the metaphor now to describe a rigid determination to make evidence fit a particular theoretical perspective, so that only an elite few can qualify as true disciples. I worry that sometimes there is a tendency within the whole language movement to "size" its novices. Discouragement can stem, not from archaic educational policies, but from some of the whole language change-agents themselves.

Sometimes it's a workshop leader's rigidity that causes distress. An upset colleague called me recently to describe a reprimand she had received from a whole language presenter during a conference. My friend, herself a sensitive whole language teacher, had suggested that there were circumstances when recording some of a child's rough-draft writing in standard spelling would be appropriate. The leader was absolute, saying that under *no* circumstances should standard spelling *ever* be put on a child's writing. She said her students wouldn't dare ask her for a word in standard spelling because they knew she would never give it to them.

This is not an isolated incident. I hear such absolutisms frequently. If an alternate term for the whole language model is the "home model," as I believe it should be, then such rigidity is actually counter to that model. Good parents don't "never" their children like that. They are flexible when they make decisions about risk-taking versus safety-netting, assessing the circumstance, the fatigue level, sibling differences in style, and future needs. Workshop leaders need to treat the questions, comments, wonderings, suggestions, and criticisms of the participants in the same way they would treat such input from their classroom learners—not by becoming critical and overbearing in their responses, which shuts off communication and causes tension at best, polarization at worst—but by accepting the learner's stage of development, then gently carrying him or her from that place to the next. We all have our "zone of proximal development"—that place in our mental growth that we can't reach on our own but that we can access with help from others (Vygotsky 1962).

Sometimes the absolutisms come from the literature. For example, I read that we mustn't share "techniques" with teachers because all they need is the philosophy to be able to "do it." Vygotsky (1978, p. 57) said, "All the higher [mental] functions *originate* [emphasis mine] as actual relations between human individuals." Every function that we learn in our cultural development we learn socially first. Gradually we internalize and transform those functions so that they become part of our inner processing systems. Many teachers have been philosophically whole language teachers for a long time. All they needed was the support of an organized and articulated movement to back their practices. But many teachers are "emergent" learners on the threshold of a new concept. Their understanding of whole

Margaret Yatsevitch Phinney teaches first grade at the Smith College Campus School in Northampton, Massachusetts. She has taught in Canada and the United States, working with children from preschool through ninth grade as a reading resource person. While serving in the Peace Corps (1966–1968), she and her husband helped build a school in a South American barrio.

language may develop only very slowly, by "successive approximations," in the same way concepts take shape for young learners.

Most of my student teachers are terrified of whole language after their first days of observation, and the terror is magnified when they try managing their first sessions. "I can't keep track of so much. I don't know what's going on. I can't sort anything out of the chaos. I had no idea teaching and learning were so complicated." These are some of the comments I hear, in spite of hours of theoretical and practical preparation and moment-by-moment safety-netting. It is only by *doing*, by being immersed in the interactions day after day, that they begin to understand whole language principles. They use, at first, *my* techniques, systems, strategies, and curricula, then gradually explore their own ways of doing and being. "*Now* I see what you meant by... when I did ... !" they say. "Now I understand why we did that!" when children respond as the theory predicted.

Inservice teachers are no less insecure when challenged to change their belief systems. Workshops and resources that share what whole language teachers do, while emphasizing the theoretical reasons for those practices, provide the safety nets from which teachers can explore the complexities of supporting literacy development. Many teachers need to start from the concrete, then shift back and forth between theory and practice as they work through the new idea.

Yes, we do have to beware of what David Bloome (1983) calls "procedural display," the acting out of practices without understanding their theoretical foundations. The solution to that, as Unsworth (1988) points out, is to keep teachers up to date on theoretical developments so that they can continue to refine their practice. That means providing release time for reading and attendance at conferences and discussion groups. It means hiring principals who are good *teacher's* principals, as well as being good administrator's principals—people who will go beyond the politics and paperwork, get into their classrooms, and *help* teachers find their way to understanding whole language. If we want whole language practice to look the way it does in Australia and New Zealand, we have to work to provide the same kind of support systems found in those countries.

Emergent whole language teachers also suffer from overly abrupt changes in policy. I know of instances where administrators, amidst praise from the whole language clubs, have declared their administrative unit "whole language," provided a summer workshop for the teachers, and promptly removed all basals and similar materials. One teacher in such a circumstance told me her school was to institute both whole language and *Mathematics Their Way* within the upcoming school year! Because there *isn't* the kind of support for staff development that is provided in Australia and New Zealand, where the movement has evolved slowly over many years, sometimes teachers here are left floundering, parents become worried, even angry, and administrators declare the movement a failure before it's had a proper chance to prove itself.

Those of us who proselytize need to remember the flexibility and variability of the home model. We must be careful not to be perfectly right or perfectly righteous in the expression of our beliefs. We are all driven by curiosity, by the natural drive to learn and to explore. But we are also susceptible to social pressure, to fear of humiliation, of being "wrong," of being a failure. As Frank Smith (1988) has made clear on many occasions, when people sense they are being excluded from a club, they reject that club. For whole language to succeed, we will need to proceed slowly and gently with teachers.

➔ See: Holdaway, p. 44; Krause, p. 396; Mothering, p. 357; Stevenson, p. 271; White, p. 395.

References
Bloome, D. 1983. "Definitions and functions of reading in two middle school classrooms." Paper presented at a meeting of the American Educational Research Association, Montreal, Canada.
Smith, F. 1988. *Joining the literacy club.* Portsmouth, NH: Heinemann.
Unsworth, L. 1988. "Whole language or procedural display? The social context of popular whole language activities." *Australian Journal of Reading* 2(2).
Vygotsky, L. S. 1978. *Mind in society.* Cambridge: Harvard University Press.
———. 1962. *Thought and language.* Cambridge: MIT Press.

Further Reading by Margaret Yatsevitch Phinney
◆ "Invented Spelling." *Mothering*, Spring 1987.
◆ *We're Off to Thunder Mountain.* Horwitz-Grahame, 1987.
◆ "Whole Reading." *Mothering*, Winter 1987.
◆ *Baba Yaga.* Horwitz-Grahame, 1988.
◆ *Reading with the Troubled Reader.* Scholastic TAB, 1988

Resource: Periodical

Rethinking Schools

$10 year (4 issues) individual; $25 year institutional
1001 E. Keefe Ave.
Milwaukee, WI 53212
1-414-964-9646

Read *Rethinking Schools*, and you'll begin to rethink your role as a professional educator. The quotation below explains who they are and what they are trying to do.

LBB

❝ Who We Are

Rethinking Schools is a quarterly published by Milwaukee area classroom teachers and educators. It is an independent journal dedicated to popularizing progressive ideas about education and giving teachers, parents and students a voice in the struggle for equal and humane schools. Discussion of educational matters is often dominated by administrators and consultants. We strive to give those directly *affected* by public schools a place to share their interests, debate alternatives and unite in the effort to better public education.

"Our central intentions are: to promote dialogue about education; to offer a rigorous analysis of current public schools policies and attitudes; to pose creative policy alternatives; and to serve as an arena for the exchange of specific teaching ideas found to be successful in the classroom. We know of no other periodical that deals with such a variety of ideas from both theoretical and practical vantage points. ❞

Cornerstone: Steven W. Graham

Whole Language: How Do We Spread the Word?

Large numbers of teachers received their formal education some time ago and may not be well versed in whole language. For example, a recent survey of over 2,000 midwestern educators enrolled in continuing education courses indicated that 45 percent of them had received their highest degree more than 10 years earlier.

So the challenge really becomes "How do we get teachers and school districts involved in whole language?" Teachers interested in learning about whole language are often active, assertive, and energetic—the types who provide leadership for their peers. In short noncredit workshops and courses, I've found that once these teachers connect to the excitement of other whole language educators, they become their strongest allies. They want to start whole language teacher groups, they seek new materials, and they talk with curriculum consultants and principals to encourage more reading activities. Once the enthusiasm begins to spread, it becomes infectious. Soon the classroom teachers are scheduling credit courses for their districts, rounding up their colleagues to enroll in them, and pressuring their administrators for more professional development.

It is also important to get local administrators involved in the process. In districts where administrators have been involved in whole language workshops, they have provided moral

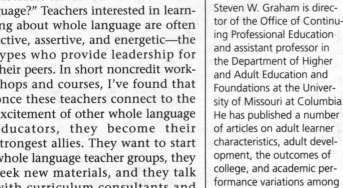

Steven W. Graham is director of the Office of Continuing Professional Education and assistant professor in the Department of Higher and Adult Education and Foundations at the University of Missouri at Columbia. He has published a number of articles on adult learner characteristics, adult development, the outcomes of college, and academic performance variations among college students. He serves as a research and evaluation consultant to business and industry.

support, financial backing for workshops and conference programs, and organized formal credit courses. They have integrated whole language into the core values of the district. One of the best ways to get administrators behind the efforts is to show them results. This includes getting them into the classrooms, where they can directly experience the enthusiasm and energy emerging from teachers and students.

The most useful initial activities are likely to be special after-school or half-day workshops. Ideally, these can be designed as a series that allows follow-ups on certain topics and on concerns that arise in implementation. Credit courses, taken out to the school districts, allow for in-depth coverage and for extended contact with teachers, as well as provide opportunities to make materials available and to establish long-term rapport. Once a successful course has been offered in an area, it often inspires the development of other courses. At several sites we have offered a series of whole language courses, in which each one built upon the others and covered specific topics in great detail.

One of the most important aspects in generating interest is to get energetic local people involved. No number of slick brochures, flyers, or gimmicks can take the place of one or two committed local teachers. They have credibility with their peers.

Short summer institutes also provide avenues for teaching about whole language instruction. Teachers from a variety of areas across the state can come together, share ideas, and develop a support system. Successful summer institute programs have often served as the impetus for full semester courses offered in the local school districts.

Conference programs are another way to spread the word about whole language. One- to five-day conferences bring teachers together from a wide geographical area. While each geographical area has its own characteristics, the following elements should be kept in mind: (1) solid program development, which should include a sound theoretical base and dynamic speakers who can inspire participants; (2) an abundance of practical ideas and suggestions, which helps to make the instruction real to the teachers; (3) keeping mailing lists updated. Such a list helps follow-up on participants; and (4) being prepared for energetic and demanding teachers.

In conclusion, whole language professional development offers an excellent opportunity to have an immediate impact in the classroom.

➜ See: Buchanan, p. 409; Christine, p. 410; Kaltenbach, p. 395; A Letter to Teachers Who Are New to Whole Language, p. 10; White, p. 395.

Further Reading by Steven W. Graham
◆ "Assessing the Learning Outcomes for Adults Participating in Formal Credit Programs." *Continuing Higher Education Review* 53(2), 1989.
◆ "College Outcome Assessment Factors: An Empirical Approach," with I. Cockriel. *College Student Journal* 23(3), 1989.
◆ "Enhancing the Appeal of Teletraining," with J. Wedman. *Journal of Instructional Psychology* 16(4), 1989.
◆ "Adult Life Roles: A New Approach to Adult Development," with J. Hughes. *Journal of Continuing Higher Education*, in press.
◆ "An Assessment of the Perceived Utility of Various College Majors," with I. Cockriel. *NACADA Journal*, in press.

As Teachers See It
by Karen Sabers Dalrymple

In the Name of Whole Language

In 1985 at IRA in New Orleans, Ken Goodman warned us not to get involved in "wholier than thou" behavior—he suggested that we consider our work as whole language teachers so valuable for our students and cautioned us about becoming judgmental of other whole language teachers' work. I was impressed with Ken's request for compassion among us and appreciated the call and time for teachers to work together supporting one another.

Now, several years later, I ache. I have witnessed, seen, read, and heard some rather appalling and dismaying examples of "whole language" at work. It would have been better not to have the label of whole language than to have it used simultaneously with or as a descriptor of activities that do not encourage language love, language use, or language meaning.

As an educational consultant, as an administrator, and as a teacher networking with many teachers around the country, I have opportunities to view a variety of school districts and many classroom teachers. I have thought with some dismay about the activities I see committed in the name of whole language. Observing and evaluating these activities makes me wonder if teachers, administrators, and publishers are using the term *whole language* without a full understanding of the philosophy.

Some of the activities that have occurred in the name of whole language include:

• 379 Thermofax Masters and 30 reams of ditto paper used by one "whole language" teacher in six months of school.
• Assigned worksheets sent home in thick packets; these papers showed no indication of teacher response, comments, or communication.
• Silent "whole language" classrooms.
• "String-along" activities that carry on for weeks in primary classrooms.
• Publishers who use the term *whole language* for isolated skill work or teacher-directed activities that ignore the intelligence of children.

I shudder. I hear "whole language" teachers discussing their students: "They're quiet, but they are not one bit creative," "I wish the kids were more enthused about learning," (this from a teacher using a group behavior management plan for primary students), and "This group just doesn't know how to listen so I quit reading aloud to them."

I'm concerned about the name of whole language. And I'm just as concerned about young children's spirits and their attitudes toward learning as I was before the term *whole language* appeared in educational literature.

Now I want to question, "Aren't some activities wholier than others? Isn't that better?"

Before Ken Goodman warned us about judging "wholiness," he had outlined a marvelous set of descriptors for whole language learning and teaching. Those descriptors included authentic speech and literacy activities, use of a wide range of materials that are easily accessible to students, and informing and involving parents in children's education. These are criteria we can use in planning and evaluating our work and in controlling our purchases. We must use the criteria as we promote literacy education. We need to know and understand the criteria that establish us as whole language educators.

Years ago a friend of mine was agonizing over her discovery that an organization for which she had volunteered years of service was, in fact, racist. She knew she had to resign her membership; she was hurt and confused, as well as angry. I surely hope that we whole language educators aren't faced with this dilemma—I certainly hope that we are able to develop within ourselves and other teachers a deep understanding of whole language. I hope whole language teachers are able to discuss, cuss, and support one another as we become strong and good educators. We must be able to question, to argue, or to be appalled *in the name of whole language* so that we might influence literacy education for all students.

➜ See: Dalrymple, pp. 63, 142, 204, 210; Goodman, p. 119; Mooney, p. 120; Owen, p. 414; Peetoom, p. 415; Watson, p. 427.

Karen Sabers Dalrymple is a teacher at Eagle Valley Middle School, Eagle, CO.

Viewpoint: Dorothy J. Watson

Reflections on Whole Language: Past, Present, & Potential

Recently I sat in the lounge of an elementary school listening to a friend talk about her fifth-grade class and about herself. With genuine enthusiasm she told all about the reading and writing her students were doing. She told anecdote after anecdote, pointing up marvelous child logic and instances in which children helped each other rather than competed with each other in order to learn. And then she began to reflect on her own first shaky steps into a whole language literacy program. Just a year ago she felt that she didn't have a firm grasp on the theoretical base that supports a whole language program and therefore felt very unsure of herself as a whole language teacher. To add to her uneasiness, she knew that for some in her school district whole language either was unknown or was unpopular—just hearing the words was like waving a red flag. On the other hand, she realized some advocates of whole language occasionally uttered the words in the self-righteous way a chip is placed on a shoulder—dare you to knock it off!—dare you to disagree with all I know about language and language learning.

Nevertheless, the literature supporting whole language was compelling for this teacher; it rang true, and, even more important, her students confirmed that it made sense to them. Within a year, with the help of not only her students but also colleagues in her teacher support group, this teacher came to understand that a whole language (or meaning-centered, student-focused, literature-based) program meant that she and her students could become a community of learners in control of their own ways of knowing.

As the teacher told me what had happened to her and her students during the year, I began to think about other teachers and of my own path toward whole language. It occurred to me, that, in keeping with whole language tradition and theory, whole language teachers have similar but never identical stories to tell. Our pasts, our presents, our potentials, are unique.

Reflections on what is happening day in and day out in our classrooms confirm and strengthen our beliefs, but they also help us think through what it was that brought us to that assumption. And those reflections not only give clarity to what we know, but they help put the future in focus and give life to it.

It's been observed that once a teacher begins to understand the power of whole language s/he will be changed. For some the change seems to be 180 degrees overnight. For others the change is considerably slower. There is room for both the tortoise and the hare in whole language.

I dream that:

1. Schools of Education will recognize the new knowledge about language learning and offer that perspective in an integrated curriculum, as an alternative to a skills model of literacy.
2. School systems will stop pandering to the uninformed teachers—rather they will recognize teachers who know what they are doing—and allow those teachers to take back the curriculum and the classroom for the sake of students. I'm not asking that whole language be mandated. I'm asking that it be a real alternative.
3. Assessment will become consistent with the curriculum and the theory on which the curriculum is based. It is tokenism, a nod at whole language, to say that teachers can develop whole language curriculum, but the children must pass the skills tests. Whole language teachers know how to gather and maintain that chain of evidence that assuredly describes learners. I look forward to the day when assessment begins with teachers asking themselves at the end of the day, "Did everything that went on in this classroom today make sense to the students and did it make sense to me?"

4a. We afford all those educators who are attempting whole language the same patience, support, and information that we have received—or should have received. In Ken Goodman's words (1986), we don't take a "wholier than thou" stance with teachers who are moving slowly into a whole languageprogram.

4b. On the other hand, I hope we will take a wholier than thou attitude with publishing companies, curriculum engineers—those who advocate the whole language basal, and other profiteers who tell us that all of whole language can be boxed and labeled. We must take a wholier than thou stand against those who would use

Dorothy J. Watson is a professor of Education at the University of Missouri at Columbia. She is the first president of the Whole Language Umbrella, the 1987 recipient of the International Reading Association's Teacher Educator of the Year Award, former director of NCTE's Commission on Reading, and past president of the Center for Expansion of Language and Thinking. She is an active member of local and national teacher support groups and sponsor of the Mid-Missouri Student Reading Association.

themselves rather than the students as our curriculum informants.

The whole language future? Our potential lies in the individual, the personal, the "this is me." Our potential lies in the partnership, the collaboration, the team support and effort, the "this is us." Our potential lies in the stories, those stories lovingly and carefully crafted by authors of literature for children and youth. Our potential lies in the parent, in the administrator, in the researcher, in the theorists . . . but our potential *will be realized* through the efforts of the teacher with the student. For it is the teacher who can open the book, unfold the story, and invite the reader. It is the teacher who can create the safe harbor where students can share their lives and their literacy. And it is the teacher, above all, who can join hands with the learners.

→ See: Dalrymple, p. 426; Ideas and Insights, p. 304; Watson, pp. 40, 408; Whole Language: Inquiring Voices, p. 215; Zinke, p. 408.

Reference
Goodman, K. S. 1986. *What's whole in whole language?* Portsmouth, NH: Heinemann.

Excerpted from *Oregon English* 11(1), Fall 1988.

Further Reading by Dorothy J. Watson
◆ "Defining and Describing Whole Language." *Elementary School Journal* 90(2), 1989.
◆ *Findings of Research in Miscue Analysis: Classroom Implications,* with P. D. Allen.
◆ *Reading Miscue Analysis: Alternative Procedures,* with Y. Goodman and C. Burke.
◆ *Whole Language: Inquiring Voices,* with C. Burke and J. Harste. Scholastic, 1989.

Resource: Publication

Holistic Education Review

$16/year (4 issues) for individuals;
$24/year for institutions from:
P.O. Box 1476
Greenfield, MA 01302

Ron Miller, the main author of our Pioneers feature, publishes *Holistic Education Review,* which provides a critical assessment of holistic education. What is holistic education? Ron provides a lucid answer below.

LBB

Resource Essay

Defining Holistic Education
by Ron Miller

1. Holistic education seeks to nurture the development of the whole person. It is not enough to educate for academic achievement and vocational skills alone; the human personality is an integrated complex of intellectual, physical, social, moral, emotional, and spiritual possibilities. All of these must be taken into account in the education of children. The manner in which our culture has selected a narrow range of human possibilities to be educated (and even force-fed) is a lopsided and ultimately impoverished conception of human potential.

Holistic education is a spiritual worldview rather than a materialist one. It is a belief in, and a reverence for, a self-directing life force that lies beyond our rational, intellectual understanding. It seeks to support and nourish the natural unfolding of the human soul within the lives of individuals. But spirituality does not imply particular religious beliefs and rituals; a more empirical spirituality may use terms such as "self-actualization" or "creativity" to refer to the same natural unfolding of human personality.

2. Holistic education involves a new relationship between teacher and student; in more general terms, between the adult generation and the young. Authoritarian practices are replaced by dialogue, cooperation, friendship, and respect. Time-honored educational goals such as discipline, order, and academic excellence often mask more authoritarian interests on the part of adults, as demonstrated by the use of corporal punishment and "anti-hyperactivity" drugs. In holistic education, students are valued for their individuality, not solely for their conformity to authoritative standards. Their distinctive styles of learning and their personal interests and questions about life need to be honored.

3. Holistic education offers an alternative. A holistic philosophy emphasizes *experience,* not "great books" or a few "basic skills." Experience is as profound and unlimited and exciting as the universe itself. Why limit students to a curriculum of academic subjects when the entire cosmos is at hand? Education, as John Dewey so eloquently argued, must not be seen as "preparation" for life—it *is* life. Education is growth, discovery, and a widening of horizons. This is just the opposite of traditional educational goals—high test scores and good behavior—which aim to prepare young people for the limited world that adults have created.

4. Holistic education is, at least implicitly, a critical perspective on modern culture. Once we seek to nurture the finer potentials of the human spirit, it becomes evident that the competitive, hierarchical, violent, materialistic, and hedonistic tendencies of the contemporary Western worldview are highly destructive of these potentials. The corrupt power of the state, the consuming greed that fuels our economic systems, and the mindless violence and hedonism glorified by the mass media all work against our spiritual unfolding. We are severely alienated in this culture. The holistic perspective is an inclusive, phenomenological,

(Continued on next page)

As I See It:
Kenneth S. Goodman

Vive la Difference: Long Live Diversity!

One of the exciting things about whole language is that it brings together a growing community of teachers, administrators, researchers, writers, scholars, teacher educators, and publishers. This has led to a dynamic development of whole language theory and practice.

Teachers hear speakers, visit other teachers' classrooms, join support groups, read new and old books, and get new ideas for their teaching. But rather than simply plugging them in, they interpret, modify, embellish, and adapt. And then they, in turn, present at conferences or write articles, books, or blurbs in newsletters. There is no cloning or imitation in whole language teaching. But there is a lot of collaborative innovation.

Researchers visit classrooms, talk with teachers, read research reports, and then they design new studies which they eventually report. Teachers and others use the research insights or offer expansions based on their own classroom experience.

In this community roles shift and merge and overlap. Teachers and researchers collaborate, administrators teach, and teachers lead; and an oral discourse in teachers' rooms and conference sessions and in living room meetings of support groups spills over into print, where it moves in widening circles and then back into oral dialogue and discourse again. And as it moves, it takes new forms, adds new color, draws on new experiences in new contexts.

In this dynamic community of inquiring voices there is a free market of ideas, practice, innovation, and dispute. No one holds a patent or copyright on whole language. And the net result is that whole language expands as a movement, builds and extends the evidence of its value and validity, and moves on to new frontiers, new controversies, new issues, and new arguments. New and better theory and new and better practice result.

From an outsider's point of view all this diversity, all this activity, all this variability, makes it hard to identify the "essence" of whole language. Outsiders look at a single characteristic or manifestation of whole language, and they think they know what whole language is. It's a literature-based reading program; it's an integrated language arts program; it's a holistic view of curriculum; it's the fun part of learning.

But when they visit more than one class or more than one school, when they hear more than one speaker, when they read more than one whole language book, they find variety, diversity, and even disagreement.

And those of us in whole language must explain that we like it that way. There's a lot on which we agree—a growing consensus is emerging from the expanding whole language community. There is a solid core of shared belief and values among whole language advocates.

But we also cherish our differences. We glory in the dynamic diversity of whole language. We enjoy the noise and dissonance produced by all of the inquiring voices. And we're willing to risk that some will go off on non-productive tangents. We're even willing to risk that whole language will evolve into something none of us can now quite imagine.

If we all agreed completely, then whole language would be another orthodoxy. Instead of growing and expanding, it would become rigid and stagnant. Instead of welcoming new voices we would require them to prove their orthodoxy and demonstrate their conformity.

Part of what we agree on is that every whole language teacher must build his or her own understanding and each must make a personal commitment to whole language. So there can be no seven-step, whole language scripted method, no mandates handed down from on high, no gurus with pronouncements that must be obeyed.

We will build whole language together. We will learn from each other. We will welcome new inquiring voices to our widening community. And out of our personal and social explorations, discussions, and disagreements will emerge an expanded consensus and a deeper level of understanding of learning and teaching and the potential of whole language.

Vive la difference; long live diversity in whole language! May we never cease to learn, to change, to grow.

➔ See: Goodman, p. 390; Phinney, p. 425; Turbill, p. 424.

📷 WHOLE LANGUAGE CAMERA

Vive la difference!

(Continued from previous page)
ecological, global perspective that seeks to encompass all aspects of human experience.

The holistic approach represents a serious rethinking of yet unsolved educational problems. And we are deliberately child-centered, in order to honor the new life that comes through the child, not to abandon moral judgment or adult guidance of the young.

Certainly holistic educators have issues to work out, and legitimate criticisms may be made about many holistic ideas and practices. One purpose of *Holistic Education Review,* in fact, is to serve as a forum for such thoughtful criticism. But holistic education is a radical break from traditional ways of understanding human development. The holistic philosophy is far more original, and far more subtle, than most educational policymakers realize. They do not understand that the holistic approach represents a new paradigm. In essence, it is the educational approach of a new culture—an emerging postindustrial, posttechnocratic civilization, in which the whole human being may yet be nurtured.

Book Note

What Are Schools For? Holistic Education in American Culture

Ron Miller
1990; 200 pp.; $14.95
Brandon, VT: Holistic Education Press

In this engaging study, Miller fully achieves his stated purpose: to explore and evaluate the nature of education. Through a scholarly, readable overview of the work of a diverse, influential group of educators, Miller shows that in spite of the centuries and continents that separate them, they are remarkably unified in their visions of the true meaning of education.

He examines the lives of some of the greatest thinkers in education, including Rousseau, Pestalozzi, Dewey, Montessori, John Holt, and Rudolf Steiner, against a sociopolitical backdrop of unfolding world history. Miller defines as "holistic" the common theme that runs through their work: Education should be a joyful experience in which the learner is respected and trusted as a capable, creative, whole individual who functions best in a stimulating, nurturing learning community.

He contends that holistic education is not simply nother way of teaching children, but a radically different way of viewing the world and our reason for being. In other words, Miller believes that we are in the midst of a transition from the industrial age, driven by materialistic, competitive, technocratic values, into a more global, humanistic, spiritual, ecologically sound perspective. Since schools are social microcosms they change only as society changes. As to the necessity of such changes, Miller does not mince words. "Humankind must soon choose between total destruction of the ecosystem or a new world view which strives for peace, cooperation and justice based upon reverence for life. There is no more room for compromise."

Reading this book was for me a moving experience. It is a deeply thoughtful, beautifully organized and written exposition of holistic educational philosophy and will surely appeal to all who are concerned with fundamental changes in our schools.

LBB

Resource: Organization/Periodical

Center for Restructuring

Radius

Free/bimonthly from:
Center for Restructuring
American Federation of Teachers
555 New Jersey Ave., NW
Washington, DC 20001
1-202-879-4559

This organization is one of several committed to restructuring public education. It publishes *Radius.* If you've read this periodical, write us with your reaction to it.

LBB

Resource: Periodical

VOL. 3, NO. 3   JUNE/JULY/AUGUST 1988

DEMOCRATIC SCHOOLS

Democratic Schools

$8.50/year for individual subscription; $20/year to become a correspondent (includes subscription) from:
The Public Education Information Network
438 N. Skinker Blvd.
St. Louis, MO 63130

Democratic Schools is written and published by a grass roots collaborative of individuals and independent organizations and networks committed to school-level change. Correspondents are full participating associates of the collaborative as providers and users of materials and resources. They write, edit, and plan issues of *Democratic Schools;* help coordinate the information exchange; and participate in organizing meetings and conferences. A unique experiment in independent publishing, it is a forum for sharing knowledge and learning about the work of others.

Public Education Information Network
LBB

Literature Reference List

Please note: This is not intended as a core literature list or a recommended reading list; it is simply an index of all the literature books to which our contributors referred in their essays. Page numbers refer to *The Whole Language Catalog*.

—LBB

Running Features

This lists all titles by running feature.
—LBB

As I/We See It

Kidwatching

Viewpoint

Cornerstone

Whole Language Internacional

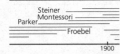

Pioneers

Education In Turin: A Romance

As Teachers See It

Principals Speak Out

Parents Perspective

As Kids See It

Classroom Demonstrations

Great Teachers

Great Schools

Resource Essays

Network

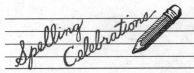

Becoming Literate

Breakthroughs

In The Mail

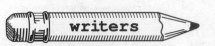

writers

Language Stories

MarveLous INVeNTioNs

I Used to Be... But Now I...

 ### The Funny Side

 ### It Shouldn't Happen to Kids

Well-Said

WHOLE LANGUAGE CAMERA

YOUNG ARTISTS

Resources and Books

Want to look up a specific resource? This index, divided into seventeen subject categories, is your best bet. Keep in mind that whole language is not easily categorized. If you don't find the resource in the first category you choose, try another.
—LBB

Art, Music, and Drama

Classroom Community
(discipline, cooperative learning)

Curriculum
(general)

Early Childhood

English/Language Arts
(includes reading and writing)

Research and Theory

Social, Political, and Environmental Issues

(censorship, sexism, racism, peace education, restructuring schools, environmental education)

Science

Second Language Learning

Social Studies

(geography, history, global education)

Special Education

Subject/Author Index

(Acknowledgments continued from p. 2).

Lucy Calkins: "A Metaphor for Teaching" is a revised version of the dedication to *Living Between the Lines,* by Lucy Calkins, Heinemann Educational Books, Inc., copyright © 1991.

Center for Establishing Dialogue in Teaching and Learning, Inc.: "Bookwords," by Maryann Eeds, from *Centerspace,* vol. 2, no. 5, May/June 1988; excerpted from "Centering Teaching and Learning," by Carol Christine, from *Centerspace,* vol. 3, no. 6, July 1989; book review by Carol Christine of *Teachers as Intellectuals: Toward a Critical Pedagogy of Learning,* by Henry A. Giroux, from *Centerspace,* vol. 3, no. 5, May/June 1989; "Testing in Arizona Schools," from *Centerspace,* vol. 1, no. 5, May/June 1987. © Centerspace, the newsletter and bulletin for members of the Center for Establishing Dialogue in Teaching and Learning, Inc. Reprinted by permission.

Central Park East Secondary School: "Labeling Students 'Easy-to-Teach'," by Deborah W. Meier, from *Changing Schools, CPEES Newsletter #17,* Central Park East Secondary School, New York City. Reprinted by permission.

Centre for Teaching & Research in Literacy, Charles Sturt University-Riverina: "Quality Classrooms," by Fred Gollasch and Chris Weckert. Excerpted from *Micro-Computers in the Whole Language Classroom,* by Fred Gollasch. Adapted from *Never Let a Chance Go By,* by Mark Brennan and Brian, Riverina College of Advanced Education. Excerpted from *A Researcher Learns to Listen: Lessons for Conferencing,* by Barbara Kamler. "Written Conversation," by Margie Leys, from *Literacy, Literature and Learning,* vol. 2, no. 1, Spring 1988. Adapted from *Developing Literature-based Programmes: Getting Kids 'Inside' Books,* by Trevor Cairney, 1987. Excerpted from "A Collection of Letters About Books, Children and the Joys of Sharing," by Ann Pulvertaft. "Peace" by Nicole Black from *Pieces of Our World: An Anthology of Poetry and Prose Written by the Children of the Riverina,* edited by Trevor H. Cairney, 1988. All selections reprinted by permission of the Centre for Teaching & Research in Literacy, Charles Sturt University-Riverina, New South Wales.

Chicago Tribune: Excerpted from "Kids' Fantasies Set the Stage for Play," by Eileen Ogintz, from *Chicago Tribune,* 9 February 1987. © Copyrighted, Chicago Tribune Company, all rights reserved, used with permission.

Child-Centered Experience-Based Learning: "When Is Language Too Much Too Soon?," by Dorothy Watson. Previously printed in *Connections* (a C.E.L. Inc., Winnipeg publication), vol. 4, no. 1, Spring 1989. Reprinted by permission.

Kittye Copeland: "A Message from Kittye Copeland to TAWL Members," from *Mid-Missouri TAWL Newsletter,* 25 September 1989. Adapted and reprinted by permission of the author.

Amanda Cornwall: "Book Review of Treasures 2: Stories and Art by Students in Oregon," by Amanda Cornwall, from *Shoe Tree Magazine,* vol. 4, no. 4, Spring/Summer 1989, National Association for Young Writers. Reprinted by permission of the author.

Courier: Excerpted from "Storyteller Awele Makeba: Making the World a Better Place," by Gwenne Culpepper, from *Courier,* 15 January 1989. Reprinted by permission of the *Courier,* Waterloo, Iowa.

Susan E. Davis: Excerpted from "Computers: A Book Revolution," by Susan E. Davis, from *San Francisco Sunday Examiner and Chronicle,* 17 September 1989. © Susan E. Davis, 1989. Reprinted by permission of the author.

Democratic Schools News Collaborative: Adaptation of "The Sherman School Story: An Interview with Dennis Doyle," from *Democratic Schools,* vol. 3, no. 3, June/July/August 1988. Adapted and reprinted by permission.

The Dewey Center Community Writing Project: Excerpted from Introduction, "A Giving Woman," by Mianne Adufutse, and "George McMahon: Life Stew," by Toby K. Curry, from *Corridors: Stories from Inner City Detroit.* Copyright © 1989. Reprinted by permission of The Dewey Center Community Writing Project.

Doubleday and The Wendy Weil Agency, Inc.: Excerpted from "Reading to Vote: The Citizenship Schools," from *The Long Haul,* by Myles Horton, with Judith Kohl and Herbert Kohl. Copyright © 1990 by Myles Horton, Judith Kohl, and Herbert Kohl. Reprinted by permission of Doubleday, a division of Bantam, Doubleday, Dell Publishing Group, Inc., and The Wendy Weil Agency, Inc.

Education Department of South Australia: Excerpted from "Some Sources of Difficulty and the Implications for Teaching," by Judy Peters, from *ELAN (English Language Arts Newsletter),* no. 4, November 1987. Reprinted by permission of English Language Arts Projects, Education Department of South Australia. "A Course Where Teachers Learn from Their Students: Learner as Informant," by Phil Cormack and Kevin Comber, eds., from *LLIMY Times,* no. 2, October 1987. Literacy and Learning in the Middle Years Project, a cooperative project involving the South Australian College of Advanced Education, Education Dept. of South Australia, Catholic Education Office, and participating Independent Schools. Reprinted by permission.

DiAnn Waskul Ellis: Excerpted from "The Child as Composer," by Dorothy S. Strickland; Chart, "Contrast Between Literature Study Sessions and 'High-Level' Reading Comprehension Sessions," by Carole Edelsky; and "An Interview with Donald Graves," by DiAnn Waskul Ellis, from *The California Reader,* vol. 21, no. 3, March-April, 1988. Reprinted by permission.

The English Centre: Excerpted from "The Miscue Head (Interview with the Goodmans)," by Michael Simons and Bronwyn Mellor from *The English Magazine,* 16, Spring 1986, published by The Inner London Education Authority English Centre. Reprinted by permission.

English Speaking Union: Excerpted from "How I'm Different From the Rest of the Kids," by Juana Arcelia Sainez, from *San Francisco Chronicle,* Spring 1987. 1987 winning essay of the San Francisco Branch English Speaking Union Essay Contest. Reprinted by permission.

Farrar, Straus & Giroux, Inc.: Excerpted from "Naftali the Storyteller & His Horse, Sus" from *Stories from Children* by Isaac Bashevis Singer. Copyright © 1973, 1976 by Isaac Bashevis Singer. Reprinted by permission of Farrar, Straus & Giroux, Inc., and Lescher & Lescher, Ltd.

Barbara M. Flores and Eddie Hernandez and Center for Applied Linguistics: Text excerpts and artwork from "A Bilingual Kindergartner's Sociopsychogenesis of Literacy and Biliteracy," by Barbara M. Flores and Eddie Hernandez, from *Dialogue,* vol. V, no. 3, December 1988, Handbook Press. Reprinted by permission of the authors and Center for Applied Linguistics.

The Foxfire Fund, Inc.: "Foxfire Teacher Outreach Programs," excerpted from The Foxfire Fund brochure, copyright 1990. Reprinted by permission.

Richard Gartner: "Music for Children," by Richard Gartner. Copyright © 1990 by Richard Gartner. All rights reserved. Used by permission of Richard Gartner, Silver String Productions, Chico, CA.

Glide Memorial United Methodist Church: Poem by Matt Dudley from *I Have Something to Say About This Big Trouble: Children of the Tenderloin Speak Out,* collected by Reverend Cecil Williams and Janice Mirikitani, Glide Word Press. Copyright © 1989 by Glide Memorial United Methodist Church. Reprinted by permission of Matt Dudley.

The Granite State Integrated Language Network: "Anecdotal Recording: Writing to Learn," by Donna Cerny, from *Network News,* vol. 1, no. 3, Summer 1989. Copyright © July 1989. Reprinted by permission.

Greenwood Publishing Group, Inc.: Excerpted from *Literacy: Reading the Word and the World,* by Paulo Freire and Donaldo Macedo, Bergin & Garvey. Copyright © 1987. Reprinted by permission.

Guilderland Central School District: "Readers' Workshop," excerpted from "Reading—It's Taking on a Whole New Meaning," by Judy Cox, from *School's In!,* December 1988. Reprinted by permission of Guilderland Central School District, Guilderland, NY.

Ulrich H. Hardt: Excerpted from "Reflections on Whole Language: Past, Present and Potential," by Dorothy Watson, from *Oregon English,* vol. XI, no. 1, Fall 1988. Reprinted with permission of Ulrich H. Hardt, editor, *Oregon English.*

Steve Harlow and Holistic Education Review: "The Medicalization of the Classroom: The Constriction of Difference in Our Schools," by Steve Harlow, from *Holistic Education Review,* vol. 2, no. 2, Summer 1989. Copyright 1989 *Holistic Education Review.* Reprinted by permission of the author and publisher.

Harvard University Press: photograph and text excerpted from *Mind in Society,* by L. S. Vygotsky, Michael Cole, editor. Copyright © 1978 by the President and Fellows of Harvard College. Reprinted by permission of Harvard University Press, Cambridge, MA.

Heinemann Educational Books, Inc.: Excerpted from "The Double Agenda of Evaluation," by Yetta M. Goodman; excerpted from "Evaluation in Whole Language," by Kenneth S. Goodman; and excerpted from "Evaluation of Students —srehcaeT fo noitaulavE," by Yetta M. Goodman, from *The Whole Language Evaluation Book,* Heinemann Educational Books, Portsmouth, NH. Copyright © 1988. Reprinted with permission from Yetta M. Goodman, Kenneth S. Goodman, and Wendy J. Hood and the publisher.

Highlights for Children, Inc.: art and text excerpted from "So You Want to Be a Writer," by Aileen Fisher, copyright © 1980. Used by permission of Highlights for Children, Columbus, OH. The excerpt includes "An Egg" from *I Wonder How, I Wonder Why,* by Aileen Fisher, Abelard-Schuman, NY. Copyright © 1962 by Aileen Fisher. Used by permission of Aileen Fisher. All rights reserved.

Marvin Hoffman: Excerpted from "Four Days," by Marvin Hoffman, a selection from *The Year of the Teacher,* a book-length manuscript. All rights reserved. Used by permssion of the author.

Henry Holt and Company, Inc.: Excerpted from *Understood Betsy,* rev. ed., by Dorothy Canfield. Copyright 1946 Henry Holt and Co., Inc., renewed copyright © 1974 by Sarah Fisher Scott. Reprinted by permission of Henry Holt and Co., Inc.

Home and School Institute: "Helping Parents Help Their Children Learn," by Dorothy Rich, from *Educational Leadership,* 1984. Copyright © 1984 Dorothy Rich. Reprinted by permission of Dr. Dorothy Rich and the nonprofit Home and School Institute, Washington, DC.

International Reading Association: Excerpted from foreword by Gordon Wells from *Teachers and Research: Language Learning in the Classroom,* by Gay Su Pinnell and Myna L. Matlin, eds. Copyright © 1989 by International Reading Association. Reprinted by permission of Gordon Wells and the International Reading Association. Excerpted from "Creative Applications of Computer Assisted Reading and Writing Instruction," by Claire Doyle, from *Journal of Reading,* December 1989. Copyright © 1989 by International Reading Association. Reprinted by permission of the author and the International Reading Association.

Anna Joyce: Excerpted from "Journey Books and Memory Quilts," by Anna Joyce, from *Mothering,* vol. 49, Fall 1988. Reprinted by permission of the author and publisher.

Herbert Kohl: "Education in Turin: A Romance," by Herbert Kohl, a revised and condensed version of a work previously published as part of *Basic Skills* by Herbert Kohl, Little, Brown, copyright © 1982 by Herbert Kohl. Used by permission of the author.

KQED-ITV: "Meet Fair Oaks School, Literary All-Stars," by Janet Nielsen, from *Vision,* Winter 1989. Reprinted by permission from *Vision,* the KQED Instructional Television Newsletter, San Francisco, CA.

La Escuela Fratney: "Right On, Fratney," by Barbara Miner, and excerpts from "A Historical Account: Constructing a Special School, La Escuela Fratney," and "The Pine Cone Story," by Robert E. Peterson, from *La Escuela Fratney: Year One,* Milwaukee Public Schools, Duplication Department. Copyright © 1989 by La Escuela Fratney. Reprinted by permission of the authors and La Escuela Fratney.

Nancy Larrick: Excerpted from "To Ride A Butterfly," by Nancy Larrick, from *Reading in Virginia,* vol. XIV, Spring 1989. Reprinted with permission from the author and *Reading in Virginia,* the journal of the Virginia State Reading Association. "Tribute to Alvina Treut Burrows," by Nancy Larrick, first appeared in the July 1989 Newsletter of the Reading Hall of Fame. Reprinted by permission of the author.

The Lexington Herald-Leader: "Dedicated Teachers Bring Change to State Classrooms," from *Lexington Herald-Leader,* Sunday, 26 February 1989. Reprinted by permission of The Lexington Herald-Leader, Lexington, KY.

Lower Mainland Society for Literacy and Employment: "Life in Prison," by Toby Taylor, from *Voices: New Writers for New Readers,* vol. 1, no. 2, Winter 1989. "Finding My Real Voice," by Linda Calahan and "Collaborative Writing," by Gary Pharness and Lee Weinstein, from *Voices: New Writers for New Readers,* vol. 2, no. 1, Fall 1989. Excerpted from"Writing Set Me Free," interview with Jack Hutchison, from *Voices: New Writers for New Readers,* vol. 2, no. 1, Fall 1989. Excerpted from"Working with Peter," by Mark McCue, from *Voices: New Writers for New Readers,* vol. 1, no. 2, Fall 1989. Reprinted by permission of Lower Mainland Society for Literacy and Employment, Surrey, British Columbia, and the authors.

Ann Manicom: Excerpted from "Interview with Susan Church, Ruth Gamberg and Jim Rice on 'Whole Language in Nova Scotia,' Part 1, Benefits, Difficulties and Potential," by Ann Manicom, from *Our Schools, Our Selves,* vol. 1, no. 2, January 1989. Reprinted by permission of the author and Our Schools/Ourselves Education Foundation.

Bill Martin Jr: Adapted from "Saturday Night at the Fair," by Bill Martin Jr and John Archambault, from *Sounds of Laughter,* DLM, Allen, TX. Copyright © 1990. Used by permission of the author.

Ministry of Education, Learning Media: Excerpted from "Selecting Books for Use in Reading Programs," from *Developing Life-long Readers,* by Margaret Mooney, Department of Education, Wellington, New Zealand, 1989. Reprinted by permission of Ministry of Education, Wellington, New Zealand.

James Moffett: "Whole Language, Whole Learner," by James Moffett. Used by permission of James Moffett.

The Mott's Apple Awards: "Reading Is Even Better," by Reena Maria Ghosh; "Swimming in Books," by David Updegraff; "Why I Love to Read," by Matthew Taylor; "Your Room Can Wait," by Timothy Cooper; "I Don't Know Which Road to Take," by Adam Sidaway; and "Books Are Full of Adventures," by Elizabeth Archibald, 1989 National Winners, Mott's Apple Awards, a national public service reading program. Reprinted by permission.

National Association for the Education of Young Children: Excerpted from "Testing of Young Children: Concerns and Cautions" from NAEYC brochure # 6582, 1988. Reprinted by permission of NAEYC.

National Coalition of Alternative Community Schools: "Wonderland," by Arwen Bunce; "Magic Bird," by Madeline Friedman; and "I Make My Little Puddings," by Christine Wright, from *A Book of Fantasy and Adventures,* by 100 students from Alternative Community Schools, National Coalition of Alternative Community Schools, 1982. Reprinted by permission.

National Council of Teachers of English: Excerpted from "Dancing on the Edge," by Yvonne Mersereau, Mary Glover, Meredith Cherland, from *Language Arts,* vol. 66, no. 2, February 1989. Copyright 1989 by the National Council of Teachers of English. "Understanding Complex Issues: *The Island of the Skog* Revisited," by Laura S. Robb, from *Language Arts,* vol. 65, no. 3, March 1988. Copyright 1988 by the National Council of Teachers of English. "Explorations: Journey Through a Novel, a Screenplay, and a Film," a revised version of "Exploring Sounder: The Novel, the Screenplay, and the Film," by Heinz Senger and B. M. Lynn Archer, from *English Journal,* December 1989. Copyright © 1989 by the National Council of Teachers of English. Reprinted by permission of the National Council of Teachers of English.

New College of California: Statement from the President by Peter Gabel from New College of California Catalog. Adapted and reprinted by permission of New College of California, San Francisco, CA.

Susan Ohanian: "Love, Leslie," by Susan Ohanian. Copyright © by Susan Ohanian. Used by permission.

Susan Ohanian and Education Week: Excerpted from "How to Create a Generation of 'Alliterates'," by Susan Ohanian, from *Education Week,* vol. VIII, no. 6, 12 October 1988. Reprinted by permission of the author and publisher.

Oregon Students Writing and Art Foundation: "Little Lies," by Meredith Proost from *Treasures: Stories & Art by Students in Oregon,* comp. by Chris Weber, copyright © 1985. "Mrs. Laxcie," by Leonila Bonifacio; "Snowflake," by Harmony Jones; "For Now," by Natasha L. Osborn; "Spring," by Hang Nguyen; "Boats" by Chau Vu, from *Treasures 2: Stories & Art by Students in Oregon,* comp. by Chris Weber, copyright © 1988. Reprinted by permission of the Oregon Students Writing and Art Foundation.

Oregonian Publishing Co.: Excerpted from "Treasures, Oregon Students Writing and Art Foundation," by Judy McDermott, from *The Sunday Oregonian,* 4 September 1988. Copyright © 1988 Oregonian Publishing Co. Reprinted by permission.

Richard C. Owen Publishers, Inc.: "My Word! A Good Book Is a Good Book Anywhere," by Margaret Mooney, from *Teachers Networking,* vol. 8, no. 2, December 1987. Adapted version of Preface to *Report Card on Basal Readers.* Copyright © 1988 by Richard C.Owen Publishers, Inc. Excerpted from "My Escape from Basals," by Patricia Yencho and from "Questions and Answers Concerning Emerging Readers," by Sharon Broadhead, from *Becoming a Whole Language School: The Fair Oaks Story,* edited by Lois Bridges Bird. Copyright © 1989 by Richard C. Owen Publishers, Inc. "Language in Personal Knowing," by Kenneth Goodman; excerpted from "Dialect Differences in School Programs," by Kenneth Goodman; "The Dialects of English," by Kenneth Goodman; "Coming to Know," by Kenneth Goodman, from *Language and Thinking in School,* 3d ed., by Kenneth Goodman et al. Copyright © 1987 by Richard C. Owen Publishers, Inc. "Grid of Reading Materials," from *Reading Strategies: Focus on Comprehension,* Copyright © 1980 by Richard C. Owen Publishers, Inc.. "Literature-based or Literature: Where Do We Stand?" by Yvonne S. Freeman, from *Teachers Networking,* Summer 1989. Reprinted by permission of Richard C. Owen Publishers, Inc., New York.

Public Affairs Television, Inc.: Excerpted from interview with Sarah Lawrence Lightfoot, by Bill Moyers, from Bill Moyers' World of Ideas, 12 October 1988, Show #123 transcript. Copyright © 1988 Public Affairs Television, Inc. Reprinted by permission.

Jerline Quintal-Finell and Peter Ballantyne Band: "Grandfather's Gun," by Ted Custer, from *Three Generations Speak,* Jerline Quintal-Finell and Peter Ballantyne Band, 1985. All rights reserved. Reprinted by permission of Jerline Quintal-Finell and Peter Ballantyne Band, Pelican Narrows, Saskatchewan, Canada.

Reflections Magazine: "Holocaust," by Alicia Brashear and "Broken Trust," by Susannah Loehr, from *Reflections,* vol. 8, issue 2, June 1989. Copyright 1989 by *Reflections* Magazine. Reprinted by permission of *Reflections.*

Becky L. Reimer: Excerpted from "But It Doesn't Say Much," by Becky Reimer and Linda Hunsacker, from *Contemporary Issues in Reading,* Fall 1987. Reprinted with permission of the authors and Utah Council of the International Reading Association.

The Saginaw News: Excerpted from "Book-learning at its Best," by Tara Ransom, from *The Saginaw News,* 9 June 1988. Copyright © 1988 The Saginaw News. Reprinted by permission of *The Saginaw News.*

San Francisco Chronicle: "Children's Poems from Tenderloin Streets," by Perry Lang, from the *San Francisco Chronicle,* 11 September 1989. Copyright © 1989 *San Francisco Chronicle.* Reprinted by permission of the *San Francisco Chronicle.*

The Sentinel: "Students Get New Perspective," by Ed Levenson, from *The Evening Sentinel.* © 1983 The Sentinel, Carlisle, PA. Reprinted by permission of *The Sentinel.*

JoAnn Shaheen and Institute for Democracy in Education: Excerpted from "Children Speak Up for Fairness," by JoAnn Shaheen, from *Democracy and Education: The Bulletin of the Institute for Democracy in Education,* vol. 2, no. 4, June 1987. Reprinted by permission of the author and publisher.

The Shoe String Press, Inc.: Excerpted from *They All Want to Write: Written English in the Elementary School,* 4th ed., by Alvina Treut Burrows, Shoe String Press, Hamden, CT, 1984. Reprinted by permission of The Shoe String Press, Inc.

Simon & Schuster, Inc.: Excerpted from *Our Children and Our Schools,* by Lucy Sprague Mitchell. Copyright © 1950, 1979, by Lucy Sprague Mitchell. Reprinted by permission of Simon & Schuster, Inc.

S.M.I.L.E.: Excerpted from "New Ways to Use the News? Tying Your Teaching Together with a Class Newspaper!" by Jeff LaBenz, from S.M.I.L.E. Newsletter IV, 1988. Reprinted by permission.

Mary Lee Smith and Phi Delta Kappa: Excerpted from "What Doesn't Work: Explaining Policies of Retention in the Early Grades," by Mary Lee Smith and Lorrie A. Shepard, from *Phi Delta Kappan,* October 1987. Reprinted by permission of the authors and Phi Delta Kappa.

Dorothy S. Strickland: Excerpted from "The Child as Composer," by Dorothy S. Strickland, from *The California Reader,* vol. 21, no. 3, March/April 1988. Reprinted with permission of the author and publisher.

Teachers & Writers Collaborative: "Meeting Louis Untermeyer," by Francelia Butler from *Teachers and Writers,* vol. 18, no. 2, November-December 1986. Copyright © 1986 by Teachers & Writers Collaborative. Reprinted by permission of the author and publisher. "Memory," by Julie Patton from *Time Made My Grandmother's Hair Turn Grey,* copyright © 1989 Teachers and Writers Collaborative. Poem by Bessie Babits from *Return of the River of No Return,* copyright © 1989 by Teachers & Writers Collaborative. Reprinted by permission of the publisher.

Times Tribune: "Nature Gets Top Billing," by Phyllis Lee, from *Times Tribune,* 31 March 1989. Reprinted by permission of the *Times Tribune.*

Mike Torbe: An early form of "Learning About Language: A Thoughtful Panic" appeared in *Education 3-13,* vol 10, no. 2, Autumn 1982. Used by permission of the author.

Utah Arts Council: "From the Inside Out: Starting with the Maincourse," from *Inside Out: Creative Writing in the Classroom,* by Marjorie Coombs. Copyright © 1989. Used with the permission of the Utah Arts Council.

Dorothy Watson: "Message from the President," by Dorothy Watson, from *Whole Language Umbrella,* vol. 1, no. 1, Fall 1989. Reprinted by permission of the author.

Constance Weaver: "Whole Language as Good Education" is based upon Chapter 1 of *Understanding Whole Language: From Principles to Practice* by Constance Weaver (Heinemann Educational Books, Inc., forthcoming 1990). Used by permission of the author.

Lillian Weber and Human Sciences Press, Inc.: Excerpted from "Comments on Language by a Silent Child," by Lillian Weber, from *Urban Review,* Fall 1976. Reprinted by permission of the author and Human Sciences Press, Inc.

Angela Wegner: Excerpted from "Testing My Patience: A Kindergarten Teacher's Diary," by Angela Wegner, from *Rethinking Schools,* vol. 3, no. 3, May 1989. Reprinted by permission of the author.

Whole Language Special Interest Group of the International Reading Association: Excerpted from "Five Tough Questions That Whole Language Teachers Ask," by Bess Altwerger, from *WLSIG Newsletter,* vol. 2, no. 1, Fall 1988. Reprinted by permission.

The Whole Language Teachers Association: Excerpted from "A School in Transition," by Barbara Siaki, from the newsletter of The Whole Language Teachers Association, Sudbury, MA, Fall 1989. Reprinted by permission. "Suggestions for Organizing a Whole Language Networking Group," by Nancy Areglado and Laura Stevick, from *Teacher's Networking,* vol. 8, no. 4, May 1988. Prepared by the Whole Language Teachers Association in Massachusetts. "Towards Joyful Language Teaching Through Homely Models," by Don Holdaway from the newsletter of the Whole Language Teachers Association, Sudbury, MA, Fall 1988. Reprinted by permission.

Sandra Wilde: "Spelling Celebrations," "Spelling's Greatest Hits: A Top Twelve List," "Tears in Teacher Education," and "Trusting the Learner: Elaine learns to punctuate," by Sandra Wilde. Copyright © by Sandra Wilde. Used by permission.

Well-Said Acknowledgments

Virginia M. Axline: *Dibs in Search of Self,* by Virginia M. Axline (Boston: Houghton Mifflin, 1964).

William Boyd: *The Educational Theory of Jean-Jacques Rousseau,* by William Boyd, Longman, Green, 1911.

Kenneth Clark: *Education Almanac, 1987–1988,* by Kenneth Clark (Alexandria, VA: NAES).

Edith Hamilton: *The Greek Way,* by Edith Hamilton (New York: W. W. Norton, 1930).

Edmund Huey: *The Psychology and Pedagogy of Reading,* by Edmund Huey (Cambridge: MIT Press, 1908, 1968).

Ulric Neisser: *Cognition and Reality: Principles and Implications of Cognitive Psychology,* by Ulric Neisser (New York: W. H. Freeman, 1976).

William Zinsser: *Writing to Learn: How to Write and Think Clearly About Any Subject at All,* by William Zinsser (New York: Harper & Row, 1989).

Photography Credits

Amerelo, Odete: 351
AP/Wide World Photos: 378
Banks, Lynda: 65
Bird, Lois: 377
Brown, Joel: 29, 84, 99, 115, 123, 125, 137, 143, 151, 165, 167, 215, 225, 239, 249, 253, 258, 264, 279, 287, 288, 299, 300, 303, 305, 329, 331, 333, 339, 343, 362, 377
Carry, Del: 284, 285
Clebsch, Carolyn: 11, 20, 81, 85, 95, 103, 209, 291, 298, 312, 322, 323, 332, 333, 335, 340, 341, 363, 377, 380, 381
Courier: 186
Cole, Carolyn: 334
Cummings, Judy: 45, 135, 161, 243, 352, 368
DeCarlo, Beverly: 201
DeLawter, Jayne: 26, 261
Doman, Brooke: 221
Ebury Teachers Centre: 100, 101
Fearn, Gloria Wilbur: 372, 373
Foxfire Fund: 221
Freire, Paolo: 100
Guilderland School District: 175
Heisey, Adriel: 128, 207
Henderson, Anne: 294, 301, 319
Howard, Catherine: 302
Hutchison, Ronald W: 258, 275
International Reading Association: 403
Jamieson, John: 284, 285
Jan, L. Wing: 152
Johnston, Jeri: 38
Lexington, Ann Ringwood: 44
Lockard, Louise: 202
Lubens, Pauline: 205, 229, 236, 237, 377
Luke, Carlen: 80, 92
Malkin, Arlene: 302
McGuffee, Mike: 317, 318
Mooney, Margaret: 187, 344
Motsinger, Cynthia: 194, 297, 327,
Muller, Dot: 289
Owen, Richard C: 120
Page, Patricia: 203
Peterson, Bob: 291, 349
PLUS Project Literacy US: 93
Riley, Owen: 286
Salzer, Dick: 109, 170, 208, 259, 272, 303
Saginaw News: 289
Schuchardt, Maria: 160
Shor, Ira: 222
Sorbo, Brian/The Darkroom: Book covers
Standerfer, Jan: 103, 164, 166, 280
Sunday Oregonian: 162
Walen, Elizabeth: 294, 301, 319

Illustration Credits

Cover: Michael Surles
Running Feature icons:
Illustrations: Ben Dann, DJ Simison
Computer interpretation: Myrna Vladic, Marsha Godfrey
"Education in Turin: A Romance":
Michael Surles, DJ Simison: 33, 55, 109, 139, 169, 204, 225, 243, 245, 303, 311, 366, 375, 393, 413
Ashisha, 357
Danz, David: 206
DLM, 96
Johnson, Bob: 371
Kowolski, Michael: 66
Lipsack, Cathy Blaski: 336, 348
Surles, Michael: 12
Smith, Jay: 163
Vladic, Myrna: 39

Historical Photographs and Art

American Montessori Society: 367
Bancroft Library: 376
Bettman Archives: 393
Harvard University Press: 413
Hill-Jaroff, Nancy: 169
Historical Pictures Service: 29, 33, 54, 139, 169, 204, 219, 243, 311, 393
State Historical Society of Wisconsin: 74
The Granger Collection: 109.

Become a Contributor to *The Catalog*

As you were reading *The Whole Language Catalog*, did you find yourself wishing you could publish your views, your experience? Do you know a better way to organize for literature study? Did you look and not find your favorite social studies resource? Do something about it! Become a *Whole Language Catalog* contributor.

"Whole language teachers share their best," says Dorothy Watson. We hope that *The Catalog* can serve as a clearinghouse for resources and materials, and as a sounding board for holistic educational theory and practice, and enable *you* to share your best. But we won't know what you know unless you write us.

We welcome your reaction—positive or negative—to everything in the *Catalog*. If you find misinformation or omissions, please drop us a card and let us know. We're especially interested in your reaction to the books and resources we've listed.

Guidelines for Contributors

Use this first edition as a model. You'll notice that space is at a premium, so short is usually better than long. Send us your best and keep the rest! When you send material, please follow these guidelines as closely as possible:

Essays and Reviews

What form should your writing take? That's up to you. Write for one of the features included in this edition or introduce something new. Here are some of our specific needs:

- Resources or professional books that we didn't include and that you recommend; write a review or send us the name and the address where it may be obtained and we'll look into it. Please write longer and more substantive reviews than our Resources and Book Notes in the current *Catalog*. A note to suppliers: we invite you to suggest your own goods. Please send samples or a review copy.

- The name, address, and, if possible, phone number of a great whole language teacher, school, or district. Write a description for us using the profiles in this *Catalog* as models, or provide us with a name and address and we'll follow up.

- Language stories; humorous anecdotes; breakthroughs.

- Political stories: are you fighting for your right to use whole language? What strategies have you found that work?

- Great invented spellings: be sure to identify the writers and include their ages.

- Your or your students' writing across genre.

- How do you organize for and support whole language learning? What practical suggestions can you share with other teachers, parents, administrators, teacher educators?

- Thematic units and hands-on, community-oriented projects.

- Information about your teacher support group: history, goals, how you are effecting change in your area.

- Your own ideas.

NOTE: Since manuscripts and photographs cannot be returned, please retain a copy for yourself. We will return original artwork.

References for Essays

Please give complete references for all quotations and book titles, including titles of children's and adolescent literature. A complete reference includes title, author, copyright date, publisher, and place of publication.

Reprints

If you send a reprint, please include with it a photocopy of the title and copyright pages of the original source.

Photographs

Black and white or color will do. Please send (1) a print, and (2) a photocopy of the print which includes the following information: when and where the photograph was taken, name of photographer, names of those in the photo, ages of any children, and your brief explanation of what's happening. Please also have the parents or guardians of any children pictured sign a permission statement like the one below:

> I _____ (designate parent or guardian) of _____ (name of child) grant permission to the authors of *The Whole Language Catalog* to publish the photograph of_____ (name of child) taken at_____ (place and date).

Artwork

Please send (1) original artwork, and (2) a photocopy of it which includes the following information: name and age of the artist, location of his/her school or home. Please also attach a permission statement like the one below:

> I _____ (designate parent or guardian) of _____ (name of child) grant permission to the authors of *The Whole Language Catalog* to publish original artwork by_____ (name of child) submitted by_____ on_____ (date).

Send all contributions with your name, address, phone number, and, if appropriate, the grade level you teach, and the name and location of your school to:

Lois Bridges Bird, Editor
The Whole Language Catalog
PO Box 51807
Palo Alto, CA 94303

• •

Reader Response

Dear Reader,

We hope that you enjoy *The Whole Language Catalog*. We would be most grateful if you would take a moment to let us know your reaction to it and your suggestions for improving it. Your comments will help shape the next edition.

Sending in this form will identify you as a *Whole Language Catalog* user. The personal data is for our files only, and will simply enable us to send you any updates regarding the *Catalog* as they become available.

Name _____

Place of work _____

Work address _____

City _____

State _____ Zip _____

Phone _____

Occupation/Title _____

Home address _____

City _____

State _____ Zip _____

Phone _____

Send to:
Lois Bridges Bird, Editor
The Whole Language Catalog
PO Box 51807, Palo Alto, CA 94303

General reaction to *The Whole Language Catalog*:

_____
_____
_____
_____
_____
_____
_____
_____
_____
_____
_____
_____

(continue on back, if you wish)

What would make *The Catalog* more useful to you?

_____
_____
_____
_____
_____
_____
_____
_____
_____
_____
_____

(continue on back, if you wish)

> **If the Order Form has been used and you want to order the *Whole Language Catalog*:**
>
> **Send orders to:**
>
> ★ ★ ★ ★ ★
> **AMERICAN SCHOOL PUBLISHERS**
>
> Macmillan/McGraw-Hill
>
> 1221 Farmers Lane, Suite C
> Santa Rosa, CA 95405
>
> **For ordering and price information:**
> Call Toll Free
> **1-800-882-2502**
>
> Call between 8:30 am–3:30 pm
> Pacific Time
>
> P.S. If you have friends who might want to order, why not copy the Order Form?

The Whole Language Catalog
Order Form for Credit Card Purchases

Send orders to:

★ ★ ★ ★ ★
AMERICAN SCHOOL PUBLISHERS

Macmillan/McGraw-Hill

1221 Farmers Lane, Suite C
Santa Rosa, CA 95405

For ordering and price information:

Call Toll Free

1-800-882-2502

Call between 8:30 am–3:30 pm
Pacific Time

Ship to: (please print)

NAME

SCHOOL / SCHOOL DISTRICT

ADDRESS

CITY

STATE   ZIP

TELEPHONE

Sold to: (please print)

NAME

SCHOOL / SCHOOL DISTRICT

ADDRESS

CITY

STATE   ZIP

TELEPHONE

All orders must be prepaid via credit card.
Charges to include local sales tax, and 8% for shipping & handling.
All orders will be shipped UPS/RPS only.

☐ MasterCard #

☐ Visa #

Expiration Date

Signature

Quantity	Product Number	Title	Price	Total
	87-020102	The Whole Language Catalog		
		8% Shipping and Handling		
		Grand Total		

Make a statement, have an impact. Give a copy of *The Whole Language Catalog* to your school principal, school board member, concerned parent, favorite colleague.

The Whole Language Catalog
Order Form for Schools/School Districts
Using Purchase Orders

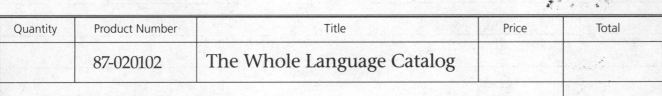

Send orders to:

★★★★★
AMERICAN SCHOOL PUBLISHERS

Macmillan/McGraw-Hill

1221 Farmers Lane, Suite C
Santa Rosa, CA 95405

For ordering and price information:

Call Toll Free

1-800-882-2502

Call between 8:30 am–3:30 pm
Pacific Time

Quantity	Product Number	Title	Price	Total
	87-020102	The Whole Language Catalog		
		8% Shipping and Handling		
		Grand Total		
		Purchase Order No:		

Make a statement, have an impact. Give a copy of *The Whole Language Catalog* to your school principal, school board member, concerned parent, favorite colleague.

_____
AUTHORIZED SIGNATURE

Ship to: (please print)

_____
SCHOOL

_____
STREET

_____
CITY

_____
STATE   ZIP

_____
NAME

_____
TITLE

Sold to: (please print)

_____
SCHOOL

_____
STREET

_____
CITY

_____
STATE   ZIP

_____
NAME

_____
TITLE